SUMMARY OF CONTENTS

PART C

EXPANDING THE FRAMEWORK OF LITIGATION: ADDITIONAL CLAIMS AND PARTIES   889

CONTENTS

PART A

THE CONSTITUTIONAL FRAMEWORK FOR U.S. LITIGATIONS   71

II. PERSONAL JURISDICTION   77

III. SUBJECT MATTER JURISDICTION OF THE FEDERAL COURTS

IV.   THE *ERIE* PROBLEM   261

EXPANDING THE FRAMEWORK OF
LITIGATION: ADDITIONAL CLAIMS
AND PARTIES

PREFACE

Process lies at the core of our legal system: it expresses many of our culture's basic ideas about the meaning of fairness; it determines the victor in close cases; and it further determines which cases will be close ones. Procedure is also the area of law least understood and most maligned by lay observers. We root for underdogs and insist that rules not be stacked against them. But we are equally quick to condemn a case for having been decided on a "legal technicality," a phrase commonly signifying that a procedural rule has come into operation.

A similar ambivalence pervades debate about the behavior of courts and lawyers. As a society we demonstrate a strong belief in the efficacy of lawsuits to solve social, business, and personal problems, and we extol the rule of law as a distinguishing virtue of our culture. But at the same time we worry about what many believe is an excessive willingness to seek legal solutions. The ensuing debate ranges from the role of courts in restructuring social institutions to the question of whether lawyers exacerbate disputes and waste social resources by reflexively behaving in competitive, adversarial ways.

All these issues are procedural. Lawyers thus need to understand process as a tool of their trade, as a constitutive element of the legal system, and as a focus of debate about social values. Yet civil procedure is, by most accounts, a difficult and frustrating first-year course. Students come to law school with little experience in thinking explicitly about procedure and with an impression that cases simply arrive at the point of decision. Moreover, students sense that procedure may be the area in which lawyers' skill counts most; the notion that meritorious cases can be lost because of bad lawyering outrages their sense of justice even as it creates anxiety.

This book seeks to show procedure as an essential mechanism for presenting substantive questions and as a system that itself often raises fundamental issues regarding social values. I hope that students will begin to appreciate that lawyers move the system and that, to a large extent, clients' fates depend on the wisdom, skill, and judgment of their lawyers. Moreover, although all would agree that cases should not be decided on the basis of "mere" technicalities, fierce debate quickly arises when one tries to distinguish rules that merely direct traffic from those that guard the boundaries of fairness.

In addition to considering such theoretical issues, the book has some practical goals. It seeks to give students a working knowledge of the procedural system and its sometimes arcane terminology. The course also introduces the techniques of statutory analysis. It should give students a better understanding of the procedural context of the decisions they read in other courses. To these ends I have tried to select cases that are factually interesting and do not involve substantive matters beyond the experience of first-year students. The problems following the cases are intended to be answerable by first-year students and to present real-life issues. Finally, the book incorporates a number of dissenting opinions to dispel the notion that most procedural disputes present clear-cut issues.

The organization of the book adapts it to the most common sequences in contemporary procedure courses. After a brief overview of the procedural system in Chapter I, some courses will initially consider the materials in Part A, which covers jurisdiction and choice of law. Other courses will begin with discussion of remedies, pleading, discovery, resolution without trial, identifying the trier, trial, appeal, and former adjudication which are addressed in Part B. Part C, on joinder and complex litigation, recapitulates much of the material in Parts A and B and can be used either as a culmination of the course or as an insertion that follows pleading.

Cases have been severely edited to eliminate citations (without indicating their omission), and they read somewhat differently from real case reports; I hope they err in the direction of smoothness. Citations are retained only when they seem significant. Footnotes have been eliminated without indication. Those that survive retain their original numbers, while the editor's footnotes employ symbols. We have used several special citation forms: F. James, G. Hazard, and J. Leubsdorf, Civil Procedure (4th ed. 1992), is cited as James, Hazard, and Leubsdorf; C. Wright, Federal Courts (5th ed. 1994), is cited as Wright, Federal Courts; J. Moore, Federal Practice and Procedure (1969), is cited as Moore; C. Wright, A. Miller, and E. Cooper, Federal Practice and Procedure (1969), is cited as Wright and Miller.

We gratefully acknowledge the permissions granted to reproduce the following materials. The excerpts from Brazil, The Adversary Character of Civil Discovery: A Critique and Proposals for Change, 31 Vand. L. Rev. 1295 (1978), are reprinted by permission of the Vanderbilt Law Review (copyright © 1978 by the Vanderbilt Law Review). The passages from Kamp, The History Behind Hansberry v. Lee, 20 U.C. Davis L. Rev. (1987), are reprinted by permission of the author and the Regents of the University of California (copyright © 1987 by the Regents of the University of California).

Those whose assistance was acknowledged in the preface of earlier editions built the foundations on which this book rests. This revision has incurred additional debts of its own, including the suggestions received from teachers and students using the book. This edition has benefited greatly from the perceptive comments of Allen M. Katz, Esq. A distinguished litigator, Mr. Katz has shared his insights about the way in which doctrine matters in the shaping of a lawsuit and has offered many valuable suggestions, particularly about pleading, discovery, and trial. Without giving him any responsibility for the errors that doubtless still remain, I also want to thank him for having read and commented on the draft of each chapter. I want also to thank Professors Richard D. Friedman, Lawrence W. Moore, and Philip Schrag for their detailed, thoughtful, and constructive comments. This edition has also benefited from the help of Heather Deetjen and Richard Kim, who tracked down citations, indexed, and improved the book's comprehensibility.

This edition bears the name of only one author. In many respects, however, it continues to be the work of Jonathan Landers and the late James Martin, on whose intellectual framework and approach I have continued to build; though neither bears any responsibility for errors of judgment or detail, both should get credit for much that is right and helpful about the book.

Stephen C. Yeazell

January 2000

CIVIL PROCEDURE

AN OVERVIEW OF PROCEDURE

I

A. The Idea and the Practice of Procedure

1. Locating Procedure

Civil procedure is about truth and justice — about how we define those words, how we seek those principles, and how we sometimes lose them. Civil procedure is also about lawyers — about their relation to their clients, to their profession, and to the courts. It is also, inevitably, a course about greed, venality, and oppression, and the running battle waged against these eternal human characteristics.

Mixed with these lofty themes are the minutiae of lawyers' work. Most of the first year of law school concerns what lawyers call substantive law, the rules governing behavior in ordinary life: property, criminal law, torts, and contract. Everyone needs to know at least a little about these topics simply to function in the everyday world. But procedure is insiders' law, of special importance to those administering the legal system.

Those insiders turn to procedure to describe steps in the elaborate game called litigation. At one level, procedure is the etiquette of ritualized battle, defining the initiation, development, and conclusion of a lawsuit. What does one have to say to get a court to pay attention? From whom may a person with a grievance seek relief? What kind of relief? If I believe my adversary has information that would help me to develop my case, may I demand it of her? All these questions — involving what lawyers would call pleading, joinder, remedies, and discovery — are dealt with in a course in civil procedure. The answers to such questions are important to any lawyer who needs to help a client in a lawsuit. Because these answers sometimes enable prediction of the probable results of suits, they are equally important to clients who want to stay out of litigation. Lawyers need to know this body of esoteric knowledge; it is part of what makes them lawyers.

If procedure were no more than a set of rules about the etiquette of

1

lawsuits, however, it would be hard to justify its place in the first-year curriculum. Another facet of procedure justifies that place: Procedure mirrors our most basic notions of fairness and about the meaning of justice. Procedure tries to capture our ideas about the acceptable forms of settling disputes — about whether we most desire peace or truth. Procedure in this aspect embodies not just the rules governing "the way we do things here" but the *reasons* we do them that way. If coming to a quick decision were all that mattered, we could flip coins to decide lawsuits. We don't flip coins because solving an important dispute without reference to its merits strikes us as unfair: The decision, we believe, ought to reflect more than chance. This belief that procedure ought to promote decisions on the merits informs the resolution of procedural questions ranging from the global — why does the system generally require a hearing before reaching a decision? — to the minute — how much time should a defendant have to reply to a complaint?

Many of the values embodied in current procedural law are now under renewed scrutiny. Lay observers, lawyers, and judges argue that our procedural system's obsession with permitting the adversarial airing of grievances has created a monster. Proposed solutions range from the streamlining of adjudication to nonadjudicative dispute resolution. The system's defenders have not been silent, arguing both that the critics overstate the problem and that adjudication has proved to be a major force for social justice and political stability over the past two centuries. Such issues lurk in the background at every turning of our path.

If the foregoing suggests the importance of procedure, it remains only to explain an obstacle to its mastery. In most of your other courses, you will deal with questions as to whose answers you will have intuitions because you can imagine yourself in similar situations. A promises to give B a present but then reneges: Should the law enforce the promise? Should C be liable for insulting D? If E finds a watch lying on the sidewalk, may he keep it? May F be punished criminally for injuring G if F believed (wrongly, as it turned out) that G was about to attack her? As you will discover, most of your substantive courses turn on such questions. You will frequently find that your first reaction differs from the law's answer, but you will usually have at least *some* initial reaction.

Your response to procedure, however, especially at the beginning, may be quite different. Consider a procedural question: If A has sued B for damage to A's car in an auto collision, may A bring a separate lawsuit to recover her medical bills? Courts in different states give different answers to that question. But your first reaction to the question may be that you don't *have* a reaction. That uncertainty flows partly from procedure's status as insider's law; at this point in your legal studies you are still an outsider. Only as you learn how the system works will you see why the answer matters. You will, for example, recognize that if we force A to bring all her claims at once it may make for more efficient adjudication, but it may also pressure parties and their lawyers to expand the size and scope of lawsuits — a result that may be undesirable.

This chapter seeks to give you some feel for procedural issues while offering you a first view of the life cycle of a civil lawsuit. It will raise more questions than it answers, but it will offer you a sense of the course of civil litigation and a taste of the kind of problems lawyers describe as procedural.

We start with a simple and plausible fact situation: Peters, a student at the University of Michigan, spent his winter vacation at his parents' home in Champaign, Illinois. While there, he was seriously injured in an automobile accident with Dodge, a lifelong resident of Champaign. The remainder of this chapter deals with issues that might flow from this everyday occurrence.

2.   Procedure, Lawyers, and Clients

Consider first whether and how this accident might enter the formal legal system. Keep in mind that most such episodes will never get near lawyers or courts. If Peters had adequate medical insurance and no lost wages, he might have little reason to sue Dodge. Alternatively, Dodge (or his insurer) might well offer Peters a satisfactory settlement before suit was filed. Or, Peters might be interested in a lawsuit but be unable to find a lawyer who would take the case. These three alternatives account for most disputes that arise in our society, with the consequence that they will never enter the official judicial system. For the rest of this book — and for the rest of law school — you will be dealing with the exceptional instances, the disputes that do find their way into the official mechanism.

How would that happen? The first step would probably involve Peters's finding a lawyer. (In the United States individuals can prosecute their cases themselves — *in pro. per.* or *pro se*, in the jargon of the law* — but

---

* *In pro. per.* is an abbreviation for the Latin in propria persona, meaning "in his or her own person" (rather than by an agent or attorney). *Pro se* means "for him- or herself." Like most Latin terms in law, they don't convey very important concepts but instead serve as shorthand.

most find lawyers worthwhile for litigation.) Having a lawyer to represent Peters has substantial consequences. Peters will hire the lawyer for her expert knowledge of the legal system and, in particular, the procedural system. Peters wants the lawyer to navigate the procedural system to bring him to his goal — in this case a recovery of damages to compensate Peters for his injuries. The lawyer presumably shares that goal, but she will also have other goals: her other cases, her professional success, and her nonprofessional interests — family, friends, religious obligations, and the like. Most of the time lawyers are able to represent clients without serious interference from these potentially divided loyalties. But when the conflict of interest between lawyer and client surfaces, it frequently does so in ways that affect the procedural system.

In order for legal representation to work, the legal system has to treat the lawyer's choices as if they were Peters's choices. For example, if Lawyer files a suit seeking recovery for Peters's personal injuries but not for damage to his car, the legal system will treat that choice as if Peters himself had made it. But what if Lawyer's behavior results not from Peters's choice but from Lawyer's own carelessness — her failure to ask Peters whether his car was damaged? In that situation, the procedural system faces a dilemma. If the system allows Lawyer to correct her mistake by later adding the claim for property damage, it will thereby harm Dodge, who may have been relying on the original claim to be a complete statement of Peters's grievance. But if the procedural system insists that Peters stand by the original version of the claim — without the property damages — it will thereby harm Peters, by forcing him to forgo compensation for his damaged car.

The system has hit on two solutions to this essentially insoluble problem — both of which you will see repeatedly in procedural cases. The first is a legal malpractice action: Peters can sue his lawyer if her negligence has caused him to forgo part of his recovery. The second is procedural flexibility: If the procedural system allows Peters's lawyer to fix her mistake, then Peters will again be adequately represented. Each solution to the dilemma has a corresponding drawback. If the system insists that Peters is bound by his lawyer's slip — and that his only remedy is a malpractice action — it will force him to start a second lawsuit (against his lawyer), with all the attendant uncertainty and delay. If the system allows Peters's lawyer to cure her slip by amending the complaint, it will undermine the efficiency that flows from treating lawyers' actions as those of their clients and will inflict the costs of Peters's lawyer's sloppiness on Dodge.

Because neither solution is very attractive and because procedural choices have consequences for clients, you will repeatedly encounter the procedural system resolving this dilemma. As you do, consider whether the choices it has made are correct.

B.   Where Can the Suit Be Brought?

Once Peters has selected a lawyer, that lawyer will have to begin making procedural choices, each of which may have consequences — sometimes unforeseeable ones — for the outcome of the suit. One of the first such choices is where to bring the action. The 50 states and the federal government all operate systems of courts, and Peters's lawyer must find out whether she can bring his suit in one or more state courts or in a federal court. If she has a choice, she will have to decide which would be most advantageous.

Why should Peters's lawyer care which court hears his suit? A complete answer to that question could take one deep into the tactics of lawyering, but a sketch of the possibilities should suffice as background to the next case. Convenience provides one possible answer: if Peters (and his lawyer) are both in Ann Arbor, Michigan, it may be cheaper and more convenient to have a court (state or federal) hear the case there rather than in Champaign, Illinois — if the court has the power to do so. All things being equal, most lawyers would rather try a case where they know the small folkways of the court and perhaps some of the judges, and are generally comfortable with the system. Moreover, convenience for Peters is likely to mean inconvenience for Dodge, a factor that may not make Peters's lawyer unhappy. Beyond convenience lies tactics. Will a Champaign jury be more sympathetic to Peters or to Dodge? Do courts in one state or the other have large case backlogs that would delay Peters's claim?

The choice between state and federal courts turns in part on these factors and brings some new elements into the calculation. First, the fact that all federal judges are appointed for life (Article III of the U.S. Constitution permits their removal only by impeachment) can be important in a case in which judicial insulation from political pressure may play a role (not likely in the Dodge-Peters case). Second, in some districts federal courts have smaller case loads than their state court counterparts and are therefore likely to bring a case to trial faster. For Peters, anxious to collect a judgment or settlement, that will be a plus; for Dodge, it may be a minus. Third, tactical factors may influence the lawyer: Sometimes the belief that the opponent will be unfamiliar with the greater formality or faster pace of federal court litigation will lead a lawyer to seek that forum. Finally, a number of idiosyncratic factors — ranging from the greater freedom to question prospective jurors in state courts to the desire to obtain or avoid a particular judge in the case — may influence the lawyer. While reading Gordon v. Steele, infra, you might speculate about why the plaintiff's lawyer sought a federal court when state courts would have been available for the claim.

With a sense of where she might prefer to bring suit in mind, the lawyer now needs to know what the possibilities are. The rules governing where a suit can be brought come under the headings of subject matter jurisdiction, personal jurisdiction, and venue.

1. Subject Matter Jurisdiction

Subject matter jurisdiction is the term used to denote whether a court can hear a particular type of dispute. For example, a small claims court has subject matter jurisdiction over claims below a set amount (for example, $25,000). If a suit for $50,000 were brought in such a court, the court would lack subject matter jurisdiction. Similarly, a family court may have jurisdiction over matters relating to marital status, child custody, name change, and other matters affecting families or family status. Such a court would lack subject matter jurisdiction over Peters's claim against Dodge, a claim that has nothing to do with the intrafamily relations of either party.

To describe the subject matter jurisdiction of a court, two different terms are used. Some courts are said to be courts of *general jurisdiction*. This means that they can hear any kind of claim between any persons unless there is legal authority saying that they cannot hear a particular kind of case. For example, it is common for probate matters (wills, trusts, and so on) to be excluded from the purview of courts of general jurisdiction. Other courts are said to be courts of *limited jurisdiction*. These courts can hear only those cases that are specifically authorized by the statutes that set up the particular court.

To return now to the question whether Peters may bring his case in federal or state court, it is helpful to know that all states have at least one court of general jurisdiction that would be competent to hear Peters's claim. In Illinois and Michigan, that court is the circuit court, but in other states it may be called a district court, superior court, court of common pleas, or, in New York, the supreme court. Thus, one alternative open to Peters is the Circuit Court of Illinois; another is the Circuit Court of Michigan.

Can Peters also bring his case in a federal court? Unlike state courts, the federal courts are *only* courts of limited jurisdiction. The outer bounds of that jurisdiction are set by Article III, Section 2 of the Constitution. There is, however, no requirement that the federal courts be granted the broadest jurisdiction allowable under the Constitution. Instead, it is up to Congress to decide the precise subject matter jurisdiction of the federal courts. The only limitation is that Congress cannot grant more subject matter jurisdiction than is permitted by the Constitution. Congress has enacted a number of statutes authorizing subject matter jurisdiction. The most important at this point are 28 U.S.C. §§1331 and 1332.

You will note from these sections that the subject matter jurisdiction of the federal courts is based on two kinds of considerations. Certain claims may be brought in the federal courts because of the nature of the claim — "arising under" the Constitution, laws, or treaties of the United States. Other claims may be brought in the federal courts because of the citizenship of the parties to the suit.

To decide whether Peters can bring his suit in the federal courts, determine whether §1331 or §1332 applies to the case. Once you have identified the section, what is the problem in applying it? Does the following case help you in any respect?

Gordon v. Steele
376 F. Supp. 575 (W.D. Pa. 1974)

Knox, J.

The problems of students have lately become numerous with respect to their legal status. . . . It was inevitable that the federal courts would soon feel the impact of this litigation with respect to problems arising under diversity jurisdiction.[1] Thinking of the courts in this area is probably colored by numerous constitutional and statutory provisions in various states to the effect that no one shall be deemed to have gained or lost a residence by attendance at an institution of higher learning.

The thinking is also colored by the traditional rule that the fact that a college student is supposedly maintained by his or her parents is a strong circumstance indicating no gain of residence in the college town, . . . and this is in accord with Restatement of Conflicts of Laws, Section

---

1. Citing 28 U.S.C. §1332, Diversity of Citizenship:

(a) The district courts shall have original jurisdiction of all civil actions where the matter in controversy exceeds the sum or value of $10,000 [at the time of the case, now $75,000 — Ed.], exclusive of interest and costs, and is between —

(1) citizens of different States;

(2) citizens of a State, and foreign states or citizens or subjects thereof; and

(3) citizens of different States and in which foreign states or citizens or subjects thereof are additional parties.

30, that a minor child has the same domicile as its father. In these days when nearly all the state legislatures have reduced the age of majority to 18, this poses a more pressing problem with respect to college students who can no longer be put off with the explanation that those under 21 are minors and hence continue their residence with their parents. See the various acts of the Pennsylvania Legislature approved June 16, 1972, particularly 73 Purdon's Pa. Stats. §2021 permitting persons 18 years of age and older to enter into legal contracts and depriving such persons of the defense of minority.

The plaintiff Susan Gordon is one of those who was benefited by the provisions of the aforesaid emancipation acts of June 16, 1972. She was born November 20, 1953 and hence was 18 years of age at the time the cause of action hereinmentioned arose and was 19 at the time this action was brought, April 10, 1973.

The action is one for malpractice against two physicians and an osteopathic hospital in Erie County, Pennsylvania. All of the defendants are citizens of Pennsylvania. There seems little question that prior to August 9, 1972, the plaintiff was also a citizen of Pennsylvania, residing at 227 Goodrich Street, Erie, Pennsylvania, with her parents and if this continued to be her address, her suit must fail for lack of diversity jurisdiction.

She complains that she suffered an injury to her wrist on February 25, 1972, and there was wrongful diagnosis as to the existence of fractures in the bones by the defendants at that time. She claims that they concluded that there were no such fractures and that as a result she endured continuing pain and disability resulting in hospitalization and medical attention and that her wrist and right hand remain at least partly disabled as the result of the alleged malpractice.

On August 9, 1972, plaintiff enrolled in Ricks College at Rexburg, Idaho where she rented an apartment which she has retained ever since. Defendants on January 21, 1974, moved to dismiss for lack of diversity. Briefs have been filed, arguments held and the court postponed decision on the matter until further depositions of the plaintiff could be taken. The matter is now before the court for disposition.

We approach the problem recognizing, of course, that it is citizenship at the time of filing suit, in this case April 10,1973, which is controlling. Further, the rule is unquestioned that where plaintiff is challenged on her claim of diversity, the burden is upon her to show by convincing evidence that diversity jurisdiction exists.

As is required in all of such cases, we must reckon up the indicators pointing for and against acquisition of a new domicile for diversity jurisdiction purposes. Defendant claims that the following indicate that plaintiff

is still a citizen of Pennsylvania and has not acquired a new residence
or citizenship in Idaho:

(1) At the time of application for admission to the college at Rexburg,
Idaho, she gave her address as Erie, Pennsylvania.

(2) The college records dated in 1972 show her address as Erie, Pennsylvania. The same is true of the college records dated May 4, 1973.

(3) During summer vacations, she worked in Erie, Pennsylvania.

(4) She held a Pennsylvania Driver's License and had a bank account
in Erie.

(5) She came to Erie for Christmas vacations.

(6) While Ricks College is a Mormon Church Institution, the supplemental depositions which were taken at the request of the court indicate
that females unlike males are generally not required to participate in the
missionary activity of the church and that she has no present intentions
of participating in such missionary work which, of course, might take
her to any part of the world.

On the other side of the ledger, plaintiff points to the following:

(1) Her expressed intention is not to return to Pennsylvania. This, of
course, is a very strong factor in a situation where subjective intent plays
a part in determining what is her animo manendi.

(2) She has an apartment in Rexburg which she regards as her residence
and this is not sublet during various times of the year but remains hers.

(3) She states she came back to Erie only one summer in 1973 [sic]
because of her eye problems and that she took eye treatment in Erie
and Cleveland.

(4) She claims that her purpose in visiting at Christmas 1973 was to
be deposed and for medical appointments. She has not returned to Erie
during Spring or Thanksgiving vacations.

(5) Her religious desires as a sincere Mormon are to further her faith
and insure that she marries in a Mormon Temple to someone of her
faith. At the present time, she has no present plans of marrying anyone
but she does desire to marry in her faith and claims that the opportunities
for such a marriage in Erie are very small and that she would be unable
to marry in a Temple here.

(6) She has introduced exhibits showing that she is a member of the
Blue Cross of Idaho, becoming a subscriber in 1972.

(7) She claims she may locate after graduation in any other of the 49
states or abroad. She may, of course, return to Pennsylvania. She, like
many other females, has vague intentions of marrying some day but does
not know to whom and in such case it is likely that she would follow
her husband where his work may take him.

We recognize that the problem of students' residence is not altogether a new one but has concerned the federal courts since Chicago and Northwestern Railway Company v. Ohle, 117 U.S. 123 (1886), where the court held that determinations of a domicile were a matter to be determined by the trier of fact.

The most recent exposition of the law on this subject for our edification by the Third Circuit is found in Krasnov v. Dinan, from which we quote at length:

> It is the citizenship of the parties at the time the action is commenced which is controlling. Brough v. Strathmann Supply Co., 358 F.2d 374 (3d Cir. 1966). One domiciled in a state when a suit is begun is "a citizen of that state within the meaning of the Constitution, art. 3, §2, and the Judicial Code. . . ." . . . *The fact of residency must be coupled with a finding of intent to remain indefinitely.* Proof of intent to remain permanently is not the test. "If the new state is to be one's home for an *indefinite period of time, he has acquired a new domicile.*" Gallagher v. Philadelphia Transp. Co. *Where jurisdictional allegations are traversed, as here, "the burden of showing . . . that the federal court has jurisdiction rests upon the complaints.*" Gibbs v. Buck, 307 U.S. 66, 72. "In determining whether a party has intended to establish a domicile in the state to which he has moved, the fact finder will look to such circumstances as his declarations, exercise of political rights, payment of personal taxes, house of residence, and place of business." Wright, Federal Courts §26, at 87 (2d ed. 1970); Mitchell v. United States, 88 U.S.(21 Wall.) 350, 353. . . .
>
> Applying these principles to the evidence before the fact finder, we cannot construe, as clearly erroneous, its finding that the defendant "intended to remain in the Commonwealth for an indefinite period of time." *Because animo manendi[*] is at best a subjective manifestation, Dinan's own declarations of intent are important, as were his explanations of the lack of compulsion in religious order assignments and his failure to obtain a Pennsylvania driver's license.*

We also have further instruction on this subject in the case in Judge Hastie's opinion in Gallagher v. Philadelphia Transportation Company, in which the lower court was criticized as putting too much emphasis on permanence of the attachment to a given state. We also quote at length from this decision:

> The emphasis of the court on the permanence of the anticipated attachment to a state, in our opinion, required too much of the plaintiff. . . . It is enough to intend to make the new state one's home. Restatement, Conflict of Laws(1934)§§19, 20; Chicago & Northwestern Ry. Co. v. Ohle,

* [Intent to remain. — ED.]

1885, 117 U.S. 123. It is not important if there is within contemplation a vague possibility of eventually going elsewhere, or even of returning whence one came. Goodrich, Handbook of the Conflict of Laws (3d ed. 1949) §28. If the new state is to be one's home for an indefinite period of time, he has acquired a new domicile. Mid-Continent Pipe Line Co. v. Whitely, 10 Cir. 1940, 116 F.2d 871. Finally, it is the intention at the time of arrival which is important. The fact that the plaintiff may later have acquired doubts about remaining in her new home or may have been called upon to leave it is not relevant, so long as the subsequent doubt or the circumstance of the leaving does not indicate that the intention to make the place the plaintiff's home never existed.

In the light of the foregoing and in view of the current tendency to treat students 18 years of age and above as emancipated and particularly in view of the fact that in this case the plaintiff has rented an apartment in Rexburg and with due regard for Judge Goodrich's statement from his Handbook of the Conflict of Laws that the possibility of eventually going elsewhere or even returning whence one came does not defeat the acquisition of a new domicile, we conclude upon the *facts of this case* considering the student's connection with Idaho and her subjective intention of not returning to Pennsylvania in the foreseeable future that she is a citizen of Idaho for the purpose of diversity jurisdiction and the motion to dismiss must be denied.

NOTES AND PROBLEMS

1. How did the court reach its conclusion?

a. Would the result have been the same if Ms.Gordon had lived in a dormitory?

b. Would the result have changed if defendants had found out that Ms.Gordon had an Idaho Blue Cross card only because the college had required her to do so?

c. What would happen if Ms.Gordon moved back to Erie six months after filing suit? What about six days?

2. Put yourself in the position of Gordon's lawyer as he thought about the significance of the questions above. His goal was to achieve a satisfactory outcome to his client's claim for medical malpractice.

a. Filing in federal court was one possible route. What advantages might such a filing have?

i. Speed might be one: Some federal courts have shorter waiting times to trial than do state courts.

ii. Tactical advantage might be another: There is one federal district judge in Erie, so Gordon's lawyer would know in advance who would be hearing the case.

b. What was the alternative to filing in federal district court?

3. Did Gordon's lawyer take a risk by filing in federal rather than in state court, where jurisdiction would have been clear? Suppose the court had reached the opposite conclusion — that Ms. Gordon was a Pennsylvania resident.

a. The federal district court would have dismissed the case, ending the lawsuit.

b. Could Gordon's lawyer then have refiled in a state court? The answer is a bit complex, but he probably could not: Given the length of time it took to process the federal lawsuit, the statute of limitations would likely have expired; if so, Gordon's state court suit would be barred.

c. If the scenario described in Note 3b occurred, would Gordon have a remedy? Against whom?

4. On the basis of the preceding case, you decide to bring Peters's case in a federal court. Peters will return to school next week. Do you think that it is a better idea to file the case now or to wait? If you think waiting is a good idea, do you have any advice concerning things Peters might do when he returns to school?

2.   Personal Jurisdiction

After deciding whether to file Peters's suit in a federal or state court, we still have to decide in which state to bring the case. Whether the suit is commenced in a state court or in a federal court located in a particular state, it may be brought only in a state where the defendant is subject to *personal jurisdiction*. That is, the state court or federal court in that state must have the power to render a judgment against this particular defendant — Dodge, in our hypothetical case. For present purposes, you may assume that the personal jurisdiction of a federal court within a given state is the same as that of a state court in the same state. Federal Rule of Civil Procedure 4(k)(1)(A).* That is, if Peters can obtain personal jurisdiction over Dodge in the state court in a given state, he can also obtain personal jurisdiction in a federal court in the same state.

---

* Hereafter, we will simply cite these as Rule _____. The Federal Rules of Civil Procedure, which govern procedure in the district courts, are promulgated by the U.S. Supreme Court pursuant to 28 U.S.C. §2072.

Traditionally, obtaining personal jurisdiction over a defendant required service of process on such defendant (that is, someone's handing to the defendant papers containing the complaint and an order to come to court to explain his conduct) within the particular state. Today, courts assert jurisdiction over persons who were not personally served within the state. For example, a person permanently residing in Illinois is subject to jurisdiction in that state even if served outside of its borders. Courts have also held that persons who engaged in certain types of activities in a state are subject to jurisdiction for claims arising from those activities. For example, in the early part of this century, many states enacted so-called nonresident motorist statutes, which provided that any nonresident who drove within a state was subject to personal jurisdiction in the state for claims arising from accidents. The notion of personal jurisdiction has since expanded far beyond that, as you will see in Chapter II.

NOTES AND PROBLEMS

1. So far as federal subject matter jurisdiction is concerned, Peters could sue Dodge in a federal court anywhere in the nation.

2. How does the doctrine of personal jurisdiction narrow Peters's choice of courts?

  a. Is Dodge subject to personal jurisdiction in Illinois?

  b. Is Dodge subject to personal jurisdiction in Michigan?

3. Venue

There is a third set of rules regulating the place where Peters can bring his action, and these are rules of *venue*. The term "venue" means, quite simply, "place of trial," and venue rules are an attempt to allocate business among those courts that have subject matter and personal jurisdiction. A suit lies open to a defendant's challenge unless the court has subject matter jurisdiction, personal jurisdiction, *and* venue.

Where would venue be proper if Peters brought his suit in a federal court? To apply the federal venue rules, a brief word must be said about the structure of the federal court system. There are three levels of federal courts. Actions are commenced and tried in the *district courts*. A district sometimes comprises part of a state and sometimes the entire state. Thus, Illinois has three districts; Michigan, two districts; California, four districts; and Kansas, a single district. The intermediate federal courts, called the *courts of appeals*, hear appeals from the district courts. The courts of appeals hear cases from district courts in regions covering several states, each region being called a "circuit." There are 11 circuits covering the 50 states, a twelfth for the District of Columbia, and a thirteenth, the Court of Appeals for the Federal Circuit, which hears appeals in certain specialized cases — patent actions, for example. Thus the Court of Appeals for the Second Circuit hears cases from the district courts in Connecticut, Vermont, and New York; the Court of Appeals for the Seventh Circuit hears cases from the district courts in Indiana, Illinois, and Wisconsin. Atop the courts of appeals is the *Supreme Court of the United States.*

Assume we have decided to file our case in a federal court in Illinois, which is divided into three districts — the Northern District (the northern part of the state, including Chicago); the Central District (the southeastern part of the state, including Champaign); and the Southern District (the southwestern part of the state).

NOTES AND PROBLEMS

1. Examine 28 U.S.C. §1391(a). On the facts of Peters v. Dodge, where will venue be proper ("lie" in lawyer's jargon)?
2. Why won't venue lie in the Eastern District of Michigan (which includes Ann Arbor, Michigan, where Peters attends school)?

If Peters's case had been brought in a state court, we would encounter similar venue rules. Most often, the states have set up a number of judicial districts with one court of general jurisdiction for each district. Usually the judicial districts are set up along county lines, although for less populous counties, one judicial district may cover several counties. The state venue rules would tell us in which judicial district to bring the case. Although state venue rules vary widely, most permit the case to be brought where either party resides, where the claim arose, or where a defendant is doing business. Thus, if our case had been brought in the Circuit Court of Illinois, proper venue would lie in the Circuit Court for Champaign County.

4. Service of Process

Once we (as advisers to Peters's lawyer) have decided where to bring the suit, we must begin the action and notify the defendant that it has begun. The first thing to do is to draft a *complaint*. See Forms 9-12 for examples of common sorts of claims.* A copy of the complaint must be filed with the court. Rule 3.

Then the plaintiff's lawyer must decide how to notify the defendant. Rule 4 sets forth two basic means of notice, one inexpensive and informal, the other more expensive and formal. The inexpensive method, called waiver of service, involves mailing the defendant the complaint and Forms 1A and 1B; if the defendant mails back a signed copy of Form 1B, the suit can proceed. The expensive method, used if the defendant refuses to cooperate, requires the lawyer to draft a *summons* (see Form 1), and take it to the clerk of the court, who will sign and seal it. See Rule 4(a) and (b). The summons and complaint must then be "served" — that is, delivered to the defendant in one of the ways authorized by Rule 4 — by private process servers or, in exceptional cases, a federal marshal. See Rule 4(c).

C. Stating the Case

1. The Lawyer's Responsibility

The preceding paragraphs referred in passing to the lawyer's drafting of a complaint. Do not be misled by that casual reference: A complaint asks the formal legal system to use governmental power to grant plaintiff relief. Those invoking that system also bear the responsibility not to invoke it for improper purposes. Lawyers bear special burdens in this respect. Read Rule 11 and consider it in connection with the next case.

Bridges v. Diesel Service, Inc.
1994 U.S. Dist. LEXIS 9429 (E.D. Pa. 1994)

HUYETT, J.

I. Background

James Bridges ("Plaintiff") commenced this action against Diesel Service, Inc. ("Defendant") under the Americans with Disabilities Act ("ADA"),

---

* The drafters of the Federal Rules have compiled an Appendix of Forms for use with the Rules. See Rule 84. These will be cited as Form ___.

42 U.S.C. §12101 et seq. [Bridges alleged that Diesel Service dismissed him from his job as a result of a disability and thus violated the ADA.] By Order dated June 29, 1994, the Court dismissed Plaintiff's Complaint without prejudice for failure to exhaust administrative remedies. In particular, Plaintiff did not file a charge with the Equal Employment Opportunity Commission ("EEOC") until after commencement of this action. Defendant now moves for sanctions pursuant to Fed. R. Civ. P. 11. . . .

II.   Discussion

. . . [A]s explained in this Court's June 29 Order, the filing of a charge with the EEOC is . . . a condition precedent to maintenance of a discrimination suit under the ADA. The parties do not dispute that administrative remedies must be exhausted before commencement of an action under the ADA. Indeed, Plaintiff's counsel stated that it would stipulate to dismissal of the Complaint without prejudice provided Defendant does not explicitly retain the right to move for sanctions under Fed. R. Civ. P. 11. . . .

Rule 11 "imposes an obligation on counsel and client analogous to the railroad crossing sign, 'Stop, Look and Listen.' It may be rephrased, 'Stop, Think, Investigate and Research' before filing papers either to initiate the suit or to conduct the litigation." Gaiardo v. Ethyl Corp., 835 F.2d 479, 482 (3d Cir. 1987). Rule 11 is violated only if, at the time of signing, the signing of the document filed was objectively unreasonable under the circumstances. "The Rule does not permit the use of the 'pure heart and an empty head' defense." Gaiardo, 835 F.2d at 482. Rather, counsel's signature certifies the pleading is supported by a reasonable factual investigation and "a normally competent level of legal research." Lieb v. Topstone Industries, Inc., 788 F.2d 151, 157 (3d Cir. 1986).

The Court is not convinced that Plaintiff's counsel displayed a competent level of legal research. A brief review of case law would have revealed the EEOC filing requirement. Further, an award of sanctions for failure to exhaust administrative remedies is not unprecedented.

Notwithstanding, the Court will not grant sanctions. Rule 11 is not intended as a general fee-shifting device. The prime goal of Rule 11 sanctions is deterrence of improper conduct. In this case, monetary sanctions are not necessary to deter future misconduct. Plaintiff's counsel immediately acknowledged its error and attempted to rectify the situation by filing a charge with the EEOC and moving to place this action in civil suspense. In fact, the Complaint has been dismissed without prejudice. The Court expects that Plaintiff's counsel has learned its lesson and will demonstrate greater diligence in future.

Further, Rule 11 sanctions should be reserved for those exceptional circumstances where the claim asserted is patently unmeritorious or frivolous. The mistake in the present case was procedural rather than substantive. It is also possible that Plaintiff's counsel was confused by the different interpretations of the Supreme Court's holding in [a case interpreting the EEOC filing requirement]. Finally, the Court is aware of the need to avoid "chilling" Title VII litigation.

III. Conclusion

For the above stated reasons, Defendant's motion pursuant to Fed. P. Civ. P. 11 is DENIED. However, this Opinion should not be read as condoning the conduct of Plaintiff's counsel. As stated above, the standard of pre-filing research was below that required of competent counsel. Plaintiff's case has been dismissed without prejudice. If the action is refiled, the Court fully expects to see a high standard of legal product from Plaintiff's counsel — in particular attorney London, who signed the Complaint.

NOTES AND PROBLEMS

1. What did the plaintiff's lawyer do wrong according to the court? What should she have done? What provision of Rule 11(b) was violated?

2. The court concludes that the plaintiff's lawyer violated Rule 11 by signing and filing a complaint that was "objectively unreasonable under the circumstances." But the court nevertheless declines to impose a sanction. What word in Rule 11(c) gives the court this discretion?

3. The judge, the defendant, and the plaintiff agree that the complaint was defective *and* that it will be easy to cure the defect by filing the right piece of paper with the Commission. If the defect is so minor and so easy to cure, why did the defendant bother to file a motion for sanctions?

a. One possibility is that the defendant hoped to collect fees for the relatively small amount of time necessary to bring the preceding motion to dismiss. Possible, but not likely: Most judges would view such a motion as a waste of time — and think ill of the defendant's lawyer for imposing on the court.

b. Consider another possibility. Many employment discrimination lawyers would say that the EEOC filing requirement as a precondition of suit was quite elementary, and that a lawyer unfamiliar with it was likely not familiar with this area of the law. Supposing such an assessment to be correct, consider what signals the defendant's lawyer would be sending to the judge with such a motion. Are there signs in the opinion that the judge has heard those between-the-lines signals?

2.   The Complaint

Bridges illustrates one facet of a lawyer's responsibility in drafting a complaint. But even if Peters's lawyer is entirely comfortable that the claim is well grounded in fact and in law, she must still confront the task of setting forth that claim in a formal document. What should be in a complaint? Should it contain a simple statement that Peters is suing Dodge for injuries suffered in an accident, a detailed recitation of what each party did on the day of the accident, and a blow-by-blow account of plaintiff's injuries and recovery, or something else? The model forms furnish some guidance. See, for example, Form 9.

Bell v. Novick Transfer Co.
17 F.R.D. 279 (D. Md. 1955)

THOMPSEN, J.

In this tort action, originally filed in the Court of Common Pleas of Baltimore City, and removed to this court pursuant to 28 U.S.C. §§1441 and 1446, defendants have moved to "dismiss the Declaration" because (1) it "fails to state a claim against the defendants and each of them upon which relief can be granted"; (2) it "alleges only that an accident occurred due to the negligence of the defendants as a result of which the plaintiffs were injured"; and (3) it "fails to allege the specific acts of negligence by the defendants of which the plaintiffs complain."

The [complaint, known in Maryland as a] declaration[,] alleges that [1] "on or about August 14, 1954, while the Infant Plaintiff, Ronald Bell, was riding in an automobile headed in a northerly direction on Race Road at its intersection with Pulaski Highway, both said road and highway being public highways of Baltimore County, State of Maryland, the automobile in which the infant plaintiff was riding was run into and struck by an automobile tractor-trailer outfit owned by the Defendants, Novick Transfer Company, Inc., and Katie Marie Parsons, and operated at the time by their agent, servant or employee, the Defendant, Morris Jarrett Coburn, III, in a careless, reckless and negligent manner, in a westerly direction on Pulaski Highway at the intersection aforesaid, [2] so that" the infant plaintiff was injured. The declaration also alleges the injuries and damage, and that they were "the direct result of the negligence on the part of the defendants" without any negligence on the part of the plaintiffs contributing thereto.

Although this declaration may not be sufficient under Maryland practice, Jeter v. Schwind Quarry Co., it meets the requirements of Rule 8,
Fed. Rules Civ. Proc., which requires only "a short and plain statement
of the claim showing that the pleader is entitled to relief." See Official
Form 9 in Appendix to Rules.

Nor is defendant entitled in this case to "a more definite statement"
by motion under Rule 12(e). Although some courts have held that such
a motion is the correct procedure to follow if a party needs further
information to prepare his defense, the better rule of law is that such
information should be obtained by interrogatories under Rule 33, or
other discovery procedure, unless it is really necessary to enable the party
to frame his responsive pleading.

Defendant may obtain by interrogatories or other discovery procedure
the facts upon which plaintiff based its allegations that the truck was
being operated in a careless, reckless and negligent manner, and that
such negligence was the direct cause of the injury to the infant plaintiff.

The motion is hereby overruled.

NOTES AND PROBLEMS

1. To understand what this fight is about, reread the second paragraph
of the opinion, which quotes the significant parts of the complaint, which
are preceded by numbers in square brackets (e.g., [1]). Imagine yourself
in the position of the defendant. What other information would defendant
want the complaint to contain?

a. If the plaintiff knew this information, why not require him to state
it in the complaint?

b. If the plaintiff did not know this information, would filing the
complaint violate Rule 11? (The case arose before the current version
of Rule 11.)

2. Notice that the plaintiff alleged that his own negligence did not
contribute to the accident.

a. Was this necessary? Rule 8(c).

b. Supposing it was not necessary, why might the plaintiff nevertheless
want to include it in a complaint?

3. The court in passing notes that the complaint was not sufficiently
detailed to pass muster under the then-prevailing Maryland state court
pleading rules.

a. Where was the suit originally filed?

b. How did it get to federal court? The case tells us it was "removed."
As you will see, under some circumstances it is possible for a defendant
to second-guess plaintiff's original choice of a court. Defendant here did

so, by "removing" the case to federal district court. Does the outcome of this case suggest that doing so was a mistake?

On the basis of *Novick Transfer Co.*, Peters's attorney has drafted the following complaint:

United States District Court for the Central District of Illinois

Paul Peters,
        Plaintiff

COMPLAINT FOR NEGLIGENCE

v.

File No. _____

Dan Dodge,
        Defendant

Plaintiff, Paul Peters, for his complaint, alleges as follows:

1. Plaintiff, Paul Peters, is a citizen of the state of Michigan, and defendant, Dan Dodge, is a citizen of the state of Illinois. The matter in controversy exceeds $75,000, exclusive of interest and costs.

2. On January 1, 2000, Paul Peters was operating his car on Main Street in Champaign, Illinois.

3. At 4:00 P.M. on that date, a car owned and operated by defendant Dan Dodge negligently collided with plaintiff's car, causing damage to plaintiff's car and injury to plaintiff's person.

4. Plaintiff suffered a sprained neck, broken arm, and numerous bruises and lacerations, and incurred medical expenses in the amount of $25,000.

WHEREFORE, plaintiff demands judgment for $100,000, together with the costs of this action.

Ursula Sands
Attorney for Plaintiff
123 Church Street
Champaign, Illinois 61820
217/353-5775

3. The Response — Motions and Answer

Once the defendant has been properly notified of the claim, attention shifts to his response — the defense of the action. Although it would be possible to have a system in which defendant was not required to do anything until trial, both the Federal Rules and state codes of procedure require some response by the defendant. Generally, that response takes one of two forms: a *motion* attacking the summons and complaint in some way or a responsive pleading (usually called an *answer*).

Theoretically, six types of responses are available to a defendant. They are outlined briefly below:

Preanswer Motions

Motions are simply requests to the court that it do something; lawyers speak of "moving" or of "making a motion" to have the court take some step — dismiss the case, enter judgment on a verdict, and so on. As you will see, most procedural topics express themselves through appropriate motions. At the early stages of the complaint, there are various motions that a defendant may make to end the case or to alter its shape.

1. There may be reasons, having nothing to do with the claim itself, why the action should not proceed. These reasons typically relate to the court in which the action is brought or the method by which the defendant was brought into that court. For example, the defendant may contend that the case should be dismissed because it does not belong in federal court (subject matter jurisdiction); such a motion brought forth the opinion in Gordon v. Steele, the first case in this chapter. See Rule 12(b)(1). Or the defendant might argue that the court had no power over the person of the defendant (personal jurisdiction), that venue was improper, or that the summons was defective or was improperly served. See Rule 12(b)(1)-(5). A somewhat related response (because again it assumes the truth of plaintiff's complaint) is the claim that plaintiff has failed to join a party whose presence is vital to the case. See Rule 12(b)(7).

2. The defendant may say that, even if everything in the complaint is true, under the substantive law plaintiff has no right to relief. The typical elementary example is a complaint that alleges that the defendant made a face at the plaintiff or that the defendant drove a car of an offensive color. At common law, the defendant would *demur* to such claims; now we say that the complaint fails to state a claim upon which relief can be granted. See Rule 12(b)(6). Bell v. Novick Transfer was written in response to the defendant's Rule 12(b)(6) motion.

3. The defendant may be unsure of what is being asserted, finding the complaint either vague or confused and complicated. In this case, defendant might want a "more definite statement" of the complaint.

See Rule 12(e). (Defendant in Bell v. Novick Transfer made a Rule 12(e) motion.)

The Answer

Notice an important characteristic of the motions described above: *they take no position on the truth or falsity of plaintiff's allegations.* By contrast, an *answer*, as the name suggests, does respond to the allegations of the complaint. There are only two essential variations on the answer:

1. In the most common response to a complaint the defendant denies the truth of one or more of the allegations of the complaint, or, if the defendant does not know whether an allegation is true, he may deny the allegation until he finds out. See Rule 8(b).

2. The defendant may want to assert additional matters that will wholly or partially defeat plaintiff's claim. For example, the defendant may claim that the applicable statute of limitations has run or that the plaintiff has released her claim. We call such assertions *affirmative defenses.* See Rule 8(c).

These five categories of motions and answers exhaust most possible responses to the complaint. It is common, however, for the defendant to want to assert his own claims against the plaintiff, another defendant, or a new party. Such claims are called, respectively, *counterclaims, cross-claims,* and *third-party claims.* See Rules 13(a), (b), (g), and 14. We will discuss this sixth category of responses in a subsequent section.

In modern procedure a defendant may respond to the complaint using several of the categories sketched above. For example, the defendant in Bell v. Novick Transfer made both Rule 12(b)(6) and Rule 12(e) motions. With a little effort one can hypothesize situations in which a defendant would want to assert all six possible responses to the complaint.

Once you have digested this catalogue of responses to the complaint, it is important to know that there is still one procedural distinction among them. The Rules (and analogous state procedural systems) permit the defendant to make the first three kinds of response in a *pre-answer motion.* Rule 12(a). The remaining responses may be made only in an answer. This distinction matters because in an answer, unlike a pre-answer motion, the defendant must take a position as to the truth of the plaintiff's allegations. To take such a stance will often require expensive factual investigation, so if a pre-answer motion is available, defendants often find it attractive.

NOTES AND PROBLEMS

1. If the defendant makes a pre-answer motion, what does she want the court to do? (Consider Gordon v. Steele and Bell v. Novick Transfer

as examples.) If the court grants the motion, why is the defendant not required to answer the complaint?

    2. Can the defendant make a pre-answer motion on the ground

    a. that everything the plaintiff alleges is false?

    b. that she was not properly served with a copy of the complaint?

    c. that venue is improper?

Suppose that in our hypothetical case Dodge wants to have the case dismissed on the ground that he and Peters are not of diverse citizenship. To accomplish that goal Dodge might file the following papers:

United States District Court for the Central District of Illinois

Paul Peters,
               Plaintiff

   v.

Dan Dodge,
               Defendant

File No. _____

NOTICE OF MOTION TO DISMISS;
MEMORANDUM OF POINTS AND
    AUTHORITIES;
AND DECLARATION OF DAN
    DODGE

To Plaintiff Paul Peters and Ursula Sands, his attorney of record:

    You and each of you will please take notice that on February 1, 2000 at 9:00 A.M. in the courtroom of the Hon. Even Hand, Defendant Dan Dodge will move the court for an order dismissing the complaint in the above-titled matter.

    Said motion will be made pursuant to Federal Rule 12(b)(1) on the ground that this Court lacks subject matter jurisdiction because no diversity of citizenship exists between Plaintiff Paul Peters and Defendant Dan Dodge.

    Said motion will be based on this notice and on the accompanying memorandum of points and authorities and declaration of Dan Dodge.

Memorandum of Points and Authorities

    1. A federal district court lacks diversity jurisdiction under 28 U.S.C. §1332(a)(1) when plaintiff and defendant are citizens of the same state. Gordon v. Steele, 376 F. Supp. 575 (W.D. Pa. 1974).

2. A person is a citizen of a state if such person resides there with the intent to remain indefinitely. Id.

3. In determining whether a person is a citizen of a given state, objective indicia as well as the person's own declarations of intent are important. Id.

4. In paragraph one of his complaint, plaintiff asserts that he is a citizen of Michigan and that defendant is a citizen of Illinois.

5. The attached declaration of Dan Dodge and the certified public records attached thereto demonstrate that Paul Peters maintains a residence in Illinois, is registered to vote there, maintains his car registration there, and lists Illinois as his home on his auto insurance policy.

6. Accordingly, plaintiff Paul Peters is a citizen of Illinois, and plaintiff and defendant are therefore citizens of the same state. Diversity of citizenship is therefore lacking and the case should be dismissed.

Yvonne O. Upton
Attorney for Defendant
125 Church St.
Champaign, IL
217/353-7531

The attached declaration, probably drafted by Dodge's lawyer, would contain assertions by Dodge, sworn under penalty of perjury, to the effect stated in paragraph 5 of the Memorandum of Points and Authorities. In drafting this declaration, Dodge's lawyer would have to make sure that the declaration set forth facts that are admissible under the rules of evidence. Although the law of evidence is complex (and is covered in a separate course), speaking generally one can say that it would allow Dodge to assert only matters that Dodge or whoever signed the declaration observed first-hand (such as the address listed on the insurance records Peters gave to Dodge at the scene of accident) and matters proved by certified public records (such as Peters's voter and auto registration).

NOTES AND PROBLEMS

1. Notice that the document above — a very short but otherwise realistic example — has several parts:

a. A notice of the motion — which simply tells the other side that the defendant plans to make a motion, what that motion is (here, a motion to dismiss for want of subject matter jurisdiction), and the time and place at which the motion will be heard by the judge;

b. The memorandum of points and authorities. This is the legal and factual basis for the argument.

2. The judge will typically have read the "motion papers" before the hearing and will usually hear oral argument from the lawyers. She may decide the motion on the spot or she may "reserve" her ruling, making it after additional thought or research.

3. If Dodge wins this motion, what will the court do?

If the defendant does not make a pre-answer motion or if the court denies a pre-answer motion, the defendant must then answer. See Rules 7(a), 12(a). Generally, the defendant can include any or all of the possible responses in his answer.* Thus a defendant may claim that the complaint does not state a claim upon which relief can be granted, deny various allegations of the complaint, and allege various affirmative defenses. See Form 20. The defendant cannot now respond that he needs a more definite statement. Why is that?

Turning to Peters's case, one can surmise that Dodge's attorney will conclude that there is no question relating to personal jurisdiction or venue and that there are no problems with the process itself or service of process. On the other hand, Dodge may very well question the subject matter jurisdiction of the court; it may be that Peters's case is distinguishable from *Gordon* or that this district may not agree with *Gordon*. And Dodge probably will want to deny certain allegations of the complaint, such as the allegation that defendant was negligent, and also may want to allege various affirmative defenses. For example, in such a case it is quite common for a defendant to claim that the plaintiff's contributory negligence was, at least in part, the cause of the accident. In all states, such contributory negligence will act as a complete or partial defense to recovery.

Before drafting our answer, we also must ask whether defendant wants to make any claim of his own, which would have to be included in the answer. There are three such possibilities: counterclaims, cross-claims, and third-party claims.

Counterclaims. It may well be that Dodge has a claim against Peters. For example, if Dodge was injured in the same accident, Dodge might want to sue Peters for his injuries. Such claims are called *counterclaims*.

---

* There are exceptions if the defendant has made a pre-answer motion and has not included certain defenses. See Rule 12(g), (h). We shall save these more intricate rules for later.

Rule 13 divides counterclaims into two categories: *compulsory counter-claims* and *permissive counterclaims.* A compulsory counterclaim is one that arises out of the same "transaction or occurrence" as plaintiff's claim, and a permissive counterclaim is one that does not arise out of the same transaction or occurrence as plaintiff's claim.

NOTES AND PROBLEMS

1. Within what category does Dodge's claim for personal injuries in the collision fall?

2. If Dodge's claim is compulsory and he does not include it in this action, what do you think the consequences will be?

3. What if Dodge had earlier lent Peters money, and Peters had not repaid it. Can Dodge bring a claim for the debt as a counterclaim? What kind of counterclaim?

Cross-claims.   Often, a plaintiff will sue several defendants; one of those defendants might then want to sue another for claims arising out of the same transaction. For example, if a pedestrian had been injured in the Peters-Dodge auto accident, he might sue both Peters and Dodge. In such a case, Peters might deny the pedestrian's claim of negligence and also may claim that Dodge was at fault and is liable to Peters for his injuries in the same accident. If Peters asserted such a claim against Dodge, it would be called a *cross-claim.* See Rule 13(g). Counterclaims involve parties on opposite sides of the "v." that divides plaintiff from defendant in the name of the lawsuit; cross-claims involve parties on the same side of the "v."

NOTES AND PROBLEMS

1. On the facts just noted, can Peters cross-claim against Dodge for breach of a contract for the sale of goods?

2. In the original Peters-Dodge action, there will not be any cross-claims because there is only one party on each side of the lawsuit, and cross-claims are possible only when there are at least two parties on the same side of the suit.

Third-party claims.   In some cases, a defendant may want to assert a claim against a party not in the action. Rule 14 would permit Dodge to file a *third-party complaint* against (*implead*) any party that is liable to

Dodge for Peters's claim against Dodge. Suppose Dodge was engaged on an assignment for Tucker at the time of the accident and Tucker had agreed to indemnify Dodge for any liabilities Dodge incurred in performing this mission. Dodge could implead Tucker as a third-party defendant. In such a suit, Peters would be the plaintiff, Dodge would be the defendant and third-party plaintiff, and Tucker would be the third-party defendant.*

After considering the possible responses and possible counterclaims, cross-claims, and third-party claims, Dodge's attorney has drafted the following answer to Peters's complaint.

United States District Court for the Central District of Illinois

Paul Peters,	
Plaintiff	ANSWER AND COUNTERCLAIM
v.	
	File No. _____
Dan Dodge,	
Defendant	

Defendant, Dan Dodge, answers the complaint of plaintiff herein as follows:

1. Admits that defendant is a citizen of the state of Illinois, and, except as admitted, denies the allegations of paragraph 1 of the complaint.

2. Admits that, at approximately 4:00 PM on January 1, 2000, plaintiff was operating a car on Main Street in Champaign, Illinois, and, except as admitted, states that defendant is without information or belief sufficient to form a belief as to the truth of the allegations in paragraph 2 of the complaint and, on that basis, denies the allegations of paragraph 2 of the complaint.

3. Admits that, at approximately 4:00 PM on January 1, 2000, there was a collision between a car owned and operated by defendant and a car owned and operated by plaintiff and that plaintiff's vehicle was damaged and plaintiff suffered some injury as a result of said

---

* If a third party is brought in, it may be possible for each of the parties to make claims against the others. We will save discussion of issues related to such multiple claims until later.

collision and, except as admitted, defendant denies the allegations
of paragraph 3 of the complaint.

4. Defendant states that he is without information sufficient to
form a belief as to the truth of the allegations in paragraph 4 of the
complaint and, on that basis, denies the allegations of paragraph 4
of the complaint.

FIRST DEFENSE
5. The court lacks jurisdiction over the subject matter of this
action because plaintiff and defendant are not citizens of different states.

SECOND DEFENSE
6. Defendant alleges that plaintiff drove his car carelessly and
recklessly, and that such careless and reckless operation was a cause
of the accident.

COUNTERCLAIM
7. On January 1, 2000, at approximately 4:00 PM at Main Street
in Champaign, Illinois, Paul Peters drove a car in a careless, reckless,
and negligent manner and thereby caused said car to collide with
a car owned and operated by Dan Dodge.

8. As a result of said collision, Dodge's car was damaged, and
Dodge also suffered a whiplash injury, as well as numerous cuts
and bruises, and incurred expenses for medical treatment of $1,800.

WHEREFORE, defendant demands judgment dismissing Peters's action and judgment against Peters on the counterclaim in
the amount of $12,000, together with the costs thereof.

Yvonne O. Upton
Attorney for Defendant
125 Church Street
Champaign, Illinois 61820
217/353-7531

NOTES AND PROBLEMS

1. Contrast this answer with the Motion to Dismiss illustrated in the
previous section.

a. Note first the difference in scope. Unlike the motion, the answer
responds to all the allegations of the complaint, rather than selecting
one or two vulnerable aspects.

b. Unlike the motion, the answer seeks no immediate relief from the court; instead it sets the stage for various future battles. For example, if Dodge had not made a pre-answer motion on this basis, he could, on the basis of his first defense, seek to have the case dismissed for want of subject matter jurisdiction, but the answer itself does not seek this immediate termination of the lawsuit.

c. The motion consists of an assertion — that there is no subject matter jurisdiction — and then both factual (Dodge's declaration) and legal (the memorandum of points and authorities) material backing up this assertion. By contrast, the answer, like the complaint, consists entirely of assertions and leaves to later stages of the lawsuit the development of factual and legal material backing up these assertions.

2. What would happen if the answer failed to respond to some of the allegations of the complaint? See Rule 8(d).

3. What is the purpose and effect of stating that the defendant lacked information or belief sufficient to admit or deny some of the allegations of the complaint? See Rule 8(b).

4. Reread paragraph 3 of the complaint. Explain why Dodge could not have made a blanket denial of this paragraph on the grounds that he thought he wasn't negligent. See Rule 8(b).

5. Are the allegations in paragraph 7 of the answer ambiguous? What exactly is Dodge alleging? Having filed such a counterclaim, could Dodge seek to introduce evidence that Peters's brakes failed because he had not properly maintained them?

6. Now that Yvonne Upton has drafted the answer, what should she do with it? See Rule 5(a), (d).

4. Amendment of Pleadings

The Federal Rules reject the view that the case is "set in stone" once the pleadings are completed. Instead, the Rules reflect a liberal policy toward changes (called *amendments*) to the pleadings. In fact, the discovery rules, which enable parties to gather information about the case, would mean little if new information could not be reflected in amended pleadings.

Rule 15(a) sets forth the basic amendment rules and states that "leave to amend shall be freely given when justice so requires." Rule 15(c) deals with amendments that are interposed after the statute of limitations on the "new" claim has run. Rule 15(b) deals with amendments interposed during the course of trial to reflect the introduction of evidence that is not within the scope of the pleadings.

D.   Parties to the Lawsuit

Our Peters-Dodge lawsuit is an action by a single plaintiff against a single defendant, but litigation often is not so simple; the events giving rise to a lawsuit may affect more than two persons, sometimes many more. The procedural issues raised by the involvement of multiple parties are discussed under a variety of headings. First, who *may* be joined as a plaintiff or a defendant in the lawsuit? See Rule 20. Second, who *must* be joined as a plaintiff or a defendant in the lawsuit? See Rule 19. Third, are there persons who are not in the lawsuit who can be joined as parties if they so choose? See Rule 24. Fourth, may some of the parties in the lawsuit represent others who are not in the lawsuit, so that the final decision will determine the rights of all? See Rule 23. There are other party issues as well, but these will give you their flavor.

1.   Permissive Joinder

Rule 20 governs *permissive joinder*. Note that the plaintiff has a choice of whom to join as a coplaintiff as well as whom to join as a codefendant. Imagine that Peters was riding in the car with Passenger, and that the car had been struck by two other vehicles, one driven by Dodge and the other by Dusty. Assume Peters and Passenger decided to bring suit together against Dodge and Dusty. What happens if Dodge is dissatisfied with the defendant lineup and thinks that Dusty should not be in the suit? Dodge may claim that Dusty was not properly joined, Rule 21, or that the suits against Dodge and Dusty should be severed, Rule 42. Otherwise, Dodge must accept plaintiffs' choice of defendants.

NOTES AND PROBLEMS

1. Herman is driving a car in which his wife Wilma is a passenger. That car collides with a car driven by Dillon and owned by Owens. Consult Rule 20 to answer the following questions:
   a. May Herman and Wilma join as plaintiffs against Dillon?
   b. May Herman join both Dillon and Owens as defendants?
   c. May Herman join Dillon and General Motors (manufacturer of the car) as defendants if Herman is suing Dillon for driving too fast and GM for using defective brakes?

2. Assume that Herman meets with Dillon to attempt a settlement of claims arising from the accident, and Dillon's son, Sidney, punches Herman. May Herman join both Dillon and Sidney as defendants, suing

Dillon for injuries sustained in the accident and Sidney for battery? Or do these claims arise from different transactions?

Returning to our hypothetical case, what happens if the reason for Dodge's dissatisfaction with the defendant lineup is that he believes Daniels, who serviced Dodge's car, should also be in the lawsuit? Under some conditions Dodge may bring in Daniels as a third-party defendant pursuant to Rule 14(a). The Rule's text permits such joinder when Daniels "is or may be liable to [Dodge] for all or part of the plaintiff's claim against him." Such a situation might occur if Dodge alleged that his failure to stop resulted from Daniels's faulty adjustment of the car's brakes. Under those circumstances, Dodge, as the driver of the car, would be liable to Peters, but he could seek to pass that liability on to Daniels.

2. Compulsory Joinder

All the joinder rules surveyed thus far involve the question of when parties to a lawsuit *may* bring another party into the action. The third party might not be happy about the prospect of being brought in, but from the standpoint of those parties already in the suit, joinder is permissive — that is, they voluntarily sought to bring an additional party into the action. *Compulsory joinder*, on the other hand, involves bringing a party into a lawsuit by order of the court, even though the opposing party might not want him there. The subject has a convoluted history. Born of an important realization — that lawsuits may affect persons who are not formally parties — the principles of compulsory joinder aim at bringing into suits those who may be affected by their results. Rule 19 represents the present codification of this idea, an idea that has proved both difficult and controversial.

In general, courts call for joinder when the underlying substantive law in a suit involves rights or liabilities that are joint, when two or more parties are claiming the same property, or when granting relief to one party would necessarily affect the rights of another party. Common examples arise in cases involving property that is jointly owned or whose ownership is disputed. If Husband and Wife own property together, then they should both be joined as plaintiffs in a lawsuit for injury to the property, or as defendants in a lawsuit against them for misuse of the property. Similarly, if Trustee is unsure whether to give an antique vase to Son or Daughter, both should be joined in any litigation involving ownership of the vase.

The difficulty with compulsory joinder is that its impulse to do entire justice, and to do it in one lawsuit, runs afoul of two other principles:

the principle of party autonomy (the idea that it is the parties in the lawsuit who should control their own claims and their own litigative strategy); and the principle that courts should seek to decide the claims of the parties now before them. The next case shows a court wrestling with these irreconcilable principles.

Temple v. Synthes Corp.
498 U.S. 5, rehg. denied, 498 U.S. 1092 (1990)

Per Curiam.

Petitioner Temple, a Mississippi resident, underwent surgery in October 1986 in which a "plate and screw device" was implanted in his lower spine. The device was manufactured by respondent Synthes, Ltd. (U.S.A.) (Synthes), a Pennsylvania corporation. Dr. S. Henry LaRocca performed the surgery at St. Charles General Hospital in New Orleans, Louisiana. Following surgery, the device's screws broke off inside Temple's back.

Temple filed suit against Synthes in the United States District Court for the Eastern District of Louisiana. The suit, which rested on diversity jurisdiction, alleged defective design and manufacture of the device. At the same time, Temple filed a state administrative proceeding against Dr. LaRocca and the hospital for malpractice and negligence. At the conclusion of the administrative proceeding, Temple filed suit against the doctor and the hospital in Louisiana state court.

Synthes did not attempt to bring the doctor and the hospital into the federal action by means of a third-part complaint, as provided in Federal Rule of Civil Procedure 14(a). Instead, Synthes filed a motion to dismiss Temple's federal suit for failure to join necessary parties pursuant to Federal Rule of Civil Procedure 19. Following a hearing, the District Court ordered Temple to join the doctor and the hospital as defendants within twenty days or risk dismissal of the lawsuit. According to the court, the most significant reason for requiring joinder was the interest of judicial economy. The court relied on this Court's decision in Provident Tradesmens Bank & Trust Co. v. Patterson, 390 U.S. 102 (1968), wherein we recognized that one focus of Rule 19 is "the interest of the courts and the public in complete, consistent, and efficient settlement of controversies." When Temple failed to join the doctor and the hospital, the court dismissed the suit with prejudice.

Temple appealed, and the United States Court of Appeals for the Fifth Circuit affirmed. The court deemed it "obviously prejudicial to the defendants to have the separate litigations being carried on," because Synthes' defense might be that the plate was not defective but that the doctor and the hospital were negligent, while the doctor and hospital, on the other hand, might claim that they were not negligent but that the plate was defective. The Court of Appeals found that claims over-lapped and that the District Court therefore had not abused its discretion in ordering joinder under Rule 19. A petition for rehearing was denied.

In his petition for certiorari to this Court, Temple contends that it was error to label joint tortfeasors as indispensable parties under Rule 19(b) and to dismiss the lawsuit with prejudice for failure to join those parties. We agree. Synthes does not deny that it, the doctor, and the hospital are potential joint tortfeasors. It has long been the rule that it is not necessary for all joint tortfeasors to be named as defendants in a single lawsuit. Nothing in the 1966 revision of Rule 19 changed that principle. The Advisory Committee Notes to Rule 19(a) explicitly state that "a tortfeasor with the usual 'joint-and-several' liability is merely a permissive party to an action against another with like liability." Advisory Committee's Notes on Fed. Rule Civ. Proc. 19, 28 U.S.C. App., p. 594, at 595. There is nothing in Louisiana tort law to the contrary. See Mullins v. Skains, 252 La. 1009, 1014, 215 So. 2d 643, 645 (1968); La. Civ. Code Ann., Arts. 1794, 1975 (West 1987).

The opinion in *Provident Bank,* supra, does speak of the public interest in limiting multiple litigation, but that case is not controlling here. There, the estate of a tort victim brought a declaratory judgment action against an insurance company. We assumed that the policyholder was a person "who, under . . . [Rule 19](a), should be joined if 'feasible.' " 390 U.S., at 108, and went on to discuss the appropriate analysis under Rule 19(b), because the policyholder could not be joined without destroying diversity. After examining the factors set forth in Rule 19(b), we determined that the action could proceed without the policyholder; he therefore was not an indispensable party whose absence required dismissal of the suit.

Here, no inquiry under Rule 19(b) is necessary, because the threshold requirements of Rule 19(a) have not been satisfied. As potential joint tortfeasors with Synthes, Dr. LaRocca and the hospital were merely per-missive parties. The Court of Appeals erred by failing to hold that the District Court abused its discretion in ordering them joined as defendants and in dismissing the action when Temple failed to comply with the court's order. For these reasons, we grant the petition for certiorari, reverse the judgment of the Court of Appeals for the Fifth Circuit, and remand for further proceedings consistent with this opinion.

It is so ordered.

NOTES AND PROBLEMS

1. The opinion does not dispute the lower courts' conclusion that it would be more efficient to have all the litigation in a single forum. It

nevertheless holds that it was reversible error to dismiss the case. Moreover, the opinion was *per curiam* (by the court as a whole, rather than signed by an individual justice). Such brief, anonymous opinions are often used in cases for which the court believes the principles are clear beyond doubt and require no extended discussion. What principle is the court valuing more highly than the obvious efficiency of consolidating the cases?

2. What does the court mean when it notes that "Synthes did not attempt to bring the doctor and the hospital into the federal action by means of a third-party complaint, as provided in Federal Rule of Civil Procedure 14(a)." How would Synthes have done so, and what would the result have been?

3. If the plaintiff had wanted to sue both defendants in the same action, how would he have done so?

4. Why might the plaintiff have wanted to conduct separate lawsuits?

a. One obvious possibility — collecting twice for the same injuries — will not work: The legal system bars double compensation for the same injury.

b. Would there be any tactical advantages to having two bites at the apple?

3. Intervention

The rules on intervention mirror those on permissive and compulsory joinder. As noted, it is for the plaintiff to decide whom to join in the first instance, and the defendant can "force" parties into the lawsuit who should be present to avoid possible prejudice to both existing and excluded parties. But if the plaintiff does not wish to join a party, and the defendant either does not wish to join a party or is unable to convince a court that the party should be joined, the absent party can still seek to come into the suit. We call this *intervention*. Rule 24 divides intervention into two categories: *intervention as of right* and *permissive intervention*. Crudely put, a party has a right to intervene when a lawsuit conducted without him has the potential to inflict real hardship on him.

NOTES AND PROBLEMS

1. There is a collision between cars driven by Peters and Dodge. Peters sues Dodge. Passenger, who was riding in Dodge's car, seeks to intervene to assert a claim against Dodge. Although such a mode of proceeding might seem efficient, it interferes with Peters's autonomy. Consequently

courts will typically refuse to allow intervention under such circumstances, reasoning that Passenger is free to bring his own lawsuit.

2. Intervention is common in land-use litigation. Suppose the city of Dogpatch refuses a request by M that the city rezone certain land from residential/single-family to residential/multifamily, so that M could use the land to build garden apartments. M sues the city, claiming that the refusal is arbitrary and capricious. Use your intuition to decide who among the following should be permitted to intervene:

a. N, who lives next door to the proposed apartment complex;

b. T, who lives two blocks away and claims that the apartment complex will lower the value of his property (estimated at $250,000);

c. the Sierra Club of Dogpatch; and

d. the Board of Realtors of Dogpatch.

4.   Class Actions

The idea of a *class action* is simple enough. Assume that a given claim or claims involve a large number of plaintiffs or defendants. It would theoretically be possible to join all the plaintiffs or defendants in accordance with Rule 20. But if the number is large enough — for example, over 30 — the multiplicity of parties (and lawyers) would make the action cumbersome indeed. To the extent that the claims of the plaintiffs or defendants are similar, it would seem to make little sense to require joinder of such an excessive number of parties. Thus the solution: Allow some parties to stand in for the entire group.

The subject of class actions attracted comparatively little attention prior to 1966; in that year, however, Rule 23 of the Federal Rules was extensively revised, and that revision served as a catalyst for the development of a vast amount of legal learning and case development of issues surrounding class actions. Indeed, shortly after Professor Wright noted that it would be possible to write a book on class actions of the length of his treatise on federal courts (more than 550 pages), another author proved his estimate decidedly low by writing no fewer than six full volumes.*

The development of the class action has received mixed reviews, some arguing that in the class action lies the solution to the role of law in a mass society, others contending that it represents at best a nuisance, at worst an abuse of the judicial process. The debate over the merit of class actions reflects the uncertainty surrounding the question of what it means

---

* Herbert B. Newberg, Newberg on Class Actions (1977).

to represent another person — an important and troubling question that is fundamental to the idea of procedure in an adversarial system. These issues are too large to be addressed in this introductory survey. Students should scan Rule 23 to know that it exists, but should recognize however, that scanning will provide little of the flavor of the disputes that have raged around its text.

E.   Factual Development — Discovery

Questions of jurisdiction, pleading, and parties typically arise at what may be called the pleading stage of a lawsuit. In order to draft a complaint or answer, the parties must have some understanding of the facts underlying the suit. They can gather those facts in any of the ways in which ordinary citizens, unaided by official sanction, find out about things — through observation, personal knowledge, or conversations with anyone who will talk to them. Before the Federal Rules, factual development largely came about through such efforts of the parties. Much of it still does. Such private inquiry is difficult to "study" in law school, and is consequently often overlooked in civil procedure courses. The limits of such self-help inquiries are not well defined; use your common sense and intuition on the following problems.

NOTES AND PROBLEMS

1. In the Peters-Dodge case, assume that one of the issues in the suit is the seriousness of Peters's injuries and that Peters has been active in college athletics. Upton (Dodge's counsel) wishes to speak to coaches and the athletic department about Peters's pre-accident and postaccident performance. Can Upton question these people on the issue and, if so, how should she go about it?

2. Same facts except that Upton knows that Fred McGolf, an assistant coach, will be a major witness for plaintiff on the issue of Peters's injuries. Can Upton question McGolf?

3. Upton wants to know whether it is proper for her to employ a photographer for either of the following purposes:

a. to stand on the edge of the field where Peters's team practices (on university property, which is open to the public) to photograph Peters while he practices;

b. to sit in a car on the street outside Peters's dormitory to do "surveillance" videotaping.

In many cases, private inquiry by the parties simply won't work. For example, neither Peters nor Dodge is likely to voluntarily provide information to opposing counsel, and the prospects for obtaining information from witnesses such as Peters's parents, friends, or coach are low. People are sometimes reluctant to become involved in litigation or to produce pertinent information in the absence of legal compulsion. Accordingly, the Rules provide mechanisms for a party to obtain information about the case both from other parties in the case and from third parties not in the case. These rules are grouped under the heading of *discovery*.

The discovery rules, which compel the parties and others involved in a lawsuit to cooperate in the unearthing of factual background, are a major innovation of modern procedure (though they have antecedents in earlier practices). They are also a source of much dispute, both among the parties seeking and resisting discovery and among the commentators debating whether the effort and expense involved in discovery yields real returns either to the judicial system or to the parties.

There are five primary means of discovery. First, unless the court otherwise orders, the parties must, without being asked, reveal to each other certain basic information about the case — names of witnesses, the existence of documents, bases for damage calculations, and the like. See Rule 26(a)(1). Beyond these *disclosures*, the parties may seek additional information through several means.

Probably most important is the request for the production or *inspection of documents*. See Rules 34 and 45(a)(1)(C). "Documents" in this sense includes everything from printed and written papers to photographs, videotapes, sound recordings, and email. In most cases such records — often in the hands of third parties — will provide the backbone of evidence; in virtually every case such documents will be significant. In Peters v. Dodge, such records might include medical bills and receipts for car maintenance. If the records are in the hands of the opposing party, the requesting party uses Rule 34 to demand the production of "specified" documents, and the opposing party must produce the documents at the appointed time and place. Frequently, significant records will be in the hands of nonparties — financial institutions, physicians and hospitals, law enforcement authorities, and the like. If so, Rule 34 will not help because it applies only to parties. But documents can be obtained from other witnesses by subpoena pursuant to Rule 45 or, in the case of public agencies, by a simple request for public records. In Peters v. Dodge, such a document might be the police report of the accident.

Armed with such documents, the parties may want to conduct *oral depositions*. See Rules 30, 45. An oral deposition may be loosely described as a procedure for questioning a witness under oath in the absence of a judge. Anyone with information about the lawsuit may be deposed. To begin the process, the attorney taking the deposition serves a notice (and perhaps a subpoena), the person to be questioned shows up (often with an attorney) at the appointed time and place (usually the office of the questioning party), and takes an oath; questions are then asked of and answered by the witness, and the responses are recorded either by audio- or videotape or by a stenographer. There are procedures for handling objectionable questions and for terminating the deposition if it becomes abusive or exceeds the bounds of propriety. In Peters v. Dodge, it's likely that lawyers will want to depose at least the two parties, Peters and Dodge.

Next in importance are *written interrogatories*. See Rule 33. These are written questions to be answered, also in writing, by the opposing party. Written interrogatories can be used only against a party, not against nonparty witnesses. As might be expected, the party's lawyer plays a substantial role in formulating the answers. The most frequently productive use of such interrogatories is to locate relevant documents. In Peters v. Dodge, the parties might ask each other for the location of any records regarding maintenance of their cars and about the existence of medical records and treating physicians.

Finally, there are *physical and mental examinations*. See Rule 35. This discovery device differs from the others in that a motion first must be made to obtain the desired examination. Also, the party seeking the examination must demonstrate that the condition to be examined is in controversy and that there is good cause for the examination. Often, the existence of good cause is not seriously disputed. For example, physical examinations are allowed almost as a matter of course when the plaintiff seeks damages for personal injuries, thereby putting his physical condition at issue. It is much more difficult to obtain an examination for purposes other than showing physical injury. Note, too, that physical and mental examinations are permitted only against parties or those persons in their control (such as children). If there were a significant dispute about the extent of injuries in Peters v. Dodge, the parties might seek such a physical examination.

Rule 26 applies generally to all discovery methods. Read Rule 26(b)(2) and (c) and the following case. As with all discovery cases, frame the issues by asking yourself what is sought to be discovered and why you think the party is seeking that information.

Butler v. Rigby
1998 U.S. Dist. LEXIS 4618 (E.D. La. 1998)

SARAH VANCE, J.

American Medical Group ("AMG") and Midtown Health Care ("MHC") object to Magistrate Judge Chasez's ruling of February 20, 1998. For the reasons that follow, Magistrate Judge Chasez's order is affirmed in part, and reversed in part.

I. Background

This lawsuit arises out of an automobile accident. . . . AMG and MHC are not parties to this lawsuit, but doctors from both groups provided medical treatment to all of the plaintiffs. Defendants filed identical notices of depositions on AMG and MHC, in which defendants requested certain documents and information. Pertinent to this motion, defendants asked for the following:

> 2) Any and all documents, computer printouts, records, charts, accounting records, tax records, canceled checks, written contracts, letters of guarantee, correspondence and any and all other tangible evidence which reflects:
>> a) A listing of the total number of patients treated at your facility which are involved in litigation since January 1992.
>> b) A listing of the total number of patients treated at your facility that have been referred to you by attorneys since January 1992.
>> c) A listing of the total number of patients/patient accounts for individuals referred you by Evan Tolchinsky, . . . Jose Castro, and/ or the Personal Injury Law Center. . . .
>> e) Any and all letters of guarantee or contracts with attorneys or law firms relating to individuals seen, treated, or examined at your facility since 1992.

AMG and MHC moved the Court for a protective order prohibiting defendants from discovering the information requested in 2(a)–(e) on the grounds that it is not relevant to the lawsuit, some of it is protected by the health care provider-patient privilege, and the request is overly burdensome. Magistrate Judge Chasez concluded that most of the information was discoverable. . . .

AMG and MHC object to the Magistrate Judge's ruling. They insist that the information is not relevant to the lawsuit, it is unduly burdensome to non-parties, and some of the information is privileged. . . .

II.   Discussion. . .

B.   Scope of Discovery in General

The Federal Rules contemplate liberal discovery and provide for a flexible treatment of relevance. Under Rule 26(b)(1) of the Federal Rules of Civil Procedure, the scope of discovery includes any matter, not privileged, that is relevant to the subject matter involved in the pending action. The range of relevant matters is broad and may be related to "the claim or defense of the party seeking discovery or to the claim or defense of any other party, including the existence, description, nature, custody, condition, and location of any books, documents, or other tangible things and the identity and location of persons having knowledge of any discoverable matter." Fed. R. Civ. P. 26(b)(1). The rules make clear that the discovery need not be admissible at trial "if the information sought appears reasonably calculated to lead to the discovery of admissible evidence." Id.

Discovery may be limited by the court if it determines that "the discovery sought is unreasonably cumulative or duplicative." Fed. R. Civ. P. 26(b)(2). The court may also restrict discovery if it concludes that "the burden or expense of the proposed discovery outweighs its likely benefit, taking into account the needs of the case, the amount in controversy, the parties['] resources, the importance of the issues at stake in the litigation, and the importance of the proposed discovery in resolving the issues." Id. Further, the federal rules provide that the court "may make any order which justice requires to protect a party or person from annoyance, embarrassment, oppression, or undue burden or expense." Fed. R. Civ. P. 26(c).

C.   The Discovery in Dispute

1.   *A listing of the total number of patients referred to AMG and/or MHC by Castro, Tolchinsky, and/or the PILC*

AMG and MHC argue that this information has no relevance to plaintiffs' lawsuit, and the request is unduly burdensome. Defendants contend that they seek this information in order to show that the medical groups receive substantial income from the attorneys who initially represented the plaintiffs in this matter, and they argue that such evidence is relevant to show potential bias.

Magistrate Judge Chasez's conclusion that the sought after information was discoverable was not contrary to law. Evidence of a special relationship between an expert witness and legal counsel is relevant to demonstrate the possible bias of the expert witness, and discovery that is reasonably calculated to lead to such evidence should be permitted. . . .

Further, it was not clearly erroneous for Magistrate Judge Chasez to conclude that the expense or burden of producing this information did not outweigh its likely benefits. . . . However, in light of the medical groups' concerns of time and expense and the sworn affidavit that states that compiling the requested information would require that each individual chart be manually pulled and reviewed, the Court orders that defendants shall pay one-half the costs associated with composing the list of the total number of patients. . . .

3. A computer printout of AMG's and MHC's current patients

Magistrate Judge Chasez ordered that the medical groups are to provide defendants with a computer printout listing their current patients as well as any patient lists that were previously generated. AMG and MHC insist that lists of their current or past patients are privileged from discovery pursuant to La. R.S. 13:3734. The Court agrees and concludes that the magistrate judge's ruling was contrary to law. Rule 501 of the Federal Rules of Evidence provides that [the state law of privilege — here, that of Louisiana — shall govern in diversity cases.] . . .

. . . Louisiana courts have broadly interpreted the scope of the health care provider-patient privilege. [Louisiana's] First Circuit Court of Appeal has concluded that "when an individual walks into a doctor's office and opens his mouth, that everything spilling out of it, whether it be his identity or his false teeth . . . , is presumptively privileged and beyond the reach of discovery." Sarphie v. Rowe, 618 So. 2d 905, 908 (La. App. 1st Cir.), writ. denied, 620 So. 2d 1324 (La. 1993). . . .

In light of this precedent, the Court concludes that the AMG/MHC lists of current and/or past patients is privileged, and the information is therefore not discoverable. Moreover, this Court does not see how the identity of these patients could be relevant to this litigation in any event. Magistrate Judge Chasez's order compelling AMG and MHC to disclose their patient lists was contrary to law, and it is reversed.

For all of the foregoing reasons,

IT IS ORDERED that Magistrate Judge Chasez's ruling of February 20, 1998 is affirmed in part, and reversed in part, in accordance with the Court's conclusions as set forth above.

NOTES AND PROBLEMS

1. From whom is defendant seeking discovery? By what procedural means did defendant seek the documents in question? See Rules 34(a), (c); 45(a)(1)(C), (c)(2)(B).

2. Why is defendant seeking this information?

a. Try to hypothesize information that would help defendant's case.

b. Perhaps defendants seek this information less because they believe it will help their case than because they think it will impede the plaintiffs' efforts. How did the plaintiffs try, unsuccessfully, to object that the discovery sought more to harass than to produce useful information?

3. The court denies defendants access to the names of current and past patients: Why?

a. At the end of the opinion the court says it "does not see how the identity of these patients could be relevant to this litigation. . . ." That statement is probably too hasty. Suppose defendants, armed with these names, interview some of the former patients, who describe how the physicians exaggerated their injuries in order to increase recoverable damages. That would surely be relevant information; would it therefore be discoverable?

b. The answer to the preceding question is no: relevance does not render something discoverable *if it is privileged,* as the court says that these names are under Louisiana law. Another way to put it is to say that privilege usually protects disclosure of even highly relevant information.

c. Consider why. The legal system has devised such privileges as the doctor-patient and lawyer-client privileges and the privilege against self-incrimination, to list only a few well-known ones. What is the justification for barring the introduction of highly relevant evidence?

F. Pretrial Disposition — Summary Judgment

Under the Federal Rules, it is uncommon for cases to be dismissed at the pleading stage. A combination of relaxed pleading rules and a policy that readily permits amendment of defective pleadings tends to minimize the role of pleadings in disposing of cases before trial. Indeed, the provisions for broad discovery implicitly suggest that dismissals should not be granted before each party has had a full opportunity to obtain factual information about the case.

Despite such a policy, orderly and efficient procedure requires some mechanism for deciding cases without trials, if possible. A trial involves substantial financial and social costs, and little purpose is served by having one unnecessarily. In consequence, the Federal Rules have adopted the device of *summary judgment* to provide a mechanism for deciding cases for which a trial is not necessary and would serve no purpose. Of course, deciding when a trial is not necessary and would serve no purpose is no mean task.

Rule 56 regulates summary judgment. Although a party may make a motion for summary judgment at any stage of the proceedings, within the scheme of the Federal Rules such motions are not ordinarily granted until after the factual development of the case is complete — that is, after discovery. In fact, Rule 56(f) specifically contemplates that the decision on a motion for summary judgment will be delayed if an opposing party has not been able to complete discovery.

When may it be said, as required by Rule 56(c), that there is "no genuine issue as to any material fact"? For example, suppose in the Peters v. Dodge case that Dodge moves for summary judgment and asserts that the collision occurred at the intersection of Massachusetts Avenue and Boylston Street, that Peters was driving down Massachusetts and Dodge down Boylston, and that the light was red for Massachusetts traffic and green for Boylston traffic. To support the motion, Dodge submits his own affidavit stating that the Boylston light was green and submits the affidavit of a truck driver who was immediately behind Peters on Massachusetts saying that the light on Massachusetts was red. On this showing, with nothing contrary in the record, most courts would grant summary judgment for Dodge.

By contrast, if in response to these affidavits from Dodge, Peters submitted his own affidavit in opposition stating that *he* had the green light, this would show the presence of a factual issue for trial: Who was accurately perceiving and telling the truth about the traffic lights? In such a situation, a court would deny Dodge's motion for summary judgment. The court would reason that summary judgment is not for weighing evidence but for determining whether there is any evidence to weigh; the conflicting affidavits would establish that there was an issue for trial.

Often, however, it is not as easy to tell whether there is a factual issue for trial. Consider the following case.

Houchens v. American Home Assurance Co.

927 F. 2d 163 (4th Cir. 1991)

Ervin, C.J.

Alice Houchens brought suit against American Home Assurance Company ("American") for breach of contract involving two insurance policies

in the United States District Court for the Eastern District of Virginia.
American made a motion for summary judgment,[1] and a hearing was
held on the motion. The district court granted American's motion for
summary judgment,[1] and Houchens appealed. Finding no error in the
granting of summary judgment in favor of American, we affirm.

I

Coulter Houchens disappeared in August 1980 and has not been heard
from since. His wife, Alice Houchens, is trying to collect upon either
of two life insurance policies issued by American, which covered Mr.
Houchens. One policy was an occupational accidental injury and death
insurance policy. The other policy was a non-occupational accident
insurance policy. . . . Both policies required that the insured's death be
caused by accident in order to be covered.

Evidence shows that Mr. Houchens was . . . [employed by the] International Civil Aviation Organization in Montreal, Canada (ICAO) . . .
[and] stationed in Dharan, Saudi Arabia.

Sometime around August 14, 1980, Mr. Houchens received a week
of vacation leave. He traveled to Bangkok, Thailand on or before
August 14 via Thai Airlines. Immigration records show that he arrived
in Bangkok on August 15, 1980. His entry permit was valid through
August 29, 1980.

No one has heard from Mr. Houchens since that time. The State
Department, the FBI, ICAO, Mrs. Houchens, and the Red Cross have
searched for him to no avail. In 1988, Mrs. Houchens brought an action
to declare Mr. Houchens legally dead under Virginia law. On April 29,
1988, an order was issued by the Circuit Court of Loudoun County,
Virginia, declaring that Mr. Houchens is presumed to have died between
August 15 and August 29, 1980.

Houchens sued American for breach of contract because American
refused to pay under either of two accidental death policies covering
Mr. Houchens, which were issued by American. Both policies provided

---

1. The court stated its reasoning as follows:

Under the *Celotex* Case, of course, when met with a motion for summary judgment
such as this it is incumbent upon the plaintiff to come forward with evidence that
would allow a fact finder to infer that the death resulted from an injury which
was caused by accident. I don't think that the plaintiff has met that burden. The
disappearance, and that is really all we have here, of the decedent is not, in my
opinion, disappearance and not being found, is all that the plaintiff really can
show here. I don't think they are such from which a jury or other fact finder could
infer a death caused or accidental injury caused by an accident which resulted
in death.

coverage in the event of death by accident. American maintained that there was no evidence of Mr. Houchens' death, nor was there evidence of *accidental* death. American moved for summary judgment, and the district court granted the motion. This appeal followed. . . .

III

Section 64.1-105 of the Virginia Code provides that a person who has been missing for 7 years is presumed to be dead. Va. Code Ann. §64.1-105 (1987). Therefore, Mr. Houchens is presumed to be dead, and Mrs. Houchens is entitled to that presumption. However, in order for Mrs. Houchens to recover under the American policies, she must prove that Mr. Houchens died as a result of an accident. The term "accident" is not defined in the policies. In such cases, the courts of Virginia have said that an accident is an "event that takes place without one's foresight or expectation; an undesigned, sudden, and unexpected event." Harris v. Bankers Life & Cas. Co., 222 Va. 45, 46, 278 S.E.2d 809, 810 (1981) (quoting Ocean Accident & Guaranty Corp. v. Glover, 165 Va. 283, 285, 182 S.E. 221, 222 (1935)).

"Under the general rule . . . a beneficiary who makes a death claim under an accident policy or the double indemnity clause of a life policy, has the burden of proving that the insured's death was caused by violent, external and accidental means within the terms of the policy." Life & Cas. Ins. Co. of Tennessee v. Daniel, 209 Va. 332, 335, 163 S.E.2d 577, 580 (1968). Therefore, the burden is on Mrs. Houchens to prove that her husband died by accidental means.

The district court granted summary judgment to American in this case under the rationale of Celotex Corp. v. Catrett, 477 U.S. 317 (1986). The Supreme Court set out the standard for granting summary judgment as follows:

> In our view, the plain language of Rule 56(c) mandates the entry of summary judgment, after adequate time for discovery and upon motion, against a party who fails to make a showing sufficient to establish the existence of an element essential to that party's case, and on which that party will bear the burden of proof at trial.

Celotex, 477 U.S. at 322. We elaborated on that standard in Helm v. Western Maryland Ry. Co.:

> The appellate court, therefore, must reverse the grant of summary judgment if it appears from the record that there is an unresolved issue of material fact; the inferences to be drawn from the underlying facts contained in the materials before the trial court must be viewed in the light most favorable to the party opposing the motion.

838 F.2d 729, 734 (4th Cir. 1988). On this appeal, then, we must view the evidence in the light most favorable to Houchens to ascertain whether she made a sufficient showing that Mr. Houchens died accidentally.

Mrs. Houchens asserts that the presumption that Mr. Houchens is dead somehow translates into the presumption that he died accidentally; therefore, she made a sufficient showing. She relies upon three cases from the western part of the country as support for the fact that she met her burden. The first case is Martin v. Insurance Co. of America, 1 Wash. App. 218, 460 P.2d 682 (1969). There, the "deceased" had been seen hunting elk in the American River Ridge. He was last seen alive at 9 A.M. at 3,000 foot level, without the aid of a compass, asking for directions. Conditions were inclement: snow on the ground, fog obscuring vision, and steep and wooded mountainside. The court explained the issue as follows:

> Defendant contends that because of the two-fold nature of the ultimate fact — both of which are dependent upon circumstantial evidence — the jury was first asked to infer death from the proven facts and thereafter to infer the manner of death — and that this process constitutes "the piling of inferences upon inferences." If this process constituted plaintiff's logical development of the ultimate fact, we would be obliged to affirm the judgment. . . . A jury will not be permitted to extrapolate conjecturally beyond a legal conclusion which is itself arrived at circumstantially by inference from a proven fact. But a given set of facts may radially project two (or more) separate inferences. In such event, one inferential conclusion is not pyramided upon another; each is drawn independently from the same evidence.

Martin, 460 P.2d at 684-85. The Martin court was persuaded that the surrounding circumstances of the missing person's disappearance gave rise to two separate inferences: (1) that he was dead; and (2) that the death was caused by accident. The plaintiff there was not piling inferences on inferences. Rather, the evidence gave rise to two separate inferences.

The other two cases Houchens relies upon have equally bizarre and telling circumstances surrounding the disappearances. In Englehart v. General Electric Co., 11 Wash. App. 922, 527 P.2d 685 (1974), the missing person told some people that he was going fishing. His car was discovered at the yacht club. His boat was found adrift with the ignition on, throttle at one-quarter speed in a forward running position. His children testified that he was not a good swimmer, and that the boat had recently had some problems requiring their father to lean over the back of the boat or to get into the water behind the boat in order to repair the problems. The court held that an inference of accidental death could be drawn from the circumstances surrounding his disappearance. . . .

In Valley Natl. Bank of Arizona v. J. C. Penney Ins. Co., 628 P.2d 991, 129 Ariz. 108 (Ct. App. 1981), the missing person disappeared while camping in California with his wife and step-daughter. They all three disappeared. The deceased's skeletal remains were discovered at a camp-site, with bullet casings nearby. The court relied upon the bizarre circumstances of his death to infer that the death was accidental.

These three cases are readily distinguishable from the case at bar. Here, there is only evidence of a disappearance. Mr. Houchens went to Bangkok and was never heard from again. There are no bizarre circumstances surrounding his disappearance. He was not last seen in a position of peril as in *Martin*. He simply vanished. The circumstances surrounding his disappearance do not give us a clue that he actually died, as did the circumstances in *Martin*, *Englehart*, and *Valley National*. Viewed in the light most favorable to Mrs. Houchens, we can only conclude that Mr. Houchens disappeared, and then presume that he died under Virginia law. We cannot conclude that he died accidentally. To do so would be to pile inferences on inferences.

This is a case where the inferences show equal support for opposing conclusions. Mr. Houchens might have died accidentally. However, it is equally likely that he was murdered, that he died of natural causes, that he took his own life, or that he just went away somewhere and lives yet. . . . The ultimate fact at issue here is whether the death occurred by accident. We cannot conclude that there is a greater probability that the death was caused by accident than by other means. . . .

IV

To summarize, Houchens relies on the presumption given her by §64-1.105 of the Virginia Code to establish that Mr. Houchens is dead. She then relies upon the facts surrounding his disappearance as a basis for a jury finding that his death was accidental. However, the meager circumstances would not allow a jury to reasonably conclude that it is more likely that Mr. Houchens died from an accident than in some other manner. Because of the sparse evidence concerning his disappearance, we cannot say that the district court erred in granting summary judgment in favor of American under the *Celotex* standard. Therefore, the order of the district court is affirmed. . . .

NOTES AND PROBLEMS

1. Be sure that you understand what it means to move for summary judgment. What pieces of paper did defendant's lawyer use? What did

he do with them? What pieces of paper did Mrs. Houchens's lawyer use? What did he do with them?

2. The court says that it can distinguish the cases cited by plaintiff because in those cases the circumstances of the deaths suggested accidents. Is that a fair reading of those cases or should the court simply concede that it is not following them?

3. Surely it would not be irrational to conclude that Mr. Houchens died accidentally. If such a conclusion would not be irrational, why did the court not permit the case to go to trial? What does its ruling tell us about the function of a trial and the burdens placed on the parties?

4. To understand summary judgment, one needs to understand what additional evidence would have enabled Mrs. Houchens to avoid summary judgment. Consider several possibilities; in each the question is whether there is a genuine issue of material fact, making summary judgment improper.

a. Suppose Mrs. Houchens produced a witness, a former college friend of Mr. Houchens who had not seen him for more than 10 years. The friend is prepared to testify that, while vacationing in Thailand during the time in question, he saw Mr. Houchens (or someone who looked like him) hit by a bus in a busy intersection. He caught only a brief glimpse; moreover, his vision is not good. The Thai police have no record of a bus accident on the day in question. Can Mrs. Houchens avoid summary judgment with this showing?

b. What if, in response to Mrs. Houchens's production of the witness above, the insurance company comes forward with two affidavits of its own. From two Thai government officials, the affidavits state that Mr. Houchens was shot and killed by Thai police when they intercepted a drug smuggling effort. (Assume that such a death would not be accidental, as the Virginia courts define that term.) In support of these affidavits, the Thai officials state that they are prepared to produce Mr. Houchens's passport. The judge, then, is faced with conflicting affidavits — one from the near-sighted former roommate, the other from Thai government officials. Summary judgment for the insurer?

c. Finally, what if, as in *Houchens* itself, neither side had been able to find information about the circumstances of Mr. Houchens's death. But assume that Virginia law specified that seven years' unexplained absence would give rise to a presumption of death, and, in the absence of contrary evidence, such presumed death would be further presumed to be accidental. Summary judgment for the insurer? For Mrs. Houchens?

There are other methods of pretrial disposition that should be briefly mentioned here. In some cases, defendant will fail to answer the complaint entirely, or will otherwise fail to defend, and a *default judgment* will be granted. See Rule 55. Similarly, if plaintiff does not obey an order of the court during the proceedings, a *dismissal* may be granted. The most common reasons for dismissal are persistent failure to comply with discovery orders, failure to prosecute the case, and failure to appear for calendar calls, motions, or pretrial conferences. See Rule 41(b). In addition, plaintiff may seek a so-called voluntary dismissal of the case if, for some reason, he thinks that he would be better off starting over. See Rule 41(a). We will discuss these matters in more detail later; for now, the student simply should be aware of their existence.

There are also two devices for streamlining the trial that may be mentioned here. One is the *request for admission.* See Rule 36. Although nominally a discovery device, it may be used most effectively to seek either the admission of known facts or acknowledgment of the genuineness of documents. The other is the *pretrial conference.* See Rule 16. Although courts differ widely in their use of the pretrial conference, some courts formulate rather elaborate pretrial orders that supersede the pleadings and govern the conduct of the trial. The pretrial conference may also provide a party with an opportunity to discuss settlement without giving the appearance of having initiated the conversation (this being a supposed sign of weakness).

G. Trial

All pretrial activities, from pleading through summary judgment, anticipate the ultimate trial, yet few cases actually reach that point. Fewer than 5 percent of all cases commenced in the federal courts go to trial, and a sizable number of the remainder are settled during trial or even at the appellate stage. Nevertheless, the trial process acts as a dominant influence on pretrial because pretrial is, by definition, an attempt to prepare for trial and also because a party's estimate of what is likely to happen at the trial has an important bearing on its pretrial preparation and its approach to settlement.

To summarize a typical trial process, we shall assume that the Peters-Dodge case is now ready for trial. The first step, which has an important effect on mechanics, is simply for the court to notify the lawyers of the trial date. In some courts, there is no fixed trial date; instead, the lawyers are told that the case will be called within a given one- or two-week period. Obviously, this strains the lawyer's ability to "peak" preparation at the correct moment and may create serious scheduling problems for active trial lawyers and for cases involving out-of-town and expert witnesses.

Once the case is called, the first step is to select the *jury*. Methods of choosing the jury pool and the jurors for a particular case differ widely. From those called to hear the particular case, twelve (or six) will be seated in the jury box (the *panel*). Generally, someone (usually the judge, but sometimes a jury clerk or the attorneys) will tell the jurors something about the case, the names of parties and witnesses, and any other information that may help to identify persons who might not be suitable jurors. For example, Peters, Dodge, and their attorneys and witnesses will be identified so that jurors who know any of them might be excluded. Since Dodge might be protected by insurance and the insurer might be defending the action, persons with some relation to insurance carriers may also be excluded.* Then the jurors are questioned as a group and individually; the questioning is by the judge, the lawyers, or both. Both parties may challenge jurors for cause (that is, for a stated legally sufficient reason), and each has a number of so-called peremptory challenges, for which reasons need not be stated. The method of using challenges and the timing of challenges differs widely among courts.

Once the jury is selected, the actual trial starts. In trial the parties' lawyers typically take turns at each stage of the proceeding. Peters's attorney begins the trial with an *opening statement*, which provides the jury with an overview of the case. Then Dodge's attorney may either deliver her opening statement or delay making it until later in the case.

Then Peters puts on his case-in-chief. As each witness is called, that witness is *examined* by Peters's attorney and *cross-examined* by Dodge's attorney. Thereafter, Peters's attorney offers *redirect testimony*, then *recross*, and so on. During the testimony various documents are introduced, and these are either accepted into evidence or excluded. When Peters is finished, he rests his case.

At this point, Dodge may make a motion for a *judgment as a matter of law* (also called a *directed verdict*). See Rule 50(a). What this motion says, in effect, is that even if all the evidence that plaintiff has offered is true and all legitimate inferences from such evidence are made, there is no right to relief. Some courts say that, in such cases, plaintiff has failed to prove a *prima facie case*. In deciding this motion, the judge must assume that what the witnesses have said is true and then decide whether a reasonable person could find for Peters. If the answer is negative, the motion is granted; otherwise, Dodge proceeds with his case.

---

* The process of excluding jurors who are related to insurance companies without letting the jurors know that the defendant is insured is, as might be expected, a tricky business.

If Dodge's attorney did not present her opening statement after Peters's attorney, she does so at this point. The defense then presents its case, with the same sequence of direct examination, cross-examination, redirect, recross, and so on. At the conclusion of Dodge's case, she rests. It is now open to plaintiff to move for a directed verdict, although in the typical case in which plaintiff has the burden of proof, this is rarely granted.

It is now the plaintiff's turn to rebut the defendant's case, then for the defendant to rebut the plaintiff's rebuttal, and so on. Technically, each rebuttal phase is limited to refuting new matters raised during the prior phase, but the judge may exercise some discretion to permit introduction of matters into evidence that were inadvertently overlooked during earlier phases. It is fair to say, however, that the trial judge is likely to insist on concluding the case after each party has had his turn and is not likely to be sympathetic to the introduction of new lines of inquiry or major witnesses during the rebuttal stages. Finally, both parties rest their cases.

At this point, either party may move for *judgment as a matter of law*. See Rule 50(a). Most often, the defendant makes the motion, claiming that plaintiff has not satisfied her burden of proof. The judge may grant the motion, although typically he reserves judgment.

The case concludes with the *arguments to the jury* and the judge's instructions to the jury (*charge*). Closing arguments provide the attorneys with an important opportunity to bring together all the evidence, marshal it in logical order, and present it in a light most favorable to their particular points of view. These arguments also provide an opportunity to persuade, cajole, humor, and win the sympathy of the jurors. Generally, attorneys are given considerable leeway in summing up, although they are bound to adhere to the evidence in the case and not go beyond the bounds of propriety.

After the arguments, the judge charges the jury. The charge tells the jury what law applies to the evidence received. Beforehand, the parties usually have the opportunity to propose jury instructions, and the judge rules on such proposed charges before making the actual charge. The attorneys must listen carefully to the charge as delivered because failure to object promptly to anything that they think is erroneous usually means waiver of the right to raise the error as a ground for appeal. See Rule 51.

Then the jury retires to deliberate and informs the judge when it has reached a *verdict*. The verdict is read in open court, and the jurors are ordinarily polled (asked) to make sure that they agree with the verdict as read. At this point, the jury is dismissed (usually with the court's thanks), and the trial ends.

The losing party is not without hope. Within ten days of an adverse verdict, the loser may again move for a *judgment as a matter of law* (at this stage sometimes called a *judgment notwithstanding the verdict* or a j.n.o.v.*), or a new trial, or both. See Rules 50(b), 59. The motion for judgment as a matter of law asserts that even if all the winner's evidence is true and the winner is given all reasonable inferences from that evidence, the loser is entitled to a verdict as a matter of law. The motion for a new trial may be based either on an error of law, such as the erroneous admission or rejection of evidence, on an erroneous charge, or on so-called discretionary grounds, such as misconduct of counsel, newly discovered evidence, or the verdict being against the weight of the evidence.

The losing party may also *appeal* the decision. It is not necessary to make a postverdict motion in order to appeal, but it is usually necessary for the loser to have perfected at least one ground for appeal by raising the point at a proper time in the proceedings in the trial court.

There is one other option open to the loser, although even a statement of it tends to overstate its availability. In limited cases it may be possible for a party against whom a judgment has been rendered to make a motion under Rule 60(b) to *set aside* the judgment. The grounds for setting aside a judgment are limited, and even those grounds are construed narrowly. For example, while it might be possible to have a judgment set aside on the ground that the judge had been bribed, it will not be set aside on the ground that the loser has now thought of a better closing argument. The major way to correct errors is, of course, on appeal, not by a motion under Rule 60(b).

Both the Seventh Amendment of the U.S. Constitution and comparable provisions in state constitutions demonstrate a strong commitment to the idea of jury trial. This commitment makes it difficult to define the circumstances under which the jury ought not to be permitted to decide the case. That is, when should the court enter judgment as a matter of law before a jury verdict, and when should the court set aside a verdict in favor of one side and enter a judgment as a matter of law in favor of the other? There is general agreement that if a party who has the burden of proof on an issue offers no evidence at all on that issue, judgment must be directed against him. There is similar agreement in cases in which the party with the burden of proof offers evidence that is simply too weak to be worthy of belief. But what about a case involving evidence that, although weak, conceivably could be credited? Courts are

---

* The "n.o.v." comes from the Latin phrase for "notwithstanding the verdict," *non obstante veredicto.*

scrupulous in asserting that it is the jury's job to evaluate the credibility of witnesses and that, in passing on motions for judgments as a matter of law and judgments n.o.v., they will not consider whether witnesses are telling the truth. Courts are equally firm, however, in their belief that the function of judgment as a matter of law is to avoid jury trials in cases in which a jury could reasonably come to only one verdict. The next case involves a collision of these two principles.

Norton v. Snapper Power Equipment
806 F.2d 1545 (11th Cir. 1987)

CLARK, J.

Plaintiff James L. Norton was injured while using a riding lawn mower manufactured by defendant Snapper Power Equipment. The issue on appeal is whether the district court erred in granting a judgment notwithstanding the verdict to Snapper on Norton's strict liability claim. We reverse.

I. Facts

Norton was, and still is, in the commercial lawn mowing business. He bought a Snapper riding mower in July 1981. On January 24, 1983, Norton was using this mower to clear leaves from a yard . . . adjacent to a creek. At the end of his third circular route through the yard, he drove up an incline, traveling in the direction away from the creek. Norton testified that as he reached the top of the incline, approximately six feet from the creek, the mower began to slide backwards toward the creek. Norton says he applied the brakes, but he continued to slide backwards. The lawn mower, with Norton still aboard, crashed into the creek. Norton testified that he kept both hands on the handle bars until the impact of the mower hitting the water knocked him off the seat. . . . [A]t some point during this crash, Norton's hand was caught in the lawn mower's blades, thereby amputating four of his fingers. It is not known . . . precisely how the injury occurred. . . .

At the close of the plaintiff's case, and again at the close of all evidence, Snapper moved for a directed verdict. The court dismissed Norton's negligence and warranty claims, but left the strict liability "defect" claim for the jury. The jury returned a verdict for Norton, holding Snapper liable for 80% of the injuries.

Immediately after dismissing the jury, the district court indicated it would enter a judgment notwithstanding the verdict:

The Court:

All right. . . . The court at this time must give a judgment notwithstanding
the verdict of the jury for the defense. The court cannot allow this case
to proceed under any of the present law in this case. The court finds that
the jury could not have considered in 1981 that the equipment used in
the normal course of the equipment as it was designed could have had a
defect which was the legal cause of this injury . . . and there is not
sufficient evidence presented which a jury could find that there was an
inherent defect in the product at that time. So the court must overturn
the jury's verdict. . . .

II.   Substantive Objections to Judgment Notwithstanding the Verdict

The test for granting a judgment notwithstanding the verdict is the same
as the test for granting a directed verdict. The court considers the evidence
in the light most favorable to the non-moving party and should grant the
judgment notwithstanding the verdict only where the evidence so strongly
and so favorably points in the favor of the moving party that reasonable
people could not arrive at a contrary verdict. . . .

The issues in this case were: (1) whether the failure to install "dead
man" devices rendered the 1981 Snapper mower defective; and (2) if
the lawn mower was defective, whether the lack of a "dead man" control
caused Norton's injury. Snapper claims that there was little or no evidence
to support the jury's verdict. . . .

[After reviewing the law on product defects, the appellate court concluded that the jury could reasonably have found the mower defective.]

B.   Causation

. . . Since Norton did not know exactly when or how his hand got
caught in the blades, and since a reconstruction of the accident was
impossible, Snapper contends that the jury could not determine whether a
blade stopping device would have eliminated or lessened Norton's injury.

Snapper correctly points out that "plaintiffs are not entitled to a verdict
based on speculation and conjecture." Fenner v. General Motors Corp.,
657 F.2d 647, 651 (5th Cir. 1981), cert. denied, 455 U.S. 942 (1982).
. . . The jury is, however, permitted to "reconstruct the series of events
by drawing an inference upon an inference." Id. at 650.

In Fenner, plaintiff contended his automobile veered off the highway
because of a defective steering mechanism. The steering problem would
only manifest itself if a stone got caught in the steering mechanism.

Because plaintiff's vehicle was not examined by any experts and since plaintiff's experts were only able to say that theoretically the accident could have been caused by a stone in the steering mechanism, the district court entered a judgment notwithstanding the verdict for defendant. . . .

The causation evidence in this case, although circumstantial, was far more impressive than the evidence presented in *Fenner*. Norton testified that the lawn mower slid six feet from the top of the hill into the creek. . . . Expert testimony revealed that when Norton applied the brakes, an effective dead man device could have stopped the blades in as little as .7 seconds. The blades on the 1981 Snapper would continue to spin for three to five seconds. . . . Each of Snapper's experts testified that, given the amount of time the mower would have taken to slide six feet and given Norton's testimony that both of his hands were on the handle bars until the mower hit the creek, a two or three second difference in blade stopping time would have avoided the injury. . . . Snapper was given every opportunity to point out the weaknesses in Norton's proof, but apparently was unpersuasive. . . .

Reversed and Remanded.

NOTES AND PROBLEMS

1. Keep in mind that in a case involving a motion for judgment as a matter of law or a judgment notwithstanding the verdict, the court is deciding whether a reasonable jury could reach a verdict in favor of the party opposing the motion. In this case the jury's verdict for plaintiff depended on its finding that the absence of a device on the lawn mower capable of quickly stopping the mower blades caused Norton's injury. The trial court concluded that there was insufficient evidence for the jury to reach this decision; the court of appeals ruled that the jury could reasonably have reached its verdict. Who is right?

2. Is the case really distinguishable from *Fenner*? In *Fenner* the plaintiff's experts testified that a stone in the steering device could have caused the car to crash; in *Norton* the plaintiff and his experts testified that Norton's injuries could have been caused by the blades' failure to stop spinning quickly enough. But isn't it equally possible that the injury could have occurred even if the blades stopped sooner? Norton, after all, did not remember just how the accident happened.

3. Is *Norton* distinguishable from *Houchens*? That question can be addressed on two levels — of procedural theory and of factual inference.

a. Start with procedural theory. *Houchens* was decided on a motion for summary judgment, under Rule 56; *Norton* was decided after trial on a motion for judgment notwithstanding the verdict (now called a motion for judgment as a matter of law), under Rule 50. Both result in a judge's decision that one party is entitled to victory because there just isn't any evidence to support the other side. But the two motions come at different stages: The summary judgment motion asserts that there just isn't any conflicting evidence that a trial could resolve; a motion for judgment as a matter of law comes during trial when the evidence for one or both sides has already been presented.

If the two motions cover similar ground, why is there ever any need for the judgment as a matter of law? Shouldn't summary judgment have been granted if there really was no evidence to support one side? Logically, that question makes sense. Practically, however, it often happens that what looks at the pretrial stage like an evidentiary conflict evaporates at trial: A witness fails to appear or tells a different story at trial than in the lawyer's office. In that situation the motion for judgment as a matter of law serves as a back-up to summary judgment.

b. Now turn to the facts of the two cases. In *Houchens* the court affirmed a grant of summary judgment while conceding it was *possible* that Houchens had died accidentally. Does the jury verdict in *Norton* rest on more than a finding that the absence of a dead-man mechanism *might* have caused the accident?

4. What will happen to this case now that the court of appeals has reversed and remanded?

H.   Former Adjudication

Most of us are vaguely familiar with the criminal law notion of double jeopardy, which prevents a person from being tried twice for the same crime. Not surprisingly, there is a similar notion in civil procedure: A plaintiff who brings a case, or a defendant who defends one, should not be able to try again if he is not satisfied with the result. This principle is easy enough to state, but it is often difficult to determine which claims and issues should be permitted to be litigated in a second action. Lawyers speak of such questions under the general heading of former adjudication or, in its Latin equivalent, res judicata (literally, (some)thing adjudicated); they subdivide former adjudication into *claim preclusion* and *issue pre-clusion*.

To take the easiest case of claim preclusion, if plaintiff sues for personal injuries suffered in a car accident with defendant and loses or is dissatisfied with the amount of damages awarded by the jury, she may not sue again. Similarly, if plaintiff wins, the defendant cannot bring a second action to set aside the first judgment. In such a case, we say that the first claim precludes the second (or is res judicata to the second).

For claim preclusion to apply, the claim must be the same in both the first and second action. As might be expected, deciding what is and is not the same claim is sometimes difficult. For example, there is general agreement that an injured party cannot sue for damage to his arm in one action and to his leg in another. But, as the next case demonstrates, not all courts agree that plaintiff's claims for personal injuries and property damage arising out of the same accident are part of the same claim.

The doctrine of former adjudication also encompasses issue preclusion. Suppose *A* sues *B* on a promissory note, and *B* defends on the ground of fraud. *A* wins, the court ruling that there was no fraud. *A* then sues *B* on another promissory note executed at the same time, and *B* again claims fraud based on the same events as those in the first suit. *A*'s claim would not be precluded (because the law sees the second note as involving a distinct claim), but under the doctrine of issue preclusion *B* would be precluded from claiming fraud a second time because that issue was determined in the first litigation between the parties.

The next case involves a court wrestling with a problem involving both claim and issue preclusion. The court uses older but still common terminology in its discussion, calling claim preclusion (and also the whole topic of former adjudication) *res judicata* and issue preclusion *collateral estoppel*. The latter term derives from the idea that the litigant is being precluded (estopped) from relitigating an issue in a second (that is, collateral) proceeding. The opinion — like many you will encounter in law school and practice — is written in a somewhat opaque style; see if you can discern the real issue being debated.

Rush v. City of Maple Heights

167 Ohio St. 221, 147 N.E.2d 599, cert. denied, 358 U.S. 814 (1958)

[Plaintiff owned a motorcycle. While her husband was driving, she was injured after being thrown to the ground when the motorcycle ran into a hole in the road. Plaintiff first sued the City for damage to the motorcycle. The Municipal Court found that the City was negligent in not repairing the road and that such negligence was the proximate cause of the accident; it awarded plaintiff damages of $100. That judgment was affirmed by the Court of Appeals and the Supreme Court.

Subsequently, plaintiff commenced the present action to recover damages for personal injuries suffered in the same accident. The trial court held that the issues of negligence and proximate cause had been determined in the prior action against the defendant and were binding. At a trial solely on the question of damages, the jury awarded plaintiff $12,000. The Court of Appeals affirmed this judgment.]

HERBERT, J.

The eighth error assigned by the defendant is that "the trial and appellate courts committed error in permitting plaintiff to split her cause of action and to file a separate action in the Cleveland Municipal Court for her property damage and reduce same to judgment, and, thereafter, to proceed, in the Cuyahoga County Common Pleas Court, with a separate action for personal injuries, both claims arising out of a single accident." . . .

In the case of Vasu v. Kohlers, Inc., 145 Ohio St. 321, 61 N.E.2d 707, 709, 166 A.L.R. 855, plaintiff operating an automobile came into collision with defendant's truck, in which collision he suffered personal injuries and also damage to his automobile. At the time of collision, plaintiff had coverage of a $50 deductible collision policy on his automobile. The insurance company paid the plaintiff a sum covering the damage to his automobile, whereupon, in accordance with a provision of the policy, the plaintiff assigned to the insurer his claim for such damage.

In February 1942, the insurance company commenced an action . . . against Kohlers, Inc., the defendant in the reported case to recoup the money paid by it to cover the damage to Vasu's automobile.

In August 1942, Vasu commenced an action in the same court against Kohlers, Inc., to recover for personal injuries which he suffered in the same collision.

In March 1943, in the insurance company's action, a verdict was rendered in favor of the defendant, followed by judgment.

Two months later an amended answer was filed in the Vasu case, setting out as a bar to the action for recovery of damages for the personal injuries suffered by plaintiff the judgment rendered in favor of defendant in the insurance company case. A motion to strike that defense having been sustained, . . . [a] trial of the action resulted in a verdict for plaintiff, upon which judgment was entered.

On appeal to the Court of Appeals the defendant claimed that the Court of Common Pleas erred in sustaining plaintiff's motion to strike from the defendant's answer the defense of res judicata claimed to have arisen by reason of the judgment in favor of the defendant in the action by the insurance company.

The Court of Appeals reversed the judgment of the Court of Common Pleas and entered final judgment in favor of defendant.

This court reversed the judgment of the Court of Appeals, holding in the syllabus, in part, as follows:

1. If the owner of a single cause of action arising out of a single tortious act brings an action against his tort-feasor, he may have but one recovery; and, in case he fails to recover, he may not maintain a subsequent action on the same cause of action, even though he has failed to include his entire cause of action or elements of damage in his original action.

2. If an owner of a single cause of action has a recovery thereon, the cause of action is merged in the judgment; but if he fails to recover on his claimed cause of action and judgment goes against him, such judgment is res judicata and a bar to a second action on the same cause of action. . . .

4. Injuries to both person and property suffered by the same person as a result of the same wrongful act are infringements of different rights and give rise to distinct causes of action, with the result that the recovery or denial of recovery of compensation for damages to the property is no bar to an action subsequently prosecuted for the personal injury, unless by an adverse judgment in the first action issues are determined against the plaintiff which operate as an estoppel against him in the second action.

5. A right, question or fact in issue which was necessarily determined by a court of competent jurisdiction in a judgment which has become final, cannot be disputed or litigated in a subsequent suit between the same parties, although the subsequent suit is based upon a different cause of action. . . .

The foregoing syllabus is set forth at considerable length for subsequent reference herein. The first two paragraphs, although not pertinent there because of the fourth paragraph, are not only applicable but persuasive in our determination here. . . .

[C]ases distinguishing and explaining the *Vasu* case have not changed the rule established in paragraph four of the syllabus of the latter case, holding that injuries to both person and property suffered by the same person as a result of the same wrongful act are infringements of different rights and give rise to distinct causes of action.

However, it is contended here that that rule is in conflict with the great weight of authority in this country and has caused vexatious litigation. The following quotation from 1 American Jurisprudence, 494, Section 114, states this question well:

It sometimes happens that a single wrongful or negligent act causes damage in respect of both the person and the property of the same individual, as, for instance, where the owner of a vehicle is injured in a collision which also damages the vehicle. In such a case, the question arises as to whether there are two causes of action or only one, and the authorities are in conflict concerning it. The majority rule is that only one cause of action arises, the reason of the rule being that as the defendant's wrongful act is single, the cause of action must be single, and that the different injuries occasioned by it are merely items of damage proceeding from the same wrong. . . .

In other jurisdictions, the rule is that two causes of action result from a negligent act which inflicts injury on a person and his property at the same time. This conclusion has been reached in different jurisdictions by different lines of reasoning.

Upon examination of decisions of courts of last resort, we find that the majority rule is followed in the following cases in each of which the action was between the person suffering injury and the person committing the tort, and where insurers were not involved, as in the case here. . . .

[The court cited 20 cases supporting the majority rule and five cases supporting the minority rule.]

The reasoning behind the majority rule seems to be well stated in the case of Mobile & Ohio Rd. Co. v. Matthews, as follows:

> The negligent action of the plaintiff in error constituted but one tort. The injuries to the person and property of the defendant in error were the several results and effects of one wrongful act. A single tort can be the basis of but one action. It is not improper to declare in different counts for damages to the person and property when both result from the same tort, and it is the better practice to do so where there is any difference in the measure of damages, and all the damages sustained must be sued for in one suit. This is necessary to prevent multiplicity of suits, burdensome expense, and delays to plaintiffs, and vexatious litigation against defendants. . . .
>
> Indeed, if the plaintiff fails to sue for the entire damage done him by the tort, a second action for the damages omitted will be precluded by the judgment in the first suit brought and tried.

The minority rule would seem to stem from the English case of Brunsden v. Humphrey (1884), 14 Q.B. 141. The facts in that case are set forth in the opinion in the *Vasu* case concluding with the statement:

> The Master of the Rolls, in his opinion, stated that the test is "whether the same sort of evidence would prove the plaintiff's case in the two actions," and that, in the action relating to the cab, "it would be necessary to give evidence of the damage done to the plaintiff's vehicle. In the present action it would be necessary to give evidence of the bodily injury occasioned to the plaintiff, and of the sufferings which he has undergone, and for this purpose to call medical witnesses. This one test shows that the causes of action as to the damage done to the plaintiff's cab, and as to the injury occasioned to the plaintiff's person, are distinct."

The fallacy of the reasoning in the English court is best portrayed in the dissenting opinion of Lord Coleridge, as follows: ". . . [I]t seems to me a subtlety not warranted by law to hold that a man cannot bring two actions, if he is injured in his arm and in his leg, but can bring two, if besides his arm and leg being injured, his trousers which contain his leg, and his coat sleeve which contains his arm, have been torn."

There appears to be no valid reason in these days of code pleading to adhere to the old English rule as to distinctions between injuries to the person and damages to the person's property resulting from a single tort. It would seem that the minority rule is bottomed on the proposition that the right of bodily security is fundamentally different from the right of security of property and, also, that, in actions predicated upon a negligent act, damages are a necessary element of each independent cause of action and no recovery may be had unless and until actual consequential damages are shown.

Whether or not injuries to both person and property resulting from the same wrongful act are to be treated as injuries to separate rights or as separate items of damage . . . a plaintiff may maintain only one action to enforce his rights existing at the time such action is commenced. . . .

Upon further examination of the cases from other jurisdictions, it appears that in those instances where the courts have held to the majority rule, a separation of causes of action is almost universally recognized where an insurer has acquired by an assignment or by subrogation the right to recover for money it has advanced to pay for property damage. . . .

The reason why the exception is recognized that, where the plaintiff has recovered from an insurance company a part of his damage, he is not estopped from prosecuting his own action, is well stated in the North Carolina case of Underwood v. Dooley, as follows:

> It cannot be held as law in this state that the owner of an automobile, who, as the result of the wrong or tort of another, has sustained damages both to his automobile and to his person, and whose automobile is insured against the loss or damage which he has sustained because of injuries to his automobile, is put to an election whether or not he shall, in order to maintain an action against the wrongdoer to recover damages for injuries to [his] person, release the insurance company from all liability to him under its policy. He does not lose his right of action to recover for the injuries to his person, by accepting from the insurance company the amount for which it is liable to him.

Apparently, much of the vexatious litigation, with its attendant confusion, which has resulted in recent years from the filing of separate petitions by the same plaintiff, one for personal injuries and one for property damage although sustained simultaneously, has grown from that one decision, this case presenting a good example.

In the light of the foregoing, it is the view of this court that the so-called majority rule conforms much more properly to modern practice, and that the rule declared in the fourth paragraph of the syllabus in the *Vasu* case, on a point not actually at issue therein, should not be followed.

We, therefore, conclude and hold that, where a person suffers both personal injuries and property damage as a result of the same wrongful act, only a single cause of action arises, the different injuries occasioned thereby being separate items of damage from such act. It follows that paragraph four of the syllabus in the *Vasu* case must be overruled. . . .

Judgment reversed and final judgment for defendant.

WEYGANDT, C.J., and STEWART, TAFT, MATTHIAS and BELL, J.J., concur.

STEWART, J. (concurring).

In the case of Vasu v. Kohlers, Inc., Judge Hart stated in part: "The rule at common law and in a majority of the states of the union is that damages resulting from a single wrongful act, even though they include both property and personal injury damages, are, when suffered by the same person, the subject of only one action against the wrongdoer."

However, he referred to the fact that there were a number of state jurisdictions which followed the English rule, laid down in Brunsden v. Humphrey, L.R., 14, Q.B. Div., 141, and known as the two-causes-of-action rule, and then proceeded to announce that rule as the Ohio rule, and it was written into the fourth paragraph of the syllabus of the *Vasu* case. If it had been necessary to decide the question whether a single tort gives rise to two causes of action as to the one injured by such tort, I would be reluctant to disturb that holding. However, neither the discussion in the *Vasu* case as to whether a single or double cause of action arises from one tort nor the language of the fourth paragraph of the syllabus was necessary to decide the issue presented in the case, and obviously both such language and such paragraph are obiter dicta and, therefore, are not as persuasive an authority as if they had been appropriate to the question presented. . . .

ZIMMERMAN, J. (dissenting).

I am not unalterably opposed to upsetting prior decisions of this court where changing conditions and the lessons of experience clearly indicate the desirability of such course, but, where those considerations do not obtain, established law should remain undisturbed in order to insure a stability on which the lower courts and the legal profession generally may rely with some degree of confidence. . . .

NOTES AND PROBLEMS

1. Both plaintiff and defendant were asserting that the first action affected the second in some way.

a. How did plaintiff think the first case should affect the second?

b. How did defendant think the first case should affect the second?

c. Which of the parties was arguing for issue preclusion? Which for claim preclusion?

2. Do you think that a court would reach the same result in this case if plaintiff's husband had sued to recover for his own injuries?

3. If plaintiff had lost the first action because the court found that the city was not negligent in maintaining the street and plaintiff's husband then sued for his own injuries, do you think that the decision in the first action would be binding on him?

4. Normally a court will follow earlier decisions on principles of law, even though the parties currently before the court were not parties to the earlier case. For example, assume that, in plaintiff's action, the court established a rule that the city is not liable for holes in the pavement unless it has actual notice of the holes (as opposed to mere reason to know). That rule ordinarily would be followed not only in an action by plaintiff's husband but also in one by an unrelated plaintiff whose cycle fell into a different hole, on a different street, on a different day. This principle is called *stare decisis*. The majority and the concurring and dissenting opinions in *Rush* are arguing in part about whether the court is departing from *stare decisis* in their treatment of *Vasu*.

a. Is it?

b. If so, is the departure justified?

5. Imagine that Ms. Rush, before she filed the property damage claim, consulted her lawyer, who told her that it was well established law in Ohio that one could bring separate claims for property damage and personal injury. She (and her lawyer) now know that advice was wrong. Can she recover from her lawyer for malpractice? Very unlikely: To prevail on such a claim, Rush must show two things: (a) that a lawyer of ordinary competence would have known that Ohio was likely to change its rule of former adjudication; and (b) that, but for the lawyer's error, she would have prevailed in the original lawsuit. Under the circumstances of *Rush*, the second showing will be easy — after all, she prevailed in the property damage action before it was reversed. But it isn't likely that a court will let a jury find that Rush's lawyer was negligent for failing to predict the Ohio Supreme Court's reversal of *Vasu* — ordinary competence doesn't include pre-science. Where does that leave Ms. Rush?

I. Appeals

Our judicial system permits a losing party to appeal an adverse judgment of the trial court to a higher court, but the right of appeal does not ensure the "correctness" of trial court rulings. To understand this apparent contradiction, one must understand the interaction of procedural rules that determine: (1) when in the course of a given lawsuit an adverse ruling can be appealed; and (2) how closely an appellate court will scrutinize any alleged error. To comprehend their interaction, imagine that a trial judge has made an important discovery ruling, one that both parties believe will affect the outcome of the case. Further, suppose that the ruling is at least questionable and that the party on the losing end of the ruling appeals. The next case shows what will happen.

Apex Hosiery Co. v. Leader
102 F.2d 702 (3d Cir. 1939)

PER CURIAM.

The defendants in an action for treble damages under the Sherman Anti-Trust Act note, have appealed from an order of the court below made under Federal Rule of Civil Procedure 34 for the discovery and production by them of documents for inspection, copying and photographing by the plaintiff for use at the trial of the action. An order of this nature is interlocutory and, therefore, not appealable. This has been expressly decided by the Supreme Court in Cogen v. United States, 278 U.S. 221 (1929). In the former case Mr. Justice Brandeis said ([278 U.S.] 223, 224): "The disposition made of the motion will necessarily determine the conduct of the trial and may vitally affect the result. In essence, the motion resembles others made before or during a trial to secure or to suppress evidence, such as applications to suppress a deposition; to compel the production of books or documents; for leave to make physical examination of a plaintiff; or for a subpoena duces tecum. The orders made upon such applications, so far as they affect the rights only of parties to the litigation, are interlocutory. It is only when disobedience happens to result in an order punishing criminally for contempt, that a party may have review by appellate proceedings before entry of the final judgment in the cause." Union Tool Co. v. Wilson, 259 U.S. 107, 110, 111 [1922]."

While the appeal must be dismissed for want of jurisdiction, we think it may fairly be said that the order entered by the learned District Judge was most carefully drawn to prevent the plaintiff from unduly prying into the defendants' affairs.

Appeal dismissed.

NOTES AND PROBLEMS

1. Be sure you understand what has happened in this case.

a. Did the court rule on defendants' contention that discovery was improper? What did it do? Why?

b. Notice the court's discomfort with this disposition, discomfort evident in the second-to-last sentence ("While the appeal must be dismissed. . . ."). Having said it has no jurisdiction over the appeal, the court nevertheless tries to reassure the losing side that the lower court has not been careless. This sentence is dictum of the purest sort — since the court has just said it has no jurisdiction over the case. Why does the court write this sentence?

2. The *final judgment* rule (as the doctrine expressed in *Apex Hosiery* is called) finds its current statutory expression in 28 U.S.C. §1291, which gives the federal courts of appeals jurisdiction "of appeals from all final decisions" of the federal district courts. The negative corollary is just as important: that the courts of appeal have no jurisdiction over appeals from judgments or rulings that are not final. Such nonfinal rulings are called *interlocutory* orders.

One can justify the final judgment rule in several ways. Probably the most telling argument is that many trial court decisions that seem wrong at the time turn out not to matter because the party on the losing end of that decision goes on to prevail. Another justification is that a rule permitting interlocutory appeals from every trial decision would enormously protract litigation and that it is more important to bring litigation to an end than to assure that every trial court ruling was perfectly correct.

The argument against the final judgment rule relies on a different kind of pragmatic reasoning. Most cases will not end in a judgment of any sort: The parties will settle. Judicial rulings that precede settlements are not appealable, but those rulings may have dictated the terms of the settlement — by greatly advantaging one party. In those cases — the majority of all cases — it seems unjust to allow what may be practically dispositive judicial rulings to escape appellate review. Some states, New York most notable among them, have adopted this reasoning by providing for liberal interlocutory appeal of significant trial court rulings. Others (the federal courts included) weasel a bit with judge-made doctrines that slightly soften the final judgment rule. It is nevertheless still fair to say that the rule poses an insuperable barrier to immediate appeal of most trial court rulings.

3. Apply the final judgment rule to some of the cases we have already considered in this chapter. From which of the following decisions would an immediate appeal lie, according to 28 U.S.C. §1291:

a. A trial court order granting a dismissal for want of subject matter jurisdiction?

b. A trial court order refusing to dismiss for want of subject matter jurisdiction (as in Gordon v. Steele)?

c. A trial court order denying a 12(b)(6) motion (as in Bell v. Novick Transfer)?

d. A trial court order granting a 12(b)(6) motion?

e. A trial court order denying requested discovery (as in Butler v. Rigby)?

4. With these exercises in mind, consider how the final judgment rule affects the dynamics of litigation. Plaintiff files a lawsuit and defendant, before answering, makes a modest settlement offer. Plaintiff's lawyer advises plaintiff to reject the offer, which he does. Plaintiff then seeks discovery of some information vital to the lawsuit, but the defendant resists and the judge refuses to grant discovery. Plaintiff cannot appeal unless the case goes to final judgment, but it will cost plaintiff considerable time and money to get to that stage. Will the defendant's original settlement offer look better? Will defendant still be willing to make even that modest offer, having won the battle over discovery?

5. The final judgment rule affects the timing of appeals. Other doctrines affect how the courts of appeals will decide those cases that do reach final judgment. Put in very simplified form, existing doctrine tells the appellate courts that they should scrutinize trial court rulings in two different ways: (a) findings of fact should be affirmed unless "clearly erroneous"; (b) by contrast, rulings of law should be subject to reversal if wrong in any respect — so long as the error affected the outcome of the lawsuit.

a. Consider what it means to say that a trial judge may be reversed by an appellate court only when factual findings are "clearly erroneous." Doesn't that standard imply that it's permissible for a trial judge to be "a little wrong," so long as her error is factual? How would one defend such a standard?

b. Conversely, why should the appellate courts be so concerned that the trial judge get the law exactly right? What is at stake?

6. Consider how the final judgment rule and the "clearly erroneous" rule operate together. Recall Gordon v. Steele, in which the defendants challenged subject matter jurisdiction and the court ruled that Susan Gordon was a citizen of Idaho for diversity purposes. That ruling was not immediately appealable because it did not result in a final judgment. If the case continued and the defendants persisted until a final judgment and wanted to raise the jurisdictional ruling on appeal, they would have to show that the court's finding of fact as to Ms. Gordon's intent to

remain in Idaho was not merely debatable or even wrong, but clearly erroneous. If you were defendant's counsel and believed that Judge Knox had erred in finding diversity, could you conscientiously counsel your clients to refrain from making a settlement offer because you were sure to win on appeal?

NOTE ON APPELLATE STRUCTURE AND JURISDICTION

In this and other law school courses you will read a good many appellate opinions from state and federal courts. What determines which court will hear such an appeal?

In the federal system, parties who lose in the district court can appeal to the court of appeals. Parties who lose in the court of appeals do not, in most cases, have an automatic right to appeal to the U.S. Supreme Court. Instead, they must apply to the U.S. Supreme Court to have the case heard, which they do by asking the Court to grant a *writ of certiorari*.

Most states have a similar appellate structure — a trial court of general jurisdiction, an intermediate appellate court to which all cases may be appealed, and a state supreme court* that has discretion over which cases it will hear. In some states, however, there is no intermediate appellate court, so appeals go directly to the state supreme court. If the case is not brought in a court of general jurisdiction but in an inferior court (for example, a court whose jurisdiction is limited to claims under $10,000), there may be a different and more limited appellate structure. Finally, some decisions of the highest state court can be reviewed by the U.S. Supreme Court.

As the preceding discussion indicates, the U.S. Supreme Court can hear cases that have originated in either the federal or the state system. But an important caveat is necessary: The U.S. Supreme Court can hear cases that arise in the state system *only* if they present an issue of federal law. It cannot hear cases from the state supreme court that involve solely questions of state law. For example, assume that a case is brought in the state courts of Florida and that on appeal the Florida Supreme Court adopts a rule to the effect that a retailer is liable for criminal acts suffered by customers on adjacent premises, if reasonably foreseeable. The Supreme Court of the United States cannot review this ruling because the issue

---

* New York has particularly challenging terminology: The state calls its trial court of general jurisdiction the "Supreme Court," its intermediate appellate court the "Appellate Division," and its highest court the "Court of Appeals."

is one of state tort law. On the other hand, if the Florida Supreme Court were to rule that a person attempting to sell magazines on a private college campus is not protected by the First Amendment, that ruling would present an issue of federal constitutional law, which could be reviewed by the U.S. Supreme Court. Supreme Court review is governed by 28 U.S.C. § §1253-1258; in exercising its power of review, the Court enjoys broad discretion in selecting which cases it will hear. An important, though widely misunderstood, point is that a decision by the Supreme Court not to review a case does not signify approval of the decision rendered by the court below. The Court's members may roundly disapprove of both the law applied and the results reached by the lower court but nevertheless determine not to grant review because, for example, they think the issue is not sufficiently important to warrant review.

NOTE: CIVIL PROCEDURE IN YOUR SUBSTANTIVE COURSES

In the course of the year you will encounter repeated discussion of procedural issues in various substantive courses. Discussing a case in contracts, your instructor may ask about the procedure by which the case reached the appellate court; a torts class may focus on the question of what additional evidence would have enabled plaintiff to avoid defendant's motion for a directed verdict. A property class may explore the defects in plaintiff's complaint for trespass that led the court to sustain a demurrer. These scenarios do not represent efforts by your other instructors to seize pedagogical territory by conquest. Instead they reflect the role that substantive law plays in procedural decisions and that procedure plays in substantive law.

Lawsuit grow from disputes. Parties may dispute what happened and what consequences the law attaches to those happenings. At several stages of litigation procedure establishes hurdles that a party must jump. Demurrers or Rule 12(b)(6) motions are one such hurdle; motions for summary judgment, a directed verdict, or a judgment n.o.v. are others. All these procedural devices require the judge to reflect on the substantive law that applies to the case and to describe the way in which that law applies to the facts as they then appear.

Focusing on the procedural stance of the case clarifies two points. First, seeing that the case arises on an appeal from a demurrer, an objection to jury instructions, or the like explains why the judge is engaging in a recitation of the substantive law. Second, understanding the procedural stance of the case enables you to see how much of what the court says depends purely on a legal assessment of the case and how much depends on a factual assessment. For example, on a demurrer or Rule 12(b)(6) motion, the court considers whether the plaintiff's allegations, if proved, would entitle him to the court's help; it does not consider whether it is likely that the plaintiff could prove the truth of the statements. On a motion for summary judgment or a directed verdict, by contrast, the court must consider both the law that applies to the case and the evidence that the parties have presented. These propositions might take concrete form in a case in which plaintiff claimed that defendant had injured him by shooting him with a ray gun. However unlikely such a claim sounds, it would survive a demurrer — even if the judge firmly believed that plaintiff's injuries were figments of an overworked imagination — because a demurrer asks whether the alleged facts, *if they were true*, would form the basis for relief. That same claim might well succumb to a motion for summary judgment or a motion for a directed verdict, not because the law of ray-gun-inflicted injuries had changed but because, for instance, doctors' examinations had revealed that, although plaintiff might be slightly deranged, he had suffered no physical injury.

Procedure will thus play two roles in your substantive courses. First, various procedural hurdles will provide the occasion for judicial expositions of the law of torts, property, contract, and crimes. Second, by understanding the procedural stage at which the issue under discussion arose, you will also understand the extent to which the court is considering the facts of the particular case. Comprehending this dual role will enable you to see both the way in which procedure shapes substantive law and the reason procedural discussions will often play a central role in learning that substantive law.

PART A

THE CONSTITUTIONAL
FRAMEWORK FOR
U.S. LITIGATION

A. Approaching Civil Procedure

One can study the procedural system from the top down or from the bottom up. The top-down approach examines the constitutional environment in which the individual lawsuit exists. That approach takes the student into both the history and the current interpretation of the Constitution of the United States. Studying the Constitution reveals several limits on the ways in which state and federal court systems conduct their business — limits that have major consequences for individual litigants. The bottom-up approach examines how an individual lawsuit develops: how the parties intially state their grievances, develop information about them, and bring them to resolution. This approach emphasizes features and problems of the contemporary procedural system, which is in many respects a bold experiment. Studying the process of litigation reveals how these features shape and constrain the litigants' responsibilities and choices.

As you have probably already guessed, anyone wanting to become a lawyer has to understand *both* approaches, to comprehend the constitutional environment as well as the modes for processing disputes. This book accordingly contains materials about both approaches, and most courses will examine both. But one can with equal validity start at the top and look down or begin at the bottom and work up. The three parts of this book are labeled to emphasize these different starting points. Some courses may begin with Part A: The Constitutional Framework for U.S. Litigation, comprising Chapters II-IV. This starting point represents the "top-down" approach. Other classes may move first to Part B: The Process of Litigation, comprising Chapters V-XII and representing the "bottom-

71

up" approach. The last part of this book, Part C: Expanding the Framework of Litigation: Additional Claims and Parties, combines significant elements of both the other parts and may be studied either at the end of the course, as a reprise, or in conjunction with either of the other two parts. The next three chapters represent an approach to litigation starting at the top — with the constitutional framework.

B.   Constitutional Limits in Litigation

The U.S. Constitution dictates many fundamental aspects of a lawsuit — not only in landmark cases but in ordinary civil litigation. For example, someone looking at the U.S. system from outside might conclude that it would be more efficient to have a single, unitary court system for all disputes rather than 51 separate systems (one for each state and one for the federal government). Efficient it might be, but it would also be unconstitutional, for reasons you will come to understand. The next three chapters develop several of the most important ways the Constitution shapes litigation in the United States. Two of those ways involve "jurisdiction," a protean and important word in U.S. litigation; the third involves "choice of law."

1.   The Idea of Jurisdiction

No legal system in the world claims the power to decide all disputes arising anywhere. Which cases, then, will a legal system resolve? Consider this question concretely. Imagine that you live in Illinois and come to California to attend law school. A particularly contentious sort, you become involved in two disputes during your first year there: You think your landlord is failing to maintain your apartment, and you question a grade assigned by one of your instructors. In the first case, you might start by complaining to the landlord; in the second, to the instructor or the dean. You probably would *not* seek relief from the landlord of the building next door or from the dean of another law school. You would not do so because the landlord of the other building and the dean of the other school have no power over the conditions in your apartment or school. Putting the matter very loosely, one could say the condition of your apartment and the marks assigned in your school fall outside of their *jurisdictions*: Say what they might about the poor state of garbage collection or the unfairness of the grade, they are powerless to remedy either.

You will repeatedly encounter the concept of jurisdiction while studying law and will soon discover that the term is used in several different ways. More or less literally, "jurisdiction" means the power to declare the law. By extension, it has acquired several other meanings. Lawyers may speak of "the law of a jurisdiction" or of a suspected felon's having "fled the jurisdiction," using the term in both instances to signify a state or territory. In civil procedure it has a narrower meaning. Lawyers sometimes refer to jurisdiction in this narrower sense as "judicial jurisdiction": the power of a court to render a judgment that other courts and government agencies will recognize and enforce.

You might encounter jurisdiction in this narrower legal sense if your two imaginary disputes escalated and you sued either the landlord or the instructor. If during the dispute with your landlord you returned to Illinois for the summer and there filed an action against your California landlord, you might well be met with the defense that courts in Illinois had no jurisdiction over the landlord. If you filed suit in federal court in California against either the instructor or the law school, a different kind of jurisdiction question might arise. While conceding that both the instructor and the school could be sued in California, the defendants might challenge the jurisdiction of *federal* courts over the lawsuit: Whether the challenge was successful would depend on whether you could either frame your unfair grading complaint as a claim "arising under federal law" or convince the court that you were still a "citizen" of Illinois and that you and the defendant(s) were of diverse citizenship.

2. Jurisdiction and the Constitution

The next two chapters explore the ways in which courts in the United States conceive of and resolve questions like those raised in the preceding hypothetical case. Exploring the topic will be easier if you have some sense of both the terminology and the context in which jurisdictional issues arise. The basic terminology requires the student to distinguish between "personal" jurisdiction, the focus of Chapter II, and "subject matter" jurisdiction, the focus of Chapter III. Lawyers would describe the challenge to the Illinois suit against your California landlord as involving a question of *personal jurisdiction* — the power of an Illinois court to render a judgment binding someone who may have never set foot in Illinois. They would describe the challenge to the federal courts' power to decide the question of your grade as raising the issue of federal courts' *subject matter jurisdiction* — the power of federal (as opposed to state) courts to decide certain kinds of cases. The terminology is slightly misleading (sometimes subject matter jurisdiction depends on, for example, the citizenship of the parties to a lawsuit), but at the outset you need only bear in mind that personal and subject matter jurisdiction are *both* necessary ingredients of any court's power to render a binding decision in a case; that is, a court must have both subject matter *and* personal jurisdiction to render a valid judgment.

The nearly obsessive concern with jurisdiction ranks high among the distinguishing characteristics of the Anglo-American legal system. The concept has special significance in the United States, where government power is divided among states and between the states as a whole and the federal government: No single government entity has plenary power. This system of limited and overlapping authority means that government agencies — including courts — must repeatedly decide which agency has the power to exercise authority in a given situation. Because the federal Constitution defines the lines of authority among the competing centers of power, courts look to the Constitution for their basic framework in deciding issues of judicial jurisdiction. This aspect of civil procedure will be for many students their first law school encounter with the Constitution, the text of which appears in the Rules supplement that accompanies the casebook.

Three parts of the Constitution bear on jurisdiction. Article III authorizes the establishment of the system of federal courts and in Section 2 sets the limits of federal judicial authority. Federal courts cannot exceed those jurisdictional boundaries, and Congress has the power in many instances to restrict the scope of federal judicial authority more narrowly than does the Constitution. The constraints imposed by Article III and the legislation implementing it are the focus of Chapter III, on subject matter jurisdiction.

Article IV, Section 1 requires that "Full Faith and Credit . . . be given in each State to the . . . judicial proceedings of every other State." The Supreme Court has interpreted this clause to require that State *A* recognize and enforce judgments of State *B*, but, as you are about to see, the clause has an important unstated condition — such judgments are entitled to full faith and credit only if the court rendering them had jurisdiction to do so. Finally, Section 1 of the Fourteenth Amendment provides that no "State [shall] deprive any person of life, liberty or property without due process of law." This clause, known as the Due Process Clause, has proved one of the cornerstones of modern constitutional and procedural theory. It derives its relation to jurisdiction from Pennoyer v.

Neff, a case that might be termed the great-grandparent of personal jurisdiction, the topic of Chapter II. As you will see, *Pennoyer* made the question of what we now call personal jurisdiction part of the Constitution.

3.   The Constitution and Choice of Law

Beyond personal and subject matter jurisdiction, the Constitution shapes U.S. litigation in a third way: It often dictates which set of laws a court must apply to a dispute. There are two key ways in which the Constitution dictates choice of law. First, Article VI provides that the Constitution and federal laws "shall be the supreme Law of the Land; and the Judges in every State shall be bound thereby, any Thing in the Constitution or Laws of any State to the Contrary notwithstanding." This provision is commonly referred to as the Supremacy Clause. Although the import of the Supremacy Clause is typically covered in a Constitutional Law class rather than in Civil Procedure, for present purposes it is enough to understand that the clause means that if Congress has enacted a statute dealing with a particular subject, both federal and state courts are required to enforce the federal statute, regardless of whether there is a contrary state statute or state common law rule.

The second key way in which the Constitution dictates choice of law is that, in the absence of a controlling federal statute, the federal court system is required to respect both the statutory and common law rules of the several states. For an example of how such an issue might arise, imagine that your hypothetical dispute with your California landlord found its way to a federal court. What law would the court apply to the dispute? Would it be bound by the California law of landlord and tenant? Or would it be free to apply what it thought was a more sensible or just system of regulation to the dispute before it? That question is the focus of Chapter IV, on the *Erie* problem, so-called from the name of its leading case, Erie Railroad v. Tompkins. *Erie* is a case of constitutional dimensions — or so it insists — but, unlike personal or subject matter jurisdiction, one cannot readily locate the constitutional provisions from which it flows; that enigma itself is part of the problem. Together with personal and subject matter jurisdiction, the Supremacy Clause and the *Erie* doctrine shape the environment in which U.S. litigation operates.

PERSONAL JURISDICTION

II

A. The Origins

Personal jurisdiction is a part of U.S. constitutional law because of Pennoyer v. Neff, a case whose deceptively simple facts spawned a truly splendid doctrinal elaboration. To understand those facts you need to have some background. One of the more difficult parts of a lawsuit often comes at its end, when a victorious plaintiff tries to collect the judgment from the defendant, who declines to pay. When this happens, the plaintiff may obtain a writ of execution from the court, which will authorize the sheriff to seize any property belonging to the defendant, sell it, and give the resulting money to the plaintiff (up to the amount of the judgment). When that sale occurs, the sheriff gives to whomever buys the defendant's property a "sheriff's deed" as evidence of title. The second piece of background you need for *Pennoyer* concerns the idea of "constructive" notice. In law "constructive" generally means "fictional" or "pretend." As you have already seen, defendants generally receive service of process, but what happens if no one can find the defendant? Under those conditions many states provide for a notice in a newspaper — in those fine-print columns no one reads. Under such conditions service is "constructive" because it is highly unlikely that the defendant will actually see it. Finally, you need to know that "attachment" is the legal term for an officially sanctioned seizure of property: Real estate, cars, and other property may be "attached." Sometimes "attachment" means literal seizure; other times it means posting notices on property or on records of title so that prospective buyers know it cannot be sold.

Pennoyer v. Neff
95 U.S. 714 (1877)

Mr. Justice FIELD delivered the opinion of the Court.

[The case concerned two lawsuits, the first in the state courts of Oregon, the second in federal court. In the first lawsuit Mitchell, a lawyer, sued his client, Neff, for unpaid legal fees. At the time Neff was, in the court's words, "a non-resident of the State [who] was not personally served with process, and did not appear [i.e., did not come to court or otherwise resist the lawsuit]. . . . [J]udgment was entered upon his default in not answering the complaint, upon a constructive service of summons by publication." *After* this default judgment, Neff acquired 300 acres of land in Oregon from the federal government. To satisfy his judgment Mitchell had the sheriff seize and sell the land. Pennoyer bought it and received a sheriff's deed as evidence of title. The sheriff then turned the sale proceeds over to Mitchell. Sometime after these events Neff reappeared, and when he discovered what had become of his land, brought the second lawsuit with which *Pennoyer* is concerned. Neff sued Pennoyer "to recover the possession of [the] tract of land." As evidence of their respective titles, Neff pointed to the original government deed, and Pennoyer pointed to the sheriff's deed. In this second suit the court thus had to decide whether the first lawsuit and the sheriff's sale had extinguished Neff's title. The opinion begins with an analysis of the form of notice in the first suit.]

The Code of Oregon provides for such [constructive] service when an action is brought against a non-resident and absent defendant, who has property within the State. It also provides, where the action is for the recovery of money or damages, for the attachment of the property of the non-resident. And it also declares that no natural person is subject to the jurisdiction of a court of the State, "unless he appear in the court, or be found within the State, or be a resident thereof, or have property therein; and, in the last case, only to the extent of such property at the time the jurisdiction attached." Construing this latter provision to mean that, in an action for money or damages where a defendant does not appear in the court, and is not found within the State, and is not a resident thereof, but has property therein, the jurisdiction of the court extends only over such property, the declaration expresses a principle of general, if not universal, law. The authority of every tribunal is necessarily restricted by the territorial limits of the State in which it is established. Any attempt to exercise authority beyond those limits would be deemed in every other forum, as has been said by this court, an illegitimate assumption of power, and be resisted as mere abuse. D'Arcy v. Ketchum et al., 11 How. 165. In the case against the plaintiff, the property here in controversy sold under the judgment rendered was not attached, nor in any way brought under the jurisdiction of the court. Its first connection with the case was caused by a levy of the execution. It was not, therefore, disposed of pursuant to any adjudication, but only in enforcement of a personal judgment, having no relation to the property, rendered against a non-resident without service of process upon him in the action, or his appearance therein. The court below did not consider that an attachment of the property was essential to its jurisdiction or to the validity of the sale, but held that the judgment was invalid from defects in the affidavit upon which the order of publication was obtained, and in the affidavit by which the publication was proved.

There is some difference of opinion among the members of this court as to the rulings upon these alleged defects. [The disagreement centered on whether the statute required an affidavit from the "printer," as the statute specified, or whether one from the editor would suffice.]

If, therefore, we were confined to the rulings of the court below upon the defects in the affidavits mentioned, we should be unable to uphold its decision. But it was also contended in that court, and is insisted upon here, that the judgment in the State court against the plaintiff was void for want of personal service of process on him, or of his appearance in the action in which it was rendered, and that the premises in controversy could not be subjected to the payment of the demand of a resident creditor except by a proceeding in rem; that is, by a direct proceeding against the property for that purpose. If these positions are sound, the ruling of the Circuit Court as to the invalidity of that judgment must be sustained, notwithstanding our dissent from the reasons upon which it was made. And that they are sound would seem to follow from two well-established principles of public law respecting the jurisdiction of an independent State over persons and property. The several States of the Union are not, it is true, in every respect independent, many of the rights and powers which originally belonged to them being now vested in the government created by the Constitution. But, except as restrained and limited by that instrument, they possess and exercise the authority of independent States, and the principles of public law to which we have referred are applicable to them. One of these principles is, that every State possesses exclusive jurisdiction and sovereignty over persons and property within its territory. As a consequence, every State has the power to determine for itself the civil status and capacities of its inhabitants; to prescribe the subjects upon which they may contract, the forms and solemnities with which their contracts shall be executed, the rights and obligations arising from them, and the mode in which their validity shall be determined and their obligations enforced; and also to regulate the manner and conditions upon which property situated within such territory, both personal and real, may be acquired, enjoyed, and transferred. The other principle of public law referred to follows from the one mentioned; that is, that no State can exercise direct jurisdiction and authority over persons or property without its territory. Story, Confl. Laws, c. 2; Wheat. Int. Law, pt. 2, c. 2. The several States are of equal dignity and authority, and the independence of one implies the exclusion of power from all others. And so it is laid down by jurists, as an elementary principle, that the laws of one State have no operation outside of its territory, except so far as is allowed by comity; and that no tribunal established by it can extend its process beyond that territory so as to subject either persons or property to its decisions. "Any exertion of authority of this sort beyond this limit," says Story, "is a mere nullity, and incapable of binding such persons or property in any other tribunals." Story, Confl. Laws, sect. 539.

But as contracts made in one State may be enforceable only in another State, and property may be held by non-residents, the exercise of the jurisdiction which every State is admitted to possess over persons and property within its own territory will often affect persons and property without it. To any influence exerted in this way by a State affecting persons resident or property situated elsewhere, no objection can be justly taken; whilst any direct exertion of authority upon them, in an attempt to give ex-territorial operation to its laws, or to enforce an ex-territorial jurisdiction by its tribunals, would be deemed an encroachment upon the independence of the State in which the persons are domiciled or the property is situated, and be resisted as usurpation.

Thus the State, through its tribunals, may compel persons domiciled within its limits to execute, in pursuance of their contracts respecting property elsewhere situated, instruments in such form and with such solemnities as to transfer the title, so far as such formalities can be complied with; and the exercise of this jurisdiction in no manner interferes with the supreme control over the property by the State within which it is situated.

So the State, through its tribunals, may subject property situated within its limits owned by non-residents to the payment of the demand of its own citizens against them; and the exercise of this jurisdiction in no respect infringes upon the sovereignty of the State where the owners are domiciled. Every State owes protection to its own citizens; and, when non-residents deal with them, it is a legitimate and just exercise of authority to hold and appropriate any property owned by such non-residents to satisfy the claims of its citizens. It is in virtue of the State's jurisdiction over the property of the non-resident situated within its limits that its tribunals can inquire into that non-resident's obligations to its own citizens, and the inquiry can then be carried only to the extent necessary to control the disposition of the property. If the non-residents have no property in the State, there is nothing upon which the tribunals can adjudicate. . . .

If, without personal service, judgments *in personam*, obtained *ex parte* against non-residents and absent parties, upon mere publication of process, which, in the great majority of cases, would never be seen by the parties interested, could be upheld and enforced, they would be the constant instruments of fraud and oppression. Judgments for all sorts of claims upon contracts and for torts, real or pretended, would be thus obtained, under which property would be seized, when the evidence of the transactions upon which they were founded, if they ever had any existence, had perished.

Substituted service by publication, or in any other authorized form, may be sufficient to inform parties of the object of proceedings taken where property is once brought under the control of the court by seizure or some equivalent act. The law assumes that property is always in the possession of its owner, in person or by agent; and it proceeds upon the theory that its seizure will inform him, not only that it is taken into the custody of the court, but that he must look to any proceedings authorized by law upon such seizure for its condemnation and sale. Such service may also be sufficient in cases where the object of the action is to reach and dispose of property in the State, or of some interest therein, by enforcing a contract or a lien respecting the same, or to partition it among different owners, or, when the public is a party, to condemn and appropriate it for a public purpose. In other words, such service may answer in all actions which are substantially proceedings in rem. But where the entire object of the action is to determine the personal rights and obligations of the defendants, that is, where the suit is merely in personam, constructive service in this form upon a non-resident is ineffectual for any purpose. Process from the tribunals of one State cannot run into another State, and summon parties there domiciled to leave its territory and respond to proceedings against them. Publication of process or notice within the State where the tribunal sits cannot create any greater obligation upon the non-resident to appear: Process sent to him out of the State, and process published within it, are equally unavailing in proceedings to establish his personal liability. . . .

[The court explained that to acquire jurisdiction by attachment Oregon would have had to attach the property before the lawsuit; doing so afterward did not suffice to establish jurisdiction.]

The force and effect of judgments rendered against non-residents without personal service of process upon them, or their voluntary appearance, have been the subject of frequent consideration in the courts of the United States and of the several States, as attempts have been made to enforce such judgments in States other than those in which they were rendered, under the provision of the Constitution requiring that "full faith and credit shall be given in each State to the public acts, records, and judicial proceedings of every other State"; and the act of Congress [current version at 28 U.S.C. §1738] providing for the mode of authenticating such acts, records, and proceedings, and declaring that, when thus authenticated, "they shall have such faith and credit given to them in every court within the United States as they have by law or usage in the courts of the State from which they are or shall be taken." In the earlier cases, it was supposed that the act gave to all judgments the same effect in other States which they had by law in the State where rendered. But this view was afterwards qualified so as to make the act applicable only when the court rendering the judgment had jurisdiction of the parties and of the subject-matter, and not to preclude an inquiry into the jurisdiction of the court in which the judgment was rendered, or the right of the State itself to exercise authority over the person or the subject-matter. M'Elmoyle v. Cohen, 13 Pet. 312. . . .

Since the adoption of the Fourteenth Amendment to the Federal Constitution, the validity of such judgments may be directly questioned, and their enforcement in the State resisted, on the ground that proceedings in a court of justice to determine the personal rights and obligations of parties over whom that court has no jurisdiction do not constitute due process of law. Whatever difficulty may be experienced in giving to those terms a definition which will embrace every permissible exertion of power affecting private rights, and exclude such as is forbidden, there can be no doubt of their meaning when applied to judicial proceedings. They then mean a course of legal proceedings according to those rules and principles which have been established in our systems of jurisprudence for the protection and enforcement of private rights. To give such proceedings any validity, there must be a tribunal competent by its constitution — that is, by the law of its creation — to pass upon the subject-matter of the suit; and, if that involves merely a determination of the personal liability of the defendant, he must be brought within its jurisdiction by service of process within the State, or his voluntary appearance.

Except in cases affecting the personal status of the plaintiff, and cases in which that mode of service may be considered to have been assented to in advance, as hereinafter mentioned, the substituted service of process by publication, allowed by the law of Oregon and by similar laws in other States, where actions are brought against non-residents, is effectual only where, in connection with process against the person for commencing the action, property in the State is brought under the control of the court, and subjected to its disposition by process adapted to that purpose, or where the judgment is sought as a means of reaching such property or affecting some interest therein; in other words, where the action is in the nature of a proceeding in rem. As stated by Cooley in his Treatise on Constitutional Limitations, 405, for any other purpose than to subject the property of a non-resident to valid claims against him in the State, "due process of law would require appearance or personal service before the defendant could be personally bound by any judgment rendered." . . .

It follows from the views expressed that the personal judgment recovered in the State court of Oregon against the plaintiff herein, then a non-resident of the State, was without any validity, and did not authorize a sale of the property in controversy.

To prevent any misapplication of the views expressed in this opinion, it is proper to observe that we do not mean to assert, by anything we have said, that a State may not authorize proceedings to determine the status of one of its citizens towards a non-resident, which would be binding within the State, though made without service of process or personal notice to the non-resident. The jurisdiction which every State possesses to determine the civil status and capacities of all its inhabitants involves authority to prescribe the conditions on which proceedings affecting them may be commenced and carried on within its territory. The State, for example, has absolute right to prescribe the conditions upon which the marriage relation between its own citizens shall be created, and the causes for which it may be dissolved. . . .

Neither do we mean to assert that a State may not require a non-resident entering into a partnership or association within its limits, or making contracts enforceable there, to appoint an agent or representative in the State to receive service of process and notice in legal proceedings instituted with respect to such partnership, association, or contracts, or to designate a place where such service may be made and notice given, and provide, upon their failure, to make such appointment or to designate such place that service may be made upon a public officer designated for that purpose, or in some other prescribed way, and that judgments rendered upon such service may not be binding upon the non-residents both within and without the State. . . . Nor do we doubt that a State, on creating corporations or other institutions for pecuniary or charitable purposes, may provide a mode in which their conduct may be investigated, their obligations enforced, or their charters revoked, which shall require other than personal service upon their officers or members. Parties becoming members of such corporations or institutions would hold their interest subject to the conditions prescribed by law.

In the present case, there is no feature of this kind, and, consequently, no consideration of what would be the effect of such legislation in enforcing the contract of a non-resident can arise. The question here respects only the validity of a money judgment rendered in one State, in an action upon a simple contract against the resident of another, without service of process upon him, or his appearance therein.

Judgment affirmed.

[Mr. Justice HUNT dissented.]

NOTES AND PROBLEMS

1. Before considering anything else, look back at the facts.

a. Do we know whether Neff ever learned about the existence of Mitchell's original lawsuit?

b. If not, isn't the absence of notice a telling objection to the way in which the first lawsuit was conducted?

c. Did the court discuss this objection?

2. The case operates on two levels — simple facts and lofty doctrine. According to the opinion, what facts would have to be different for the Oregon courts to have had jurisdiction to enter a valid judgment in Mitchell's original suit against Neff?

3. Much of the lofty doctrine has to do with dividing the world into two jurisdictional categories: *in personam* and *in rem*. The case assumes that jurisdiction is about power and that one can divide power into two apparently distinct categories — power over persons and power over property. Making that distinction implied that one could sensibly think about Oregon's having power over Neff's property (had it gone about acquiring it in the proper way) as a question separate from its having power over Neff himself. Power over Neff himself came to be known as jurisdiction *in personam* (over the person); power over his property came to be known as jurisdiction *in rem* (over the thing). Modern legal scholars have tended to believe that the distinction doesn't hold up. The best critique appears in Geoffrey C. Hazard, Jr., A General Theory of State Court Jurisdiction, 1965 S. Ct. Rev. 241. As you will see, in recent years the Supreme Court has also reconsidered this distinction.

a. *In personam* jurisdiction looks, at first, refreshingly simple. To obtain jurisdiction over a person one must personally serve that person with process within the borders of the state in question. In *Pennoyer's* view, serving him by other means in other places does not work. Working with the facts of *Pennoyer*, explain why the Oregon court did not obtain *in personam* jurisdiction over Neff.

b. *In rem* jurisdiction, the more obscure category, seems to flow from a problem created by the rules for *in personam* jurisdiction: People sometimes own property distant from their usual personal residence.

What happens if the title to property is disputed while the alleged owner is out of the state — perhaps for years at a time? If *in personam* jurisdiction is the only possibility, nothing can be done until the owner returns and can be served with process. Unwilling to see that result, the court created a procedure by which a court located in the same state as the property could enter a judgment disposing of that property — by seizing it before beginning the lawsuit. *Pennoyer* calls that procedure *in rem* jurisdiction. Working with the facts of *Pennoyer*, explain why the Oregon court did not obtain *in rem* jurisdiction over Neff.

4. In sorting out the case's doctrine, it may be helpful to think of the opinion as having three sections.

a. It begins with a recitation of the facts, here summarized in brackets. Spend some time becoming very clear about these facts; they will matter, here and in subsequent cases.

b. It proceeds to paint, in very broad strokes, the principles of personal jurisdiction, explaining along the way why Oregon's courts obtained no jurisdiction over Neff in the first lawsuit. The basic proposition is that the procedure used in Mitchell v. Neff fell between two stools, achieving neither *in rem* nor *in personam* jurisdiction. Implicit in this doctrinal discussion is that these two jurisdictional categories are mutually exclusive and that they exhaust the universe of possibilities.

c. Finally, starting with the paragraph that begins "To prevent any misapplication. . . ," the opinion qualifies and retracts some of the broad statements it makes in the second section. Can you explain how this section changes some of the jurisdictional principles (or at least the way in which they will be applied in practice) of the second section?

5. Mitchell's original suit against Neff occurred in 1866. The Fourteenth Amendment — part of a revolution in state-federal relations following the Civil War — was not ratified until 1868. Is it surprising to find that amendment applied retroactively?

6. *Pennoyer* established fundamental jurisdictional doctrine whose main outlines prevailed for a century and which is still good law in many fundamental respects. *Pennoyer* proclaims that its holding rests on the Constitution, and the opinion mentions both the Due Process and the Full Faith and Credit clauses. That assertion has two implications. First, because the Due Process Clause restricts the power of state governments, the boundaries of personal jurisdiction proclaimed by the Supreme Court bind state courts.

Pennoyer's mention of the Full Faith and Credit Clause (U.S. Const. Art. IV, §1) pointed to a second constitutional issue. The opinion links full faith and credit to jurisdiction: the courts of State Y need not heed a judgment entered by the courts of State X if X lacked personal jurisdiction over the defendant. That proposition is sometimes described as the doctrine of *collateral attack:* A defendant may under some circumstances attack in a second — collateral — proceeding a judgment rendered without jurisdiction. What circumstances? It is difficult in a brief space to sketch all the variations, but, at a minimum, it is possible to attack collaterally a judgment entered without personal jurisdiction if the challenging party did not appear at all in the proceedings that led to the assertedly invalid judgment. Explain how this proposition applied to Neff in *Pennoyer.*

7. To test your understanding of *Pennoyer's* general principles and its specific holding, consider the following variations. To which does *Pennoyer* give a clear answer? In each assume that A, a resident of Minnesota, is suing B, a resident of North Dakota, in Minnesota (where B owns some land).

a. A serves B in North Dakota; B moves to dismiss the Minnesota action for lack of personal jurisdiction.

b. Same as (a) except that instead of appearing to object to the Minnesota court's jurisdiction, B defaults and the court enters judgment against her. A then takes that judgment to North Dakota to enforce; B appears in the enforcement proceeding and argues that the judgment is invalid and should not be enforced.

c. A serves B while B is traveling on business in Minnesota; B moves to dismiss for lack of personal jurisdiction.

d. Same as (c) except that instead of moving to dismiss, B defaults; A recovers a default judgment, which he then takes to North Dakota to enforce; B appears in the enforcement proceeding and argues that the judgment is invalid and should not be enforced.

e. A attaches B's land in Minnesota and obtains a judgment against B. A then seeks to have the land sold to satisfy the judgment. B sues to enjoin the sale, arguing that the court lacked jurisdiction over her or her land because she was not personally served.

f. Without attaching B's land, A serves B by publication, obtains a default judgment, and sues to enforce that judgment in North Dakota. B appears in North Dakota and objects.

g. A and B are married, and the suit is for divorce. A notifies B in North Dakota. B's lawyer moves to dismiss on the ground that the Minnesota court lacks personal jurisdiction.

h. Same facts as in (g), except that, in addition to a divorce, A seeks child support and alimony.

i. Finally, consider a question that *Pennoyer* does not answer: A attempts to serve B while B is on a fishing trip on the Minnesota-Wisconsin border. B moves to dismiss the Minnesota suit, claiming she was served in Wisconsin. B loses the motion to dismiss. A then gets a judgment and sues on the judgment in North Dakota. *B* appears in the North Dakota enforcement proceeding and argues that the judgment should not be enforced because the Minnesota court lacked jurisdiction — because she, *B*, was not in Minnesota when served with process. In principle, how should the court in this second enforcement action respond to *B*'s argument?

8. As befits an important case, *Pennoyer* had a colorful cast of characters:

> Mitchell was a well-known Portland lawyer specializing in land litigation and railroad right-of-way cases. In 1872 Mitchell was elected a United States Senator. Allegations of vote fraud were made against Mitchell, and indictments were sought but later dismissed. Interestingly, Judge Deady — who rendered the lower court decision in *Pennoyer* — actively supported the attempts to seek indictments for vote fraud. It is somewhat surprising that Mitchell was ever elected to public office given his somewhat sordid past. At the age of 22, Mitchell was forced to marry a fifteen-year-old girl "he had seduced and made pregnant." He soon abandoned his first wife and took up with a "schoolmarm." Mitchell next entered a bigamous marriage, and eventually fell "in love with his wife's sister and carr[ied] on an open affair for many years." [Citing and quoting from E. MacColl, The Shaping of a City 201-203 (1976).]
>
> Pennoyer was also active in public life. Educated at Harvard, he was both governor of Oregon and mayor of Portland. Something of a political maverick, Pennoyer proclaimed Oregon's Thanksgiving Day holiday one week later than the rest of the Nation.

Silberman, Shaffer v. Heitner: The End of an Era, 53 N.Y.U.L. Rev. 33, 44 n.53 (1978).

9. Focus on *Pennoyer*'s conceptual scheme. That scheme appears to involve three elements: power, consent, and notice. Each element persists, though in altered form, as a theme in today's jurisdictional cases.

a. *Power.* We have already considered the main outlines of *Pennoyer*'s division of power into two categories, *in personam* and *in rem* jurisdiction (see Note 3, supra). *In personam* jurisdiction, suggested *Pennoyer*, was necessary when one wanted to obtain either a money judgment or injunctive relief against a defendant; it would also suffice to decide the ownership of property. As already noted, *in rem* jurisdiction was available if one wanted to decide the ownership of property when one could not acquire *in personam* jurisdiction over a defendant claiming title. By extension, *in rem* jurisdiction could also be used to adjudicate claims unrelated to the property itself. For example, in *Pennoyer*, Mitchell's claim was for legal fees; he was interested in Neff's property only as a way of satisfying his contract claim. Some courts refer to this extended use of *in rem* jurisdiction as *quasi in rem*.

While it lasted, such *quasi in rem* jurisdiction created some striking doctrinal possibilities. The most unexpected elaboration of this branch of *Pennoyer* came in a series of cases holding that plaintiffs could obtain jurisdiction by seizing not only tangible property — land and chattels — but also debts owed to the defendant. Harris v. Balk, 198 U.S. 215 (1905), is probably the most bizarre of this line of cases. Harris owed Balk money, and Balk owed Epstein money; Balk lived in North Carolina, Epstein in Maryland. Harris journeyed from North Carolina to Maryland. While Harris was in Maryland, Epstein had him served with process, and a Maryland court entered a judgment saying that Harris should pay the money he owed Balk to Epstein instead. Balk challenged the Maryland court's power to enter this judgment (arguing that only personal service on him in Maryland would have justified such a judgment), but the Supreme Court upheld it. The consequence of *Harris* was that a state could acquire jurisdiction over persons whenever their debtors were present in that state by "attaching" the debts. The result was to make creditors liable (to the extent of amounts owed them) in any state in which their debtors set foot.

Pennoyer, as if anticipating the problems its absolute scheme would create, immediately softened it by establishing a number of exceptions. One such exception is the mysterious jurisdiction over the "status of one of its citizens toward a nonresident." The reference, as the remainder of the discussion makes clear, is to marriage and family relations. Even under the strictest interpretation of *Pennoyer*, a deserted spouse could sue for divorce — though not alimony or child support — even if the absent wife or husband could not be served within the state. See notes 7(g) and 7(h) above.

More obscure was the question of whether *Pennoyer*'s language about service of process as a requirement of *in personam* jurisdiction applied to *residents* of the state in question. Would Oregon have jurisdiction over a lifelong resident who could not be located and served with process? Was domicile — actual residence combined with the intent to remain indefinitely — enough to establish jurisdiction? With its attention focused on nonresidents, the opinion did not directly answer this question, although parts hint that the answer might be yes. We shall consider these questions in more detail later.

b. *Consent.*   *Pennoyer* allowed one other escape from the rigors of its jurisdictional scheme, an escape whose importance depended on how loosely one interprets the idea of consent. In several parts of the opinion the Court indicated that nonresidents who had no property in the state were nevertheless subject to its jurisdiction if they had consented to its exercise — for example, by designating an agent in the state who would accept service of process on their behalf. The penultimate paragraph of the opinion goes further, saying that the state might *require* persons and organizations to appoint such agents (and thereby to "consent" to jurisdiction). If that rather loose idea of consent were taken far enough, a state could obtain jurisdiction over a wide variety of nonresidents by requiring them to agree to jurisdiction as a condition of engaging in various sorts of transactions in the state. For corporations, such required consent became a widespread way of obtaining jurisdiction; for persons, it was much more problematic because other portions of the Constitution give persons the right to travel between states and to do business: Could a state require someone to "consent" to jurisdiction as the price of doing something he had a constitutional right to do in any case? For example, could Oregon require that any person — such as Neff — contracting for legal services to be rendered in that state had "consented" to jurisdiction for claims arising from that contract? Again, we shall return to that theme later.

c. *Notice.*   The final, almost concealed strand of *Pennoyer* dealt with notice, a topic about which the court appears to have contradictory ideas. On the one hand, the opinion contains a paragraph ("If without personal service. . . .") suggesting the importance of notice in *in personam* actions. On the other hand, it is perfectly willing to permit notice by publication in *in rem* actions. This judicial schizophrenia led to two lines of apparently contradictory decisions.

For *in personam* actions, the terms of *Pennoyer*'s scheme almost guaranteed that defendants would receive notice: So long as personal service of process was the primary way of obtaining *in personam* jurisdiction, the questions of notice and power would collapse into one inquiry. By personally serving a person with process within its borders, a state would simultaneously give notice and assert power. Only after states attempted service by means other than personal service did the questions of notice and power separate themselves. We shall consider the question of the constitutional sufficiency of notice in Mullane v. Central Hanover Bank & Trust, infra page 175.

For *in rem* actions the court lapsed into wishful thinking and fictions. Justifying notice by publication, *Pennoyer* says, "Substituted service by publication, or in any other authorized form, may be sufficient to inform parties of the object of proceedings taken where property is once brought under the control of the court by seizure or some equivalent act. The law assumes that property is always in the possession of its owner, in person or by agent; and it proceeds upon the theory that its seizure will inform him. . . ." Using this rationale, courts for almost a century upheld very scanty notice, so long as the action in question could be called *in rem*. As we shall see, Mullane v. Central Hanover Bank & Trust ended this scheme.

10. Pennoyer *in a modern economy*. *Pennoyer* has its feet planted in a pre-industrial world with uncertain communications. The Court seemed to assume that the instance of the nonresident defendant would be only an occasional problem that could be averted in most cases by the availability of property as an alternative basis of jurisdiction. The Court proved a poor prophet; the decade following *Pennoyer* saw enormous railroad construction. The last quarter of the nineteenth century also witnessed both a great expansion of industrial production and the proliferation of often interlocking corporations organizing that production. Within 50 years of the decision other developments — the automobile, telegraph, and telephone — had nationalized economic life and even leisure activities in a way unforeseen by *Pennoyer's* authors. In consequence, many of the most difficult problems facing the courts after *Pennoyer* dealt with entities and situations to which *Pennoyer* only passingly alluded.

To solve them the Court repeatedly resorted to two concepts that appeared in *Pennoyer:* consent and presence. Under *Pennoyer* a state could acquire jurisdiction over a defendant who consented to its assertion of power; likewise over a defendant present in the state when served with process. For 70 years after *Pennoyer*, the courts stretched these ideas of consent and presence considerably.

a. *"Consent."*   Consent had its easiest application to corporations. Initially, courts held that corporations could be subject to service where they were incorporated, and this view found support in a Supreme Court dictum that "a corporation can have no legal existence out of the boundaries of the sovereignty by which it is created." Bank of Augusta v. Earle, 38 U.S. (13 Pet.) 519 (1839). Later it was held that corporations could operate outside the state that created them, but that the "host" state could place conditions on foreign corporations (meaning U.S. corporations operating outside their home state). The condition most important for present purposes was that of requiring consent to jurisdiction. Such consent might be express or implied, but if implied it was limited to suits arising from the transaction of business in the state.

With persons, the notion of consent was less clear. Thus, in Flexner v. Farson, 248 U.S. 289 (1919), the Supreme Court held that Kentucky did not have jurisdiction over a partnership doing business in Kentucky through an agent. The Court noted that the "consent" was a "mere fiction, founded upon the accepted doctrine that States could exclude foreign corporations altogether" and could therefore require their consent as a condition to business activity. Since partnerships could not be excluded (because partnerships are not separate legal entities and therefore enjoy the rights of the individual partners), implied consent could not be found. But eight years later, in Hess v. Pawloski, 274 U.S. 352 (1927), the Court sustained jurisdiction over a nonresident defendant who had been involved in an accident on the Massachusetts highways. The statute involved provided that

> the acceptance by a nonresident of the rights and privileges [of driving on the Massachusetts highways] shall be deemed equivalent to the appointment [of a local official] upon whom may be served all lawful processes . . . growing out of any accident or collision in which said nonresident may be involved while operating a motor vehicle on such a way, and said acceptance or operation shall be a signification of his agreement that any such process against him . . . shall be of the same legal force and validity as if served on him personally.

The Court sustained the statute based on the implied consent of the nonresident, the rather dubious power to exclude nonresidents absent consent, and the "state's power to regulate the use of its highways." Later, the *Hess* doctrine was applied to authorize jurisdiction over a nonresident who was selling securities in Iowa; such an activity had been heavily regulated by the state. Henry L. Doherty & Co. v. Goodman, 294 U.S. 623 (1935).

b. *"Presence."*   A corporation does not have a physical existence that permits personal service where it is located. Initially the problem was solved by *Bank of Augusta,* supra, which held that a state could exact "consent" to jurisdiction as a price of permitting a corporation to operate. Then courts began to reject the *Bank of Augusta* dictum and held that a corporation was "present" (that is, subject to jurisdiction) if it conducted a certain level of activity in the state. Once present, the corporation was subject to jurisdiction for all claims (just as under *Pennoyer* an individual was subject to jurisdiction for all claims if personally served in the forum).

The courts used both consent and presence alternatively; the confusion was compounded because they used the same test—doing business—to determine both issues. That is, a corporation doing business might be held either to have "consented" to jurisdiction or to be "present" in the state. Such manipulation of consent and presence achieved bearable results—states could by and large regulate activities conducted within their borders—but getting to those results required some rather creaky doctrinal machinery. The modern reworking of that machinery is the focus of the next section.

NOTE ON THE MECHANICS OF JURISDICTION:
CHALLENGE AND WAIVER

Before further exploring the development of personal jurisdiction, the
student will find it useful to understand how lawyers bring jurisdictional
challenges to bear on actual cases. The workings of such procedures
grow from *Pennoyer* and expose some otherwise hidden assumptions
about the meaning of jurisdiction.

Assume Abe, a resident of Illinois, sues Barbara, a resident of California,
in Illinois, and Barbara thinks that she is not subject to personal jurisdiction. How does she proceed?

The simplest but riskiest course is for Barbara to do nothing. If she is
very sure indeed that the court lacks jurisdiction, she may simply decline
to appear, suffer a default judgment, and attack the judgment only when
Abe seeks to enforce it in a subsequent proceeding. Even before *Pennoyer*,
that route — known as collateral attack — lay open. D'Arcy v. Ketchum,
52 U.S. 165 (1850). It carries, however, a serious risk, for if the second
court rejects the jurisdictional challenge, Barbara can raise no other
defenses on the merits. Jurisdiction, but *only* jurisdiction, is open to
collateral attack.

What happens if Barbara wishes to pursue a less heroic course of
action; how does she raise jurisdictional objections in the first proceeding?

a. Under the Federal Rules (and state statutes patterned on them),
Barbara must raise the defense in a pre-answer motion if she makes one.
If she makes no pre-answer motion, she must include the objection of
personal jurisdiction as a defense in her answer. Making an appearance
or litigating other issues but failing to challenge personal jurisdiction in
one of these two ways results in waiver of the jurisdictional defense. See
Rule 12(b), (g), (h). If Barbara raises the objection at the proper time,
she does not waive it by joining it with other defenses or objections.
Moreover, she must litigate the claim promptly. This happens as a matter
of course if she makes a pre-answer motion. If she makes no such motion
but challenges jurisdiction in her answer, she must promptly move for
dismissal on this ground. Although the Rules do not say so, courts will
not look kindly on a defendant who waits until the end of discovery
before moving to dismiss for want of personal jurisdiction.

b. In a few state systems (and in many older cases), Barbara would
raise the jurisdictional claim by making a "special appearance." See, for
example, 735 Ill. Comp. Stat. 5/2-301(b) (West 1992); Tex. R. Civ. P.
120a (1999). The procedure is "so-called" for reasons you can now
understand: In *Pennoyer*'s scheme, a defendant who "appeared" might

be held to have consented to the state's exercise of power. What was needed was a form of "appearance" that would not be equated with "presence" or consent. A "special" appearance permitted the defendant to object to jurisdiction without the action of objecting being itself the basis for jurisdiction. Finally, what happens if the defendant has availed herself of the system's opportunity to challenge jurisdiction but loses? May she immediately appeal that decision? Some states do permit such an immediate appeal. Other states and the federal system treat a jurisdictional defense like other pretrial rulings and require that an appeal await final judgment. If you were a defendant with a jurisdictional defense, which pattern would you prefer? If you were a plaintiff, which would you prefer?

NOTES AND PROBLEMS

1. Defendants can easily — even by inattention — waive objections to personal jurisdiction. What does that say about the nature of this defense?

2. Rule 12(b) allows a defense of lack of personal jurisdiction to be raised by motion, prior to answering the plaintiff's complaint. Why would a defendant choose to answer by motion rather than in her answer to the complaint? To get an idea of one possible reason, read Rules 8(b) and 11, which puts the lawyer's professional standing — and also her pocketbook — behind the allegations of an answer. Rule 13 supplies another reason: It requires that an answer contain any counterclaim arising out of the same transaction as the claim.

3. Other preliminary matters may also be raised by motion before answering the complaint. See Rule 12(b). Therein lies a trap for the unwary, for Rule 12(h) provides that objections to the court's jurisdiction are waived unless they are made by motion or by answer and are waived if a Rule 12 motion is made raising other issues but not raising the jurisdictional issue, even though it is put in the answer. Why is such a premium placed upon arguing the jurisdictional issue at the same time as or before other issues?

Consider the following scenarios. Each assumes that the plaintiff has filed a complaint and the defendant then makes one of the following responses. The question is whether the defendant has preserved her jurisdictional objection.

a. Defendant makes a pre-answer 12(b)(6) motion; upon its denial she files an answer containing both a defense on the merits and a 12(b)(2) motion to dismiss for want of personal jurisdiction.

b. Defendant makes a 12(f) motion to strike a scandalous allegation from the complaint; she then makes a 12(b)(2) motion.

c. Defendant moves to transfer venue under 28 U.S.C. §1404; after transfer is denied she moves to dismiss under 12(b)(2).

4. Other actions by the defendant, apart from motions under Rule 12(b) and answers to the complaint, may result in waiver of the jurisdictional issue, and a defendant who wishes to object to personal jurisdiction must carefully consider any litigation activity preceding such an objection. For example, litigating the propriety of a preliminary injunction or filing a permissive counterclaim before answer or 12(b) motion have sometimes been held to constitute waiver. See Wright, Federal Courts 463.

B. The Modern Constitutional Formulation of Power

Each of the elements found in *Pennoyer* — power, consent, and notice — continues to play a role in modern jurisdictional thought. But each has taken on a different shape, one that sometimes makes the original assumptions difficult to recognize. The remainder of this section on personal jurisdiction traces the evolution of these three themes in the modern law of personal jurisdiction.

1. Redefining Constitutional Power

Operating under the framework established by *Pennoyer,* state and federal courts encountered several situations for which its schema seemed ill-adapted. One of the most frequent involved *in personam* jurisdiction over the defendant corporation. The corporate form of business enterprise presented problems because corporations have neither physical reality nor wills. Thus, to speak either of corporate "presence" or corporate "consent" becomes difficult. Yet *Pennoyer* had said that such presence or consent was generally a prerequisite to jurisdiction. Courts coped with such difficulties by attributing the activities of various employees and agents to the corporation, finding that enough such activities constituted corporate "presence" or "consent." The following landmark case rearranges the landscape of personal jurisdiction; most contemporary debate concerns its application and interpretation, and it thus bears careful study.

International Shoe Co. v. Washington
326 U.S. 310 (1945)

Mr. Chief Justice STONE delivered the opinion of the Court.

The questions for decision are (1) whether, within the limitations of the due process clause of the Fourteenth Amendment, the appellant, a Delaware corporation, has by its activities in the State of Washington rendered itself amenable to proceedings in the courts of that state to recover unpaid contributions to the state unemployment compensation fund enacted by state statutes, Washington Unemployment Compensation Act, and (2) whether the state can exact those contributions consistently with the due process clause of the Fourteenth Amendment.

The statutes in question set up a comprehensive scheme of unemployment compensation, the costs of which are defrayed by contributions required to be made by employers to a state unemployment compensation fund. The contributions are a specified percentage of the wages payable annually by each employer for his employees' services in the state. The assessment and collection of the contributions and the fund are administered by appellees. Section 14(c) of the Act authorizes appellee Commissioner to issue an order and notice of assessment of delinquent contributions upon prescribed personal service of the notice upon the employer if found within the state, or, if not so found, by mailing the notice to the employer by registered mail at his last known address. . . .

In this case notice of assessment for the years in question was personally served upon a sales solicitor employed by appellant in the State of Washington, and a copy of the notice was mailed by registered mail to appellant at its address in St. Louis, Missouri. Appellant appeared specially before the office of unemployment and moved to set aside the order and notice of assessment on the ground that the service upon appellant's salesman was not proper service upon appellant; that appellant was not a corporation of the State of Washington and was not doing business within the state; that it had no agent within the state upon whom service could be made; and that appellant is not an employer and does not furnish employment within the meaning of the statute. . . .

The facts as found by the appeal tribunal and accepted by the state Superior Court and Supreme Court, are not in dispute. Appellant is a Delaware corporation, having its principal place of business in St. Louis, Missouri, and is engaged in the manufacture and sale of shoes and other footwear. It maintains places of business in several states, other than Washington, at which its manufacturing is carried on and from which its merchandise is distributed interstate through several sales units or branches located outside the State of Washington.

Appellant has no office in Washington and makes no contracts either for sale or purchase of merchandise there. It maintains no stock of merchandise in that state and makes there no deliveries of goods in intrastate commerce. During the years from 1937 to 1940, now in question, appellant employed eleven to thirteen salesmen under direct supervision and control of sales managers located in St. Louis. These salesmen resided in Washington; their principal activities were confined to that state; and they were compensated by commissions based upon the amount of their sales. The commissions for each year totaled more than $31,000. Appellant supplies its salesmen with a line of samples, each consisting of one shoe of a pair, which they display to prospective purchasers. On occasion they rent permanent sample rooms, for exhibiting samples, in business buildings, or rent rooms in hotels or business buildings temporarily for that purpose. The cost of such rentals is reimbursed by appellant.

The authority of the salesmen is limited to exhibiting their samples and soliciting orders from prospective buyers, at prices and on terms fixed by appellant. The salesmen transmit the orders to appellant's office in St. Louis for acceptance or rejection, and when accepted the merchandise for filling the orders is shipped f.o.b. from points outside Washington to the purchasers within the state. All the merchandise shipped into Washington is invoiced at the place of shipment from which collections are made. No salesman has authority to enter into contracts or to make collections.

The Supreme Court of Washington was of the opinion that the regular and systematic solicitation of orders in the state by appellant's salesmen, resulting in a continuous flow of appellant's product into the state, was sufficient to constitute doing business in the state so as to make appellant amenable to suit in its courts. But it was also of opinion that there were sufficient additional activities shown to bring the case within the rule frequently stated, that solicitation within a state by the agents of a foreign corporation plus some additional activities there are sufficient to render the corporation amenable to suit brought in the courts of the state to enforce an obligation arising out of its activities there. The court found such additional activities in the salesmen's display of samples sometimes in permanent display rooms, and the salesmen's residence within the state, continued over a period of years, all resulting in a substantial volume of merchandise regularly shipped by appellant to purchasers within the state. . . .

Appellant . . . insists that its activities within the state were not sufficient to manifest its "presence" there and that in its absence the state courts were without jurisdiction, that consequently it was a denial of due process for the state to subject appellant to suit. It refers to those cases in which it was said that the mere solicitation of orders for the purchase of goods within a state, to be accepted without the state and filled by shipment of the purchased goods interstate, does not render the corporation seller amenable to suit within the state. And appellant further argues that since it was not present within the state, it is a denial of due process to subject it to taxation or other money exaction. It thus denies the power of the state to lay the tax or to subject appellant to a suit for its collection.

Historically the jurisdiction of courts to render judgment in personam is grounded on their de facto power over the defendant's person. Hence his presence within the territorial jurisdiction of a court was prerequisite to its rendition of a judgment personally binding him. Pennoyer v. Neff. But now that the capias ad respondendum has given way to personal service of summons or other form of notice, due process requires only that in order to subject a defendant to a judgment in personam, if he be not present within the territory of the forum, he have certain minimum contacts with it such that the maintenance of the suit does not offend "traditional notions of fair play and substantial justice."

Since the corporate personality is a fiction, although a fiction intended to be acted upon as though it were a fact, it is clear that unlike an individual its "presence" without, as well as within, the state of its origin can be manifested only by activities carried on in its behalf by those who are authorized to act for it. To say that the corporation is so far "present" there as to satisfy due process requirements, for purposes of taxation or the maintenance of suits against it in the courts of the state, is to beg the question to be decided. For the terms "present" or "presence" are used merely to symbolize those activities of the corporation's agent within the state which courts will deem to be sufficient to satisfy the demands of due process. Those demands may be met by such contacts of the corporation with the state of the forum as to make it reasonable, in the context of our federal system of government, to require the corporation to defend the particular suit which is brought there. An "estimate of the inconveniences" which would result to the corporation from a trial away from its "home" or principal place of business is relevant in this connection.

"Presence" in the state in this sense has never been doubted when the activities of the corporation there have not only been continuous and systematic, but also give rise to the liabilities sued on, even though no consent to be sued or authorization to an agent to accept service of process has been given. Conversely it has been generally recognized that the casual presence of the corporate agent or even his conduct of single or isolated items of activities in a state in the corporation's behalf are not enough to subject it to suit on causes of action unconnected with the activities there. To require the corporation in such circumstances to defend the suit away from its home or other jurisdiction where it carries on more substantial activities has been thought to lay too great and unreasonable a burden on the corporation to comport with due process.

While it has been held, in cases on which appellant relies, that continuous activity of some sorts within a state is not enough to support the demand that the corporation be amenable to suits unrelated to that activity, there have been instances in which the continuous corporate operations within a state were thought so substantial and of such a nature as to justify suit against it on causes of action arising from dealings entirely distinct from those activities.

Finally, although the commission of some single or occasional acts of the corporate agent in a state sufficient to impose an obligation or liability on the corporation has not been thought to confer upon the state authority to enforce it, other such acts, because of their nature and quality and the circumstances of their commission, may be deemed sufficient to render the corporation liable to suit. True, some of the decisions holding the corporation amenable to suit have been supported by resort to the legal fiction that it has given its consent to service and suit, consent being implied [sic] from its presence in the state through the acts of its authorized agents. But more realistically it may be said that those authorized acts were of such a nature as to justify the fiction.

It is evident that the criteria by which we mark the boundary line between those activities which justify the subjection of a corporation to suit, and those which do not, cannot be simply mechanical or quantitative. The test is not merely, as has sometimes been suggested, whether the activity, which the corporation has seen fit to procure through its agents in another state, is a little more or a little less. Whether due process is satisfied must depend rather upon the quality and nature of the activity in relation to the fair and orderly administration of the laws which it was the purpose of the due process clause to insure. That clause does not contemplate that a state may make binding a judgment in personam against an individual or corporate defendant with which the state has no contacts, ties, or relations.

But to the extent that a corporation exercises the privilege of conducting activities within a state, it enjoys the benefits and protection of the laws of that state. The exercise of that privilege may give rise to obligations, and, so far as those obligations arise out of or are connected with the activities within the state, a procedure which requires the corporation to respond to a suit brought to enforce them can, in most instances, hardly be said to be undue.

Applying these standards, the activities carried on in behalf of appellant in the State of Washington were neither irregular nor casual. They were systematic and continuous throughout the years in question. They resulted in a large volume of interstate business, in the course of which appellant received the benefits and protection of the laws of the state, including the right to resort to the courts for the enforcement of its rights. The obligation which is here sued upon arose out of those very activities. It is evident that these operations establish sufficient contacts or ties with the state of the forum to make it reasonable and just, according to our traditional conception of fair play and substantial justice, to permit the state to enforce the obligations which appellant has incurred there. Hence we cannot say that the maintenance of the present suit in the State of Washington involves an unreasonable or undue procedure.

We are likewise unable to conclude that the service of the process within the state upon an agent whose activities establish appellant's "presence" there was not sufficient notice of the suit, or that the suit was so unrelated to those activities as to make the agent an inappropriate vehicle for communicating the notice. It is enough that appellant has established such contacts with the state that the particular form of substituted service adopted there gives reasonable assurance that the notice will be actual. Nor can we say that the mailing of the notice of suit to appellant by registered mail at its home office was not reasonably calculated to apprise appellant of the suit. . . .

Appellant having rendered itself amenable to suit upon obligations arising out of the activities of its salesmen in Washington, the state may maintain the present suit in personam to collect the tax laid upon the exercise of the privilege of employing appellant's salesmen within the state. For Washington has made one of those activities, which taken together establish appellant's "presence" there for purposes of suit, the taxable event by which the state brings appellant within the reach of its taxing power. The state thus has constitutional power to lay the tax and to subject appellant to a suit to recover it. The activities which establish its "presence" subject it alike to taxation by the state and to suit to recover the tax.

Affirmed.

Mr. Justice BLACK delivered the following opinion. . . .

I believe that the Federal Constitution leaves to each State, without any "ifs" or "buts," a power to tax and to open the doors of its courts for its citizens to sue corporations whose agents do business in those States. Believing that the Constitution gave the States that power, I think it a judicial deprivation to condition its exercise upon this Court's notion of "fair play," however appealing that term may be. Nor can I stretch the meaning of due process so far as to authorize this Court to deprive a State of the right to afford judicial protection to its citizens on the ground that it would be more "convenient" for the corporation to be sued somewhere else.

There is a strong emotional appeal in the words "fair play," "justice," and "reasonableness." But they were not chosen by those who wrote the original Constitution or the Fourteenth Amendment as a measuring rod for this Court to use in invalidating State or Federal laws passed by elected legislative representatives. No one, not even those who most feared a democratic government, ever formally proposed that courts should be given power to invalidate legislation under any such elastic standards. . . .

True, the State's power is here upheld. But the rule announced means that tomorrow's judgment may strike down a State or Federal enactment on the ground that it does not conform to the Court's idea of natural justice. . . .

NOTES AND PROBLEMS

1. *International Shoe* is an unusual case in two respects.

a. The opinion is remarkably vague about the application of the principles it announces to the facts before it. Can you infer what facts would have to change for the Court to have reached a different result?

b. In most cases the briefs and the ensuing opinion occupy the same conceptual universe — that is, the parties and the court agree, for example, that this is a contract case and that the central issue is whether the "offer" was definite enough to be accepted. *International Shoe* is different. The parties briefed and argued the case in the then-traditional categories of "presence" and "consent." The Court responded in quite different terms, with a conceptual scheme focusing on "minimum contacts" and "substantial justice and fair play." Should a court tell the parties in advance that it is contemplating such a doctrinal shift?

2. When the Court writes that, to be subject to a state's jurisdiction, a defendant must "have certain minimum contacts with it such that the maintenance of suit does not offend 'traditional notions of fair play and substantial justice,'" does it provide a workable standard for the lower courts to follow in deciding future cases? In later cases, if the salespeople in question are freelancers who work for several companies, will each of

the companies be subject to the jurisdiction of the State of Washington under the *International Shoe* rationale? What if their activities are not confined to Washington but also take them to Oregon and California? One commentator has suggested that the basic test of *International Shoe* is a good one but that because of its generality it must be subjected to a process of "arbitrary particularization" in order to come up with workable rules. Geoffrey C. Hazard, Jr., A General Theory of State-Court Jurisdiction, 1965 Sup. Ct. Rev. 241, 283.

3. *General and specific jurisdiction.* Consider the following paragraph of *International Shoe*:

> While it has been held, in cases on which appellant relies, that continuous activity of some sorts within a state is not enough to support the demand that the corporation be amenable to suits *unrelated to that activity*, there have been instances in which the continuous corporate operations within a state were thought so substantial and of such a nature as to justify suit against it on causes of action arising from dealings *entirely distinct from those activities.* (Emphasis added.)

Many have implied from this sentence an entire vision of jurisdiction.

a. In this view some cases will be relatively easy instances of *general jurisdiction* in which the defendant's contacts with the forum state are sufficiently "substantial" to support jurisdiction even over claims unrelated to those contacts. For example, General Motors has its chief place of business in Michigan. Under the theory of general jurisdiction, General Motors could be sued in Michigan even over contracts or torts concluded or committed in Idaho or Germany. *International Shoe* did nothing to disturb the rule that when a corporation is doing business in a state such that its contacts are "substantial," even cases unrelated to the corporation's activities within the state may be brought against the corporation there. Such cases fall within the category described above as instances "in which the continuous corporate operations within a state were thought so substantial and of such a nature as to justify a suit against it on causes of action arising from dealings entirely distinct from those activities." As the Court put it in Helicopteros Nacionales de Colombia v. Hall, 466 U.S. 408, 414(1984), "Even when the cause of action does not arise out of or relate to the foreign corporation's activities in the forum State, due process is not offended by a State's subjecting the corporation to its in personam jurisdiction when there are sufficient contacts between the State and the foreign corporation."

b. By contrast, where the defendant's activities fall short of general jurisdiction, the minimum contacts analysis of *International Shoe* becomes important. In those cases courts worry about the relation between the defendant's contacts and the claim on which plaintiff is suing. Commentators describe such cases as instances of *specific jurisdiction*, in which jurisdiction exists for the specific claim in question but not necessarily for other claims. All other things being equal, the more closely related the contacts and the facts giving rise to the claim, the more likely the court is to uphold jurisdiction.

The most elaborate and influential discussion of this jurisdictional scheme is that of Arthur von Mehren and Donald Trautman, Jurisdiction to Adjudicate: A Suggested Analysis, 79 Harv. L. Rev. 1121 (1966).

4. For practice in using the concepts of specific and general jurisdiction, consider the following variations on the facts in *International Shoe*. As stated in the case, assume that International Shoe is incorporated in Delaware and has its headquarters and principal manufacturing operations in Missouri. Further assume that International Shoe has no salespeople in Wyoming, sells no shoes there, buys no cowhide there, and does no business there of any sort — except use the roads for transporting its wares to other states.

a. A truck loaded with shoes, owned by International Shoe Co. and driven by one of its employees, traveled through Wyoming on its way to the State of Washington. While in Wyoming, the truck collided with a pickup driven by a rancher, who was injured in the accident. The rancher filed suit against International Shoe in Wyoming, alleging negligence by the International Shoe driver. Jurisdiction?

b. In Wyoming there also lives a former employee of International Shoe. Alleging that she was wrongfully discharged from her job in Missouri, she files suit against International Shoe in Wyoming. Jurisdiction?

What is the rationale on which one could explain a different jurisdictional outcome in 4a and 4b?

c. Same facts except the plaintiff sues in Missouri. In this instance would it make any difference whether the plaintiff was the rancher in 4a or the former employee in 4b?

d. Same facts except the plaintiff sues in Delaware. Would it make any difference whether the plaintiff was the rancher or the former employee?

e. Same facts as 4a, except that plaintiff rancher owns some shares of International Shoe bonds on which the corporation has failed to pay interest when due. He brings suit on two claims — personal injury and for the unpaid interest. Suppose there is jurisdiction as to the claim for personal injury; does it follow that the rancher can also sue for the bond interest?

5. *Domicile, incorporation, and jurisdiction.* If one accepts the notion of general jurisdiction, a question arises: Do easily identifiable circumstances exist in which a defendant invariably may be sued for all claims?

a. The circumstances most closely approaching such a rule are incorporation (for corporations) and domicile (for individuals). It is generally accepted that a corporation may be sued in its state of incorporation for all claims, even though that state serves primarily as an address of convenience — as Delaware does for many modern corporations. The result is sometimes justified by pointing out that the incorporating state has "created" the corporation (by granting its charter) and therefore can put whatever conditions it wishes on that grant. Can you see the shadow of *Pennoyer*'s notion of induced consent lurking here?

b. An analogous rule applies to the domicile (place of permanent residence) for individuals. Thus, in Milliken v. Meyer, 311 U.S. 457, 462-464 (1940), plaintiff sued Meyer, a permanent resident of Wyoming, in Wyoming courts. Meyer was served with process, but not in Wyoming, and, taking at face value *Pennoyer*'s suggestion that service effected outside the state would not suffice to confer jurisdiction, he challenged the Wyoming court's power to enter a binding judgment. The U.S. Supreme Court upheld jurisdiction:

> Domicile in the state is alone sufficient to bring an absent defendant within the reach of the state's jurisdiction. . . . As in the case of the authority of the United States over its absent citizens, the authority of a state over one of its citizens is not terminated by the mere fact of his absence from the state. The state which accords him privileges and affords protection to him and his property by virtue of his domicile may also exact reciprocal duties. . . . One such incident of domicile is amenability to suit within the state . . . where the state has provided and employed a reasonable method for apprising such an absent party of the proceedings against him.

2. Absorbing *In Rem* Jurisdiction

International Shoe provided a new framework for thinking about *in personam* jurisdiction over corporations. But the case left open other jurisdictional questions. *International Shoe* involved a corporate defendant (as did many of the most difficult jurisdictional questions), and it therefore did not discuss the applicability of its approach to jurisdiction over individuals. The second issue left untouched by *International Shoe* was *in rem* jurisdiction. Under the line of cases descended from *Pennoyer* and Harris v. Balk, the presence of property could be the basis for jurisdiction over claims of any sort. Recall that "property" included the debts that anyone owed to the defendant. For example, if Alfred Manhattanhite had lent money to his friend Jane Gotham and she took a trip to Florida, that state had the power to enter a judgment directing Jane to pay someone besides Alfred the money she owed him — if Jane's debt to Alfred were "attached" during her visit.

These two issues — the applicability of *International Shoe* to individuals and the role of *in rem* jurisdiction — came together in Shaffer v. Heitner, the most important jurisdictional case since *International Shoe*. A bit of substantive law background will help the jurisdictional point emerge more clearly. Directors of corporations are trustees, charged with guiding the corporation's affairs in a prudent manner. Like other trustees, they can be sued by their beneficiaries. But because the corporation is the beneficiary and is controlled by the directors, the prospect of such a suit to enforce the directors' fiduciary duties is nil — unless a representative of the corporation who is independent of the directors may sue. American law has developed such a procedure, called the shareholder's derivative suit. In a derivative action, a shareholder steps forward and sues the directors or officers in the name of the corporation, alleging some breach of fiduciary duty. If the suit is successful, the proceeds go to the corporation. Such suits have spawned numerous complex issues of procedural and corporate law as well as a good deal of controversy.

Shaffer v. Heitner
433 U.S. 186 (1977)

Mr. Justice MARSHALL delivered the opinion of the Court.

The controversy in this case concerns the constitutionality of a Delaware statute that allows a court of that State to take jurisdiction of a lawsuit by sequestering any property of the defendant that happens to be located in Delaware. Appellants contend that the sequestration statute as applied in this case violates the Due Process Clause of the Fourteenth Amendment both because it permits the state courts to exercise jurisdiction despite the absence of sufficient contacts among the defendants, the litigation, and the State of Delaware and because it authorizes the deprivation of defendants' property without providing adequate procedural safeguards. We find it necessary to consider only the first of these contentions.

I

Appellee Heitner, a nonresident of Delaware, is the owner of one share of stock in the Greyhound Corporation, a business incorporated under the laws of Delaware with its principal place of business in Phoenix, Ariz. On May 22, 1974, he filed a shareholder's derivative suit in the

Court of Chancery for New Castle County, Del., in which he named as defendants . . . 28 present or former officers or directors of one or both of the corporations. In essence, Heitner alleged that the individual defendants had violated their duties to Greyhound by causing it and its subsidiary to engage in actions that resulted in the corporation's being held liable for substantial damages in a private antitrust suit and a large fine in a criminal contempt action. The activities which led to these penalties took place in Oregon.

Simultaneously with his complaint, Heitner filed a motion for an order of sequestration of the Delaware property of the individual defendants pursuant to 10 Del. C. §366. This motion was accompanied by a supporting affidavit of counsel which stated that the individual defendants were nonresidents of Delaware. The affidavit identified the property to be sequestered as

> common stock, 3% Second Cumulative Preferenced Stock and stock unit credits of the Defendant Greyhound Corporation, a Delaware corporation, as well as all options and all warrants to purchase said stock issued to said individual Defendants and all contractual [sic] obligations, all rights, debts or credits due or accrued to or for the benefit of any of the said Defendants under any type of written agreement, contract, or other legal instrument of any kind whatever between any of the individual Defendants and said corporation.

The requested sequestration order was signed the day the motion was filed. Pursuant to that order, the sequestrator "seized" approximately 82,000 shares of Greyhound common stock belonging to 19 of the defendants, and options belonging to another two defendants. These seizures were accomplished by placing "stop transfer" orders or their equivalents on the books of the Greyhound Corporation. So far as the record shows, none of the certificates representing the seized property was physically present in Delaware. The stock was considered to be in Delaware, and so subject to seizure, by virtue of 8 Del. C. §169, which makes Delaware the situs of ownership of all stock in Delaware corporations.

All 28 defendants were notified of the initiation of the suit by certified mail directed to their last known addresses and by publication in a New Castle County newspaper. The 21 defendants whose property was seized (hereafter referred to as appellants) responded by entering a special appearance for the purpose of moving to quash service of process and to vacate the sequestration order. They contended that the *ex parte* sequestration procedure did not accord them due process of law and that the property seized was not capable of attachment in Delaware. In addition, appellants asserted that under the rule of International Shoe

Co. v. Washington, they did not have sufficient contacts with Delaware to sustain the jurisdiction of that State's courts.

[The Delaware courts rejected all of defendants' arguments. They distinguished seizure for jurisdictional purposes from other forms of *ex parte* seizure. And they contended that the assertion of jurisdiction need not meet *International Shoe* standards because Delaware was asserting in rem, rather than in personam, jurisdiction.]

II

The Delaware courts rejected appellants' jurisdictional challenge by noting that this suit was brought as a quasi in rem proceeding. Since quasi in rem jurisdiction is traditionally based on attachment or seizure of property present in the jurisdiction, not on contacts between the defendant and the State, the courts considered appellants' claimed lack of contacts with Delaware to be unimportant. This categorical analysis assumes the continued soundness of the conceptual structure founded on the century-old case of Pennoyer v. Neff.

[The Court discussed the development of jurisdictional ideas from the time of Pennoyer v. Neff. In reviewing *International Shoe* itself, the opinion explained in footnote 19 that "the *International Shoe* court believed that the standard it was setting forth governed actions against natural persons as well as corporations, and we see no reason to disagree. The differences between individuals and corporations may, of course, lead to the conclusion that a given set of circumstances establishes State jurisdiction over one type of defendant but not over the other."]

[T]he relationship among the defendant, the forum, and the litigation, rather than the mutually exclusive sovereignty of the States on which the rules of *Pennoyer* rest, became the central concern of the inquiry into personal jurisdiction.[20] The immediate effect of this departure from *Pennoyer's* conceptual apparatus was to increase the ability of the state courts to obtain personal jurisdiction over nonresident defendants.

No equally dramatic change has occurred in the law governing jurisdiction in rem. There have, however, been intimations that the collapse of the in personam wing of *Pennoyer* has not left that decision unweakened

---

20. Nothing in Hanson v. Denckla [infra page 117] is to the contrary. The *Hanson* Court's statement that restrictions on state jurisdiction "are a consequence of territorial limitations on the power of the respective states," simply makes the point that the States are defined by their geographical territory. After making this point, the Court in *Hanson* determined that the defendant over which personal jurisdiction was claimed had not committed any acts sufficiently connected to the State to justify jurisdiction under the *International Shoe* standard.

as a foundation for in rem jurisdiction. [The court cited lower court opinions, commentators, and oblique hints in Supreme Court cases.] . . .

It is clear, therefore, that the law of state-court jurisdiction no longer stands securely on the foundation established in *Pennoyer*. We think that the time is ripe to consider whether the standard of fairness and substantial justice set forth in *International Shoe* should be held to govern actions in rem as well as in personam.

III

The case for applying to jurisdiction in rem the same test of "fair play and substantial justice" as governs assertions of jurisdiction in personam is simple and straightforward. It is premised on recognition that "[t]he phrase, 'judicial jurisdiction over a thing,' is a customary elliptical way of referring to jurisdiction over the interests of persons in a thing." Restatement (Second) of Conflict of Laws §56, introductory note. This recognition leads to the conclusion that in order to justify an exercise of jurisdiction in rem, the basis for jurisdiction must be sufficient to justify exercising "jurisdiction over the interests of persons in a thing."[23] The standard for determining whether an exercise of jurisdiction over the interests of persons is consistent with the Due Process Clause is the minimum contacts standard elucidated in *International Shoe*.

This argument, of course, does not ignore the fact that the presence of property in a State may bear on the existence of jurisdiction by providing contacts among the forum State, the defendant, and the litigation. For example, when claims to the property itself are the source of the underlying controversy between the plaintiff and the defendant, it would be unusual for the State where the property is located not to have jurisdiction. In such cases, the defendant's claim to property located in the State would normally indicate that he expected to benefit from the State's protection of his interest. The State's strong interests in assuring the marketability of property within its borders and in providing a procedure for peaceful resolution of disputes about the possession of that property would also support jurisdiction, as would the likelihood that important records and witnesses will be found in the State.[28] The presence of property may also favor jurisdiction in cases, such as suits for injury

23. It is true that the potential liability of a defendant in an in rem action is limited by the value of the property but that limitation does not affect the argument. The fairness of subjecting a defendant to state-court jurisdiction does not depend on the size of the claim being litigated.

28. We do not suggest that these illustrations include all the factors that may affect the decision, nor that the factors we have mentioned are necessarily decisive.

suffered on the land of an absentee owner, where the defendant's ownership of the property is conceded but the cause of action is otherwise
related to rights and duties growing out of that ownership.

It appears, therefore, that jurisdiction over many types of actions which
now are or might be brought in rem would not be affected by a holding
that any assertion of state-court jurisdiction must satisfy the *International
Shoe* standard. For the type of quasi in rem action typified by Harris v.
Balk and the present case, however, accepting the proposed analysis
would result in significant change. These are cases where the property
which now serves as the basis for state-court jurisdiction is completely
unrelated to the plaintiff's cause of action. Thus, although the presence
of the defendant's property in a State might suggest the existence of other
ties among the defendant, the State, and the litigation, the presence of
the property alone would not support the State's jurisdiction. If those
other ties did not exist, cases over which the State is now thought to
have jurisdiction could not be brought in that forum.

Since acceptance of the *International Shoe* test would most affect this
class of cases, we examine the arguments against adopting that standard
as they relate to this category of litigation. Before doing so, however, we
note that this type of case also presents the clearest illustration of the
argument in favor of assessing assertions of jurisdiction by a single standard. For in cases such as *Harris* and this one, the only role played by
the property is to provide the basis for bringing the defendant into court.
Indeed, the express purpose of the Delaware sequestration procedure is
to compel the defendant to enter a personal appearance. In such cases,
if a direct assertion of personal jurisdiction over the defendant would
violate the Constitution, it would seem that an indirect assertion of the
jurisdiction should be equally impermissible.

It might also be suggested that allowing in rem jurisdiction avoids the
uncertainty inherent in the *International Shoe* standard and assures a
plaintiff of a forum.[37] We believe, however, that the fairness standard of
International Shoe can be easily applied in the vast majority of cases.
Moreover, when the existence of jurisdiction in a particular forum under
International Shoe is unclear, the cost of simplifying the litigation by
avoiding the jurisdictional question may be the sacrifice of "fair play and
substantial justice." That cost is too high.

We are left, then, to consider the significance of the long history of
jurisdiction based solely on the presence of property in a State. . . .

---

37. This case does not raise, and we therefore do not consider, the question whether
the presence of a defendant's property in a State is a sufficient basis for jurisdiction when
no other forum is available to the plaintiff.

"[T]raditional notions of fair play and substantial justice" can be as readily offended by the perpetuation of ancient forms that are no longer justified as by the adoption of new procedures that are inconsistent with the basic values of our constitutional heritage. Cf. Sniadach v. Family Finance Corp. The fiction that an assertion of jurisdiction over property is anything but an assertion of jurisdiction over the owner of the property supports an ancient form without substantial modern justification. Its continued acceptance would serve only to allow state court jurisdiction that is fundamentally unfair to the defendant.

We therefore conclude that all assertions of state court jurisdiction must be evaluated according to the standards set forth in *International Shoe* and its progeny.[39]

IV

The Delaware courts based their assertion of jurisdiction in this case solely on the statutory presence of appellants' property in Delaware. Yet that property is not the subject matter of this litigation, nor is the underlying cause of action related to the property. Appellants' holdings in Greyhound do not, therefore, provide contacts with Delaware sufficient to support the jurisdiction of that State's courts over appellants. If it exists, that jurisdiction must have some other foundation.

Appellee Heitner did not allege and does not now claim that appellants have ever set foot in Delaware. Nor does he identify any act related to his cause of action as having taken place in Delaware. Nevertheless, he contends that appellants' positions as directors and officers of a corporation chartered in Delaware provide sufficient "contacts, ties, or relations," International Shoe Co. v. Washington, with that State to give its courts jurisdiction over appellants in this stockholder's derivative action. This argument is based primarily on what Heitner asserts to be the strong interest of Delaware in supervising the management of a Delaware corporation. That interest is said to derive from the role of Delaware law in establishing the corporation and defining the obligations owed to it by its officers and directors. In order to protect this interest, appellee concludes, Delaware's courts must have jurisdiction over corporate fiduciaries such as appellants.

This argument is undercut by the failure of the Delaware Legislature to assert the state interest appellee finds so compelling. Delaware law

39. It would not be fruitful for us to re-examine the facts of cases decided on the rationales of *Pennoyer* and *Harris* to determine whether jurisdiction might have been sustained under the standard we adopt today. To the extent that prior decisions are inconsistent with this standard, they are overruled.

bases jurisdiction not on appellants' status as corporate fiduciaries, but rather on the presence of their property in the State. Although the sequestration procedure used here may be most frequently used in derivative suits against officers and directors, the authorizing statute evinces no specific concern with such actions. Sequestration can be used in any suit against a nonresident, and reaches corporate fiduciaries only if they happen to own interests in a Delaware corporation, or other property in the State. But as Heitner's failure to secure jurisdiction over seven of the defendants named in his complaint demonstrates, there is no necessary relationship between holding a position as a corporate fiduciary and owning stock or other interests in the corporation. If Delaware perceived its interest in securing jurisdiction over corporate fiduciaries to be as great as Heitner suggests, we would expect it to have enacted a statute more clearly designed to protect that interest. . . .

Appellee suggests that by accepting positions as officers or directors of a Delaware corporation, appellants performed the acts required by Hanson v. Denckla. He notes that Delaware law provides substantial benefits to corporate officers and directors, and that these benefits were at least in part the incentive for appellants to assume their postions. It is, he says, "only fair and just" to require appellants, in return for these benefits, to respond in the State of Delaware when they are accused of misusing their powers.

But like Heitner's first argument, this line of reasoning establishes only that it is appropriate for Delaware law to govern the obligations of appellants to Greyhound and its stockholders. It does not demonstrate that appellants have "purposefully avail[ed themselves] of the privilege of conducting activities within the forum State," Hanson v. Denckla, in a way that would justify bringing them before a Delaware tribunal. Appellants have simply had nothing to do with the State of Delaware. Moreover, appellants had no reason to expect to be haled before a Delaware court. Delaware, unlike some States, has not enacted a statute that treats acceptance of a directorship as consent to jurisdiction in the State. And "[i]t strains reason . . . to suggest that anyone buying securities in a corporation formed in Delaware 'impliedly consents' to subject himself to Delaware's . . . jurisdiction on any cause of action." Appellants, who were not required to acquire interests in Greyhound in order to hold their positions, did not by acquiring those interests surrender their right to be brought to judgment only in States with which they had "minimum contacts."

The Due Process Clause "does not contemplate that a state may make binding a judgment . . . against an individual or corporate defendant with which the state has no contacts, ties, or relations." International

Shoe Co. v. Washington, supra, at 319. Delaware's assertion of jurisdiction over appellants in this case is inconsistent with that constitutional limitation on state power. The judgment of the Delaware Supreme Court must, therefore, be reversed.

It is so ordered.

Mr. Justice REHNQUIST took no part in the consideration or decision of this case.

Mr. Justice POWELL, concurring.

I agree that the principles of International Shoe Co. v. Washington should be extended to govern assertions of in rem as well as in personam jurisdiction in state court. I also agree that neither the statutory presence of appellants' stock in Delaware nor their positions as directors and officers of a Delaware corporation can provide sufficient contacts to support the Delaware courts' assertion of jurisdiction in this case.

I would explicitly reserve judgment, however, on whether the ownership of some forms of property whose situs is indisputably and permanently located within a State may, without more, provide the contacts necessary to subject a defendant to jurisdiction within the State to the extent of the value of the property. In the case of real property, in particular, preservation of the common law concept of quasi in rem jurisdiction arguably would avoid the uncertainty of the general *International Shoe* standard without significant cost to "traditional notions of fair play and substantial justice."

Subject to that reservation, I join the opinion of the Court.

Mr. Justice STEVENS, concurring in the judgment.

The Due Process Clause affords protection against "judgments without notice." International Shoe Co. v. Washington (opinion of Black, J.). . . .

One who purchases shares of stock on the open market can hardly be expected to know that he has thereby become subject to suit in a forum remote from his residence and unrelated to the transaction. As a practical matter, the Delaware sequestration statute created an unacceptable risk of judgment without notice. . . . I therefore agree with the Court that on the record before us no adequate basis for jurisdiction exists and that the Delaware statute is unconstitutional on its face.

How the Court's opinion may be applied in other contexts is not entirely clear to me. . . . My uncertainty as to the reach of the opinion, and my fear that it purports to decide a great deal more than is necessary to dispose of this case, persuade me merely to concur in the judgment.

Mr. Justice BRENNAN, concurring and dissenting.

I join Parts I-III of the Court's opinion. I fully agree that the minimum contacts analysis developed in International Shoe Co. v. Washington represents a far more sensible construct for the exercise of state court jurisdiction than the patchwork of legal and factual fictions that has been generated from the decision in Pennoyer v. Neff. It is precisely because the inquiry into minimum contacts is now of such overriding importance, however, that I must respectfully dissent from Part IV of the Court's opinion. . . .

I am convinced that as a general rule a state forum has jurisdiction to adjudicate a shareholder derivative action centering on the conduct and policies of the directors and officers of a corporation chartered by that State. Unlike the Court, I therefore would not foreclose Delaware from asserting jurisdiction over appellants were it persuaded to do so on the basis of minimum contacts.

It is well settled that a derivative lawsuit as presented here does not inure primarily to the benefit of the named plaintiff. . . . "The cause of action which such a plaintiff brings before the court is not his own but the corporation's. . . . Such a plaintiff often may represent an important public and stockholder interest in bringing faithless managers to book."

Viewed in this light, the chartering State has an unusually powerful interest in insuring the availability of a convenient forum for litigating claims involving a possible multiplicity of defendant fiduciaries and for vindicating the State's substantive policies regarding the management of its domestic corporations. I believe that our cases fairly establish that the State's valid substantive interests are important considerations in assessing whether it constitutionally may claim jurisdiction over a given cause of action.

In this instance, Delaware can point to at least three interrelated public policies that are furthered by its assertion of jurisdiction. First, the State has a substantial interest in providing restitution for its local corporations that allegedly have been vicitimized by fiduciary misconduct, even if the managerial decisions occurred outside the State. . . . Second, state courts have legitimately read their jurisdiction expansively when a cause of action centers in an area in which the forum state possesses a manifest regulatory interest. . . . Finally, a State like Delaware has a recognized interest in affording a convenient forum for supervising and overseeing the affairs of an entity that is purely the creation of that State's law. . . .

I, therefore, would approach the minimum contacts analysis differently than does the Court. Crucial to me is the fact that appellants voluntarily associated themselves with the State of Delaware, "invoking the benefits and protections of its laws," Hanson v. Denckla; International Shoe Co. v. Washington, by entering into a long term and fragile relationship with one of its domestic corporations. They thereby elected to assume powers and to undertake responsibilities wholly derived from that State's rules and regulations, and to become eligible for those benefits that Delaware law makes available to its corporations' officials. E.g., 8 Del. C. §§143 (interest-free loans); 145 (indemnification). While it is possible that countervailing issues of judicial efficiency and the like might clearly favor a different forum, they do not appear on the meager record before us; and, of course, we are concerned solely with "minimum" contacts, not the "best" contacts. I thus do not believe that it is unfair to insist that appellants make themselves available to suit in a competent forum that Delaware might create for vindication of its important public policies directly pertaining to appellants' fiduciary associations with the State.

NOTES AND PROBLEMS

1. Do not let the corporate context of this suit mislead you into assuming that jurisdiction over the corporation was at issue. The defendants challenging jurisdiction were the 21 individual members of Greyhound's board of directors, none of whom were residents of Delaware. No one suggested that Delaware lacked jurisdiction over Greyhound itself, which was a Delaware corporation.

2. Did *Shaffer* decide:

a. That property is irrelevant to the existence of jurisdiction?

b. That stock is not property?

c. That directors of a corporation cannot be sued in the state of incorporation?

d. That Greyhound's board of directors had not "consented" to be sued in Delaware?

e. That attachment of property is an unconstitutional way for a state to assert its jurisdiction?

3. If all these statements are misreadings of the case, what did *Shaffer* decide? Approach that question by imagining two variations on *Pennoyer*.

a. Neff, who has never been to Oregon, inherits property there. Mitchell, from whom Neff has borrowed money, sues Neff for the unpaid debt, asserting jurisdiction by attaching the property.

b. Neff, who has never been to Oregon, hires Mitchell to help him buy some property. Mitchell does so, but Neff fails to pay Mitchell's fees. Mitchell sues Neff. Jurisdiction?

4. Why does the majority, in the second-to-last paragraph of its opinion, suggest that Delaware could have required the corporate officers to submit to Delaware jurisdiction as a condition of becoming corporate officers?

Wasn't that whole line of reasoning rejected in *International Shoe*, which said at one point, "True, some of the decisions holding the corporation amenable to suit have been supported by resort to the legal fiction that it has given its consent to service and suit, consent being implied [sic] from its presence in the state through the acts of its authorized agents. But more realistically it may be said that those authorized acts were of such a nature as to justify the fiction."

After the decision in *Shaffer*, the Delaware legislature enacted a statute purporting to give its courts jurisdiction over officers and directors of Delaware corporations in cases related to their corporate activities. See 10 Del. Code §3114. The Delaware Supreme Court upheld the statute against constitutional attack in Armstrong v. Pomerance, 423 A.2d 174 (Del. 1980). Does *Shaffer* permit Delaware to assert such jurisdiction regardless of the extent of directors' and officers' other contacts with the state?

5. Notice Justice Brennan's contention that one ought to take into account not only the defendant's circumstances but the interests of the forum state. As you will see in subsequent cases, the Court has not entirely agreed about how to take this factor into account. Notice that it will usually favor the assertion of jurisdiction and the plaintiff, who is likely to be at least a temporary resident of the forum state.

6. Footnote 37 of the Court's opinion suggests that attachment jurisdiction might still be available when "no other forum is open to the plaintiff." When would that be the case? When the defendant is domiciled outside the country? Would that discriminate against foreign defendants?

7. In Carolina Power & Light Co. v. Uranex, 451 F. Supp. 1044 (N.D. Cal. 1977), the plaintiff sought to garnish a debt owed by a California corporation to Uranex, a French company. (Garnishment is a form of attachment in which the property attached is in the hands of a third party.) Plaintiff was already arbitrating a contract dispute against Uranex in New York. Plaintiff feared, however, that even if it won the arbitration, it would be unable to collect the award against Uranex, which had few assets in the United States. Plaintiff therefore filed a suit in California to attach a debt owed Uranex by another corporation. Uranex argued that *Shaffer* forbade the seizure of the debt in question. The court disagreed, noting that while *Shaffer* forbade adjudication of the merits of a case simply on the basis of the presence of property, in the present case plaintiff was seeking seizure of the property not to determine the merits but rather to have security for the New York determination on the merits. We will see in Chapter V that such cases of prejudgment seizure of property, even when there are minimum contacts, may require prior notice and hearing to the owner of the property.

8. Because the defendants in *Shaffer* were individuals (even though the case arose in a corporate context), a necessary implication of the holding (as well as of footnote 19, quoted supra page 106) is that *International Shoe* applies to individuals as well as to corporations. But what exactly does that statement mean? One part of the picture is clear enough: In order for a state to exercise jurisdiction over a person not present in the state, contacts are necessary. Those contacts may include the ownership of property, but mere ownership of property does not conclusively establish jurisdiction, as it did under the regime of *Pennoyer* and Harris v. Balk.

The picture gets murkier if the question is whether the mere physical presence of the defendant — without any other contacts — is sufficient to establish jurisdiction for all claims. For a long time before *Shaffer* the answer was yes. The Restatement (Second) of Conflict of Laws §28 (1971) said so: "A state has power to exercise judicial jurisdiction over an individual who is present within its territory, whether permanently or temporarily." A series of colorful cases took this view; the most striking of them, Grace v. MacArthur, 170 F. Supp. 442 (E.D. Ark. 1959), upheld Arkansas jurisdiction over a defendant who was served with process in an airplane flying over that state. Do those cases upholding this rule of so-called transient jurisdiction survive *Shaffer*? Consider this question again after reading Burnham v. Superior Court, infra page 150.

3. Specific Jurisdiction: The Modern Cases

Having understood how Shaffer v. Heitner eliminated *in rem* jurisdiction and consolidated the regime of *International Shoe*, the student needs to think about two issues. First, one needs practice in applying the concepts of *International Shoe* and its two strands — specific and general jurisdiction. Specific jurisdiction has produced more recent Supreme Court cases, and in those cases the Court has shown some restlessness with the doctrinal categories of *International Shoe*. The Court's restlessness raises the second question, one you should consider as you work through the intricacies of modern jurisdictional doctrine: do we need the doctrine at all? Consider the following comment, made by an experienced litigator:

> Born in a world in which travel and communication were expensive and uncertain and in which trial was the dominant mode of adjudication, *Pennoyer* (or something like it) made sense. Does it continue to do so in an environment of the internet, the cell phone, and the jet plane — and a procedural environment in which most litigation ends before trial? Defen-

dants retain lawyers to represent them in suits; parties rarely attend any proceedings except trial itself. Lawyers are available everywhere there are courts. Defendants typically communicate with their lawyers by phone, fax and e-mail. They might spend some minimal time meeting them in person, but in today's world, most contacts with lawyers are not "live." Courts are even starting to have telephonic hearings in some cases. It is just as easy and almost as cheap for a defendant to maintain contact with his lawyer in another state as with a lawyer who works in the same city where the defendant resides. There is the issue of where discovery should be taken, but that should be handled by other rules (if a California resident were sued in New York, the plaintiff might be required to go to California to take the defendant's deposition rather than require the defendant to travel to New York for the deposition.) The only serious burden on the defendant arises at trial, but 96% of cases are decided without a trial. And you could allow the defendant to recover costs of travel to trial as a taxable cost if the plaintiff loses. Is the law of personal jurisdiction an example of the legal system persisting in retaining and elaborating doctrines that made sense when originally adopted, but have been outgrown by technological changes in the way in which people interact and do business?

Is this a fair critique? Before you can answer that question with confidence, you need a better sense of what modern jurisdictional doctrine looks like. The cases that follow represent a sampling of the Supreme Court's cases in the years since *International Shoe*. As you read them, work on two levels of analysis. Intially, consider the analytical framework the Court is applying: To what extent is it working within, and to what extent modifying or departing from, the framework of *International Shoe*? Second, try to understand how the particular facts of each case led to its holding; what is the smallest alteration in facts that would lead the Court to a different result? We start with two cases that pre-date *Shaffer* and which represent paradigmatic instances of the issues that arise in applying *International Shoe*.

McGee v. International Life Insurance Co.

355 U.S. 220 (1957)

Opinion of the Court by Mr. Justice BLACK, announced by Mr. Justice DOUGLAS.

The material facts are relatively simple. In 1944, Lowell Franklin a resident of California, purchased a life insurance policy from [an insurer subsequently bought by respondent, who] then mailed a reinsurance certificate to Franklin in California offering to insure him. . . . He accepted this offer and from that time until his death in 1950 paid premiums by mail from his California home to respondent's Texas office. [When the beneficiary notified International Life of Franklin's death,] it refused to pay claiming that he had committed suicide. It appears that neither [the original insurer] nor respondent has ever had any office or agent in California. . . .

Looking back over this long history of [jurisdiction cases] a trend is clearly discernible toward expanding the permissible scope of state jurisdiction over foreign corporations and other nonresidents. In part this is attributable to the fundamental transformation of our national economy. . . . With this increasing nationalization of commerce has come a great increase in the amount of business conducted by mail across state lines. At the same time modern transportation and communication have made it much less burdensome for a party sued to defend himself in a State where he engages in economic activity. Turning to this case we think it apparent that the Due Process Clause did not preclude the California court from entering a judgment binding on respondent. It is sufficient for purposes of due process that the suit was based on a contract which had substantial connection with that State. The contract was delivered in California, the premiums were mailed from there and the insured was a resident of that State when he died. It cannot be denied that California has a manifest interest in providing effective means of redress for its residents when their insurers refuse to pay claims. These residents would be at a severe disadvantage if they were forced to follow the insurance company to a distant State in order to hold it legally accountable. . . . There is no contention that respondent did not have adequate notice of the suit or sufficient time to prepare its defenses and appear.

Hanson v. Denckla

357 U.S. 235 (1958)

Mr. Chief Justice WARREN delivered the opinion of the Court.

[The case arose from a family fight over the assets of Mrs. Donner, a deceased mother who had established a trust in Delaware and some years later moved to Florida, where she died. The contest was whether Florida or Delaware courts had jurisdiction over the trust assets; that issue turned on whether Florida could acquire jurisdiction over the Delaware trustee. If Florida had jurisdiction, one daughter got the entire estate; if it didn't, three daughters shared equally. The Supreme Court said Florida had no jurisdiction.]

. . . [P]rogress in communications and transportation has made the defense of a suit in a foreign tribunal less burdensome. In response to these changes, the requirements for personal jurisdiction over nonresidents have evolved from the rigid rule of Pennoyer v. Neff to the flexible standard of International Shoe Co. v. Washington. But it is a mistake to assume that this trend heralds the eventual demise of all restrictions on the personal jurisdiction of state courts. Those restrictions are more than a guarantee of immunity from inconvenient or distant litigation. They are a consequence of territorial limitations on the power of the respective States. However minimal the burden of defending in a foreign tribunal, a defendant may not be called upon to do so unless he has had the "minimal contacts" with that State that are a prerequisite to its exercise of power over him. See International Shoe Co. v. Washington.

We fail to find such contacts in the circumstances of this case. The defendant trust company has no office in Florida, and transacts no business there. . . . [T]he record discloses no solicitation of business in that State either in person or by mail. . . .

The first relationship Florida had to the agreement was years later when [Mrs. Donner] became domiciled there, and the trustee remitted the trust income to her in the State. From Florida Mrs. Donner carried on several bits of trust administration. . . . But the record discloses no instance in which the *trustee* performed any acts in Florida. . . .

The unilateral activity of those who claim some relationship with a nonresident defendant [Mrs. Donner] cannot satisfy the requirement of contact with the forum State. The application of that rule will vary with the quality and nature of the defendant's activity, but it is essential in each case that there be some act by which the defendant purposefully avails itself of the privilege of conducting activities within the forum State, thus invoking the benefits and protections of its laws. International Shoe Co. v. Washington. . . .

[Justices BLACK, BURTON, BRENNAN, and DOUGLAS dissented, the latter separately.]

NOTES AND PROBLEMS

1. *McGee* and *Hanson*, decided a year apart, come to different conclusions about jurisdiction on remarkably similar facts: business conducted by mail with an out-of-state financial institution, which was then sued in plaintiff's state. Notice as well the emphasis both case place on modern transport and communication.

a. *McGee* is often thought to represent a high-water mark of jurisdictional aggressiveness. Was its result justified?

b. Can you identify a factual difference that justifies the difference in outcomes in the two cases?

2. *McGee* and *Hanson* represent one model of national and international transactions — a continuing relationship with a financial institution.

That model has numerous applications, ranging from catalog sales to the Internet. But the economy has changed substantially since the mid-1950s, and contemporary jurisdictional cases often have an international character, like that presented in two of the next three cases. Notice that the problem is not unique to the United States: so long as economic relations cross jurisdictional boundaries, courts will have to decide how far their power reaches and what principles ought to control it. The next three cases grapple with the problem.

World-Wide Volkswagen Corp. v. Woodson
444 U.S. 286 (1980)

Mr. Justice WHITE delivered the opinion of the Court.

The issue before us is whether, consistently with the Due Process Clause of the Fourteenth Amendment, an Oklahoma court may exercise in personam jurisdiction over a nonresident automobile retailer and its wholesale distributor in a products-liability action, when the defendants' only connection with Oklahoma is the fact that an automobile sold in New York to New York residents became involved in an accident in Oklahoma.

I

Respondents Harry and Kay Robinson purchased a new Audi automobile from petitioner Seaway Volkswagen, Inc. (Seaway) in Massena, N.Y., in 1976. The following year the Robinson family, who resided in New York, left that State for a new home in Arizona. As they passed through the State of Oklahoma, another car struck their Audi in the rear, causing a fire which severely burned Kay Robinson and her two children.[1]

The Robinsons subsequently brought a products-liability action in the District Court for Creek County, Okla. claiming that their injuries resulted from defective design and placement of the Audi's gas tank and fuel system. They joined as defendants the automobile's manufacturer, Audi NSU Auto Union Aktiengesellschaft (Audi); its importer, Volkswagen of America, Inc. (Volkswagen); its regional distributor, petitioner World-Wide Volkswagen Corporation (World-Wide); and its retail dealer, petitioner Seaway. Seaway and World-Wide entered special appearances,[3]

---

1. The driver of the other automobile does not figure in the present litigation.

3. Volkswagen also entered a special appearance in the District Court, but unlike World-Wide and Seaway did not seek review in the Supreme Court of Oklahoma and is not a petitioner here. Both Volkswagen and Audi remain as defendants in the litigation pending before the District Court in Oklahoma.

claiming that Oklahoma's exercise of jurisdiction over them would offend the limitations on the State's jurisdiction imposed by the Due Process Clause of the Fourteenth Amendment.

The facts presented to the District Court showed that World-Wide is incorporated and has its business office in New York. It distributes vehicles, parts and accessories, under contract with Volkswagen, to retail dealers in New York, New Jersey, and Connecticut. Seaway, one of these retail dealers, is incorporated and has its place of business in New York. Insofar as the record reveals, Seaway and World-Wide are fully independent corporations whose relations with each other and with Volkswagen and Audi are contractual only. Respondents adduced no evidence that either World-Wide or Seaway does any business in Oklahoma, ships or sells any products to or in that State, has an agent to receive process there, or purchases advertisements in any media calculated to reach Oklahoma. In fact, as respondents' counsel conceded at oral argument, there was no showing that any automobile sold by World-Wide or Seaway has ever entered Oklahoma with the single exception of the vehicle involved in the present case. . . .

The Supreme Court of Oklahoma denied the writ. . . . The Court's rationale was contained in the following paragraph:

> In the case before us, the product being sold and distributed by the petitioners is by its very design and purpose so mobile that petitioners can foresee its possible use in Oklahoma. This is especially true of the distributor, who has the exclusive right to distribute such automobile in New York, New Jersey and Connecticut. The evidence presented below demonstrated that goods sold and distributed by the petitioners were used in the State of Oklahoma, and under the facts we believe it reasonable to infer, given the retail value of the automobile, that the petitioners derive substantial income from automobiles which from time to time are used in the State of Oklahoma. This being the case, we hold that under the facts presented, the trial court was justified in concluding that the petitioners derive substantial revenue from goods used or consumed in this State.

We granted certiorari to consider an important constitutional question with respect to state-court jurisdiction and to resolve a conflict between the Supreme Court of Oklahoma and the highest courts of at least four other States. We reverse.

II

. . . As has long been settled, and as we reaffirm today, a state court may exercise personal jurisdiction over a nonresident defendant only so long as there exist "minimum contacts" between the defendant and the forum State. International Shoe Co. v. Washington. The concept of minimum contacts, in turn, can be seen to perform two related, but distinguishable functions. It protects the defendant against the burdens of litigating in a distant or inconvenient forum. And it acts to ensure that the States, through their courts, do not reach out beyond the limits imposed on them by their status as coequal sovereigns in a federal system.

The protection against inconvenient litigation is typically described in terms of "reasonableness" or "fairness." We have said that the defendant's contacts with the forum State must be such that maintenance of the suit "does not offend 'traditional notions of fair play and substantial justice.' " International Shoe Co. v. Washington, quoting Milliken v. Meyer. The relationship between the defendant and the forum must be such that it is "reasonable . . . to require the corporation to defend the particular suit which is brought there." Implicit in this emphasis on reasonableness is the understanding that the burden on the defendant, while always a primary concern, will in an appropriate case be considered in light of other relevant factors, including the forum State's interest in adjudicating the dispute; the plaintiff's interest in obtaining convenient and effective relief, at least when that interest is not adequately protected by the plaintiff's power to choose the forum, cf. Shaffer v. Heitner; the interstate judicial system's interest in obtaining the most efficient resolution of controversies; and the shared interest of the several States in furthering fundamental substantive social policies.

The limits imposed on state jurisdiction by the Due Process Clause, in its role as a guarantor against inconvenient litigation, have been substantially relaxed over the years. As we noted in McGee v. International Life Ins. Co., this trend is largely attributable to a fundamental transformation in the American economy. . . .

The historical developments noted in *McGee*, of course, have only accelerated in the generation since that case was decided. Nevertheless, we have never accepted the proposition that state lines are irrelevant for jurisdictional purposes, nor could we and remain faithful to the principles of interstate federalism embodied in the Constitution. The economic interdependence of the States was foreseen and desired by the Framers. In the Commerce Clause, they provided that the Nation was to be a common market, a "free trade unit" in which the States are debarred from acting as separable economic entities. But the Framers also intended that the States retain many essential attributes of sovereignty, including, in particular, the sovereign power to try causes in their courts. The sovereignty of each State, in turn, implied a limitation on the sovereignty of all of its sister States — a limitation express or implicit in both the original scheme of the Constitution and the Fourteenth Amendment. . . .

Thus, the Due Process Clause "does not contemplate that a state may make binding a judgment in personam against an individual or corporate defendant with which the state has no contacts, ties, or relations." International Shoe Co. v. Washington. Even if the defendant would suffer minimal or no inconvenience from being forced to litigate before the tribunals of another State; even if the forum State has a strong interest in applying its law to the controversy; even if the forum State is the most convenient location for litigation, the Due Process Clause, acting as an instrument of interstate federalism, may sometimes act to divest the State of its power to render a valid judgment. Hanson v. Denckla.

III

Applying these principles to the case at hand, we find in the record before us a total absence of those affiliating circumstances that are a necessary predicate to any exercise of state-court jurisdiction. Petitioners carry on no activity whatsoever in Oklahoma. They close no sales and perform no services there. They avail themselves of none of the privileges and benefits of Oklahoma law. They solicit no business there either through salespersons or through advertising reasonably calculated to reach the State. Nor does the record show that they regularly sell cars at wholesale or retail to Oklahoma customers or residents or that they indirectly, through others, serve or seek to serve the Oklahoma market. In short, respondents seek to base jurisdiction on one, isolated occurrence and whatever inferences can be drawn therefrom: the fortuitous circumstance that a single Audi automobile, sold in New York to New York residents, happened to suffer an accident while passing through Oklahoma.

It is argued, however, that because an automobile is mobile by its very design and purpose it was "foreseeable" that the Robinsons' Audi would cause injury in Oklahoma. Yet "foreseeability" alone has never been a sufficient benchmark for personal jurisdiction under the Due Process Clause. In Hanson v. Denckla, supra, it was no doubt foreseeable that the settlor of a Delaware trust would subsequently move to Florida and seek to exercise a power of appointment there; yet we held that Florida courts could not constitutionally exercise jurisdiction over a Delaware trustee that had no other contacts with the forum State. . . .

If foreseeability were the criterion, a local California tire retailer could be forced to defend in Pennsylvania when a blowout occurs there; a Wisconsin seller of a defective automobile jack could be haled before a distant court for damage caused in New Jersey; or a Florida soft drink concessionaire could be summoned to Alaska to account for injuries happening there. Every seller of chattels would in effect appoint the chattel his agent for service of process. His amenability to suit would travel with the chattel. We recently abandoned the outworn rule of Harris v. Balk, that the interest of a creditor in a debt could be extinguished or otherwise affected by any State having transitory jurisdiction over the debtor. Shaffer v. Heitner. Having interred the mechanical rule that a creditor's amenability to a quasi in rem action travels with his debtor, we are unwilling to endorse an analogous principle in the present case.

This is not to say, of course, that foreseeability is wholly irrelevant. But the foreseeability that is critical to due process analysis is not the mere likelihood that a product will find its way into the forum State. Rather, it is that the defendant's conduct and connection with the forum State are such that he should reasonably anticipate being haled into court there. The Due Process Clause, by ensuring the "orderly administration of the laws,"gives a degree of predictability to the legal system that allows potential defendants to structure their primary conduct with some minimum assurance as to where that conduct will and will not render them liable to suit.

When a corporation "purposefully avails itself of the privilege of conducting activities within the forum State," it has clear notice that it is subject to suit there, and can act to alleviate the risk of burdensome litigation by procuring insurance, passing the expected costs on to customers, or, if the risks are too great, severing its connection with the State. Hence if the sale of a product of a manufacturer or distributor such as Audi or Volkswagen is not simply an isolated occurrence, but arises from the efforts of the manufacturer or distributor to serve, directly or indirectly, the market for its product in other States, it is not unreasonable to subject it to suit in one of those States if its allegedly defective merchandise has there been the source of injury to its owner or to others. The forum State does not exceed its powers under the Due Process Clause if it asserts personal jurisdiction over a corporation that delivers its products into the stream of commerce with the expectation that they will be purchased by consumers in the forum State.

But there is no such or similar basis for Oklahoma jurisdiction over World-Wide or Seaway in this case. Seaway's sales are made in Massena, N.Y. World-Wide's market, although substantially larger, is limited to dealers in New York, New Jersey, and Connecticut. There is no evidence of record that any automobiles distributed by World-Wide are sold to retail customers outside this tri-State area. It is foreseeable that the purchasers of automobiles sold by World-Wide and Seaway may take them to Oklahoma. But the mere "unilateral activity of those who claim some relationship with a nonresident defendant cannot satisfy the requirement of contact with the forum State." Hanson v. Denckla.

In a variant on the previous argument it is contended that jurisdiction can be supported by the fact that petitioners earn substantial revenue from goods used in Oklahoma. The Oklahoma Supreme Court so found, drawing the inference that because one automobile sold by petitioners had been used in Oklahoma, others might have been used there also. While this inference seems less than compelling on the facts of the instant case, we need not question the Court's factual findings in order to reject its reasoning.

This argument seems to make the point that the purchase of automobiles in New York, from which the petitioners earn substantial revenue, would not occur but for the fact that the automobiles are capable of use in distant States like Oklahoma. Respondents observe that the very purpose of an automobile is to travel, and that travel of automobiles sold by petitioners is facilitated by an extensive chain of Volkswagen service centers throughout the Country, including some in Oklahoma.[12] However, financial benefits accruing to the defendant from a collateral relation to the forum State will not support jurisdiction if they do not stem from a constitutionally cognizable contact with that State. In our view, whatever marginal revenues petitioners may receive by virtue of the fact that their products are capable of use in Oklahoma is far too attenuated a contact to justify that State's exercise of in personam jurisdiction over them.

Because we find that petitioners have no "contacts, ties, or relations" with the State of Oklahoma, the judgment of the Supreme Court of Oklahoma is reversed.

Mr. Justice BRENNAN, dissenting.

. . . Because I believe that the Court reads *International Shoe* and its progeny too narrowly, and because I believe that the standards enunciated by those cases may already be obsolete as constitutional boundaries, I dissent.

I

The Court's opinions focus tightly on the existence of contacts between the forum and the defendant. In so doing, they accord too little weight to the strength of the forum State's interest in the case and fail to explore whether there would be any actual inconvenience to the defendant. . . .

12. As we have noted, petitioners earn no direct revenues from these service centers.

II . . .

B

[T]he interest of the forum State and its connection to the litigation is strong. The automobile accident underlying the litigation occurred in Oklahoma. The plaintiffs were hospitalized in Oklahoma when they brought suit. Essential witnesses and evidence were in Oklahoma. See Shaffer v. Heitner. The State has a legitimate interest in enforcing its laws designed to keep its highway system safe, and the trial can proceed at least as efficiently in Oklahoma as anywhere else.

The petitioners are not unconnected with the forum. Although both sell automobiles within limited sales territories, each sold the automobile which in fact was driven to Oklahoma where it was involved in an accident. It may be true, as the Court suggests, that each sincerely intended to limit its commercial impact to the limited territory, and that each intended to accept the benefits and protection of the laws only of those States within the territory. But obviously these were unrealistic hopes that cannot be treated as an automatic constitutional shield.[9]

An automobile simply is not a stationary item or one designed to be used in one place. An automobile is intended to be moved around. Someone in the business of selling large numbers of automobiles can hardly plead ignorance of their mobility or pretend that the automobiles stay put after they are sold. It is not merely that a dealer in automobiles foresees that they will move. The dealer actually intends that the purchasers will use the automobiles to travel to distant States where the dealer does not directly "do business." The sale of an automobile does *purposefully* inject the vehicle into the stream of interstate commerce so that it can travel to distant States. . . .

The Court accepts that a State may exercise jurisdiction over a distributor which "serves" that State "indirectly" by "deliver[ing] its products into the stream of commerce with the expectation that they will [be] purchased by consumers in other States." It is difficult to see why the Constitution should distinguish between a case involving goods which reach a distant State through a chain of distribution and a case involving

9. Moreover, imposing liability in this case would not so undermine certainty as to destroy an automobile dealer's ability to do business. According jurisdiction does not expand liability except in the marginal case where a plaintiff cannot afford to bring an action except in the plaintiff's own State. In addition, these petitioners are represented by insurance companies. They not only could, but did, purchase insurance to protect them should they stand trial and lose the case. The costs of the insurance no doubt are passed on to customers.

goods which reach the same State because a consumer, using them as the dealer knew the customer would, took them there. In each case the seller purposefully injects the goods into the stream of commerce and those goods predictably are used in the forum State. . . .

III

It may be that affirmance of the judgments in these cases would approach the outer limits of *International Shoe's* jurisdictional principle. But that principle, with its almost exclusive focus on the rights of defendants, may be outdated. . . .

The Court's opinion suggests that the defendant ought to be subject to a State's jurisdiction only if he has contacts with the State "such that he should reasonably anticipate being haled into court there."[18]. . .

I would also, however, strip the defendant of an unjustified veto power over certain very appropriate fora — a power the defendant justifiably enjoyed long ago when communication and travel over long distances were slow and unpredictable and when notions of state sovereignty were impractical and exaggerated. But I repeat that that is not today's world. If a plaintiff can show that his chosen forum State has a sufficient interest in the litigation (or sufficient contacts with the defendant), then the defendant who cannot show some real injury to a constitutionally protected interest should have no constitutional excuse not to appear.[21]. . .

[Two dissenting opinions, one by Justice MARSHALL, joined by Justice BLACKMUN, and another by Justice BLACKMUN writing separately, are omitted.]

NOTES AND PROBLEMS

1. To help you clarify what the case did and didn't decide:

a. Which defendants were before the Supreme Court?

b. Audi, the manufacturer, did not challenge personal jurisdiction; Volkswagen of America, the national distributor, originally objected to the Oklahoma court's jurisdiction, but did not appeal the trial court's

---

18. The Court suggests that this is the critical forseeability rather than the likelihood that the product will go to the forum State. But the reasoning begs the question. A defendant cannot know if his actions will subject him to jurisdiction in another State until we have declared what the law of jurisdiction is. . . .

21. Frequently, of course, the defendant will be able to influence the choice of forum through traditional doctrines, such as venue or forum non conveniens, permitting the transfer of litigation.

rejection of that defense. If these two parties had challenged jurisdiction, how would the U.S. Supreme Court have ruled on their objections? The Supreme Court decision does not hold that these parties are subject to jurisdiction, but the case hints that they would be:

> Hence if the sale of a product of a manufacturer or distributor such as Audi or Volkswagen is not simply an isolated occurrence, but arises from the efforts of the manufacturer or distributor to serve, directly or indirectly, the market for its product in other States, it is not unreasonable to subject it to suit in one of those States if its allegedly defective merchandise there has been the source of injury to others. . . .

c. Apply the case to the following hypothetical: Assume that, as purchased, the Robinsons' car lacked a radio. Before leaving on the trip to Arizona, they went to a Massena, N.Y., retailer who specialized in sound equipment for cars and purchased a sound system for the Audi. The system was manufactured in Japan and sold all over the United States. The national distributor was located in California. Further assume that the cause of the car fire was traced to defective wiring in the sound system. If the Robinsons sue in Oklahoma, naming the Massena retailer, the Japanese manufacturer, and the California distributor, who will be subject to personal jurisdiction?

2. If the manufacturer and importer are subject to jurisdiction in Oklahoma but the regional distributor and dealer are not, does the result of *World-Wide Volkswagen* promote an unnecessary multiplicity of lawsuits — one in Oklahoma and another in New York?

a. Such multiplicity will not be a problem if the suit — as in *World-Wide Volkswagen* — is for a design defect, for which the manufacturer would ultimately be liable.

b. But what if the cause of the fire was uncertain? Suppose, for example, that the car bought by the Robinsons was defectively manufactured but that Audi had sent a service bulletin to Seaway and World-Wide requiring them to correct the problem. The failure of those two to correct the defect might not be a defense in the Robinsons' actions against Audi, but it might be the basis for requiring Seaway and World-Wide to indemnify Audi. Under these circumstances, Audi would have to sue Seaway and World-Wide separately, probably in New York. Once more it would be necessary to litigate the causes of the accident, with the possibility that the factfinder in New York might not conclude that the car was defectively designed.

3. Why did the Robinsons name Seaway and World-Wide Volkswagen in a design-defect suit when they knew that Oklahoma had jurisdiction over the importer and manufacturer, both presumably having deep

enough pockets? And why didn't they sue the driver who hit them from behind, causing the accident? The story behind the case, as told by Charles W. Adams in World-Wide Volkswagen v. Woodson — The Rest of the Story, 72 Neb. L. Rev. 1122 (1993) is both dramatic and complex.

a. Prof. Adams begins with the other driver:

> Lloyd Hull knew he had a serious drinking problem. Ever since his retirement from the Navy two years before, it seemed as though he needed to get a little high, or better, every day. After getting off work on September 21, 1977, in Berryville, Arkansas, Lloyd was on his way to visit his older sister on Okarche, Oklahoma. Next to the bottle of Jim Beam on the front seat was a loaded .22 Magnum pistol for shooting jack rabbits on his sister's farm. . . .
>
> As he drove along, Lloyd took shots from the bottle of bourbon. . . . Later he assumed he must have been driving too fast on account of the liquor. Lloyd did not notice the small car ahead of him until he was nearly on top of it. . . .
>
> Lloyd Hull was an obvious defendant, but he had no liability insurance. . . .

Id. at 1122-1123, 1127.

b. This part of Prof. Adams's account explains the absence of the other driver. More intricate procedural tactics explain the presence of World-Wide and Seaway as defendants. The suit was filed in Creek County, Oklahoma, "a blue collar community that had become known to personal injury lawyers throughout the state as being particularly sympathetic to personal injury plaintiffs." Id. at 1128.

Having made this choice of forum, the Robinsons' lawyer anticipated that the defendants, none of them Oklahoma citizens, would try to get the case into federal district court, which would not be in Creek County. As you will see in the next chapter, noncitizen defendants may "remove" to federal court an action if the requisites of diversity have been met.

But were they met? For diversity jurisdiction to exist, none of the defendants can be of the same state as the plaintiffs (a principle explored more fully in the next chapter). The Robinsons' lawyer argued that the Robinsons, although they were on their way to Arizona, remained New York citizens. Hence the importance of naming World-Wide and Seaway, both New York corporations, as defendants: So long as they remained in the lawsuit, the case could not be removed to federal court and would therefore be tried before a Creek County jury. Do you now understand why there was such a fierce battle about personal jurisdiction over two apparently irrelevant defendants?

c. Given this background, what would you expect to be the remaining defendants' next procedural move after the case has been sent back to Oklahoma courts with the holding that there is no jurisdiction over Seaway and World-Wide?

4. *World-Wide Volkswagen* is emblematic of the modern economy. A car is a complicated product, assembled from components made by many "upstream" manufacturers and then sold through a national network of "downstream" distributors and dealers. Many goods — from simple ones like toasters and bicycles to complex ones like autos, electronic equipment — have similar profiles. When something goes wrong with such a product and a lawsuit results, the legal system has to answer the question of who will be subject to suit.

Part of the answer lies in substantive law, which has evolved dramatically over the last hundred years. Another part is jurisdictional. Everyone seems to agree that the manufacturer of the product — the entity that designed and assembled it (like Audi in *World-Wide Volkswagen*) — will be subject to suit where that product causes injury. The hard question comes when one thinks about those who precede and follow the manufacturer — the potential upstream and downstream defendants. The *World-Wide Volkswagen* case itself dealt with those downstream parts of the network. Suppose that, as the suit against World-Wide proceeded, attention had focused on the manufacturer of the gas tank — a Polish company, let us imagine. Could Audi have joined this "upstream" component manufacturer in the Oklahoma litigation? The next case responds to that question.

Asahi Metal Industry Co. v. Superior Court
480 U.S. 102 (1987)

Justice O'CONNOR announced the judgment of the Court and delivered the unanimous opinion of the Court with respect to Part I; the opinion of the Court with respect to Part II-B, in which THE CHIEF JUSTICE, J[ustices] BRENNAN, WHITE, MARSHALL, BLACKMUN, POWELL, and STEVENS join; and an opinion with respect to Parts II-A and III, in which THE CHIEF JUSTICE, Justice[s] POWELL and SCALIA join.

This case presents the question whether the mere awareness on the part of a foreign defendant that the components it manufactured, sold, and delivered outside the United States would reach the forum State in the stream of commerce constitutes "minimum contacts" between the defendant and the forum State such that the exercise of jurisdiction "does not offend 'traditional notions of fair play and substantial justice.'" International Shoe Co. v. Washington, quoting Milliken v. Meyer.

I

On September 23, 1978, on Interstate Highway 80 in Solano County, California, Gary Zurcher lost control of his Honda motorcycle and collided with a tractor. Zurcher was severely injured, and his passenger and wife, Ruth Ann Moreno, was killed. In September 1979, Zurcher filed a product liability action in the Superior Court of the State of California in and for the County of Solano. Zurcher alleged that the 1978 accident was caused by a sudden loss of air and an explosion in the rear tire of the motorcycle, and alleged that the motorcycle tire, tube, and sealant were defective. Zurcher's complaint named, inter alia, Cheng Shin Rubber Industrial Co., Ltd. (Cheng Shin), the Taiwanese manufacturer of the tube. Cheng Shin in turn filed a cross-complaint [that is, what the Federal Rules would call a third-party complaint] seeking indemnification from its codefendants and from petitioner, Asahi Metal Industry Co., Ltd. (Asahi), the manufacturer of the tube's valve assembly. Zurcher's claims against Cheng Shin and the other defendants were eventually settled and dismissed, leaving only Cheng Shin's indemnity action against Asahi.

California's long-arm statute authorizes the exercise of jurisdiction "on any basis not inconsistent with the Constitution of this state or of the United States." Cal. Code Civ. Proc. Ann. §410.10 (West 1973). Asahi moved to quash Cheng Shin's service of summons arguing the State could not exert jurisdiction over it consistent with the Due Process Clause of the Fourteenth Amendment.

. . . Asahi is a Japanese corporation. It manufactures tire valve assemblies in Japan and sells the assemblies to Cheng Shin, and to several other tire manufacturers, for use as components in finished tire tubes. . . . Cheng Shin bought and incorporated into its tire tubes [between 100,000 and 500,000 assemblies annually in the years from 1978 to 1982; those sales] accounted for 1.24 percent of Asahi's income in 1981 and 0.44 percent in 1982. Cheng Shin alleged that approximately 20 percent of its sales in the United States are in California. Cheng Shin purchases valve assemblies from other suppliers as well, and sells finished tubes throughout the world.

. . . An affidavit of a manager of Cheng Shin whose duties included the purchasing of component parts stated: " 'In discussions with Asahi regarding the purchase of valve stem assemblies the fact that my Company sells tubes throughout the world and specifically the United States has been discussed. I am informed and believe that Asahi was fully aware that valve stem assemblies sold to my Company and to others would end up throughout the United States and in California.' " An affidavit of the president of Asahi, on the other hand, declared that Asahi " 'has never contemplated that its limited sales of tire valves to Cheng Shin in Taiwan would subject it to lawsuits in California.' " The record does not include any contract between Cheng Shin and Asahi.

Primarily on the basis of the above information, the Superior Court denied the motion to quash summons, stating that "Asahi obviously does business on an international scale. It is not unreasonable that they defend claims of defect in their product on an international scale."

We granted certiorari and now reverse.

II

A

. . . Applying the principle that minimum contacts must be based on an act of the defendant, the Court in World-Wide Volkswagen Corp. v. Woodson rejected the assertion that a *consumer's* unilateral act of bringing the defendant's product into the forum State was a sufficient constitutional basis for personal jurisdiction over the defendant. Since *World-Wide Volkswagen*, lower courts have been confronted with cases in which the defendant acted by placing a product in the stream of commerce, and the stream eventually swept defendant's product into the forum State, but the defendant did nothing else to purposefully avail itself of the market in the forum State. Some courts have understood the Due Process Clause, as interpreted in *World-Wide Volkswagen*, to allow an exercise of personal jurisdiction to be based on no more than the defendant's act of placing the product in the stream of commerce. Other courts have understood the Due Process Clause and the above-quoted language in *World-Wide Volkswagen* to require the action of the defendant to be more purposefully directed at the forum State than the mere act of placing a product in the stream of commerce.

The reasoning of the Supreme Court of California in the present case illustrates the former interpretation of *World-Wide Volkswagen*. The Supreme Court of California held that, because the stream of commerce eventually brought some valves Asahi sold Cheng Shin into California, Asahi's awareness that its valves would be sold in California was sufficient to permit California to exercise jurisdiction over Asahi consistent with the requirements of the Due Process Clause. The Supreme Court of California's position was consistent with those courts that have held that mere foreseeability or awareness was a constitutionally sufficient basis for personal jurisdiction if the defendant's product made its way into the forum State while still in the stream of commerce.

Other courts, however, have understood the Due Process Clause to require something more than that the defendant was aware of its product's entry into the forum State through the stream of commerce in order for the state to exert jurisdiction over the defendant. . . .

We now find this latter position to be consonant with the requirements of due process. The "substantial connection," between the defendant and the forum State necessary for a finding of minimum contacts must come about by *an action of the defendant purposefully directed toward the forum State.* The placement of a product into the stream of commerce, without more, is not an act of the defendant purposefully directed toward the forum State. Additional conduct of the defendant may indicate an intent or purpose to serve the market in the forum State, for example, designing the product for the market in the forum State, advertising in the forum State, establishing channels for providing regular advice to customers in the forum State, or marketing the product through a distributor who has agreed to serve as the sales agent in the forum State. But a defendant's awareness that the stream of commerce may or will sweep the product into the forum State does not convert the mere act of placing the product into the stream into an act purposefully directed toward the forum State.

[R]espondents have not demonstrated any action by Asahi to purposefully avail itself of the California market. . . . On the basis of these facts, the exertion of personal jurisdiction over Asahi by the Superior Court of California* exceeds the limits of due process.

B

The strictures of the Due Process Clause forbid a state court from exercising personal jurisdiction over Asahi under circumstances that would offend "traditional notions of fair play and substantial justice." International Shoe v. Washington, quoting Milliken v. Meyer.

We have previously explained that the determination of the reasonableness of the exercise of jurisdiction in each case will depend on an evaluation of several factors. A court must consider the burden on the defendant,

---

* We have no occasion here to determine whether Congress could, consistent with the Due Process Clause of the Fifth Amendment, authorize federal court personal jurisdiction over alien defendants based on the aggregate of national contacts, rather than on the contacts between the defendant and the State in which the federal court sits. See Max Daetwyler Corp. v. R. Meyer, 762 F.2d 290, 293-295 (CA3 1985); DeJames v. Magnificence Carriers, Inc., 654 F.2d 280, 283 (CA3 1981); see also Born, Reflections on Judicial Jurisdiction in International Cases, to be published in 17 Ga. J. Intl. & Comp. L. 1 (1987); Lilly, Jurisdiction Over Domestic and Alien Defendants, 69 Va L. Rev. 85, 127-145 (1983).

the interests of the forum state, and the plaintiff's interest in obtaining relief. It must also weigh in its determination "the interstate judicial system's interest in obtaining the most efficient resolution of controversies; and the shared interest of the several States in furthering fundamental substantive social policies." *World-Wide Volkswagen.*

A consideration of these factors in the present case clearly reveals the unreasonableness of the assertion of jurisdiction over Asahi, even apart from the question of the placement of goods in the stream of commerce.

Certainly the burden on the defendant in this case is severe. Asahi has been commanded by the Supreme Court of California not only to traverse the distance between Asahi's headquarters in Japan and the Superior Court of California in and for the County of Solano, but also to submit its dispute with Cheng Shin to a foreign nation's judicial system. The unique burdens placed upon one who must defend oneself in a foreign legal system should have significant weight in assessing the reasonableness of stretching the long arm of personal jurisdiction over national borders.

When minimum contacts have been established, often the interests of the plaintiff and the forum in the exercise of jurisdiction will justify even the serious burdens placed on the alien defendant. In the present case, however, the interests of the plaintiff and the forum in California's assertion of jurisdiction over Asahi are slight. All that remains is a claim for indemnification asserted by Cheng Shin, a Taiwanese corporation, against Asahi. The transaction on which the indemnification claim is based took place in Taiwan; Asahi's components were shipped from Japan to Taiwan. Cheng Shin has not demonstrated that it is more convenient for it to litigate its indemnification claim against Asahi in California rather than in Taiwan or Japan.

Because the plaintiff is not a California resident, California's legitimate interests in the dispute have considerably diminished. . . . The possibility of being haled into a California court as a result of an accident involving Asahi's components undoubtedly creates an additional deterrent to the manufacture of unsafe components; however, similar pressures will be placed on Asahi by the purchasers of its components as long as those who use Asahi components in their final products, and sell those products in California, are subject to the application of California tort law.

World-Wide Volkswagen also admonished courts to take into consideration the interests of the "several States," in addition to the forum State, in the efficient judicial resolution of the dispute and the advancement of substantive policies. In the present case, this advice calls for a court to consider the procedural and substantive policies of other *nations* whose interests are affected by the assertion of jurisdiction by the California court. . . . "Great care and reserve should be exercised when extending our notions of personal jurisdiction into the international field." United States v. First National City Bank.

Considering the international context, the heavy burden on the alien defendant, and the slight interests of the plaintiff and the forum State, the exercise of personal jurisdiction by a California court over Asahi in this instance would be unreasonable and unfair.

III

Because the facts of this case do not establish minimum contacts such that the exercise of personal jurisdiction is consistent with fair play and substantial justice, the judgment of the Supreme Court of California is reversed, and the case is remanded for further proceedings not inconsistent with this opinion. It is so ordered.

[Justice BRENNAN, with whom Justices WHITE, MARSHALL, and BLACK-MUN joined, concurred in part and concurred in the judgment.]

I do not agree with the interpretation in Part II-A of the stream-of-commerce theory, nor with its conclusion that Asahi did not "purposely avail itself of the California market." I do agree, however, with the Court's conclusion in Part II-B that the exercise of personal jurisdiction over Asahi in this case would not comport with "fair play and substantial justice." *International Shoe.* This is one of those rare cases in which "minimum requirements inherent in the concept of 'fair play and substantial justice' . . . defeat the reasonableness of jurisdiction even [though] the defendant has purposefully engaged in forum activities." Burger King Corp. v. Rudzewicz. I therefore join Parts I and II-B of the Court's opinion, and write separately to explain my disagreement with Part II-A.

[Justice Brennan argued that injecting goods into a stream of commerce should suffice to support jurisdiction.] The endorsement in Part II-A of what appears to be the minority view among Federal Courts of Appeals represents a marked retreat from its analysis in World-Wide Volkswagen v. Woodson. . . .

. . . Accordingly, I cannot join the plurality's determination that Asahi's regular and extensive sales of component parts to a manufacturer it knew was making regular sales of the final product in California is insufficient to establish minimum contacts with California.

[Justice STEVENS, joined by Justices WHITE and BLACKMUN, concurred in part and concurred in the judgment.]

The judgment of the Supreme Court of California should be reversed for the reasons stated in Part II-B of the Court's opinion. While I join

Parts I and II-B, I do not join Part II-A for two reasons. First, it is not necessary to the Court's decision. An examination of minimum contacts is not always necessary to determine whether a state court's assertion of personal jurisdiction is constitutional. See Burger King Corp. v. Rudzewicz. Part II-B establishes, after considering the factors set forth in World-Wide Volkswagen Corp. v. Woodson, that California's exercise of jurisdiction over Asahi in this case would be "unreasonable and unfair." This finding alone requires reversal; this case fits within the rule that "minimum requirements inherent in the concept of 'fair play and substantial justice' may defeat the reasonableness of jurisdiction even if the defendant has purposefully engaged in forum activities." *Burger King* (quoting International Shoe Co. v. Washington). Accordingly, I see no reason in this case for the Court to articulate "purposeful direction" or any other test as the nexus between an act of a defendant and the forum State that is necessary to establish minimum contacts.

Second, even assuming that the test ought to be formulated here, Part II-A misapplies it to the facts of this case. The Court seems to assume that an unwavering line can be drawn between "mere awareness" that a component will find its way into the forum State and "purposeful availment" of the forum's market. Over the course of its dealings with Cheng Shin, Asahi has arguably engaged in a higher quantum of conduct than "[t]he placement of a product into the stream of commerce, without more. . . ." Whether or not this conduct rises to the level of purposeful availment requires a constitutional determination that is affected by the volume, the value, and the hazardous character of the components. In most circumstances I would be inclined to conclude that a regular course of dealing that results in deliveries of over 100,000 units annually over a period of several years would constitute "purposeful availment" even though the item delivered to the forum state was a standard product marketed throughout the world.

NOTES AND PROBLEMS

1. First, sort out holding and dicta, majority and concurrences.

a. Somewhat unusually, the Court agreed unanimously on a result but split sharply on the reasoning leading to its conclusion. What parts of Justice O'Connor's opinion commanded a majority? (Note that *only* these parts are precedent.)

b. Can you infer the views of the majority that endorsed the result but declined to join Parts II-A and III?

c. Can you infer the position of Justice Scalia, who endorsed Parts II-A and III but *not* Part II-B, which the other eight Justices signed?

d. What do lower courts do when the U.S. Supreme Court produces such a split opinion on a frequently litigated topic like personal jurisdiction? *U.S. Law Week* reported the following reaction:

> *Asahi Metal* . . . failed to produce a majority opinion. Subsequently, the circuits have divided over the appropriate test to draw from *Asahi Metal:* the Fifth and Eighth circuits have adopted the test advocated by Justice Brennan; the First Circuit has adopted the test advocated by Justice O'Conner; the other circuits have not adopted a specific test; and the Eleventh Circuit has issued conflicting decisions. For its part, the Third Circuit [has] recognized this division of authority but found it unnecessary to choose a specific test.

Circuit Split Roundup, 67 *U.S. L. Wk.* 2158 (1998). One imagines similar confusion among state courts. Should such results persuade the justices to do everything they can to arrive at a majority opinion?

2. Would the outcome have been different:

a. If Asahi had been a U.S. manufacturer of tire valves that had sold them to a U.S. tire manufacturer for incorporation in motorcycles manufactured in the United States?

b. If Asahi had been one of the primary defendants rather than a third-party defendant?

c. If the suit against the primary defendants had not been settled?

d. If Asahi also sold some of its tire valves to tire stores in California, for sale as replacements?

e. If Cheng Shin had presented evidence that, because of a chill in foreign relations, Japan's courts were closed to Taiwanese plaintiffs?

3. Put *World-Wide Volkswagen* and *Asahi* together. Both grew from tort actions involving a complicated product assembled from many components and sold nationally. Both assume without so holding that the manufacturer — Audi and Honda — can be sued wherever the product is sold. Both limit jurisdiction over those who precede and follow the manufacturer in the "stream of commerce."

Assume that Volvo, a Swedish car maker partly owned by General Motors, buys brake components from BrakeCo, a U.S. manufacturer located in Illinois. Volvo has a national distributor, located in New Jersey, and a network of dealers throughout the United States. Consumer buys a Volvo in Florida; the brakes fail and it crashes. Consumer brings suit in Florida against Volvo, BrakeCo, National Distributor, and Dealer. Who will be subject to personal jurisdiction? What more facts do you want to know — and why?

4. Doctrinally, *Asahi* is interesting because of its suggestion that "substantial justice and fair play" is not a synonym for minimum contacts but

an independent requirement. In *Asahi* the substantial justice requirement defeated jurisdiction, even though a majority of the justices seemed prepared to say that Asahi did have minimum contacts with California, the forum state. The next case suggests that substantial justice may also play a positive role — pushing the court toward assumption of jurisdiction, even when contacts are quite thin.

Burger King Corp. v. Rudzewicz
471 U.S. 462 (1985)

Justice BRENNAN delivered the opinion of the Court.

[Burger King operates an extensive fast food franchise system in which it trains franchisees and regulates their operations in great detail. Headquarters are in Florida, but regional offices supervise franchisees in their areas.]

The instant litigation grows out of Burger King's termination of one of its franchisees, and is aptly described by the franchisee as "a divorce proceeding among commercial partners." The appellee John Rudzewicz, a Michigan citizen and resident, is the senior partner in a Detroit accounting firm. In 1978, he was approached by Brian MacShara, the son of a business acquaintance, who suggested that they jointly apply to Burger King for a franchise in the Detroit area. MacShara proposed to serve as the manager of the restaurant if Rudzewicz would put up the investment capital; in exchange, the two would evenly share the profits. Believing that MacShara's idea offered attractive investment and tax-deferral opportunities, Rudzewicz agreed to the venture.

Rudzewicz and MacShara jointly applied for a franchise to Burger King's Birmingham, Michigan, district office in the autumn of 1978. Their application was forwarded to Burger King's Miami headquarters, which entered into a preliminary agreement with them in February 1979. During the ensuing four months it was agreed that Rudzewicz and MacShara would assume operation of an existing facility in Drayton Plains, Michigan. MacShara attended the prescribed management courses in Miami during this period, and the franchisees purchased $165,000 worth of restaurant equipment from Burger King's Davmor Industries division in Miami. Even before the final agreements were signed, however, the parties began to disagree over site-development fees, building design, computation of monthly rent, and whether the franchisees would be able to assign their liabilities to a corporation they had formed. During these disputes Rudzewicz and MacShara negotiated both with the Birmingham district office and with the Miami headquarters. With some misgivings, Rudzewicz and MacShara finally obtained limited concessions from the Miami headquarters, signed the final agreements, and commenced operations in June 1979. By signing the final agreements, Rudzewicz obligated himself personally to payments exceeding $1 million over the 20-year franchise relationship.

[Shortly after the agreement was signed, business at the franchise began to deteriorate. When rent payments fell behind, Burger King first negotiated, then sued in federal district court in Florida, invoking both diversity and trademark jurisdiction. Rudzewicz and MacShara challenged personal jurisdiction. The district court rejected their challenge. The case went to trial, at which the judge awarded Burger King both damages and injunctive relief. A divided] panel of [the Eleventh] Circuit reversed the judgment, concluding that the District Court could not properly exercise personal jurisdiction over Rudzewicz pursuant to Fla. Stat. §48.193(1)(g) (Supp. 1984) because "the circumstances of the Drayton Plains franchise and the negotiations which led to it left Rudzewicz bereft of reasonable notice and financially unprepared for the prospect of franchise litigation in Florida." [W]e . . . reverse.

II

A

The Due Process Clause protects an individual's liberty interest in not being subject to the binding judgments of a forum with which he has established no meaningful "contacts, ties, or relations." International Shoe Co. v. Washington.[13] By requiring that individuals have "fair warning that a particular activity may subject [them] to the jurisdiction of a foreign sovereign," Shaffer v. Heitner (Stevens, J., concurring in judgment), the Due Process Clause "gives a degree of predictability to the legal system that allows potential defendants to structure their primary conduct with some minimum assurance as to where that conduct will and will not render them liable to suit," World-Wide Volkswagen Corp. v. Woodson.

Where a forum seeks to assert specific jurisdiction over an out-of-state defendant who has not consented to suit there, this "fair warning" requirement is satisfied if the defendant has "purposefully directed" his activities at residents of the forum and the litigation results from alleged injuries that "arise out of or relate to" those activities. . . .

13. Although this protection operates to restrict state power, it "must be seen as ultimately a function of the individual liberty interest preserved by the Due Process Clause" rather than as a function "of federalism concerns." Insurance Corp. of Ireland, Ltd. v. Compagnie des Bauxites de Guinée, 456 U.S. 694, 702-703, n.10 (1982).

. . . Although it has been argued that foreseeability of causing *injury* in another State should be sufficient to establish such contacts there when policy considerations so require, the Court has consistently held that this kind of foreseeability is not a "sufficient benchmark" for exercising personal jurisdiction. World-Wide Volkswagen Corp. v. Woodson. Instead, "the foreseeability that is critical to due process analysis . . . is that the defendant's conduct and connection with the forum State are such that he should reasonably anticipate being haled into court there." Id. In defining when it is that a potential defendant should "reasonably anticipate" out-of-state litigation, the Court frequently has drawn from the reasoning of Hanson v. Denckla:

> The unilateral activity of those who claim some relationship with a nonresident defendant cannot satisfy the requirement of contact with the forum State. The application of that rule will vary with the quality and nature of the defendant's activity, but it is essential in each case that there be some act by which the defendant purposefully avails itself of the privilege of conducting activities within the forum State, thus invoking the benefits and protections of its laws. . . .

Once it has been decided that a defendant purposefully established minimum contacts within the forum State, these contacts may be considered in light of other factors to determine whether they comport with "fair play and substantial justice." International Shoe Co. v. Washington. . . . These considerations sometimes serve to establish the reasonableness of jurisdiction upon a lesser showing of minimum contacts than would otherwise be required. On the other hand, where a defendant who purposefully has directed his activities at forum residents seeks to defeat jurisdiction, he must present a compelling case that the presence of some other considerations would render jurisdiction unreasonable. Most such considerations usually may be accommodated through means short of finding jurisdiction unconstitutional. For example, the potential clash of the forum's law with the "fundamental substantive social policies" of another State may be accommodated through application of the forum's choice-of-law rules. Similarly, a defendant claiming substantial inconvenience may seek a change of venue. Nevertheless, minimum requirements inherent in the concept of "fair play and substantial justice" may defeat the reasonableness of jurisdiction even if the defendant has purposefully engaged in forum activities. World-Wide Volkswagen Corp. v. Woodson. As we previously have noted, jurisdictional rules may not be employed in such a way as to make litigation "so gravely difficult and inconvenient" that a party unfairly is at a "severe disadvantage" in comparison to his opponent.

B

(1)

Applying these principles to the case at hand, we believe there is substantial record evidence supporting the District Court's conclusion that the assertion of personal jurisdiction over Rudzewicz in Florida for the alleged breach of his franchise agreement did not offend due process. At the outset, we note a continued division among lower courts respecting whether and to what extent a contract can constitute a "contact" for purposes of due process analysis. If the question is whether an individual's contract with an out-of-state party alone can automatically establish sufficient minimum contacts in the other party's home forum, we believe the answer clearly is that it cannot. . . . A "contract" is "ordinarily but an intermediate step serving to tie up prior business negotiations with future consequences which themselves are the real object of the business transaction." [Hoopeston Canning Co. v. Cullen.] It is these factors — prior negotiations and contemplated future consequences, along with the terms of the contract and the parties' actual course of dealing — that must be evaluated in determining whether the defendant purposefully established minimum contacts within the forum.

In this case, no physical ties to Florida can be attributed to Rudzewicz other than MacShara's brief training course in Miami. Rudzewicz did not maintain offices in Florida and, for all that appears from the record, has never even visited there. Yet this franchise dispute grew directly out of "a contract which had a *substantial* connection with that State." McGee v. International Life Insurance Co. Eschewing the option of operating an independent local enterprise, Rudzewicz deliberately "reach[ed] out beyond" Michigan and negotiated with a Florida corporation for the purchase of a long-term franchise and the manifold benefits that would derive from affiliation with a nationwide organization. Upon approval, he entered into a carefully structured 20-year relationship that envisioned continuing and wide-reaching contact with Burger King in Florida. In light of Rudzewicz's voluntary acceptance of the long-term and exacting regulation of his business from Burger King's Miami headquarters, the "quality and nature" of his relationship to the company in Florida can in no sense be viewed as "random," "fortuitous," or "attenuated." Hanson v. Denckla. . . . Rudzewicz most certainly knew that he was affiliating himself with an enterprise based primarily in Florida. The contract documents themselves emphasize that Burger King's operations are conducted and supervised from the Miami headquarters, that all relevant notices and payments must be sent there, and that the agreements were made in and enforced from Miami. Moreover, the parties' actual course of dealing repeatedly confirmed that decision making authority was vested in the Miami headquarters and that the district office served largely as an intermediate link between the headquarters and the franchisees. When problems arose over building design, site-development fees, rent computation, and the defaulted payments, Rudzewicz and MacShara learned that the Michigan office was powerless to resolve their disputes and could only channel their communications to Miami. . . .

Moreover, we believe the Court of Appeals gave insufficient weight to provisions in the various franchise documents providing that all disputes would be governed by Florida law. The franchise agreement, for example, stated:

> This Agreement shall become valid when executed and accepted by BKC at Miami, Florida; it shall be deemed made and entered into in the State of Florida and shall be governed and construed under and in accordance with the laws of the State of Florida. The choice of law designation does not require that all suits concerning this Agreement be filed in Florida.

. . . As Judge Johnson argued in his dissent below, Rudzewicz "purposefully availed himself of the benefits and protections of Florida laws" by entering into contracts expressly providing that those laws would govern franchise disputes.[24]

The Court of Appeals . . . concluded, however, that the parties' dealings involved "a characteristic disparity, of bargaining power" and "elements of surprise," and that Rudzewicz "lacked fair notice" of the potential for litigation in Florida because the contractual provisions suggesting to the contrary were merely "boilerplate declarations in a lengthy printed contract." Rudzewicz presented many of these arguments to the District Court, contending that Burger King was guilty of misrepresentation, fraud, and duress, that it gave insufficient notice in its dealings with him, and that the contract was one of adhesion. After a 3-day bench trial, the District Court found that Burger King had made no misrepresentations, that Rudzewicz and MacShara "were and are experienced and sophisticated businessmen," and that "at no time" did they "ac[t] under economic duress or disadvantage imposed by" Burger King. Federal Rule of Civil Procedure 52(a) requires that "[f]indings of fact shall not be set aside

---

24. In addition, the franchise agreement's disclaimer that the "choice of law designation does not *require* that all suits concerning this Agreement be filed in Florida" (emphasis added) reasonably should have suggested to Rudzewicz that by negative implication such suits *could* be filed there. . . .

unless clearly erroneous," and neither Rudzewicz nor the Court of Appeals have pointed to record evidence that would support a "definite and firm conviction" that the District Court's findings are mistaken. . . .

III

Notwithstanding these considerations, the Court of Appeals apparently believed that it was necessary to reject jurisdiction in this case as a prophylactic measure, reasoning that an affirmance of the District Court's judgment would result in the exercise of jurisdiction over "out-of-state consumers to collect payments due on modest personal purchases" and would "sow the seeds of default judgments against franchisees owing smaller debts." We share the Court of Appeals' broader concerns and therefore reject any talismanic jurisdictional formulas; "the facts of each case must [always] be weighed" in determining whether personal jurisdiction would comport with "fair play and substantial justice." Kulko v. California Superior Court. . . . We also have emphasized that jurisdiction may not be grounded on a contract whose terms have been obtained through "fraud, undue influence, or overweening bargaining power" and whose application would render litigation "so gravely difficult and inconvenient that [a party] will for all practical purposes be deprived of his day in court." The Bremen v. Zapata Off-Shore Co. Cf. Fuentes v. Shevin; National Equipment Rental, Ltd. v. Szukhent (1964) (Black, J., dissenting) (jurisdictional rules may not be employed against small consumers so as to "crippl[e] their defense"). Just as the Due Process Clause allows flexibility in ensuring that commercial actors are not effectively "judgment proof" for the consequences of obligations they voluntarily assume in other States, McGee v. International Life Insurance Co., so too does it prevent rules that would unfairly enable them to obtain default judgments against unwitting customers.

For the reasons set forth above, however, these dangers are not present in the instant case. . . . The judgment of the Court of Appeals is accordingly reversed, and the case is remanded for further proceedings consistent with this opinion.

Justice POWELL took no part in the consideration or decision of this case.

Justice STEVENS, with whom Justice WHITE joins, dissenting.

In my opinion there is a significant element of unfairness in requiring a franchisee to defend a case of this kind in the forum chosen by the franchiser. It is undisputed that respondent maintained no place of business in Florida, that he had no employees in that State, and that he was not licensed to do business there. Respondent did not prepare his french fries, shakes, and hamburgers in Michigan, and then deliver them into the stream of commerce "with the expectation that they [would] be purchased by consumers in" Florida. To the contrary, respondent did business only in Michigan, his business, property, and payroll taxes were payable in that state, and he sold all of his products there.

Throughout the business relationship, respondent's principal contacts with petitioner were with its Michigan office. Notwithstanding its disclaimer, the Court seems ultimately to rely on nothing more than standard boilerplate language contained in various documents, to establish that respondent "'purposefully availed himself of the benefits and protections of Florida's laws.'" Such superficial analysis creates a potential for unfairness not only in negotiations between franchisers and their franchisees but, more significantly, in the resolution of the disputes that inevitably arise from time to time in such relationships.

Judge Vance's opinion for the Court of Appeals for the Eleventh Circuit adequately explains why I would affirm the judgment of that court. I particularly find the following more persuaive than what this Court has written today:

> Nothing in the course of negotiations gave Rudzewicz reason to anticipate a Burger King suit outside of Michigan. The only face-to-face or even oral contact Rudzewicz had with Burger King throughout months of protracted negotiations was with representatives of the Michigan office. . . .
>
> Just as Rudzewicz lacked notice of the possibility of suit in Florida, he was financially unprepared to meet its added costs. The franchise relationship in particular is fraught with potential for financial surprise. The device of the franchise gives local retailers the access to national trademark recognition which enable them to compete with better-financed, more efficient chain stores. This national affiliation, however, does not alter the fact that the typical franchise store is a local concern serving at best a neighborhood or community. Neither the revenues of a local business nor the geographical range of its market prepares the average franchise owner for the cost of distant litigation. . . .
>
> The particular distribution of bargaining power in the franchise relationship further impairs the franchisee's financial preparedness. In a franchise contract, "the franchiser normally occupies [the] dominant role." . . .
>
> We discern a characteristic disparity of bargaining power in the facts of this case. There is no indication that Rudzewicz had any latitude to negotiate a reduced rent or franchise fee in exchange for the added risk of suit in Florida. He signed a standard form contract whose terms were non-negotiable and which appeared in some respects to vary from the more favorable terms agreed to in earlier discussions. In fact, the final contract required a minimum monthly rent computed on a base far in excess of that discussed in oral negotiations. Burger King resisted price

concessions, only to sue Rudzewicz far from home. In doing so, it severely impaired his ability to call Michigan witnesses who might be essential to his defense and counterclaim.

In sum, we hold that the circumstances of the Drayton Plains franchise and the negotiations which led to it left Rudzewicz bereft of reasonable notice and financially unprepared for the prospect of franchise litigation in Florida. Jurisdiction under these circumstances would offend the fundamental fairness which is the touchstone of due process.

Accordingly, I respectfully dissent.

NOTES AND PROBLEMS

1. Consider first the significance of *Burger King*.

a. Short of not entering into the franchise agreement, is there any way that Rudzewicz could have avoided Florida jurisdiction?

b. If you were advising Burger King, would you tell them that the opinion means that they can henceforth sue any franchisee in Florida courts? Or would you have qualifications?

c. You are a lawyer who has read *Burger King*. You are consulted by another Burger King franchisee who is in a dispute with the franchise and who foresees litigation. You want to avoid the Florida forum, thinking another venue may be more sympathetic. What can you do?

2. Can you distinguish *Burger King* from *World-Wide Volkswagen*? Why is the local automobile dealer not subject to jurisdiction in Oklahoma, while the local hamburger dealer is subject to jurisdiction in Florida?

3. Compare *Burger King* with *Asahi*. Both cases turn on "substantial justice and fair play," one of the central formulations in *International Shoe*. Describe the role that the concept plays in the two cases.

4. Toward the end of the opinion the majority responds to the court of appeals' concern that a victory for Burger King would "result in the exercise of jurisdiction over 'out-of-state consumers to collect payments due on modest personal purchases.'" The majority indicates, without explanation, that its holding does not stretch that far. Even if one takes the Court at its word, however, it is unclear whether the key word in the quoted phrase is "consumer" or "modest." National financial institutions are beginning to enter previously local mortgage markets. Picture a Colorado homeowner who arranges financing with a lender in New Jersey (whose rates are lower than those of local banks). The expected duration of the loan contract might be more than that of the Burger King franchise, and the amount in question almost as much.

Under those circumstances, could the lender bring suit in New Jersey against a homeowner who fell behind in payments?

5. Unlike *World-Wide Volkswagen* and *Asahi*, *Burger King* was initiated in a federal court. The *Burger King* opinion silently assumes that the analysis is identical — that the jurisdictional reach of a federal court matches that of a state court sitting in the same state. The reason for that assumption at one level is straightforward: Federal Rule of Civil Procedure 4(k)(1)(A) confines the jurisdictional reach of federal courts to the state in which they sit, except when either a specific federal statute or a state long-arm statute authorizes long-arm jurisdiction.

a. Exceptions to this provision occur when a specific federal statute or Rule authorizes more extensive personal jurisdiction. Rule 4(k)(1)(B)-(D). In several notable instances Congress has purported to give the federal courts expansive powers of personal jurisdiction. For example, the Federal Interpleader Act, 28 U.S.C. §2361, gives federal courts the power to serve process anywhere in the nation, a power that has been interpreted to include personal jurisdiction. Various laws regulating federal securities do the same. Is such jurisdictional reach constitutional? Under a jurisdictional model deriving from *Pennoyer*, the question was fairly simple. If jurisdictional power flowed from sovereignty, and if the federal government was in some sense sovereign within the borders of the nation, then jurisdiction existed: The only restraint lay in Congress's self-denial, the limitations of venue, and the doctrine of forum non conveniens.

b. *International Shoe* (and its reaffirmation in *Shaffer* and subsequent cases) made the question much harder. If personal jurisdiction was a matter of inconvenience to the defendant, then was it not equally possible for that inconvenience to exist in a federal as in a state forum? Of course, if the defendant in question has the sort of contacts with a state or judicial district that would suffice under *International Shoe,* the problem is again easy. But what happens if the defendant doesn't? That is, suppose a state court could not constitutionally exercise jurisdiction because to do so would violate due process? May a federal court, sitting in the same state, disregard that limitation? (A small technical note: The Constitution contains two due process clauses, one in the Fourteenth Amendment, applying to state governments, and one in the Fifth Amendment, applying to the federal government; courts have generally interpreted them in identical ways.)

6. Recapitulate your understanding of personal jurisdiction by considering two problems drawn from a number of recent cases about jurisdictional contacts and the Internet. Both involve claims by a plaintiff that an Internet posting violates trademark laws and both seek to use the

accessibility of the defendant's Web site in the forum state as the basis for jurisdiction.

a. A New York nightclub calls itself The Green Note and has federally registered that trademark, under which it operates other clubs around the world. Richard Duke lives in Columbia, Missouri, where he owns a "small club," also called The Green Note. Columbia, Missouri is a college town and Duke, thinking that students might be attracted by a Web page, creates such a page and posts it. The site contains information about coming events and the places — all in Columbia, Missouri — where tickets can be obtained. The site is not interactive: No tickets can be ordered or additional information sought through the site. The Web is, of course, available internationally, and Duke's page is read in, among other places, New York City, by those who operate The Green Note there. The New York nightclub operators sue in federal court alleging, let us suppose validly, that the Missouri Green Note infringes their federal trademark. Suit is brought in the federal court for the Southern District of New York; jurisdiction is based on the availability of the Web site in New York.

b. Zippo Co. manufactures cigarette lighters in Pennsylvania. Zippo Dot Com, Inc., based in California, operates an Internet Web site and Internet news service and has obtained an exclusive right to the "zippo. com" and similar domain names. The Internet Zippo offers subscriptions to its services over the Internet, selling them interactively: Would-be subscribers fill out their names and address and supply a credit card number for payment. The Internet Zippo has about 3,000 subscribers in Pennsylvania. The lighter Zippo sues the Internet Zippo for trademark infringement in Pennsylvania, alleging that the use of its federally pro-tected name in the domain site constitutes infringement. As in the preced-ing case, the Web activity in Pennsylvania was used as the jurisdictional basis for the suit.

c. Should personal jurisdiction be available in either suit? In both?

d. As between the two cases, in which is the case for jurisdiction stronger? Why? Compare Bensusan Restaurant Corp. v. The Blue Note, 937 F. Supp. 295 (S.D.N.Y. 1996) (no jurisdiction) with Zippo Mfg. Co. v. Zippo Dot Com, Inc., 952 F. Supp. 1119 (W.D. Pa. 1997) (jurisdiction).

4. General Jurisdiction

The cases in the previous section all concerned the relationship to the forum state necessary to support specific jurisdiction. For example, *Burger King* holds that Florida had jurisdiction to hear a lawsuit against

Mr. Rudzewicz arising out of his dealings with Burger King; the case does not stand for the proposition that Florida could hear a lawsuit brought by Mr. Rudzewicz's Michigan neighbor claiming that his tree roots had clogged the neighbor's drains, or a suit by an Iowa motorist claiming that Rudzewicz had collided with her on a Colorado road.

Under what circumstances will defendant be subject to jurisdiction for all claims — even those without any connection to the forum state? In passing, *International Shoe* suggests that at least for U.S. defendants, there will always be a state in which suit may be brought on all claims. For corporations, the state of incorporation will be such a forum; so will the state that is the principal place of business (if different from the state of incorporation). To return to an example used in a previous section, General Motors, incorporated in Delaware and with its principal place of business in Michigan, may be sued in either of those states even for claims unrelated to its activities there. Thus an Oregon automobile owner claiming injuries due to a defectively designed GM vehicle could sue in either Michigan or Delaware. That would be true even if the vehicle had been manufactured at a GM plant in Texas, Mexico, or Germany.

A similar situation holds true for individuals. As already noted, Milliken v. Meyer (supra page 103) stands for the proposition that individuals can be sued in the state of their domicile for all claims. Thus Mr. Rudzewicz could be sued in Michigan for claims arising out of an auto accident that occurred while he was vacationing in Colorado.

The states of domicile (for individuals) and incorporation and principal place of business (for corporations) comprise the easy instances of general jurisdiction, instances where defendants are being sued in what is self-evidently their "base of operations." The language of *International Shoe* and the cases elaborating on it suggest that the principle of general jurisdiction extends further than this, and that, given some absolute level of activity, a defendant may be subject to suit beyond this base of operations. But contemporary cases so holding are surprisingly difficult to find. No one litigates the easy cases — domicile and state of incorporation — because they are so easy. And the expansion of specific jurisdiction in recent decades provides a jurisdictional basis for lawsuits that once might have relied on general jurisdiction. One sees many cases that reject assertions of general jurisdiction and specific jurisdiction as well, but virtually none that reject specific jurisdiction while finding general jurisdiction. This section explores the limits of this doctrine with two cases. Both involve defendants sued outside their home states on claims unrelated to the activities conducted in the forum states. In one the court rejects general jurisdiction; in the other the court upholds it: Why?

Washington Equipment Manufacturing Co. v. Concrete Placing Co.

85 Wash. App. 240, 931 P.2d 170 (1997)

SWEENEY, C.J.

A foreign corporation must obtain a certificate of authority to do business and appoint a registered agent to transact business in Washington. RCW 23B.15.010(1), .070(1)(b). Concrete Placing Company, Inc., is an Idaho corporation. It obtained a certificate of authority and appointed a registered agent in order to build two roads in Walla Walla County [in Washington] in 1985 and 1986. In 1994, it bought a concrete placing machine and a concrete paving plant from Washington Equipment Manufacturing Company, Inc., a Washington corporation. Concrete Placing refused to pay the full purchase price. Washington Equipment sued for the balance of the purchase price in Washington. The trial court dismissed the complaint for lack of jurisdiction. Washington Equipment appeals.

The question presented is one of first impression. Does a foreign corporation consent to general personal jurisdiction by securing a certificate of authority to do business and appointing a registered agent? . . .

Consent to General Personal Jurisdiction

Washington Equipment first argues that Concrete Placing consented to general personal jurisdiction by obtaining a certificate of authority to do business and appointing a registered agent. This first contention presents a question of general jurisdiction over this foreign corporation not specific jurisdiction. Specific jurisdiction is appropriate when a particular cause of action arises out of, or relates to, the foreign corporation's activities in this state. General jurisdiction, on the other hand, is unrelated to the corporation's specific activities in this state. General jurisdiction focuses instead on whether the foreign corporation's general business activities in Washington are substantial and continuous. . . .

Washington Equipment argues that by obtaining a certificate of authority to do business and appointing a registered agent, a foreign corporation consents to the imposition of general jurisdiction. Underlying Washington Equipment's argument is the legal fiction that by registering to do business in Washington, a foreign corporation consents to jurisdiction. We read Washington's statutory scheme differently. . . .

[A] foreign corporation doing business in Washington, such as Concrete Placing's road jobs in Walla Walla County during 1985 and 1986, must appoint a registered agent and have a registered office in Washington. RCW 23B.15.030, .070. Nothing, however, in the Washington Business Corporation Act (RCW 23B) states, or implies, that by complying with these mandatory requirements a foreign corporation consents to general jurisdiction in Washington.

Indeed, when the Legislature has wanted to impose jurisdiction because of a foreign corporation's activity, it has said so. For example, members and managers of a foreign limited liability company doing business in Washington submit to the personal jurisdiction of this state. RCW 25.15.310(3). Consent, including consent to general jurisdiction, requires some knowing and voluntary act. A foreign corporation should not be deemed to have knowingly consented to general jurisdiction by doing an act required by the state obtaining a certificate of authority to do business and appointing a registered agent absent legislative intent. . . .

Waiver

Washington Equipment next argues that Concrete Placing waived the jurisdiction issue by asserting forum non conveniens. A defendant waives any objection to personal jurisdiction by a claim for affirmative relief. The claim of forum non conveniens was . . . not a claim for affirmative relief.

Dismissal with Prejudice

Washington Equipment finally claims the court erred in dismissing its claim with prejudice. But dismissing a claim with prejudice because of a lack of jurisdiction only affects Washington Equipment's ability to renew the claim in Washington. It should not deprive Washington Equipment from reinstituting the action in an appropriate forum.

NOTES AND PROBLEMS

1. What should plaintiff do now?

2. Most states have similar foreign corporation statutes, requiring out-of-state firms to register with some state agency. These statutes have several purposes — regulatory, fiscal (tax authorities often want to tax income from in-state business), and informational.

3. Does the court interpret the constitutional cases correctly?

a. The opinion speaks of "consent" to general jurisdiction, but the consent of which it speaks is fictional, for the case conducts its analysis as if the only thing that mattered was legislative intent — not the intent of the defendant.

b. Treating the question as one of statutory interpretation, the court implies that if the Washington legislature had made clear its intent to subject all registering foreign corporations to general jurisdiction, that would have been permissible. If that's correct (and the legislature had made its intent clear), then a disgruntled former employee could sue the Idaho firm in Washington on a claim unrelated to any business in that state. Would that be constitutional?

c. To answer the preceding question and to review your mastery of the material on specific jurisdiction, contrast the result in *Washington Equipment* with that in Hess v. Pawloski, 274 U.S. 352 (1927), supra page 91. In *Hess*, which involved a nonresident motorist statute, the court held that operating a motor vehicle in the state constituted an "appointment" of a state official to receive service of process for claims arising from operation of the vehicle. Reconcile that holding with the ruling in *Washington Equipment*.

4. In many business transactions involving smaller corporations, an officer of the corporation personally guarantees a debt: The officer pledges to pay out of his personal assets if the company does not pay. Suppose that the president of Concrete Placing had personally guaranteed the sales price of the equipment. While the dispute is pending, he visits Washington to attend a football game. He is there served with process. Is there jurisdiction? The next case considers the question.

Burnham v. Superior Court
495 U.S. 604 (1990)

Justice SCALIA announced the judgment of the Court and delivered an opinion in which the CHIEF JUSTICE and Justice KENNEDY joined, and in which Justice WHITE joined as to Parts I, II-A, II-B, and II-C.

The question presented is whether the Due Process Clause of the Fourteenth Amendment denies California courts jurisdiction over a nonresident, who was personally served with process while temporarily in that State, in a suit unrelated to his activities in the State.

I

Petitioner Dennis Burnham married Francie Burnham in 1976, in West Virginia. In 1977 the couple moved to New Jersey, where their two children were born. In July 1987 the Burnhams decided to separate. They agreed that Mrs. Burnham, who intended to move to California, would take custody of the children. Shortly before Mrs. Burnham departed for California that same month, she and petitioner agreed that she would file for divorce on grounds of "irreconcilable differences."

In October 1987, petitioner filed for divorce in New Jersey state court on grounds of "desertion." Petitioner did not, however, obtain an issuance of summons against his wife, and did not attempt to serve her with process. Mrs. Burnham, after unsuccessfully demanding that petitioner adhere to their prior agreement to submit to an "irreconcilable differences" divorce, brought suit for divorce in California state court in early January 1988.

In late January, petitioner visited southern California on business, after which he went north to visit his children in the San Francisco Bay area, where his wife resided. He took the older child to San Francisco for the weekend. Upon returning the child to Mrs. Burnham's home on January 24, 1988, petitioner was served with a California court summons and a copy of Mrs. Burnham's divorce petition. He then returned to New Jersey.

Later that year, petitioner made a special appearance in the California Superior Court, moving to quash the service of process on the ground that the court lacked personal jurisdiction over him because his only contacts with California were a few short visits to the State for the purpose of conducting business and visiting his children. The Superior Court denied the motion, and the California Court of Appeal denied mandamus relief, rejecting petitioner's contention that the Due Process Clause prohibited California courts from asserting jurisdiction over him because he lacked "minimum contacts" with the State. The court held it to be "a valid jurisdictional predicate for in personam jurisdiction" that the "defendant [was] present in the forum state and personally served with process." We granted certiorari.

II

A

. . . To determine whether the assertion of personal jurisdiction is consistent with due process, we have long relied on the principles traditionally followed by American courts in making out the territorial limits of each State's authority. That criterion was first announced in Pennoyer v. Neff, in which we stated that due process "mean[s] a course of legal proceedings according to those rules and principles which have been established in our systems of jurisprudence for the protection and enforcement of private rights," including the "well-established principles of public law respecting the jurisdiction of an independent State over persons and property." In what has become the classic expression of the criterion, we said in International Shoe Co. v. Washington, 326 U.S. 310 (1945), that a State Court's assertion of personal jurisdiction satisfies the Due Process Clause if it does not violate "'traditional notions of fair play and substantial justice'" [quoting Milliken v. Meyer]. See also Insurance Corp. of Ireland v. Compagnie des Bauxites de Guinée [infra page 160]. Since *International Shoe*, we have only been called upon to decide whether these "traditional notions" permit States to exercise jurisdiction over absent defendants in a manner that deviates from the rules of jurisdiction applied in the 19th century. We have held such deviations permissible, but only with respect to suits arising out of the absent defendant's contacts with the State.[1] The question we must decide today is whether due process requires a similar connection between the litigation and the defendant's contacts with the State in cases where the defendant is physically present in the State at the time process is served upon him.

B

Among the most firmly established principles of personal jurisdiction in American tradition is that the courts of a State have jurisdiction over nonresidents who are physically present in the State. The view developed early that each State had the power to hale before its courts any individual who could be found within its borders, and that once having acquired jurisdiction over such a person by properly serving him with process, the State could retain jurisdiction to enter judgment against him, no matter how fleeting his visit. See, e.g., Potter v. Allin, 2 Root 63, 67 (Conn. 1793); Barrell v. Benjamin, 15 Mass. 354 (1819). That view had antecedents in English common-law practice, which sometimes allowed "transitory" actions, arising out of events outside the country, to be maintained against seemingly nonresident defendants who were present in England. . . .

Recent scholarship has suggested that English tradition was not as clear [as Supreme Court Justice and treatise writer Joseph Story thought

1. We have said that "[e]ven when the cause of action does not arise out of or relate to the foreign corporation's activities in the forum state, due process is not offended by a State's subjecting the corporation to its *in personam* jurisdiction when there are sufficient contacts between the state and the foreign corporation." Helicopteros Nacionales de Colombia v. Hall, 466 U.S. at 414. Our only holding supporting that statement, however, involved "regular service of summons upon [the corporation's] president while he was in [the forum state] acting in that capacity." See Perkins v. Benguet Consolidated Mining Co., 342 U.S. 437 (1952). It may be that whatever special rule exists permitting "continuous and systematic" contacts . . . to support jurisdiction with respect to matters unrelated to activity in the forum, applies *only* to corporations, which have never been fitted comfortably within a jurisdictional regime based primarily upon "de facto power over the defendant's person." *International Shoe*. . . . We express no views on these matters — and, for simplicity's sake, omit reference to this aspect of "contacts"-based jurisdiction in our discussion.

it was.] . . . . Accurate or not, however, judging by the evidence of contemporaneous . . . decisions, one must conclude that Story's understanding was shared by American courts at the crucial time for present purposes: 1868, when the Fourteenth Amendment was adopted.

C

Despite this formidable body of precedent, petitioner contends, in reliance on our decisions applying the *International Shoe* standard, that in the absence of "continuous and systematic" contacts with the forum, see note 1, supra, a nonresident defendant can be subjected to judgment only as to matters that arise out of or relate to his contacts with the forum. This argument rests on a thorough misunderstanding of our cases. . . .

[Cases following *International Shoe* upheld jurisdiction over defendants who were *not* present in the forum state.]

Nothing in *International Shoe* or the cases that have followed it, however, offers support for the very different proposition petitioner seeks to establish today: that a defendant's presence in the forum is not only unnecessary to validate novel, nontraditional assertions of jurisdiction, but is itself no longer sufficient to establish jurisdiction. . . .

The short of the matter is that jurisdiction based on physical presence alone constitutes due process because it is one of the continuing traditions of our legal system that define the due process standard of "traditional notions of fair play and substantial justice." That standard was developed by analogy to "physical presence," and it would be perverse to say it could now be turned against that touchstone of jurisdiction.

D

Petitioner's strongest argument, though we ultimately reject it, relies upon our decision in Shaffer v. Heitner.

It goes too far to say, as petitioner contends, that *Shaffer* compels the conclusion that a State lacks jurisdiction over an individual unless the litigation arises out of his activities in the State. *Shaffer*, like *International Shoe*, involved jurisdiction over an absent defendant, and it stands for nothing more than the proposition that when the "minimum contact" that is a substitute for physical presence consists of property ownership it must, like other minimum contacts, be related to the litigation. Petitioner wrenches out of its context our statement in *Shaffer* that "all assertions of state-court jurisdiction must be evaluated according to the standards set forth in *International Shoe* and its progeny." 433 U.S., at 212. When read together with the two sentences that preceded it, the meaning of this statement becomes clear:

> The fiction that an assertion of jurisdiction over property is anything but an assertion of jurisdiction over the owner of the property supports an ancient form without substantial modern justification. Its continued acceptance would serve only to allow state-court jurisdiction that is fundamentally unfair to the defendant.
>
> "We *therefore conclude* that all assertions of state-court jurisdiction must be evaluated according to the standards set forth in *International Shoe* and its progeny." Ibid. (emphasis added).

Shaffer was saying, in other words, not that all bases for the assertion of in personam jurisdiction (including, presumably, in-state service) must be treated alike and subjected to the "minimum contacts" analysis of *International Shoe*; but rather that quasi in rem jurisdiction, that fictional "ancient form," and in personam jurisdiction, are really one and the same and must be treated alike — leading to the conclusion that quasi in rem jurisdiction, i.e., that form of in personam jurisdiction based upon a "property ownership" contact and by definition unaccompanied by personal, in-state service, must satisfy the litigation-relatedness requirement of *International Shoe*. . . . *International Shoe* confined its "minimum contacts" requirement to situations in which the defendant "be not present within the territory of the forum," and nothing in *Shaffer* expands that requirement beyond that.

It is fair to say, however, that while our holding today does not contradict *Shaffer*, our basic approach to the due process question is different. . . . While in no way receding from or casting doubt upon the holding of *Shaffer* or any other case, we reaffirm today our time-honored approach. For new procedures, hitherto unknown, the Due Process Clause requires analysis to determine whether "traditional notions of fair play and substantial justice" have been offended. *International Shoe*. But a doctrine of personal jurisdiction that dates back to the adoption of the Fourteenth Amendment and is still generally observed unquestionably meets that standard. . . .

III

A few words in response to Justice Brennan's opinion concurring in the judgment. . . .

The subjectivity, and hence inadequacy, of [Justice Brennan's] approach becomes apparent when the concurrence tries to explain why the assertion of jurisdiction in the present case meets its standard. . . .

Justice Brennan lists the "benefits" Mr. Burnham derived from the State of California—the fact that, during the few days he was there, "[h]is health and safety [were] guaranteed by the State's police, fire, and emergency medical services; he [was] free to travel on the State's roads and waterways; he likely enjoy[ed] the fruits of the State's economy." Three days' worth of these benefits strike us as powerfully inadequate to establish, as an abstract matter, that it is "fair" for California to decree the ownership of all Mr. Burnham's worldly goods acquired during the 10 years of his marriage, and the custody over his children. We daresay a contractual exchange swapping those benefits for that power would not survive the "unconscionability" provision of the Uniform Commercial Code. . . .

Suppose . . . that a defendant in Mr. Burnham's situation enjoys not three days' worth of California's "benefits," but 15 minutes' worth. Or suppose we remove one of those "benefits"—"enjoy[ment of] the fruits of the State's economy"—by positing that Mr. Burnham had not come to California on business, but only to visit his children. . . .

. . . What if Mr. Burnham were visiting a sick child? Or a dying child? Cf. Kulko v. Superior Court of California, City and County of San Francisco, 436 U.S. 84, 93 (1978) (finding the exercise of long-arm jurisdiction over an absent parent unreasonable because it would "discourage parents from entering into reasonable visitation agreements"). . . .

The difference between us and Justice Brennan has nothing to do with whether "further progress [is] to be made" in the "evolution of our legal system." It has to do with whether changes are to be adopted as progressive by the American people or decreed as progressive by the Justices of this Court. . . .

[Justice WHITE's concurrence is omitted.]

Justice BRENNAN, with whom Justice MARSHALL, Justice BLACKMUN, and Justice O'CONNOR join, concurring in the judgment.

I agree with Justice Scalia that the Due Process Clause of the Fourteenth Amendment generally permits a state court to exercise jurisdiction over a defendant if he is served with process while voluntarily present in the forum State.[1] I do not perceive the need, however, to decide that a jurisdictional rule that "'has been immemorially the actual law of the land,'" quoting Hurtado v. California, 110 U.S. 516, 528 (1884), automatically comports with due process simply by virtue of its "pedigree." Although I agree that history is an important factor in establishing whether

1. I use the term "transient jurisdiction" to refer to jurisdiction premised solely on the fact that a person is served with process while physically present in the forum State.

a jurisdictional rule satisfies due process requirements, I cannot agree that it is the only factor such that all traditional rules of jurisdiction are, ipso facto, forever constitutional. Unlike Justice Scalia, I would undertake an "independent inquiry into the . . . fairness of the prevailing in-state service rule." I therefore concur in the judgment.

I

I believe that the approach adopted by Justice Scalia's opinion today — reliance solely on historical pedigree — is foreclosed by our decisions in International Shoe Co. v. Washington, 326 U.S. 310 (1945), and Shaffer v. Heitner, 433 U.S. 186 (1977). . . . In *Shaffer*, we stated that *"all* assertions of state-court jurisdiction must be evaluated according to the standards set forth in *International Shoe* and its progeny." 433 U.S. at 212 (emphasis added). The critical insight of *Shaffer* is that all rules of jurisdiction, even ancient ones, must satisfy contemporary notions of due process. . . .

II

. . . Tradition, though alone not dispositive, is of course *relevant* to the question. . . .

. . . [T]he historical background [is] relevant because, however murky the jurisprudential origins of transient jurisdiction, the fact that American courts have announced the rule for perhaps a century (first in dicta, more recently in holdings) provides a defendant voluntarily present in a particular State *today* "clear notice that [he] is subject to suit" in the forum. Regardless of whether Justice Story's account of the rule's genesis is mythical, our common understanding now, fortified by a century of judicial practice, is that jurisdiction is often a function of geography. The transient rule is consistent with reasonable expectations and is entitled to a strong presumption that it comports with due process. . . . "If I visit another State, . . . I knowingly assume some risk that the State will exercise its power over my property or my person while there. My contact with the State, though minimal, gives rise to predictable risks." *Shaffer*, 433 U.S., at 218 (Stevens, J., concurring in judgment). . . .[11]

By visiting the forum State, a transient defendant actually "avail[s]" himself of significant benefits provided by the State. His health and safety

---

11. As the Restatement suggests, there may be cases in which a defendant's involuntary or unknowing presence in a State does not support the exercise of personal jurisdiction over him. The facts of the instant case do not require us to determine the outer limits of the transient jurisdiction rule.

are guaranteed by the State's police, fire, and emergency medical services; he is free to travel on the State's roads and waterways; he likely enjoys the fruits of the State's economy as well. Moreover, the Privileges and Immunities Clause of Article IV prevents a state government from discriminating against a transient defendant by denying him the protections of its law or the right of access to its courts. . . . Without transient jurisdiction, an asymmetry would arise: a transient would have the full benefit of the power of the forum State's courts as a plaintiff while retaining immunity from their authority as a defendant.

The potential burdens on a transient defendant are slight. " '[M]odern transportation and communications have made it much less burdensome for a party sued to defend himself' " in a State outside his place of residence. *Burger King*, 471 U.S. at 474, quoting McGee v. International Life Insurance Co. That the defendant has already journeyed at least once before to the forum — as evidenced by the fact that he was served with process there — is an indication that suit in the forum likely would not be prohibitively inconvenient. . . .

In this case, it is undisputed that petitioner was served with process while voluntarily and knowingly in the State of California. I therefore concur in the judgment.

Justice STEVENS, concurring in the judgment.

As I explained in my separate writing, I did not join the Court's opinion in Shaffer v. Heitner because I was concerned by its unnecessarily broad reach. The same concern prevents me from joining either Justice Scalia's or Justice Brennan's opinion in this case. For me, it is sufficient to note that the historical evidence and consensus identified by Justice Scalia, the considerations of fairness identified by Justice Brennan, and the common sense displayed by Justice White, all combine to demonstrate that this is, indeed, a very easy case.*

NOTES AND PROBLEMS

1. As in *Asahi*, the Court in *Burnham* is unanimous as to the result but cannot agree as to how to reach that result.

a. If they agree about the result, what are they disagreeing about?

b. Should they have agreed about the result? Justice Stevens characterizes *Burnham* as an easy case; was it? Which Justice's views could you most easily turn into a dissent?

---

* Perhaps the adage about hard cases making bad law should be revised to cover easy cases.

c. Perhaps the answer to the preceding question turns on how broadly one reads *Burnham*: as a marital property case or a case applicable to all settings. If one limits *Burnham* to its domestic relations context, it begins to look easy. After all, there are only two possible states that could take jurisdiction (New Jersey, where the husband lives, and California, where the wife lives); isn't one as reasonable as the other? Moreover, Mr. Burnham, having allegedly reneged on his preseparation agreement to divide marital property equally with Mrs. Burnham, was not entirely sympathetic.

d. Nothing in the opinion suggests such a limitation. Read broadly, it revives "tag" jurisdiction, in which mere presence and service with process conclusively establishes jurisdiction. Is that a good rule?

2. Apply the broad reading of *Burnham* to a hypothetical variation on the facts in *Washington Equipment*: Having personally guaranteed the payment for his company's machines, the owner of Washington Equipment travels to Washington to attend a sporting event. There he is served with process.

a. Jurisdiction?

b. If not, can you distinguish *Burnham*? If you think there is jurisdiction, can you justify a world in which the owner is subject to jurisdiction but his company is not?

3. Could Mr. Burnham (or his lawyer) have avoided this outcome?

a. Recall that Mr. Burnham had filed a divorce action in New Jersey, but he had not served Mrs. Burnham. If he had done so — and divorce and marital property litigation was underway in another state — California courts would not have proceeded with the action. Could New Jersey have acquired jurisdiction over the absent Mrs. Burnham based on the substantial duration of the marriage and location of at least some of the marital property in that state?

b. According to one study, most states now have some form of long-arm statute that applies to marital property and child custody. Note, The Georgia Domestic Relations Long-Arm Statute: An Appraisal, 189 Ga. L. Rev. 691, 692 (1984). Most such statutes require that the parties had their marital domicile in the state in the period immediately preceding the separation and often require that the plaintiff spouse continue to live there. Such a statute would not have provided a basis for Mrs. Burnham's suing Mr. Burnham in California, but it would permit Mr. Burnham to bring such a suit in New Jersey.

4. *Burnham* concerns an individual defendant.

a. What if a registered agent of a corporation were served with process, the corporation having no other contacts with the state? Siemer v. Learjet Acquisition Corp., 966 F.2d 179 (5th Cir. 1992), cert. denied, 506 U.S.

1080 (1993) (*Burnham* not applicable to corporate defendants.) Compare also *Washington Equipment Mfg. Co.*, supra page 148 (registering to do business as a foreign corporation does not subject out-of-state-corporation to general jurisdiction).

b. Is it fair to subject the casual visitor to general jurisdiction but not the corporation that does unrelated business in the state?

5. *Burnham* suggests that the courts applying its principles will need to confront an issue that arose regularly under the regime of *Pennoyer:* When does service of process obtained by force or fraud confer jurisdiction? Consider the following examples.

a. If the defendant were kidnapped, brought across state borders, served with process, and then released, would that establish jurisdiction? A number of cases assert that under such conditions service of process did not establish jurisdiction, although the situation seems to have arisen so infrequently in civil suits that it is difficult to locate a holding on point.

b. What would have happened if Mrs. Burnham had called Mr. Burnham had falsely told him one of the children was seriously ill, and, when he arrived to visit the "sick" child, had served him with process? On analogous facts the court in Wyman v. Newhouse, 93 F.2d 313 (2d Cir.), cert. denied, 303 U.S. 664 (1937), held that the court lacked personal jurisdiction. See also Voice Systems Marketing Co. v. Appropriate Technology Corp., 153 F.R.D. 117 (E. D. Mich. 1994) (called to state to resolve customer problems, defendant was asked to extend stay for a day for a "meeting," at which he was served with process; service quashed).

c. What would be the result if the defendant were present in the state to participate in court proceedings, whether as a lawyer, a party, a witness, or a criminal defendant? By and large U.S. courts have given witnesses immunity from service of process. They have wavered on parties to civil actions (some courts granting immunity to nonresident defendants but not to nonresident plaintiffs) and on criminal defendants (some courts distinguishing between the defendants who voluntarily surrender and those who are extradited). See James, Hazard, and Leubsdorf §2.15.

d. Is the necessity to work out rules in such cases an argument against reverting to the rule of *Pennoyer?* Or is the clarity of the rule sufficient to outweigh the occasional attempted abuse?

5. The Outer Limits of Jurisdictional Power: Jurisdiction to Determine Jurisdiction

Many of the jurisdictional cases presented thus far share two characteristics that sometimes create tension. On one hand, under *International*

Shoe determining jurisdiction in each case often depends on developing facts about the defendant's contacts with the forum state. On the other hand, a challenge to a court's jurisdiction questions the court's power to order disclosure of the very facts on which jurisdiction may depend. Those two elements collided in Insurance Corporation of Ireland v. Compagnie des Bauxites de Guinée.

If you have not yet studied discovery (dealt with in Chapter VII), some background information will make the case clearer. Discovery is the generic term for devices used to gather information about a case and prepare for trial, such as taking depositions of witnesses (including one's opponent) or requiring one's opponent to produce relevant documents. Discovery may serve to obtain information not only about the substantive aspects of a case but also about jurisdictional issues. When the court rules on the issue of jurisdiction before trial, as it ordinarily will, how does it obtain the facts on which to determine the existence of "minimum contacts"? The answer is usually through discovery engaged in by the parties. But what happens if a party resists discovery designed to determine the facts necessary to establish minimum contacts? May a party disobey discovery orders on the ground that minimum contacts are lacking, thereby depriving the court of any authority over that party? May the court say to the party disobeying a discovery order (on the ground that there is no authority for the order because there is no jurisdiction) that jurisdiction will be presumed?

Insurance Corp. of Ireland, Ltd. v. Compagnie des Bauxites de Guinée

456 U.S. 694 (1982)

Justice WHITE delivered the opinion of the Court.

Rule 37(b), Federal Rules of Civil Procedure, provides that a District Court may impose sanctions for failure to comply with discovery orders. Included among the available sanctions is:

> An order that the matters regarding which the order was made or any other designated facts shall be taken to be established for the purposes of the action in accordance with the claim of the party obtaining the order.

Rule 37(b)(2)(A).

The question presented by this case is whether this rule is applicable to facts that form the basis for personal jurisdiction over a defendant. May a District Court, as a sanction for failure to comply with a discovery order directed at establishing jurisdictional facts, proceed on the basis that personal jurisdiction over the recalcitrant party has been established?

Petitioners urge that such an application of the Rule would violate Due Process: If a court does not have jurisdiction over a party, then it may not create that jurisdiction by judicial fiat. They contend also that until a court has jurisdiction over a party, that party need not comply with orders of the court; failure to comply, therefore, cannot provide the ground for a sanction. In our view, petitioners are attempting to create a logical conundrum out of a fairly straightforward matter.

[Plaintiff/respondent Compagnie des Bauxites de Guinée (CBG) arranged to obtain insurance against business interruption. When such an interruption allegedly occurred and the insurers refused to pay, CBG brought suit in federal district court in Pennsylvania. The insurers, a group of foreign insurance companies, challenged personal jurisdiction. In order to respond to this challenge, plaintiff made certain requests for discovery. The excess insurers refused to comply with the discovery requests on the grounds that the requests were too burdensome (at one point defendants claimed that plaintiffs had requested 8 million documents, all of them abroad). CBG sought an order to comply, which the district court granted. A series of further moves failed to produce the required material. Finally the district court warned defendants that it would assume that there was jurisdiction, as a sanction pursuant to Rule 37, unless there was compliance. There was no compliance, and the court entered an order finding in personam jurisdiction.

Meanwhile, the insurers had filed suit in England to rescind the policies. At CBG's instance, the Pennsylvania federal district court enjoined the insurers from pursuing the English lawsuit; the insurers appealed from the injunction under 28 U.S.C. §1292(a)(1). Whether the injunction was valid turned on whether there was personal jurisdiction over defendants.]

II

In McDonald v. Mabee, 243 U.S. 90 (1917), another case involving an alleged lack of personal jurisdiction, Justice Holmes wrote for the Court, "great caution should be used not to let fiction deny the fair play that can be secured only by a pretty close adhesion to fact." Petitioners' basic submission is that to apply Rule 37(b)(2) to jurisdictional facts is to allow fiction to get the better of fact and that it is impermissible to use a fiction to establish judicial power, where, as a matter of fact, it does not exist. In our view, this represents a fundamental misunderstanding of the nature of personal jurisdiction.

The validity of an order of a federal court depends upon that court's having jurisdiction over both the subject matter and the parties. [The

Court discussed the nature of subject matter jurisdiction, including its nonwaivability and the fact that it may be raised sua sponte by the court.]

None of this is true with respect to personal jurisdiction. The requirement that a court have personal jurisdiction flows not from Art. III, but from the Due Process Clause. The personal jurisdiction requirement recognizes and protects an individual liberty interest. It represents a restriction on judicial power not as a matter of sovereignty, but as a matter of individual liberty.[10] . . .

Because the requirement of personal jurisdiction represents first of all an individual right, it can, like other such rights, be waived. . . . [R]egardless of the power of the State to serve process, an individual may submit to the jurisdiction of the Court by appearance. A variety of legal arrangements have been taken to represent express or implied consent to the personal jurisdiction of the court. . . . [U]nlike subject-matter jurisdiction, which even an appellate court may review sua sponte, under Rule 12(h), Fed. Rules Civ. Proc., "[a] defense of lack of jurisdiction over the person . . . is waived" if not timely raised in the answer or a responsive pleading.

. . . The plaintiff's demonstration of certain historical facts may make clear to the court that it has personal jurisdiction over the defendant as a matter of law — i.e., certain factual showings will have legal consequences — but this is not the only way in which the personal jurisdiction of the court may arise. The actions of the defendant may amount to a legal submission to the jurisdiction of the court, whether voluntary or not.

The expression of legal rights is often subject to certain procedural rules: The failure to follow those rules may well result in curtailment of the rights. Thus, the failure to enter a timely objection to personal jurisdiction constitutes, under Rule 12(h)(1), a waiver of the objection.

---

10. It is true that we have stated that the requirement of personal jurisdiction, as applied to state courts, reflects an element of federalism and the character of state sovereignty vis-à-vis other states. . . . Contrary to the suggestion of Justice Powell, our holding today does not alter the requirement that there be "minimum contacts" between the nonresident defendant and the forum State. Rather, our holding deals with how the facts needed to show those "minimum contacts" can be established when a defendant fails to comply with court-ordered discovery. The restriction on state sovereign power described in World-Wide Volkswagen Corp., however, must be seen as ultimately a function of the individual liberty interest preserved by the Due Process Clause. That Clause is the only source of the personal jurisdiction requirement and the clause itself makes no mention of federalism concerns. Furthermore, if the federalism concept operated as an independent restriction on the sovereign power of the court, it would not be possible to waive the personal jurisdiction requirement: Individual actions cannot change the powers of sovereignty, although the individual can subject himself to powers from which he may otherwise be protected.

A sanction under Rule 37(b)(2)(A) consisting of a finding of personal jurisdiction has precisely the same effect. As a general proposition, the Rule 37 sanction applied to a finding of personal jurisdiction creates no more of a due process problem than the Rule 12 waiver. Although "a court cannot conclude all persons interested by its mere assertion of its own power," not all rules that establish legal consequences to a party's own behavior are "mere assertions" of power.

Rule 37(b)(2)(A) itself embodies the standard established in Hammond Packing Co. v. Arkansas, 212 U.S. 322 (1909), for the Due Process limits on such rules. There the Court held that it did not violate due process for a state court to strike the answer and render a default judgment against a defendant who failed to comply with a pretrial discovery order. Such a rule was permissible as an expression of

> the undoubted right of the lawmaking power to create a presumption of fact as to the bad faith and untruth of an answer begotten from the suppression or failure to produce the proof ordered. . . . The preservation of due process was secured by the presumption that the refusal to produce evidence material to the administration of due process was but an admission of the want of merit in the asserted defense. . . .

Petitioners argue that a sanction consisting of a finding of personal jurisdiction differs from all other instances in which a sanction is imposed, including the default judgment in *Hammond Packing,* because a party need not obey the orders of a court until it is established that the court has personal jurisdiction over the party. If there is no obligation to obey a judicial order, a sanction cannot be applied for the failure to comply. Until the court has established personal jurisdiction, moreover, any assertion of judicial power over the party violates due process.

This argument again assumes that there is something unique about the requirement of personal jurisdiction, which prevents it from being established or waived like other rights. A defendant is always free to ignore the judicial proceedings, risk a default judgment and then challenge that judgment on jurisdiction grounds in a collateral proceeding. By submitting to the jurisdiction of the court for the limited purpose of challenging jurisdiction, the defendant agrees to abide by that court's determination on the issues of jurisdiction: That decision will be res judicata on that issue in any further proceedings. As demonstrated above, the manner in which the court determines whether it has personal jurisdiction may include a variety of legal rules and presumptions, as well as straightforward fact-finding. A particular rule may offend the due process standard of *Hammond Packing,* but the mere use of procedural rules does not in itself violate the defendant's due process rights.

[The Court concluded by finding that the sanction imposed by the district court was not an abuse of discretion under the facts of the case.]

Justice POWELL, concurring in the judgment. . . .

In my view the Court's broadly theoretical decision misapprehends the issues actually presented for decision. Federal courts are courts of limited jurisdiction. Their personal jurisdiction, no less than their subject matter jurisdiction, is subject both to constitutional and to statutory definition. When the applicable limitations on federal jurisdiction are identified, it becomes apparent that the Court's theory could require a sweeping but largely unexplicated revision of jurisdictional doctrine. . . . Fair resolution of this case does not require the Court's broad holding. Accordingly, although I concur in the Court's judgment, I cannot join its opinion. . . .

A

Under traditional principles, the due process question in this case is whether "minimum contacts" exist between petitioners and the forum State that would justify the State in exercising personal jurisdiction. By finding that the establishment of minimum contacts is not a prerequisite to the exercise of jurisdiction to impose sanctions under Fed. Rule Civ. Proc. 37, the Court may be understood as finding that "minimum contacts" no longer is a constitutional requirement for the exercise by a state court of personal jurisdiction over an unconsenting defendant. Whenever the Court's notions of fairness are not offended, jurisdiction apparently may be upheld.

Before today, of course, our cases had linked minimum contacts and fair play as *jointly* defining the "sovereign" limits on state assertions of personal jurisdiction over unconsenting defendants. See World-Wide Volkswagen Corp. v. Woodson, Hanson v. Denckla. The Court appears to abandon the rationale of these cases in a footnote. See n.10. . . .

B

Alternatively, it is possible to read the Court opinion, not as affecting the state jurisdiction, but simply as asserting that Rule 37 of the Federal Rules of Civil Procedure represents a congressionally approved basis for the exercise of personal jurisdiction by a federal district court. On this view Rule 37 vests the federal district courts with authority to take jurisdiction over persons not in compliance with discovery orders. . . .

. . . There is nothing in Rule 37 to suggest that it is intended to confer a grant of personal jurisdiction. Indeed, the clear language of Rule 82 seems to establish that Rule 37 should *not* be construed as a jurisdictional grant: "These rules shall not be construed to extend . . . the jurisdiction of the United States district courts or the venue of actions therein." Moreover, assuming that minimum contacts remain a constitutional predicate for the exercise of a State's in personam jurisdiction over an unconsenting defendant, constitutional questions would arise if Rule 37 were read to permit a plaintiff in a diversity action to subject a defendant to a "fishing expedition" in a foreign jurisdiction. A plaintiff is not entitled to discovery to establish essentially speculative allegations necessary to personal jurisdiction. Nor would the use of Rule 37 sanctions to enforce discovery orders constitute a mere abuse of discretion in such a case. For me at least, such a use of discovery would raise serious questions as to the constitutional as well as the statutory authority of a federal court — in a diversity case — to exercise personal jurisdiction absent some showing of minimum contacts between the unconsenting defendant and the forum State.

II

In this case the facts alone — unaided by broad jurisdictional theories — more than amply demonstrate that the District Court possessed personal jurisdiction to impose sanctions under Rule 37 and otherwise to adjudicate this case. I would decide the case on this narrow basis. . . .

As recognized both by the District Court and the Court of Appeals, the respondent adduced substantial support for its jurisdictional assertions. By affidavit and other evidence, it made a prima facie showing of "minimum contacts." . . .

Where a plaintiff has made a prima facie showing of minimum contacts, I have little difficulty in holding that its showing was sufficient to warrant the District Court's entry of discovery orders. And where a defendant then fails to comply with these orders, I agree that the prima facie showing may be held adequate to sustain the court's finding that minimum contacts exist, either under Rule 37 or under a theory of "presumption" or "waiver." . . .

NOTES AND PROBLEMS

1. The majority enunciates two rationales for its holding: a "waiver" theory and a "presumption" theory. The majority suggests that either theory would have supported a finding of personal jurisdiction.

a. What is the waiver theory?

b. What is the presumption theory? (Focus on the second sentence in the quoted excerpt from *Hammond Packing*.) How does it apply to the facts of *Insurance Corp. of Ireland*?

c. Justice Powell rejects both of these rationales yet concurs in the holding. How does he reach that conclusion?

2. Would it violate due process for the court to require that the defendant submit to the ordinary processes of the court for the purpose of deciding whether the court had jurisdiction?

3. If the defendants had made no appearance at all, even to contest jurisdiction, the court might have entered a judgment against them; the judgment, however, would have been subject to collateral attack — that is, a second court, asked to enforce the judgment, would have been required to inspect the jurisdictional contacts afresh and make its own determination. On the facts of *Insurance Corp. of Ireland*, however, collateral attack is presumably not permitted. How can the Court justify worse treatment for the defendants who show up but don't cooperate fully than for those who don't cooperate at all by failing to show up?

4. What drove the parties' litigative strategies?

a. Plaintiff could presumably have sued on the defendant's turf (Insurance Corporation of Ireland is headquartered in Dublin). It chose a U.S. forum: Why? One possibility is that it sought any forum *other* than the defendant's home country. Another is that it believed that it wanted a jury and that jury trial of civil cases is, practically speaking, available only in the United States. A third is that in this multidefendant case (there were other insurers involved) it wanted some forum where all could be sued at once.

b. Defendant could have defaulted and presented its jurisdictional defense when plaintiff sought to enforce the judgment. That tactic is most attractive when the jurisdiction defense is the only — or the strongest — defense. If defendant thought it also had a reasonable defense on the merits, default becomes unattractive.

NOTE ON PROCEDURE IN INTERNATIONAL LITIGATION

Insurance Corporation of Ireland represents not only a wrinkle in jurisdictional doctrine but a kind of case in which one or both of the parties is not a U.S. citizen or entity. With the growth of world trade, such cases comprise a significant part of U.S. litigation and pose some special issues.

Jurisdiction

As you have already seen, foreign defendants can be called to respond to complaints filed in U.S. courts. The jurisdictional standards developed in *International Shoe* apply to foreign as well as to domestic defendants. Besides *Insurance Corporation of Ireland*, recall Asahi Metal Industry v. Superior Court, supra page 129, and *World-Wide Volkswagen*, supra page 119. Though both state and federal courts can hear cases involving foreign defendants, many such cases find their way ultimately to federal courts because defendants who sued in state courts remove to federal court, invoking diversity jurisdiction. (The next chapter will explore the principles of removal.) Although one might surmise that a foreign defendant, such as Insurance Company of Ireland, would suffer from nationalistic bias, there is some empirical evidence that foreign defendants are quite successful, at least in federal courts. Kevin Clermont & Theodore Eisenberg, Xenophilia in American Courts, 109 Harv. L. Rev. 1120(1996) ("foreign plaintiffs and defendants win substantially more often than domestic litigants"). Abroad, U.S. defendants, whether individual or corporate, can similarly sue or be sued in foreign tribunals, whose jurisdictional reach is controlled by applicable foreign law — Chinese, German, Chilean, etc.

Choice of Law

Note that subjection to jurisdiction does not mean that jurisdiction's law will govern the dispute. For example, even though the federal district court in Philadelphia had jurisdiction to hear *Insurance Corporation of Ireland*, Irish or English or French or some other body of contract and insurance law might apply to the interpretation of the insurance policies in dispute. See Rule 44.1, which requires parties to give the court early notice that foreign law may apply to the suit. Similarly, given appropriate circumstances, a Japanese court might apply U.S. law to a dispute it is hearing. Such *choice of law* might be governed by the contract itself or by a body of legal principles to which the course in Conflict of Laws is devoted.

Enforcement of Judgments

Suppose that plaintiff prevailed in *Insurance Company of Ireland*, recovering a money judgment against defendant. How would it collect such a judgment? If the defendant had U.S. assets — bank accounts or other financial holdings — they could be attached just as with any other judgment. Suppose, however, that the defendant had insufficient U.S. assets to satisfy the judgment. In such cases the plaintiff would probably seek to enforce the United States judgment abroad — in a nation, perhaps

Ireland, where the defendant had assets. Foreign recognition and enforcement of judgments could be governed by treaty — and in many nations it is; for example, the European Union nations have agreed to enforce each other's judgments. To date, though, the United States has not been able to negotiate such a treaty, in part because many foreign nations are wary of enforcing what they perceive to be excessively large U.S. damage awards. (The United States and most other major trading partners *do* have such an agreement for the enforcement of arbitrators' awards.) As a result, enforcement of judgments occurs on a case-by-case basis. Foreign and U.S. courts typically will recognize and enforce foreign judgments that they perceive to be the result of fundamentally fair procedures, so long as enforcement does not contravene public policy. But in the absence of a treaty, litigators and transaction planners must take into account that enforcing a foreign judgment will always involve some uncertainty.

C.   Consent as a Substitute for Power

Recall *Pennoyer*'s indication that either power or consent could establish jurisdiction. That proposition remains true today: A defendant may, either at the outset of the lawsuit itself or before it, consent to jurisdiction in a forum. But the significance of consent as a basis for jurisdiction long remained buried. Before *International Shoe* the cases that spoke of consent often referred to consent implied from presence, or from what modern jurisdictional analysis would refer to as contacts. Such contacts can provide a perfectly adequate basis for jurisdiction, but they are not consent in any strong sense of the word. Since *International Shoe* recharacterized implied consent cases in terms of contacts, it has once again become possible to focus on what one might call "real" consent, a specific agreement to submit to jurisdiction.

The starting point is National Equipment Rental v. Szukhent, 375 U.S. 311 (1964). The Szukhents, Michigan farmers, leased farm equipment from a New York concern. On the back of the lease form was a clause saying that the Szukhents "designate[ ] Florence Weinberg [at a New York City address] as agent for the purpose of accepting service of process." When the Szukhents defaulted on the lease, plaintiff sued in New York, serving process on Ms. Weinberg (who notified defendants of the suit), and basing jurisdiction on such service. The Supreme Court upheld this procedure, treating the quoted clause as consent to personal jurisdiction and holding that under the circumstances the clause did not violate due process.

In *National Equipment Rental* the parties manipulated jurisdictional rules contractually, the Szukhents consenting to a New York jurisdiction that would not likely have existed without that clause. Notice, however, that the clause in *National Equipment Rental* permitted, but did not *require*, suit to be brought in New York; so far as the contract was concerned, the Szukhents could have sued National Equipment Rental in Michigan. The next case takes matters further. (A word about substantive background may ease understanding: Federal courts have jurisdiction over admiralty matters, which include the interpretation of contracts calling for carriage of passengers by sea.)

Carnival Cruise Lines, Inc. v. Shute

499 U.S. 585 (1991)

Justice BLACKMUN delivered the opinion of the Court.

In this admiralty case we primarily consider whether the United States Court of Appeals for the Ninth Circuit correctly refused to enforce a forum-selection clause contained in tickets issued by petitioner Carnival Cruise Lines, Inc., to respondents Eulala and Russel Shute.

I

The Shutes, through an Arlington, Wash., travel agent, purchased passage for a 7-day cruise on petitioner's ship, the Tropicale. Respondents paid the fare to the agent who forwarded the payment to petitioner's headquarters in Miami, Fla. Petitioner then prepared the tickets and sent them to respondents in the State of Washington. The face of each ticket, at its left-hand lower corner, contained this admonition: "SUBJECT TO CONDITIONS OF CONTRACT ON LAST PAGES IMPORTANT! PLEASE READ CONTRACT—ON LAST PAGES 1, 2, 3"

The following appeared on "contract page 1" of each ticket:

Terms and Conditions of Passage Contract Ticket. . . .

3. (a) The acceptance of this ticket by the person or persons named hereon as passengers shall be deemed to be an acceptance and agreement by each of them of all of the terms and conditions of this Passage Contract Ticket. . . .

8. It is agreed by and between the passenger and the Carrier that all disputes and matters whatsoever arising under, in connection with or incident to this Contract shall be litigated, if at all, in and before a Court located in the State of Florida, U.S.A., to the exclusion of the Courts of any other state or country.

The last quoted paragraph is the forum-selection clause at issue.

II

Respondents boarded the Tropicale in Los Angeles, Cal. The ship sailed to Puerto Vallarta, Mexico, and then returned to Los Angeles. While the ship was in international waters off the Mexican coast, respondent Eulala Shute was injured when she slipped on a deck mat during a guided tour of the ship's galley. Respondents filed suit against petitioner in the United States District Court for the Western District of Washington, claiming that Mrs. Shute's injuries had been caused by the negligence of Carnival Cruise Lines and its employees.

Petitioner moved for summary judgment, contending that the forum clause in respondents' tickets required the Shutes to bring their suit against petitioner in a court in the State of Florida. . . .

III

We begin by noting the boundaries of our inquiry. First, this is a case in admiralty, and federal law governs the enforceability of the forum-selection clause we scrutinize. Second, we do not address the question whether respondents had sufficient notice of the forum clause before entering the contract for passage. Respondents essentially have conceded that they had notice of the forum-selection provision. Brief for Respondents 26 ("The respondents do not contest the incorporation of the provisions nor [sic] that the forum selection clause was reasonably communicated to the respondents, as much as three pages of fine print can be communicated."). . . .

Within this context, respondents urge that the forum clause should not be enforced because, contrary to this Court's teachings in *The Bremen* [v. Zapata Off-Shore Co., 407 U.S. 1 (1972)], the clause was not the product of negotiation, and enforcement effectively would deprive respondents of their day in court. . . .

IV

A

. . . [R]espondents' passage contract was purely routine and doubtless nearly identical to every commercial passage contract issued by petitioner and most other cruise lines. In this context, it would be entirely unreasonable for us to assume that respondents — or any other cruise passenger — would negotiate with petitioner the terms of a forum-selection clause in an ordinary commercial cruise ticket. Common sense dictates that a ticket of this kind will be a form contract the terms of which are not subject to negotiation, and that an individual purchasing the ticket will not have bargaining parity with the cruise line. . . .

Including a reasonable forum clause in a form contract of this kind well may be permissible for several reasons: First, a cruise line has a special interest in limiting the fora in which it potentially could be subject to suit. Because a cruise ship typically carries passengers from many locales, it is not unlikely that a mishap on a cruise could subject the cruise line to litigation in several different fora. Additionally, a clause establishing ex ante the forum for dispute resolution has the salutary effect of dispelling any confusion about where suits arising from the contract must be brought and defended, sparing litigants the time and expense of pretrial motions to determine the correct forum and conserving judicial resources that otherwise would be devoted to deciding those motions. Finally, it stands to reason that passengers who purchase tickets containing a forum clause like that at issue in this case benefit in the form of reduced fares reflecting the savings that the cruise line enjoys by limiting the fora in which it may be sued. . . .

It bears emphasis that forum-selection clauses contained in form passage contracts are subject to judicial scrutiny for fundamental fairness. In this case, there is no indication that petitioner set Florida as the forum in which disputes were to be resolved as a means of discouraging cruise passengers from pursuing legitimate claims. Any suggestion of such a bad-faith motive is belied by two facts: Petitioner has its principal place of business in Florida, and many of its cruises depart from and return to Florida ports. Similarly, there is no evidence that petitioner obtained respondents' accession to the forum clause by fraud or overreaching. Finally, respondents have conceded that they were given notice of the forum provision and, therefore, presumably retained the option of rejecting the contract with impunity. In the case before us, therefore, we conclude that the Court of Appeals erred in refusing to enforce the forum-selection clause. . . .

Justice STEVENS, with whom Justice MARSHALL joins, dissenting. . . .

Forum-selection clauses in passenger tickets involve the intersection of two strands of traditional contract law that qualify the general rule that courts will enforce the terms of a contract as written. Pursuant to the first strand, courts traditionally have reviewed with heightened scrutiny the terms of contracts of adhesion, form contracts offered on a take-or-leave basis by a party with stronger bargaining power to a party with weaker power. Some commentators have questioned whether contracts of adhesion can justifiably be enforced at all under traditional contract theory because the adhering party generally enters into them without manifesting knowing and voluntary consent to all their terms. . . .

The second doctrinal principle implicated by forum-selection clauses is the traditional rule that "contractual provisions, which seek to limit the place or court in which an action may . . . be brought, are invalid as contrary to public policy." Although adherence to this general rule has declined in recent years, particularly following our decision in The Bremen v. Zapata Off-Shore Co., 407 U.S. 1 (1972), the prevailing rule is still that forum-selection clauses are not enforceable if they were not freely bargained for, create additional expense for one party, or deny one party a remedy. . . .

NOTES AND PROBLEMS

1. To see the effect of the forum selection clause in this case, begin by imagining that the ticket had contained no such clause. Under such circumstances the questions that arise are a recapitulation of the material in the preceding sections of this chapter:

a. Where might the lawsuit plausibly have been brought?

b. What jurisdictional issues would arise in each of those jurisdictions?

2. Now consider the forum selection clause. One of the hallmarks of U.S. law is the extent to which the rules of procedure are "default" rules, rules that govern if the parties have not agreed to something else. Forum selection clauses provide an example of the parties' ability to make agreements that displace ordinary procedural rules. The clause is a contractual provision. As Justice Stevens's dissent suggests, courts approaching such clauses will always have at least two questions to consider:

a. As a matter of contract law, is the clause enforceable?

b. Apart from the law of contract, is there some overriding reason that such clauses should not be enforceable?

c. On the facts of *Carnival Cruise Lines*, which of these two issues provided the better argument against enforcement of the clause? Can you summarize the reasons the majority rejected this argument?

d. Does the majority suggest any circumstances under which it would have been unwilling to enforce a forum selection clause?

3. *Carnival Cruise Lines* stands as evidence of the Court's willingness to enforce forum selection clauses. Until the middle of this century, courts often looked on forum selection and similar clauses skeptically; *Carnival Cruise Lines* is one of a number of cases that accept such clauses, thereby opening the door to substantial party choice about forum and procedure.

a. Consider the personal jurisdiction cases you have already read; in which of them could the jurisdictional dispute have been eliminated by a forum selection clause?

b. After *Carnival Cruise Lines,* does a lawyer commit malpractice if she does not consider such a clause in any important agreement?

4. A forum selection clause lies in the middle of a spectrum of contractual provisions that affect procedure:

a. Choice of law clauses do not purport to say where suit shall be brought but do provide that the substantive law of a particular jurisdiction will govern disputes arising under the contract. The contract in *Burger King* (supra page 137) contained such a clause, which specified that Florida law would govern the agreement.

b. Consent-to-jurisdiction clauses say that the parties (or one of the parties) consents to suit in a particular place, thus waiving challenges to personal jurisdiction. Such clauses permit, but do not require, that the suit be brought in the consented-to place. The Supreme Court upheld such a clause in National Equipment Rental v. Szukhent, described supra page 168.

c. Forum selection clauses, exemplified in *Carnival Cruise Lines,* take things one step further, limiting the forum to a single location.

d. Arbitration clauses (discussed in Chapter VIII infra) take disputes out of the hands of the judicial system altogether and place them in an arbitration procedure.

e. *Cognovit* clauses represent the outer limits of the parties' ability to contract out of procedural law. The cognovit is a contract that

> authorizes an attorney to confess judgment against the person or persons signing it. It is written authority of a debtor and a direction by him for the entry of a judgment against him if the obligation set forth in the note is not paid when due. Such a judgment may be taken by any person . . . holding the note, and it cuts off every defense which the maker of the note may otherwise have. It likewise cuts off all rights of appeal from any judgment taken on it.

Jones v. John Hancock Mutual Life Ins. Co., 289 F. Supp. 930, 935 (W. D. Mich. 1968). The cognovit thus involves not only consent to jurisdiction but also a waiver of the right to assert a defense and the right to trial and appeal. Notice that the cognovit need not deprive the signer of a hearing, but it does mean that any hearing will come only if that signer brings an action to set aside the judgment authorized by the cognovit. The person who would ordinarily be the defendant becomes the plaintiff in such an action, and assumes the burden of instituting litigation and of producing evidence to show that entry of judgment was not warranted. In D. H. Overmyer Co. v. Frick Co., 405 U.S. 174 (1972), the Court upheld the constitutionality of a cognovit, but did so in a way suggesting the device will be limited to circumstances in which the party signing the note understands its effect and receives something in exchange for consent.

D. The Constitutional Requirement of Notice

Pennoyer established an analytic scheme with three branches — power, consent, and notice. This exploration of personal jurisdiction has so far focused on the first two of these branches. Before taking up notice, it may help to refine the relationship of power and consent. Reflecting on the case law examined so far, one could conclude that in order to exercise jurisdiction over a defendant a forum state must have *either* power (flowing from the kind of relationships discussed in the contacts cases) *or* the defendant's consent. Consent may come either in the form of a prelitigation agreement (as in Carnival Cruise Lines v. Shute) or by waiver (when defendant appears but fails to challenge jurisdiction).

The facts of *Pennoyer*, however, suggested another basic objection to the exercise of a state's power. In Mitchell v. Neff, the lawsuit preceding Pennoyer v. Neff, the only notice given to the defendant was a small-print advertisement appearing in the pages of a legal newspaper. In the lower courts Neff argued that the statute authorizing notice in this form had not been complied with, and the lower court had reversed on this ground. The U.S. Supreme Court split on the question of statutory interpretation and went on to rest its decision on the absence of power. Because the Court equated power with personal service of process, the question of notice was for some decades buried: Personal service of process on the defendant within the state simultaneously asserted power and gave notice.

The issues of power and notice began to diverge as states expanded the concept of consent. For example, in Wuchter v. Pizzutti, 276 U.S. 13 (1928), a precursor of Mullane v. Central Hanover Bank & Trust, infra, the Supreme Court considered a New Jersey nonresident motorist statute. It treated the use of the state's roads by nonresidents as consent to both jurisdiction and to the appointment of the Secretary of State as the agent of the defendant for service of process. But the statute did not explicitly direct the Secretary to give notice to the nonresident driver. Even though the defendant had in fact received notice, the Court struck down the statute.

Cases like *Wuchter* made it clear that individuals being sued in personam must receive some form of notice. But again recall the distinction, established by *Pennoyer*, between in personam and in rem jurisdiction. As the *Pennoyer* Court saw things, because it was perfectly permissible for a state to assume that people kept an eye on their property, a state could presume that the seizure of property (a necessary prerequisite to in rem jurisdiction, you will recall) would also accomplish notice. Lying behind this rather cavalier assumption may have been an understandable concern. If states were to exercise control over land titles, they had to have some method of rendering binding judgments; a rule that permitted landowners to avoid jurisdiction simply by wandering off without leaving an address would be intolerable. The willingness to presume notice from seizure was a rough but effective way of insuring that this situation did not arise. But it also posed a potentially troubling question — could a state also dispense with notice if the whereabouts of the property owner *were* known? The next case, a constitutional landmark, addresses that question.

Mullane v. Central Hanover Bank & Trust Co.
339 U.S. 306 (1950)

Mr. Justice JACKSON delivered the opinion of the Court.

This controversy questions the constitutional sufficiency of notice to beneficiaries on judicial settlement of accounts by the trustee of a common trust fund established under the New York Banking Law. . . .

Common trust fund legislation is addressed to a problem appropriate for state action. Mounting overheads have made administration of small trusts undesirable to corporate trustees. In order that donors and testators of moderately sized trusts may not be denied the service of corporate fiduciaries, the District of Columbia and some thirty states other than New York have permitted pooling small trust estates into one fund for investment administration. The income, capital gains, losses and expenses of the collective trust are shared by the constituent trusts in proportion to their contribution. By this plan, diversification of risk and economy of management can be extended to those whose capital standing alone would not obtain such advantage.

Statutory authorization for the establishment of such common trust funds is provided in the New York Banking Law. . . . [which provides] for accountings twelve to fifteen months after the establishment of a fund and triennially thereafter. The decree in each such judicial settlement of accounts is made binding and conclusive as to any matter set forth in the account upon everyone having any interest in the common fund or in any participating estate, trust or fund.

In January, 1946, Central Hanover Bank and Trust Company established a common trust fund in accordance with these provisions, and in March, 1947, it petitioned the Surrogate's Court for settlement of its first account as common trustee. During the accounting period a total of 113 trusts, approximately half inter vivos and half testamentary, participated in the common trust fund, the gross capital of which was nearly three million dollars. The record does not show the number or residence of the beneficiaries, but they were many and it is clear that some of them were not residents of the State of New York.

The only notice given beneficiaries of this specific application was by publication in a local newspaper in strict compliance with the minimum requirements of N.Y. Banking Law § 100-c(12): "After filing such petition [for judicial settlement of its account] the petitioner shall cause to be issued by the court in which the petition is filed and shall publish not less than once in each week for four successive weeks in a newspaper to be designated by the court a notice or citation addressed generally without naming them to all parties interested in such common trust fund and in such estates, trusts or funds mentioned in the petition, all of which may be described in the notice or citation only in the manner set forth in said petition and without setting forth the residence of any such decedent or donor of any such estate, trust or fund." Thus the only notice required, and the only one given, was by newspaper publication setting forth merely the name and address of the trust company, the name and the date of establishment of the common trust fund, and a list of all participating estates, trusts or funds.

At the time the first investment in the common fund was made on behalf of each participating estate, however, the trust company, pursuant to the requirements of § 100-c(9), had notified by mail each person of full age and sound mind whose name and address were then known to it and who was "entitled to share in the income therefrom . . . [or] . . . who would be entitled to share in the principal if the event upon which such estate, trust or fund will become distributable should have occurred at the time of sending such notice." Included in the notice was a copy of those provisions of the Act relating to the sending of the notice itself and to the judicial settlement of common trust fund accounts.

Upon the filing of the petition for the settlement of accounts, appellant was, by order of the court pursuant to § 100-c(12), appointed special guardian and attorney for all persons known or unknown not otherwise appearing who had or might thereafter have any interest in the income of the common trust fund; and appellee Vaughan was appointed to represent those similarly interested in the principal. There were no other appearances on behalf of any one interested in either interest or principal.

Appellant appeared specially, objecting that notice and the statutory provisions for notice to beneficiaries were inadequate to afford due process under the Fourteenth Amendment, and therefore that the court was without jurisdiction to render a final and binding decree. Appellant's objections were entertained and overruled, the Surrogate [*] holding that the notice required and given was sufficient. A final decree accepting the accounts has been entered, affirmed by the Appellate Division of the Supreme Court and by the Court of Appeals of the State of New York.

The effect of this decree, as held below, is to settle "all questions respecting the management of the common fund." We understand that every right which beneficiaries would otherwise have against the trust company, either as trustee of the common fund or as trustee of any individual trust, for improper management of the common trust fund during the period covered by the accounting is sealed and wholly terminated by the decree.

We are met at the outset with a challenge to the power of the State — the right of its courts to adjudicate at all as against those beneficiaries who reside without the State of New York. It is contended that the proceeding is one in personam in that the decree affects neither title to nor possession of any res, but adjudges only personal rights of the beneficiaries to surcharge their trustee for negligence or breach of trust. Accordingly, it is said, under the strict doctrine of Pennoyer v. Neff, the Surrogate is without jurisdiction as to nonresidents upon whom personal service of process was not made.

Distinctions between actions in rem and those in personam are ancient and originally expressed in procedural terms what seems really to have been a distinction in the substantive law of property under a system quite unlike our own. The legal recognition and rise in economic importance of incorporeal or intangible forms of property have upset the ancient simplicity of property law and the clarity of its distinctions, while new forms of proceedings have confused the old procedural classification. American courts have sometimes classed certain actions as in rem because personal service of process was not required, and at other times have held personal service of process not required because the action was in rem.

Judicial proceedings to settle fiduciary accounts have been sometimes termed in rem, or more indefinitely quasi in rem, or more vaguely still,

---

* [In New York the court with jurisdiction over trusts and estates is the Surrogate's Court; its judges are known as Surrogates. — ED.]

"in the nature of a proceeding in rem." It is not readily apparent how the courts of New York did or would classify the present proceeding, which has some characteristics and is wanting in some features of proceedings both in rem and in personam. But in any event we think that the requirements of the Fourteenth Amendment to the Federal Constitution do not depend upon a classification for which the standards are so elusive and confused generally and which, being primarily for state courts to define, may and do vary from state to state. Without disparaging the usefulness of distinctions between actions in rem and those in personam in many branches of law, or on other issues, or the reasoning which underlies them, we do not rest the power of the State to resort to constructive service in this proceeding upon how its courts or this Court may regard this historic antithesis. It is sufficient to observe that whatever the technical definition of its chosen procedure the interest of each state in providing means to close trusts that exist by the grace of its laws and are administered under the supervision of its courts is so insistent and rooted in custom as to establish beyond doubt the right of its courts to determine the interests of all claimants, resident or nonresident, provided its procedure accords full opportunity to appear and be heard.

Quite different from the question of a state's power to discharge trustees is that of the opportunity it must give beneficiaries to contest. Many controversies have raged about the cryptic and abstract words of the Due Process Clause but there can be no doubt that at a minimum they require that deprivation of life, liberty or property by adjudication be preceded by notice and opportunity for hearing appropriate to the nature of the case.

In two ways this proceeding does or may deprive beneficiaries of property. It may cut off their rights to have the trustee answer for negligent or illegal impairments of their interests. Also, their interests are presumably subject to diminution in the proceeding by allowance of fees and expenses to one who, in their names but without their knowledge, may conduct a fruitless or uncompensatory contest. Certainly the proceeding is one in which they may be deprived of property rights and hence notice and hearing must measure up to the standards of due process.

Personal service of written notice within the jurisdiction is the classic form of notice always adequate in any type of proceeding. But the vital interest of the State in bringing any issues as to its fiduciaries to a final settlement can be served only if interests or claims of individuals who are outside of the State can somehow be determined. A construction of the Due Process Clause which would place impossible or impractical obstacles in the way could not be justified.

Against this interest of the State we must balance the individual interest sought to be protected by the Fourteenth Amendment. This is defined by our holding that "The fundamental requisite of due process of law is the opportunity to be heard." This right to be heard has little reality or worth unless one is informed that the matter is pending and can choose for himself whether to appear or default, acquiesce or contest.

The Court has not committed itself to any formula achieving a balance between these interests in a particular proceeding or determining when constructive notice may be utilized or what test it must meet. Personal service has not in all circumstances been regarded as indispensable to the process due to residents, and it has more often been held unnecessary as to nonresidents. We disturb none of the established rules on these subjects. No decision constitutes a controlling or even a very illuminating precedent for the case before us, but a few general principles stand out in the books.

An elementary and fundamental requirement of due process in any proceeding which is to be accorded finality is notice reasonably calculated, under all the circumstances, to apprise interested parties of the pendency of the action and afford them an opportunity to present their objections. The notice must be of such nature as reasonably to convey the required information, and it must afford a reasonable time for those interested to make their appearance. But if with due regard for the practicalities and peculiarities of the case these conditions are reasonably met, the constitutional requirements are satisfied. . . .

But when notice is a person's due, process which is a mere gesture is not due process. The means employed must be such as one desirous of actually informing the absentee might reasonably adopt to accomplish it. The reasonableness and hence the constitutional validity of any chosen method may be defended on the ground that it is in itself reasonably certain to inform those affected, or, where conditions do not reasonably permit such notice, that the form chosen is not substantially less likely to bring home notice than other of the feasible and customary substitutes.

It would be idle to pretend that publication alone, as prescribed here, is a reliable means of acquainting interested parties of the fact that their rights are before the courts. It is not an accident that the greater number of cases reaching this Court on the question of adequacy of notice have been concerned with actions founded on process constructively served through local newspapers. Chance alone brings to the attention of even a local resident an advertisement in small type inserted in the back pages of a newspaper, and if he makes his home outside the area of the newspaper's normal circulation the odds that the information will never reach him are large indeed. The chance of actual notice is further reduced when, as here, the notice required does not even name those whose attention it is supposed to attract, and does not inform acquaintances who might call it to attention. In weighing its sufficiency on the basis of equivalence with actual notice, we are unable to regard this as more than a feint.

Nor is publication here reinforced by steps likely to attract the parties' attention to the proceeding. It is true that publication traditionally has been acceptable as notification supplemental to other action which in itself may reasonably be expected to convey a warning. The ways of an owner with tangible property are such that he usually arranges means to learn of any direct attack upon his possessory or proprietary rights. Hence, libel of a ship, attachment of a chattel or entry upon real estate in the name of law may reasonably be expected to come promptly to the owner's attention. When the state within which the owner has located such property seizes it for some reason, publication or posting affords an additional measure of notification. A state may indulge the assumption that one who has left tangible property in the state either has abandoned it, in which case proceedings against it deprive him of nothing, or that he has left some caretaker under a duty to let him know that it is being jeopardized. . . .

In the case before us there is, of course, no abandonment. On the other hand these beneficiaries do have a resident fiduciary as caretaker of their interest in this property. But it is their caretaker who in the accounting becomes their adversary. Their trustee is released from giving notice of jeopardy, and no one else is expected to do so. Not even the special guardian is required or apparently expected to communicate with his ward and client, and, of course, if such a duty were merely transferred from the trustee to the guardian, economy would not be served and more likely the cost would be increased.

This Court has not hesitated to approve of resort to publication as a customary substitute in another class of cases where it is not reasonably possible or practicable to give more adequate warning. Thus it has been recognized that, in the case of persons missing or unknown, employment of an indirect and even a probably futile means of notification is all that the situation permits and creates no constitutional bar to a final decree foreclosing their rights.

Those beneficiaries represented by appellant whose interests or whereabouts could not with due diligence be ascertained come clearly within this category. As to them the statutory notice is sufficient. However great the odds that publication will never reach the eyes of such unknown parties, it is not in the typical case much more likely to fail than any of the choices open to legislators endeavoring to prescribe the best notice practicable.

Nor do we consider it unreasonable for the State to dispense with more certain notice to those beneficiaries whose interests are either conjectural or future or, although they could be discovered upon investigation, do not in due course of business come to knowledge of the common trustee. Whatever searches might be required in another situation under ordinary standards of diligence, in view of the character of the proceedings and the nature of the interests here involved we think them unnecessary. We recognize the practical difficulties and costs that would be attendant on frequent investigations into the status of great numbers of beneficiaries, many of whose interests in the common fund are so remote as to be ephemeral; and we have no doubt that such impracticable and extended searches are not required in the name of due process. The expense of keeping informed from day to day of substitutions among even current income beneficiaries and presumptive remaindermen, to say nothing of the far greater number of contingent beneficiaries, would impose a severe burden on the plan, and would likely dissipate its advantages. These are practical matters in which we should be reluctant to disturb the judgment of the state authorities.

Accordingly we overrule appellant's constitutional objections to published notice insofar as they are urged on behalf of any beneficiaries whose interests or addresses are unknown to the trustee.

As to known present beneficiaries of known place of residence, however, notice by publication stands on a different footing. Exceptions in the name of necessity do not sweep away the rule that within the limits of practicability notice must be such as is reasonably calculated to reach interested parties. Where the names and post-office addresses of those affected by a proceeding are at hand, the reasons disappear for resort to means less likely than the mails to apprise them of its pendency.

The trustee has on its books the names and addresses of the income beneficiaries represented by appellant, and we find no tenable ground for dispensing with a serious effort to inform them personally of the accounting, at least by ordinary mail to the record addresses. Certainly sending them a copy of the statute months and perhaps years in advance does not answer this purpose. The trustee periodically remits their income to them, and we think that they might reasonably expect that with or apart from their remittances word might come to them personally that steps were being taken affecting their interests.

We need not weigh contentions that a requirement of personal service of citation on even the large number of known resident or nonresident beneficiaries would, by reasons of delay if not of expense, seriously interfere with the proper administration of the fund. Of course personal service even without the jurisdiction of the issuing authority serves the end of actual and personal notice, whatever power of compulsion it might lack. However, no such service is required under the circumstances. This type of trust presupposes a large number of small interests. The individual interest does not stand alone but is identical with that of a class. The rights of each in the integrity of the fund and the fidelity of the trustee are shared by many other beneficiaries. Therefore notice reasonably certain to reach most of those interested in objecting is likely to safeguard the interests of all, since any objection sustained would inure to the benefit of all. We think that under such circumstances reasonable risks that notice might not actually reach every beneficiary are justifiable. "Now and then an extraordinary case may turn up, but constitutional law like other mortal contrivances has to take some chances, and in the great majority of instances no doubt justice will be done."

The statutory notice to known beneficiaries is inadequate, not because in fact it fails to reach everyone, but because under the circumstances it is not reasonably calculated to reach those who could easily be informed by other means at hand. However it may have been in former times, the mails today are recognized as an efficient and inexpensive means of communication. Moreover, the fact that the trust company has been able to give mailed notice to known beneficiaries at the time the common trust fund was established is persuasive that postal notification at the time of accounting would not seriously burden the plan.

In some situations the law requires greater precautions in its proceedings than the business world accepts for its own purposes. In few, if any, will it be satisfied with less. Certainly it is instructive, in determining the reasonableness of the impersonal broadcast notification here used, to ask whether it would satisfy a prudent man of business, counting his pennies but finding it in his interest to convey information to many persons whose names and addresses are in his files. We are not satisfied that it would. Publication may theoretically be available for all the world to see, but it is too much in our day to suppose that each or any individual beneficiary does or could examine all that is published to see if something may be tucked away in it that affects his property interests. We have before indicated in reference to notice by publication that, "Great caution should be used not to let fiction deny the fair play that can be secured only by a pretty close adhesion to fact." McDonald v. Mabee.

We hold that the notice of judicial settlement of accounts required by the New York Banking Law §100-c(12) is incompatible with the requirements of the Fourteenth Amendment as a basis for adjudication depriving known persons whose whereabouts are also known of substantial property rights. Accordingly the judgment is reversed and the cause remanded for further proceedings not inconsistent with this opinion.

NOTES AND PROBLEMS

1. To see the force of *Mullane*, be prepared to explain the following:

a. Imagine the thought processes of the drafters of the New York Banking Law: What led them to think that the published form of notice would be constitutionally adequate?

b. What was wrong with their thinking, according to the Court?

2. What does the decision mean in practical terms? After the decision, what steps would have to occur to assure that the proceeding would bind the beneficiaries? How, in light of this decision, should New York have amended its statute to create a constitutionally valid procedure for examining and approving trustees' accounts? See N. Y. Banking Law §100-c(6)(Consol. 1990).

3. Written in broad terms, *Mullane* is a central case for the meaning of due process in civil litigation. But, like many well-written cases, it is less explicit about its implications than about its holding:

a. In *Mullane* mass mailings were deemed satisfactory. The Court acknowledged that some letters would not get through to their intended recipients but reasoned that under the particular circumstances, in which all intended recipients had the same interests, contacting a certain number of people in the group would serve approximately the same function as contacting them all. How would this principle apply to ordinary litigation, in which only a few parties are involved: Is mail adequate then? The answer matters because mail notice reduces the cost of serving process while also increasing the risk that the mail will not arrive. One court has suggested *Mullane* prohibits service of process by ordinary mail. Miserandino v. Resort Properties, Inc., 691 A. 2d 208 (Md.), cert. denied, 118 S. Ct. 397 (1997). Is that an accurate reading of *Mullane*?

b. Does *Mullane* require individual notice whenever one can identify and locate a person whom litigation may affect — even if the cost of such notice will be high? The issue matters greatly in class actions — where both sides in the debate cite *Mullane*, one stressing its requirement of individual notice, the other stressing its emphasis on practicality. Who's right?

4. Although the *Mullane* court dropped some broad hints, many courts and lawyers thought it did not answer the question whether notice was required in traditional in rem actions. In Walker v. Hutchinson, 352

U.S. 112 (1956), the Court applied *Mullane* to require that personal notice be given a landowner whose property was being taken by condemnation and whose name and address were listed in the city's land records. Similar reasoning was applied in Schroeder v. City of New York, 371 U.S. 208 (1962) (planned diversion of water; published notice not sufficient when property owner's address known) and in Tulsa Professional Collection Services, Inc. v. Pope, 485 U.S. 478 (1985) (settlement of decedent's estate; published notice to creditors in general insufficient when estate knew of claim of particular creditor). Given this line of cases, should a lawyer assume that published notice will never suffice for a defendant whose identity and whereabouts are known and who is not seeking to evade service?

5. The student should be alert to a potential confusion that arises when courts or statutes speak of service of process and personal jurisdiction.

a. In speaking of "service of process," courts sometimes refer to the way in which the defendant is given notice of the action — the question with which *Mullane* deals. At other times they refer instead to the issues involving the extent of a court's adjudicatory power — minimum contacts and the like. This blending occurs because, unless transient jurisdiction is no longer valid, service of process within a state's borders may confer jurisdiction (as in Burnham v. Superior Court, supra page 150). There is thus a tendency in some contexts to speak of "service of process" although what is meant is jurisdiction or a combination of jurisdiction and service. (The Federal Interpleader Act, 28 U.S.C. §2361, for example, speaks in terms of nationwide process rather than nationwide jurisdiction.)

b. Conversely, courts that conclude that a defendant did not receive constitutionally adequate notice (as in *Mullane*) will sometimes express that conclusion by saying that the court lacked "jurisdiction"; that is, it lacked one of the constitutional requisites for exercising adjudicatory power: proper notice.

NOTES AND PROBLEMS ON SERVICE OF PROCESS

1. Assuming that some constitutionally adequate notice is required, one must then decide what form notice must take. That form is widely regulated by statute. Rule 4 provides that regulation in federal courts. The current Rule 4 consolidates a gradual informalizing of the practice of service of process that has taken place over the last few decades, an evolution enabled in part by *Mullane*'s suggestion that forms of notice other than personal service would satisfy due process. In pursuit of informality, Rule 4 makes service by an officer of the court (a U.S. marshal)

exceptional rather than ordinary. In its place the Rule provides for service by any individual who is not a party and is at least eighteen years old.

More fundamentally, Rule 4 proposes to replace even this personal but "unofficial" service with a still less formal procedure called "waiver of service" (see Rule 4(d)). Waiver of service uses first-class mail to send a copy of the complaint to the defendant, together with a request that the defendant return by mail a form (Form 1B) waiving formal service of a summons. If the defendant does return that form, the case proceeds as if process had been served. If the defendant does not return the form within the time specified in the Rule, the plaintiff must then proceed to have a summons served more formally, using the procedures set forth in Rule 4(e)-(j). The defendant who waives service does not thereby waive objections to venue or jurisdiction, or any defenses to the merits of the lawsuit. By waiving service the defendant does, however, give up any objections to the sufficiency of the summons or the method by which it was served (Rule 12(b)(4) and (5)).

Why should the defendant want to make things easy for the plaintiff by waiving formal service of process? Rule 4 provides two answers to that question — a stick for failing to waive and a carrot for doing so. The Rule imposes on defendants the "duty to save costs of service." Enforcing that duty is a provision of Rule 4(d)(2) requiring a "defendant located within the United States" to pay the costs of subsequent service if he has without good cause refused to waive service of process. On the other hand, the Rule gives defendants additional time to answer the complaint if they do waive service — extending the time from twenty to sixty days for domestic defendants and from twenty to ninety days for foreign defendants. The accompanying notes reflect a hope that this combination of procedural sticks and carrots will make waiver the predominant form of "service" in federal litigation.

If the defendant fails to waive service, Rule 4 goes on to specify various means by which a plaintiff may serve defendants. Plaintiff must also use these means to serve defendants from whom a waiver of service cannot be demanded. Such defendants include the U.S. government, infants and incompetents, and others whose service is thought to require special formality so as to reduce the possibility of inadvertent default.

Where such formal service is required, its form depends on the nature of the defendant — individuals and corporations, domestic and foreign defendants, and federal and state government entities all have sections. The amended Rule specifies the means of serving foreign defendants, a source of special problems and growing concern as the volume of international business increases. Rules 4(f) and (h) set forth a list of ways in which such foreign defendants may be served, incorporating the provisions of the Hague Service Convention of 1969, an important international treaty.

2. Read Rule 4 and answer the following questions:

a. Plaintiff wishes to sue an individual located in the United States and wants to commence the suit at minimum cost. What steps should she take?

b. Defendant, located in the United States, receives a complaint together with copies of Forms 1A and 1B, requesting waiver of summons. Defendant seeks advice from Lawyer about the effect of ignoring this request. What should Lawyer tell defendant?

c. Defendant, located in the United States, receives a complaint together with copies of Forms 1A and 1B, requesting waiver of summons. The request is dated September 1. If defendant wishes to waive summons, by when must she respond? See Rule 4(d)(2)(F).

d. Defendant, located in the United States, receives a complaint together with copies of Forms 1A and 1B, requesting waiver of summons. The request is dated September 1; defendant signs and returns Form 1B by September 20 but does not file an answer to the complaint. On October 20 plaintiff moves to enter a default, citing Rule 12(a), which requires defendant to answer the complaint within 20 days. How should the court rule on plaintiff's motion?

e. Defendant, located in the United States, receives a complaint together with copies of Forms 1A and 1B, requesting waiver of summons. The request is dated September 1. Three months elapse, and plaintiff has received no response. What should plaintiff do?

f. Plaintiff wishes to sue defendant, located in the United States, on a claim in diversity jurisdiction on which the statute of limitations will run in 45 days. Should plaintiff request a waiver of service from defendant? Why?

g. Plaintiff requests a waiver of summons from a defendant located in the United States, receives no waiver, and incurs the costs of personal service. After service has been completed, plaintiff moves pursuant to Rule 4(d)(2) to recover the increased costs from defendant. Defendant resists the motion, arguing that the underlying lawsuit is without merit and that it denies him due process of law to require him to help his adversary bring a meritless action. How should plaintiff respond to this argument?

h. Plaintiff wishes to sue the United States. May plaintiff request a waiver of summons from this defendant?

i. Plaintiff wishes to sue a defendant located in the United States who has failed to return the request for a waiver of summons within a reasonable time. What information must plaintiff have in order to know what form of service to employ?

3. Service of process gives defendant notice and thus overcomes what would otherwise be a constitutional obstacle to a valid judgment. Service may also avoid a defense based on the statute of limitations; in many states the statute is satisfied not by filing the suit but by serving defendant with process. For claims based on federal law, Rule 3 provides that the statute of limitations stops running when the complaint is filed with the court. But defendant must still be notified; how long does plaintiff have to do so? Read Rule 4(m) and respond to the following questions.

a. Suppose a claim is based on federal law. Plaintiff has filed his complaint with the court but has been unable to serve process because defendant has gone into hiding. Time is running out on the 120-day period for service of process; what should plaintiff do?

b. Can a court extend the time for service *without* a showing of good cause? The second half of Rule 4(m) contains a good cause requirement; the first half, which allows a court to "direct that service be effected within a specified time," contains no such requirement.

4. The current Rule 4 also makes explicit one proposition that has been implicit since Pennoyer v. Neff and another that the Rules have long skirted: the nature of the relation between personal jurisdiction and service of process and the relation between the reach of personal jurisdiction of the state and federal courts.

a. On the first issue, Rule 4(k)(1) states that service (or waiver) establishes jurisdiction over defendants subject to personal jurisdiction. That formula is as important for what it does not say as for what it does. It does not say that service establishes jurisdiction. That had been the assumption of *Pennoyer*, at least for defendants served in the forum state. Instead, the Rule states that *if* the requisites of personal jurisdiction exist, proper service establishes jurisdiction. Thus a defendant who waives process, or who has been properly served, remains free to challenge the existence of personal jurisdiction.

b. How does waiver of service interact with tag jurisdiction under *Burnham*? Plaintiff wishes to sue defendant, who has no constitutionally adequate contacts with the forum state but has recently visited the state. Had plaintiff served defendant with process while he was in the state, *Burnham* suggests that jurisdiction would be established. Can plaintiff request a waiver and argue that the forum state has jurisdiction because he *could* have served defendant while in the forum state? Or is this a bit too cute?

c. On the second issue — the personal jurisdiction of federal courts — Rule 4 establishes a four-tier scheme. First, it says that federal courts, at a minimum, have personal jurisdiction over any defendant over whom the state court of the forum state would have such jurisdiction (Rule

4(k)(1)(A)). To that extent — and this provision covers the vast majority of all cases — the personal jurisdiction of state and federal courts "match." Thus a federal court sitting in California or Georgia has the same jurisdictional reach as a state court in that state — no less, but also no more.

The three remaining provisions deal with situations in which the Rule defines a longer jurisdictional reach for the federal courts than the state courts would have. One occurs when a party is joined to litigation under Rule 14 or 19; in these instances the Rules provide for a "100-mile bulge" in the personal jurisdiction of a federal district court, even if a state court would not have had such jurisdiction (Rule 4(k)(1)(B)). This provision is particularly useful where federal district courts lie close to state lines: the Southern and Eastern Districts of New York (Manhattan and Brooklyn) and the district courts in Washington, D.C., Philadelphia, and Delaware provide examples.

The second special situation arises when federal legislation specifically provides for broad, national power of a federal court. One example is a federal statute providing for nationwide service of process (for example, see 28 U.S.C. §1335); another is the enforcement of a civil contempt order arising from litigation involving a federal question (Rule 4.1(b)).

Finally, the Rule purports to define a new form of personal jurisdiction, limited to federal claims against defendants no subject to personal jurisdiction in any state. Such defendants will inevitably be foreign persons or entities that have insufficient contacts with any single state to create personal jurisdiction. In that situation, Rule 4(k)(2) provides:

> If the exercise of jurisdiction is consistent with the Constitution and laws of the United States, serving a summons or filing a waiver of service is also effective, with respect to claims arising under federal law, to establish personal jurisdiction over the person of any defendant who is not subject to the courts of general jurisdiction of any state. . . .

This provision seems to rest on the proposition that the Due Process Clause permits aggregation of the defendant's contacts with the United States as a whole for jurisdictional purposes.

5. As international litigation grows with international business, more lawyers find themselves faced with the necessity to serve process on foreign defendants. When they do, they discover that matters can quickly become complicated. This note cannot be comprehensive, but it can sketch the issues.

a. The Hague Service Convention, an important international treaty covering service of process, aims at clarifying the means of serving judicial process abroad. The Hague Convention would, for example, guide a Japanese firm seeking to serve an American defendant in a suit brought in Japanese courts; it would also guide a U.S. plaintiff seeking to sue a Spanish defendant. The Convention provides that each signatory nation must designate a "Central Authority"* responsible for serving process on its nationals. So long as a plaintiff submits its request to this Central Authority in proper form, the Authority assumes responsibility for serving process in whatever way plaintiff directs.

b. Unfortunately, the Convention's flexibility sometimes creates complications, and other complications arise from the interaction of the Convention and Rule 4. For example, the Convention permits the Central Authority to serve process in any of three ways: (1) in any manner specified by the receiving nation for its own civil litigation (thus the United States might employ Rule 4); (2) in a manner specified by the plaintiff, so long as that manner does not violate the receiving nation's laws; or (3) by the defendant's voluntarily accepting service. If one asks the Central Authority to use the first of these procedures, it is clear that one must submit translations of all the relevant documents; under the remaining two that requirement is less clear. The difference matters because translations involve expense and delay. The question matters because if one does not effect proper service, the nation in question may refuse to enforce any subsequent judgment.

c. Lawyer represents plaintiff, a former wife domiciled in the United States, who seeks to collect delinquent child support from her former husband, who now resides in Italy but has assets in the United States. The courts of plaintiff's state permit mail service on defendants located out of state. Italy does not allow mail service in its courts. How should plaintiff proceed? See Rule 4(f). What risks does plaintiff run if she uses mail service? Are those risks worth running? How would your answer change if defendant had assets only in Italy?

d. Nations' rules for voluntary acceptance of service differ; for example, in some countries the defendant must retrieve process from the local police station. Rule 4(d) allows foreign defendants to waive service of process by mail. Suppose a product liability suit against a foreign manufacturer, who waives service under Rule 4(d). The suit goes to judgment with defendant suffering a money judgment against it. Plaintiff now seeks to enforce the judgment abroad. Do you see what defense the defendant might raise?

6. Assuming one knows the proper mode of service, questions still arise over whether the attempt has complied with a suitable mode. For example, has the process server left process with a "person of suitable

---

* In the United States the Central Authority is a division of the U.S. Department of Justice.

age and discretion" as required by Rule 4(e)(2)? Or what if the process server submits an affidavit that the defendant was served, but defendant denies it? Such questions will often require a hearing and judicial resolution. They may arise, for example, in a motion made under Rule 60(b) to set aside a judgment. They may also arise in those states in which the statute of limitations does not stop running until process is served. And, ironically, service may be quashed on defendant's motion at the preliminary stages of the case for improprieties of form even though the service has performed its chief function — that of notifying the defendant of the commencement of the case.

a. Failure to deliver service may be to the benefit of the process server if his failures are not caught, because he can collect the fees and not do the work. Such intentional failure to serve process, accompanied by a false affidavit of service, is called "sewer service" by reference to the place where process eventually finds itself. Such abuses may also benefit the plaintiff, who may be able to collect a default judgment based on the sewer service because the defendant was intimidated by the judgment collection process, was ignorant of his rights, or could not afford a lawyer.

b. On the other side of the coin, defendants may sometimes take unfair advantage of service-of-process rules. Wily prospective defendants have sometimes dodged process for long periods, thereby requiring process servers to display ingenuity and sometimes even physical bravery. What should be done with such defendants, who refuse to waive service and then evade the process server? Rule 4(d), which imposes the duty to minimize costs of service on defendants and shifts those costs to a defendant who makes expensive personal service necessary, is one response; Rule 4(m), extending the time for service "for good cause," is another. But such a defendant must be served as a prerequisite even for collecting those costs of service, not to speak of the relief sought on the merits of the lawsuit. The provision of Rule 4(e) allowing process to be left at the defendant's home is a partial answer. Some states permit notice by publication in such circumstances. Another solution is found in Michigan Gen. Ct. R. 105.8, which empowers the judge in any case to "allow service of process to be made upon a defendant in any other manner which is reasonably calculated to give him actual notice of the proceedings and an opportunity to be heard, if an order permitting such service is entered before service of process is made upon a showing to the court that service of process cannot reasonably be made in the manner provided for under other rules."

c. Finally, one case involving service of process should not go unnoticed. In United States ex rel. Mayo v. Satan and His Staff, 54 F.R.D. 282 (W.D. Pa. 1971), plaintiff complained that the defendant had "on numerous occasions caused plaintiff misery" and that the defendant had caused his downfall. The court refused to allow the plaintiff to proceed in forma pauperis in part because he had failed to include in his complaint instructions for service of process on the defendant.

E. Self-Imposed Restraints on Jurisdictional Power: Long-Arm Statutes, Venue, and Discretionary Refusal of Jurisdiction

Our discussion of jurisdiction has thus far proceeded as if the only relevant questions are constitutional power and notice. Each case has silently assumed that the state or federal court in question was authorized to assert jurisdiction if doing so was constitutionally permissible. The issue has been whether the Constitution permitted such an assertion of jurisdiction. We now go behind that assumption in three settings: long-arm statutes, venue laws, and the doctrine of forum non conveniens. Each represents a situation in which the legislature or courts have framed rules that restrict where a lawsuit may take place — even when the Constitution would pose no obstacles.

1. Long-Arm Statutes as a Restraint on Jurisdiction

A court may exercise jurisdiction over a defendant only when the state or federal government authorizes it to do so (and the authorization must be constitutional as applied to the case in question). In the world of *Pennoyer* such authorization was usually a simple matter: Had the state provided for service of process on a defendant in this situation? As the doctrines of personal jurisdiction expanded (especially in the years after *International Shoe*), many states began to authorize service (often by mail) on defendants beyond their borders. Because *Pennoyer* had conceived of such extensions of state court jurisdiction as near-physical exertions of state power, statutes authorizing courts to reach beyond their own borders came to be known as "long-arm" statutes: states were extending their jurisdictional "arms." The name has stuck.

Some states have enacted long-arm statutes that reach for as much jurisdiction as the Constitution allows. California provides a well-known example:

California Code of Civil Procedure §410.10 (West 1991)

A Court of this state may exercise jurisdiction on any basis not inconsistent with the Constitution of this state or of the United States.

Under such a statute there is no separate problem of analyzing the coverage of the long-arm statute: If jurisdiction is constitutional, it is also authorized by the statute. (A variation on this pattern occurs when the words of the statute appear to limit jurisdiction to specified instances but the state's courts have construed the statute to permit jurisdiction whenever constitutionally permissible.) Other states have long-arm statutes limiting jurisdiction to specified occurrences. The next case exemplifies the inquiry that must occur in interpreting such a statute.

Gibbons v. Brown

716 So. 2d 868 (Fl. Dist. Ct. App. 1998)

PER CURIAM.

[In 1994 Martine Gibbons and Mr. and Mrs. Brown were driving together in Montreal, Canada. Ms. Gibbons gave allegedly faulty directions to Mr. Brown, who was driving, causing him to turn the wrong way onto a one-way street, resulting in a head-on collision that injured both passengers. In 1995 Ms. Gibbons, a Texas resident, sued Mr. Brown in Florida; Mrs. Brown was not a party. Two years later Mrs. Brown, seeking to recover for her own injuries, brought this Florida action against Ms. Gibbons.]

In her complaint. . . Mrs. Brown alleged 1) that she is a resident of Florida; 2) that Ms. Gibbons has subjected herself to the personal jurisdiction of the Florida court by bringing [the prior] lawsuit. . . . In her motion to quash service of process and, alternatively, motion to dismiss, Ms. Gibbons . . . challenged the allegations in the 1997 complaint as . . . inadequate to satisfy the strict requirements of the Florida long-arm statute. . . .

Obtaining in personam jurisdiction over a non-resident defendant requires a two-pronged showing. First, the plaintiff must allege sufficient jurisdictional facts to bring the defendant within the coverage of the long-arm statute, section 48.193, Florida Statutes. If that prong is satisfied, then the second inquiry is whether sufficient "minimum contacts" are shown to comply with the requirements of due process. International Shoe Co. v. Washington. Generally speaking, Florida's long-arm statutes are of a class that requires more activities or contacts to allow service of process than are currently required by the decisions of the United States Supreme Court.

As to the first part of the inquiry, Mrs. Brown contends that the allegations in her complaint satisfy section 48.193(2), Florida Statutes (1995), which states:

A defendant who is engaged in substantial and not isolated activity within this state, whether such activity is wholly intrastate, interstate, or otherwise, is subject to the jurisdiction of the courts of this state, whether or not the claim arises from that activity.

The parties agree that as a general rule in Florida, a plaintiff, by bringing an action, subjects herself to the jurisdiction of the court and to subsequent lawful orders entered regarding the same subject matter of that action. Mrs. Brown broadly construes this general rule to mean that by initiating the 1995 action, Ms. Gibbons subjected herself to Florida jurisdiction with respect to any "lawful orders" that were entered subsequently regarding "the subject matter of the action." On the other hand, Ms. Gibbons notes that her prior suit was brought in 1995, whereas Mrs. Brown did not file her complaint until October 20, 1997. Although Ms. Gibbons acknowledges that her prior action arose from the same vehicular accident as Mrs. Brown's instant suit, Ms. Gibbons notes that Mrs. Brown was not a party in the earlier action. Furthermore, several years separate the filing of the two proceedings. For purposes of the resolution of the question on appeal, we assume that the 1995 proceedings were over by the time Mrs. Brown brought her 1997 suit.

In Milberg Factors, Inc. v. Greenbaum, 585 So. 2d 1089 (Fla. 3d DCA 1991) . . . [o]bserving that an entity cannot control where its account debtors choose to relocate, the court stated that "the filing of lawsuits unrelated to this action against account debtors in Florida does not subject Milberg to the jurisdiction of our courts."

Even if we assume (without deciding) that bringing an action in a Florida court can constitute a "substantial and not isolated activity" in some instances, we nevertheless note that Mrs. Brown has not shown that Ms. Gibbons "is engaged" in any activity in this state whatsoever other than defending the present suit. A current defendant's prior decision to bring a suit in Florida should not act indefinitely as a sword of Damocles hanging perilously over the head of that defendant if she later challenges jurisdiction in a separate suit (albeit a suit arising from the same subject matter). . . . Given the length of time between the two actions and the fact that the prior suit named as the defendant a non-party in the instant proceedings, we conclude that Mrs. Brown has not alleged a satisfactory ground for personal jurisdiction pursuant to statutory subsection (2). The appellee does not suggest, nor do we find, that the appellant's filing the 1995 action in the Florida court would, by itself, satisfy any of the alternative grounds for jurisdiction set forth in section 48.193(1)(a)-(1)(h). . . .

Absent sufficient jurisdictional allegations to show that Ms. Gibbons' acts satisfy the prerequisites in the Florida long-arm statute . . . the trial court is directed to DISMISS Mrs. Brown's complaint.

NOTES AND PROBLEMS

1. Be sure you understand why the opinion printed above does *not* say that it would be unconstitutional for Florida to assert personal jurisdiction over Ms. Gibbons.

a. Why does Ms. Gibbons's activity not satisfy the Florida statute?

b. Suppose Florida had a long-arm statute like that of California (quoted supra), extending state court jurisdiction to the boundaries permitted by the Due Process Clause. On the facts of this case, would it have been constitutional for Florida to exercise jurisdiction over Ms. Gibbons? What bearing does *World-Wide Volkswagen* have on such a case? *Hanson v. Denckla?*

c. In answering the preceding question, it may help to compare the facts of *Gibbons* to those of Adam v. Saenger, 303 U.S. 59 (1938). Saenger, a Texas citizen, brought suit in California against Adam, a California resident. Adam counterclaimed against Saenger, whereupon Saenger abandoned his action. Adam then recovered a default judgment on the counterclaim against Saenger. When Adam sued in Texas to enforce his judgment, Saenger defended on the ground that the California court lacked personal jurisdiction. So far as the record showed, Saenger's one and only contact with California was the filing of the lawsuit in question. That was enough, held the U.S. Supreme Court: "The plaintiff having, by his voluntary act in demanding justice from the defendant, submitted himself to the jurisdiction of the court, there is nothing arbitrary or unreasonable in treating him as being there for all purposes for which justice to the defendant demands his presence." Id. at 67-68. Is *Gibbons* distinguishable?

2. *Gibbons* points out that "Florida's long-arm statutes are of a class that requires more activities or contacts to allow service of process than are currently required by the decisions of the United States Supreme Court."

a. New York is another populous state that has decided not to extend its jurisdictional reach to the full extent permitted by the constitution. As described in a recent case,

> [NY]CPLR 302 (a) (3), the provision of New York's long-arm statute at issue here, permits a court to exercise personal jurisdiction over a nondomiciliary who:
>
> "3. commits a tortious act without the state causing *injury* to person or property *within the state* . . . if he
>
> "(i) *regularly* does or solicits business, or engages in any other persistent course of conduct, or derives substantial revenue from goods used or consumed or services rendered, *in the state,* or

"(ii) expects or should reasonably expect the *act to have consequences in the state* and derives substantial revenue from *interstate* or international *commerce*"

(CPLR 302[a][3] [emphasis supplied]).

Under this provision, the appellant must show both that an injury occurred "within the state," and that the elements of either clause (i) or (ii) have been satisfied. It is appropriate to point out that establishment of long-arm jurisdiction in connection with a New York injury under either clause does not implicate constitutional due process concerns. "[T]he subdivision [302 (a) (3)] was not designed to go to the full limits of permissible jurisdiction. The limitations contained in subparagraphs (i) and (ii) were deliberately inserted to keep the provision 'well within constitutional bounds' " (1 Weinstein-Korn-Miller, NY Civ Prac P 302.14, quoting 12th Ann Report of NY Jud Conf, at 341).

Ingraham v. Carroll, 90 N.Y.2d 592, 596 (1997) Which portions of the quoted statute would you amend to make its limits congruent with the Due Process Clause?

b. Apply the New York statute to the following facts. Mrs. Ingraham "was a patient of Community Health Plan (CHP), a New York HMO with clinic located in Hoosick Falls, New York," near the Vermont border. On several occasions her HMO physicians referred her to Dr. Carroll, who practices in Bennington, Vermont. Dr. Carroll is not under contract with CHP for consultation services. However, he frequently sees CHP patients on an ad hoc/fee-for-service basis, on referral. Dr. Carroll allegedly misdiagnosed Mrs. Ingraham, whose survivors sued in New York. Assuming that defendant's contacts satisfied the Due Process Clause, did they fall within the New York Statute? Held, no. Ingraham v. Carroll, 90 N.Y.2d 592 (1997).

3. What is the relation between long-arm statutes and the Due Process Clause?

a. Analytically, the two involve distinct inquiries. The Constitution sets the outer boundaries of personal jurisdiction, but nothing requires that a state assert all the jurisdiction permitted by the Constitution. A legislature might decide that it did not want to be as jurisdictionally aggressive as the Constitution would permit. As in *Gibbons*, a court convinced that the long-arm statute does not cover the facts would simply stop there, without needlessly deciding the constitutionality of asserting personal jurisdiction. Only if one decides that the long-arm statute *does* reach the facts of the lawsuit must one make the second, constitutional inquiry.

b. Why would a state want to restrict its jurisdictional reach more than the Constitution already requires? Imagine advising a state legislative committee revising a long-arm statute. Having read the cases in this chapter, can you develop an argument that a state ought to adopt a rule more restrictive than the Constitution requires?

c. Encountering a long-arm statute that appears to be more restrictive than the Constitution, the lawyer must be careful not to assume that it is as limited as the text suggests. State courts have often interpreted such statutes to reach beyond what the text implies. For example, see Sifers v. Horen, 385 Mich. 195 (1971) (interpreting "transaction of any business within the state" as expressing legislative intent to go to limits of Due Process Clause).

4. *Gibbons* is a state case and applies a state long-arm statute. How do long-arm statutes apply in the federal courts? Mrs. Brown was apparently a Florida citizen, and Ms. Gibbons a citizen of Texas. As you will see in the following chapter, if more than $75,000 was in controversy, Ms. Gibbons could have sued in federal district court, invoking diversity jurisdiction. Suppose she had; would the Florida long-arm statute still apply? Reread Rule 4(k)(1)(A).

5. In several notable instances Congress has enacted federal long-arm statutes, which purport to give the federal courts expansive powers of personal jurisdiction. Provisions of the federal securities laws provide one example. Another is the Federal Interpleader Act, 28 U.S.C. §2361, which gives federal courts the power to serve process anywhere in the nation, a power that has been interpreted to include personal jurisdiction.

a. Is such an extended federal jurisdictional reach constitutional?

b. Suppose a defendant is properly served under such a "nationwide service" statute attached to a federal claim. Plaintiff also brings related state-law claims against the same defendant. The federal long-arm statute is constitutional as applied to defendant and reaches far enough to bring defendant into the federal court, but the state's statute doesn't reach as far as the federal long-arm statute. May plaintiff bring the state-law claims, invoking what some have called "pendent personal jurisdiction"? One court has so held:

> [W]e recognize pendent personal jurisdiction of a district court which has obtained personal jurisdiction over a defendant by reason of a federal claim to adjudicate state claims properly within the court's subject matter jurisdiction, even though that state's long-arm statute could not authorize service over the defendants with respect to the state claims. . . . Once a court has a constitutional case, in the Article III sense, properly before it, service by a court sufficient to assert personal jurisdiction over a defendant by any authorized mechanism consistent with due process may be held to apply to the entire constitutional case.

ESAB Group, Inc. v. Centricut Inc., 126 F.3d 617, 628-629 (4th Cir. 1997). Can you frame an argument that this result runs counter to the last fifty years of jurisdictional doctrine? Is it nonetheless the right result?

2. Venue as a Further Localizing Principle

Venue, like personal jurisdiction, determines where litigation will take place. Unlike personal jurisdiction, venue flows solely from statutory rather than constitutional sources. The general federal venue statute is 28 U.S.C. §1391. Surveying this statute will show that it typically tries to place suits in areas connected either to the parties or to the events giving rise to the action. See, for example, the portions of 28 U.S.C. §1391(a) and (b), which put venue "where any defendant resides" or where "a substantial part of the events or omissions giving rise to the claim occurred." In many respects, then, the inquiries necessary under present venue statutes duplicate those involved in personal jurisdiction questions.

Why, then, have both a law of personal jurisdiction and one of venue? At a technical level the answer to that question is easy: Unlike personal jurisdiction, venue locates litigation not just in a state but in a particular federal judicial district within that state. For example, suppose a defendant is clearly subject to personal jurisdiction in Florida, which has three federal judicial districts. See 28 U.S.C. §133(a). Principles of jurisdiction tell plaintiff that she can sue in Florida, but the venue statutes and cases interpreting them will tell her in which of the three districts venue will lie.

The federal venue statute took its present form in 1990, following a century-long evolution during which it was sometimes impossible to find a judicial district in which venue lay even when there was both personal and subject matter jurisdiction over the case and parties. Of the present statute one commentator has remarked: "It is still possible to conceive of cases in which there will be no federal district in which suit can be brought, but those cases are more likely to arise in classroom hypotheticals than in real life." Wright, Federal Courts 262. The following problems survey a range of common federal venue problems under the current statute; we shall concentrate on what Professor Wright calls the "real life" problems, saving a few of the other sort for the end.

NOTES AND PROBLEMS

After reviewing 28 U.S.C. §§1391-1392, answer the following questions by deciding the states (or districts) in which venue lies. (You may assume that all requirements of federal subject matter jurisdiction have been met.) Notice that §1391 (a) and (b) differ slightly and that their application depends on whether the case contains any claim based on federal law.

1. Plaintiff sues defendant, a resident of the Southern District of New York, on a claim of breach of contract. The contract called for the manufacture and delivery of a machine. The machine was designed in New Mexico and assembled in the Northern District of Illinois from parts made in Ohio, California, and Pennsylvania.

a. Where will venue certainly lie?

b. What additional information would one need to decide whether there were other available venues?

2. Plaintiff sues A, a resident of the Southern District of New York, and B, who resides in New Jersey but conducts his business from an office in the Southern District of New York, on a claim of breach of contract. The contract called for the manufacture and delivery of a machine in Japan, from parts made in Mexico.

3. The problems thus far have assumed that the defendants are individuals. For corporations, §1391(c) provides a more expansive definition of "jurisdiction": Quite simply, a corporate defendant is deemed, for venue purposes, to reside wherever it is subject to personal jurisdiction.

4. Special venue provisions apply to aliens:

a. C, a Canadian citizen, wishes to sue D, a resident of the Eastern District of California, alleging personal injury damages arising from an automoblie accident in Nevada. Where will venue lie?

b. D, a resident of the Eastern District of California, wishes to sue C, a Canadian citizen, alleging personal injury damages arising from an automobile accident in Nevada. Where will venue lie?

c. Section 1391(d) also applies to alien corporations, subjecting them to suit not just where they do business, but in any judicial district.

d. Before deciding that §1391(d) is extremely harsh on aliens, consider how doctrines of personal jurisdiction will limit its application. In Problem 4b, venue will lie in any judicial district in the United States; assuming that C is a tourist who has since returned to Canada, where will personal jurisdiction lie?

5. What is the difference between §1391(a)(3) and §1391(b)(3)? Section 1391 (a)(3) requires that a defendant be subject to personal jurisdiction in a district; §1391 (b)(3) allows for venue whenever a defendant "may be found" in that district. Is "be[ing] found" a less rigorous test than being subject to personal jurisdiction? May a defendant ever be "found" in a district in which personal jurisdiction is unavailable? After Burnham v. Superior Court, supra, the answer may be "never" in the case of an individual. If service of process on an individual satisfies the requirements of jurisdiction, being "found" will be the same as being

subject to personal jurisdiction, at least if one is "found" by a process server. The next case wrestles with the problem:

Dee-K Enterprises, Inc., v. Heveafil Sdn. Bhd.
982 F. Supp. 1138 (E.D. Va. 1997)

ELLIS, J.

In this antitrust action, two American purchasers of extruded rubber thread sue various foreign manufacturers and distributors of the thread alleging an international conspiracy to restrain trade in, and fix prices of, the thread in the United States. Defendants' several motions to dismiss raise the following threshold issues:

(1) whether there is personal jurisdiction over an Indonesian manufacturer-defendant that consummates its sales of thread in Indonesia;

(2) whether venue is proper in the Eastern District of Virginia; . . . .

[Plaintiffs Dee-K and Asheboro, Virginia and North Carolina corporations respectively, bought rubber thread from defendants to make, among other things, bungee cords. Plaintiffs sued a number of corporations producing the rubber thread, corporations in Malaysia (including defendants Heveafil, Rubfil, and Rubberflex), in Indonesia (defendants Bakrie and Perkebunan), and in Thailand. Plaintiffs alleged a broad conspiracy among defendants to fix prices and restrain competition in rubber thread. Defendants challenged jurisdiction and venue.]

The prerequisites for obtaining personal jurisdiction are well established. . . . First, the plaintiff must point to a statute (usually a state's long-arm statute) or rule that authorizes service of process over the defendant. Second, the service of process pursuant to the specified statute or rule must comport with due process. . . .

In the instant circumstances, the first prerequisite is met both by §12 of the Clayton Act, 15 U.S.C. §22, and by Rule 4(k)(2), Fed. R. Civ. P. Section 12 of the Clayton Act provides for nationwide — indeed worldwide — service of process when the antitrust defendant is a corporation. See 15 U.S.C. §22 (providing for service "wherever [defendant] may be found").[9] Further, under Rule 4(k)(2), a defendant not subject to the jurisdiction of any state court that is served with process is subject to personal jurisdiction in the federal courts as long as the assertion of jurisdiction (i) is consistent with federal law, and (ii) does not offend the Constitution.

---

9. Of course, §12 provides only that service may be effected worldwide; it does not prescribe the proper means for accomplishing the service. In that regard, a plaintiff must comply with Rule 4, Fed. R. Civ. P.

In this case, Bakrie was properly served in Indonesia pursuant to Rule 4(f)(2)(C)(ii), Fed. R. Civ. P. Because the Clayton Act provides for worldwide service, service in Indonesia was consistent with federal law. Thus, plaintiffs need only show under Rule 4 that the service effected did not offend the Constitution. . . . Thus, under either the Clayton Act or Rule 4, any challenge to personal jurisdiction is governed by the familiar constitutional test of "fair play and substantial justice." *International Shoe*. In essence, the statutory analysis regarding service of process collapses into the constitutional inquiry. . . .

[Applying *International Shoe* to the facts, the court found that due process was satisfied by defendants' appointment of exclusive U.S. sales agents and its customizing of its products for the U.S. market.]

Next, there is the matter of venue. Defendants contend that even if in personam jurisdiction is established on the basis of aggregated, national contacts, venue in the Eastern District of Virginia is improper.

Section 12 of the Clayton Act lays venue in any district where the defendant is "found" or where it "transacts business." At first blush this would seem to be an insurmountable obstacle to suit in this district, as the foreign defendants here apparently cannot be found in any judicial district in the United States because they conduct their business abroad. Yet, this is not fatal to venue, for the Supreme Court has held that 28 U.S.C. §1391(d), which provides that aliens may be sued in any district, overrides any special venue statute (such as the one contained in 12 of the Clayton Act). Thus, §1391(d) eliminates any venue impediment to suit in this district with respect to the foreign defendants because they, as aliens, may be sued in any federal judicial district.

As to the American defendants, [under 28 U.S.C. §1391(b)] venue is proper in (1) a judicial district where any defendant resides, if all defendants reside in the same State, (2) a judicial district in which a substantial part of the events or omissions giving rise to the claim occurred . . . or (3) a judicial district in which any defendant may be found, if there is no district in which the action may otherwise be brought. In the case at bar, neither (1) nor (2) applies; thus, venue is proper as to all the American defendants in any district where one of them may be found.[24]

24. The fact that the foreign defendants can be *sued* in this district pursuant to 28 U.S.C. §391(d) does not mean that they can also be *found* in this district, thereby creating a basis for proper venue as to the domestic defendants pursuant to 1391(b)(3). Were this not so, in a case involving foreign and domestic defendants, 1391(d) could be used as to the foreign defendants to circumvent the requirements of 1391(b) as to the domestic defendants. Neither the statute as a whole, nor sensible policy, permits such a result. When, as here, there are both foreign and domestic defendants, 1391(b) must be satisfied as to the domestic defendants.

Plaintiffs have alleged some Virginia-related contacts of defendants, but the allegations are quite sparse. In addition to the boilerplate statement that defendants "are found or do business in the district or the state," Second Amended Complaint P 2, plaintiffs assert that Heveafil sold its rubber thread in Virginia; that Rubfil had customers in Virginia and sold to them with the aid of its subsidiary, Rubfil-USA; that Rubberflex sold its thread in Virginia with the aid of its subsidiaries Flexfil (RI) and Flexfil (NC); and that Consortium sold Perkebunan's product in this state. Several defendants contend — and plaintiffs have yet to dispute — that these Virginia contacts were located in the Western District of Virginia, not the Eastern District, and thus that venue here is improper. Not all defendants, however, have objected to venue being laid in this district. That fact might suggest that there are indeed sufficient contacts with this district such that at least one of the American distributors can be "found" here, thus satisfying 1391(b)(3). Yet no specific allegation to that effect is found in the second amended complaint. At this time, therefore, it is unclear whether venue is proper in the Eastern District of Virginia. Accordingly, plaintiffs must show that venue in this district is proper, or the action may be transferred to the Western District of Virginia. . . .

NOTES AND PROBLEMS

1. *Dee-K Enterprises* reviews many of the topics considered in this chapter as it illustrates how they relate to each other.

a. Explain why "the statutory analysis regarding service of process collapses into the constitutional inquiry" in this case.

b. The opinion says that process was served under Rule 4(f)(2)(C)(ii) — certified mail with return receipt. Why not under the Hague Service Convention, described supra at page 188? Indonesia had not signed the Convention.

2. Wrap yourself around footnote 24, which explores the relationship of §§1391(b)(3) and (d).

a. If this suit were solely against Bakrie, the Indonesian defendant, where would venue lie?

b. Why, in the court's view, does this change when Bakrie is joined with the other defendants?

c. The opinion ends by sending the parties out to develop additional information about domestic defendants' contacts with the Eastern District of Virginia. Why?

3. Having surveyed the basic issues of the contemporary federal venue statute, we can reconsider the overlap between personal jurisdiction and venue: Why have both? At a basic level, the question of whether venue is redundant has no easy answer. Historically, venue statutes preceded concepts of personal jurisdiction and were, until Pennoyer v. Neff, the only law regulating the place where suit might be brought. Moreover, until a few decades ago venue was in some respects more restrictive than the law of personal jurisdiction. But as the requirements for venue have come ever more closely to approximate those of personal jurisdiction, it is fair to ask whether we need both doctrines, or would jurisdiction alone suffice? Note that because venue is statutory, one could contemplate its abolition: It is safe to say that the abolition of venue requirements might cause some housekeeping problems but would not violate the Due Process Clause.

When an action is brought in state court, federal venue statutes are irrelevant; they apply only to actions originally brought in the federal courts. (Cases removed to the federal courts from state courts are similarly not subject to federal venue requirements; venue lies in the district encompassing the state court from which the case is removed.) States, however, have their own venue statutes that indicate in which county an action must be brought. Professors James, Hazard, and Leubsdorf have summarized the state venue rules as follows:

> In transitory actions, state venue rules follow variegated patterns that employ one or more of the following tests: (a) where the cause of action, or part thereof, arose or accrued; (b) where some fact is present or happened; (c) where the defendant resides; (d) where the defendant is doing business; (e) where the defendant has an office or place of business, or an agent, or representative, or where an agent or officer of defendant resides; (f) where the plaintiff resides; (g) where the plaintiff is doing business; (h) where the defendant may be found; (i) where the defendant may be summoned or served; (j) in the county designated in the plaintiffs complaint; (k) in any county; (l) where the seat of government is located. The tests that give plaintiff the widest choice are often applicable only where defendant is a nonresident of the state. The defendant's residence is the most common provision for venue.*

Another principle that is sometimes given the label "venue" is the local-action rule for certain causes of action, chiefly those involving real property. The rule states that only the courts of the state where land is

----

* James, Hazard, and Leubsdorf 97, citing Stevens, Venue Statutes: Diagnosis and Proposed Cure, 49 Mich. L. Rev. 307, 310-315 (1951).

located will hear cases that raise any question concerning title to the land. In the early case of Livingston v. Jefferson, 15 F. Cas. 660 (C.C.D. Va. 1811)(No, 8,411), Livingston sought to sue Thomas Jefferson for trespass to land located in Louisiana. As Jefferson was a resident of Virginia and not subject to jurisdiction elsewhere, and as the court ruled that under English common law the action was local and had to be brought where the land was located, the plaintiff was effectively left without a remedy. The rule has since been changed by statute in many states and was rejected by court decision in Reasor-Hill Corp. v. Harrison, 220 Ark. 521, 249 S.W. 2d 994 (1952). Another traditional local action is an action by a state to collect taxes, although increasingly that restriction has been abandoned. E.g., Oklahoma ex rel. Oklahoma Tax Committee v. Neely, 225 Ark. 230, 282 S.W. 2d 150 (1955).

3.   Declining Jurisdiction: Transfer and Forum Non Conveniens

Both state and federal courts possess the power to decline to exercise jurisdiction even though they possess it. You have already encountered one example of this power: long-arm statutes that do not extend as far as the Constitution would permit. As personal jurisdiction has expanded under modern analyses and as state and federal courts perceive themselves to be working with greater caseloads, the power of declining to hear cases has been exercised more frequently. This section examines two of the rationales for declining to exercise jurisdiction. One — transfer among federal judicial districts under 28 U.S.C. §1404 — has special significance for federal courts because they are located throughout the United States and its possessions. The other — forum non conveniens — affects both state and federal courts.

Both §1404(a) transfer and forum non conveniens dismissals flow from the same perception: that there will be circumstances in which a court has the power to hear a case but, for reasons of justice or efficiency, should not do so. One might think that for a court applying the jurisdictional principles enunciated in *International Shoe*, such situations would be rare. They can, however, occur. For example, the judge may conclude that although jurisdiction is clear, a strong local prejudice against one of the parties will make a fair trial difficult to achieve. Or the preponderance of witnesses, perhaps some of them severely disabled, will have to travel long distances to testify. Under these or similar circumstances, a federal court may decide to either transfer the case to another federal court under §1404(a) or dismiss it under the forum non conveniens doctrine for trial in another country. A state court might take a similar action, transferring (under a state statute analogous to §1404(a)) to another court in the same state or dismissing under the forum non conveniens doctrine for refiling in another state or country. We start with the more basic doctrine, *forum non conveniens*.

a.   *Forum Non Conveniens*

Piper Aircraft v. Reyno
454 U.S. 235 (1981)

Justice MARSHALL delivered the opinion of the Court. . . .

I

A

In July 1976, a small commercial aircraft crashed in the Scottish highlands during the course of a charter flight from Blackpool to Perth. The pilot and five passengers were killed instantly. The decedents were all Scottish subjects and residents, as are their heirs and next of kin. There were no eyewitnesses to the accident. At the time of the crash the plane was subject to Scottish air traffic control.

The aircraft, a twin-engine Piper Aztec, was manufactured in Pennsylvania by petitioner Piper Aircraft Co. (Piper). The propellers were manufactured in Ohio by petitioner Hartzell Propeller, Inc. (Hartzell). . . . [The aircraft was owned and maintained by Air Navigation and] was operated by McDonald Aviation, Ltd. (McDonald), a Scottish air taxi service. Both Air Navigation and McDonald were organized in the United Kingdom. The wreckage of the plane is now in a hanger in Farnsborough, England.

[A] British Department of Trade [report] . . . found no evidence of defective equipment and indicated that pilot error may have contributed to the accident. The pilot, who had obtained his commercial pilot's license only three months earlier, was flying over high ground at an altitude considerably lower than the minimum height required by his company's operations manual.

In July 1977, a California probate court appointed respondent Gaynell Reyno administratrix of the estates of the five passengers. Reyno is not related to and does not know any of the decedents or their survivors; she was a legal secretary to the attorney who filed this lawsuit. Several days after her appointment, Reyno commenced separate wrongful-death actions against Piper and Hartzell in the Superior Court of California, claiming negligence and strict liability. . . . Reyno candidly admits that the action against Piper and Hartzell was filed in the United States because its laws regarding liability, capacity to sue, and damages are more favorable to her position than are those of Scotland. Scottish law does not recognize strict liability in tort. Moreover, it permits wrongful-death actions only when brought by a decedent's relatives. The relatives may sue only for "loss of support and society."

[The defendants first removed to federal district court in California, then successfully sought §1404(a) transfer to the Middle District of Pennsylvania, where Piper does business. Then defendants sought to dismiss the case on grounds of forum non conveniens.]

B

. . . The District Court granted these motions in October 1979. It relied on the balancing test set forth by this Court in Gulf Oil Corp. v. Gilbert, 330 U.S. 501 (1947), and its companion case, Koster v. Lumbermens Mut. Cas. Co., 330 U.S. 518 (1947). In those decisions, the Court stated that a plaintiff's choice of forum should rarely be disturbed. However, when an alternative forum has jurisdiction to hear the case, and when trial in the chosen forum would "establish . . . oppressiveness and vexation to a defendant . . . out of all proportion to plaintiff's convenience," or when the "chosen forum [is] inappropriate because of considerations affecting the court's own administrative and legal problems," the court may, in the exercise of its sound discretion, dismiss the case. To guide trial court discretion, the Court provided a list of "private interest factors" affecting the convenience of the litigants, and a list of "public interest factors" affecting the convenience of the forum.[6]

[The Third Circuit reversed, on the ground that dismissal for forum non conveniens is never appropriate where the law of the alternative forum is less favorable to the plaintiff.]

---

6. The factors pertaining to the private interests of the litigants included the "relative ease of access to sources of proof; availability of compulsory process for attendance of unwilling, and the cost of obtaining attendance of willing, witnesses; possibility of view of premises, if view would be appropriate to the action; and all other practical problems that make trial of a case easy, expeditious and inexpensive." Gilbert, 330 U.S., at 508. The public factors bearing on the question included the administrative difficulties flowing from court congestion; the "local interest in having localized controversies decided at home"; the interest in having the trial of a diversity case in a forum that is at home with the law that must govern the action; the avoidance of unnecessary problems in conflict of laws, or in the application of foreign law; and the unfairness of burdening citizens in an unrelated forum with jury duty.

II

The Court of Appeals erred in holding that plaintiffs may defeat a motion to dismiss on the ground of forum non conveniens merely by showing that the substantive law that would be applied in the alternative forum is less favorable to the plaintiffs than that of the present forum. The possibility of a change in substantive law should ordinarily not be given conclusive or even substantial weight in the forum non conveniens inquiry.

We expressly rejected the position adopted by the Court of Appeals in our decision in Canada Malting Co. v. Paterson Steamships, Ltd., 285 U.S. 413 (1932). . . .

The Court of Appeals' decision is inconsistent with this Court's earlier forum non conveniens decisions in another respect. Those decisions have repeatedly emphasized the need to retain flexibility. . . .

[I]f conclusive or substantial weight were given to the possibility of a change in law, the forum non conveniens doctrine would become virtually useless. Jurisdiction and venue requirements are often easily satisfied. As a result, many plaintiffs are able to choose from among several forums. Ordinarily, these plaintiffs will select that forum whose choice-of-law rules are most advantageous. Thus, if the possibility of an unfavorable change in substantive law is given substantial weight in the forum non conveniens inquiry, dismissal would rarely be proper. . . .

Upholding the decision of the Court of Appeals would result in other practical problems. At least where the foreign plaintiff named an American manufacturer as defendant, a court could not dismiss the case on grounds of forum non conveniens where dismissal might lead to an unfavorable change in law. The American courts, which are already extremely attractive to foreign plaintiffs, would become even more attractive. The flow of litigation into the United States would increase and further congest already crowded courts.[19] . . .

We do not hold that the possibility of an unfavorable change in law should never be a relevant consideration in a forum non conveniens

19. In holding that the possibility of a change in law unfavorable to the plaintiff should not be given substantial weight, we also necessarily hold that the possibility of a change in law favorable to defendant should not be considered. Respondent suggests that Piper and Hartzell filed the motion to dismiss, not simply because trial in the United States would be inconvenient, but also because they believe the laws of Scotland are more favorable. She argues that this should be taken into account in the analysis of the private interests. We recognize, of course, that Piper and Hartzell may be engaged in reverse forum-shopping. However, this possibility ordinarily should not enter into a trial court's analysis of the private interests. If the defendant is able to overcome the presumption in favor of plaintiff by showing that trial in the chosen forum would be unnecessarily burdensome, dismissal is appropriate — regardless of the fact that defendant may also be motivated by a desire to obtain a more favorable forum.

inquiry. Of course, if the remedy provided by the alternative forum is so clearly inadequate or unsatisfactory that it is no remedy at all, the unfavorable change in law may be given substantial weight; the district court may conclude that dismissal would not be in the interests of justice. In these cases, however, the remedies that would be provided by the Scottish courts do not fall within this category. Although the relatives of the decedents may not be able to rely on a strict liability theory, and although their potential damages award may be smaller, there is no danger that they will be deprived of any remedy or treated unfairly. . . .

III

The Court of Appeals also erred in rejecting the District Court's *Gilbert* analysis. . . .

A

The District Court acknowledged that there is ordinarily a strong presumption in favor of the plaintiff's choice of forum, which may be overcome only when the private and public interest factors clearly point towards trial in the alternative forum. It held, however, that the presumption applies with less force when the plaintiff or real parties in interest are foreign.

The District Court's distinction between resident or citizen plaintiffs and foreign plaintiffs is fully justified. In *Koster*, the Court indicated that a plaintiff's choice of forum is entitled to greater deference when the plaintiff has chosen the home forum. When the home forum has been chosen, it is reasonable to assume that this choice is convenient. When the plaintiff is foreign, however, this assumption is much less reasonable. Because the central purpose of any forum non conveniens inquiry is to ensure that the trial is convenient, a foreign plaintiff's choice deserves less deference.

B

The forum non conveniens determination is committed to the sound discretion of the trial court. It may be reversed only when there has been a clear abuse of discretion. . . .

(1)

In analyzing the private interest factors, the District Court stated that the connections with Scotland are "overwhelming." This characterization may be somewhat exaggerated. Particularly with respect to the question of relative ease of access to sources of proof, the private interests point in both directions. As respondent emphasizes, records concerning the design, manufacture, and testing of the propeller and plane are located in the United States. She would have greater access to sources of proof relevant to her strict liability and negligence theories if trial were held here.[25] However, the District Court did not act unreasonably in concluding that fewer evidentiary problems would be posed if the trial were held in Scotland. A large proportion of the relevant evidence is located in Great Britain. . . .

The District Court correctly concluded that the problems posed by the inability to implead potential third-party defendants clearly supported holding the trial in Scotland. Joinder of the pilot's estate, Air Navigation, and McDonald is crucial to the presentation of petitioners' defense. If Piper and Hartzell can show that the accident was caused not by a design defect, but rather by the negligence of the pilot, the plane's owners, or the charter company, they will be relieved of all liability. . . .

(2)

The District Court's review of the factors relating to the public interest was also reasonable. On the basis of its choice-of-law analysis, it concluded that if the case were tried in the Middle District of Pennsylvania, Pennsylvania law would apply to Piper and Scottish law to Hartzell. It stated that a trial involving two sets of laws would be confusing to the jury. It also noted its own lack of familiarity with Scottish law. Consideration of these problems was clearly appropriate under *Gilbert.* . . .

Scotland has a very strong interest in this litigation. The accident occurred in its airspace. All of the decedents were Scottish. Apart from Piper and Hartzell, all potential plaintiffs and defendants are either Scottish or English. As we stated in *Gilbert,* there is "a local interest in having localized controversies decided at home." Respondent argues that American citizens have an interest in ensuring that American manufacturers are deterred from producing defective products, and that additional deterrence might be obtained if Piper and Hartzell were tried in the United States, where they could be sued on the basis of both negligence and strict liability. However, the incremental deterrence that would be gained if this trial were held in American court is likely to be insignificant. The American interest in this accident is simply not sufficient to justify the enormous commitment of judicial time and resources that would inevitably be required if the case were to be tried here.

25. In the future, where similar problems are presented, district courts might dismiss subject to the condition that defendant corporations agree to provide the records relevant to the plaintiff's claims.

IV

The Court of Appeals erred in holding that the possibility of an unfavorable change in law bars dismissal on the ground of forum non conveniens. It also erred in rejecting the District Court's *Gilbert* analysis. The District Court properly decided that the presumption in favor of the respondent's forum choice applied with less than maximum force because the real parties in interest are foreign. It did not act unreasonably in deciding that the private interests pointed towards trial in Scotland. Nor did it act unreasonably in deciding that the public interests favored trial in Scotland. Thus, the judgment of the Court of Appeals is

Reversed.

[Justices POWELL and O'CONNOR took no part in the decision of these cases. The concurring opinion of Justice WHITE and the dissent of Justices STEVENS and BRENNAN are omitted.]

NOTES AND PROBLEMS

1. Be sure you understand the issue at stake. Defendants were not challenging the court's personal jurisdiction; what were they arguing?

2. What change in facts should lead to a different outcome — that is, the denial of the motion to dismiss for forum non conveniens?

   a. If the decedents had been U.S. citizens?

   b. If the plane had crashed into the sea, making it unavailable for examination?

   c. If Scotland permitted no recovery for wrongful death?

3. What will happen now that the case has been dismissed? One possibility is that the plaintiffs, deprived of the advantageous U.S. product liability law, will drop the lawsuit. Another possibility is that they will refile in Scotland. But what if, in the meantime, the statute of limitations has run? It seems unfair to permit a defendant to move for dismissal on the grounds that forum A is less convenient than forum B, only to raise a defense that makes forum B entirely unavailable.

   a. To obviate this unfairness, courts regularly require that a defendant moving to dismiss on grounds of an inconvenient forum agree in advance to waive the statute of limitations defense in the alternative forum.

   b. The same requirement sometimes applies to personal jurisdiction and venue: Occasionally defendants will argue that a forum lacking either jurisdiction or venue is more convenient. When courts accept such arguments, they often condition dismissal on an agreement to waive jurisdictional or venue defenses in the new forum.

4. The opinion hints at the possibility that dramatic differences in procedure in the alternative forum would make dismissal inappropriate. How different would a foreign legal system have to be for a U.S. court to refuse to dismiss on grounds that there was no adequate alternative forum? How much weight should a court accord the following factors:

a. The absence of the right to a jury trial? The United States stands almost alone in using juries in civil cases.

b. The inability of lawyers to conduct fact investigation and discovery without judicial participation? No other legal system gives civil parties the power to conduct discovery as broad and as deep as that available in the United States.

c. The absence of the right to cross-examine witnesses? In many legal systems judges do more and lawyers less examining of witnesses.

d. The absence of the right to appeal? Most civil law legal systems provide more by way of appellate supervision of lower courts than does the United States; would such increased review compensate for the absence of other procedural features?

5. Margaret Stewart, in her article Forum Non Conveniens: A Doctrine in Search of a Role, 74 Cal. L. Rev. 1259, 1263 (1986), argues that in cases like *Piper*, "the doctrine of forum non conveniens had outlived its usefulness." She contends that if there are sufficient contracts to permit a court to both hear a case and apply its law to the case, the court in question should decide the lawsuit; if either of these conditions is absent, the case should be dismissed for want of jurisdiction.

Texas seems to have taken Professor Stewart's advice. In a case that, like *Piper*, involved claims brought by foreign citizens against a U.S. defendant for injuries suffered abroad, the Supreme Court of Texas held that the Texas legislature had abolished the doctrine of forum non conveniens in wrongful death and injury actions arising out of incidents in foreign countries. Dow Chemical Co. v. Alfaro, 786 S.W. 2d 674 (Tex. 1990), cert. denied, 498 U.S. 1024 (1991) (reversing lower court dismissal). *Alfaro* was a 4-to-3 decision, with dissents colorfully noting that " 'Texas has constituted itself the world's forum of last resort . . .' " and predicting that " our residents [will be forced] to wait in the corridors of our courthouses while foreign causes of action are tried."

b.   Transfer under 28 U.S.C. §§1404, 1406, and 1631

Reading *Piper* carefully, one notices that before seeking dismissal under forum non conveniens, the defendants first removed to federal court and then sought *transfer* to a different judicial district under 28 U.S.C. §1404. That statute permits transfer"[f]or the convenience of parties and witnesses, in the interest of justice." It thus gives to federal courts the ability to move cases within the system without the necessity for dismissal and refiling, which would be necessary under the doctrine of forum non conveniens.

NOTES AND PROBLEMS

1. *Piper* was filed in a California state court, then removed to federal court in California, where the defendants made the §1404 motion. Using the facts in the opinion, reconstruct the arguments defendants would have made in support of their motion to transfer the case to the Middle District of Pennsylvania.

2. Why could defendants not invoke §1404(a) when they sought to move the litigation to Scotland?

3. Although the statutory scheme of §1404(a) closely resembles the common law doctrine of forum non conveniens, there are differences worth noting:

a. Section 1404(a) governs only in the federal courts. State courts may make use of the forum non conveniens doctrine to dismiss a case or of state statutes analogous to §1404(a) to transfer between districts within the state, but they lack power to transfer a case to another state.

b. Forum non conveniens dismissal is available only to the defendant, because the plaintiff may voluntarily dismiss the first action, which he brought. But plaintiffs may seek transfer under §1404. Ferens v. John Deere Co., 494 U.S. 516 (1990).

c. The district judge has a bit more discretion under §1404 than under the forum non conveniens doctrine. In Norwood v. Kirkpatrick, 349 U.S. 29 (1955), the Supreme Court upheld a transfer even though the plaintiff was a resident of the district in which he had brought suit. The traditional deference to the plaintiff's choice of forum (if jurisdiction and venue were proper) meant that forum non conveniens was unavailable in such circumstances.

4. Section 1404 does not exhaust the possibilities of transfer within the federal system.

a. Section 1406 allows transfer from a district in which venue is improper. (Dismissal is also allowed.)

b. When venue is proper but jurisdiction is lacking, 28 U.S.C. §1631 permits transfer to a court with jurisdiction. In such a case, the statute specifies that "the action . . . shall proceed as if it had been filed in

. . . the court to which it is transferred." It further stipulates that the transferred action relates back to date of the original filing.

5. Section 1407 of 28 U.S.C. sets up a judicial panel on multidistrict litigation and authorizes it to transfer cases pending in different districts to a single district for coordinated or consolidated pretrial proceedings. The transferee district need not be one in which venue was originally proper. The theory underlying such consolidation is efficiency: It is needless to have multiple courts deciding identical pretrial motions and numerous parties conducting duplicative discovery. This quest for efficiency halts, however, at the threshold of trial, as §1407 proceedings are limited to the pretrial stage. Trial takes place in the original district in which the action is brought (unless it is transferred under §1404 or §1406). Lexecon v. Milberg Weiss, 118 S Ct. 96 (1998) (assigned multidistrict court cannot "transfer" case to itself for trial). Typical cases for the application of §1407 are airplane crash cases.

This chapter has explored the elaborate law developed to answer a single question: Can this lawsuit against this defendant be brought in this court? The complexity of the doctrine answering that question testifies both to its practical importance and to the constitutional structure that divides power among units of government in the United States. The practical importance results from the autonomy given to the units of government by the constitutional structure. Simply put: It matters whether Alabama or California courts will hear a case because the constitutional structure gives to Alabama and California courts the last word on many important questions. But — the student may ask — why can't the case be heard instead in a federal court? The next chapter explores the answer to that question.

SUBJECT MATTER JURISDICTION OF THE FEDERAL COURTS

III

A. The Idea and the Structure of Subject Matter Jurisdiction

The law of personal jurisdiction limits courts in relation to particular defendants. If the defendant lacks the requisite connection with the forum state, due process prevents courts sitting in that state from rendering a judgment that will bind that defendant. The Constitution thereby guards the boundary between fair and unfair assertions of judicial power over a particular defendant by courts in a given geographic location.

Courts in the United States must also cope with a second and quite different jurisdictional boundary. The Constitution created a federal government but made the federal government supreme only in certain areas. In other areas the states are sovereign, and in still others federal and state governments share power. The 200 years since the ratification of the Constitution have seen numerous political struggles and a major war fought over the location of the line between state and federal power. That continuing struggle is reflected in the realm of civil procedure. Because both state and federal governments possess court systems, litigants, their lawyers, and judges need to know which kinds of cases belong in which courts. Lawyers describe this sorting of cases between court systems as "subject matter jurisdiction."

A sketch of constitutional history reveals that several political compromises shape the structure of federal judicial jurisdiction. Read Article III, the portion of the Constitution devoted to the judiciary. You will readily discover that §1 of this Article establishes a Supreme Court. Section 1 also authorizes, but does not require, Congress to establish lower federal courts — what we know today as the courts of appeals and the district courts. Putting the question of lower federal courts into Congress's hands represented a compromise between those who feared an overly

213

powerful federal government and those who viewed the establishment of federal courts as one of the most important goals of the new government. The compromise left the issue subject to changeable legislative wishes. In fact, the first Congress created lower federal courts, and their existence has never been in serious question since.

Section 2 of Article III contains a second compromise, one whose terms have been fiercely litigated for more than 200 years. Article III limits federal courts' jurisdiction to the list set forth in §2: By implication a case not there enumerated may not be heard in a federal court. Such a case could be heard only in a state court. Within the boundaries of Article III, however, Congress remains free to bestow all or some of the constitutionally permissible jurisdiction on the lower federal courts.

This history has implications even in ordinary lawsuits. Because the federal courts are courts of *limited jurisdiction*, two questions lurk at the threshold of every federal case: Does the case fall within one of the enumerated categories of Article III, §2; and has Congress further authorized the lower federal courts to assume that jurisdiction? Rule 8(a) reflects these questions in that it requires every federal complaint to begin with a "short and plain statement of the grounds upon which the court's jurisdiction depends." In judging those jurisdictional statements, the courts look to three bodies of law — the Constitution, the statutes conferring jurisdiction, and the case law construing both.

Skimming the jurisdictional statutes, one might not suspect a very important feature: Federal courts share most of their jurisdiction with state courts. Look, for example, at the so-called general federal question statute, 28 U.S.C. §1331. It grants federal courts jurisdiction over cases that arise under federal law. That federal courts have such jurisdiction does not seem surprising, but it may be surprising to learn that they do not have *exclusive* jurisdiction over such cases. So far as Congress and the Constitution are concerned, cases arising under federal law can be brought in state as well as federal courts. Lawyers speak of such shared jurisdiction as *concurrent*. Like general federal question cases, diversity jurisdiction (28 U.S.C. §1332) is also concurrent. In some instances Congress has made federal jurisdiction exclusive. See, for example, 28 U.S.C. §§1333 (admiralty), 1334 (bankruptcy), and 1337 (antitrust). For an example of a statute carefully discriminating between grants of concurrent and exclusive federal jurisdiction, read 28 U.S.C. §1338. Can you construct a theory on which Congress made patent and copyright jurisdiction exclusive but trademark jurisdiction concurrent?

Why would a lawyer or a litigant care whether a state or federal court heard her case? Assuming some court is available, why should it matter which one? The answer has both practical and political dimensions. As a tactical matter, the reasons for seeking federal rather than state court range from the mundane (some federal courts presently have shorter waiting times until trial than their state counterparts) to the strategic (is the defendant likely to get a more sympathetic hearing from the local state judge than from the federal judge in the nearest large city; will a federal jury, drawn from a different population than a state jury, be likely to award higher — or lower — damages; if a jury awards large damages, will a federal judge — insulated by lifetime tenure — be more likely to reduce it; are federal judges more inclined to enforce arbitration agreements than state judges?) to the crafty (is the opposing lawyer uncomfortable with the generally more formal conduct and faster pace of federal litigation?).

On a somewhat different plane, one might note that Article III, §1 gives federal judges lifetime tenure, a protection that is supposed to shield them from certain sorts of political pressure. The limited jurisdiction of the federal courts also shields them, however, from certain kinds of cases: Family law disputes, for example, are not part of the federal docket. These dual insulations — from political pressure and from a broad caseload — may work in opposite directions. Arguing that federal courts possess a range of virtues ranging from greater competence to "class based predilections favorable to constitutional enforcement," one civil rights litigator has argued in virtually every conceivable situation the federal courts would be more hospitable to his clients' claims. Bert Neuborne, The Myth of Parity, 90 Harv. L. Rev. 1105 (1977). Another has argued that for his gay and lesbian clients, the state courts' closer ties both to the local community and their broad range of cases make them the superior forum. William Rubenstein, The Myth of Superiority, 16 Const. Commentary 599 (2000). For us the significance of the debate lies in the fact that experienced lawyers could believe it matters whether a state or a federal court hears the case — even in instances when the two courts would be applying the same law. This proposition sets the stage for an exploration of federal subject matter jurisdiction.

B.   Federal Question Jurisdiction

Although most Americans today assume that federal trial courts have jurisdiction to hear all cases involving federal law, that assumption has not been true for most of the nation's history and is true today only in a limited and sometimes counterintuitive form. The first Congress passed a Judiciary Act that exercised the option given it by Article III to expand the federal judiciary beyond the Supreme Court. In choosing to create what the Constitution calls "inferior" federal courts, Congress bestowed on those courts some but not all of the jurisdiction allowed under Article III. Among the most important grants of jurisdiction were diversity and admiralty. Most striking from a modern perspective, however, is the absence of any general federal question jurisdiction. Individual statutes contained jurisdictional grants — patents and federal pension laws are two early examples — but no general power was given to federal courts to entertain claims based on federal law. Consider what that meant: Unless it fell under one of these narrowly drawn statutes, a claim based directly on the Constitution or a federal statute could not be brought in federal court; the federal question would come to a federal forum (the Supreme Court) only on appeal from a state court judgment. Not until after the Civil War had reshaped the understanding of federalism and, in particular, the federal courts' role in the enforcement of civil rights, did Congress in 1875 enact a general federal question statute. Its contemporary successor is found in 28 U.S.C. §1331.

The key provision of that statute gives district courts jurisdiction over cases "arising under" the Constitution, statutes, or treaties of the federal government. The difficulty comes in deciding what it means for a case to "arise under" federal law. About the interpretation of that phrase, one scholar has said, "Though the meaning of this phrase has attracted the interest of such giants of the bench as Marshall, Waite, Bradley, the first Harlan, Holmes, Cardozo, Frankfurter, and Brennan, and has been the subject of voluminous scholarly commentary, it cannot be said that any clear test has yet been developed to determine which cases 'arise under' the Constitution, laws or treaties of the United States." Wright, Federal Courts 101. Before you despair, bear in mind that the basics are quite straightforward and that the difficult problems arise in a narrow band of cases. As a preface to our exploration, consider the following two cases.

1. Worker contends that Employer has violated the federal Fair Labor Standards Act, which, among other things, establishes a minimum wage for certain employees. Employer does not contest the applicability of the statute or the amount of the minimum wage but instead asserts that Worker has overstated the number of hours he has worked and is for that reason not entitled to the pay he seeks. Consider what issues will be contested.

2. Plaintiff claims that Newspaper has libeled her. Newspaper's defense rests on a body of law that the courts have elaborated from the First Amendment. Specifically, it relies on the theory that media defendants in libel cases may prevail — even if they have published false and injurious

information — so long as they have not been negligent in, for example, checking their sources. Newspaper concedes the inaccuracy of its article but nevertheless believes that it has such a First Amendment defense. Consider what the contested issues in the second case will be.

As an intuitive matter, which, if either, of these cases should be in federal court? Why? Now consider how the following case affects the answers to those questions.

Louisville & Nashville Railroad v. Mottley
211 U.S. 149 (1908)

[The Mottleys were injured in a railway accident. To settle their claims, the railroad in 1871 gave them a lifetime pass good for free transportation on the line. Several decades later, Congress, believing that railroads were using free transportation to bribe public officials, made free passes unlawful. The railroad thereupon refused to honor the Mottleys' passes, citing the new federal legislation. The Mottleys sued in federal court seeking specific performance of their contract. "The bill [, that is the complaint,] further alleges: First, that the act of Congress referred to does not prohibit the giving of passes under the circumstances of this case; and, second, that if the law is to be construed as prohibiting such passes, it is in conflict with the Fifth Amendment of the constitution, because it deprives the plaintiffs of their property without due process of law. The defendant demurred to the bill." [The federal trial court overruled the demurrer and granted the Mottleys the relief they had requested. Defendant railroad appealed to the Supreme Court.]

Mr. Justice MOODY . . . delivered the opinion of the court.

Two questions of law were raised by the demurrer to the bill, were brought here by appeal, and have been argued before us. They are, first, whether that part of the act of Congress of June 29, 1906 (34 Stat. 584), which forbids the giving of free passes or the collection of any different compensation for transportation of passengers than that specified in the tariff filed, makes it unlawful to perform a contract for transportation of persons, who in good faith, before the passage of the act, had accepted such contract in satisfaction of a valid cause of action against the railroad; and, second, whether the statute, if it should be construed to render such a contract unlawful, is in violation of the Fifth Amendment of the Constitution of the United States. We do not deem it necessary, however, to consider either of these questions, because, in our opinion, the court below was without jurisdiction of the cause. Neither party has questioned that jurisdiction, but it is the duty of this court to see to it that the jurisdiction of the Circuit Court, which is defined and limited by statute, is not exceeded. This duty we have frequently performed of our own motion.

There was no diversity of citizenship and it is not and cannot be suggested that there was any ground of jurisdiction, except that the case was a "suit . . . arising under the Constitution and laws of the United States.", [Citing the "arising under" jurisdiction statute.] It is the settled interpretation of these words, as used in this statute, conferring jurisdiction, that a suit arises under the Constitution and laws of the United States only when the plaintiff's statement of his own cause of action shows that it is based upon those laws or that Constitution. It is not enough that the plaintiff alleges some anticipated defense to his cause of action and asserts that the defense is invalidated by some provision of the Constitution of the United States. Although such allegations show that very likely, in the course of the litigation, a question under the Constitution would arise, they do not show that the suit, that is, the plaintiff's original cause of action, arises under the Constitution. In Tennessee v. Union & Planters' Bank, 152 U.S. 454, the plaintiff, the State of Tennessee, brought suit in the Circuit Court of the United States to recover from the defendant certain taxes alleged to be due under the laws of the State. The plaintiff alleged that the defendant claimed an immunity from the taxation by virtue of its charter, and that therefore the tax was void, because in violation of the provision of the Constitution of the United States, which forbids any State from passing a law impairing the obligation of contracts. The cause was held to be beyond the jurisdiction of the Circuit Court, the court saying, by Mr. Justice Gray, "a suggestion of one party, that the other will or may set up a claim under the Constitution or laws of the United States, does not make the suit one arising under that Constitution or those laws." Again, in Boston & Montana Consolidated Copper & Silver Mining Company v. Montana Ore Purchasing Company, 188 U.S. 632, the . . . cause was held to be beyond the jurisdiction of the Circuit Court, the court saying, by Mr. Justice Peckham:

> It would be wholly unnecessary and improper in order to prove complainant's cause of action to go into any matters of defence which the defendants might possibly set up and then attempt to reply to such defence, and thus, if possible, to show that a Federal question might or probably would arise in the course of the trial of the case. To allege such defence and then make an answer to it before the defendant has the opportunity to itself plead or prove its own defence is inconsistent with any known rule of pleading so far as we are aware, and is improper.
>
> The rule is a reasonable and just one that the complainant in the first instance shall be confined to a statement of its cause of action, leaving to

the defendant to set up in his answer what his defence is and, if anything more than a denial of complainant's cause of action, imposing upon the defendant the burden of proving such defence.

Conforming itself to that rule the complainant would not, in the assertion or proof of its cause of action, bring up a single Federal question. The presentation of its cause of action would not show that it was one arising under the Constitution or laws of the United States.   •

The only way in which it might be claimed that a Federal question was presented would be in the complainant's statement of what the defence of defendants would be and complainant's answer to such defence. Under these circumstances the case is brought within the rule laid down in Tennessee v. Union & Planters' Bank, 152 U.S. 454. That case has been cited and approved many times since. . . .

. . . The application of this rule to the case at bar is decisive against the jurisdiction of the circuit court.

It is ordered that the judgment be reversed and the case remitted to the circuit court with instructions to dismiss for want of jurisdiction.

NOTES AND PROBLEMS

1. Explain why the federal trial court lacked jurisdiction.

a. How did the federal issue arise in *Mottley*?

b. Look back at the two hypothetical cases in the text preceding *Mottley*. Under the principle applied in *Mottley*, which case will "arise under" federal law?

2. Who raised the question of federal jurisdiction in *Mottley*?

a. If both parties were prepared to argue the merits of the case, how could a court justify dismissal on a ground unrelated to those merits? See Federal Rule 12(h)(3) for another example of the importance federal courts attach to their subject matter jurisdiction.

b. After suffering dismissal in the Supreme Court, the Mottleys refiled their suit in state court; it again made its way to the U.S. Supreme Court. The Mottleys lost again, this time on the merits. 219 U.S. 467 (1911). Is this any way to run either a railroad or a judicial system? Before answering, consider the next two notes.

3. *Mottley* represents one rather rigid approach to a difficult problem. Can one justify this approach? An enormous number of claims have some federal ingredient in their background. For example, as Charles Wright points out, land title in most western states can be traced back to U.S. land grants. Wright, Federal Courts 102. Large numbers of checks clear through federal reserve banks. Does every question of land title or

every suit on a bad check arise under federal law? If one answers that question "no," then one has to find a principled way of sorting claims in which federal questions have some central importance from those in which they are merely background assumptions.

Mottley chooses to sort roughly, based on the pleadings. That choice has at least one important advantage: It permits the sorting to occur at the opening of the lawsuit before the parties and court have invested much time. To see the force of this point, consider the opposite extreme: One could, theoretically, postpone a decision on jurisdiction until after trial, to see whether an important question of federal law had emerged, and dismiss if it had not. Not too surprisingly, not even the fiercest critic of *Mottley* has suggested taking things this far.

There are also some disadvantages to the *Mottley* approach. First, one eliminates cases, like *Mottley* itself, in which the central issue of federal law was a defense rather than a part of the plaintiff's claim. Second, the rule may make less sense now than it did when framed. In 1908, pleadings (under either common law or code pleading regimes, discussed in Chapter VI) required considerably more detail than do the Federal Rules. Under the current notice pleading regime, in some cases it may be quite difficult to apply the approach used in *Mottley*.

4. It is clear that the restrictive reading *Mottley* (and numerous other cases) gives to "arising under" is not constitutionally required. Why? After all, both Article III and §1331 speak of cases "arising under" federal law; how could that phrase mean different things in the Constitution and in the statute? It is not possible to give an entirely satisfying answer to that question, but the Supreme Court in several cases has said that the meaning of "arising under" in Article III is broader than the same phrase in §1331. The different constitutional and statutory constructions of "arising under" have several implications.

a. Because the constitutional meaning of "arising under" is broader than its statutory meaning, the Supreme Court (operating under the broader constitutional definition) had jurisdiction to hear and decide *Mottley* the second time around, even though it previously decided that the district court (operating under the narrower statutory definition) did not have jurisdiction.

b. As a further corollary, Congress could change the result in *Mottley* by amending §1331. It might, for example, provide that the district courts have original jurisdiction over cases "in which an essential element either of a claim or defense rests on federal law." Should Congress do so?

5. When a defendant challenges federal question jurisdiction, one of three questions commonly arises:

a. Is there a federal issue at all? If the plaintiff's claim is based on some federal statute or regulation, the problem consists in interpreting legislation. If the plaintiff claims the right to relief under federal common law, the question is whether such federal common law exists. As we will see in Chapter IV, the scope of federal common law is less extensive than that of state common law.

b. Assuming there is a federal issue, does it "give rise to" plaintiff's claim? That is the question in *Mottley.*

c. If there is a federal issue that is not, strictly speaking, part of the basis for plaintiff's claim, is it sufficiently important to "federalize" the case?

6. *Mottley's* bright-line test suggests that the answer to 5c is simple: No. But alongside this broad and tightly channeled main stream flows a narrow and meandering rivulet. In this second line of cases the federal courts have assumed "arising under" jurisdiction on the basis of something less — or different — than a claim depending on federal law.

a. Smith v. Kansas City Title & Trust Co., 255 U.S. 180 (1921), is the poster child of this more expansive view. In *Smith* the plaintiff alleged that the defendant bank had violated a state law allowing it to invest only in legal securities. Thus stated, the suit would seem to arise entirely under state law. But the allegedly "illegal" securities were bonds issued by a federal agency under a federal law that plaintiff claimed was unconstitutional. Held: "arising under" jurisdiction. Is *Mottley* distinguishable?

b. With *Smith* contrast T.B. Harms Co. v. Eliscu, 339 F.2d 823 (2d Cir. 1964), another well-known case in the *Mottley* tradition, which beautifully summarizes the problem:

A layman would doubtless be surprised to learn that an action wherein the purported sole owner of a [federal] copyright alleged that persons claiming partial ownership had recorded their claim in the Copyright Office and had warned his licensees against disregarding their interests was not one "arising under any Act of Congress relating to copyrights" over which 28 U.S.C. §1338 gives the federal courts exclusive jurisdiction. Yet precedents going back for more than a century teach that lesson and lead us to affirm Judge Weinfeld's dismissal of the complaint.

The litigation concerns four copyrighted songs[, but the issue raised by the complaint was not whether the copyright had been infringed — a federal question — but whether the owner of the copyright had assigned it to another — a question of property and contract arising under state law.] Defendants moved to dismiss the complaint for failure to state a claim on which relief can be granted and for lack of federal jurisdiction; voluminous affidavits were submitted. The district court dismissed the complaint for want of federal jurisdiction. . . .

. . . [T]he jurisdictional statute does not speak in terms of infringement, and the undoubted truth that a claim for infringement "arises under" the Copyright Act does not establish that nothing else can. Simply as a matter of language, the statutory phrasing would not compel the conclusion that an action to determine who owns a copyright does not arise under the

Copyright Act, which creates the federal copyright with an implied right
to license and an explicit right to assign. But the gloss afforded by history
and good sense leads to that conclusion as to the complaint in this
case. . . .

Just as with western land titles, the federal grant of a patent or copyright
has not been thought to infuse with any national interest a dispute as to
ownership or contractual enforcement turning on the facts or on ordinary
principles of contract law. Indeed, the case for an unexpansive reading of
the provision conferring exclusive jurisdiction with respect to patents and
copyrights has been especially strong since expansion would entail depriving the state courts of any jurisdiction over matters having so little federal significance.

In an endeavor to explain precisely what suits arose under the patent
and copyright laws, Mr. Justice Holmes stated that "(a) suit arises under
the law that creates the cause of action"; in the case sub judice, injury to
a business involving slander of a patent, he said, "whether it is a wrong
or not depends upon the law of the State where the act is done" so that
the suit did not arise under the patent laws. American Well Works Co. v.
Layne & Bowler Co., 241 U.S. 257, 260 (1916). . . .

Having thus found that appropriate pleading of a pivotal question of
federal law may suffice to give federal jurisdiction even for a "state-created"
claim, we cannot halt at questions hinging only on the language of the
Copyright Act. For a new and dynamic doctrine, taking its name from
Clearfield Trust Co. v. United States, 318 U.S. 363 (1943), instructs us
that even in the absence of express statute, federal law may govern what
might seem an issue of local law because the federal interest is dominant.
Sola Elec. Co. v. Jefferson Elec. Co., 317 U.S. 173 (1942), is relevant
here, not only for its holding that the radiations of the antitrust laws
governed an estoppel question in a patent license case but also for the
Court's unwillingness to say whether the estoppel rule would have been
"local" or "federal" even if the antitrust laws had not been invoked. If
this "federal common law" governed some disputed aspect of a claim to
ownership of a copyright or for the enforcement of a license, federal
jurisdiction might follow . . . . But there is not the slightest reason to
think that any legal question presented by Harms' complaint falls in the
shadow of a federal interest suggested by the Copyright Act or any other
source. . . .

c. What's going on in the "broader" Smith line of cases? One way of
explaining is to say that the courts thought the federal law interests were
very important. How important? A monumentally important case with a
federal ingredient will likely make its way to the Supreme Court, which,
you'll recall, has a broader "arising under" jurisdiction than do the district
courts. But the Supreme Court hears only about a hundred cases a year,
so as a practical matter most federal interests litigated in state courts have

little chance of federal review. The battle in the statutory "arising under" cases is fought over which federal interest cases should be heard in federal trial and intermediate appellate courts. One thoughtful analysis puts the question like this:

> Federal issues might be raised in a large number of cases, but the claimants of federal rights are often wrong in their view that federal law protects them. They would therefore lose on the federal issue, and they could win only on state law grounds. If "arising under" were interpreted expansively, many cases in federal court on the basis of "arising under" jurisdiction would be disposed of on state law grounds. . . . What is needed is a test that will screen out cases in which federal interests are unlikely to be strongly implicated. Can the following considerations be combined to produce a "test"? (i) What is the national interest in disposing of the case as a whole — with federal fact-finding [in the district courts] — in the federal courts, as compared to the interest of disposing it in the state courts? (ii) How likely is it that the national interest will in fact be implicated? (iii) How likely is it that the Supreme Court will use its limited resources to decide the federal issue where the record is made in the state court?

Howard Fink & Mark Tushnet, Federal Jurisdiction: Policy and Practice 473 (1984). Recall that these questions — if these are the right questions — must be decided at a very early stage, with nothing more than the pleadings before the court, and you will understand why courts and scholars have struggled over the question for a century.

7. As you will see in Chapter V, under the federal Declaratory Judgment Act, 28 U.S.C. §§2201-2202, the federal courts are empowered to hear certain cases in which a potential defendant seeks not a coercive remedy but a declaration of rights. Thus, for example, an insurance company might seek a declaration of nonliability under an insurance contract. How does one apply the well-pleaded complaint rule to such cases? The question is made more difficult by a well-established understanding that the Declaratory Judgment Act did not expand the jurisdiction of the federal courts.

a. Some cases are simple. Suppose a patent-holder believes that a competing business is infringing his patent. He could sue for damages or file an injunction, and such a suit would "arise under" federal law. Believing that proof of damages or of the requisites for injunctive relief would be expensive to prove, he simply sues for a declaration that the competitor is infringing his patent. The claim for relief arises under federal law.

b. Reverse the situation. This time Competitor sues, seeking a declaration that she is not infringing the patent, perhaps so she can convince a bank or investor to give her funds to expand her factory. It's well established that a federal district court has jurisdiction to hear Competitor's claim for relief. Wright, Federal Courts 111. Why? Before the Declaratory Judgment Act, the suit couldn't have been brought in federal district court; if we now say there is federal jurisdiction, haven't we allowed the Act to expand federal question jurisdiction? The standard answer is that the exact issue — patent validity and scope — could have been tried, although in a suit brought by the patent-holder, so the Act isn't really "expanding" jurisdiction. This approach reverses the normal "plaintiff" and "defendant" labels, asking whether the federal court would have had jurisdiction if the defendant had brought a coercive suit in the declaratory action.

c. Now a harder case. Suppose "a party seeks a declaration that it is immune, by virtue of federal law, from a nonfederal claim that the other party may have." Wright, Federal Courts 112. For example, imagine that the Louisville & Nashville Railroad had brought a declaratory action against the Mottleys (seeking a declaration that their refusal of passage was lawful). Would that action have been within the jurisdiction of the federal courts? As Professor Wright puts it,

> On the narrow view [the railroad] could not, for absent the declaratory procedure, the federal claim would arise only as a defense to the passholders' [state law] action for breach of contract, and the only possible coercive action, that by the Mottleys for specific performance, would raise no federal question. The broader view would permit the declaratory action since in that suit the railroad's federal claim of an immunity to the [state law] action would appear on the face of the railroad's complaint.

Wright, Federal Courts 111. After some struggle, the Supreme Court appears to have taken the narrower view, though conceding that it reached its view "for reasons involving perhaps more history than logic. . . ." Franchise Tax Board v. Construction Laborers Vacation Trust for Southern California, 463 U.S. 1, 4 (1983).

8. A case can start out as a federal case, but after a judgment or settlement lose its federal status.

a. Plaintiffs sue defendants on a claim arising under federal law. The parties then settle the case by signing an agreement. The case is dismissed in an order that makes no reference to the settlement agreement. Plaintiff then sues defendant for violation of the agreement. Is there federal question jurisdiction? The Fourth Circuit ruled "no" in Fairfax Countywide Citizens Association v. County of Fairfax, 571 F.2d 1299 (4th Cir.), cert. denied, 439 U.S. 1047 (1978). The settlement agreement is an ordinary contract, whose breach does not arise under federal law. But if the agreement were embodied in the court's judgment of dismissal, its breach would arise under federal law, because federal courts have jurisdiction to enforce their own judgments. What should plaintiff have done to ensure continuing federal jurisdiction over the settlement?

b. Sally borrowed money from Frank, giving him a mortgage as security. She then declared bankruptcy, and, in a federal bankruptcy proceeding, Frank's interest was transferred to Joe. (Recall that there is exclusive federal jurisdiction over bankruptcy.) Through an error, however, the transfer to Joe was never properly recorded. Frank now sues Joe, alleging that he still holds a mortgage on the property. Joe seeks to remove the case to federal district court, arguing that Frank's lawsuit calls into question the validity of the federal bankruptcy judgment and thus "arises under" federal law. Held: No, in Rivet v. Regions Bank, 522 U.S. 470 (1998) (claim preclusion based on a prior federal judgment is a defense, so the claim does not arise under federal law, citing *Mottley*).

NOTE: CHALLENGING FEDERAL SUBJECT MATTER JURISDICTION

Suppose you represent a defendant in a case filed in federal court and you think that there isn't a basis for federal subject matter jurisdiction. How do you get the court to dismiss the case? The obvious answer seems to be to make a motion under Rule 12(b)(1), asserting the absence of federal subject matter jurisdiction. In diversity cases the obvious method is also the correct method. In federal question cases there is a special twist, however. Because "arising under" jurisdiction depends on the substance of the plaintiff's claim, one can think of the challenge as attacking either the *claim* (there's no federal claim, therefore no federal jurisdiction) or jurisdiction (there's no jurisdiction *because* there's no claim arising under federal law). In fact, the Court has said that if there's any arguable basis for a federal claim, the district court should examine the federal question not as a matter of jurisdiction but on a Rule 12(b)(6) motion to dismiss the substantive claim. Why does it matter how that question is decided?

Bell v. Hood, 327 U.S. 67, 939 (1946), is often taken as indicating that if a complaint comes close enough to presenting a federal claim that the court has trouble in deciding that it doesn't, dismissal of that claim should be for "failure to state a claim upon which relief can be granted" rather than for lack of jurisdiction. . . . The only apparent consequence of Bell v. Hood as applied to this case is that if the complaint is close enough to the line to give "jurisdiction," the court may have power to adjudicate a "pendent" or "ancillary" state claim. But a federal court need not try such a state claim when the non-existence of the federal claim has been determined on motion prior to trial on the merits — and the case against its doing so is particularly strong when, as here, a prior suit for the same relief is pending in a state court.

T.B. Harms v. Eliscu, 339 F.2d 823, 828-829 (1964). Pendent and ancillary jurisdiction are now subsumed under the concept of supplemental jurisdiction, discussed later in this chapter.

But suppose that the defendant does not move to dismiss under either Rule 12(b)(2) or 12(b)(6). Is jurisdiction waived? No: As *Mottley* demonstrates, and Note 2, supra, also points out, the requirement of subject matter jurisdiction is held to be so fundamental that a court is required to raise the issue *sua sponte* (on the court's own motion) and dismiss if it finds a lack of jurisdiction. Moreover, the case must be dismissed even if the lack of jurisdiction is discovered for the first time at the appellate stage. Thus, in Capron v. Van Noorden, 6 U.S. 126 (1804), plaintiff sued defendant in federal court and lost. On appeal in the Supreme Court (there was no court of appeals at the time), plaintiff suggested a lack of jurisdiction because of lack of diversity. The Supreme Court dismissed the case, leaving the plaintiff free to bring suit in state court (assuming that the statute of limitations had not yet run).

With *Capron* contrast Caterpillar, Inc. v. Lewis, infra page 252. Lewis sued Caterpillar for personal injuries, invoking diversity jurisdiction. At the start of the suit there were nondiverse parties. Caterpillar nevertheless removed, over Lewis's objection, but the district court erroneously ruled that there was diversity jurisdiction. During pretrial proceedings the nondiverse parties settled and thus vanished from the party configuration. After losing at trial, Lewis renewed his objections to jurisdiction. The Supreme Court affirmed Caterpillar's trial court victory. True, Lewis should have prevailed in seeking to have the case remanded to state court, but by the time the trial occurred there was diversity; the values of efficiency and finality overcame the validity of Lewis's timely objections. Explain how one can distinguish *Capron* and *Caterpillar*.

In one respect *Capron* and *Caterpillar* agree: Both treat challenges to subject matter jurisdiction in a way that differs sharply from personal jurisdiction. On one hand, personal jurisdiction may be waived by failing to raise it at the threshold of litigation: Imagine the outcome in *Capron* if the objection to personal jurisdiction had been raised for the first time on appeal. On the other hand, Lewis, the defendant in *Caterpillar*, would have won on appeal had his challenge been to personal jurisdiction. Does the difference in treatment make sense? Consider the differences in the values protected by personal and subject matter jurisdiction.

Given draconian rules about the nonwaivability of federal subject matter jurisdiction, one might ask if it would be easy to mount a collateral attack on a judgment alleged to be without federal jurisdiction. In fact, the answer is "probably not," though the few cases that have dealt with this question have not been resolved consistently. Moreover, the legal principles have been slowly evolving. In 1940, First Restatement of Judgments took the position that collateral attack was presumptively available. In 1982 the Restatement (Second) Judgments took the position collateral attack was presumptively unavailable — justified only by special circumstances. To get a feel for the problem, consider three situations: (1) defendant appears, challenges subject matter jurisdiction and loses; (2) defendant appears, fails to challenge subject matter jurisdiction, and loses on the merits; (3) defendant defaults.

Parties who appear, challenge the subject matter jurisdiction of a federal court, and lose are bound by that determination; just as with personal jurisdiction, they may not thereafter challenge the judgment in a second action. Stoll v. Gottlieb, 305 U.S. 165 (1938).

Similarly, and again as with personal jurisdiction, parties who have appeared but failed to challenge the subject matter jurisdiction of a district court may *generally* not thereafter attack its judgment in another court, state or federal, for lack of diversity or federal question jurisdiction. Chicot County Drainage District v. Baxter State Bank, 308 U.S. 371 (1939); Durfee v. Duke (infra, page 872). To this general principle the Supreme Court has also added an exception of indeterminate size. In the same term in which the Supreme Court decided *Chicot County Drainage District* came Kalb v. Feuerstein, 308 U.S. 433 (1940). *Kalb* held that a state court foreclosure proceeding against a farmer during the pendency of federal bankruptcy proceedings was not binding on the federal court because Congress had divested the state courts of jurisdiction. The result would follow, the Court indicated, even if the jurisdictional issue had been litigated in the state court in favor of that court's jurisdiction. This allowance of collateral attack, the Court said, was simply an application of legislative intent: Congress had meant to permit such collateral challenges to foreclosure proceedings. The difficulty arises because Congress had not in so many words decreed that result; it was rather implied from the general circumstances of the legislation.

What about defendants who entirely default? Were they objecting to personal jurisdiction, they would be entitled to attack collaterally under the doctrine of *Pennoyer*. May they collaterally attack subject matter jurisdiction in the same way? Here one cannot be certain. If one extends *Chicot County Drainage District*, one concludes that collateral attack is not available — that a party wishing to challenge subject matter jurisdiction must appear. *Kalb*, however, points in the opposite direction: A party who had appeared (in the foreclosure proceeding) was nevertheless able to raise a collateral challenge. To be sure, *Kalb* involved a statute that, as the Court saw things, permitted collateral challenge. The only entirely safe statement is that the Court has not clearly resolved that question. As one commentator put it:

> The proverbial case involves a justice of the peace who has undertaken to grant a divorce [thus clearly overstepping his jurisdictional power]. [W]ould [one] require the respondent in such a case to appear before the justice under penalty that otherwise the divorce would be legally valid [?] I cannot believe that any court would hold that.

Geoffrey C. Hazard, Jr., Revisiting the Second Restatement of Judgments: Issue Preclusion and Related Problems, 66 Cornell L. Rev. 564, 591 (1981).

Finally, what about defendants who combine challenges to subject matter and personal jurisdiction? If either challenge is well-founded, the case will be dismissed. But a dismissal will have different consequences for a refiled suit, depending on which ground is used for dismissal. If a case is dismissed for want of federal subject matter jurisdiction, a plaintiff is free to refile the suit in state court. If dismissed for want of personal jurisdiction, a plaintiff is precluded from refiling in state court because the federal court's decision that personal jurisdiction is lacking will bind the state court under the principles of issue preclusion. Under those circumstances, should a federal court faced with motions to dismiss on both grounds always take subject matter jurisdiction first, because that will have the narrowest subsequent effect? No, the Supreme Court has said; the discretion of a trial court to handle its docket allows it to dismiss for want of personal jurisdiction if that is the most obvious ground. Ruhrgas AG v. Marathon Oil Co., 119 S. Ct. 1653 (1999).

C.   Diversity Jurisdiction

Diversity jurisdiction was among the earliest congressional grants to the lower federal courts. The underlying justification, however, has remained obscure, and the grant has come under considerable attack. The following excerpt from a congressional committee report sums up the standard learning.

> Federal diversity of citizenship jurisdiction is made possible by Article III of the Constitution which was drafted to permit, but not mandate, Federal court jurisdiction based on "controversies between citizens of different States" and "between a State, or the citizens thereof, and foreign States, citizens or subjects." The framers did not make this grant self-executing.

Article III also provides that "the judicial power of the United States shall be vested in one Supreme Court, and in such inferior courts as the Congress may from time to time ordain and establish."

Thus, Federal court jurisdiction is almost entirely permissive. The Constitution does not mandate the creation of inferior Federal courts and it clearly granted the power to decide whether, and to what extent, there should be diversity jurisdiction.

The debates of the Constitutional Convention are unclear as to why the Constitution made provision for such jurisdiction; nor is pertinent legislative history much aid as to why the First Congress exercised its prerogative to vest diversity jurisdiction in the Federal courts.

Many legal scholars who have researched this issue have concluded that it was based on a fear that State courts would be biased or prejudiced against those from out of State. A minority view is that the Nation's early lawmakers shared misgivings as to whether at least some of the State courts would be fair to the interests of creditors, out-of-staters or in-staters. Another position is that, the Federal courts being better than the State, it was preferable to route as many cases into the former as possible.

Abolition of Diversity of Citizenship Jurisdiction, H.R. Rep. No. 893, 95th Cong., 2d Sess. 2 (1978). In the midst of this uncertainty about the basis for diversity jurisdiction, courts must nevertheless decide whether it exists. The next two cases demonstrate some of the problems.

Mas v. Perry

489 F.2d 1396 (5th Cir. 1974)

AINSWORTH, J.

This case presents questions pertaining to federal diversity jurisdiction under 28 U.S.C. §1332, which, pursuant to article III, section II of the Constitution, provides for original jurisdiction in federal district courts of all civil actions that are between, inter alia, citizens of different States or citizens of a State and citizens of foreign states and in which the amount in controversy [requirement is satisfied.*]

Appellees Jean Paul Mas, a citizen of France, and Judy Mas were married at her home in Jackson, Mississippi. Prior to their marriage, Mr. and Mrs. Mas were graduate assistants, pursuing coursework as well as performing teaching duties, for approximately nine months and one year, respectively, at Louisiana State University in Baton Rouge, Louisiana. Shortly after their marriage, they returned to Baton Rouge to resume their duties as graduate assistants at LSU. They remained in Baton Rouge

---

* [The statutory amount has risen over time: When Mas v. Perry was decided it was $10,000; currently it is $75,000 — ED]

for approximately two more years, after which they moved to Park Ridge, Illinois. At the time of the trial in this case, it was their intention to return to Baton Rouge while Mr. Mas finished his studies for the degree of Doctor of Philosophy. Mr. and Mrs. Mas were undecided as to where they would reside after that.

Upon their return to Baton Rouge after their marriage, appellees rented an apartment from appellant Oliver H. Perry, a citizen of Louisiana. This appeal arises from a final judgment entered on a jury verdict awarding $5,000 to Mr. Mas and $15,000 to Mrs. Mas for damages incurred by them as a result of the discovery that their bedroom and bathroom contained "two-way" mirrors and that they had been watched through them by the appellant during three of the first four months of their marriage.

At the close of the appellees' case at trial, appellant made an oral motion to dismiss for lack of jurisdiction. The motion was denied by the district court. Before this Court, appellant challenges the final judgment below solely on jurisdictional grounds, contending that appellees failed to prove diversity of citizenship among the parties and that the requisite jurisdictional amount is lacking with respect to Mr. Mas. Finding no merit to these contentions, we affirm. Under section 1332(a)(2), the federal judicial power extends to the claim of Mr. Mas, a citizen of France, against the appellant, a citizen of Louisiana. Since we conclude that Mrs. Mas is a citizen of Mississippi for diversity purposes, the district court also properly had jurisdiction under section 1332(a)(1) of her claim.

It has long been the general rule that complete diversity of parties is required in order that diversity jurisdiction obtain; that is, no party on one side may be a citizen of the same State as any party on the other side. Strawbridge v. Curtiss, 7 U.S. 267 (1806). This determination of one's State citizenship for diversity purposes is controlled by federal law, not by the law of any State. As is the case in other areas of federal jurisdiction, the diverse citizenship among adverse parties must be present at the time the complaint is filed. Jurisdiction is unaffected by subsequent changes in the citizenship of the parties. The burden of pleading the diverse citizenship is upon the party invoking federal jurisdiction, and if the diversity jurisdiction is properly challenged, that party also bears the burden of proof. To be a citizen of a State within the meaning of section 1332, a natural person must be both a citizen of the United States and a domiciliary of that State. For diversity purposes, citizenship means domicile; mere residence in the State is not sufficient.

A person's domicile is the place of "his true, fixed, and permanent home and principal establishment, and to which he has the intention of returning whenever he is absent therefrom. . . ." A change of domicile may be effected only by a combination of two elements: (a) taking up residence in a different domicile with (b) the intention to remain there.

It is clear that at the time of her marriage, Mrs. Mas was a domiciliary of the State of Mississippi. While it is generally the case that the domicile of the wife — and, consequently, her State citizenship for purposes of diversity jurisdiction — is deemed to be that of her husband, we find no precedent for extending this concept to the situation here, in which the husband is a citizen of a foreign state but resides in the United States. Indeed, such a fiction would work absurd results on the facts before us. If Mr. Mas were considered a domiciliary of France — as he would be since he had lived in Louisiana as a student-teaching assistant prior to filing this suit — then Mrs. Mas would also be deemed a domiciliary [of France] and thus . . . would not be a citizen of any State and could not sue in a federal court on that basis; nor could she invoke the alienage jurisdiction to bring her claim in federal court, since she is not an alien. On the other hand, if Mrs. Mas's domicile were Louisiana, she would become a Louisiana citizen for diversity purposes and could not bring suit with her husband against appellant, also a Louisiana citizen, on the basis of diversity jurisdiction. These are curious results under a rule arising from the theoretical identity of person and interest of the married couple.

An American woman is not deemed to have lost her United States citizenship solely by reason of her marriage to an alien. 8 U.S.C. §1489. Similarly, we conclude that for diversity purposes a woman does not have her domicile or State citizenship changed solely by reason of her marriage to an alien.

Mrs. Mas's Mississippi domicile was disturbed neither by her year in Louisiana prior to her marriage nor as a result of the time she and her husband spent at LSU after their marriage, since for both periods she was a graduate assistant at LSU. Though she testified that after her marriage she had no intention of returning to her parents' home in Mississippi, Mrs. Mas did not effect a change of domicile since she and Mr. Mas were in Louisiana only as students and lacked the requisite intention to remain there. Until she acquires a new domicile, she remains a domiciliary, and thus a citizen, of Mississippi.[2] . . .

2. The original complaint in this case was filed within several days of Mr. and Mrs. Mas's realization that they had been watched through mirrors, quite some time before they moved to Park Ridge, Illinois. Because the district court's jurisdiction is not affected by actions of the parties subsequent to the commencement of the suit, the testimony concerning Mr. and Mrs. Mas's moves after that time is not determinative of the issue of diverse citizenship, though it is of interest so far as it supports their lack of intent to remain permanently in Louisiana.

Thus the power of the federal district court to entertain the claims of appellees in this case stands on two separate legs of diversity jurisdiction: a claim by an alien against a State citizen; and an action between citizens of different States. We also note, however, the propriety of having the federal district court entertain a spouse's action against a defendant, where the district court already has jurisdiction over a claim, arising from the same transaction, by the other spouse against the same defendant. In the case before us, such a result is particularly desirable. The claims of Mr. and Mrs. Mas arise from the same operative facts, and there was almost complete interdependence between their claims with respect to the proof required and the issues raised at trial. Thus, since the district court had jurisdiction of Mr. Mas's action, sound judicial administration militates strongly in favor of federal jurisdiction of Mrs. Mas's claim.

Affirmed.

NOTES AND PROBLEMS

1. Start by supposing that Jean-Paul Mas alone sued Oliver Perry.

a. Does §1332 grant the district court jurisdiction over such a case?

b. What would be the theory underlying that jurisdiction?

c. How might the last sentence in §1332(a) affect Jean-Paul Mas? What additional information would one want to have?

2. Now suppose that Judy Mas alone had sued Oliver Perry.

a. Before she went to college she was clearly a citizen of Mississippi.

b. But then she left home, went across the river to school, presumably attained the age of majority, and married. How does the court avoid the conclusion that she had become a citizen of Louisiana? Can one reconcile the ruling in Mas with Gordon v. Steele in Chapter I?

c. In a context other than diversity, the rule that a woman's domicile is that of her husband has been ruled unconstitutional when it operates to deprive her of the right to hold a job with the government of a county in which she claimed to be domiciled but in which her husband was not domiciled. The rule was said to operate whether the couple was living apart or "happily married." Brathol v. Milwaukee County, 4 Fam. L. Rep. 2538 (Wis. Cir. Ct. 1978).

3. Now put the hypothetical cases in Notes 1 and 2 together. Jean-Paul and Judy Mas both sue Perry.

a. Why is there a problem?

b. Why isn't it clear that the court has jurisdiction under §1332(a)(2)?

4. The hinge on which Mas turns is the "rule of complete diversity." Although 28 U.S.C. §1332 does not by its terms require that each plaintiff

be diverse from each defendant, that interpretation was attached to the predecessor statute by Chief Justice Marshall in Strawbridge v. Curtiss, 7 U.S. 267 (1806).

a. Some question remained after *Strawbridge* as to whether the constitutional language of Article III, from which the statutory language was taken, required the same interpretation. It is now settled that the Constitution, as opposed to §1332, requires only minimal diversity, that is, at least one claimant diverse in citizenship from another. State Farm v. Tashire, 386 U.S. 523 (1967). The principle matters in applying statutes not requiring complete diversity—for example, the Federal Interpleader Act, 28 U.S.C. §1335.

b. In 1990 Congress enacted 28 U.S.C. §1367, providing for "supplemental" jurisdiction as extensive as that allowed by Article III. Read §1367(a) and (b). Does the text of these sections allow one to argue that they repeal the rule of complete diversity in some cases? The relatively brief legislative history does not suggest that Congress meant to achieve such a result; did it inadvertently do so?

5. Does—and should—the rule of complete diversity apply to aliens as well as to citizens of U.S. states?

a. It is clear that there is no diversity jurisdiction in a suit between a citizen of Mexico and a citizen of Japan; it simply doesn't fall within any of the categories of §1332.

b. It is equally clear that there is diversity jurisdiction over a suit in which a citizen of California sues citizens of Mexico and Japan—or in which those citizens sue the citizen of California. §1332(a)(2).

c. Similarly, there is diversity jurisdiction when a citizen of California and a citizen of Mexico sue a citizen of New York and a citizen of Japan. See §1332(a)(3).

d. Finally, suppose things are as in the preceding problem, and the citizen of New York drops out. At that point a citizen of California and a citizen of Mexico are suing a citizen of Japan. The case no longer falls within §1332(a); do you see why? Should diversity jurisdiction extend to this situation? In what might be called a strong dictum, the Supreme Court has suggested not. Ruhrgas AG v. Marathon Oil, 119 S. Ct. 1563 (1999) ("Marathon joined an alien plaintiff (Norge) as well as an alien defendant (Ruhrgas). If the joinder of Norge is legitimate, the complete diversity required by 28 U.S.C. S 1332 (1994 ed. and Supp. III), but not by Article III, . . . is absent.").

6. If the *Mas* court had concluded that Mrs. Mas was not of diverse citizenship, would the entire case have had to be dismissed? Newman-Green, Inc. v. Alfonzo-Larrain, 490 U.S. 826 (1989), permitted a court to retain jurisdiction by dismissing a party not held to be indispensable.

See Rule 19 and infra page 928: Could the court have permitted the case to proceed with only Mr. Mas as a plaintiff?

d. A quick reading of the diversity statute might suggest that everyone and every entity falls into one of its categories — a citizen of a state, a citizen of a foreign country, a foreign country, etc. In fact, U.S. citizens permanently domiciled abroad are neither citizens of a state nor citizens of foreign countries, and therefore cannot sue or be sued under the diversity jurisdiction rules. Newman-Greene, Inc. v. Alfonzo-Lorrain, supra Note 4c. What does this tell us about the function of diversity jurisdiction?

7. For diversity purposes, partnerships are not considered as entities but as collections of individuals; thus the citizenship of each of the members of a partnership must be considered. In a state court the State of Wisconsin sues a New York law firm for malpractice. The defendant firm would like to remove to federal court, where it believes that a jury pool drawn from a wider area will be more sympathetic to its defense. The firm, with more than 250 partners, has no offices and no partners in Wisconsin but has several U.S. offices and several located overseas. Each of these overseas offices has at least one U.S. citizen partner assigned to it. What issue will determine whether defendant can invoke diversity jurisdiction to remove to federal court?

8. Beyond the requirement of complete diversity, the other principal difficulty presented by diversity jurisdiction has to do with determining the citizenship of a corporation. The rules for determining such citizenship for diversity purposes are set out in 28 U.S.C. §1332(c).

a. The corporation has dual citizenship: where it is incorporated and where it has its chief place of business. The purpose of the dual citizenship is to prevent what Congress thought were essentially local state claims between a citizen and a local corporation, incorporated elsewhere for convenience, from burdening the federal courts. Many corporations incorporate under the law of a state deemed to have more permissive corporation laws than those of the state of their chief place of business. Delaware, for example, is more often the legal "home" of corporations than is their chief place of business.

b. The chief place of business of a corporation is said to be a question of fact. Though there can be only one such chief place of business, there are various tests for locating it. One is to emphasize the corporate "nerve" center where the executive and administrative functions are controlled. Another is to concentrate on the everyday business activities of the company — sometimes called the "muscle" in an extension of the anatomical metaphor. Many courts look to both; for example, see Northeast Nuclear Energy Co. v. General Electric Co., 435 F. Supp. 344 (D. Conn. 1977).

Northeast Nuclear referred to the purpose of diversity jurisdiction — to avoid prejudice against outsiders — in order to emphasize the place where the company has its greatest contact with the public. How would one apply that test to a company such as an airline that might be incorporated in Delaware, have chief executive offices in New York, have its greatest number of flights out of O'Hare Airport in Chicago, have training facilities in Kansas City, and have its greatest number of employees living in Kansas City and Chicago?

9. *Strawbridge's* rule of complete diversity limits the scope of §1332 beyond what one would expect from reading its text. Another doctrine has a similar effect. In Ankenbrandt v. Richards, 504 U.S. 689 (1992) the Court reaffirmed a nineteenth century decision holding that suits for divorce, alimony, or child custody fell outside the scope of diversity jurisdiction, even if the spouses were citizens of different states when suit was brought. *Ankenbrandt* went on to hold that some "domestic" cases could invoke diversity; for example, one former spouse could sue the other in tort for child abuse. It is fair to say that neither *Ankenbrandt* nor its nineteenth century predecessor, Barber v. Barber, 62 U.S. 582 (1858), are masterpieces of judicial persuasion. *Ankenbrandt* essentially says that *Barber* was wrong when decided but that its holding has become settled practice without congressional response, so that the passage of time has made bad law into good law.

a. Does the federal judiciary's reluctance to hear "domestic" cases, even in the face of a statute that suggests such actions fall within its jurisdiction, flow from gender bias — the idea that such cases are "beneath" the federal judiciary. See Judith Resnik, "Naturally" Without Gender: Women, Jurisdiction, and the Federal Courts, 66 N.Y.U.L. Rev. 1682 (1991).

b. Against the backdrop of agonizing child custody disputes, Congress has enacted 28 U.S.C. §1738A (the Parental Kidnapping Prevention Act), which sets forth criteria for the interstate recognition and modification of child custody decrees. The statute does not confer federal jurisdiction but instead purports to tell state courts when they must heed and when they can modify a sister state's decree.

c. Notice that §1738A will only come into effect when there is diversity between the parties — when the custodial and noncustodial parents are in different states. Should Congress have solved this problem by creating diversity jurisdiction for these cases instead of telling the state courts what to do?

10. Section 1359 of 28 U.S.C. deprives district courts of jurisdiction in those cases in which a party has been "improperly or collusively . . . joined" to invoke diversity jurisdiction. The courts are not unanimous

in what is "improper." The statute resolves one situation: For diversity purposes the representative of a child, an incompetent, or a deceased person (appointed to administer the estate) has the same citizenship as the individual represented. 28 U.S.C. §1332(a)(2).

11. Is a citizen of the District of Columbia (or of Puerto Rico, Guam, or another American territory not a state) a citizen of a "state" for diversity purposes? 28 U.S.C. §1332(d) says so, and its constitutionality was upheld in National Mutual Ins. Co. v. Tidewater Transfer Co., 337 U.S. 582 (1949).

12. As suggested in Note 1c above, the last sentence of §1332(a) might have affected the outcome of *Mas* if it had been in effect at the time of the lawsuit. Added to the statute in 1988, this provision treats permanent resident aliens as citizens of a state for diversity purposes. If Mr. Mas had held such a status, there would have been no diversity between him and Mr. Perry: Both would have been citizens of Louisiana for diversity purposes. Does this amendment to the statute also expand diversity? Suppose Mr. Mas, a Louisiana "citizen" under §1332(a), sued a fellow French citizen; would there be jurisdiction?

Saadeh v. Farouki

107 F.3d 52 (D.C. Cir. 1997)

ROGERS, J.

[Mr. Farouki, a businessman with wide international investments, borrowed funds from Mr. Saadeh and defaulted on the loan. By the time suit was filed, Farouki, a Jordanian citizen residing in Maryland, had achieved "permanent resident" immigration status in the United States. Saadeh, a Greek citizen, brought suit on the several written contracts allegedly breached, invoking diversity jurisdiction. While the litigation was underway, Farouki became a citizen of the United States. The district court rendered a judgment for Saadeh, and Farouki appealed on the merits. The Court of Appeals asked that the parties brief jurisdiction and, in the opinion that follows, without reaching the merits ordered the case dismissed for lack of subject matter jurisdiction.]

. . . Article III of the Constitution . . . requires only minimal diversity, that is, diversity of citizenship between any two parties on opposite sides of an action, regardless of whether other parties may be co-citizens. Congress has never granted the district courts the full measure of diversity jurisdiction permitted by the Constitution, however. . . . The Supreme Court has never addressed the scope of the complete diversity rule in cases involving alien parties. Prior to 1988, however, this court held, as have others, that the diversity statute did not confer jurisdiction over a lawsuit involving an alien on one side, and an alien and a citizen on the other side.

. . . Congress amended the diversity statute in 1988 to add what now appears as the last sentence of 28 U.S.C. §1332(a). This sentence provides in pertinent part that for the purposes of §1332(a) "an alien admitted to the United States for permanent residence shall be deemed a citizen of the State in which such alien is domiciled." Under this amendment, diversity of citizenship no longer exists in an action between a citizen of State A and an alien admitted to the United States for permanent residence who resides in State A. Read literally, however, the amended statute would create diversity between Saadeh and . . . Farouki[]. As permanent residents of Maryland at the time Saadeh filed his complaint, Mr. . . . and Mrs. Farouki would be "deemed" citizens of Maryland. Thus the amended statute would also appear to abrogate partially the rule of complete diversity by permitting a non-resident alien and a resident alien to be present on opposite sides of this lawsuit. Courts and commentators have differed as to whether this latter result is permissible under the amended statute.

[The opinion first affirmed the principle that citizenship at the time suit is filed is the relevant test, so that Farouki's subsequent acquisition of U.S. citizenship did not create diversity.]

Thus, the remaining question is whether, at the time Saadeh filed his complaint, Farouki qualified as a "citizen of a State" under the 1988 amendment to §1332. In resolving a question of statutory interpretation, a court's starting point is always the language of the statute. . . .

A literal reading of the 1988 amendment to §1332(a) would produce an odd and potentially unconstitutional result. It would both partially abrogate the longstanding rule of complete diversity, and create federal diversity jurisdiction over a lawsuit brought by one alien against another alien, without a citizen of a state on either side of the litigation. The judicial power of the United States does not extend to such an action under the Diversity Clause of Article III. Hodgson v. Bowerbank, 9 U.S. 303 (1809). Under the circumstances, it behooves the court to examine the legislative history of the 1988 amendment in order to determine congressional intent.

The 1988 alienage amendment was added to the Judicial Improvements Act during the Senate debate, and the legislative history consists of what is in the Congressional Record. So far as appears, the idea for the addition of an alienage provision originated in a recommendation of the Judicial Conference of the United States. The Judicial Conference supported the addition of the alienage provision in order to restrict diversity jurisdiction:

> There is no reason why actions involving persons who are permanent residents of the United States should be heard by federal courts merely because one of them remains a citizen or subject of a foreign state or has not yet become a citizen of the United States. Accordingly, the Conference agreed to recommend that Congress amend 28 U.S.C. §1332(a) to treat a permanent resident alien as a citizen of the state of his or her domicile.

The intentions of the Judicial Conference are mirrored by the comments of Senator Heflin, the sponsor of the Senate bill, during the debate on the Judicial Improvements Act. Referring to Title II, on diversity jurisdiction, he stated:

> The provisions of this title make modest amendments to reduce the basis for Federal court jurisdiction based solely on diversity of citizenship. . . .

A section-by-section analysis introduced into the Congressional Record similarly reveals the intent to reduce diversity jurisdiction through the alienage provision. Describing Title II as "making modest adjustments to the scope of diversity jurisdiction to relieve the caseload pressures on the Federal Courts," the analysis paralleled the language of the Judicial Conference report. . . .

Given the reasoning underlying the recommendation for the alienage provision and the general expressions of legislative intent for the Judicial Improvements Act, in the absence of contrary evidence, we conclude that Congress intended to contract diversity jurisdiction through the 1988 amendment to §1332(a), not to expand it by abrogating the longstanding rule that complete diversity is destroyed in lawsuits between aliens. . . . [W]e do not view these concerns about the workload of the federal judiciary and the burdens imposed by diversity jurisdiction as consistent with the conclusion that Congress intended what a literal reading of the statute suggests. It would be illogical to conclude that Congress intended to eliminate diversity jurisdiction in cases between a citizen and an alien permanently residing in the same state, but simultaneously intended to expand diversity jurisdiction in cases between an alien permanently residing in one state and an alien permanently residing in another state. Despite the plain language of §1332(a), the alienage amendment "clearly appears to have been intended only to eliminate subject matter jurisdiction of cases between a citizen and an alien living in the same state." Lloyds Bank v. Norkin, 817 F. Supp. at 419. There is no reason to conclude, however, that the amendment was intended to create diversity jurisdiction where it did not previously exist. . . .

[T]his appears to be one of those rare cases where the most literal interpretation of a statute is at odds with the evidence of Congressional
intent and a contrary construction is necessary to avoid "formidable
constitutional difficulties." 491 U.S. at 463, 466.

NOTES AND PROBLEMS

1. *Saadeh* is another case in which an appellate court, rather than the
parties, raised the jurisdictional question even though neither party did.
Why would Farouki, who had objected to jurisdiction at the outset of
the case, abandon this argument and brief only the merits of the case
on appeal?

a. By the time of the appeal, three circumstances had changed: (a)
the other parties who were nondiverse had been dropped from the case;
(b) Farouki had become a U.S. citizen; (c) Farouki had lost on the merits
at trial. Explain how these events might lead Farouki's lawyer to ignore
the jurisdictional question.

b. What do you suppose Saadeh's lawyer will do after reading this case?

2. The opinion proceeds on several levels. Most obviously it is a case
about the interpretation of §1332(a) and of Article III of the Constitution.

a. The court says that if it construes the statute to mean what it appears
to mean — and upholds jurisdiction in this case — that interpretation presents "'formidable constitutional difficulties.'" Explain what those difficulties are.

b. Can you construct an argument — apparently one not made in
Congress — that the sentence in question should be construed evenhand-
edly to deprive resident aliens of diversity jurisdiction in suits against the
fellow residents of their home state but to grant them diversity in suits
against foreign nationals?

3. At a second level, this opinion deals with conflicting approaches to
statutory interpretation. In courts and academic circles a debate rages
about the circumstances — if there are any — in which a court should
look beyond the text of a statute to consider the legislative history.

a. A dissenting opinion in a different case captures the conflicting
views of statutory interpretation:

Well, what if anything can we judges do about this mess? The answer lies
in the shadow of a jurisprudential disagreement that is not less important
by virtue of being unavowed by most judges. It is the disagreement between
the severely positivistic view that the content of law is exhausted in clear,
explicit, and definite enactments by or under express delegation from

legislatures, and the natural lawyer's or legal pragmatist's view that the practice of interpretation and the general terms of the Constitution (such as "equal protection of the laws") authorize judges to enrich positive law with the moral values and practical concerns of civilized society. Judges who in other respects have seemed quite similar, such as Holmes and Cardozo, have taken opposite sides of this issue. Neither approach is entirely satisfactory. The first buys political neutrality and a type of objectivity at the price of substantive injustice, while the second buys justice in the individual case at the price of considerable uncertainty and, not infrequently, judicial willfulness. It is no wonder that our legal system oscillates between the approaches.

United States v. Marshall, 908 F.2d 1312, 1334-1335 (Posner, J., dissenting) (7th Cir. 1990) (en banc). Recently the most prominent champion of "textualism," a methodology relying solely on statutory language, has been Justice Antonin Scalia of the U.S. Supreme Court. For a thoughtful survey of the debate, which has ramifications far beyond diversity jurisdiction, see William Eskridge, Jr., The New Textualism, 37 UCLA L. Rev. 621 (1990).

b. Other courts have reached different conclusions about the statutory language in question. As *Saadeh* noted:

> The Third Circuit reached a contrary conclusion in *Singh* [v. Daimler Benz], 9 F.3d 303. It reasoned that although "Congress may not have intended to enlarge diversity jurisdiction, . . . the possible unintended effect of permitting a permanent resident alien to invoke diversity jurisdiction when that party could not have done so before the amendment is not sufficient reason for us to torture or limit the statutory language." The Third Circuit concluded that the legislative history of the Judicial Improvements Act did not provide an "overriding reason" to depart from the plain language of §1332(a). In particular, the court rejected the claim that the overall purpose of the Act was to "to reduce diversity jurisdiction to relieve caseload pressures."

107 F.3d 52, 60 (D.C. Cir. 1997).

c. Is the opinion in *Saadeh* convincing in its conclusion that one should look to the legislative history in this case? Might someone think that a court should be most wary of invoking legislative history when: (a) Part of that history was drafted by judges (who comprise the entire membership of the Judicial Conference); and (b) the statute in question involves the court's own jurisdiction?

4. The opinion also gives us a glimpse of the concern of some members of the federal judiciary about caseloads, which in recent decades have risen faster than the number of judges. One result has been recommenda-

tions by such bodies as the Judicial Conference, the administrative voice of the federal judiciary, to restrict federal judicial jurisdiction.

a. Very roughly speaking, one could keep caseloads at manageable levels in three ways: by increasing the number of judges to keep pace with caseloads; by restricting jurisdiction and thus reducing the number of cases; and by ending cases at an early stage of litigation. One can find all three themes in recent law. Which one thinks is preferable may depend in part on one's notion of the functions of the federal judiciary and on the nature of civil litigation.

b. For a case making the caseload concern very explicit and attaching specific numbers to the concern, see Lockhart v. Patel, infra page 605.

5. Finally, the opinion gives us a glimpse of the continuing debate about the existence of diversity jurisdiction.

a. Although diversity was among the first of the jurisdictional grants to be passed by Congress, since the 1960s regular proposals to abolish or limit it have been introduced in Congress. The argument against diversity generally has two prongs. The first is that diversity cases constitute a substantial portion of the federal courts' civil caseload — ranging between 20 and 25 percent in recent years. So, if those courts are feeling pressed by caseloads, as they increasingly have been since the mid-1960s, diversity is an obvious candidate for elimination — unless, of course, it serves a vital function.

The second prong of the argument is that diversity serves no such function. The argument is that prejudice based on state citizenship is simply no longer an important factor in contemporary U.S. society. As a congressional report put the matter, "although there is still far too much prejudice in the United States (especially on grounds of race, religion, economic class, sex, nationality and age), it is . . . doubtful that prejudice against an individual because he is from another State is any longer a significant factor in this country's State courts." H.R. Rep. No. 893, 95th Cong., 2d Sess. 3-5 (1978).

Supporters of diversity argue that prejudice in state courts continues to exist, that a system of concurrent jurisdiction results in a beneficial interplay between state and federal procedures, that federal judges benefit from the regular exposure to run-of-the-mill state law, and that federal courts are superior to state courts.

b. While unwilling to eliminate diversity jurisdiction, Congress has been willing to limit its availability by increasing the required amount in controversy and by restricting the availability of supplemental jurisdiction in diversity cases. One can read Saadeh as another case in this tradition.

NOTE: AMOUNT IN CONTROVERSY

Besides diversity, §1332 requires an amount greater than $75,000 in controversy. Congress has from time to time increased this amount, most recently in 1997, from $50,000 to the present figure. The courts have treated this requirement in much the same way as they have the issue of federal question jurisdiction — that is, they have viewed the allegations of the pleading as all but controlling, rather than engaging in judicial guessing about the likelihood that the plaintiff would succeed in collecting as much as he had prayed for. The leading Supreme Court case, St. Paul Mercury Indemnity Co. v. Red Cab Co., 303 U.S. 283, 289 (1938), stated as follows:

> It must appear to a legal certainty that the claim is really for less than the jurisdictional amount to justify dismissal. The inability of plaintiff to recover an amount adequate to give the court jurisdiction does not show his bad faith or oust the jurisdiction. Nor does the fact that the complaint discloses the existence of a valid defense of the claim. But if, from the face of the pleadings, it is apparent, to a legal certainty, that the plaintiff cannot recover the amount claimed, or if, from the proofs, the court is satisfied to a like certainty that the plaintiff never was entitled to recover that amount, and that his claim was therefore colorable for the purpose of conferring jurisdiction, the suit will be dismissed.

Other significant issues in determining the amount in controversy for jurisdictional purposes are:

1. What should be done if the plaintiff asks for an injunction rather than money damages? At least four approaches have been used: Determine the value of the injunction to the plaintiff; determine the cost to the defendant of complying; determine the cost or value to the party invoking federal jurisdiction (the plaintiff, if the action is brought in federal court, and the defendant, if the action was brought in state court and defendant is attempting to remove); and allow jurisdiction if any of the tests above yields a figure of the statutory amount. For a discussion of these approaches (and an application of the fourth), see McCarty v. Amoco Pipeline Co., 595 F.2d 389 (7th Cir. 1979).

2. May a plaintiff aggregate claims? In some circumstances, different claims may be aggregated to meet the statutory amount; saying when that can happen is harder:

> The law on aggregation . . . is in a very unsatisfactory state. The traditional rules in this area evolved haphazardly and with little reasoning. They serve no apparent policy and "turn on a mystifying conceptual test." . . . Thus it is not altogether easy to say what the law is in this area and it is quite hard to say why it is as it seems to be.

Wright, Federal Courts 209. Some guidelines from the case law:

a. A single plaintiff with two or more unrelated claims against a single defendant may aggregate claims to satisfy the statutory amount.

b. If two plaintiffs each have claims against a single defendant, they may not aggregate if their claims are regarded as "separate and distinct."

c. If one plaintiff has a claim in excess of the statutory amount and a second plaintiff has a claim for less than the statutory amount, both against the same defendant, the first plaintiff can sue in federal court. What about the second? In Stromberg Metal Works, Inc. v. Press Mechanical, 77 F.3d 928 (7th Cir. 1996), the court allowed the second plaintiff to invoke supplemental jurisdiction under 28 U.S.C. §1367, where the claims were related.

d. In situations involving multiple plaintiffs or multiple defendants with a common undivided interest and single title or right, the value of the total interest will be used to determine the amount in controversy. This is not the case if the various claims are considered several and distinct, and they may be so considered even though the claims arose from a single instrument or the parties have a community of interest.

e. The preceding rules have been extended to cover class actions. Simply aggregating the claims of all the class members cannot satisfy the amount in controversy; at least some members must have claims that individually satisfy the jurisdictional amount. Snyder v. Harris, 394 U.S. 332 (1969). One case held that *each* class member had to have a claim that satisfied the jurisdictional amount. Zahn v. International Paper Co., 414 U.S. 291 (1973). But several lower courts have now held that the 1990 enactment of §1367, discussed in the next section, changed this result — permitting a class action as long as the class representative satisfies the jurisdictional limit. Free v. Abbott Labs., 51 F.3d 524 (5th Cir. 1995); Garza v. National American Ins. Co., 807 F. Supp. 1256 (1992).

3. Counterclaims are treated differently, depending on their classification under Rule 13 as either compulsory or permissive. Basically, when a plaintiff's claim exceeds $75,000 (the statutory amount), a compulsory counterclaim may be heard regardless of amount, while a permissive counterclaim requires an independent jurisdictional basis. The law is unsettled, however, when plaintiff's claim falls short of $75,000 but defendant's counterclaim increases the amount in controversy to more than $75,000. See generally Wright, Federal Courts 216-221.

4. Apply these principles to some common cases; in each, assume that the requisite diversity exists and only the amount in controversy is an issue.

a. Mas sues Perry for $75,000 for invasion of privacy.

b. Mas sues Perry for $100,000 for invasion of privacy; Perry counterclaims for unpaid rent in the amount of $5,000.

c. Perry sues Mas on two claims: unpaid rent in the amount of $5,000 and an unrelated promissory note for $72,000.

d. Mas and Friend sue Perry. Mas alleges invasion of privacy and seeks $60,000. Friend, alleging that Perry's parking garage collapsed while he was visiting Mas, crushing Friend's expensive car, seeks $40,000.

e. Jean-Paul and Judy Mas both sue Perry for invasion of privacy, each seeking $50,000.

D.   Supplemental Jurisdiction

Thus far we have examined aspects of federal subject matter jurisdiction that narrow the doors to federal courts in ways that the texts of the Constitution and the statutes might not suggest. We turn now to a doctrine that broadens federal jurisdiction, in equally unexpected ways. This doctrine, now known as *supplemental jurisdiction*, originated in case law and has recently taken statutory form.

Supplemental jurisdiction originated in decisions that stretched federal jurisdiction to cover parts of cases that, if brought independently, would not have fit within the district courts' subject matter jurisdiction. Because of the case law origins of the principles, we shall first examine a leading case and then consider how it was codified and altered in 28 U.S.C. §1367. Before this codification, the courts used two different terms to describe the concept that §1367 calls supplemental jurisdiction: pendent jurisdiction and ancillary jurisdiction. The next case is the leading prestatutory exposition of thinking about supplemental jurisdiction, — one that, as you will see, shaped the subsequent statute.

United Mine Workers v. Gibbs
383 U.S. 715 (1966)

Mr. Justice BRENNAN delivered the opinion of the Court.

[In the midst of a dispute between the United Mine Workers and the rival Southern Labor Union over representation of miners, respondent Paul Gibbs was hired to run a mine and to haul coal.] On August 15 and 16, 1960, armed members of Local 5881 forcibly prevented the opening of the mine, threatening respondent and beating an organizer for the rival union. The members of the local believed Consolidated had promised them the jobs at the new mine; they insisted that if anyone would do the work, they would. At this time, no representative of the UMW, their international union, was present. George Gilbert, the

UMW's field representative for the area including Local 5881, was away at Middlesboro, Kentucky, attending an Executive Board meeting when the members of the local discovered Grundy's plan; he did not return to the area until late in the day of August 16. There was uncontradicted testimony that he first learned of the violence while at the meeting, and returned with explicit instructions from his international union superiors to establish a limited picket line, to prevent any further violence, and to see to it that the strike did not spread to neighboring mines. There was no further violence at the mine site; a picket line was maintained there for nine months; and no further attempts were made to open the mine during that period. . . .

Respondent lost his job as superintendent, and never entered into performance of his haulage contract. He testified that he soon began to lose other trucking contracts and mine leases he held in nearby areas. Claiming these effects to be the result of a concerted union plan against him, he sought recovery not against Local 5881 or its members, but only against petitioner, the international union. The suit was brought in the United States District Court for the Eastern District of Tennessee, and jurisdiction was premised on allegations of secondary boycotts under §303, [a federal labor statute]. The state law claim, for which jurisdiction was based upon the doctrine of pendent jurisdiction, asserted "an unlawful conspiracy and an unlawful boycott aimed at him and [Grundy] to maliciously, wantonly and willfully interfere with his contract of employment and with his contract of haulage."

[Gibbs sued the union, bringing two claims: one under the §303 of the federal Labor Management Relations Act and the other a state law conspiracy claim. The federal district court heard both claims.] The trial judge . . . held that union pressure [on Gibb's employer] to discharge respondent as supervisor . . . was not cognizable under [federal labor law]. Interference with the employment relationship was cognizable as a state claim, however. . . .

I

A threshold question is whether the District Court properly entertained jurisdiction of the claim based on Tennessee law. . . .

. . . The Court held in Hurn v. Oursler that state law claims are appropriate for federal court determination if they form a separate but parallel ground for relief also sought in a substantial claim based on federal law. The Court distinguished permissible from nonpermissible exercises of federal judicial power over state law claims by contrasting "a case where two distinct grounds in support of a single cause of action are alleged, one only of which presents a federal question, and a case where two separate and distinct causes of action are alleged, one only of which is federal in character. In the former, where the federal question averred is not plainly wanting in substance, the federal court, even though the federal ground be not established, may nevertheless retain and dispose of the case upon the non-federal *ground*; in the latter it may not do so upon the non-federal *cause of action.*" The question is into which category the present action fell.

Hurn was decided in 1933, before the unification of law and equity by the Federal Rules of Civil Procedure. At the time, the meaning of "cause of action" was a subject of serious dispute; the phrase might "mean one thing for one purpose and something different for another." United States v. Memphis Cotton Oil Co. . . .

With the adoption of the Federal Rules of Civil Procedure and the unified form of action, Fed. Rule Civ. Proc. 2, much of the controversy over "cause of action" abated. The phrase remained as the keystone of the *Hurn* test, however, and, as commentators have noted, has been the source of considerable confusion. Under the Rules, the impulse is toward entertaining the broadest possible scope of action consistent with fairness to the parties; joinder of claims, parties and remedies is strongly encouraged. Yet because the *Hurn* question involves issues of jurisdiction as well as convenience, there has been some tendency to limit its application to cases in which the state and federal claims are, as in *Hurn*, "little more than the equivalent of different epithets to characterize the same group of circumstances."

This limited approach is unnecessarily grudging. Pendent jurisdiction, in the sense of judicial power, exists whenever there is a claim "arising under [the] Constitution, the Laws of the United States, and Treaties made, or which shall be made, under their Authority. . . .," U.S. Const., Art III, §2, and the relationship between that claim and the state claim permits the conclusion that the entire action before the court comprises but one constitutional "case." The federal claim must have substance sufficient to confer subject matter jurisdiction on the court. The state and federal claims must derive from a common nucleus of operative fact. But if, considered without regard to their federal or state character, a plaintiff's claims are such that he would ordinarily be expected to try them all in one judicial proceeding, then, assuming substantiality of the federal issues, there is *power* in federal courts to hear the whole.[13]

13. While it is commonplace that the Federal Rules of Civil Procedure do not expand the jurisdiction of federal courts, they do embody "the whole tendency of our decisions . . . to require a plaintiff to try his . . . whole case at one time," Baltimore S. S. Co. v. Phillips, [274 US. 316], and to that extent emphasize the basis of pendent jurisdiction.

That power need not be exercised in every case in which it is found to exist. It has consistently been recognized that pendent jurisdiction is a doctrine of discretion, not of plaintiff's right. Its justification lies in considerations of judicial economy, convenience and fairness to litigants; if these are not present a federal court should hesitate to exercise jurisdiction over state claims, even though bound to apply state law to them, Erie R. Co. v. Tompkins. Needless decisions of state law should be avoided both as a matter of comity and to promote justice between the parties, by procuring for them a surer-footed reading of applicable law. Certainly, if the federal claims are dismissed before trial, even though not insubstantial in a jurisdictional sense, the claims should be dismissed as well. Similarly, if it appears that the state issues substantially predominate, whether in terms of proof, of the scope of the issues raised, or of the comprehensiveness of the remedy sought, the state claims may be dismissed without prejudice and left for resolution to state tribunals. There may, on the other hand, be situations in which the state claim is so closely tied to questions of federal policy that the argument for exercise of pendent jurisdiction is particularly strong. In the present case, for example, the allowable scope of the state claim implicates the federal doctrine of pre-emption; while this interrelationship does not create statutory federal question jurisdiction, Louisville & N.R. Co. v. Mottley, its existence is relevant to the exercise of discretion. Finally, there may be reasons independent of jurisdictional considerations, such as the likelihood of jury confusion in treating divergent legal theories of relief, that would justify separating state and federal claims for trial, Fed. Rule Civ. Proc. 42(b). If so, jurisdiction should ordinarily be refused.

The question of power will ordinarily be resolved on the pleadings. But the issue whether pendent jurisdiction has been properly assumed is one which remains open throughout the litigation. Pretrial procedures or even the trial itself may reveal a substantial hegemony of state law claims, or likelihood of jury confusion, which could not have been anticipated at the pleading stage. Although it will of course be appropriate to take account in this circumstance of the already completed course of the litigation, dismissal of the state claim might even then be merited. For example, it may appear that the plaintiff was well aware of the nature of his proofs and the relative importance of his claims; recognition of a federal court's wide latitude to decide ancillary questions of state law does not imply that it must tolerate a litigant's effort to impose upon it what is in effect only a state law case. Once it appears that a state claim constitutes the real body of a case, to which the federal claim is only an appendage, the state claim may fairly be dismissed.

We are not prepared to say that in the present case the District Court exceeded its discretion in proceeding to judgment on the state claim. . . . [T]he state and federal claims arose from the same nucleus of operative fact and reflected alternative remedies. . . .

It is true that the [federal] §303 claims ultimately failed and that the only recovery allowed respondent was on the state claim. We cannot confidently say, however, that the federal issues were so remote or played such a minor role at the trial that in effect the state claim only was tried. . . . Moreover, the question whether the permissible scope of the state claim was limited by the doctrine of pre-emption afforded a special reason for the exercise of pendent jurisdiction; the federal courts are particularly appropriate bodies for the application of pre-emption princi-ples. We thus conclude that although it may be that the District Court might, in its sound discretion, have dismissed the state claim, the cir-cumstances show no error in refusing to do so. . . .

[Turning to the merits, the Court then decided that plaintiff could not recover for conspiracy under Tennessee law on the facts in the record.]

NOTES AND PROBLEMS

1. *Gibbs* contains both an important constitutional holding and a principle for the exercise of judicial discretion. Both aspects of the case appear in 28 U.S.C. §1367.

2. Consider first the constitutional aspect of *Gibbs*.

a. Why was it not a violation of Article III of the Constitution for the district court to hear and decide a claim based entirely on state law even though the parties were not of diverse citizenship? What phrase in Article III authorizes the court to hear a state law claim where the parties are not of diverse citizenship?

b. How is that constitutional holding reflected in the text of §1367(a)?

c. United Mine Workers v. Gibbs espouses a principle that may look surprising at first glance. Its rationale emerges more clearly if one recalls that a central feature of the Federal Rules is the ease with which they permit joinder of claims. See, e.g., Rule 18(a). It would be logically possible, but awkward, to permit parties to join closely connected claims but then deny the federal courts power over claims that did not bring their own jurisdictional basis with them. In such situations, whichever court (state or federal) tried the related claim second would have to engage in elaborate analyses of which issues were precluded in the first lawsuit.

3. *Gibbs* suggests that courts need not exercise supplemental jurisdiction even when they have the constitutional power to do so.

a. What are the circumstances in which Gibbs suggests that such an exercise might be inappropriate?

b. Compare §1367(c) to the discretionary aspects of *Gibbs*. Does the statute include all the factors suggested? Does it add any? The circuits are split on whether §1367(c) codifies the discretionary aspects of *Gibbs* or limits courts' discretion more than *Gibbs* did. The "codifiers" point to the "shall" language of the statute; the "restricters" point to some of the modifiers: "*substantially* predominates" and "*exceptional* circumstances." The Supreme Court has in passing suggested that §1367 "codifies" *Gibbs*. City of Chicago v. International College of Surgeons, 522 U.S. 156 (1997).

c. *Gibbs* and §1367(c) speak of refraining from the exercise of jurisdiction in cases in which "state issues substantially predominate." What does this mean? Why was *Gibbs* not such a case?

d. Federal courts have sometimes been reluctant to dismiss state law claims once the suit was well under way for fear that, during the pendency of the suit in federal court, the applicable state statute of limitations would have run, thus preventing refiling in state court. How does §1367 address that issue?

4. Arthur, a citizen of New York, sues Barbara, a citizen of Pennsylvania, in federal district court. He alleges several claims: federal antitrust violations, federal securities law violations, and state law breach of contract. He prays more than $100,000 in damages for each claim. Will the district court have to analyze how closely related the federal and state law claims are for purposes of deciding whether supplemental jurisdiction exists or whether any of the reasons in §1367(c) for declining to exercise jurisdiction apply? Why not?

5. The impulse toward sweeping related claims into a single pile has led the federal courts to some rather dramatic extensions of supplemental jurisdiction. The following two cases illustrate the Supreme Court's prestatutory stance toward such extensions of jurisdiction; in reading them, consider which result was changed by the enactment of §1367.

a. In Owen Equipment & Erection Co. v. Kroger, 437 U.S. 365 (1978), the Court faced what had begun as an ordinary diversity suit. Mrs. Kroger (an Iowa citizen) based a claim against the Omaha Public Power Dept. (not surprisingly, a Nebraska citizen) on the alleged wrongful death of her husband, who had been killed in a construction accident. Omaha Power then impleaded Owen Equipment, the operator of the crane whose contact with a power line had caused Mr. Kroger's death. Although at the time the suit was filed everyone thought that Owen, like Omaha Power, was a Nebraska citizen, as the suit progressed it emerged that Owen was in fact an Iowa citizen for diversity purposes because it had its principal place of business in that state. That change in citizenship assumed a crucial role once Mrs. Kroger added to her original claim against Omaha Power a claim against Owen, the impleaded third-party defendant. The Supreme Court held that there was no jurisdiction to support that claim. Ancillary jurisdiction extended to cover counterclaims, cross-claims, and third-party claims, but it did not permit the plaintiff to sue a defendant whom she could not have named as a party to the original lawsuit. We shall look at *Owen Equipment* more carefully when we consider impleader in Chapter XIII.

b. Finley v. United States, 490 U.S. 545 (1989), presented the court with a claim involving a "pendent party." Airline passengers died when a plane struck a power line while landing. Passengers' representatives sued the United States, alleging that the Federal Aviation Administration had been negligent; such claims arise under federal law by virtue of the Federal Tort Claims Act. But plaintiffs also wished to sue the power company, alleging that it had negligently located the lines. There was no independent basis for federal jurisdiction over the power company, but claims against both parties would have involved many overlapping factual questions. The Supreme Court firmly rejected the notion that the power company could be joined:

> Analytically, petitioner's case is fundamentally different from *Gibbs* in that it brings into question what has become known as pendent-*party* jurisdiction, that is, jurisdiction over parties not named in any claim that is independently cognizable by the federal court. . . . Our cases show, however, that with respect to the addition of parties, as opposed to the addition of only claims, we . . . will not read jurisdictional statutes broadly. . . .
>
> . . . As we noted at the outset our cases do not display an entirely consistent approach with respect to the necessity that jurisdiction be explicitly conferred. The *Gibbs* line of cases was a departure from prior practice, and a departure that we have no intent to limit or impair. . . . What is of paramount importance is that Congress be able to legislate against a clear background of interpretive rules, so that it may know the effect of language it adopts.

Id. at 549, 556.

c. Which result — that in *Owen Equipment* or that in Finley — does §1367 alter? What might have led Congress to alter that result but not the other?

d. Why would Congress be stingier with the supplemental jurisdiction bestowed by §1367(a) than with that in (b)?

E. Removal

Jurisdictional statutes give plaintiffs an initial choice of federal courts for cases in which federal and state court jurisdiction overlap. Congress has also given defendants the power to second-guess plaintiffs through a process known as *removal*. The basic text is 28 U.S.C. §1441; consider its operation in the following problems.

NOTES AND PROBLEMS

Which of the following cases would be removable?

1. *P* sues *D* for defamation in state court; *D* believes the statement she published is protected under the First Amendment.

2. *P* sues *D* for copyright infringement in state court.

3. *P* sues *D* in state court, alleging violation of *P*'s rights under the equal protection clause of the U.S. Constitution.

4. *P*, a citizen of Florida, sues *D*, a citizen of New Jersey, on a personal injury claim in New Jersey state court, seeking $100,000 in damages.

5. The facts are as in Problem 4, except that *P* adds a claim that *D* has violated her federal civil rights.

6. *P*, a citizen of Florida, sues *D*, a citizen of New Jersey, and *E*, a citizen of New York, on a personal injury claim in New York state court, seeking $100,000 in damages.

7. *P*, a citizen of California, sues *D*, a citizen of California, for infringement of copyright. *P* brings the suit in California state courts. *D* seeks to remove. Until 1988 there was an unexpected result: Although the federal courts have exclusive jurisdiction over copyright claims, *D* could not remove — because the California courts never had jurisdiction. There was no validly pending "case" which could be removed to federal court. In 1988 Congress amended §1441, adding what is now section (e). What result in the case just posed?

8. The procedure for removal is set forth in 28 U.S.C. §1446; that for challenging removal in §1447. Read these statutes and apply them to the following questions.

a. Plaintiff, a citizen of Pennsylvania, files a complaint in Pennsylvania state court naming Danielle as defendant and seeking $100,000 in damages. Danielle is a citizen of Georgia. If Danielle wishes to remove, what must her petition say?

b. If in her removal petition Danielle falsely states that she is a citizen of Georgia, what risks does she run?

c. Danielle files her removal petition two months after being served with the state court complaint. Assuming that the conditions for diversity exist, can she remove?

d. Same problem as in (a), except that plaintiff's initial complaint seeks only $10,000 in damages. Six months later, after some discovery, plaintiff amends his state complaint to add an additional cause of action, so he now seeks $85,000 in damages. May Danielle now remove?

e. Same problem as in (d), except the damage prayer is well below the jurisdictional amount. Danielle seeks to remove, claiming that if she is liable, which she denies, the damages are far more than the jurisdictional amount. May she remove?

f. Same problem as in (d), except that plaintiff amends his complaint a year after the original complaint. No removal is possible, even though the requisites of diversity jurisdiction are met. Why?

g. Finally, §1447 (c) contains a pair of provisions concerning remand to the state courts. The first, remand for "any defect in removal procedure," has a 30-day time limit. The second requires remand if the "district court lacks subject matter jurisdiction." What's the difference? Courts have interpreted the first to apply to problems that would prevent removal but would not have destroyed federal jurisdiction — for example, if one or more of the defendants seeking removal was a citizen of the state where suit was brought. See §1441(b). The second refers to facts that negate federal subject matter jurisdiction — for example, the absence of diversity or a federal question.

The problems discussed above deal with the basic situations in which removal is available. There are, however, more difficult situations, illustrated by the next case.

Caterpillar, Inc. v. Lewis
519 U.S. 61 (1996)

Justice GINSBURG delivered the opinion of the Court.

This case, commenced in a state court, involves personal injury claims arising under state law. The case was removed to a federal court at a time when . . . complete diversity of citizenship did not exist among the parties. Promptly after the removal, the plaintiff moved to remand the case to the state court, but the District Court denied that motion. Before trial of the case, however, all claims involving the nondiverse defendant were settled, and that defendant was dismissed as a party to the action. Complete diversity thereafter existed. The case proceeded to trial, jury verdict, and judgment for the removing defendant. The Court of Appeals vacated the judgment, concluding that, absent complete diversity at the time of removal, the District Court lacked subject-matter jurisdiction.

The question presented is whether the absence of complete diversity at the time of removal is fatal to federal-court adjudication. We hold that a district court's error in failing to remand a case improperly removed is not fatal to the ensuing adjudication if federal jurisdictional requirements are met at the time judgment is entered.

Respondent James David Lewis, a resident of Kentucky, filed this lawsuit in Kentucky state court on June 22, 1989, after sustaining injuries while operating a bulldozer. Asserting state-law claims based on defective manufacture, negligent maintenance, failure to warn, and breach of warranty, Lewis named as defendants both the manufacturer of the bulldozer — petitioner Caterpillar Inc., a Delaware corporation with its principal place of business in Illinois — and the company that serviced the bulldozer — Whayne Supply Company, a Kentucky corporation with its principal place of business in Kentucky.

Several months later, Liberty Mutual Insurance Group, the insurance carrier for Lewis' employer, intervened in the lawsuit as a plaintiff. A Massachusetts corporation with its principal place of business in that State, Liberty Mutual asserted subrogation claims against both Caterpillar and Whayne Supply for workers' compensation benefits Liberty Mutual had paid to Lewis on behalf of his employer.

Lewis entered into a settlement agreement with defendant Whayne Supply less than a year after filing his complaint. Shortly after learning of this agreement, Caterpillar filed a notice of removal, on June 21, 1990, in the United States District Court for the Eastern District of Kentucky. Grounding federal jurisdiction on diversity of citizenship, Caterpillar satisfied with only a day to spare the statutory requirement that a diversity-based removal take place within one year of a lawsuit's commencement, see 28 U.S.C. §1446(b). Caterpillar's notice of removal explained that the case was nonremovable at the lawsuit's start: Complete diversity was absent then because plaintiff Lewis and defendant Whayne Supply shared Kentucky citizenship. Proceeding on the understanding that the settlement agreement between these two Kentucky parties would result in the dismissal of Whayne Supply from the lawsuit, Caterpillar stated that the settlement rendered the case removable.

Lewis objected to the removal and moved to remand the case to state court. Lewis acknowledged that he had settled his own claims against Whayne Supply. But Liberty Mutual had not yet settled its subrogation claim against Whayne Supply, Lewis asserted. Whayne Supply's presence as a defendant in the lawsuit, Lewis urged, defeated diversity of citizenship. Without addressing this argument, the District Court denied Lewis' motion to remand on September 24, 1990, treating as dispositive Lewis' admission that he had settled his own claims against Whayne Supply.

In June 1993, [Liberty Mutual and Whayne settled]. . . . With Caterpillar as the sole defendant adverse to Lewis, the case proceeded to a 6-day jury trial in November 1993, ending in a unanimous verdict for Caterpillar. . . .

We note, intially, two "givens" in this case as we have accepted it for review. First, the District Court, in its decision denying Lewis' timely motion to remand, incorrectly treated Whayne Supply, the nondiverse defendant, as effectively dropped from the case prior to removal. Second, the Sixth Circuit correctly determined that the complete diversity requirement was not satisfied at the time of removal. We accordingly home in on this question: Does the District Court's initial misjudgment still burden and run with the case, or is it overcome by the eventual dismissal of the nondiverse defendant? . . . .

Beyond question, as Lewis acknowledges, there was in this case complete diversity, and therefore federal subject-matter jurisdiction, at the time of trial and judgment. . . . Caterpillar maintains that this change cured the threshold statutory misstep, i.e., the removal of a case when diversity was incomplete.

Caterpillar moves too quickly over the terrain we must cover. The jurisdictional defect was cured, i.e., complete diversity was established before the trial commenced. Therefore, the Sixth Circuit erred in resting its decision on the absence of subject-matter jurisdiction. But a statutory flaw — Caterpillar's failure to meet the §1441 (a) requirement that the case be fit for federal adjudication at the time the removal petition is filed — remained in the unerasable history of the case.

And Lewis, by timely moving for remand, did all that was required to preserve his objection to removal. An order denying a motion to remand, "standing alone," is "obviously . . . not final and [immediately] appealable" as of right. Chicago, R. I. & P. R.Co.v. Stude, 346 U.S. 574, 578 (1954). Nor is a plaintiff required to seek permission to take an interlocutory appeal pursuant to 28 U.S.C. §1292(b) in order to avoid waiving whatever ultimate appeal right he may have. . . .

Having preserved his objection to an improper removal, Lewis urges that an "all's well that ends well" approach is inappropriate here. He maintains that ultimate satisfaction of the subject-matter jurisdiction requirement ought not swallow up antecedent statutory violations. The course Caterpillar advocates, Lewis observes, would disfavor diligent plaintiffs who timely, but unsuccessfully, move to check improper removals in district court. Further, that course would allow improperly removing defendants to profit from their disregard of Congress' instructions, and their ability to lead district judges into error.

Concretely, in this very case, Lewis emphasizes, adherence to the rules Congress prescribed for removal would have kept the case in state court. Only by removing prematurely was Caterpillar able to get to federal court inside the 1-year limitation set in §1446(b). Had Caterpillar waited until the case was ripe for removal, i.e., until Whayne Supply was dismissed as a defendant, the 1-year limitation would have barred the way, and plaintiff's choice of forum would have been preserved.[14]

These arguments are hardly meritless, but they run up against an overriding consideration. Once a diversity case has been tried in federal court, with rules of decision supplied by state law under the regime of Erie R. Co. v. Tompkins, 304 U.S. 64 (1938), considerations of finality, efficiency, and economy become overwhelming. . . .

Our view is in harmony with a main theme of the removal scheme Congress devised. Congress ordered a procedure calling for expeditious superintendence by district courts. The lawmakers specified a short time, 30 days, for motions to remand for defects in removal procedure, 28 U.S.C. §1447(c), and district court orders remanding cases to state courts generally are "not reviewable on appeal or otherwise," §1447(d). Congress did not similarly exclude appellate review of refusals to remand. But an evident concern that may explain the lack of symmetry relates to the federal courts' subject-matter jurisdiction. Despite a federal trial court's threshold denial of a motion to remand, if, at the end of the day and case, a jurisdictional defect remains uncured, the judgment must be vacated. See Fed. Rule Civ. Proc. 12(h)(3) ("Whenever it appears by suggestion of the parties or otherwise that the court lacks jurisdiction of the subject matter, the court shall dismiss the action.") In this case, however, no jurisdictional defect lingered through judgment in the District Court. To wipe out the adjudication postjudgment, and return to state court a case now satisfying all federal jurisdictional requirements, would impose an exorbitant cost on our dual court system, a cost incom-

---

14. Lewis preferred state court to federal court based on differences he perceived in, inter alia, the state and federal jury systems and rules of evidence.

patible with the fair and unprotracted administration of justice. Lewis ultimately argues that, if the final judgment against him is allowed to stand, "all of the various procedal requirements for removal will become unenforceable"; therefore, "defendants will have an enormous incentive to attempt wrongful removals." Brief for Respondent 9. In particular, Lewis suggests that defendants will remove prematurely "in the hope that some subsequent developments, such as the eventual dismissal of nondiverse defendants, will permit the case to be kept in federal court." We do not anticipate the dire consequences Lewis forecasts.

The procedural requirements for removal remain enforceable by the federal trial court judges to whom those requirements are directly addressed. Lewis' prediction . . . rests on an assumption we do not indulge — that district courts generally will not comprehend, or will balk at applying, the rules on removal Congress has prescribed. The prediction furthermore assumes defendants' readiness to gamble that any jurisdictional defect, for example, the absence of complete diversity, will first escape detection, then disappear prior to judgment. The well-advised defendant, we are satisfied, will foresee the likely outcome of an unwarranted removal — a swift and nonreviewable remand order, see 28 U.S.C. §1447(c), (d), attended by the displeasure of a district court whose authority has been improperly invoked. The odds against any gain from a wrongful removal, in sum, render improbable Lewis' projection of increased resort to the maneuver.

For the reasons stated, the judgment of the Court of Appeals is reversed, and the case is remanded for proceedings consistent with this opinion. . . .

NOTES AND PROBLEMS

1. *Caterpillar*, written by a former civil procedure teacher,* splendidly illustrates the pitfalls of removal.

a. Explain why removal was improper at the time Caterpillar attempted it.

b. Explain why removal would still have been improper had Caterpillar waited until the point in the lawsuit when complete diversity existed.

c. Explain why Lewis, faced with an erroneous ruling by the district court (that diversity existed), could not immediately appeal it.

2. The opinion suggests that Lewis did everything right, raising objections in a timely and cogent fashion, but he nevertheless found himself

---

* Justice Ginsburg taught civil procedure for more than a decade before being appointed to the bench.

trapped in this procedural nightmare, with the Supreme Court conceding that he was right at the time but loses now. Is there anything he could have done to get himself back into state court?

a. The opinion mentions an interlocutory appeal under 28 U.S.C. §1292(b). Perhaps. Such appeals by discretion require both the district court and circuit court to agree that the question is important and doubtful enough to warrant appealing. That doesn't happen very often: Out of almost 40,000 federal appeals filed annually, only about 100 cases see successful interlocutory appeals.

b. Could Lewis, having suffered an undeserved defeat on his jurisdictional motion, stage the procedural equivalent of a sit-down strike, refusing to comply with judicial orders until his case was dismissed, and then appeal on the grounds that it should have been dismissed earlier on jurisdictional grounds? Perhaps, but, again it's risky. Recall *Insurance Corp. of Ireland,* supra page 160, which held that the district court properly entered an order assuming jurisdiction over a defendant who refused to cooperate with discovery on the ground that personal jurisdiction was lacking. True, the federal courts have been much more cautious about subject matter than about personal jurisdiction. But they are almost equally protective about their own powers to conduct proceedings.

3. Removal is not an entirely popular idea, either with states or with the litigants who choose their courts.

a. Why did Congress place a one-year "statute of limitations" on removal petitions in diversity cases — even in cases where the basis for removal did not present itself until after that date? See §1446(b). Notice that in some cases this time limit allows plaintiffs an opportunity to manipulate jurisdiction, joining non-diverse parties and then dropping them after a year. A low prayer for damages that is amended after the year has passed will accomplish the same thing.

b. Ohio sought to discourage removal by enacting a statute providing that any out-of-state insurer that removed a case to federal court was barred from doing business in the state for three years. Held: unconstitutional. International Insurance Co. v. Duryee, 96 F 3d 837 (6th Cir. 1996).

4. In Capron v. Van Noorden, supra page 226, the Supreme Court dismissed a case in which plaintiff had improperly invoked diversity jurisdiction, then lost at trial. On appeal, plaintiff pointed to the lack of jurisdiction — and won. Contrast *Caterpillar,* in which the defendant properly and accurately objected to removal. But the *Caterpillar* Court, acknowledging that diversity did not exist at the time of filing, nevertheless rejected defendant's challenge. Why?

5. Subsection (c) of §1441 poses unexpected difficulties. Until 1990 this subsection contained a snarl of statutory construction (involving its application to diversity cases) so tangled that we shall not try to describe

it. Congress cut this knot by specifying that subsection (c) applies only to federal question cases. But when *can* §1441(c) apply to a federal question case? Consider two possible constructions:

a. In a suit in which the parties are not of diverse citizenship, plaintiff brings a pair of claims, one based on federal law, the other on state law. Defendant seeks to remove. If the two claims are closely related, defendant can remove without regard to subsection (c); the two claims are part of the same constitutionally related "case or controversy." Recall *Gibbs* and 28 U.S.C. §1367, which say that a federal court has jurisdiction over state law claims that are closely related to federal claims. In that situation the entire case would be removable under §1441 (*b*) because it would be "a civil action of which the district courts have original jurisdiction." If, however, the two claims are entirely unrelated, they will not be part of the same case or controversy and therefore will be beyond the constitutional reach of the federal courts' jurisdiction. If jurisdiction under those circumstances is unconstitutional, a mere statute cannot alter the situation. Under this analysis §1441(c) is either unnecessary or unconstitutional.

b. Now imagine the same situation, with the two claims unrelated to each other. But imagine that one of the claims contains a federal element; for example, a fired employee sues, invoking a state law barring religious discrimination and, in addition, a federal law claim for alleged violations of the federal pension laws. The pension claim, let us imagine, arises directly under federal law and would thus be removable if brought alone; the state law discrimination claim is not removable, however. Nor are the two claims sufficiently related to be removable under the *Gibbs* test. Does §1441(c) give the courts jurisdiction over a "separate and independent" claim with a federal ingredient, even if that ingredient would not suffice for federal jurisdiction if brought separately? See Wisconsin Dept. of Corrections v. Schacht, 524 U.S. 381 (1998) (federal court retains jurisdiction over remaining claim).

c. One can cut this Gordian knot by supposing that the federal court will promptly determine that the unrelated state claim should be remanded to the state courts. At a pragmatic level this solves the problem; at a conceptual level the statute still appears to give federal courts temporary jurisdiction over cases they cannot constitutionally hear.

6. In addition to 28 U.S.C. §1441, which is the general removal statute, there are statutes permitting removal in specific cases. For example, §1442 permits removal of suits by federal officers or agencies sued for the performance of their duties. By contrast, some actions that otherwise would be removable under §1441 are made specifically nonremovable by §1445. Examine that statute and consider why Congress might have

made such actions nonremovable and thus allowed plaintiffs to dictate the choice between state and federal court.

7. Finally, consider an interesting use of removal that takes us full circle back to the premises of *Mottley*, with which this chapter began. The Securities Litigation Uniform Standards Act of 1998 does three things. First, it preempts state securities class actions alleging fraud in the sales of securities; it provides, in other words, that in such cases federal law displaces otherwise applicable state law. 15 U.S.C. §77p(b). Second, it provides that securities fraud class actions based entirely on state law "shall be removable to the federal district court for the district in which the action is pending. " 15 U.S.C. §77p(c). Finally, it orders dismissal of the removed class actions. This three-step process provides a review of much of this chapter.

a. The first step is substantive and takes us beyond the boundaries of procedure. Without going into great detail, one can conclude that Congress could constitutionally displace — preempt — all state securities law. If Congress can do that, can it take a half-way step — of allowing state law to continue to exist in suits brought by individual plaintiffs but preempting state law in securities class actions?

b. If one assumes that Congress has the power suggested in (a), one reaches the procedural curiosity. The Securities Litigation Act has created a federal defense to a state law claim — the defense of preemption. Ordinarily the system relies on state courts to recognize federal defenses. If state courts err, the remedy — the only remedy — is review by the U.S. Supreme Court. One can think of *Mottley* in these terms: the Supreme Court dismissed the case, requiring the Mottleys to refile in state court and to await review by the Supreme Court as the only way to get a federal court to pass on the federal question involved. Notice that this scheme creates some slippage; if the U.S. Supreme Court had not reviewed the case the second time around, the Mottleys would have hung onto their free pass even though federal law outlawed it.

c. The Securities Litigation Uniform Standards Act eliminates this slippage. The statute does two things: It creates a federal defense to certain state law claims, and then it creates removal based on that defense. Recall from the start of the chapter that the well-pleaded complaint rule as interpreted in *Mottley* is a statutory rather than a constitutional matter and that Congress can statutorily create a broader jurisdiction for the federal courts under removal than under original jurisdiction. It has done so here. As a consequence, one can expect that all such claims will be removed — and dismissed — by federal district courts.

d. Should Congress use this technique more widely? For all federal defenses? Should Congress use it at all?

THE *ERIE* PROBLEM

IV

Recall the theme of this section — the constitutional framework for U.S. litigation. The two preceding chapters have illustrated the two principal means by which the Constitution creates that framework: It limits the powers of states, and it enumerates (thereby limiting) the powers of the federal government. The first limitation appears in the doctrines of personal jurisdiction, the second in those of federal subject matter jurisdiction. The Constitution thus requires state courts to share power with one another and with a federal judiciary. This chapter explores an entailment of that shared power: How does the Constitution ensure that these two court systems respect each other's spheres of power?

The question arises because state and federal courts not only share power, but they exercise overlapping jurisdiction. For example, under modern understandings of personal jurisdiction, several different states may have jurisdiction to hear a case against a particular defendant. Similarly, state courts can hear cases arising under federal law, and federal courts, sitting in diversity, can hear cases that could also be tried in state courts. Under these circumstances both state and federal courts frequently face a question that arises from this overlapping jurisdiction: What law applies to the case before us?

Seen abstractly, this question has many applications. Must a state court in a criminal trial apply federal constitutional law? Must a state court, hearing a question arising under federal law, follow the Federal Rules of Civil Procedure instead of its usual procedural code? The *Erie* problem, from which this chapter takes its title, involves a very specific subset of these questions: When a federal court sits in diversity jurisdiction, where does it look for its sources of law?

This question, though phrased narrowly, opens the door onto a much larger set of questions about the relations of state and federal courts and of constitutional interpretation. Speaking about part of this problem, one distinguished commentator has written, "No issue in the whole field of federal jurisprudence has been more difficult. . . ."* This chapter will seek to explain why someone might take that view — but also to make the problems less difficult than this quotation implies.

A.   State Courts as Lawmakers in a Federal System

1.   The Issue in Historical Context

To understand how the issue arises, one needs a very brief historical introduction. The first judiciary act contained a section now codified at 28 U.S.C. §1652 and known as the Rules of Decision Act:

> The laws of the several states, except where the Constitution or Acts of Congress otherwise require or provide, shall be regarded as rules of decisions in civil actions in the courts of the United States, in cases where they apply.

On its face, one might think that that statute, in effect since the earliest days of the Republic, would resolve the question — telling the federal courts to follow state law in diversity cases. The story is not that simple, however, because people have disagreed sharply about what "the laws of the several states" means.

The leading pre-*Erie* case, the case *Erie* overrules, was Swift v. Tyson, 41 U.S. 1 (1841). The case involved a "bill of exchange," a halfway step between a promissory note and a modern check. With promissory notes, there are numerous defenses assertable by anyone sued for breach; with checks those defenses are much more limited. The substantive issue in *Swift* was how many defenses could be asserted and thus how much like a contract and how much like a check the "bill" was. Procedurally and jurisprudentially (the aspect with which we shall be concerned), the issue was how one decided which law applied to the substantive question. *Swift* was a diversity case filed in a federal court sitting in New York. New York courts had spoken on the substantive issue, ruling that bills were subject to a number of defenses. Were these New York cases part of "the laws" of that state and thus binding on the federal district court? No, held the U.S. Supreme Court; the New York precedents were not

---

* Wright, Federal Courts 369.

"laws"; instead, the federal courts sitting in diversity were free to ignore them:

> But, admitting the doctrine to be fully settled in New York, it remains to be considered whether it is obligatory upon this court if it differs from the principles established in the general commercial law. It is observable that the Courts of New York do not found their decisions upon this point upon any local statute, or positive, fixed, or ancient usage; but they deduce the doctrine from the general principles of commercial law. It is, however, contended that [the Rules of Decision Act] furnishes a rule obligatory on this Court to follow the decisions of state tribunals in all cases to which they apply. . . . In order to maintain the argument, it is essential . . . that the word "laws" [in the Rules of Decision Act] includes within the scope of its meaning the decisions of local tribunals. In the ordinary use of language it will hardly be contended that the decisions of Courts constitute laws. They are at most evidence of what the laws are; and are not themselves laws. . . . The laws of a state are more usually understood to mean the rules and enactments promulgated by the legislative authority thereof. . . . [The court said it would be bound by state legislation and by state judge-made law on matters of peculiarly "local usages," generally understood to involve land title, but not on more general topics.] Undoubtedly, the decisions of the local tribunals upon such subjects are entitled to, and will receive, the most deliberate attention and respect of this Court; but they cannot furnish positive rules on conclusive authority. . . .

Swift went on to reach a conclusion different from that reached by the New York courts in similar cases.

In the next century *Swift* came to be seen by many not only as momentous but also as pernicious, not because of its holding on the negotiability of bills of exchange, but because of its treatment of state law. For many federal courts *Swift* became a charter of judicial independence, a declaration that they could ignore state law even when sitting in cases that were not explicitly governed by federal law. Often decisions in the *Swift* line of cases seemed to favor business interests. One commentary argues:

> The furor can only be understood against the background of 19th-century mercantile expansion westward, although it is rarely presented so. In the latter part of the 19th century, and the early part of the 20th, the federal courts came to be seen as protectors of mercantile and corporate interests against agrarian and workingmen's interests. . . .*

Notice that *Swift* reached its conclusion as an interpretation of the Rules of Decision Act, which Congress could have amended during the

---

* Howard Fink and Mark V. Tushnet, Federal Jurisdiction: Policy and Practice 168 (1984).

ensuing century. Congress did not amend the Act. The next step in the story took matters out of Congress's hands.

2. Constitutionalizing the Issue

This step grew out of homely circumstances. On Thursday, July 26, 1934, Harry Tompkins visited his mother-in-law's house in Hughestown, Pennsylvania, a village of 2,800 people. He received a ride part of the way home and walked the remaining distance along the railroad tracks of the Erie Railroad, keeping several feet between himself and the tracks. A train passed, and an open door on a refrigerator car struck him and knocked him partially under the train. His right arm was severed. After recovering from his injuries, he sought a lawyer and found 27-year-old Bernard Nemeroff. Hoping to benefit from Swift v. Tyson, Nemeroff and his partner, 21-year-old Aaron Danzig, chose to bring suit against the railroad in the federal District Court for the Southern District of New York.

Under Pennsylvania law, for whose application the railroad's lawyer argued, Tompkins was a trespasser, and the railroad was therefore liable only for "wanton" negligence, a finding unlikely given the facts. The judge, relying on the freedom given by Swift v. Tyson, instructed the jury according to the "general law," that the railroad was liable even if it was guilty of only "ordinary" negligence. The jury returned a verdict for Tompkins in the amount of $30,000. The railroad appealed, but the Second Circuit upheld Tompkins's verdict. The railroad then sought a writ of certiorari from the Supreme Court. In the meantime the railroad asked Justice Cardozo to stay the judgment until the Supreme Court could consider the certiorari petition, and Justice Cardozo obliged. The railroad then made Tompkins a settlement offer — $7,500 plus the withdrawal of its certiorari petition — but Danzig and Nemeroff talked him out of accepting and then hid him from the railroad's lawyers.

The Supreme Court granted certiorari, even though it rarely did so in negligence cases. On April 25, 1938, the Supreme Court decided the case in one of the last opinions written by Justice Brandeis. The decision went unnoticed until Justice Stone wrote privately to Arthur Krock of the *New York Times* calling to his attention "the most important opinion since I have been on the court."*

---

* This summary comes from Younger, Observation: What Happened in *Erie*, 56 Tex. L. Rev. 1011 (1978), and Rizzi, Erie Memoirs Reveal Drama, Tragedy, 63 Harv. L. Record 2 (Sept. 24, 1976).

Erie Railroad v. Tompkins

304 U.S. 64 (1938)

Mr. Justice BRANDEIS delivered the opinion of the Court.

The question for decision is whether the oft-challenged doctrine of Swift v. Tyson shall now be disapproved. . . .

The Erie insisted that its duty to Tompkins was no greater than that owed to a trespasser. It contended, among other things, that its duty to Tompkins, and hence its liability, should be determined in accordance with the Pennsylvania law. . . .

The Erie had contended that application of the Pennsylvania rule was required, among other things, by [the Rules of Decision Act].

Because of the importance of the question whether the federal court was free to disregard the alleged rule of the Pennsylvania common law, we granted certiorari.

First. Swift v. Tyson held that federal courts exercising jurisdiction on the ground of diversity of citizenship need not, in matters of general jurisprudence, apply the unwritten law of the State as declared by its highest court; that they are free to exercise an independent judgment as to what the *common* law of the State is — or should be; and that, as there stated by Mr. Justice Story:

> [T]he true interpretation of the [Rules of Decision Act] limited its applica-
> tion to state laws strictly local, that is to say, to the positive statutes of the
> state, and the construction thereof adopted by the local tribunals, and to
> rights and titles to things having a permanent locality, such as the rights
> and titles to real estate, and other matters immovable and intraterritorial
> in their nature and character. It never has been supposed by us, that the
> section did apply, or was intended to apply, to questions of a more general
> nature, not at all dependent upon local statutes or local usages of a fixed
> and permanent operation, as, for example, to the construction of ordinary
> contracts or other written instruments, and especially to questions of gen-
> eral commercial law, where the state tribunals are called upon to perform
> the like functions as ourselves, that is, to ascertain upon general reasoning
> and legal analogies, what is the true exposition of the contract of instrument,
> or what is the just rule furnished by the principles of commercial law to
> govern the case.

The Court in applying the [Rules of Decision Act] to equity cases, in Mason v. United States said: "The statute, however, is merely declarative of the rule which would exist in the absence of the statute." The federal courts assumed, in the broad field of "general law," the power to declare rules of decision which Congress was confessedly without power to enact as statutes. Doubt was repeatedly expressed as to the correctness of the

construction given [the Act], and as to the soundness of the rule which
it introduced. But it was the more recent research of a competent scholar,
who examined the original document, which established that the construction given to it by the Court was erroneous; and that the purpose
of the section was merely to make certain that, in all matters except those
in which some federal law is controlling, the federal courts exercising
jurisdiction in diversity of citizenship cases would apply as their rules of
decision the law of the State, unwritten as well as written.[5]

Criticism of the doctrine became widespread after the decision of
Black & White Taxicab Co. v. Brown & Yellow Taxicab Co. There,
Brown and Yellow, a Kentucky corporation owned by Kentuckians, and
the Louisville and Nashville Railroad, also a Kentucky corporation, wished
that the former should have the exclusive privilege of soliciting passenger
and baggage transportation at the Bowling Green, Kentucky, railroad
station; and that the Black and White, a competing Kentucky corporation,
should be prevented from interfering with that privilege. Knowing that
such a contract would be void under the common law of Kentucky, it
was arranged that the Brown and Yellow reincorporate under the law of
Tennessee, and that the contract with the railroad should be executed
there. The suit was then brought by the Tennessee corporation in the
federal court for Western Kentucky to enjoin competition by the Black
and White; and injunction issued by the District Court was sustained
by the Court of Appeals; and this Court, citing many decisions in which
the doctrine of Swift v. Tyson had been applied, affirmed the decree.

Second. Experience in applying the doctrine of Swift v. Tyson had
revealed its defects, political and social; and the benefits expected to flow
from the rule did not accrue. Persistence of state courts in their own
opinions on questions of common law prevented uniformity; and the
impossibility of discovering a satisfactory line of demarcation between
the province of general law and that of local law developed a new well
of uncertainties.

On the other hand, the mischievous results of the doctrine had become
apparent. Diversity of citizenship jurisdiction was conferred in order to
prevent apprehended discrimination in State courts against those not
citizens of the State. Swift v. Tyson introduced grave discrimination by
non-citizens against citizens. It made rights enjoyed under the unwritten
"general law" vary according to whether enforcement was sought in the
state or in the federal court; and the privilege of selecting the court in

5. Charles Warren, New Light on the History of the Federal Judiciary Act of 1789,
37 Harv. L. Rev. 49, 51-52, 81-88, 108 (1923).

which the right should be determined was conferred upon the non-citizen. Thus, the doctrine rendered impossible equal protection of the law. In attempting to promote uniformity of law throughout the United States, the doctrine had prevented uniformity in the administration of the law of the State.

The discrimination resulting became in practice far-reaching. This resulted in part from the broad province accorded to the so-called "general law" as to which federal courts exercised an independent judgment. In addition to questions of purely commercial law, "general law" was held to include the obligations under contracts entered into and to be performed within the State, the extent to which a carrier operating within a State may stipulate for exemption from liability for his own negligence or that of his employee; the liability for torts committed within the State upon persons resident or property located there, even where the question of liability depended upon the scope of a property right conferred by the State; and the right to exemplary or punitive damages. Furthermore, state decisions construing local deeds, mineral conveyances, and even devises of real estate were disregarded.

In part the discrimination resulted from the wide range of persons held entitled to avail themselves of the federal rule by resort to the diversity of citizenship jurisdiction. Through this jurisdiction individual citizens willing to remove from their own State and become citizens of another might avail themselves of the federal rule. And, without even change of residence, a corporate citizen of the State could avail itself of the federal rule by re-incorporating under the laws of another State, as was done in the *Taxicab* case.

The injustice and confusion incident to the doctrine of Swift v. Tyson have been repeatedly urged as reasons for abolishing or limiting diversity of citizenship jurisdiction. Other legislative relief has been proposed. If only a question of statutory construction were involved, we should not be prepared to abandon a doctrine so widely applied throughout nearly a century. But the unconstitutionality of the course pursued has now been made clear and compels us to do so.

Third. Except in matters governed by the Federal Constitution or by Acts of Congress, the law to be applied in any case is the law of the State. And whether the law of the State shall be declared by its Legislature in a statute or by its highest court in a decision is not a matter of federal concern. There is no federal general common law. Congress has no power to declare substantive rules of common law applicable in a State whether they be local in their nature or "general," be they commercial law or a part of the law of torts. And no clause in the Constitution

purports to confer such a power upon the federal courts. As stated by
Mr. Justice Field when protesting in Baltimore & Ohio R. Co. v. Baugh,
against ignoring the Ohio common law of fellow servant liability:

> I am aware that what has been termed the general law of the country —
> which is often little less than what the judge advancing the doctrine thinks
> at the time should be the general law on a particular subject — has been
> often advanced in judicial opinions of this court to control a conflicting
> law of a State. I admit that learned judges have fallen into the habit of
> repeating this doctrine as a convenient mode of brushing aside the law of
> a State in conflict with their views. And I confess that, moved and governed
> by the authority of the great names of those judges, I have, myself, in many
> instances, unhesitatingly and confidently, but I think now erroneously,
> repeated the same doctrine. But, notwithstanding the great names which
> may be cited in favor of the doctrine, and notwithstanding the frequency
> with which the doctrine has been reiterated, there stands, as a perpetual
> protest against its repetition, the Constitution of the United States, which
> recognizes and preserves the autonomy and independence of the States —
> independence in their legislative and independence in their judicial de-
> partments. Supervision over either the legislative or the judicial action of
> the States is in no case permissible except as to matters by the Constitution
> specifically authorized or delegated to the United States. Any interference
> with either, except as thus permitted, is an invasion of the authority of the
> State and, to that extent, a denial of its independence.

The fallacy underlying the rule declared in Swift v. Tyson is made
clear by Mr. Justice Holmes. The doctrine rests upon the assumption
that there is "a transcendental body of law outside of any particular State
but obligatory within it unless and until changed by statute," that federal
courts have the power to use their judgment as to what the rules of
common law are; and that in the federal courts "the parties are entitled
to an independent judgment on matters of general law":

> [B]ut law in the sense in which courts speak of it today does not exist
> without some definite authority behind it. The common law so far as it
> is enforced in a State, whether called common law or not, is not the
> common law generally but the law of that State existing by the authority
> of that State without regard to what it may have been in England or
> anywhere else. . . . The authority and only authority is the State, and if
> that be so, the voice adopted by the State as its own [whether it be of its
> Legislature or of its Supreme Court] should utter the last word.

Thus the doctrine of Swift v. Tyson is, as Mr. Justice Holmes said,
"an unconstitutional assumption of powers by courts of the United States
which no lapse of time or respectable array of opinion should make

us hesitate to correct." In disapproving that doctrine we do not hold unconstitutional §34 of the Federal Judiciary Act of 1789 or any other Act of Congress. We merely declare that in applying the doctrine this Court and the lower courts have invaded rights which in our opinion are reserved by the Constitution to the several States.

Fourth. The defendant contended that by the common law of Pennsylvania as declared by its highest court in Falchetti v. Pennsylvania R. Co., 160 A. 859, the only duty owed to the plaintiff was to refrain from willful or wanton injury. The plaintiff denied that such is the Pennsylvania law. In support of their respective contentions the parties discussed and cited many decisions of the Supreme Court of the State. The Circuit Court of Appeals ruled that the question of liability is one of general law; and on that ground declined to decide the issue of state law. As we hold this was error, the judgment is reversed and the case remanded to it for further proceedings in conformity with our opinion.
Reversed.

Mr. Justice REED.

I concur in the conclusion reached in this case, in the disapproval of the doctrine of Swift v. Tyson, and in the reasoning of the majority opinion except insofar as it relies upon the unconstitutionality of the "course pursued" by the federal courts.

The "doctrine of Swift v. Tyson," as I understand it, is that the words "the law" as used in [the Rules of Decision Act], do not include in their meaning "the decisions of the local tribunals." Mr. Justice Story, in deciding that point, said: "Undoubtedly, the decisions of the local tribunals upon such subjects are entitled to, and will receive, the most deliberate attention and respect of this Court; but they cannot furnish positive rules, or conclusive authority, by which our own judgments are to be bound up and governed."

To decide the case now before us and to "disapprove" the doctrine of Swift v. Tyson requires only that we say that the words "the laws" include in their meaning the decisions of the local tribunals. As the majority opinion shows, by its reference to Mr. Warren's researches and the first quotation from Mr. Justice Holmes, that this Court is now of the view that "laws" includes "decisions," it is unnecessary to go further and declare that the "course pursued" was "unconstitutional," instead of merely erroneous.

The "unconstitutional" course referred to in the majority opinion is apparently the ruling in Swift v. Tyson that the supposed omission of Congress to legislate as to the effect of decisions leaves federal courts free to interpret general law for themselves. I am not at all sure whether, in the absence of federal statutory direction, federal courts would be compelled to follow state decisions. There was sufficient doubt about the matter in 1789 to induce the first Congress to legislate. No former opinions of this Court have passed upon it. Mr. Justice Holmes evidently saw nothing "unconstitutional" which required the overruling of Swift v. Tyson, for he said in the very opinion quoted by the majority, "I should leave Swift v. Tyson undisturbed, as I indicated in Kuhn v. Fairmont Coal Co., but I would not allow it to spread the assumed dominion into new fields." Black & White Taxicab Co. v. Brown & Yellow Taxicab Co. If the opinion commits this Court to the position that the Congress is without power to declare what rules of substantive law shall govern the federal courts, that conclusion also seems questionable. The line between procedural and substantive law is hazy but no one doubts federal power over procedure. The Judiciary Article and the "necessary and proper" clause of Article One may fully authorize legislation, such as this section of the Judiciary Act.

In this Court, stare decisis, in statutory construction, is a useful rule, not an inexorable command. It seems preferable to overturn an established construction of an Act of Congress, rather than, in the circumstances of this case, to interpret the Constitution.

There is no occasion to discuss further the range or soundness of these few phrases of the opinion. It is sufficient now to call attention to them and express my own nonacquiescence.

[Dissenting opinion of Justices BUTLER and MCREYNOLDS is omitted.]

NOTES AND PROBLEMS

1. Upon remand to the Court of Appeals, judgment for the railroad was entered. Plaintiff took nothing. What is the connection between this result and the doctrine announced in the decision?

a. Under the circumstances of this case, why did it matter to Harry Tompkins (or to the Erie Railroad) whether *Swift* was overruled?

b. Tompkins won in the trial court. The U.S. Supreme Court seems to assume that if the tort law of Pennsylvania applied to the facts of the case, the railroad would owe Tompkins only the duty of refraining from wanton or willful negligence. Tompkins had a better chance of preserving his verdict if the railroad owed him a higher degree of care. Tompkins's lawyers pointed to a different source of law, one requiring such a higher standard of care. What was that source?

2. With the practical consequences framed, turn to the doctrine.

a. According to the opinion, what is the source of the federal courts' duty to follow Pennsylvania judge-made law in this case?

b. The most obvious answer is to point to the Rule of Decision Act, requiring federal courts to apply state law in appropriate cases. Why won't that work as a fair reading of *Erie*?

c. The *Erie* Court says that it is handing down a constitutional decision. Does the opinion ever identify a part of the Constitution that leads to its holding?

d. If *Erie* isn't a constitutional decision, Congress could change its result. How?

3. Since *Erie* was decided, lawyers and political scientists have argued about whether it was a constitutional decision, and, if so, how it ought to be understood. One plausible candidate is the opinion's statement that "Congress has no power to declare substantive rules of common law applicable in a State whether they be local in their nature or 'general,' be they commercial law or a part of the law of torts."

a. Assume for the moment that this statement is accurate as a matter of constitutional law. Congress has no power to make general tort law, and nothing in Article III gives the federal courts that power either. It would therefore follow that a federal court, like the district court in *Erie*, that purported to be declaring substantive law in such a setting would be acting unconstitutionally — because it would be exercising a power not given it by any part of the Constitution.

b. Now alter the assumption about Congressional power. Understandings of constitutional law have changed considerably since the *Erie* decision was handed down. Today's Supreme Court would likely uphold a federal statute establishing rules for liability for injury incurred along the right-of-way of a railroad engaged in interstate commerce. Indeed, Congress has gone much further than that: To choose just one example, a federal statute regulating debt collectors purports to specify venue for a state law lawsuit seeking to enforce a simple debt, governed by state contract law. 15 U.S.C. §1692i(a). If such statutes are constitutional, should *Erie*, though not overruled, be considered obsolete because its underlying assumptions have been eroded?

c. One answer to the preceding question is to distinguish between Congress's power to make such a law and the federal courts' power to do so. Because of its structure (giving each state a voice), Congress gives considerable deference to state interests; the courts have no such structural characteristics. One might therefore think that it continues to be unconstitutional for the federal courts to displace state law, even if the federal government as a whole could do so. Does the mere grant of diversity jurisdiction to the district courts include the power to legislate — judicially — whenever Congress itself could do so?

d. Test your understanding of the constitutional issues by trying to restate — briefly — the constitutional argument set forth by this note.

4. There have been a very few instances in which the Court has taken a grant of jurisdiction to include the power to set forth substantive law. In Textile Workers Union of America v. Lincoln Mills, 353 U.S. 448 (1957), the Supreme Court was faced with an attack on the constitutionality of §301 of the Taft-Hartley Act, 29 U.S.C. §185 (1982). The statute was challenged on the ground that it purported to confer jurisdiction on the federal courts for disputes arising between employers and labor unions, without suggesting substantive rules to govern such disputes. The problem arose in this case because there was neither obvious federal question jurisdiction nor diversity of citizenship among the parties. The Court said Congress must have intended by the grant of jurisdiction in §301 to give the federal courts substantive rulemaking power in the area — in other words, the courts were to develop a federal common law under the Taft-Hartley Act (often by borrowing from state contract law and the like).

In light of *Lincoln Mills*, could Congress amend the Rules of Decision Act to provide that the federal courts can form their own common law? Or is a narrower grant, limited to a single field like labor law, a necessary condition for such a delegation?

5. Note that the *Erie* case was brought in the Southern District of New York, yet the Court assumed that Pennsylvania law had to be applied. Why?

a. Each state has a body of law called its conflict of laws rules, which specify the circumstances in which courts of that state should follow laws of other jurisdictions, such as those of other states, federal law, or foreign law. Two inferences are possible from the *Erie* Court's silence on this point. The Court might have thought it absolutely clear that New York courts would have applied Pennsylvania law, or the Court might have thought that the New York conflict of laws rules were irrelevant.

b. In the latter case, conflict of laws rules would themselves be an exception to *Erie* — that is, the federal courts on their own would be free to choose which state's law would apply to a case connected to more than one state. Some have suggested that the federal courts, as a neutral forum, would be well-suited to decide which state's law should apply.

c. Such speculation was laid to rest, however, in Klaxon Co. v. Stentor Elec. Mfg. Co., 313 U.S. 487 (1941), in which the Supreme Court applied *Erie* principles to conflicts rules: Under *Erie* a federal court sitting in diversity must apply the conflicts principles of the forum state. Failure to refer to New York conflicts rules in *Erie* presumably came about because in the simple case presented by *Erie*, all states' conflicts rules (at the time) pointed to the law of Pennsylvania.

6. Much of the Court's discussion in *Erie* is devoted to the evils of forum-shopping. By "forum-shopping" the Court seems to mean the practice of a litigant's selecting one rather than another court in which to sue, in the hope that the court will in some way treat the litigant more favorably than another court that might have heard the case. For example, under Swift v. Tyson there were several circumstances in which federal courts would enforce contracts that state courts would have refused to enforce. In such an instance, a plaintiff hoping to enforce such an agreement would "shop" for a forum (in this case the federal courts) that would enforce it.

a. What's wrong with different outcomes? If a federal judge believes that she has come up with the just and proper solution to a particular legal problem, doesn't it deny justice to the parties to rule to the contrary simply to imitate the state court's predicted result? Isn't that behaving as if two wrongs will somehow make a right?

b. What's wrong with forum-shopping? *Erie* seems to assume that forum-shopping between state and federal courts is the major problem; what about forum-shopping among states? Seven years after *Erie*, the Court decided *International Shoe*, thus giving its constitutional blessing to an extended jurisdictional reach for state courts. With this extension, plaintiffs will often have a choice of several different states in which to sue a defendant, states that may have different substantive laws. Indeed, even at the time of *Erie*, Tompkins could have sued the railroad in Pennsylvania, in New York, and perhaps in several other states where it did business; each of those states would likely have taken a slightly different approach to his case. So, if forum-shopping is both inevitable and constitutionally permissible, why does it become unconstitutional in *Erie*?

7. Consider two perspectives on *Erie*:

a. *Erie* increases the significance of state court decisions by commanding federal judges sitting in diversity to abide by those decisions. That was a tactful thing for the Court to do and maybe was constitutionally required, but in the years since *Erie* the number of questions left to state judges has decreased significantly. First, state legislatures are more active than they were in the period before *Erie*, so that state statutes (which controlled even in the regime of Swift v. Tyson) have left fewer areas in the discretion of state judges' lawmaking power. Second, in the wake of the New Deal and the civil rights era, Congress has exerted much more control over a number of areas that were once left to the states. The combination of these two factors has diminished the significance of *Erie*: It commands federal courts to respect state court lawmaking, but state court lawmaking matters less than it did in 1938. The upshot is that *Erie* commands federal judges to pay careful attention to their state counterparts even as those counterparts' decisions matter less and less.

b. *Erie* was a sensible decision. The mistake came three years later, in Klaxon v. Stentor, Note 5c supra. *Klaxon* surrendered the only really useful role federal courts might have played in conflicts between citizens of different states: that of providing a neutral forum for deciding *which* state's law should apply to the case. As things stand, we have left to the state courts the task of deciding whether their own law or that of a sister state should apply. For example, if a citizen of Ohio sues a citizen of New York on a claim arising in Pennsylvania, there could be a question of whose statute of limitations or whose damage rules apply — those of New York, Pennsylvania, or Ohio? In making such decisions it is difficult for state courts to be impartial: They will too often pick either their own rules or the rule that favors their citizen. Federal courts could provide a less partisan forum. Moreover, independent, federal choice of law rules created by federal courts would become a particularly important form of federal common law, one that would bind the state courts as well under the Supremacy Clause of the Constitution.

8. *Erie* was the first civil case heard by Judge Mandelbaum, the trial judge. Judge Mandelbaum, born in Poland, was a product of Tammany politics and, over strong protest from the bar, was appointed to the bench by President Roosevelt. Before his appointment Mandelbaum had visited the federal courthouse only once, to see what it looked like. Do you agree with his notes, penned in the margin of his copy of the Supreme Court's *Erie* opinion and reported in Younger, Observation: What Happened in *Erie*, 56 Tex. L. Rev. 1011, 1030 (1978): "Because the Swift Tyson case although before this case I never knew of its existence to be truthful and for the confusion this decision brought about, it might have been better to leave it alone and stand by good old Swifty"?

NOTE: *ERIE* AND THE PERSISTENCE OF FEDERAL COMMON LAW

Erie says that "there is no federal general common law." One can easily understand this sentence to mean more than it does. In fact, federal common law continues to flourish. *Erie* holds only that "general" federal common law may not displace that of the states in areas in which the

Constitution grants lawmaking power to the states. The Constitution grants substantive lawmaking power to the federal government; because the courts are part of that government, and because courts in the United States have traditionally exercised lawmaking powers, the Constitution thus grants potential lawmaking power to the federal courts in many areas.

The grant of judicial power in admiralty and maritime cases under Article III invites federal courts to create common law for such cases. Federal statutes may also provide an opportunity for federal common law to fill gaps in the statutory scheme. Much of antitrust law, for example, is judge-made law that fills the gaps left by vague and general statutes. Perhaps the most famous case in which the Court has found the existence of a jurisdictional statute authority for the federal courts to elaborate a body of federal common law is Textile Workers Union of America v. Lincoln Mills, discussed in Note 4 supra. In *Lincoln Mills* the Court held that the jurisdictional provisions of the Taft-Hartley Act, regulating labor unions, was an invitation for the federal courts to fashion federal common law in the labor area.

B. The Limits of State Power in Federal Courts

Having struggled with the constitutional ambiguities, the student will be distressed to learn that, constitutional basis aside, *Erie* was an easy case for the application of the principle it announced. The remainder of this chapter will consider decisions in which the issue is whether and how to apply the *Erie* doctrine — decisions that require a much more subtle look at what that case held.

Erie established that federal courts sitting in a diversity action were bound to replicate state practice in some circumstances: What were those circumstances? Though *Erie* did not say so, its setting suggested that at the very least federal courts sitting in diversity should observe state substantive law, whether made by legislatures or by judges. But what about other "laws"? For example, were federal courts sitting in diversity bound to apply state statutes of limitations? If the courts of the state in question did not generally enforce arbitration agreements, could federal courts nevertheless do so if authorized by a federal statute? If a suit in state court could be decided only by a judge, was a federal court precluded from using a jury? If a state statute required personal service of process, did that requirement also apply to process served in a federal diversity action? If a state court were bound to refuse to honor a contractual forum selection clause, were federal courts sitting in that state required to do likewise? If a state legislature orders its appellate courts to reduce excessive damages awarded by juries, does a federal appellate court have the same power?

In the years since *Erie* the Supreme Court has addressed each of these questions (as well as others) in an effort to mediate between two opposing principles: that *Erie* requires deference to state courts as lawmaking bodies, and that federal courts are an independent judicial system with the autonomy that statement implies. Justice Reed's concurrence in *Erie* raised but did not resolve the question: "The line between procedural and substantive law is hazy, but no one doubts federal power over procedure." Notice that many of these questions involve issues that could be described as "procedural." As you read the next cases, consider whether it is true that "no one doubts" federal power over procedure.

1. Interpreting the Constitutional Command of *Erie*

Guaranty Trust Co. v. York
326 U.S. 99 (1945)

Mr. Justice FRANKFURTER delivered the opinion of the Court. . . .

[Plaintiffs sued a bond trustee in a federal diversity action alleging misrepresentation and breach of trust. New York substantive law governed. Among other defenses, defendant invoked the New York statute of limitations. Plaintiffs argued that the statute of limitations did not bar the suit because it was on the "equity side" of federal court. The courts of equity had traditionally considered the length of time elapsing between the maturing of a claim and the bringing of suit but had not thought themselves strictly bound by statutes of limitations. Referring to that equitable tradition, the Second Circuit ruled that plaintiffs' suit was not barred. The Supreme Court disagreed.]

Our starting point must be the policy of federal jurisdiction which Erie R. Co. v. Tompkins embodies. In overruling Swift v. Tyson, Erie R. Co. v. Tompkins did not merely overrule a venerable case. It overruled a particular way of looking at law which dominated the judicial process long after its inadequacies had been laid bare. Law was conceived as a "brooding omnipresence" of Reason, of which decisions were merely evidence and not themselves the controlling formulations. Accordingly, federal courts deemed themselves free to ascertain what Reason, and therefore Law, required wholly independent of authoritatively declared State law, even in cases where a legal right as the basis for relief was created by State authority and could not be created by federal authority and the case got into a federal court merely because it was "between Citizens of different States" under Art. III, §2 of the Constitution of the United States. . . .

And so this case reduces itself to the narrow question whether, when no recovery could be had in a State court because the action is barred by the statute of limitations, a federal court in equity can take cognizance of the suit because there is diversity of citizenship between the parties. Is the outlawry, according to State law, of a claim created by the States a matter of "substantive rights" to be respected by a federal court of equity when that court's jurisdiction is dependent on the fact that there is a State-created right, or is such statute of "a mere remedial character," which a federal court may disregard?

Matters of "substance" and matters of "procedure" are much talked about in the books as though they defined a great divide cutting across the whole domain of law. But, of course, "substance" and "procedure" are the same key-words to very different problems. . . . Each implies different variables depending on the particular problem for which it is used. . . .

And so the question is not whether a statute of limitations is deemed a matter of "procedure" in some sense. The question is whether such a statute concerns merely the manner and the means by which a right to recover, as recognized by the State, is enforced, or whether such statutory limitation is a matter of substance in the aspect that alone is relevant to our problem, namely, does it significantly affect the result of a litigation for a federal court to disregard a law of a State that would be controlling in an action upon the same claim by the same parties in a State court?

It is therefore immaterial whether statutes of limitation are characterized either as "substantive" or "procedural" in State court opinions in any use of those terms unrelated to the specific issue before us. Erie R. Co. v. Tompkins was not an endeavor to formulate scientific legal terminology. It expressed a policy that touches vitally the proper distribution of judicial power between State and federal courts. In essence, the intent of that decision was to insure that, in all cases where a federal court is exercising jurisdiction solely because of the diversity of citizenship of the parties, the outcome of the litigation in the federal court should be substantially the same, so far as legal rules determine the outcome of a litigation, as it would be if tried in a State court. The nub of the policy that underlies Erie R. Co. v. Tompkins is that for the same transaction the accident of a suit by a non-resident litigant in a federal court instead of in a State court a block away should not lead to a substantially different result. And so, putting to one side abstractions regarding "substance" and "procedure," we have held that in diversity cases the federal courts must follow the law of the State as to burden of proof, as to conflict of laws, Klaxon Co. v. Stentor Co., as to contributory negligence. Erie R. Co. v. Tompkins has been applied with an eye alert to essentials in avoiding disregard of State law in diversity cases in the federal courts. A policy so important to our federalism must be kept free from entanglements with analytical or terminological niceties. . . .

The judgment is reversed and the case is remanded for proceedings not inconsistent with this opinion.

So ordered.

[The dissenting opinion of Justice RUTLEDGE is omitted.]

NOTES AND PROBLEMS

1. *Guaranty Trust* displays a ferocity that impedes analysis.

a. The opinion sharply attacks the proposition that if something is "procedural" it is not governed by the rule in *Erie*. Why? The main opinion in *Erie* had asserted no such proposition; is Justice Frankfurter disputing Justice Reed's statement about federal power over procedure?

b. Even in the midst of this attack, however, Justice Frankfurter conceded that federal courts need not follow state law that "concern[ed] merely the manner and means by which a right to recover is . . . enforced." Isn't this saying that Justice Reed was right?

c. As you read the rest of the cases in the *Erie* line, consider whether they don't come down to the question of defining "the manner and means by which a right to recover is . . . enforced." (A procedure casebook can be excused for omitting "merely" from the phrase.)

2. To solve the problem of distinguishing between such "manner and mode" issues and the other (dare one say "substantive"?) kind, *Guaranty Trust* proposed what came to be known as the "outcome-determinative test." A state rule that was outcome-determinative was to be followed, no matter how it might be labeled.

What does that mean? At one time, the federal government used paper measuring 8 × 10½ inches. The standard sizes are 8½ × 11 and 8½ × 14. If a litigant offered the clerk of a federal district a complaint typed on 8½ × 14 inch paper, but the clerk refused to accept it on the grounds that the rules required shorter paper and the filing cabinets couldn't hold paper 14 inches long, would you call the rule invoked by the clerk substantive because it was outcome-determinative? After all, the plaintiff might very well win in state court but can hardly win in federal court if the complaint can't be filed. If you conclude that the "paper size" rule is not substantive for *Erie* purposes, how would you modify the outcome-determinative rule to exclude cases of this sort?

3. *Guaranty Trust* not only decided a lawsuit; it also asserted that *Erie* marked a revolution in legal thought, a rejection of "Law . . . as a 'brooding omnipresence' of Reason," a view presumably attributed to those judges (perhaps especially to Justice Story) who had adhered to Swift v. Tyson. *Erie* and *Guaranty Trust* asserted that such a view was not only jurisprudentially bankrupt but historically false — that the understanding of the Rules of Decision Act held by its framers was in accordance with that enunciated by *Guaranty Trust* and *Erie*.

a. Historians of American law have vigorously debated this question, and a number have kinder words to say about Justice Story's interpretation than does *Guaranty Trust*. One study argues that the Rules of Decision Act meant just what Story thought it did, and that its reference to "laws of the several states" was meant precisely to refer to "general law" rather than to the laws of the individual states. Patrick Borchers, The Origins of Diversity Jurisdiction, the Rise of Legal Positivism, and a Brave New World for *Erie* and *Klaxon*, 72 Tex. L. Rev. 79 (1993). Others have argued that Justice Story was primarily interested in using diversity jurisdiction to create a uniform national law of commercial transactions or in seeking to fulfill the parties' expectations about how their agreement would be interpreted. Compare T. A. Freyer, Harmony and Dissonance: The *Swift & Erie* Cases in American Federalism 17-34 (1981), with R. Bridwell and R. U. Whitten, The Constitution and the Common Law 1-5 (1977).

b. Does the difference in historical interpretation matter? Perhaps: If *Swift* was a defensible use of federal courts' lawmaking power, then *Erie* is not a constitutional decision. Instead it is simply a case in which the Supreme Court in 1938 (when the American economy was irrevocably national in scope) thought that it was no longer appropriate to interpret the Rules of Decision Act as *Swift* had. One implication of this view is that Congress would be free to change its mind and grant the general courts sitting in diversity lawmaking power.

4. In reaching its decision that the federal courts were bound to apply the state statute of limitations, the *Guaranty Trust* majority rejected an argument that *Erie* did not apply to the equity practice of federal courts. Federal courts for much of the preceding century had exercised a powerful independent equity jurisdiction. There had been two sets of equity rules (promulgated by the Supreme Court in 1843 and 1912), which freed the federal courts from adhering to state procedures in equity cases. Such a tradition might have been a basis for drawing a distinction between federal obligation to follow state "law" while allowing some room for

divergent practices in equity. But consider two arguments against drawing such a distinction. First, 1938, the date of the *Erie* decision, was also the year in which the Federal Rules were first promulgated, and one of the Rules' most important achievements was the merger of law and equity. It would look odd for the federal courts to be insisting that they no longer drew a distinction between legal and equitable remedies and procedures while disregarding state practices on the basis of such a distinction. Second, the existence of federal equity doctrines had been a prime reason for some litigants to seek federal courts in pre-*Erie* days. If forum-shopping was one of the concerns of *Erie*, it would be strange to leave intact one of the federal judicial practices that had provided a major reason for such preference of federal courts.

5. After *Guaranty Trust* the Supreme Court for more than a decade regularly upheld state practices (whether called substantive or procedural) whenever they conflicted with the practice the federal court would have used in the absence of *Erie*. All these cases involved conflicts between a federal statute or Rule of Civil Procedure and a state practice:

a. Ragan v. Merchants Transfer & Warehouse Co., 337 U.S. 530 (1949), held that state law, rather than federal, would determine when an action was "commenced" for purposes of satisfying the state statute of limitations. Federal Rule 3 provides that an action is commenced by filing a complaint; the state rule provided that a case was commenced by service on the defendant. *Guaranty Trust* was invoked as controlling.

b. Cohen v. Beneficial Indus. Loan Corp., 337 U.S. 541 (1949), held that federal diversity cases must apply a state statute allowing a corporation to require plaintiff to post a bond for the expenses of defense of a shareholder's derivative suit; the corporation could recover its expenses if the plaintiff lost. Federal Rule 23 (now 23.1) did not require such a bond. The purpose of the bond and requirement that the plaintiff was to pay expenses was to discourage so-called strike suits brought to coerce settlements rather than win on the merits.

c. Bernhardt v. Polygraphic Co. of America, 350 U.S. 198 (1956), narrowly construed the federal arbitration statute (which requires federal courts to enforce arbitration agreements in contracts affecting interstate commerce) and held, under the influence of *Erie*, that state law concerning the enforceability of arbitration agreements should control in a diversity action.

d. Woods v. Interstate Realty Co., 337 U.S. 535 (1949), held that a state statute closing the doors of the state courts to out-of-state corporations that had not qualified to do business (by paying taxes) in Mississippi would close the Mississippi federal courts to those same corporations. *Woods* did not consider the effect of Rule 17(b), which says that the state of incorporation, and by inference *not* the forum state, should determine the capacity of a corporation to sue.

6. The cases in Note 5 are remarkable for several reasons:

a. They represent a high-water mark of *Erie*-compelled deference to state courts. Starting only two years after *Bernhardt Polygraphic*, the last of the series, the Court began to retreat from its almost reflexive bowing to state law.

b. Each involved a conflict between a state practice and an arguably applicable federal statute or rule of procedure. Such conflicts have characterized the *Erie* cases for the past forty years.

c. Finally, one can ask whether all — or any — of these cases described in Note 5 are correctly decided. As you will see, the *Erie* cases from the late 1950s onward broke with the pattern of invariably favoring state practice. They also suggested a different framework for analyzing the *Erie* problem and in the process began to retreat from *Guaranty Trust*.

Byrd v. Blue Ridge Rural Electric Cooperative
356 U.S. 525 (1958)

Mr. Justice BRENNAN delivered the opinion of the Court.

[Plaintiff was injured while on a construction job for defendant; he sued in tort. Although plaintiff was employed by an independent contractor, defendant contended plaintiff was doing the same work as defendant's regular employees and, therefore, was a "statutory" employee whose exclusive remedy was under the South Carolina Workmen's Compensation Act.]

[Presenting evidence on the statutory employee defense,] respondent's manager testified on direct examination that three of its substations were built by the respondent's own construction and maintenance crews. When pressed on cross-examination, however, his answers left his testimony in such doubt as to lead the trial judge to say, "I understood he changed his testimony, that they had not built three." But the credibility of the manager's testimony, and the general question whether the evidence in support of the affirmative defense presented a jury issue, became irrelevant because of the interpretation given [the state statute] by the trial judge.

[The Court first decided that the lower courts had incorrectly interpreted the state statute.]

II

A question is also presented as to whether on remand the factual issue is to be decided by the judge or by the jury. The respondent argues on the basis of the decision of the Supreme Court of South Carolina in Adams v. Davison-Paxon Co., that the issue of immunity[*] should be decided by the judge and not by the jury. . . . .

The respondent argues that this state-court decision governs the present diversity case and "divests the jury of its normal function" to decide the disputed fact question of the respondent's immunity under §72-111. This is to contend that the federal court is bound under Erie R. Co. v. Tompkins to follow the state court's holding to secure uniform enforcement of the immunity created by the State.

First. It was decided in Erie R. Co. v. Tompkins that the federal courts in diversity cases must respect the definition of state-created rights and obligations by the state courts. We must, therefore, first examine the rule in Adams v. Davison-Paxon Co. to determine whether it is bound up with these rights and obligations in such a way that its application in the federal court is required.

The Workmen's Compensation Act is administered in South Carolina by its Industrial Commission. The South Carolina courts hold that, on judicial review of actions of the Commission under §72-111, the question whether the claim of an injured workman is within the Commission's jurisdiction is a matter of law for decision by the court, which makes its own findings of fact relating to that jurisdiction. The South Carolina Supreme Court states no reasons in Adams v. Davison-Paxon Co. why, although the jury decides all other factual issues raised by the cause of action and defenses, the jury is displaced as to the factual issue raised by the affirmative defense under §72-111. . . . We find nothing to suggest that this rule was announced as an integral part of the special relationship created by the statute. Thus the requirement appears to be merely a form and mode of enforcing the immunity, Guaranty Trust Co. v. York, and not a rule intended to be bound up with the definition of the rights and obligations of the parties. . . .

Second. But cases following *Erie* have evinced a broader policy to the effect that the federal courts should conform as near as may be — in the absence of other considerations — to state rules even of form and mode where the state rules may bear substantially on the question whether the litigation would come out one way in the federal court and another way in the state court if the federal court failed to apply a particular local rule. E.g., Guaranty Trust Co. v. York; Bernhardt v. Polygraphic Co. Concededly the nature of the tribunal which tries issues may be important in the enforcement of the parcel of rights making up a cause of action or defense, and bear significantly upon achievement of uniform enforce-

---

[* The employer would be immune from a tort suit if the worker were covered by Workers' Compensation, which bars tort actions against employers. — ED.]

ment of the right. It may well be that in the instant personal-injury case the outcome would be substantially affected by whether the issue of immunity is decided by a judge or a jury. Therefore, were "outcome" the only consideration, a strong case might appear for saying that the federal court should follow the state practice.

But there are affirmative countervailing considerations at work here. The federal system is an independent system for administering justice to litigants who properly invoke its jurisdiction. An essential characteristic of that system is the manner in which, in civil common-law actions, it distributes trial functions between judge and jury and, under the influence — if not the command[10] — of the Seventh Amendment, assigns the decisions of disputed questions of fact to the jury. The policy of uniform enforcement of state-created rights and obligations, see, e.g., Guaranty Trust Co. v. York, supra, cannot in every case exact compliance with a state rule[12] — not bound up with rights and obligations — which disrupts the federal system of allocating functions between judge and jury. Thus the inquiry here is whether the federal policy favoring jury decisions of disputed fact questions should yield to the state rule in the interest of furthering the objective that the litigation should not come out one way in the federal court and another way in the state court.

We think that in the circumstances of this case the federal court should not follow the state rule. It cannot be gainsaid that there is a strong federal policy against allowing state rules to disrupt the judge-jury relationship in the federal courts. . . . Perhaps even more clearly in light of the influence of the Seventh Amendment, the function assigned to the jury "is an essential factor in the process for which the Federal Constitution provides." . . .

Third. We have discussed the problem upon the assumption that the outcome of the litigation may be substantially affected by whether the issue of immunity is decided by a judge or a jury. But clearly there is not present here the certainty that a different result would follow, cf. Guaranty Trust Co. v. York, supra, or even the strong possibility that this would be the case. There are factors present here which might reduce that possibility. The trial judge in the federal system has powers denied the judges of many States to comment on the weight of evidence and credibility of witnesses, and discretion to grant a new trial if the verdict appears to him to be against the weight of the evidence. We do not think

10. Our conclusion makes unnecessary the consideration of — and we intimate no view upon — the constitutional question whether the right of jury trial protected in federal courts by the Seventh Amendment embraces the factual issue of statutory immunity when asserted, as here, as an affirmative defense in a common-law negligence action.

12. This Court held in Sibbach v. Wilson & Co. that Federal Rule of Civil Procedure 35 should prevail over a contrary state rule.

the likelihood of a different result is so strong as to require the federal practice of jury determination of disputed factual issues to yield to the state rule in the interest of uniformity of outcome. . . .

Reversed and remanded.

[The opinions of Justices WHITTAKER, FRANKFURTER, and HARLAN are omitted.]

NOTES AND PROBLEMS

1. State the holding of *Byrd*.

2. *Byrd* could have been decided under the criterion of *Guaranty Trust*: Unlike previous cases in which the outcome-determinative test had been applied, using a jury rather than a judge in these circumstances might, but would not necessarily, determine the outcome of the case. The Court thus seemed to be going out of its way to find another analysis by which to approach *Erie* problems. That process continued in the next case in this line, to which we now turn.

2. De-Constitutionalizing *Erie*

Under both *Guaranty Trust* and *Byrd*, *Erie* questions are constitutional matters; whether federal courts should follow the state practice is a constitutional question. That framing of the issue is consistent with *Erie* itself, which rejected the invitation to reach its decision as an interpretation of the Rules Enabling Act rather than the Constitution. The next case, while purporting to overrule none of the cases in the *Erie* line, reframes the issue as one of statutory rather than constitutional interpretation.

Hanna v. Plumer
380 U.S. 460 (1965)

Mr. Chief Justice WARREN delivered the opinion of the Court.

The question to be decided is whether, in a civil action where the jurisdiction of the United States district court is based upon diversity of citizenship between the parties, service of process shall be made in the manner prescribed by state law or that set forth in Rule 4(d)(1) of the Federal Rules of Civil Procedure.

On February 6, 1963, petitioner, a citizen of Ohio, filed her complaint in the District Court for the District of Massachusetts, claiming damages in excess of $10,000 for personal injuries resulting from an automobile accident in South Carolina, allegedly caused by the negligence of one Louise Plumer Osgood, a Massachusetts citizen deceased at the time of the filing of the complaint. Respondent, Mrs. Osgood's executor and also a Massachusetts citizen, was named as defendant. On February 8, service was made by leaving copies of the summons and the complaint with respondent's wife at his residence, concededly in compliance with [the version of] Rule 4(d)(1) [then in effect]. . . .

Respondent filed his answer on February 26, alleging, inter alia, that the action could not be maintained because it had been brought "contrary to and in violation of the provisions of Massachusetts General Laws (Ter. Ed.) Chapter 197, Section 9." That section provides:

> Except as provided in this chapter, an executor or administrator shall not be held to answer to an action by a creditor of the deceased which is not commenced within one year from the time of his giving bond for the performance of his trust, or to such an action which is commenced within said year unless before the expiration thereof the writ in such action has been served by delivery in hand upon such executor or administrator or service thereof accepted by him or a notice stating the name of the estate, the name and address of the creditor, the amount of the claim and the court in which the action has been brought has been filed in the proper registry of probate. . . . Mass. Gen. Laws Ann., c. 197, §9 (1958).

On October 17, 1963, the District Court granted respondent's motion for summary judgment, citing Ragan v. Merchants Transfer Co. and Guaranty Trust Co. v. York in support of its conclusion that the adequacy of the service was to be measured by §9, with which, the court held, petitioner had not complied. On appeal, petitioner admitted noncompliance with §9, but argued that Rule 4(d)(1) defines the method by which service of process is to be effected in diversity actions. The Court of Appeals for the First Circuit, finding that "[r]elatively recent amendments [to §9] evince a clear legislative purpose to require personal notification within the year,"[1] concluded that the conflict of state and federal rules

---

1. Section 9 is in part a statute of limitations, providing that an executor need not "answer to an action . . . which is not commenced within one year from the time of his giving bond. . . ." This part of the statute, the purpose of which is to speed the settlement of estates, is not involved in this case, since the action clearly was timely commenced. . . .

Section 9 also provides for the manner of service. Generally, service of process must be made by "delivery in hand," although there are two alternatives: acceptance of service by the executor, or filing of a notice of claim, the components of which are set out in the statute, in the appropriate probate court. The purpose of this part of the statute, which is involved here, is, as the court below noted, to insure that executors will receive actual notice of claims. Actual notice is of course also the goal of Rule 4(d)(1); however, the Federal Rule reflects a determination that this goal can be achieved by a method less cumbersome than that prescribed in §9. In this case the goal seems to have been achieved; although the affidavit filed by respondent in the District Court asserts that he had not been served in hand nor had he accepted service, it does not allege lack of actual notice.

was over" a substantive rather than a procedural matter," and unanimously affirmed. Because of the threat to the goal of uniformity of federal procedure posed by the decision below, we granted certiorari.

We conclude that the adoption of Rule 4(d)(1), designed to control service of process in diversity actions, neither exceeded the congressional mandate embodied in the Rules Enabling Act nor transgressed constitutional bounds, and that the Rule is therefore the standard against which the District Court should have measured the adequacy of the service. Accordingly, we reverse the decision of the Court of Appeals.

The [version of the] Rules Enabling Act, 28 U.S.C. §2072 [then in effect] provide[d] in pertinent part:

> The Supreme Court shall have the power to prescribe, by general rules, the forms of process, writs, pleadings, and motions, and the practice and procedure of the district courts of the United States in civil actions.
>
> Such rules shall not abridge, enlarge or modify any substantive right and shall preserve the right of trial by jury. . . . [*]

Under the cases construing the scope of the Enabling Act, Rule 4(d)(1) clearly passes muster. Prescribing the manner in which a defendant is to be notified that a suit has been instituted against him, it relates to the "practice and procedure of the district courts." "The test must be whether a rule really regulates procedure — the judicial process for enforcing rights and duties recognized by substantive law and for justly administering remedy and redress for disregard or infraction of them." Sibbach v. Wilson & Co. . . .

Thus were there no conflicting state procedure, Rule 4(d)(1) would clearly control. However, respondent, focusing on the contrary Massachusetts rule, calls to the Court's attention another line of cases, a line which — like the Federal Rules — had its birth in 1938. Erie R. Co. v. Tompkins, overruling Swift v. Tyson, held that federal courts sitting in diversity cases, when deciding questions of "substantive" law, are bound by state court decisions as well as state statutes. The broad command of *Erie* was therefore identical to that of the Enabling Act: federal courts are to apply state substantive law and federal procedural law. However, as subsequent cases sharpened the distinction between substance and procedure, the line of cases following *Erie* diverged markedly from the line construing the Enabling Act. . . .

Respondent, by placing primary reliance on *York* and *Ragan,* suggests that the *Erie* doctrine acts as a check on the Federal Rules of Civil Procedure, that despite the clear command of Rule 4(d)(1), *Erie* and its progeny demand the application of the Massachusetts rule. Reduced to

[* The current version of §2072 is substantially identical in all respects relevant to this case — ED.]

essentials, the argument is: (1) *Erie*, as refied in *York*, demands that federal courts apply state law whenever application of federal law in its stead will alter the outcome of the case. (2) In this case, a determination that the Massachusetts service requirements obtain will result in immediate victory for respondent. If, on the other hand, it should be held that Rule 4(d)(1) is applicable, the litigation will continue, with possible victory for petitioner. (3) Therefore, *Erie* demands application of the Massachusetts rule. The syllogism possesses an appealing simplicity, but is for several reasons invalid.

In the first place, it is doubtful that, even if there were no Federal Rule making it clear that in-hand service is not required in diversity actions, the *Erie* rule would have obligated the District Court to follow the Massachusetts procedure. "Outcome-determination" analysis was never intended to serve as a talisman. Byrd v. Blue Ridge Cooperative. Indeed, the message of *York* itself is that choices between state and federal law are to be made not by application of any automatic, "litmus paper" criterion, but rather by reference to the policies underlying the *Erie* rule.

The *Erie* rule is rooted in part in a realization that it would be unfair for the character or result of a litigation materially to differ because the suit had been brought in a federal court. . . . The decision was also in part a reaction to the practice of "forum-shopping" which had grown up in response to the rule of Swift v. Tyson. That the *York* test was an attempt to effectuate these policies is demonstrated by the fact that the opinion framed the inquiry in terms of "substantial" variations between state and federal litigation. Not only are nonsubstantial, or trivial, variations not likely to raise the sort of equal protection problems which troubled the Court in *Erie*; they are also unlikely to influence the choice of a forum. The "outcome-determination" test therefore cannot be read without reference to the twin aims of the *Erie* rule: discouragement of forum-shopping and avoidance of inequitable administration of the laws.[9]

---

9. The Court of Appeals seemed to frame the inquiry in terms of how "important" §9 is to the State. In support of its suggestion that §9 serves some interest the State regards as vital to its citizens, the court noted that something like §9 has been on the books in Massachusetts a long time, that §9 has been amended a number of times, and that §9 is designed to make sure that executors receive actual notice. See note 1, supra. The apparent lack of relation among these three observations is not surprising because it is not clear to what sort of question the Court of Appeals was addressing itself. One cannot meaningfully ask how important something is without first asking "important for what purpose?" *Erie* and its progeny make clear that when a federal court sitting in a diversity case is faced with a question of whether or not to apply state law, the importance of a state rule is indeed relevant, but only in the context of asking whether application of the rule would make so important a difference to the character or result of the litigation that failure to enforce it would unfairly discriminate against citizens of the forum State, or whether application of the rule would have so important an effect upon the fortunes of one or both of the litigants that failure to enforce it would be likely to cause a plaintiff to choose the federal court.

The difference between the conclusion that the Massachusetts rule is applicable, and the conclusion that it is not, is of course at this point "outcome-determinative" in the sense that if we hold the state rule to apply, respondent prevails, whereas if we hold that Rule 4(d)(1) governs, the litigation will continue. But in this sense *every* procedural variation is "outcome-determinative." For example, having brought suit in a federal court, a plaintiff cannot then insist on the right to file subsequent pleadings in accord with the time limits applicable in the state courts, even though enforcement of the federal timetable will, if he continues to insist that he must meet only the state time limit, result in determination of the controversy against him. So it is here. Though choice of the federal or state rule will at this point have a marked effect upon the outcome of the litigation, the difference between the two rules would be of scant, if any, relevance to the choice of a forum. Petitioner, in choosing her forum, was not presented with a situation where application of the state rule would wholly bar recovery;[10] rather, adherence to the state rule would have resulted only in altering the way in which process was served.[11] Moreover, it is difficult to argue that permitting service of defendant's wife to take the place of in-hand service of defendant himself alters the mode of enforcement of state-created rights in a fashion sufficiently "substantial" to raise the sort of equal protection problems to which the *Erie* opinion alluded.

There is, however, a more fundamental flaw in respondent's syllogism: the incorrect assumption that the rule of Erie R. Co. v. Tompkins constitutes the appropriate test of the validity and therefore the applicability of a Federal Rule of Civil Procedure. The *Erie* rule has never been invoked to void a Federal Rule. It is true that there have been cases where this Court has held applicable a state rule in the face of an argument that the situation was governed by one of the Federal Rules. But the holding of each such case was not that *Erie* commanded displacement of a Federal Rule by an inconsistent state rule, but rather that the scope of the Federal Rule was not as broad as the losing party urged, and therefore, there being no Federal Rule which covered the point in dispute, *Erie* commanded the enforcement of state law. . . . (Here, of

10. Similarly, a federal court's refusal to enforce the New Jersey rule involved in Cohen v. Beneficial Loan Corp., 337 U.S. 541, requiring the posting of security by plaintiffs in stockholders' derivative actions, might well impel a stockholder to choose to bring suit in the federal, rather than the state, court.

11. We cannot seriously entertain the thought that one suing an estate would be led to choose the federal court because of a belief that adherence to Rule 4(d)(1) is less likely to give the executor actual notice than §9, and therefore more likely to produce a default judgment. Rule 4(d)(1) is well designed to give actual notice, as it did in this case. See note 1, supra.

course, the clash is unavoidable; Rule 4(d)(1) says — implicity, but with unmistakable clarity — that in-hand service is not required in federal courts.) At the same time, in cases adjudicating the validity of Federal Rules, we have not applied the *York* rule or other refinements of *Erie*, but have to this day continued to decide questions concerning the scope of the Enabling Act and the constitutionality of specific Federal Rules in light of the distinction set forth in *Sibbach*.

Nor has the development of two separate lines of cases been inadvertent. The line between "substance" and "procedure" shifts as the legal context changes. . . . It is true that both the Enabling Act and the *Erie* rule say, roughly, that federal courts are to apply state "substantive" law and federal "procedural" law, but from that it need not follow that the tests are identical. For they were designed to control very different sorts of decisions. When a situation is covered by one of the Federal Rules, the question facing the court is a far cry from the typical, relatively unguided *Erie* choice: the court has been instructed to apply the Federal Rule, and can refuse to do so only if the Advisory Committee, this Court, and Congress erred in their prima facie judgment that the Rule in question transgresses neither the terms of the Enabling Act nor constitutional restrictions.

We are reminded by the *Erie* opinion that neither Congress nor the federal courts can, under the guise of formulating rules of decision for federal courts, fashion rules which are not supported by a grant of federal authority contained in Article I or some other section of the Constitution; in such areas state law must govern because there can be no other law. But the opinion in *Erie*, which involved no Federal Rule and dealt with a question which was "substantive" in every traditional sense (whether the railroad owed a duty of care to Tompkins as a trespasser or a licensee), surely neither said nor implied that measures like Rule 4(d)(1) are unconstitutional. For the constitutional provision for a federal court system (augmented by the Necessary and Proper Clause) carries with it congressional power to make rules governing the practice and pleading in those courts, which in turn includes a power to regulate matters which, though falling within the uncertain area between substance and procedure, are rationally capable of classification as either. Neither *York* nor the cases following it ever suggested that the rule there laid down for coping with situations where no Federal Rule applies is coextensive with the limitation on Congress to which *Erie* had adverted. . . .

Erie and its offspring cast no doubt on the long-recognized power of Congress to prescribe housekeeping rules for federal courts even though some of those rules will inevitably differ from comparable state rules. . . . Thus, though a court, in measuring a Federal Rule against the standards contained in the Enabling Act and the Constitution, need not wholly blind itself to the degree to which the Rule makes the character and result of the federal litigation stray from the course it would follow in state courts, it cannot be forgotten that the *Erie* rule, and the guidelines suggested in *York*, were created to serve another purpose altogether. To hold that a Federal Rule of Civil Procedure must cease to function whenever it alters the mode of enforcing state-created rights would be to disembowel either the Constitution's grant of power over federal procedure or Congress' attempt to exercise that power in the Enabling Act. Rule 4(d)(1) is valid and controls the instant case.

Reversed.

Mr. Justice BLACK concurs in the result.

Mr. Justice HARLAN, concurring. . . .

Erie was something more than an opinion which worried about "forum-shopping and avoidance of inequitable administration of the laws," although to be sure these were important elements of the decision. I have always regarded that decision as one of the modern cornerstones of our federalism, expressing policies that profoundly touch the allocation of judicial power between the state and federal systems. *Erie* recognized that there should not be two conflicting systems of law controlling the primary activity of citizens, for such alternative governing authority must necessarily give rise to a debilitating uncertainty in the planning of everyday affairs.[1] And it recognized that the scheme of our Constitution envisions an allocation of law-making functions between state and federal legislative processes which is undercut if the federal judiciary can make substantive law affecting state affairs beyond the bounds of congressional legislative powers in this regard. Thus, in diversity cases *Erie* commands that it be the state law governing primary private activity which prevails.

The shorthand formulations which have appeared in some past decisions are prone to carry untoward results that frequently arise from oversimplification. The Court is quite right in stating that the "outcome-determinative" test of Guaranty Trust Co. v. York, if taken literally, proves too much, for any rule, no matter how clearly "procedural," can affect the outcome of litigation if it is not obeyed. In turning from the "outcome" test of *York* back to the unadorned forum-shopping rationale of *Erie*, however, the Court falls prey to like oversimplification, for a simple forum-shopping rule also proves too much; litigants often choose a federal

---

1. Since the rules involved in the present case are parallel rather than conflicting, this first rationale does not come into play here.

forum merely to obtain what they consider the advantages of the Federal Rules of Civil Procedure or to try their cases before a supposedly more favorable judge. To my mind the proper line of approach in determining whether to apply a state or a federal rule, whether "substantive" or "procedural," is to stay close to basic principles by inquiring if the choice of rule would substantially affect those primary decisions respecting human conduct which our constitutional system leaves to state regulation.[2] If so, *Erie* and the Constitution require that the state rule prevail, even in the face of a conflicting federal rule.

The Court weakens, if indeed it does not submerge, this basic principle by finding, in effect, a grant of substantive legislative power in the constitutional provision for a federal court system, and through it, setting up the Federal Rules as a body of law inviolate. . . . So long as a reasonable man could characterize any duly adopted federal rule as "procedural," the Court, unless I misapprehend what is said, would have it apply no matter how seriously it frustrated a State's substantive regulation of the primary conduct and affairs of its citizens. Since the members of the Advisory Committee, the Judicial Conference, and this Court who formulated the Federal Rules are presumably reasonable men, it follows that the integrity of the Federal Rules is absolute. Whereas the unadulterated outcome and forum-shopping tests may err too far toward honoring state rules, I submit that the Court's "arguably procedural, ergo constitutional" test moves too fast and far in the other direction.

The courts below relied upon this Court's decisions in Ragan v. Merchants Transfer Co. and Cohen v. Beneficial Loan Corp. Those cases deserve more attention than this Court has given them. . . .

. . . *Ragan* . . . was wrong. At most, application of the Federal Rule [3] would have meant that potential Kansas tort defendants would have to defer for a few days the satisfaction of knowing that they had not been sued within the limitations period. The choice of the Federal Rule would have had no effect on the primary stages of private activity from which torts arise, and only the most minimal effect on behavior following the commission of the tort. In such circumstances the interest of the federal system in proceeding under its own rules should have prevailed. . . .

The proper view of *Cohen* is, in my opinion, that the statute was meant to inhibit small stockholders from instituting "strike suits," and thus it was designed and could be expected to have a substantial impact on

---

2. See Hart and Wechsler, The Federal Courts and the Federal System 678. Byrd v. Blue Ridge Rural Electric Coop. indicated that state procedures would apply if the State had manifested a particularly strong interest in their employment. However, this approach may not be of constitutional proportions.

private primary activity. Anyone who was at the trial bar during the period when *Cohen* arose can appreciate the strong state policy reflected in the statute. I think it wholly legitimate to view Federal Rule 23[.1] as not purporting to deal with the problem. But even had the Federal Rules purported to do so, and in so doing provided a substantially less effective deterrent to strike suits, I think the state rule should still have prevailed. That is where I believe the Court's view differs from mine; for the Court attributes such overriding force to the Federal Rules that it is hard to think of a case where a conflicting state rule would be allowed to operate, even though the state rule reflected policy considerations which, under *Erie*, would lie within the realm of state legislative authority.

It remains to apply what has been said to the present case. The Massachusetts rule provides that an executor need not answer suits unless in-hand service was made upon him or notice of the action was filed in the proper registry of probate within one year of his giving bond. The evident intent of this statute is to permit an executor to distribute the estate which he is administering without fear that further liabilities may be outstanding for which he could be held personally liable. If the Federal District Court in Massachusetts applies Rule 4(d)(1) of the Federal Rules of Civil Procedure instead of the Massachusetts service rule, what effect would that have on the speed and assurance with which estates are distributed? As I see it, the effect would not be substantial. It would mean simply that an executor would have to check at his own house or the federal courthouse as well as the registry of probate before he could distribute the estate with impunity. As this does not seem enough to give rise to any real impingement on the vitality of the state policy which the Massachusetts rule is intended to serve, I concur in the judgment of the Court.

NOTES AND PROBLEMS

1. Briefly explain why the federal court could disregard the state practice in this case.

2. *Byrd* and *Hanna* reach similar results: Both hold that the federal court need not behave as a state court would if it were hearing the case. Moreover, both enunciate multi-tiered "tests" for determining whether federal or state practice should prevail. And they complement each other in one respect: *Hanna*, narrowly construed, tells a federal court what to do when a Rule or federal statute dictates the federal practice; *Byrd* deals with a federal practice not dictated by a specific federal statute or Rule. However similar in result, the two cases diverge sharply in their texture.

Byrd is nuanced, "soft," and, in many cases, indeterminate — and grounds its analysis directly in the Constitution. *Hanna* is hard-edged and more determinate — and insists that a statute — the Rules Enabling Act — is as important as the Constitution in many *Erie* cases.

3. Analytically it is easier to begin with *Hanna's* framework. Start with the proposition that one faces an *Erie* problem only when a federal court, left to its own devices, would ordinarily behave differently from a state court: At that point a federal court sitting in diversity must decide whether it should follow its usual practice. According to *Hanna*, one's analysis of the problem differs, depending on the source of the federal practice.

a. *Hanna* says that the answer to that question is relatively easy if the federal practice in question is dictated by a Federal Rule of Civil Procedure (or, by extension, a federal statute). If so, one has to ask whether the statute itself is constitutional. One can hear in this question an echo of *Erie*, with its assertion that Congress could not constitutionally dictate tort law to the states. The converse proposition is that Congress *can* dictate rules of procedure to the federal courts it creates. If the statute is constitutional and tells a federal court to do something, the court must follow the dictates of that statute. At that point, the *"Erie"* issue ceases to be directly constitutional, becoming instead a matter of statutory construction: What does the governing statute tell the federal court to do?

In the case of a Federal Rule of Civil Procedure, the analysis requires two steps, because the Rules are not themselves statutes but a delegation to the Supreme Court to make statute-like rules. Theoretically, one must consider whether the initial delegation (in the Rules Enabling Act, 28 U.S.C. §2072) was constitutional; the few cases to consider the question have said it is. E.g., Sibbach v. Wilson, 312 U.S. 1 (1941). As a practical matter, the open questions thus become: (a) whether the Rule promulgated under the authority of the Rules Enabling Act in fact fits its description, "rules of practice and procedure" and (b) whether the Rule itself is constitutional. If the Rule passes both these tests, then it must be applied, even if it differs from the state practice in a significant way.

If the Rule fails either test (that is, if it is not "procedural" as the Rules Enabling Act uses that term) or if it is unconstitutional, then the state practice applies. No case has ever held a Rule to be beyond the scope of the Rules Enabling Act, though some have suggested that particular Rules come close to the line. Jonathan M. Landers, Of Legalized Blackmail and Legalized Theft: Consumer Class Actions and the Substance Procedure Dilemma, 47 S. Cal. L. Rev. 842 (1974). Nor has any Rule ever been held unconstitutional, though several have been revised in light of constitutional developments that might have made them subject to attack. See., e.g., Rule 65(b).

b. To test your understanding of this scheme, apply it to the facts of *Hanna* itself, explaining the source of the conflict between state and federal practice and the reason for following the federal practice.

c. Now extend that application. Assume that the issue is whether the statute of limitations has expired. Plaintiff filed a federal complaint within the relevant statute of limitations, but did not serve defendant until after the running of the statute. Under state practice, the statute is satisfied only by *serving* defendant with the complaint; contrast Rule 3. Now apply *Hanna* to this situation: According to *Hanna*, should the federal court sitting in diversity conclude that the statute has run? Compare your conclusion with the holding of Ragan v. Merchants Transfer & Warehouse Corp., described in Note 5a, following *Guaranty Trust* and criticized by Justice Harlan in his *Hanna* concurrence. Criticized or not, *Ragan* was reaffirmed in Walker v. Armco Steel Corp., 446 U.S. 740 1980), largely on the grounds of stare decisis.

d. *Hanna*'s principle will yield a result different from *Guaranty Trust* whenever the federal practice is dictated by a federal statute or Rule (so long as the statute or Rule is constitutional and within the scope of the Rules Enabling Act). Explain why this first part of *Hanna*'s doctrine would not have yielded a different result in *Guaranty Trust* itself.

4. Consider now the second part of *Hanna*'s doctrine, the problem with which *Byrd* deals: What if the usual federal practice is not dictated by a specific statute or Rule, but has its roots either in the common law of federal procedure or in mere custom? How then should a court think about whether to follow the federal or the state practice? One example would be the issue in *Byrd* itself—whether a question would be decided by a judge or submitted to a jury. Another might be differences in the manner in which prospective jurors were questioned: Many states, either by law or custom, permit extensive colloquies between jurors and lawyers during jury selection; no statute or Rule governs the matter, but in many federal courts judges do all the questioning and do so very quickly. In a clash, should state or federal practice prevail? *Byrd* and *Hanna* approach that question in different ways.

a. For *Byrd* there are three questions: (1) is the state practice "bound up with the definition of the rights and obligations of the parties?"; if so, state law governs; (2) even if it isn't part of the substantive rights and obligations, would its application determine the outcome of the case?; (3) if so, are there "affirmative countervailing" considerations of federal judicial administration present? The *Byrd* Court assumes that if the first question is answered affirmatively, state practice should prevail. The idea seems to be that some procedural practices are so much a part of the substantive law that they should be followed; burden of proof would supply an example. *Byrd*'s distinctive doctrinal contribution lies in its third question, which requires courts to balance state against federal interests. As with all balancing tests, the results will be fact-bound.

b. Under the same circumstances (in the absence of a federal Rule or statute dictating federal practice), *Hanna* asks a different question: Would following the federal practice lead to forum-shopping or inequitable administration of the laws? The implication is that if one finds either of these likely, the state rather than the federal practice should prevail. One difficulty in applying this standard lies in knowing what those two phrases mean. In some respect these terms seem to be *Hanna*'s rephrasing of what *Guaranty Trust* and *Byrd* called "outcome-determination." It remains to be seen if the rephrasing is helpful. Forum-shopping refers to the practice, widely followed by lawyers, of seeking a court that will be most hospitable to the client's claims or defenses. As suggested earlier, almost any imaginable procedural difference in systems could lead to such a choice; perhaps one should therefore limit the inquiry to differences that, before the lawsuit began, seem significant enough to cause forum-shopping. Does even that version give state practice too much power? "Inequitable administration of the laws" is more difficult. It seems to refer to patterns of federal practice that regularly result in different applications of what is nominally the same substantive law, such as federal courts' pre-*Erie* willingness to enter injunctions in situations where state courts would not.

The problem with both of *Hanna*'s criteria is that for federal diversity jurisdiction to have any usefulness, it *should* sometimes lead to different results, and if lawyers can predict that, their obligation to their clients *requires* them to shop for the most advantageous forum.

c. *Hanna* did not overrule *Byrd*, which it cited with approval. Both cases suggest an approach to a federal practice not dictated by a federal statute or Rule. Which is preferable? One finds courts citing both.

3. Determining the Scope of Federal Law: Avoiding and Accommodating *Erie*

Under *Hanna*'s reading of *Erie*, many "*Erie*" questions will not require resort to the Constitution because Congress by statute will have told federal courts what to do in the situation. So long as the statute is constitutional and one knows what the statute requires, the choice of law problem is solved. Because the constitutionality of the major procedural statutes seems clear, this route to the solution of *Erie* problems has proved tempting — perhaps too tempting. So long as a judge can find a federal statute governing the situation, it prevails over the state practice, and a difficult, perhaps indeterminate, *Erie* analysis is unnecessary.

Under this analysis, much hangs on finding that a federal Rule or statute applies. Deciding that it does is usually tantamount to deciding that federal law will prevail over a contrary state rule. Consider three cases decided within a decade. In each there was a state practice — sometimes statutory, sometimes common law — that could be characterized as procedural but which carried significant substantive overtones. In each there was an arguably pertinent federal provision (one a Rule, one a statute, and one a provision of the Constitution); interpreted in one way that federal provision came into conflict with the state practice. In one of these cases the federal practice triumphed outright; in one the state law was reduced to a factor that the federal court might consider — or ignore; and in one the Court crafted a compromise that left a four-person dissent arguing that the result did violence both to the state law and the Constitution. Consider how these cases interpret *Erie*.

Burlington Northern Railroad v. Woods
480 U.S. 1 (1987)

[An Alabama statute provided:]

> When a judgment or decree is entered or rendered for money, . . . and the same has been stayed on appeal by the execution of a bond . . . if the appellate court affirms the judgment of the court below, it must also enter judgment against all [the appellants] for the amount of the affirmed judgment, 10 per cent damages thereon, and the costs of the appellate court. . . .

[The federal courts have no such practice; they ordinarily award "costs" to the winner of an appeal, but nothing further unless they conclude that the appeal is frivolous. In such a case, Federal Rule of Appellate Procedure 38 applies. It reads in its entirety: "If a court of appeals shall determine that an appeal is frivolous, it may award just damages and single or double costs to the appellee."

Burlington Northern, defendant-appellant in a diversity case, had lost on appeal, and the successful plaintiff asked for the statutory bonus. Burlington Northern argued that the imposition of a penalty for appealing without regard to the merits of the appeal violated both the Due Process and the Equal Protection clauses. Notice the premise of these constitutional challenges: that the state statute applied, presumably under the command of *Erie*.

The Supreme Court avoided these constitutional challenges as well as *Erie*, holding that Federal Rule of Appellate Procedure 38 conflicted with the statute and, under *Hanna*, controlled. In so ruling the Court rejected plaintiff's interpretation that Rule 38 did not conflict with the statute because a court could award the mandatory 10 percent penalty for an unsuccessful appeal and, as a matter of discretion, additional damages and costs if it believed the appeal was frivolous.]

Stewart Organization, Inc. v. Ricoh
487 U.S. 22 (1988)

[Plaintiff, a local franchisee of a national corporation selling photocopiers, became involved in a dispute with the national organization and, invoking diversity jurisdiction, filed a lawsuit in federal district court in Alabama, alleging breach of the dealership contract as well as other theories. The dealership contract contained a forum selection clause requiring any litigation arising out of the agreement to be brought in "any appropriate state or federal district court located in the Borough of Manhattan, New York City, New York." The defendant invoked the forum selection clause and moved for transfer of the case, or in the alternative dismissal for improper venue. Plaintiff opposed this move, pointing out that Alabama, in a series of state court decisions, had refused to enforce such forum selection clauses; plaintiff argued that the federal district court sitting in diversity was bound to honor that state law.

The Supreme Court disagreed:]

We hold that federal law, specifically §1404(a), governs the District Court's decision whether to give effect to the parties' forum selection clause and transfer this case to a court in Manhattan.[11]

[Discussed in Chapter II, §1404 provides:

> For the convenience of the parties, in the interest of justice, a district
> court may transfer any civil action to any other district or division where
> it might have been brought.

Guiding the lower courts on remand, the Supreme Court suggested that, in deciding how to apply §1404, the courts were free to take into account the state's antipathy to forum selection clauses—but only as one factor, and perhaps not a dispositive one.]

Gasperini v. Center for Humanities, Inc.
116 S. Ct. 2211 (1996)

Justice GINSBURG delivered the opinion of the Court.

Under the law of New York, appellate courts are empowered to review the size of jury verdicts and to order new trials when the jury's award

---

11. Because a validly enacted Act of Congress controls the issue in dispute, we have no occasion to evaluate the impact of federal judge-made law on the 'twin-aims' that animate the *Erie* doctrine.

"deviates materially from what would be reasonable compensation." Under the Seventh Amendment, which governs proceedings in federal court, but not in state court . . . "no fact, tried by a jury, shall be otherwise reexamined in any Court of the United States, than according to the rules of the common law." The compatibility of these provisions [in a diversity case] is the issue we confront. . . .

[Plaintiff-petititioner had won a jury verdict that was attacked as unreasonably high on appeal. Defendant argued that the state statute was substantive and must be applied under *Erie*, allowing the federal circuit court to reduce the damage award; plaintiff responded that the state statute controlled procedure and was therefore trumped by federal procedural law, including the Reexamination Clause of the Seventh Amendment. The federal Court of Appeals applied the New York statute reducing the jury verdict.

Reversing, the majority held (a) that the Reexamination clause barred a federal appellate court from directly applying the New York statute; (b) but the *district* court could initially apply the statute; (c) the appellate court could then review the district court's application of the statute for abuse of discretion.]

New York's dominant interest can be respected, without disrupting the federal system, once it is recognized that the federal district court is capable of performing the checking function [in the New York statute.]

[Justice STEVENS dissented on the grounds that nothing in the Seventh Amendment prevented federal appellate courts from applying the New York statute.

Justices SCALIA and THOMAS and the CHIEF JUSTICE dissented on the grounds that both parts of the majority opinion were wrong: Rule 59 controlled the power of a federal district judge to review jury verdicts and prevailed over the state law; the Seventh Amendment prohibited all federal courts from reexamining jury verdicts in the way proposed by the New York statute.]

NOTES AND PROBLEMS

1. Notice the common analytic problems presented by these three cases. In each there is a state practice at variance with federal practice. These state practices all seem to have some weight. Two cases, *Ricoh* and *Gasperini*, have unmistakable substantive aims — the former seeking not to disadvantage home-state litigants, the latter seeking to hold down tort damages. *Burlington Northern*'s provision is more difficult to characterize, but it has a clear pro-plaintiff effect: It operates as a penalty on unsuccessful defendants' appeals.

2. In each case the Supreme Court located a provision of federal law in arguable conflict with the state practice. That step involves at least two moves. First, one has to find that there is pertinent federal law. Second, one has to find that the federal law conflicts with state practice and that federal law controls. Neither step is always obvious.

a. In *Burlington Northern* the Court read a Federal Rule of Appellate Procedure dealing with frivolous appeals as if it also addressed nonfrivolous but unsuccessful appeals, the subject of the state statute. According to the Court, Rule 38 deals with all appeals, and its silence about nonfrivolous appeals therefore displaces the contrary state statute. The plaintiff argued that both the state and the federal provision could be applied — with "costs" to the prevailing party, but with the 10 percent penalty added in cases to which the state statute applied.

b. In *Ricoh* the Court read §1404, usually thought to address questions of forum non conveniens, as if it also covered — and therefore displaced — state law on the enforcement of forum selection clauses. Again, there was an obvious argument that §1404 applied only in the usual case, in which there was neither a forum selection clause nor a state law forbidding the enforcement of such clauses.

c. In *Gasperini* the federal law was more obviously applicable: Both the Reexamination Clause and the case law suggested that there was a serious question of whether federal appellate courts could exercise the verdict reduction power.

3. How far should a federal court stretch to find an applicable and conflicting federal law?

a. Taken too far, the technique does violence to state lawmaking in any area touching on procedure. Used this way, *Hanna* eradicates *Byrd* and *Guaranty Trust*. Is that happening in *Ricoh*? The Court in *Ricoh* rested its holding on a federal statute. But the statute is a very thin fig leaf. Written in very general terms, the statute, according to *Ricoh*, does two things: (1) it provides that federal rather than state law will govern; but (2) it gives immense discretion to the federal courts, including the discretion to enforce the forum selection clause when state courts would be bound not to enforce it. That conclusion represents very nearly a full circle back to *Swift v. Tyson*.

b. On the other hand, unless the federal courts preserve some independent procedural space, they cease to exist as independent tribunals when sitting in diversity, thus obviating the point of diversity jurisdiction. That may be one justification for *Burlington Northern*. Congress and the federal judiciary (in its rulemaking capacity) have reached a judgment that appeal ought to be relatively inexpensive. To apply the Alabama statute penalizing appeals distorts that judgment in a way that compromises the independence and procedural integrity of the federal judicial system. If that is the reasoning underlying *Burlington Northern*, however, the holding should have been based on the same sort of reasoning as *Byrd*, rather than resting on the weak support given by a Rule of Appellate Procedure.

4. How does *Gasperini* fit into this pattern?

a. If one accepts the majority's analysis, *Gasperini* differs from the other two cases in that there was a constitutional argument on *both* sides. Plaintiff argued that the Reexamination Clause of the Seventh Amendment prevented federal courts from behaving as the New York legislature commanded. Defendant argued that *Erie* required federal courts to do so.

b. The majority tries to accommodate both interests. Does the accommodation work? Consider the difference between the structure of trial and appellate courts. Can you frame an argument that the New York legislature that enacted the statute in question would not have been satisfied by the Supreme Court's compromise?

c. Suppose the New York legislature in fact doesn't like the *Gasperini* compromise. Is there anything it can do about it?

5. A true believer in *Erie* might be pardoned for condemning the approach taken in *Burlington Northern* and *Ricoh*: Find a federal statute dealing with the same general topic (the vaguer the statute the better), declare that the statute covers the area thus displacing state law, and then interpret the statute to give the federal courts maximum discretion. The result, though technically consistent with *Erie*, would probably induce apoplexy in Justices Brandeis and Frankfurter. But, keeping in mind that one should not condemn another before walking a mile in his shoes, consider the problem facing a federal judge who conscientiously decides that state law *does* govern — except that no one knows what the state law is. The next section describes the problem.

4. Determining the Scope of State Law: an Entailment of *Erie*

Erie requires federal courts sitting in a diversity action to use state law under various circumstances. That holding requires the federal court to declare state law. *State* courts face such questions all the time; a state trial judge must often decide what law applies to the case before her. Sometimes determining the answer will be a simple matter: A recent supreme court case has carefully defined it, or the matter is covered in an authoritative statute.

But the question can be far more difficult. What happens if there is no precedent on point, or the only available precedent is some years old, and the area of law has recently shown signs of change? Or what if the question is complicated by a horizontal choice of law problem like the one that brought forth Judge Henry Friendly's quip: "Our principal task, in this diversity of citizenship case, is to determine what the New York courts would think the California courts would think on an issue about which neither has thought." Nolan v. Transocean Air Lines, 276 F.2d 280, 281 (2d Cir. 1960). For a state trial judge, such a situation presents difficulties, but she at least has the assurance that if she is wrong, the state appellate courts will straighten things out. Federal judges, compelled to follow *Erie*, generally lack that assurance.

What, then, should the federal judge do? Should she predict what the state court would probably do under such circumstances? Should she act as she thinks a state court should act in these circumstances, even if she thinks they would not behave that way? For that matter, which state court should the federal district court seek to resemble — the state trial court, which is often hesitant to depart from precedent — or the state supreme court? The district court judge must exercise his best judgment about how the state courts would resolve the issue, but appeal from his decision lies only within the federal system.

The same predicament faces the federal courts of appeals. On appeal from the district court's judgment, a federal court of appeals must do its best to decide what the state appellate courts would do when faced with the same appeal. Nor may the courts of appeals simply defer to the district court (on the ground that district judges are more likely to be familiar with state practice). Salve Regina College v. Russell, 499 U.S. 225 (1991) (federal court of appeals required to review de novo district court's determination of state law).

Under such circumstances, one finds federal courts of appeals making such statements as, "Because we are persuaded by a careful review of the Ohio decisional law, as well as other relevant sources,[*] that the Supreme Court of Ohio would not construe its statute of limitations so as to preclude recovery in this case, we [do likewise]." McKenna v. Ortho Pharmaceutical Corp., 622 F.2d 657, 659 (3d Cir. 1980). Holdings based on such predictions of state court views are awkward, particularly if the predictions later turn out to be wrong.

Consider, for example, the tangle in Pierce v. Cook & Co., 518 F.2d 720 (10th Cir. 1975), cert. denied, 423 U.S. 1079 (1976). Driver and three passengers were involved in a collision with a truck driven by an independent contractor hauling wheat for Cook. Driver and Passengers

[* What other sources *could* be relevant? Presumably only ones that the Ohio appellate courts themselves would find persuasive. — ED.]

each brought actions. Two of the suits were removed to federal courts; the third remained in state courts. In the federal court actions defendants won a summary judgment on the basis of thirty-year-old precedent making Cook not responsible for the negligence of an independent contractor, and the case was affirmed on appeal. Meanwhile, the state trial court had also granted summary judgment — on the basis of the same precedent — but plaintiff appealed to the state supreme court, which overruled the precedent. The state supreme court decision became final more than three years after the original federal appeal.

Six months later, the two federal plaintiffs moved to vacate the federal appellate decision under Rule 60(b), which permits the reopening of a final judgment under limited circumstances (see Chapter XII). In setting aside the federal judgment, the court of appeals emphasized that there had been "divergent results from a common vehicular accident," that plaintiffs had been forced into the federal courts, and that plaintiffs had received substantially different results in the federal courts than they would have in the state courts, in violation of the *Erie* principle. *Pierce* received considerable attention. See Note, Pierce v. Cook & Co.: Rule 60(b)(6) Relief from Judgment for Change of State Law in a Diversity Case, 62 Va. L. Rev. 414 (1976) (raising the question whether it is rational to limit the rule to common-accident cases); Note, Federal Rule of Civil Procedure 60(b): Standards for Relief from Judgments Due to Changes in Law, 43 U. Chi. L. Rev. 646 (1976).

Contrast DeWeerth v. Baldinger, 38 F.3d 1266 (2d Cir. 1994), cert. denied, 115 S. Ct. 512 (1994), with *Pierce*. In 1987 plaintiff sued a New York art dealer to recover a Monet painting stolen from his family during World War II. The federal court ruled that DeWeerth had failed to satisfy what they understood to be a required showing of reasonable diligence in locating stolen property. Four years later the New York courts in a similar case held that a showing of reasonable diligence was not required under the relevant statute. DeWeerth moved to reopen his federal judgment under Rule 60(b), the same Rule used in *Pierce*. The Second Circuit sharply rejected the attempt:

> *Erie* simply does not stand for the proposition that a plaintiff is entitled to reopen a federal court case that has been closed for several years in order to gain the benefit of a newly announced decision of a state court, a forum in which she specifically declined to litigate her claim.

In an effort to render cases like *Pierce* and *DeWeerth* less frequent, several states have adopted a process called certification. In certification the federal court asks the state supreme court for an answer to a question about state law. There are, however, several defects in this system. First, the state must have a certification procedure; many do not. Even when the procedure is available and is used, the results are not always satisfactory.

Where certification is not available and where a federal court believes the state law is unclear, what should the federal court do? In England v. Louisiana State Board of Medical Examiners, 375 U.S. 411 (1964), the Supreme Court rejected the plausible argument that federal courts were always required to accept cases within the statutory jurisdiction conferred upon them by Congress. Instead, under *England*, abstention from deciding the case would be appropriate when state law was uncertain and when the effect of misinterpreting state law might be drastic. Such a case might arise, for example, when the plaintiff seeks a declaration in federal court that a state licensing procedure is unconstitutional but the court thinks that the state courts might interpret state rules or statutes in such a way as to avoid the constitutional issue. Federal courts are not to abstain routinely; doing so requires "special circumstances." Baggett v. Bullitt, 377 U.S. 360, 375 (1964) (disapproving abstention). The greater the state concern with the state law in question, the more appropriate abstention is likely to be. Reetz v. Bozanich, 397 U.S. 82 (1970) (reversing in an action where the federal district court failed to abstain; the issue was fishing rights and was treated in the state's constitution). There are several procedural pitfalls in the abstention doctrine — pitfalls beyond the scope of this note.

Does abstention conflict with the grant of diversity jurisdiction to the federal courts? Does the grant of diversity, combined with *Erie*, suggest that there will be times when a federal court is required, however uncertainly, to rule on questions of state law?

PART B

THE PROCESS OF LITIGATION

A. Approaching Civil Procedure

In studying the procedural system used in U.S. courts one can take at least two different paths. One path starts from the bottom, examining the way in which an individual lawsuit develops: how the parties state cases, develop information about them, and bring them to resolution. This approach emphasizes features and problems of the contemporary procedural system, which is in many respects a bold experiment. Studying the process of litigation reveals how these features shape and constrain the litigants' responsibilities and choices. The other approach starts from the top, examining the constitutional environment in which the individual lawsuit exists. That approach takes the student into both the history and the current interpretation of the Constitution of the United States. Studying that document reveals several limits on the ways in which state and federal court systems conduct their business, limits that have major consequences for individual litigants.

Anyone wanting to become a lawyer has to understand *both* approaches, comprehending the constitutional environment as well as the modes for processing disputes. This book accordingly contains materials about both, and most courses will examine both. But one can with equal validity start at the top and look down or begin at the bottom and work up. The three Parts of this book are labeled to emphasize those different starting points. Some courses may begin with this section, "Part B: The Process of Litigation," comprising Chapters V-XII and representing the "bottom-up" approach. Other classes may start with "Part A: The Constitutional Framework for U.S. Litigation," comprising Chapters II-IV, the "top-down" approach.

The third part of this book, "Part C: Expanding the Framework of Litigation — Additional Claims and Parties" combines significant elements of both the other parts and may be studied either at the end of the course, as a reprise, or in conjunction with either of the other two parts.

B.   Choosing Procedure

Beginning with the process of litigation, one finds oneself exploring the development of the individual lawsuit. The themes here transcend boundaries of time and culture. Since disputing began (which, according to several religious traditions, was shortly after the first humans appeared on the face of the earth), disputants and whoever helped them resolve their disputes have been faced with procedural choices. One way of framing the choices is as between speed and quality. Everyone wants disputes to be decided quickly; everyone also wants them to be decided correctly—after full exploration of the facts and careful weighing of the law. But even in a world of unlimited resources these two goals are in conflict, and ours is hardly a world of unlimited resources. Another way to frame the conflict is as between fairness and justice. Everyone wants the judge to be fair as between the parties; everyone also wants the judge to decide in favor of the party on whose side truth lies. But in some cases these goals will conflict; the party who makes the best presentation of the evidence may not be the side that should win.

These conflicts force those who design procedure (legislators, lawyers, judges) to choose; moreover, they must choose not just once but at every stage of the process. Should all cases go to trial—on the ground that trials may best uncover the truth—or should we weed out most cases before trial, thus speeding the resolution of disputes while increasing the risk of error? Should plaintiffs have to state their cases in detail—in the hope that we can sort weak from strong cases at an early stage—or does a requirement of detailed pleading trip up plaintiffs with good cases who need access to facts possessed by the defendant? How much discovery should we permit, bearing in mind that free access to discovery will turn up more information but also increase cost and delay?

Behind all these questions lies another, more generalized issue: Is a lawsuit a quest for truth or is it primarily a means of settling a dispute? The more we think litigation is an inquiry into truth, the more likely we are to want judges rather than the adversaries to control the inquiry. The more confident we are that litigation reveals the truth, the more likely we are to extend the results of one lawsuit into other, similar ones. Conversely, the more we see litigation as a battle between the parties, the greater our comfort with giving the parties control over the terms of that battle, but the less we shall be inclined to think that the personalized battle yields the truth.

These and similar questions lie just beneath the surface of contemporary procedural rules; each rule, and often even innocuous-looking individual words and phrases within rules, represent a choice among procedural values. In exploring the development of a lawsuit, we shall be doing at least two things: seeing how a procedural system has made particular choices; and looking beneath those choices at the values they imply. That exploration is particularly apt because the procedural system we shall explore — that set forth in the Federal Rules of Civil Procedure — represents a self-conscious choice of flexibility. The drafters of the Rules (and those who have since amended them) sought above all to break free from what they thought were rigidities of earlier procedural systems. They largely succeeded, but critics have begun to ask whether lawsuits have become unstructured, expensive monsters as a result.

C. A Roadmap for Exploring Choices

This book explores the answers to such questions by following the development of a lawsuit in roughly chronological order. The first chapter in this section (Chapter V) looks at why people litigate. The chapter explores both the arsenal of remedies courts can grant and the way in which those remedies are administered, including a look at the cost of litigation. Having decided to commence a lawsuit, one needs to know how to get things started; Chapter VI — on pleading — does that. Logically, one can proceed in two ways at this point. One approach moves from pleading (the setting forth of claims) to the exploration of facts underlying those claims — that is discovery, explored in Chapter VII. The other direction explores a second aspect of pleading, how one adds additional parties and additional claims to a lawsuit (joinder, the topic of Chapter XIII in Part C) before examining discovery.

Most modern lawsuits reach the discovery stage; the real question is whether they will go further. Chapter VIII examines a variety of official and unofficial ways in which lawsuits can end at this stage. If they do not end here, they proceed to trial. Chapter IX examines the doctrines that determine who will participate in that trial — whether it is a judge alone or a judge and jury and, further, which judge or which jury. Chapter X examines a central issue in the trial itself — the law's efforts to assure a rational result. Once the trial is over, the loser may appeal; the availability of and limits on appeals constitute Chapter XI. Whether a lawsuit ends on appeal or at some earlier stage, there may come a quite difficult question: Just what is it that the concluded lawsuit has decided? That question, which goes under several doctrinal names, is explored in Chapter XII, Respect for Judgments.

INCENTIVES TO LITIGATE

V

People don't litigate for fun. Lawsuits cost money. Worse, they are for most participants miserable experiences whether one wins or loses. In considering the litigation process, one might therefore begin asking why anyone brings a lawsuit. That inquiry should extend as well to those who defend lawsuits: In almost every civil lawsuit, the plaintiff is seeking something in defendant's power to grant; one can ask why defendant chooses to add the insult of litigation to what may be the eventual injury of an adverse judgment. And to make the inquiry complete, one should also ask whether the expense and unpleasantness of litigation are desirable or undesirable. Should it be easier to commence or defend a lawsuit, or is it already too easy? Lawyers give two labels to these inquiries: *remedies* (comprising the question of what courts can do to and for litigants) and *access to justice* (the question of whether barriers to litigation are too high or too low).

A. Litigation in the United States at the End of the Twentieth Century

1. How Much Litigation?

Answering any of the inquiries posed above is silly without at least a sketch of the existing litigation system. For one's answer to the question of whether litigation should be easier — or whether it is already too easy — should turn on one's view of the way things are now. There is, for example, presently a debate conducted in legislatures, editorial pages, and scholarly journals about whether the United States is experiencing a "litigation explosion." Some of this debate turns on factual premises. To be a participant in this debate or a well-informed lawyer one needs to know how much litigation there is in the contemporary United States, what it consists of, and how long it takes.

Because of jurisdictional limits on the federal courts, more than 99 percent of litigation in the United States occurs in state courts. In 1995, about 85 million cases were filed in the United States.* If the population of the United States is about 275 million, that is one case per year for about every 3.2 persons. Of the 85 million state court cases, 51 million — three-fifths — are traffic and other ordinance violations. Some of these cases can have significant effects on people's lives — lost driving licenses, towed cars, and increased insurance premiums — but they are not typically what we think of when we think of serious litigation.

The remaining 34 million cases could be thought of as "serious." They consist of two large groups — civil and criminal cases — and one much smaller one — juvenile cases. In the most recent year for which hard data are available there were about 13 million criminal cases in state courts (about 38 percent of the nontraffic cases) and about 1.9 million juvenile cases (about 5 percent) of such cases. That leaves us with 19 million civil filings (55 percent of the nontraffic cases), or about one civil lawsuit for every 14 persons. Again, before concluding that this number either proves or disproves the "litigation explosion" hypothesis, it helps to have a picture of the composition of these cases. About 20 percent of the civil filings — 3.9 million cases — are domestic relations cases: marital dissolutions and property distributions, and child custody and support. Some of these cases represent real and bitter disputes; others are in court only because one cannot dissolve a marriage without filing a lawsuit to do so. Omitting domestic relations cases, one has about one civil lawsuit for every nineteen persons.

Another way of subdividing the 34 million nontraffic cases is to distinguish between those filed in courts of general jurisdiction (typically the more serious cases: for example, criminal felony charges and civil lawsuits seeking substantial damages or injunctive relief) and those filed in courts of limited jurisdiction (municipal or justice courts typically hear criminal misdemeanor charges and civil suits seeking small amounts of damages). If one makes this final division, almost 60 percent of the civil cases and two-thirds of the criminal cases disappear. From this process of elimination

* State court statistics in this discussion come from Brian J. Ostrom et al., Examining the Work of State Courts, 1995: A National Perspective from the Court Statistics Project (National Center for State Courts 1996). Federal statistics come from the Annual Report, Administrative Office of the United States Courts 1998, on line at http://www.uscourts.gov/dirrpt98/index.html.

emerges a picture of the nontraffic filings in the courts of general jurisdiction, the most serious cases:

Civil lawsuits:	40%	(6,300,000)
Criminal charges:	27%	(4,200,000)
Domestic relations:	24%	(3,700,000)
Juvenile cases:	8%	(1,300,000)

Focusing on the civil lawsuits within this group, one can ask what they are about. They are almost evenly divided between tort and contract actions, at 49 percent and 48 percent respectively, with real property actions bringing up the rear at 3 percent. Among the tort actions, about 30 percent are motor vehicle cases, with no other single identifiable category making up more than 2 percent. Among the contract cases about a quarter involve a seller plaintiff—probably suing for an unpaid purchase price; 6 percent involve a buyer plaintiff—probably complaining about undelivered or poor-quality goods. One percent involve employment claims and 16 percent are unclassified.

What happens to these cases? They aren't tried: only 3.3 percent of filed civil cases are resolved by trials, about evenly divided between jury and non-jury ("bench") trials; for criminal cases the rate is only slightly higher: Nationally 4 percent of criminal cases go to trial—two-thirds of those go to juries. That overall average for civil cases conceals regional variations, with states ranging between trial rates of 1 percent and 8.6 percent.

Be clear about what trial rates do and do not mean. Although most civil cases will not end in trial, many will end with a judicial decision—about jurisdiction, about the sufficiency of pleadings, about discovery issues, about summary judgment—even though there is no trial. For example, in the federal system, for which we have elaborate statistics, such rulings are dispositive (that is, case-ending) in about a third of all filings. So a low trial rate does not mean a low "decision" rate. As you will see, a good part of the contemporary litigation process involves such pretrial rulings. It may not be a great exaggeration to say that contemporary litigation *is* the pretrial process. Indeed, some cases end almost as soon as they begin, with a default judgment: about 14 percent of the total cases and about a quarter of the contract cases end with default judgments, probably because a debtor has no defense to a claim for breach of contract.

How fast are these numbers growing? For the last decade the rate of filings has been increasing faster than the population, in part because litigation growth rates track economic activity as well as population. While overall filings have grown by about 21 percent in the past decade, the areas of growth differ substantially. Domestic relations and juvenile filings have grown the most — by 70 percent and 55 percent respectively, criminal filings by 38 percent and civil filings the least — by 28 percent. Breaking down the civil filings, one finds that tort filings in courts of general jurisdiction have leveled off in the past decade and contract filings are *down* by 16 percent in the same period. What's happening? The growth in divorce, juvenile, and criminal filings are part of larger social changes, the assessment of which would take us far outside the boundaries of civil procedure. Part of the story of torts has to do with legal changes — limiting of joint and several liability, caps on damages — that change incentives to sue. Another part has to do with the fact that even before these changes, tort growth was slower than one might have gathered from reading the newspapers. The decline in contract filings in courts of general jurisdiction may be largely an accident of jurisdictional change: if courts increase the minimum level of damages required to get access to general jurisdiction courts, they will drive some contract litigation into the lower tier of courts.

Whatever the growth rate, however, in some places it is outpacing growth in the court system. Judicial administrators speak of "clearance" rates: if 100,000 cases are filed in a given year and 100,000 disposed of, the clearance rate is 100 percent. (Notice that the cases "cleared" needn't be the same ones filed; a clearance rate measures not speed of disposition but whether the system as a whole is gaining ground or falling behind.) A few states are gaining ground; most are barely keeping pace, and a few are losing substantial ground. About half the states "clear" (dispose of, by adjudication, settlement, or abandonment) 98 percent of the cases filed in a given year. Only seven states have clearance rates below 90 percent — falling behind at a rate of 10 percent per year or more. So regional variation is again considerable, and national extrapolation based on how the local court system is doing may be deceptive.

How long does it take for cases to work their way through the system? And is that too slow? The answer to the second question will depend on one's expectations. The answer to the first varies considerably by type of litigation and by the court location. Urban areas have slower clearance times. As a group, contract cases, many of which, you may recall, are uncontested, move faster than tort cases. A typical uncontested contract case is completed in about five months; a contested contract case in a year. Most would say that is reasonably speedy justice. By contrast, just over 25 percent of tort cases in urban areas are still unresolved after three years. Such averages conceal large regional variations: If one drives the few hours north from Chicago to Milwaukee, one moves from the nation's longest median disposition time (861 days) for a tort case to the shortest (217).

NOTES AND PROBLEMS

1. Consider some implications of the statistical picture sketched above:

a. Legislation is introduced to streamline litigation by reducing the amount of time spent in jury selection. Explain why the legislation, though it may make jurors' lives more pleasant, will have no effect on the time of disposition of an average case.

b. State court administrators and judges, staggering under heavy caseloads, sometimes oppose federal legislation that would limit federal diversity jurisdiction on the grounds that the state courts already have too many cases and the "dumped" federal cases would overwhelm them. Explain why that argument is weak.

c. A civil trial lawyer complains that her breach of contract case will never get to court because "all courts do these days is try drug cases." Explain why she's wrong.

d. You represent a tort plaintiff with a strong case who is eager to get a quick judgment or settlement. The auto accident giving rise to the claim occurred in a mountain resort; the defendant lives in a big city, where juries often award larger damages than do rural juries. Where should the plaintiff file suit?

e. A legislative committee is trying to plan for courts in the future. It has population statistics, together with fairly reliable projections of population growth. Explain what further information the committee needs.

2. The raw numbers do little to highlight the relationship between the civil and the criminal cases.

a. In the present climate, most of those arguing that we have too much civil litigation are likely to reverse their views as one changes the topic from civil to criminal. Those decrying the "litigation explosion" in civil cases are thus quite likely to favor "tougher" law enforcement—and therefore more criminal cases. Those on the opposite side of the political spectrum often view rising criminal dockets as evidence of threats to civil liberty but see the growth of civil cases as either benign or desirable (a way for the "little people" to get redress).

b. The civil and criminal dockets battle each other in another way: They compete for judicial time and courtroom space. Any given judge can at any given moment hear either a criminal or a civil case. The U.S. Constitution gives criminal defendants a right to a speedy trial; charges must be dropped against a defendant who has not been given a speedy trial. To avoid this result, statutes enforcing the speedy trial rule give priority to criminal cases. Thus, if a criminal and a civil case are filed the same day, it is very likely that the criminal case will be heard first.

c. In states or localities where there are large numbers of criminal cases, it is possible for civil cases to be pushed permanently to the end of the line — to be in an endless holding pattern, waiting either for a decline in criminal filings or the appointment of more judges.

3. Notice that most civil cases end in an event that is ambiguous: settlement or abandonment. These events may represent a response to the merits: As facts are uncovered, the plaintiff or defendant recognizes that what he thought was a strong case has a fatal flaw. Alternatively, settlement or abandonment may represent surrender to financial exigency: A plaintiff gives up a strong case because she cannot afford to litigate any further; a defendant offers something to make a plaintiff with a trumped up claim go away because defeating the claim on the merits will cost more than the settlement offered. When financial exigency rather than the merits of the claim dictate the result, one confronts the central topic of this chapter, the relation of the incentives and costs of litigation to the merits of the claims involved.

2. Why Litigate?

The people filing 19 million civil lawsuits (six million of which are "big" cases) each year want something; the people against whom they are filed want to know what they stand to lose. To a lawyer, those questions translate into inquiries about what *remedies* a court will order — what acts it will require of the defendant if plaintiff prevails on the merits. Remedies in our legal system aim to "cure" a legal harm. Remedies can be divided into two groups — those that seek to restore directly and specifically that which the defendant has taken from the plaintiff (*specific* remedies) and those that seek to provide the plaintiff with a reasonable substitute (*substitutionary* remedies). If, for example, defendant takes plaintiff's car unlawfully, a specific remedy would be an order (either to the defendant or the sheriff) commanding the return of the car; a substitutionary remedy would be a judgment that defendant pay plaintiff an amount sufficient to purchase an equivalent car. In some cases, the two remedies merge: If a debtor owes a creditor money, a judgment for money is simultaneously a specific and a substitutionary remedy because money is fungible. One of the issues we shall examine below is the extent to which plaintiffs have a choice between these two forms of remedies.

Aside from what courts can do for them, clients are interested in how much it will cost them to get that relief. Most of the bar in the United States is private and charges its clients fees for its services. In addition to attorneys' fees are other costs: filing fees, the fees of court reporters, the cost of expert witnesses, and the like. Such costs can form a significant barrier to litigation such that the harmed plaintiff finds the costs of litigation greater than the potential recovery. To that extent there are legal rights for which there is no practical remedy. That anomaly resolves itself if the successful plaintiff can recover attorneys' fees as part of the remedy. Since the mid-1970s, large changes have occurred in the extent to which such costs can be shifted to the other side of the lawsuit.

B. Substitutionary Remedies

Most remedies in the modern U.S. legal system are substitutionary. This predominance occurs because most suits seek money damages, making damages also the most common substitutionary remedy. This frequency of money damages has several sources. One is that in a credit economy many claims are for debts, and a successful debt claim will always result in a damage judgment. Second, for many common claims specific remedies are impossible: Defendant cannot precisely replace an injured limb or erase the pain of disfigurement or insult. Under such conditions money may be a poor substitute, but only a substitute is possible. Because damages are a substitute, however, the law encounters difficulty in deciding how to measure them. In settlement negotiations the parties bargain directly about how much (or how little) they would accept to dispose of the case. In trials, courts must resort to less direct methods for estimating the value of a substitute. Many of these methods depend on the existence of a market in which the substitute can be priced. The next case tests the limits of such a market-oriented model of damages.

1. Compensatory Damages

United States v. Hatahley

257 F.2d 920 (10th Cir.), cert. denied, 358 U.S. 899 (1958)

[Plaintiffs were members of the Navajo tribe. They lived, and for some time grazed their burros and horses, on federal range land. They used these burros and horses to tend cattle, sheep, and goats, which they also raised. The government and white ranchers alleged that the Navajo cattle were not entitled to graze on federal lands and filed a lawsuit to stop the practice. Before that suit was decided, federal agents rounded up the Navajo burros and horses and sold them to a glue factory. The Navajos sued under the Federal Tort Claims Act to recover the value of the burros and horses as well as to recover damages to their cattle, sheep and goat herds, whose reduction, they contended, resulted from the loss of the Navajos' burros and horses. The Tort Claims Act permits plaintiffs to recover against the United States for behavior that would violate state tort law if done by private citizens. The U.S. Supreme Court, in Hatahley v. United States, 351 U.S. 173 (1956), held that the killing of the horses was a trespass under Utah law and therefore a violation of the Tort Claims Act. The Court sent the case back to the district court for a determination of damages. The following opinion came after the district court had determined those damages. Under the Federal Tort Claims Act all questions are tried to a judge, and it is that judge's calculation of damages that is under review.]

PICKETT, J. . . .

Upon remand, the District Court took additional evidence on the issue of consequential damages, and . . . entered a judgment against the United States for the total sum of $186,017.50. The value of each horse or burro was fixed at $395; each plaintiff was awarded $3,500 for mental pain and suffering; and damages were given for one-half the value of the diminution of the individual herds of sheep, goats, and cattle between the date the horses and burros were taken in 1952 and the date of the last hearing in 1957. . . .

The fundamental principle of damages is to restore the injured party, as nearly as possible, to the position he would have been in had it not been for the wrong of the other party. Applying this rule, the plaintiffs were entitled to the market value, or replacement cost, of their horses and burros as of the time of taking, plus the use value of the animals during the interim between the taking and the time they, acting prudently, could have replaced the animals.

The plaintiffs did not prove the replacement cost of the animals, but relied upon a theory the animals taken were unique because of their peculiar nature and training, and could not be replaced. The trial court accepted this theory, and relying upon some testimony that a horse or a burro could be traded among Indians for sheep, goats, or cattle worth a stated price, together with the owner's testimony of the value, arrived at a market value of $395 per head. No consideration was given to replacement cost. The court rejected evidence of the availability of like animals in the immediate vicinity, and their value. This, we think, was error. It is true that animals of a particular strain and trained for a special purpose are different from animals of another strain and not so trained, but that does not mean that they cannot be replaced by animals similarly developed and trained, or which may be trained after acquisition. Ordinarily every domestic animal is developed and trained for the purpose to which the owner intends to use it. This development and training adds to its usefulness and generally increases the market value of the animal. In arriving at a fair market value of trained animals, the court should consider the availability of like animals, together with all other elements which go to make up market value. In proper instances parties and witnesses may be cross-examined on this subject.

Likewise we think the court applied an erroneous rule, wholly unsupported by the evidence, in arriving at the amount of loss of use damage. There was testimony by the plaintiffs that because of the loss of their horses and burros they were not able to maintain and look after as much livestock as they had been able to before the unlawful taking, consequently the size of their herds was reduced. If the unlawful taking of the animals was the proximate cause of the herd reductions, the measure of damages would be the loss of profits occasioned thereby.

. . . For example, the plaintiff Sakezzie had 600 sheep and goats and 101 head of cattle when his horses and burros were taken in 1952. At the date of the last hearing in 1957, he had 160 head of sheep and goats and 39 head of cattle. The dollar value of the difference at $15 per head for the sheep and goats, and $150 per head for the cattle, amounted to $15,900. The court found that "approximately fifty percent of this amount represents damages to the plaintiff proximately caused by deprivation of the use of plaintiff's horses . . ." The result . . . was arbitrary, pure speculation, and clearly erroneous. In United States v. Huff[, a similar case,] . . . the court said:

> Moreover, there has been no sufficient showing of how much of the damage from the loss of the sheep and goats was proximately caused by the Government [] . . . and how much of the damage resulted from other causes. There is no testimony whatever as to the specific dates of the loss of the sheep and goats, or as to their age, weight, condition and fair market value. . . . It therefore becomes patent that the evidence as to the loss of these animals fails to rise above mere speculation and guess.

Plaintiffs' evidence indicated that the loss of their animals made it difficult and burdensome for them to obtain and transport needed water, wood, food, and game, and curtailed their travel for medical care and to tribal council meetings and ceremonies. Plaintiffs also testified that because of the loss of their animals they were not able to grow crops and gardens as extensively as before. These were factors upon which damages for loss of use could have been based. This does not exclude the right to damages for loss of profits which may have resulted from reduction of the number of livestock, or actual loss of the animals, if the unlawful acts of the defendant agents were the proximate cause of the loss and were proved to a reasonable degree of certainty.

But the right to such damages does not extend forever, and it is limited to the time in which a prudent person would replace the destroyed horses and burros. The law requires only that the United States make full reparation for the pecuniary loss which their agents inflicted. . . .

The District Court awarded each plaintiff the sum of $3,500 for mental pain and suffering. . . . There was evidence that because of the seizure of their animals and the continued activity of government agents and white ranchers to rid the ranges of trespassers, the plaintiffs and their families were frightened, and after the animals were taken, they were "sick at heart, their dignity suffered, and some of them cried." There was considerable evidence that some of the plaintiffs mourned the loss of their animals for a long period of time. We think it quite clear that the sum given each plaintiff was wholly conjectural and picked out of thin air. The District Court seemed to think that because the horses and burros played such an important part in the plaintiffs' lives, the grief and hardship was the same as to each of them. . . .

. . . Pain and suffering is an individual matter, not a common injury, and must be so treated. . . . Reversed, and remanded for a new trial as to damages only.

[In remanding the court also recommended that the district judge, whom it described as "incensed and embittered, perhaps understandably so, by the general treatment over a period of years of the plaintiffs and other Indians in southeastern Utah," recuse himself from further proceedings in the case.]

NOTES AND PROBLEMS

1. Imagine that the plaintiffs could have shown that the destroyed horses belonged to a centuries-old lineage and that the federal agents' actions had destroyed the last of the breed? Would that eliminate the need to show damages by referring to a market price?

2. The court recites a black-letter statement of the purpose of compensatory damages: "The fundamental principle of damages is to restore the injured party, as nearly as possible, to the position he would have been

in had it not been for the wrong of the other party." Later the opinion also says, "the right to such damages does not extend forever, and is limited to the time in which a prudent person would replace" whatever had been lost.

a. Are these two statements consistent with each other?

b. Is the second statement a rule about damages or about substantive law?

3. To what extent do rules of damages like those announced in *Hatahley* presuppose a functioning market in whatever has been taken or injured, a market that includes credit available to injured plaintiffs?

a. Should the rules be different if such markets do not exist?

b. For example, would the outcome be different if the Navajos could show that they had no significant assets other than the destroyed animals and that no one would lend them money for replacements pending the result of their lawsuit? See Valencia v. Shell Oil Co., 23 Cal. 2d 840, 845, 147 P.2d 558, 560 (1944): "The duty to minimize damages does not require an injured person to do what is unreasonable or impracticable, and, consequently, when expenditures are necessary for minimization of damages, the duty does not run to a person who is financially unable to make such expenditures."

4. Cases like *Hatahley* (in which the plaintiffs may attach a subjective value different from the market price) test the goals of a damage remedy. In ascertaining damages courts do not simply ask the plaintiffs how much it would take to compensate them for the harm they have suffered. One reason for not doing so is the parties' temptation to exaggerate the amount. Sometimes, however, one finds evidence of subjective valuation that seems trustworthy. Does that matter? For example, suppose one of the Navajo plaintiffs had, the day before the horses were unlawfully rounded up, offered to buy one for $395 (the price the court of appeals said wasn't supported by the evidence). Would that evidence be sufficient to support such a valuation for *that* plaintiff? Probably not, unless the plaintiff could show that others shared this value — that there was, in effect, a "special" market. Otherwise, most courts would do what the *Hatahley* court does — insist that the goods be valued on the general open market. The theory is that the general market price reflects the average value placed on the goods or services in question. Note that such a rule of damage calculations suggests that damages aim at compensating the harm suffered not by the exact plaintiff but by the *average* plaintiff. Does that practice conflict with the stated goal of "restoring the injured party . . . to the position he would have been in had it not been for the wrong of the other party"?

5. The opinion requires that the Navajo plaintiffs prove the precise value of livestock herds lost as a result of the loss of the horses. Note the position in which this requirement puts plaintiffs. All agree that the

defendant is liable. But if plaintiffs cannot produce evidence of such things as "specific dates of loss . . . , age, weight, condition and fair market value at the time of the alleged loss," they may encounter difficulty in recovering anything—because they cannot prove damages with the required precision. Such rulings are common. Do they make recordkeeping, in effect, a requirement of the substantive law? Is this what courts mean when they refer to proof of damages as one of the elements of a claim?

6. The *Hatahley* court also reflects a concern with individualization of damages. It rejects the trial court's efforts to make estimates of the average amount of emotional pain and suffering. Such insistence on individualization of damages reflects the goal of what might be called the "perfect remedy"—that which provides an exact compensation for the harm suffered by *this* plaintiff. The goal is noble, but it has its costs, chiefly in the time it takes to establish the precise level of harm.

a. A litigation technique popular among attorneys required to offer such "proof" in physical pain and suffering cases is to ask the jury how much it would take to compensate the plaintiff for a single hour's (or day's) suffering, and then to multiply that number by the expected duration of the pain—sometimes a lifetime. In Beagle v. Vasold, 65 Cal. 2d 166, 417 P.2d 673, 53 Cal. Rptr. 129 (1966), a trial court was reversed for abuse of discretion because it had refused to permit such an argument. How else would the plaintiff make the sort of individualized demonstration required?

b. In analogous circumstances we accept rough guesses about the extent of harm: Many so-called accident insurance policies offer their insured stated sums for certain kinds of injuries—so much for death, so much for the loss of an arm or leg, and so on. Some jurisdictions have statutes specifying *maximum* amounts recoverable for wrongful death. Would such estimates of pain and suffering be worth the savings in time to prove damages individually?

7. The *Hatahley* court evinces great concern to calculate the proper way to measure the loss of the destroyed animals, but it does not mention the cost of vindicating the legal right to compensation—court fees, attorneys' fees, and the like. The reason for this omission is simple: As you will see in Section E of this chapter, American courts do not typically compensate successful litigants for the cost of litigation. This feature of remedial law means that an award of compensatory damages, no matter how precisely calculated, will always fall short of full compensation. Is there a justification for this rule?

8. Consider the length of time that elapsed between the harm and the damage judgment in *Hatahley*. When the plaintiffs do recover, will they recover the sums necessary to replace the horses at present prices or at

the prices prevailing years earlier when the horses were taken? The way courts usually make such adjustments is to add interest to the damages. Rules for awarding interest vary depending on whether it is calculated from the time the claim accrues (*prejudgment* interest) or only during the time between the entry of judgment and the moment when the judgment amount is paid (*postjudgment* interest).

a. In most jurisdictions, the naturè of the harm sued for will determine whether prejudgment interest accrues. The Restatement (Second) of Torts §913 provides for prejudgment interest for the taking of property and for other pecuniary harms if necessary to avoid injustice, but not for bodily injury, emotional distress, or reputational harms. How would that formula apply to *Hatahley?* What theory underlies such a distinction? The Restatement (Second) of Contracts, §354 provides for prejudgment interest on actions brought to enforce a sum certain (for example, a promissory note), and for interest on other contracts if justice requires.

b. After judgment is entered, most jurisdictions provide for interest to accrue until the judgment is paid, but the rate of interest varies considerably. Federal law (28 U.S.C. §1961) ties such postjudgment interest to the rate of one-year U.S. Treasury Bills. Some states, however, have fixed rates, which may be above or below the prevailing rate (for example, 10 percent in California. Civ. Proc. Code §685.010 (West 1991)).

2. Liquidated, Statutory, and Punitive Damages

Given the difficulty of calculating compensatory damages, in some situations the parties try to agree beforehand about price of the harm. The most common such situations are contractual, in which the parties may agree to such *liquidated* damages for breach of contract. Their power to so agree is limited in several ways. First, they may not agree to liquidated damages unless the actual damages would be difficult to calculate. The parties could not, for example, agree to liquidated damages of $1,000 for failure to repay a $500 debt. An example of a statute simultaneously permitting and limiting liquidated damages is UCC §2-718(1):

> Damages for breach by either party may be liquidated in the agreement but only at an amount which is reasonable in light of the anticipated or actual harm caused by the breach, the difficulties of proof of harm caused by the breach, the difficulties of proof of loss, and the inconvenience or nonfeasibility of otherwise obtaining an adequate remedy. A term fixing unreasonably large liquidated damages is void as a penalty.

Using a logic somewhat resembling that of liquidated damage clauses, statutes sometimes set minimum damages not specifically tied to the amount of the loss suffered. For example, the Copyright Act gives holders whose rights have been infringed a choice between proving lost profits and accepting *statutory* damages in an amount between $500 and $20,000 for a negligent violation and up to $100,000 for a willful violation. 17 U.S.C. §504(c); Feltner v. Columbia Pictures Television, Inc., 523 U.S. 340 (1998) (holding that a jury must set the amount of statutory damages between the applicable minimum and maximum). Minimum damage provisions (often coupled with separate provisions for attorneys' fees) also arise in the context of small transactions (bad-check statutes provide a common example); they are designed to offset the costs of litigation over matters that are often small in dollar amount and to encourage plaintiffs to enforce public policy by bringing suit.

The theory underlying minimum damage amounts is also partly punitive. *Punitive damages*, by contrast, aim entirely at punishment. Specifically designed to punish the defendant for wrongful behavior, they provide an exception to the general rule that damages serve only to compensate the plaintiff. Both substantive law and rules of evidence reflect the change in emphasis. For example, mere negligence will generally not support an award of punitive damages; "willfulness" or some malicious intent is generally required. Because punitive damages aim to punish defendants rather than compensate plaintiffs, in some jurisdictions plaintiffs seeking punitive damages may introduce testimony as to the defendant's net worth; the idea is that one has to know the defendant's wealth in order to decide how much a given award will hurt—a monetary instance of suiting the punishment to the criminal.

The increased willingness of courts and juries to award punitive damages has led to litigation challenging the constitutionality of punitive damages alleged to be excessive. For ten years the U.S. Supreme Court repeatedly struggled with this question and decided five cases in which it tried to find a congenial approach to the question.

The sequence started with Browning-Ferris Indus. v. Kelco Disposal, 492 U.S. 257 (1989), in which the Court said that "[t]here is some authority in our opinions for the view that the Due Process Clause places outer limits on the size of a civil damages award made pursuant to a statutory scheme." The second sentence of §1 of Fourteenth Amendment to the U.S. Constitution forbids "any State" from "depriv[ing] any person of life, liberty, or property without due process of law." Known as the Due Process Clause, these words have been the subject of thousands of cases and pages of commentary. They forbid summary executions and imprisonment without trial; they also bar state seizure of property without a hearing. But the difficult questions begin when one asks what advantages constitute "property" and how elaborate process must be before it is "due process."

The Court had to confront those questions when litigants seized the hint in *Browning-Ferris Industries* and in a series of cases challenged particular impositions of punitive damages. After two false starts (Pacific Mut. Life Ins. Co. v. Haslip, 499 U.S. 1 (1991); TXO Production Corp. v. Alliance Resources Corp., 509 U.S. 443 (1993)), in which the justices affirmed punitive damage awards without explaining very precisely why they were doing so, the Court within three years decided a pair of cases that set forth contrasting and complementary approaches to the problem.

Honda Motor Co. v. Oberg
512 U.S. 415 (1994)

Justice STEVENS delivered the opinion of the Court.

An amendment to the Oregon Constitution prohibits judicial review of the amount of punitive damages awarded by a jury "unless the court can affirmatively say there is no evidence to support the verdict." The question presented is whether that prohibition is consistent with the Due Process Clause of the Fourteenth Amendment. We hold that it is not.

I

Petitioner manufactured and sold the three-wheeled all-terrain vehicle that overturned while respondent was driving it, causing him severe and permanent injuries. Respondent brought suit alleging that petitioner knew or should have known that the vehicle had an inherently and unreasonably dangerous design. The jury found petitioner liable and awarded respondent $919,390.39 in compensatory damages and punitive damages of $5,000,000. . . . On appeal, relying on our then recent decision in Pacific Mut. Life Ins. Co. v. Haslip, petitioner argued that the award of punitive damages violated the Due Process Clause of the Fourteenth Amendment, because the punitive damages were excessive and because Oregon courts lacked the power to correct excessive verdicts. . . .

II

Our recent cases have recognized that the Constitution imposes a substantive limit on the size of punitive damage awards. *Haslip; TXO Production Corp.* . . . In the case before us today we are not directly concerned with the character of the standard that will identify unconstitutionally excessive awards; rather we are confronted with the question of what procedures are necessary to ensure that punitive damages are not imposed in an arbitrary manner. . . .

The opinions in both *Haslip* and *TXO* . . . suggest that our analysis in this case should focus on Oregon's departure from traditional procedures. We therefore first contrast the relevant common law practice with Oregon's procedure, which that State's Supreme Court once described as "a system of trial by jury in which the judge is reduced to the status of a mere monitor." Van Lom v. Schneiderman, 187 Ore. 89, 113, 210 P.2d 461, 471 (1949). We then examine the constitutional implications of Oregon's deviation from established common law procedures.

III

Judicial review of the size of punitive damage awards has been a safeguard against excessive verdicts for as long as punitive damages have been awarded. One of the earliest reported cases involving exemplary damages, Huckle v. Money, 95 Eng. Rep. 768 (C. P. 1763), arose out of King George III's attempt to punish the publishers of the allegedly seditious North Briton, No. 45. The King's agents arrested the plaintiff, a journeyman printer, in his home and detained him for six hours. Although the defendants treated the plaintiff rather well, feeding him "beef-steaks and beer, so that he suffered very little or no damages," 95 Eng. Rep., at 768, the jury awarded him £300, an enormous sum, almost three hundred times the plaintiff's weekly wage. . . . While the court denied the motion for new trial, the Chief Justice explicitly rejected plaintiff's absolute rule against review of damages amounts. Instead, he noted that when the damages are "outrageous" and "all mankind at first blush must think so," a court may grant a new trial "for excessive damages." In accord with his view that the amount of an award was relevant to the motion for a new trial, the Chief Justice noted that "upon the whole, I am of opinion the damages are not excessive."

Subsequent English cases, while generally deferring to the jury's determination of damages, steadfastly upheld the court's power to order new trials solely on the basis that the damages were too high. . . .

Common law courts in the United States followed their English predecessors in providing judicial review of the size of damage awards. They too emphasized the deference ordinarily afforded jury verdicts, but they recognized that juries sometimes awarded damages so high as to require correction. . . .

IV

There is a dramatic difference between the judicial review of punitive damages awards under the common law and the scope of review available in Oregon. An Oregon trial judge, or an Oregon Appellate Court, may order a new trial if the jury was not properly instructed, if error occurred during the trial, or if there is no evidence to support any punitive damages at all. But if the defendant's only basis for relief is the amount of punitive damages the jury awarded, Oregon provides no procedure for reducing or setting aside that award. . . .

V

Oregon's abrogation of a well-established common law protection against arbitrary deprivations of property raises a presumption that its procedures violate the Due Process Clause. As this Court has stated from its first Due Process cases, traditional practice provides a touchstone for constitutional analysis. Murray v. Hoboken Land & Improvement Co., 18 How. 272 (1856). . . . Because the basic procedural protections of the common law have been regarded as so fundamental, very few cases have arisen in which a party has complained of their denial. In fact, most of our Due Process decisions involve arguments that traditional procedures provide too little protection and that additional safeguards are necessary to ensure compliance with the Constitution.

Nevertheless, there are a handful of cases in which a party has been deprived of liberty or property without the safeguards of common law procedure. When the absent procedures would have provided protection against arbitrary and inaccurate adjudication, this Court has not hesitated to find the proceedings violative of Due Process. . . .

Punitive damages pose an acute danger of arbitrary deprivation of property. Jury instructions typically leave the jury with wide discretion in choosing amounts, and the presentation of evidence of a defendant's net worth creates the potential that juries will use their verdicts to express biases against big businesses, particularly those without strong local presences. Judicial review of the amount awarded was one of the few procedural safeguards which the common law provided against that danger. Oregon has removed that safeguard without providing any substitute procedure and without any indication that the danger of arbitrary awards has in any way subsided over time. For these reasons, we hold that Oregon's denial of judicial review of the size of punitive damage awards violates the Due Process Clause of the Fourteenth Amendment.[10] . . .

10. This case does not pose the more difficult question of what standard of review is constitutionally required. Although courts adopting a more deferential approach use different verbal formulations, there may not be much practical difference between review which focuses on "passion and prejudice," "gross excessiveness," or whether the verdict was "against the great weight of the evidence." All of these may be rough equivalents of the standard this Court articulated in Jackson v. Virginia, 443 U.S. 307, 324 (1979) (whether "no rational trier of fact could have" reached the same verdict).

The judgment is reversed, and the case is remanded to the Oregon Supreme Court for further proceedings not inconsistent with this opinion.

It is so ordered.

[Justice SCALIA's concurring opinion is omitted].

Justice GINSBURG, with whom the CHIEF JUSTICE joins, dissenting.

In product liability cases, Oregon guides and limits the factfinder's discretion on the availability and amount of punitive damages. The plaintiff must establish entitlement to punitive damages, under specific substantive criteria, by clear and convincing evidence. Where the fact-finder is a jury, its decision is subject to judicial review to this extent: The trial court, or an appellate court, may nullify the verdict if reversible error occurred during the trial, if the jury was improperly or inadequately instructed, or if there is no evidence to support the verdict. Absent trial error, and if there is evidence to support the award of punitive damages, however, Oregon's Constitution, Article VII, §3, provides that a properly instructed jury's verdict shall not be reexamined. Oregon's procedures, I conclude, are adequate to pass the Constitution's due process threshold. I therefore dissent from the Court's judgment upsetting Oregon's disposition in this case. . . .

[The dissent found Oregon's procedural protections to be at least as strong as those approved in *Haslip* and *TXO* and disagreed with the majority's reading of the historical record, finding that eighteenth and nineteenth century appellate courts were deferential to jury awards.]

BMW of North America v. Gore

517 U.S. 559 (1996)

Justice STEVENS delivered the opinion of the Court.

The Due Process Clause of the Fourteenth Amendment prohibits a State from imposing a "grossly excessive" punishment on a tortfeasor. The wrongdoing involved in this case was the decision by a national distributor of automobiles not to advise its dealers, and hence their customers, of predelivery damage to new cars when the cost of repair amounted to less than 3 percent of the car's suggested retail price. The question presented is whether a $2 million punitive damages award to the purchaser of one of these cars exceeds the constitutional limit.

[While awaiting shipment to the U.S., some of BMW's vehicles suffered paint damage from acid rain. After they arrived, BMW had them repainted and sold them as new cars. Upon discovering that his vehicle had been repainted, Gore sued, on behalf of himself and nearly 1000 other BMW owners throughout the nation. A jury found that the diminution in value was $4,000 per car. To this amount it added $4 million in punitive damages. On appellate review the Alabama Supreme Court reduced this punitive award to $2 million, an amount the U.S. Supreme Court found still to be so excessive as to violate due process.]

Because we believed that a review of this case would help to illuminate "the character of the standard that will identify unconstitutionally excessive awards" of punitive damages, we granted certiorari.

II

Punitive damages may properly be imposed to further a State's legitimate interests in punishing unlawful conduct and deterring its repetition. In our federal system, States necessarily have considerable flexibility. . . . Only when an award can fairly be categorized as "grossly excessive" in relation to these interests does it enter the zone of arbitrariness that violates the Due Process Clause of the Fourteenth Amendment. . . .

[The Court reviewed the means by which various states regulated automobile sales practices, concluding that various means were constitutional.] But by attempting to alter BMW's nationwide policy, Alabama would be infringing on the policy choices of other States. [To the extent, therefore, that the punitive damage award punished BMW for its conduct in states other than Alabama, it was unconstitutional.]

III

Elementary notions of fairness enshrined in our constitutional jurisprudence dictate that a person receive fair notice not only of the conduct that will subject him to punishment, but also of the severity of the penalty that a State may impose. Three guideposts, each of which indicates that BMW did not receive adequate notice of the magnitude of the sanction that Alabama might impose for adhering to the nondisclosure policy adopted in 1983, lead us to the conclusion that the $2 million award against BMW is grossly excessive: [1] the degree of reprehensibility of the nondisclosure; [2] the disparity between the harm or potential harm suffered by Dr. Gore and his punitive damages award; and [3] the difference between this remedy and the civil penalties authorized or imposed in comparable cases. . . .

In this case, none of the aggravating factors associated with particularly reprehensible conduct is present. The harm BMW inflicted on Dr. Gore was purely economic in nature. The presale refinishing of the car had no effect on its performance or safety features, or even its appearance for at least nine months after his purchase. BMW's conduct evinced no indifference to or reckless disregard for the health and safety of others. . . .

The $2 million in punitive damages awarded to Dr. Gore by the Alabama Supreme Court is 500 times the amount of his actual harm as determined by the jury. Moreover, there is no suggestion that Dr. Gore or any other BMW purchaser was threatened with any additional potential harm by BMW's nondisclosure policy. The disparity in this case is thus dramatically greater than those considered in *Haslip* and *TXO*. . . .

Comparing the punitive damages award and the civil or criminal penalties that could be imposed for comparable misconduct provides a third indicium of excessiveness. . . . The maximum civil penalty authorized by the Alabama Legislature for a violation of its Deceptive Trade Practices Act is $2,000; other States authorize more severe sanctions, with the maxima ranging from $5,000 to $10,000. . . .

As in *Haslip*, we are not prepared to draw a bright line marking the limits of a constitutionally acceptable punitive damages award. Unlike that case, however, we are fully convinced that the grossly excessive award imposed in this case transcends the constitutional limit. Whether the appropriate remedy requires a new trial or merely an independent determination by the Alabama Supreme Court of the award necessary to vindicate the economic interests of Alabama consumers is a matter that should be addressed by the state court in the first instance. . . .

[Reversed.]

[Justice BREYER wrote a brisk concurrence (joined by Justices O'CONNOR and SOUTER) in which he contended that Alabama's standards of judicial review, vague to begin with, were pushed over the border of unconstitutionality by the Alabama courts' lax scrutiny of punitive awards.]

[Justices SCALIA, THOMAS, GINSBURG, and Chief Justice REHNQUIST all dissented, the former two on the grounds that the Court had no constitutional power to review punitive damage awards, the latter two on the grounds that the Court, though it had the power to do so, was unnecessarily and unwisely interfering with state autonomy.]

NOTES AND PROBLEMS

1. What was wrong with the punitive damage award in *Oberg*?

a. What did Oregon do that was unconstitutional?

b. What government institution would have to initiate the changes? What would they be?

2. What was wrong with the punitive damage award in *Gore?*

a. What did Alabama do that was unconstitutional?

b. Is the problem one that could have been remedied legislatively?

c. If not, what would the trial or appellate courts have had to do to make the award lawful?

3. Putting the string of five cases together, what has the Court said about punitive damages?

a. That they are, as a matter of due process, subject to constitutional scrutiny. Consider what this means: that every punitive damage award in the United States faces potential U.S. Supreme Court scrutiny. According to one statistical survey, "punitive damages are included in 6% of all general civil cases with a monetary award."* In practice such review will occur only rarely: the U.S. Supreme Court has in recent years decided only about a hundred cases a year.

b. But, according to the same survey, review may be unnecessary in most cases. The amounts awarded show an enormous range, with the median award $50,000 but the mean (arithmetic average) $859,000, which demonstrates that a very few enormous awards (which get substantial press coverage and are more likely to draw appellate scrutiny) are statistical outliers. Is the need for review confined to those cases, or could a small award still be disproportional?

c. When the state and federal appellate courts do scrutinize such awards, what will be the bases on which they will do so? Can you briefly outline the circumstances that should result in reversal or reduction of a punitive damages award? In Atlas Food Systems v. Crane National Vendors, Inc., 99 F.3d 587 (4th Cir. 1996) the court upheld a district court's reduction of punitive damages even after a second jury had returned a punitive verdict even higher than the first.

4. *Oberg* and *Gore* are cases not only about punitive damages but also about due process, but they display two quite different faces of due process.

a. As the opinion in *Oberg* points out, it is an unusual due process case. Most due process cases ask when some traditional form of process is inadequate in light of contemporary conditions and standards. Fuentes v. Shevin, considered later in this chapter, infra page 369, is an example of such a case, as is Mullane v. Central Hanover Bank & Trust in Chapter II, supra page 175. By contrast, *Oberg* strikes down a state law for departing from the procedures traditionally used by common law courts. Why

*Statistical information in these notes comes from Brian J. Ostrom et al., Examining the Work of State Courts, 1995: A National Perspective from the Court Statistics Project at 36-38 (National Center for State Courts 1996).

is old process due process? Specifically, if one could demonstrate that modern jury instructions are more precise and that the modern law of evidence provides much more protection against prejudicial information reaching the jury, why should that not be thought of as a protection for a defendant roughly equivalent to the common law courts' rarely exercised power of appellate review?

b. *Oberg* is about what lawyers call, with apparent redundancy, "procedural due process": A party claims that she is due some process that has not been afforded her. In such cases is one can specify a change in the procedure of the case that would cure the constitutional defect. *Gore* is different. The Court faced a procedure that it had approved in *Haslip*, and the opinion doesn't suggest that Alabama needed to add or modify its punitive damage procedures. Instead, the Court said the award was just unfair — it was too much under all the circumstances. Courts in the United States have recently been rather wary of such pronouncements — they smack too much of rule by judicial fiat. Did the *Gore* court sufficiently explain how it reached its conclusion?

5. *Oberg*, *Gore*, and the preceding three cases ask whether a punitive damage award might be disproportionately large or insufficiently constrained by standards. One can ask the converse question: Can punitive damages be *too* constrained? In McBride v. General Motors Corp., 737 F. Supp. 1563 (M.D. Ga. 1990), the district court held unconstitutional Georgia's effort to curb punitive damages. The statute in question limited punitive damage awards to one per defendant, regardless of the number of people affected by defendant's behavior, and allowed the state to collect 75 percent of any punitive damage award in a product liability suit.

C. Specific Remedies

1. The Idea of Specific Relief

Though damages are the most commonly sought remedy, they are not the only available one. Courts may order parties to do things or to refrain from doing them; they also can enlist the help of officials in recapturing personal or real property from defendants wrongfully possessing or occupying it. Legal writers sometimes refer to such remedies as *specific* (as opposed to *substitutionary*) remedies. The plaintiffs in *Hatahley* sought to recover for the loss of their horses, a substitutionary remedy. If they had sued before the horses had been destroyed, would they have been able to obtain a specific remedy — the return of the actual animals? The answer is almost certainly yes: A successful action of *replevin* will result in the sheriff's or marshal's taking the horses (or car or diamond or painting) from the defendant and giving them to the person declared to be the rightful owner. Had the *Hatahley* plaintiffs been wrongfully occupying the government land on which the horses grazed, the United States would have been able to employ another specific remedy, *ejectment*, to have them removed. In recent times many of the most interesting and controversial remedies have been specific: racial integration of schools and places of employment; changes in the operation of prisons, hospitals, and other institutions.

Given the existence of both substitutionary and specific remedies, a lawyer who is thinking about filing a lawsuit must consider which among the array of potential remedies is actually available in this case. To answer this, some historical background is needed.

2.   An Excursus on Equity and Specific Relief

The English legal system, whose structure and suppositions the colonies inherited, had in the sixteenth and seventeenth centuries (when the founders of those colonies emigrated) not one or two but a group of court systems, each with a rather specialized jurisdiction. The most significant of these systems were the courts of common law and the Court of Chancery (sometimes referred to as a court of equity). You will explore more fully the workings of the common law system in Chapter VI, but a few words about its relationship to equity — the system administered by the Court of Chancery — are necessary at this stage. For our purposes the important point is that each court administered different remedies. Courts of common law administered legal remedies; the Court of Chancery administered equitable remedies. To call a remedy "equitable" thus simply means that it would, historically, have been granted by the Court of Chancery rather than by one of the common law courts.

A brief account of equitable remedies may help underline the point. *Injunctions* are by far the most prevalent form of equitable relief. They can range from a simple order to a defendant to stop burning garbage on his land to a complex restructuring of a school system. But the fact that injunctions are common should not blind you to their potentially dramatic effects. One of the consequences of a court's issuing an injunction is that it is prepared to enforce it if the party to whom it is directed does not comply. Injunctions are enforced by *contempt* proceedings. A party who is held in contempt of court for refusing to obey an injunction may be fined or put in jail until she obeys the order. That makes the

injunction an extremely powerful weapon; one writer has compared it
to a criminal statute drafted and enforced at the behest of a party to
civil litigation.*

Although injunctions are the most frequently sought form of equitable
relief, there are others that remain important. A party may seek the
declaration of a *constructive trust* over funds a defendant has wrongfully
diverted. A party to a contract may seek *rescission* of the contract or its
cancellation, or may seek to have it *reformed* to comply with the true
intent of the parties. In complex financial transactions in which it is
impossible for the plaintiff to calculate his actual money damages, he
may ask the court to require an *accounting* of the defendant in order to
determine what is owed. And an owner in possession of land may seek
to *quiet title* to it or to *remove clouds from the title.*

This list of equitable remedies can easily — but wrongly — lead you to
assume that all specific remedies are equitable. In fact, several legal
remedies are specific rather than substitutionary. As already noted, an
action in *replevin* to recover personal property is classified as legal, as is
an action in *ejectment* to recover land wrongfully in the possession of
another. The *writ of mandamus*, through which a court orders a lower
court or a public official to perform an act required by law, is also officially
categorized as legal. So is *habeas corpus* (a civil writ, though it has its
most frequent use in criminal cases). The reason for the "legal" label in
these cases is, again, simply historical: Courts of law (rather than Chancery, the court of equity) had jurisdiction to grant those forms of relief.

Unfortunately, the distinction between legal and equitable remedies
was not founded on any neat concept. As the list in the preceding
paragraph makes clear, it is not true, for example, that equity granted
only specific remedies and common law only substitutionary remedies.
Just as the courts of law administered several specific remedies, so Chancery sometimes ordered the payment of damages as part of its decrees, thus
administering substitutionary remedies. By and large, however, Chancery
issued orders directing defendants to act or refrain from acting — to perform the contract, stop dumping waste on the plaintiff's land, hand over
the deed to Blackacre, render an accounting to the beneficiary of the
trust, and the like. And, by and large (with the notable exceptions just
listed), the common law awarded damages — to pay the plaintiff the
amount promised, compensate him for injuries inflicted, and so on.

With law and equity operating as separate courts, the system required
some rules of priority. Was the choice between legal and equitable

---

* Owen Fiss, The Civil Rights Injunction 7-37 (1978).

remedies (and the two court systems that delivered those remedies) entirely up to the plaintiff? Could law and equity undo each other's decrees — equity granting injunctions against the enforcement of damage awards and law awarding damages to undo the effect of injunctions? In 1616 the problem rose to a fever pitch in what came to be known as the Coke-Ellesmere dispute (named after the judges involved rather than the litigants). In that case, King James I himself rendered a judgment that worked a truce between the two systems. If courts of equity and courts of law were to continue to coexist, one had to defer to the other. Equity did the deferring. The accepted maxim was that in order to be entitled to an equitable remedy, the plaintiff had to show that her legal remedy was "inadequate" — that some injustice would result if Chancery (equity's court) did not come to the rescue.

In Great Britain and in most judicial systems in the United States the two court systems have merged. Rule 1 accomplishes such a merger for the federal system. Merger makes things much easier for the litigant and lawyer in one respect: No longer need they worry which court system can grant relief. And no longer need the sovereign referee fights between the two systems. The question remains whether there is still a need for a remedial hierarchy — and whether one exists.

3. Is There a Remedial Hierarchy?

One frequently encounters statements suggesting that a hierarchy of remedies persists, that courts prefer legal to equitable remedies. Courts sometimes refer to the requirement that a plaintiff seeking an equitable remedy (usually an injunction) demonstrate that the legal remedy (usually damages) is inadequate. Other times courts will insist that the plaintiff demonstrate that the harm is "irreparable," meaning that money damages will not provide an adequate remedy. In such standard doctrinal formulations the plaintiff who prevails on the merits will receive the equitable remedy only if she demonstrates the irreparability of the harm or the inadequacy of the legal remedy, a showing amounting to the same thing.

Despite these statements, one writer has denied that, in practice, U.S. courts still insist that legal remedies be preferred to equitable ones:

> The . . . statement [that] damages [are] the rule and specific relief "a most extraordinary exception". . .is not the law. It is not even close to the law. It is merely a spectacular example of the confusion created by one of our archaic "rules" for choosing among remedies. It states an extreme but recognizable version of the most general and most misleading

of those rules—the irreparable injury rule. But it is wildly wrong as a
description of what courts do.*

Others would disagree with the broad form of this statement, but even
they acknowledge that courts are readier than they once were to grant
injunctive relief and other forms of equitable remedies:

> The courts have altered their application of the inadequacy prerequisite
> without changing their terminology. More and more plaintiffs seek injunc-
> tions to protect statutory, common law, and constitutional entitlements to
> less and less palpable interests. Commentators note that litigants raise the
> inadequacy prerequisite less frequently and that contemporary judges grant
> more injunctions than their predecessors. The inadequacy prerequisite has
> been eroded, operating today in a less formidable, more limited fashion.**

Neither statement should be understood to mean that all plaintiffs
who win on the merits and want injunctions get them. Courts regularly
deny injunctions for a variety of reasons. Sometimes they describe those
reasons by asserting that the legal remedy is adequate or that the plaintiff's
harm is not irreparable. A classic example is the proposition that a court
will not enjoin a libelous publication. Is that because the legal remedy,
damages, is truly adequate? Or because the injunction will be *too* effective,
interfering with other values (free speech and press) that we think valuable
as well? A similar reason for denying injunctive relief is that the injunction
will work too great a hardship on the defendant. The next case considers
and rejects such an argument.

Sigma Chemical Co. v. Harris
605 F. Supp. 1253 (E.D. Mo. 1985)

NANGLE, C.J.

This case was tried to this Court sitting without a jury. This Court
. . . hereby makes the following findings of fact and conclusions of law
as required by Rule 52 of the Federal Rules of Civil Procedure.

A. Findings of Fact

1. Sigma Chemical Company . . . is a Missouri corporation . . . selling
16,000 esoteric or fine chemicals used in research, production and analy-

---

* Douglas Laycock, The Death of the Irreparable Injury Rule, 103 Harv. L. Rev.
688 (1990).

** Doug Rendleman, The Inadequate Remedy at Law Prerequisite for an Injunction,
33 U. Fla. L. Rev. 346, 347 (1981).

sis in laboratories, universities and hospitals. . . . Of these 16,000 chemicals, 10,000 are purchased from supplies in the United States and all over the world. . . . Purchases are made from 2,300 suppliers, many of whom are small "mom and pop" operations. The heart of Sigma's business is matching the right supplier with the product sold by Sigma. Although Sigma's suppliers send out catalogues and advertisements to many buyers, including Sigma's competitors, and although the chemicals and their names are in the public domain, Sigma's knowledge of which supplier sells a particular chemical of a certain quality that satisfies a particular purpose at the right price is not in the public domain. . . .

[Foster Harris, the defendant, went to work for Sigma in 1979, after signing an agreement that he would not work for a competitor for two years after leaving Sigma and even after that period would not disclose any confidential information acquired from Sigma.]

19. After becoming dissatisfied with Sigma, Harris started sending out resumes to pharmaceutical companies . . . [including] ICN . . . one of Sigma's five major competitors. . . .

20. Harris accepted a job with ICN as a purchasing agent and began employment on November 29, 1983. Prior to leaving Sigma, Harris lied about the identity of his future employer. . . .

[Harris used information acquired during his employment at Sigma, suggesting to ICN new sources of various chemicals. He also violated the terms of a temporary restraining order by continuing to do work for ICN after being ordered to stop.]

B. Conclusions of Law

This Court has subject matter jurisdiction because the parties are of diverse citizenship and the amount in controversy exceeds [the statutory minimum]. . . .

1. Validity of Restrictive Covenant

The benchmark in determining the validity of a restrictive covenant is whether it is reasonable. . . . Reasonableness has three components: 1) the covenant must be reasonably necessary to protect the employer's legitimate interest; 2) the convenant must be reasonable in terms of temporal scope; and 3) the covenant must be reasonable in terms of geographic scope. . . . [After a detailed analysis the court concluded that the covenant Harris signed was valid and enforceable.]

2. Propriety of Permanent Injunctive Relief

The principles which guide this court in determining whether permanent injunctive relief is appropriate in this case are well known. "[T]he determination whether to issue an injunction involves a balancing of the interests of the parties who might be affected by the Court's decision — the hardship on plaintiff if relief is denied as opposed to the hardship to defendant if it is granted. . . ." 11 C. Wright & A. Miller, Federal Practice and Procedure: Civil §2942 at 366-67 (1973). Moreover, "the main prerequisite to obtaining injunctive relief is a finding that plaintiff is being threatened by some injury for which he has no adequate legal remedy." Id. at 368-69. In the opinion of this Court, Sigma is entitled to permanent injunctive relief in this case.

First, it is clear that Harris is violating or would violate the restrictive covenant in his employment contract by working for ICN as a purchasing agent. Given Harris' responsibilities and activities at ICN. . . . Harris is contributing his knowledge to a service or product which is competitive with and similar to a service or product on which Harris worked at Sigma. In addition, Harris is in a position where it is very likely that he will, directly or indirectly, use or disclose trade secret information that Harris learned from Sigma's product files. Under these circumstances, there is a strong threat of irreparable injury to Sigma. Plaintiff stands to lose part of a competitive edge that has taken over forty years to develop. The threat that Harris poses to Sigma is particularly great in view of defendant's own testimony that he had memorized some information through daily use and that he was the "best source person" at Sigma. . . .

On the other hand, the harm that would occur to Harris if a permanent injunction were granted is not insubstantial. By the terms of the restrictive covenant Harris will be prevented from working for ICN until November 22, 1985. In addition, Harris may be barred from utilizing his knowledge of Sigma's sources in the fine chemical business, so long as Sigma's trade secret information remains secret. . . . The potential harm to Harris is . . . diminished by the fact that other Sigma former employees have not had difficulty obtaining other employment [with employers that did] not compete with Sigma. Further, the balance of the equities do not favor Harris because he was aware of the restrictions imposed on him by his contract with Sigma and he took a voluntary, knowing and calculated risk by deciding to violate that contract.

On balance, it is the opinion of this Court that the threat of harm to Sigma if an injunction were not granted greatly outweighs the threat of harm to Harris if an injunction were granted. Accordingly, Sigma is entitled to permanent injunctive relief. . . .

IT IS HEREBY ORDERED, ADJUDGED and DECREED that defendant be and is hereby restrained and enjoined from: 1) rendering services directly or indirectly to or for ICN Pharmaceuticals, Inc., as a purchasing agent involved in the purchase of, or the selection of sources of supply for, chemicals which are also sold by Sigma, until November 22, 1985, or further Order of this Court, whichever first occurs; and 2) using or disclosing any trade secret or other confidential information that is the property of plaintiff which defendant acquired by reason of his employment with plaintiff.

NOTES AND PROBLEMS

1. One might cite *Sigma Chemical* as an example both for those who think that the irreparable injury rule has disappeared and for those who think it persists.

a. Those who think it persists could point to the fact that the court refers to the rule at one point.

b. Those who think it has disappeared could point to the sparse analysis of the reasons Sigma's legal remedy was inadequate. In *Sigma*, as in many inadequacy-of-remedy cases, the court reaches a conclusion without truly analyzing the alternative legal remedies, which here would be damages. Consider what such an analysis might have looked like:

> The damage remedy in this case would have consisted of the profits Sigma lost as a result of ICN's acquiring its trade secrets about suppliers. Two circumstances make this remedy awkward and unrealizable: First, it would be very difficult to calculate just how much business ICN took away from its competitor as a result of Harris's actions; second, even if that calculation could be made, defendant Harris would be extremely unlikely to have the money to pay such damages. In ruling that the legal remedy is inadequate, this court concludes that awarding damages would be a nuisance, and probably a futile nuisance at that. We prefer the equitable remedy because it's simpler and it will work.

Does this imaginary analysis make some sense out of the "inadequacy" requirement?

2. In discussing the propriety of issuing an injunction, the court mentions two factors: the inadequacy of the legal remedy and the balance of hardships to the two parties. What is the relationship between these two factors? If the denial of an injunction works crushing hardship to the plaintiff, that presumably demonstrates the inadequacy of the legal remedy. But if the legal remedy is inadequate, why does it matter whether

the defendant will be disadvantaged by the issuance of the injunction? Remedies always inflict hardship on defendants, and courts generally don't stop ordering them on that account alone. For the hardship standard to make sense, it has to mean that the court might choose the legal remedy if the equitable remedy is *too* adequate. Is the idea behind the phrase "equitable discretion" beginning to take shape?

3. Assuming hardship does matter, how much would there have to be to change the decision in *Sigma*?

a. Notice the terms of the injunction: how has the court arguably taken Harris's hardship into account?

b. On appeal the injunction was modified. Harris could work for ICN, but not as a purchasing agent. Moreover, the case was remanded so the district court could modify the injunction so that it forbade the disclosure of proprietary information only for so long as it would "take a 'legitimate competitor' to independently reproduce the information contained in the product and vendor files." Sigma was unsuccessful in its argument on cross-appeal, contending that Harris should not have been allowed to work for ICN in any capacity. Sigma Chemicals v. Harris, 794 F.2d 371 (8th Cir. 1986). Is this an adequate remedy? Is it enforceable?

4. Notice who decided this case in the trial court: the judge. Historically, cases in equity were decided not by a jury but by the judge (the chancellor and various assistant judges). Even after merger that tradition persists; as you will see in Chapter IX, cases seeking solely equitable relief (like the injunction in *Sigma Chemical*) are tried to judges. The choice of a remedy can therefore determine not only what relief the plaintiff will get but also what trier will decide on whether he gets any relief.

D.   Declaratory Relief

Occasionally a party has a legal problem that neither damages nor an equitable remedy can solve. Imagine, for example, that Alice, whose signature appears on a promissory note due in five years, denies the note's validity. How is Sam, holding the note, to determine whether he has a valuable asset or a worthless piece of paper? He cannot sue for damages until the note is due, and there is no claim for injunctive relief on the facts stated. Or suppose a theater owner wants to show a film declared obscene by the local prosecutor, who has threatened to prosecute anyone who exhibits the film. Thinking that the film is not obscene, the owner wishes to show it. He wants to abide by the law, however, and doesn't want to risk a jail sentence as the price of guessing wrong about the law of obscenity.

Under the federal Declaratory Judgment Act, 28 U.S.C. §§2201 and 2202, and similar legislation in almost every state, parties in such circumstances may seek a declaration of their rights. The procedure for *declaratory judgment* in the federal courts is governed by Rule 57.

Who actually uses declaratory judgments? "Declaratory judgments are probably sought most often in insurance and patent litigation, but they are available and used in all types of civil litigation" with two exceptions: state and federal taxes. Wright, Federal Courts 715. Declaratory judgment actions are also used for testing the constitutionality of legislation, though the Supreme Court has demonstrated some reluctance to adjudicate public issues without the factual record that often accompanies suits for coercive relief.

The only real controversy about declaratory judgments concerns the line between a hypothetical case and a concrete factual controversy. In the federal courts, Article III of the Constitution is viewed as limiting the availability of declaratory judgments to actual cases or controversies; hypothetical questions may not be answered by the courts. "Necessarily the difference between an abstract question and an actual controversy is one of degree, and where there is a substantial dispute touching some real and proximate interest of the party, the fact that he has taken action in order to provoke a test case does not make the case inappropriate for a declaratory judgment." Wright, Federal Courts 714.

Unlike equitable relief, which is available only in the absence of adequate legal remedies, declaratory relief may be chosen by a party even though other avenues are open to her. See Rule 57. For that and other reasons, modern declaratory relief is considerably broader in scope than its predecessors in equity, the actions to quiet title or remove clouds from title.

Declaratory relief raises some peculiar procedural problems flowing from the fact that the declaratory judgment action converts the party who ordinarily would be the defendant into the plaintiff. For example, is there a "federal question" for purposes of jurisdiction in the federal district courts when *P* seeks a declaration that he holds a valid patent and that *D* is infringing it? That *D* holds a patent that is invalid under federal law and that *P* therefore is not infringing it? That *D* claims that *P* owes her a contractual duty under state law but that the contract is invalid under federal antitrust law? The state of the law is unsettled. Some lower courts have held that a plaintiff seeking declaratory relief may base federal jurisdiction on an anticipated federal defense, but the

Supreme Court has frowned on such an expansion of "arising under" jurisdiction. See Note 7, supra page 223.

What about nonjurisdictional issues? If P sues D for breach of contract, P bears the burden of producing evidence and the burden of persuasion. But if D sues P for a declaration that D has not violated the contract in question, who should bear these burdens? The case law is again muddled on the subject. And if D sues P for a declaration that D has not breached a contract on which P might have sued either for damages or for specific performance, is either entitled to a jury trial? See Chapter IX. And finally, what happens if P sues D for a declaration of nonliability on an insurance contract and loses, but D does not counterclaim for damages under the contract? Is D forever barred under Rule 13(a) from collecting the money to which the court's judgment implies he is entitled? As a practical matter, must the defendant in a declaratory judgment action always counterclaim in a jurisdiction with a compulsory counterclaim statute?

E.   Financing Litigation

To understand litigation, one has to understand who is paying for it. That might not be true in a world in which the state absorbed all litigation costs, but that world is not ours. Both the conduct and the results of litigation are driven by financing systems.

Lawsuits cost money. Some of the expenses — the courtroom, the judge, clerical staff, and bailiffs — are borne by society generally, paid for by taxes. Other expenses take the form of fees paid directly either to a court (filing fees, jury fees, fees for a marshal to serve process) or to nonlawyers who perform some service (expert witnesses, private investigators, court reporters). Today, attorneys' fees account for most of the cost of litigation in the United States; those fees are often substantial. Relatively high legal fees result in part from the design of the U.S. legal system, which assigns to parties (and their lawyers) much of the responsibility for conducting the suit: Not only pleading but discovery and virtually every other step of the lawsuit occurs because the lawyer on one side or the other takes some initiative. In other societies a judge or similar official paid by the state assumes some of these responsibilities, resulting in lower legal fees and higher taxes.

Legal fees shape contemporary litigation. Any fee system in which the parties bear any costs of litigation will cause cases to be brought, abandoned, or settled on bases other than their legal and factual merits. Financing systems will affect not only how many suits are brought but also which ones; for example, the availability of punitive damages in a particular case category, combined with contingent fees, will, all other things being equal, move legal resources toward such cases. Understanding civil litigation therefore requires comprehending the incentives and barriers to litigation posed by the way in which lawyers are paid. That understanding is particularly important because the fee system is changing in ways that affect those incentives. In thinking about fee systems, consider two sorts of incentives: those for the client (when will a prospective litigant be encouraged or discouraged?) and those for the lawyer (how will the fee system affect the lawyer's work on the case once it is under way?).

1. The "American" Rule

Who pays for lawyers' work? Essentially there are three possibilities: the client, the opposing party, and society generally (via subsidies), though within these three patterns there are combinations and nuances. In this century the most common answer has been the client. The lawyer bills the client for legal services at a flat or an hourly rate. In the United States hourly fees range from fifty to hundreds of dollars; one study done at the end of the 1980s found that the median hourly rate for legal fees was $83 in smaller communities and $103 in larger ones, but these averages mask wide variations.

The system in which each party pays its own legal fees has come to be known as the *American Rule*. It is so called to distinguish it from the *English Rule*, under which (in its purest form) the losing party pays both its own fees and those of the other side. In practice, to an increasing extent someone other than the client pays U.S. legal fees, and in Great Britain less than the full amount of actual fees is generally taxed to the other side. Thus these two "rules" do not accurately describe present practice in either country; they are, however, useful as models with which to explore the subject.

The English Rule in its pure form fully compensates the winner: She gets both the damages (or other remedy) and the costs of litigation. By contrast, under the pure American Rule, a winning litigant has to subtract from any damages the amount charged by his lawyer, and is to that extent made less than whole. Defenders of the American Rule point out that it permits litigants, typically plaintiffs, with tenable but less-than-certain cases to invoke the legal system without fear of having to bear the expense both of their own and the opposition's attorney. That incentive may be particularly important in a political system in which the courts play a significant role (as they do not in Britain) in protecting the constitutional rights of unpopular groups. One might not wish to burden an unsuccessful effort to protect a constitutional right with the legal fees of the victor.

Let us begin to explore the structure of fee arrangements with a common situation — the client who agrees to pay the lawyer's fee. Often, but not always, agreements take the form of a written contract between lawyer and client, sometimes called "a retainer letter" (from the still-occasional practice of requiring a deposit — a retainer — from a client). In some states such written agreements are required in some categories of cases. One common form of agreement calls for the client to pay the lawyer at a specified hourly rate for legal services, plus various costs — photocopying, telephone calls, and the like. Hourly rate billing is a common way of financing litigation.

NOTES AND PROBLEMS

1. What incentives does the American Rule create for litigants?

a. Andy has a claim for $1,000 arising out of a dispute with a merchant. A competent lawyer estimates that handling the claim in even the most economical way will take 20 hours. What will Andy do?

b. Irma's Grocery is a small family business that does not carry liability insurance. One day Irma receives a summons and complaint from a customer who alleges injuries from a slip and fall. Irma remembers the episode and strongly doubts the customer was injured at all, much less seriously. But when she consults a lawyer she learns that it will cost perhaps $7,000 to defend the claim. The plaintiff's lawyer tells Irma his client is willing to settle for $1,500. What will Irma do?

2. How does one defend a legal system in which some meritorious claims and defenses are simply too expensive to vindicate?

3. Nor are matters simple even if one posits a claim that is economical to bring or defend. Assume that the client hires a lawyer, engaging her on an hourly fee basis. Consider the incentives that such a payment system creates for the lawyer. Some argue that such a payment scheme encourages the lawyer to invest unneeded hours in the case because each hour can be billed. Such undesirable incentives may not operate if the lawyer has other work on her desk; nevertheless, fear of such incentives can cause clients to spend time and money monitoring legal fees to try to detect unnecessary expenditure.

4. Given the American Rule, legal rules that increase the amount of damages potentially available will increase the availability of lawyers to take a claim. For example, if a fraud claim can be added to a breach of contract action, the availability of punitive damages may make it economi-

cal to bring a claim that would otherwise be irrational to pursue. By the same token, the potential for such "super-damages" may enable a plaintiff to pursue a claim marginal on the merits.

Another financing system is the flat rate: a set amount for an uncontested divorce, a will, a stock offering, and so on. Some lawyers use such a system or use it in combination with other kinds of compensation. It has the obvious advantage of a predictable, guaranteed fee. Its disadvantages are equally clear. Underestimates are possible: What begins as an uncomplicated will can turn into a nightmare of legal research into the Rule against Perpetuities. Yet if the lawyer tries to allow for such contingencies, she risks charging more than the matter warrants. Few lawyers will handle contested litigation on a flat-rate basis because litigation is unpredictable. As a consequence, flat rates are most often used for kinds of work that the lawyer thinks will have predictable investments of time: Wills are probably the most common example.

2.   Insurance and the Contingent Fee

Thus far, the discussion has assumed that the client will pay legal fees directly out of current assets. Often, however, that will not be the case. Consider an everyday occurrence — an automobile accident in which Driver A sues Driver B for injuries and property damage. In that very frequent source of litigation in the United States it is unlikely that *either* side will pay its legal expenses directly. Both plaintiff and defendant will probably have their fees paid through schemes that spread the costs among other similarly situated persons. Take first the defendant. If he has liability insurance (required in some states), the insurance company will provide the defense as part of the policy benefits. Thus large numbers of vehicle owners have purchased a form of legal insurance. Homeowners' and tenants' insurance policies typically contain similar provisions for claims arising from household accidents, thereby creating a widespread form of legal insurance for potential defendants.

NOTES AND PROBLEMS

1. Most liability policies that undertake to pay eventual damage claims (including those for legal and medical malpractice) also promise to undertake the insured's legal defense and require that the insurer's lawyers conduct the lawsuit.

a. Can you imagine why an insurance company would be reluctant to issue such a policy if it did not contain such a clause?

b. For some categories of liability insurance, insurers write policies to provide that *both* legal fees and the amount of the judgment or settlement are subject to the policy limits — this is, for example, a common term in legal malpractice insurance. Under such a policy, $1 million in coverage would support a $200,000 defense and an $800,000 settlement but would not cover all of a $100,000 defense and a $1 million judgment.

2. In addition to such legal insurance included within liability policies, a small but increasing number of people have "pure" legal insurance. Such policies typically provide for a limited amount of prepaid office or telephone consultation and a few standard services at a flat rate. Almost none of them will cover the expenses of any form of litigation. Why not?

What about the plaintiff in the automobile accident scenario? Her automobile liability policy will provide a *defense* against any counter-claim the other driver may bring, but it will not finance her claim as a plaintiff. A uniquely American fee arrangement — the contingent fee — may, however, perform a similar function. In the contingent fee system, the lawyer typically agrees to provide legal representation, with the fee to be paid from the proceeds of any settlement or recovery. A standard contingent fee arrangement might provide that the lawyer will receive 20 percent of a settlement reached before filing suit, 25 percent if suit is filed but no further steps taken, 33 percent if the case goes to trial, and perhaps 50 percent if the case goes to appeal. In return for these hefty chunks taken from the plaintiff's recovery, the lawyer agrees to forgo a fee entirely if there is no recovery: The plaintiff thus eliminates the risk of paying legal fees in a losing cause. For the client with limited funds the idea is often inviting — he pays only if he recovers something. No recovery means no fee. Most individual plaintiffs seeking damages for personal injuries enter into contingent fee arrangements.

People sometimes praise or malign the contingent fee system without understanding it. To do so one must consider several perspectives: that of the individual client, the lawyer's other clients, and the lawyer. The client gains the assurance that he will not suffer out-of-pocket expenses, which may make the client more willing to bring a case where recovery is doubtful: He risks no loss and he may gain. Some have criticized and others have praised the system for this characteristic. This assurance (of a risk-free lawsuit) comes at a cost that becomes apparent if one considers the position of the lawyer and the lawyer's other clients. The lawyer, to be sure, does not charge the plaintiff any fees if the case is lost, but the lawyer has incurred expenses on the case — if only such overhead items as rent and secretarial services. Those expenses must be paid, and the only source of payment is the fees generated by clients who have recovered or settled. In setting fees, the lawyer must take the probability of success into account; fees from successful cases must cover the expenses incurred in unsuccessful cases. To that extent *contingent fees cause the successful clients to bear part of the costs attributable to the unsuccessful clients.* To describe it thus is not to condemn the arrangement; the winners are only going to pay legal fees if in fact they recover something, and the guarantee of no fee if they lose may be an assurance for which they would willingly pay the higher fee if they win. Indeed, the prevalence of such arrangements may suggest that all concerned find them satisfactory.

NOTES AND PROBLEMS

1. One can think of the contingent fee in several ways. For medieval and early modern lawyers it was an antisocial charge that stirred up dissension and disserved society. This view, still prevalent in most of the world today, makes a contingent fee a form of criminal activity.

2. Alternatively, one can see the contingent fee as a form of insurance in which the payment of the premium is delayed and discounted. Each client pools his risk with that of the other clients of the same lawyer. So long as the lawyer is a good estimator of risks (or has a sufficiently large inventory of cases), the winners and the losers will balance out.

3. One can also think of the contingent fee as a credit system in which the client borrows from the lawyer and repays him only when (and if) there is a recovery.

a. Because repayment is contingent on success, the rate of interest is considerably higher than it would be if the money were borrowed directly.

b. Theoretically, a meritorious claim could serve as collateral for an ordinary bank loan. In practice, a banker would have apoplexy if a client walked into a bank and announced, "I have a perfectly splendid little lawsuit, and I'd like you to lend me some money to pursue it."

In practice, that does happen, only it happens indirectly. One reason for the banker's hypothesized reaction is that bankers are not very expert in assessing the merits of legal claims. Lawyers, however, are, and it therefore makes sense for the lawyer to assess the claim. But the lawyer will typically need to pay the rent and support her family while the suit is in progress; to get this working capital she is quite likely to seek a line of credit from a bank. When the bank lends in such a situation, it is indirectly lending against the expected proceeds, not from a single lawsuit, but from the lawyer's whole inventory of claims. As one banker who writes loans to lawyers put it:

> One thing we do is to look at a firm's collateral base — its receivables, its inventory, how much it makes. . . . With a plaintiffs' firm, there is no asset base. What they offer is an income stream of several types of cases that will come in over time. So you research their reputation in the marketplace, the size of the organization, the number of cases coming in. . . .
>
> If a lawyer tells you, "I'm going to invest $1 million in this case and it's the only one I have, and I'm sure I'll get paid on June 30," we know that's not how it always works. We are more inclined to lend money to someone who says, "I have seven cases and a business plan that includes a worst-case scenario of what may happen to them."

Michael Grinfeld, Justice on Loan, 19 Calif. Lawyer 39, 40 (1999).

4. A fourth way of thinking about the contingent fee is as a partnership entered into by the lawyer and the client. Each brings something to the partnership: The client has a potentially valuable asset; the lawyer has human capital in the form of her education and experience. They agree ahead of time to divide the proceeds of this mutual investment in a particular way. If there are no proceeds, the two "partners" go their separate ways, sadder but wiser. (Note that this theoretical model of the contingent fee is technically illegal: Most rules of professional ethics make it unlawful for a lawyer to practice law in partnership with a nonlawyer: "A lawyer shall not form a partnership with a nonlawyer if any of the activities of the partnership consist of the practice of law." ABA Model Rules of Prof. Conduct 5.4(b).)

5. An alternative to the contingent fee would be the purchase and assignment of legal claims. In theory, a client might go to a lawyer and describe the claim, whereupon the lawyer would buy it outright, paying client immediate cash; the lawyer would then prosecute the case in his own name. Such a system would work only if it were possible for the client to sell ("assign") claims to the lawyer. With a limited set of exceptions, such purchases are illegal (and have been since the Middle Ages, when they were known as "champerty").

a. An interesting recent exception to the champerty laws has appeared. There are now several firms that will "buy" part of a damage judgment on appeal. According to a press account, it works like this: After a plaintiff has won a damage judgment but while the case is on appeal, the law firm examines the record and briefs and then offers to "invest" in the judgment. For example, one such lender paid $200,000 for a $400,000 share of a $1.5 million compensatory damage award. Large Verdicts for

Sale, Nat'l L.J., at Jan. 11, 1999, at 1. As in a contingency fee contract, if the damage judgment is reversed on appeal, the lender gets nothing; if the judgment is affirmed and paid, at least to the tune of $400,000, the lender gets that amount. The advantage for the plaintiff is that the immediate proceeds may enable him to wait out a protracted appeals process rather than settling for a smaller amount.

b. Should such a scheme be extended to the trial level so that prospective plaintiffs could borrow directly on the strength of their claims? Or does the contingent fee system already do that?

Consider now the contingent fee from the lawyer's perspective as she evaluates a prospective client. Ideally, she would like to minimize the number of unsuccessful clients; unlike the hourly-fee lawyer, each such client costs her money. She may screen her cases differently from the hourly-fee lawyer and seek to eliminate those in which a recovery is unlikely or damages are likely to be low or uncollectible. Does the effect of this screening offset the greater incentives of contingent fee clients to sue? The question would be very hard to answer with any assurance; at this point it is important for the student to see that this fee system involves complex and offsetting incentives.

Another of those incentives may affect the lawyer's behavior once she takes the contingent fee case. All lawyers owe their clients the duties of loyalty and competence; financial self-interest sometimes creates a tension with these ethical obligations. We have already seen that the hourly-fee lawyer may have some incentive to spend too much time on the case. At first glance, one might think that the contingent fee would correct this tendency by linking the lawyer's fee to the client's recovery. Recall, however, that the lawyer's economic interest lies not in the maximum absolute fee, but in the maximum profit after subtracting the cost of time and overhead, and, if she has a desk full of work, at the maximum fee per hour of her time.

NOTES AND PROBLEMS

1. The contingent fee lawyer can approach cases in two rather different ways: a large inventory of cases with varying merit or a small inventory of carefully screened cases. Either approach may yield a steady income for the lawyer, but the two approaches will have different consequences for the client and different ethical challenges for the lawyer.

a. The low-volume, high-screening approach would be to accept only those cases in which the chances of recovery seem high. At its most extreme, this approach involves taking only those cases in which liability is clear and in which damages are the only issue. Such a lawyer will devote substantial time to each case, knowing he has a high probability of success. Correspondingly, he will refuse many unpromising cases.

b. The high-volume, low-screening approach would be to accept almost all cases in which there is any prospect of a money recovery. The lawyer will then devote modest amounts of time to each case, hoping that a sufficient percentage of the cases will yield a sufficient recovery to result in an acceptable hourly rate of compensation.

c. If we think of the lawyer as an "investor" in cases, both methods are defensible. The first relies on "stock-picking," with the lawyer hoping that careful research will identify winners in which he will then invest his time heavily. The second relies on "indexing," with the lawyer hoping that small amounts invested in a broad "portfolio" will yield good results on average — with diversification offering some protection against bad picks.

2. Even if both approaches are defensible from the lawyer's standpoint, they have different consequences for the client and bring with them corresponding ethical issues.

a. Consider first the ethical challenges to the lawyer who does substantial screening of his cases. Some have criticized contingent fees under such circumstances on the ground that the fee is really not contingent. If the lawyer has carefully screened his clients, there is a high probability of recovery in each case. Such lawyers, the argument continues, cannot justify the increased-percentage fee for successive stages of litigation.

One proposal to deal with this criticism is to allow defendants to make offers to settle at an early stage of the litigation. If the plaintiff accepted the offer, the lawyer would be entitled only to fees for the hours worked plus a small percentage of the settlement (10 percent or less). If the offer was refused, the lawyer would be entitled to a contingent fee *only if the amount recovered was greater than the original offer.* Lester Brickman, Michael Horowitz, and Jeffrey O'Connell, Rethinking Contingency Fees (Manhattan Institute 1994). No jurisdiction has thus far adopted this proposal: Should it be adopted?

b. Now consider the challenges confronting the lawyer who does minimal screening. A lawyer has agreed to take a case on a sliding scale: 25 percent if it settled before the complaint is filed or 33 percent for any settlement short of trial itself. After three hours of work — interviewing the client and ascertaining some basic facts — the lawyer calls the prospective defendant, who makes a settlement offer of $10,000. If the client accepted that settlement, the lawyer's share would be $2,500, or more than $800 per hour for the lawyer's time. Client asks what the lawyer expects from the case. Lawyer believes that with about 300 hours of work, the case will settle on the courthouse steps for about $100,000. The lawyer's share of that recovery will be $33,000, a per hour return of $110. Which scenario is more profitable for lawyer if she has other, equally profitable cases on her desk? Recall that the lawyer owes her client the duties of loyalty and competence.

3. Client comes to you with a story involving a serious injury for which it appears a solvent prospective defendant is responsible. You do almost all such representation on a contingent fee basis. Client asks you if you would represent him at an hourly rate instead and also asks you to explain what difference it might make. What should you tell him? Should you explain that it might be to his financial advantage to hire you on an hourly basis? Cf. N.J. Gen. Ct. R. 1-21-7(b) (West 1998) (requiring that lawyer raise possible hourly-rate alternatives to prospective contingent fee client).

4. One form of the sliding contingent fee scale — in which the fee increases as later stages of litigation are reached — is described supra. Some states have by statute enacted a different form of contingency arrangement in which the lawyer is entitled to a decreasing percentage of the recovery or settlement as the absolute amount increases — for example, 33-1/3 percent of damages up to $500,000, 30 percent on the next $500,000, 25 percent on the next, 20 percent on the next, and a fee set by the court on any recovery above $2,000,000. See N.J. Gen. Ct. R. 1:21-7(c) (West 1998); Cal. Bus. & Prof. Code §6146 (Deering 1999) (applying only to medical malpractice actions). What would be the justification for such statutes?

3. Public Subsidies and Professional Charity

Insurance will help only those who have it. Contingent fee systems will help only those who seek to recover as plaintiffs. That leaves substantial numbers of people who could benefit from legal counsel but who have no means to pay for it. How substantial those numbers are is a debated professional and political question. Much depends on how the question is asked. Some would ask how many people would benefit — in the sense of improving their present position — from legal advice or representation but do not think they can spare the money for such assistance. Others

would ask how many people handed say, $1,000 would choose to spend
it on legal fees. The response to the first question yields a picture of
widespread unmet legal need; the response to the second suggests that
the demand is far more modest. Much debate occurs over which form
of the question is the appropriate one.

Whatever the measure of need, various local, state, and national efforts
are in place to address it, with varying degrees of success. Some of these
services are staffed with volunteers — lawyers who donate time either as a
professional obligation (some bar associations have established minimum
amounts of donated time to be an obligation of membership) or as a
personal act of charity. Another form of subsidized legal services is that
formed around a cause — an ethnic or religious group or those who have
some agenda for social change. Still other efforts, the greatest part, are
funded with tax dollars, typically a network of federal, state, and local
money. They are often generically referred to as "legal aid," borrowing
the name of one of the most widespread and successful such plans. Most
focus on people of small means who find themselves in the position of
defendants faced with eviction or with creditors' suits. The theory is that
for most suits that would yield a money recovery, it is possible to find a
lawyer who would take the matter on a contingency basis. Some challenge
that assumption — one that often represents a concession to segments of
the local bar that opposed the establishment of Legal Aid as unnecessary.
Others have argued that such a defensive posture robs Legal Aid of the
ability to challenge the conditions that underlie poverty and oppression
in the United States.

One result of such debate has been some notable exceptions to the
predominantly reactive posture of legal assistance programs. In several,
such programs have mounted major challenges to social, political, and
economic systems ranging from racial segregation to school finance.
Evans v. Jeff D., the next case in this section, was conducted by Legal Aid;
the last case in this chapter, Fuentes v. Shevin, was a major constitutional
challenge to a centuries-old common law procedure. The challenge was
conceived and financed by Legal Aid lawyers. Such challenges have
sometimes created opposition, especially when publicly subsidized lawyers question some part of the existing political order. In some instances
legislatures have responded by trying to limit the kinds of legal work
publicly subsidized lawyers can perform for their clients — for example,
by forbidding them to sue state and local governments.

Finally, note that *every* lawsuit receives some public subsidy: the
amounts necessary to maintain the judicial establishment — everything
from judges' salaries to the electricity bill for the courthouse. Each federal

district judgeship (including law clerks, secretarial help, and bailiffs) costs in excess of $250,000 annually just in salaries. This amount does not include either real estate costs, the central clerks' office, or general overhead. State judgeships, which are less well supported, would typically have lower costs. No litigant pays for these direct costs of adjudication. Moreover, the amount of the subsidy falls unevenly. For the great majority of litigants who file a complaint, engage in modest procedural maneuvering, and then settle, the subsidy is small. For litigants who proceed to trial, the subsidy is quite large.

4.   From Fee Spreading to Fee Shifting

Thus far we have examined means of spreading litigation costs. Contingent fees and insurance spread costs among particular groups of litigants; public subsidies spread costs among all citizens. There is one more spreading device that begins to shade into fee shifting.

a.   The Common Fund

Plaintiff brings a lawsuit that benefits him, but in the process also benefits other similarly situated persons. Should those others have an obligation to contribute to the plaintiff's attorneys' fees? The origin of this theory came in a suit in which a bondholder sued the bond issuer to force payment of the bond. The plaintiff won and in the process established that the issuer had to pay other similarly situated bondholders: He had, by vindicating his interest, helped others to win a valuable legal right. In that case the court held that the original plaintiff could recover part of his attorney's fee from the *fund* that his efforts had created — the sum from which the other bondholders would be paid. Trustees v. Greenough, 105 U.S. 527 (1881). Notice that this *common fund* theory requires that the plaintiff's efforts create some fund from which the lawyer's fee can be deducted. This judicially created doctrine has proved very important in financing class actions, in which one party or a few parties may represent a class of many thousands. If in such a case the class representatives win a judgment or settlement for money damages, they regularly seek a contribution to their fees from the fund created for the benefit of the class. Observe that the common fund theory does not itself shift fees from one party to the other; instead it requires that all who benefit from the recovery share its cost. The common fund theory *shares* fees among similarly situated persons rather than shifting them to the opposing party in a lawsuit.

NOTES AND PROBLEMS

In which of the following situations will the common fund theory apply?

1. Student A sues the Regents of State University, alleging that they have without legal authority increased tuition payments; she sues on behalf of all students and recovers $4 million in excess tuition payments, to be distributed among those paying the excess tuition.

2. Student B sues the Regents of State University, alleging that the tuition increase about to go into effect is unauthorized. He prevails, and the court enters an injunction forbidding the tuition increase. If Student B had not brought this suit, all students would have been required to pay a higher tuition, the total sum amounting to some $4 million.

Because the common fund theory depends on a fund created by a judgment or settlement against the adversary, it straddles the line between fee spreading and fee shifting. We turn now to purer forms of fee shifting, in which the losing party pays the winner's attorneys' fees. When that happens, the so-called American Rule begins to shade into something closer to the English Rule. Since the early 1970s, an increasing amount of U.S. litigation has involved the possibility for such fee shifting, a circumstance that has in turn created sublitigation about the conditions and circumstances for such shifting. Notice that such systems fall into two groups. In their purest form, such fee shifts are symmetrical; that is, the loser pays the winner's fees. An increasingly common form is asymmetrical (also called "one-way fee shifting"), in which a prevailing plaintiff collects at least partial fees from a defendant, but a prevailing defendant does not collect fees from a losing plaintiff unless the plaintiff has sued in bad faith.

b.   By Contract

In the contemporary United States, a common form of symmetrical fee shifting arises from contractual agreements. Parties to contracts may provide that if litigation over the contract arises, the loser will pay the winner's legal fees. Such agreements may in theory be asymmetrical (tenant pays landlord's lawyer if evicted; landlord doesn't have to pay tenant's lawyer if effort to evict fails), but courts and legislatures have often required that such asymmetrical clauses be interpreted as symmetrical — loser pays winner's lawyer. Loan agreements and leases often contain such clauses. When a landlord sues a tenant for rent, the tenant may be ordered to pay both the rent and the fee of the landlord's lawyer. The reverse would be true if the tenant sued the landlord for constructive eviction. If the tenant's lease had such a clause, how would it affect her incentives to sue or defend? One often finds such clauses in contracts where the amount in dispute will be relatively small. Do you see the reason for that pattern?

c. By Common Law

Even when the parties have not agreed to shift fees, there are exceptions to the American Rule. A well-established situation in which one side may pay the other's legal fee occurs when a plaintiff has groundlessly brought a suit; in most states one element of damages in a subsequent action for *malicious prosecution* is attorneys' fees for defending the first suit. Beyond any specific statutory authority lies the inherent power of the court to control behavior designed to thwart the just operation of the legal system. Chambers v. NASCO, Inc., 501 U.S. 32 (1991) (upholding imposition of nearly $1 million in fees on party acting in bad faith).

In an influential opinion, the U.S. Supreme Court said that it would not create a generalized common law doctrine shifting fees in "public interest" cases but said that the legislature remained free to do so. Alyeska Pipeline Service v. Wilderness Society, 421 U.S. 240, 257 (1975).

d. By Statute

Over the past few decades legislatures have accepted the invitation in *Alyeska*. Several hundred federal and several thousand state statutes shift attorneys' fees in various categories of cases. Those "exceptions" to the American Rule have now grown so numerous that some have asked whether the rule still exists in the country that supplied its name. That assessment probably stretches things — in the most common forms of litigation, fees will still not shift — but it properly highlights the importance of such statutes.

In their most general form, such statutes authorize courts to award fees to parties "in any action which has resulted in the enforcement of an important right affecting the public interest." Cal. Code Civ. P. §1021.5 (Deering 1999). Most legislatures have been less sweeping, en-

acting fee shifting statutes to cover particular substantive areas. Such
statutes cover many topics — mine safety, truth in lending, consumer
product safety, endangered species — but among the most important such
federal statutes have been those concerning the enforcement of civil
rights. The basic provision is contained in 42 U.S.C. §1988(b):

> In any action or proceeding to enforce. . . [various listed civil rights
> statutes]. . . , the court, in its discretion, may allow the prevailing party,
> other than the United States, a reasonable attorney's fee as part of the costs.

The quoted statute speaks of a "prevailing party" being entitled to fees.
One might think such language created symmetrical fee shifting — that
an employee who unsuccessfully sues her employer alleging job discrimination will not only lose the suit but also have to pay the defendant's
legal fees. Not so, held Christianburg Garment Co. v. Equal Employment
Opportunity Commission, 434 U.S. 412 (1978). In light of the legislative
history suggesting that Congress wanted to make it easier, not harder, to
enforce civil rights, the *Christianburg* court interpreted such statutes to
permit routine attorneys' fees awards to prevailing *plaintiffs* but not to
defendants. The exception, in which a two-way shift was permissible,
occurred only when the plaintiff's claim was "frivolous, unreasonable,
or groundless, or that the plaintiff continued to litigate after it clearly
became so." *Christianburg* at 422. *Christianburg* has had an important
influence: It has meant that the predominant form of fee shifting statute
in the United States has been one-way shifting.

Another important fee-shifting statute applies only in civil litigation
against the United States. 28 U.S.C. §2412. The Equal Access to Justice
Act provides that, unless a specific statute prohibits it, a court shall award
fees to a party that prevails against the United States, unless
the government's position was "substantially justified." 28 U.S.C.
§2412(d)(1)(A). The statute is complex (it limits fee awards to individuals
and businesses below a certain size, exempts tort actions, and caps fees
at $125 an hour) and growing (it has been amended six times in the last
fifteen years). Its exception for "substantially justified" litigative positions
suggests an interesting alternative to 42 U.S.C. §1988(b). The same
phrase appears in Rule 37(a)(4), governing sanctions for failure to comply
with discovery.

NOTES AND PROBLEMS

1. Consider the effect of fee shifting on the filing and conduct of
litigation. Client has been recently discharged from her job. Your investi-

gation suggests a breach of the employment contract. There is also a possible racial discrimination claim, which is much more difficult to prove. The potential amounts at stake are not large. Does the choice make any difference so far as the financing of the case is concerned?

2. Suppose you and your client decide to press both claims, with the client agreeing to a contingent fee for any sums recovered. In spite of your best efforts the employment discrimination claim is dismissed at an early stage. How will this affect your estimate of whether this case will pay for itself? Professional ethics limit the ability of a lawyer to withdraw from representation once it has begun but allow a lawyer to withdraw from representation if "the representation will result in an unreasonable financial burden on the lawyer." Model Rule 1.16(a)(5). Losing money on a case in which the lawyer thought he would make money probably does not qualify as an unreasonable financial burden. Could the lawyer have avoided this situation?

5.   Fee Shifting and Settlement

Financing systems affect not only what litigation is brought but how it ends; they also affect the parties' negotiation strategies. That proposition is particularly true in cases where there is a potential for shifting fees. On one hand, such shifts mean that in a case in which the defendant thinks the plaintiff is likely to prevail, each hour of legal work done by the plaintiff's lawyer increases the potential judgment against the defendant — a circumstance that may lead the defendant to settle sooner rather than later. Defendants seeking to counteract this effect have two procedural weapons in their arsenal.

a.   Rule 68

Suppose that early in a lawsuit the defendant offers to settle with the plaintiff, but the plaintiff rejects the offer. The case proceeds to judgment, and the plaintiff wins, but the amount recovered is less than the defendant's settlement offer. In those circumstances one can in hindsight say two things: that the plaintiff should have accepted the settlement and that the litigation wasted costs on both sides. Rule 68 addresses that situation by visiting consequences on the plaintiff who refuses what turns out to have been a good offer.

Understanding Rule 68 requires a little background. The winning party in a lawsuit generally gets not only the damage or injunctive relief that she has sought but also "costs" (fees of the clerk, marshal, and court reporter, photocopying fees, witness fees, and printing bills). See Rule 54(d)(1); 28 U.S.C. §1920. To that extent the loser is penalized for litigating what turned out to be a losing case.

Rule 68 alters this scheme by permitting defendants to make formal settlement offers and creating incentives for plaintiff to accept them. The Rule provides that if defendant makes a Rule 68 offer and plaintiff rejects the offer and then recovers less than the offered amount, (1) plaintiff may not collect his own costs incurred after the offer, and (2) plaintiff must pay defendant's costs incurred after the offer. As we have already seen, in American courts those "costs" do not *ordinarily* include attorneys' fees.

How does Rule 68 apply to a case in which the plaintiff, if she prevailed, would be entitled to attorneys' fees by virtue of a fee shifting statute? The starting point is the propostition that, when a fee shifting statute defines attorneys' fees as part of costs, the costs affected by a Rule 68 offer *do* include attorneys' fees. More explicitly, a successful Rule 68 offer will stop post-offer accrual of fees for a prevailing plaintiff; it will *not*, however, cause the unsuccessful plaintiff to pay defendant's attorneys' fees. Marek v. Chesney, 473 U.S. 1 (1985). Consider how this reading of the statute plays out.

NOTES AND PROBLEMS

1. To have a concrete example in mind, consider again the hypothetical employment discrimination claim used in the preceding section. If plaintiff prevailed on that claim, she would be entitled to her attorneys' fees. Suppose that defendant, early in the case, makes a Rule 68 offer of $50,000. At the time of that offer plaintiff has incurred $5,000 in attorneys' fees. The case goes to trial and plaintiff recovers a verdict of $75,000, having reasonably expended attorneys' fees in the amount of $35,000. To what attorneys' fees will plaintiff be entitled?

2. Now suppose the case goes to trial and plaintiff recovers a verdict of $40,000. To what attorneys' fees is plaintiff entitled?

a. Five thousand dollars — the amount reasonably expended before the settlement offer. Because one reads attorneys' fees into the Rule 68 definition of "costs" when a fee shifting statute applies, the offer cut off the entitlement to costs incurred after its date.

b. Will plaintiff be liable for defendant's fees after rejecting the offer? No: Defendant will have to pay post-offer costs, but those costs do not include fees. As interpreted by the courts, Rule 68 stops *plaintiff's* fees from accruing as costs but does not shift defendant's fees.

3. Finally, suppose that the defendant puts its offer in the following form: "I'm prepared to offer you $60,000, but that's a package that *includes* your lawyers' fees." At the time of the offer plaintiff had incurred $10,000 in attorneys' fees.

a. There is the initial question of whether that was an offer that is valid under Rule 68. In Marek v. Chesney, 473 U.S. 1 (1985), the Court held that it was.

b. Plaintiff turns down the offer just described, goes to trial, and recovers $10,000 in damages. Plaintiff has prevailed, but the amount recovered is less than the settlement offer, so plaintiff is entitled only to attorneys' fees incurred before the offer.

c. What if plaintiff recovered $50,000, by which time she had reasonably expended another $50,000 in fees? The amount recovered is less than the offer of $60,000, but the offer included fees. To calculate whether the judgment is greater than the offer, should one add the fees to the verdict, on the grounds that the offer did just that?

4. Rule 68 is a powerful sword, but it has two edges, as the defendant in Perkins v. U.S. West Communication, 138 F.3d 336 (8th Cir. 1998) learned. Defendant made the offer. The court, not knowing of the offer, granted summary judgment for defendant on the merits. Plaintiff, having learned of the court's ruling and before the ten-day period for accepting the offer had elapsed, accepted it. Held: The accepted offer, not the judgment, prevails.

5. Rule 68 allows defendants but not plaintiffs to make offers. Plaintiffs can make informal offers, but they do not carry the sanctions and incentives of Rule 68. Some states permit either party to make an offer of settlement, whose rejection then subjects the other side to the same kind of liability as Rule 68. See, e.g., Cal. Code Civ. P. §998 (West 1990). Should Rule 68 be similarly symmetrical?

b.   Separating Lawyer and Client

In exploring financing systems, we have already seen that all such systems pose potential conflicts of interest between lawyer and client. Fee shifting statutes create another issue: the opportunity for the opponent to use settlement offers to drive a wedge between lawyer and client. The next case illustrates the dynamics. In *Jeff D.* the underlying action was based on 42 U.S.C. §1983, one of the civil rights statutes enumerated in the fee shifting provisions of 42 U.S.C. §1988(b). See how the defendant used Rule 68 and §1988(b).

Evans v. Jeff D.
475 U.S. 717 (1986)

Justice STEVENS delivered the opinion of the Court.

The Civil Rights Attorney's Fees Awards Act of 1976 (Fees Act) provides that "the court, in its discretion, may allow the prevailing party . . . a reasonable attorney's fee" in enumerated civil rights actions. 42 U.S.C. §1988(b).

. . . In this case, we consider the question whether attorney's fees must be assessed when the case has been settled by a consent decree granting prospective relief to the plaintiff class but providing that the defendants shall not pay any part of the prevailing party's fees or costs. We hold that the District Court has the power, in its sound discretion, to refuse to award fees. . . .

I

[The plaintiff class of emotionally and mentally handicapped children sued the State of Idaho seeking injunctive relief that would improve the treatment of institutionalized class members. Johnson, the class's attorney, was employed by the Idaho Legal Aid Society; his representation agreement with the class representatives contained no provision covering legal fees.]

[O]ne week before trial, petitioners presented respondents with a new settlement proposal . . . "offer[ing] virtually all of the injunctive relief . . . sought in the[] complaint[,]" [but] includ[ing] a provision for a waiver by respondents of any claim to fees or costs. Originally, this waiver was unacceptable to the Idaho Legal Aid Society, which had instructed Johnson to reject any settlement offer conditioned upon a waiver of fees, but Johnson ultimately determined that his ethical obligation to his clients . . . "forced," [him] by an offer giving his clients "the best result [they] could have gotten in this court or any other court," to waive his attorney's fees.[6] The District Court, however, evaluated the waiver in the context of

6. Johnson's oral presentation to the District Court reads in full as follows:

In other words, an attorney like myself can be put in the position of either negotiating for his client or negotiating for his attorney's fees, and I think that is pretty much the situation that occurred in this instance. I was forced, because of what I perceived to be a result favorable to the plaintiff class, a result that I didn't the entire settlement and rejected the ethical underpinnings of Johnson's argument. . . .

. . . Rule 23(e) wisely requires court approval of the terms of any settlement of a class action, but the power to approve or reject a settlement negotiated by the parties before trial does not authorize the court to require the parties to accept a settlement to which they have not agreed. . . . The question we must decide, therefore, is whether the District Court had a duty to reject the proposed settlement because it included a waiver of statutorily authorized attorney's fees.

That duty, whether it takes the form of a general prophylactic rule or arises out of the special circumstances of this case, derives ultimately from the Fees Act rather than from the strictures of professional ethics. Although respondents contend that Johnson, as counsel for the class, was faced with an "ethical dilemma" when petitioners offered him relief greater than that which he could reasonably have expected to obtain for his clients at trial (if only he would stipulate to a waiver of the statutory fee award), and although we recognize Johnson's conflicting interests between pursuing relief for the class and a fee for the Idaho Legal Aid Society, we do not believe that the "dilemma" was an "ethical" one in the sense that Johnson had to choose between conflicting duties under the prevailing norms of professional conduct. Plainly, Johnson had no ethical obligation to seek a statutory fee award. His ethical duty was to serve his clients loyally and competently.[14] Since the proposal to settle the merits was more favorable than the probable outcome of the trial, Johnson's decision to recommend acceptance was consistent with the highest standards of our profession. The District Court, therefore, correctly concluded that approval of the settlement involved no breach of ethics in this case.

---

want to see jeopardized by a trial or by any other possible problems that might have occurred. And the result is the best result I could have gotten in this court or any other court and it is really a fair and just result in any instance and what should have occurred years earlier and which in fact should have been the case all along. That result I didn't want to see disturbed on the basis that my attorney's fees would cause a problem and cause that result to be jeopardized.

14. Generally speaking, a lawyer is under an ethical obligation to exercise independent professional judgment on behalf of his client; he must not allow his own interests, financial or otherwise, to influence his professional advice. ABA, Model Code of Professional Responsibility EC 5-1, 5-2 (as amended 1980); ABA, Model Rules of Professional Conduct 1.7(b), 2.1 (as amended 1984). Accordingly, it is argued that an attorney is required to evaluate a settlement offer on the basis of his client's interest, without considering his own interest in obtaining a fee; upon recommending settlement, he must abide by the client's decision whether or not to accept the offer, see Model Code of Professional Responsibility EC 7-7 to EC 7-9; Model Rules of Professional Conduct 1.2(a).

The defect, if any, in the negotiated fee waiver must be traced not to the rules of ethics but to the Fees Act. Following this tack, respondents argue that the statute must be construed to forbid a fee waiver that is the product of "coercion." They submit that a "coercive waiver" results when the defendant in a civil rights action (1) offers a settlement on the merits of equal or greater value than that which plaintiffs could reasonably expect to achieve at trial but (2) conditions the offer on a waiver of plaintiffs' statutory eligibility for attorney's fees. Such an offer, they claim, exploits the ethical obligation of plaintiffs' counsel to recommend settlement in order to avoid defendant's statutory liability for its opponents' fees and costs. . . .

III

The text of the Fees Act provides no support for the proposition that Congress intended to ban all fee waivers offered in connection with substantial relief on the merits. On the contrary, the language of the Act, as well as its legislative history, indicates that Congress bestowed on the "prevailing party" (generally plaintiffs) a statutory eligibility for a discretionary award of attorney's fees in specified civil rights actions. It did not prevent the party from waiving this eligibility anymore than it legislated against assignment of this right to an attorney, such as effectively occurred here. . . . The statute and its legislative history nowhere suggest that Congress intended to forbid all waivers of attorney's fees — even those insisted upon by a civil rights plaintiff in exchange for some other relief to which he is indisputably not entitled[20] — anymore than it intended to bar a concession on damages to secure broader injunctive relief. . . .

In fact, we believe that a general proscription against negotiated waiver of attorney's fees in exchange for a settlement on the merits would itself impede vindication of civil rights, at least in some cases, by reducing the

20. Judge Wald has described the use of attorney's fees as a "bargaining chip" useful to plaintiffs as well as defendants. In her opinion concurring in the judgment in Moore v. National Assn. of Security Dealers, Inc., she wrote:

> On the other hand, the *Jeff D.* approach [taken by the 9th Circuit] probably means that a defendant who is willing to grant immediate prospective relief to a plaintiff case, but would rather gamble on the outcome at trial than pay attorneys' fees and costs up front, will never settle. In short, removing attorneys' fees as a "bargaining chip" cuts both ways. It prevents defendants, who is Title VII cases are likely to have greater economic power than plaintiffs, from exploiting that power in a particularly objectionable way; but it also deprives plaintiffs of the use of that chip, even when without it settlement may be impossible and the prospect of winning at trial may be very doubtful.

762 F.2d, at 1112.

attractiveness of settlement. [As we said in] Marek v. Chesney, 473 U.S. 1 (1985) . . . [:]

> . . . Some plaintiffs will receive compensation in settlement where, on trial, they might not have recovered, or would have recovered less than what was offered. And, even for those who would prevail at trial, settlement will provide them with compensation at an earlier date without the burdens, stress, and time of litigation. In short, settlements rather than litigation will serve the interests of plaintiffs as well as defendants.

. . . We conclude, therefore, that it is not necessary to construe the Fees Act as embodying a general rule prohibiting settlements conditioned on the waiver of fees in order to be faithful to the purposes of that Act.

IV

The question remains whether the District Court abused its discretion in this case by approving a settlement which included a complete fee waiver. As noted earlier, Rule 23(e) wisely requires court approval of the terms of any settlement of a class action. The potential conflict among members of the class — in this case, for example, the possible conflict between children primarily interested in better educational programs and those primarily interested in improved health care — fully justifies the requirement of court approval.

The Court of Appeals, respondents, and various amici supporting their position, however, suggest that the court's authority to pass on settlements, typically invoked to ensure fair treatment of class members, must be exercised in accordance with the Fees Act to promote the availability of attorneys in civil rights cases. . . .

[The court rejected this proposition, holding that the question was instead the overall fairness of the settlement agreement; in deciding whether to approve such a settlement, the court could consider the demand for a fee waiver.]

Remarkably, there seems little disagreement on these points. . . . The Solicitor General, for example, has suggested that a fee waiver need not be approved when the defendant had "no realistic defense on the merits," or if the waiver was part of a "vindictive effort . . . to teach counsel that they had better not bring such cases." . . .

[The court found no such evidence.]

In light of the record, respondents must — to sustain the judgment in their favor — confront the District Court's finding that the extensive structural relief they obtained constituted an adequate quid pro quo for their waiver of attorney's fees. . . .

What the outcome of this settlement illustrates is that the Fees Act has given the victims of civil rights violations a powerful weapon that improves their ability to employ counsel, to obtain access to the courts, and thereafter to vindicate their rights by means of settlement or trial. For aught that appears, it was the "coercive" effect of respondents' statutory right to seek a fee award that motivated petitioners' exceptionally generous offer. Whether this weapon might be even more powerful if fee waivers were prohibited in cases like this is another question,[34] but it is in any event a question that Congress is best equipped to answer. Thus far, the Legislature has not commanded that fees be paid whenever a case is settled. Unless it issues such a command, we shall rely primarily on the sound discretion of the district courts to appraise the reasonableness of particular class-action settlements on a case-by-case basis, in the light of all the relevant circumstances. In this case, the District Court did not abuse its discretion in upholding a fee waiver which secured broad injunctive relief, relief greater than that which plaintiffs could reasonably have expected to achieve at trial. . . .

[Justice BRENNAN'S dissent is omitted.]

NOTES AND QUESTIONS

1. Start by recognizing the circumstances in which Johnson, the lawyer for the plaintiff class found himself.

a. Recall that Johnson was working for the Legal Aid Society. In most areas such organizations work on perennially tight budgets. Imagine the following quite plausible scenario. After interviewing his clients, Johnson consults his supervising attorney, who, after discussing the case for a bit, tells him that the society is very strapped for personnel and funds right now, but, with some misgivings, she'll let Johnson take the case *because* it has the potential for generating at least enough fees to pay the overhead on the case.

---

34. We are cognizant of the possibility that decisions by individual clients to bargain away fee awards may, in the aggregate and in the long run, diminish lawyers' expectations of statutory fees in civil rights cases. If this occurred, the pool of lawyers willing to represent plaintiffs in such cases might shrink, constricting the "effective access to the judicial process" for persons with civil rights grievances which the Fees Act was intended to provide. H.R. Rep. No. 94-1558, p. 1 (1976). That the "tyranny of small decisions" may operate in this fashion is not to say that there is any reason or documentation to support such a concern at the present time. Comment on this issue is therefore premature at this juncture. We believe, however, that as a practical matter the likelihood of this circumstance arising is remote.

b. Now comes the settlement offer. The court tells us that Johnson faced no ethical dilemma because the professional ethics are quite clear that the lawyer is obliged to pursue his client's interest, not his own or that of his employer (the Legal Aid Society). What kind of dilemma did Johnson face? Should that dilemma, of whatever sort it is, have any bearing on the outcome of the case?

2. The opinion hints that Johnson had found himself in this dilemma because his clients had not instructed him to refuse any settlement requiring a waiver of fees.

a. If one pursues the implications of that suggestion, lawyers wishing to avoid such a problem will simply ask their clients to sign a standard form instructing the lawyer to refuse all settlement offers that do not provide for attorneys' fees.

b. Is it that simple? Model Rule of Professional Responsibility 1.7(b) provides that:

> A lawyer shall not represent a client if the representation of that client may be materially limited by the lawyer's responsibility to another client . . . or by the lawyer's own interests unless:
>> (1) the lawyer reasonably believes the representation will not be adversely affected; and
>> (2) the client consents after consultation. . . .

Put yourself in Johnson's shoes at two stages. First, imagine how you would explain to the clients what you were asking them to sign. Can you meet the two conditions of Model Rule 1.7(b) (quoted above)? Second, suppose your clients do sign and Idaho now makes its offer. Assume you believe that the settlement (fees aside) is as good a job as you can do for the handicapped children. On the other hand, you realize that Legal Aid might do much for your other clients with the fees received if you can bargain your way into some. Are the free, by refusing to accept the settlement offer (as the agreement with your clients provides), to trade off the interests of your present clients against other clients?

F. Provisional Remedies

A remedy that comes too late is useless — worse than useless if the client has incurred costs to obtain it. In the federal system currently the median time to trial (for those cases that do go to trial) is about a year and a half; in state systems the wait can be much longer. Litigants cannot always wait for the ponderous mechanisms of the law. Interest added to money judgments is one recognition of the importance of timing. But life sometimes demands speed from the legal system. The battered spouse needs a protective order immediately, not after a year's wait for trial. The small business threatened by a competitor's unlawful action will be bankrupt if it has to wait for full-blown adjudication. Provisional remedies — relief pending final adjudication of the dispute — are the legal system's response to this need.

But provisional remedies present a problem: Because, by definition, they must be granted or denied before the case has been heard on the merits, they will often be based on incomplete information, and the court will often be asked to act without the benefit of the adversarial exchange that would accompany a trial. The stage of the proceedings at which the issue arises and the need for a quick resolution pose at least two problems: (1) How should a court decide whether to grant temporary relief when all the relevant information is not yet available? (2) When does the curtailment of ordinary procedures in granting provisional relief amount to a denial of due process?

1. Preliminary Injunctions and Temporary Restraining Orders: The Basic Problem

William Inglis & Sons Baking Co. v. ITT Continental Baking Co.

526 F.2d 86 (9th Cir. 1976)

SKOPIL, J.

In 1971 William Inglis & Sons Baking Co. (Inglis) and four other wholesale baking companies filed this antitrust action against various competitors within relevant geographic markets in Washington, Oregon, and California. The complaint charged violations of §§1 and 2 of the Sherman Act, 15 U.S.C. §§1 and 2; §2(a) of the Robinson-Patman Act, 15 U.S.C. §13(a); §§3 and 7 of the Clayton Act, 15 U.S.C. §§14 and 18; and applicable state laws.

In 1974 Inglis moved for a preliminary injunction in the Northern California market against five of the defendants: ITT Continental Baking Co., Inc., American Bakeries Company, Rainbo Baking Co. of Sacramento Valley, Kilpatrick's Bakeries, Inc., and San Joaquin Bakeries, Inc. The latter three defendants are subsidiaries of defendant Campbell Taggart, Inc. The preliminary injunction sought involved only alleged violations of §2(a) of the Robinson-Patman Act and §17000 et seq. of the California UPA [Unfair Practices Act].

The district court conducted extensive hearings on the motion, reviewed voluminous briefs submitted by the parties, and ordered preparation of cost studies by the defendants. On January 21, 1975, the court issued a memorandum opinion and order denying issuance of the preliminary injunction requested by Inglis. Plaintiff appeals from that denial pursuant to 28 U.S.C. §1292(a)(1). We vacate and remand.

Our disposition of this case makes a detailed discussion of the facts unnecessary. Basically, plaintiff contends that the defendants are guilty of discriminatory and below-cost pricing of their "private label" bread products.[1] As one of their defenses to these allegations, defendants assert that their bread prices were established in a good faith effort to meet competition. The meeting competition defense is a statutory defense to violations of both §2(a) of the Robinson-Patman Act and the UPA.

The district court stated that a plaintiff is entitled to a preliminary injunction only if the court finds that (1) the plaintiff will suffer irreparable injury if injunctive relief is not granted, (2) the plaintiff will probably prevail on the merits, (3) in balancing the equities, the defendants will not be harmed more than plaintiff is helped by the injunction, and (4) granting the injunction is in the public interest. The district court denied the injunction sought in this case because of its "serious reservations as to the probability of success on the merits. In brief, while the evolution of this market does indicate a tendency toward monopoly, the court is unconvinced that the purpose of defendants' conduct was to injure competition or monopolize." Even assuming that Inglis had shown a prima facie violation of §2(a) of the Robinson-Patman Act and the UPA, the court found that the defendants had adequately negated such violation by the meeting competition defense.

The grant or denial of a preliminary injunction is subject to reversal only if the lower court based its decision upon an erroneous legal premise or abused its discretion. As a court of appeals, our review is extremely limited: "An appeal from an order granting or refusing an interlocutory injunction does not invoke the judicial discretion of the appellate court. The question is not whether or not that court in the exercise of its discretion would make or would have made the order. It was to the discretion of the trial court, not to that of the appellate court, that the law entrusted the granting or refusing of these injunctions, and the only question here is: Does the proof clearly establish an abuse of that

---

1. "Private label" bread products are produced by the wholesale baker for sale under the retail grocer's own label rather than under a nationally-advertised brand label.

discretion?" The district court was faced with the difficult task of resolving conflicting evidence in an extremely complex case. We are unable to find an abuse of discretion in its conclusion that plaintiff failed to satisfy the standard for granting a preliminary injunction applied by the district court.

There is, however, an alternative test that the district court did not apply. As the Second Circuit stated in Charlie's Girls, Inc. v. Revlon, Inc.: "One moving for a preliminary injunction assumes the burden of demonstrating either a combination of probable success and the possibility of irreparable injury or that serious questions are raised and the balance of hardships tips sharply in his favor." The alternative test was also stated in one of the cases cited by the district court: "It is not necessary that the moving party be reasonably certain to succeed on the merits. If the harm that may occur to the plaintiff is sufficiently serious, it is only necessary that there be a fair chance of success on the merits." This court has adopted the alternative test.

Since the district court did not consider whether a preliminary injunction should issue under the alternative test, we remand for a consideration of that question. In the event it becomes necessary, the district court shall also consider other questions bearing upon the propriety of injunctive relief not previously reached because of its conclusion that relief was barred in any event by plaintiff's failure to establish probability of success on the merits. We wish to make it unmistakably clear that in remanding for further consideration we intimate no position whatsoever as to whether a preliminary injunction should issue.

Reversed and remanded for proceedings consistent with this opinion.

NOTES AND PROBLEMS

1. Why did Inglis want a preliminary injunction? What would its lawyer have said to the district court to persuade it to issue this extraordinary relief?

2. What is the difference between the two tests that the opinion enunciates? What parties are more likely to succeed under the second than under the first?

3. Do not be misled by the "preliminary" label. Not only in *Inglis & Sons* but in many other cases, the decision about the preliminary injunction will, as a practical matter, end the case. For example, in many business transactions, market conditions will mean that even a short delay makes the transaction financially infeasible. Raider Corporation wants to buy Sluggish Co. for several million dollars. The management of

Sluggish seeks a preliminary injunction, alleging that the acquisition will violate securities laws and mean the loss of scores of jobs if Raider tries to cut expenses. Raider opposes the injunction, contending that Sluggish's management is only trying to protect their ill-deserved salaries, and arguing that even a three-week delay (until a fuller hearing can occur) will mean the expiration of their financing for the acquisition. How should a trial court rule on such a motion? Consult Rule 65(a). Does it suggest a way to accommodate both parties' interests?

4. John Leubsdorf has analyzed the problem of the preliminary injunction as follows:

> A court considering a motion for interlocutory relief faces a dilemma. If it does not grant prompt relief, the plaintiff may suffer a loss of his lawful rights that no later remedy can restore. But if the court does grant immediate relief, the defendant may sustain precisely the same loss of his rights.
>
> The dilemma, of course, exists only because the court's interlocutory assessment of the parties' underlying rights is fallible in the sense that it may be different from the decision that ultimately will be reached. The danger of incorrect preliminary assessment is the key to the analysis of interlocutory relief. . . .
>
> The court need not consider every harm resulting from an erroneous preliminary decision, but only harm that final relief cannot address.

J. Leubsdorf, The Standard for Preliminary Injunctions, 91 Harv. L. Rev. 525, 541 (1978). If this analysis is valid, does it imply that the more certain a judge is about the correctness of the decision on the merits, the less she need worry about the special problems of a preliminary injunction?

5. If preliminary relief is granted but the court's final decision is in defendant's favor, defendant may have suffered harm during the time the preliminary injunction was in effect. For example, if the *Inglis & Sons* court had granted a preliminary injunction that later was dissolved, ITT Continental Baking Co. might have lost customers from being forced, during the pendency of the preliminary injunction, to charge higher prices. One response to this concern is to require plaintiffs seeking preliminary relief to post a bond intended to cover such losses. See Rule 65(c). Notice the problems of setting an appropriate bond on the facts of a case like *Inglis & Sons*. If one of the grounds for seeking injunctive relief in the first place is the difficulty of calculating damages, how would one decide how large the bond should be? What happens if plaintiff makes a showing of likely irreparable harm but lacks money to post the bond? In general such bonds have not proved a very effective way of compensating defendants for the harm caused by erroneously issued preliminary injunctions.

6. Though appeals in the federal courts generally lie only from final judgments of the district courts (28 U.S.C. §1291), §1292(a)(1) creates an exception allowing interlocutory appeals from orders "granting, continuing, modifying, refusing or dissolving injunctions, or refusing to dissolve or modify injunctions." Preliminary injunctions are "injunctions" for purposes of the statute. Do the circumstances of *Inglis* explain why Congress permitted immediate appeals?

7. Preliminary injunctions are a provisional form of injunctive relief. There are also processes that are in effect provisional monetary relief — attachment and garnishment. The first involves seizure of property (in the case of real property the "seizure" may be accomplished by anything from physical occupation of the land to the symbolic posting of a notice at the recorder's office). Garnishment involves asking some third party — often the defendant's bank or employer — not to pay defendant money due him because the plaintiff has a claim on it. The justification for these provisional remedies resembles that for the preliminary injunctions: Without them the plaintiff may suffer severe hardship, in some cases extreme enough to render a final remedy meaningless. A plaintiff seeking damages may believe that the defendant will, if given enough time, either dissipate or conceal the assets from which a judgment could be satisfied. Under such circumstances, the plaintiff needs relief before a final judgment. That relief comes, however, at a price to the defendant. As with preliminary injunctive relief, these remedies can work great hardship on the defendant and give significant power to the plaintiff who obtains such an order. Not only does the attachment or garnishment guarantee the plaintiff that there will be some assets from which a judgment may be satisfied, but it may also provide significant leverage in settlement negotiations.

2.   Provisional Remedies and Due Process

Preliminary injunctions exist because final remedies can be too slow. Is it possible for provisional remedies to be too fast?

The problem arises because in some situations, the very procedural steps required to obtain a preliminary injunction will cause or exacerbate the threatened harm. For example, a defendant served with notice of an application for an order garnishing her bank account may transfer the assets abroad or flee the jurisdiction to avoid service of process. A defendant accused of battering a spouse might instigate new violence if served with a notice of hearing on a preliminary injunction. In these and similar cases the desire for an effective remedy collides with another principle, the guarantee of due process. The next case illustrates the collision; it is important in its own right and as a reminder that all procedures are subject to examination under the Due Process Clause.

Fuentes v. Shevin
407 U.S. 67 (1972)

Mr. Justice STEWART delivered the opinion of the Court.

We here review the decisions of two three-judge federal District Courts that upheld the constitutionality of Florida and Pennsylvania laws authorizing the summary seizure of goods or chattels in a person's possession under a writ of replevin. Both statutes provide for the issuance of writs ordering state agents to seize a person's possessions, simply upon the ex parte application of any other person who claims a right to them and posts a security bond. Neither statute provides for notice to be given to the possessor of the property, and neither statute gives the possessor an opportunity to challenge the seizure at any kind of prior hearing. The question is whether these statutory procedures violate the Fourteenth Amendment's guarantee that no State shall deprive any person of property without due process of law.

I

The appellant in No. 5039, Margarita Fuentes, is a resident of Florida. She purchased a gas stove and service policy from the Firestone Tire and Rubber Co. (Firestone) under a conditional sales contract calling for monthly payments over a period of time. A few months later, she purchased a stereophonic phonograph from the same company under the same sort of contract. The total cost of the stove and stereo was about $500, plus an additional financing charge of over $100. Under the contracts, Firestone retained title to the merchandise, but Mrs. Fuentes was entitled to possession unless and until she should default on her installment payments.

For more than a year, Mrs. Fuentes made her installment payments. But then, with only about $200 remaining to be paid, a dispute developed between her and Firestone over the servicing of the stove. Firestone instituted an action in a small-claims court for repossession of both the stove and the stereo, claiming that Mrs. Fuentes had refused to make her remaining payments. Simultaneously with the filing of that action and before Mrs. Fuentes had even received a summons to answer its complaint, Firestone obtained a writ of replevin ordering a sheriff to seize the disputed goods at once.

In conformance with Florida procedure, Firestone had only to fill in the blanks on the appropriate form documents and submit them to the clerk of the small-claims court. The clerk signed and stamped the documents and issued a writ of replevin. Later the same day, a local deputy sheriff and an agent of Firestone went to Mrs. Fuentes' home and seized the stove and stereo. . . .

The appellants in No. 5138 filed a very similar action in a federal district court in Pennsylvania, challenging the constitutionality of that State's prejudgment replevin process. . . .

II

Under the Florida statute challenged here, "[a]ny person whose goods or chattels are wrongfully detained by any other person . . . may have a writ of replevin to recover them. . . ." Fla. Stat. Ann. §78.01 (Supp. 1972-1973). There is no requirement that the applicant make a convincing showing before the seizure that the goods are, in fact, "wrongfully detained." Rather, Florida law automatically relies on the bare assertion of the party seeking the writ that he is entitled to one and allows a court clerk to issue the writ summarily. It requires only that the applicant file a complaint, initiating a court action for repossession and reciting in conclusory fashion that he is "lawfully entitled to the possession" of the property, and that he file a security bond

> in at least double the value of the property to be replevied conditioned that plaintiff will prosecute his action to effect and without delay and that if defendant recovers judgment against him in the action, he will return the property, if return thereof is adjudged, and will pay defendant all sums of money recovered against plaintiff by defendant in the action. Fla. Stat. Ann. §78.07 (Supp. 1972-1973).

On the sole basis of the complaint and bond, a writ is issued "command[-ing] the officer to whom it may be directed to replevy the goods and chattels in possession of defendant . . . and to summon the defendant to answer the complaint." If the goods are "in any dwelling house or other building or enclosure," the officer is required to demand their delivery; but if they are not delivered, "he shall cause such house, building or enclosure to be broken open and shall make replevin according to the writ. . . ."

Thus, at the same moment that the defendant receives the complaint seeking repossession of property through court action, the property is seized from him. He is provided no prior notice and allowed no opportunity whatever to challenge the issuance of the writ. *After* the property has been seized, he will eventually have an opportunity for a hearing, as the defendant in the trial of the court action for repossession, which the plaintiff is required to pursue. And he is also not wholly without recourse in the meantime. For under the Florida statute, the officer who seizes the property must keep it for three days, and during that period the defendant may reclaim possession of the property by posting his own security bond in double its value. But if he does not post such a bond, the property is transferred to the party who sought the writ, pending a final judgment in the underlying action for repossession. . . .

The Pennsylvania law differs, though not in its essential nature, from that of Florida. . . .

IV

For more than a century the central meaning of procedural due process has been clear: "Parties whose rights are to be affected are entitled to be heard; and in order that they may enjoy that right they must first be notified." It is equally fundamental that the right to notice and an opportunity to be heard "must be granted at a meaningful time and in a meaningful manner."

The primary question in the present cases is whether . . . procedural due process in the context of these cases requires an opportunity for a hearing *before* the State authorizes its agents to seize property in the possession of a person upon the application of another.

The constitutional right to be heard is a basic aspect of the duty of government to follow a fair process of decision making when it acts to deprive a person of his possessions. The purpose of this requirement is not only to ensure abstract fair play to the individual. Its purpose, more particularly, is to protect his use and possession of property from arbitrary encroachment—to minimize substantively unfair or mistaken deprivations of property, a danger that is especially great when the State seizes goods simply upon the application of and for the benefit of a private party. So viewed, the prohibition against the deprivation of property without due process of law reflects the high value, embedded in our constitutional and political history, that we place on a person's right to enjoy what is his, free of governmental interference. . . .

If the right to notice and a hearing is to serve its full purpose, . . . it must be granted at a time when the deprivation can still be prevented. At a later hearing, an individual's possessions can be returned to him if they were unfairly or mistakenly taken in the first place. Damages may even be awarded to him for the wrongful deprivation. But no later hearing and no damage award can undo the fact that the arbitrary taking that was subject to the right of procedural due process has already occurred. "This Court has not . . . embraced the general proposition that a wrong may be done if it can be undone."

This is no new principle of constitutional law. The right to a prior hearing has long been recognized by this Court under the Fourteenth and Fifth Amendments. Although the Court has held that due process tolerates variances in the *form* of a hearing "appropriate to the nature of the case," Mullane v. Central Hanover Tr. Co., and "depending upon the importance of the interests involved and the nature of the subsequent proceedings [if any]," Boddie v. Connecticut, the Court has traditionally insisted that, whatever its form, opportunity for that hearing must be provided before the deprivation at issue takes effect. "That the hearing required by due process is subject to waiver, and is not fixed in form does not affect its root requirement that an individual be given an opportunity for a hearing *before* he is deprived of any significant property interest, except for extraordinary situations where some valid governmental interest is at stake that justifies postponing the hearing until after the event." Boddie v. Connecticut, supra.

The Florida and Pennsylvania prejudgment replevin statutes fly in the face of this principle. To be sure, the requirements that a party seeking a writ must first post a bond, allege conclusorily that he is entitled to specific goods, and open himself to possible liability in damages if he is wrong, serve to deter wholly unfounded applications for a writ. But those requirements are hardly a substitute for a prior hearing, for they test no more than the strength of the applicant's own belief in his rights.[13] Since his private gain is at stake, the danger is all too great that his confidence in his cause will be misplaced. Lawyers and judges are familiar with the phenomenon of a party mistakenly but firmly convinced that his view of the facts and law will prevail, and therefore quite willing to risk the costs of litigation. . . .

The minimal deterrent effect of a bond requirement is, in a practical sense, no substitute for an informed evaluation by a neutral official. More specifically, as a matter of constitutional principle, it is no replacement for the right to a prior hearing that is the only truly effective safeguard

---

13. They may not even test that much. For if an applicant for the writ knows that he is dealing with an uneducated, uninformed consumer with little access to legal help and little familiarity with legal procedures, there may be a substantial possibility that a summary seizure of property—however unwarranted—may go unchallenged, and the applicant may feel that he can act with impunity.

against arbitrary deprivation of property. While the existence of these other, less effective, safeguards may be among the considerations that affect the form of hearing demanded by due process, they are far from enough by themselves to obviate the right to a prior hearing of some kind.

V

The right to a prior hearing, of course, attaches only to the deprivation of an interest encompassed within the Fourteenth Amendment's protection. In the present cases, the Florida and Pennsylvania statutes were applied to replevy chattels in the appellants' possession. The replevin was not cast as a final judgment; most, if not all, of the appellants lacked full title to the chattels; and their claim even to continued possession was a matter in dispute. Moreover, the chattels at stake were nothing more than an assortment of household goods. Nonetheless, it is clear that the appellants were deprived of possessory interests in those chattels that were within the protection of the Fourteenth Amendment.

A

[The Court ruled that even temporary deprivation of property, so long as it was significant, was subject to the constraints of due process.] The Fourteenth Amendment draws no bright lines around three-day, 10-day or 50-day deprivations of property. Any significant taking of property by the State is within the purview of the Due Process Clause. While the length and consequent severity of a deprivation may be another factor to weigh in determining the appropriate form of hearing, it is not decisive of the basic right to a prior hearing of some kind.

B

[Nor did the fact that those possessing the goods had not fully paid for them, and that they were being seized by persons (the sellers) claiming that partial ownership justify the seizures.] The Fourteenth Amendment's protection of "property," however, has never been interpreted to safeguard only the rights of undisputed ownership. Rather, it has been read broadly to extend protection to "any significant property interest," including statutory entitlements. . . .

Their ultimate right to continued possession was, of course, in dispute. If it were shown at a hearing that the appellants had defaulted on their contractual obligations, it might well be that the sellers of the goods would be entitled to repossession. But even assuming that the appellants had fallen behind in their installment payments, and that they had no other valid defenses, that is immaterial here. The right to be heard does not depend upon an advance showing that one will surely prevail at the hearing. "To one who protests against the taking of his property without due process of law, it is no answer to say that in his particular case due process of law would have led to the same result because he had no adequate defense upon the merits." It is enough to invoke the procedural safeguards of the Fourteenth Amendment that a significant property interest is at stake, whatever the ultimate outcome of a hearing on the contractual right to continued possession and use of the goods.[18]

C

[The Court refused to limit the protection to "necessities" (however these might be defined) on the grounds that "under our free enterprise system, an individual's choices in the market place are respected, however unwise they may seem to someone else. It is not the business of a court adjudicating due process rights to make its own critical evaluation of those choices and protect only the ones that, by its own rights, are 'necessary.' "]

VI

There are "extraordinary situations" that justify postponing notice and opportunity for a hearing. These situations, however, must be truly unusual.[22] Only in a few limited situations has this Court allowed outright

18. The issues decisive of the ultimate right to continued possession, of course, may be quite simple. The simplicity of the issues might be relevant to the formality or scheduling of a prior hearing.

22. A prior hearing always imposes some costs in time, effort, and expense, and it is often more efficient to dispense with the opportunity for such a hearing. But these rather ordinary costs cannot outweigh the constitutional right. Procedural due process is not intended to promote efficiency or accommodate all possible interests: it is intended to protect the particular interests of the person whose possessions are about to be taken.

The establishment of prompt efficacious procedures to achieve legitimate state ends is a proper state interest worthy of cognizance in constitutional adjudication. But the Constitution recognizes higher values than speed and efficiency. Indeed, one might fairly say of the Bill of Rights in general, and the Due Process Clause in particular, that they were designed to protect the fragile values of a vulnerable citizenry from the overbearing concern for efficiency and efficacy that may characterize praiseworthy government officials no less, and perhaps more, than mediocre ones.

Stanley v. Illinois, 405 U.S. 645, 656.

seizure[23] without opportunity for a prior hearing. First, in each case, the seizure has been directly necessary to secure an important governmental or general public interest. Second, there has been a special need for very prompt action. Third, the State has kept strict control over its monopoly of legitimate force: the person initiating the seizure has been a government official responsible for determining, under the standards of a narrowly drawn statute, that it was necessary and justified in the particular instance. Thus, the Court has allowed summary seizure of property to collect the internal revenue of the United States, to meet the needs of a national war effort, to protect against the economic disaster of a bank failure, and to protect the public from misbranded drugs and contaminated food.

The Florida and Pennsylvania prejudgment replevin statutes serve no such important governmental or general public interest. They allow summary seizure of a person's possessions when no more than private gain is directly at stake[29]. . .

Nor do the broadly drawn Florida and Pennsylvania statutes limit the summary seizure of goods to special situations demanding prompt action.

23. Of course, outright seizure of property is not the only kind of deprivation that must be preceded by a prior hearing. In three cases, the Court has allowed the attachment of property without a prior hearing. In one, the attachment was necessary to protect the public against the same sort of immediate harm involved in the seizure cases—a bank failure. Coffin Bros. & Co. v. Bennett, 277 U.S. 29. Another case involved attachment necessary to secure jurisdiction in state court—clearly a most basic and important public interest. Ownbey v. Morgan, 256 U.S. 94. It is much less clear what interests were involved in the third case, decided with an unexplicated per curiam opinion simply citing Coffin Bros. and Ownbey. McKay v. McInnes, 279 U.S. 820. As far as essential procedural due process doctrine goes, McKay cannot stand for any more than was established in the Coffin Bros. and Ownbey cases on which it relied completely.

29. By allowing repossession without an opportunity for a prior hearing, the Florida and Pennsylvania statutes may be intended specifically to reduce the costs for the private party seeking to seize goods in another party's possession. Even if the private gain at stake in repossession actions were equal to the great public interests recognized in this Court's past decisions, the Court has made clear that the avoidance of the ordinary costs imposed by the opportunity for a hearing is not sufficient to override the constitutional right. See n.22, supra. The appellees argue that the cost of holding hearings may be especially onerous in the context of the creditor-debtor relationship. But the Court's holding in Sniadach v. Family Finance Corp., [395 U.S. 337] indisputably demonstrates that ordinary hearing costs are no more able to override due process rights in the creditor-debtor context than in other contexts.

In any event, the aggregate cost of an opportunity to be heard before repossession should not be exaggerated. For we deal here only with the right to an opportunity to be heard. Since the issues and facts decisive of rights in repossession suits may very often be quite simple, there is a likelihood that many defendants would forgo their opportunity, sensing the futility of the exercise in the particular case. And, of course, no hearing need be held unless the defendant, having received notice of his opportunity, takes advantage of it.

There may be cases in which a creditor could make a showing of immediate danger that a debtor will destroy or conceal disputed goods. But the statutes before us are not "narrowly drawn to meet any such unusual condition." And no such unusual situation is presented by the facts of these cases.

The statutes, moreover, abdicate effective state control over state power. Private parties, serving their own private advantage, may unilaterally invoke state power to replevy goods from another. No state official participates in the decision to seek a writ; no state official reviews the basis for the claim to repossession; and no state official evaluates the need for immediate seizure. There is not even a requirement that the plaintiff provide any information to the court on these matters. The State acts largely in the dark.[30]

VII

Finally, we must consider the contention that the appellants who signed conditional sales contracts thereby waived their basic procedural due process rights. The contract signed by Mrs. Fuentes provided that "in the event of default of any payment or payments, Seller at its option may take back the merchandise. . . ." The contracts signed by the Pennsylvania appellants similarly provided that the seller "may retake" or "repossess" the merchandise in the event of a "default in any payment." These terms were parts of printed form contracts, appearing in relatively small type and unaccompanied by any explanations clarifying their meaning.

In D. H. Overmyer Co. v. Frick Co., 405 U.S. 174, the Court recently outlined the considerations relevant to determination of a contractual waiver of due process rights. Applying the standards governing waiver of constitutional rights in a criminal proceeding—although not holding that such standards must necessarily apply—the Court held that, on the

---

30. The seizure of possessions under a writ of replevin is entirely different from the seizure of possessions under a search warrant. First, a search warrant is generally issued to serve a highly important governmental need—e.g., the apprehension and conviction of criminals—rather than the mere private advantage of a private party in an economic transaction. Second, a search warrant is generally issued in situations demanding prompt action. The danger is all too obvious that a criminal will destroy or hide evidence or fruits of his crime if given any prior notice. Third, the Fourth Amendment guarantees that the State will not issue search warrants merely upon the conclusory application of a private party. It guarantees that the State will not abdicate control over the issuance of warrants and that no warrant will be issued without a prior showing of probable cause. Thus, our decision today in no way implies that there must be opportunity for an adversary hearing before a search warrant is issued. But cf. Quantity of Books v. Kansas, 378 U.S. 205.

particular facts of that case, the contractual waiver of due process rights was "voluntarily, intelligently, and knowingly" made. The contract in *Overmyer* was negotiated between two corporations; the waiver provision was specifically bargained for and drafted by their lawyers in the process of these negotiations. As the Court noted, it was "not a case of unequal bargaining power or overreaching. The Overmyer-Frick agreement, from the start, was not a contract of adhesion." Both parties were "aware of the significance" of the waiver provision.

The facts of the present cases are a far cry from those of *Overmyer*. There was no bargaining over contractual terms between the parties who, in any event, were far from equal in bargaining power. The purported waiver provision was a printed part of a form sales contract and a necessary condition of the sale. The appellees made no showing whatever that the appellants were actually aware or made aware of the significance of the fine print now relied upon as a waiver of constitutional rights. . . .

The conditional sales contracts here simply provided that upon a default the seller "may take back," "may retake" or "may repossess" merchandise. The contracts included nothing about the waiver of a prior hearing. They did not indicate *how* or *through what process* — a final judgment, self-help, prejudgment replevin with a prior hearing, or prejudgment replevin without a prior hearing — the seller could take back the goods. Rather, the purported waiver provisions here are no more than a statement of the seller's right to repossession upon occurrence of certain events. The appellees do not suggest that these provisions waived the appellants' right to a full post-seizure hearing to determine whether those events had, in fact, occurred and to consider any other available defenses. By the same token, the language of the purported waiver provisions did not waive the appellants' constitutional right to a preseizure hearing of some kind.

VIII

We hold that the Florida and Pennsylvania prejudgment replevin provisions work a deprivation of property without due process of law insofar as they deny the right to a prior opportunity to be heard before chattels are taken from their possessor. Our holding, however, is a narrow one. We do not question the power of a State to seize goods before a final judgment in order to protect the security interests of creditors so long as those creditors have tested their claim to the goods through the process of a fair prior hearing. The nature and form of such prior hearings, moreover, are legitimately open to many potential variations and are a subject, at this point, for legislation — not adjudication.[33] Since the essential reason for the requirement of a prior hearing is to prevent unfair and mistaken deprivations of property, however, it is axiomatic that the hearing must provide a real test. "[D]ue process is afforded only by the kinds of 'notice' and 'hearing' that are aimed at establishing the validity, or at least the probable validity, of the underlying claim against the alleged debtor before he can be deprived of his property. . . ." Sniadach v. Family Finance Corp. (Harlan, J., concurring).

For the foregoing reasons, the judgments of the District Courts are vacated and these cases are remanded for further proceedings consistent with this opinion.

It is so ordered.

Vacated and remanded.

Mr. Justice POWELL and Mr. Justice REHNQUIST did not participate in the consideration or decision of these cases.

[The dissenting opinion of Justice WHITE is omitted.]

NOTES AND PROBLEMS

1. What did the court hold in *Fuentes*? One way of getting at that answer is to imagine yourself on the staff of a Florida or Pennsylvania legislative committee shortly after the statutes had been held unconstitutional. What changes in the procedures of those states would render them constitutional?

2. Can the parties negotiate around the requirements of *Fuentes*? The Court discusses the possibility of a waiver of the rights of the defendant. Can you draft a waiver clause that would stand up to the Court's discussion in *Fuentes*? Would it make a difference if the appliance store offered stoves at two prices — one, the regular "with hearing" price and a second, discounted price available if the customer signed a waiver?

3. Compare *Fuentes* with Honda Motors v. Oberg, earlier in this chapter, supra page 323.

a. In *Fuentes* the court strikes down a procedure that had been part of the common law for half a millennium, holding that it violated due process. At a minimum such a result suggests that "due" means more than simply "ordinary" or "regular." It means that an ordinary form of procedure can be unconstitutional. That fact in turn means that one can

33. Leeway remains to develop a form of hearing that will minimize unnecessary cost and delay while preserving the fairness and effectiveness of the hearing in preventing seizures of goods where the party seeking the writ has little probability of succeeding on the merits of the dispute.

ask about *all* aspects of civil procedure: Is this constitutional? Why? In return for a promise that you won't be tortured with that question as to each aspect of procedure, be prepared to explain why preliminary injunctions are not violations of due process.

b. In *Oberg* the court struck down Oregon's punitive damage procedure because it failed to grant defendants protections that the court thinks were traditional at common law. Can one reconcile the two cases by positing that defendants are entitled at *least* to traditional legal protections but perhaps to more as well?

4. *Fuentes* is important in its own right and also as a representative of many circumstances in which due process regulates government actions. In the debtor-creditor context the cases have established the proposition that, except in unusual circumstances, prejudgment seizure of a debtor's property without notice and an opportunity for a hearing is unconstitutional. Mitchell v. W.T. Grant Co., 416 U.S. 600 (1974); North Georgia Finishing Inc. v. Di-Chem, Inc., 419 U.S. 601 (1975). But collection attempts do not begin to exhaust the circumstances in which one must consider the meaning of due process.

a. Connecticut v. Doehr, 501 U.S. 1 (1991), considered a due process challenge to a Connecticut statute permitting the attachment of real estate at the instance of a plaintiff in any civil action. The lawsuit was a battery action unrelated to the real estate. The "attachment" consisted of the filing of a lien against the property rather than physical occupation or deprivation of the land; the defendant continued to live in the house throughout the attachment. The Court nevertheless held that, without either a pre-attachment hearing or a bond, there was too serious a risk of error in depriving defendant of a significant asset. On the basis of *Doehr,* can one say that any seizure without the opportunity for a hearing needs special justification?

b. In United States v. Good, 510 U.S. 43 (1993), the Court held that the exigency of a civil forfeiture action — in which property used for unlawful purposes is seized and forfeited to the government — did not justify the seizure without notice of real property.

c. By contrast, in City of West Covina v. Perkins, 119 S. Ct. 678 (1998), the Court held that due process does *not* require that the notice left with the owner of property seized on a search warrant give detailed notice of state procedures for the return of seized property.

d. Louisiana enforces its mandatory vehicle insurance requirement by permitting a law enforcement officer to impound any vehicle whose driver cannot produce the required insurance certificate. The statute allows owners to reclaim vehicles by presenting valid certificates within three days of the seizure. Rejecting a due process challenge to the statute, the Louisiana Supreme Court held that the post-deprivation processes were adequate in light of the state's strong interest in enforcing the insurance requirement. Fields v. State ex rel. Dept. of Public Safety, 714 So. 2d 1244 (La. 1998).

5. The injunctive equivalent of a seizure without a hearing is a *temporary restraining order* (or TRO). TROs may be issued with even less process than preliminary injunctions. Indeed, under limited circumstances a TRO may be issued ex parte — that is, without the presence or knowledge of the other party. Situations that might call for such drastic action include those in which there is not time to schedule a hearing (for example, bulldozers are about to excavate an area in which rare and legally protected Native American artifacts have just been discovered) or in which notice itself might trigger the action to be restrained (for example, in the case of a battering spouse).

a. How can such an ex parte TRO be squared with the principles of due process established in cases like *Fuentes*?

b. Read Rule 65(b), which governs the issuance of TROs in the federal courts. Which of its provisions are constitutionally required?

c. Plaintiff appears in court seeking an ex parte TRO to restrain defendant from conducting excavations by dynamite on defendant's adjacent land. The affidavits submitted with the application say that plaintiff's poultry (of which there are many thousands) will have their laying cycles seriously disrupted by such activities and that a two-day delay will enable the plaintiff to move them and prevent this harm. With which requirement of Rule 65(b) does plaintiff's affidavit fail to comply?

6. *Fuentes* says situations in which the state may seize property without prior notice or hearing are "truly unusual." Consider some situations in which there is government action but no judicial involvement. One can think of these as informal due process cases.

a. The state health department inspects a restaurant, finds inadequate refrigeration and rampant Salmonella infestation, and orders immediate closure. Is that act unconstitutional because there was no opportunity for a prior hearing? Would the answer be different if the only defect identified by the inspector was a rusty knife blade?

b. Many cities have responded to persistent parking violators by attaching to their car wheels a "Denver Boot," a device that locks the wheels in place, preventing the car from being moved. Driver challenges this deprivation of his property, alleging his entitlement to prior notice and a hearing. Patterson v. Cronin, 650 P.2d 531 (Colo. 1982), rejected this claim but held that the city had violated due process because the post-seizure hearing was insufficiently prompt.

7. Review footnote 23 of *Fuentes*. Note that attachment for the purpose of obtaining jurisdiction is upheld on the basis of a compelling public interest. If a long-arm statute is available as an alternative means for obtaining jurisdiction, can the need for attachment be said to be compelling? After Shaffer v. Heitner (see Chapter II), does it follow that prejudgment attachment without hearing for the purpose of obtaining jurisdiction should no longer be available in a state whose long-arm statute reaches the limits of due process? Consider: There either are or are not minimum contacts. If there are, the long-arm statute should be available and there exists no compelling need for attachment. *Fuentes* thus forbids the attachment. If there are not, *Shaffer* forbids the use of attachment for obtaining jurisdiction.

Even if a state's statute does not reach the limits of due process, may a state argue that its need for attachment for jurisdictional purposes is therefore compelling when the state has the option of extending its statute?

8. One of the ironies of the *Fuentes* line of cases, with its emphasis on judicial control as justifying prejudgment seizure, is that private repossession, entirely unsupervised by the judiciary, does not violate the Fourteenth Amendment's Due Process Clause because the clause forbids only a "state" from denying due process. Self-help repossession, authorized by UCC §9-503 when it can be accomplished without breach of the peace, does not involve state action.

9. Keep in mind that the issue in these cases was the constitutionality of *prejudgment* remedies. Attachment, garnishment, and the like continue to be widely used as means for victorious plaintiffs to collect their judgments.

This chapter has explored the reasons people litigate. That exploration has taken us from the global and statistical to the minutely doctrinal. We have begun to examine the lawyer's role in litigation by considering the fee system and its potential for linking or separating lawyer and client, but we have not yet begun to examine what lawyers actually do in litigation. The next chapter begins that inquiry by looking at the first step in a lawsuit—the ancient and honorable practice of pleading.

PLEADING

VI

Why should the plaintiff need to allege anything to start a lawsuit? The plaintiff could serve a summons and notice upon the defendant that the action had been commenced, leaving until later a description of the claim being asserted. Or the plaintiff might be required to identify the transaction or occurrence that is the subject of the lawsuit in only general terms — for example, "This action arises out of my purchase of a car from you," or "This action arises out of our accident on Wall Street." Such general statements of claim are permitted in small claims courts and sometimes in state courts of limited jurisdiction.

Customarily, however, the plaintiff has been required to say something more about his case, and the question usually has been, "How much more?" Must all elements of the claim be stated? Must plaintiff offer a theory of recovery, such as negligence or breach of contract? With what degree of detail must plaintiff allege the facts underlying the action? How specifically must plaintiff state damages? The answers to these questions depend, to some extent, on the function of pleadings. Over the last thousand years, pleadings have been used: (1) to give notice of the nature of the claim, (2) to state the relevant facts, (3) to narrow the issues to be addressed at later stages of the litigation process, (4) to serve as guides for later discovery and trial, (5) to expose insubstantial claims, and (6) to separate disputes over the facts from disputes over the law. Today, only the first and to a lesser extent the second of these functions dominate. Other procedural devices now serve the remaining functions. This chapter explores the development of pleading, a development in which pleading has moved from the center of the procedural stage to an important, but supporting, role.

Modern procedure blends two approaches to the resolution of disputes. These two approaches derive from two rival systems of adjudication that coexisted, sometimes uneasily, for almost five centuries: the system of common law and that of equity. Common law excelled in defining the dispute between the parties but had a rather primitive method for gathering information about factual disputes and suffered from the inability to handle disputes involving more than two parties. By contrast, equity prided itself on its ability to gather information before trial and to handle disputes with several parties. But equity's effort to produce a complete resolution of the dispute led to often-interminable proceedings and uncertainty about whether any resolution had been reached.

The Federal Rules (and most state systems) combine elements of both systems. The drafters of the Rules self-consciously sought to borrow the best from the competing systems: While retaining the procedures and doctrines that brought lawsuits to a conclusion, modern procedure permits extensive gathering of pretrial information (in discovery) and broadens the joinder of claims and of parties. Some have argued, however, that we have chosen badly, either because we borrowed too many features from one system or because the two approaches to litigation are fundamentally incompatible. In particular, some argue that modern procedure erred by rejecting the practices in common law that brought disputes to a conclusion. Preeminent among these was common law pleading, the topic of the next section. After looking at that system and at equity's alternative model, we'll examine modern pleading regimes.

A.   Rival Procedural Systems

1.   Common Law Pleading in Theory and Practice

No American jurisdiction now uses the common law system of pleading in its full complexity. Why, then, study such an archaic topic? Its usefulness to modern lawyers derives from three circumstances. First, although legislatures and rulemakers have formally abolished the system of common law pleading, it continues to exercise profound influence on the way judges and lawyers think — not just about pleading, but about the legal system itself. The most famous expression of this idea comes from the eminent historian of the common law, F.W. Maitland, who remarked, "[t]he forms of action we have buried, but they rule us still from their graves."* His point was that the system of common law pleading expressed a system of categories, a way of thinking about legal rights and injuries to those rights that has persisted in legal systems deriving from the common law. For example, modern lawyers may debate whether a claim "sounds" in tort or in contract, perhaps for the purpose of deciding

* Frederic W. Maitland, The Forms of Action at Common Law 1 (1909).

what statute of limitations applies or which remedies are available. Their question asks, essentially, which medieval form of pleading would have been used to bring the claim. As a consequence, trying to learn the contemporary U.S. legal system without having some idea how earlier procedure worked is like trying to learn to dance by watching professional dancers execute fancy variations on a waltz step: The watcher might eventually catch on, but knowing the basic pattern makes things much easier.

Second, the idea behind common law pleading remains attractive. If people can agree about the nature of their dispute, resolution may come much faster and cheaper. Achieving such agreement was the principal aim of common law pleading. Did we throw out the baby with the bath water when we abolished common law pleading? Recent suggestions for the reform of civil procedure have said as much; assessing these suggestions requires some idea of the regime to which they refer.

Third, the development of common law pleading reflected three ideas of profound importance: that government power is shared among several different jurisdictions, none of which has plenary power, and that courts have the power to reshape law. All of these propositions persist in modern U.S. law, but both would strike lawyers from many other legal systems as peculiar and questionable.

a. The First Premise of Common Law: Divided Judicial Power

Common law pleading, like the common law itself, derived from a system of medieval English government. Accustomed to contrasting the checks and balances characteristic of contemporary democracies with monarchic absolutism, we risk misunderstanding medieval English justice. At its base lay both the fact and the political premise that royal judicial power was limited. Medieval England had numerous court systems: some local, some operated by the aristocracy, others by various ecclesiastical authorities. The king's courts, from which the common law system evolved, were at first the extraordinary, not the ordinary, everyday courts. Just as most litigation in the contemporary United States occurs in state rather than in federal courts, so in early medieval England most suits took place in local rather than in royal courts. Only when local justice failed, or when something happened that required the king's attention, did royal power come into play.

An aggrieved subject who wished to invoke royal judicial power therefore had to explain, first of all, why her grievance was one about which the king's judges should concern themselves. Pleadings, no matter what else they said, explained why the case was one for a royal court. What allegations were likely to attract attention? The most basic was an allegation that the peace had been broken. However violent medieval life was in practice, medieval kings in theory strove to maintain peace in their realm, and a breach of the peace was also an act against the king. What we would now call crimes — homicide, robbery, assault — would attract royal attention.

This jurisdiction over crimes against the peace of the realm opened the door for certain forms of civil liability. Imagine a defendant who had done something that, in addition to offending the peace of the realm, also inflicted special damage on the plaintiff. Assault provides a common example. Could the plaintiff ask the king's justices to give him a remedy in addition to inflicting whatever criminal penalties might flow from the offense? The answer was yes; in anachronistically modern terms, the plaintiff who alleged such facts had stated a claim that lay within the jurisdiction of the royal courts. Such a claim was called, in the Latin of common law pleadings, "trespass *vi et armis*." "Trespass" in this context has a much broader meaning than its modern one; it signifies any wrong, not just the unauthorized entry of land. "Vi et armis" means "with force and arms," or, translating more idiomatically, "the defendant was armed and violent." The point of alleging armed violence was jurisdictional: Because armed violence was a breach of the king's peace, such an action lay within the power of royal courts. By alleging armed violence, the plaintiff was explaining why the king's courts, rather than some other court, should hear the case.

Originally the claims underlying the various writs were what the writs stated them to be. In the thirteenth century, if Abigail Adams filed a declaration in trespass *quare clausum fregit* ("by which he broke the 'close,' i.e., invaded my land") alleging that John Jones had forcibly entered her land and destroyed her crops, one might have assumed that Abigail Adams was really claiming that John Jones had entered her land and destroyed crops. By the nineteenth century, however, the recitations had in many cases become formulas that bore little relationship to the facts of the suit. By that time trespass "q.c.f." (as the writ was abbreviated) was often used not to collect for damages to land but to determine title.

To illustrate the system in action, consider a more textured example. Suppose that Abigail Adams and John Jones were neighboring farmers. Suppose that there was a field located between Adams's and Jones's farms. Suppose that Jones had been peacefully occupying and farming that field for some time, believing that he owned it. Then suppose that Adams claimed that *she* owned the field. What type of lawsuit would Adams bring to resolve the dispute? She would bring a trespass q.c.f. action against Jones, the allegedly wrongful occupier. When Jones responded to allegations of trespass by saying he owned the land and therefore was not a trespasser, Adams would try to show that she, not Jones, had the true title. What would the complaint in such an action have looked like? In order to invoke the royal court's jurisdiction, Adams would still allege in her declaration that Jones entered her land "with force and arms" and caused great damage to her land. But the declaration would nowhere state that the real dispute between the parties was not over damage to the land but over who had title to the land.

Because royal justice was speedier and usually more evenhanded than local justice, most plaintiffs sought to bring their cases into royal courts, even when they did not apparently belong there. Recall that the earliest civil jurisdiction of the royal courts focused on peacekeeping, requiring allegations that defendant had committed violence (trespass vi et armis). But what would occur if the defendant didn't commit armed violence? If, for example, she merely cheated the defendant or failed to keep her promise, was an action against her within the jurisdiction of royal courts? Answering that question precisely would require much detail. Roughly speaking, however, one can say that the common law began to expand royal jurisdiction by stretching the categories that grew out of the core cases of violence. Judges, construing pleadings that tested the limits of royal jurisdiction, often expanded these limits by holding that the pleading in question was sufficiently close to a recognized category to fall within the scope of royal justice. For example, some of the early examples of what we would now call breach of contract occurred in allegations that blacksmiths had committed assaults on horses, thereby injuring them. Unless one assumes that a sudden fit of cruelty afflicted blacksmiths in the fourteenth century, the probable explanation is that these cases were for breach of contract or for what we would now call negligence. The smith had slipped, injuring the horse in the process.

Why were such fictions necessary? Why didn't the plaintiff simply allege the smith's carelessness or breach of promise? The answer lies in our starting point: Royal courts were courts of limited and extraordinary jurisdiction, and the pleader had to explain why his case lay within the royal power. Moreover, at some point the number of categories that would invoke royal justice became fixed. Each category had its own "writ," a document issued by part of the king's small bureaucracy (called the chancery). Each writ contained a formula that described a category of behavior with which the royal courts would concern themselves. Because the number and kind of writs, which had grown rapidly in the thirteenth century, later became frozen, a person with a grievance (or her lawyer) had to fit that grievance into one of the categories of existing writs and describe the behavior in question in the language of the writs.

The catalogue of writs thus became, in time, a somewhat haphazard catalogue of substantive law. The names of these writs — trespass (with several different subcategories), debt (to recover sums owed), covenant (to remedy breaches of written, sealed contracts), ejectment (to recover land unlawfully occupied), trover and replevin (to recover for unlawful takings of personal property), and assumpsit (meaning "he (or she) promised" and used to recover for breaches of informal, generally oral contracts) — became the names for categories of substantive law. But recall that the beginnings were much humbler: These were simply the words used by early royal bureaucrats to describe the kinds of wrongs with which the royal courts would concern themselves. The writ was a command to the sheriff to summon the defendant to respond to the plaintiff's grievance.

The differences among the forms of action reflected differences far greater than variations in the language of initiating writs. The entire ensuing procedure depended on which form of action the plaintiff had chosen. A modern analogy may help to illuminate the importance of variations among the forms of action. Today all U.S. jurisdictions use different rules of procedure for civil and criminal cases. Early common law carried this one step further by having separate procedures for different writs. These procedures differed in the way of commencing suit and proving disputed facts and offered different remedies. It is as if there were different Federal Rules of Civil Procedure — setting forth different processes — for different kinds of claims. The writ system thus reflected a very sophisticated and specialized conception of procedure in which each claim had its own form of procedure.

This specialization meant that a prospective plaintiff had to think about not only whether her claim fit the contours of some form of action but also, if it potentially fit several, which of those forms provided the most advantageous form of process. Consider, for example, the choice between the writ of debt and of assumpsit. A medieval plaintiff who had lent money could, if the debtor did not pay, bring a writ of debt. But the writ of debt, although it was a common law writ, did not use a jury as a factfinding body. Instead, a defendant required to answer a writ of debt could "wage his law," a procedure in which, on the day appointed for trial, the defendant appeared with "oath helpers," who would recite an oath that the defendant did not owe the debt. If the defendant produced the proper number of oath helpers and if each of them recited the oath precisely, judgment went to the defendant; no other form of testimony was needed — or permitted. Such a system may have been reliable in small, stable communities, where plaintiff's neighbors might have been very reluctant to swear such an oath unless they were quite sure the debt was not owed. Creditors became quite unenthusiastic about actions of debt, however, when oath helpers, bribed with the price of a drink, could be recruited from pubs surrounding the courts. They consequently sought to bring a different writ — a form of action that would not carry with it the wager of law as a factfinding method. By the early seventeenth century, creditors had convinced the royal courts that one of the trespass writs — indebitatus assumpsit — was available to collect a debt. That mattered because in trespass the use of a jury, not the wager of law, was the factfinding method, and the defendant could not make use of oath helpers.

NOTES AND PROBLEMS

1. Because the royal courts were courts of limited jurisdiction, a plaintiff needed first to invoke royal power and then to put her case before the court. One sees a similar pattern in modern courts of limited jurisdiction, including the federal courts. Examine Rule 8(a)(1).

2. Imagine the problems of a defendant served with a writ filled with time-honored but uninformative formulas. Read Rule 8(a)(2); how does it address this problem?

b. The Second Premise: Framing the Issue for Decision

Once the royal courts had concluded that the case belonged to them, they faced a second decision: what to do with it. To help with this decision, they put the litigants through an elaborate dance of pleading. It is sometimes said that common law pleading aimed at defining precisely the issue in contention between the parties. That assertion is only partly true. Common law pleading aimed, above all, at separating two different kinds of disputes: those that focused on law and those that focused on fact. Disputes about law were supposed to be settled by judges; those about fact by juries. Introduced in part because early English kings did not have enough trained personnel to handle cases from start to finish, juries became a distinctive feature of common law adjudication — a feature that persists in the modern U.S. (though not the British*) legal system. The pleading system isolated the area of dispute sufficiently so that judges could determine, first, whether there was a factual dispute for the jury to hear, and, second, what that dispute was.

To perform this isolating function, the pleading system put the parties to a series of stark choices. Unlike contemporary pleading, early common

---

* Great Britain currently uses the jury regularly in criminal cases but in only a handful of civil actions.

law pleading forced parties to stake their whole case on either law or
fact, in an elaborate dance in which the parties traded responses until
they had, in effect, agreed on what they were disagreeing about. In the
very early days of common law pleading this exchange was oral, as the
pleaders appeared before judges to discuss the nature of the claims. These
oral exchanges apparently had a good deal of flexibility. In time, however,
pleading became a written exchange and in the process became more
rigid.

In principle, common law pleading permitted a limited number of
quite simple responses to allegations. In response to a pleading by either
side, the opposing party could make the following responses (paraphrased
in contemporary vernacular to emphasize their simple nature):

1. Challenges to the *jurisdiction* of the court. Translated into contemporary colloquialism, these pleas said, "Not here."
2. *Pleas in suspension* challenged the plaintiff's right to bring the
   action until some problem was resolved; for example, an ex-
   communicated or outlawed plaintiff could not bring an action until
   the disability was removed. "Not now," such pleas said.
3. *Pleas in abatement* challenged some defect in the pleading itself;
   for example, the failure to name an absent party. "Not like this,"
   such a plea responded.

These first three pleas have something in common: None of them
approaches the merits of the case. They take no position on either the
facts or the law. As a consequence, they were known as "dilatory pleas,"
responses that delayed the suit, perhaps permanently but did not constitute
a resolution of its merits. A defendant could make multiple dilatory pleas,
but they had to be presented one at a time in a specified order. Dilatory
pleas made too late were waived.

If a defendant could not dispose of a pleading through a dilatory plea,
he had to make a series of choices. Essentially, these choices forced the
pleader to decide between resting on the facts and resting on the law,
and, as to the facts, between denying the other side's facts and pleading
additional facts of one's own. To continue the list of possible pleas, the
pleading could respond with:

4. A *demurrer,* which conceded the truth of the opponent's factual
   allegations but challenged their legal sufficiency. "So what?" serves
   as a rough translation of the demurrer.
5. A *traverse,* the opposite of a demurrer, conceded the legal sufficiency
   of the plea but denied its factual allegations. "Not true," captures
   the idea behind a traverse.

6. A *plea of confession and avoidance* conceded the legal sufficiency and the factual truth of the preceding plea, but alleged additional facts that changed their significance. "Yes but," serves as a rough paraphrase of the confession and avoidance. For example, if the plaintiff pleaded trespass quare clausum fregit, the defendant might, by way of confession and avoidance, plead that the plaintiff had granted him an easement on the land. This plea conceded that there was a cause of action for trespass q.c.f. and that the defendant had entered the plaintiff's land but, by alleging the grant of an easement, sought to "avoid" the effect of these concessions.

These last three responses were called "peremptory" pleas; unlike pleas in abatement they grappled with the merits of the claim.

NOTES AND PROBLEMS

1. The system of common law pleading has vanished, but its structure remains. Read Federal Rules of Civil Procedure 8(b), (c), 12(b).

a. Which of the enumerated defenses correspond to the dilatory pleas at common law?

b. Which are modern versions of the peremptory pleas?

2. Read Federal Rule of Civil Procedure 12(b)(6). What was its common law analogue?

3. Consider which of the common law pleas the defendant should enter in each of the following circumstances:

a. Plaintiff alleges that defendant insulted him in public; defendant believes that the law does not permit recovery for verbal insults unaccompanied by violence.

b. Plaintiff alleges that defendant struck her; defendant says he was not present at the time and place alleged.

c. Plaintiff alleges that defendant and plaintiff signed a contract, whose terms defendant then violated. Defendant contends that she refused to honor the agreement because the plaintiff forced her to sign at gunpoint.

4. Explain why a defendant, in deciding whether to demur or traverse, was also choosing who would decide the case.

2. Chancery and Its Procedure: the Procedural Alternative

Recall the hypothetical dispute involving Abigail Adams and John Jones. Although Adam's declaration might allege trespass, the underlying dispute was not really about simple trespass and damage to crops but about who owned the field in question, located between Adams's and Jones's farms. If Adams and Jones both understand the basis of their rival claims of title and have access to all the relevant evidence, a jury trial might do a good job of deciding the case. But imagine that Adams, while knowing that Jones claims the land, does not know the basis for that claim — Jones being a notoriously uncommunicative and churlish neighbor. Or imagine that Adams knows that Jones claims title and possesses a deed, but Adams alleges that the deed is fraudulent. Or imagine that Jones and his sister, Edith, both claim title to the land (having inherited it — they say — from their father), but Edith lives in another county. In any of these situations, common law might bring the lawsuit to an unsatisfactory conclusion — either because the judgment would be based on an incomplete factual record or because the common law courts would not hear testimony to contradict a properly attested deed, or because the judgment would not bind Edith, who could continue to challenge Adams's claim to the land.

In each of these settings the very strengths of common law — its ability, by limiting the scope of the dispute and the kinds of evidence to be heard, to come to a resolution of the claim — were also a source of weakness. To remedy these weaknesses, litigants could seek relief from another royal court, the court of chancery.

Chancery has a rich and often misunderstood history. For the student concerned solely with mastering modern American law, it is necessary to bear only a few points in mind. First, chancery was, like the courts of common law, a royal court, whose power came from the monarch. Chancery was headed by the chancellor, a powerful royal official who, until well into the nineteenth century, had a number of important political duties in addition to presiding over the court of chancery. (If one seeks a modern analogy, it would be as if the White House chief of staff also presided over a special court.) Second, everyone agreed that chancery's job was to deal with cases that, for a variety of reasons, were not adequately handled by the ordinary royal courts.

What were the cases that fell within chancery jurisdiction? One makes a mistake by looking for an entirely coherent theory of chancery power. Maitland once explained that one could comprehend chancery jurisdiction only by listing all the claims the chancellor would recognize and the remedies he would grant. Blackstone, writing in the eighteenth century, was more optimistic; after rejecting a number of fallacious distinctions, he summarized the distinction between chancery and the common law as "principally consist[ing] in different modes of administering justice in each; in the mode of proof, the mode of trial, and the mode of relief."*

---

* William Blackstone, Commentaries on the Laws of England *436 (1768).

In other words, the distinctions were primarily procedural. One can understand this statement by seeing that chancery's jurisdiction, even more than that of the common law, grew by happenstance: To the extent there is any common theme in this description of chancery jurisdiction, it is that chancery often acted when something about the common law seemed to result in unacceptable results. Frequently these unacceptable results flowed from an aspect of common law procedure.

For example, chancery sometimes administered special *remedies* for claims as to which common law courts had jurisdiction. The best known examples of such remedies are decrees of specific performance for contracts and injunctions against torts. If one sought money damages, the common law courts could give the plaintiff what he wanted; if injunctive decrees were sought, the claim had to be brought in chancery. In judging such cases, chancery sometimes developed what eventually came to be seen as substantive rules. For example, in deciding cases seeking specific performance (a form of injunctive relief), chancery developed the rule that the buyer of a parcel of land was entitled to a decree of specific performance — an order that the seller convey the land.

Another of chancery's specialties was remedies for fraud. At common law — especially early common law — a formal, sealed written contract had enormous significance. If a debtor paid his debt but failed to get the physical contract canceled or destroyed, he could be sued again. Or a contract arrived at by fraud could be enforced so long as it had actually been signed by the parties in question. Common law enforced these agreements, perhaps because it feared to turn such questions over to juries, or perhaps because at early common law the parties could not themselves testify under oath, thus making it harder to get at the truth of the matter. The chancery court, where parties could be forced to testify under oath and where the chancellors sat without juries, dared to make those judgments, which it enforced by rescinding contracts for fraud. That meant that a plaintiff alleging fraud would, before the eighteenth century, have had to seek relief in chancery to get that remedy. In Adams's claim against Jones, she might go to chancery to have his "deed" *rescinded* for fraud, thus clarifying her title to the land.

Another large group of cases came to chancery because they involved the administration of *trusts,* over which chancery had jurisdiction. The trust is a device with its roots in a medieval tax evasion scheme that has given rise to a number of important modern institutions. The basic principle underlying a trust is that the trustee holds legal title and exercises control over property, but the benefits of that property go to the beneficiary. Chancery's jurisdiction over trusts, as with fraud, may have originated in the need to examine parties under oath. Because many wealthy families tied up their property in complex trusts, the beneficiaries of these trusts — and their creditors — spent a good deal of time in chancery litigation. In administering the trust, chancery developed new substantive law and a new remedy. The substantive law was the high standard of honesty and care to which trustees were held: the fiduciary obligation. The new remedy was the *constructive trust*. The constructive trust treated misused trust assets as if they were still held in trust. For example, if a trustee took trust assets and purchased land for himself, chancery would impose a constructive trust on the land. The result would be that if the land were worth more than the original assets, the beneficiary would recover not just the original assets but a more valuable asset — here, the land — into which those assets had been transformed.

Having argued that chancery procedures were often the reason cases came to that court, we should sketch those processes. Like courts of common law, chancery had its own procedures, many of which contrasted sharply with those of the common law. Some have already been mentioned. Chancery used no jury; judges — the chancellor and a small number of lesser officials — deciding all the cases themselves.* Chancery's pleadings, instead of consisting of the formulas of common law, often went into enormous detail. Where common law insisted on live witnesses testifying in open court, chancery forbade live testimony, relying instead on extensive written depositions, the ancestors of our modern discovery practice. Where common law forbade the parties from testifying under oath, chancery insisted on it. Where common law depended on the parties' ability to persuade witnesses to testify, chancery employed the subpoena, which compelled testimony, making it possible to compel reluctant witnesses. Where common law often sharply limited the number of parties who could participate in a suit, chancery prided itself on including all those who were concerned, even to the point of refusing to act at all unless the optimum number of parties could be joined. As you examine modern American process more closely, you will see that at a number of points it has blended common law and chancery procedures. A point sometimes disputed is whether we have chosen the most attractive features of the two systems.

Whatever their differences, common law and equity agreed on a point of pleading. As with an action at common law, a suit in equity required the pleader to state facts that brought him within the jurisdiction of chancery. In chancery, that allegation required that the pleader state both that a claim was within royal power generally and that it was one

---

* Chancery judges would sometimes require that an issue of fact first be tried by a jury by bringing a common law action; then, aided by the jury's decision of the question of fact, chancery would conduct further proceedings.

for which the ordinary royal courts — the common law courts — afforded no adequate remedy. That requirement has persisted in modern pleading: A party seeking an injunction, for example, must allege that she has no adequate legal remedy. What did — and what *does* — that mean? At the height of the system (say, the seventeenth century) it meant that the courts of common law could not grant an injunction (they simply lacked the power to give such a remedy), that the court of chancery had such power, and — this is the crucial point — that the case was one in which money damages (the ordinary legal remedy) would not be a sufficient remedy. Just what those circumstances are is the subject not only of part of Chapter V but also of several substantive courses. For present purposes the point is that equity, like the common law, required pleadings that properly invoked its jurisdiction, and behind these invocations of jurisdiction lay the idea that power, even royal power, was limited and divided.

NOTES AND PROBLEMS

1. Plaintiff complains of breach of contract. She seeks to have the contract reformed to conform to the parties' agreement and then to collect damages for defendant's breach of that agreement.

a. Up until the middle of the nineteenth century plaintiff would have to bring two separate lawsuits to achieve this goal. Explain where and in what order she would have to file her actions.

b. Read Rules 1, 2, and 8(a)(3) and explain how they affect plaintiff's lawsuit today.

2. Equity as a separate jurisdiction has almost vanished. (Delaware maintains such a system primarily as a way of providing a specialized court for the many enterprises incorporated in that state.) But, according to one commentator, the disappearance of equity's name masks its continued importance. In an essay provocatively titled, How Equity Conquered the Common Law: The Federal Rules of Civil Procedure in Historical Perspective,* Stephen Subrin argues that contemporary procedure has adopted the most salient aspects of chancery procedure: discovery, broad joinder, remedial flexibility — and with these a tendency to protracted, indecisive proceedings. The genius of the common law, argues Subrin, was its penchant for ending disputes, and he contends that contemporary procedure is deficient in this virtue. As you encounter modern pretrial practice — including procedure — reflect on whether it would be possible

* 135 U. Pa. L. Rev. 909 (1987).

to have a system that combined common law's decisiveness (assuming that is an accurate characterization) and equity's flexibility.

3. Reforming Process

By the nineteenth century both common law and chancery procedure were under attack from several directions. Chancery was attacked for its interminable proceedings, most famously by Charles Dickens in Bleak House, a splendid novel whose opening chapter is called "In Chancery," which describes a lawsuit "so complicated, that no man alive knows what it means." Common law came in for equally fierce criticism. Jeremy Bentham assailed it for its intricacies known only to the legal profession, whose members Bentham collectively referred to as "Judge and Company," thus suggesting a closed, self-interested trade guild. One strand of criticism focused on an issue one might think to be the strong point of common law pleading — its aim of narrowing the precise issues at stake. Not so, said many critics. Because broadly phrased writs had been pressed into service for several sorts of claims and because courts permitted many defendants to plead "the general issue" as a defense, it was often impossible for either party to know in advance of trial what the real dispute involved. Other critics raised the converse problem, contending that pleading rules aimed at a precision that was unrealistic.

These criticisms, from both without and within the profession, coalesced in the nineteenth century to bring about major changes in common law procedure on both sides of the Atlantic. In the United States the change came as state legislatures adopted the Field Code, named after their drafter, David Dudley Field.* Reform came more slowly to the federal system, which adopted the Federal Rules only in 1938.

Though details differed widely, the reforms had two common themes: They simplified pleading and they merged law and equity into a single system. Consider some statutes accomplishing this change:

California Code of Civil Procedure §307 (West 1999)

There is in this State but one form of civil actions for the enforcement or protection of private rights and the redress or prevention of private wrongs.

---

* The source was to be the legislature (enacting statutes, called "codes"), not the courts. For a legal profession accustomed to having judge-made rules, this was a novel and controversial idea. Lawyers of the day focused on this new rule source as a leading characteristic of the new process, calling it "code pleading." When lawyers speak today of "code pleading" they refer to these codes and their successors. They generally designate by such a reference the model of procedure promulgated in these early codes.

New York Civil Practice Law & Rules 103(a) (Consol. 1999)

There is only one form of civil action. The distinction between actions at law and suits in equity, and the forms of those actions and suits, have been abolished.

Federal Rules of Civil Procedure 1 and 2

These rules govern the procedure in the United States district courts in all suits of a civil nature whether cognizable as cases at law or in equity. . . .
    There shall be one form of action, known as "civil action."

NOTES AND PROBLEMS

1. What was the point of saying that there should be "one form of action"? What was the alternative?

2. In many respects the blending of law and equity and the combining of the forms of action is historically curious. Seen from a distant perspective, the modern age has been one of increasing specialization of function. Imagine that one knew nothing of the legal history sketched above but was told that at one time there was a "one size fits all" legal procedure and that at another time there were specialized procedures for different kinds of claims. Would not most of us guess that the specialized procedures were the modern and the single procedure the "primitive" form?

Having rejected the forms of action and the separation of law and equity, the reformers then tried to address the deficiencies of common law pleading. The first attempted solution, typically found in the Field codes, was to require the plaintiff simply to state the "dry, naked actual facts." J. Pomeroy, Code Remedies §423, at 640 (5th ed. 1929). Such a factual statement enabled the court to determine whether the plaintiff had a valid claim, the defendant to determine what points were disputed, and a later court (in the event of a second lawsuit) to determine what matters were tried in the first action. Again, consider the analogous provisions of two Code pleading states, California and Nebraska:

California Code of Civil Procedure (West 1999)

§421. The forms of pleading in civil action, and the rules by which the sufficiency of the pleadings is to be determined, are those prescribed in this Code.

§425.10. A complaint or cross-complaint shall contain both of the following:

(a) A statement of the facts constituting the cause of action, in ordinary and concise language.

(b) A demand for judgment for the relief to which the pleader claims he is entitled. . . .

§452. In the construction of a pleading, for the purpose of determining its effect, its allegations must be liberally construed, with a view to substantial justice between the parties.

Nebraska Revised Statutes (1995)

§25-802. The rules of pleading formerly existing in civil actions are abolished and hereafter the forms of pleading of civil actions in courts of record, and the rules by which their sufficiency may be determined are those prescribed by this code.

§25-804. The petition must contain . . . a statement of the facts constituting the cause of action, in ordinary and concise language, and without repetition; and . . . a demand for the relief to which the party supposes himself entitled. . . .

The Codes replaced the formulas of the writs with "facts" and the forms of actions with the "cause of action." Both changes aimed at correcting what was thought to be a major failing of the common law system, but each created problems of its own. Thus, despite the reforms, pleading litigation did not go away. One source of the litigation was the fact that, although technical pleading had been abolished, the substantive law as incorporated into the forms of action had not. Moreover, courts interpreted the phrase "cause of action" to refer to this substantive law and treated each cause of action as mutually exclusive. For example, one finds a court insisting that a complaint setting forth the elements of a fraud claim could be treated *only* as a fraud claim, even if plaintiff proved breach of contract. Ross v. Mather, 51 N.Y. 108 (1872).

Another source of litigation was the requirement for stating "*facts* constituting the cause of action" (emphasis added). Assuming one knew what the cause of action was, when were allegations considered either too specific ("mere evidence," as the cases sometimes called them) or too general ("mere conclusions") to fit the requirement of "facts"? Either failing could lead to the sustaining of a demurrer to the complaint. For example, in Gillispie v. Goodyear Service Stores, 258 N.C. 487, 128 S.E.2d 762 (1963), the court upheld the dismissal of a complaint in trespass, noting that the plaintiff alleged, "in a single sentence, that defendants, 'without cause or just excuse and maliciously,' trespassed upon premises occupied by [plaintiff] as a residence." The court ruled that "[t]he complaint states no facts upon which these legal conclusions may be predicated." 128 S.E.2d at 765-766.

Seeking to avoid such difficulties, the drafters of the Federal Rules engaged in a masterful bit of evasion:

Federal Rule of Civil Procedure 8(a)

Claims for Relief. A pleading which sets forth a claim for relief . . . shall contain (1) [an allegation of jurisdiction], (2) a short and plain statement of the claim showing that the pleader is entitled to relief, and (3) a demand for judgment for the relief the pleader seeks. Relief in the alternative or of several different types may be demanded.

NOTES AND PROBLEMS

1. The Rules contain an Appendix of Forms, drafted to illustrate how short and plain various pleadings might be. Consult Forms 3-9 for examples of brief pleadings.

2. In the past several decades most courts, even in code pleading states, have abandoned the effort to discriminate among "evidentiary facts," "ultimate facts," and "mere conclusions." They have become more accepting of generalized allegations, influenced in part by the model proposed in the Federal Rules, and in part by despair at their inability to make such distinctions between different sorts of "facts." Nevertheless, courts in Code pleading states occasionally will insist that pleaders set forth the elements of a claim with more precision than one might expect a federal court to require.

3. Note that lawyers, for reasons of strategy, will often wish to tell their clients' stories in considerably more detail than the Rules require. Recall that the complaint is the first opportunity to set before one's opponent and the judge the story of wrong done the plaintiff: If the facts are good, why not make the most of them?

B. Pleading in a Modern Regime

No longer do pleaders need to concern themselves about which writ lies on a given set of facts. But the unification of law and equity and the progressive simplification of pleading have not entirely eliminated difficulties. Indeed, they have created some that did not exist in earlier times.

1.   Why Pleading Matters

At the risk of having the reader skip immediately to the next chapter, let us reveal a not-very-secret truth about modern pleading: It is no longer the hinge of procedure. In most cases its importance comes from its role as a gatekeeper to the next stage of process, discovery. In modern litigation, most cases will end during this next stage. This will happen for several reasons, important among which is the power of discovery to uncover information relevant to the case and, equally, its power to inflict costs on one's adversary. But discovery is available only if one can file a valid complaint. For a plaintiff it becomes very important to be able to move beyond the pleading stage into discovery. For a defendant, faced with what she believes is a meritless lawsuit, the ability to end the suit before being subject to the often lengthy and expensive discovery stage is equally important. For judges, seeking to give meritorious claims a fair hearing by clearing dockets of unmeritorious litigation, the issues are similar. These facts of procedural life often lead to fierce maneuvering over constraints on pleading.

Having understood that pleading is no longer the center of procedure, one must be careful not to dismiss it as trivial. In a substantial number of cases pleading battles will eliminate some claims, changing the scope of discovery and the value of the lawsuit. Imagine, for example, a landlord-tenant dispute. A claim of unpaid rent and a defense of constructive eviction might lie at the core of the case; these claims would be unlikely to disappear at the pleading stage because they will be very fact-bound. But suppose the tenant has alleged harassment by the landlord, claiming intentional infliction of emotional distress, for which punitive damages are available. If that claim survives the pleading stage, the stakes in the case are much larger. Conversely, if the landlord can eliminate that claim, both the scope of discovery and the potential damages will be much more limited. So even if pleading is no longer the center of procedure, it often has substantial importance.

2.   Stating a Claim: General Principles

Even if pleading bears less procedural weight than it once did, the lawyer needs to understand how it works and how to avoid the pitfalls that can still be fatal. The student embarking on this exploration needs to bear a distinction in mind — that between allegations and proof. Pleading is about allegations; later stages of litigation — discovery, summary adjudication, and trial — are about proof. Allegations — the stuff of pleading — are statements that the party says are true, but at the pleading stage their truth or falsity are open questions. If all goes well for the pleader, she may be able to demonstrate that what she says (alleges) is indeed so, but having said it does not make it so. Pleading, then, is the rhetoric of grievances rather than evidence of historical events.

A legal claim consists of two elements: (1) It invokes some body of law (contracts, civil rights, negligence, battery, and so on); and (2) it relates a set of facts that fall under the umbrella of the body of law. A claim will succeed if it invokes a valid body of law and if it recites facts that, under the body of law invoked, entitle the plaintiff to recovery.

Claims fail for one of two reasons: either (1) the law permits recovery on the underlying facts but the lawyer has stated those facts ineptly; or (2) the law does not afford any remedy on the underlying facts. In the first instance the lawyer has failed his client inexcusably. In the second case the law, not the lawyer, is responsible for the dismissed claim. In this section we shall examine both problems. Let us begin by focusing on avoidable mistakes — on understanding when failures of form doom a complaint that might otherwise succeed. Modern pleading systems are caught between two worthy but conflicting goals. On the one hand, they seek to assure that technical quibbles and matters of form do not end cases before any investigation of their factual merits. On the other hand, they aim at giving defendants fair notice of the claim against which they are defending and, where possible, to terminate meritless lawsuits at an early stage.

The two major extant pleading systems, — Code pleading and the Federal Rules — have taken slightly different stances toward the goals of pleading. The Code states have historically asked for more factual detail in their pleading; the Rules emphasize a "short plain statement." For the Rules, the classical statement of the level of required detail comes in Conley v. Gibson, 355 U.S. 41, 45–46 (1957): "[W]e follow," the Court said, "the accepted rule that a complaint should not be dismissed for failure to state a claim unless it appears beyond doubt that the plaintiff can prove no set of facts in support of his claim which would entitle him to relief." One critical commentator has described this often-quoted phrase from Conley as "turn[ing] Rule 8 on its head by holding that a claim is insufficient only if the insufficiency appears from the pleading itself." Geoffrey Hazard, From Whom No Secrets Are Hid, 76, Texas L. Rev. 1665, 1682 (1998). Even if Hazard's description is an overstatement, he has captured a leaning of Rules-pleading courts — a preference for not resolving cases on the pleadings.

By contrast, Code pleading states often "require more precision and detail than is required in notice pleading jurisdictions. . . ." Robert

Weil & Ira Brown, California Practice Guide: Civil Procedure Before
Trial 6-1 (Rutter Group 1998). In many respects the older punctilious-
ness has melted away, and what is left is sometimes described in atti-
tudinal rather than doctrinal terms, but the emphasis still lies on notice
to the defendant: "The distinction [between Code and Rule pleading]
is not at all clear and involves at most a matter of degree. . . . What is
important is that the complaint as a whole contain sufficient facts to
apprise the defendant of the basis upon which the plaintiff is seeking relief. . . ." Perkins v. Superior Court, 117 Cal. App. 3d 1, 6
(1981).

Knowing that a complaint must invoke law and recite facts falling
within that law, one might think that both of those would occur explicitly.
Some pleading systems do just that. Historically, each writ specifically
invoked a body of substantive law, so that if one saw a writ headed
"trespass quare clausum fregit," one knew what the legal elements of the
claim were. Recently, for reasons of convenience rather than history,
some jurisdictions have returned to such a system, publishing "check a
box" form pleadings that bear titles describing the body of law involved.
Consider one such form, promulgated by the Judicial Council of California, reproduced on page 403.

NOTES AND PROBLEMS

Imagine that you are consulted by the Hernandezes, who were severely
injured when they were struck by a vehicle that had crossed over the
dirt median strip of a multi-lane highway. Assume that your research
leads you to conclude that, under California law, the state (which is
responsible for the design and maintenance of the highway in question)
may be liable for injuries sustained on that highway under certain conditions: (1) that the highway was "dangerous"; (2) that the dangerous
condition caused the plaintiffs' injuries; (3) that the risk of injury was a
foreseeable risk of the kind of dangerous condition involved; and (4) that
the state had created the dangerous condition or knew of it. Your theory
is that a concrete or metal center divider would have prevented the
accident and that such a divider was called for given the amount of traffic
on the highway.

1. What boxes would you check on the form reproduced above?
2. Write a paragraph of factual allegations suitable for the top of the
form ("description of premises and circumstances of injury").
3. Compare your description to that composed by the plaintiffs' lawyer
in the next case.

Rule 982.1(5)   Cause of Action — Premises Liability

SHORT TITLE:	CASE NUMBER

_____ **CAUSE OF ACTION—Premises Liability**   Page _____
(number)

ATTACHMENT TO ☐ Complaint ☐ Cross-Complaint

(Use a separate cause of action form for each cause of action.)

Prem.L-1.   Plaintiff *(name):*
alleges the acts of defendants were the legal (proximate) cause of damages to plaintiff.
On *(date):*   plaintiff was injured on the following premises in the following fashion *(description of premises and circumstances of injury):*

Prem.L-2.   ☐ **Count One—Negligence** The defendants who negligently owned, maintained, managed and operated the described premises were *(names):*

   ☐ Does _____ to _____

Prem.L-3.   ☐ **Count Two—Willful Failure to Warn** [Civil Code section 846] The defendant owners who willfully or maliciously failed to guard or warn against a dangerous condition, use, structure, or activity were *(names):*

   ☐ Does _____ to _____
   Plaintiff, a recreational user, was ☐ an invited guest ☐ a paying guest.

Prem.L-4.   ☐ **Count Three—Dangerous Condition of Public Property** The defendants who owned public property on which a dangerous condition existed were *(names):*

   ☐ Does _____ to _____
   a. ☐ The defendant public entity had ☐ actual ☐ constructive notice of the existence of the dangerous condition in sufficient time prior to the injury to have corrected it.
   b. ☐ The condition was created by employees of the defendant public entity.

Prem.L-5.   a. ☐ **Allegations about Other Defendants** The defendants who were the agents and employees of the other defendants and acted within the scope of the agency were *(names):*

   ☐ Does _____ to _____
   b. ☐ The defendants who are liable to plaintiffs for other reasons and the reasons for their liability are ☐ described in attachment Prem.L-5.b ☐ as follows *(names):*

People ex rel. Department of Transportation v. Superior Court

5 Cal. App. 4th 1480 (Cal. App. 2d Dist. 1992)

GILBERT, J.

Are Judicial Council form complaints invulnerable to a demurrer? No. . . .

Facts. . . .

A section of the form complaint with the heading "Prem.L-1" provides space for a plaintiff to fulfill the requirement to supply a "description of premises and circumstances of injury."

[Plaintiffs] describe the circumstances of the injury as follows: "U.S. Highway 101 approximately 1,652 feet north of the Arroyo Hondo Bridge in the County of Santa Barbara, State of California. Plaintiff Ernesto Verdeja was driving his 1979 Datsun northbound at said time and place. Plaintiffs Elizabeth Hernandez and Luis Fabian Hernandez were passengers in his car. Another vehicle driven by defendant Seth R. Wood traveling southbound crossed over the dirt center divider and struck plaintiff's vehicle head-on."

On October 17, 1991, CalTrans filed a demurrer to the first amended complaint. It claimed that the complaint did not set forth adequate " 'circumstances of injury' "and " 'reasons for liability' " as required in a suit for dangerous condition of public property. (See Code Civ. Proc. §425.10; Gov. Code §835.)

On November 6, 1991, the superior court judge overruled the demurrer. In making his ruling, the judge said, "I will make it easy. Regardless of its deficiencies and by whatever else the Code of Civil Procedure or prior Supreme Court or Court of Appeal rules have given us as to the sufficiency of pleadings, all this aside, if you use a Judicial Council form, it is non-demurrable. Okay. That is my order and take it up, please."

CalTrans followed this advice and seeks a writ of mandate. In Omaha Indemnity Co. v. Superior Court, 209 Cal. App. 3d 1266, 1272 [258 Cal. Rptr. 66] (1989), we held that extraordinary writs not be granted "at the drop of a hat" lest they overburden the crowded dockets of appellate courts. "Were reviewing courts to treat writs in the same manner as they do appeals, these courts would be trapped in an appellate gridlock." Here, however, the judge's view of the case put CalTrans in the fast lane of review. The issue tendered in its petition is worthy of review by extraordinary writ and we have granted an alternative writ of mandate. . . .

Discussion

Government Code section 68511 provides that "the Judicial Council may prescribe by rule the form and content of forms used in the courts of this state." (See also Code Civ. Proc. §425.12.) The Judicial Council has adopted a pleading form for a complaint for personal injury. (Cal. Rules of Court, rule 982.1.)

The Judicial Council pleading forms have simplified the art of pleading, and have made the task of drafting much easier. Nevertheless, in some cases more is required than merely placing an "X" in a box. Weil & Brown, [Civil Procedure before Trial (1991)], at §6:105, p. 6-24.) "Adoption of Official Forms for the most common civil actions has not changed the statutory requirement that the complaint contain 'facts constituting the cause of action.' " (Id., at §6:103, p. 6-23.5.) Thus, in order to be demurrer-proof, a form "complaint must contain whatever ultimate facts are essential to state a cause of action under existing statutes or case law." (Ibid.)

A cause of action for dangerous condition of public property must allege:

1. a dangerous condition of public property;
2. a proximate causal connection between the condition and the injury sustained;
3. a reasonably foreseeable risk that the kind of injury that occurred would result from the dangerous condition; and
4. the entity either created the condition, or had actual notice or constructive notice of its existence, and there was sufficient time before the injury for it to have taken remedial action.

[The plaintiffs] have merely alleged that a motorist crossed a dirt median of Highway 101 and struck their vehicle.

[Plaintiffs] argue that the "inescapable conclusion from the allegations of paragraph Prem.L-1 is 'but for' the failure by CalTrans to properly isolate the north and southbound lanes of Highway 101 in the vicinity of the accident, the head-on collision would not have occurred." They believe that the existence of a median barrier would have prevented the accident.

It is true that the allegations in a complaint must be liberally construed. (Code Civ. Proc. §452.) It is also true that " ' . . . the essence is fairness in pleading in order to give the defendant sufficient notice of the cause of action stated against him so that he will be able to prepare his case. . . .' " (Fuhrman v. California Satellite Systems (1986).) Therefore, we must not so liberally construe the allegations of the complaint so as to deny the defendant adequate notice to defend the case.

A while ago, Justice Field lamented, "in numerous instances before us, pleadings [are] filled with recitals, digressions and stories, which only tend to prolixity and obscurity." (Green v. Palmer (1860) 15 Cal. 411, 414.) The Judicial Council went a long way in answering Justice Field's lament. Brevity is the soul of a well-pled complaint. Providing too many details obscures rather than enlightens. On the other hand, too little information confounds and obfuscates. In either case the environment is cloudy and justice cannot shine.

The problem with the allegations in Prem.L-1 is that they do not tell enough. [Plaintiffs] argue that the allegations necessarily indicate the absence of a barrier contributed to the accident. Although that may be a possible inference to draw from the allegations, it is not the only one. The median may have had nothing to do with the accident. For example, other factors, such as a wet or slick highway, could have contributed to the accident.

[Plaintiffs] have an obligation to give CalTrans more information. The complaint fails to tell CalTrans in what manner the existence of the dirt median was hazardous. It fails to state whether a proper median barrier was lacking, and it fails to inform CalTrans about the nature of the relationship between the condition of the median and the injuries suffered by real parties.

Relief against a public entity is limited to those theories set forth in the complaint. Here, the inadequate pleadings prevent CalTrans from determining under what theory [plaintiffs] are seeking relief. This deprives CalTrans of certain possible defenses. It also prevents CalTrans from determining whether [plaintiffs'] basis for recovery is at variance with their Board of Control claim.

In some cases, merely checking a box on a Judicial Council form complaint will be sufficient. In other cases, such as this one, where specific allegations need be alleged, the form complaint is like a partially completed painting. It is up to the pleader to add the details that complete the picture. The form complaint here, standing alone, is no more immune to demurrer than any other complaint that fails to meet essential pleading requirements to state a cause of action.

Conclusion

Let a writ of mandate issue commanding respondent superior court to set aside its order overruling the demurrer and to enter a new order sustaining the demurrer with leave to amend.

STONE, P.J., and YEGAN, J., concurred.

NOTES AND PROBLEMS

1. The defendant demurred to the complaint. What does that mean?

a. The standard response says that a demurrer is the motion by which a defendant challenges the "sufficiency" of the complaint. If the complaint is sufficient, the trial court denies the motion; if it is insufficient, the trial court "sustains the demurrer," dismissing the case.

b. "Sufficiency" refers to the concepts described above — the invocation of a legal framework that would warrant relief and the recitation of factual allegations that fit within the framework.

c. Consider the two ways, discussed above, in which a pleading might fail: because the claim was not adequately described, or because the law simply does not grant any form of relief on the underlying facts. With which of these problems is this case dealing?

2. Why does the appellate court say the pleading is insufficient? Consider one theory of pleading — not the only one, as you will see:

> Pleadings should tell defendants the kind of case they are facing; details can come later, but the complaint should give the outlines of the claim. Even though the complaint stated that a vehicle "crossed over the dirt center divider and struck plaintiff's vehicle head-on," the appellate court says that it is a possible inference from the complaint that "the median may have had nothing to do with the accident."

If this captures the court's view, consider what the complaint means:

a. That the accident might have happened even if there was a median barrier?

b. That the plaintiff might be contending that some dangerous condition other than the absence of a median barrier caused the accident? Imagine conditions that could have caused this accident other than the absence of a median barrier.

In light of such other possible scenarios, did the complaint give the defendant fair notice to defend the case?

3. Although it held that the trial court should have granted the demurrer, the appellate court also held that the trial court should have given the plaintiff "leave to amend."

a. When a plaintiff has invoked a valid body of law and when the facts of the complaint sound as if they might, with some additional work, fit within the framework, a trial court will almost always grant leave to amend; failure to grant such leave is itself a basis for appellate reversal. The idea behind this second (or third or fourth) chance for a plaintiff is that cases should not be lost because of technical defects in a pleading; they should only be dismissed at the complaint stage after plaintiff has had a chance to fix his pleading.

b. The consequence of such liberally granted leave to amend is that, with most garden-variety claims, the only result of a demurrer will be a delay and the education of plaintiff's counsel. Only when the plaintiff cannot ethically amend the complaint to satisfy the legal framework will a demurrer result in the final dismissal of the lawsuit.

c. In light of the opinion in People ex rel. Department of Transp. v. Superior Court, can you redraft the factual allegations so that they would meet the requirements enunciated in the case?

d. If it is this easy to fix a complaint, why did the defendant (the State of California) bother to demur? The answer may lie in the closing paragraphs of the opinion, which notes a special pleading requirement applicable to claims against the state: Unlike ordinary cases, a plaintiff may receive relief only for theories pleaded in the complaint. Such a requirement means that the defendant wants to pin down the plaintiff to one or more specific theories.

e. In oral argument before the appellate court, plaintiff's counsel was quick to explain that it was plaintiff's theory that the dangerous condition was the absence of a median barrier. Why didn't plaintiff's counsel simply offer to amend the complaint so to state when the defendant demurred in the trial court?

3. How did this case get to the appellate court? Under the final judgment rule, the denial of a motion to dismiss would not be immediately appealable. Instead, defendants used an extraordinary remedy, *mandamus* or, in English, a write of mandate. In such a proceeding the applicant asserts to the appellate court that a trial court has acted so improperly that the error is both obvious and important to remedy immediately. Such writs are infrequently granted.

a. Can you identify anything about this case that might have persuaded the appellate court to hear the case before a final judgment?

b. Notice that if the appellate court had not granted the writ, defendant would have had to wait until a final judgment — assuming no settlement occurred — before appealing.

4. Are you beginning to reach the conclusion that not many cases will ultimately be dismissed on grounds that the complaint was insufficient? "Not many" does not, however, mean none. Consider the next section, in which we discuss the plaintiff's complaint. We then go to three decisions construing that complaint, the district court's order granting the motion to dismiss the complaint for failure to state a claim for relief, then to the Court of Appeals's decision affirming the district court, and then to the Supreme Court's decision reversing the Court of Appeals. As you read the materials, note the following:

a. Unlike the previous case, this one arises under the Federal Rules.

The Rules do not employ check-a-box forms that specifically identify the legal theory invoked by the plaintiff. In some instances the reader of a complaint must infer the legal theory from the facts alleged. For example, if a complaint alleged that A was driving a car, that A had negligently failed to observe traffic, and that the result of that failure was a collision that injured B, the reader of the complaint could infer that the plaintiff was proceeding on a theory of common law negligence, even if the complaint did not specifically so state. Where the complaint fails to identify a legal theory, the complaint can fail because the facts do not bring to mind any body of law applicable to the facts that would entitle the plaintiff to recover.

b. Although the Rules do not require the complaint to identify the legal theories the plaintiff is pursuing, it is common practice to do so. Where the complaint does identify the plaintiff's legal theories, the complaint can still fail if it omits one or more facts necessary to the body of law invoked. As you read the complaint below, think about what bodies of substantive law it is invoking and how, if you are the defendant, you might attack the complaint.

In the United States District Court for the Southern District of Georgia

MICHAEL A. HADDLE,
    Plaintiff

vs.   Civ. No. 96-00029-CV-1-AAA

JEANETTE G. GARRISON [et al.]
    Defendants.

COMPLAINT FOR DAMAGES PURSUANT TO 42 U.S.C. §1985(2) (THE CIVIL RIGHTS ACT OF 1871), THE GEORGIA RICO STATUTE AND GEORGIA LAW OF TORTIOUS INTERFERENCE AND FRAUDULENT CONVEYANCE

NOW COMES Plaintiff MICHAEL A. HADDLE and for this his complaint against Defendants JEANETTE G. GARRISON ("Garrison"), DENNIS KELLY ("Kelly"), PETER MOLLOY ("Molloy"), HEALTHMASTER, INC. ("Healthmaster"), and shows as follows:

INTRODUCTORY STATEMENT

1. Plaintiff is a citizen and resident of the State of Georgia.

2. Defendant Garrison is a resident of the State of South Carolina.

3. Defendants Molloy [and] Kelly are residents of the Southern District of Georgia.

4. Defendant Healthmaster is a corporation organized and existing under the laws of the State of Georgia with its principal place of business within the Southern District of Georgia.

5. Jurisdiction is proper in this Court over Count I of this Complaint (the Civil Rights Act of 1871) by virtue of 28 U.S.C. s 1331. Jurisdiction over Count II (Georgia RICO), Count III (Tortious Interference) and Count IV (Fraudulent Conveyance) is proper in this Court because these Counts are pendent to Count I.

6. Venue is proper in this Court in that most Defendants reside within the Southern District of Georgia and in that the actions of all Defendants as alleged below occurred within the Southern District of Georgia.

GENERAL FACTUAL ALLEGATIONS

7. From September 22, 1986 until approximately April 13, 1995, Plaintiff was employed by Defendant Healthmaster.

8. From approximately April 13, 1995 until his discharge as alleged below, Plaintiff was employed by Healthmaster Home Health Care, Inc., a Georgia corporation whose stock is owned entirely by Defendant Healthmaster.

9. Defendant Garrison has at all relevant times owned 50% of the stock of Healthmaster and controlled Healthmaster until April or May, 1995, when a trustee was appointed for Healthmaster, then a debtor in possession under Chapter II of the federal Bankruptcy Code, by the United States Bankruptcy Court for the Southern District of Georgia.

10. The individual Defendants herein have all served in various capacities as corporate officers and directors of Defendant Healthmaster and of Healthmaster Home Health Care, Inc.

11. Defendant Molloy has at all relevant times been employed by Defendant Healthmaster or Healthmaster Home Health Care, Inc.

12. On March 8, 1995, a grand jury convened in the United States District Court for the Southern District of Georgia, Augusta Division, filed an indictment against Defendants Garrison, Kelly, Healthmaster and others charging a total of 133 counts of fraud

against various defendants, which indictment is enumerated as number CR-195-11 in this Court.

13. Although not indicted, Defendant Molloy was, on information and belief, a target of the ongoing criminal investigation.

14. Plaintiff cooperated with the investigation by federal agents which preceded this indictment and testified pursuant to subpoena before said grand jury and appeared pursuant to subpoena to testify before said grand jury, although his testimony was not actually taken due to the press of time.

15. As a result of their indictment, Defendants Garrison and Kelly were banned from any participation in the affairs of Healthmaster Home Health Care, Inc., by order of said Bankruptcy Court.

16. On June 21, 1995, after Defendants had become aware that Plaintiff would appear as a witness at the criminal trial of Indictment No. CR 195-11, Defendant Molloy, who was then President of Defendant Healthmaster, having been retained in said position by the trustee, but acting at the direction of Defendants Garrison and Kelly and pursuant to a prior understanding and agreement between these three persons, terminated Plaintiff from his employment at Healthmaster Home Health Care, Inc.

COUNT I — CONSPIRACY IN VIOLATION OF
42 U.S.C.§1985(2)
(THE CIVIL RIGHTS ACT OF 1871)

17. The allegations contained in paragraphs numbered "1" through "16" are incorporated herein by reference.

18. The decision to terminate Plaintiff was made by Defendants and others, not in furtherance of the business interests of Defendant Healthmaster, but instead for the purpose of retaliating against Plaintiff for his cooperation with federal agents and his testimony under subpoena to the federal grand jury, and in order to intimidate Plaintiff and others from cooperating with federal agents or testifying in any criminal matters against them including said indictment.

19. Defendants participated in and carried out the decision to terminate Plaintiff, not in furtherance of the business interests of Defendant Healthmaster, but rather to protect themselves as criminal defendants or potential criminal defendants.

20. By means of the described actions, and their agreement and plan to do the same, Defendants have violated 42 U.S.C. §1985(2), in that they have conspired within the State of Georgia to deter, by force, intimidation or threat, a party or witness in the United

States District Court for the Southern District of Georgia, from attending such court, or from testifying in any matter pending therein, freely, fully, and truthfully, or to injure such party or witness in his person or property on account of his having so attended or testified, or to influence the verdict, presentment, or indictment of the grand jurors of such court.

21. Plaintiff has been injured in his person and property by the acts of Defendants in violation of 42 U.S.C. §1985(2), and Plaintiff is entitled to recover his damages occasioned by such injury and deprivation against Defendants jointly and severally.

22. Because said Defendants' acts were willful, intentional and malicious, Plaintiff is entitled to recover punitive damages against Defendants jointly and severally.

23. Pursuant to 42 U.S.C. §1988, Plaintiff is entitled to recover his expenses of litigation including a reasonable attorney's fee from said Defendants jointly and severally.

[The Counts alleging statutory and common law claims under Georgia state law are omitted.]

PRAYER FOR RELIEF

WHEREFORE, Plaintiff demands trial by jury on all counts and judgment as to all Defendants jointly and severally for money damages in such amount for actual damages as the evidence may show and as to all Defendants, jointly and severally, judgment for punitive damages and reasonable attorneys' fees and expenses of litigation, together with all costs of Court and such other and further relief as the Court may deem equitable and just.

NOTES AND PROBLEMS

1. To grasp the issue raised by this complaint, one must start with the text and history of 42 U.S.C. §1985(2). The statute was enacted in the wake of the Civil War and aimed at those who sought to intimidate newly freed former slaves by preventing them from using courts to enforce newly granted constitutional rights.

a. The statute provides:

If two or more persons in any State or Territory conspire to deter, by force, intimidation, or threat, any party or witness in any court of the United

States from attending such court, or from testifying to any matter pending therein, freely, fully, and truthfully, or to injure such party or witness in his person or property on account of his having so attended or testified . . . the party so injured or deprived may have an action for the recovery of damages, occasioned by such injury or deprivation, against any one or more of the conspirators.

b. As with any statute creating a claim, one has to analyze the terms in which the claim is created, considering which, if any, of them will raise issues on the facts alleged. To use an easy example, on the facts as alleged no problem of pleading arises as to the number of conspirators: If all happened as plaintiffs alleged, "two or more persons" — as required by the statute — conspired to have Michael Haddle fired. Is there a problem with the pleading insofar as it alleges that the firing was retaliation for Haddle's testimony before the grand jury? Does the statutory phrase "attend[] any court . . . [and] testify[] to any matter" cover such a situation?

2. Focus now on the statutory phrase "to injure such party or witness in his person or property on account of his having so attended or testified."

a. Haddle does not allege that anyone threatened him physically, so we can disregard the statutory phrase "in his person." His claim must be that the firing injured him "in his . . . property." What "property"?

b. Now consider Georgia's law of employment. Under the relevant Georgia labor statutes, any employment agreement that is not for a specified term is considered to be at will — that is, terminable by the employer for any reason or for no reason at all.

c. Construct an argument for the defendants that — however unadmirable their actions may have been — those actions did not violate the federal civil rights statute quoted above.

d. Consider how the district court responded to the defendants' contention that the complaint did not state a claim on which relief could be granted.

Haddle v. Garrison

Unpublished Opinion. Docket No. 96-00029-CV-1 (S.D. Ga. 1996)

ALAIMO, J.

Plaintiff, Michael A. Haddle, has brought the current litigation seeking damages under Section 1985(2) of Title 42 of the United States Code, and state law. Presently before the Court are four [defendants'] motions to dismiss for failure to state a claim upon which relief can be granted under Rule 12(b)(6) of the Federal Rules of Civil Procedure. For the reasons stated below, Defendants' motions will be GRANTED.

Facts

Haddle is a former employee of Healthmaster Home Health Care, Inc. He claims that he was improperly discharged from his employment by Defendants in an attempt to deter his participation as a witness in a Federal criminal trial. At the times relevant to this litigation, Haddle concedes that he was an at-will employee.

Discussion

I. Rule 12(b)(6)

Rule 12(b)(6) permits a defendant to move to dismiss a complaint on the grounds that the plaintiff has failed to state a claim upon which relief can be granted. A motion under Rule 12(b)(6) attacks the legal sufficiency of the complaint. In essence, the movant says, "Even if everything you allege is true, the law affords you no relief." Consequently, in determining the merits of a 12(b)(6) motion, a court must assume that all of the factual allegations of the complaint are true. A court should not dismiss a complaint for failure to state a claim unless it is clear that the plaintiff can prove "no set of facts in support of his claim which would entitle him to relief." Conley v. Gibson, 355 U.S. 41, 45-46 (1957).

II.   42 U.S.C. §1985(2). . . .

In the case at bar, Haddle asserts that he can maintain an action under Section 1985(2) despite the fact that he was defined as an at-will employee during the term of his employment. This is directly contrary to binding precedent of the Eleventh Circuit. Case law states:

> [T]o make out a cause of action under §1985(2) the plaintiff must have suffered an actual injury. Because [Plaintiff] was an at-will employee . . . he has no constitutionally protected interest in continued employment. Therefore, [Plaintiff's] discharge did not constitute an actual injury under this statute.

Morast v. Lance, 807 F.2d 926, 930 (11th Cir. 1987). Given the clear language of Morast, the Court is required to DISMISS Haddle's claim under Section 1985(2).

[The district court declined to exercise supplemental jurisdiction over the state law claims.]

Conclusion

The Court has determined that, under Rule 12(b)(6) Haddle has failed to state a federal claim upon which relief can be granted. His claim under Section 1985(2) is DISMISSED with respect to the above named Defendants. Additionally, all state law claims are DISMISSED WITHOUT PREJUDICE.

NOTES AND PROBLEMS

1. In what respect did the district court find that Haddle's case was deficient?

a. Did the district court make a factual determination that Haddle had not been fired? That he had not cooperated with the federal investigation? That he had not agreed to testify before the grand jury? That he had not been fired because of his cooperation with the federal investigation and prosecution?

b. If not, why was the complaint dismissed? The necessary elements of the federal claim are set forth in the district court's order. Which element did the district court find to be missing from the complaint?

2. The district court cites well-settled law that, in deciding a motion under Rule 12(b)(6), the "court must assume that all of the factual allegations of the complaint are true." That phrase is the key to understanding what a 12(b)(6) motion, or its analogue, the demurrer, is about.

a. Is the allegation in Paragraph 21 that Haddle was "injured in his person or property" a factual allegation?

b. If it is a factual allegation, should the district court have dismissed the complaint? If it is not a factual allegation, what is it?

3. The district court's order states that Haddle conceded he was an at-will employee.

a. Does the complaint itself state that Haddle was an at-will employee?

b. Is it reasonable to treat the complaint as conceding that Haddle was an at-will employee because it does not allege that his employment was for a specified term? Is it possible that the concession the district court refers to was made somewhere other than in the complaint itself? Imagine oral argument on the motion to dismiss, at which the judge asked Haddle's lawyer if he was contending that his client had some form of protected employment. The lawyer says no. At that point the judge could, technically, ask that the complaint be amended to make that clear or simply treat the concession as part of the pleading as it stood.

4. To distinguish a 12(b)(6) motion from other attacks on plaintiff's claim, imagine some alternative scenarios. Suppose the defendants had moved to dismiss on the ground that Haddle had quit his job and had not been fired, and defendants had submitted in support of the motion a letter signed by Haddle admitting he had quit. Explain why, in such a scenario, the district court could not have granted a motion to dismiss under Rule 12(b)(6) on the ground that Haddle had quit and not been fired. See the second sentence of Rule 12(c).

5. Is there anything Haddle's lawyer could have put into the complaint that would have cured the problem that led the district court to dismiss?

a. Suppose Haddle's lawyer concluded that the judge was about to dismiss his complaint because he had not alleged that his client held a job more permanent than at-will employment—that, for example, he had a contract stating that the employer could dismiss him only for "good cause."

b. Imagine a conversation between a law student and Haddle's lawyer:

Student: Let me see if I understand what's going on. The case was dismissed because the complaint failed to allege some things—that Mr. Haddle had a certain kind of clause in his employment contract or understanding with his employer that he would be fired only for good cause.

Lawyer: Right.

Student: Do you have to prove things in a complaint?

Lawyer: No; proof comes later—during discovery, summary judgment, and trial, if things come to that. Complaints are just allegations—things you write down on paper, not evidence.

Student: So what's the problem? As I understand it, a judge will almost always allow leave to amend either before or after a 12(b)(6) dismissal. Now that you know what you should have alleged, all you need to do is to get leave to amend, and then write down the things—about Haddle's terms of employment—that will satisfy the judge. Just say that he had a written contract guaranteeing that he would be fired only for good cause. Why the fuss?

Lawyer: Hold on. It's not quite that simple. Read Rule 11(b) before you tell me to do that. Do you see what would happen if I took your advice?

Student: I guess it's not quite as simple as I thought.

6. Probably because of the constraints suggested in the preceding note, plaintiff did not seek to amend the complaint, and it was dismissed. Plaintiff appealed.

a. If plaintiff did not seek to amend, why did he appeal? What was he trying to accomplish?

b. The Court of Appeals gave short shrift to Haddle's appeal. The following is the entire text of its unpublished opinion:

Garrison v. Haddle

Unpublished Opinion. Docket No. 96-8856 (11th Cir. 1997)

PER CURIAM:

Michael A. Haddle appeals following the district court's dismissal of his 42 U.S.C. §1985(2) claim for failure to state a claim. We conclude that Haddle's arguments on appeal are foreclosed by this court's decision in Morast v. Lance, 807 F.2d 926 (11th Cir. 1987). The judgment of the district court is therefore affirmed.

NOTES AND PROBLEMS

1. Why might the 11th Circuit have thought this was such an easy case that it could be disposed of in a three-sentence per curiam opinion, one perhaps drafted by a law clerk.

2. Plaintiff sought a writ of certiorari from the U.S. Supreme Court, which granted certiorari, heard argument, and issued the following opinion.

Haddle v. Garrison

119 S. Ct. 489 (1998)

Chief Justice REHNQUIST delivered the opinion of the Court.

Petitioner Michael A. Haddle, an at-will employee, alleges that respondents conspired to have him fired from his job in retaliation for obeying a federal grand jury subpoena and to deter him from testifying at a federal criminal trial. We hold that such interference with at-will employment may give rise to a claim for damages under the Civil Rights Act of 1871, Rev. Stat §1980, 42 U.S.C. §1985(2).

According to petitioner's complaint, a federal grand jury indictment in March 1995 charged petitioner's employer, Healthmaster, Inc., and respondents Jeanette Garrison and Dennis Kelly, officers of Healthmaster, with Medicare fraud. Petitioner cooperated with the federal agents in the investigation that preceded the indictment. He also appeared to testify before the grand jury pursuant to a subpoena, but did not testify due to the press of time. Petitioner was also expected to appear as a witness in the criminal trial resulting from the indictment.

Although Garrison and Kelly were barred by the Bankruptcy Court from participating in the affairs of Healthmaster, they conspired with G. Peter Molloy, Jr., one of the remaining officers of Healthmaster, to bring about petitioner's termination. They did this both to intimidate petitioner and to retaliate against him for his attendance at the federal-court proceedings.

Petitioner sued for damages in the United States District Court for the Southern District of Georgia, asserting a federal claim under 42 U.S.C. §1985(2) and various state-law claims. Petitioner stated two grounds for relief under §1985(2): one for conspiracy to deter him from testifying in the upcoming criminal trial and one for conspiracy to retaliate against him for attending the grand jury proceedings. As §1985 demands, he also alleged that he had been "injured in his person or property" by the acts of respondents in violation of §1985(2) and that he was entitled to recover his damages occasioned by such injury against respondents jointly and severally.

Respondents moved to dismiss for failure to state a claim upon which relief can be granted. Because petitioner conceded that he was an at-will employee, the District Court granted the motion on the authority of Morast v. Lance, 807 F.2d 926 (1987). In Morast, the Eleventh Circuit held that an at-will employee who is dismissed pursuant to a conspiracy proscribed by §1985(2) has no cause of action. The Morast court explained that "to make out a cause of action under §1985(2) the plaintiff must have suffered an actual injury. Because Morast was an at-will employee, he had no constitutionally protected interest in continued employment. Therefore, Morast's discharge did not constitute an actual injury under this statute." Relying on its decision in Morast, the Court of Appeals affirmed.

The Eleventh Circuit's rule in Morast conflicts with the holdings of the First and Ninth Circuits. We therefore granted certiorari, to decide whether petitioner was "injured in his property or person" when respondents induced his employer to terminate petitioner's at-will employment as part of a conspiracy prohibited by §1985(2).

The statute provides that if one or more persons engaged in such a conspiracy "do, or cause to be done, any act in furtherance of the object of such conspiracy, whereby another in injured in his person or property,

. . . the party so injured . . . may have an action for the recovery of damages occasioned by such injury . . . against any one or more of the conspirators." §1985(3).

Petitioner's action was dismissed pursuant to Federal Rule Civil Procedure 12(b)(6) because, in the Eleventh Circuit's view, he had not suffered an injury that could give rise to a claim for damages under §1985(2). We must, of course, assume that the facts as alleged in petitioner's complaint are true and that respondents engaged in a conspiracy prohibited by §1985(2). Our review in this case is accordingly confined to one question: Can petitioner state a claim for damages by alleging that a conspiracy proscribed by §1985(2) induced his employer to terminate his at-will employments.

We disagree with the Eleventh Circuit's conclusion that petitioner must suffer an injury to a "constitutionally protected property interest" to state a claim for damages under §1985(2). Nothing in the language or purpose of the proscriptions in the first clause of §1985(2), nor in its attendant remedial provisions, establishes such a requirement. The gist of the wrong at which §1985(2) is directed is not deprivation of property, but intimidation or retaliation against witnesses in federal-court proceedings. The terms "injured in his person or property" define the harm that the victim may suffer as a result of the conspiracy to intimidate or retaliate. Thus, the fact that employment at will is not "property" for purposes of the Due Process Clause, does not mean that loss of at-will employment may not "injur[e] [petitioner] in his person or property" for purposes of §1985(2).

We hold that the sort of harm alleged by petitioner here — essentially third-party interference with at-will employment relationships — states a claim for relief under §1985(2). Such harm has long been a compensable injury under tort law, and we see no reason to ignore this tradition in this case. As Thomas Cooley recognized:

> One who maliciously and without justifiable cause, induces an employer to discharge an employee, by means of false statements, threats or putting in fear, or perhaps by means of malevolent advice and persuasion, is liable in an action of tort to the employee for the damages thereby sustained. *And it makes no difference whether the employment was for a fixed term not yet expired or is terminable at the will of the employer.*

2. T. Cooley, Law of Torts 589-591 (3d ed. 1906) (emphasis added). This Court also recognized in Truax v. Raich, 239 U.S. 33 (1915):

> The fact that the employment is at the will of the parties, respectively, does not make it one at the will of others. The employee has manifest interest in the freedom of the employer to exercise his judgment without

illegal interference or compulsion and, by the weight of authority, the unjustified interference of third persons is actionable although the employment is at will.

The kind of interference with at-will employment relations alleged here is merely a species of the traditional torts of intentional interference with contractual relations and intentional interference with prospective contractual relations. See Restatement (Second) of Torts s 766, Comment g, pp. 10-11 (1977); see also id., §766B, Comment c, at 22. This protection against third-party interference with at-will employment relations is still afforded by state law today. See W. Keeton, D. Dobbs, R. Keeton, & D. Owen, Prosser and Keaton on Law of Torts §129, pp. 995-996, and n. 83 (5th ed. 1984) (citing cases). For example, the State of Georgia, where the acts underlying the complaint in this case took place, provides a cause of action against third parties for wrongful interference with employment relations.

Thus, to the extent that the terms "injured in his person or property" in §1985 refer to principles of tort law, see 3 W. Blackstone, Commentaries on *493 the Laws of England 118 (1768) (describing the universe of common law torts as "all private wrongs, or civil injuries, which may be offered to the rights of either a man's person or his property"), we find ample support for our holding that the harm occasioned by the conspiracy here may give rise to a claim for damages under §1985(2).

The judgment of the Court of Appeals is reversed, and the case is remanded for further proceedings consistent with this opinion.

NOTES AND PROBLEMS

1. Why did the Supreme Court reverse?

a. Did the Supreme Court take issue with the district court's application of the standard for granting a motion to dismiss under Rule 12(b)(6)? If not, what aspect of the two lower court decisions was the Supreme Court rejecting?

b. The Supreme Court's opinion was unanimous. Does that circumstance suggest that the Eleventh Circuit was too hasty in its per curiam decision of the case without oral argument? Or is the Supreme Court's disagreement with the Circuit about an issue as to which more deliberate consideration would have made no difference?

2. Suppose yourself hired by the defendant in Haddle v. Garrison to argue in the Supreme Court. You conclude that you have a client whose factual circumstances are unattractive: It is hard to be sympathetic to a defendant accused first of engaging in criminal activity and then of firing

an employee who cooperated with the prosecution in exposing those activities. (And recall that you cannot argue, however truthfully, that your client didn't do any of the things he was accused of: The case arises on a 12(b)(6) motion — on which, as the Supreme Court notes, "We must, of course, assume that the facts as alleged in petitioner's complaint are true. . . .) In such circumstances many lawyers would say that the best argument focuses not on this client, but on the bad consequences of a legal principle resulting from a decision against this client.

a. Can you frame an argument focusing on such a rule of law? Suppose — as actually happened — that the decision goes against the defendant. Can you predict a series of claims brought by other plaintiffs? How might those plaintiffs be less attractive than Michael Haddle?

b. You are a Supreme Court justice considering how to decide Haddle v. Garrison. The plaintiff stresses the intuitive justice of his client's case: shouldn't one interpret the statute to provide a remedy for an honest employee fired for cooperating with a criminal investigation of his employer? In briefs and in oral argument defendant's counsel takes a different tack, stressing the flood of trivial or unattractive cases that will result from a decision in plaintiff's favor. How should a judge think about the relation between the specific case before the court and the long-term consequences of a rule of law?

3. The complaint in Haddle v. Garrison is fairly detailed. Compare it to the skeletal complaints set forth in forms 3-17 of the Rules, none of which occupies more than a page of text. How detailed must a complaint be to survive a motion to dismiss? Conley v. Gibson, the leading case on specificity, cited and quoted in the district court opinion, says: "[T]he Federal Rules of Civil Procedure do not require a claimant to set out in detail the facts upon which he bases his claim." That hardly resolves the matter. What by way of detail should we ask of a plaintiff?

a. A fundamental problem in federal pleading arises from the fact that Rule 8 tells pleaders they need not be detailed, but it also tells pleaders that they must state a claim. At some high level of generality, the two points merge.

b. Consider a complaint that, after properly invoking federal subject matter jurisdiction, simply says, "The defendant's behavior has been reprehensible and illegal, and I demand relief." That complaint fails — but why? One can describe the difficulty either as failure to state a claim or as providing insufficient detail and conclusory allegations. Which it is depends on whether one is looking just at the complaint or at the behavior behind the complaint. If the basis for the complaint were the defendant's negligent infliction of a physical injury on plaintiff, one would be inclined to say that plaintiff had a claim but that her lawyer had failed to describe it in sufficient detail. But if one looks just at the complaint's language, one can't tell the difference between that set of facts and the case of a plaintiff who has simply taken an irrational dislike to the defendant.

c. Another way to put the issue is to ask whether *Department of · Transportation* and *Haddle*, the two preceding cases, are distinguishable. Is one about "substance" and the other about "form" in pleading?

d. Substantive rules of law can be thought of in logical terms: "If A, B, C, and D, then defendant is liable to plaintiff." How specifically must plaintiff allege A, B, C, and D? Is it enough that plaintiff's allegations appear to be invoking a particular substantive rule? For example, in order to recover for fraud, plaintiff must establish representation, falsity, scienter (defendant's knowledge that it was false), intent to induce reliance, and damage. What happens if a complaint "sounds" in fraud but does not allege scienter? Does the following observation help to answer this question? "A plaintiff will not be thrown out of court for failing to plead facts in support of every arcane element of his claim. But when a complaint omits facts that, if they existed, would clearly dominate the case, it seems fair to assume that those facts do not exist." O'Brien v. Di Grazia, 544 F.2d 543 (1st Cir. 1976), cert. denied, 431 U.S. 914 (1977).

4. A complaint can be too detailed. In Gordon v. Green, 602 F.2d 743 (5th Cir. 1979), plaintiff's complaints in five consolidated securities fraud cases totaled 4,000 pages, occupied eighteen volumes, and required a handtruck or cart to move. After finding noncompliance with Rule 8 and noting that such pleadings would "hasten the speed at which our country's trees are being transformed into sheets of legal jargon," the court dismissed the complaint with leave to file an amended complaint. According to the court, counsel were lucky that the discipline was not akin to that meted out by the chancellor in 1596 who "decided to make an example of a particularly prolix document filed in his court. The chancellor first ordered a hole cut through the center of the document, all 120 pages of it. Then he ordered that the person who wrote it should have his head stuffed through the hole, and the unfortunate fellow was led around to be exhibited to all those attending court at Westminster Hall."

NOTE: CONSISTENCY IN PLEADING

A common law pleader had to worry about the consistency of his complaint. If plaintiff said defendant trespassed on Blackacre, defendant could not simultaneously deny that he had entered the land in question and assert that he had an easement. The attractiveness of this insistence on a single consistent story is obvious: We expect people in ordinary life not to vary their version of the facts from moment to moment. A person may legitimately assert either that she made a promise or she didn't; that she kept her promise or she didn't; but not that she didn't make a promise *and* that she kept it.

Yet modern pleading rules, of which Rule 8(e)(2) is one example, permit just this sort of apparent duplicity: "[a] party may set forth two or more statements of a claim or defense alternately or hypothetically [and a] party may also state as many separate claims or defenses as he has regardless of consistency." As a result, a defendant may deny that she ever entered into a contract with plaintiff and at the same time assert that she kept her side of the bargain; similarly, a plaintiff may seek to recover on the ground that a written contract provides "X" and simultaneously seek to have the court reform the contract so that the crucial clause reads "not X" rather than "X."

Understanding why the Federal Rules condone behavior that one would condemn in everyday life requires the student to recall the role of the pleadings in the lawsuit. First, pleadings come very early in the case, often before the parties know all that they will by the time the case comes to trial or to the point of serious settlement discussions. The lawyer is therefore often setting forth what seem to her to be the possible versions of the law and the facts that appear plausible at the time the pleading is filed. Second, allegations in pleadings are tempered by burdens of proof. Thus a lawyer who entirely believes her client's story that he had, but lost, a signed, written contract may allege that in her pleadings but, as a safety net, may also seek to recover on a quantum meruit count in case she decides she cannot convince a jury that the written contract existed. Finally, one has to remember that however inconsistent and contradictory the pleadings, the lawyer will often have to settle on a single version of the story before the case comes to trial. Both judge and jury are likely to look with disfavor on a case that rests on logically inconsistent versions of the facts. (In a multiparty defendant case the plaintiff might conceivably try different versions of the facts against different defendants, but this tactic has its limits.) Thus inconsistent pleadings reflect not lawyers' propensity to talk out of both sides of their mouths but a pleading system that requires lawyers to make allegations before they are certain of the facts and the law. Inconsistent pleadings represent alternative drafts of a story, one version of which the advocate hopes ultimately will persuade a judge or jury.

The fact that inconsistent pleading does not rise to the level of a moral offense, however, does not give the lawyer complete license in the matter. Consider, for example, the lawyer retained by the family of an injured, unconscious person. Knowing only that his client was hurt in an automo-

bile accident and the name of the other driver, could the lawyer file a
complaint alleging, alternatively, that the other driver was negligent and
that he intentionally ran down the plaintiff? Delay your response until
after reading the next section.

3.   Ethical Limitations and Disfavored Claims

Given the breadth and apparent ease of notice pleading under the
federal regime and the apparent fluidity of theories and stories made
possible by Rule 8(e)(2), the student may wonder what the limits are:
Short of incoherence or allegations that do not come close to describing
a claim, what would constitute a bad pleading? The answer to that
question involves an examination both of ethical constraints on lawyers
and of disfavored claims on which the federal courts seem to impose
higher pleading standards.

a.   Ethical Principles as a Limitation

This section looks at principles that stiffen not the formal pleading
requirements but the requirements for the factual and legal investigation
that lie behind the pleading. As you saw in Bridges v. Diesel Service
Inc. in Chapter I, Rule 11 restricts the lawyer's ability to file a pleading
when he has no more than a hope that favorable facts or law will emerge
as the case progresses. Rule 11 is probably the most important constraint
on lawyers' behavior during litigation, but it is not the only one. Apart from
procedural statutes and rules, courts have inherent powers to discipline
misbehaving lawyers. And rules of professional conduct make lawyers
accountable to bar associations and clients as well as to judges and
adversaries. We shall here focus on Rule 11 because it is a procedural
rule that manifests itself within the lawsuit. Consider two cases that
punish lawyers and clients for different kinds of violations of Rule 11.

Business Guides v. Chromatic Communications Enterprises
498 U.S. 533 (1991)

Justice O'CONNOR delivered the opinion of the Court. . . .

Business Guides, Inc., a subsidiary of a leading publisher of trade
magazines and journals, publishes directories for 18 specialized areas of
retail trade. In an effort to protect its directories against copying, Business
Guides deliberately plants in them bits of false information, known as

"seeds." Some seeds consist of minor alterations in otherwise accurate listings — transposed numbers in an address or zip code, or a misspelled name — while others take the form of wholly fictitious listings describing nonexistent businesses. Business Guides considers the presence of seeds in a competitor's directory to be evidence of copyright infringement.

On October 31, 1986, Business Guides, through its counsel Finley, Kumble, Wagner, Heine, Unterberg, Manley, Myerson, and Casey (Finley, Kumble), filed an action in the United States District Court for the Northern District of California against Chromatic Communications Enterprises, Inc., claiming copyright infringement, conversion, and unfair competition, and seeking a temporary restraining order (TRO). The TRO application was signed by a Finley, Kumble attorney and by Business Guides' president on behalf of the corporation. Business Guides submitted under seal affidavits in support of the application. These affidavits charged Chromatic with copying, as evidenced by the presence of 10 seeds in Chromatic's directory. One affidavit, that of sales representative Victoria Burdick, identified the 10 listings in Business Guides' directory that had allegedly been copied, but did not pinpoint the seed in each listing.

A hearing on the TRO was scheduled for November 7, 1986. Three days before the hearing, the District Judge's law clerk phoned Finley, Kumble and asked it to specify what was incorrect about each listing. Finley, Kumble relayed this request to Business Guides' Director of Research, Michael Lambe. This was apparently the first time the law firm asked its client for details about the 10 seeds. Based on Lambe's response, Finley, Kumble informed the court that Business Guides was retracting its claims of copying as to three of the seeds. The District Court considered this suspicious and so conducted its own investigation into the allegations of copying. The District Judge's law clerk spent one hour telephoning the businesses named in the "seeded" listings, only to discover that 9 of the 10 listings contained no incorrect information.

Unaware of the District Court's discovery, Finley, Kumble prepared a supplemental affidavit of Michael Lambe, identifying seven listings in Chromatic's directory and explaining precisely what part of each listing supposedly contained seeded information. Lambe signed this affidavit on the morning of the November 7 hearing. Before doing so, however, Lambe crossed out reference to a fourth seed that he had determined did not in fact reflect any incorrect information but which Finley, Kumble had not retracted.

At the hearing, the District Court, based on its discovery that 9 of the original 10 listings contained no incorrect information, denied the application for a TRO. More importantly, the judge stayed further proceedings and referred the matter to a Magistrate to determine whether

Rule 11 sanctions should be imposed. The Magistrate conducted two evidentiary hearings, at which he instructed Business Guides and Finley, Kumble to explain why 9 of its 10 charges of copying were meritless. Both claimed it was a coincidence. Doubting the good faith of these representations, the Magistrate recommended that both the law firm and the client be sanctioned.

Later, claiming to have uncovered the true source of the errors, the parties asked for and received a third hearing. Business Guides explained that in compiling its "master seed list," it had departed from its normal methodology. Usually, letters and numbers were transposed deliberately and recorded on the seed list before the directory was published. In this case, the company had compiled the master seed list after publication by looking for unintended typographical errors in the directory. To locate such errors, sales representative Victoria Burdick had compared the final version of the directory against initial questionnaires that had been submitted to Business Guides by businesses that wanted to be listed. When Burdick discovered a disparity between a questionnaire and the final directory, she included it on the seed list. She assumed, without investigating, that the information on the questionnaires was accurate. As it turned out, the questionnaires themselves sometimes contained transposed numbers or misspelled names, which other employees had corrected when proofreading the directory prior to publication. Consequently, many of the seeds appearing on the master list contained no false information. The presence of identical listings in a competitor's directory thus would not indicate copying, but rather accurate research.

The Magistrate accepted this explanation, but determined that sanctions were nonetheless appropriate. First, he found that Business Guides, in filing the initial TRO application, had "failed to conduct a proper inquiry, resulting in the presentation of unreasonable and false information to the court." The Magistrate did not recommend that Finley, Kumble be sanctioned for the initial application, however, as the firm had been led to believe that there was an urgent need to act quickly and thus relied on the information provided by its sophisticated corporate client. Next, the Magistrate recommended that both Business Guides and Finley, Kumble be sanctioned for having failed to inquire into the accuracy of the remaining seeds following Michael Lambe's discovery, based on only a few minutes of investigation, that 3 of the 10 were invalid. Finally, the Magistrate recommended that both the law firm and its client be sanctioned for their conduct at the first two evidentiary hearings. Instead of investigating the cause of the errors in the seed list, Business Guides and Finley, Kumble had relied on a "coincidence" defense. The Magistrate determined that "no reasonable person would have been satisfied with these explanations. . . . Finley, Kumble and Business

Guides did not need this court to point out the blatant errors in the logic of their representations."

The District Court agreed with the Magistrate, stating: "The standard of conduct under Rule 11 is one of objective reasonableness. Applying this standard to the circumstances of this case, it is clear that both Business Guides and Finley, Kumble have violated the Rule." 119 F.R.D. 685, 688-689 (N.D. Cal. 1988). . . .

. . . Citing "the rather remarkable circumstances of this case, and the serious consequences of Business Guides' improper conduct," [the district court] dismissed the action with prejudice. Additionally, it imposed $13,865.66 in sanctions against Business Guides, the amount of Chromatic's legal expenses and out-of-pocket costs. . . .

[The Court held that sanctions could be levied against Business Guides under these circumstances.]

Religious Technology Center v. Gerbode

1994 U.S. Dist. LEXIS 6432 (C.D. Cal. 1994)

TASHIMA, Judge.

This case is the continuation of long-standing and acrimonious litigation between plaintiff Religious Technology Center (RTC) and defendants David Mayo, Julie Mayo and the Church of the New Civilization. Plaintiffs allege that defendants violated the Racketeer Influenced and Corrupt Organization Act (RICO), 18 U.S.C. §1961 et seq., by engaging in acts of mail fraud and wire fraud in connection with the formation and operation of purportedly non-profit corporations. . . .

Defendants now seek attorneys' fees from plaintiffs and their attorneys Bowles & Moxon, and Cooley, Manion, Moore & Jones in the amount of $80,030 for having to defend against this action. The motion is based on F.R. Civ. P. 11, 28 U.S.C. §1927 and on the court's inherent powers. In this case, the court concludes that proceeding under either §1927[*] or its inherent powers adds nothing to the outcome of the motion. Therefore, this motion shall be treated as a motion made under Rule 11[2]. . . .

Plaintiffs first contend that the motion should not be considered because it was filed in violation of the "safe harbor" provision of the amended rule. Rule 11(c)(1)(A) now provides that a motion for sanctions under the rule shall not be filed until 21 days after it is served on opposing

---

* [Section 1927 permits a judge to impose costs and attorneys' fees on a lawyer "who so multiplies the proceedings . . . as to increase costs unreasonably and vexatiously." — ED.]

2. Moreover, the court finds that defendants have not established the "bad faith" component required for the imposition of sanctions under either §1927 or the court's inherent powers.

counsel and the challenged paper "is not withdrawn or appropriately corrected." It would not be "practicable" to require compliance with the "safe harbor" provision in this case.[6] Amended Rule 11 became effective on the same date that this action was dismissed. Thus, it would be futile to now require defendants to comply with the "safe harbor" provision.

II. Merits. . . .

[B]y the time the amended complaint was filed, [the leading case on the legal question presented — whether "a plaintiff's alleged RICO injury must be proximately caused by the predicate acts"] was "established law" which reasonable inquiry (i.e., basic legal research) would have disclosed. This RICO complaint does not pass muster under Rule 11(b)(2) that the claims be "warranted by existing law."[8] Neither is any "nonfrivolous argument" made "for the extension, modification, or reversal of existing law" in support of plaintiffs' RICO theory. No logical argument does or can support plaintiffs' contention that the creation of fraudulent tax-exempt organizations for the purpose of evading income taxes proximately caused plaintiffs' injury in having to defend the . . . litigation. The claims are frivolous.[9]

Alleging the RICO claims in the amended complaint was objectively unreasonable under the circumstances.

III. Appropriate Sanction

A. Nature and Amount of Sanctions

Both amended Rule 11(c)(2) and the Advisory Committee's Notes which accompany the December 1, 1993, amendment indicate that

6. It would appear to be problematical to comply with the "safe harbor" provision in any case involving a challenge to a complaint. Even if the frivolousness is immediately apparent on the face of the pleading at the time of service, does service of a motion for sanctions under Rule 11 toll the 20-day period to answer under Rule 12(a)(1)(A)? If not, what purpose does compliance with the "safe harbor" provision serve if the complaint must be responded to before the 21-day waiting period expires? If the frivolousness is not immediately apparent and the Rule 11 motion is not made until after the complaint is dismissed, what useful purpose is served by compliance with the "safe harbor" provision at that point? Certainly, by that juncture, it is too late for the complaint to be "withdrawn or appropriately corrected."

8. This substantive standard under Rule 11(b)(2) remains unchanged from the pre-amendment version in effect at the time the amended complaint was filed.

9. Because the court finds the amended complaint to be sanctionable as frivolous, under Rule 11(b)(2), it does not explore defendants' further contention that it was filed for an improper purpose, in violation of Rule 11(b)(1).

attorney's fees should not automatically be imposed for a Rule 11 violation and that the court should explore the adequacy of non-monetary sanctions as an effective deterrent. However, the rule authorizes the award of attorney's fees if "warranted for effective deterrence."

Here, because of the long and acrimonious history of repeated litigation between these parties, the court finds that a partial award of attorneys' fees is necessary as a deterrent to the bringing of further frivolous actions. Further, because the case has been concluded by dismissal of the amended complaint, other sanctions, which might be effective in the context of ongoing litigation, are unavailable. Because only partial fees are being awarded, as authorized by Rule 11(c)(2), the court also imposes a monetary penalty to be paid to the court as an additional deterrent equal to that portion of reasonable fees not awarded to defendants.

Defendants seek attorneys' fees in the amount of $80,030. The hours on which this amount is based, however, include all hours expended in defending against this case in its entirety. Attorney Helena K. Kobrin, who signed the amended complaint, and her law firm Bowles & Moxon, did not associate in as counsel of record until April 19, 1993, when this action was transferred to this district. . . . Attorney Kobrin and Bowles & Moxon cannot be held responsible for the costs of defending the action before they became attorneys of record for plaintiffs. . . .

Rule 11(c)(1)(A) now makes it discretionary with the court as to whether or not to award attorneys' fees to the prevailing party "incurred in presenting or opposing the motion." The rule does not require the presence of any exceptional circumstances for the award of such fees, but only that the award be "warranted." Again, because of the long-standing and acrimonious litigation between the parties, the court finds that the award of fees for the preparation of the Rule 11 motion is warranted in this case.

In calculating the reasonable fees in this case, the court employs the lodestar method.* Commencing with their first telephone conference on October 12, 1993, to discuss the amended complaint, defense counsel incurred, respectively, a total of 47.1 hours (for Mr. Fagelbaum) and 39.3 hours (for Mr. Bright), plus an additional 49.2 hours of a law clerk's time, to the conclusion of the case, including work on the pending motion. The court finds these hours to be reasonable.

Defendants seek an award based on an hourly rate of $225 for the work of Jerold Fagelbaum. While the court agrees that this rate is well within the range of fees charged by competent attorneys in the community

[*The "lodestar method" is a system of calculating attorneys' fees in which the court guides itself by the "lodestar" of the attorneys' usual hourly rates, which it then adjusts up or down as various circumstances warrant—ED.]

for similar work, for this case, the court finds that it is somewhat inflated. Mr. Fagelbaum has represented the same parties in the related litigation. He is very familiar with the context of this litigation. The work in this case and on this motion was not unusual or complex. The court finds that an hourly rate of $200 is a reasonable hourly rate for Mr. Fagelbaum's work, especially when compared to the rate awarded below for the work of Mr. Bright. . . .

[The court went on to examine the hourly rates charged by another lawyer and a law clerk and found that the defendant had reasonably expended $17,775.00 in legal fees.]

The court awards to defendants as a sanction under Rule 11 and in partial reimbursement of the costs they incurred in defending against the frivolous amended complaint one-half of the lodestar amount, or $8,887.50. A like amount is assessed as a monetary penalty and shall be payable to the Clerk of the Court.

B. Persons to Be Sanctioned

Amended Rule 11(c)(2)(A) now prohibits the imposition of monetary sanctions on a represented party, such as RTC, for a violation of Rule 11(b)(2).[13] Therefore, to the extent sanctions are sought against plaintiff RTC, the motion must be denied.

However, amended Rule 11(c) now authorizes sanctions to be imposed on law firms, as well as the particular attorney who signs the offending pleading.[14] More specifically, Rule 11(c)(1)(A) goes on to provide that "Absent exceptional circumstances, a law firm shall be held jointly responsible for violations committed by its partners, associates, and employees."

There are no such "exceptional circumstances" here. . . .

The motion also seeks sanctions against the law firm of Cooley, Manion, Moore & Jones, P.C. That law firm, as well as the law firm of Wilson, Ryan & Campilongo, along with Bowles & Moxon, appears as counsel of record for plaintiffs on the amended complaint. However, it was Attorney Kobrin of Bowles & Moxon who signed the complaint.

Rule 11(c) provides that the court may "impose an appropriate sanction upon the attorneys, law firms, or parties that have violated subdivision (b) or are responsible for the violation." While this language, standing alone, does not clearly indicate that the rule is intended to catch within

13. This amendment restricts the scope of Business Guides, Inc. v. Chromatic Communications Enter., Inc., 498 U.S. 533 (1991).

14. This amendment overrules Pavelic & LeFlore v. Marvel Entertainment Group, 493 U.S. 120 (1989), which construed the language of Rule 11 before the 1993 amendment as authorizing sanctions only against the attorney who signed the offending pleading.

its sweep a co-counsel law firm which did not actually sign the offending pleading, the Advisory Committee's Notes do provide some clarification[:]

> The revision permits the court to consider whether other attorneys in the firm, co-counsel, other law firms, or the party itself should be held accountable for their part in causing a violation.

It, thus, appears that the court has the authority to sanction a co-counsel law firm, as well as the primary offending firm, even though co-counsel did not sign the offending pleading. In order to do so, however, the record must show that firm's culpability — in the Committee's words, evidence of its "part in causing a violation." Here, the court finds that the record is insufficient to establish that any law firm besides Bowles & Moxon was responsible for the drafting and filing of the amended complaint. Therefore, the motion will be denied as against Cooley, Manion, Moore & Jones. . . .

NOTES AND PROBLEMS

1. *Business Guides* and *Gerbode* illustrate a characteristic of many Rule 11 cases: The courts applying sanctions often find it easier to be clear about the procedural issues (to which persons does the rule apply? does it apply to law firms as well as to individuals?) than about the underlying substantive standards (how much investigation of facts is necessary? when is a legal contention "nonfrivolous?"). The notes below use *Business Guides* and *Gerbode* as a taking-off point to discuss four aspects of the Rule: (1) substantive standards (what behavior violates the Rule?); (2) enforcement procedure (what procedural mechanisms attend the invocation of the Rule?); (3) appropriate sanctions (what punishment is apppropriate for a violation of the Rule?); and (4) appellate review (when appellate courts review the application of the Rule, how what standards will guide them?).

Substantive standards

2. Start by comparing the nature of the violation in *Business Guides* and in *Gerbode*.

a. What provision of the current Rule did the plaintiffs in *Business Guides* violate?

b. What provision of the current Rule did the plaintiffs in *Gerbode* violate?

3. Focus first on *Business Guides*. In that case the initial hearings occurred before the law firm representing Business Guides declared bankruptcy and was dropped from the case. At those initial hearings the

magistrate judge* considered whether to impose sanctions on the law firm for its original failure to investigate the facts underlying the complaint. The magistrate judge decided not to do so, on the grounds that "the firm had been led to believe that there was an urgent need to act quickly [to get the temporary restraining order before the competing directory was published] and thus relied on the information provided by its sophisticated corporate client."

a. Is that an appropriate interpretation of the current Rule, whose relevant provision requires an "inquiry reasonable under the circumstances"? How much time would have to have been available before the firm's failure to investigate violated the Rule?

b. Did the district court and Supreme Court correctly apply this "under the circumstances" standard to Business Guides itself? No one argued that Business Guides consciously filed a frivolous lawsuit; those responsible for initiating the lawsuit were not aware that Victoria Burdick, the sales representative who had compiled the "seeds," had departed from the usual practice in doing so. Moreover, the managers of Business Guides knew that their competitor, who they honestly (but incorrectly) believed was about to infringe their copyright, was about to publish its competing guide. Explain why the Rule punishes honest beliefs that turn out to be mistaken. Make an argument that this standard is the correct one, even though some honest people will be punished under it.

4. Lawyer files an answer alleging the statute of limitations as an affirmative defense. At the time Lawyer filed the answer, she reasonably believed that the facts warranted such a response. Lawyer later learns that a salient event occurred later than she previously thought, and that the statute of limitations therefore has not run. Does Lawyer violate the Rule by failing to file an amended answer? Does Lawyer violate the Rule by orally asserting this defense at a subsequent pretrial conference?

5. *Business Guides* deals with a common basis for Rule 11 sanctions, the failure to investigate underlying facts sufficiently. But what if those facts are in the possession of the other side? Discovery will uncover them, but discovery is available only if one can file a pleading. The current version of the Rule tries to address this problem in section (b)(3), which permits a litigant to allege facts that, though lacking present support, "are likely to have evidentiary support after a reasonable opportunity for further investigation and discovery." The same section requires the pleader specifically to identify such allegations. If construed too broadly,

---

* Magistrate judges, whose jurisdiction is described in 28 U.S.C. §636, assist federal district judges in the pretrial phases of civil litigation. In many districts they have primary responsibility for discovery rulings.

this provision becomes a loophole that renders the Rule meaningless; if construed too narrowly, this provision blocks access to discovery for meritorious lawsuits. What should it mean that an allegation is "likely" to have evidentiary support?

6. We have thus far been considering problems relating to inadequate factual bases for claims and defenses. Now shift to the violation in *Gerbode*. What did the plaintiffs do wrong? How is their violation different from that of the plaintiffs in *Business Guides*?

a. Why were the *Gerbode* lawyers punished for filing the complaint?

b. Suppose Judge Tashima in *Gerbode* had learned at the sanctions hearing that the plaintiffs themselves — sophisticated clients, let us assume — had urged their lawyers to allege the unfounded RICO claims, hoping to frighten defendants into a quick settlement. Explain why, even on these facts, the judge could not have imposed sanctions on the clients under Rule 11.

7. If the lawyer's problem in the *Business Guides* situation is knowing how much investigation is enough, the analogous problem in the *Gerbode* situation is knowing when a legal contention is warranted, or is at least "nonfrivolous."

a. Again, courts tend to describe offenses in rather conclusory terms:

> [Lawyer] represented his law firm . . . in this action. His representations to the Court concerning the law in the Third Circuit on the legal certainty test [for whether the amount of damages requisite to qualify for diversity jurisdiction], the critical issue on the summary judgment motion, were less than complete and reflect careless research. . . .
>
> As an experienced attorney, he should have evaluated his legal position concerning the availability of punitive damages more carefully. Furthermore, as an experienced attorney, he should have realized that the Release Agreement would preclude any recovery against [defendant] for fraudulent misrepresentation. . . .

Furman & Halpern v. Nexgen Software Corp., 1994 U.S. Dist. LEXIS 8686, *17-*18 (E.D. Pa. 1994).

b. That isn't very helpful, is it? But is it possible to be more specific?

8. *Furman & Halpern* wrestles with applying the standard of frivolousness to particular circumstances. What is that standard? The Advisory Committee notes report that the standard is objective: Would a competent lawyer think the argument was a decent one? Most of the cases imposing sanctions for violations of this provision have been extreme — sanctioning lawyers for failing to do any research whatsoever (*Gerbode*), or for relying on argumentation that was little more than assertion: "Plaintiff's counsel has advanced the arguments contained in his law review article to the Ninth, First, Fifth, and District of Columbia Circuits with no success,

and has provided this court with no arguments that the Second Circuit would receive these arguments with any more favor. . . ." Knipe v. Skinner, 146 F.R.D. 58 (N.D.N.Y. 1993).

9. Having surveyed the kinds of behavior punished by Rule 11, one needs to understand the circumstances that trigger its application. Consider the following scenarios and decide whether the behavior is subject to Rule 11:

a. Party calls Opponent on the telephone, threatening her with a lawsuit that Party knows to be groundless. May Party be sanctioned under Rule 11? Is there a different result if Lawyer rather than Party makes the telephone call?

b. Party files groundless discovery motion. May Party be sanctioned under Rule 11? (See Rule 11(d).)

Enforcing Rule 11

10. Besides illustrating one form of behavior that violates Rule 11, *Gerbode* discusses several of the procedures attending its enforcement. One of the most significant, in Rule 11(c)(1)(A), is a "safe harbor" provision.

a. Be sure you understand how the safe-harbor provision works in an ordinary case. Your adversary signs and files a meritless paper. If you wish to invoke Rule 11 against her, what steps must you take?

b. Rule 11 was drafted with complaints (as well as other papers and pleadings) in mind, but Judge Tashima believes that the safe-harbor provision sometimes does not work well when the document is a complaint. Follow his reasoning. Under ordinary circumstances, how long does a defendant have before she must answer a complaint? See Rule 12(1)(A). Why is it a problem that the defendant must answer the complaint before the plaintiff's time for withdrawing it has expired?

c. Consider now another wrinkle, introduced by Rule 4(d)(3) and Rule 12(a)(1)(B): a defendant who waives service of process (a procedure described in Chapter II) thereby extends the time to answer from twenty to sixty days. Does that suggest a paradox: that a defendant served with what he believes to be an entirely meritless complaint ought to waive service of process? Explain the tactical reasoning behind such a decision.

d. Note that the safe-harbor provision does not apply to sanctions imposed by the court on its own initiative. Rule 11(c)(1)(B). *Business Guides* was such a case. But the *Business Guides* court did something quite unusual when it initiated an independent inquiry into the factual bases of the complaint. One would expect to find Rule 11(c)(1)(B) invoked more frequently as to legal than as to factual contentions, because judges are likely to recognize absurd legal contentions when they see them.

Sanctions

11. Assume that either the judge or the opposition believes a lawyer has violated one of the provisions of Rule 11(b). After the appropriate procedural opportunities (notice and a chance to withdraw, opportunity to respond to charges), the judge finds that the lawyer has violated the rule. What follows from that finding? See Rule 11(c)(2).

a. Need the court impose any sanction at all? Rule 11(c) provides that "the court *may* . . . impose an appropriate sanction. . . ."

b. The current version of the Rule requires that sanctions be "limited to what is sufficient to deter repetition" of the offending conduct and mentions nonmonetary sanctions (presumably such as requiring the lawyers to take additional training). Some appellate courts have urged trial courts to consider "which sanction 'constitutes the least severe sanction that will adequately deter the undesirable conduct.' " Kirk Capital Corp. v. Bailey, 16 F.3d 1485, 1490 (8th Cir. 1994) (quoting Pope v. Federal Express, 974 F.2d 982, 984 (8th Cir. 1992).

One district court, faced with the prospect of invoking Rule 11 under these circumstances, remarked, "This Court is disinclined to bring Rule 11's mechanisms into play to consider the imposition of nonmonetary sanctions on [Opponent] or her lawyer (an action that would most likely compel [Opponent] to send good money after bad by having to become involved in such proceedings) — it is enough that the publication of this opinion labels [Opponent's] counsel's effort for what it is." Pierre v. Inroads, Inc., 858 F. Supp. 769, 775 (N.D. Ill. 1994).

c. Even if awarded, monetary sanctions are presumptively to be paid to the court — like a criminal fine — rather than to the adversary — like a civil damage award. *Gerbode* illustrates this procedure in action. These changes thus effectively shift the focus from compensation of the adversary to deterrence of future conduct.

d. In spite of this presumption, a court may, and some courts have, concluded that an award of attorneys' fees to the other side was the only appropriate sanction. *Gerbode* again provides an example.

12. Consider the incentives created by the current Rule. Party files a groundless paper. Opponent challenges it, giving Party the required notice and 21-day period before filing the Rule 11 motion; Party perseveres in groundless paper. Opponent makes the necessary substantive motion to defeat the groundless paper (12(b)(6) motion — Rule 56 motion, etc.). Ideally, Party would like to be able to collect its legal fees for opposing the groundless paper. But the court need not impose any sanction at all; if it does, that sanction may not require any payment to Party. Moreover, Party cannot combine its Rule 11 motion with the substantive motion because of the separate-motion requirement. Under those circumstances, if Party has already won the underlying lawsuit, is it worth the effort to

bring a separate Rule 11 motion? Will Rule 11 motions be confined to "grudge matches" between lawyers who have developed strong personal animosity in the course of litigation?

13. Rule 11 does not exhaust a court's power to impose punishment for improper behavior. In Chambers v. NASCO, Inc., 501 U.S. 32 (1991), the Court upheld a district court's "inherent power" to impose nearly $1 million in fees and costs on a litigant. After agreeing to sell a television station, Chambers changed his mind. When the buyer sued for specific performance, Chambers took a series of actions designed to thwart the court's ability to order the transfer: He transferred the property to others; failed to disclose the transfer to the court; refused to permit plaintiff to inspect records; engaged in a series of meritless motions, depositions, and the like; sought to persuade other government agencies to block the transfer; and disconnected equipment. The district court ordered the party, not his lawyer, to pay the fees, finding specifically that some of the punished behavior would not have been covered by Rule 11.

a. Is there conduct one could punish under Rule 11 that could not be punished under *Chambers*?

b. Lockary v. Kayfetz, 974 F.2d 1166 (9th Cir. 1992), invoked inherent powers to punish an entity that had been neither the party nor the lawyer in the lawsuit. The entity, a nonprofit foundation, had organized and financed the underlying litigation, which the court had found to be without merit. Explain why a court could not reach this result under Rule 11.

b.   Disfavored Claims?

Even if a lawyer has carefully adhered to the requirements of Rule 11, complaints in some categories get closer scrutiny. The question in such cases is whether that heightened scrutiny violates either the letter or the spirit of Rule 8.

(1)   Fraud

Olsen v. Pratt & Whitney Aircraft
136 F.3d 273 (2d Cir. 1998)

JACOBS, J.

Andrew Olsen sued his former employer, Pratt & Whitney ("P & W"), claiming that P & W beguiled him with promises of job security into revoking his participation in a special early retirement plan, and then broke its promises by firing him soon thereafter. The complaint alleged a variety of claims, all of which were dismissed. . . .

On appeal, Olsen advances a single argument: that the district court erred in dismissing his common law fraud claim (with prejudice) on the ground that it is preempted by the Employee Retirement Income Security Act of 1974 ("ERISA"). We affirm the district court's dismissal of Olsen's fraud claim on other grounds and do not reach the issue of whether the claim is preempted by ERISA. We conclude that Olsen's fraud claim fails to satisfy the pleading requirements of Fed. R. Civ. 9(b), and we remand to permit Olsen one more opportunity to seek leave from the district court to file a well-pleaded amended complaint. . . .

Olsen was employed by P & W from 1956 to 1992. When he left, he was a Fire Lieutenant in the Fire and Security Department.

On November 1, 1991, P & W notified Olsen, then age 54, that he was eligible to participate in the company's Voluntary Retirement Incentive Program ("VRIP"). The program granted special retirement benefits, including an increased pension and a $10,000 lump-sum cash payment, to eligible employees who agreed to take early retirement and to waive certain claims against the company, including any right to sue under the Age Discrimination in Employment Act ("ADEA").

On December 18, 1991, Olsen enrolled in the VRIP, signed the required waiver of claims, and agreed to retire on March 31, 1992. He alleges that soon afterward, P & W employees represented to him that his job was secure and recommended that he revoke his participation in the VRIP. On January 2, 1992, Olsen revoked his participation in the VRIP, allegedly in reliance on these representations. On September 7, 1992, Olsen was terminated, a step that P & W ascribes to a reduction in force.

The complaint alleged six claims. Four (an ADEA claim, a breach of contract claim, and two claims of violations of the seniority system) have no bearing on this appeal. The fifth, asserted under ERISA, alleged that the document which purported to revoke Olsen's participation in the VRIP was void because it was signed after the contractual and statutory period for revocation expired, and that P & W "violated . . . ERISA by breaching the waiver contract and not providing any of the consideration falling under ERISA." The district court dismissed this ERISA claim, and Olsen has not challenged that dismissal on appeal. Olsen's sole ground for appeal is the dismissal of his common law fraud claim, which alleges that he relied, "to his detriment, on the defendant's inducements of job security when he agreed to continue to work for the defendant" and give up the VRIP benefits. The district court dismissed the fraud claim with prejudice, finding that it was preempted by ERISA. The court noted:

> The [fraud] count. . . . is essentially a common law claim of misrepresentation and is a reformulation of the [ERISA] count. Olsen asserts that he was induced to revoke the VRIP based on false promises of future job security. . . . The court finds that this count relates to the VRIP plan, as "the alleged misconduct is intertwined with the refusal to pay benefits". . . .

On appeal, Olsen challenges the district court's dismissal of his state common law fraud claim. . . .

It is well settled that "we may affirm on any grounds for which there is a record sufficient to permit conclusions of law, including grounds not relied upon by the district court." We agree with P & W that Olsen's fraud allegations fail to comply with the heightened pleading requirements of Fed. R. Civ. P. 9(b). . . .

We have held that "when a complaint charges fraud, it must (1) detail the statements . . . that the plaintiff contends are fraudulent, (2) identify the speaker, (3) state where and when the statements . . . were made and (4) explain why the statements . . . are fraudulent."

Olsen's allegations of fraud are conclusory and lacking in particulars. He alleges that "the defendant, through its agents, servants, and employees, advised, counseled, and recommended to Olsen" that he revoke his participation in the VRIP and "represented and warranted" that "he had the right to the continued expectation that he would not be terminated involuntarily." Compl. ¶33. Further, Olsen alleges that he "never was told by [P & W] that if [he] continued to work, he would be terminated shortly thereafter." He claims that he relied on these false representations and misleading omissions in revoking his participation in the VRIP. Olsen does not specify what was said, or the terms of the advice, counsel, and recommendations (as opposed to the mere gist); who said it, and what positions were held by these "agents, servants and employees" whose words are alleged to bind or be imputed to the company; where and when these words of advice, counsel, and recommendation were imparted to the plaintiff; and why these predictions of future events were fraudulent (as opposed to wrong prognostications). Thus the complaint falls far short of the requirements of Fed. R. Civ. P. 9(b), and must be dismissed.

The deficiencies in Olsen's complaint obscure the contours of this fraud claim, its relation to the ERISA plan, or even whether Olsen can actually sufficiently plead his claim. Given the complicated nature of the ERISA preemption inquiry, and its ramifications, we will not attempt to resolve it without a properly pleaded claim.

Plaintiffs whose complaints are dismissed pursuant to Rule 9(b) are typically given an opportunity to amend their complaint. Accordingly, although we agree with the district court that the complaint should have been dismissed, we vacate the judgment and remand with directions to the district court to afford the plaintiff the opportunity to file an amended complaint that complied with Rule 9(b). . . .

NOTES AND PROBLEMS

1. The district court did not rule on whether the fraud count was pleaded with sufficient particularity. Why not? And why did the appellate court do so?

a. In many areas both state and federal law operate; environmental regulation provides one example. In others, either state or federal law is supreme, leaving no room for regulation by the other unit of government. "Preemption" describes a situation in which federal law entirely occupies an area, leaving no room for supplementary state law. Whether federal legislation (here, ERISA) preempts state law will often be a question of legislative intent: Did Congress mean to occupy the area entirely, or does the legislation leave room for state law?

b. Why did the appellate court decide the case based on Rule 9(b) without reaching the issue on which the district court had decided the case?

c. What will happen to the case after this decision?

2. What allegations were omitted improperly from the complaint?

a. When plaintiff is given an opportunity to amend, what kind of allegations should he try to include?

b. Rule 9(b) most often functions to doom complaints that would survive scrutiny under Rule 8(a) standards. Here Rule 9(b) operates to rescue — perhaps temporarily — a complaint that might otherwise have been dismissed. The rescue occurs because of a well-established principle that a plaintiff who has any prayer of conforming his complaint to pleading requirements should be given a chance to amend the pleading. The opinion refers to this practice in regard to Rule 9(b), but it applies to virtually all complaints. As a consequence, a district court will almost always be reversed for abuse of discretion if it fails to allow a plaintiff who wants to amend at least one opportunity to do so.

3. Why does Rule 9(b) require more specificity in pleading? Consider a fraud claim from two vantage points, that of plaintiff and that of defendant.

a. For plaintiff the problem is that, if fraud occurred, plaintiff is likely still to be in the dark about some of the salient facts. Consider what

Olsen's lawyer might want to find out from Pratt & Whitney. Plaintiff wants to get to discovery to uncover those facts and prove that defendant was misrepresenting the facts. But discovery will be unavailable if the complaint is dismissed for failure to plead with sufficient specificity to comply with Rule 9(b).

b. For defendant the problem is that fraud cases are both serious (as intentional torts they carry punitive damages) and time-consuming. Consider how *Olsen*'s settlement value to the defendant changes if plaintiff can successfully plead it as a fraud suit. Inquiry into all the potentially material facts surrounding a transaction will involve a great deal of discovery, and punitive damages are a risky wild card for defendants. Defendants will therefore argue for a high threshold for fraud complaints, a threshold suggesting that plaintiff has a good case, before opening up discovery.

c. Does Rule 9(b) properly resolve this conflict?

4. Why doesn't the rationale of Rule 9(b) apply to other cases as well? Why shouldn't plaintiffs seeking to recover for negligence have to allege in detail the acts asserted to constitute lack of due care?

5. Rule 9 is the only federal Rule setting forth special pleading rules for a disfavored kind of claim. Other jurisdictions have found other ways to prevent or discourage some kinds of claims. For example, California Code of Civil Procedure §425.13(a) (Deering 1995) provides that no complaint may state a claim for punitive damages against a health care provider "unless the court enters an order allowing an amended pleading," and that the court may enter such an order only after "supporting and opposing affidavits [show] that the plaintiff has established that there is a substantial probability that the plaintiff will prevail. . . ." Like Rule 9(b), such procedures seek to prevent insubstantial claims from advancing to discovery. Are such provisions desirable? Would the California approach (amend after presenting evidence) be preferable to the federal approach (plead specifically)?

6. Congress has concluded that for some fraud claims Rule 9(b) does not go far enough. The Private Securities Litigation Reform Act of 1995 sets forth elaborate pleading requirements that apply to claims alleging fraud under federal securities statutes.

a. Among those requirements are that the complaint "shall specify each statement alleged to have been misleading, the reason or reasons why the statement is misleading, and, if an allegation regarding the statement or omission is made on information and belief, the complaint shall state with particularity all facts on which that belief is formed." 15 U.S.C. §78u-4(b)(1)(B). The same statute modifies the requirements of Rule 9(b) as to states of mind, requiring that a plaintiff "state with particularity facts giving rise to a strong inference that the defendant acted with the required state of mind." Id. at (b)(2). The Act also requires the district court to stay any discovery until any challenge to the pleadings has been decided.

b. Specificity and length are not synonymous. As one court noted, after dismissing a long complaint that appended 62 newspaper articles, "A complaint can be long-winded, even prolix, without pleading with particularity. Indeed, such a garrulous style is not an uncommon mask for an absence of detail. The amended complaint here, although long, states little with particularity." Williams v. WMX Technologies Inc., 112 F.3d 175 (5th Cir. 1997).

(2)   Civil rights

Since the 1950s a number of new bases of civil liability have evolved. Among the most important and interesting are claims based on violation of the plaintiff's civil rights — rights that encompass discrimination based on race, religion, ethnicity, gender, age, and disability. Some of these rights have flowed from detailed statutes; others have evolved from judicial decisions construing the Constitution itself and more general statutes. One of the most important of these general statutes, 42 U.S.C. §1983, permits a suit against those who act "under color of law" (that is, in some official or quasi-official capacity) to deprive persons of constitutional rights. We shall encounter this statute, which has a broad reach, in several cases; it has proved an especially fertile source of pleading disputes. It has also been treated in ways that sometimes look as if courts are disfavoring civil rights claims.

An important aspect of the statute concerns the liability of various government officials. In a complex series of cases, the Supreme Court has said: (a) that such officials are liable if their actions or orders violate constitutional rights but (b) that they enjoy a "qualified immunity" if those actions took place under a reasonable misapprehension of the law. To use an example, a school principal who unlawfully ordered the search of student lockers would be able to avoid liability if, when she gave the order to search, she reasonably believed that the order was constitutional, even if it was not. This "immunity," the Supreme Court has said, is more than an ordinary defense; it is "the right not to stand trial," and, in particular, the right not to be subjected to discovery proceedings. Mitchell v. Forsyth, 472 U.S. 511, 526 (1985). Some courts have enforced such immunities by requiring more specific pleading, so that plaintiff can show that the official could not reasonably have believed his acts to be constitutional. The next case involves a struggle between these substantive rules of immunity and the pleading standards of Rule 8(a).

Leatherman v. Tarrant County Narcotics Intelligence & Coordination Unit

507 U.S. 163 (1993)

Chief Justice REHNQUIST delivered the opinion of the Court.

We granted certiorari to decide whether a federal court may apply a "heightened pleading standard" — more stringent than the usual pleading requirements of Rule 8(a) of the Federal Rules of Civil Procedure — in civil rights cases alleging municipal liability under 42 U.S.C. §1983. We hold it may not.

We review here a decision granting a motion to dismiss, and therefore must accept as true all the factual allegations in the complaint. This action arose out of two separate incidents involving the execution of search warrants by local law enforcement officers. Each involved the forcible entry into a home based on the detection of odors associated with the manufacture of narcotics. One homeowner claimed that he was assaulted by the officers after they had entered; another claimed that the police had entered her home in her absence and killed her two dogs. Plaintiffs sued several local officials in their official capacity and the county and two municipal corporations that employed the police officers involved in the incidents, asserting that the police conduct had violated the Fourth Amendment to the United States Constitution. The stated basis for municipal liability under Monell v. New York City Dept. of Social Services was the failure of these bodies to adequately train the police officers involved.

The United States District Court for the Northern District of Texas ordered the complaints dismissed because they failed to meet the "heightened pleading standard" required by the decisional law of the Court of Appeals for the Fifth Circuit. . . . [W]e granted certiorari, to resolve a conflict among the Courts of Appeals concerning the applicability of a heightened pleading standard to §1983 actions alleging municipal liability. . . . We now reverse.

Respondents seek to defend the Fifth Circuit's application of a more rigorous pleading standard on two grounds. First, respondents claim that municipalities' freedom from respondeat superior liability necessarily includes immunity from suit. In this sense, respondents assert, municipalities are no different from state or local officials sued in their individual capacity. Respondents reason that a more relaxed pleading requirement would subject municipalities to expensive and time-consuming discovery in every §1983 case, eviscerating their immunity from suit and disrupting municipal functions. This argument wrongly equates freedom from liability with immunity from suit. . . . These decisions make it quite clear that, unlike various government officials, municipalities do not enjoy immunity from suit. . . . In short, a municipality can be sued under §1983, but it cannot be held liable unless a municipal policy or custom caused the constitutional injury. We thus have no occasion to consider whether our qualified immunity jurisprudence would require a heightened pleading in cases involving individual government officials. . . .

Second, respondents contend that the Fifth Circuit's heightened pleading standard is not really that at all. According to respondents, the degree of factual specificity required of a complaint by the Federal Rules of Civil Procedure varies according to the complexity of the underlying substantive law. To establish municipal liability under §1983, respondents argue, a plaintiff must do more than plead a single instance of misconduct. This requirement, respondents insist, is consistent with a plaintiff's Rule 11 obligation to make a reasonable prefiling inquiry into the facts.

But examination of the Fifth Circuit's decision in this case makes it quite evident that the "heightened pleading standard" is just what it purports to be: a more demanding rule for pleading a complaint under §1983 than for pleading other kinds of claims. . . : "[W]e require of trial judges that they demand that the plaintiff's complaints state with factual detail and particularity the basis for the claim which necessarily includes why the defendant-official cannot successfully maintain the defense of immunity." Elliott v. Perez, 751 F.2d 1472, 1473 (5th Cir. 1985). . . .

We think that it is impossible to square the "heightened pleading standard" applied by the Fifth Circuit in this case with the liberal system of "notice pleading" set up by the Federal Rules. Rule 8(a)(2) requires that a complaint include only "a short and plain statement of the claim showing that the pleader is entitled to relief." In Conley v. Gibson, 355 U.S. 41, 47 (1957), we said in effect that the Rule meant what it said:

> The Federal Rules of Civil Procedure do not require a claimant to set out in detail the facts upon which he bases his claim. To the contrary, all the Rules require is "a short and plain statement of the claim" that will give the defendant fair notice of what the plaintiff's claim is and the grounds upon which it rests.

Rule 9(b) does impose a particularity requirement in two specific instances. It provides that "in all averments of fraud or mistake, the circumstances constituting fraud or mistake shall be stated with particularity." Thus, the Federal Rules do address in Rule 9(b) the question of the need for greater particularity in pleading certain actions, but do not include among the enumerated actions any reference to complaints alleging municipal liability under §1983. *Expressio unius est exclusio alterius.*[*]

The phenomenon of litigation against municipal corporations based on claimed constitutional violations by their employees dates from our decision in *Monell*, where we for the first time construed §1983 to allow such municipal liability. Perhaps if Rules 8 and 9 were rewritten today, claims against municipalities under §1983 might be subjected to the added specificity requirement of Rule 9(b). But that is a result which must be obtained by the process of amending the Federal Rules, and not by judicial interpretation. In the absence of such an amendment, federal courts and litigants must rely on summary judgment and control of discovery to weed out unmeritorious claims sooner rather than later.

The judgment of the Court of Appeals is reversed. . . .

NOTES AND PROBLEMS

1. At one level *Leatherman* is very easy — maybe deceptively easy — to understand.

a. Of course no court is free to ignore the Rules, and the Rules set forth a well-known generally applicable standard of pleading — the "short, plain statement of a claim."

b. Why then was the Fifth Circuit engaging in an apparent act of lawlessness by requiring more detail? As noted in the text introducing *Leatherman*, the law of official immunities and defenses to civil rights claims is both elaborate and formidable. The immunities create a problem because they limit but do not entirely bar suits against officials.

c. We run a litigation system premised on the notion that most cases will sort themselves out only in discovery. Discovery and summary judgment thus seem to be the obvious stages at which to sort out immunity claims. But the Supreme Court has repeatedly said that the immunity enjoyed by individual defendants is not just a defense to the lawsuit but the "right not to be sued" — a "right" that includes freedom from the entanglements of discovery. How then can courts respect these immunities?

d. If one cannot use discovery, to sort out these suits, pleading is the only available tool. Such reasoning has led several Circuits besides the Fifth to impose heightened pleading requirements on plaintiffs suing

[*A canon of statutory construction: Expressing only one of two related ideas implies the exclusion of the other. — ED.]

individual governmental officials. See, e.g., Branch v. Tunnell, 937 F.2d 1382, 1386 (9th Cir. 1991):

> In order to survive a motion to dismiss [certain civil rights claims], plaintiffs must state in their complaints nonconclusory allegations setting forth evidence of unlawful intent. The allegations of facts must be specific and concrete enough to enable the defendants to prepare a response and, where appropriate, a motion for summary judgment.

Notice that *Leatherman* carefully avoids the question of heightened pleading requirements for individual — as opposed to municipal — defendants. After *Leatherman* the Ninth Circuit concluded that heightened pleading for individual defendants was still lawful. Branch v. Tunnell, 14 F.3d 449 (9th Cir. 1994), cert. denied, 512 U.S. 1219 (1994). The Fifth Circuit, perhaps a bit wary after being unanimously reversed in *Leatherman*, was more cautious. In Schultea v. Wood, 47 F.3d 1427 (5th Cir. 1995) (en banc), that Circuit decided that it would allow plaintiffs bringing §1983 suits against officials to plead broadly in conformity with Rule 8(a) but would then require a seldom-used pleading, the "reply" to the answer, in which the plaintiff would have to set out the attack on official immunity more specifically. See Rule 7(a). Who is right? Is there a solution short of a change in the substantive law or an amendment to the Rules?

2. At the end of the opinion the Court speculates that a revision of Rule 9 might be in order, with official immunities added to the cases required to be pleaded with specificity. Should that happen? Or should Rule 9(b) simply be repealed, allowing fraud and civil rights defendants required to take their chances with everyone else?

4. Allocating the Elements

Thus far we have considered the regime of notice pleading and its requirements and the added considerations introduced by Rule 11. An important piece of the picture is still missing. The substantive law tells the parties in general what issues matter in the lawsuit: In a contract claim, whether the parties agreed, whether the agreement reflected a bargain, and so on; in a negligence claim, whether the defendant fell below ordinary standards of care, whether that carelessness caused harm to the plaintiff, and so on. But knowing what issues will matter in the suit does not answer all the questions in a system driven by party initiative, for one must also ask which party has the responsibility for which of those issues. To put that question into technical procedural terms, which party has the *burden* of pleading, producing evidence, or proving a particular element of a claim?

The U.S. legal system assigns these tasks to the parties and penalizes them for their failure to fulfill their assignments. As the next case demonstrates, logic does not entirely explain the system of assigning burdens to parties. One could imagine a system in which the plaintiff identified the general contours of the claim and then left it to the judge to direct whatever investigations were necessary. Many civil law countries operate under such a system, and at early common law the jury was told to decide the claims based on its own knowledge of events or to conduct whatever inquiries seemed likely to uncover the truth. Those two systems do not need to allocate burdens between the parties. Only when trials become a structured contest between two adversaries, each of whom tries to demonstrate the truth or falsity of various propositions, does a second-order question emerge: Which party bears initial responsibility for which element of a given claim? That question arises at several points in litigation and first surfaces at the pleading stage. Where the burden of pleading and proving particular elements of a claim rests may be important, both as a procedural and a substantive matter.

One final note is in order. Lawyers usually distinguish among three burdens: the burden of pleading, the burden of production, and the burden of persuasion. To have the burden of pleading means that one must allege that element of the claim or defense; one cannot expect the other party to do so. To have the burden of production means that at trial one must produce evidence — witnesses, documents, and the like — that tend to demonstrate the proposition at stake. To have the burden of persuasion in a civil case means, generally, that one must persuade the trier of fact that one's version of the facts is more likely than not to be true. Usually, though not invariably, the three burdens go together: The party with the burden of pleading an element will also have the burden of producing evidence to prove that element, and, assuming the facts are disputed, of persuading the trier that its version of the facts is more likely than not to be true. Gomez v. Toledo purports to be only about the first of these burdens, that of pleading. For the reader of this text, *Gomez* has another feature: it was the case that gave to defendants the burden of pleading good faith immunity in §1983 cases, thus creating the tension explored in *Leatherman* and its sequels.

Gomez v. Toledo

446 U.S. 635 (1980)

Mr. Justice MARSHALL delivered the opinion of the Court.

The question presented is whether, in an action brought under 42 U.S.C. §1983 against a public official whose position might entitle him to qualified immunity, a plaintiff must allege that the official has acted in bad faith in order to state a claim for relief or, alternatively, whether the defendant must plead good faith as an affirmative defense.

I

Petitioner Carlos Rivera Gomez brought this action against respondent, the Superintendent of the Police of the Commonwealth of Puerto Rico, contending that respondent had violated his right to procedural due process by discharging him from employment with the Police Department's Bureau of Criminal Investigation. Basing jurisdiction on 28 U.S.C. §1343(3),[2] petitioner alleged the following facts in his complaint.[3] Petitioner had been employed as an agent with the Puerto Rican police since 1968. In April 1975, he submitted a sworn statement to his supervisor in which he asserted that two other agents had offered false evidence for use in a criminal case under their investigation. As a result of this statement, petitioner was immediately transferred from the Criminal Investigation Corps for the Southern Area to Police Headquarters in San Juan, and a few weeks later to the Police Academy in Gurabo, where he was given no investigative authority. In the meantime respondent ordered an investigation of petitioner's claims, and the Legal Division of the Police Department concluded that all of petitioner's factual allegations were true.

In April 1976, while still stationed at the Police Academy, petitioner was subpoenaed to give testimony in a criminal case arising out of the evidence that petitioner had alleged to be false. At the trial petitioner, appearing as a defense witness, testified that the evidence was in fact false. As a result of this testimony, criminal charges, filed on the basis of information furnished by respondent, were brought against petitioner for the allegedly unlawful wiretapping of the agents' telephones. Respondent suspended petitioner in May 1976 and discharged him without a hearing in July. In October, the District Court of Puerto Rico found no probable cause to believe that petitioner was guilty of the allegedly unlawful wiretapping and, upon appeal by the prosecution, the Superior Court affirmed. Petitioner in turn sought review of his discharge before the Investigation, Prosecution, and Appeals Commission of Puerto Rico, which, after a hearing, revoked the discharge order rendered by respondent and ordered that petitioner be reinstated with back pay.

---

2. That section grants the federal district courts jurisdiction "[t]o redress the deprivation, under color of any State law, statute, ordinance, regulation, custom or usage, of any right, privilege or immunity secured by the Constitution of the United States or by any Act of Congress providing for equal rights of citizens or of all persons within the jurisdiction of the United States."

3. At this stage of the proceedings, of course, all allegations of the complaint must be accepted as true.

Based on the foregoing factual allegations, petitioner brought this suit for damages, contending that his discharge violated his right to procedural due process, and that it had caused him anxiety, embarrassment, and injury to his reputation in the community. In his answer, respondent denied a number of petitioner's allegations of fact and asserted several affirmative defenses. Respondent then moved to dismiss the complaint for failure to state a cause of action, see Fed. Rule Civ. Proc. 12(b)(6), and the District Court granted the motion. Observing that respondent was entitled to qualified immunity for acts done in good faith within the scope of his official duties, it concluded that petitioner was required to plead as part of his claim for relief that, in committing the actions alleged, respondent was motivated by bad faith. The absence of any such allegation, it held, required dismissal of the complaint. The United States Court of Appeals for the First Circuit affirmed.

We granted certiorari to resolve a conflict among the courts of appeals.

II

Section 1983 provides a cause of action for "the deprivation of any rights, privileges, or immunities secured by the Constitution and laws" by any person acting "under color of any statute, ordinance, regulation, custom, or usage, of any State or Territory."[6] This statute, enacted to aid in " 'the preservation of human liberty and human rights,' " Owen v. City of Independence, 445 U.S. 622, 636 (1980), reflects a congressional judgment that a "damages remedy against the offending party is a vital component of any scheme for vindicating cherished constitutional guarantees." As remedial legislation, §1983 is to be construed generously to further its primary purpose.

In certain limited circumstances, we have held that public officers are entitled to a qualified immunity from damages liability under §1983. This conclusion has been based on an unwillingness to infer from legislative silence a congressional intention to abrogate immunities that were both "well-established at common law" and "compatible with the purposes of the Civil Rights Act." Finding of immunity have thus been "predicated upon a considered inquiry into the immunity historically accorded the relevant official at common law and the intentions behind

---

6. Section 1983 provides in full: "Every person who, under color of any statute, ordinance, regulation, custom, or usage, of any State or Territory, subjects, or causes to be subjected, any citizen of the United States or other person within the jurisdiction thereof to the deprivation of any rights, privileges, or immunities secured by the Constitution and laws, shall be liable to the person injured in an action at law, suit in equity, or other proper proceeding for redress."

it." Imbler v. Pachtman, 424 U.S. 409, 421 (1976). In Pierson v. Ray, 386 U.S. 547, 555 (1967), for example, we concluded that a police officer would be "excus[ed] from liability for acting under a statute that he reasonably believed to be valid but that was later held unconstitutional, on its face or as applied." And in other contexts we have held, on the basis of "[c]ommon-law tradition . . . and strong public-policy reasons," Wood v. Strickland, 420 U.S. 308, 318 (1975), that certain categories of executive officers should be allowed qualified immunity from liability for acts done on the basis of an objectively reasonable belief that those acts were lawful. See Procunier v. Navarette, 434 U.S. 555 (1978) (prison officials); O'Connor v. Donaldson, 422 U.S. 563 (1975) (superintendent of state hospital); Wood v. Strickland, 420 U.S. 308 (1975) (local school board members); Scheuer v. Rhodes, 416 U.S. 232 (1974) (state Governor and other executive officers). Cf. Owen v. City of Independence, supra (no qualified immunity for municipalities).

Nothing in the language or legislative history of §1983, however, suggests that in an action brought against a public official whose position might entitle him to immunity if he acted in good faith, a plaintiff must allege bad faith in order to state a claim for relief. By the plain terms of §1983, two — and only two — allegations are required in order to state a cause of action under that statute. First, the plaintiff must allege that some person has deprived him of a federal right. Second, he must allege that the person who has deprived him of that right acted under color of state or territorial law. Petitioner has made both of the required allegations. He alleged that his discharge by respondent violated his right to procedural due process, and that respondent acted under color of Puerto Rican law.

Moreover, this Court has never indicated that qualified immunity is relevant to the existence of the plaintiff's cause of action; instead we have described it as a defense available to the official in question. Since qualified immunity is a defense, the burden of pleading it rests with the defendant. See Fed. Rule Civ. Proc. 8(c) (defendant must plead any "matter constituting an avoidance or affirmative defense"); 5 C. Wright & A. Miller, Federal Practice and Procedure §1271 (1969). It is for the official to claim that his conduct was justified by an objectively reasonable belief that it was lawful. We see no basis for imposing on the plaintiff an obligation to anticipate such a defense by stating in his complaint that the defendant acted in bad faith.

Our conclusion as to the allocation of the burden of pleading is supported by the nature of the qualified immunity defense. As our decisions make clear, whether such immunity has been established depends on facts peculiarly within the knowledge and control of the defendant. Thus we have stated that "[i]t is the existence of reasonable grounds for the belief formed at the time and in light of all the circumstances, coupled with good-faith belief, that affords a basis for qualified immunity of executive officers for acts performed in the course of official conduct." Scheuer v. Rhodes. The applicable test focuses not only on whether the official has an objectively reasonable basis for that belief, but also on whether "[t]he official himself [is] acting sincerely and with a belief that he is doing right." Wood v. Strickland. There may be no way for a plaintiff to know in advance whether the official has such a belief or, indeed, whether he will even claim that he does. The existence of a subjective belief will frequently turn on factors which a plaintiff cannot reasonably be expected to know. For example, the official's belief may be based on state or local law, advice of counsel, administrative practice, or some other factor of which the official alone is aware. To impose the pleading burden on the plaintiff would ignore this elementary fact and be contrary to the established practice in analogous areas of the law.[8]

The decision of the Court of Appeals is reversed, and the case is remanded to that court for further proceedings consistent with this opinion.

It is so ordered.

Mr. Justice REHNQUIST joins the opinion of the Court, reading it as he does to leave open the issue of the burden of persuasion, as opposed to the burden of pleading, with respect to a defense of qualified immunity.

NOTES AND PROBLEMS

1. As a point of departure for analyzing the case, test your understanding of demurrers and Rule 12(b)(6) motions by briefly explaining why the assertion in footnote 3 is true.

2. With the fundamentals in mind, the first difficulty in understanding this case is seeing what the fight was about. The difference between a complaint that Toledo would have found sufficient and the one actually filed might have been a matter of a single sentence. Consider the following: "In taking the actions alleged in paragraphs 1-6, Defendant Toledo acted in bad faith." Plaintiff could have added such a sentence when he was given leave to amend by the district court. Instead he incurred many thousands of dollars in costs and fees by taking the case to the Supreme Court.

8. As then-Dean Charles Clark stated over forty years ago, "It seems to be considered only fair that certain types of things which in common law pleading were matters in confession and avoidance — i.e., matters which seemed more or less to admit the general complaint and yet to suggest some other reason why there was no right — must be specifically pleaded in the answer, and that has been a general rule."

a. Why? Recalling that pleadings generally serve as a blueprint for trial, consider what plaintiff might have thought was at stake.

b. Recalling that discovery would be the next stage of the case, consider what defendant may have thought was at stake.

c. And, with the advantage of hindsight gained from *Leatherman*, supra page 442, one can see that the battle in *Gomez* was a mere hint at the pleading battles to come.

3. Once one understands why the parties thought this issue was worth disputing, one then has to confront the Court's resolution of it.

a. What does the Court mean when it calls good faith an affirmative defense? What consequences does that have for the parties and for future parties bringing or defending such a claim?

b. Why should "qualified immunity for actions in good faith" be an affirmative defense rather than a part of plaintiff's claim?

c. Much scholarly and some judicial analysis of burdens suggests that courts resolve most disputes about burdens of pleading and proof by using value-free analyses. While courts sometimes write in value-free terms (there are hints of such language in *Gomez*), such discourse is deceptive. At root, decisions about burdens of pleading and proof are decisions about which party, in a close case, should win. The answer to that question is anything but value-free. Yet courts frequently express only the value-neutral features of their decisions, and the student accordingly needs to master that discourse.

4. *Gomez* predates *Leatherman*, supra page 442, and Schultea v. Wood, noted at page 445 (holding that while plaintiff may plead a §1983 case generally, once defendant asserts good faith immunity as a defense, plaintiff must reply to the answer). All deal with the same issue, the immunity defense available to an official defendant sued under §1983. Consider how the three cases would interact today.

a. Officer Gomez files his complaint, in which he may allege in general terms (recall *Leatherman*) the claim that he was denied due process.

b. Superintendent Toledo must plead good faith immunity as a defense.

c. Now what? After *Schultea*, what should be Superintendent Toledo's next move, and what should the judge do? After *Schultea*, is the plaintiff any better off than he would have been if *Gomez* court had held that the plaintiff had the burden of pleading bad faith?

5. At the time of *Gomez* the good faith defense consisted of two elements: (1) that the defendant subjectively believed in the propriety of his actions; and (2) that such a belief was objectively reasonable. In *Gomez*, defendant Toledo could have maintained such a defense only if he showed that: (1) he believed that he did not need to give Gomez a hearing; and (2) this belief was reasonable. Since *Gomez*, the Court has redefined the good faith defense. It now consists only of the objective

reasonableness of the defendant's actions. Harlow v. Fitzgerald, 457 U.S. 800 (1982). If one believed that the Court's primary reason for assigning the burden of pleading good faith to the defendant was that he had easier access to his own mental processes, the changed definition of "good faith" might lead one to expect that the plaintiff would now have the burden of showing bad faith. That has not occurred so far. Does that tell us something about the real reasons for assigning burdens?

6. Try your hand at a couple of run-of-the-mill problems in assigning burdens. Where should the burden of pleading lie in these cases? On what theory?

a. Adams, a lawyer, sues his cousin, Davis, for professional services. Who must allege that the services were (or were not) intended as a gift?

b. Bellows, a disc jockey, sues his employer, WFCP, for failure to pay the amount of overtime compensation required by the Fair Labor Standards Act. Who must allege that Bellows is (or is not) a professional employee and therefore is not (or is) subject to the act?

7. A typical construction contract contains a number of promises by the contractor. If a contractor sues a homeowner for failure to make the payments under the contract, must the contractor allege specific performance of those conditions that are the subject of the homeowner's complaints or must he allege something else? See Rule 9(c).

8. Assume E sues R for breach of an oral employment contract, but the statute of frauds requires all employment contracts to be in writing. Or assume P sues D for damages suffered in an accident that occurred in 1992, and the statute of limitations for negligence actions is two years. Although both the statute of frauds and statute of limitations are listed as affirmative defenses in Rule 8(c), the complaints may be said to include "built-in" affirmative defenses — that is, the basis for the affirmative defense is clear from the complaint. In such a case, plaintiff may be required to negate the built-in defense by an additional allegation, such as fraud, estoppel, or waiver.

C.   Responding to the Complaint

We already have observed that no a priori reason compels the defendant to respond to the plaintiff's complaint. Instead, defendant simply could be assumed to deny the significant allegations, and no further response would be required. In such a system, any objections to the bringing of the lawsuit or further clarification of issues would be left to a later pretrial stage (for example, by requiring defendant to file a piece of paper at a later date), the pretrial hearing, or the trial itself. In fact, this is precisely the procedure that is followed by small claims courts as well as by some informal dispute settlement mechanisms (for example, arbitration).

Despite this possibility, neither the federal nor state courts have chosen to stop the formal statement of issues with the plaintiff's complaint. Instead, the defendant typically has two opportunities to respond to the complaint. The *pre-answer motion* permits defendant to raise certain types of objections to the action at a very early stage of the litigation. If the defendant makes no such motion or if it is denied, the defendant must file an additional pleading, usually called an *answer*. The answer responds to the allegations of the complaint and asserts any additional information or affirmative claims that the defendant may have against the plaintiff.

NOTES AND PROBLEMS

1. Who draws up the answer?
2. What does he do with the answer once it is drawn up? See Rules 12(a)(2) and 5(a).
3. How long does he have to do it? See Rule 12(a)(1).

1. Pre-Answer Motion

We already have had a chance to consider defendant's possible responses to plaintiff's complaint. Briefly, these responses include: (a) reasons why the court should not proceed with the action; (b) questions as to whether the complaint, even if true, provides a basis for legal relief or whether plaintiff has joined an essential party; (c) denials; (d) affirmative defenses; and (e) requests for clarification and more information. This section will discuss methods by which a defendant can raise and present such responses.

All these responses but (e) — a request for clarification or more information — may be included in the defendant's answer. In addition, Rule 12(b) permits certain defenses to be raised by a pre-answer motion. Read Rule 12(b).

The previous section presented examples of how pre-answer motions can be used both to object to plaintiff's failure to state a claim upon which relief can be granted, Rule 12(b)(6), and to assert the need for a more definite statement of plaintiff's complaint, Rule 12(e). Chapters II and III showed pre-answer motions being used to raise objections to jurisdiction, venue, and service of process. Chapter XIII contains examples of pre-answer motions used to raise questions relating to the failure to join necessary and indispensable parties. Each of these instances concerns questions such as whether the complaint stated a claim, whether jurisdiction was proper, whether other parties may or must be joined and so on, rather than with the actual mechanics of making the motion. Let us now turn to this latter point.

What is a "motion"? Rule 7 states that a motion is a request to the court for an order. Rule 7 does not specify what kinds of documents constitute the motion. Ordinarily a motion consists of four different documents, although in many districts several may be combined in one document. First is the motion itself or, in other words, a request for the specific relief sought. Form 19 is an example of a motion. Second is the notice of the motion. This document tells the opposing party when the motion will be heard. Form 19 is an example of a notice of the motion. In some districts, such as the Southern District of New York, the motion and the notice are combined in a single document. Third, if the motion in question requires or permits affidavits setting forth any factual information necessary for granting the motion, they will be included. (As a test of your understanding, explain why one would not expect a 12(b)(6) motion to have any affidavits.) The affidavit ordinarily will be made by one of the parties or by an attorney for the moving party. Fourth is a memorandum of law explaining, with reference to supporting authorities, the legal basis for the motion.

NOTES AND PROBLEMS

1. A motion — any motion — is a request for a court to make an order of some kind.

a. What kind of order does a defendant seek in a pre-answer motion?

b. When must a pre-answer motion be made?

2. What happens to the defendant's obligation to answer the complaint if he makes a pre-answer motion?

3. Scan Rules 12(b) and 8(c).

a. Does the subject matter of the 12(b) defenses suggest a reason why they are permitted at an early stage of the litigation?

b. Are the issues in 12(b) motions ordinarily factual or legal in nature?

c. Are the factual issues likely to be disputed or to be complex? In answering this question, consider how factual evidence will "get in" the case.

4. What happens if the 12(b) motion is denied?

5. What happens if the 12(b) motion is granted?

6. Rule 12(e), the motion for a more definite statement, is best understood in historical terms. Under early common law and Code pleading systems, the complaint bore much of the weight of narrowing the parties' contentions and exposing the issues in dispute. Under such circumstances it was frequently a fair request, as well as a good tactic, to ask the pleader to "make more definite and certain" his contentions. Such motions served as a form of discovery not otherwise permitted. Though it seems inconsistent with the idea of notice pleading, an analogous motion was carried over into the original Federal Rules; there it proved to be the subject of more judicial rulings than any other part of the Federal Rules, often at the hands of judges unfamiliar with the philosophy underlying the Rules. At present, Rule 12(e) is rarely, and almost never successfully, invoked. If the claim is truly so vague as to make a response impossible, it will be subject to a 12(b)(6) motion. In the far more frequent circumstance, in which the pleader has a good idea what the claim is about but wants to know more about the precise nature of the pleader's case, discovery beckons.

7. Another pre-answer motion, likewise of limited use, is the motion to strike any "redundant, immaterial, impertinent, or scandalous matter." Rule 12(f). Such a motion may be granted if allegations in the complaint have no relation to the case or are unnecessarily confusing: if the complaint is overly long and detailed (especially if it contains excessive evidentiary information) or if allegations are unnecessarily derogatory. See, e.g., Hughes v. Kaiser Jeep Corp., 40 F.R.D. 89, 93 (D.S.C. 1966) (reference to car as "death trap"); Budget Dress Corp. v. ILGWU, 25 F.R.D. 506 (S.D.N.Y. 1959) (defenses based on alleged conspiracy between plaintiff and underworld elements described as "strong arm men" and "racketeers"). It is frequently argued that such motions are not favored, waste time, should not be granted as to background information, and should not be granted if the court is at all in doubt. See, e.g., Fuchs Sugars & Syrups, Inc. v. Amstar Corp., 402 F. Supp. 636 (S.D.N.Y. 1975). Accordingly, the decision to strike may depend on whether the allegations are likely to prejudice the moving party, which might occur if the pleadings will be read or given to the jury, and, if so, whether limiting instructions will be given. Rule 12(f) is necessarily limited by the general pleading standards of Rule 8 and may not be used to enforce technical pleading rules of a bygone era. See generally 5 Wright and Miller §§1382, 1383.

8. Rule 12(f) has a substantive role as well. Assume A's wife is killed in an accident with B, and A sues for wrongful death and seeks punitive damages. If, under the applicable tort law, punitive damages are not recoverable, defendant may move to strike the allegations relating to punitive damages. See Mills v. Fox, 421 F. Supp. 519 (E.D.N.Y. 1976).

In this sense, it is analogous to a Rule 12(b)(6) motion directed to a single allegation. See Fry v. Lamb Rental Tools, 275 F. Supp. 283 (W.D. La. 1967) (claimed damages for sorrow, grief, loss of love, affection, and companionship not recoverable under state law).

9. Rule 12 sets out a fairly elaborate set of "consequences" of making and not making a Rule 12 motion. Rule 12(g) and (h). These consequences can be explored by a careful reading of Rule 12 and the following questions.

a. A sues B. Before answering, B moves to dismiss for failure to state a claim upon which relief can be granted. The motion is denied.

(1) Can B now move to dismiss for improper venue?

(2) Can B now move to dismiss for failure to join an indispensable party?

(3) Can B now move, under Rule 12(e), for a more definite statement?

(4) Can B include the defense of insufficiency of service of process in his answer?

(5) Can B include the defense of failure to join an indispensable party in his answer?

(6) Can B now move to dismiss for lack of subject matter jurisdiction?

b. C sues D. Without making a pre-answer motion, D answers. The answer consists solely of denials of the material elements of the complaint.

(1) Can D move to dismiss for improper venue?

(2) D wants to have the complaint dismissed for failure to state a claim upon which relief can be granted. Rule 12(h)(2) preserves this defense, but it is too late for a pre-answer motion. How does D achieve the desired result? See Rule 12(h)(2) and 12(c).

(3) Can D move three months later to amend her answer to include the defense of improper service of process? See Rule 15(a).

c. E sues F, and, within the proper time, F answers, denying the material elements of the complaint and including the defense of improper venue. What happens to that defense from here on? See Rule 12(d).

2. Answer

If the defendant cannot demur to the complaint (or make an equivalent 12(b)(6) motion) or dispose of it on any of the grounds listed in 12(b), she must respond to its factual allegations. At common law the most common responses were the traverse and the plea in confession and avoidance; they live on, though under their less colorful modern names of denial and affirmative defense. The ensuing sections explore the contours of each.

a. Denials

In most cases, the defendant denies many of the allegations of the complaint. Rule 8(b) and (d). In essence, Rule 8(b) requires the defendant to deny only those allegations that he actually disputes, and Rule 8(d) provides that any allegation that is not denied is deemed admitted.

As in other areas of the law, though, history has tended to affect practices in this area as much as have the rules themselves. At common law, the form of plea called the *general issue* was permitted for many forms of action, especially cases in assumpsit; this plea placed all allegations of the declaration at issue. The modern analogue is the *general denial*, an allegation that denies each and every allegation of the complaint. A more limited form of general denial denies each and every allegation of a specific paragraph or group of paragraphs.

There is nothing bad in theory about the general denial. The problem is that extremely few cases arise in which the defendant can plausibly deny each and every allegation or, as is more common, each and every allegation not relating to the names and citizenship of the parties. Nevertheless, it is still not uncommon for parties to interpose a general denial when they deny the major operative allegations of the complaint. Courts condemn casual, blanket denials because they require parties to spend needless time ferreting out the real items in dispute. A defendant who enters such a general denial may well find himself on the wrong end of a Rule 11 inquiry.

The next case deals with the converse problem — the inclusion of an absolutely accurate denial that proves, however, to be remarkably deceptive. The case asks you to consider the purpose of denials in litigation.

Zielinski v. Philadelphia Piers, Inc.

139 F. Supp. 408 (E.D. Pa. 1956)

VAN DUSEN, J.

Plaintiff requests a ruling that, for the purposes of this case, the motor-driven fork lift operated by Sandy Johnson on February 9, 1953, was owned by defendant and that Sandy Johnson was its agent acting in the course of his employment on that date. The following facts are established by the pleadings, interrogatories, depositions and uncontradicted portions of affidavits:

1. Plaintiff filed his complaint on April 28, 1953, for personal injuries received on February 9, 1953, while working on Pier 96, Philadelphia,

for J.A. McCarthy, as a result of a collision of two motor-driven fork lifts.

2. Paragraph 5 of this complaint stated that "a motor-driven vehicle known as a fork lift or chisel, owned, operated and controlled by the defendant, its agents, servants and employees, was so negligently and carelessly managed . . . that the same . . . did come into contact with the plaintiff causing him to sustain the injuries more fully hereinafter set forth."

3. The "First Defense" of the Answer stated "Defendant . . . (c) denies the averments of paragraph 5. . . ."

4. The motor-driven vehicle known as a fork lift or chisel, which collided with the McCarthy fork lift on which plaintiff was riding, had on it the initials "P.P.I."

5. On February 10, 1953, Carload Contractors, Inc. made a report of this accident to its insurance company, whose policy No. CL 3964 insured Carload Contractors, Inc. against potential liability for the negligence of its employees contributing to a collision of the type described in paragraph 2 above.

6. By letter of April 29, 1953, the complaint served on defendant was forwarded to the above-mentioned insurance company. This letter read as follows:

Gentlemen:

As per telephone conversation today with your office, we attach hereto "Complaint in Trespass" as brought against Philadelphia Piers, Inc. by one Frank Zielinski for supposed injuries sustained by him on February 9, 1953.

We find that a fork lift truck operated by an employee of Carload Contractors, Inc. also insured by yourselves was involved in an accident with another chisel truck, which, was alleged [sic], did cause injury to Frank Zielinski, and same was reported to you by Carload Contractors, Inc. at the time, and you assigned Claim Number OL 0153-94 to this claim.

Should not this Complaint in Trespass be issued against Carload Contractors, Inc. and not Philadelphia Piers, Inc.?

We forward for your handling.

7. Interrogatories 1 to 5 and the answers thereto, which were sworn to by defendant's General Manager on June 12, 1953, and filed on June 22, 1953, read as follows:

1. State whether you have received any information of an injury sustained by the plaintiff on February 9, 1953, South Wharves. If so, state when and from whom you first received notice of such injury. A. We were first notified of this accident on or about February 9, 1953 by Thomas Wilson.

2. State whether you caused an investigation to be made of the circumstances of said injury and if so, state who made such investigation and when it was made. A. We made a very brief investigation on February 9, 1953 and turned the matter over to (our insurance company) for further investigation. . . .

8. At a deposition taken August 18, 1953, Sandy Johnson testified that he was the employee of defendant on February 9, 1953, and had been their employee for approximately fifteen years.

9. At a pre-trial conference held on September 27, 1955, plaintiff first learned that over a year before February 9, 1953, the business of moving freight on piers in Philadelphia, formerly conducted by defendant, had been sold by it to Carload Contractors, Inc. and Sandy Johnson had been transferred to the payroll of this corporation without apparently realizing it, since the nature or location of his work had not changed. . . .

11. Defendant now admits that on February 9, 1953, it owned the fork lift in the custody of Sandy Johnson and that this fork lift was leased to Carload Contractors, Inc. It is also admitted that the pier on which the accident occurred was leased by defendant.

12. There is no indication of action by either party in bad faith and there is no proof of inaccurate statements being made with intent to deceive. Because defendant made a prompt investigation of the accident . . . its insurance company has been representing the defendant since suit was brought, and this company insures Carload Contractors, Inc. also, requiring defendant to defend this suit, will not prejudice it. Under these circumstances, and for the purposes of this action, it is ordered that the following shall be stated to the jury at the trial:

It is admitted that, on February 9, 1953, the towmotor or fork lift bearing the initials "P.P.I." was owned by defendant and that Sandy Johnson was a servant in the employ of defendant and doing its work on that date.

This ruling is based on the following principles:

1. Under the circumstances of this case, the answer contains an ineffective denial of that part of paragraph 5 of the complaint which alleges that "a motor driven vehicle known as a fork lift or chisel (was) owned, operated and controlled by the defendant, its agents, servants and employees."

F.R. Civ. P. 8(b), 28 U.S.C. provides:

A party shall state in short and plain terms his defenses to each claim asserted and shall admit or deny the averments upon which the adverse party relies. . . . Denials shall fairly meet the substance of the averments denied. When a pleader intends in good faith to deny only a part or a qualification of an averment, he shall specify so much of it as is true and material and shall deny only the remainder.

For example, it is quite clear that defendant does not deny the averment in paragraph 5 that the fork lift came into contact with plaintiff, since it admits, in the answers to interrogatories, that an investigation of an occurrence of the accident had been made and that a report dated February 10, 1953, was sent to its insurance company stating "While Frank Zielinski was riding on bumper of chisel and holding rope to secure cargo, the chisel truck collided with another chisel truck operated by Sandy Johnson causing injuries to Frank Zielinski's legs and hurt head of Sandy Johnson." Compliance with the above-mentioned rule required that defendant file a more specific answer than a general denial. A specific denial of parts of this paragraph and specific admission of other parts would have warned plaintiff that he had sued the wrong defendant.

Paragraph 8.23 of Moore's Federal Practice (2nd Edition) Vol. II, p. 1680, says: "In such a case, the defendant should make clear just what he is denying and what he is admitting." This answer to paragraph 5 does not make clear to plaintiff the defenses he must be prepared to meet.

Under circumstances where an improper and ineffective answer has been filed, the Pennsylvania courts have consistently held that an allegation of agency in the complaint requires a statement to the jury that agency is admitted where an attempt to amend the answer is made after the expiration of the period of limitation. Although the undersigned has been able to find no federal court decisions on this point, he believes the principle of these Pennsylvania appellate court decisions may be considered in view of all the facts of this case, where jurisdiction is based on diversity of citizenship, the accident occurred in Pennsylvania, and the federal district court is sitting in Pennsylvania. . . .

2. Under the circumstances of this case, principles of equity require that defendant be estopped from denying agency because, otherwise, its inaccurate statements and statements in the record, which it knew (or had the means of knowing within its control) were inaccurate, will have deprived plaintiff of his right of action.

If Interrogatory 2 had been answered accurately[10] by saying that employees of Carload Contractors, Inc. had turned the matter over to the insurance company,[11] it seems clear that plaintiff would have realized his mistake. The fact that if Sandy Johnson had testified accurately, the plaintiff could have brought its action against the proper party defendant within the statutory period of limitations is also a factor to be considered, since defendant was represented at the deposition and received knowledge of the inaccurate testimony.

At least one appellate court has stated that the doctrine of equitable estoppel will be applied to prevent a party from taking advantage of the statute of limitations where the plaintiff has been misled by conduct of such party. See, Peters v. Public Service Corporation. In that case, the court said, "Of course, defendants were under no duty to advise complainants' attorney of his error, other than by appropriate pleadings, but neither did defendants have a right, knowing of the mistake, to foster it by its acts of omission."

This doctrine has been held to estop a party from taking advantage of a document of record where the misleading conduct occurred after the recording, so that application of this doctrine would not necessarily be precluded in a case such as this where the misleading answers to interrogatories and depositions were subsequent to the filing of the answer, even if the denial in the answer had been sufficient.

Since this is a pre-trial order, it may be modified at the trial if the trial judge determines from the facts which then appear that justice so requires.

NOTES AND PROBLEMS

1. Start by getting clear about the real problem in this case and how it arose.

a. For purposes of tort law, an employer is responsible for the negligent torts of an employee. Whoever ran the business — "operated and controlled" the forklift, in the language of the complaint — was therefore responsible if Sandy Johnson had been negligent.

---

10. At least one federal district court case has suggested that a contempt proceeding under 18 U.S.C. §401 is the proper procedure to compensate the attorneys for one party who had been misled to their pecuniary damage by inaccurate answers to interrogatories. It suggested the imposition of a fine to be paid as civil liability to the attorneys for the complaining party. . . .

11. Pages 73 and 85 of the depositions of October 14, 1955, indicate that the answer to Interrogatory 2 was also inaccurate in saying that defendant made the investigation of the accident; but actually the employees of Carload Contractors, Inc. made the investigation.

b. When plaintiff read the answer, what do you suppose he thought defendant meant by denying the allegations of ¶5 of the complaint (quoted in ¶2 of the opinion)?

c. At some point before trial, the confusion about who was responsible for the forklift became obvious to both parties. Why didn't plaintiff at that point simply voluntarily dismiss the suit against Philadelphia Piers (Rule 41(a) permits such dismissals) and file a new complaint naming the correct defendant, Carload Contractors?

2. Now focus on the court's dilemma.

a. Wasn't the denial by Philadelphia Piers that it operated and controlled the forklift "true"? If so, the judge's order is forcing the defendant at trial to admit something that is false: Why?

b. The court's action would be easy to understand if the court had found that the defendant purposely misled the plaintiff, but that explanation fails on two accounts. First, the opinion specifically rejects that possibility: "There is no indication of action by either party in bad faith and there is no proof of inaccurate statements being made with intent to deceive." Second, as between the parties, what argument can one make that it was *plaintiff's* fault that the denial was deceptive? Redraft the complaint in a way that would make it much less likely that a hastily drafted answer would unintentionally deceive.

3. What change in facts would have led the court to permit Philadelphia Piers to stand by its deceptive but truthful denial?

4. *Zielinski* is a case in which defendant with complete certainty could have denied the allegation of operation and control, had it focused on that allegation. What happens if defendant is not sure or if she believes that plaintiff's allegations may be true? Some defendants seek to evade the requirements of Rule 8 by "putting plaintiff to his proof." That practice, at odds with the spirit of Rule 8(b), drew a spirited rebuke from one federal judge who had seen it tried in one case too many:

> This is it. For too many years and in too many hundreds of cases this Court has been reading, and has been compelled to order the correction of, allegedly responsive pleadings that are written by lawyers who are either unaware of or who choose to depart from Rule 8(b)'s plain roadmap. It identifies only three alternatives as available for use in an answer to the allegations of a complaint: to admit those allegations, to deny them or to state a disclaimer (if it can be made in the objective and subjective good faith demanded by Rule 11) in the express terms of the second sentence of Rule 8(b), which then entitles the pleader to the benefit of a deemed denial.
>
> Here [defendants'] counsel has engaged in a particularly vexatious violation of that most fundamental aspect of federal pleading. It is hard to imagine, but fully 30 of the Response's 35 paragraphs . . . contain this nonresponse, in direct violation of Rule 8(b)'s express teaching:

> Neither admit nor deny the allegations of said Paragraph — but demand strict proof thereof.

It is time for this Court to follow the Rules itself, in this instance Rule 8(d):

> Averments in a pleading to which a responsive pleading is required, other than those as to the amount of damage, are admitted when not denied in the responsive pleading.

> . . . Accordingly all of the allegations of Complaint ¶¶6–12, 17, 25–26 and 33–34 are held to have been admitted by [defendants], and this action will proceed on that basis.

King Vision Pay Per View, Ltd. v. J.C. Dimitri's Restaurant, Inc., 180 F.R.D. 332 (N.D. Ill. 1998)

5. In light of the excerpt above, consider how a defendant would respond in the following situation. Suppose A, a jogger, is injured when B's car swerves off the road and hits A. A sues B. After reviewing the text of Rule 11(b), decide how B should respond to the following allegations:

a. The complaint alleges that B has not had his car serviced for the past two years. Although this allegation is true, B knows that it will be impossible for A to prove it.

b. The complaint alleges that A was running north (the same direction B was driving). B does not doubt that this is true but did not actually see A running.

c. Same as in (b), except that X, a friend of A, has told B that he was standing 20 feet away and saw A running north.

b. Affirmative Defenses

Zielinski demonstrates that the traverse lives on in the form of the general or specific denial. The following case asks where the borderline lies between a denial and an affirmative defense — the old plea in confession and avoidance.

Layman v. Southwestern Bell Telephone Co.
554 S.W.2d 477 (Mo. Ct. App. 1977)

WEIER, J.

This court-tried case comes to us on appeal from a judgment in favor of defendants Southwestern Bell Telephone Company and Wright Tree Service of Iowa, Inc., and against the plaintiff Eileen Layman. Plaintiff's petition contained two counts. In Count I she alleged that she was the owner of real estate in Jefferson County, Missouri, and that the defendants had trespassed upon this land and had installed underground telephone wires and cables without her consent. She further alleged that the defendants continued to enter upon this land and maintained the wires and cables. As to damages she stated that by reason of the trespass the property had depreciated in value in the amount of $7,500. She prayed judgment for this sum together with $2,000 for punitive damages because of the willful and forceful nature of the acts of defendants. In Count II she realleged the same facts, prayed for the same damages and added as additional relief that she be restored to possession of the real property. After hearing the evidence, there being no request for findings of fact and conclusions of law, the court rendered judgment in favor of defendants stating that there was "insufficient evidence to establish the trespass pleaded and sought to be proved."[1] . . .

The evidence indicated that plaintiff had received a title to the 10.3 acres of land by deed on March 8, 1956. Although unsupported by record evidence, in cross-examination, she admitted conveying a remainder interest in the land in 1967 without consideration to her son and daughter retaining a life estate. On July 11, 1973, she saw some men and equipment digging across the south boundary of her land and destroying trees. They dug a trench about a foot wide and some three feet deep and anywhere from eight to twelve feet from the south boundary line. Mrs. Layman testified that prior to July 11, 1973, the fair market value of her property was $35,000 and that thereafter, after telephone wires had been laid in the ditch and covered up, the market value was $20,000 or a difference of $15,000. By answers to interrogatories directed to Southwestern Bell Telephone Company, this defendant admitted that it had employed Wright Tree Service to perform the work of installing the telephone wires on the property of the plaintiff. Defendant Wright Tree Service also admitted installing the wires under contract with Southwestern Bell Telephone Company.

The theory of the defendants in defense of their action in going upon plaintiff's property and installing a telephone cable beneath the surface of the ground was that defendant Southwestern Bell Telephone Company had received an assignment of an easement originally executed by owners of the land prior to the conveyance to plaintiff Layman and further that Mrs. Layman had given her permission for the installation of the cable across her land. In support of their easement defense, a recorded instrument entitled "Easement" executed by Ferdinand Kramme and his wife to Union Electric Company of Missouri dated March 1, 1946, was intro-

---

1. Although this case has been considered as a trespass case by both parties and the court, because permanent damages were sought and proven under the value formula, it would actually seem to be a suit in the nature of inverse condemnation.

duced in the evidence. Defendants claimed assignment of this easement by a document entitled "Joint Use Agreement" between Southwestern Bell Telephone Company and Union Electric Company. It is in the introduction of these documents, the easement to Union Electric and the alleged assignment of the easement rights of Union Electric to Southwestern Bell by the Joint Use Agreement, that plaintiff's contentions on appeal are grounded. . . .

Plaintiff's first point relied on to reverse the trial court contends that the court erred when it permitted the defendant Southwestern Bell to introduce evidence of an easement when it had pleaded only a general denial and not an affirmative defense of easement to plaintiff's claim of trespass. It was the theory of Southwestern Bell that it had a right of easement across plaintiff's land and that this right of easement was supported by two documents. As previously described, one was an easement which had been granted to Union Electric Company and the other was an assignment of this easement right by a joint use agreement. When defendant Southwestern Bell attempted to introduce the easement as its first exhibit, plaintiff objected on the grounds that an easement is an affirmative defense and that the answers of both Southwestern Bell and Wright Tree Service failed to set this defense out affirmatively. The court overruled the objection and allowed the introduction of the easement. The question now posed is whether right of entry by easement is an affirmative defense in an action for trespass.

Rule 55.08 [similar to Rule 8(c)] specifies that certain named affirmative defenses shall be pleaded to a preceding pleading. In addition to those named, which does not include "easement," the rule specifies "and any other matter constituting an avoidance or affirmative defense." In applying Rule 55.08 and in determining what defenses must be affirmatively pleaded as a condition to the admissibility of such evidence at the trial, the test applied is whether the defendant intends to rest his defense upon some fact not included in the allegations necessary to support the plaintiff's case. A general denial places in issue all of the material allegations contained in plaintiff's petition necessary to support his claim and the defendant is entitled to prove any fact which tends to show plaintiff's cause of action never had any legal existence. On the other hand, if the defendant has a defense in the nature of a confession of the facts of the plaintiff's petition but avers that the plaintiff's theory of liability even though sustained by the evidence does not apply to it because of additional facts which place defendant in a position to avoid any legal responsibility for its action, then such defense must be set forth in his answer. It seems clear that the right of defendant to enter upon the land to which plaintiff has indisputable possessory right would have to be proven by some compe-

tent evidence which would give that right to defendant. This would not
be in derogation of plaintiff's claim by way of showing that her claim
was nonexistent but rather that despite her claim, the defendant had a
positive right to enter and disturb the possessory rights of the plaintiff.
Thus it is the obligation of a defendant in an action for trespass to
affirmatively plead and prove matters in justification. It should also be
noted that another form of authority, to go upon land, that is a license,
is specifically mentioned in Rule 55.08 as an affirmative defense. The
conclusion is therefore inescapable that plaintiff's objection to the introduction of the easement evidence when it was not pleaded in justification
of the trespass should have been sustained. . . .

The judgment is reversed and the cause remanded for new trial.

NOTES AND PROBLEMS

1. Start by seeing the role that pleading plays in this case.

a. At what stage of the litigation did the plaintiff object?

b. Why, at this stage, did the court refer all the way back to the pleadings
to decide the issue raised by plaintiff's objection?

2. What did defendant do wrong?

a. Would the court have reached the same result if the defendant had
simply denied trespass, but, in response to an interrogatory about the
basis for its denial, had produced a copy of the purported easement?

b. One can find numerous cases that, if not directly contradicting
Layman, at least appear inconsistent with it. For example, Denham v.
Cuddeback, 210 Or. 485, 311 P.2d 1014 (1957), held that defendants
who had denied the allegations in a trespass action would be permitted
to prove title by adverse possession.

3. In ruling on cases like *Layman* and *Denham*, courts tend to make
broad pronouncements about how one aspect of proof or another is
inherently part (or not part) of the elements of the claim — and therefore
(or therefore not) put at issue by a general denial. It may prove more
helpful to think about the role that pleading plays in modern litigation.

a. For an example of a case taking such an approach, consider Harris
v. Secretary, U.S. Dept. of Veterans' Affairs, 126 F.3d 339 (D.C. Cir.
1997). Plaintiff, suing the Department alleging racial discrimination in
employment, filed her complaint after the statute of limitations had run.
Defendant failed to assert the statute of limitations as an affirmative
defense, as required in Rule 8(c), but after discovery did so in a motion
for summary judgment. Like *Layman*, the *Harris* court insisted that
defendant had erred by not pleading the statute; unlike *Layman*, the

Harris court gave a reason for this rule and suggested that some flexibility might be in order on remand:

> Rule 8(c) means what it says: affirmative defenses must be raised in a responsive pleading, not a dispositive motion. This requirement permits the parties to chart the course of litigation in advance of discovery and motions thereon. Because the Department did not raise the defense in a responsive pleading and did not apply to the District Court for leave to amend its answer under Rule 15(a), the Court should not, without more, have considered the defense of untimeliness. However, this procedural error need not necessarily cause loss of the defense. On remand, the government may seek leave to amend its answers.

b. To the extent that discovery and pretrial conferences expose the areas of controversy, it shouldn't matter a great deal whether something is pleaded as a denial or an affirmative defense. It does matter in a case in which little discovery or other pretrial process has occurred; there the pleadings will bear the entire burden of exposing the issues in dispute, as they did at common law. *Layman* may be such a case: The small amount at stake makes it likely that neither party did much discovery or conferring, in which case the plaintiff may have been genuinely surprised by the evidence produced at trial.

Is it possible to frame any general principle to cover such situations? Consider the ordinary contract case in which defendant pleads a general denial. The plaintiff will expect defendant to try to show that the negotiations did not amount to an agreement or that the agreement was performed. Much less expected would be an assertion by defendant that the parties had already entered into a binding settlement of the dispute. Look at the list of affirmative defenses in Rule 8(c): Is the list really one of "unexpected" defenses? Section 3018(b) of N.Y. Civ. Prac. L. & R. (McKinney 1974 & Supp. 1987), which requires pleading of "all matters which if not pleaded would be likely to take the adverse party by surprise or would raise issues of fact not appearing on the face of a prior pleading," makes such a principle explicit.

4. If the "surprise" principle were in effect, which of the following would have to be pleaded as an affirmative defense?

a. Plaintiff sues for damages caused by water that overflowed from a dam on defendant's land. Defendant claims that the overflow was caused by an "act of God" and that an even higher dam would have been inadequate.

b. Plaintiff sues for damages caused when defendant's car suddenly swerved into plaintiff's lane. Defendant claims he swerved to avoid hitting a child.

c. Plaintiff sues for medical malpractice resulting from an operation. Defendant claims that plaintiff planned the lawsuit before the surgery and that she faked the injury.

d. Plaintiff sues for damages caused in an automobile accident. Defendant claims that the negligence of X, rather than his own, was the proximate cause of the accident.

e. Plaintiff sues defendant for repayment of a loan. Defendant claims that she and plaintiff formed a joint venture to purchase property and that the funds were plaintiff's contribution to the capital of the venture.

f. Plaintiff sues for breach of contract and seeks recovery of certain expenses incurred in performing the contract. Defendant claims that such expenses are not mentioned in the contract and that recovery is barred by the parol evidence rule.

5. The defendant faces a dilemma in each of the preceding cases. What happens if the defendant decides to take the "safe" course and plead the particular issue as an affirmative defense but later learns that a denial would have been adequate? Has the defendant lost anything by pleading it as an affirmative defense? At common law the answer was clear: A plea of confession and avoidance (see supra page 391) expressly admitted the facts constituting the "confession." That is no longer true, but some courts take the view that by pleading the matter as an affirmative defense, the defendant has assumed the burden of proof on the issue, even though defendant would not have had such a burden had he pleaded a denial. In fact, modern writers urge that defendants plead any doubtful matters as affirmative defenses in order to avoid the possibility of a waiver. See 5 Wright and Miller §1278, at 344. A third, somewhat older view is that by pleading the matter as an affirmative defense, the defendant has assumed has assumed the burden of proof on that issue, even though the defendant would not have had such a burden had he pleaded a denial.

6. There are a few special situations in which the plaintiff must allege a certain matter, and the defendant must allege the opposite in the form of an affirmative defense, rather than simply denying plaintiff's allegation. For example, the plaintiff in a defamation suit must allege the falsity of the statement, but the truth of the statement is an affirmative defense that must be pleaded. Similarly, although a plaintiff suing on a debt must allege nonpayment, the defendant must assert payment as an affirmative defense. The rationale for these quirks seems to be that the facts in question are such an integral part of the claim that the plaintiff must make the initial allegation, but courts have applied the allocation rules discussed earlier in such a way as to place responsibility for pleading and proving such matters upon the defendant.

7. Assume *A* sues *B* on a negligence claim, and *B*'s answer pleads the affirmative defense of release. *A* does not believe that he signed a release but also wants to assert that any release he did sign was procured by fraud.

a. Can *A* reply to the answer? See Rule 7(a).

b. Will *A* be able to rely on both contentions at the trial? See Rule 8(d).

8. Assume *P* sues *D* for breach of an oral contract, and *D* interposes the affirmative defense of statute of frauds. What happens if *P* claims that *D*'s affirmative defense does not state a valid defense to *P*'s claim because the statute of frauds does not apply to the contract alleged by *P*? A procedural device is available to *P* that is analogous to the defense of failure to state a claim: *P* may make a motion to strike the affirmative defense. See Rule 12(f). This device allows *P* to attack the legal sufficiency of *D*'s affirmative defense.

3. Reply

In most cases, the pleadings stop with the answer. This is true whether the answer simply denies certain allegations of the complaint or contains new matter in the form of various affirmative defenses. We have already noted that allegations relating to such new matter are considered as "denied or avoided."

There is another rarely employed pleading: the reply. Rule 7(a) requires a reply if the answer contains "a counterclaim denominated as such." In other words, a reply is required only if the answer contains a counterclaim that is labeled as a counterclaim. If the answer contains an ostensible counterclaim that is not a counterclaim but an affirmative defense, then a reply technically is not required, although a cautious lawyer may well decide to reply. Similarly, if the answer contains allegations that are labeled as affirmative defenses, then no reply is required even though such matters should have been labeled as counterclaims. Professor Wright has suggested that when a reply to a counterclaim is required, such reply should be only to the counterclaim. Wright, Federal Courts 456-457. Frequently, however, lawyers will reply to all new matter to avoid a possible inadvertent admission.

In addition to mandatory replies, Rule 7(a) permits the court to order a reply on its own motion or on the motion of a party. In practice, replies rarely are ordered, and the mere fact that the answer raises affirmative defenses ordinarily is an insufficient basis on which to order a reply. One court has suggested the reply as a solution to the tension between substantive law and pleading rules in the civil rights/official immunity cases. In Schultea v. Wood, 47 F.3d 1427 (5th Cir. 1995) (en banc), the court suggested that it was possible to reconcile *Leatherman*, supra page 442, with the substantive law of civil rights cases by permitting the plaintiff initially to plead generally, but if the defendant then raised an official immunity defense, to require that the plaintiff reply to the answer and in the reply to supply the specificity that *Leatherman* said was not required by Rule 8. Is this a fair solution? Is it true to *Gomez*? To *Leatherman*?

4. Amendments

Pleadings provide at least a preliminary definition of what a lawsuit is about. Because that definition may change as the suit develops, particularly as discovery reveals facts unknown at the time of the original pleadings, parties may seek to change their stories. Rule 15 governs such amendments. A reading of the Rule suggests a tension between two goals: easy amendment, which allows the pleadings to reflect the parties' changed view of the case as it develops; and the notion of "prejudice," which reflects the idea that at some point a party ought to be able to pin down the other side. The cases below reflect this tension.

a. The Basic Problem: Prejudice

Beeck v. Aquaslide 'N' Dive Corp.

562 F.2d 537 (8th Cir. 1977)

BENSON, J.

This case is an appeal from the trial court's exercise of discretion on procedural matters in a diversity personal injury action.

Jerry A. Beeck was severely injured on July 15, 1972, while using a water slide. He and his wife, Judy A. Beeck, sued Aquaslide 'N' Dive Corporation (Aquaslide), a Texas corporation, alleging it manufactured the slide involved in the accident, and sought to recover substantial damages on theories of negligence, strict liability and breach of implied warranty.

Aquaslide initially admitted manufacture of the slide, but later moved to amend its answer to deny manufacture; the motion was resisted. The district court granted leave to amend.[2] On motion of the defendant, a

---

2. Beeck v. Aquaslide 'N' Dive Corp., 67 F.R.D. 411 (S.D. Iowa 1975).

separate trial was held on the issue of "whether the defendant designed, manufactured or sold the slide in question." This motion was also resisted by the plaintiffs. The issue was tried to a jury, which returned a verdict for the defendant, after which the trial court entered summary judgment of dismissal of the case. Plaintiffs took this appeal, and stated the issues presented for review to be:

> Where the manufacturer of the product, a water slide, admitted in its answer and later its answer to interrogatories both filed prior to the running of the statute of limitations that it designed, manufactured and sold the water slide in question, was it an abuse of the trial court's discretion to grant leave to amend to the manufacturer in order to deny these admissions after the running of the statute of limitations?
>
> After granting the manufacturer's motion for leave to amend in order to deny the prior admissions of design, manufacture and sale of the water slide in question, was it an abuse of the trial court's discretion to further grant the manufacturer's motion for a separate trial on the issue of manufacture?

I. Facts

A brief review of the facts found by the trial court in its order granting leave to amend, and which do not appear to have been in dispute, is essential to a full understanding of appellants' claims.

In 1971 Kimberly Village Home Association of Davenport, Iowa, ordered an Aquaslide product from one George Boldt, who was a local distributor handling defendant's products. The order was forwarded by Boldt to Sentry Pool and Chemical Supply Co. in Rock Island, Illinois, and Sentry forwarded the order to Purity Swimming Pool Supply in Hammond, Indiana. A slide was delivered from a Purity warehouse to Kimberly Village, and was installed by Kimberly employees. On July 15, 1972, Jerry A. Beeck was injured while using the slide at a social gathering sponsored at Kimberly Village by his employer, Harker Wholesale Meats, Inc. Soon after the accident investigations were undertaken by representatives of the separate insurers of Harker and Kimberly Village. On October 31, 1972, Aquaslide first learned of the accident through a letter sent by a representative of Kimberly's insurer to Aquaslide, advising that "one of your Queen Model #Q-3D slides" was involved in the accident. Aquaslide forwarded this notification to its insurer. Aquaslide's insurance adjuster made an on-site investigation of the slide in May 1973, and also interviewed persons connected with the ordering and assembly of the slide. An inter-office letter dated September 23, 1973, indicates that Aquaslide's insurer was of the opinion the "Aquaslide in question was definitely manufactured by our insured." The complaint was filed October 15, 1973.[3] Investigators for three different insurance companies, representing Harker, Kimberly and the defendant, had concluded that the slide had been manufactured by Aquaslide, and the defendant, with no information to the contrary, answered the complaint on December 12, 1973, and admitted that it "designed, manufactured, assembled and sold" the slide in question.[4]

The statute of limitations on plaintiff's personal injury claim expired on July 15, 1974. About six and one-half months later Carl Meyer, president and owner of Aquaslide, visited the site of the accident prior to the taking of his deposition by the plaintiff.[5] From his on-site inspection of the slide, he determined it was not a product of the defendant. Thereafter, Aquaslide moved the court for leave to amend its answer to deny manufacture of the slide.

II.   Leave to Amend

Amendment of pleadings in civil actions is governed by Rule 15(a), F.R. Civ. P., which provides in part that once issue is joined in a lawsuit, a party may amend his pleading "only by leave of court or by written consent of the adverse party; and leave shall be freely given when justice so requires."

In Foman v. Davis, 371 U.S. 178(1962), the Supreme Court had occasion to construe that portion of Rule 15(a) set out above:

> Rule 15(a) declares that leave to amend "shall be freely given when justice so requires"; this mandate is to be heeded. . . . If the underlying facts or circumstances relied upon by a plaintiff may be a proper subject of relief, he ought to be afforded an opportunity to test his claim on the merits. In the absence of any apparent or declared reason — such as undue delay, bad faith or dilatory motive on the part of the movant, repeated failure to cure deficiencies by amendments previously allowed, undue prejudice to the opposing party by virtue of allowance of the amendment, futility of amendment, etc. — the leave sought should, as the rules require, be "freely given." Of course, the grant or denial of an opportunity to amend is within the discretion of the district court. . . .

This court in Hanson v. Hunt Oil Co. held that "[p]rejudice *must be shown*." (Emphasis added). The burden is on the party opposing the amendment to show such prejudice. In ruling on a motion for leave to

---

3. Aquaslide 'N' Dive Corporation was the sole defendant named in the complaint.

4. In answers to interrogatories filed on June 3, 1974, Aquaslide again admitted manufacture of the slide in question.

5. Plaintiffs apparently requested Meyer to inspect the slide prior to the taking of his deposition to determine whether it was defectively installed or assembled.

amend, the trial court must inquire into the issue of prejudice to the opposing party, in light of the particular facts of the case.

Certain principles apply to appellate review of a trial court's grant or denial of a motion to amend pleadings. First, as noted in Foman v. Davis, allowance or denial of leave to amend lies within the sound discretion of the trial court and is reviewable only for an abuse of discretion. The appellate court must view the case in the posture in which the trial court acted in ruling on the motion to amend.

It is evident from the order of the district court that in the exercise of its discretion in ruling on defendant's motion for leave to amend, it searched the record for evidence of bad faith, prejudice and undue delay which might be sufficient to overbalance the mandate of Rule 15(a), F.R. Civ. P., and Foman v. Davis, that leave to amend should be "freely given." Plaintiffs had not at any time conceded that the slide in question had not been manufactured by the defendant, and at the time the motion for leave to amend was at issue, the court had to decide whether the defendant should be permitted to litigate a material factual issue on its merits.

In inquiring into the issue of bad faith, the court noted the fact that the defendant, in initially concluding that it had manufactured the slide, relied upon the conclusions of three different insurance companies,[6] each of which had conducted an investigation into the circumstances surrounding the accident. This reliance upon investigations of three insurance companies, and the fact that "no contention has been made by anyone that the defendant influenced this possibly erroneous conclusion," persuaded the court that "defendant has not acted in such bad faith as to be precluded from contesting the issue of manufacture at trial." The court further found "[t]o the extent that 'blame' is to be spread regarding the original identification, the record indicates that it should be shared equally."

In considering the issue of prejudice that might result to the plaintiffs from the granting of the motion for leaving to amend, the trial court held that the facts presented to it did not support plaintiffs' assertion that, because of the running of the two-year Iowa statute of limitations on personal injury claims, the allowance of the amendment would sound the "death knell" of the litigation. In order to accept plaintiffs' argument, the court would have had to assume that the defendant would prevail at trial on the factual issue of manufacture of the slide, and further that plaintiffs would be foreclosed, should the amendment be allowed, from proceeding against other parties if they were unsuccessful in pressing

---

6. The insurer of Beeck's employer, the insurer of Kimberly Village, as well as the defendant's insurer had each concluded the slide in question was an Aquaslide.

their claim against Aquaslide. On the state of the record before it, the trial court was unwilling to make such assumptions,[7] and concluded "[u]nder these circumstances, the court deems that the possible prejudice to the plaintiffs is an insufficient basis on which to deny the proposed amendment." The court reasoned that the amendment would merely allow the defendant to contest a disputed factual issue at trial, and further that it would be prejudicial to the defendant to deny the amendment.

The court also held that defendant and its insurance carrier, in investigating the circumstances surrounding the accident, had not been so lacking in diligence as to dictate a denial of the right to litigate the factual issue of manufacture of the slide.

On this record we hold that the trial court did not abuse its discretion in allowing the defendant to amend its answer.

III.   Separate Trials

After Aquaslide was granted leave to amend its answer, it moved pursuant to Rule 42(b), F. R. Civ. P. for a separate trial on the issue of manufacture of the slide involved in the accident. The grounds upon which the motion was based were:

(1) a separate trial solely on the the issue of whether the slide was manufactured by Aquaslide would save considerable trial time and unnecessary expense and preparation for all parties and the court, and
(2) a separate trial solely on the issue of manufacture would protect Aquaslide from substantial prejudice.

The court granted the motion for a separate trial on the issue of manufacture, and this grant of a separate trial is challenged by appellants as being an abuse of discretion.

A trial court's severance of trial will not be disturbed on appeal except for an abuse of discretion.

The record indicates that Carl Meyer, president and owner of Aquaslide, designs the slides sold by Aquaslide. The slide which plaintiff Jerry

---

7. The district court noted in its order granting leave to amend that plaintiffs may be able to sue other parties as a result of the substituting of a "counterfeit" slide for the Aquaslide, if indeed this occurred. The court added:

[A]gain, the court is handicapped by an unclear record on this issue. If, in fact, the slide in question is not an Aquaslide, the replacement entered the picture somewhere along the Boldt to Sentry, Sentry to Purity, Purity to Kimberly Village chain of distribution. Depending upon the circumstances of its entry, a cause of action sounding in fraud or contract might lie. If so, the applicable statute of limitations period would not have run. Further, as defendant points out, the doctrine of equitable estoppel might possibly preclude another defendant from asserting the two-year statute as a defense.

A. Beeck was using at the time of his accident was very similar in appearance to an Aquaslide product, and was without identifying marks. Kimberly Village had in fact ordered an Aquaslide for its swimming pool, and thought it had received one. After Meyer's inspection and Aquaslide's subsequent assertion that it was not an Aquaslide product, plaintiffs elected to stand on their contention that it was in fact an Aquaslide. This raised a substantial issue of material fact which, if resolved in defendant's favor, would exonerate defendant from liability.

Plaintiff Jerry A. Beeck had been severely injured, and he and his wife together were seeking damages arising out of those injuries in the sum of $2,225,000.00. Evidence of plaintiffs' injuries and damages would clearly have taken up several days of trial time, and because of the severity of the injuries, may have been prejudicial to the defendant's claim of non-manufacture. The jury, by special interrogatory, found that the slide had not been manufactured by Aquaslide. That finding has not been questioned on appeal. Judicial economy, beneficial to all the parties, was obviously served by the trial court's grant of a separate trial. We hold the Rule 42(b) separation was not an abuse of discretion.

The judgment of the district court is affirmed.

NOTES AND PROBLEMS

1. Rule 15 says that "leave [to amend] shall be freely given when justice so requires." The courts have read this phrase to mean: (a) that the would-be amender should have a good reason for not getting the pleading right the first time; and (b) that allowing the change now shouldn't hurt the other side too much. That latter requirement is often captured in the not very illuminating word "prejudice."

a. State simply how the court concluded that the first requirement was met.

b. Without deciding whether the prejudice to the plaintiff was too much, explain simply what it was. How was plaintiff hurt by permitting this amendment to the answer?

2. Is it true, as the court suggests, that the parties are equally to blame for the misidentification of the slide?

a. First assume, as the district court found, that Aquaslide and its insurers acted in completely good faith and that it was in fact difficult to tell the real from the counterfeit slide. Surely the defendant was in a better position to find this out than was the plaintiff. Moreover, once Aquaslide had admitted manufacture in its answer, could one expect any rational plaintiff to invest additional effort in making sure that the admission was accurate?

b. Was Aquaslide on notice that identification was a problem? Later phases of this lawsuit revealed that Aquaslide and its president were aware that other manufacturers had been copying their slides; there had been several other lawsuits in which it had turned out that the slides were made by competitors. Beeck v. Aquaslide 'N' Dive Corp. 350 N. W. 2d 149 (Iowa 1984). Assume that information had been presented to the court in this lawsuit. Under those circumstances would it have been an abuse of discretion had the trial court denied permission to amend?

3. If one accepts the argument implicit in the preceding two notes, the case presents a problem. The defendant has questionable excuse for having mispleaded in the first place, and the plaintiff will suffer crushing prejudice if amendment is allowed. The court nevertheless permitted amendment. Perhaps the court was simply wrong. But before you conclude that, consider whether there is another, deeper justification for the court's decision.

a. One answer appears if one conducts a thought experiment. Assume the amendment had been denied, and the wrong defendant had remained in the case. How would defendant have responded to the claim of negligent manufacture? Would it have shown its own design, testing, manufacturing, and safety procedures or those of the actual manufacturer? Assuming the latter, what would happen if it didn't know who manufactured the slide? How, in other words, could the defendant have conducted itself during litigation if it had been forced to stand by its erroneous admission of manufacture?

b. Compare *Beeck* to Zielinski v. Philadelphia Piers, which appears earlier in this chapter. In that case the court required the defendant to admit an allegation that was demonstrably false. Is *Zielinski* a persuasive analogy? What key fact differed between the circumstances of that case and those of *Beeck*?

4. The *Beeck* opinion reproduced above did not end this litigation. The Beecks filed a second suit in state court, still against Aquaslide. This time, however, they did not claim a defective product but reckless misrepresentation made in the pleadings in the federal litigation. Plaintiffs theory was that misrepresentations in the answer (inaccurately admitting that the product was made by Aquaslide) had caused the Beecks to lose their chance to sue the real manufacturer. The Beecks presented evidence summarized in Note 2b — showing that Aquaslide should have been on notice that there were counterfeit slides on the market. Plaintiffs argued that defendants were reckless in admitting manufacture without a more complete investigation.

The case came before the Iowa Supreme Court twice, once in 1981 and again in 1984. That court upheld a recovery based on a misrepresentation theory. However, in analogizing the Beecks' claim to a legal malpractice action, the court also said that, in order to prevail, the plaintiffs would have to show not only that they would have recovered a judgment against the actual manufacturer but also that the judgment would have been collectible. Beeck v. Aquaslide 'N' Dive Corp., 350 N.W.2d 149 (Iowa 1984). Does this outcome suggest that the Eighth Circuit should have ruled as the *Zielinski* court did—forcing the defendant to stay with its original answer, even though it was inaccurate?

b. Statutes of Limitations and Relation Back

Beeck v. Aquaslide derived its bite from the possibility that the plaintiff, having suffered a dismissal, would be unable to refile its complaint against the right defendant before the statute of limitations had run. Rule 15(c) gives plaintiffs some leeway in this respect, but the flexibility is not limitless, as the next cases demonstrate. Central to the decision is the question of what constitutes a "claim," a question that takes us back to the beginning of this chapter. Compare the approach taken by the next two cases: Are they consistent?

Moore v. Baker
989 F.2d 1129 (11th Cir. 1993)

MORGAN, Senior Circuit Judge.
[Judith Moore consulted Dr. Baker about a blockage of her carotid artery. Baker recommended surgery and warned her about its risks. Moore signed a consent form. The operation went badly and left Moore severely and permanently disabled. Moore sued Dr. Baker. The initial complaint alleged that he had violated Georgia's informed consent law by failing to advise her of an alternative therapy.]
On August 6, 1991, Dr. Baker filed a motion for summary judgment on the issue of informed consent. On August 26, 1991, Moore moved to amend her complaint to assert allegations of negligence by Dr. Baker in the performance of the surgery and in his post-operative care of Moore. . . .

I

Moore claims that the district court abused its discretion by . . . denying Moore's motion to amend her complaint. . . . In the instant case, the lower court denied leave to amend on the ground that the newly-asserted claim was barred by the applicable statute of limitations and that allowing the amendment would, therefore, be futile. If correct, the district court's rationale would be sufficient to support a denial of leave to amend the complaint.

Moore filed her original complaint on the last day permitted by Georgia's statute of limitations. Accordingly, the statute of limitations bars the claim asserted in Moore's proposed amended complaint unless the amended complaint relates back to the date of the original complaint. An amendment relates back to the original filing "whenever the claim or defense asserted in the amended pleading arose out of the conduct, transaction, or occurrence set forth or attempted to be set forth in the original pleading." Fed. R. Civ. P. 15(c). The critical issue in Rule 15(c) determinations is whether the original complaint gave notice to the defendant of the claim now being asserted.

Moore relies heavily on Azarbal v. Medical Center of Delaware, Inc., 724 F. Supp. 279 (D. Del. 1989), which addressed the doctrine of relation back in the context of a medical malpractice case. In *Azarbal*, the original complaint alleged negligence in the performance of an amniocentesis on the plaintiff, resulting in injury to the fetus. After the statute of limitations had expired, the plaintiff sought to amend the complaint to add a claim that the doctor failed to obtain her informed consent prior to performing a sterilization procedure on her because the doctor did not tell her that the fetus had probably been injured by the amniocentesis. The district court found that "the original complaint provided adequate notice of any claims Ms. Azarbal would have arising from the amniocentesis, including a claim that Dr. Palacio should have revealed that the procedure had caused fetal injury." *Azarbal*, supra at 283.

The instant case is clearly distinguishable from *Azarbal*. Unlike the complaint in *Azarbal*, the allegations asserted in Moore's original complaint contain nothing to put Dr. Baker on notice that the new claims of negligence might be asserted. Even when given a liberal construction, there is nothing in Moore's original complaint which makes reference to any acts of alleged negligence by Dr. Baker either during or after surgery.[1] The original complaint focuses on Baker's actions before Moore

---

1. Moore's original complaint is very specific and focuses solely on Dr. Baker's failure to inform Moore of EDTA therapy as an alternative to surgery. Although the complaint recounts the details of the operation and subsequent recovery, it does not hint that Dr. Baker's actions were negligent. In fact, the only references in the original complaint relating to the surgery or postoperative care suggest that Dr. Baker acted with reasonable care. The complaint states that "the nurses noticed a sudden onset of right sided weakness of which they immediately informed Defendant Baker." (Complaint, P 18). "Upon being informed of this [right sided weakness], Defendant Baker immediately caused Plaintiff to be returned to the operation suite . . . . Although the clot was promptly removed by Defendant Baker. . . ." (Complaint, P 19).

decided to undergo surgery, but the amended complaint focuses on Baker's actions during and after the surgery. The alleged acts of negligence occurred at different times and involved separate and distinct conduct. In order to recover on the negligence claim contained in her amended complaint, Moore would have to prove completely different facts than would otherwise have been required to recover on the informed consent claim in the original complaint.

We must conclude that Moore's new claim does not arise out of the same conduct, transaction, or occurrence as the claims in the original complaint. Therefore, the amended complaint does not relate back to the original complaint, and the proposed new claims are barred by the applicable statute of limitations. Since the amended complaint could not withstand a motion to dismiss, we hold that the district court did not abuse its discretion in deying Moore's motion to amend her complaint. . . .

Bonerb v. Richard J. Caron Foundation
159 F.R.D. 16 (W.D.N.Y. 1994)

CAROL E. HECKMAN, Magistrate Judge. . . .

In this diversity action, plaintiff seeks damages for personal injuries allegedly sustained when he slipped and fell while playing basketball on defendant's recreational basketball court on November 29, 1991. Defendant is a not-for-profit corporation licensed and doing business as a drug and alcohol rehabilitation facility in Westfield, Pennsylvania. Plaintiff is a resident of Western New York.

The original complaint, filed on October 1, 1993, alleges that plaintiff was injured while he was a rehabilitation patient at defendant's Westfield facility, and was participating in a mandatory exercise program. Plaintiff claims that the basketball court was negligently maintained by defendant.

On July 25, 1994, this court granted plaintiffs motion for substitution of new counsel. On September 1, 1994, plaintiff moved to amend his complaint to add a new cause of action for "counseling malpractice" (Item 16, Mahoney Aff., P 4). According to plaintiff's counsel, investigation and discussions undertaken after his substitution as counsel indicated to him that a malpractice claim was warranted under the circumstances (id.). Defendant objects to the amendment on the grounds that the counseling malpractice claim does not relate back to the original pleading and is therefore barred by Pennsylvania's two-year statute of limitations.

Discussion

Rule 15 of the Federal Rules of Civil Procedure provides that once time for amending a pleading as of right has expired, a party may request leave of court to amend, which "shall be freely given when justice so requires." Fed. R. Civ. P. 15(a). This provision has been liberally construed, and leave to amend should be granted absent undue prejudice to the party opposing the amendment, undue delay on the part of the party seeking the amendment, or bad faith. Foman v. Davis, 371 U.S. 178, 182 (1967). However, an amendment which seeks to add a time-barred claim would be futile, and should not be allowed unless the otherwise untimely claim "relates back" to the date of the original pleading. . . .

In determining whether a claim relates back, courts look to the "operational facts" set forth in the original complaint to determine whether the defendant was put on notice of the claim that the plaintiff later seeks to add.

The relation back doctrine is based upon the principle that one who has been given notice of litigation concerning a given transaction or occurrence has been provided with all the protection that statutes of limitation are designed to afford. Thus, if the litigant has been advised at the outset of the general facts from which the belatedly asserted claim arises, the amendment will relate back even though the statute of limitations may have run in the interim.

An amendment which changes the legal theory of the case is appropriate if the factual situation upon which the action depends remains the same and has been brought to the defendant's attention by the original pleading. . . .

In this case, the original complaint alleges that plaintiff was injured when he slipped and fell on a wet, muddy basketball court "while participating in a mandatory exercise program. . . ." at defendant's rehabilitation facility (Item 1, P 8). Plaintiff alleges several instances of defendant's negligent conduct, such as failure to maintain the premises safely, failure to warn, failure to inspect and failure to "properly supervise and/or instruct plaintiff. . . ." (id., P 9). The proposed amendment seeks to allege that plaintiff "was caused to fall while playing in an outdoor basketball court . . . in an exercise program mandated as part of his treatment in the rehabilitation program. . . ." (Item 16, Ex. A, P 20), and that "the rehabilitation and counseling care rendered . . . was negligently, carelessly and unskillfully performed" (id., P 21).

The allegations in the original and amended complaints derive from the same nucleus of operative facts involving injury suffered by plaintiff on November 29, 1991. It is true that a claim for professional malpractice invokes an entirely different duty and conduct on the part of the defendant than does a claim for negligent maintenance of the premises. However, the original complaint advised defendant of the same transaction or occurrence giving rise to these different theories of negligence. Indeed, the original complaint alleged that participation in the exercise program was mandatory, and that the injury was caused by defendant's failure to "properly supervise and/or instruct plaintiff. . . ." These allegations not only gave defendant sufficient notice of the general facts surrounding the occurrence, but also alerted defendant to the possiblity of a claim based on negligent perfomance of professional duties. See, e.g., Crossland Savings FSB v. Rockwood Insurance Co., 700 F. Supp. 1274, 1279 (S.D.N.Y. 1988). This is all that is required for relation back under Rule 15(c).

Defendant contends that it will be unduly prejudiced by the amendment because it will have to return to the drawing board to prepare an entirely new defense. However, as plaintiff points out, the period for discovery has not yet expired, depositions of defendant's personnel have not yet been taken, and expert witness information has not been exchanged. In addition, the parties have consented to trial before the undersigned, thereby simplifying any further supervision of discovery and the conduct and review of pretrial matters and dispositive motions.

Finally, there has been no showing of undue delay or bad faith on the part of plaintiff. . . .

NOTES AND PROBLEMS

1. Relation-back cases test our belief in statutes of limitations and our idea of a claim.

a. What are statutes of limitations for? Why do we have them?

b. How is that justification linked to the relation-back doctrine? One could, theoretically, have a doctrine that permitted relation back of any subsequent amendment, no matter how unrelated to the original claim. What is the argument against such a doctrine?

2. If one has decided that relation back applies only to "related" claims, the question is how to define "relatedness." One possibility would be on the basis of legal theory: Any tort claim could be joined to an initial claim for a tort, and so on. As a review of this chapter, explain why such a theory is incompatible with the idea of notice pleading.

3. That leaves us with Rule 15(c), which defines the line between permitted and unpermitted amendments in terms of "the conduct, transaction, or occurrence set forth or attempted to be set forth in the original pleading." That language is purposely general, and courts will inevitably perceive "conduct, transaction, [and] occurrence" in different-sized packages.

4. In Moore v. Baker, the court finds that the allegations of medical malpractice did not relate back to the allegations of failure to get informed

consent for the operation. In Bonerb v. Richard J. Caron Foundation, the court finds that the claim of "counselling malpractice" did relate back to the allegations of negligent maintenance of the basketball court.

a. Are the cases distinguishable? Does it matter that the attempted amendment in *Moore* came after considerable discovery and a summary judgment motion, while that in *Bonerb* came earlier in the litigation?

b. Is either one correctly decided? Make an argument that both should come out the other way — Ms. Moore permitted to amend and Mr. Bonerb not permitted.

5. Among the most spectacular relation-back cases occur when the plaintiff wants to change not just a legal theory, but the party sued. Even such an amendment can relate back under some conditions. Read carefully Rule 15(c)(3).

a. The ordinary version of such cases involves a corporation sued under the wrong name or an individual whose name is misspelled. In such instances the "right" defendant knows of the suit, and the courts have often allowed such amendments to relate back.

b. More dramatic are the cases where the real defendant wasn't served with process. In those cases courts wrestle with the question of whether the newly named party knew enough about the suit that she won't be prejudiced in her defense and knew that she would have been named but for a mistake of the plaintiff. Among the most difficult of these are suits against institutions where the plaintiff initially names the institution but for various reasons decides later to sue individuals within that institution — for example, specific police officers rather than the police department or city. Consider, for example, Worthington v. Wilson, 790 F. Supp. 829 (C.D. Ill. 1992), in which the court concluded that the defendant officers had known of the suit — and thus had received the requisite notice — but that the failure to name the officers had not been a "mistake" and that the amended complaint therefore did not relate back.

c. Apply Rule 15(c)(3) to the facts of Zielinski v. Philadelphia Piers, supra page 457. The present version of this Rule was not in effect at the time *Zielinski* was decided. Suppose it had been? Could the court have avoided the awkward step of forcing the defendants to admit a false statement by instead permitting an amendment to change the defendant? Do you need any additional facts to decide whether this approach would work?

As we have seen, modern pleading has eliminated most of the rigidities and trapdoors that characterized its common law predecessors. Pleading is no longer a technical game. It continues, however, to serve two central functions. First, it can often eliminate some legal theories and thereby enable the parties to reach converging estimates of a case's values. Second, it can define the ground to be covered in the ensuing discovery phase. Equally important is what modern pleading does not do. It does not sharply define the dispute. And it does not convey substantial factual information about the case.

This situation requires other procedural devices to convey information about the lawsuit and to end meritless cases short of trial. The following two chapters describe the answers modern procedure has given to the problems posed by contemporary pleading. The next chapter, on discovery, displays the system's response to the scanty information conveyed by pleading. The one after that, on resolution without trial, discusses ways in which contemporary litigators can seek to eliminate meritless claims and defenses. As you consider these topics, bear in mind that they are in substantial part responses to decisions made about the pleading system.

DISCOVERY

VII

A hundred years ago, if a complaint survived demurrer, the case would go to trial if the plaintiff wanted it to. That is no longer true. In contemporary litigation the chief significance of a complaint's surviving dismissal is that it enables the plaintiff to reach the "pretrial" stage — the intermediate stage between pleading and trial. Today, most lawsuits end at this pretrial stage. In part, they end at this stage *because* of the procedural device explored in this chapter — discovery. Discovery ends lawsuits for two reasons; one of them good, the other not. First, discovery produces information about the merits of the lawsuit and permits parties to make informed judgments about the strength of their and their opponent's positions; such information can end either in settlement or in summary judgment, both of which are explored in the next chapter. Second, because discovery costs time and money, it also enables one of the parties simply to wear the other down — or both sides to wear each other down — without regard to the merits of the case. This chapter explains why discovery has both these potentials and explores ways in which the Rules try to maximize the first reason and minimize the second reason that lawsuits can end at this stage.

A. Modern Discovery

Contemporary discovery permits parties to compel the disclosure of witnesses, evidence, documents, and other matters before trial. Under previous practice, only a limited range of discovery devices was available and only against some persons, and in some kinds of actions. Discovery was not always a matter of right, and was often limited to a scope narrower than the issues relevant at trial. This recipe could produce good courtroom drama, but not, critics argued, truth or justice.

The institution of modern discovery has changed that picture. Both state courts and the federal system have adopted broad civil discovery rules that permit a lawyer to uncover, in advance of trial, enormous amounts of information. The scope and depth of modern U.S. discovery practice make it unique among today's legal systems. This scope permits the bringing and defense of claims where all or much of the relevant information lies in the possession of the other side. Outside the U.S., neither common law nor civil law systems permit the searching scrutiny of material in the possession of the opposing party, and American lawyers often encounter strong resistance when they seek to use discovery techniques in multinational litigation.

Have these changes have made litigation "better"? Since the 1970s a debate on this point has developed between critics and defenders of modern discovery. Critics tell nightmarish anecdotes of lawyers burying each other under piles of form interrogatories and waves of requests for documents; defenders cite instances in which discovery worked smoothly to uncover facts that otherwise would not have emerged and those in which discovery led to no disputes. Several empirical studies undertaken to resolve this debate have instead confirmed *both* hypotheses. The data suggest that in regard to discovery, civil cases form a spectrum, with ends defined by the ordinary case and the giant or mega-case. At one end is most litigation: the lawsuit growing from an automobile accident, the small contract dispute between businesses, the employment discrimination case brought by an individual employee. At the other end are the big antitrust cases (the federal government's attacks on Microsoft and AT&T are paradigms) and certain kinds of product liability or disaster litigation. The studies suggest that in many ordinary cases no formal discovery at all takes place; when it does occur, discovery works fairly well with relatively few disputes, modest use of the discovery devices, and rather little judicial time consumed in refereeing squabbles. Those characteristics are reversed in big cases: There, discovery can consume years, produce reams of material that scores of lawyers and paralegals struggle to digest, and occupy many hours of judicial time in deciding disputes. Between these poles lies midsized litigation, in which discovery is sometimes a useful tool, sometimes a daunting obstacle.

B.   The Possibilities and Limits of Discovery: Relevance and Privilege

Both the power and the destructive potential of discovery hinge on the principles governing its use. Rule 26(b)(1) gives the parties a right to discover "any matter, not *privileged*, which is *relevant* to the subject matter involved in the pending action" (emphasis added). A proposed revision of this section would authorize discovery of "any matter, not privileged, that is relevant to the claim or defense of any party." In either version the concept of relevance both grants and limits power; privilege operates solely as a limitation.

1.   Relevance

To be discoverable, information must be relevant. Relevance is simultaneously a branch of the law of evidence and a matter of common sense. It defines a relationship between pieces of information: how I tie my shoelaces is irrelevant to whether it will rain today, but how the sky looks is highly relevant to the same question. For a piece of information to be relevant to a legal proposition means, according to the governing substantive law, that the information tends to prove or disprove something that matters according to the applicable substantive law. For example, if, in a contract dispute, the defendant contends that he failed to pay for goods because the goods were defective, the condition of the goods will be relevant, but if he contends that he failed to pay for the goods because he used the money to support a sick relative, the state of the relative's health would be irrelevant. Its irrelevance flows from the law of contract, which says that one's motives for breaching a contract don't matter. The next two cases illustrate the relation among substantive law, relevance, and discoverability.

Blank v. Sullivan & Cromwell
16 Fair Empl. Prac. Cas. (BNA) 87 (S.D.N.Y. 1976)

MOTLEY, J.

[Plaintiffs were female lawyers who had unsuccessfully applied for positions as associates in the law firm around 1970. They sued, alleging sexual discrimination in hiring.]

Plaintiffs have moved for a rehearing and modification of so much of this court's order of May 24, 1976 as denied plaintiffs the discovery sought in Interrogatories 60(f) and (g), 61, 62, and 63 of their First Interrogatories[1] (filed in court on April 18, 1976). That order adopted the report

---

1. "60. Identify each and every female permanent associate at Sullivan & Cromwell prior to August 30, 1970 and indicate as to each: . . .
(f) whether each was offered an opportunity to become a partner; and
(g) whether each became a partner.

of Magistrate Harold J. Raby, to whom plaintiffs' Rule 37 motion had previously been referred, but modified the report insofar as it had recommended compliance with the Interrogatories here in question. Specifically, with respect to these Interrogatories (and certain others not in issue on the motion for rehearing), the court held that "the defendant need not respond in any form to such interrogatories since the information sought therein relates to defendant's partners and employees who became partners, and is not relevant to the subject matter of the suit before this court." However, upon reconsideration and upon careful examination of the arguments submitted by plaintiffs, defendant, and amicus Equal Employment Opportunity Commission, the court has decided to order defendants to respond to the interrogatories here in issue. . . .

In reversing its prior ruling, this court also is mindful of the fact that a plaintiff may not sue for injuries that he or she has not suffered, and he or she may not sue on behalf of a class of which he or she is not a member. Plaintiff, therefore, cannot represent in this action those who may be aggrieved by defendant's partner selection criteria. However, defendant is incorrect in suggesting that because the individual plaintiff here has not alleged that she was denied partnership due to her sex, she is not entitled to the requested discovery.

Under Rule 26, Fed. R. Civ. P., a party is entitled to discovery, not only of material which is relevant and admissible at trial, but also of information which "appears reasonably calculated to lead to the discovery of admissible evidence." More specifically, in Title VII cases, in which a plaintiff alleges discriminatory employment practices, both the Supreme Court, in McDonnell Douglas Corp. v. Green, 411 U.S. 792, 804-805 (1973), and the Second Circuit in Kohn v. Royall, Koegel & Wells, 496 F.2d 1094, 1101 (1974) have ruled that general information on defendant's labor hierarchy may be reflective of restrictive or exclusionary hiring practices within the contemplation of the statute.

Thus, the narrow inquiry is whether the information requested is so unrelated to plaintiffs' claim that women are discriminated against by

---

61. State the average length of service at the firm as an associate, of all associates who were offered partnerships in the firm between 1961 and the present date.

62. If any person listed in answer to Question 60 was not offered an opportunity to become a partner within the average length of service period noted in answer to Question 61, state the reason why she was not extended such an offer.

63. State the name of each male attorney hired by the firm after the earliest date listed in answer to Question 60(b) who was offered an opportunity to become a partner at the firm, and indicate:

    (a) the date when each person started work at the firm;

    (b) the date on which each person was offered the opportunity to become a partner; and

    (c) the area of specialization of each person."

defendant on account of sex that it cannot be said to be "relevant" within the expansive meaning of that term in Rule 26. In the court's view, this connection is not nearly so tenuous as defendant suggests.

By order dated June 13, 1975, this court ruled that "the class represented by plaintiff is defined to include all women qualified to hold legal positions at the law firm of Sullivan and Cromwell who have been or would be denied employment because of their sex." Judge Lasker of this Court dealt with a plaintiff class similarly constituted in a suit against the law firm of Royall, Koegel & Wells. By order dated January 7, 1975, he granted plaintiffs in that suit similar discovery with respect to advancement to partnership, endorsing the recommendation of Magistrate, now Judge Goettel, who had commented as follows: "It is difficult to conceive of anything more telling with respect to whether or not these [female] associates are being subject to employment discrimination than whether they proceed on to partnerships in the firm in the same manner as male attorneys with similar capabilities."

The court is, of course, aware that the numerous factors which bear upon the admission to partnership make it impossible to equate that decision with the decision to hire an associate. However, it does not follow from that recognition that a firm's practices in advancing, or failing to advance, associates to partnership have no probative bearing upon allegations of improper discrimination in hiring associates. Even assuming arguendo, that Title VII does not proscribe the use of sex as a criterion for admission to partnership, that legal conclusion does not necessarily indicate that evidence of sexually oriented discrimination at that level might not be probative of a similar pattern in the selection of associates, where it would be illegal.

Accordingly, defendant is directed to answer the Interrogatories referred to above.

Steffan v. Cheney

920 F.2d 74 (D.C. Cir. 1990)

PER CURIAM.

Joseph C. Steffan resigned from the United States Naval Academy in 1987, after an administrative board recommended that he be discharged. The board's recommendation was based solely upon Steffan's statements proclaiming himself a homosexual; he was not charged with any homosexual conduct. In 1988 he filed this action, claiming that he was constructively discharged and challenging the constitutionality of the regulations that provided for the discharge of admitted homosexuals. The factual and procedural background of the case is set out in the opinion of the district court, and will not be repeated in detail here.

The matter is before this court now because Steffan, claiming his Fifth Amendment privilege against self-incrimination, refused to answer deposition questions directed to whether he had engaged in homosexual conduct during or after his tenure as a midshipman. He also objected that the questions were not relevant to the legality of his separation. The district court, having issued a prior warning, dismissed Steffan's action for failure to comply with its discovery order, see Fed. R. Civ. P. 37(b)(2), and Steffan appeals. Although the district court has broad discretion in choosing a sanction under Rule 37, no sanction may be upheld if its imposition was based upon an error of law. Because this is such a case, we reverse.

The district court acknowledged that "the record is clear that [Steffan] was separated from the Naval Academy based on his admissions that he is a homosexual rather than on any evidence of misconduct." Nevertheless, the court thought that the questions about homosexual conduct were "highly relevant" because, it believed, the Navy could "refuse reinstatement on the grounds that an individual has engaged in homosexual acts." The court held that "in seeking reinstatement and award of his diploma, [Steffan] through his claims has placed in issue whether he is qualified for such relief."

Judicial review of an administrative action is confined to "the grounds . . . upon which the record discloses that [the] action was based." SEC v. Chenery Corp., 318 U.S. 80, 87 (1943). This rule applies with equal force to judicial review of administrative actions by the military.

Here Steffan is challenging the Navy's administrative determination that he is unfit for continued service because he stated that he is a homosexual. That he seeks reinstatement as relief for an allegedly invalid separation does not put into issue the question whether he engaged in potentially disqualifying conduct unless such conduct was a basis for his separation. See White v. Secretary of the Army, 878 F.2d 501, 505 (D.C. Cir. 1989).* If Steffan was discharged wrongfully, he "has never been discharged[;] . . . in the eyes of the law, [he] remains in service." Dilley v. Alexander, 627 F.2d 407, 411 (D.C. Cir. 1980).

The district court therefore erred in finding the inquiry into homosexual conduct vel non to be relevant on the ground asserted in its opinion. Should the district court find that the questions are relevant on

---

* The Government now argues that Steffan's admission of homosexuality raised a "rebuttable regulatory presumption that he had a predilection [sic] to commit, and had committed, homosexual acts." This argument, not raised in the district court, finds no support in the record. Cf. Ben-Shalom v. Marsh, 881 F.2d 454, 457 (7th Cir. 1989) (soldier given written notice of presumption).

any other ground, it must of course balance anew the interests of the parties before deciding upon a sanction. We reverse the judgment of the district court and remand for further proceedings consistent with this opinion.

So ordered.

NOTES AND PROBLEMS

1. How does one explain the different results in the two cases? In both cases one party (plaintiffs in *Blank,* the defendant in *Steffan*) asked a broad question; in one case the court orders an answer, in the other it refuses to order Steffan to answer. Why?

2. Focus on the procedural moves that led these two courts to issue their discovery rulings.

a. Which actions by which parties led the district court to issue its ruling?

b. How did *Steffan* reach an appellate court?

c. Suppose the defendant in *Blank* wanted to challenge the district court ruling. Could it have appealed?

d. What do your answers tell you about the power of district courts in discovery matters?

3. Develop your understanding of the concept of relevance by working through the following problems:

a. Albert and Barbara are involved in an automobile collision. Albert sues Barbara, alleging negligence. Barbara denies liability. Barbara seeks to discover the size of Albert's bank account. (Assume Barbara is interested because she wishes to know whether Albert will be able to finance protracted litigation.) Is this information relevant and thus discoverable?

b. Same facts as in Problem 3a. Now Albert seeks to discover the size of Barbara's bank account. (He wants to know whether she will be capable of satisfying a damage judgment.) Is this information relevant to the question of liability and thus discoverable?

c. Same facts as in Problem 3a, except that in addition to asserting negligence, Albert alleges that Barbara intentionally collided with him. Intentional torts carry with them punitive damages, and in many jurisdictions a jury asked to award punitive damages may consider the wealth of the defendant, the idea being that the punishment should be tailored to the defendant's circumstances. Albert again seeks to discover the size of Barbara's bank account. Is it now relevant and thus discoverable?

d. Same lawsuit as in Problem 3a — that is, a negligence action, with no allegations of intentional harm. Albert, fearing that Barbara may lack assets to pay damages, seeks to discover whether Barbara has a liability insurance policy that would be available to satisfy a damage judgment if he wins the suit. If one considers only relevance, is the policy discoverable? Now consider how Rule 26(a)(1)(D) changes this result. What might justify this exception to the ordinary rules of relevance?

4. Now consider a variation on this problem, one in which you begin to confront some of the techniques of discovery. The current version of Rule 26 provides for a two-stage discovery process. In the first, set forth in Rule 26(a), the parties come forward with certain basic information; in the second stage, they may ask each other for additional information under the guidelines described in Rule 26(b)(1). Read those provisions and answer the following questions:

a. Albert alleges that Barbara "negligently collided" with his car; Barbara's answer has denied negligence. (For an example of such an exchange of general pleadings, see pages 20 and 23.) Barbara's lawyer has interviewed her and knows the name and address of a mechanic who can testify about the maintenance of her car, her boss (with whom she had a major argument just before the accident), and a bystander who saw the accident.

b. Explain how each of these witnesses might have information relevant to the lawsuit.

c. Which of their names must Barbara's lawyer supply at the time appropriate for the disclosure required in Rule 26(a)(1)(A)?

5. The preceding problem grows from three interlocking Rules: 8, 11, and 26. Rule 8(a) requires only a "short and plain statement of the claim." The disclosure provisions of Rule 26 do not change that standard. They do, however, change a party's incentives to plead more specifically, for specific allegations will trigger both sides' obligation to disclose. In the case of Albert v. Barbara, for example, a complaint alleging that negligently maintained brakes caused the accident would presumably trigger Barbara's obligation to disclose a witness with information about the brakes.

But such allegations cannot be made casually. Rule 11 requires that all allegations of fact "have evidentiary support" as to which the certifying party has made an "inquiry reasonable under the circumstances." Rule 11(b)(3), however, permits a party to allege something lacking evidentiary support if it "is likely to have evidentiary support after a reasonable opportunity for further investigation or discovery." Would that provision allow Albert, without any basis for so believing, to allege that Barbara's brakes and steering mechanism were negligently maintained — in the hopes that such allegations would trigger some disclosure on which Albert could build a case?

6. Once one grasps the basic concept of relevance, a question arises: How weak can the link between information sought and the proposition to be proved become before the information becomes irrelevant?

a. In a suit attacking the reserve clause of player contracts of the National Football League, discovery was permitted into the method of management and financial affairs of all twenty-six teams on the theory that the subject matter of the suit was "football and the business of conducting it." Is this too broad?

b. Peters was killed while operating a back hoe manufactured by DigTrench Manufacturing Co. He was digging to locate a water main when the backhoe flipped over and crushed him. There were no witnesses to the accident, and it is unclear why the backhoe flipped over. Mrs. Peters commences a products liability action against DigTrench and serves interrogatories asking about other accidents with a similar model backhoe. The law of evidence, based on the rationale of not wanting to discourage repairs and redesign of dangerous conditions, says that a plaintiff cannot introduce evidence of subsequent repairs to show that the defendant acknowledged the dangerousness of the condition. DigTrench answers the interrogatories by saying that no similar accidents occurred before the one resulting in Peter's death, and objects to the interrogatory insofar as it seeks evidence of later accidents on the ground that evidence of such accidents is inadmissible. What result? Construct an argument about how information about such accidents might lead to admissible evidence.

2.   Privilege

Rule 26(b)(1) contains an explicit exception: It makes discoverable "any matter, *not privileged*, which is relevant. . . ." (emphasis added). The law of evidence creates privileges — protections for information *from certain sources*. For example, in a criminal case the prosecutor cannot call the defendant to the stand and ask her if she committed the crime; such an action would violate the constitutional privilege against self-incrimination. Notice first that this objection on the grounds of a privilege has nothing to do with relevance: Whether the defendant committed the crime is highly relevant. Second, note that privileges typically block information from a particular source; privileges are not meant to block the underlying facts. Thus the prosecution in a criminal case, though barred by the Fifth Amendment from asking the defendant about her guilt, can introduce evidence from other, unprivileged sources.

Some of the more common privileges are attorney-client, doctor-patient, and psychotherapist-patient. Discussing all of the privileges and the conditions for their invocation is far beyond the scope of a course in civil procedure. Our focus instead is on the interaction of privileges and discovery in civil lawsuits.

NOTES AND PROBLEMS

1. Albert and Barbara are involved in an automobile collision. Albert sues Barbara, alleging that Barbara intentionally drove her car into Albert's. Barbara denies liability. In a deposition Albert's lawyer asks Barbara, "Did you intentionally collide with Albert?"

a. Can Barbara object on the grounds that the question is irrelevant?

b. Barbara objects on grounds of privilege. What privilege?

2. Often the existence of a privilege only begins an inquiry. All privileges can be waived, either explicitly by the party entitled to use it or implicitly by an action inconsistent with the privilege. Moreover, privileges cannot be abused.

a. For example, a criminal defendant invoking a privilege against self-incrimination may waive that privilege by taking the stand and denying the crime. Having started to testify about the crime, he cannot then invoke the privilege when the prosecution seeks to cross-examine. Or a client can waive the attorney-client privilege by disclosing to some third party the contents of his statements to his lawyer — statements that would otherwise be privileged.

b. Same lawsuit as in Problem 1, except that in addition to negligence and battery, Albert alleges that Barbara intentionally inflicted emotional distress. Barbara's answer denies causation and her lawyer plans to argue at trial that Albert has been emotionally unstable for years. During discovery, Barbara's lawyer learns that Albert has been in psychotherapy for some time. (The state in question recognizes a privilege for patient-psychotherapist communications.) Should Albert be allowed to claim privilege as a basis for refusing to answer questions about his therapy?

3. The discussion above contrasts relevance and privilege. In a few unusual cases a party has plausible objections on both grounds. Recall Steffan v. Cheney, in which the Navy sought to depose Steffan about his sexual behavior. Steffan objected on grounds both of relevance and privilege.

a. As a review, explain why relevance was a plausible objection given the law governing the case.

b. Because the court found the question irrelevant, it did not have to decide on the claim of privilege. Assume that the court reached a different decision on relevance. Construct Steffan's argument based on privilege.

4. One evidentiary privilege arises frequently in a discovery context and deserves special note. The attorney-client privilege protects communications between lawyers and clients concerning the matters the lawyer is handling for the client. Such a privilege does not, of course, prevent discovery of underlying facts ("How fast were you driving, Ms. Defendant?"), but it does prevent inquiries about communications to one's lawyer ("What did you tell your lawyer about how fast you were driving?"). The scope of the attorney-client privilege in corporate contexts forms the center of a case with significant discovery implications. In Upjohn Co. v. United States, 449 U.S. 383, 391-393 (1981), the Court held that the corporation's attorney-client privilege extended beyond the "control group" (top management):

> Middle-level — and indeed lower-level — employees can, by actions within the scope of their employment, embroil the corporation in serious legal difficulties, and it is only natural that these employees would have the relevant information needed by corporate counsel if he is adequately to advise the client with respect to such actual or potential difficulties. . . .
>
> The control group test adopted by the court below thus frustrates the very purpose of the privilege by discouraging the communication of relevant information by employees of the client to attorneys seeking to render legal advice to the client corporation. The attorney's advice will also frequently be more significant to noncontrol group members than to those who officially sanction the advice, and the control group test makes it more difficult to convey full and frank legal advice to the employees who will put into effect the client corporation's policy. . . .

a. Notice an implication of the Upjohn holding: Suppose an individual and a firm in litigation with each other on a matter in which the proper accounting treatment of a particular transaction is in dispute. The corporation's lawyer interviews the accountant, who is an employee of the firm. The individual's lawyer interviews the individual's accountant, a professional who, like the lawyer, works for many clients. Now suppose that each lawyer seeks to discover the contents of the opposing lawyer's interview with the accountant. Will the corporation's lawyer's conversation be privileged? Will that of the individual's lawyer? (As you will see later in this chapter, there may be other barriers to discovery in the latter situation, but not the attorney-client privilege.)

b. Recognize the limitations of the Upjohn holding as well: Suppose that, before any litigation is in sight, both the corporation and the individual consulted their respective accountants about how to treat the transaction. When litigation is underway, both sides are deposed. In the deposition the opposing lawyer states, "Describe your conversation with the accountant concerning this transaction." Explain why neither side can claim a privilege in this situation.

C.   Surveying Discovery: Procedures and Methods

Lawyers need to understand the interplay of relevance, privilege, and judicial discretion in discovery. They also need to understand the more specific workings of the discovery rules. The easiest way to grasp these rules is first to read Federal Rules 26-37; then, refer again to specific rules as this survey touches them. As you read, consider why the discovery rules contain more detail than, say, the pleading rules.

Rule 26 is the master rule: It provides a catalogue of disclosure and discovery methods (in 26(a) and (b)) and defines the ground rules. These ground rules come in two parts: a requirement of mandatory disclosure (in 26(a)) and for further discovery (in 26(b)).

1.   Required Disclosures

Rule 26(a)(1) describes the first stage, which it calls "required disclosures." Early in the suit the parties must meet; within 10 days of that meeting, each party must offer the other side the names of witnesses and descriptions of documents "relevant to disputed facts alleged with particularity in the pleadings," as well as calculations of damages, and copies of insurance agreements. The parties must exchange such information without its having been requested by their opponent. Once these initial disclosures have occurred, the parties may then request additional information using interrogatories, depositions, requests for inspection of documents and physical objects, requests for physical and mental examinations, and for admissions. All this requires cooperation by the lawyers, a timetable, and mechanisms for enforcing discovery and disclosure obligations.

NOTES AND PROBLEMS

1. Your client, Baker, gives you a complaint served on him by Alice, who alleges that Baker agreed to sell her his car and then refused to go through with the transaction. Alice seeks $5,000 in damages. Baker tells you that he and Alice discussed such a possibility, but that they never agreed. In response to your questions, Baker tells you no one witnessed their discussion. You file an answer denying that there was a contract. You know that Rule 26(a)(1) requires some disclosures.

a. Given the allegations in the pleadings and the requirements of Rule 26(a)(1), what information would you have to prepare for disclosure?

b. On this state of the pleadings, what would be the only information you would be confident Alice would have to disclose to you?

2. Assuming a party must make some disclosure, when must that disclosure occur? Answering this question requires a close reading of Rules 4, 16(b), 26(a)(1), and 26(f). Together these provisions establish a time line that starts when the defendant has been served or has "appeared" in the lawsuit. Service occurs when the defendant has been served or when the defendant, pursuant to Rule 4(d), has waived formal service. "Appearance" refers to the defendant's filing some paper or motion that evinces its participation in the lawsuit; it would include an answer as well as various Rule 12(b) motions.

At this point a series of time sequences that govern pretrial procedure begins to run. One requirement appears in Rule 16(b), which provides that within 90 days after a defendant's appearance and 120 days after service the judge shall hold a "scheduling conference" to discuss the way discovery and other pretrial matters should proceed. Rule 26(f) requires the parties meet each other without the judge to discuss the case "as soon as practicable and in any event at least 14 days before a scheduling conference is held." Finally, to complete the link to disclosure, Rule 26(a)(1) requires the parties, at this meeting or within 10 days after it, to exchange disclosure lists.

These interlocking provisions require the parties to exchange the required disclosures at least four days before the scheduling conference and, at the latest, four months after the complaint is served on defendant. More commonly, where defendant has appeared, the disclosure will occur no later than 85 days after that appearance.

3. The disclosures required by Rule 26(a)(1) occur unless the parties have otherwise agreed or the court has otherwise ordered. The first clause of Rule 26(a) permits the parties by agreement, or the court by a local rule applying to categories of cases, or an order entered in the particular case, to dispense with required disclosure. The advisory committee notes to the amended Rule suggest that courts may wish to exempt cases such as Social Security claims, where the amounts at stake are typically small and the facts are well known to both parties.

4. Rule 26(d) says that the parties may not use other forms of discovery — depositions, interrogatories, etc — until after the meeting required by Rule 26(f). In districts employing disclosure, the exchange of disclosures must closely follow the Rule 26(f) meeting. In such districts the other forms of discovery usually come into play only after the initial disclosures. In districts not using disclosure, the Rule 26(f) meeting usually triggers the first round of discovery requests.

Rule 26 defines the broad guidelines for discovery. Rules 27-36 spell out the ways to obtain information and the protocol for using each of the discovery devices. Finally, Rules 26(g) and 37 provide for enforcement of the discovery rules.

There are generally three ways of obtaining information: by asking questions; by examining documents, physical objects, and persons; and by asking one's opponent to admit contentions. Each method has its advantages and problems.

2.   Asking Questions: Interrogatories and Depositions (Rules 28, 30, 31, 32, 33, and 37)

One may send one's opponent a list of questions to answer (interrogatories) or one may take a witness's deposition ("depose" him or her). What is the difference between the two? The answer usually involves balancing utility and cost; in discovery one often gets what one pays for.

Interrogatories (Rule 33) are typically much cheaper for the interrogator (the "propounder" of the interrogatories) because one can inexpensively frame a set of appropriate questions, send it to an adverse party, and sit back and wait for the answers. The recipient (and his lawyer) must either answer the questions or object to them. A drawback to interrogatories is that, because the questioner cannot follow up evasive answers with questions designed to pin things down, interrogatories that go beyond fairly routine specific information, such as the names and addresses of witnesses, may yield little valuable information. And because such routine information will ordinarily emerge as part of the disclosure required by Rule 26(a)(1), there may be limited situations in which interrogatories serve a useful role. Moreover, parties must seek permission of the court — or a stipulation from their opponents — before propounding more than 25 questions. Note also that interrogatories may be sent only to a party; nonparty witnesses may be deposed but need not answer written interrogatories.

Depositions (Rules 28, 30, 31, 32) present the opposite balance of cost and usefulness. A deposition is like questioning a witness at trial without the judge: Depositions often occur in lawyers' offices, and the lawyers are present, as is the witness and a court reporter or recording device. The lawyers ask questions that the witness must answer under oath. The advantage is that the lawyer can ask a series of questions that force the witness to take a position as to the matters at issue, and the lawyer can follow up with further questions if the witness is evasive, or if the witness's testimony opens up new avenues of inquiry. The disadvantage is the expense to all concerned. In a full-blown deposition, both sides have their lawyers there; even if the witness is not one of the parties he or she may be represented by a lawyer. In addition, the deposing party must arrange for some form of recording or transcription of the deposition. In a case with multiple parties, each hour of deposition time may amount to thousands of dollars in legal fees and costs. As with interrogatories, the Rules place limits on depositions. Without seeking permission, the total number of depositions taken by one side (plaintiff(s), defendant(s), third-party defendant(s)) may not exceed 10, and no person may be deposed a second time without the permission of the court or the other side.

Halfway between interrogatories and a deposition is a deposition on written questions (Rule 31). In this rarely used procedure the lawyer writes down the questions and sends them to the court reporter presiding at the deposition, who asks the questions and records the witness's answers. This is a good deal cheaper than a deposition on oral examination. It often, however, yields less information than a "live" deposition. To understand the reason for this low yield, think how difficult it would be to compose such a set of questions: The first one or two inquiries are straightforward, but how does one frame follow-up questions without knowing what the witness will say to the initial inquiry?

What happens if there is a disagreement about whether a question in a deposition or an interrogatory is justified? The procedure differs according to the device being used. Read Rules 30(d) and 33(b), together with Rule 37(a)(2) and (4), and apply them to the questions below.

PROBLEMS

1. Having sustained injuries from a household appliance, Cora sues Manufacturer in a district using the disclosure regime of Rule 26(a). The required discovery conference and the ensuing disclosures occur. Cora then serves 55 interrogatories on Manufacturer and 20 interrogatories on Department Store, which sold her the product. Both Store and Manufacturer refuse to answer.

a. Assuming the questions are relevant and not privileged, must Store answer? By what procedural step might Cora induce Store to answer?

b. Can Cora get a court to compel Manufacturer's answers?

2. Pursuant to Rule 30(b)(6), Cora serves on Manufacturer a request to depose an employee or officer responsible for the "design and safety engineering" of the appliance in question. Manufacturer designates Geraldine Chen, a vice president for product design. At the deposition, Cora's lawyer asks Chen a series of questions about her qualifications and responsibilities. She then asks Chen a question about the financial structure of the company. Manufacturer's lawyer believes that question is outside the subject matter specified in the Rule 30(b)(6) notice (and Chen is therefore less well prepared to answer).

a. May Manufacturer's lawyer advise Chen not to answer the line of questions to which he objects? See Rule 30(d)(1).

b. What should Manufacturer's lawyer do? See Rule 30(d)(3).

3. Later in the same deposition, Cora's lawyer asks Chen a series of questions that Manufacturer's lawyer believes constitute violations of the attorney-client privilege ("Have you consulted with counsel about potential liability for a product with this design characteristic?"). Many lawyers would respond to such a question by advising their client not to answer it, a course of action explicitly permitted by Rule 30(d)(1). Having elicited this response to a series of similar questions, Cora's lawyer moves to another subject and thereafter ends the deposition. If Cora's lawyer believes that some of the unanswered questions were not subject to any privilege, how should she proceed to require answers?

4. One should not overlook the deposition as a source of unintentional humor. Consider the following excerpts, collected by Mary Louise Gilman, the editor of *National Shorthand Reporter* and published in Richard Lederer, Anguished English (1987):

Q. Doctor, did you say he was shot in the woods?
A. No, I said he was shot in the lumbar region.

Q. What is your name?
A. Ernestine McDowell.
Q. And what is your marital status?
A. Fair.

Q. Mrs. Smith, do you believe that you are emotionally unstable?
A. I should be.
Q. How many times have you committed suicide?
A. Four times.

Q. When he went, had you gone and had she, if she wanted to and were able, for the time being excluding all the restraints on her not to go, gone also, would he have brought you, meaning you and she, with him to the station?
Mr. Brooks: Objection. That question should be taken out and shot.

Finally, consider what Professor Richard Friedman reports as "an actual trial transcript," whose accuracy he has confirmed with one of the lawyers:

The Court: Next witness.
Ms. Olschner: Your Honor, at this time I would like to swat Mr. Buck in the head with his client's deposition.

The Court: You mean read it?

Ms. Olschner: No, sir. I mean to swat him [in] the head with it. Pursuant to Rule 32, I may use the deposition "for any purpose" and that is the purpose for which I want to use it.

The Court: Well, it does say that.

(Pause.)

The Court: There being no objection, you may proceed.

Ms. Olschner: Thank you, Judge Hanes.

(Whereupon Ms. Olschner swatted Mr. Buck in the head with a deposition.)

Mr. Buck: But Judge. . . .

The Court: Next witness.

Mr. Buck: We object.

The Court: Sustained. Next witness.

3. Examining Things and People: Production and Inspection of Documents and Things; Physical and Mental Examinations (Rules 34 and 35)

Sometimes a lawsuit turns on the condition of a physical object (the wrecked automobile, the allegedly defective computer chip); sometimes the condition of land is at issue (How deep is the hole into which plaintiff fell? Is it concealed by grass?). Rule 34 permits inspection of land and objects. In addition, documents often provide important evidence, and discovery in most lawsuits will include requests for documents in the possession of the opposing party, or third parties. It is important to keep in mind that the term "documents" is a bit of a misnomer, as it includes not only what we traditionally think of as documents (sheets of paper such as letters, notes, drafts, and manuals), but any medium for recording data or information. An email message stored on a computer's hard drive, or on a backup tape made for crash-recovery purposes is a "document," as is a photograph or videotape.

Documents frequently relate to issues of damages. Medical records, for example, are typically the backbone of damage discovery in personal injury cases, whereas accounting records would be the core of discovery in a case involving a claim of lost profits. Documents may also be critical to liability issues. In a contract dispute over the interpretation of an ambiguous provision of a contract, for example, each side will want to see any drafts, memos, or notes that might reflect the other side's interpretation of the disputed provision, and will want to use such documents in the depositions it might take of the opposing side's witnesses.

Note the procedure for requesting documents differs slightly according to whether one is requesting them from a party or a nonparty. For a party, one simply sends a Rule 34 request, specifying the documents sought. For a nonparty, one makes a similar request but embodies it in a subpoena issued under Rule 45(a)(1)(C). As with both depositions and interrogatories, requests for documents from parties may not be made before the disclosures required by Rule 26(a). It is also important to bear in mind that, unlike interrogatories and depositions, the number of document requests is not limited by the Rules. Because of the central role that documents play, parties will typically want to make comprehensive document requests and want to review the documents produced in response to the request before proceeding with depositions. For such an instance and one court's response to it, see Chudasama v. Mazda Motor Corp. at the end of this chapter (infra page 549).

The difficulties surrounding requests for documents can resemble those that might be encountered in a large library staffed by hostile librarians who respond to research queries only if asked precisely the right question. Some document production disputes are akin to those in interrogatory practice: How exactly must the requester identify the record in question? In practice, very broad requests are usually allowed, because the party propounding the request does not know what records the responding party has. A typical request might seek all documents in the custody or control of the responding party that "refer, relate or pertain in any manner" to subject X. Such broad requests might end up calling for hundreds, thousands, or even millions of documents, only a small portion of which bear even the remotest potential relevance to the lawsuit. The responding party might then object to the request on the grounds that it is overbroad, or begin a negotiation process whereby it seeks to have the propounding party redefine or narrow the request. The propounding party, however, is suspicious that the responding party is seeking to have the request redrawn in a manner that will insulate the production of relevant and damaging evidence. *Chudasama* again provides an example of such a pattern. To the extent that such documents fall within the disclosures required by Rule 26(a), these problems may subside slightly.

Other difficulties with Rule 34 requests arise from issues of who will bear the cost of production: May the party on whom the discovery request is served simply point to a warehouse full of files (or to a computer data bank)? Note that the last sentence of Rule 34(b) requires that the producing party produce the documents "as they are kept in the usual course of business or shall organize and label them to correspond with the categories in the request."

One of the more delicate Rule provisions concerns the physical and mental examinations of parties. Unlike other discovery provisions, Rule 35 requires a special application to the court and a showing of "good cause." The disputes here focus on what constitutes "good cause."

PROBLEMS

1. Alice brings suit against Centerville Village, claiming that its police officers assaulted her during an afternoon political demonstration. Her complaint alleges that the assault "severely injured her." The city attorney assigned to the case uncovers a photograph of Alice, taken the night after the incident, showing her participating enthusiastically in a local dance contest. At the Rule 26(f) conference with Alice's lawyer, Centerville's lawyer learns that she will contend that the police assault injured her leg.

a. Must the defendant produce the photograph as part of the disclosures required within ten days of the lawyers' conference? Read Rule 26(a)(1)(B).

b. Assume that the defendant concludes that Alice's injury was not pleaded with sufficient particularity and does not disclose the existence of the photograph. Thereafter Alice makes a Rule 34 demand that Centerville produce "all documents, memoranda, and reports relating to the incident." As attorney for Centerville, must you now produce the photograph?

c. If you do not produce the photograph either as part of the required disclosure or in response to the later request but later seek to introduce it as evidence at trial, what risk do you run?

2. Randolph files suit for damages after being injured in an accident with a truck owned and operated by Craven. Randolph has reason to think that Craven's truck was serviced at Elaine's Garage and wants to see the service record. Randolph doubts Elaine will produce it voluntarily. What steps can Randolph take to obtain the documents?

3. Pat is injured in an automobile crash with Dunham; Pat sues. Dunham seeks to have Pat examined by a physician.

a. Should the court grant permission?

b. If the examination takes place, is Pat entitled to see a copy of the physician's report to Dunham?

c. Pat requests a copy of the physician's report and receives it. Dunham then requests from Pat copies of *her* physician's reports on her injury. Is Dunham entitled to these?

4. Rather than move for a physical examination, Dunham's lawyer in the Rule 26(f) conference suggests that Pat submit voluntarily to a physical examination. If Pat's attorney agrees, can he obtain a copy of the report? Can he take the examining doctor's deposition?

5. A key witness in Pat's suit against Dunham is Jones, who allegedly saw "everything that happened" from a position more than 100 feet away. Can Dunham require Jones to take an eye examination? What happens if Jones is an employee of Dunham?

6. Elizabeth Learned, who holds a doctorate in English from Stateville University, applies for but is denied a teaching position at Stateville. Learned sues Stateville alleging gender discrimination. Stateville moves to have a mental examination of Learned to support its defense that it refused to hire her because she was mentally unstable. Attached to the motion is an affidavit of Professor Pigge to the effect that feminists have severe emotional problems and that he observed Elizabeth Learned acting "psychotic" at a meeting of women English students at Stateville. Should the examination be granted? Why?

4.   Asking Your Opponent to Admit Things: Requests for Admission (Rule 36)

One can consider Rule 36 as much a pleading rule as a discovery device: It does not uncover evidence so much as it makes evidence irrelevant by taking an issue out of controversy. Notice that, because of Rule 37(c), Rule 36 has teeth. Rule 36 has functioned best when used to eliminate essentially undisputed issues — for example, that the defendant is incorporated in Washington or that at the time in question the automobile was registered to Martha. In a regime that required detailed pleading, these issues might be disposed of at the pleading stage. The adoption of notice pleading makes a device like Rule 36 useful.

The disputes over Rule 36 have arisen when, either by design or inadvertence, one party has asked the other to admit a fact that seemed to be at the core of the case. One type of such a question might be normative: "Were you driving negligently?" "Did defendant breach the contract?" Another type might be historical: "Were you driving 50 M.P.H. at the time of the accident?" "Did defendant on February 22 deliver the 500 rolls of paper?" In either case the question may lie at the center of the case. How should a party respond to such a question?

Matters become worse when the party served with such a request has simply let the time for reply elapse without responding. Read literally, the Rule suggests that the requested facts should be deemed admitted, and occasionally courts have so held. For example, see Morast v. Auble,

164 Mont. 100, 519 P.2d 157 (1974). Other courts have ignored the literal language or have glossed it with an interpretation suggesting that admissions were meant to deal with peripheral rather than central issues in the case. See Pickens v. Equitable Life Assurance Society, 413 F.2d 1390 (5th Cir. 1969). The Rule states that such an interpretation is erroneous and that a party who wishes in good faith to contest an issue may, if the facts permit, deny it and thereby put the other side to its proof.

PROBLEMS

1. Could plaintiff ask defendant to admit that there was a contract and defendant had breached it, and then, if defendant refused to admit that and plaintiff won the ensuing trial, ask for attorneys' fees for all the legal work done after the refusal to admit? Cf. Marchand v. Mercy Medical Center, 22 F.3d 933 (9th Cir. 1994) (imposing $205,000 attorneys' fees and costs on physician who failed to admit that he was negligent in treating plaintiff).

2. Greg is injured on a scout outing when he stumbles on a tent wire after returning from a late night raid on the campsite of another troop. He brings suit against the Boy Scouts of America, Inc. A young boy tells defense counsel he saw four other boys trip over the same wire. Plaintiff serves a notice to admit that, prior to this incident, four boys had stumbled on the same wire. Must defendant admit this "fact"?

3. Assume that defendant makes the admission, and one of the other trippers sues. Is the admission binding on defendant?

4. What is the difference between the effect of an interrogatory asking defendant some question and a request for an admission as to the same thing? The answer will emerge if one remembers that an admission is very much like a pleading, while an interrogatory is merely a bit of evidence. An admission takes a matter entirely out of controversy, while an interrogatory answer is a piece of evidence that may be contradicted by other pieces of evidence.

5.   Ensuring Compliance

All the discovery methods discussed above need enforcement mechanisms. The rules contain two — a general provision in Rule 26(g) and more specific provisions in Rule 37. Parties engaged in discovery often want information, and Rule 37 sets forth a series of devices designed either to elicit the information or to respond to parties' refusal to supply

it. Under Rule 37, a court may impose punishments ranging from awards
of expenses to dismissals of an entire case or the entry of a default
judgment. Under Rule 37(d) and (g), some sanctions are available on the
occurrence of misbehavior. Under Rule 37(b), however, other sanctions
cannot be sought until after the court orders a party to comply. (Put
another way, Rule 37(b) sanctions come into play not when a party
initially fails to comply with some discovery rule but when the party
refuses to comply with a specific court order.) If this feature is a weakness,
it is partially remedied by Rule 26(g), which (like Rule 11) requires
parties to sign disclosures, discovery requests, and objections and punishes
the parties for unjustified requests and refusals even when the parties'
behavior does not violate a court order. Unlike Rule 11, Rule 26(g)
suggests that attorneys' fees will be an appropriate sanction for most
violations of its obligations. Reread Rules 26(g) and 37 and consider their
operation in the following problems.

PROBLEMS

1. In a judicial district using disclosure, Producer Corp. sues Supplier,
Inc., alleging failure to fulfill the conditions of a contract. Supplier denies
the allegations of the complaint and counterclaims for Producer's alleged
failure to pay for goods delivered. As soon as pleadings have closed and
before the disclosures have occurred, Producer *notices* (that is, notifies
of the intention to take) the depositions of several of Supplier's officers
and employees.

a. Explain why Supplier can object to this course of action? See
Rule 26(g)(3).

b. After the initial round of disclosures, Producer again seeks to depose
the officers and employees. Supplier objects to this course of action,
believing that without more groundwork having been laid, these depositions will prove a waste of time and expense — and will have to be repeated
later in the action once Producer has developed more information. Can
Supplier refuse to attend the depositions and avoid sanctions on the
grounds that Producer should first have built a stronger foundation for
an efficient use of deposition time? If not, what can Supplier do? See
Rule 26(b)(2) and Rule 26(c).

2. In the lawsuit described in Problem 1, Producer's disclosures fail
to list a former officer who was present at the negotiations of the agreement
and who could testify as to the parties' intent. At trial Producer seeks
to have this person testify. What objection can Supplier make? See
Rule 37(c)(1).

3. Suppose the same situation as in the preceding problem, except that Producer does not wish to have the former officer testify at trial because she will give testimony damaging to Producer. Further assume that Supplier has, through other discovery means, found out about her existence. Is there any sanction the court can impose on Producer for its failure to disclose the identity of this witness?

4. As the lawsuit described in Problem 1 proceeds, Supplier serves Producer with a request to produce documents relevant to the suit.

a. First suppose that Producer simply fails to respond to the requests for documents. What steps must Supplier follow to force Producer either to comply or suffer sanctions? Read carefully Rule 37(a)(1)-(2). See Shuffle Master Inc. v. Progressive Games, Inc., 170 F.R.D. 166 (D. Nev. 1996) (refusing to order sanctions in the absence of a certificate demonstrating good faith effort to confer with adversary).

b. Now suppose two of the documents sought are letters from Producer's lawyer to Producer that answer questions about the interpretation of the contract in question; Producer believes that both documents are protected by the attorney-client privilege. How should Producer raise such a contention? See Rules 26(c) and 37(a). What tactical advantages might accrue from using Rule 26(c) rather than 37(a) as the setting in which to raise the privilege?

c. Producer's response to Supplier's request states simply, "The requested documents have not been produced because they are protected by the attorney-client privilege." What should Supplier do? See Rules 26(b)(5), 37(a)(2)(B).

Despite the provision for judicial supervision and sanctions in Rules 26(g) and 37, what is most remarkable about discovery is the extent to which the parties run the system without court supervision. Rule 26(f) requires parties to confer about the case and about discovery plans as a prelude to a subsequent scheduling conference with the judge. Rules 26(a) and 29 give the parties the power to write their own discovery rules.

Finally, it is well worth remembering that the formal devices for discovery do not exhaust the possibilities for factual investigation. Independent factual investigation is entirely possible and in many cases is far more important than formal discovery. Legwork, telephone calls, informal interviews, examination of public records, and the like will often yield enormous amounts of information. It is important for the beginning lawyer not to become so mesmerized by the tool kit of formal discovery as to forget the existence of other means of gathering information.

D. Discovery and Privacy

Discovery aims at uncovering truth and permitting lawsuits to be decided on their merits. But truth sometimes hurts, and one can ask as to any given disclosure whether the gain in relevant information offsets the embarrassment, pain, and possible consequences of revealing tangentially relevant information.

The system seeks to shield parties from such excessive discovery. The question of what discovery is excessive is of course difficult. The general proposition underlying the discovery rules is that people can be required to reveal relevant information, even when the information is embarrassing or "confidential," in the ordinary sense of that word. But the Rules also recognize that sometimes a zealous or ill-meaning adversary will use discovery not to uncover relevant information but to harass. Beyond the general provisions in Rule 26(g) forbidding abusive discovery, the Rules use two devices to control such behavior. Rule 26(c) permits a party to seek a protective order and gives the judge broad power to prevent abusive discovery. Rule 35 places special limits on the use of discovery to compel physical or mental examinations. This section explores both provisions.

1. The General Problem of Privacy

Rule 26(c) gives a judge power to enter "any order which justice requires to protect a party or person from annoyance, embarrassment, oppression, or undue burden or expense." Those terms are broad and undefined. The next case wrestles with what they might mean in the context of a specific case raising sensitive personal issues.

Stalnaker v. Kmart Corp.

71 Fair Empl. Prac. Cas. (BNA) 705 (D. Kan. 1996)

RUSHFELT, Magistrate Judge.

Under consideration is Defendant's First Motion For Protective Order. Pursuant to Fed. R. Civ. P. 26(c), defendant thereby seeks an order protecting non-party witnesses Lea Rozenberg, Rhonda Hyde, Gloria Olivares, and Lonny Casaert from discovery concerning voluntary romantic conduct or their sexual-related [sic] activities. Plaintiff has noticed depositions for these witnesses. She opposes the motion.

Plaintiff claims sexual harassment. She alleges that Donald Graves, an employee in the Receiving Department of defendant, created a hostile working environment and sexually harassed her by inappropriate touching. She has made no allegations against any of the proposed deponents.

Defendant asserts that plaintiff has not alleged that any of the witnesses had romantic or sexual involvement with her, created or contributed to the alleged hostile work environment, or otherwise wronged her. It further states that none of them have complained to it of sexual harassment. It contends that any voluntary romantic or sexual activities of the witnesses are irrelevant. It suggests, furthermore, that inquiry into such activities will invade their privacy rights. It argues that the embarrassment, humiliation, and invasion of privacy which would result from such inquiry substantially outweighs the probative value, if any, of such activities. It contends that Fed. R. Evid. 412 bars inquiry into such activities.

Plaintiff asserts that investigation has revealed potential harassment by Mr. Graves towards Ms. Rozenberg. Plaintiff suggests that the other witnesses may possess relevant information about sexual harassment at Kmart. She would agree to a protective order preventing dissemination of discovery to third parties. She suggests that such an order would alleviate the concern for privacy. She claims no intent to violate Fed. R. Evid. 412. . . .

Fed. R. Civ. P. 26(b) permits a broad scope of discovery. It provides in pertinent part that "[p]arties may obtain discovery regarding any matter, not privileged, which is relevant to the subject matter involved in the pending action." Fed. R. Civ. P. 26(b)(1). The information sought need not be admissible at trial if it appears reasonably calculated to lead to the discovery of admissible evidence. Despite the broad scope of permissible discovery, the court may enter protective orders totally prohibiting certain discovery or limiting the scope of discovery to certain matters. Fed. R. Civ. P. 26(c)(1) and (4).

Whether to enter a protective order is within the sound discretion of the court. Fed. R. Civ. P. 26(c) provides that the court, upon a showing of good cause, "may make any order which justice requires to protect a party or person from annoyance, embarrassment, oppression, or undue burden or expense." "[A] party is entitled to request a protective order to preclude any inquiry into areas that are clearly outside the scope of appropriate discovery." Caldwell v. Life Ins. Co. of N. Am., 165 F.R.D. 633, 637 (D. Kan. 1996). The party seeking a protective order, however, has the burden to show good cause for it. To establish good cause, that party must submit "a particular and specific demonstration of fact, as distinguished from stereotyped and conclusory statements." Gulf Oil Co. v. Bernard, 452 U.S. 89, 102 n.16 (1981).

Even when a motion arises in the context of discovery under Rule 26 of the Federal Rules of Civil Procedure, the Court must remain mindful of Rule 412 and its implications. Fed. R. Evid. 412(a) provides that "[e]vidence offered to prove that any alleged victim engaged in other sexual behavior" or "to prove any alleged victim's sexual predisposition" is not admissible in any civil or criminal proceeding involving alleged sexual misconduct except as provided in subdivisions (b) and (c). . . .

. . . [R]ule [412] aims to safeguard the alleged victim against the invasion of privacy, potential embarrassment and sexual stereotyping that is associated with public disclosure of intimate sexual details and the infusion of sexual innuendo into the factfinding process. By affording victims protection in most instances, the rule also encourages victims of sexual misconduct to institute and to participate in legal proceedings against alleged offenders. . . .

Although Fed. R. Evid. 412 applies generally to sexual harassment cases, the court does not find it controlling the present motion for protective order. The rule does not apply . . . "unless the person against whom the evidence is offered can reasonably be characterized as a 'victim of alleged sexual misconduct.' "Fed. R. Civ. P. advisory committee notes (1994 Amend.). . . .

Fed. R. Evid. 412 aside, defendant has demonstrated good cause to bar discovery of voluntary romantic and sexual activities of the four non-party witnesses to the extent they have no relationship to the allegations against Kmart. Those activities appear generally irrelevant to any issue in this action. Any sexual harassment by Graves is relevant, however, whether of plaintiff or of others. Consequently, the court will not preclude inquiry about any voluntary romantic or sexual activities with Mr. Graves to the extent they show any conduct on his part to encourage, solicit, or influence any employee of defendant to engage or continue in such activities. Such discovery is potentially embarrassing and annoying, both to the deponents and to defendant. The parties shall use such discovery, therefore, only for purposes of this litigation and shall not disclose it to anyone outside this litigation.

For the foregoing reasons the court sustains in part and overrules in part Defendant's First Motion For Protective Order. Plaintiff may not pursue discovery from Lea Rozenberg, Rhonda Hyde, Gloria Olivares, or Lonny Casaert about any voluntary romantic or sexual activities, except to the limited extent indicated in this order. The parties, furthermore, shall use discovery from such witnesses only for purposes of this litigation and shall not otherwise disclose it.

IT IS SO ORDERED.

NOTES AND PROBLEMS

1. Be clear about the procedural setting and the nature of the argument.

a. What information was the plaintiff seeking?

b. Why did plaintiff think that information was relevant?

c. Was the defendant claiming that the information was privileged?

2. What did the protective order forbid?

a. Imagine that you are at the deposition of Ms. Rozenberg. What type of questions about her relationship, if any, with Mr. Graves would be allowed under the order? What type of questions would not be allowed?

b. Would it be proper for plaintiff's counsel to begin the deposition by asking "Did you ever have a romantic or sexual relationship with Mr. Graves?"

c. What about asking "Did you ever have a romantic or sexual relationship with Mr. Graves that he in any way encouraged or solicited?" Is there any difference between these two questions?

3. The court took note that the proposed deponents had not themselves sought a protective order. Is it fair to infer that they didn't care about providing the type of information the plaintiff was seeking?

4. Consider the tactics of discovery employed in *Stalnaker*.

a. Plaintiff had a plausible argument for the relevance of the information sought. But think about what other purposes, beyond that of winning on the merits, plaintiff might have hoped to gain from seeking this information.

b. Suppose Rozenberg, the proposed deponent, after being informed of the court's order, retains you as her attorney, telling you she doesn't want to answer questions about her romantic or sexual activities with Mr. Graves. What would you advise her to do? See Rule 26(c).

c. What would happen if she refused to show up for her deposition, or refused to answer questions about her relationship with Mr. Graves? See Rules 37(a),(d).

5. Suppose the plaintiff's or defendant's lawyer disagrees with the magistrate judge's ruling in *Stalnaker*. Can he appeal? The answer to that question requires one to understand the judicial office of the person who makes discovery rulings.

a. If the ruling were made by a district judge, the answer to the question would be easy: No. A nonfinal order cannot be appealed. 28 U.S.C. §1291.

b. The *Stalnaker* ruling, however, was made by a magistrate judge, whose jurisdiction is defined by 28 U.S.C. §§636 et seq. One of the provisions of that jurisdiction is that a magistrate judge may hear nondispositive motions. 28 U.S.C. §636(b)(1)(A). (A dispositive motion is a motion that has the potential to end the case. Discovery orders serve as a prime example of nondispositive motions. Consequently many magistrates hear most or all discovery matters in many cases.

c. The section defining the magistrate's jurisdiction also provides for limited review of the magistrate's orders by *the district court judge*: "A judge of the [district] court may reconsider any pretrial matter under this subparagraph [providing for magistrate judges' jurisdiction over nondispositive motions] where it has been shown that the magistrate's order is clearly erroneous or contrary to law."

6. Because Rule 26(c) and similar provisions in state procedural rules are cast in terms of the courts' discretion, one cannot set forth clear rules for the granting or denying of protective orders. Consider how you, as the district court or magistrate judge, would respond to a request for a protective order in the following hypothetical case:

Nancy Clark has an abortion at Thomas Jefferson Hospital (TJH) and afterward suffers various complications that lead to a hysterectomy. Clark brings suit against TJH and the operating doctor, claiming that the hysterectomy was made necessary by the negligent treatment that she received after the abortion. The complaint seeks damages for being rendered sterile and for severe mental depression. Defendant seeks information on the name of the putative father, Clark's social relationships, and other facts relating to her emotional state. Does she have to answer the questions? If the doctor and hospital are asked to identify prior patients who have undergone abortions, must they do so? What if such information is revealed and either Clark or the hospital wants to depose one of the former patients to learn of any side effects?

7. The preceding problem illustrates an easily misunderstood point: how the discovery system treats information that is relevant and unprivileged (and not covered by a protective order) but which is confidential. Does Rule 26 exclude confidential information from discovery? Consider some situations in which such an issue might arise.

a. Plaintiffs sue Blood Bank, alleging negligent testing resulted in the transfusion of HIV-contaminated blood. Plaintiff seeks disclosure of the identity of the donor so that plaintiffs can discover from him facts bearing on their contention that Blood Bank failed to screen donors properly. Blood Bank argues that donors will not give blood if they believe their personal lives will thereby become the subject of lawsuits. How should the court rule? See Long v. American Red Cross, 145 F.R.D. 658 (S.D. Ohio 1993) (ruling that discovery — with unspecified protective order — permissible in part because deceased donor had diminished privacy interest).

b. A dismissed professor sues University alleging wrongful refusal to grant tenure. The plaintiff professor seeks to discover confidential tenure review files of others granted tenure at the same time, alleging that comparison will show that he was better qualified than they. The other professors intervene to seek a protective order. See Blum v. Schlegel, 150 F.R.D. 38 (W.D.N.Y.) (granting protective order to prevent discovery of embarrassing "sensitive, scholarly critiques . . . [and] personal observations" of reviewers).

c. At State University, Abrams and Braun have an altercation that results in serious injuries to Abrams. The dean recommends that Braun be suspended for one semester; pursuant to the student code, a hearing is to be held before the student court. The dean tells all parties to testify freely and calls attention to a provision in the student code that all testimony given at the hearing will be "privileged and confidential." As attorney for Braun, should you permit him to testify?

8. Protective orders will not solve all clashes between the broad scope of discovery and clients' interests in keeping certain matters confidential. An example arose in connection with Coca-Cola Bottling Co. v. Coca-Cola Co., 107 F.R.D. 288 (D. Del. 1985), in which Coca-Cola bottlers sued the manufacturer over the division of profits from Diet Coke. The primary issue in contention was "whether the contractual term 'Coca-Cola Bottler's Syrup' includes the syrup used to make Diet Coke." Id. at 289. The bottlers contended that the question could be resolved by discovering the ingredients used in both drinks. The defendant manufacturer strongly resisted the effort, for reasons the opinion explains:

> The complete formula for Coca-Cola is one of the best kept trade secrets in the world. . . . The ingredient that gives Coca-Cola its distinctive taste is a secret combination of flavoring oils and ingredients known as "Merchandise 7X." The formula for Merchandise 7X has been tightly guarded since Coca-Cola was first invented and is known by only two persons within The Coca-Cola Company. . . . The only written record of the secret formula is kept in a security vault . . . which can only be opened upon a resolution from the Company's Board of Directors.

Id. at 289. The court, ruling that the formula was relevant and unprotected by any privilege, ordered disclosure but also scheduled hearings on ways in which to protect the trade secret from disclosure to third parties. Defendant still refused to comply:

> By letter . . . counsel for the Company informed the Court that the Company would not disclose its formulae, "[i]n light of the overriding commercial importance of the secrecy of the formulae to the entire Coca-Cola system . . . even under the terms of a stringent protective order. . . ."

Coca-Cola Bottling Co. v. Coca-Cola Co., 110 F.R.D. 363, 366 (D. Del. 1986). The court held a hearing on sanctions and concluded that it would not impose a default judgment but would order that plaintiffs were entitled to any favorable inference from the assumption that the formulas were identical. It also ordered the defendant to pay attorneys' fees and costs on the motion to compel, though not the costs related to its original resistance to discovery.

9. A frequent reason for requesting protective orders is to prevent discovery in one case from being available in another, similar case. Suppose attorney represents plaintiff in a suit alleging a defect in a widely sold automobile. In discovery defendant produces much information about the design and testing of the vehicle.

a. Attorney A wants to use the discovery in other cases he is handling. As a practical matter, it scarcely matters what rule one frames about this situation. Even if one formally prohibits the lawyer from using the information directly, she knows exactly which questions to ask in other cases.

b. Can Attorney A disseminate the information to other lawyers? Lawyers with expertise in particular areas of litigation often give seminars for other lawyers, charging sometimes-hefty fees for their knowledge. Can Attorney A "sell" the discovery information in this way?

c. One answer to the last question is that attempts to sell information will fail if it is available free in court records where other lawyers can review it if they know of its existence. In some jurisdictions depositions and interrogatories must be filed with the court and are therefore available for inspection unless the court issues a protective order.

d. Can a defendant obtain a protective order to prevent such collateral use of discovery? See Jochims v. Isuzu Motors Ltd., 148 F.R.D. 624 (S.D. Iowa 1993) (car manufacturer entitled to protective order for trade secrets but not for information relevant to other lawsuits on same topic; plaintiffs' lawyers in other suit entitled to intervene for purpose of contesting motion for protective order).

10. Finally, consider a common effort to achieve a privately negotiated protective order. Suppose the parties settle the case. One of the terms of the settlement agreement calls for the plaintiff's lawyers to return all originals and copies of discovery documents and not to disclose their contents to any other person. The agreement provides that breach of this term gives rise to liquidated damages of $25,000. Such an agreement is a contract between the parties and is enforceable like any other contract unless one of its terms violates public policy. Alternatively, the parties may seek to have such an agreement made part of a consent judgment and thus enforceable by contempt power. Should the court enter such a judgment?

a. Should the Rules or legislation prohibit such agreements?

b. Such questions have two sides. On the one hand, any term that protects defendants against future liability will encourage them to settle and will result in a higher settlement payment to plaintiffs. (Think how reluctant defendants would be to settle if the terms of each settlement and the underlying information were automatically available to the public.) On the other hand, some discovery will apply to many similar lawsuits, and it is inefficient to require each set of new parties to go through the same discovery routine. How should courts weigh such matters of public concern against the desires of the plaintiff and defendant before the court — both of whom are, for different reasons, seeking to prevent disclosure of the discovery information?

c. In Baker v. General Motors, 522 U.S. 222 (1997), the Supreme Court faced a variation on the questions posed in this and the preceding question. Elwell, an engineer dismissed from GM, became involved in litigation with his former employer. As part of a settlement of that suit — a settlement embodied in a consent decree entered by a Michigan court — Elwell was enjoined from "testifying, without the prior written consent of [GM], . . . as . . . a witness of any kind . . . in any litigation . . . involving [GM] as an owner, seller, manufacturer, and/or designer. . . ." Sometime after this decree, the Bakers sued GM in federal court in Missouri alleging a design defect in one of their vehicles. Plaintiffs subpoenaed Elwell to testify about some of his design work while employed at GM. GM argued that the subpoena, by failing to respect the injunction in the Michigan consent decree, violated the Full Faith and Credit Clause. No, said the U.S. Supreme Court, in a somewhat opaque opinion: Although there is no "public policy exception" to the Full Faith and Credit Clause (as the plaintiffs had argued), "Michigan's judgment cannot reach beyond [that] controversy to control proceedings against GM brought in other states. . . ." Id. at 238.

2.   A Special Instance: Physical and Mental Examinations

All uses of discovery conflict with the values of privacy, if one uses that term in a broad sense. The previous section explores how judges must balance this broad interest in privacy against the goals of discovery. Our culture places the highest value on privacy, however, when the question involves individual bodily or psychic integrity, and here the tension between the goals of disclosure and those of privacy seems greatest. Read Rule 35, which attempts to balance those interests, and consider this clash in the next case.

Schlagenhauf v. Holder

379 U.S. 104 (1964)

Mr. Justice GOLDBERG delivered the opinion of the Court. . . .

I

An action based on diversity of citizenship was brought in the District Court seeking damages arising from personal injuries suffered by passengers of a bus which collided with the rear of a tractor-trailer. The named defendants were The Greyhound Corporation, owner of the bus; petitioner, Robert L. Schlagenhauf, the bus driver; Contract Carriers, Inc., owner of the tractor; Joseph L. McCorkhill, driver of the tractor; and National Lead Company, owner of the trailer. Answers were filed by each of the defendants denying negligence.

Greyhound then cross-claimed against Contract Carriers and National Lead for damage to Greyhound's bus, alleging that the collision was due solely to their negligence in that the tractor-trailer was driven at an unreasonably low speed, had not remained in its lane, and was not equipped with proper rear lights. Contract Carriers filed an answer to this cross-claim denying its negligence and asserting "[t]hat the negligence of the driver of the . . . bus [petitioner Schlagenhauf] proximately caused and contributed to . . . Greyhound's damages."

Pursuant to a pretrial order, Contract Carriers filed a letter — which the trial court treated as, and we consider to be, part of the answer — alleging that Schlagenhauf was "not mentally or physically capable" of driving a bus at the time of the accident.

Contract Carriers and National Lead then petitioned the District Court for an order directing petitioner Schlagenhauf to submit to both mental and physical examinations by one specialist in each of the following fields:

(1) Internal medicine;
(2) Ophthalmology;
(3) Neurology; and
(4) Psychiatry.

For the purpose of offering a choice to the District Court of one specialist in each field, the petition recommended two specialists in internal medicine, ophthalmology, and psychiatry, respectively, and three specialists in neurology — a total of nine physicians. The petition alleged that the mental and physical condition of Schlagenhauf was "in controversy" as it had been raised by Contract Carriers' answer to Greyhound's cross-claim. This was supported by a brief of legal authorities and an affidavit of Contract Carriers' attorney stating that Schlagenhauf had seen red lights 10 to 15 seconds before the accident, that another witness had seen the rear lights of the trailer from a distance of three-quarters to one-half mile, and that Schlagenhauf had been involved in a prior accident. . . .

While disposition of this petition was pending, National Lead filed its answer to Greyhound's cross-claim and itself "cross-claimed" against Greyhound and Schlagenhauf for damage to its trailer. The answer asserted generally that Schlagenhauf's negligence proximately caused the accident. The cross-claim additionally alleged that Greyhound and Schlagenhauf were negligent

> [b]y permitting said bus to be operated over and upon said public highway by the said defendant, Robert L. Schlagenhauf, when both the said Greyhound Corporation and said Robert L. Schlagenhauf knew that the eyes and vision of the said Robert L. Schlagenhauf were impaired and deficient.

The District Court, on the basis of the petition filed by Contract Carriers, and without any hearing, ordered Schlagenhauf to submit to nine examinations — one by each of the recommended specialists — despite the fact that the petition clearly requested a total of only four examinations.[3]

Petitioner applied for a writ of mandamus in the Court of Appeals against the respondent, the District Court judge, seeking to have set aside the order requiring his mental and physical examinations. The Court of Appeals denied mandamus, one judge dissenting.

We granted certiorari to review undecided questions concerning the validity and construction of Rule 35. . . .

III

Rule 35 on its face applies to all "parties," which under any normal reading would include a defendant. Petitioner contends, however, that the application of the Rule to a defendant would be an unconstitutional invasion of his privacy, or, at the least, be a modification of substantive rights existing prior to the adoption of the Federal Rules of Civil Procedure and thus beyond the congressional mandate of the Rules Enabling Act.

These same contentions were raised in Sibbach v. Wilson & Co., 312 U.S. 1 (1941), by a plaintiff in a negligence action who asserted a physical injury as a basis for recovery. The Court, by a closely divided vote,

---

3. After the Court of Appeals denied mandamus, the order was corrected by the District Court to reduce the number of examinations to the four requested.

sustained the Rule as there applied. Both the majority and dissenting opinions, however, agreed that Rule 35 could not be assailed on constitutional grounds.

The division in the Court was on the issue of whether the Rule was procedural or a modification of substantive rights. The majority held that the Rule was a regulation of procedure and thus within the scope of the Enabling Act — the dissenters deemed it substantive. Petitioner does not challenge the holding in *Sibbach* as applied to plaintiffs. He contends, however, that it should not be extended to defendants. We can see no basis under the *Sibbach* holding for such a distinction. Discovery "is not a one-way proposition." Hickman v. Taylor. Issues cannot be resolved by a doctrine of favoring one class of litigants over another.

We recognize that, insofar as reported cases show, this type of discovery in federal courts has been applied solely to plaintiffs, and that some early state cases seem to have proceeded on a theory that a plaintiff who seeks redress for injuries in a court of law thereby "waives" his right to claim the inviolability of his person.

However, it is clear that *Sibbach* was not decided on any "waiver" theory. As Mr. Justice Roberts, for the majority, stated, one of the rights of a person "is the right not to be injured in one's person by another's negligence to redress infraction of which the present action was brought." For the dissenters, Mr. Justice Frankfurter pointed out that "[o]f course the Rule is compulsive in that the doors of the federal courts otherwise open may be shut to litigants who do not submit to such a physical examination."

These statements demonstrate the invalidity of any waiver theory. The chain of events leading to an ultimate determination on the merits begins with the injury of the plaintiff, an involuntary act on his part. Seeking court redress is just one step in this chain. If the plaintiff is prevented or deterred from this redress, the loss is thereby forced on him to the same extent as if the defendant were prevented or deterred from defending against the action.

Moreover, the rationalization of *Sibbach* on a waiver theory would mean that a plaintiff has waived a right by exercising his right of access to the federal courts. Such a result might create constitutional problems. Also, if a waiver theory is espoused, problems would arise as to a plaintiff who originally brought his action in a state court (where there was no equivalent of Rule 35) and then has the case removed by the defendant to federal court.

We hold that Rule 35, as applied to either plaintiffs or defendants to an action, is free of constitutional difficulty and is within the scope of the Enabling Act. . . .

Petitioner contends that even if Rule 35 is to be applied to defendants, which we have determined it must, nevertheless it should not be applied to him as he was not a party in relation to Contract Carriers and National Lead — the movants for the mental and physical examinations — at the time the examinations were sought.[11] The Court of Appeals agreed with petitioner's general legal proposition, holding that the person sought to be examined must be an opposing party vis-à-vis the movant (or at least one of them).

While it is clear that the person to be examined must be a party to the case,[12] we are of the view that the Court of Appeals gave an unduly restrictive interpretation to that term. Rule 35 only requires that the person to be examined be a party to the "action," not that he be an opposing party vis-à-vis the movant. There is no doubt that Schlagenhauf was a "party" to this "action" by virtue of the original complaint. Therefore, Rule 35 permitted examination of him (a party defendant) upon petition of Contract Carriers and National Lead (co-defendants), provided, of course, that the other requirements of the Rule were met. Insistence that the movant have filed a pleading against the person to be examined would have the undesirable result of an unnecessary proliferation of cross-claims and counterclaims and would not be in keeping with the aims of a liberal, nontechnical application of the Federal Rules. . . .

Petitioner next contends that his mental or physical condition was not "in controversy" and "good cause" was not shown for the examinations, both as required by the express terms of Rule 35. . . .

It is notable, however, that in none of the other discovery provisions is there a restriction that the matter be "in controversy," and only in Rule 34 is there Rule 35's requirement that the movant affirmatively demonstrate "good cause."[*]

---

11. We have already pointed out that at the time of the first petition, Schlagenhauf was a named defendant in the original complaint but was not a named cross-defendant in any pleadings filed by Contract Carriers or National Lead.

12. Although petitioner was an agent of Greyhound, he was himself a party to the action. He is to be distinguished from one who is not a party but is, for example, merely the agent of a party. This is not only clear in the wording of the Rule, but is reinforced by the fact that this Court has never approved the Advisory Committee's proposed amendment to Rule 35 which would include within the scope of the Rule "an agent or a person in the custody or under the legal control of a party." Advisory Committee on Rules for Civil Procedure, Report of Proposed Amendments, 41-43 (1955). It is not now necessary to determine to what extent, if any, the term "party" includes one who is a "real party in interest" although not a named party to the action. [Rule 35 was amended in 1970 to include "a person in the custody or under the legal control of a party." — ED.]

[* Before 1970, Rule 34, governing production of documents, required "good cause." In 1970 this requirement was deleted. — ED.]

This additional requirement of "good cause" was reviewed by Chief Judge Sobeloff in Guilford National Bank of Greensboro v. Southern Ry. Co. in the following words:

> Subject to . . . [the restrictions of Rules 26(b) and 30(b) and (d)], a party may take depositions and serve interrogatories without prior sanction of the court or even its knowledge of what the party is doing. Only if a deponent refuses to answer in the belief that the question is irrelevant, can the moving party request under Rule 37 a court order requiring an answer.
>
> Significantly, this freedom of action, afforded a party who resorts to depositions and interrogatories, is not granted to one proceeding under Rules 34 and 35. Instead, the court must decide as an initial matter, and in every case, whether the motion requesting production of documents or the making of a physical or mental examination adequately demonstrates good cause. The specific requirement of good cause would be meaningless if good cause could be sufficiently established by merely showing that the desired materials are relevant, for the relevancy standard has already been imposed by Rule 26(b). Thus, by adding the words" . . . good cause. . . ," the Rules indicate that there must be greater showing of need under Rules 34 and 35 than under the other discovery rules.

The courts of appeals in other cases have also recognized that Rule 34's good cause requirement is not a mere formality, but is a plainly expressed limitation on the use of that Rule. This is obviously true as to the "in controversy" and "good cause" requirements of Rule 35. They are not met by mere conclusory allegations of the pleadings — nor by mere relevance to the case — but require an affirmative showing by the movant that each condition as to which the examination is sought is really and genuinely in controversy and that good cause exists for ordering each particular examination. Obviously what may be good cause for one type of examination may not be so for another. The ability of the movant to obtain the desired information by other means is also relevant.

Rule 35, therefore, requires discriminating application by the trial judge, who must decide, as an initial matter in every case, whether the party requesting a mental or physical examination or examinations has adequately demonstrated the existence of the Rule's requirements of "in controversy" and "good cause.". . .

Of course, there are situations where the pleadings alone are sufficient to meet these requirements. A plaintiff in a negligence action who asserts mental or physical injury, cf. Sibbach v. Wilson & Co., supra, places that mental or physical injury clearly in controversy and provides the defendant with good cause for an examination to determine the existence and extent of such asserted injury. This is not only true as to a plaintiff, but applies equally to a defendant who asserts his mental or physical condition as a defense to a claim. . . . Here, however, Schlagenhauf did not assert his mental or physical condition either in support of or in defense of a claim. His condition was sought to be placed in issue by other parties. Thus, under the principles discussed above, Rule 35 required that these parties make an affirmative showing that petitioner's mental or physical condition was in controversy and that there was good cause for the examinations requested. This, the record plainly shows, they failed to do.

The only allegations in the pleadings relating to this subject were the general conclusory statement in Contract Carriers' answer to the cross-claim that "Schlagenhauf was not mentally or physically capable of operating" the bus at the time of the accident and the limited allegation in National Lead's cross-claim that, at the time of the accident, "the eyes and vision of . . . Schlagenhauf were impaired and deficient."

The attorney's affidavit attached to the petition for the examinations provided:

> [T]hat . . . Schlagenhauf, in his deposition . . . admitted that he saw red lights for 10 to 15 seconds prior to a collision with a semi-tractor trailer unit and yet drove his vehicle on without reducing speed and without altering the course thereof.
>
> The only eye-witness to this accident known to this affiant . . . testified that immediately prior to the impact between the bus and truck that he had also been approaching the truck from the rear and that he had clearly seen the lights of the truck for a distance of three-quarters to one-half mile to the rear thereof.
>
> . . . Schlagenhauf has admitted in his deposition . . . that he was involved in a [prior] similar type rear end collision. . . .

This record cannot support even the corrected order which required one examination in each of the four specialties of internal medicine, ophthalmology, neurology, and psychiatry. Nothing in the pleadings or affidavit would afford a basis for a belief that Schlagenhauf was suffering from a mental or neurological illness warranting wide-ranging psychiatric or neurological examinations. Nor is there anything stated justifying the broad internal medicine examination.[16]

The only specific allegation made in support of the four examinations ordered was that the "eyes and vision" of Schlagenhauf were impaired. Considering this in conjunction with the affidavit, we would be hesitant

---

16. Moreover, it seems clear that there was no compliance with Rule 35's requirement that the trial judge delineate the "conditions, and scope" of the examinations. Here the examinations were ordered in very broad, general areas. The internal medicine examination might for example, at the instance of the movant or its recommended physician extend to such things as blood tests, electrocardiograms, gastrointestinal and other X-ray examinations. It is hard to conceive how some of these could be relevant under any possible theory of the case.

to set aside a visual examination if it had been the only one ordered. However, as the case must be remanded to the District Court because of the other examinations ordered, it would be appropriate for the District Judge to reconsider also this order in light of the guidelines set forth in this opinion. . . .

Vacated and remanded.

Justice BLACK, with whom Justice CLARK joins, concurring in part and dissenting in part.

I agree with the Court that under Rule 35(a): (1) a plaintiff and a defendant have precisely the same right to obtain a court order for physical or mental examination of the other party or parties to a lawsuit; (2) before obtaining such an order it must be shown that physical or mental health is "in controversy" as to a relevant and material issue in the case; and (3) such an order "may be made only on motion for good cause shown" after "notice to the party to be examined and to all other parties." Unlike the Court, however, I think this record plainly shows that there *was* a controversy as to Schlagenhauf's mental and physical health and that "good cause" *was* shown for a physical and mental examination of him, unless failure to deny the allegations amounted to an admission that they were true. While the papers filed in connection with this motion were informal, there can be no doubt that other parties in the lawsuit specifically and unequivocally charged that Schlagenhauf was not mentally or physically capable of operating a motor bus at the time of the collision, and that his negligent operation of the bus caused the resulting injuries and damage. The other parties filed an affidavit based on depositions of Schlagenhauf and a witness stating that Schlagenhauf, driving the bus along a four-lane highway in what apparently was good weather, had come upon a tractor-trailer down the road in front of him. The tractor-trailer was displaying red lights visible for at least half a mile, and Schlagenhauf admitted seeing them. Yet after coming in sight of the vehicle Schlagenhauf continued driving the bus in a straight line, without slowing down, for a full 10 or 15 seconds until the bus struck the tractor-trailer. Schlagenhauf admitted also that he had been involved in the very same kind of accident once before. Schlagenhauf has never at any time in the proceedings denied and he does not even now deny the charges that his mental and physical health and his eyes and vision were impaired and deficient.

In a collision case like this one, evidence concerning very bad eyesight or impaired mental or physical health which may affect the ability to drive is obviously of the highest relevance. It is equally obvious, I think, that when a vehicle continues down an open road and smashes into a truck in front of it although the truck is in plain sight and there is ample time and room to avoid collision, the chances are good that the driver has some physical, mental or moral defect. When such a thing happens twice, one is even more likely to ask, "What is the matter with that driver? Is he blind or crazy?" Plainly the allegations of the other parties were relevant and put the question of Schlagenhauf's health and vision "in controversy." The Court nevertheless holds that these charges were not a sufficient basis on which to rest a court-ordered examination of Schlagenhauf. It says with reference to the charges of impaired physical or mental health that the charges are "conclusory." I had not thought there was anything strange about pleadings being "conclusory" — that is their function, at least since modern rules of procedure have attempted to substitute simple pleadings for the complicated and redundant ones which long kept the common-law courts in disrepute. . . .

Justice DOUGLAS, dissenting in part.

While I join the Court in reversing this judgment, I would, on the remand, deny all relief asked under Rule 35.

I do not suppose there is any licensed driver of a car or a truck who does not suffer from some ailment, whether it be ulcers, bad eyesight, abnormal blood pressure, deafness, liver malfunction, bursitis, rheumatism, or what not. If he or she is turned over to the plaintiff's doctors and psychoanalysts to discover the cause of the mishap, the door will be opened for grave miscarriages of justice. When the defendant's doctors examine plaintiff, they are normally interested only in answering a single question: Did plaintiff in fact sustain the specific injuries claimed? But plaintiff's doctors will naturally be inclined to go on a fishing expedition in search of *anything* which will tend to prove that the defendant was unfit to perform the acts which resulted in the plaintiff's injury. And a doctor for a fee can easily discover something wrong with any patient — a condition that in prejudiced medical eyes might have caused the accident. Once defendants are turned over to medical or psychiatric clinics for an analysis of their physical well-being and the condition of their psyche, the effective trial will be held there and not before the jury. There are no lawyers in those clinics to stop the doctor from probing this organ or that one, to halt a further inquiry, to object to a line of questioning. And there is no judge to sit as arbiter. The doctor or the psychiatrist has a holiday in the privacy of his office. The defendant is at the doctor's (or psychiatrist's) mercy; and his report may either overawe or confuse the jury and prevent a fair trial. . . .

Neither the Court nor Congress up to today has determined that any person whose physical or mental condition is brought into question during some lawsuit must surrender his right to keep his person inviolate. Congress did, according to *Sibbach*, require a plaintiff to choose between his privacy and his purse; but before today it has not been thought that any other "party" had lost this historic immunity. Congress and this Court can authorize such a rule. But a rule suited to purposes of discovery against defendants must be carefully drawn in light of the great potential of blackmail. . . .

NOTES AND PROBLEMS

1. Rule 35 contains two requirements in addition to those in the general provisions of Rule 26. The first is that the mental or physical condition be "in controversy"; the second is that the party seeking such discovery show "good cause."

   a. How does *Schlagenhauf* deal with each of these requirements?

   b. What does it mean for a physical or mental condition to be in controversy?

   c. If such condition is in controversy, what *additional* showing does a party have to make to demonstrate good cause?

2. *Schlagenhauf* is unusual in an important respect: it reached an appellate court while discovery was still going on.

   a. Why won't that happen in the great majority of cases?

   b. In *Schlagenhauf* the appellant used an extraordinary writ, *mandamus*. Mandamus is, technically, not an appeal but an independent action against the court or judge, alleging that the order is unlawful. The granting of such writs is in the discretion of the appellate courts, and they are rarely granted. Why do you suppose it was granted in this case?

3. Pat is injured in a collision with a truck owned by Dunham and sues for personal injuries. Dunham moves to take Pat's physical examination.

   a. Can Pat's lawyer or doctor attend the physical examination? Justice Douglas, in his dissent, assumes not. Compare Langefeldt-Haaland v. Saupe Enterprises, 768 P.2d 1144 (Alaska 1989) (presence of attorney during physical exam ordered), with Wheat v. Biesecker, 125 F.R.D. 479 (N.D. Ind. 1989) (attorney had no right to be present during exam), and Di Bari v. Incaica Cia Armadora, S. A., 126 F.R.D. 12 (E.D.N.Y. 1989) (magistrate denied request for attorney's presence but allowed stenographer).

   b. What happens if Pat claims that it violates her religious principles to be examined by a doctor not of her sect, and she attaches appropriate supporting documents attesting to this religious belief?

   c. What happens if Pat agrees that there is good cause for a physical examination but contends that the form of examination proposed will place dangerous stress on her weak heart?

4. Assume the Pat-Dunham litigation is settled. Pat's husband, Mike, brings an action against Dunham for loss of consortium (affection and sexual relations between spouses). Can Dunham obtain a physical or mental examination of Pat?

E.   Discovery in an Adversary System

The preceding section examined two situations in which discovery rules balance the privacy of witnesses and parties against the other goals of discovery. Another problem arises because discovery lies within a system in which the opposing parties must represent their own interests while conducting the case in conformity with the Rules. Discovery thus poses a question about what it means to be an "adversary" in litigation. Some lawyers have difficulty reconciling the required disclosure of potentially harmful information to one's adversary with the competitive stance that adversarial litigation otherwise fosters. Moreover, the present scheme of discovery often requires opposing counsel to cooperate with each other. This section will examine several contexts in which discovery clashes with adversarial impulses and with other social goals.

1.   Privilege and Trial Preparation Material

Hickman v. Taylor is the leading discovery case. It may be helpful to note that the original Rules had no provision covering trial preparation materials. (Rule 26(b)(3) did not become effective until 1970.)

Hickman v. Taylor
329 U.S. 495 (1947)

Mr. Justice MURPHY delivered the opinion of the Court.

This case presents an important problem under the Federal Rules of Civil Procedure, as to the extent to which a party may inquire into oral and written statements of witnesses, or other information, secured by an adverse party's counsel in the course of preparation for possible litigation after a claim has arisen. Examination into a person's files and records, including those resulting from the professional activities of an attorney, must be judged with care. It is not without reason that various safeguards have been established to preclude unwarranted excursions into the privacy of a man's work. At the same time public policy supports reasonable and necessary inquiries. Properly to balance these competing interests is a delicate and difficult task.

On February 7, 1943, the tug "J.M. Taylor" sank while engaged in helping to tow a car float of the Baltimore & Ohio Railroad across the Delaware River at Philadelphia. The accident was apparently unusual in nature, the cause of it still being unknown. Five of the nine crew members were drowned. Three days later the tug owners and the underwriters employed a law firm, of which respondent Fortenbaugh is a member, to defend them against potential suits by representatives of the deceased crew members and to sue the railroad for damages to the tug.

A public hearing was held on March 4, 1943, before the United States Steamboat Inspectors, at which the four survivors were examined. This testimony was recorded and made available to all interested parties. Shortly thereafter, Fortenbaugh privately interviewed the survivors and took statements from them with an eye toward the anticipated litigation; the survivors signed these statements on March 29. Fortenbaugh also interviewed other persons believed to have some information relating to the accident and in some cases he made memoranda of what they told him. At the time when Fortenbaugh secured the statements of the survivors, representatives of two of the deceased crew members had been in communication with him. Ultimately claims were presented by representatives of all five of the deceased; four of the claims, however, were settled without litigation. The fifth claimant, petitioner herein, brought suit in a federal court under the Jones Act on November 26, 1943, naming as defendants the two tug owners, individually and as partners, and the railroad.

One year later, petitioner filed 39 interrogatories directed to the tug owners. The 38th interrogatory read: "State whether any statements of the members of the crews of the Tugs 'J.M. Taylor' and 'Philadelphia' or of any other vessel were taken in connection with the towing of the car float and the sinking of the Tug 'John M. Taylor.' Attach hereto exact copies of all such statements if in writing, and if oral, set forth in detail the exact provisions of any such oral statements or reports."

Supplemental interrogatories asked whether any oral or written statements, records, reports or other memoranda had been made concerning any matter relative to the towing operation, the sinking of the tug, the salvaging and repair of the tug, and the death of the deceased. If the answer was in the affirmative, the tug owners were then requested to set forth the nature of all such records, reports, statements or other memoranda.

The tug owners, through Fortenbaugh, answered all of the interrogatories except No. 38. and the supplemental ones just described. While admitting that statements of the survivors had been taken, they declined to summarize or set forth the contents. They did so on the ground that such requests called "for privileged matter obtained in preparation for litigation" and constituted "an attempt to obtain indirectly counsel's private files." It was claimed that answering these requests "would involve practically turning over not only the complete files, but also the telephone records and, almost, the thoughts of counsel."

In connection with the hearing on these objections, Fortenbaugh made a written statement and gave an informal oral deposition explaining the circumstances under which he had taken the statements. But he was not expressly asked in the deposition to produce the statements. The District Court for the Eastern District of Pennsylvania, sitting en banc, held that the requested matters were not privileged. The court then decreed that the tug owners and Fortenbaugh, as counsel and agent for the tug owners, forthwith "Answer Plaintiff's 38th interrogatory and supplemental interrogatories; produce all written statements of witnesses obtained by Mr. Fortenbaugh, as counsel and agent for Defendants; state in substance any fact concerning this case which Defendants learned through oral statements made by witnesses to Mr. Fortenbaugh whether or not included in his private memoranda and produce Mr. Fortenbaugh's memoranda containing statements of fact by witnesses or to submit these memoranda to the Court for determination of those portions which should be revealed to Plaintiff." Upon their refusal, the court adjudged them in contempt and ordered them imprisoned until they complied.

The Third Circuit Court of Appeals, also sitting en banc, reversed the judgment of the District Court. It held that the information here sought was part of the "work product of the lawyer" and hence privileged from discovery under the Federal Rules of Civil Procedure. The importance of the problem, which has engendered a great divergence of views among district courts, led us to grant certiorari.

The pre-trial deposition-discovery mechanism established by Rules 26 to 37 is one of the most significant innovations of the Federal Rules of Civil Procedure. Under the prior federal practice, the pre-trial functions of notice-giving issue-formulation and fact-revelation were performed primarily and inadequately by the pleadings. Inquiry into the issues and the facts before trial was narrowly confined and was often cumbersome in method. The new rules, however, restrict the pleadings to the task of general notice-giving and invest the deposition-discovery process with a vital role in the preparation for trial. The various instruments of discovery now serve (1) as a device, along with the pre-trial hearing under Rule 16, to narrow and clarify the basic issues between the parties, and (2) as a device for ascertaining the facts, or information as to the existence or whereabouts of facts, relative to those issues. Thus civil trials in the federal courts no longer need be carried on in the dark. The way is now clear, consistent with recognized privileges, for the parties to obtain the fullest possible knowledge of the issues and facts before trial.

[The Court noted that plaintiff had sought Fortenbaugh's memoranda pursuant to Rules 33 and 34, but neither Rule was appropriate under the circumstances. Rule 33 was improper because it permitted a party to seek information but not documents. Rule 34 was improper because it applied only to a party, and Fortenbaugh was not a party. The proper procedure, according to the Court, was to take Fortenbaugh's deposition and "to attempt to force Fortenbaugh to produce the materials by use of a subpoena duces tecum in accordance with Rule 45." The Court then declined to rest its decision on this "procedural" irregularity.] Having noted the proper procedure, we may accordingly turn our attention to the substance of the underlying problem.

In urging that he has a right to inquire into the materials secured and prepared by Fortenbaugh, petitioner emphasizes that the deposition-discovery portions of the Federal Rules of Civil Procedure are designed to enable the parties to discover the true facts and to compel their disclosure wherever they may be found. It is said that inquiry may be made under these rules, epitomized by Rule 26, as to any relevant matter which is not privileged; and since the discovery provisions are to be applied as broadly and liberally as possible, the privilege limitation must be restricted to its narrowest bounds. On the premise that the attorney-client privilege is the one involved in this case, petitioner argues that it must be strictly confined to confidential communications made by a client to his attorney. And since the materials here in issue were secured by Fortenbaugh from third persons rather than from his clients, the tug owners, the conclusion is reached that these materials are proper subjects for discovery under Rule 26.

As additional support for this result, petitioner claims that to prohibit discovery under these circumstances would give a corporate defendant a tremendous advantage in a suit by an individual plaintiff. Thus in a suit by an injured employee against a railroad or in a suit by an insured person against an insurance company the corporate defendant could pull a dark veil of secrecy over all the pertinent facts it can collect after the claim arises merely on the assertion that such facts were gathered by its large staff of attorneys and claim agents. At the same time, the individual plaintiff, who often has direct knowledge of the matter in issue and has no counsel until some time after his claim arises, could be compelled to disclose all the intimate details of his case. By endowing with immunity from disclosure all that a lawyer discovers in the course of his duties, it is said, the rights of individual litigants in such cases are drained of vitality and the lawsuit becomes more of a battle of deception than a search for truth.

But framing the problem in terms of assisting individual plaintiffs in their suits against corporate defendants is unsatisfactory. Discovery concededly may work to the disadvantage as well as to the advantage of individual plaintiffs. Discovery, in other words, is not a one-way proposition. It is available in all types of cases at the behest of any party, individual or corporate, plaintiff or defendant. The problem thus far transcends the situation confronting this petitioner. And we must view that problem in light of the limitless situations where the particular kind of discovery sought by petitioner might be used.

We agree, of course, that the deposition-discovery rules are to be accorded a broad and liberal treatment. No longer can the time-honored cry of "fishing expedition" serve to preclude a party from inquiring into the facts underlying his opponent's case. Mutual knowledge of all the relevant facts gathered by both parties is essential to proper litigation. To that end, either party may compel the other to disgorge whatever facts he has in his possession. The deposition-discovery procedure simply advances the stage at which the disclosure can be compelled from the time of trial to the period preceding it, thus reducing the possibility of surprise. But discovery, like all matters of procedure, has ultimate and necessary boundaries. As indicated by Rules 30(b) and (d) and 31(d) [now Rules 26(c) and 30(d)], limitations inevitably arise when it can be shown that the examination is being conducted in bad faith or in such a manner as to annoy, embarrass or oppress the person subject to the inquiry. And as Rule 26(b) provides, further limitations come into existence when the inquiry touches upon the irrelevant or encroaches upon the recognized domains of privilege.

We also agree that the memoranda, statements and mental impressions in issue in this case fall outside the scope of the attorney-client privilege and hence are not protected from discovery on that basis. It is unnecessary here to delineate the content and scope of that privilege as recognized in the federal courts. For present purposes, it suffices to note that the protective cloak of this privilege does not extend to information which an attorney secures from a witness while acting for his client in anticipation of litigation. Nor does this privilege concern the memoranda, briefs, communications and other writings prepared by counsel for his own use in prosecuting his client's case; and it is equally unrelated to writings which reflect an attorney's mental impressions, conclusions, opinions or legal theories.

But the impropriety of invoking that privilege does not provide an answer to the problem before us. Petitioner has made more than an ordinary request for relevant, non-privileged facts in the possession of his adversaries or their counsel. He has sought discovery as of right of oral and written statements of witnesses whose identity is well known and whose availability to petitioner appears unimpaired. He has sought production of these matters after making the most searching inquiries of his opponents as to the circumstances surrounding the fatal accident, which inquiries were sworn to have been answered to the best of their information and belief. Interrogatories were directed toward all the events prior to, during and subsequent to the sinking of the tug. Full and honest answers to such broad inquiries would necessarily have included all pertinent information gleaned by Fortenbaugh through his interviews with the witnesses. Petitioner makes no suggestion, and we cannot assume, that the tug owners or Fortenbaugh were incomplete or dishonest in the framing of their answers. In addition, petitioner was free to examine the public testimony of the witnesses taken before the United States Steamboat Inspectors. We are thus dealing with an attempt to secure the production of written statements and mental impressions contained in the files and the mind of the attorney Fortenbaugh without any showing of necessity or any indication or claim that denial of such production would unduly prejudice the preparation of petitioner's case or cause him any hardship or injustice. For aught that appears, the essence of what petitioner seeks either has been revealed to him already through the interrogatories or is readily available to him direct from the witnesses for the asking.

The District Court, after hearing objections to petitioner's request, commanded Fortenbaugh to produce all written statements of witnesses and to state in substance any facts learned through oral statements of witnesses to him. Fortenbaugh was to submit any memoranda he had made of the oral statements so that the court might determine what portions should be revealed to petitioner. All of this was ordered without any showing by petitioner, or any requirement that he make a proper showing, of the necessity for the production of any of this material or any demonstration that denial of production would cause hardship or injustice. The court simply ordered production on the theory that the facts sought were material and were not privileged as constituting attorney-client communications.

In our opinion, neither Rule 26 nor any other rule dealing with discovery contemplates production under such circumstances. That is not because the subject matter is privileged or irrelevant, as those concepts are used in these rules. Here is simply an attempt, without purported necessity or justification, to secure written statements, private memoranda and personal recollections prepared or formed by an adverse party's counsel in the course of his legal duties. As such, it falls outside the arena of discovery and contravenes the public policy underlying the orderly prosecution and defense of legal claims. Not even the most liberal of discovery theories can justify unwarranted inquiries into the files and the mental impressions of an attorney.

Historically, a lawyer is an officer of the court and is bound to work for the advancement of justice while faithfully protecting the rightful interests of his clients. In performing his various duties, however, it is essential that a lawyer work with a certain degree of privacy, free from unnecessary intrusion by opposing parties and their counsel. Proper preparation of a client's case demands that he assemble information, sift what he considers to be the relevant from the irrelevant facts, prepare his legal theories and plan his strategy without undue and needless interference. That is the historical and the necessary way in which lawyers act within the framework of our system of jurisprudence to promote justice and to protect their clients' interests. This work is reflected, of course, in interviews, statements, memoranda, correspondence, briefs, mental impressions, personal beliefs, and countless other tangible and intangible ways — aptly though roughly termed by the Circuit Court of Appeals in this case as the "work product of the lawyer." Were such materials open to opposing counsel on mere demand, much of what is now put down in writing would remain unwritten. An attorney's thoughts, heretofore inviolate, would not be his own. Inefficiency, unfairness and sharp practices would inevitably develop in the giving of legal advice and in the preparation of cases for trial. The effect on the legal profession would be demoralizing. And the interests of the clients and the cause of justice would be poorly served.

We do not mean to say that all written materials obtained or prepared by an adversary's counsel with an eye toward litigation are necessarily free from discovery in all cases. Where relevant and non-privileged facts remain hidden in an attorney's file and where production of those facts is essential to the preparation of one's case, discovery may properly be had. Such written statements and documents might, under certain circumstances, be admissible in evidence or give clues as to the existence or location of relevant facts. Or they might be useful for purposes of impeachment or corroboration. And production might be justified where the witnesses are no longer available or can be reached only with difficulty. Were production of written statements and documents to be precluded under such circumstances, the liberal ideals of the deposition-discovery portions of the Federal Rules of Civil Procedure would be stripped of much of their meaning. But the general policy against invading the privacy of an attorney's course of preparation is so well recognized and so essential to an orderly working of our system of legal procedure that a burden rests on the one who would invade that privacy to establish adequate reasons to justify production through a subpoena or court order. That burden, we believe, is necessarily implicit in the rules as now constituted.

Rule 30(b) [now Rule 26(c)], as presently written, gives the trial judge the requisite discretion to make a judgment as to whether discovery should be allowed as to written statements secured from witnesses. But in the instant case there was no room for that discretion to operate in favor of the petitioner. No attempt was made to establish any reason why Fortenbaugh should be forced to produce the written statements. There was only a naked, general demand for these materials as of right and a finding by the District Court that no recognizable privilege was involved. That was insufficient to justify discovery under these circumstances and the court should have sustained the refusal of the tug owners and Fortenbaugh to produce.

But as to oral statements made by witnesses to Fortenbaugh, whether presently in the form of his mental impressions or memoranda, we do not believe that any showing of necessity can be made under the circumstances of this case so as to justify production. Under ordinary conditions, forcing an attorney to repeat or write out all that witnesses have told him and to deliver the account to his adversary gives rise to grave dangers of inaccuracy and untrustworthiness. No legitimate purpose is served by such production. The practice forces the attorney to testify as to what he remembers or what he saw fit to write down regarding witnesses' remarks. Such testimony could not qualify as evidence; and to use it for impeachment or corroborative purposes would make the attorney much less an officer of the court and much more an ordinary witness. The standards of the profession would thereby suffer.

Denial of production of this nature does not mean that any material, non-privileged facts can be hidden from the petitioner in this case. He need not be unduly hindered in the preparation of his case, in the discovery of facts or in his anticipation of his opponents' position. Searching interrogatories directed to Fortenbaugh and the tug owners, production of written documents and statements upon a proper showing and direct interviews with the witnesses themselves all serve to reveal the facts in Fortenbaugh's possession to the fullest possible extent consistent with public policy. Petitioner's counsel frankly admits that he wants the oral statements only to help prepare himself to examine witnesses and to make sure that he has overlooked nothing. That is insufficient under the circumstances to permit him an exception to the policy underlying the privacy of Fortenbaugh's professional activities. If there should be a rare situation justifying production of these matters, petitioner's case is not of that type.

We fully appreciate the wide-spread controversy among the members of the legal profession over the problem raised by this case. It is a problem that rests on what has been one of the most hazy frontiers of the discovery process. But until some rule or statute definitely prescribes otherwise, we are not justified in permitting discovery in a situation of this nature as a matter of unqualified right. When Rule 26 and the other discovery rules were adopted, this Court and the members of the bar in general certainly did not believe or contemplate that all the files and mental processes of lawyers were thereby opened to the free scrutiny of their adversaries. And we refuse to interpret the rules at this time so as to reach so harsh and unwarranted a result.

We therefore affirm the judgment of the Circuit Court of Appeals.

Affirmed.

Mr. Justice JACKSON, concurring. . . .

"Discovery" is one of the working tools of the legal profession. It traces back to the equity bill of discovery in English Chancery practice and seems to have had a forerunner in Continental practice. See Ragland, Discovery Before Trial (1932) 13-16. Since 1848 when the draftsmen of New York's Code of Procedure recognized the importance of a better system of discovery, the impetus to extend and expand discovery, as well as the opposition to it, has come from within the Bar itself. It happens in this case that it is the plaintiff's attorney who demands such unprecedented latitude of discovery and, strangely enough, amicus briefs in his support have been filed by several labor unions representing plaintiffs as a class. It is the history of the movement for broader discovery, however, that in actual experience the chief opposition to its extension has come from lawyers who specialize in representing plaintiffs because defendants have made liberal use of it to force plaintiffs to disclose their cases in advance. Discovery is a two-edged sword and we cannot decide this problem on any doctrine of extending help to one class of litigants. . . .

To consider first the most extreme aspect of the requirement in litigation here, we find it calls upon counsel, if he has had any conversations with any of the crews of the vessels in question or of any other, to "set forth in detail the exact provision of any such oral statements or reports." Thus the demand is not for the production of a transcript in existence but calls for the creation of a written statement not in being. But the statement by counsel of what a witness told him is not evidence when written. Plaintiff could not introduce it to prove his case. What, then, is the purpose sought to be served by demanding this of adverse counsel?

Counsel for the petitioner candidly said on argument that he wanted this information to help prepare himself to examine witnesses, to make sure he overlooked nothing. He bases his claim to it in his brief on the view that the Rules were to do away with the old situation where a law suit developed into "a battle of wits between counsel." But a common law trial is and always should be an adversary proceeding. Discovery was hardly intended to enable a learned profession to perform its functions either without wits or on wits borrowed from the adversary.

The real purpose and the probable effect of the practice ordered by the district court would be to put trials on a level even lower than a "battle of wits." I can conceive of no practice more demoralizing to the Bar than to require a lawyer to write out and deliver to his adversary an account of what witnesses have told him. Even if his recollection were perfect, the statement would be his language permeated with his inferences. Every one who has tried it knows that it is almost impossible so fairly to record the expressions and emphasis of a witness that when he testifies in the environment of the court and under the influence of the leading question there will not be departures in some respects. Whenever the testimony of the witness would differ from the "exact" statement the lawyer had delivered, the lawyer's statement would be whipped out to impeach the witness. Counsel producing his adversary's "inexact" statement could lose nothing by saying, "Here is a contradiction, gentlemen of the jury. I do not know whether it is my adversary or his witness who is not telling the truth, but one is not." Of course, if this practice were adopted, that scene would be repeated over and over again. The lawyer who delivers such statements often would find himself branded a deceiver afraid to take the stand to support his own version of the witness's conversation with him, or else he will have to go on the stand to defend his own credibility — perhaps against that of his chief witness, or possibly even his client.

Every lawyer dislikes to take the witness stand and will do so only for grave reasons. This is partly because it is not his role; he is almost invariably a poor witness. But he steps out of professional character to do it. He regrets it; the profession discourages it. But the practice advocated here is one which would force him to be a witness, not as to what he has seen or done but as to other witnesses' stories, and not because he wants to do so but in self-defense. . . .

It is true that the literal language of the Rules would admit of an interpretation that would sustain the district court's order. . . . But all such procedural measures have a background of custom and practice which was assumed by those who wrote and should be by those who apply them. . . . Certainly nothing in the tradition or practice of discovery up to the time of these Rules would have suggested that they would authorize such a practice as here proposed. . . .

Mr. Justice FRANKFURTER joins in this opinion.

NOTES AND PROBLEMS

1. It is easy to miss the point of *Hickman* unless one focuses on the precise question decided.

a. What information was sought?

b. Was it relevant?

c. Was it privileged?

d. Why wasn't it discoverable?

e. How do the majority and concurrence differ in the reasons given for the result?

2. At the time of *Hickman*, Rule 26 did not deal specifically with the topic of trial preparation materials. It now does. Read Rule 26(b)(3) and answer the following questions:

a. Does the doctrine apply to nonlawyers, such as insurance adjusters and investigators?

b. What if a party or witness makes a written statement to the lawyer? Is that discoverable?

c. What about factual information, as opposed to mental impressions — is that undiscoverable if the facts were uncovered by a lawyer?

d. Unlike privileges, which are absolute unless waived, trial preparation material is sometimes discoverable: When?

e. Most of the following problems deal with the variations on these themes. Work through the problems to see how Rule 26 applies in litigation settings.

3. Start with a routine setting. *P* was injured when struck by a bus owned by *B* Bus Co.; *P* then sued *B*. The litigation raises the following discovery issues:

a. Immediately after the accident, a vice president of *B* went to the scene and made a full investigation, including interviews with witnesses and measurements of the accident location. He then made a written report to the directors of *B*. Can *P* obtain the report? Would it make any difference if *B* has a claims department and the vice president is "attached" to that department? See Rakus v. Erie-Lackawanna Railroad, 76 F.R.D. 145 (W.D.N.Y. 1977) (employees' accident reports to claims department are discoverable); Spaulding v. Denton, 68 F.R.D. 342 (D. Del. 1975) (marine surveyors' report, made in regular course of business without attorney's legal expertise when insurers were trying to find out about unusual accident, is discoverable).

b. Through the expenditure of more than $10,000, *B*'s attorney has uncovered another eyewitness to the accident. *P* serves an interrogatory asking for the names of all eyewitnesses, and *B* objects on the ground of "trial preparation materials." Must *B* disclose the witness's name?

4. In *Hickman*, Fortenbaugh interviewed the witnesses and took notes but apparently did not ask the witnesses to write out statements or tape-record the witnesses' statements. Many lawyers will do so in order to have a basis for subsequent examination or impeachment of the witness. Are such statements discoverable? See Rule 26(b)(3).

a. Boris is seriously injured in an automobile accident with Charles. In the hospital Boris is visited by an investigator for State Farm Insurance Co., which had insured Charles's car. Boris thinks he gave a videotaped statement to the investigator and knows that he talked to the investigator about the accident. As attorney for Boris, (a) can you find out whether Boris gave a statement?; (b) if so, can you obtain a copy of the statement before Boris's scheduled deposition next month?; and (c) if Boris did not give a statement, can you find out what he told the investigator?

b. In Boris's suit against Charles, Frank, a friend of Boris, will testify on his behalf. Frank gave a written, signed statement to Charles's attorney but does not remember what he said. As attorney for Boris, can you obtain the statement? How?

5. What does it take to overcome a claim of work product? How special must the circumstances be?

a. Try first two variations on the facts of *Hickman*. What if Fortenbaugh had interviewed the crew members in the hospital, and they had died before giving their testimony?

b. What if the crew members were still alive but there had been no public hearing on the accident, and the witnesses claimed not to be able to remember events clearly?

c. Plaintiff claims personal injuries in a bus crash. Defendant assigns an investigator to film plaintiff scuba diving while on vacation. Plaintiff seeks both the film and the investigator's report. Substantial need and undue hardship? Freiman v. USAIR Group, Inc., 1994 U.S. Dist. LEXIS 16994 (1994) (work product protection overcome for videotape but not for investigator's report, since he could be deposed). Gibson v. National Rail Pass. Corp., 170 F.R.D. 408 (E.D. Pa. 1997) (surveillance reports discoverable only if defendant plans to offer in evidence, but defendant must disclose a reasonable time before trial whether it plans to offer surveillance in evidence).

6. A common work product problem is the so-called contention inter-rogatory, in which one party seeks to discover the facts that underlie broad allegations. Thus, for example, in an auto negligence case like Bell v. Novick Transfer (see Chapter I), the defendant might ask plaintiff whether he contended that defendant had driven too fast, failed to main-tain his brakes, or failed to heed a traffic signal. The purpose of such interrogatories is to expand on the generalities of the pleading and to prepare for the lines of proof one will need to meet at trial. But do

such questions delve impermissibly into the opposing lawyer's mental impressions and legal theories? Sometimes the recipients of such interrogatories refuse to answer on the grounds that such questions reveal their theory of the case and therefore constitute protected work product. Is such an objection justified? Consider how Rule 33(c) bears on your answer:

> An interrogatory otherwise proper is not necessarily objectionable merely because an answer to the interrogatory involves an opinion or contention that relates to fact or the application of law to fact, but the court may order that such an interrogatory need not be answered until after designated discovery has been completed or until a pre-trial conference or other later time.

Does this modify what might otherwise be the effect of Rule 26(b)(3) on such an interrogatory? See Rifkind v. Good, 227 Cal. Rptr. 2d 822 (CA 2d Dist. 1994) (in action between attorneys on fee dispute, proper to seek by interrogatory list of documents supporting affirmative defenses; not proper to ask same question in deposition).

7. This chapter does not seek to explore the doctrines of evidentiary privilege, but you should know that one U.S. Supreme Court opinion on privilege significantly affects discovery. In Upjohn Co. v. United States, 449 U.S. 393 (1981), noted supra on page 495, the Court held that the attorney-client privilege extended to communications between counsel and all corporate employees, not just managers.

a. Recall that *Hickman* rejected the claim that the crew's conversations with Fortenbaugh came under the attorney-client privilege. Explain why, under *Upjohn*, the tugboat company in *Hickman* might have had a stronger argument for privilege. And recall that privilege, unlike trial preparation protection, cannot be pierced by a showing of need. Privilege, unless waived, is absolute.

b. If corporate employees are "clients," another rule, this one concerning lawyers' ethical responsibilities, comes into play. To prevent overreaching and back-door negotiations, professional rules prohibit lawyers from communicating directly with a party represented by another lawyer, unless that lawyer consents. See, e.g., Model Rule of Professional Conduct 4.2.

c. As a review of this section, consider the facts of *Hickman* after *Upjohn*. What new argument against disclosure of the interview notes does Fortenbaugh now have? At one point in *Hickman*, in explaining why plaintiff's lawyer cannot have Fortenbaugh's notes, the Court points out that the plaintiff's lawyer can simply interview the surviving crew members himself. How is this argument complicated after *Upjohn*? Finally, does anything in *Hickman* or *Upjohn* prevent plaintiff's lawyer from deposing the crew members? Why not?

2.   Expert Information

In many cases the parties hire experts to analyze the case and, perhaps, to testify. Such experts range from the standard professionals —
physicians, accountants, engineers — to exotics who claim expertise in
"accident reconstruction" and "brand name identification." Experts typically testify to the inferences one can draw about causes of an event by
applying their special knowledge to the evidence available. Before a court
will let an expert testify, the party presenting such testimony must establish
that he or she *is* an expert and that the expertise is relevant to contested issues.

The problems posed by expert testimony resemble those of the work
product doctrine. Both involve relevant, unprivileged information "produced" by the efforts of one of the adversaries. The clash is between two
assumptions of the system: We hope that each side will do its own
preparation and neither will "freeload" on the efforts of the other. On
the other hand, we want parties to have access before trial to information on which the trial outcome may turn. Issues posed by expert testimony have become especially heated as more experts testify at trials.
The other problem with expert testimony flows from the special difficulties of conducting cross-examination of an expert. Many lawyers believe that it is almost impossible to conduct such a cross-examination
effectively unless one has had a prior opportunity to depose the expert
and unless one has access to the reports and documents on which she
bases her opinion.

Two portions of Rule 26 speak to the problems of expert testimony.
Rule 26(a)(2) requires, as part of the initial disclosures, information about
experts who may testify and about the basis for their testimony, including
a requirement that the adversary receive "a written report prepared and
signed by the witness . . . contain[ing] a complete statement of all
opinions to be expressed and reasons therefor. . . . Rule 26(b)(4) provides
for additional discovery from experts: The Rule requires that testifying
experts submit to pretrial deposition but erects special barriers around
the opinions of nontestifying experts.

NOTES AND PROBLEMS

1. Before dealing with borderline cases, consider some straightforward
applications of the discovery provisions on experts. Perhaps the most
significant but nonobvious point is that the Rule grants its protections
not to experts per se but to experts who have developed their information
in preparation for litigation. The rule is in that respect like the trial

preparation doctrine, which shields not the underlying facts but only the mental processes of those who are using those facts to prepare for litigation.

2. John is seriously injured in an automobile accident and is taken to Coral Hospital for emergency care. In the emergency room, he is examined by Dr. Kildare, who subsequently operates on John's back. Three months later, John's back is examined by Dr. Welby, an orthopedic specialist. One year after the accident John brings suit against Mary, the driver of the other car. Dr. Welby has been hired by John's lawyer and has prepared a report on John's condition.

a. John's lawyer expects to call both physicians to testify at trial. What information must John's lawyer give to Mary's as part of the initial disclosure required by Rule 26(a)? Can Dr. Kildare be required to prepare a written report on his findings?

b. John's lawyer does not plan to call Dr. Welby at trial. What information must John's lawyer give to Mary's as part of the initial disclosure?

c. John's lawyer does plan to call Dr. Welby at trial. May Mary's lawyer depose him?

3. Assume that John's lawyer decides that because Dr. Welby will not testify, his report need not be disclosed. Does he nevertheless have to list Dr. Welby's name as someone with information about relevant facts, as required in Rule 26(a)(1)(A)? Mary's lawyer will be quite interested in this information, because one can fairly infer that the failure to call Dr. Welby as a witness means that his testimony will not favor John. And, for the same reason, we can assume that John's lawyer will be as interested in not divulging his name.

a. Does the qualification in Rule 26(a)(1)(A) that limits disclosure to "*discoverable* information relevant to facts alleged with particularity" help John?

b. If not — that is, if John must disclose Dr. Welby's name — can John's lawyer get a protective order forbidding Mary from deposing Dr. Welby or from calling him as a witness? What would be the grounds for such an order?

4. The most difficult questions arise in connection with Rule 26(b)(4)(B), which tries to balance the adversaries' abilities to prepare their cases against the possibility that a nontestifying expert may have the only access to facts. The next two cases deal with such situations.

Thompson v. The Haskell Co.

65 F. Empl. Prac. Cas. (BNA) 1088 (M.D. Fla. 1994)

SNYDER, Magistrate Judge.

This cause is before the Court on Plaintiff's Motion for Protective Order filed on May 13, 1994 (hereinafter Motion). Plaintiff seeks to shield from discovery documents related to her in the possession of Lauren Lucas, Ph.D., a psychologist. She contends that Rule 26(b)(4) of the Federal Rules of Civil Procedure (FRCP) protects the psychological records in Dr. Lucas' possession. In particular, Plaintiff represents Dr. Lucas was retained by her prior counsel to perform a diagnostic review and personality profile, and that, after seeing Plaintiff on one occasion on June 15, 1992, Dr. Lucas prepared a report for her prior counsel.[1]

Rule 26(b)(4)[(B)] of the FRCP provides:

> A party may, through interrogatories or by deposition, discover facts known or opinions held by an expert who has been retained or specially employed by another party in anticipation of litigation or preparation for trial and who is not expected to be called as a witness at trial only as provided in Rule 35(b) or upon a showing of exceptional circumstances under which it is impracticable for the party seeking discovery to obtain facts or opinions on the same subject by other means.

Assuming arguendo that Dr. Lucas' report is covered by Rule 26(b)(4), it would nevertheless be discoverable under the circumstances presented in this case. In the instant lawsuit, Plaintiff alleges that, as a result of sexual harassment by co-defendant Zona, a supervisor in the employ of the Defendant, she was "reduced to a severely depressed emotional state and her employment was terminated when she did not acquiesce to the advances of [Zona]." Complaint, filed on September 23, 1993, at 6. According to a complaint filed with the Jacksonville Equal Opportunity Commission, Plaintiff apparently was terminated from her position with Defendant Haskell Company on June 5, 1992. Thus, her mental and emotional state ten days later on June 15, 1992, the date on which she was examined by Dr. Lucas, is highly probative with regard to the above-quoted allegation, which is essential to her case.

This highly probative information is discoverable notwithstanding Rule 26(b)(4), moreover, given the nature of the report at issue. Apparently, no other comparable report was prepared during the weeks immediately following Plaintiff's discharge. Thus, the Defendant could not obtain the information contained in Dr. Lucas' report by other means. In a case almost on all fours with the instant one, the Court recognized that even "independent examinations. . .pursuant to Rule 35 would not contain equivalent information." Dixon v. Cappellini, 88 F.R.D. 1, 3 (M.D. Pa.

---

1. Plaintiff also relies on Rule 26(b)(3) of the Federal Rules of Civil Procedure, which is inapplicable since, by its own terms, it is "subject to the provisions of subdivision (b)(4) of this rule. . . ." Even if Rule 26(b)(3) could apply in situations covered by Rule 26(b)(4), the considerations outlined herein justifying disclosure under the latter provision would also justify disclosure under the former.

1980). Under these facts, it appears there are exceptional circumstances favoring disclosure of Dr. Lucas' report, and that the Defendant could not obtain comparable information by other means. Accordingly, the Motion is DENIED. . . .

Chiquita International Ltd. v. M/V Bolero Reefer
1994 U.S. Dist. LEXIS 5820 (S.D.N.Y. 1994)

FRANCIS, Magistrate Judge.

This is a maritime action in which the shipper, Chiquita International Ltd. ("Chiquita"), sues the carrier, International Reefer Services, S.A. ("International Reefer"), for cargo loss and damage. Chiquita alleges that International Reefer was engaged to transport 154,660 boxes of bananas from Puerto Bolivar, Ecuador to Bremerhaven, Germany aboard the M/V Bolero Reefer. However, because of alleged malfunctions of the vessel's loading cranes and side-ports, only 111,660 boxes were loaded. Thus, 43,000 boxes of bananas were left on the wharf and were later disposed of. The cargo that did arrive in Germany was allegedly in poor condition.

International Reefer has submitted a letter in support of an application to compel discovery of Joseph Winer. Mr. Winer is a marine surveyor who examined the vessel and loading gear at Chiquita's request shortly after the vessel arrived in Bremerhaven. International Reefer seeks Mr. Winter's deposition and production of the file he assembled in connection with his inspection. Chiquita has objected to these demands on the ground that Mr. Winer is a non-testifying expert as to whom discovery is closely circumscribed by Rule 26(b)(4)(B) of the Federal Rules of Civil Procedure. International Reefer replies that Mr. Winer is a fact witness rather than an expert. Moreover, even if he is an expert, International Reefer argues that the fact that he is the only surveyor who observed the vessel shortly after it docked is an exceptional circumstance warranting discovery. . . .

[The opinion quoted Rule 26(b)(4)(B).]

Thus, a non-testifying expert is generally immune from discovery.

Mr. Winer qualifies as such an expert. He is a marine engineer who was specifically engaged by Chiquita to examine the vessel in connection with the cargo loss claim. He is clearly an "expert" in that he brought his technical background to bear in observing the condition of the gear and offering his opinion to Chiquita. He does not forfeit this status merely because he made a personal examination of the vessel and therefore learned "facts," rather than simply offering an opinion based on the observations of others. Rule 26(b)(4)(B) generally precludes discovery of

"facts known or opinions held" by a non-testifying expert, and so it
anticipates that such an expert may make his or her own investigation.
Thus, the relevant distinction is not between fact and opinion testimony
but between those witnesses whose information was obtained in the
normal course of business and those who were hired to make an evaluation
in connection with expected litigation. See Harasimowicz v. McAllister,
78 F.R.D. 319, 320 (E.D. Pa. 1978) (medical examiner subject to ordinary
discovery on routine autopsy); Congrove v. St. Louis-San Francisco Railway, 77 F.R.D. 503, 504-05 (W.D. Mo. 1978) (treating physician subject
to ordinary discovery); Duke Gardens Foundation, Inc. v. Universal Resto-
ration, Inc., 52 F.R.D. 365, 366-67 (S.D.N.Y. 1971) (expert retained in
connection with litigation could be examined regarding prior work for
party). Here, Mr. Winer falls into the latter category and Rule 26(b)(4)(B)
therefore applies.

International Reefer nevertheless contends that discovery should be
permitted under the "exceptional circumstances" clause of the rule, since
no other marine surveyor viewed the vessel shortly after docking. This
argument would have merit if International Reefer had been precluded
from sending its own expert to the scene by forces beyond its control.
Thus, for example, in Sanford Construction Co. v. Kaiser Aluminum &
Chemical Sales, Inc., 45 F.R.D. 465, 466 (E.D. Ky. 1968), the court
found there to be exceptional circumstances where the plaintiff allowed
its own expert to examine the item at issue while barring the defendant's
experts until the item was no longer accessible.

However, that is not the case here. The vessel and equipment were
at least as available to International Reefer as to Chiquita from the
time of loading. Indeed, during the three-week voyage to Bremerhaven,
International Reefer's employees had the exclusive opportunity to examine the loading cranes. Under these circumstances, the failure of International Reefer to engage its own marine surveyor in a timely manner
should not be rewarded by permitting discovery of Chiquita's expert. To
do so would permit the exceptional circumstances exception to swallow
Rule 26(b)(4)(B).

Finally, International Reefer maintains that even if it is foreclosed
from deposing Mr. Winer, it should be given access to his file. However,
Rule 26(b)(4)(B) applies to document discovery as well as to depositions.
Nevertheless, International Reefer is correct that information does not
become exempt from discovery merely because it is conveyed to a non-
testifying expert. Thus, while the file may contain Mr. Winer's recorded
observations and opinions which need not be disclosed, it may also
include discoverable information provided to Mr. Winer by others. Such
documents shall be produced.

Conclusion

For the reasons set forth above, International Reefer's application to take the deposition of Joseph Winer is denied. By May 13, 1994, Chiquita shall produce from Mr. Winer's file those documents that do not reflect his observations and opinions or are otherwise privileged. Chiquita shall prepare a log of any documents withheld, identifying them with the specificity required by Local Rule 46(e).

SO ORDERED.

NOTES AND PROBLEMS

1. Focus first on what was being sought in each case:

a. What was the defendant seeking in *Thompson*?

b. What was the plaintiff's argument in *Thompson* that the report was undiscoverable?

c. What was the defendant seeking in *Chiquita*?

d. What did the court order discovered in *Chiquita*? Why?

2. *Thompson* and *Chiquita* deal with similar information, which the respective courts concede is relevant and unprivileged. But the *Thompson* court orders disclosure, the *Chiquita* court denies disclosure.

a. Why?

b. What facts would one change about each case to reach a different result?

c. In *Chiquita* the views of someone familiar with crucial facts are suppressed. How does one justify that result, given the general thrust toward disclosure of the discovery rules?

3. In *Chiquita* the court suggests there is no question that Mr. Winer is a Rule 26(b)(4) expert. In *Thompson* the court suggests in passing that Dr. Lucas might not be: "Assuming arguendo that Dr. Lucas' report is covered by Rule 26(b)(4), it would nevertheless be discoverable under the circumstances presented in this case." If Dr. Lucas's report weren't covered by 26(b)(4), what else would be? See Problem 2, page 539.

4. *Thompson* and *Chiquita* deal with attempts to discover the reports of nontestifying experts. What if the parties try to go one step further and, having obtained the reports, try actually to compel the opposition's experts to testify at trial? The argument for doing so looks straightforward: These people have unprivileged information relevant to the case. The law is anything but straightforward, as it jumbles together considerations of litigative fairness with a sense that the expert "owns" the subject of her expertise:

As at least one commentator has noted, the case law dealing with the question whether a party to a lawsuit may obtain discovery of or testimony from an expert consulted by the other, but not to be called at trial by the consulting party, is confused at best. Note, Must the Show Go On? Defining When One Party May Call or Compel An Opposing Party's Consultative Expert to Testify, 78 Minn. L. Rev. 1191, 1199-1203 (1994).

Experts enjoy no constitutional or statutory immunity from compulsory process. Moreover, the desire for all probative information in service of the overall search for truth weighs in favor of compelled testimony and, indeed, discovery even from consultative experts. On the other hand, several considerations may cut the other way, depending upon the particular circumstances.

First, there is an important interest in allowing counsel to obtain the expert advice they need in order properly to evaluate and present their clients' positions without fear that every consultation with an expert may yield grist for the adversary's mill. This policy underlies Fed. R. Civ. P. 26(b)(4)(B)'s severe limitation on the discovery of consultative, as opposed to testifying, experts. . . .

Second, the Federal Rules of Civil Procedure reflect a view that it would be unfair to allow a party to benefit from the effort and expense incurred by the other in preparing its case. In other words, the general policy, which is not without exceptions, is that each side should prepare its own case at its own expense.

Third, there are concerns peculiar to the issue of compelled testimony from nontestifying experts. Some have suggested that allowing the use of compulsion might diminish the willingness of experts to serve as consultants and, in any case, that it is unfair to the experts. . . .

Fourth, and perhaps most pertinent, permitting one party to call an expert previously retained or consulted by the other side entails a risk of very substantial prejudice stemming from the fact of the prior retention, quite apart from the substance of the testimony. One leading commentator aptly has characterized the fact of the prior retention by the adversary as "explosive." 8 C. Wright et al., Federal Practice and Procedure: Civil §2032, at 447 (1994).

Rubel v. Eli Lilly & Co., 1995 U.S. Dist. LEXIS 3456 (S.D.N.Y. 1995).

F.   Ensuring Compliance and Controlling Abuse of Discovery

Even with the preceding doctrinal framework in mind, one of the hardest concepts for the student to grasp is the "culture" of discovery. *Hickman's* fears that the advent of discovery would mean the demise of the adversary system appear to have been greatly exaggerated. Instead, discovery has become the field on which some of unrestrained advocacy's least attractive features have displayed themselves. Delay, evasiveness, abusive use of various discovery devices, use of discovery to buy time or to force a hard-pressed opponent to settle for less, and the like appear on lawyers' lists of such tactics. One study, reprinted in part below, catalogues some common abuses.

Interrogatories and Document Productions

Attorneys drafting interrogatories do not view them primarily as means of openly exploring the data . . . [but] as weapons to be used in the manner that best advances the competitive interests of their client. . . . Many litigators feel compelled to use written interrogatories as weapons for purely tactical purposes. . . . Some attorneys serve lengthy sets of "canned" interrogatories if they perceive some advantage to be gained by psychologically or economically harassing an opposing party or counsel. Litigators may also use interrogatories to pressure or manipulate opposing counsel into doing such initial case preparation as factual investigation and legal research and analysis that properly should be undertaken by the propounding counsel and paid for by that counsel's client. . . .

The responding adversary's first impulse is to construe all inquiries and requests as narrowly as possible, thereby limiting the amount of useful information that must be divulged. . . . Nor will litigators necessarily answer a request even if they have construed it as narrowly as possible and have objected to every arguable technical deficiency. Responding counsel's next line of defense is built on the use of privileges and the work product doctrine. . . .

When responding to document production demands, litigators sometimes resort to the obstructive device of burying significant documents in mounds of irrelevant or innocuous materials. . . . If the tactics discussed above fail to conceal damaging information, counsel may feel constrained to refuse to respond to interrogatories or document production requests until compelled to do so. The first ploy is to ignore the original discovery probe and its deadlines. At least among seasoned litigators the fear of sanctions for missing one deadline is not great. . . .

Depositions

An aggressive litigator bent on straining the resources and testing the will of an adversary can notice numerous depositions and can prolong each examination for extended periods of time . . . [with the effect of] harassing and embarrassing adverse parties or witnesses and . . . disrupting their lives and businesses. . . .

Brazil, The Adversary Character of Civil Discovery: A Critique and Proposals for Change, 31 Vand. L. Rev. 1295, 1320-1324, 1329 (1978).

Such depressing observations have several sources, some of which lie in the design of the discovery system itself. The Federal Rules envisioned discovery's operating largely without judicial supervision, and the Rules therefore speak of lawyers exchanging various discovery requests without intervention by the court. Judges become involved only when the system breaks down — for example, in the event of a motion for a protective order, a request to compel discovery, or a motion for sanctions. But when such judicial intervention comes, the judge must step into a dispute about which she may know little, and may therefore be inclined to tread rather warily. Moreover, many judges routinely assign discovery matters to federal magistrate judges and hear only appeals from their orders. Thus judges faced with discovery battles often have very little feel for the dispute before them.

1. An Anatomy of Discovery Abuses

The discovery rules seek to address these complaints in Rules 26(g) and 37. The first seeks to control abuse by establishing rules for lawyers' behavior, the second by giving judges tools to punish abuses. Before assessing the effectiveness of these efforts, it may help to construct an anatomy of discovery abuses. There are three basic patterns: too little discovery, too much discovery, and mismatched discovery. The first, sometimes called "stonewalling," occurs when one party refuses or resists appropriate requests for discovery. The second occurs when one party seeks more discovery than the case justifies so as to discourage or hamper the opponent. The last pattern, "mismatched" discovery, occurs when the two parties have significantly unequal wealth; the richer party, even if it does not abuse discovery, may seem to have an unfair advantage.

The Rules offer partial solutions to the first two problems but deal less well with the third. Refusal to cooperate with justifiable discovery requests can subject a party to sanctions. Read Rules 26(g) and 37. Note the range of propositions to which the signature of the lawyer certifies under 26(g), particularly the assertion that discovery is not "unreasonable or unduly burdensome or expensive, given the needs of the case." Too much discovery gives the opponent a choice of responses. If the information requested is irrelevant or privileged, one may simply decline to answer. If it is instead excessive because it is cumulative or burdensome, Rule 26(c) permits any party to seek a protective order. That Rule permits a court to limit discovery, even though the information sought might otherwise be discoverable, if it would produce "annoyance, embarrassment, oppression, or undue burden or expense." For problems that do not fit neatly into any of these categories, one might consider a discovery conference (under Rule 16), which involves the judge in the framing of a discovery plan. Such a conference may be convened by the court on its own motion. Judges who wish to manage discovery may use such conferences as a tool.

PROBLEMS

1. Having filed a complaint against Baxter Corp. for breach of contract and having received the required disclosures, Arthur Corp. sends Baxter a set of additional interrogatories seeking some routine information about the details of company organization, such as which officers and employees are responsible for which aspects of the company's affairs. Baxter refuses to answer any of the questions, noting in its response that these matters are not relevant to the claims and defenses of the action. Arthur's lawyer believes that such questions are entirely proper because they enable her to decide which officers to depose — and that they are thus included within Rule 26(b)(1) as "reasonably calculated to lead to the discovery of admissible evidence."

a. How should Arthur's lawyer proceed to get answers to its interrogatories?

b. Can Arthur seek sanctions? Under what Rule(s)?

2. Baxter serves a notice to take the deposition of Alice Arthur, the president of Arthur Corp. On the appointed day, Arthur doesn't show up. As attorney for Baxter, what remedies would you seek? See Rule 37(d).

3. When Baxter seeks sanctions, Arthur claims that Baxter purposefully scheduled the deposition at an extremely inconvenient place and requests that the location be changed. Should that argument, if true, block or mitigate sanctions?

4. Arthur and Baxter serve a series of requests for discovery on each other, including interrogatories, notices of depositions, and various requests for the production of documents. Arthur believes that it has responded in good faith to Baxter's requests but that Baxter has been systematically uncooperative: raising many barely tenable objections, declining to produce documents until threatened with a court order, producing incomplete sets of documents, then producing overwhelming quantities of documents in which the relevant material is buried, and similar tactics. What should Arthur do?

5. The amount at stake in Arthur v. Baxter is $100,000, all but $5,000 of that amount representing Arthur's claim against Baxter. In connection with its counterclaim, Baxter serves on Arthur notices for a series of depositions of Arthur's officers. When Arthur's lawyer calls Baxter's lawyer to discuss the scheduling of these depositions, Arthur's lawyer learns that

the series of depositions will take thirty hours to complete. Given the billing rates of the two attorneys and the cost of a stenographer, the cost of such a series of depositions could exceed $10,000. Is that troubling? Is there anything Arthur's lawyer can do about it?

We have not yet addressed one of the more difficult discovery problems: how the legal system should cope with substantial imbalance in the parties' wealth. Because discovery is conducted by the parties' lawyers, the litigants must bear the costs. Some of the more elaborate forms, particularly depositions, can cost a lot. Can the wealthier party prevail simply by dint of greater resources? The problem has two versions. First, what happens if one party lacks resources to do adequate discovery? The most troubling case would arise if most of the likely evidence was in defendant's hands and the case suggested that assembly of evidence would be complex, such as in a product liability or environmental hazard claim. Without access to discovery, such a claim has no chance of succeeding. Although the Rules nowhere address this problem specifically, several possibilities present themselves. The party with fewer resources may be able to conduct discovery from various public sources — government or public documents, press sources, Internet searches, and the like. Also, a disciplined discovery scheme making maximum use of "cheap" discovery (such as document requests and interrogatories) may yield a good deal. With large public and private institutions, well-planned document requests can produce rich veins of information. Finally, it may be possible to ride free on the discovery efforts of other parties if they are involved: A deposition conducted by one party will often yield useful information. None of these responses may be entirely adequate, but they offer some hope.

2. Sanctions as a Remedy

The ultimate incentive to comply with discovery obligations is the court's power to punish violations of the discovery rules. Even though the rules give district courts a broad range of options — from dismissal or a default judgment to requiring a litigant to pay an opponent's costs and expenses incurred as a result of a failure to make discovery — there remains a widespread sense that much discovery abuse goes unchecked. Some observers suggest that judges tend to accept delay and lame excuses on the part of litigants and their attorneys until the court is provoked beyond endurance, at which point the court punishes one side or the other with a termination of the lawsuit by default or dismissal. Judges may be reluctant to mete out less draconian orders for "routine" discovery abuse for fear that such would only compound the burden of discovery disputes by adding a contest over cost-shifting to every underlying discovery problem. Finally, discovery disputes tend to be very fact-intensive and time-consuming for judges. It is often difficult for a judge to figure out which side is being unfair or unreasonable in any particular dispute. The following case demonstrates how matters can go awry.

Chudasama v. Mazda Motor Corp.
123 F.3d 1353 (11th Cir. 1997).

TJOFLAT, Circuit Judge:

This case illustrates the mischief that results when a district court effectively abdicates its responsibility to manage a case involving contentious litigants and permits excessive and dilatory discovery tactics to run amok. Not only did the district court fail to manage discovery in this case, it in effect delegated the duty to manage to the plaintiffs' counsel. To protect themselves from the plaintiffs' inevitable overreaching, the defendants resorted to self-help and did not provide full discovery. Their tactic resulted in draconian sanctions, including the entry of a default under Rules 26 and 37 of the Federal Rules of Civil Procedure. Finding that the district court abused its discretion, we vacate the order imposing sanctions and direct that the case be assigned on remand to another district judge. . . .

I

On May 16, 1991, Bhupendra Chudasama and his wife, Gunvanti B., appellees, purchased a used 1989 Mazda MPV minivan (the "MPV minivan") from Jays Dodge City, a Columbus, Georgia Dodge dealer. On the morning of October 15, 1991, Gunvanti Chudasama was injured when Bhupendra Chudasama lost control of the minivan and it collided with a utility pole. Mrs. Chudasama sustained a broken pelvis and broken facial bones; Mr. Chudasama was uninjured. Mrs. Chudasamas' medical bills totaled approximately $13,000, and she lost approximately $5,000 in wages. The accident left the MPV minivan, worth approximately $11,000, beyond repair.

On April 30, 1993, the Chudasamas filed a products liability action against the appellants . . . in the United States District Court for the Middle District of Georgia. The complaint pointed to two alleged defects in the MPV minivan as the cause of the Chudasamas' accident and resulting injuries: (1) the brakes were likely to cause "the driver's unexpected loss of control . . . in the highway environment of its expected use," and (2) the "doors, side panels and supporting members [were] inadequately designed and constructed, and failed to provide a reasonable degree of occupant safety so that they [were] unreasonably likely to crush and deform into the passenger compartment."

Their complaint contained four counts: three standard products liability counts — strict liability, breach of implied warranty, and negligent design and manufacture — and one count of fraud. Each count sought compensatory damages to cover Mrs. Chudasama's medical bills and lost wages, to compensate her for pain and suffering, to compensate Mr. Chudasama for his loss of his wife's "society, companionship and services," and to cover the loss of the vehicle. All but the breach of implied warranty count also sought punitive damages.

Over the next two years, the parties engaged in protracted discovery disputes. As has become typical in recent years, both sides initially adopted extreme and unreasonable positions; the plaintiffs asked for almost every tangible piece of information or property possessed by the defendants, and the defendants offered next to nothing and took several steps to delay discovery. In this case, however, the district court never attempted to resolve the parties' disputes and force the parties to meet somewhere in the middle of their respective extreme positions. As a result, what began as a relatively common discovery dispute quickly deteriorated into unbridled legal warfare.

We see no useful purpose in describing the drawn-out discovery battle in detail; a relatively brief summary will suffice. On July 28, 1993, the Chudasamas served Mazda with their first interrogatories and requests for production. Both documents were models of vague and overly broad discovery requests. The production requests, for example, contained 20 "special instructions," 29 definitions, and 121 numbered requests (some containing as many as 11 subparts). Similarly, the interrogatories contained 18 "special instructions," 29 definitions, and 31 numbered interrogatories. "One" interrogatory included five separate questions that applied to each of the 121 numbered requests for production, arguably expanding the number of interrogatories to 635.

The production requests all but asked for every document Mazda ever had in its possession and then some. For example, the Chudasamas sought detailed information about practically all of Mazda's employees worldwide. They requested production of "all documents relating to organizational charts, books or manuals of Mazda . . . which will or may assist in identifying an[d] locating those operating divisions, committees, groups, departments, employees, and personnel involved in the conception, market analysis, development, testing, design safety engineering and marketing of the product for all years during which the product has been developed, designed, manufactured and marketed."

They also sought "all documents relating to any organizational chart or structure for each of Mazda['s] . . . committees, sub-committees, boards, task forces, and technical groups which took any part in overseeing the design, market analysis, cost/benefits analysis, economic feasibility analysis, development, testing and safety engineering of the product."

The scope of these requests becomes apparent only after reading the Chudasamas' definition of the term "product":

> This word means the Mazda MPV Minivan involved in the incident and all vehicles similar, though not necessarily identical, to that Minivan. The word includes all variations of 1989 Mazda MPV Minivan vehicles, as well as all variations of the MPV Minivan vehicles produced by Mazda . . . in all years before and after the incident. The term should be construed to include each and every component part of the vehicle and more specifically the related components of the assemblies and subassemblies of the vehicle's chassis, wheelbase, steering system, suspension system, braking system, side and side supporting system.

The Chudasamas thus asked for production of nearly every document ever made that would list or assist in finding every person that ever had anything to do with any component of any year model of the MPV minivan "and all vehicles similar."

Another representative example of the breadth of discovery sought by the Chudasamas involves Mazda's advertising campaigns. They requested production of all documents relating to any print and broadcast media advertisements, catalogues, sales brochures, product inserts, or promotional information of any kind, relating to the product issued by or on behalf of Mazda . . . for the purpose of marketing the product to consumers in the United States . . . [or] in any other country where the product was marketed.

In other words, the Chudasamas wanted every document related to any form of advertising anywhere in the world of any year Mazda MPV minivan and "all vehicles similar" and all components thereof. . . .

In response to the Chudasamas' excessively broad discovery requests, Mazda adopted four different strategies. First, it objected to almost every production request and interrogatory on almost every imaginable ground. While some of its objections were clearly boilerplate and bordered on being frivolous, many were directly on point and raised bona fide questions of law. On ten different occasions from September 7, 1993, until November 21, 1994, Mazda filed written objections to the Chudasamas' discovery requests. Moreover, during three different hearings in January, August, and September of 1994, Mazda asked the district court to rule on its objections no fewer than twenty-five times, all to no avail. Finally, on November 4, 1994, counsel for Mazda sent a letter to the court imploring it to rule on three specific aspects of the Chudasamas' discovery requests. Mazda apparently hoped that such rulings would limit the scope of discovery or, at the very least, clarify its duties. The district court never directly ruled on any of these objections or requests for rulings; nor did it ever give any indication that it had considered them in even the most cursory fashion. Accordingly, the Chudasamas continued their broad demands, unchecked by the district court.

On October 21, 1993, Mazda began pursuing a second strategy for countering the Chudasamas' vague and overbroad discovery requests. It filed a motion to dismiss their fraud count for failure to plead fraud with particularity, pursuant to Fed. R. Civ. P. 9(b). Mazda contended that the Chudasamas had failed to point to any specific misrepresentation made by Mazda.

The Chudasamas' fraud claim is based on the Federal Motor Vehicle Safety Standards, promulgated by the National Highway and Traffic Safety Administration. They alleged in their complaint that the MPV minivan only satisfied the standards that applied to "multipurpose" vehicles (the "multipurpose standards") and not the standards applicable to "passenger cars" (the "car standards"). Mazda "defrauded and deceived the American consuming public, including the plaintiffs and others similarly situated," the Chudasamas alleged, because it marketed the MPV minivan "as a family passenger car or vehicle intended to be used primarily for transporting adults and children." This marketing scheme was fraudulent according to the complaint because Mazda "well knew" that the MPV minivan only met the multipurpose standards and not the car standards. . . .

Mazda recognized that the fraud count substantially widened the scope of discovery. Absent the fraud count, the only information that the Chudasamas would be entitled to discover would be information related to the 1989 MPV minivan's brakes and side structure. The fraud count, however, arguably widened the scope of discovery to include information relating to Mazda's intentions in designing and marketing the MPV minivans, and possibly other "vehicles similar." Therefore, if Mazda could convince the district court to dismiss the fraud count, discovery would become substantially more manageable. . . .

Despite the fact that both parties fully briefed Mazda's motion to dismiss, the district court never ruled on it. . . .

Mazda's third strategy was to seek a protective order. Much of the information requested by the Chudasamas involved confidential documents that went to the heart of Mazda's business. They sought, inter alia, marketing studies, internal memoranda, and documentation on the history of the development and design of the MPV minivan and other vehicles. Fearing disclosure of this information to its competitors or to other potential plaintiffs, Mazda sought a "non-sharing" protective order that would keep the information under seal and prohibit the Chudasamas from sharing Mazda's proprietary information with anyone. They filed a motion for such a protective order on August 16, 1994. The Chudasamas objected, but indicated that they would accept a "sharing" protective order that would allow them to share the information with similarly situated plaintiffs, but not with anyone else. . . .

Perhaps because it realized that the district court had no intention of ruling on its motion to dismiss the fraud count or its various objections, Mazda adopted a fourth strategy; it withheld a substantial amount of information that it later conceded was properly discoverable. . . .

On November 12, 1993, the Chudasamas filed a motion to compel Mazda to respond "fully and completely" to a laundry list of their interrogatories and requests for production. They also sought attorneys' fees. The motion alleged that Mazda had only provided "evasive and incomplete" responses and that Mazda's objections were all too general, improperly asserted, or simply without merit.

The district court held a hearing on January 21, 1994, to address the discovery disputes. Counsel for the Chudasamas and counsel for Mazda discussed the various disputed issues at the hearing, and Mazda repeatedly asked the court to rule on its objections. The district court remained silent throughout most of the hearing, and at the end of the hearing made it clear that it did not want to rule on any objections or motions relating to discovery and warned that, if forced to rule, it would be inclined to issue sanctions "on somebody." Instead of managing the disputes itself, the court wanted the parties to confer and settle the disputes on their own. The hearing thus ended without any rulings from the bench. . . .

After Mazda disclosed the withheld discovery, the district court held another status conference on September 30. Like the previous two hearings, the court spent most of the hearing simply listening to the attorneys present their grievances. This time, however, the court indicated about halfway through the hearing that it was not interested in hearing Mazda's objections, but simply wanted counsel for the Chudasamas to summarize the state of discovery on each of the discovery requests in dispute. Although Mazda again made clear that it needed a ruling on its various objections, this conference ended like the previous two — without a ruling from the bench.

As mentioned previously, counsel for Mazda wrote a letter to the court on November 4, imploring the court to rule on three specific issues. Mazda received no response. On November 28, counsel for the Chudasamas wrote a letter complaining about Mazda's responses. This letter contained a new laundry list of discovery requests to which they had not received satisfactory responses from Mazda. They thus sought an order to compel Mazda to respond. Unlike the letter from Mazda's counsel, this letter received prompt treatment by the district court. Three days later, on December 1, 1994, the court granted the Chudasamas' motion and entered a compel order incorporating the laundry list set out in the November 28 letter.

The order contained three paragraphs. The first excoriated Mazda for its conduct in the discovery disputes. The second paragraph contained the details of the order. It directed Mazda to "make complete, proper, non-evasive responses to" the listed interrogatories and production requests. The order directed that Mazda comply within fifteen days of the date of the order and concluded in its final paragraph with the warning: "Upon failure of the Defendants to comply with this order it will be the Court's intention to impose the ultimate sanction of judgment by default."

December 1 was clearly a turning point in the case. Although the order made no mention of Mazda's objections or motion to dismiss, Mazda assumed that all of its objections had been implicitly overruled. The Chudasamas' broad and vague discovery requests were no longer simply the initial, unreasonable discovery demands that had become commonplace. They had been transformed undiluted into the court's unqualified mandate. Although the listed discovery requests were practically impossible to satisfy with any degree of certainty, Mazda had no more than fifteen days in which to satisfy the Chudasamas' excessive demands, on pain of a default judgment.

While it certainly could not hope to satisfy the plaintiffs, Mazda made a near-Herculean effort to comply. . . .

Not only did the Chudasamas' counsel refuse to accept Mazda's responses after five o'clock on the day they were due, he drafted a motion for sanctions that very day. The motion requested that the court strike Mazda's answers and enter a default judgment against Mazda on all four counts of the complaint, leaving damages as the only issue to be litigated on the merits. . . .

On June 26, 1995, the court issued an opinion and order granting the Chudasamas' motion for sanctions. . . .

Mazda sought appellate review. . . . [I]t moved for a stay of the vacatur of the protective order pending appeal and for certification under 28 U.S.C. §1292(b). . . . The district court denied the stay but [certified the case for interlocutory appeal under §1292(b). The 11th Circuit accepted the interlocutory appeal and reinstated the protective order pending decision of the appeal].

II

[The Court of Appeals decided that its acceptance of the certified appeal gave it jurisdiction not only to consider the portion of the district court's order vacating the protective order, but also the entire sanctions order as well as the underlying motion to compel.]

III

The district court based its decision to impose sanctions on Rules 37(b)(2) and 26(g) of the Federal Rules of Civil Procedure. Although the order contained several sanctions, it gave no indication as to which sanctions were imposed under which rule. Because the framework for imposing sanctions differs under the two [R]ules, we analyze the propriety of the entire order under both [R]ules. The order must stand unless it cannot be supported by either [R]ule. . . .

Rule 37 authorizes a district court to impose such sanctions "as are just" against a party that violates an order compelling discovery. Fed. R. Civ. P. 37(b)(2). Included in the rule's list of possible sanctions is an order striking a defendant's answer and entering a default. Fed. R. Civ. P. 37(b)(2)(C). District courts enjoy substantial discretion in deciding whether and how to impose sanctions under Rule 37. We accordingly review such orders for abuse of discretion. When reviewing an order striking a defendant's pleadings, our "review should be particularly scrupulous lest the district court too lightly resort to this extreme sanction, amounting to judgment against the defendant without an opportunity to be heard on the merits."

To the extent that the district court based its sanctions order on Rule 37(b), the propriety of that order depends in large part on the propriety of the earlier compel order. We review orders compelling discovery under the same abuse of discretion standard. In evaluating whether a district court abuses its discretion when it imposes severe sanctions upon a party that violates an order, we believe that an important factor is whether the entry of that order was itself an abuse of discretion. . . .[34]

A

We find that the district court's decision to compel discovery in this case was an abuse of discretion. We draw this conclusion based on the district court's failure adequately to manage this case. District courts must take an active role in managing cases on their docket.

We recognize that district courts enjoy broad discretion in deciding how best to manage the cases before them. This discretion is not unfettered, however. When a litigant's rights are materially prejudiced by the district court's mismanagement of a case, we must redress the abuse of discretion. The mismanagement of two key parts of this case — Mazda's motion to dismiss the Chudasamas' fraud claim and Mazda's resistance to the Chudasamas' discovery requests — indicates that the district court abused its discretion.

1

Failure to consider and rule on significant pretrial motions before issuing dispositive orders can be an abuse of discretion. . . . Facial challenges to the legal sufficiency of a claim or defense, such as a motion to dismiss based on failure to state a claim for relief, should . . . be resolved before discovery begins. Such a dispute always presents a purely legal question; there are no issues of fact because the allegations contained in the pleading are presumed to be true. . . .

Although mechanisms for effective discovery are essential to the fairness of our system of litigation, they also carry significant costs. . . .

If the district court dismisses a nonmeritorious claim before discovery has begun, unnecessary costs to the litigants and to the court system can be avoided. Conversely, delaying ruling on a motion to dismiss such a claim until after the parties complete discovery encourages abusive discovery and, if the court ultimately dismisses the claim, imposes unnecessary costs. . . .

Turning to the facts of the instant case, we note that even the most cursory review of the Chudasamas' shotgun complaint reveals that it contains a fraud count that is novel and of questionable validity. Upon reading the complaint, the district court should have noted that the fraud

34. Because we expect litigants to obey all orders, even those they believe were improvidently entered, sanctions will very often be sustained, particularly when the infirmity of the violated order is not clear and the sanctions imposed are moderate. This case presents neither of these circumstances.

count dramatically enlarged the scope of the Chudasamas' case. Without the fraud theory, the scope of discovery likely would have been limited to information tending to show that the MPV minivan was a defective product and that Mazda was negligent in designing it. With the fraud theory in the case, on the other hand, the scope of discovery broadened to include, inter alia, Mazda's marketing strategies and safety testing. As a result, the Chudasamas could seek much broader discovery with the fraud count in the complaint than without it. The presence of the fraud count accordingly contributed greatly to the discovery disputes. Furthermore, as long as the fraud claim remained in the case without a dispositive ruling from the bench, any analysis of "the needs of the case," as required of the court by Rule 26(b)(2) and of the litigants by Rule 26(g)(2)(C), would be hindered. As a result, Mazda faced significant uncertainty in certifying that any of its responses were "complete, proper, and non-evasive."

Many, if not most, of these problems could have been solved had the district court simply ruled on Mazda's motion to dismiss the fraud claim. Had it granted the motion, then the Chudasamas would have been forced to narrow the scope of their discovery requests considerably. Had it denied the motion and ruled that the Chudasamas had stated a claim for fraud, then Mazda would have been forced to accept a broader view of discoverable information.

2

By and large, the Federal Rules of Civil Procedure are designed to minimize the need for judicial intervention into discovery matters. They do not eliminate that need, however. . . . When the parties to a case inform the court that there are objections to discovery requests that they cannot resolve, the court should provide rulings on the objections. . . .

Filtering out overly burdensome discovery requests before issuing dispositive orders serves many of the same purposes as eliminating nonmeritorious claims for relief that unnecessarily broaden the scope of discovery. To the extent that such requests unduly broaden the scope of discovery, rejecting them saves significant costs to the parties, the court, and other litigants. To the extent the requests unduly increase the parties' costs of compliance, rejecting them will result in more equitable and more efficient discovery management and will discourage further abuse.

Our review of the record in this case convinces us that Mazda filed and argued numerous good-faith objections based on persuasive grounds. Although we express no opinion as to whether the objections should have been sustained, we are deeply concerned by the district court's failure either to explain why it granted the compel order over Mazda's objections or otherwise to indicate that it had taken the objections into consideration. As with the court's refusal to rule on the motion to dismiss, we find that this mismanagement by the court strongly suggests that the court abused its discretion in issuing the compel order. When both instances of the court's mismanagement are viewed together, any doubt that the court abused its discretion in issuing the compel order disappears. That order must be vacated.

B

Having determined that the district court abused its discretion in ordering Mazda to respond to the Chudasamas' requests, we turn to the subsequent sanctions order to determine whether it fell within the district court's broad discretion. The answer is fairly clear: the district court would have been hard pressed to fashion sanctions more severe than those included in its order. Mazda lost nearly everything that was at stake in the litigation and more. In addition to granting costs and attorneys' fees to the Chudasamas, the court struck Mazda's answer and ordered that a default be entered on all claims, reserving damages as the only issue to be tried on the merits. Moreover, it vacated its previously entered protective order. This may have been as prejudicial a sanction as it could adopt. Not only could Mazda's commercial competitors gain access to the design documents, marketing materials, and other proprietary information which Mazda had already disclosed, the order made it clear that Mazda had to disclose even more sensitive information to assist the Chudasamas in the looming trial on damages. These sanctions were so unduly severe under the circumstances as to constitute a clear abuse of discretion. . . .

IV

As noted, the district court also based its sanctions order on Rule 26(g). This rule requires that discovery-related filings bear the signature of an attorney of record. This signature certifies that the filing conforms to the discovery rules, is made for a proper purpose, and does not impose undue burdens on the opposing party in light of the circumstances of the case. Fed. R. Civ. P. 26(g)(2). If the court finds that "without substantial justification a certification is made in violation of the rule," then it must impose on the offending party "an appropriate sanction, which may include an order to pay" the other party's expenses including attorneys' fees. Fed. R. Civ. P. 26(g)(3).

The decision whether to impose sanctions under Rule 26(g)(3) is not discretionary. Once the court makes the factual determination that a discovery filing was signed in violation of the rule, it must impose "an appropriate sanction." The decision of what sanction is appropriate, however, is committed to the district court's discretion. Fed. R. Civ. P. 26(g) advisory committee's note (1983 amend.) ("The nature of the sanction is a matter of judicial discretion to be exercised in light of the particular circumstances."). When reviewing a sanctions order entered pursuant to Rule 26(g)(3), we therefore review the court's factual finding that a certification was made in violation of Rule 26(g) for clear error and the court's decision of the appropriate sanction for an abuse of discretion.

The record does contain some evidence that Mazda abused the discovery procedures, withheld admittedly relevant information, and engaged in dilatory tactics. Accordingly, the court's determination that Mazda certified its discovery responses and objections in violation of Rule 26(g) is not clearly erroneous. Contrary to the Chudasamas' assertions, however, this evidence is not enough to support the severe sanctions order. First, the majority of Mazda's misconduct was due to the court's utter failure to exercise its discretion in managing the case. While we do not condone self-help, under the circumstances here, we find the entry of a default and the vacatur of the protective order to be undue punishment. . . .

Finally and most importantly, in exercising its discretion under Rule 26(g)(3) for determining an appropriate sanction, the district court must analyze the needs of the case. See Fed. R. Civ. P. 26(g)(2)(C). As our earlier analysis demonstrates, the court clearly failed to do this. . . . Although sanctions may have been appropriate, the severe sanctions imposed were clearly excessive, and the court's determination of the "appropriate sanction" under Rule 26(g)(2)(C) was therefore an abuse of discretion.[45] Because the sanctions order cannot stand under either Rule 37(b) or Rule 26(g), it must be vacated. . . .

For the foregoing reasons, we VACATE both the district court's order compelling discovery and its order granting the appellee's amended motion for sanctions and REMAND this case with the instruction that the Chief Judge of the Middle District of Georgia reassign the case to a different district judge for further proceedings consistent with this opinion.

NOTES AND PROBLEMS

1. The Court of Appeals' opinion excoriates the district court. Is that the right place to put the blame?

a. What, according to the opinion, did the district judge do wrong? Be specific. Why was the district judge wrong to impose sanctions on a

---

45. We note that the imposition of costs and attorneys' fees probably would not have been an abuse of discretion. Rule 26(g)(3) suggests just such a sanction.

party that had, according to the appellate court, willfully refused to supply discoverable information?

b. Seen from another perspective — perhaps that taken by the district judge — the failure was that of the lawyers. What did each of them do wrong? Be specific.

c. From still another perspective, one hinted at by the opinion, the Rules, rather than the lawyers or the judge, bear responsibility for this mess. The Rules, after all, put discovery initially in the hands of the lawyers and ask the lawyers to behave cooperatively. The opinion itself suggests a structural rather than an individual problem: "As has become typical in recent years, both sides initially adopted extreme and unreasonable positions. . . ." If this assessment is accurate — and some would say it is not — does that suggest a response more global than administering a tongue-lashing to a hapless district court judge? What sort of response?

2. The opinion illustrates the linkage of pleading and discovery. Much of the court of appeals' criticism of the district court revolves around the district court's failure to rule on the motion to dismiss the fraud claim. What explanation other than inattention is there for the district court's deferring ruling on the motion to dismiss?

a. What argument did defendant make in the motion to dismiss?

b. What argument did plaintiffs make in opposition? How does that argument bear on the ensuing discovery?

c. If the district court had granted the motion to dismiss and barred discovery on the issues it raised, what risks would it have been taking? (Note that dismissal of the fraud counts would not have constituted an appealable final judgment, because the remaining counts would still be valid.)

3. The opinion at one point suggests that Mazda's failure to disclose discoverable documents could be explained — though not justified — by the court's and the plaintiff's behavior.

a. Is it a defense to a motion for sanctions under either Rule 37(b) or Rule 26(g) that the opposing party itself has violated its discovery obligations or engaged in unreasonable discovery tactics? Should the moving party's "unclean hands" be a defense to a motion for sanctions? Why not?

b. Does the opinion say that one can avoid discovery sanctions if the district court is very lax in pretrial management?

4. Mazda was able to appeal the sanctions order because the district court certified the order for interlocutory review under 28 U.S.C. §1292(b).

a. The grant of interlocutory review is itself unusual: Very few discovery cases come to the appellate court in a pretrial phase because of the final judgment rule.

b. Suppose the district court had not certified the case for interlocutory appeal. When (if ever) could Mazda have sought judicial review of the sanctions order? The opinion emphasizes the importance that Mazda attached to its marketing strategy and its consequent reluctance to disclose documents laying out those plans. Assuming that this importance was real and not merely a ploy, what do you think Mazda would have done had the trial judge refused to certify the appeal?

5. If we set aside the punitive damages, the amounts at stake look relatively modest. One of the plaintiffs in *Chudasama* allegedly suffered $13,000 in medical expenses and $5,000 in lost wages as a result of the defendants' alleged wrongdoing.

a. Should the amount of compensatory damages at stake in the litigation play a role in the district court's determination as to the appropriate scope of discovery? Should more discovery be allowed in a case where a plaintiff died than in a case where the plaintiff suffered only minor damages?

b. Look at Rule 26(b)(2) and note that it applies only to depositions and interrogatories. Is there any reason it should not apply to document requests?

6. Suppose the district judge had not certified an interlocutory appeal. Further suppose that Mazda, perhaps fearing "copycat" litigation, refused to settle. Further suppose that it had continued with its "fourth strategy [of] withh[olding] a substantial amount of information" properly discoverable.

a. One possibility — quite common — is that someone reveals the nondisclosure. As to almost every document in almost every large organization, there is (1) another copy (perhaps in a computer file) and (2) someone (besides the opposing party) in whose interest it is to reveal it. That person could be another lawyer working on the case who understands that his or her career is at risk for failure to make court-ordered disclosure. It can also be someone in the client organization.

b. Consider some possible consequences, suggested by Rozier v. Ford Motor Co., 573 F.2d 1332 (5th Cir. 1978). In wrongful death/product liability litigation, plaintiff requested engineering analyses from Ford, which responded that there were no documents making certain comparisons of fuel tank placements. Defendants won a jury verdict. Ten months later, a document came to light that arguably fit the description of the requested documents. The Court of Appeals held that the trial court abused its discretion in failing to reopen the judgment under Rule 60(b)(3) because plaintiff had, under that Rule, shown defendant's "fraud . . . , misrepresentation, or other misconduct." The case was remanded for a new trial. Notice that an undisclosed document will often look worse in retrospect. What should Ford's lawyer — if we assume him genuinely uncertain about whether the document was covered by the discovery request — have done?

c. Consequences can reach well beyond the case:

> The most famous example occurred in the complex antitrust litigation instituted by Berkey Photo Inc. against Eastman Kodak Co. in the 1970s in the Southern District of New York. There, during the course of protracted litigation, Mahlon F. Perkins Jr., one of Kodak's outside trial attorneys and a member of a prestigious Wall Street law firm, lied to presiding Southern District Judge Marvin E. Frankel, saying that he had destroyed certain documents which otherwise would had to have been produced during discovery. When Perkins' law partner, John Doar, learned that Perkins had lied to the court and had, instead, withheld the documents, the facts were made known to Judge Frankel. In turn, Judge Frankel wrote to U.S. Attorney Robert E. Fiske Jr., an act which, in a very closely watched case, resulted in the prosecutor instituting criminal contempt charges against Perkins under 18 U.S.C. §§401(1) and (3) and Rule 42(b) of the Federal Rules of Criminal Procedure. Perkins pleaded guilty. While he was sentenced by Southern District Judge Robert J. Ward to a term of imprisonment of one month and had suffered a humiliating resignation from his law firm, he was spared disbarment. . . . A disciplinary sanction of "severe censure" was imposed on Perkins for his conduct.

Perjury and Fraud In Civil Proceedings, N.Y.L.J. Jan. 25, 1994, at 1. Why shouldn't Perkins also be disbarred?

7. What causes the kind of lawyer behavior that results in sanctions? Putting aside humankind's propensity for evil, one can point to two characteristics of modern American legal practice. First, the U.S. bar has been growing younger since the 1970s, as new lawyers starting their careers outnumber older practitioners. Lawyers in Society: The Common Law World 198 (Abel & Lewis eds. 1988). That increased youth means, of course, that the average level of experience (and attendant professional socialization) has decreased. Second, the larger size of the profession means that any two lawyers facing each other in litigation are less likely ever to encounter each other again. Such "one shot" encounters may increase the lawyers' propensity to engage in unattractive forms of behavior, especially in high-stakes lawsuits (the sort most likely to have significant discovery). This propensity to gamble may be reinforced by the rarity and, some would say, the haphazard incidence of sanctions.

Having looked at some of the obstacles to the smooth functioning of discovery, step back and consider its place in the larger scheme. If pleading and discovery do their job, the lawsuit will be in a paradoxical state: It will be ready for trial, but trial will probably not occur. The next three chapters focus on those outcomes and explain the paradox. Chapter VIII looks at formal and informal ways in which the parties may avoid trial. Chapters IX and X look at trial itself.

The paradoxical consequences of discovery come from its dual role. It aims to prevent surprise at trial and to assure that cases will be resolved justly on their merits. Surprise witnesses make good courtroom drama but do not reassure us that justice has been done. In this trial-oriented role, discovery aims at laying bare both the parties' positions and the facts of the case.

In its other guise, discovery aims to put the parties in a position from which they can realistically assess the merits. In an ideal world such assessments would match (that is, the parties would both accurately predict the results of a trial). When that happens, the parties will often settle. The next chapter explores the dynamics of settlement. When the parties' assessments of the merits are inaccurate or mismatched, settlement is unlikely, but other mechanisms, like summary judgment, may use the products of discovery to end the case.

Still other parties may be so averse to the litigation process — including abuses of discovery — that they seek to take themselves outside the adjudicatory system. United States law gives them amazing freedom to do so in recognizing a number of contractual alternatives to litigation.

The next chapter explores both the voluntary and involuntary ways in which litigation may be avoided altogether or in which it can end without a trial.

RESOLUTION WITHOUT TRIAL

VIII

"A trial is a failure,"* write two lawyers. What they might mean and whether they are right will provide the focus of this chapter. Applied to contemporary U. S. litigation, the quoted statement looks in two directions. It can refer, as the authors of the statement intended, to the parties' inability to settle or, failing that, their inability to agree on a method of resolving their dispute outside the formal litigation processes. Alternatively, it can refer to the procedures that the formal litigation process itself uses to end lawsuits without a trial.

Both paths build on the pretrial stage and on discovery in particular. Discovery will sometimes produce information that enables the parties to reach converging estimates of the outcome of the lawsuit. When that happens, they can both save time and money by agreeing to a settlement. Discovery, however, particularly if it produces acrimony, can also drive the parties further apart. When that happens, litigation may be the only way to settle the dispute. But even in this situation there may be faster ways to resolve the conflict. Some of these ways exist within the litigation system; others take the parties outside that system to other methods of resolution. This chapter explores both the "inside" and the "outside" alternatives to trial.

The nineteenth century was the age of trial. As common law pleading disintegrated, disputes that did not settle could be adjudicated only at trial. With the coming of discovery, however, trials have become expensive and time-consuming. In the last half of this century procedural systems have consequently sought to avoid them. In this aim they largely succeed; in the last fifty years the civil trial rate in the federal courts has fallen from about 20 percent — one in five filed suits — to just over 4 percent — one in twenty-five filed suits. Nationally, the rate of trial for

* Samuel Gross & Kent Syverud, Getting to No: A Study of Settlement Negotiations and the Selection of Cases for Trial, 90 Mich. L. Rev. 319 (1991).

civil lawsuits ranges between 1 and 9 percent, with the mean at 3.3 percent, of filings.*

What happens to the rest of the lawsuits? Two answers emerge, one for cases that remain within the courts, another for cases outside the courts. For the cases within the system, you should be careful not to equate trial with adjudication: Many filed cases end with adjudicated dispositions other than trial — for example, by a dismissal on the pleadings or through summary judgments. Although trial rates have dropped, the rate of adjudicated cases has remained constant for about fifty years, at about 30 percent of filed cases.

The remainder, almost three-quarters of all cases, end by some means other than an adjudicated decision. As we shall see, even this statistic understates the rate of unadjudicated resolutions, because it fails to capture the large number of disputes where formal litigation is never begun. Both this latter group and the cases that begin in the litigation system but do not reach adjudication exist in an alternative world of disputing. This world, which some say is replacing ordinary litigation, presents both the best and worst of potential human creativity. On the one hand, it suggests that people can resolve disputes economically and creatively. On the other hand, it demonstrates one-sidedness, avarice, and disregard for basic human fairness.

We start and end with the official litigation system, venturing outside it after we have established some baselines and some points of connection between the official and the alternative systems.

A.   The Pressure to Choose Adjudication or an Alternative

Why do lawsuits ever proceed beyond the complaint? Defendants accused of wrongdoing might just ignore the allegations, were there not a way of forcing a response. Conversely, plaintiffs might file meritless suits that they would leave hanging over defendants' heads were there not some way of forcing them to proceed to a conclusion. The procedural devices that force the parties to engage and respond to each other are the bookends of an adversarial system in which the parties rather than the court have primary responsibility for the progress of litigation. There are two such devices, the default judgment — designed to goad the defendant into action — and the involuntary dismissal, which is intended to keep the

---

* Brian Ostrom & Neal Kauder, Examining the Work of State Courts, 1995: A National Perspective from the Court Statistics Project 22 (Natl. Center for State Courts 1996).

plaintiff from going to sleep at the litigative switch. One version of such principles is found in Rules 55 (for default judgments) and Rule 41(b) (involuntary dismissal). Default typically occurs when a defendant refuses to respond to his litigative cues. Involuntary dismissal occurs when a plaintiff initiates a suit but then fails to respond to one of the defendant's initiatives or disobeys court orders.

1. Default and Default Judgments

Read Rule 55 and consider the following problems.

NOTES AND PROBLEMS

1. Your client, Paula Houston, is involved in an automobile accident with Darlene Magnus. Darlene's insurance carrier, Ace Insurance Company, contacts your client after the accident. You discuss the case with Ace and exchange some letters and medical reports. About six months after the accident, you conclude that the case can't be settled without litigation, and you bring a claim in the appropriate federal district court.

a. You serve Magnus with process. Read Rule 12(b)(1)(A). Twenty days pass, and you have not heard from defendant. What, if anything, should you do? See First Interstate Bank v. Service Stores of America, 128 F.R.D. 679 (W.D. Okla. 1989) (unprofessional conduct to take default on first possible day).

b. You request a waiver of service (see Rule 4(d) and Form 1A), and the defendant signs and returns the waiver form (see Form 1B). How long must you wait before being justified in seeking a default judgment?

2. It is now three months after filing the complaint and serving Magnus, and you still have heard nothing. You decide to take a default judgment.

a. State precisely the steps you must take to obtain it.

b. Rule 55(a) provides that the clerk may "enter [a] . . . default" against a party who has failed "to plead or otherwise defend." Rule 55(b)(1) provides that a "default judgment" for a sum certain may be entered against a defendant who "has been defaulted for failure to appear." Rule 55(b)(2) has a similar reference to "appearance." What does it mean to "appear" in an action where one has failed to plead or defend?

3. Assume you obtain a default judgment. What does it actually accomplish? See Rules 55(c) and 60(b).

4. In some civil law systems, default operates as a general denial — that is, the plaintiff must still satisfy the court that the facts justify granting relief. By contrast, in the United States a default operates as an admission

of liability. See Hughes Tool Co. v. Trans World Airlines, 409 U.S. 363 (1973).

a. What does this contrast say about party responsibility, the role of the court, and the concept of a lawsuit?

b. Even though a default judgment resolves the question of liability, questions can arise when the court is asked to grant relief. See Rule 55(b)(2).

c. In an action to recover a debt, for example, the judgment will be for the amount owed plus statutory or contractual interest. The situation becomes more complicated when the amount of damages is uncertain, as in a typical accident case. Under these circumstances, the plaintiff must then "prove up" damages. See Rule 55(b)(2). In *Hughes Tool*, supra, a special master heard extensive testimony before awarding $145 million in antitrust damages after the defendant defaulted by refusing to cooperate with discovery.

d. Tension can arise, however, between the idea that default establishes liability and the need for proof of damages. Rule 55(b)(2) provides that a defendant who has "appeared" (see Note 2b, supra), must receive notice of the plaintiff's intention to ask for judgment. Having received such notice, the defendant can appear and contest damages; indeed, Rule 55(b)(2) goes on to say that the parties may have a right to trial by jury at this "prove-up" stage. How far can a defendant who has defaulted on the merits go in contesting damages? For example, suppose in a libel case a defendant seeks to minimize damages by showing that there was no libel. Allowable?

5. Despite the system's reliance on default to force the defendant to get on with the job, the courts display real discomfort at entering judgment for reasons that fall so far short of the merits. The next case explores limits on the courts' power to force the parties toward adjudication on the merits.

Peralta v. Heights Medical Center
485 U.S. 80 (1988)

Justice WHITE delivered the opinion of the Court.

Heights Medical Center, Inc. (hereafter appellee) sued appellant Peralta in February 1982, to recover some $5600 allegedly due under appellant's guarantee of a hospital debt incurred by one of his employees. Citation issued, the return showing personal, but untimely, service. Appellant did not appear or answer, and on July 20, 1982, default judgment was entered for the amount claimed, plus attorney's fees and costs.

In June 1984, appellant began a bill of review proceeding in the Texas courts to set aside the default judgment and obtain the relief. In the second amended petition, it was alleged that the return of service itself showed a defective service[2] and that appellant in fact had not been personally served at all. The judgment was therefore void under Texas law. It was also alleged that the judgment was abstracted and recorded in the county real property records, thereby creating a cloud on appellant's title, that a writ of attachment was issued, and that, unbeknownst to him, his real property was sold to satisfy the judgment and for much less than its true value. Appellant prayed that the default judgment be vacated, the abstract of judgment be expunged from the county real property records, the constable's sale be voided, and that judgment for damages be entered against the Medical Center and Mr. and Mrs. Paul Seng-Ngan Chen, the purchasers at the constable's sale and appellees here.

Appellee filed a motion for summary judgment asserting that in a bill of review proceeding such as appellant filed, it must be shown that the petitioner had a meritorious defense to the action in which judgment had been entered, that petitioner was prevented from proving his defense by the fraud, accident, or wrongful act of the opposing party, and that there had been no fault or negligence on petitioner's part. Although it was assumed for the purposes of summary judgment that there had been defective service and that this lapse excused proof of the second and third requirement for obtaining a bill of review, it was assertedly necessary, nevertheless, to show a meritorious defense, which appellant had conceded he did not have. . . .

. . . "An elementary and fundamental requirement of due process in any proceeding which is to be accorded finality is notice reasonably calculated, under the circumstances, to apprise interested parties of the pendency of the action and afford them the opportunity to present their objections." Mullane v. Central Hanover Bank & Trust Co. [supra page 175] Failure to give notice violates "the most rudimentary demands of due process of law."Armstrong v. Manzo, 380 U.S. 545, 550 (1965). See also . . . Pennoyer v. Neff.

The Texas courts nevertheless held, as appellee urged them to do, that to have the judgment set aside, appellant was required to show that he had a meritorious defense, apparently on the ground that without a defense, the same judgment would again be entered on retrial and hence appellant had suffered no harm from the judgment entered without notice. But this reasoning is untenable. As appellant asserts, had he had

2. The petition alleged that the record contained a return of service of process, showing that service was effected more than 90 days after its issuance, contrary to Texas Rule of Civil Procedure 101. . . . Texas courts have held that service after the 90th day is a nullity, depriving the court of personal jurisdiction over the defendant.

notice of the suit, he might have impleaded the employee whose debt had been guaranteed, worked out a settlement, or paid the debt. He would also have preferred to sell his property himself in order to raise funds rather than to suffer it sold at a constable's auction.

Nor is there any doubt that the entry of the judgment itself had serious consequences. It is not denied that the judgment was entered on the county records, became a lien on appellant's property, and was the basis for issuance of a writ of execution under which appellant's property was promptly sold, without notice. Even if no execution sale had yet occurred, the lien encumbered the property and impaired appellant's ability to mortgage or alienate it; and state procedures for creating and enforcing such liens are subject to the strictures of due process. Here, we assume that the judgment against him and the ensuing consequences occurred without notice to appellant, notice at a meaningful time and in a meaningful manner that would have given him an opportunity to be heard. . . .

. . . The Texas court held that the default judgment must stand absent a showing of a meritorious defense to the action in which judgment was entered without proper notice to appellant, a judgment that had substantial adverse consequences to appellant. By reason of the Due Process Clause of the Fourteenth Amendment, that holding is plainly infirm.

Where a person has been deprived of property in a manner contrary to the most basic tenets of due process, "it is no answer to say that in his particular case due process of law would have led to the same result because he had no adequate defense upon the merits." Coe v. Armour Fertilizer Works, 237 U.S. 413, 424 (1915). As we observed in Armstrong v. Manzo, supra, at 552, only "wip[ing] the slate clean . . . would have restored the petitioner to the position he would have occupied had due process of law been accorded to him in the first place." The Due Process Clause demands no less in this case.

The judgment below is reversed.

NOTES AND PROBLEMS

1. *Peralta* has several layers.

a. As the court frames the case, Mr. Peralta received no notice of the pending action. Thus framed, the argument for setting aside any resulting judgment seems easy. Recall the facts of Pennoyer v. Neff that are cited in the opinion: So far as the record showed, Neff had never received notice of Mitchell's first lawsuit. Could *Pennoyer* have been dealt with in the same way as *Peralta*, without the need to invent the law of personal jurisdiction?

b. The *Peralta* court has to work hard to frame the issue that way, since, as the case's first paragraph and footnote 2 suggest, Mr. Peralta apparently did receive actual notice of the suit. Because the service took place beyond the 90-day period in which Texas deems the service to be effective it was, however, under Texas law "a nullity."If one views the case as one in which actual notice — though not valid service — was received, the case becomes harder. If one assumes that Mr. Peralta did receive such notice, does it really deny him due process to require that he show a meritorious defense as a prerequisite to setting aside the default judgment?

c. The court's answer to that question is phrased in terms of "might haves": Mr. Peralta might have impleaded the employee; he might have worked out a settlement; he might have paid the debt; he might have sold the property himself. Would it be unconstitutional to ask Peralta to show that any of these events were likely? Would it be fair to ask him why he had ignored the summons?

2. *Peralta* demonstrates that courts, while prepared to enter default judgments, greatly prefer to see the parties engage on the merits of the dispute.

a. This preference means that parties seeking relief from defaults get them set aside if they can show some plausible reason (such as illness or family emergency) for failing to respond to the summons. See Rule 55(c).

b. Rule 55(c) also points to Rule 60(b), which permits the reopening of the case even after judgment is entered on a default. The easy Rule 60(b) cases are situations in which the defendant can show that she did not receive notice. Much harder are the cases in which the defendant is served and retains a lawyer — who then fails to respond to the complaint or to judicial orders. The defendant client who suffers as a result of such lawyer neglect has a claim in malpractice against his lawyer. But lawyers who habitually fail clients in such elementary ways are disproportionately likely to be uninsured or otherwise judgment-proof. Should the court relieve the defendant of the default, thus burdening the plaintiff, who may have changed his position in reliance on the default judgment?

3. One circumstance distinguishes Mr. Peralta from that of other defendants who suffer default judgments: He challenged it. The vast number of such judgments are entered and not challenged; frequently these defendants do not consult lawyers. A typical case involves a creditor's suit over an unpaid consumer debt. The debate is over the number of these defendants who have plausible defenses or counterclaims. If the number of such defenses is very low (if, that is, most defendants would inevitably suffer an adverse judgment), then the default judgment represents merely a shorter, cheaper route to that result. If, however, substantial

numbers of these defendants have viable defenses, the entry of a default judgment represents a reproach to the legal system. The empirical data are scanty.

2.   Failure to Prosecute: Involuntary Dismissal

Involuntary dismissal does to plaintiffs what default does to defendants: It forces them to pursue the lawsuit to some resolution. In an ordinary lawsuit, defendant has something that plaintiff wants and can get only if the lawsuit proceeds. One might therefore think that a defendant would be quite happy to have a plaintiff who, after filing and serving the complaint, did nothing. Why might a defendant nevertheless feel aggrieved if a plaintiff commenced but then, perhaps distracted by other business, did nothing to prosecute the suit for several years? For a concrete example, imagine a variation on the facts in *Peralta*: The plaintiff files the suit, serves the defendant and puts a lien on his property, but instead of proceeding to a judgment, the plaintiff simply sits and waits. Mr. Peralta can't get the suit dismissed on the merits (recall he has no meritorious defense), but meanwhile he can't sell the property or borrow money on it because of the lien.

What can a defendant in such a situation do about it? Rule 41(b) provides for involuntary dismissal "for failure of the plaintiff to prosecute" (as well as on other grounds). Such a dismissal takes the lawsuit off the books. The question is, how lax must a plaintiff be before a judge should enter such a dismissal? In other words, when does "standard" foot-dragging become abandonment?

NOTES AND PROBLEMS

1. Consider some possible scenarios: In which ones would involuntary dismissal for failure to prosecute be justified?

a. K files suit against F in Hawaii, claiming fraud in connection with the sale of real property in California. In April 1999 the action is transferred to California; thereafter, the pretrial conference is continued several times at the request of K's local counsel (his Hawaii attorney was lead counsel). In May 2000, K's local counsel is incapacitated, and, at a hearing on June 29, 2000, he requests another continuance since he is closing his practice. The court grants the continuance, stating that the action will be dismissed if K is not ready for the pretrial conference within 60 days. On August 31, 2000, K's newly retained local counsel requests another continuance.

b. After much delay, a case is called for trial. Plaintiff's attorney claims he is sick and unable to obtain transportation and sends a substitute to seek an adjournment. The court, having reason to doubt the excuse, insists that the backup counsel pick the jury and try the case. The back-up counsel refuses to do so, pleading complete ignorance.

2. As the preceding examples suggest, the cases involve widely differing factual situations, making it hard to pin down differences in legal standards for granting or denying involuntary dismissal. Moreover, trial courts frequently do not explain why they have dismissed a case, and appellate courts often state that they simply are deciding whether the trial court properly exercised it discretion.* In addition to relying on judicial discretion, some states attempt to deal with less than diligent plaintiffs by setting absolute guidelines. The California Code of Civil Procedure (Deering 1999) contains two examples:

§583.210(a). The summons and complaint shall be served upon the defendant within three years after the action is commenced against the defendant.

§583.310. An action shall be brought to trial within five years after the action is commenced against the defendant.

Even in the face of such absolute statements, however, much litigation has occurred over whether the opposing party has explicitly or impliedly waived such a deadline.

3. Default judgments and involuntary dismissals may present both claim preclusion and issue preclusion issues if plaintiff starts over or if there is litigation on a closely related matter. If, for example, plaintiff's action is dismissed for one of the reasons already discussed, should she be free to start over? If so, what issues, if any, have been determined in the prior "litigation"? See Chapter XII.

3. Voluntary Dismissal

On the basis of the exposition so far, one might assume that both plaintiff and defendant were locked in adversarial combat until a conclusion of the suit. Not so. Rule 41(a)(1)(i) allows a plaintiff to dismiss any time before the defendant answers, and 41(a)(1)(ii) permits the plaintiff to dismiss a suit at any time if all the parties agree. Such stipulated

---

* Note that a trial court decision denying dismissal is not immediately appealable because, under 28 U.S.C. §1291, appeals lie only from "final decisions." This means that, in practice, a denial of dismissal will be reviewed only if the victorious party on the motion also wins the case on the merits. In such a case, the appellate court is most unlikely to find an abuse of discretion.

dismissals do not bar a later refiling of the suit unless there has been a previous dismissal or the dismissal itself contains a provision that bars refiling. Provisions barring refiling frequently result from successful settlement negotiations: In return for satisfaction, the plaintiff gives up her chance to pursue the suit or to refile it later.

What about the plaintiff who realizes she needs to gather more evidence? The defendant is unlikely to agree to a dismissal for such purposes. Rule 41(a)(2) authorizes a voluntary dismissal only by permission of the court.

NOTES AND PROBLEMS

1. Two kinds of questions present themselves about such cost-free voluntary dismissals. First, one can ask why they are ever permitted.

a. At common law, such dismissals made sense because they enabled a plaintiff who had a good claim but had brought the wrong writ to replead (e.g., to replead trespass instead of trespass on the case, assumpsit instead of debt).

b. The justification for such false starts is much less clear in a system that permits easy joinder of claims and easy amendment. In such a system, one could easily justify a door that locked behind the plaintiff once she had begun a lawsuit: "Either pursue it to a judgment or settlement, or, if you abandon the suit, do so irrevocably." Why do we permit even one costless voluntary dismissal?

c. One possible reason is to facilitate settlement negotiations. Plaintiff files claim; defendant immediately offers to settle; and the parties begin talking. Meanwhile the judge has set a tight discovery schedule and time is running out. The parties might ask the judge to relax the timetable (see discussion of Rule 16, later in this chapter), but it might be simpler for plaintiff to dismiss the suit, knowing that he can refile if negotiations fail. Indeed, voluntary dismissal may enable the plaintiff simultaneously to demonstrate a good faith effort to settle and to gain leverage in settlement with the implicit threat to refile if negotiations bog down. If they succeed, of course, the ensuing agreement will prohibit refiling of the suit.

d. Rule 41(a)(1)(i) allows the plaintiff voluntarily to dismiss at any time before the defendant has answered; after that point the court's permission or agreement of the other side is necessary. In one notorious case the availability of voluntary dismissal proved catastrophic for the defendant. In corporate control litigation between Texaco and Pennzoil — Texaco Inc. v. Pennzoil, 481 U.S. 1 (1987) — the plaintiff filed originally in a Delaware state court seeking a preliminary injunction.

Plaintiff opposed the injunction but did not answer the complaint. When the court denied the injunction, using language suggesting the plaintiff would lose on the merits, the plaintiff quickly took a voluntary dismissal and refiled in Texas. A Texas jury eventually awarded the plaintiff $10 billion. This maneuver by the plaintiff would have been unavailable had Texaco answered the Delaware complaint. One account described the defendant's failure to answer as "one of the most expensive tactical errors every committed in a lawsuit."* The moral, apparently, is that if a voluntary dismissal will harm your case, answer the complaint promptly and lock plaintiff into the forum.

2. Suppose the lawsuit has proceeded further than discussed in the preceding note: Can the plaintiff still dismiss and then restart the litigation? Rule 41(a)(2) gives the judge broad discretion in deciding when to grant a voluntary dismissal after the defendant has answered. The case law surrounding this discretion does not produce clear rules but suggests that plaintiffs should not be permitted to bail out simply to avoid a loss on the merits. To use an extreme example, it would be an abuse of discretion for a trial court to permit a plaintiff to dismiss the suit voluntarily after the jury has returned a verdict for the defendant but before judgment has been entered. The hard questions arise not when there have been such determinations on the merits but when significant procedural issues have been decided. Consider two cases, in both of which the plaintiff sought to dismiss voluntarily after a procedural ruling that made plaintiff's case more difficult.

a. Maurice Manshack, the employee of an electrical contractor, was severely burned while working on Utility Co.'s high-voltage electrical pole and line in Louisiana. The Manshacks filed a lawsuit in the U.S. District Court for the Eastern District of Texas. Shortly after suit was filed, Mrs. Manshack was fired from her job with Utility Co. In the pretrial stage a critical issue was whether Texas or Louisiana law would apply. Louisiana law would handle Manshack's injury under workers' compensation, barring a tort suit; Texas would permit a tort suit. After the district court ruled that Louisiana law applied, the Manshacks sought voluntarily to dismiss the suit, refiling it in Texas state courts. The Fifth Circuit affirmed a district court order permitting the voluntary dismissal. Manshack v. Southwestern Electric Power Co., 915 F.2d 172 (5th Cir. 1990).

b. A child and his parents sued a pharmaceutical company, alleging injuries as a result of the child's grandmother's ingesting a drug given

* Timothy Feltham, Tortious Interference with Contractual Relations: The Texaco Inc. v. Pennzoil Litigation, 33 N.Y.L. Sch. L. Rev. 111, 117, Note 65 (1988).

while she was pregnant with the child's mother. Ohio law applied to the case, and a diversity action was brought in federal court. Uncertain what Ohio law was on liability for preconception conduct, the district court certified the question to the Ohio Supreme Court. (For a description of certification of state law questions, see para pages 302–303). The Ohio Supreme Court held that the state recognized no such cause of action. The plaintiff thereupon sought, and the district court granted, permission to dismiss voluntarily. The plaintiff sought such a dismissal to allow him to file suit in an Ohio state court in case the state legislature changed Ohio law before the statute of limitations expired. The Sixth Circuit held that permitting a voluntary dismissal under those circumstances was an abuse of discretion. Grover v. Eli Lilly & Co., 33 F. 3d 716 (6th Cir. 1994).

c. Can *Grover* and *Manshack* be reconciled? Both deal with plaintiffs who sought to dismiss after adverse rulings on choice of law questions that had dispositive potential. Was the Ohio Supreme Court decision more dispositive than the *Manshack* decision that Louisiana law applied? Or is it bad form to fire the wife of a badly injured plaintiff and then expect the court to be generous in rulings about whether one's litigative position has been "prejudiced."

B.   Avoiding Adjudication

Faced with the products of discovery and kept in engagement by procedural rules, parties may decide that they want to avoid adjudication. Indeed, given foreknowledge about procedural rules, they may decide well before any dispute arises that they wish to avoid litigation. The contemporary U.S. legal regime offers parties a broad set of ways to avoid litigation altogether or to escape from it once involved. Some would add that these alternatives have prevailed and that for most disputes adjudication occurs only under unusual, even pathological, conditions.

These escapes from adjudication, popularly known as alternative dispute resolution (ADR), take us into a realm that lies beyond the boundaries of formal procedure. But even these alternatives depend on law for their effectiveness. They rely principally on contract: Because the courts will enforce contracts not to litigate, parties, either before or during litigation, can choose some other mechanism to resolve their disputes. By refusing to hear a lawsuit filed in breach of such an agreement, courts force parties to use the agreed-on procedure or to abandon their dispute.

As a consequence, parties have enormous freedom to write their own procedural rules. To put the matter starkly, one can think of existing procedural rules as rules that come into play only if the parties have not otherwise agreed. The remaining parts of this section explore some of the paths opened by judicial enforcement of such alternative processes.

1. Negotiation and Settlement

Since the beginning of recorded legal systems, parties have regularly settled most of their disputes informally, without adjudication. Behind this fact lies a normative question. Settlements are cheaper and faster than trials. Are they also better — or are they merely a capitulation to expediency? Some argue that settlements are not just faster and cheaper but also qualitatively better, because consent is a basic principle of justice, and because settlements can take account of nuances and subtleties in the facts and in the parties' interests that would be lost at trial. On the other side are those who argue that settlement leaves the parties less satisfied than if a trier heard their stories, permits might to triumph over right, and deprives the public of definitive adjudication of issues that may reach beyond the individual case.

Whether because settlements are good or merely because they are cheap, lawyers frequently use them. Settlement agreements require both negotiating skill and knowledge of how parties can achieve their goal once they come to agreement in principle. Unlike parties who are negotiating the sale of a building or the terms of an employment agreement, parties who are negotiating when a lawsuit is imminent or actually has been filed are likely to be somewhat annoyed with each other. One of the lawyers' contributions to the negotiation may be the interposition of a professional role that keeps the disputants from each others' throats long enough to work out an agreement.

Concerning this professional role, there are two different schools of thought and practice. One group emphasizes the sense in which negotiation is a competition or conflict in which each point gained by one side is lost by the other. Another school of thought argues that adversarial negotiators exaggerate the extent to which zero-sum situations dominate negotiation. Advocates of such a problem-solving approach to negotiation argue that focusing on the clients' goals will often yield solutions not evident to the adversarial school. Once the lawyer has found a negotiating stance with which she is comfortable, she must confront several concrete problems particular to the settlement of a threatened or actual lawsuit.

a.   Contracting to Dismiss

The simplest form of settlement is a contract (sometimes called a *release*) in which the plaintiff (or prospective plaintiff) agrees not to bring a lawsuit or to drop one already filed. Most plaintiffs want something, typically money, in return for such agreements.

NOTES AND PROBLEMS

1. Suppose, as often happens, the parties reach a settlement before suit is filed.

a. The parties might do so in a number of ways: a meeting of the lawyers, a series of telephone calls, an exchange of documents. Recently one firm has opened an Internet site dedicated to settling lawsuits. Lawyers log on to the Web site and get a password. The defendant must list three possible settlement figures, in an ascending dollar order for which she will settle. Without knowing the defendant's figures, the plaintiff must list three figures in descending order for which he will settle. The program then matches each of the rounds of offers and "settles" the case if any set of figures falls within 30 percent or $5,000 of each other. For Dueling Lawyers the Internet Is Unlikely Referee, Wall. St. J., May 12, 1999, at B1.

b. Whether they reach agreement through an old-fashioned handshake or through cyberspace, do the parties need approval of their deal? No: In an ordinary case, the judge need not examine or approve the settlement. Plaintiffs needing immediate funds may settle meritorious claims for trivial sums; defendants eager to get on with other matters may offer meritless or even fraudulent plaintiffs substantial sums to end litigation. The exceptions to this "freedom to settle" arise in class actions (where Rule 23(e) requires judicial approval of settlements), in cases involving minors, where the court is required to approve settlements (see, e.g., Cal. Prob. Code §3500(b) (West 1999), and in some multi-defendant cases (see, e.g., Cal. Code Civ. Proc. §887.6 (West 1999). What theory underlies these exceptions to the general rule of judicial indifference to the fairness of settlements?

c. Is the usual practice of judicial indifference defensible? Should judges be required to scrutinize all settlements for fairness? Before answering, imagine yourself in such a position. A suit has been filed alleging negligent operation of an automobile and seeks damages for whiplash injuries, a frequent injury that is also frequently feigned. Defendant, represented by an insurer, has answered denying liability but has offered a small settlement. You, the judge, are asked to approve or disapprove the settlement. How would you reach a decision? What information would you want to have? Would your concern be substantive (is the settlement fair?) or procedural (did both parties know the material facts?)? Would the cost of gathering and presenting this information eliminate a chief advantage of settlement, speed and cheapness?

d. As a half-way step between trying to police all settlements and leaving matters entirely to the law of contract, legislators can build procedural protections into settlements of certain kinds of claims. For example, federal legislation regulates settlements releasing Age Discrimination in Employment Act (ADEA) claims: Offers must be clearly written; they must remain in effect for stated periods of time; they must advise employees to consult a lawyer; and they must give settling employees at least a week in which to revoke a signed settlement agreement. 29 U.S.C. §626(f). In Oubre v. Entergy Operations, Inc., 522 U.S. 422 (1998), the Court held that an employee who had released ADEA claims without these procedures could, without tendering back the money paid for a settlement, bring suit under the act.

e. Although there is no general doctrine requiring judicial approval of settlements, settlements are contracts and can be attacked on any of the grounds on which one can attack any contract: fraud, duress, mistake, incapacity, unconscionability, and the like.

2. You represent a defendant employer against a former employee who threatens to bring an action for employment discrimination in federal district court, invoking Title VII — perhaps like the *Stalnaker* case in Chapter VII, supra page 508. You think the plaintiffs case is weak, but your client understands that litigating it will require hours of lost time consumed in depositions and may undermine the morale of other employees. She asks you to see if you can settle the case, inquiring what you think it will cost her.

a. How do you answer her question about cost? A good deal of it will depend on the merits of the case: How "good" or "bad" are the facts? How sympathetic and credible will the plaintiff and her supervisor be as witnesses? But some part of the response will depend on other factors. With all but the most sophisticated clients, one will need to persuade the plaintiff's lawyer as well as the plaintiff that the offer is good, if for no other reason than that the client is likely to ask the lawyer whether to accept the offer. The lawyer in turn may be influenced by such factors as how much effort he has already expended on the case. All other things being equal, the same settlement offer coming before any discovery or pretrial motions will look more attractive than it does on the eve of trial. For the same reason most defendants will offer somewhat less at the very early stages of the case.

b. After discussion, your client gives you a dollar figure she is willing to offer the plaintiff to settle. You contact the plaintiff's lawyer (ethical rules prohibit a lawyer's directly contacting a represented client), discuss a series of depositions you want to take, and, at the end of the conversation, ask whether there's any point in discussing settlement. (Some negotiation literature, and much lawyer's lore, says that one should never be the first to utter the dreaded "s" word, but you are unpersuaded by this.) The plaintiff says it might be possible, and after some haggling you reach a figure that the plaintiff's counsel is willing to recommend to his client. Assuming the plaintiff accepts, how will you actually effect the settlement?

c. The simplest way would be an oral agreement that plaintiff will drop the suit when he receives your client's check. This route is also an excellent way to assure that your former client sues you for malpractice. Why?

3. Assume now that you think you should draft a written settlement agreement. What should it say?

a. That the plaintiff should agree not to file a threatened lawsuit?

b. That, having filed suit, the plaintiff should seek a voluntary dismissal and agree not to refile the suit?

c. That, having filed suit, the plaintiff should consent to a dismissal with prejudice and, as insurance, also agree not to refile the suit?

d. That, having filed suit, the plaintiff should stipulate to a judgment against him and, as insurance, agree not to refile the suit?

4. All of these techniques are used to create settlements. Consider some of their advantages and disadvantages and the problems entailed by each.

a. Take first the prefiling agreement not to sue. In some respects this is the simplest and best form of settlement: By definition it eliminates all litigation costs. But this form of agreement also requires the lawyer carefully to define the scope of the threatened lawsuit. One common form calls for the plaintiff to relinquish any and all claims he might have against defendant as of the date of the agreement. That will work if the parties have no other plausible claims against each other. But there may be unrelated claims: Suppose that the dismissed employee had claims to a pension and that neither side wants now to calculate the value of that entitlement, which may involve complex contingencies. In such a situation, the lawyers will have to carve those other claims out of the agreement unless they can reach a global settlement.

b. Once suit has been filed, a settlement will call for an end to the lawsuit. A settlement achieved at this point saves less in the way of litigation costs, but it also has some advantages: It may save the defendant the cost and publicity of filing an answer — only the plaintiff's complaint will be on file with the court. Voluntary dismissal will end the lawsuit.

But recall that Rule 41(a) permits a plaintiff taking a voluntary dismissal to refile the suit — just the result that a settlement seeks to avoid. To avoid this result, a settlement agreement at this stage will require the plaintiff to refrain from refiling this or any related lawsuit.

What if the plaintiff nevertheless does refile? How does the defendant, having paid to settle the suit, enforce the agreement? Rule 8(c) provides that "accord and satisfaction" (an old-fashioned term for settlement) is an affirmative defense that the defendant must plead (and prove). This will require the defendant in the second suit to show that the second claim was the same as the one covered by the settlement agreement.

c. Suppose the defendant wants the lawsuit not only to go away but for the court to enter a judgment on the merits. A voluntary dismissal does not achieve that; involuntary dismissal, with prejudice, under Rule 41(b) does. An involuntary dismissal solves another problem as well: It acts as a judgment on the merits and allows the scope of the claim to be defined by the doctrines of former adjudication rather than by the contract of settlement. As you will see in Chapter XII, under modern doctrines of former adjudication, a claim adjudicated on the merits bars all related claims, whether or not they were stated in the complaint. Such a mode of dismissal also means that if the plaintiff files a second lawsuit, the defendant can invoke not just the contract of settlement but the doctrines of former adjudication to have the suit dismissed. Courts are often quite protective of suits that seem to be flouting their former judgments — an advantage to the defendant.

d. Consider one possible disadvantage of the simple dismissal with prejudice: Imagine that the settlement agreement calls for the parties to take some future action, perhaps to assist the employee to gain other employment, or perhaps to continue medical benefits for some period of time. The employer breaches that duty and the former employee wants to enforce it. Can he do so by going back to federal court?

e. Contrast two approaches to the last question. In Langley v. Jackson State University, 14 F. 3d 1070 (5th Cir. 1994), plaintiff sued her university employer alleging racial discrimination. The parties settled. A couple of years later plaintiff sued again, invoking the same federal civil rights statutes, alleging both new acts of discrimination and failure to abide by the terms of the settlement agreement. The Fifth Circuit ruled that the district court had no jurisdiction over the breach of settlement allegations. The court reasoned that the claim for breach of settlement was a contract claim that did not arise under federal law. Contrast Board of Trustees v. Madison Hotel, Inc. 97 F. 3d 1479 (D.C. Cir. 1996). Plaintiff trustees of a union pension fund sued an employer over alleged failures to comply with federal pension laws. The parties settled, with the agreement calling for an audit and payments of any sums found owing. The plaintiffs sued again, alleging that the defendant had failed to pay the funds required by the audit. The district court dismissed on the grounds that the suit was for simple breach of contract, with no basis for diversity jurisdiction. The D.C. Circuit reversed, holding that determination of the breach-of-settlement allegations would require the court to interpret federal pension law and that the case therefore fell within federal question jurisdiction. The court evinced a certain nervousness about its holding. The opinion scolded the plaintiff for failing to embody the settlement in a consent decree and for failing to provide that the district court would maintain continuing jurisdiction over the agreement.

f. If one anticipates such a problem, there is a solution, although it too has some disadvantages. One can embody the terms of the settlement in the judgment of dismissal itself, so that the judgment entered by the court sets forth the obligations of the parties — that is, in a stipulated or consent decree:

> The situation would be quite different if the parties' obligation to comply with the terms of the settlement agreement had been made part of the order of dismissal — either by separate provision (such as a provision "retaining jurisdiction" over the settlement agreement) or by incorporating the terms of the settlement agreement in the order. In that event a breach of the agreement would be a violation of the order, and ancillary jurisdiction to enforce the agreement would therefore exist.

Kokkonen v. Guardian Life Insurance Co., 511 U.S. 375 (1994).

5. Return to the facts of the hypothetical employment discrimination suit. The employer wants the terms of the settlement — and even the fact of the suit — to remain confidential if possible. The employee wants compensation and continuing health coverage until he finds new employment, and for the employer not to give him a bad reference with other prospective employers.

a. Which form of settlement would best suit the employer's interests?

b. Which form would best suit the employee's interests?

6. Suppose the parties have a commercial dispute involving breach of contract. Suit is filed in state court. As the case develops, it emerges that in the background of the dispute is disagreement about the scope of a patent. Federal courts have exclusive jurisdiction over patent litigation. One of the parties files a federal patent action. Meanwhile, the state action develops and the parties make a final effort to settle it; defendant, however, objects to any settlement that does not include the patent claim. Can they enter into such a settlement? Can they incorporate it into a consent decree in the state court action? How does the next case answer that question?

Matsushita Elec. Industrial Co. v. Epstein
516 U.S. 367 (1996)

Justice THOMAS delivered the opinion of the Court.

This case presents the question whether a federal court may withhold full faith and credit from a state-court judgment approving a class-action settlement simply because the settlement releases claims within the exclusive jurisdiction of the federal courts. The answer is no. Absent a partial repeal of the Full Faith and Credit Act, 28 U.S.C. §1738, by another federal statute, a federal court must give the judgment the same effect that it would have in the courts of the State in which it was rendered.

[The dispute arose from Matsushita's acquisition of MCA, an entertainment company. Two primary sets of lawsuits were filed on behalf of MCA shareholders — both consisting primarily of class actions. One such group of federal actions alleged breach of federal securities laws. A second group of class actions, filed in Delaware state court, alleged breaches of various state-law fiduciary responsibilities of directors. The claims in the federal actions all fell within the federal courts' exclusive jurisdiction. After the federal district court granted summary judgment to the defendants in the federal cases, but while those cases were on appeal to the Ninth Circuit, the parties to the Delaware action negotiated "a global release of all claims arising out of the Matsushita-MCA acquisition." After notifying the class members of the pending settlement, and holding the required fairness hearing, the Delaware court approved the settlement as fair. In reaching the conclusion of fairness, the Delaware chancellor engaged in a process required by state law in which he assessed the fair value of the claims — including the federal claims — that were being settled.]

The order and final judgment of the Chancery Court incorporated the terms of the settlement agreement, providing:

> All claims, rights and causes of action (state or federal, including but not limited to claims arising under the federal securities law, any rules or regulations promulgated thereunder, or otherwise), whether known or unknown that are, could have been or might in the future be asserted by any of the plaintiffs or any member of the Settlement Class . . . in connection with or that arise now or hereafter out of the Merger Agreement, the Tender Offer, the Distribution Agreement, the Capital Contribution Agreement, the employee compensation arrangements, the Tender Agreements, the Initial Proposed Settlement, this Settlement . . . including without limitation the claims asserted in the California Federal Actions . . . are hereby compromised, settled, released and discharged with preju-

dice by virtue of the proceedings herein and this Order and Final Judgment.

[Citing 28 U.S.C. §1738, Matsushita asserted the Delaware judgment embodying this settlement as a bar to the federal action.] The Ninth Circuit [before which the federal securities claims were pending, ruled that] the preclusive force of a state-court settlement judgment is limited to those claims that "could . . . have been extinguished by the issue preclusive effect of an adjudication of the state claims." [Determining that the issues in the state and federal cases were distinct, the Ninth Circuit held that adjudication of the state claims could have had no preclusive effect on issues in the federal case. Nor, because of exclusive federal jurisdiction, could Delaware courts have adjudicated the federal securities claims. Accordingly, reasoned the Ninth Circuit, Delaware's approval of the settlement could not bar litigation of the federal claims in federal court. After granting certiorari on the Ninth Circuit opinion, the Supreme Court reversed.]

II

The Full Faith and Credit Act mandates that the "judicial proceedings" of any State "shall have the same full faith and credit in every court within the United States . . . as they have by law or usage in the courts of such State . . . from which they are taken." 28 U.S.C. §1738. The Act thus directs all [federal] courts to treat a state-court judgment with the same respect that it would receive in the courts of the rendering state. Federal courts may not "employ their own rules . . . in determining the effect of state judgments," but must "accept the rules chosen by the State from which the judgment is taken." Kremer v. Chemical Constr. Corp., 456 U.S. 461(1982). Because the Court of Appeals failed to follow the dictates of the Act, we reverse. . . .

[The opinion first examined Delaware precedents and concluded that Delaware would bar the federal claims.][5] [The Court then looked to the text and statutory history of the federal securities law to determine whether, in providing for exclusive federal jurisdiction over such claims, Congress impliedly repealed 28 U.S.C. §1738 insofar as it would defeat the statutory scheme of exclusive federal jurisdiction. The Court concluded there was

5. Apart from any discussion of Delaware law, respondents contend that the settlement proceedings did not satisfy due process because the class was inadequately represented. Respondents make this claim in spite of the Chancery Court's express ruling, following argument on the issue, that the class representatives fairly and adequately protected the interests of the class. We need not address the due process claim, however, because it is outside the scope of the question presented in this Court. . . .

no such implied repeal. In reaching this conclusion the opinion noted that] state-court proceedings may, in various ways, subsequently affect the litigation of exclusively federal claims, [citing both patent and civil rights cases.]

The judgment of the Court of Appeals is reversed, and the case is remanded for proceedings consistent with this opinion.

It is so ordered.

Justice GINSBURG, [joined by Justice STEVENS] concurring and dissenting. . . .

I write separately to emphasize a point key to the application of §1738: A state-court judgment generally is not entitled to full faith and credit unless it satisfies the requirements of the Fourteenth Amendment's Due Process Clause. In the class-action setting, adequate representation is among the due process ingredients that must be supplied if the judgment is to bind absent class members. [Because the Ninth Circuit decided the case on other grounds,] that inquiry remains open for consideration on remand.

NOTES AND PROBLEMS

1. What does *Matsushita* hold?

2. Notice several points of apparent agreement:

a. The opinion did not question the parties' ability to settle any pending litigation of any sort by contract. Ordinary settlement agreements every day end cases of all sorts.

b. The opinion did not question the exclusivity of federal jurisdiction for the adjudication of the federal securities claims at issue. No one said that Delaware could *adjudicate* these claims.

c. The opinion did not question that Congress could, by appropriate legislation, have prevented state court decrees from settling federal securities claims.

3. Does the majority agree with Justice Ginsburg that the federal plaintiffs are entitled to a hearing on whether, in the state court action, they were adequately represented? Footnote 5 is the crucial text. Its second sentence suggests that the question has already been decided; its third sentence suggests that the Supreme Court isn't deciding the question.

a. In class action litigation only adequately represented class members can be bound; whether the representation was adequate is a matter of due process. See Hansberry v. Lee, Chapter XIII, page 982.

b. Footnote 5 of the majority opinion notes that the Delaware court made a finding of adequate representation. Such findings are required by Rule 23 and similar state law class action rules. But could such a finding bind an absentee class member who did not appear in the state court action? Hansberry v. Lee, supra, and Justice Ginsburg think not; the majority, though hinting otherwise, did not decide the question. How would you like to be on the panel of the Ninth Circuit to which the case was remanded?

4. That left two areas of disagreement:

a. Could a state court *judgment* (embodying a settlement agreement) settle claims that the state court had no jurisdiction to adjudicate? As to that question, there was a further area of agreement: that §1738 mandates that the effect of such a settlement depends on the respect it would be given by Delaware law. The Delaware judgment would not have settled the federal claims unless Delaware preclusion principles, as read by the U.S. Supreme Court, had purported to do so. The majority thought they did, and the concurring and dissenting justices argued only that the question ought to have been remanded to the Ninth Circuit for it to decide initially.

b. Had the members of the Delaware class in fact received adequate representation? On remand, the Ninth Circuit, in a split decision, first said no, then withdrew its opinion and said that the Supreme Court had decided that the Delaware court had decided that there was adequate representation — and that the matter was therefore closed. Epstein v. MCA, Inc., 1999 U.S. App. LEXIS 11723 (9th Cir. 1999).

5. So what was all the fuss about in *Matsushita*?

a. Didn't the settlement clause quoted in the opinion clearly state it was settling the federal claims?

b. Was the Delaware court doing something that looked very much as though it was trying the federal claims? Delaware law requires a court considering a class action settlement in this context to decide the fair value of the claims being settled. Those claims included the federal securities claims. The state judge explicitly stated that in "determining whether a settlement should be approved, a court should not try the merits of the underlying claims" and that "it is sufficient that the determination of the federal district court that the claims lack merit . . . be accorded substantial weight in determining the settlement value of those claims." Nonetheless, to decide their fair value, as Delaware law requires, the Delaware court had to engage in a process like an adjudication of those claims, deciding whether they were based on a viable interpretation of law and whether the facts available suggested defendant's liability. Is that getting too close for comfort to trespassing on exclusive federal jurisdiction over securities claims?

b. Contracting for Confidentiality

One settlement goal shared by many defendants, and some plaintiffs, is that the settlement be confidential. What they mean by confidentiality differs from case to case. At its maximum, such a desire means that the parties want not even the fact of a dispute to become public, much less the terms of its compromise. How might a settlement agreement be drafted to assure that the plaintiff keeps the details confidential? Consider one effort:

> 7. *Return of Documents.* The Plaintiffs agree to return to [Defendant] all originals and copies of all documents and data, obtained from [Defendant], directly or indirectly, at any time, by either Plaintiff, or any agent, attorney, representative, or anyone else acting or purporting to act on his or her behalf. The obligations of this Paragraph 7 are cumulative to other existing obligations that Plaintiffs have as a result of their employment with [Defendant].
>
> 8. *Confidentiality.*
>
> 8.1 Plaintiffs and their attorneys, and each of them, expressly agree that this Agreement and the terms and conditions of this Settlement are confidential, and agree not to disclose, publicize, or cause to be disclosed or publicized the fact of settlement or any of the terms or conditions of this Agreement, including but not limited to the amounts received pursuant to Paragraph 1 of this Agreement or the amounts paid in connection with the Workers' Compensation Claims, except as required by judicial process, or as otherwise required by law. Notwithstanding the foregoing, it is hereby expressly understood and agreed that the Plaintiffs and their attorneys may need to disseminate certain information concerning the settlement to their accountants, auditors, attorneys, and/or other entities as necessary in the regular course of business. While such disclosures are expressly permitted under the terms of this Agreement, Plaintiffs and their attorneys shall insure that information deemed confidential under this Agreement is treated as confidential by the recipients thereof. Except as required by judicial process, or as otherwise required by law, if any of the Plaintiffs or their attorneys or any recipient of information from Plaintiffs or their attorneys concerning the Settlement is asked about the disposition of the action, such Plaintiff, attorney, or recipient shall state the following in substance: "I am not at liberty to discuss it."
>
> 8.2 Each disclosure by Plaintiffs or their attorneys or by any recipient of information from Plaintiffs or their attorneys concerning this Settlement

other than a disclosure expressly permitted by subparagraph 8.1 shall be considered a material breach of this Agreement. For each such breach of the confidentiality provision set forth in subparagraph 8.1, the Plaintiff who breaches such confidentiality provision shall be solely liable to [Defendant] for Twenty-Five Thousand Dollars ($25,000.00) in liquidated damages. Plaintiffs, and each of them, agree that said sum represents a reasonable estimate of the actual damages which would be suffered by [Defendant] as a result of a violation of subparagraph 8.1 and that this sum is not punitive in any way. In the event [Defendant] is required to file suit or otherwise seek judicial enforcement of its rights under this paragraph 8, the Plaintiff who breaches such confidentiality provision shall be solely liable for attorneys' fees and costs incurred as a result thereof.

NOTES AND PROBLEMS

1. Consider several features of this agreement:

a. Why did the defendant's lawyer, who probably drafted this agreement, create an exception for disclosures "as required by judicial process, or as otherwise required by law"? What do you suppose the lawyer thought the courts might do with such an agreement if it did not contain such a provision?

b. Why did the defendant's lawyer insert the liquidated damages provision? How would one enforce such an agreement were there not a liquidated damages clause?

c. Why did the agreement call for the return of documents? What was the defendant worried about?

2. Should such agreements be enforceable? That question has raised a fierce academic and professional debate. This presentation cannot do justice to the nuances, but the positions can be roughly characterized:

a. Proponents: Disputes are fundamentally private matters, which courts exist to decide if the parties cannot do so themselves. We ought therefore honor any lawful agreement by the parties that ends the dispute. Confidentiality agreements have two advantages. First, they encourage settlements. Many defendants consider the confidentiality of the settlement to be even more important than the amount of the settlement; without it, they will not settle. Second, it benefits plaintiffs. Defendants wanting confidentiality will pay a premium to defendants to achieve this goal.

b. Opponents: Disputes aren't solely private matters; in many disputes the public has an interest that is defeated by confidentiality agreements. The danger of a particular product, the illegality of defendant's course of action, the efficacy of regulatory regimes — all these and more can only be judged if the contents of settlements and the underlying information (including the products of discovery) are publicly known. The public has a right to know, and the parties can't agree to waive that right, even if it is to their mutual advantage to do so.

c. Who's right?

3. As matters now stand, such confidentiality agreements are generally enforceable, but what exactly do they protect against? At a minimum, they would prohibit the plaintiff from holding a news conference to announce the terms of the settlement. What could defendant do if, after entering into such a settlement, plaintiff took such an action?

4. Do they prevent the plaintiff from disclosing information about the underlying merits of the case — even under legal compulsion? The next case considers the issue.

Kalinauskas v. Wong

151 F.R.D. 363 (D. Nev. 1993)

JOHNSTON, Magistrate Judge.

This matter was submitted to the undersigned Magistrate Judge on a Motion for a Protective Order filed by defendant Desert Palace, Inc., doing business as Caesars Palace Hotel & Casino (Caesars). . . .

The plaintiff, Ms. Lin T. Kalinauskas (Kalinauskas), a former employee of Caesars, has sued Caesars for sexual discrimination in the instant case. As part of discovery Kalinauskas seeks to depose Donna R. Thomas, a former Caesars employee who filed a sexual harassment suit against Caesars last year. Ms. Thomas's suit settled without trial pursuant to a confidential settlement agreement[,] which the court sealed upon the stipulated agreement of the parties.

This court has examined, in camera, sealed materials relating to Ms. Thomas's case and settlement. [One such sealed document provided] that the plaintiff "shall not discuss any aspect of plaintiff's employment at Caesars other than to state the dates of her employment and her job title." Identical language appears in the Protective Order and Confidentiality Order. . . .

Discussion

In general, the scope of discovery is very broad. "Parties may obtain discovery regarding *any matter, not privileged, which is relevant to the subject matter involved in the pending action.* . . . It is not ground for objection that the information sought will be inadmissible at the trial if the information sought appears *reasonably calculated to lead to the discovery of admissible evidence.*" Fed. R. Civ. P. 26(b)(1) (emphasis added). The primary goal of the court and discovery is "to secure the just, speedy, and inexpensive determination of every action." Fed. R. Civ. P.1.

The public interest favors judicial policies which promote the completion of litigation. Public interest also seeks to protect the finality of prior suits and the secrecy of settlements when desired by the settling parties. However, the courts also serve society by providing a public forum for issues of general concern. The case at bar presents a direct conflict between these crucial public and private interests.

To allow full discovery into all aspects of Ms. Thomas's case could discourage similar settlements. Confidential settlements benefit society and the parties involved by resolving disputes relatively quickly, with slight judicial intervention, and presumably result in greater satisfaction to the parties. Sound judicial policy fosters and protects this form of alternative dispute resolution. See, e.g., Fed. R. Evid. 408 which protects compromises and offers to compromise by rendering them inadmissible to prove liability. The secrecy of a settlement agreement and the contractual rights of the parties thereunder deserve court protection.

On the other hand, to prevent any discovery into Ms. Thomas's case based upon the settlement agreement results in disturbing consequences. First, as pointed out by Kalinauskas, preventing the deposition of Ms. Thomas would condone the practice of "buy[ing] the silence of a witness with a settlement agreement." This court harbors little doubt that preventing the dissemination of the underlying facts which prompted Ms. Thomas to file suit is in Caesars's interest, and formed an important part of the agreement to Caesars. Caesars avers that without the confidentiality order the Thomas case would not have settled. Yet despite this freedom to contract, the courts must carefully police the circumstances under which litigants seek to protect their interests while concealing legitimate areas of public concern. This concern grows more pressing as additional individuals are harmed by identical or similar action.

Second, the deposition of Ms. Thomas is likely to lead to relevant evidence. Preventing the deposition of Ms. Thomas or the discovery of documents created in her case, could lead to wasteful efforts to generate discovery already in existence. . . .

As in *Wilk* [v. American Medical Assoc., 635 F.2d 1295 (7th Cir. 1980)], this court faces two very similar lawsuits. Factually, and legally, Kalinauskas's case nearly duplicates Ms. Thomas's. Also, Kalinauskas is a bona fide litigant seeking access for legitimate litigation purposes. While *Wilk* examined the issue on a much larger scale because it involved prior massive discovery of an alleged nationwide conspiracy, the underlying concern about the wastefulness of repetitive discovery applies equally to Kalinauskas. Thus this court adopts the holding in *Wilk* that "where an appropriate modification of a protective order [or confidentiality agreement] can place private litigants in a position they would otherwise reach only after repetition of another's discovery, such modification can be denied only where it would tangibly prejudice substantial rights of the party opposing modification." Moreover, even after a demonstration of prejudice the court "has broad discretion in judging whether that injury outweighs the benefits of any possible modification."

Caesars's motion for a protective order preventing the deposition of Ms. Thomas rests entirely upon the confidential settlement agreement. Caesars has neither asserted an applicable privilege nor demonstrated any potential injury or prejudice which could arise from allowing the deposition.

Caesars argues that Kalinauskas must intervene in the Thomas case and seek a modification of the confidentiality order to depose Thomas. Caesars also maintains that it should be able to rely upon the confidentiality order to protect against third parties, unless extraordinary circumstances or compelling need justifies some breach of secrecy.

This court rejects Caesars's first argument regarding intervention. Intervention was appropriate in *Wilk* because that case was ongoing at the time the New York plaintiffs sought discovery. Contrastingly, in this situation the Thomas action had concluded before Kalinauskas filed her discovery motion. Hence, requiring intervention under these circumstances would be wasteful and cause needless delay, especially in light of the fact that no live controversy exists in which Kalinauskas can properly intervene.

Furthermore, intervention to seek modification is not necessary because the confidentiality agreement itself provides that a court or government agency may order either party to the confidential settlement agreement to disclose information. ¶7 on page 3 of Thomas Settlement agreement. The wording of the settlement agreement clearly indicates that the court in *Thomas* did not reserve supervisory control over the agreement and that any court has the authority to order disclosure. Consequently, this court, having inherent authority to order disclosure, will not require Kalinauskas to formally intervene in the closed *Thomas* case.

Next, the argument that Kalinauskas must show a compelling need to obtain discovery applies to discovery of the specific terms of the settlement agreement (i.e., the amount and conditions of the agreement), not [to] factual information surrounding Thomas's case. Caesars should not be able to conceal basic facts of concern to Kalinauskas in her case, and of legitimate public concern, regarding employment at its place of business.

Accordingly, keeping in mind the liberal nature of discovery, this court will allow the deposition of Ms. Thomas. Kalinauskas has already acquired information about Ms. Thomas's case gleaned through publicly available documents, including Ms. Thomas's original complaint filed in state court. Moreover, Kalinauskas' case even involves at least one Caesars supervisory employee in common with Ms. Thomas's.

The deposition of Ms. Thomas and any further discovery into the Thomas case must not, however, disclose any substantive terms of the Caesars-Thomas settlement agreement. Naturally, Ms. Thomas may answer questions regarding her employment at Caesars and any knowledge of sexual harassment.

Although the terms of the confidential settlement agreement impose penalties upon Ms. Thomas for discussing her past employment at Caesars, those penalties shall not apply to the disclosure of information for discovery purposes in furtherance of Kalinauskas's case. Indeed, the settlement agreement itself makes exception for court ordered release of information.

While settlement is an important objective, an overzealous quest for alternative dispute resolution can distort the proper role of the court. Furthermore, settlement agreements which suppress evidence violate the greater public policy.

With respect to contracts containing explicit guarantees of confidentiality, "such contracts, of course, cannot bind parties who do not sign them and may have little effect on the capacities of a non-party to discover or introduce at trial the settlement communications covered by the contract." The Hon. Wayne D. Brazil, Protecting the Confidentiality of Settlement Negotiations, 39 Hastings L. Rev. 955, 1026 (July 1988).

Order

Based on the foregoing, and good cause appearing therefore, IT IS HEREBY ORDERED that the Defendant's Motion for Protective Order (#39) is granted in part and denied in part.

IT IS FURTHER ORDERED that the Defendant's Motion for Protective Order is granted to the extent that during the deposition of Ms. Donna R. Thomas, no information regarding the settlement agreement itself shall come forth.

IT IS FURTHER ORDERED that the Defendant's Motion for Protective Order (#39) is denied as to all other requests. . . .

NOTES AND PROBLEMS

1. Caesars, the defendant in both cases, obviously did not get all of the benefit it wanted out of the confidentiality agreement.

a. Is there anything it could have done to avoid the deposition of Ms. Thomas?

b. *Should* there be anything that Caesars (or other defendants) can do in such circumstances?

c. Consider an analogue to the ruling in *Kalinauskas:* the work product doctrine. Under that doctrine, announced in Hickman v. Taylor (supra page 525) and codified in Rule 26(b)(3), a lawyer is protected against disclosure in discovery of information generated by the litigation process itself but not against disclosure of underlying historical facts. Doesn't the ruling in *Kalinauskas* achieve the same result — permitting Ms. Thomas to testify to the historical conditions of employment at Caesars but not to the terms on which the case was settled?

d. Do you suppose that Caesars would have taken the Thomas case to trial rather than settling if it had known that other plaintiffs might depose Ms. Thompson?

2. With *Kalinauskas* compare the approach taken to protective orders in two other federal cases, each of which involved state as well as federal law:

a. A police chief, disciplined for mishandling parking meter receipts, sued the city alleging violation of his civil rights. After the parties settled, their settlement agreement was reviewed by the district court, which entered an order requiring confidentiality of the settlement as part of the judgment. A newspaper sought to uncover the terms of the settlement, citing a Pennsylvania "right to know" statute. The Third Circuit held that "whether an order of confidentiality is granted at the discovery stage or any other stage of litigation, including settlement, good cause must be demonstrated to justify such orders. . . . [G]iven these facts it would be unusual if on remand the district court were to find that circumstances exist that justify the order of confidentiality being maintained over the settlement agreement." The court suggested that if the parties wanted to avoid such judicial scrutiny of confidentiality agreements, they could simply embody them in contracts rather than seeking to have them entered as judgments. It conceded, however, that a contractual term calling for confidentiality would probably yield to the state right-to-know statute. Pansy v. Borough of Stroudsburg, 23 F.3d 772 (3d Cir. 1994).

b. General Motors and Elwell, one of its engineers, had a falling out. Elwell sued GM in a Michigan court. The parties settled that case and as part of the settlement the company asked the court to enter an injunction prohibiting Elwell from "testifying, without the prior written consent of [GM], . . . as . . . a witness of any kind . . . in any litigation . . . involving [GM] as an owner, seller, manufacturer, and/or designer. . . ." As in *Kalinauskas*, a second suit occurred. In Baker v. General Motors, 118 S. Ct. 657 (1998), the Bakers brought a diversity action in federal court alleging deaths from a defectively designed GM vehicle. They sought to depose Elwell as a witness concerning the design of the vehicle. GM contended that his testimony would violate not just a settlement agreement but the Michigan injunction — and that the federal court was bound by the Full Faith and Credit Clause and 28 U.S.C. §1738 to enforce the ban on Elwell's testimony. No, said the U.S. Supreme Court, in a somewhat opaque opinion: Although there is no "public policy exception" to the Full Faith and Credit clause (as the plaintiffs had argued), "Michigan's judgment cannot reach beyond [that] controversy to control proceedings against GM brought in other states. . . ." Explain how the doctrinal question facing the court in *Baker* differed from the doctrinal question facing the *Kalinauskas* court. Did they both come to the right result?

3. As suggested by the preceding notes, states differ substantially in the stance toward confidentiality agreements. At the no-confidentiality end of the spectrum lies Texas Rule of Civil Procedure R. 76(a)(1)-(1) (1994). That rule (1) creates a presumption that court records will be open to the public, (2) classifies as court records settlement agreements that have not been filed with the court as well as unfiled discovery materials if either concerns "matters that have a probable adverse effect upon the general public health or safety, or the administration of public office, or the operation of government. . . ." Are such rules a good idea? As a practical matter, how would one go about finding out whether there were such "court records" residing in lawyers' files?

c.   Contracting for a Judgment

In *Kalinauskas*, *Pansy*, and *Baker*, the parties' efforts to have the court order confidentiality as part of the judgment raises a third possibility: to what extent are judicial pronouncements themselves malleable by agreement among the parties? Parties can always stop the court from issuing a judgment by settling. What if the court has already done so? Should the parties, by agreement, be able to bring about a retraction of the judgment? The next two cases reveal two courts, one state and one federal, reaching different answers to that question.

Neary v. University of California

3 Cal. 4th 273, 834 P.2d 119, 10 Cal. Rptr. 2d 859 (1992)

BAXTER, J. . . .

Plaintiff George Neary, a cattle rancher, obtained a jury verdict of $7 million in a libel action against the Regents of the University of California and three veterinarians employed by the University of California at Davis in its School of Veterinary Medicine (hereafter the University). The action arose from the University's publication of a report asserting that Neary had engaged in deficient ranch management practices that caused illness and death of many of Neary's cattle. Neary contended the cattle had been poisoned by a pesticide sprayed by governmental agencies to control an infestation of scabies mites. Defendants appealed, and Neary cross-appealed. While the appeals were pending, the parties agreed to settle.

Defendants would pay Neary $3 million, and in return, he joined with all defendants in a stipulation providing that: the appeals would be dismissed with prejudice, the Court of Appeal would vacate the trial court's judgment, and the action in the trial court would then be dismissed. Pursuant to this stipulation, the parties filed a joint application in the Court of Appeal asking it to reverse the trial court's judgment and remand the case to the trial court for dismissal with prejudice. The Court of Appeal rejected the request.

We . . . conclude that, as a general rule, the parties should be entitled to a stipulated reversal to effectuate settlement absent a showing of extraordinary circumstances that warrant an exception to this general rule. This presumption in favor of a stipulated reversal is sound and salutary for several reasons. The facts of this case in particular demonstrate why the settlement should be effectuated pursuant to the parties' terms, including their request for a stipulated reversal.

A.   The Efficiency of Postjudgment Settlements

This court recognized a century ago that settlement agreements " 'are highly favored as productive of peace and good will in the community,' " as well as " 'reducing the expense and persistency of litigation.' " (McClure v. McClure (1893) 100 Cal. 339, 343.) The need for settlements is greater than ever before. "Without them our system of civil adjudication would quickly break down." (Lynch, California Negotiation and Settlement Handbook (1991), p. vii [foreword by California Supreme Court Chief Justice Malcolm M. Lucas].) Settlement is perhaps most efficient the earlier the settlement comes in the litigation continuum. The benefits of settlement, however, do not evaporate when judgment is entered. . . .

The policy in favor of settlement, even when it requires a stipulated reversal, is rooted in practicality. If settlement on appeal is prohibited, the appeal must be heard and decided. If the judgment is reversed and retrial is allowed (not an unusual result), considerable future expense and trial court resources will be consumed. The present case is an excellent example of the merit of postjudgment settlements. . . .

We reject the notion, advanced by some of the amici curiae in this case, that the possibility of postjudgment settlements incorporating a stipulated reversal will reduce the frequency of pretrial settlements. This view misses the mark in several respects. First, the law review article on which the amici curiae rely claims that "the availability of vacatur [i.e., reversal] makes going to trial cost-free, apart from litigation costs." (Fisch, Rewriting History: The Propriety of Eradicating Prior Decisional Law Through Settlement and Vacatur (1991) 76 Cornell L. Rev. 589, 596.) This is rather like saying that death is only temporary, apart from its permanency. . . .

B.   Fairness to the Parties

Simple fairness requires that the first and most weighty consideration be given to the parties' interests and that they be accommodated except in the extraordinary case. The parties are the persons (or entities) most affected by a judgment, which is the ultimate product of their sustained effort and expense. Homilies about "judicial integrity" and "legal truth" will ring hollow in the ears of the parties. The courts exist for litigants. Litigants do not exist for courts. . . .

The present case is again a prime example of why the parties should be accommodated. As reflected by the complexity of the underlying defamation action, the parties will incur substantial costs on appeal and, if necessary, on retrial. Aside from continued legal costs, the parties will suffer continuing psychological burdens. . . . The defendant veterinarians in this case plausibly assert a desire for nothing more than to put this case behind them. Plaintiff Neary, now in his advanced years, also makes clear that he wants his recovery. His plea is sympathetic: "Neary has spent more than twelve years in an expensive, time-consuming, emotionally wrenching, and destructively distracting struggle which has included enough twists, turns, setbacks and victories for a novel. He has finally resolved that struggle through negotiation and voluntary agreement." Thwarting the settlement would frustrate the parties' mutual desire for an immediate end to their now 13-year-old dispute. The parties have pummeled each other long enough and have staggered to their respective corners. We choose to give them help, not the prospect of further battering. . . .

D. Integrity of the Judicial Process

The Court of Appeal opined that stipulated reversal "would trivialize the work of the trial courts and undermine the integrity of the entire judicial process." This conclusion is based on the Court of Appeal's faulty premise that litigation is a search for "legal truth," not "simply a dispositional act." This puts the abstract cart before the practical horse. The primary purpose of the public judiciary is "to afford a forum for the settlement of litigable matters between disputing parties." (Vecki v. Sorensen (1959) 171 Cal. App. 2d 390, 393.) We do not resolve abstract legal issues, even when requested to do so. We resolve real disputes between real people. This function does not undermine our integrity or demean our function. By providing a forum for the peaceful resolution of citizens' disputes, we provide a cornerstone for ordered liberty in a democratic society. . . .

Some of the amici curiae in this case contend a stipulated reversal should be denied when it would adversely affect the public interest. As an abstract matter, this conclusion cannot be rejected out of hand. There might be unusual circumstances in which the public interest would weigh dispositively against a stipulated reversal. We caution, however, that the strong presumption in favor of allowing stipulated reversals is not rebutted by some amorphous and speculative public interest. . . . To be sufficient to overcome the strong presumption in favor of allowing stipulated reversals, an asserted public interest must be specific, demonstrable, well established, and compelling. No such public interest is present in this case.

F. Potential Collateral Estoppel

Amici curiae in this case also contend a stipulated reversal should be denied whenever a judgment might give rise to collateral estoppel in a future action. Even the Court of Appeal, although it rejected the stipulation, did not rely on this factor. The reason is apparent. The parties in this case agree that no nonparty is or will be affected by the trial court judgment, and nothing in the record suggests otherwise. Collateral estoppel is not an issue in this case. We therefore need not decide, and do not decide, whether potential collateral estoppel should be a factor in deciding whether to depart from the strong presumption in favor of allowing the parties to settle their dispute by seeking a stipulated reversal. . . .

[Justice MOSK's concurrence is omitted.]

KENNARD, J. [dissenting:]

More than just a dispute resolution service, the judiciary is an integral part of our government. Working in the context of actual disputes, courts interpret and enforce the policies adopted by the legislative process, striving always to give those policies coherence and vitality. Thus, when a trial court renders judgment in a particular case, it is not just deciding who wins and who loses, who pays and who recovers. Rather, the ultimate purpose of a judgment is to administer the laws of this state, and thereby to do substantial justice.

Because a judgment embodies an act of government, its annulment must be reconciled with public as well as private interests. And because stipulated reversals tend to diminish public respect for the judiciary and to discourage prejudgment settlement, appellate courts should carefully examine the parties' reasons for seeking stipulated reversal and should attempt to determine whether the judgment sought to be annulled has value for third parties or for the public at large. . . .

[The majority's] reasoning, which allows parties to dictate an appellate court's actions, could lead to absurd results. Suppose, for example, that the parties conditioned settlement on the appellate justices wearing green robes on Saint Patrick's Day, or singing "California Here I Come" before court proceedings. Would the majority weigh the benefits of settlement against the slight inconvenience of performing the requested act, or would it instead ask whether the act itself was proper, whether it would be demeaning for courts to humor the parties' whimsical demands in this fashion?

U.S. Bancorp Mortgage Co. v. Bonner Mall
513 U.S. 18 (1994)

Justice SCALIA delivered the opinion of the Court.

The question in this case is whether appellate courts in the federal system should vacate civil judgments of subordinate courts in cases that are settled after appeal is filed or certiorari sought.

I . . .

[Bonner owned a shopping mall; Bancorp held a mortgage on the mall. The mortgage required Bonner to pay real estate taxes and provided that failure to do so was a ground for foreclosing on the mortgage.] Bonner defaulted on its real-estate taxes and Bancorp scheduled a foreclosure sale.

The day before the sale, Bonner filed a petition under Chapter 11 of the Bankruptcy Code, 11 U.S.C. §1101 et seq., in the United States Bankruptcy Court for the District of Idaho. It filed a reorganization plan that depended on the "new value exception" to the absolute priority rule.[*] [The case worked its way through the federal court system, Bancorp losing in its attack on the new value exception. The Supreme Court granted certiorari to consider the new value exception. While the case was pending in the Supreme Court,] Bancorp and Bonner stipulated to a consensual plan of reorganization, which received the approval of the Bankruptcy Court. The parties agreed that confirmation of the plan constituted a settlement that mooted the case. Bancorp, however, also requested that we exercise our power under 28 U.S.C. §2106 to vacate the judgment of the Court of Appeals. Bonner opposed the motion. We set the vacatur question for briefing and argument. . . .

III . . .

As always when federal courts contemplate equitable relief, our holding must also take account of the public interest. "Judicial precedents are presumptively correct and valuable to the legal community as a whole. They are not merely the property of private litigants and should stand unless a court concludes that the public interest would be served by a vacatur." Izumi Seimitsu Kogyo Kabushiki Kaisha v. U.S. Phillips Corp., 510 U.S. 27, 40 (1993) (Stevens, J., dissenting). Congress has prescribed a primary route, by appeal as of right and certiorari, through which parties may seek relief from the legal consequences of judicial judgments. To allow a party who steps off the statutory path to employ the secondary remedy of vacatur as a refined form of collateral attack on the judgment would — quite apart from any considerations of fairness to the parties — disturb the orderly operation of the federal judicial system. [United States v.] Munsingwear [340 U.S. 36 (1950)] establishes that the public interest is best served by granting relief when the demands of "orderly procedure" cannot be honored; we think conversely that the public interest requires those demands to be honored when they can. . . .

[* The new value exception is a bankruptcy doctrine that permits under some circumstances the owners of a bankrupt firm, who would ordinarily lose their entire investment, to retain an interest in it, even when creditors have not been paid in full. The doctrine has been controversial. — ED.]

A . . . policy justification urged by petitioner is the facilitation of settlement, with the resulting economies for the federal courts. But while the availability of vacatur may facilitate settlement after the judgment under review has been rendered and certiorari granted (or appeal filed), it may deter settlement at an earlier stage. Some litigants, at least, may think it worthwhile to roll the dice rather than settle in the district court, or in the court of appeals, if, but only if, an unfavorable outcome can be washed away by a settlement-related vacatur. And the judicial economies achieved by settlement at the district-court level are ordinarily much more extensive than those achieved by settlement on appeal. We find it quite impossible to assess the effect of our holding, either way, upon the frequency or systemic value of settlement. Although the case before us involves only a motion to vacate, by reason of settlement, the judgment of a court of appeals (with, of course, the consequential vacation of the underlying judgment of the district court), it is appropriate to discuss the relevance of our holding to motions at the court of appeals level for vacatur of district-court judgments. Some opinions have suggested that vacatur motions at that level should be more freely granted, since district-court judgments are subject to review as of right. Obviously, this factor does not affect the primary basis for our denying vacatur. Whether the appellate court's seizure of the case is the consequence of an appellant's right or of a petitioner's good luck has no bearing upon the lack of equity of a litigant who has voluntarily abandoned review. If the point of the proposed distinction is that district-court judgments, being subject to review as of right, are more likely to be overturned and hence presumptively less valid: We again assert the inappropriateness of disposing of cases, whose merits are beyond judicial power to consider, on the basis of judicial estimates regarding their merits. . . .

We hold that mootness by reason of settlement does not justify vacatur of a judgment under review. This is not to say that vacatur can never be granted when mootness is produced in that fashion. As we have described, the determination is an equitable one, and exceptional circumstances may conceivably counsel in favor of such a course. It should be clear from our discussion, however, that those exceptional circumstances do not include the mere fact that the settlement agreement provides for vacatur — which neither diminishes the voluntariness of the abandonment of review nor alters any of the policy considerations we have discussed. Of course even in the absence of, or before considering the existence of, extraordinary circumstances, a court of appeals presented with a request for vacatur of district-court judgment may remand the case with instructions that the district court consider the request, which it may do pursuant to Federal Rule of Civil Procedure 60(b). . . .

Petitioner's motion to vacate the judgment of the Court of Appeals for the Ninth Circuit is denied. The case is dismissed as moot. See this Court's Rule 46.

It is so ordered.

NOTES AND PROBLEMS

1. What is at stake in *Neary* and *Bonner Mall*? At one level the argument is quite narrow: Should an appellate court vacate a lower court judgment because the parties so request? That is narrow because so few filed cases make it to trial, much less to appeal. Compared to questions about the confidentiality of settlements, this disagreement is esoteric. However esoteric, the problem is difficult. Judith Resnik argues in Whose Judgment? Vacating Judgments, Preferences for Settlement, and the Role of Adjudication at the Close of the Twentieth Century, 41 UCLA L. Rev. 1471 (1994), that there are strong arguments on both sides. Arrayed against the courts' status as deciders of law are the interests of the parties in autonomy.

a. Resnik points out that a vacated judgment has some attractive qualities for *both* parties: It blurs the lines between total victory and total defeat, a characteristic of judicial judgments, and lets each party come away thinking it has won something valuable. In cases like *Bonner Mall*, vacatur eliminates what would otherwise be a strong precedent that one side would view as undesirable — and the other side wouldn't care about, so long as it had won its case.

b. Moreover, in cases like *Neary* the plaintiff benefits directly: The defendant is presumably willing to make a more favorable settlement with stipulated vacatur than without it. Put crudely, Mr. Neary got something in return for his agreement to join the defendant in seeking vacation of the trial court judgment. Future parties in his position lose part of their bargaining power if they cannot use stipulated vacatur as a bargaining tool.

2. The opinions in *Neary* and *Bonner Mall* open in a broad way the question implicit in Professor Resnik's title: Who "owns" the judgment of a court? In legal systems in which the judges do the primary investigation of cases (as is true in most civil law systems), the question seems to have a clear answer: The court does. In a system like that of the United States., in which the parties do most of the work involved in presenting evidence and arguing law, do they thereby gain a moral claim to "ownership" of the ensuing judgment? The work product doctrine, discussed in Chapter VII, provides a very rough analogy. The opinion in *Bonner Mall* rejects such a view, quoting from a dissent of Justice Stevens, in

which he contended that "precedents . . . are presumptively correct and valuable to the legal community as a whole. They are not merely the property of the private litigants. . . ." One could think of this statement in a number of ways. One would be as a matter of cost accounting: Court "costs" paid by litigants do not come close to paying the expense of operating the judicial system, which is heavily subsidized by tax dollars. What if they did? Should it matter that the parties offer to compensate the system for the full costs of adjudication? Would that put the parties in a better position to demand the vacation of a decision? Or would that make matters even worse?

3. *Neary* and *Bonner Mall* display two judicial systems coming to different answers to similar questions. The split raises both technical and broader issues.

a. In a federal diversity action in which California substantive law controls (by virtue of *Erie*), should the federal courts accede to state law (as enunciated in *Neary*) and permit the parties to stipulate to vacating a judgment? Or does 28 U.S.C. §2106, as interpreted in *Bonner Mall*, provide governing federal law that supersedes the state's policies?

b. Though California and the federal system have reached opposite conclusions, neither *Neary* nor *Bonner Mall* is airtight; both establish presumptive policies that allow for exceptions. What would be an exceptional situation warranting a refusal to vacate judgment in California? What would constitute an exceptional situation warranting the vacation of judgment in the federal system?

c. Which case — *Neary* or *Bonner Mall* — comes to the better result? Is it possible that both are correctly decided because their factual circumstances are distinguishable and that their respective courts erred only in writing such broad opinions?

2.   Guided Negotiation: Meditation and Coercion

Settlement negotiations sometimes fail. Generally one can trace the failure of negotiations to one of two causes. The parties may have different estimates of the result of litigation, in which case one or both is too optimistic. Alternatively, the parties may have similar guesses about the outcome of litigation but may not be communicating clearly. Either circumstance can lead to the collapse of negotiations.

Sometimes, however, negotiations that would otherwise fail can succeed if the parties have help. A variety of techniques are available and widely used to bring the parties together in their assessment of the likely outcome: reading and sharing the published reports of jury verdicts and settlements in similar cases; participation of a settlement judge who is older, more experienced, and who may therefore have a better idea of how the case will come out; summary jury trial, in which the participants present a truncated version of their case to a panel of jurors who render a nonbinding verdict, thus giving the parties more feel for how an actual jury might react.

Communication problems can be addressed with another array of tools: using a settlement judge or mediator who can, in a private conversation, get a party to reveal how much she is willing to pay (or accept); making sure the client is involved and that the pros and cons of settlement have been fully discussed with the client (lawyers are sometimes reluctant to do this); giving clients a chance to tell their stories to a neutral party even if that party cannot bindingly resolve the case; or getting a sense of whether a nonmonetary factor is involved, such as the need for a decision maker to have "cover" for settling a case.

In many of these situations a *mediator* may be able to help the parties come to an agreement. The narrowest definition of "mediation" sees it as assisted negotiation, aid in overcoming barriers to agreement. What does a mediator do? One way to describe her role is to frame it entirely in terms of process: The mediator seeks to engage the parties in a structured set of discussions leading to agreement. Because the goal is an agreement of the parties, the mediator does not rule on the rights and wrongs of the dispute or tell the parties what to do. But the mediator's limited role is also a function of the fact that she has no coercive power: The mediator succeeds only if the parties agree. The mediator typically talks with the parties (sometimes together, sometimes individually), to ferret out areas of agreement and possible starting points for negotiations, to discover the respective parties' goals, and to suggest ways to accommodate these goals. The success of mediation depends partly on the level of trust the mediator is able to establish and partly on the distance separating the parties' goals. One requisite for successful mediation is trust: If the parties, having called in a mediator because they distrust each other, feel the same way toward the mediator, a successful outcome is unlikely.

But happy results also are possible. Labor mediation on the local, state, and federal level has a long and distinguished history; mediation in racial discrimination, a shorter and less conclusive one. Recent years have seen several efforts to reduce court caseloads by urging — or requiring — parties to use mediation rather than litigation. Family law — divorce, support, and custody disputes — has been a frequent target for such efforts. In one view, the popularity of mediation in this context reflects the fact that family conflicts by their nature are ideal for mediation; in another view, it is said to reflect the low importance attached to such cases by some judges and lawyers. Bear in mind, too, that some efforts described as mediation would be more accurately described either as arbitration or as settlements arrived at under heavy pressure (sometimes called "muscle mediation"). Professional mediators differ on whether to applaud or condemn such hybrid forms.

NOTES AND PROBLEMS

1. Suppose two parties who would like to settle a claim have chosen a mediator.

a. To begin work, what would Mediator want to know from the parties?

b. After gathering and digesting this information, Mediator works out a solution that maximizes each side's interest and announces the solution to the parties. Why would they be justifiably upset with Mediator's behavior?

2. As mediation proceeds, the parties come close to an agreement. Mediator believes, however, that one side is taking unfair advantage of the other side's momentary financial weakness to drive a hard bargain.

a. Should that be a concern to Mediator if the two parties are satisfied with the agreement?

b. If so, on what theory?

3. How and when should judges act as mediators?

a. One might take the view that they never should — that judges should be adjudicators, pure and simple, and should leave any settlement to the parties.

b. Whatever the merits of such a view, current procedural law does not support it. Two bodies of law allow a judge actively to manage litigation. Rule 16 (Pretrial Conferences; Scheduling; Management) establishes as one of its objectives "establishing early and continuing control so that the case will not be protracted because of lack of management" (Rule 16(a)(2)). Rule 16(c) contains a shopping list of management techniques ranging from establishing time limits to encouraging settlement. The Alternative Dispute Resolution Act of 1998, 28 U.S.C. §§651 et seq. goes further by requiring each federal district court to "authorize[], . . . devise, and implement its own alternative dispute resolution program." 28 U.S.C. §651(b). The legislative intent becomes clear from a section instructing district courts to adopt a local rule that "require[s] litigants in all civil cases to consider the use of an alternative dispute resolution process at an appropriate state in the litigation" and to "provide litigants in all civil cases with at least one alternative dispute resolution process. . . ." The act goes on to require training of "neutrals," the legislation's term for both arbitrators and mediators. The act gives a consented-to arbitrator's award the effect of a judgment, except that it cannot be reviewed by a court of appeal. 28 U.S.C. §657. A party who does not like an arbitrator's award can request a trial de novo in the district court. The act explicitly excepts from its requirements cases seeking remedies for civil and constitutional rights and cases involving more than $150,000. The Act of 1998 replaced the Civil Justice Reform Act of 1990, which had expired under its own terms the year before. Like its predecessor, the 1998 Act encourages courts to use alternatives to adjudication and to "manage" litigation efficiently.

b. The act's reference to "early neutral evaluation" embodies a simple idea: Parties tend to have excessively optimistic evaluations of their cases; presenting one's case briefly to a neutral party who assesses its strengths and weaknesses will lead to a more realistic negotiating position. Such evaluators are typically volunteer lawyers or magistrate judges not otherwise involved in the case.

c. A variation on early neutral evaluation is nonbinding arbitration, in which, as a condition of going to trial, the parties are required to present their cases to an arbitrator, who issues a decision. This decision, however, does not bind the parties.

d. A third variation is the *summary jury trial* as a settlement device. In summary jury trials a small jury (usually of eight or fewer members) is chosen, and the parties present their cases to the jury in very abbreviated form (usually with the lawyers narrating what the evidence will show rather than calling actual witnesses). The "jury" is charged, deliberates, and returns its verdict, which, however, is not binding. Instead the verdict serves as a basis for further negotiation: The plaintiff who thought his case was worth $250,000 discovers the jury was willing to award only $50,000; the defendant who thought she would win a defense verdict finds herself stung for significant damages. Both return to the negotiating table sadder but better informed. The hope underlying all these processes is that actually "losing" a case (or winning less than was hoped for) may cause the parties to settle.

e. Consider one judge who, having used every tool he could think of, found parties who still would not settle. Did he do the right thing?

Lockhart v. Patel

115 F.R.D. 44 (E.D. Ky. 1987)

BERTELSMAN, J.

Unfortunately, the court finds it necessary in this case to discuss . . . its authority to order parties and their insurers to attend settlement conferences . . . [and] the propriety of sanctions for failure to attend.

This is a medical malpractice action in which the plaintiff, a teenager, lost the sight of one eye, allegedly due to the defendant doctor's negligence. In a summary jury trial an advisory jury awarded the plaintiff $200,000.[1]

Following the summary jury trial, the court held several formal and informal pretrial and settlement conferences, both in person and by telephone. In a telephone conference on October 30, 1986, the attorney for the defendant doctor's liability insurance carrier, St. Paul Fire & Marine Insurance Company, advised the court that he had been authorized by that company's home office to offer $125,000 and no more and not to negotiate any further. At this time, the plaintiff's demand was $175,000.

Having had some success with settlement conferences in the past, the court directed the defense attorney to attend a settlement conference on November 3 . . . and to bring with him the representative of the insurance company from the home office who had issued these instructions, or one with equal authority. The court specifically and formally admonished defense counsel: "Tell them no[t] to send some flunky who has no authority to negotiate. I want someone who can enter into a settlement in this range without having to call anyone else."

November 3 arrived, and so did the defense attorney. But the representative from St. Paul's home office did not. Instead, an adjuster from the local office appeared. She advised the court that her instructions from the officials at the home office were to reiterate the offer previously made and not to call them back if it were not accepted.

When asked by the court whether there was some misunderstanding that it had stated a representative from the home office was required to attend, the adjuster replied, "I doubt if anyone from the home office would have come down even if in fact this is what you said."

Measures in response to such clearly improper conduct seemed called for. At this point, the court made the appropriate oral findings, promptly followed by a written order, that "St. Paul had deliberately refused to obey the order of the court" and that "such disobedience was deliberately contemptuous, contumacious and purposely demonstrated disrespect and disregard for the authority of the court."

Accordingly, the court forthwith struck the pleadings of the defendant and declared him in default. The court further ordered that the trial set for the next day would be limited to damages only and that a hearing to show cause why St. Paul should not be punished for criminal contempt

---

1. For a discussion of summary jury trial procedure, see Lambros, The Summary Jury Trial and Other Alternative Methods of Dispute Resolution, 103 F.R.D. 461 (1984).

be held on December 12, 1986. Later that day, St. Paul settled with the plaintiff for $175,000.

December 12 arrived, and this time so did not one but several representatives from St. Paul's home office . . . [who] assured the court that it had all been a misunderstanding . . . [and] provid[ed] a letter of apology from its Chief Executive Officer. . . . [The court accepted these apologies and permitted St. Paul to purge itself of its contempt.]

This opinion is written, therefore, solely to discuss the authority of the court to hold meaningful settlement conferences. . . .

The authority of a federal court to order attendance of attorneys, parties, and insurers at settlement conferences and to impose sanctions for disregard of the court's orders is so well established as to be beyond doubt. . . .

Rule 16(f) was added to original Rule 16 . . . in 1983. Although the rule refers to "parties," it clearly would be meaningless if it did not also apply to a party's liability insurer. . . .

. . . Cases since the Amendment are few, perhaps because the text of the Rule is so clear as to require little interpretation. The court finds G. Heileman Brewing Company, Inc. v. Joseph Oat Corp., 107 F.R.D. 275 (W.D. Wis. 1985), worthy of note. . . :

> I do not accept the proposition that Rule 16 does not authorize a court to require the presence of parties with full authority to settle a case. . . .
> The clear intention of the recent amendments to the Federal Rules is to provide courts with the tools that are required to manage their caseloads effectively and efficiently. . . . *A settlement conference without all the necessary parties present is not productive. Neither is a conference of persons who have no authority to settle.*
>
> It is no argument that it would have been futile for Joseph Oat or National Union Fire to appear by representatives with full authority to settle, simply because these corporations had decided that they would not settle on any terms other than full dismissal of the claims against Joseph Oat. It is always possible that exposure of the decision makers to the realities of a case will bring about a reevaluation of settlement posture. . . .

107 F.R.D. at 277.

This court is in complete agreement with these observations. The normal caseload of a United States District Judge is now considered to be 400 civil cases. At this time every judge in this district has half again that many. . . . And in addition to this civil caseload the court is also expected to deal with the criminal docket, which for this court averages about 40 cases per judge per year, some taking several weeks to try.

The drafters of amended Rule 16 knew of the docket pressures to which our courts are subject, and knew that to process 400 cases you have to settle at least 350. That is why they encouraged "forceful judicial management," which is the only means of settling a high percentage of cases.

. . . The exigencies of modern dockets demand the adoption of novel and imaginative means . . . [including] compulsory arbitration, summary jury trials, imposing reasonable limits on trial time, or, as here, the relatively innocuous device of requiring a settlement conference attended by the clients as well as the attorneys.

Of course, the court cannot require any party to settle a case, whether the court thinks that party's position is reasonable or not, but it can require it to make reasonable efforts. . . .*

NOTES AND PROBLEMS

1. The opinion speaks of the judge's authority to order parties' attendance at settlement conferences as "beyond doubt" and the text of Rule 16 in this respect "so clear as to require little interpretation." That may be an overstatement.

a. Some authorities have disagreed. David L. Shapiro, Federal Rule 16: A Look at the Theory and Practice of Rulemaking, 137 U. Pa. L. Rev. 1969, 1989-1990 (1990): "I for one find it hard to read this authority into Rule 16."

b. The advisory committee on civil rules may have shared Prof. Shapiro's doubts, for in 1993 they added to Rule 16(c) the following sentence: "If appropriate, the court may require that a party or its representative be present or reasonably available by telephone to consider possible settlement of the dispute. . . ." Does the addition of that sentence settle the matter? The Advisory Committee note to the preceding sentence states: "Finally, it should be noted that the unwillingness of a party to be available, even by telephone, for a settlement conference may be a clear signal that the time and expense involved in pursuing settlement is likely to be unproductive and that personal participation by the parties should not be required."

2. Assume this revision and its accompanying comment had been in effect at the time of *Lockhart.*

[* Appended to the opinion is the text of a letter from the chairman of St. Paul Fire & Marine Insurance Company, in which he "publicly apologizes to the court . . . for the misunderstanding which occurred at the settlement conference" and assures the court that it "has never been . . . the . . . policy of St. Paul . . . to ignore the orders of this court or any other court of law" and that "[it] is the company's policy that its employees attend all settlement conferences when ordered to do so by a court of competent jurisdiction." — ED.]

a. Do they support Judge Bertelsman's actions?

b. Or do they suggest that the judge had the power to enter the order in question but should have refrained from doing so?

3. Assuming that the judge has power to order a party's attendance at a settlement conference, didn't St. Paul comply by sending an adjuster who apparently had been told that she could enter into any settlement up to $125,000? Though the opinion disclaims judicial power to force unwilling parties to settle, didn't St. Paul in fact incur displeasure for failing to send a representative with "authority to negotiate . . . a settlement in this range," when "this range" meant more than $125,000 — the amount of the previous offer? To pose the problem concretely, suppose St. Paul had sent a representative from the home office and that representative had said: "I have full authority to settle this case for any reasonable amount. After careful consideration, I have concluded that the upper limit on settlement is $125,000."

4. The *Lockhart* opinion stresses the size of the caseload as a reason justifying the insistence on settlement conferences. In the twelve months ending September 30, 1998, federal district courts disposed of 202,000 civil cases. The median time from filing to termination was eight months, with 10 percent taking less than two months, and 10 percent more than twenty-five months. Eighteen percent of the cases ended with no action at all; they ended, presumably through settlement or abandonment by the parties, in a median time of six months. An additional 69 percent terminated after some court action but before pretrial; for these cases the median time from filing to termination was seven months. Another 10 percent of the cases terminated, like *Lockhart*, during the pretrial phase; the median time from filing to termination was thirteen months. Slightly less than 3 percent of the civil filings terminated at or during trial; the median time from filing to termination for these cases was eighteen months. Annual Report of the Director of the Administrative Officer of the United States Courts, ⟨http://www.uscourts.gov/dirrpt98/c05sep98.pdf⟩ (1998). What do these statistics tell us?

a. The largest difference in time to termination is between cases that end without any court action or before pretrial (87 percent of all cases; median between six and seven months' duration) and those that involve at least pretrial (between thirteen and eighteen months).

b. In contrast, the difference between cases that end at the pretrial stage and those that end at trial is, on average, five months.

c. Do these statistics suggest that judicial intervention of the sort in *Lockhart*, which focuses on the period just before trial, comes too late to make a significant difference in the average "age" of a case? Or do they lend support to those who would intervene vigorously to save the additional five months?

3.   Contracting for Arbitration

Parties can enter contracts to settle lawsuits, and they can employ mediators to help them reach such settlements. But what if the parties cannot agree, even with the help of a mediator, or can agree only that they want to have their disputes decided by a third party. Must they then resort to the courts? No; one of the oldest and best-established alternatives to litigation is arbitration. Unlike a mediator, an arbitrator decides a dispute and issues an oral or a written decision after having heard from both sides. Arbitration, in other words, closely resembles adjudication — private, nonjudicial adjudication, but still adjudication.

Why, if it is so closely akin to adjudication, do the parties not simply use the ordinary court system? First, unlike court-controlled adjudication, arbitration permits the parties to design their own procedure. Sometimes that results in processes that are scarcely distinguishable from judicial adjudication, including the rules of evidence and various formal stages of procedure. In other cases arbitration may depart dramatically from legal process. The parties may agree that the arbitrator will be bound by precedent or that he will ignore it — with a number of intermediate variations. Second, the parties may, to an even greater extent than in courts, control the applicable substantive law — they can insist, for example, that the arbitrator will not refer to the ordinary rules of contract but instead will adhere to the traditions that have developed around this particular relationship. Third, arbitration may be faster, cheaper, and more private than ordinary adjudication. The parties may be able to dispense with the rules of discovery or with other procedural stages and insist on a quick decision of their dispute. They may also be able to insist that the arbitrator disclose neither the existence of a dispute nor his decision. Fourth, because the parties may arrange to have only experienced and known arbitrators decide their disputes, they can both ensure a decision maker who is experienced in the field (be it medical malpractice, engineering, or stockbroking) and eliminate the vagaries in outcome that a jury may introduce. In the process, however, they may also deprive one side of the larger damages a jury might award. Finally — and this may be either an advantage or a disadvantage — the arbitrator, though deciding the dispute, may decide it more "softly" than a court:

> It is said of the American commercial arbitrator that he may "do justice as he sees it, applying his own sense of the law and equity to the facts as he finds them to be and making an award reflecting the spirit rather than the letter of the agreement." Many awards resulting from such proceedings might also be described as Solomonic, halving the objects in dispute.

Paul Carrington & Paul Haagen, Contract and Jurisdiction, 1996 Sup. Ct. Rev. 331, 345, quoting Silverman v. Benmor Coats, 61 N.Y.2d 299 (1984).

These features of arbitration will emerge only if the courts are willing to require parties who have agreed to arbitrate to submit their disputes to arbitration when a question arises. Judicial attitudes toward arbitration have undergone a great swing from which the pendulum may now be returning. In the nineteenth and early twentieth centuries many courts widely refused to enforce predispute arbitration agreements; they would enforce arbitration only if the parties chose the method after the dispute had arisen. By case law and statute, however, the rule has generally been changed in favor of arbitration even if agreed to by the parties before any dispute has arisen. For example, the U.S. Supreme Court, which once viewed with suspicion the arbitration of claims arising under federal statutes, has enforced agreements to arbitrate securities claims, Shearson/ American Express Co. v. McMahon, 482 U.S. 220 (1987), and Age Discrimination in Employment Act claims, Gilmer v. Interstate/ Johnson Lane Corp., 500 U.S. 20 (1991). The Court overruled or distinguished older cases that had refused to permit arbitration of federal statutory claims. And in recent years an increasing number of employers and medical service providers — particularly health maintenance organizations — have included arbitration provisions in their employment manuals and policies.

As a consequence of such cases, parties who have entered a predispute arbitration agreement may be required to use arbitration as their exclusive forum, and a party bound by the agreement may be enjoined from litigating instead of arbitrating. The Federal Arbitration Act, 9 U.S.C. §§2 et seq., allows for enforcement of arbitration agreements in the federal courts; in several cases the Supreme Court has required state courts to enforce arbitration agreements even when they contravene state law if the underlying transaction involves interstate commerce. The result is that in any contract involving such commerce (which, given other decisions, covers most commercial transactions), arbitration clauses will be enforceable.

Recently some have argued that, whatever the virtues of arbitration, it is not a panacea and that, like other litigation alternatives, it is subject to misuse and should be prohibited, curtailed, or otherwise limited. As you will see below, the debate suggests that both enthusiasts and critics have valid points.

a. The Possibilities of Arbitration

Parties who agree to arbitrate are, at a minimum, taking their dispute outside the ordinary rules of litigation. In practice, they may be doing little else. Many arbitrators operate under procedural rules that, although less formal than those of courts, closely resemble them: There are adversary presentations; witnesses and documents presented to an arbitrator; or briefs submitted to the arbitrator, who then renders a decision (usually called an "award"), which may be in writing. But arbitration also opens the gates of procedural imagination, permitting the parties to provide rules of procedure that differ dramatically from the ones we see in courts. The next case illustrates the possibilities of that freedom.

Ferguson v. Writers Guild of America, West
226 Cal. App. 3d 1382, 277 Cal. Rptr. 450 (1991)

KLEIN (B.), J. A.*

I

Larry Ferguson appeals from a judgment of the superior court denying his petition for a writ of mandate directed to respondent Writers Guild of America, West, Inc.

Ferguson, a screenwriter, was engaged by Paramount Pictures Corporation to write a screenplay for a feature-length theatrical motion picture entitled "Beverly Hills Cop II." When the picture was completed, the Writers Guild, on April 27, 1987, determined the writing credits for the picture as follows: Screenplay by Larry Ferguson and Warren Skaaren; Story by Eddie Murphy & Robert D. Wachs.

Ferguson then commenced this proceeding by filing a petition for writ of mandate in the superior court on May 15, 1987. In his petition he asked the court to issue a peremptory writ of mandate requiring the Writers Guild to set aside its credit determination and make a new determination giving Ferguson sole screenplay credit and sole story credit. . . .

II

The process for determining writing credits for theatrical motion picture scripts is governed in this case by two documents. The first is the 369-page theatrical and television basic agreement, reached in 1985 by 241 producing companies, represented by the Alliance of Motion Picture and Television Producers, Inc.; 3 television networks; Writers Guild of America, West, Inc.; and Writers Guild of America, East, Inc. The second document is the Writers Guild West's 11-page credits manual, dated December 31, 1980.

---

* Assigned by the Chairperson of the Judicial Council.

The basic agreement contains, in a section entitled theatrical schedule A, detailed provisions concerning writing credits for feature-length theatrical photoplays. Under schedule A, the production company must notify all participating writers of its tentative credits determination. Any of the writers may then file with the production company and the Writers Guild a written request for arbitration of credits. If such a request is filed, the Writers Guild, through its arbitration committee, must determine the credits within 18 business days. . . .

Schedule A authorizes the Writers Guild's arbitration committee, prior to rendering its decision, to "make such investigations and conduct such hearings as may seem advisable to it." The credits manual, discussed below, sets forth the procedures the Writers Guild has adopted. . . .

The procedure can be summarized as follows. The credit arbitration is administered by the Writers Guild's credit arbitration secretary. When a credit arbitration is requested, this officer sends the parties to the arbitration a screen arbiter's list, containing the names of all potential arbitrators. These are Writers Guild members with credit arbitration experience or with at least three screenplay credits of their own. This list comprised at least 400 names in 1987. Each party can peremptorily disqualify a reasonable number of persons from the list. From the remaining potential arbitrators, the secretary selects three, endeavoring to select individuals experienced in the type of writing involved in the particular case.

The secretary delivers to the three arbitrators all script, outline, and story material prepared or used in the creation of the screenplay, together with source material (writings upon which the screenplay or story is based). These documents are supplied to the Writers Guild by the production company, and each participant in the credit arbitration may examine them to assure the inclusion of everything he or she has written. Any dispute over the "authenticity, identification, sequence, authorship or completeness" of literary material to be included is resolved by a special three-member committee, which conducts for that purpose a prearbitration hearing, at which all affected writers may present testimony and other evidence.

The arbitrators also receive the production company's statement of tentative credits; a copy of the credits manual; and the statements of the parties, which are confidential. The secretary designates a member of the Writers Guild's Screen Writers' credits committee to act as consultant to the arbitrators on procedure, precedent, policies, and rules, and to aid the arbitrators toward a majority decision.

The three arbitrators hold no hearing, and they deliberate independently of each other. Indeed, each remains unaware of the identity of the other two (unless, after they reach their decisions, the consultant convenes a meeting with the three). Each arbitrator notifies the secretary of his or her determination. The secretary then informs the parties of the decision of the majority of the arbitrators.

Within 24 hours thereafter, any party may request the convening of a policy review board, consisting of three members of the Writers Guild's credits committee including that committee's chairman or vice-chairman. The policy review board does not examine the script, story, or source material; indeed, its members are forbidden to read these. Its function is solely to detect any substantial deviation from the policy of the Writers Guild or from the procedure set forth in the credits manual. The policy review board has authority to direct the arbitration committee to reconsider the case or to order a fresh arbitration by a new triumvirate. The policy review board is not empowered to reverse the decision of an arbitration committee in matters of judgment. A decision of the policy review board approving a credit determination is final.

III

With his petition, Ferguson furnished the superior court with all screenplay and story materials, so the court could make the proper credit decisions under Writers Guild standards. Thus, to determine the correct story credit, the court was invited to ascertain which writings represented "a contribution distinct from screenplay and consisting of basic narrative, idea, theme or outline indicating character development and action." . . . On this appeal, Ferguson asks us to undertake the same task, then to command the Writers Guild to award him sole screenplay credit and sole story credit for the picture.

Ferguson contends, in the alternative, that the Writers Guild's credit determination process was infected by procedural improprieties and irregularities, and asks us to order the Writers Guild to conduct the credit arbitration anew. The asserted procedural defects are these: (1) the credit arbitration secretary improperly cast herself in the role of consultant to the arbitration committee and had improper substantive communications with the three arbitrators; (2) Ferguson was unfairly denied a postponement of the arbitration to assemble additional story materials and prepare his confidential statement for the arbitrators; (3) the arbitrators were given insufficient time to review the materials Ferguson submitted; (4) the Writers Guild took no steps to ensure the three arbitrators were disinterested and unbiased; (5) the arbitrators were not provided with copies of schedule A or the credits Manual; (6) the Writers Guild incorrectly treated as story material a memorandum in which Paramount executive David Kirkpatrick recounted a story idea told him orally by Murphy and

Wachs; and (7) the Writers Guild improperly denied Ferguson's request that the arbitrators be given a second memorandum in which Paramount executive Michael Roberts remarked that Paramount "threw out" the screenplay drafted by the writers it had previously engaged and hired Ferguson "to write an entirely new draft."

Ferguson presents a final contention, challenging as error the rulings of the superior court denying his requests (a) to take the deposition of Warren Skaaren, the writer awarded shared screenplay credit, and (b) to compel the Writers Guild to reveal the identity of the three arbitrators, presumably so Ferguson could take their depositions.

IV

Before ruling on these contentions, we must consider the proper scope of judicial review of the Writers Guild's credit determination in this case. We agree with the Writers Guild's position that under schedule A and the credits manual, disputes over writing credits for feature-length photoplays are nonjusticiable. As judges we are no doubt as capable as any lay person of studying screenplays, outlines, and other literary material to assess the relative contributions of the participating writers. The membership of the Writers Guild, however, have agreed among themselves (by approving the credits manual) and with the producers' association (by entering into schedule A of the basic agreement) that this delicate task is to be performed by arbitration committees composed of experienced Writers Guild members. The professional writers who constitute the Writers Guild have thus decided[,] quite appropriately we think[,] that the credit-determination process can be handled both more skillfully, more expeditiously, and more economically by Writers Guild arbitration committees than by courts. The finality provisions of schedule A and the credits manual, quoted earlier, demonstrate the Writers Guild membership's intention that credit disputes be resolved without resort to ruinously expensive litigation. (See Code Civ. Proc., §§1286-1286.8; Morris v. Zuckerman, 69 Cal. 2d 686, 691 (1968).)

V

In examining Ferguson's claims of procedural irregularities, we bear in mind that the procedures employed in the present arbitration have already been reviewed for correctness by the Writers Guild's own policy review board. The court accords considerable deference to the decision of the policy review board, because of its members' expertise in the interpretation and application of schedule A and the credits manual.

In addition, the familiar principle of exhaustion of administrative remedies prevents a litigant from pursuing a judicial remedy for procedural defects without having first asked the private organization to correct them. . . .

[Ferguson, though he requested review by the policy review board, did not specify the errors in the arbitration procedure that he later argued before the court.]

Accordingly, we hold that Ferguson has not preserved for judicial review the seven contentions listed [above], because he has not demonstrated that he presented them to the Writers Guild's policy review board.

Even were we to reach the merits of Ferguson's seven claims, we would find them devoid of merit. Judicial review of the Writers Guild's credits determination is restricted to considering whether the party challenging the determination has demonstrated a material and prejudicial departure from the procedures specified in the credits manual. Applying this standard, we have determined that the record sustains none of Ferguson's seven procedural contentions.

Ferguson's remaining grievance is that he should have been told the names of the arbitrators and permitted to interrogate them and Skaaren. We reject this position.

Skaaren was a party to the credit arbitration, and could have made any concessions he deemed appropriate in that forum; otherwise, as the trial court correctly determined, Skaaren's appraisal of his and Ferguson's relative contributions could add nothing to Ferguson's claim to sole story and screenplay credit.

With respect to the identity of the arbitrators, the credits manual unequivocally specifies that the three arbitrators are not to be informed of each other's identities, and the Writers Guild has sufficiently established that, though not also stated in the credits manual, its unvarying and well-known rule has long been that the identities of the arbitrators are also not disclosed to the parties to the arbitration nor to anyone else inside or outside the Writers Guild. The Writers Guild's insistence on this practice is supported by important and legitimate considerations, including the necessity that arbitrators be entirely freed from both real and perceived dangers of pressure, retaliation, and litigation. While it is unusual to have an arbitration procedure in which the parties cannot appear in person before the arbitrators and cannot learn the arbitrators' identities, discovery of the names of the arbitrators in a Writers Guild credit arbitration could serve no legitimate function. Ferguson apparently wishes to ask the arbitrators, inter alia, to explain and justify their conclusions regarding the various writers' contributions to the final screenplay. Even when an arbitration is conducted under more familiar rules, though, such as the commercial arbitration rules of the American Arbitration

Association, the losing party is not permitted to conduct an inquisition into the arbitrators' thought processes in reaching their award.

Appellant's request to dismiss the appeal is denied, and the judgment is affirmed. . . .

NOTES AND PROBLEMS

1. Imagine that a state legislature adopted the Writers Guild procedure for its court system: litigants limited to written submission to an anonymous panel of judges; no opportunity to appear, summon witnesses, or present testimony; and the court's judgment rendered without explanation. Would such a procedure be held to violate due process?

a. If so, why is such a process permissible here?

b. If not, does that suggest that a wide range of nontraditional processes would accord with due process?

2. Could the Guild have adopted even more streamlined procedures — eliminating, for example, the right to exercise peremptory challenges to names on the panel and the right of appeal to the policy review board?

3. If one believed the answer to the preceding question is no, how would one challenge such a process? In a judicial system the Due Process Clause lies at hand, but in private arbitration the clause does not apply because the requisite state action is absent. Because most arbitration agreements result from such contractual provisions, they are subject to attack on the same fronts as are other contractual clauses. One could, for example, attack an arbitration clause on grounds of adhesion or unconscionability in the same way one might attack consent to jurisdiction or the signing of a cognovit note. See Carnival Cruise Lines v. Shute, Chapter II, supra page 169. Ferguson did not mount such an attack. Should he have done so? Would it matter whether he could demonstrate that membership in the Guild, which includes agreeing to consent to its credit arbitration procedures, was required by the studios who buy scripts? Should it matter that the Writers Guild's members have in repeated elections endorsed the arbitration system by large majorities?

4. If a judge renders a decision, in most U.S. jurisdictions the decision can be appealed. What about arbitrators' awards? The general proposition, illustrated by *Ferguson*, is that appeal to a court is possible but not generally useful because the court will narrowly restrict the scope of its review.

a. *Ferguson* actually offers three different descriptions of judicial review of arbitration awards. At one point it says, "disputes over writing credits for feature-length photoplays are nonjusticiable." At another it describes its review as "limited to a determination whether there has been a material breach of the terms of the credits manual, which binds the Writers Guild as well as its members." Finally, it compares this review to that employed in "more traditional arbitrations": "The court does not review the merits of the arbitrators' award; it examines only whether the parties in fact agreed to submit their controversy to arbitration, whether the procedures employed deprived the objecting party of a fair opportunity to be heard, and whether the arbitrators exceeded their powers."

b. These three formulations have a similar core idea: The court's reviewing powers are limited to whether the parties actually agreed to submit this particular dispute to arbitration and to whether the arbitrator exceeded the power granted by the agreement.

c. Two cases give a sense of how hesitant courts are to review arbitration awards and of how expansively they interpret arbitrators' powers. In Advanced Micro Devices, Inc. v. Intel Corp., 36 Cal. Rptr. 2d 581 (Cal. 1994), the California Supreme Court upheld an arbitrator's award that gave not damages but a royalty-free license to the intellectual property of a competitor. Such an award would, the dissent pointed out, be beyond the powers of a court and was not specifically conferred by the contract to arbitrate. In Mastrobuono v. Shearson Lehman Hutton, 115 S. Ct. 1212 (1995), the U.S. Supreme Court upheld an arbitrator's award that gave a brokerage house customer punitive damages, despite a clause in the arbitration agreement specifying application of New York law, which does not permit arbitrators to award punitive damages. The *Mastrobuono* court ruled that the choice of law clause clearly governed the substantive law to be applied by the arbitrator but did not clearly specify that it should govern remedial choices as well; the arbitrator's award was therefore not clearly beyond the scope of his jurisdiction.

b.   The Limits of Arbitration

With so much judicial enthusiasm for arbitration, what are its limits? First, despite the increasing support of arbitration, there are disputes as to which an arbitration agreement would be unenforceable. For example, a husband and wife could not agree to have an arbitrator grant them a divorce, and courts have split about whether arbitration of child custody is permissible. See Faherty v. Faherty, 97 N.J. 99, 477 A.2d 1257 (1984). Courts have, however, permitted divorcing spouses to allow arbitration of property issues, including child support. More fundamentally, issues of public law are probably beyond the scope of arbitration: It is difficult to imagine the courts' upholding the agreement of a president and Congress to arbitrate a challenge to presidential war-making powers.

Other limitations flow from the circumstance that arbitrators are like judges — in that they decide who has the better case — but are not part of the judicial system. As a consequence, one cannot simply appeal the arbitrator's award. For some parties this is a major advantage of arbitration; for others — like Mr. Ferguson — it is a drawback. One way to achieve appellate review of quasi-arbitration proceedings is the system popularly known as Rent-A-Judge, which is permitted in some states, such as California. Under statutory authority, in this system retired judges sit as "referees." See Cal. Code Civ. P. §§638-645 (West 1991). The advantage of such a system is that it eliminates waiting for a trial and permits subsequent appeal. It has also been challenged as inequitable because only those who can afford the often-substantial fees involved can make use of such a system.

Another reason to avoid arbitration is that a litigant wants something arbitration cannot give: an authoritative, public declaration of law, a jury trial, or the advantages of formal discovery processes. Other disadvantages include the possible lack of legal training of the arbitrator, the inability to obtain review for ordinary errors made by the arbitrator, and the growing tendency of arbitration to become formalized and more "legal" in nature. This legalization can include a rather slow pace: In *Advanced Micro Devices*, noted in the previous section, the California Supreme Court observed that the "arbitration lasted four and one-half years and included three hundred and fifty-five days of hearings."

Finally, because arbitration grows from contract, one can object to arbitration on essentially contractual grounds. Consider the approach taken in the next case.

Engalla v. Permanente Medical Group, Inc.

15 Cal. 4th 951 (1997)

MOSK, J.

In this case we consider the circumstances under which a court may deny a petition to compel arbitration because of the petitioner's fraud in inducing the arbitration agreement or waiver of the arbitration agreement. . . . [Plaintiffs were the surviving family of Wilfredo Engalla, who through his employer was enrolled in Kaiser's health maintenance organization. Kaiser as part of its standard insurance agreement provided for binding arbitration with a panel of three arbitrators, one named by the plaintiff/patient, the other by Kaiser, and the third by the first two. Kaiser's arbitration clause provides that each side shall designate its arbitrator within thirty days and the third, neutral arbitrator will be named within the next thirty days. Alleging that Kaiser lost X-rays, failed to follow its physicians' recommendations, and otherwise negligently

failed to diagnose his cancer until it was inoperable, Mr. Engalla initiated arbitration.]

Prior to his death, Engalla was engaged in a medical malpractice
dispute with Kaiser, which, according to the terms of Kaiser's Group
Medical and Hospital Services Agreement (Service Agreement), was submitted to arbitration. After attempting unsuccessfully to conclude the
arbitration prior to Engalla's death, the Engallas filed a malpractice action
against Kaiser in superior court, and Kaiser filed a petition to compel
arbitration pursuant to Code of Civil Procedure section 1281.2. In opposing the petition, plaintiffs claimed that Kaiser's self-administered arbitration system was corrupt or biased in a number of respects, that Kaiser
fraudulently misrepresented the expedition of its arbitration system, and
that Kaiser engaged in a course of dilatory conduct in order to postpone
Engalla's arbitration hearing until after his death, all of which should be
grounds for refusing to enforce the arbitration agreement. . . .

The arbitration program is designed, written, mandated and administered by Kaiser. In regard to the latter, Kaiser collects funds from claimants
and holds and disburses them as necessary to pay the neutral arbitrator
and expenses approved by him or her. It monitors administrative matters
pertinent to the progress of each case including, for example, the identity
and dates of appointment of arbitrators. It does not, however, employ or
contract with any independent person or entity to provide such administrative services, or any oversight or evaluation of the arbitration program or its
performance. Rather, administrative functions are performed by outside
counsel retained to defend Kaiser in an adversarial capacity.

The fact that Kaiser has designed and administers its arbitration program from an adversarial perspective is not disclosed to Kaiser members
or subscribers. . . . In those materials, Kaiser represented that an arbitration in its program would reach a hearing within several months' time,
and that its members would find the arbitration process to be a fair
approach to protecting their rights. . . .

Kaiser received the Engallas' May 31, 1991, demand for arbitration
on June 5 or 6. . . .

[There ensued six months during which the parties designated various
arbitrators who proved to be unavailable. Toward the end of that time
Mr. Engalla died. Kaiser refused to stipulate that the arbitration would
not be prejudiced by the plaintiff's death. (Under state law the death of
the husband merged the wife's claim for loss of consortium with her
wrongful death action, potentially reducing the total amount of damages.)
Plaintiff Mrs. Engalla then broke off the arbitration and filed a medical
malpractice lawsuit. When Kaiser moved to compel arbitration, the plaintiff resisted on grounds of fraud and unconscionability.]

Statistically, delays occur in 99 percent of all Kaiser medical malpractice arbitrations. An independent statistical analysis of Kaiser-provided data of arbitration between 1984 and 1986 reveals that in only 1 percent of all Kaiser cases is a neutral arbitrator appointed within the 60-day period provided by the arbitration provision. Only 3 percent of cases see a neutral arbitrator appointed within 180 days. On average, it has taken 674 days for the appointment of a neutral arbitrator. For claimants whose cases were resolved by settlement or after a hearing, the time required to appoint a neutral arbitrator consumed more than half the total time for resolution. Furthermore, because the arbitration provision of the Service Agreement does not clearly establish a time frame for a hearing (it must be within a "reasonable time" after appointment of the neutral arbitrator), and because Kaiser claims it has no obligation to participate in a hearing until it deems itself ready, there tend to be significant additional delays after appointment of the neutral arbitrator. Thus, on average, it takes 863 days — almost 2 1/2 years — to reach a hearing in a Kaiser arbitration. The depositions of Scott Fleming and Arthur Bernstein, both of whom formerly served as Kaiser's in-house counsel, revealed that Kaiser had long been aware that widespread delays were commonplace in Kaiser arbitrations. . . .

III. Fraud in the Inducement of the Arbitration Agreement. . .

. . . Fraud is one of the grounds on which a contract can be rescinded. (Civ. Code, 1689, subd. (b)(1).) In order to defeat a petition to compel arbitration, the parties opposing a petition to compel must show that the asserted fraud claim goes specifically "to the 'making' of the agreement to arbitrate," rather than to the making of the contract in general. In the present case, the Engallas do allege, and seek to show, fraud in the making of the arbitration agreement. . . .

Here the Engallas claim, (1) that Kaiser misrepresented its arbitration agreement in that it entered into the agreement knowing that, at the very least, there was a likelihood its agents would breach the part of the agreement providing for the timely appointment of arbitrators and the expeditious progress towards an arbitration hearing; (2) that Kaiser employed the above misrepresentation in order to induce reliance on the part of Engalla and his employer; (3) that Engalla relied on these misrepresentations to his detriment. The trial court found evidence supporting those claims. We examine each of these claims in turn.

First, evidence of misrepresentation is plain. . . . As recounted above, section 8.B. of the arbitration agreement provides that party arbitrators "shall" be chosen within 30 days and neutral arbitrators within 60 days, and that the arbitration hearing "shall" be held "within a reasonable time thereafter.". . . Here there are facts to support the Engallas' allegation that Kaiser entered into the arbitration agreement with knowledge that it would not comply with its own contractual timelines, or with at least a reckless indifference as to whether its agents would use reasonable diligence and good faith to comply with them. As discussed, a survey of Kaiser arbitrations between 1984 and 1986 submitted into evidence showed that a neutral arbitrator was appointed within 60 days in only 1 percent of the cases, with only 3 percent appointed within 180 days, and that on average the neutral arbitrator was appointed 674 days — almost 2 years — after the demand for arbitration. Regardless of when Kaiser became aware of these precise statistics, which were part of a 1989 study, the depositions of two of Kaiser's in-house attorneys demonstrate that Kaiser was aware soon after it began its arbitration program that its contractual deadlines were not being met, and that severe delay was endemic to the program. Kaiser nonetheless persisted in its contractual promises of expedition. . . .

The systemwide nature of Kaiser's delay comes into clearer focus when it is contrasted with other arbitration systems. As the Engallas point out, many large institutional users of arbitration, including most health maintenance organizations, avoid the potential problems of delay in the selection of arbitrators by contracting with neutral third party organizations, such as the American Arbitration Association (AAA). These organizations will then assume responsibility for administering the claim from the time the arbitration demand is filed, and will ensure the arbitrator or arbitrators are chosen in a timely manner. . . . In sum, we conclude there is evidence to support the Engallas' claims that Kaiser fraudulently induced Engalla to enter the arbitration agreement in that it misrepresented the speed of its arbitration program, a misrepresentation on which Engalla's employer relied by selecting Kaiser's health plan for its employees, and that the Engallas suffered delay in the resolution of its malpractice dispute as a result of that reliance, despite Engalla's own reasonable diligence. The trial court, on remand, must resolve conflicting factual evidence in order to properly adjudicate Kaiser's petition to compel arbitration. . . .

V. Unconscionability

We turn then to the Engallas' unconscionability argument. We have required that "contractual arrangements for the nonjudicial resolution of disputes" must possess " 'minimum levels of integrity.' ". . .

. . . The unfairness that is the substance of the Engallas' unconscionability argument comes essentially to this: The Engallas contend that
Kaiser has established a system of arbitration inherently unfair to claimants, because the method of selecting neutral arbitrators is biased. They
claim that Kaiser has an unfair advantage as a "repeat player" in arbitration, possessing information on arbitrators that the Engallas themselves
lacked. They also argue that Kaiser, under its arbitration system, has
sought to maximize this advantage by reserving for itself an unlimited
right to veto arbitrators proposed by the other party. This method is in
contrast to arbitration programs run by neutral, third party arbitration
organizations such as the AAA, which give parties a very limited ability
to veto arbitrators from its preselected panels.

Yet none of these features of Kaiser's arbitration program renders the
arbitration agreement per se unconscionable. As noted above, section
1281.6 specifically contemplates a system whereby neutral arbitrators will
be chosen directly by the parties. The alleged problem with Kaiser's
arbitration in this case was not any defect or one-sidedness in its contractual provisions, but rather in the gap between its contractual representations and the actual workings of its arbitration program. It is the doctrines
of fraud and waiver, rather than of unconscionability, that most appropriately address this discrepancy between the contractual representation and
the reality. Thus, viewing the arbitration agreement on its face, we cannot
say it is unconscionable. . . .

[Reversed and remanded.]

KENNARD. J., concurring.

I concur in the majority opinion. I write separately to note that this
case illustrates yet again the essential role of the courts in ensuring that
the arbitration system delivers not only speed and economy but also
fundamental fairness. . . .

. . . Although the comparison is not exact, it is instructive to compare
the "speed" of Kaiser's arbitration process to the speed of judicial proceedings in Alameda County Superior Court, where this action was filed.
During the 1993-94 fiscal year that court disposed of 96 percent of its
civil cases in less than 24 months. (Judicial Council of Cal., Annual
Data Reference (1993-94) Caseload Data by Individual Courts, Table
No. 22, p. 52.) . . .

Private arbitration may resolve disputes faster and cheaper than judicial
proceedings. Private arbitration, however, may also become an instrument
of injustice imposed on a "take it or leave it" basis. The courts must
distinguish the former from the latter, to ensure that private arbitration

systems resolve disputes not only with speed and economy but also with fairness.

BROWN, J. dissenting.

The intended target of the majority's wrath — the Permanente Medical Group, Inc., Kaiser Foundation Hospitals, and the Kaiser Foundation Health Plan (hereafter Kaiser) — could not be more deserving. I write separately to represent the interests of the unintended victim of the majority's holding — private arbitration in California. . . .

. . . Make no mistake about it. The majority's decision to validate a party's unilateral withdrawal from a pending arbitration based on the conduct of its arbitration adversary will wreak havoc on arbitrations throughout the state. . . .

Almost lost in the majority's exhaustive procedural summary is one key fact — namely, the arbitration process was already underway by the time the plaintiffs unilaterally withdrew. . . .

Although the majority's desire to penalize Kaiser's obduracy is understandable, the consequences of validating a party's unilateral withdrawal from a pending arbitration based on the conduct of its arbitration adversary will reverberate far beyond the bad facts of the instant case. . . .

The inclusiveness of the language of section 1281.6 belies the notion that it contains some sort of ill-defined exception for unreasonable or bad faith delay. By its own terms, the statute comes into play whenever "the agreed method [of appointing an arbitrator] fails or for any reason cannot be followed.". . . In this case, having previously submitted their dispute to private arbitration and having already completed the arbitrator selection process, the Engallas should have sought relief for Kaiser's dilatory conduct in the pending arbitration. For example, the Engallas could have presented their fraud and waiver claims directly to the arbitrators and requested that they not enforce the arbitration provision. . . .

The one thing the Engallas should not be permitted to do, however, is to circumvent the arbitrators altogether. The consequences of validating a party's unilateral withdrawal from a pending arbitration will be dramatic. Jurisdictional disputes will inevitably arise. Suppose, for example, that following the Engallas' unilateral withdrawal, Kaiser had elected to continue to pursue the pending arbitration and that the arbitrators had ultimately entered a default judgment in favor of Kaiser. Would that default judgment have been valid? Would the same have been true if the trial court had simultaneously entered a default judgment in favor of the Engallas in the pending litigation?. . .

However well-intentioned the majority and however deserving its intended target, today's holding pokes a hole in the barrier separating private arbitrations and the courts. Unfortunately, like any such breach, this hole will eventually cause the dam to burst. Ironically, the tool the majority uses to puncture its hole is the observation that " 'those who enter into arbitration agreements expect that their dispute will be resolved without necessity for any contact with the courts.' " Because I suspect that parties to private arbitrations will be having quite a bit more contact with the courts than they ever bargained for, I dissent.

NOTES AND PROBLEMS

1. What did *Engalla* hold?

a. That Kaiser could not use arbitration clauses in its health insurance contracts?

b. That Kaiser had to tell its clients how long an average arbitration actually took?

c. That Kaiser had to hire an administrator to run its arbitration programs efficiently?

d. That Kaiser had to abandon its three-person arbitration panels?

e. That Kaiser had to spend more money on its arbitration program, money that would be paid by its patients?

f. That a four-month delay in the start of arbitration is unreasonable?

2. The majority lays heavy emphasis on how long the arbitration proceeding took in the Engallas' case. Justice Kennard in concurrence compares judicial proceedings in at least one California county favorably with the arbitration in this case.

a. Might Kaiser have thought that it was — in this case if not in others — doing rather well? It began the arbitration about six months after the complaint was filed, putting this case in the top 3 percent of all cases filed with it and eighteen months before the equivalent case would have been resolved in Alameda County, according to Justice Kennard. Most state and federal courts would be quite pleased to have brought a case to trial in the same period. Note that the California Supreme Court decided the case six years after it was filed in state courts.

b. How long would the delay have to be before it became unreasonable? Is this delay unreasonable only because of Mr. Engalla's death and Kaiser's refusal to stipulate that his death would not prejudice the case? As a test of that question, do you suppose the court would have refused to compel arbitration if Mr. Engalla had been alive at the time of the decision?

3. In the wake of this decision Kaiser consults you. The organization, ashamed about the gap between its representations and the reality, nevertheless genuinely believes that arbitration presents the best possibilities

both for its patients and for the future of affordable health care. Tell Kaiser what it has to do to create a viable — enforceable — arbitration system.

a. If one focuses on fraud — the central basis for the holding — one might advise Kaiser simply to stop making such rosy representations about its system, to stop representing it as generally faster than the litigation system. Is that what Kaiser should do? If this is really a fraud case, changing the misleading representations will eliminate any fraud.

b. Should the majority have laid less emphasis on fraud and more on unconscionability, requiring an arbitration system to be reasonably efficient and fair, regardless of the representations made about it? Compare the decision in Hooters of America, Inc, v. Phillips, 67 173 F.3d 933 (4th Cir. 1999). Employer required employees to agree to arbitration rules that company would promulgate "from time to time." Employee brought federal claim for sexual harassment, and employer sought to compel arbitration. The Fourth Circuit refused to compel arbitration, ruling that the company's arbitration procedures were so "egregiously unfair as to constitute a complete default of its contractual obligation to draft arbitration rules and to do so in good faith." "[T]heir only possible purpose is to undermine the neutrality of the proceeding." The rules required the employee to give written notice of the claim but did not require a written response from the employer. They allowed the employer but not the employee to expand the scope of the arbitration beyond the original claim. The employer had total control over the list of approved arbitrators and was free to list persons with financial or personal relations with the employer. The employer was also free to change any of the rules on thirty days' notice, including changing them in the middle of an arbitration proceeding. Notice that this result could not have been reached based on the *Engalla* fraud approach, because the company in *Hooters* had made no representation about the fairness of the rules.

c. *Engalla* refers favorably at several points to the procedures of the American Arbitration Association, a private organization of arbitrators and one of the national standard-setters for arbitration. In the wake of *Engalla* the association passed a resolution asking its arbitrators to refrain from doing any medical malpractice arbitration. Does that suggest the association is less sure than the court that arbitrators could speedily and fairly decide such cases?

4. Suppose one admired the creativity and flexibility displayed in the Writers Guild arbitration procedure but was unhappy about the side of arbitration displayed in *Engalla*. How might one retain the strengths while minimizing the weaknesses of arbitration?

a. First, there is an institutional question: If this is a problem, is it one for courts or for legislatures?

b. That depends on how one describes the problem in *Engalla*. One can plausibly describe the problem in several ways. It could be that the disproportion in sophistication between the insurer and the patient made any agreement likely to be unfair. Under that view, a flat prohibition on arbitration in such settings — health insurance, employment, small consumer contracts — would be the "cure." Such disputes would have to go to court — period.

c. That approach might, however, risk losing both baby and bathwater. Another approach might be to allow arbitration but to set forth minimum procedural requirements for "fair" arbitration in contracts of adhesion, thus leaving sophisticated repeat players like the Writers' Guild to go their own unfettered way. What would such terms be? Would it be enough to say that such arbitration had to be timely, fair, and otherwise "reasonably adapted" to its goal, or should an "arbitration code" be much more detailed?

C. Curtailed Adjudication: Summary Judgment

Suppose that the client is open to settlement, but negotiations prove fruitless. Or the client wants something that only adjudication can deliver — for example, a binding public declaration of rights. Is trial inevitable? No. Curtailed adjudication — typically known as summary judgment — is an adjudicative alternative to trial for cases so one-sided that trial would be pointless. This section explores the possibilities and limits of summary adjudication.

Rule 56 governs the making and granting of motions for summary judgment. The key provision, in Rule 56(c), provides that such motions are to be granted when the record "show[s] that there is no genuine issue as to any material fact and that the moving party is entitled to judgment as a matter of law." That terse language means that summary judgment reaches both the legal and factual merits of the case. Consider how it does so.

NOTES AND PROBLEMS

1. Start with a simple case that reflects the historical origins of summary judgment. A plaintiff sues the defendant, alleging that the defendant executed a promissory note that is now due and unpaid.

a. The defendant files a Rule 12(b)(6) motion. That motion will be denied. Why?

b. Now explain why the denial of the Rule 12(b)(6) motion does not mean that the plaintiff will prevail at trial. What does a trial test that a 12(b)(6) motion does not?

2. Assume that in this case the defendant answers the complaint with a general denial.

a. Unlike a 12(b)(6) motion, a denial puts the facts of the case at issue.

b. Under the governing substantive law, only a few factual issues are relevant on this state of the pleadings: was the note actually signed by the defendant? has the defendant repaid the money owed under the note? (Note that other issues that might arise — the defendant's contention that the plaintiff had previously sued on this same note; her allegation that the parties had agreed to arbitrate their dispute or that the plaintiff had forged defendant's signature — are specified as affirmative defenses under Rule 8(c) and therefore cannot be raised by an answer that simply denies liability.)

c. If you were a plaintiff faced with a general denial in such a case, what information would you want to find out during discovery?

3. Assume that disclosure and discovery yield the note itself, whose validity the defendant does not contest, and the defendant's answer to an interrogatory in which she does not claim to have repaid the note.

a. If the parties go to trial, the plaintiff will presumably introduce the note, testify that the defendant signed it, further testify that the defendant has not paid the money owed under the note. At that point the plaintiff will rest his case. Unless the defendant changes her story from that revealed in the interrogatory answers, she has no defense, because she acknowledges having signed the note and does not claim to have repaid it. Accordingly, the plaintiff will prevail at trial, either because the trier of fact (judge or jury) returns a verdict or judgment in his favor, or, more likely, because the judge uses Rule 50 to order "judgment as a matter of law" — the equivalent of saying that the defendant has not presented a case that would permit a jury to decide in her favor.

b. Summary judgment is designed to prevent the futility of a trial under these circumstances. If the plaintiff properly moved for summary judgment on these facts, the court would grant it, entering judgment in the plaintiff's favor and obviating the necessity of a trial. The court would take this action because, in the hypothetical case, the plaintiff established all the elements of the claim beyond genuine dispute, or, in the language of Rule 56(c), "there is no genuine issue of material fact."

4. How would a plaintiff make such a motion? What would he have to present to the court?

a. Courts decide summary judgment motions on the basis of various documents (affidavits, deposition transcripts, copies of relevant documents). No witnesses testify in court, and no jury is present. Because some of the modes by which we assess witness credibility (cross-examination, demeanor) are absent, the law responds by trying to rule out any assessments of credibility.

b. One of the most common documents in summary judgment motions is an affidavit. An affidavit is a written document in which the *affiant* swears under penalty of perjury that the statements made are true. Typically, affidavits are drafted by lawyers who review them with the affiants, who then sign them.

5. Read Rule 56(e) and answer the following questions.

a. In the hypothetical case described above, recall that one of the issues was whether the defendant had signed the promissory note. Suppose the plaintiff's lawyer presented to the court an affidavit in which the lawyer swore, "Plaintiff told me he watched the defendant personally sign the promissory note." What's the problem?

b. Suppose the plaintiff signs an affidavit whose core statement is, "I know that defendant signed the promissory note." What's the problem?

c. Suppose the plaintiff's lawyer has learned from interviewing his client that the plaintiff watched the defendant sign the note. To support the contention that the defendant signed the note, what statements should plaintiff's affidavit contain?

d. Suppose that in a deposition of the defendant, she said, "I signed the note." Could the transcript (or audio- or videotape) of that deposition be presented instead of the plaintiff's affidavit? In addition to it?

6. Finally, consider what a defendant must present to avoid summary judgment. In our hypothetical case, assume that plaintiff has presented evidence sufficient to warrant a grant of summary judgment. That evidence includes an affidavit from the plaintiff stating that he watched the defendant sign the promissory note. The defendant tells her lawyer that she did not sign the note.

a. To defeat the motion for summary judgment, can she submit an affidavit saying, "I can prove I didn't sign the note"? Why not?

b. What should her affidavit say?

c. Notice a crucial point: If in opposition to a plaintiff's motion for summary judgment, the defendant submits an affidavit denying that she signed the note, the judge will deny the plaintiff's motion. That is true even if the plaintiff bolsters his own affidavit with the deposition in which the defendant admits signing the note, and affidavits of twenty-six disinterested witnesses, each of whom swears to watching the defendant sign the note. For the defendant to prevail in opposing the plaintiff's motion for summary judgment does *not* mean that defendant will prevail at trial. It simply means that there is something to have a trial about — here, about the defendant's credibility in denying that he signed the note and about the accuracy of perception and credibility of the witnesses contradicting the defendant.

7. Having cleared this preliminary ground, let us consider summary judgment in action. We do so in two cases. The first, Celotex Corp. v. Catrett, focuses on what the party moving for summary judgment must (in the absence of any opposition) do to justify a court's granting its motion. The second case, Visser v. Packer Engineering Associates, focuses on what a party opposing the motion must do to defeat it.

Before *Celotex*, the leading case on federal summary judgment was Adickes v. S.H. Kress & Co., 398 U.S. 144 (1970). *Adickes* grew out of a civil rights demonstration in which plaintiff, refused service at a racially segregated lunch counter, sued the restaurant owner. At the time, the federal public accommodations laws provided no damages remedy for private discrimination, and the liability of the business therefore depended on whether it had acted in concert with the local authorities, thereby fulfilling the state action requirement of 28 U.S.C. §1983. All agreed that there had been a police officer in the store at the time service was refused, but plaintiff produced no evidence showing communication between the officer and any store employee. The defendant submitted affidavits and deposition transcripts from the store manager and the police officer that they had not communicated with each other and that the manager had refused service because he was concerned about "a riot." The Supreme Court held that it was inappropriate to grant summary judgment because defendant "did not carry its burden [on summary judgment] because of its failure to foreclose the possibility that . . . this policeman reached an understanding with some Kress employee that petitioner not be served." 398 U.S. at 157. For *Adickes*, then, the defendant moving for summary judgment had the burden of showing that plaintiff could not prevail at trial. The *Celotex* case asserts that it does not overrule *Adickes*. Is that correct?

Celotex Corp. v. Catrett
477 U.S. 317 (1986)

REHNQUIST, J.

. . . Respondent commenced this lawsuit in September 1980, alleging that the death . . . of her husband . . . resulted from his exposure to products containing asbestos manufactured or distributed by 15 named corporations. . . . Petitioner's motion [for summary judgment] . . . argued that summary judgment was proper because respondent had "failed to produce evidence that any [Celotex] product . . . was the proximate cause of the injuries alleged. . . ." In particular, petitioner noted that respondent had failed to identify, in answering interrogatories specifically requesting such information, any witnesses who could testify about the decedent's exposure to petitioner's asbestos products. In response to petitioner's summary judgment motion, respondent then produced three documents which she claimed "demonstrate that there is a genuine material factual dispute" as to whether the decedent had ever been exposed to petitioner's asbestos products. The three documents included a transcript of a deposition of the decedent, a letter from an official of one of the decedent's former employers whom petitioner planned to call as a trial witness, and a letter from an insurance company to respondent's attorney, all tending to establish that the decedent had been exposed to petitioner's asbestos products in Chicago. . . .

. . . The District Court granted . . . the motion . . . because "there [was] no showing that the plaintiff was exposed to the defendant Celotex's product in the District of Columbia or elsewhere within the statutory period." [The court of appeals reversed.]

. . . In our view, the plain language of Rule 56(c) mandates the entry of summary judgment, after adequate time for discovery . . . against a party who fails to make a showing sufficient to establish the existence of an element essential to that party's case, and on which that party will bear the burden of proof at trial. In such a situation, there can be "no genuine issue as to any material fact," since a complete failure of proof concerning an essential element of the nonmoving party's case necessarily renders all other facts immaterial. The moving party is "entitled to judgment as a matter of law" because the nonmoving party has failed to make a sufficient showing on an essential element of her case with respect to which she has the burden of proof. "[The] standard [for granting summary judgment] mirrors the standard for a directed verdict under Federal Rule of Civil Procedure 50(a). . . ." Anderson v. Liberty Lobby, 477 U.S. 242, 250 (1986).

Of course, a party seeking summary judgment always bears the initial responsibility of informing the district court of the basis for its motion, and identifying those portions of "the pleadings, depositions, answers to interrogatories, and admissions on file, together with the affidavits, if any" which it believes demonstrate the absence of a genuine issue of material fact. But unlike the Court of Appeals, we find no express or implied requirement in Rule 56 that the moving party support its motions with affidavits or other similar materials *negating* the opponent's claim. On the contrary, Rule 56(c), which refers to "the affidavits, *if any*," (emphasis added), suggests the absence of such a requirement. . . . One of the principal purposes of the summary judgment rule is to isolate and dispose of factually unsupported claims or defenses, and we think it should be interpreted in a way that enables it to accomplish this purpose. . . .

We do not mean that the nonmoving party must produce evidence in a form that would be admissible at trial in order to avoid summary judgment. Obviously, Rule 56 does not require the nonmoving party to depose her own witness. Rule 56(e) permits a proper summary judgment motion to be opposed by any of the kinds of evidentiary materials listed in Rule 56(c), except the mere pleadings themselves. . . .

The Court of Appeals in this case felt itself constrained, however, by language in Adickes v. S. H. Kress & Co., 398 U.S. 144 (1970). There we held that summary judgment had been improperly entered in favor of the defendant. . . . *Adickes* . . . said . . . "both the commentary on and the background of the 1963 Amendment conclusively show that it was not intended to modify the burden of the moving party . . . to show initially the absence of a genuine issue concerning any material fact." We think that this statement is accurate in a literal sense. . . . But we do not think the *Adickes* language quoted above should be construed to mean that the burden is on the party moving for summary judgment to produce evidence showing the absence of a genuine issue of material fact, even with respect to an issue on which the nonmoving party bears the burden of proof. Instead, as we have explained, the burden on the moving party may be discharged by "showing" — that is, pointing out to the District Court — that there is an absence of evidence to support the nonmoving party's case. . . .

Respondent commenced this action in September 1980, and petitioner's motion was filed in September 1981. The parties had conducted discovery, and no serious claim can be made that the respondent was in any sense "railroaded" by a premature motion for summary judgment. . . .

In this Court, respondent's brief and oral argument have been devoted as much to the proposition that an adequate showing of exposure to petitioner's asbestos products was made as to the proposition that no such showing should have been required. But the Court of Appeals declined to address either. . . . We think the Court of Appeals . . . is better suited than we are to make these determinations in the first instance.

. . . Summary judgment procedure is properly regarded not as a disfavored procedural shortcut, but rather as an integral part of the Federal Rules as a whole, which are designed "to secure the just, speedy and inexpensive determination of every action." Fed. Rule Civ. Proc. 1. Before the shift to "notice pleading" accomplished by the Federal Rules, motions to dismiss a complaint or to strike a defense were the principal tools by which factually insufficient claims or defenses could be isolated and prevented from going to trial. . . . But with the advent of "notice pleading," the motion to dismiss seldom fulfills this function any more, and its place has been taken by the motion for summary judgment. . . .

[Reversed and remanded.]

Justice WHITE, concurring.

[I agree with the holding, but] the movant must discharge the burden the rules place upon him: It is not enough to move for summary judgment without supporting the motion in any way or with a conclusory allegation that the plaintiff has no evidence to prove his case. . . .

. . . Celotex does not dispute that if respondent has named a witness to support her claim, summary judgment should not be granted without Celotex['s] somehow showing that the named witness' possible testimony raises no genuine issue of material fact. . . .

Justice BRENNAN, with whom The CHIEF JUSTICE and Justice BLACK-MUN join, dissenting.

. . . I do not disagree with the Court's legal analysis [but believe the majority gives insufficient guidance to district courts. Moreover] I believe that Celotex did not meet its burden of production under Federal Rule of Civil Procedure 56. . . .

. . . If the burden of persuasion at trial would be on the *nonmoving* party, [the *moving*] party . . . may satisfy Rule 56's burden of production in either of two ways. First, the moving party may submit affirmative evidence that negates an essential element of the nonmoving party's claim. Second, the moving party may demonstrate to the Court that the nonmoving party's evidence is insufficient to establish an essential element of the nonmoving party's claim. . . .

Where the moving party adopts this second option . . . . a conclusory assertion that the nonmoving party has no evidence is insufficient. . . . Rather, as the Court confirms, a party who moves for summary judgment on the ground that the nonmoving party has no evidence must affirmatively show the absence of evidence in the record. This may require the moving party to depose the nonmoving party's witnesses or to establish the inadequacy of the documentary evidence. [Or] the moving party may demonstrate this by reviewing for the court the admissions, interrogatories and other exchanges between the parties that are in the record. Either way, however, the moving party must affirmatively demonstrate that there is no evidence in the record to support a judgment for the nonmoving party.

. . . [T]he nonmoving party may defeat a motion for summary judgment that asserts the nonmoving party has no evidence by calling the court's attention to supporting evidence in the record that was overlooked or ignored by the moving party. . . .

[Justice BRENNAN'S dissent was based on Celotex's failure to discharge its burden as he understood it; he pointed to the failure to deal with the testimony expected to be given by plaintiff's former supervisor. Justice Brennan stated that the supervisor could "describe asbestos products to which decedent had been exposed." Justice STEVENS'S dissent is omitted.]

NOTES AND PROBLEMS

1. What was the fight about in *Celotex*?

a. Everyone agreed that, to recover, Mrs. Catrett had to show that her husband had been exposed to asbestos manufactured by Celotex. (A subsidiary issue concerned the date of that exposure. Had it been within the statue of limitations?)

b. Everyone agreed that Celotex could defeat recovery by showing that Mr. Catrett had not been exposed to asbestos manufactured by it (or one of its predecessors).

c. So what were the parties disagreeing about?

2. *Celotex* becomes easier to understand if one bears in mind that summary judgment operates to eliminate trial. At trial Celotex, the defendant, could prevail in two ways. It could prove that Mr. Catrett was *not* exposed to its asbestos. Or it could prevail if Mrs. Catrett *failed to show* that Mr. Catrett *was* exposed to its asbestos.

a. Explain why these two routes lead to the same result.

b. As a matter of practice, which of these routes to the same result is likely to be more difficult for Celotex to demonstrate?

c. According to *Celotex*, the defendant Celotex can certainly win its summary judgment motion by making the first showing — that Mr. Catrett was not exposed to its product. That is no news: *Adickes* had said as much. Can Celotex also win with the second showing — that Mrs. Catrett has failed to show that Mr. Catrett *was* exposed? Explain how this development — whether or not it overrules *Adickes* — could affect the number of cases in which courts will grant summary judgment.

3. Did *Celotex* overrule *Adickes*? The strongest reading of *Adickes* has defendant, moving for summary judgment, lose his motion because he cannot prove that plaintiff will lose at trial. By contrast, *Celotex* says that defendant should win its motion for summary judgment if a survey of evidence shows that plaintiff could not — on the state of the present evidence — win at trial. What is the difference?

a. One answer is that *Celotex* looked at the state of the evidence at the time of summary judgment, while *Adickes* was prepared to speculate about what plaintiff might uncover between summary judgment and trial or what she might be able to achieve with direct and cross-examination at trial. Notice that such a standard will make it harder to get summary judgment, because it is always possible that a witness will change a story at trial.

b. Notice the implication of *Celotex's* focus on the state of evidence at summary judgment: It will not suffice for the party resisting summary judgment to say, "I'm planning to look into that before trial." Unless the party can show that it has had insufficient time for discovery, it will lose. How would a party that believed it had had insufficient opportunity for discovery ward off summary judgment? See Rule 56(f).

c. A strong way to state the proposition explored in this note is to say that *Celotex* made effective use of discovery not just one option for a party, but virtually mandatory. See Rule 56(f) and explain.

4. Notice the *Celotex* formulation: The party that will have the burden of proof at trial has the equivalent burden at summary judgment — the burden of "mak[ing] a showing" of evidence sufficient to let a rational trier of fact find in its favor. This alignment of burdens at summary judgment with burdens at trial means that the standard for summary judgment will apply differently depending on which party is moving for summary judgment. To see this point, suppose that one of the issues in contention is whether asbestosis (as opposed to some other disease process) caused Mr. Catrett's death. Mrs. Catrett's complaint alleges that asbestosis caused her husband's death; Celotex denies that allegation in its answer. Mrs. Catrett as the plaintiff will have the burden of proof at trial on that issue.

a. First suppose that Celotex, the defendant, moves for summary judgment on this issue of causation. In its supporting papers, it reviews all the discovery documents (including experts' reports) and points out that no medically qualified expert has opined that asbestosis caused Mr. Catrett's death. In her response, Mrs. Catrett produces the affidavit of a pathologist who recites his professional qualifications, examination of the relevant tissue samples, and comes to the conclusion that the laboratory findings are "consistent with Mr. Catrett's having died as a result of asbestosis." Explain why the court should deny Celotex's motion for summary judgment.

b. Now suppose that it is Mrs. Catrett, not Celotex, who moves for summary judgment on the issue of causation. In support of this motion she produces the same affidavit. In response, Celotex produces no affidavit or other evidence contradicting plaintiff's expert. Explain why the court should deny Mrs. Catrett's motion for summary judgment.

c. Why does the same affidavit lead to different results in the two situations?

5. The Court in *Celotex* did not actually decide who should prevail on the defendant's motion for summary judgment. It contented itself instead with setting out a new standard for summary judgment and remanding for the lower courts to decide the case using that new standard. Suppose that Celotex had made an adequate initial showing under that new standard to justify the grant of summary judgment — unless plaintiff in response produced evidence that would entitle a rational trier of fact to find in its favor. Such a situation would frame a question for the lower court: Did the material presented by Mrs. Catrett in response to the motion for summary judgment suffice? That topic is the focus of the next case.

As a bridge to that case, imagine several possibilities. The key piece of evidence was a letter to which both the dissent and majority refer — a letter written by a Mr. Hoff, an executive for a company that had once employed Mr. Catrett. The issue, you recall, is whether Mr. Catrett was exposed to a Celotex asbestos product.

a. Suppose the letter said, "I bought asbestos from Celotex and gave it to Catrett for use on the job." Sufficient to avoid summary judgment? The underlying factual assertion clearly would be. But recall that the letter is not an affidavit — that is, it is not a sworn statement. Will the sufficiency of the letter turn on whether it would be admissible as evidence, as specified in Rule 56(e)?

b. Suppose the letter said, "I don't know what asbestos products Catrett used while employed here, but I think our records will contain that information." Sufficient to avoid summary judgment?

c. What if the letter said, "I wasn't in direct contact with this part of the operation, but I understand that Catrett used Celotex products." Sufficient to avoid summary judgment?

d. The next case assumes that the defendant's initial showing is sufficient to warrant summary judgment unless the plaintiff rebuts that showing and focuses on the adequacy of the plaintiff's response.

Visser v. Packer Engineering Associates
924 F.2d 655 (7th Cir. 1991) (en banc)

POSNER, J.

The Age Discrimination in Employment Act, 29 U.S.C. §§621 et seq., is a major source of federal litigation and a growing factor in American labor markets. The question of what a plaintiff in an age discrimination case must show in order to defeat the defendant's motion for summary judgment is fundamental to the administration of the Act, and hence is of large practical importance.

The district judge granted summary judgment to the defendant in this case, so we must construe the facts as favorably to the plaintiff, Philip Visser, as the record will permit. Dr. Kenneth Packer, founder, chief executive officer, and dominant personality of the defendant, Packer Engineering Associates, Inc., a consulting firm, hired Visser in 1981 as an officer of the firm, and soon afterward Visser also became a member of the firm's board of directors. Visser was 57 years old when he was hired. Years later a bitter dispute erupted within the board over Kenneth Packer's conduct. A dissident group of board members, including Visser, believed that Packer was siphoning money from the firm into his pocket and that of another company that he dominated. Visser threatened to bring a stockholder derivative suit against Packer (and eventually carried out his threat). Matters came to a head on October 1, 1987, when an anonymous memorandum that Visser admitted at his deposition having coauthored was circulated to employees of the firm, attacking Packer's leadership. The same day, the board of directors voted Visser and two other dissident members of the board out of office. The dissidents remained employees of the firm for the time being. But two and a half weeks later a group of them, not including Visser, quit to form their own competing consulting firm — which they had secretly incorporated while employed by Packer Engineering — and took with them valuable clients. The following day Kenneth Packer summoned Visser, who was not among those who had quit, to Packer's office and asked Visser to pledge his unqualified loyalty to him, Kenneth Packer. Visser refused and instead told Packer that he was unwilling to take "any further abuse" from him and demanded an apology for previous abuse. Packer fired Visser on the spot, and shortly afterward Visser joined the breakaway firm. Visser was 64 years old when he was fired — nine months short of the full vesting of his Packer Engineering pension. As a result he lost almost two-thirds of his pension benefits.

In the district court, as in this court, Visser's lawyer emphasized the impropriety of Kenneth Packer's conduct under the norms of corporation law. Packer Engineering is a corporation. It is not the personal fiefdom of Kenneth Packer. He had no right to ask Visser to pledge personal loyalty to him, as distinct from the firm. Insofar as Packer was siphoning funds from the firm, loyalty to him would have been, on Visser's part, disloyalty to his employer. He was wrongfully fired.

This may well be if the facts are as just recited, as we must assume they are because the case was decided on summary judgment. But the age discrimination law does not protect an older employee from being fired without good cause. It protects him from being fired because of his age. If the employer offers a pretext — a phony reason – for why it fired the employee, then the trier of fact is permitted, although not compelled, to infer that the real reason was age. This is just the test of McDonnell Douglas Corp. v. Green, 411 U. S. 792 (1973), transposed to the age discrimination setting. But there is no indication of pretext here. Packer fired Visser because Visser was disloyal to him. Visser concedes as much. His reply brief says that "Kenneth Packer terminated Visser because Visser was disloyal to *him* not to the corporation or its shareholders" (emphasis in original); "he was fired for his loyalty to the corporation."

Visser does not understand the meaning of "pretext" in the law of discrimination. He says "the accusation of disloyalty was an ill founded pretext, and meant only that Visser opposed illegitimate action of Kenneth Packer." A pretext, in employment law, is a reason that the employer offers for the action claimed to be discriminatory and that the court disbelieves, allowing an inference that the employer is trying to conceal a discriminatory reason for his action. It is not, as the quotation demonstrates that Visser believes, an unethical reason for action, or a mask for such a reason. If Kenneth Packer really fired Visser because Visser protested against Packer's highhanded behavior, or because Visser was a whistleblower, or because Visser's primary loyalty was, as it should have been, to Packer Engineering rather than to the person of Kenneth Packer (these are closely related points, of course), this may show that Packer is a bad man. It does not show or even tend to show that Visser was fired because of his age. It tends if anything to show the opposite, because if Visser was fired because of his disloyalty to Packer the natural though not inevitable inference is that he was not fired because of his age. Certainly his age had nothing to do with the direction of his loyalties.

But we must consider the possibility that there was more than one reason for Visser's discharge. After all, he was within months of the full vesting of his pension. One reason for firing an older employee might be to economize on the employer's pension costs. . . .

Granted, the mere existence of mixed motives — one permissible, one forbidden — is not enough to establish liability. The forbidden motive, age in this case, must be a sufficient condition, or but-for cause, of the employee's termination. . . .

So we must consider whether Visser's age may have been a substantial factor, along with his disloyalty to Kenneth Packer, in Packer's decision to fire him. There is not an iota of evidence that Visser's age per se was a substantial, or any, factor in this decision — no evidence for example that Packer is contemptuous of the ability of 64-year-olds. (Packer himself was 63 when he fired Visser, though he might of course exempt himself from infirmities that he believed afflict the rest of his age group.). . .
[T]here is no evidence that the opportunity to shave off two-thirds of

Visser's pension benefits influenced Packer's decision to fire Visser in the slightest. The proverbial "smoking gun" is not required, but there is no circumstantial evidence, either, that pension costs played a role in the decision to fire Visser. Packer did not mention such costs. And the timing of the firing is not suspicious. Its occurrence on October 20 was precipitated by the events of October 1 and October 19 rather than by the looming date of full vesting of Visser's pension. It is true that as chief executive officer and a former trustee of the pension fund Packer almost certainly knew that Visser was near to full vesting; and so we shall assume. But a trier of fact may not infer action from knowledge alone. Otherwise every worker who lost his job within months, or perhaps years, before the full vesting of his pension would have a prima facie case of age discrimination. . . . The only evidence of age discrimination is — what we have just said is not enough — Packer's knowledge of Visser's age and pension rights.

Except for the affidavits. Three of the other dissident employees of Packer Engineering filed affidavits in the district court which state that Packer fired Visser because of his age. The self-serving character of such affidavits requires no comment. But that is not in itself a ground for refusing to consider them. Nor the fact that the affidavits use almost identical words and obviously were drafted by a lawyer. Nor that the bulk of each affidavit is given over to arguing that Kenneth Packer is indeed a vengeful, vindictive man and Visser an angel. The proper ground for excluding the affidavits is that witnesses who are not expert witnesses — and these affiants were not — are permitted to testify only from their personal knowledge. Testimony about matters outside their personal knowledge is not admissible, and if not admissible at trial neither is it admissible in an affidavit used to support or resist the grant of summary judgment. Fed. R. Civ. P. 56(e). In fact Rule 56(e) incorporates evidence rule 602 in words as well as by reference, by stating that "supporting and opposing affidavits shall be made on personal knowledge." It is true that "personal knowledge" includes inferences — all knowledge is inferential — and therefore opinions. But the inferences and opinions must be grounded in observation or other firsthand personal experience. They must not be flights of fancy, speculations, hunches, intuitions, or rumors about matters remote from that experience.

The affiants say Packer knew Visser's pension situation. So far, so good. They were high-level employees of Packer Engineering. They worked closely with Packer. They should have known the extent of his knowledge concerning personnel matters at their level. But the affidavits go on to state, largely in the identical words, that Packer's motive in firing Visser, in part anyway, was to deprive Visser of his pension rights. Here is how one of the affidavits puts it: "When the three former board members resigned from Packer Engineering, Kenneth Packer needed to hurt some-one immediately. That reaction has frequently been observed by affiant. He [Packer] couldn't immediately hurt the departed so he chose to hurt Visser by depriving him of his cherished goal of a full pension. Kenneth Packer knew Visser's age, knew exactly what he was doing and acted consistent with his pattern of activity in years past. Visser's age was a significant factor in the decision." This part of the affidavits is amateur psychoanalysis. The affiants do not report admissions by Packer about his motives in firing Visser. They do not report primary facts from which a reasonable person in their position would infer that one of Packer's motives was to deprive Visser of most of his pension. They construct a psychological model of Packer and deduce from it that he must have wanted to do Visser out of a pension. He was that kind of guy. This is the kind of argumentation one expects in a closing argument. It is doubtful that a psychiatrist or psychologist would be allowed to offer it as expert testimony — it comes awfully close to arguing bad conduct from bad character, contrary to Fed. R. Evid. 404(a). It certainly exceeds the compe-tence of a lay witness.

. . . Since there was no evidence that age or pension costs played a substantial, or indeed any, factor in the firing of Visser, the district judge was right to grant summary judgment. We need not consider in what circumstances it is proper to grant summary judgment in favor of a party having the burden of persuasion. Certainly there are such cases. This might have turned into such a case if we had concluded that the plaintiff, by showing that age was a substantial factor in his termination, had succeeded in placing on the defendant the burden of persuading the trier of fact that the plaintiff would have been fired regardless. For the plaintiff has done such a good job in his brief and deposition and affidavits of painting Kenneth Packer as a monster of vengefulness as to leave little room for conjecture that Packer would have retained this "disloyal" employee even if he had been a stripling of 29, the age of his replacement. But this we need not decide. Before Visser could shift the burden of persuasion on causation to the defendant he had to show that a reasonable jury could find that age, or (we are assuming) a factor correlated with age, such as concern with the expense of a pension, was a substantial factor in Kenneth Packer's decision to fire Visser. He failed to show this.

Caution is required in granting summary judgment, especially under a statute that allows for trial by jury, as the age discrimination law does. But if no rational jury could, on the evidence presented in the summary judgment proceeding, bring in a verdict for the party opposing summary judgment — if in other words the movant would be entitled to judgment notwithstanding the verdict if the case did go to trial before a jury and he lost — then summary judgment must be granted. We are persuaded that this is such a case.

Affirmed.

FLAUM, Circuit Judge, with whom BAUER, Chief Judge, and CUDAHY, Circuit Judge, join, dissenting.

The majority concludes that "there was no evidence that age or pension costs played a substantial, or indeed any, factor" in Kenneth Packer's decision to fire Philip Visser. Because I disagree with this view of the facts before us, and with the substantive law and procedural standards this view of Visser's case leads the majority to apply, I respectfully dissent.

Unlike those who bring suit under other employment discrimination statutes, age discrimination plaintiffs enjoy the right "to a trial by jury of any issue of fact" pertinent to the statutory violation they allege. 29 U.S.C. §626(c)(2). While we apply the substantive law developed under Title VII in ADEA cases, the application of that body of law is unmistakably influenced by the difference in the parties' litigation strategy created by the availability of a jury trial in ADEA cases, but not Title VII cases. Put simply, employers and their counsel may well conclude that ADEA cases are won or lost on summary judgment, because jurors find it difficult to close their hearts to the plight of the terminated older employee but easy to open the purse strings of his employer. . . .

. . . At the summary judgment stage, an employer can prevail . . . only if the record evidence that its employment decision was not based on discrimination is so strong that a reasonable trier of fact must so conclude; in other words, there must be no genuine issue of material fact but that the employer would have made the same employment decision even absent the discriminatory motive. . . .

I am compelled to disagree with the majority's conclusion that this is one of those rare cases. . . . Visser was 64 when he was fired a few months before his pension benefits would vest. As three of his coworkers affirmed, Kenneth Packer knew that firing Visser would save the company he founded and managed the not inconsiderable expense of paying the better part of Visser's pension, a factor this court has in the past considered in assessing the strength of an ADEA claim.[2] Visser was replaced by a

---

2. The majority disparages these affidavits because their ultimate conclusion lies outside the personal knowledge of the affiants. This ignores other information contained in the affidavits as to which the three affiants did have personal knowledge. Specifically, the affidavits raised factual questions about the extent of Visser's role in the conflicts between Kenneth Packer and others that roiled Packer Engineering in the period shortly before Visser's termination. This information casts doubt on the sincerity of Kenneth Packer's concerns about Visser's loyalty. Even more helpful to Visser are the affiants' statements that Visser predicted over three months before he was fired that Kenneth Packer would find some way to deprive Visser of his pension benefits.

worker too young to be included in the class of those protected by ADEA, see 29 U.S.C. §631(a), something other courts have looked to in determining whether an ADEA plaintiff has established that the illegitimate consideration of age played a part in a termination decision. I regard this evidence, taken together and examined as befits the procedural posture of this case, to be sufficient to establish a prima facie case of employment discrimination. . . .

BAUER, Chief Judge, dissenting.

I join Judge Flaum's dissent. I confess, however, that I found great merit in the majority opinion. My dissent is really occasioned by my conviction that summary judgment is too rapid a disposition in this case, that sufficient factual questions remain that belong to a jury. And when these factual questions unfold in the trial setting there always remains a right in the court to correct or prevent a verdict that is founded, not on the law and facts, but on sympathy and prejudice. I think we have denied the plaintiff in this case a basic right of all mankind: the right to rise at least to the height of failing.

CUDAHY, Circuit Judge, dissenting.

I join fully in Judge Flaum's persuasive dissenting opinion. We should be exceedingly cautious in holding that the irascible temperament and apparently unwarranted demands for "loyalty" of a corporate executive may insulate his corporation against age discrimination charges otherwise supported by probative circumstantial evidence (and employee affidavits).

A mean personality should not provide an impregnable shield against claims that are objectively plausible. Apparently Packer would be easier to convict of age discrimination if he were a kindly and forgiving soul with a short memory.

I respectfully dissent.

NOTES AND PROBLEMS

1. Start by using the facts as a review of *Celotex*. The opinion does not tell us what Packer's lawyer submitted in support of his motion for summary judgment. We can assume it contained an affidavit from Packer himself, swearing that he did not fire Visser on account of his age. According to *Celotex*, what other evidentiary showing would the defendant need to make?

2. The opinion focuses on the adequacy of plaintiff's response to the motion. Plaintiff, to avoid summary judgment, needs to point to admissible evidence that would allow a rational jury to conclude that Packer

fired Visser on account of his age. Consider various items that Visser might have presented in opposition to Packer's motion, along with the material he actually did present.

a. Suppose Visser presented an affidavit from an employee in the payroll department who heard Packer say, in ordering that Visser's termination papers be prepared, "That guy will never get his pension." Packer's overheard statement would be admissible under one of the exceptions to the hearsay rule; would the statement suffice to avoid summary judgment?

b. Suppose that two weeks before the firing, Packer convened a meeting of the people responsible for employee benefits (which include pensions) and stated, "We have to cut back on benefit costs here." Sufficient?

c. Suppose that two weeks before the firing, Packer inquired of the benefits administrator how close to vesting his pension rights Visser was.

d. Finally, consider the three affidavits, each stating that Packer fired Visser because of his age. If they were admissible, would they be sufficient? Why did the majority opinion disregard them?

e. Can one make an argument that, even disregarding the three affidavits, there is sufficient evidence from which a jury might conclude that there was age discrimination?

3. After *Celotex* one must face the question of how much (or, perhaps how little) evidence would support a jury verdict. The author of the majority opinion in *Visser* put the matter rather bluntly in another case:

> There is latent in this discussion a further tension, however: between the orthodox view that treats the issue on summary judgment as whether the moving party would be entitled to a directed verdict if the proceeding were a trial rather than a summary judgment proceeding, and the "realist" view that treats the issue on summary judgment as whether the nonmovant has a prayer of winning at trial. . . . The issue is not whether a jury composed of experts in perceptual psychology, presided over by a judge equally expert in the field, could find for the plaintiff in the absence of evidence in the usual sense. The issue is whether a normal jury could so find. It could not.

Krist v. Eli Lilly & Co., 897 F. 2d 293, 299 (7th Cir. 1990). Is the *Visser* majority taking the "orthodox" or the "realist" stance? Does the "realist" stance turn the summary judgment motion into a quick trial without live witnesses?

D. Judicial Management of Litigation

This chapter has thus far explored two quite different ways in which litigation might end. On the one hand, the parties might employ the flexibility of a nonadjudicative resolution; on the other hand they might use the much more formal apparatus of adjudication. Procedural rules seem designed to force a choice between these two paths by building procedural walls around the arena of dispute, letting the parties leave only through two doors, one marked "Adjudication," the other marked "Settlement." These rules force the parties to engage each other in an effort to herd them toward some resolution of the dispute. These rules do not, however, dictate any particular pace of litigation, nor do they express a preference for one of the two exit doors.

Recently, courts and legislatures have sought to speed the parties' choice of one of the doors and to suggest which door they should use. The aim of such efforts is to save time and judicial effort, thus bringing litigation to a quicker (and cheaper) end and reducing the waiting time for other cases. Such efforts go by several names: "managerial judging."* "fast-track adjudication,"** and others.

1.   "Managing" Litigation

An elaborate set of studies commissioned by the Congress has found that early judicial management reduced time to disposition but increased litigation cost: Faster but more expensive litigation resulted from judicial management.† According to the cited studies, the single management technique that consistently speeded litigation (though it increased costs) was setting an early date for trial; other techniques yielded the worst of both worlds, increasing cost without speeding disposition. Many judges wishing to establish such deadlines divide cases into categories: simple cases with an early trial date, cases of "ordinary" complexity with a mid-range trial date, and complex cases with a more distant trial date. Linked to trial dates would be other deadlines: for joinder and dismissal motions, for disclosure and discovery cut-off, for pretrial conferences, accordingly. The underlying assumption is that the setting of firm trial dates will prevent counsel (and judges) from procrastinating; deviations from schedules have to be justified. Effective though they may be at speeding disposition, such schedules can yield stark results in the hands of a judge determined to enforce them.

---

* Judith Resnik, Managerial Judges, 96 Harv. L. Rev. 374 (1986).
** Calif. Gov. Code §6816 (West 1976).
† James Kakalik et al., Just, Speedy and Inexpensive? An Evaluation of Judicial Case Management Under the Civil Justice Reform Act (Rand Institute for Civil Justice 1996).

Sanders v. Union Pacific Railroad Co.

154 F. 3d 1037 (9th Cir. 1998)

PER CURIAM.

Phillip Sanders appeals the district court's dismissal of his action with prejudice for failure to comply with the court's pretrial preparation order. . . . Finding no abuse of discretion by the district court, we affirm.

Background

In June 1995, Sanders sued his employer, Union Pacific Railroad Co., under the Federal Employer's Liability Act, following a work-related back injury. The district judge set a trial date of November 19, 1996. He also scheduled a pretrial conference for November 8, 1996, and issued a form order concerning preparation for that conference. The order set forth a schedule for the filing of various motions, oppositions, proposed instructions, and other trial-related documents. The order's introduction warned the parties that a failure to comply could result in sanctions. The order repeated this admonition in its final paragraph, which stated in bold letters:

> **Sanctions. Counsel are advised that failure to comply with the procedures set forth in this order, including the duty to provide the court with updated documents as necessary, may result in sanctions, including but not limited to monetary sanctions, adverse evidentiary rulings, trial continuance, and dismissal of the action.**

Several of the items required by the order, such as the proposed pretrial order, stipulated instructions, and list of stipulated exhibits, called for joint preparation. . . . Sanders's counsel failed to comply with almost all of the requirements of the pretrial order.

The district court's order required motions in limine to be filed twenty-one days before trial. Union Pacific filed eleven motions in limine on time; Sanders's counsel filed one motion in limine six days late. The order required the parties to meet and confer regarding jury instructions, and to submit joint instructions fourteen days before trial. Sanders's counsel did not meet and confer, and submitted about fifty unilateral jury instructions. He submitted his exhibit, witness and expert witness lists two days late. The order required counsel to submit a trial brief fourteen days before trial; Sanders's counsel never submitted a trial brief. The order required joint preparation of a trial notebook, to be submitted fourteen days prior to trial; Sanders's counsel never conferred on the trial notebook and offered to submit a unilateral one only at the pretrial conference. Sanders's counsel never submitted oppositions to Union Pacific's motions in limine, which were due fourteen days before trial. At no time prior to the pretrial conference did Sanders's counsel request a continuance.

Judge Ideman's law clerk presided over the pretrial conference, without any objection by Sanders. Sanders's counsel explained during the conference that he had been representing plaintiffs in a lawsuit in Nebraska involving a multiple-death train collision. His responsibilities in that other matter had lasted longer than he could have anticipated, and he therefore was unable to meet the pretrial order's deadlines. He further asserted that Union Pacific's attorneys were partially responsible for his failure to comply with the order because they had been uncooperative with him. Sanders's counsel made it clear that he was not ready to go to trial; he had further work to do on the case. He suggested a dismissal without prejudice; Union Pacific declined to agree to one. At the conclusion of the pretrial hearing, the presiding law clerk indicated that the case would be removed from the trial calendar, and that the judge would probably take additional action.

About a week after the pretrial conference, the district court dismissed Sanders's action with prejudice as a sanction for failure to comply with the pretrial order. . . . He levied the sanction . . . because (1) Sanders's counsel had completely failed to comply with the pretrial order, (2) Union Pacific had already incurred "great pain and expense in preparing for trial," (3) other litigants before the district court would be inconvenienced by a delay in the present case, and (4) Sanders's case did not involve important questions of public policy. . . .

Discussion

Before dismissing a case for failure to comply with a court order, . . . the key factors are prejudice and availability of lesser sanctions." Wanderer v. Johnston, 910 F.2d 652, 656 (9th Cir. 1990). . . .

In the present case, by the time of the pretrial conference, Sanders's . . . multiple failures undoubtedly impaired the defendant's efforts to prepare for trial.

. . . By neglecting to alert the court or opposing counsel to his impending total failure to meet pretrial and trial deadlines, Sanders's counsel deprived the court of its best opportunity to impose lesser sanctions to force the litigation back onto track or to make timely alternative arrangements. Counsel's conduct left the court only with last-minute notice of a total failure of preparation, with a consequent disruption of the trial calendar. In these circumstances, we conclude that the district court did not abuse its discretion in rejecting lesser sanctions than dismissal. Trial judges are constantly struggling to avoid the increasing problems of delay and expense that threaten to overwhelm the courts. In our continuing efforts to achieve justice for individual litigants, we must not allow the flagrant disobedience of judges' orders to bring about further delay and expense. . . .

Sanders contends that the district court violated the Due Process Clause because it failed to notify him that a dismissal was imminent. In Link v. Wabash Railroad Co., however, the Supreme Court suggested that Rule 41(b) was itself sufficient notice of a district court's authority to dismiss a case under the appropriate circumstances. 370 U. S. 626-30 (1962). Moreover, in the present case, the court's order expressly advised Sanders that the court would consider dismissal as a sanction for failure to comply. . . . Sanders also argues that he did not receive an adequate hearing prior to the dismissal. But "a District Court may dismiss a complaint for failure to prosecute even without affording notice of its intention to do so or providing an adversary hearing before acting." Id. at 633. . . .

CANBY, Senior Circuit Judge, dissenting:

The position of the majority is understandable; district courts must be able to manage their dockets, and conduct such as that of Sanders' counsel cannot be tolerated. Dismissal, however, "is so harsh a penalty it should be imposed as a sanction only in extreme circumstances." Thompson v. Housing Authority, 782 F.2d 829, 831 (9th Cir. 1986). Although Sanders's counsel was guilty of multiple failures, they all occurred at once as part of his general failure to be ready for the pretrial conference and trial. This is not a case where the court was met with repeated instances of dilatory behavior over a span of time, nor has the litigation been inordinately delayed. In these circumstances, I believe that dismissal with prejudice was an abuse of discretion.

The dismissal was entered by the court sua sponte, which means that counsel should have been warned that a dismissal was imminent. A boilerplate warning in a preprinted order, distributed before any problem has arisen, does not advise counsel that dismissal is imminent. . . .

I would . . . reverse and remand for the imposition of other sanctions.

NOTES AND PROBLEMS

1. What was the district court's authority for the original scheduling order whose violation led to dismissal? See Rule 16(b).

2. Sanders sought an en banc rehearing by the Ninth Circuit. The en banc panel reversed the district court with terse explanation:

We decline to dissect what happened in this case and to prescribe a recipe for how and when an action may be dismissed, with or without prejudice, for failure to follow the pretrial rules. This is a unique case. Suffice it to say that where, as here, the district judge allows his law clerk to conduct the final pretrial conference, declines to give counsel an opportunity to be heard before the court, and then dismisses the action sua sponte with prejudice, we cannot let the dismissal stand.

Counsel was plainly derelict in meeting his Rule 16 obligations, but so was the district judge. In different circumstances, where the district court exercises its own discretion in a deliberate, informed and reasonable way, we would accord it considerable deference. But we cannot see how any deference is warranted in these circumstances.

Accordingly, we vacate all orders entered after the pretrial conference and remand for another district judge to consider afresh how to proceed. In so doing, we express no opinion about how the new judge's discretion should be exercised. Rather, we simply put the parties back to square one.

Sanders v. Union Pacific Railroad Co., 1999 U.S. App. Lexis 26831 (9th Cir. 1999)(en banc).

a. You are the district judge to whom the case has been newly assigned. What do you do? Can you dismiss the case, as the first judge did? Can you decide to ignore the behavior of plaintiff's lawyer and set the case for trial?

b. Who's right, the original panel or the en banc?

3. To answer the preceding question, take the case and the problem it presents in stages.

a. Begin at the point that plaintiff's lawyer saw that his Nebraska case would take longer than he had anticipated and prevent this meeting the pretrial order deadlines. What should he have done?

b. Suppose that, before any deadlines had passed, plaintiff's lawyer approached the other side and explained his problem. In the ensuing conversation the opposing lawyer tells plaintiff's lawyer that she's been working late into every night and all weekend for several weeks to comply with the deadline, and isn't inclined to stipulate to an extension just because plaintiff's lawyer took on more work than he could handle. What should plaintiff's lawyer do now?

c. Besides irritation at having worked hard to meet a deadline the other side ignored, defendant's lawyer has an argument about unfairness. Most lawyers will tell you that there's an enormous difference between simultaneous exchange of information — briefs, witness and exhibit lists, etc. — and having the luxury of being able to prepare your documents after you have already seen the other side's. Had the trial court not dismissed, plaintiff's lawyer's delay would have enabled him to prepare his trial brief after seeing the defendant's, to choose his witnesses after seeing whom the defendant was planning to introduce, and so on. Had plaintiff's lawyer moved for an extension of time, the defendant's lawyer could have averted this unfairness by withholding her materials until plaintiff had prepared his.

4. Now consider the consequences for plaintiff and his lawyer.

a. Suppose the original opinion — dismissing the case — had stood. Imagine a meeting between the plaintiff, Mr. Sanders, and his lawyer after this case. What should the lawyer tell him?

b. Further suppose that after the dismissal Mr. Sanders consulted another lawyer. What should that lawyer tell him?

5. Many lawyers think that the federal court system operates somewhat more formally, with tighter deadlines, than do state courts, though there are very wide variations among individual judges in both systems.

a. One consequence is that in many state courts it takes longer to bring a case to trial than it does in federal courts. Does that justify the harshness of an occasional case like *Sanders*?

b. Was the real failure of "due process" in *Sanders* the judge's failure to warn Sanders's lawyer (supposing he didn't already know it) that he was entering a different zone of "legal culture" than the one he was used to? Does a judge have an obligation to let lawyers know that he or she really means it when a deadline is imposed?

2.   Managing Litigation Bound for Trial: The Pretrial Order

Pretrial orders like those in *Sanders* will end some litigation, but their overt aim is different — to prepare parties for the actual trial by encouraging both a winnowing of legal theories and factual disputes and a precise identification of questions to be contested at trial. Note that practices vary among judges using the pretrial conference in this way. Some courts require parties to submit elaborate pretrial statements defining the issues and proof and specifying the admitted and disputed facts. Others conduct a number of conferences throughout the progress of the case. The hope is that such conferences will both reduce the time required for trial and enhance the eventual quality of the trial. The leading study of pretrial in negligence cases* found that only half of these hopes were realized. It concluded that trial time of pretrial cases was not reduced when the time spent in pretrial was taken into account (and that the chances for settlement were not enhanced) but that the quality of trials was improved in terms of party preparation and effective presentation.

When the pretrial conference serves this latter function, one major

---

*Maurice Rosenberg, The Pretrial Conference and Effective Justice (1964).

issue is the precise scope of pretrial and, particularly, of the pretrial order. Appellate courts, on occasion, have cautioned judges both against turning the pretrial order into a common law pleading in disguise and against overzealous attempts to encourage admissions on disputed issues. The most commonly litigated issue involves a situation in which the pretrial order specifies that certain issues will be tried, certain witnesses will testify, or certain evidentiary items will be introduced, and one party then seeks to raise matters or present evidence not within the scope of the order.

McKey v. Fairbairn

345 F. 2d 739 (D. C. Cir. 1965)

MILLER, J.

By a written contract, Levi McKey rented a dwelling house from Kenneth Fairbairn, agent for Euphemia L. Haynes, on a month-to-month basis beginning January 17, 1958. Agnes Littlejohn, McKey's mother-in-law, occupied a bedroom and other space on the second floor.

On February 20, 1958, apparently as a result of a snow storm, moisture on an area "about twice the size of a pie" was noticed on a wall of Mrs. Littlejohn's bedroom. There was no moisture on the floor. This condition was reported to the appellees and within a week their representative inspected the premises, discovered the dampness on the wall of Mrs. Littlejohn's room, but found no leak in the roof. He agreed to eliminate the cause of the dampness. On the night of February 26, 1958, an all-night rain fell, as a result of which the roof developed a leak and the floor of Mrs. Littlejohn's bedroom became wet. Upon arising the next morning and discovering the floor's condition,[1] Mrs. Littlejohn went over it twice with a mop. Having left the room for a short time, she returned to awaken her grandson, who was sleeping there, and to get her coat. She slipped on the wet floor and fell, sustaining certain injuries.

On April 24, 1959, Mrs. Littlejohn brought this suit to recover damages from the owner of the house and her agent. In her complaint, she alleged that the floor on which she slipped and fell

> was wet and dangerous due to a leaking roof which the defendants, or either of them, knew or should have known in time to have repaired said damage; that actually defendants, or either of them, had notice of said defect by February 20, 1958, and that previously there had been difficulty and trouble with the roof.

---

1. It was not a puddle, she said, and was not actually running water. She merely said, "It was wet."

Mrs. Littlejohn died May 27, 1960, from causes unrelated to the fall, and Helen McKey, her administratrix, was substituted as plaintiff.

The statement of the pretrial proceedings filed March 12, 1963, contains the following:

Plaintiff asserts that on February 27, 1958, Agnes Littlejohn slipped and fell on the wet floor in her second floor bedroom on premises 814 Constitution Avenue, N. E.; that the wet floor was caused by a leaking roof and wall; that her fall and resulting injuries and damages were caused by the following negligence of D: Failure to repair roof and eliminate dangerous condition of roof and walls allowing entry of water, after notice thereof and promise by the Ds to make such repairs, in breach of duty owed under the lease.

During the progress of the trial, the District Judge asked appellant's counsel this question:

Do you agree that the allegation of negligence in this case is as set forth in the pre-trial order, which reads as follows: Failure to repair roof and eliminate dangerous condition of roof and walls allowing entry of water, after notice thereof and promise by the defendants to make such repairs, in breach of duty owed under the lease? That is your contention?

To which he replied, "Yes, sir, Your Honor." The judge then asked:

Do you both agree on that, that is the allegation of negligence, that is the issue in the case?

Again appellant's counsel answered, "Yes, sir." Later in the trial, counsel for appellant moved to amend the pretrial order to permit him to introduce certain sections of the District of Columbia Housing Regulations, particularly Section 2507 which requires that roofs shall be leakproof, and that rain water shall be drained so as not to cause wet walls or ceilings. The trial judge denied the motion, and directed a verdict for the defendants.

The administratrix appeals, stating thus the questions presented:

1. Did the Court err in directing a verdict for appellees where evidence was presented that said appellees — landlords — had notice of a leakage in the roof, which leakage caused plaintiff to slip and suffer injuries, and where said landlords had promised to repair said condition?

2. Did the Court err in refusing to admit into evidence pertinent housing regulations where counsel for plaintiff first became aware of them during the course of trial and proffered them while still putting on plaintiff's evidence; particularly where counsel for *defendants* had admittedly been familiar with these regulations?

[The court first held that the landlord had no duty under the lease to make repairs.]

The second question presented by the appellant remains to be answered. Appellant refers to the housing regulations which she offered as "pertinent." It is suggested the proffered regulations relate only to multiple-unit dwellings and are not pertinent here. Whether so or not, we need not decide because we hold the trial judge acted within his discretion in refusing to receive the housing regulations. In the recent case of Gould v. DeBeve we said in footnote 2:

> In any event the principal ground advanced for the exclusion of Section 2608 was that no reference had been made to this section of the Code in the pre-trial statement. We enter here into the area of the trial court's justifiably large discretion in the conduct of a trial, and we cannot say that that discretion was abused in this instance.

In like manner, we hold the trial judge in this case did not abuse his "justifiably large discretion" in refusing to permit appellant to change her theory during the trial.

In addition to the foregoing, there is another reason for upholding the trial court's action in directing a verdict for the defendants. There was no possibility of constructive notice to the landlord about the wetness of the floor of Mrs. Littlejohn's room. But she was well aware of the condition, as shortly before she had mopped the floor twice. Then, on re-entering the room to awaken her grandson and get her coat, she slipped on the floor she knew was wet. She had not forgotten it,[5] but was thinking only of getting her coat to go to work. This was a frank admission that her own negligence caused the accident, for of course one can walk on a wet floor without falling if the condition is known and proper care is exercised. Thus, even if it be thought that somehow appellees were negligent, the trial judge would have been justified in instructing the jury that Mrs. Littlejohn was contributorily negligent as a matter of law. . . .

We are clear that the trial judge did not err in directing a verdict for the defendants.

Affirmed.

FAHY, J. (dissenting).

The service performed by pre-trial procedure is of unquestionable value. A case arises occasionally, however, in which the latitude granted to the trial judge by Rule 16, Fed. R. Civ. P., to depart from the pre-

---

5. When asked in her deposition if she had forgotten about the floor being wet, she said: "No, I knew it was raining and it had been wet. I didn't think about falling, and I was going to get my coat and go to work."

trial order should be used. The Rule provides that the order controls the subsequent course of the action "unless modified at the trial to prevent manifest injustice." There is no touchstone by which to determine when "manifest injustice" would be prevented by permitting modification. A case must be judged according to its circumstances. The circumstances which lead me to dissent include the important one that the law in this jurisdiction applicable to the legal obligations of a landlord to a tenant includes our decision in Whetzel v. Jess Fisher Management Co. We there held his obligations embrace those imposed by applicable Housing Regulations. Those urged to apply here were not referred to in the pre-trial order. Nevertheless they are public regulations, and Whetzel v. Fisher is a decision of this court. A question for determination at the trial should have been whether the regulations applied and, if so, whether the injury of the tenant was proximately caused by their violation. In deciding the matter of "manifest injustice," or, otherwise stated, "manifest justice," the failure of counsel specifically to bring forth this theory of liability until during the trial must be weighed against the possible prejudice to defendant in then permitting departure from the pre-trial order. The defendants could have been given opportunity to meet the case sought to be based on the regulations; but unless plaintiff were permitted to seek reliance upon them he was, of course, "out of court" entirely with respect to them.

Failure to include the regulations in the pre-trial order appears not to have been deliberate. Plaintiff is thus made to suffer from an inadvertence counsel sought to have remedied at the trial. Any possible disadvantage to experienced counsel for defendants, by permitting the requested departure from the pre-trial order, could have been obviated by a continuance if counsel so desired. In any event the disadvantage to defendants is more than outweighed, it seems to me, by the disadvantage to plaintiff in unnecessarily limiting consideration of her case to only a part of the law which might be found applicable. Manifest injustice is more likely to occur when the applicable law is precluded from consideration because not referred to in the pre-trial order than when the preclusion is of evidentiary matter which takes the adversary by surprise. . . .[1]

The court also gives as a reason for affirmance that the decedent's own negligence caused the accident. The trial court did not mention this in its direction of a verdict for defendants and it was not advanced by them

---

1. I have not sought to solve the problem on the theory, not urged, that the pre-trial order might be read to allow the inclusion of the Housing Regulations in evidence without necessity for its amendment.

on the appeal as ground for affirmance. I would not affirm on this ground; for the question of contributory negligence should be initially considered and answered in the District Court.

NOTES AND PROBLEMS

1. Be clear about the consequences of the judge's failure to amend the pretrial order. The plaintiff had, potentially, two theories of liability — one relying on the lease and the other on the housing code.

a. The plaintiff started by relying exclusively on the lease.

b. When the plaintiff, during trial, sought to introduce into evidence parts of the housing code, the judge refused to permit it. Why?

2. If plaintiff had sought to amend her pleading to allege violation of the housing code, would her motion have been granted? See Rule 15(a). If so, why could she not amend the pretrial order?

3. The conflict that gave rise to this opinion would have been avoided if, during the pretrial conference, the judge had explicitly drawn plaintiff's attention to the housing statute and pointed out that it obviated the necessity to prove negligence. Most judges will not take such an action, arguing that to do so is tantamount to "trying the party's case" for her and that it is inconsistent with the premises of the adversary system. Is there an inconsistency between the relatively active role taken by some judges in the settlement phase of pretrial conferences (exemplified by Lockhart v. Patel, supra) and the disinclination to guide the parties regarding the merits of their cases?

———————

Most lawsuits filed in U.S. courts will end by the time they have reached the stage described in this chapter. But don't stop reading: those suits will end *because* the parties know about the processes discussed in the next several chapters. One can, therefore, think about those processes in two ways. From one point of view, they will yield results so predictable that parties can settle without regret. From another point of view, they are so unpredictable and so dangerous that parties will settle even strong cases to avoid them. As you read, consider which point of view seems closest to the truth.

IDENTIFYING THE TRIER

IX

At the end of the pretrial stage and on the brink of trial, we focus on an issue that has lurked in the background throughout our consideration of the litigation process: the identity of the trier of fact. Some lawyers assert that the identity of the trier is the most important single factor in determining the outcome of the case; others go even further, asserting that it is the *only* thing that matters. Even if this view is exaggerated, in close cases it matters who holds the power of decision; small differences in perspective may determine the outcome of cases involving such questions as whether witnesses are trustworthy or what behavior is "reasonable." Notice that we have already approached this topic in exploring jurisdiction, arbitration, mediation, and settlement. Jurisdictional challenges, if successful, take a case out of one court system and put it in another. In negotiated and arbitrated disputes the parties, by taking their case out of the court system, are also taking it out of a judge's hands. This chapter examines a set of issues that arise when a dispute stays within the court system. Even within that system there can be a choice among judges, a further choice between judge and jury, and still further choices among jurors.

A. Judging Judges: Bias and Recusal

We start with the key figure in any case — the judge. The central importance of the judge derives from two circumstances. First, as we have seen, most contemporary lawsuits do not reach trial. Consequently, the potential counterbalance offered by jury trial, where that is available, will not come into play. In most cases the only decisions made by anyone other than a party will be made by a judge. That includes rulings on almost every topic addressed thus far: jurisdiction and venue, choice of law, the pleadings, discovery motions, and motions for summary judgment. Second, even if there is a jury, the judge not only rules on various challenges to jurors but also has the power of setting aside jury verdicts and ordering new trials. The identity of the judge becomes vital to the litigants, and the possibility of a biased judge can be terrifying. Professional training may help keep judges focused on factors the law defines as permissible, but judges are human, and humans are fallible. How does the system seek to protect litigants against biased judges?

Some states permit peremptory challenges of judges simply by the filing of a timely affidavit alleging in conclusory terms that the judge is prejudiced against the party. Cal. Civ. Proc. Code §170.6 (West 1998) (permitting one such peremptory challenge of a judge). Such legislation has been proposed in Congress, but at present the federal system permits challenges only for cause. The procedure and standards are set forth in 28 U.S.C.§§144 and 455. The latter statute establishes two broad categories for disqualifying a judge. One contains specific guidelines barring, for example, a judge's hearing a case "where he has served as lawyer in the matter in controversy" before becoming a judge or "[w]here he has served in governmental employment and . . . expressed an opinion concerning the merits of the particular case or controversy." It also bars decisions in cases in which a judge or her family has a financial interest. 28 U.S.C. §455(b). The other category is much broader: "Any justice, judge, or magistrate of the United States shall disqualify himself in any proceeding in which his impartiality might reasonably be questioned." 28 U.S.C. §455(a). The next case illustrates the difficulty of applying both the specific and the general standards. The facts of the case arise in criminal litigation, but §455 applies to all cases.

In re Jeffrey C. Hatcher, Sr.
150 F.3d 631 (7th Cir. 1998)

DIANE P. WOOD, Circuit Judge.

The Gangster Disciples were one of the largest and most powerful of Chicago's street gangs. On August 30, 1995, a Chicago federal grand jury returned indictments in three related cases, charging 39 members of the Gangster Disciples with a variety of federal drug and conspiracy crimes. Petitioner, Jeffrey Hatcher, was named as a co-conspirator in two of the original indictments and as a defendant in the third. Gang leader Larry Hoover, who controlled the gang's drug trafficking business from his prison cell in downstate Illinois, was one of the defendants in the Hoover indictment, and was named as a co-conspirator in the other two indictments. . . .

Prior to trial Hatcher . . . moved under 28 U.S.C. §455 to have presiding District Judge Charles Kocoras recuse himself. Hatcher pointed out that the district judge's son, while working as an intern in the U.S. Attorney's office as a third-year law student, had assisted in the Hoover trial. The judge's son, presumably acting under the authority of Northern District of Illinois General Rule 3.11 (which allows supervised third-year law students to act as attorneys), presented eight government witnesses to the jury. . . .

I

A more extensive account of this case and the ones that preceded it is necessary to understand Hatcher's recusal motion, because our resolution of the motion turns on the degree to which the Hoover case and the present case overlap for purposes of §455. . . .

The overlap between the Hoover indictment and the second Hatcher indictment is almost complete. The conspiracy alleged is, almost verbatim, the same, except that the second Hatcher indictment alleges that the conspiracy started somewhat later and adds certain allegations relating to conduct after the Hoover indictment was handed down. Of the 34 people alleged to be a member of the conspiracy in Count One of the second Hatcher case, 26 were alleged to be a member of the conspiracy in Count One of the Hoover indictment; of the 39 listed in Count One of the Hoover indictment, 26 appeared in the second Hatcher case. Jeffrey Hatcher appears in both. Even Hatcher's weapons violation — Count Five in the second Hatcher indictment — perfectly duplicates a parallel count — Count Fifteen — in the Hoover indictment.

II

We begin our analysis of Hatcher's present motion with the point he has emphasized most strongly, which we find to be without merit. During the course of the Hoover trial, Hatcher learned, Judge Kocoras spent some time sitting in the public audience section of Judge Leinenweber's courtroom, so that he could observe his son's performance. Hatcher alleges now that this gave Judge Kocoras "personal knowledge of disputed evidentiary facts" in his own case, thereby satisfying the standard for mandatory recusal under §455(b)(1).

We disagree. First, as the government pointed out in its response to Hatcher's petition, Judge Kocoras was present only as a spectator in the courtroom. He therefore learned nothing about the Gangster Disciple conspiracy that any member of the public could not also have learned by attending the trial or reading a good newspaper account of its progress.

This limited exposure is simply not the kind of personal knowledge of disputed evidentiary facts with which §455(b)(1) is concerned. Cf. Diamondstone v. Macaluso, 148 F. 3d 113 (2d Cir. 1998) (judge did not gain sufficient personal knowledge of disputed evidentiary facts "by walking past . . . peace vigils, which were only tangentially related to [plaintiff's] claims"); Easley v. University of Michigan Bd. of Regents, 906 F.2d 1143 (6th Cir. 1990) (knowledge gained by judge while serving on law school's Committee of visitors did not require recusal from suit alleging discrimination by law school). Second, Judge Kocoras has made it clear that he has no recollection of any particular evidence that was presented while he was in attendance. Like any proud parent, he was paying attention to what his son was doing, not to the details of the trial. A review of transcripts of the examination of the witnesses Judge Kocoras's son presented in the Hoover trial shows, not surprisingly, that the Assistant U.S. Attorney in charge of the case allowed the judge's son to present only witnesses of limited significance. Finally, both the judge and the government have pointed out that the judge has been supplied with transcripts from prior related trials as part of the government's proffer in the present case. Those transcripts have given him legitimate access to the same kind of information he may have heard while he was watching the earlier trial. Under these circumstances Judge Kocoras perhaps could have chosen to recuse himself under the terms of §455(b)(1) without abusing his discretion, but we hold that Hatcher has not shown that he was required to do so.

III

Next, we consider whether the participation of the judge's son in the Hoover trial was enough to require recusal under the provisions of §455(b)(5), which in relevant part reads as follows:

> [The judge] shall also disqualify himself in the following circumstances:
>
> > (5) He or his spouse, or a person within the third degree of relationship to either of them, or the spouse of such a person:
> > > (ii) Is acting as a lawyer in the proceeding;. . . .

The first question under this part of the statute is whether the relative in question is closely enough related to the judge to trigger its restrictions. . . . [I]t is clear that a judge's children fall within its purview. The next question is slightly more complex: . . . whether such students [practicing under a lawyer's supervision] are acting as lawyers for purposes of §455. While novel, this is a simple inquiry, with a simple answer — they are.

Even if the judge's son was "acting as a lawyer," we must still consider whether, for purposes of the mandatory disqualification rule of §455(b)(5)(ii), the Hoover case was the same "proceeding" as the Hatcher trial that was before Judge Kocoras. "Proceeding" is defined in §455(d)(1), to "include[ ] pretrial, trial, appellate review, or other stages of litigation." As a formal matter, Hatcher's case has never been part of the same proceeding as Hoover's. . . . No matter how closely related the two cases were factually or legally (as different aspects of the same conspiracy), the fact remains that they were separate "proceedings." . . . Precisely because §455(b) sets forth mandatory disqualification rules, courts have read its requirements strictly, so that both judges and litigants will know when a judge must step aside. Because the Hoover case in which the judge's son participated was not the same proceeding as Hatcher's present case, we conclude that Judge Kocoras was not required to recuse himself under §455(b)(5)(ii).

IV

That leaves the remaining theory for recusal, which is under the more open-ended standard of §455(a). . . .

The standard in any case for a §455(a) recusal is whether the judge's impartiality could be questioned by a reasonable, well-informed observer. . . :

> An objective standard creates problems in implementation. Judges must imagine how a reasonable, well-informed observer of the judicial system would react. . . . Drawing all inferences favorable to the honesty and care of the judge whose conduct has been questioned could collapse the appearance of impropriety standard under §455(a) into a demand for proof of actual impropriety. So although the court tries to make an external reference to the reasonable person, it is essential to hold in mind that these outside observers are less inclined to credit judges' impartiality and mental discipline than the judiciary itself will be.

In re Mason, 916 F 2d 384, 386 (7th Cir. 1990).

The question here is whether the Hoover case in which the judge's son participated is so closely related to Hatcher's case that our hypothetical reasonable person would question the judge's impartiality. Reluctantly, we conclude that the answer is yes. Conceding the point, as we have, that the Hoover prosecution and the present Hatcher case are formally separate proceedings, our examination of the two indictments leaves no doubt that functionally they are both component parts of one large prosecution of the continuing criminal enterprise, conspiracy, and drug offenses of the members of the Gangster Disciple gang. Outside observers have no way of knowing how much information the judge's son acquired about that broader prosecution while working on the Hoover case. We underscore that the admitted fact that Judge Kocoras's son actually worked on the Hoover case while he was an intern in the U.S. Attorney's office is critically important to our decision. The Advisory Committee on Judicial Activities has concluded that under Canon 3C of the Code of Conduct for United States Judges "[a] judge whose child is an Assistant United States Attorney need not for that reason alone recuse from all cases in which the United States Attorney appears as counsel, although the child may not participate in cases before the parent." Compendium §3.2-1(a)(1)(1995), citing Advisory Opinion No. 38. We are also not saying that any connection, however tenuous, between two cases would require recusal under §455(a); indeed, we [have] held to the contrary. . . . This is instead the rare case where the earlier proceedings were so close to the case now before the judge that recusal under §455(a) was the only permissible option.

. . . Last, although we regret very much the necessity of upsetting the start of a trial toward which both the judge and the parties had devoted so much time, the outcome of any criminal trial must come about through procedures that are not only fair in fact, but that are also seen to be fair by the public.

BAUER, Circuit Judge, dissenting.

I dissent. No good purpose would be served by going on at length — the matter is presently moot — but I do not think that Judge Kocoras had to recuse himself. And if it was not required, it would have been wrong to do so.

The opinion points out that the two proceedings discussed were "separate proceedings" . It also properly finds that the knowledge the judge obtained by visiting the Hoover trial did not require his recusal. For me, that ends the inquiry.

The son did not appear before Judge Kocoras in this (or any other) case. The cases were distinct and Judge Kocoras denied the motion to recuse. I disagree that a reasonable person could question his impartiality. He was right not to grant the motion to recuse; we were wrong to compel it.

NOTES AND PROBLEMS

1. Does the result in *Hatcher* make intuitive sense? Would a detached, reasonable observer question Judge Kocoras's impartiality?

2. What is the consequence of holding that recusal was required by §455(a) but not by any of the sections of §455(b)?

a. Suppose that Judge Kocoras had, before trial, called the prosecuting and defense attorneys together and disclosed to them that his son, as a law student, had participated in a related proceeding, which the judge had briefly attended. Suppose further that the two sides, after conferring with their clients, had approached the judge and said, "We understand the circumstances, but we nevertheless want you to hear the case. We're both convinced that you are impartial." Could the judge have accepted such a waiver? See §455(e).

b. Does its distinction in §455(e) between waivable and nonwaivable circumstances make sense?

3. As you might imagine, courts have found §455(b) easier than §455(a) to apply. In §455(b) there can be some borderline questions. For example, the Eleventh Circuit had to decide whether frequent flier miles accumulated by judges constituted a "financial interest" within the meaning of §455(b)(4) and (5). Delta Air Lines, Inc. v. Sasser, 127 F.3d 1296 (11th Cir. 1997) (held, no). But such cases are not common and have not proved very difficult. And if the section applies, recusal is mandatory and may not be waived by the parties.

4. By contrast, the general standard of §455(a) has caused courts great difficulty. The authorities agree that the standard is objective — that is, the individual party's belief in the judge's bias, no matter how strongly and sincerely held, does not suffice to disqualify the judge. They are equally clear that the party seeking to disqualify need not demonstrate actual bias on the judge's part. Defining the area lying between these poles has proved challenging. Consider a sampling of §455(a) cases.

a. With *Hatcher* compare O'Bannon v. Union Pacific R.R. Co., 169 F.3d. 1088 (8th Cir. 1999). During the first eight months the personal injury case was pending the judge's law clerk "lived in the same house with one of counsel for defendants." Recusal was not required: Although a judge sharing a house with defense counsel would be grounds for recusal, and a judge who knew of the law clerk's situation might well instruct the clerk not to work on the case in question, "plaintiff's argument in the present case overlooks [the fact] that cases are decided by judges, not law clerks." Fair enough, but by the same reasoning, could one argue that Judge Kocoras, not his son, was deciding *Hatcher* and that recusal was not required? Is there something else that distinguishes the cases?

b. In United States v. Cerceda, 172 F. 3d 806 (11th Cir. 1999), matters came much closer to the judge: In November 1992 the U.S. Attorney for the Southern District of Florida told Judge Moore that he was the subject of a federal grand jury investigation. That information became public knowledge about a year later, and Judge Moore then began to recuse himself sua sponte from all matters where the United States was a party. Defendants who had been tried or sentenced during the time when Judge Moore, but not the public, knew of the investigation moved to reopen their cases on grounds that the judge should have recused himself. Held, Judge Moore should have recused himself, but the risk of injustice to the defendants was not so egregious as to require retrial.

c. By contrast, in United States v. Anderson, 160 F. 3d 231 (5th Cir. 1998), a divided appeals court held both that recusal was required and that the judgment should be set aside where the judge had failed to recuse himself. Judge McBryde was presiding over a criminal trial during a period where he was under investigation by his Circuit Council for alleged acts of judicial misbehavior. See 28 U.S.C. §372 for a description of this investigatory process, which can be the first step on the road to impeachment. Defendant's counsel had testified before the Council as to the judge's behavior in a series of cases. The majority reasoned:

> As Anderson notes, many attorneys are fearful of even filing a complaint against a judge to a circuit judicial council, due to fear of retaliation. . . .
> If there is fear in merely filing a complaint against a judge, it is evident that a greater fear arises from actually testifying against a judge, who is present at that hearing. It is difficult under those circumstances not to argue that a reasonable person would not harbor any doubt about Judge McBryde's impartiality.

The dissent thought otherwise:

> The panel's principal error is to review Judge McBryde's recusal decision only in hindsight. The defendants' recusal motions must be viewed in terms of events as the parties knew them at the time. The public defenders had testified against Judge McBryde and the disciplinary hearing was over, but no decision had yet been rendered. . . . There is no reason to think that Judge McBryde would have had it in for the clients of people who were testifying against him. Every judge must develop a thick skin against criticism, and most judicial conduct complaints come to nought. . . .
> Does [the majority opinion] suggest that any aggressive lawyer who faces the prospect of a trial before a judge he dislikes could file a spurious misconduct complaint against the judge, give an unflattering interview to the press, or otherwise publicly rebuke the judge, and then seek his recusal?

5. Recusal cases on appeal often involve two questions: (1) should the judge have recused himself?; (2) if so, did the failure to recuse involve a sufficiently serious likelihood of injustice as to overturn or reopen the

case? As you can see from some of the examples just cited, courts sometimes answer the first question positively but the second negatively.

a. In In re Chevron U.S.A., 121 F.3d 163 (5th Cir. 1997), the court of appeals granted mandamus in mid-trial to consider defendant's claims that, in a racially charged case, the judge had made a number of statements suggesting racial bias in favor of the African-American plaintiffs. After condemning the statements by the judge and saying that they would cause an objective observer to suspect partiality, the court of appeals nevertheless refused to order the judge's recusal. The opinion noted that a jury had been picked and that recusal would require repeating thirty-one days of trial and the testimony of fifty-eight witnesses. The court contented itself with warning the judge to control himself and noting that it was reserving the right to reverse on appeal after final judgment.

b. The leading §455 case in the U.S. Supreme Court, Liljeberg v. Health Services Acquisition Corp., 486 U.S. 847 (1988), reopened a judgment under unusual circumstances. Judge Collins sat on the board of directors of a university that stood to profit or lose depending on the decision of the case — clear grounds for recusal under §455(b)(4). But §455(b)(4) requires that the judge know of the interest in the case. Judge Collins claimed that he had not attended the board meetings in question or opened the mail that would have revealed the university's interest and consequently lacked the requisite knowledge. A second district judge, after hearings, made factual findings in accord with Judge Collins's assertions that he lacked the actual knowledge required by §455(b)(4). The Supreme Court accepted those findings but nevertheless required reopening of the judgment, not under §455(b) but under §455(a). Essentially the Court held that, while it accepted Judge Collins's protestations of ignorance, "an objective observer would have questioned Judge Collins's impartiality," and that the judgment must therefore be set aside.

6. Notice that an unarticulated assumption stands behind every recusal motion against a federal trial or appellate court judge: that there is another judge without the asserted bias who is available to replace him or her. Consider two situations where that assumption does not hold:

a. What if a challenged judge cannot be replaced? District court and court of appeals judges can fill in for each other, even when a judge has to be brought from another district or circuit to do so. But there are only nine Supreme Court justices: unlike some state systems, the Constitution has not been thought to permit temporary appointment from a lower court. If a justice is unavailable, by reason of disability or recusal, the Court simply operates with a smaller number of justices. (In such a circumstance a tie vote affirms the result in the lower court.) Does that mean that it should be more difficult to recuse a Supreme Court justice?

The justices regularly recuse themselves from cases in circumstances in which §455(b) might apply, generally without announcing publicly their reasons for doing so. Suppose, however, a situation in which only §455(a) applies. In 1993 the Court promulgated an unusual document, a Statement of Recusal Policy, 114 S. Ct. (No. 3) cix (1993). In the statement the justices announced a policy that would govern their recusal when a relative is a lawyer at a firm involved in litigation before the Supreme Court, but where the relative is not working directly on the case involved:

> We do not think it would serve the public interest to go beyond the requirements of the statute, and to recuse ourselves, out of an excess of caution, whenever a relative is a partner in the firm before us. . . . In this court, where the absence of one justice cannot be made up by another, needless recusal deprives the litigants of the nine Justices to which they are entitled. . . .

Id. at cx. Is this the right result? Compare *Hatcher.*

b. What if a judge can be replaced, but only with a substitute who will have either the same challenged characteristic or its mirror image? A version of such a situation occurred in Blank v. Sullivan & Cromwell, supra page 487. In employment discrimination litigation, the defendant law firm moved to disqualify Judge Motley because, as a black woman, she "strongly identified with those who suffered discrimination in employment because of sex or race." Judge Motley denied the motion:

> It is beyond dispute that for much of my legal career I worked on behalf of blacks who suffered race discrimination. I am a woman, and before being elevated to the bench, was a woman lawyer. These obvious facts, however, clearly do not, ipso facto, indicate or even suggest the personal bias or prejudice required [for disqualification]. The assertion, without more, that a judge who engaged in civil rights litigation and who happens to be of the same sex as a plaintiff in a suit alleging sex discrimination on the part of a law firm, is, therefore, so biased that he or she should not hear the case, comes nowhere near the standards required for recusal. Indeed, if background or sex or race of each judge were, by definition, sufficient grounds for removal, no judge on this court could hear this case, or many others, by virtue of the fact that all of them were attorneys, of a sex, often with distinguished law firm or public service background.

Blank v. Sullivan & Cromwell, 418 F. Supp. 1, 4 (S.D.N.Y. 1975). Right result?

6. Most disqualification cases concern knowledge and attitudes gained by the judge before the litigation started. What about an attitude gained in the course of litigation itself? Can that ever be a basis for disqualification? For example, what if the facts presented in the case arouse in the judge a passionate hatred of the party?

a. Theoretically, one might not call this attitude "bias" at all:

. . . Not all unfavorable disposition towards an individual (or his case) is properly described by those terms. One would not say, for example, that world opinion is biased or prejudiced against Adolf Hitler. The words connote a favorable or unfavorable disposition or opinion that is somehow wrongful or inappropriate, either because it is undeserved, or because it rests upon knowledge that the subject ought not to possess (for example, a criminal juror who has been biased or prejudiced by receipt of inadmissible evidence concerning the defendant's prior criminal activities), or because it is excessive in degree (for example, a criminal juror who is so inflamed by properly admitted evidence of a defendant's prior criminal activities that he will vote guilty regardless of the facts).

Liteky v. United States, 510 U.S. 540, 550 (1994).

b. The U.S. Supreme Court has rejected this proposition and is pre-pared to hold that at least some judicial attitudes acquired during litigation itself ("intrajudicial" bias) can be so disproportionate as to be grounds for recusal. But it has narrowly circumscribed such cases, probably out of fear that every adverse ruling would otherwise lead to a disqualification motion. To require recusal as a result of information gained during trial, "judicial remarks" must "reveal such a high degree of favoritism or antagonism as to make fair judgment impossible." Liteky v. United States, 510 U.S. 540, 555 (1994). One would not expect to find many such cases.

7. Both §§144 and 455 of 28 U.S.C. provide for the disqualification of judges. Section 144 is short and is cast in broad language; section 455, as you have already seen, is considerably more detailed. Despite this difference in specificity, the courts have held that §144 incorporates the detailed substantive provisions of §455 such that the substantive standards for disqualification are the same under both sections. Section 144, how-ever, permits a party to seek recusal by bringing specific issues to the court's attention. Section 144 also contains a provision not found in §455: When a judge is challenged under that section, "such judge shall proceed no further therein, but another judge shall be assigned to hear such proceeding." On its face, such language might suggest that the question of *recusal* itself must be decided by another judge. The statute has not been so interpreted. The leading case, Berger v. United States, 255 U.S. 22 (1921), held that the challenged judge rules on the challenge to impartiality. In many districts judges always ask colleagues to rule on recusal motions, but that practice varies. Should Congress amend the statute to require that another judge hear the challenge?

8. Finally, as a transition to the next section, consider whether it should make a difference in §455(a) cases that in some of them — but not all — there will be another decision maker: the jury. Does this cancel out some kinds of judicial bias?

B.   Judge or Jury: The Right to a Civil Jury Trial

In the United States the jury — an ancient, almost unique, and contested institution — counterbalances the judge's power in some cases. The material that follows explores the law governing the choice and the qualifications of the jury, but at the outset you should bear in mind some demographic and structural differences between these two types of decision makers. In this country judges are still predominantly male, white, and at least middle-aged. Equally important, they are all likely to have specialized education and half a lifetime of professional experience in law — with all the habits of mind that implies — behind them. Juries, because they are drawn from the community at large and serve only for a short time, may vary widely from this profile. Juries deliberate in secret and generally announce their verdicts only in general terms They also are unburdened by the requirement that they describe each link in the chain of fact and law that leads them to their conclusions. Both trial and appellate courts are bound to give jury verdicts wide deference. It therefore makes a difference — sometimes a great difference — whether a litigant can have a jury decide her case.

1.   Historical Reconstruction and the Seventh Amendment

The civil trial jury flourishes only in the United States. Although we inherited the institution from English law, it is available there only in a few specialized cases (for example, in libel actions). But in the United States jury trials are widely available in both state and federal courts. This availability results from provisions in a state and the federal Constitution granting the right to jury trial in certain cases. In the debates attending the adoption of the federal Constitution in 1789 and the Bill of Rights in 1791, much attention was paid to the jury trial. Some opponents of the Constitution cited the omission of a jury trial provision as an argument for not ratifying the document:

> [T]he crux of the objection lay in the political significance of the jury trial. While an adequate representation in at least one branch of the legislature was indispensable at the top, law-making level, the jury trial provided the people's safeguard at the bottom, administrative, level. A [Maryland] Farmer argued, indeed, that the jury trial is more important than representation in the legislature, because "those usurpations, which silently undermine the spirit of liberty, under the sanctions of law, are more dangerous than direct and open legislative attacks. . . ."*

---

* H. J. Storing, What the Anti-Federalists Were For: The Political Thought of the Opponents of the Constitution 18-19 (1981).

Beyond its place in the structure of government, those seeking to include the right to jury trial in the Constitution believed that it would affect the outcome of certain cases. In particular, many of the jury's champions believed that juries would be sympathetic to the claims of rural debtors when sued by big-city or foreign creditors. As one authority points out:

> [I]nconveniences [of jury trial were] accepted precisely because, in impor-tant instances, through its ability to disregard substantive rules of law, the jury would reach a result that the judge either could not or would not reach. Those who favored the civil jury were not misguided tinkerers. [T]hey were, for their day, libertarians who avowed that important areas of protection for litigants . . . would be placed in grave danger unless it were required that juries sit in civil cases.*

The proponents of jury trial won an important battle: The Seventh Amendment became part of the Bill of Rights. They did not win the war, however, because the amendment did not make all cases triable to a jury. The amendment was a compromise between those who thought jury trial at best a nuisance, at worst an invitation to lawlessness, and those who thought it a vital structural and substantive principle of govern-ment. The compromise is embedded in a deceptively short text of the Seventh Amendment:

> In suits at common law, where the value in controversy shall exceed twenty dollars, the right of trial by jury shall be preserved. . . .

The language of the Seventh Amendment reflects this compromise in two phrases: "suits at common law" and "shall be preserved." Unlike other provisions of the Bill of Rights that guarantee various rights, the Seventh Amendment purports to preserve a right but does not indicate the scope of the right being preserved. As you may recall from your study of pleading, the English judicial system, whose organization was echoed by colonial courts in the period immediately before the Revolution, was divided into several jurisdictions. In courts of law, jury trial was widely available on most of the writs commonly in use by the eighteenth century. In chancery (which administered various equitable remedies), however, the judge (the chancellor) sat without a jury. The constitutional compro-mise, then, "preserved" as triable to a jury those cases that could have been brought in a court of common law. If, however, the claim would have fallen into the jurisdiction of the court of chancery, the Seventh Amendment did not extend the right to jury trial. As you will see, courts dealing with this issue distinguish between legal and equitable claims

---

* Wolfram, The Constitutional History of the Seventh Amendment, 57 Minn. L. Rev. 639, 668-705 (1973).

and remedies. By so doing they are simply using a shorthand form of reference: "Legal" in this context means a claim recognized by a court of law (where juries sat), and "equitable" means that the claim or remedy would have been in chancery (where no juries sat).

In Chapter VI we noted the development of elaborate doctrine concerning what cases could be brought in equity. The result was that remedies such as injunctions, specific performance, rescission, and accountings and procedural devices such as derivative suits, class actions, bills of peace, and bills of interpleader were within equity jurisdiction. A given plaintiff had to show that the traditional legal remedy of money damages was inadequate and that he otherwise qualified for equitable relief.

It is important to emphasize that most cases within equity jurisdiction did not wind up there because of anyone's conviction that the judge was better suited than a jury to decide a particular type of claim. Although the judge may have been more qualified to sort out fiduciary relationships, probate matters, or multiparty actions, many other branches of equity jurisdiction involved the same questions of fact — what happened, how it happened, and who was telling the truth — as legal actions. For example, injunctive actions frequently involved questions of land ownership or commission of a tort, and specific performance claims usually involved the construction and meaning of contracts. Moreover, the "clean-up" doctrine permitted an equity court to decide issues that might otherwise have been presented to a jury in an action at law. As time went on, distinctions between the two jurisdictions blurred even further: Legal claims in general assumpsit (money had and received) tended to parallel equitable remedies for restitution, and traditionally equitable defenses such as fraud, duress, and illegality came to be recognized at law. In sum, the law-equity jurisdictional distinction was far from hard and fast, and whatever distinction existed was more a result of history than of logic or function.

Given the constitutional language "preserving" rights at "common law," it is not surprising that the courts adopted a historical test for deciding the right to jury trial under the Seventh Amendment. Under the historical test, courts seek to give parties the same right of jury trial as they had in 1791. Presumably, the drafters of the Seventh Amendment were thinking of a world in which there were separate courts of law and equity, a world in which one could only "preserve" a right to jury trial in suits at common law. Because there had never been a right to jury trial in equity, there was nothing to preserve and no right to jury trial.

Consequently, courts applying the historical test do not directly inquire about jury trial. Instead, they ask a related question: whether a given claim lay within the jurisdiction of the common law courts in 1791. If so, the parties have the right to a jury; if not — if only a court of equity would have heard the claim — there is no right to a jury. Equitable jurisdiction generally turned on whether the plaintiff wanted injunctive or other relief available only in equity, wanted to use a procedural device that was available only in equity, or had a claim that could be brought only in equity. Before you despair of sorting all this out, be comforted by the thought that a very large portion of claims fit neatly into well-established historical patterns. Having mastered that pattern, you will have answers for most jury trial questions you will ever encounter. The problems that follow cover this ground.

NOTES AND PROBLEMS

In each of the following problems, the question is whether the parties are entitled to a jury trial under the Seventh Amendment. In answering the questions, assume that if the action could have been brought in a court of common law in 1791, the parties are entitled to a jury; otherwise they are not so entitled. Before answering, you may wish to review the material on common law and equity, supra pages 384–396.

1. Plaintiff and defendant sign a contract.

a. Plaintiff, alleging breach of contract, seeks money damages.

b. Plaintiff, alleging breach of contract, seeks a decree of specific performance.

c. Plaintiff contends that the agreed price of the goods in question was $200,000 but that through a typing error the contract read "$100,000." Plaintiff seeks to have the contract reformed.

d. Plaintiff, alleging that defendant tricked her into signing the contract by fraud, seeks to have the purported agreement rescinded.

2. Plaintiff and defendant own adjoining real property. Plaintiff alleges that defendant is committing a nuisance on real estate adjoining plaintiff's land.

a. Plaintiff seeks damages for harm caused by the nuisance.

b. Plaintiff seeks an injunction against the continuation of the nuisance.

3. Plaintiff alleges that defendant has taken his diamond ring.

a. Plaintiff seeks to recover its value.

b. Plaintiff seeks an order restoring the ring to his possession.

4. Plaintiff alleges that defendant wrongfully occupies Blackacre.

a. Plaintiff seeks damages resulting from defendant's wrongful possession.

b. Plaintiff seeks to eject defendant from the property.

2.   Applying the Historical Test to New Claims

Each of the claims in the preceding set of problems could have arisen in 1791. Determining the availability of jury trial for such claims is therefore a matter of recognizing the type of claim involved and knowing whether it would have been brought in a court of law or in a court of equity. That may require refreshing one's historical memory, but it presents no conceptual difficulties.

Knottier problems emerge when one considers claims that did not exist at the time the Bill of Rights was adopted, particularly those created by statute. The next case faces that difficulty, illustrating both the prevailing historical approach to such new claims and an alternative to that approach.

Chauffeurs, Teamsters & Helpers, Local No. 391 v. Terry
494 U.S. 558 (1990)

Justice MARSHALL delivered the opinion of the Court except as to Part III-A.

This case presents the question whether an employee who seeks relief in the form of back pay for a union's alleged breach of its duty of fair representation has a right to trial by jury. We hold that the Seventh Amendment entitles such a plaintiff to a jury trial.

I

McLean Trucking Company and the Chauffeurs, Teamsters, and Helpers Local Union No. 391 were parties to a collective-bargaining agreement that governed the terms and conditions of employment at McLean's terminals. The 27 respondents were employed by McLean as truckdrivers in bargaining units covered by the agreement, and all were members of the Union. In 1982 McLean implemented a change in operations that resulted in the elimination of some of its terminals and the reorganization of others. As part of that change, McLean transferred respondents to the terminal located in Winston-Salem and agreed to give them special seniority rights in relation to "inactive" employees in Winston-Salem who had been laid off temporarily.

After working in Winston-Salem for approximately six weeks, respondents were alternately laid off and recalled several times. [As a result of these layoffs and the ensuing loss of seniority, workers filed grievances with the union. The union prosecuted two of these grievances. When the workers filed a third grievance, the union refused to prosecute it, arguing that the previous grievance decisions had settled the issue. At that point the workers sued both the trucking company and the union. They alleged that the company had violated the collective bargaining agreement and that the union had violated the duty of fair representation. Before the case came to trial, the trucking company filed for bankruptcy, and plaintiffs voluntarily dismissed the case against the company.]

III

We turn now to the constitutional issue presented in this case — whether respondents are entitled to a jury trial.[3]

To determine whether a particular action will resolve legal rights, we examine both the nature of the issues involved and the remedy sought. "First, we compare the statutory action to 18th-century actions brought in the courts of England prior to the merger of the courts of law and equity. Second, we examine the remedy sought and determine whether it is legal or equitable in nature." *Tull* [v. United States, 481 U.S. 412 (1987)]. The second inquiry is the more important in our analysis. Granfinanciera, S. A. v. Nordberg, 492 U.S. 33, 47-48 (1989).[4]

A

An action for breach of a union's duty of fair representation was unknown in 18th-century England; in fact, collective bargaining was unlawful. See N. Citrine, Trade Union Law 4-7 (2d ed. 1960). We must therefore look for an analogous cause of action that existed in the 18th century to determine whether the nature of this duty of fair representation suit is legal or equitable.

3. Because the National Labor Relations Act, 49 Stat. 449, 29 U.S.C. §159(a) (1982 ed.), does not expressly create the duty of fair representation, resort to the statute to determine whether Congress provided for a jury trial in an action for breach of that duty is unavailing. Cf. Curtis v. Loether, 415 U.S. 189, 192, n. 6 (1974) (recognizing the "'cardinal principle that this Court will first ascertain whether a construction of the statute is fairly possible by which the [constitutional] question may be avoided'" (quoting United States v. Thirty-Seven Photographs, 402 U.S. 363, 369 (1971)).

4. Justice Stevens's analysis emphasizes a third consideration, namely whether "the issues [presented by the claim] are typical grist for the jury's judgment." This Court, however, has never relied on this consideration "as an independent basis for extending the right to a jury trial under the Seventh Amendment." Tull v. United States, 481 U. S. 412, 418, n. 4 (1987). . . .

The Union contends that this duty of fair representation action resembles a suit brought to vacate an arbitration award [, which would have been brought in equity in the eighteenth century].

The arbitration analogy is inapposite, however, to the Seventh Amendment question posed in this case. No grievance committee has considered respondents' claim that the Union violated its duty of fair representation; the grievance process was concerned only with the employer's alleged breach of the collective-bargaining agreement. . . .

. . . The Union next argues that respondents' duty of fair representation action is comparable to an action by a trust beneficiary against a trustee for breach of fiduciary duty. Such actions were within the exclusive jurisdiction of courts of equity. 2 Story, [Commentaries on Equity Jurisprudence], §960, p. 266 [(13th ed. 1886)]; Restatement (Second) of Trusts §199(c) (1959). This analogy is far more persuasive than the arbitration analogy. Just as a trustee must act in the best interests of the beneficiaries, a union, as the exclusive representative of the workers, must exercise its power to act on behalf of the employees in good faith. Moreover, just as a beneficiary does not directly control the actions of a trustee, an individual employee lacks direct control over a union's actions taken on his behalf.

The trust analogy extends to a union's handling of grievances. In most cases, a trustee has the exclusive authority to sue third parties who injure the beneficiaries' interest in the trust, including any legal claim the trustee holds in trust for the beneficiaries. The trustee then has the sole responsibility for determining whether to settle, arbitrate, or otherwise dispose of the claim. Similarly, the union typically has broad discretion in its decision whether and how to pursue an employee's grievance against an employer. . . .

Respondents contend that their duty of fair representation suit is less like a trust action than an attorney malpractice action, which was historically an action at law. [The Court had suggested this analogy in an earlier case.] Presented with a more complete range of alternatives, we find that. . . . [t]he attorney malpractice analogy is inadequate in several respects. Although an attorney malpractice suit is in some ways similar to a suit alleging a union's breach of its fiduciary duty, the two actions are fundamentally different. The nature of an action is in large part controlled by the nature of the underlying relationship between the parties. Unlike employees represented by a union, a client controls the significant decisions concerning his representation. Moreover, a client can fire his attorney if he is dissatisfied with his attorney's performance. This option is not available to an individual employee who is unhappy with a union's representation, unless a majority of the members of the bargaining unit share his dissatisfaction. Thus, we find the malpractice analogy less convincing than the trust analogy.

Nevertheless, the trust analogy does not persuade us to characterize respondents' claim as wholly equitable. The Union's argument mischaracterizes the nature of our comparison of the action before us to 18th-century forms of action. As we observed in Ross v. Bernhard, 396 U.S. 531 (1970), "The Seventh Amendment question depends on the nature of the *issue* to be tried rather than the character of the overall action." Id., at 538 (emphasis added) (finding a right to jury trial in a shareholder's derivative suit, a type of suit traditionally brought in courts of equity, because plaintiffs' case presented legal issues of breach of contract and negligence). As discussed above . . . , to recover from the Union here, respondents must prove both that McLean violated §301 by breaching the collective-bargaining agreement and that the Union breached its duty of fair representation. When viewed in isolation, the duty of fair representation issue is analogous to a claim against a trustee for breach of fiduciary duty. The §301 issue, however, is comparable to a breach of contract claim — a legal issue.

Respondents' action against the Union thus encompasses both equitable and legal issues. The first part of our Seventh Amendment inquiry, then, leaves us in equipoise as to whether the respondents are entitled to a jury trial.

B

Our determination under the first part of the Seventh Amendment analysis is only preliminary. In this case, the only remedy sought is a request for compensatory damages representing backpay and benefits. Generally, an action for money damages was "the traditional form of relief offered in the courts of law." Curtis v. Loether, 415 U.S. 189, 196 (1974). This Court has not, however, held that "any award of monetary relief must *necessarily* be 'legal' relief." Ibid. (emphasis added). Nonetheless, because we conclude that the remedy respondents seek has none of the attributes that must be present before we will find an exception to the general rule and characterize damages as equitable, we find that the remedy sought by respondents is legal.

First, we have characterized damages as equitable where they are restitutionary, such as in "action[s] for disgorgement of improper profits," *Tull*, 481 U.S., at 424. The backpay sought by respondents is not money wrongfully held by the Union, but wages and benefits they would have received from McLean had the Union processed the employees' grievances properly. Such relief is not restitutionary.

Second, a monetary award "incidental to or intertwined with injunctive relief" may be equitable. Because respondents seek only money damages, this characteristic is clearly absent from the case. . . .[8]

We hold, then, that the remedy of backpay sought in this duty of fair representation action is legal in nature. Considering both parts of the Seventh Amendment inquiry, we find that respondents are entitled to a jury trial on all issues presented in their suit.

IV

On balance, our analysis of the nature of respondents' duty of fair representation action and the remedy they seek convinces us that this action is a legal one. Although the search for an adequate 18th-century analog revealed that the claim includes both legal and equitable issues, the money damages respondents seek are the type of relief traditionally awarded by courts of law. Thus, the Seventh Amendment entitles respondents to a jury trial, and we therefore affirm the judgment of the Court of Appeals.

It is so ordered.

Justice BRENNAN, concurring in part and concurring in the judgment.

I agree with the Court that respondents seek a remedy that is legal in nature and that the Seventh Amendment entitles respondents to a jury trial on their duty of fair representation claims. I therefore join Parts I, II, III-B, and IV of the Court's opinion. I do not join that part of the opinion which reprises the particular historical analysis this Court has employed to determine whether a claim is a "Suit at common law" under the Seventh Amendment, because I believe the historical test can and should be simplified. . . .

8. Both the Union and the dissent argue that the backpay award sought here is equitable because it is closely analogous to damages awarded to beneficiaries for a trustee's breach of trust. Such damages were available only in courts of equity because those courts had exclusive jurisdiction over actions involving a trustee's breach of his fiduciary duties.

The Union's argument, however, conflates the two parts of our Seventh Amendment inquiry. Under the dissent's approach, if the action at issue were analogous to an 18th-century action within the exclusive jurisdiction of the courts of equity, we would necessarily conclude that the remedy sought was also equitable because it would have been unavailable in a court of law. This view would, in effect, make the first part of our inquiry dispositive. We have clearly held, however, that the second part of the inquiry — the nature of the relief — is more important to the Seventh Amendment determination. The second part of the analysis, therefore, should not replicate the "abstruse historical" inquiry of the first part, *Ross*, 396 U.S., at 538, n. 10, but requires consideration of the general types of relief provided by courts of law and equity.

I believe that our insistence that the jury trial right hinges in part on a comparison of the substantive right at issue to forms of action used in English courts 200 years ago needlessly convolutes our Seventh Amendment jurisprudence. For the past decade and a half, this Court has explained that the two parts of the historical test are not equal in weight, that the nature of the remedy is more important than the nature of the right. Since the existence of a right to jury trial therefore turns on the nature of the remedy, absent congressional delegation to a specialized decisionmaker, there remains little purpose to our rattling through dusty attics of ancient writs. The time has come to borrow William of Occam's razor and sever this portion of our analysis. . . .

To rest the historical test required by the Seventh Amendment solely on the nature of the relief sought would not, of course, offer the federal courts a rule that is in all cases self-executing. Courts will still be required to ask which remedies were traditionally available at law and which only in equity. . . .[7]

If we are not prepared to accord the nature of the historical analog sufficient weight for this factor to affect the outcome of our inquiry, except in the rarest of hypothetical cases, what reason do we have for insisting that federal judges proceed with this arduous inquiry? It is time we read the writing on the wall, especially as we ourselves put it there.

---

7. There are, to be sure, some who advocate abolishing the historical test altogether. See, e.g., Wolfram, The Constitutional History of the Seventh Amendment, 57 Minn. L. Rev. 639, 742-747 (1973). Contrary to the intimations in justice Kennedy's dissent, I am not among them. I believe that it is imperative to retain a historical test, for determining when parties have a right to jury trial, for precisely the same reasons Justice Kennedy does. It is mandated by the language of the Seventh Amendment and it is a bulwark against those who would restrict a right our forefathers held indispensable. Like Justice Kennedy, I have no doubt that courts can and do look to legal history for the answers to constitutional questions, and therefore the Seventh Amendment test I propose today obliges courts to do exactly that.

Where Justice Kennedy and I differ is in our evaluations of which historical test provides the more reliable results. That three learned Justices of the Supreme Court cannot arrive at the same conclusion in this very case, on what is essentially a question of fact, does not speak well for the judicial solvency of the current test. My concern is not merely the competence of courts to delve into this peculiarly recalcitrant aspect of legal history and certainly not, as Justice Kennedy summarizes it, the "competence of the Court to understand legal history" in general. My concern is that all too often the first prong of the current test requires courts to measure modern statutory actions against 18th-century English actions so remote in form and concept that there is no firm basis for comparison. In such cases, the result is less the discovery of a historical analog than the manufacture of a historical fiction. By contrast, the nature of relief available today corresponds more directly to the nature of relief available in Georgian England. Thus the historical test I propose, focusing on the nature of the relief sought, is not only more manageable than the current test, it is more reliably grounded in history.

Justice STEVENS, concurring in part and concurring in the judgment.

Because I believe the Court has made this case unnecessarily difficult by exaggerating the importance of finding a precise common-law analogue to the duty of fair representation, I do not join Part III-A of its opinion. Ironically, by stressing the importance of identifying an exact analogue the Court has diminished the utility of looking for any analogue.

As I have suggested in the past, I believe the duty of fair representation action resembles a common law action against an attorney for malpractice more closely than it does any other form of action. Of course, this action is not an exact counterpart to a malpractice suit. Indeed, by definition, no recently recognized form of action — whether the product of express congressional enactment or of judicial interpretation — can have a precise analogue in 17th- or 18th-century English law. Were it otherwise the form of action would not in fact be "recently recognized."

But the Court surely overstates this action's similarity to an action against a trustee. Collective bargaining involves no settlor, no trust corpus, and no trust instrument executed to convey property to beneficiaries chosen at the settlor's pleasure. Nor are these distinctions reified matters of pure form. The law of trusts originated to expand the varieties of land ownership in feudal England, and evolved to protect the paternalistic beneficence of the wealthy, often between generations and always over time. Beneficiaries are protected from their own judgment. The attorney-client relationship, by contrast, advances the client's interests in dealings with adverse parties. Clients are saved from their lack of skill, but their judgment is honored. Union members, as a group, accordingly have the power to hire, fire, and direct the actions of their representatives — prerogatives anathema to the paternalistic forms of the equitable trust. . . .

Justice KENNEDY, with whom Justice[s] O'CONNOR and SCALIA join, dissenting.

This case asks whether the Seventh Amendment guarantees the respondent union members a jury trial in a duty of fair representation action against their labor union. The Court is quite correct, in my view, in its formulation of the initial premises that must govern the case. Under Curtis v. Loether, 415 U.S. 189, 193 (1974), the right to a jury trial in a statutory action depends on the presence of "legal rights and remedies." To determine whether rights and remedies in a duty of fair representation action are legal in character, we must compare the action to the 18th-century cases permitted in the law courts of England, and we must examine the nature of the relief sought. I agree also with those Members of the Court who find that the duty of fair representation action resembles an equitable trust action more than a suit for malpractice.

I disagree with the analytic innovation of the Court that identification of the trust action as a model for modern duty of fair representation actions is insufficient to decide the case. . . . Having made this decision in favor of an equitable action, our inquiry should end. Because the Court disagrees with this proposition, I dissent. . . .

NOTES AND PROBLEMS

1. The parties fought this case to the Supreme Court over an issue that seems rather far from the merits. Why did the plaintiffs want a jury so badly? Why did the union think it worthwhile to spend many thousands of dollars resisting one? What assumptions are the parties making about the likely sympathies of a jury?

2. To understand how *Terry* illustrates the application of the historical test, follow its analytic steps:

a. The union, resisting the jury demand, first contended that the action resembled a suit brought to vacate an arbitration award. If this contention had been accepted, why would it have defeated plaintiff's demand for a jury?

b. The union's second analogy was to an action brought against a trustee. If this contention had been accepted, why would it have defeated plaintiff's demand for a jury?

c. Terry and his coplaintiffs countered with still another analogy: to a malpractice action brought against a lawyer by his clients. If this contention had been accepted (as Justice Stevens argues it should have been), why would it have assured the plaintiffs a jury?

d. Offered these three analogies, the majority finds that of the trust most apt. Why?

3. Having accepted the trust analogy, the Court might have stopped there — as Justice Kennedy thinks it should have.

a. Instead, the Court found that the trust analogy was imperfect because the facts of the case involved two claims — one against the employer for breach of contract (the collective bargaining agreement) and another against the union for breach of the duty of fair representation. To recover from the union the plaintiffs had to show, first, that they had a good contract claim against the employer and, second, that the union breached its fiduciary duty in failing to press that claim.

b. The majority fails to ask a question about this analysis: Suppose one could demonstrate that such a claim — breach of fiduciary duty by failing to pursue a contract claim held by the beneficiary — would have been handled as a single equitable action. Would that argue in favor of a no-jury result?

4. The majority doesn't take that step. Instead, it moves from a consideration of analogues to the entire action to a consideration of remedy alone. Why? Why does the Court find that the remedy sought in this case was "legal," thus entitling the plaintiffs to a jury?

5. Finally, what is Justice Brennan's position — to which only he subscribes?

6. The Supreme Court has fiercely protected the right to a jury trial, but, like other constitutional rights, the parties can waive it by failing to raise the issue. In the case of the right to trial by jury, Rule 38 reaffirms the constitutional status of jury trial while insisting on a timely demand and establishing waiver as the penalty for failing to do so. See how the Rule works in two cases:

a. Plaintiff sues, seeking damages for breach of contract. Within the twenty-day limit set forth in Rule 12(a), defendant answers, denying various allegations. Assuming no amendments to the pleadings, how long do the parties have in which to demand a jury trial?

b. Plaintiff sues, alleging breach of contract and seeking specific performance; defendant answers, denying breach and alternatively contending that specific performance is not an available remedy. Plaintiff receives leave to amend and adds a claim for damages. May defendant now demand a jury trial?

c. A party can insert a demand for a jury directly into its pleading. In Note 6a, for example, the plaintiff who sought damages for breach could have in his complaint demanded a jury trial, and the defendant could equally have done so in her answer.

7. *Terry* fits a pattern: For most newly created claims that seek money damages as a remedy, the Court has found a right to jury trial under the Seventh Amendment.

a. For example, in Curtis v. Loether, 415 U.S. 189 (1974) (cited in *Terry*), the Court found that in civil actions brought under Title VIII of the Civil Rights Act of 1968, the parties had a right to jury trial. The Court reached a similar result under the Age Discrimination in Employment Act (ADEA) in Lorillard v. Pons, 434 U.S. 575 (1978). *Lorillard* relied heavily on the fact that Congress borrowed the remedy provisions of ADEA from the Fair Labor Standards Act, which carried a right to jury trial. The Court concluded:

> This inference [that jury trial would be available] is buttressed by an examination of the language Congress chose to describe the available remedies under the [act]. Section 7(b) empowers a court to grant "*legal*

or equitable relief" and §7(c) authorizes individuals to bring actions for "*legal* or equitable relief" (emphasis added). The word "legal" is a term of art: In cases in which legal relief is available and legal rights are determined, the Seventh Amendment provides a right to jury trial. . . . We can infer, therefore, that by providing specifically for "legal" relief, Congress knew the significance of the term "legal," and intended that there would be jury trial on demand to "enforc[e] . . . liability for amounts deemed to be unpaid minimum wages or unpaid overtime compensation."

Id. at 583.

b. By contrast, Title VII, which prohibits discrimination in employment, has led a far more tortured existence. Title VII provides that:

[T]he court may enjoin the respondent from engaging in such unlawful employment practice, and order such affirmative action as may be appropriate, which may include, but is not limited to, reinstatement or hiring of employees, with or without back pay . . . , or any other equitable relief as the court deems appropriate.

If the relief sought is limited to reinstatement or promotion, courts have been uniform in concluding that the relief is equitable and thus not triable to a jury. But what about claims for back pay? The Supreme Court has thus far been silent, leaving lower courts to struggle.

Congress has also gotten into the act without bringing much more clarity to the issue. A 1991 amendment to Title VII, 42 U.S.C. §1981(c), allowing a plaintiff to seek "compensatory and punitive damages" for intentional discrimination in employment, explicitly provides that such claims for compensatory and punitive damages are to be tried to a jury. 42 U.S.C. §1981(a)c. So far, one might assume that Congress had brought Title VII into conformity with the rest of the Civil Rights Act — that all claims of employment discrimination, like suits seeking damages for discrimination in housing, accommodations, education, and the like, were all not triable to a jury. But things are not that simple, for in defining "compensatory damages" in §1981a(b)(2), the statute provides that "[c]ompensatory damages shall not include backpay. . . ." How, then, should one treat a case in which a plaintiff sought reinstatement, back pay, and damages for intentional discrimination?

8. In one notable area, the Supreme Court has appeared to cut back on the extent of jury trial. Patents existed at the time of the ratification of the Seventh Amendment and claims of patent infringement were regularly tried to juries for almost two centuries. But in Markman v. Westview Instruments, 517 U.S. 370 (1996), the Court reanalyzed patent cases in a way that dramatically reduced the jury's scope. By way of background, note that a patent applicant files with the Patent Office a

"claim," in which the inventor defines the scope of his invention — what it does and what its advantages are. *Markman* revolved around whether the jury would construe the meaning of such "claims." The Court held that it would not. The opinion had four steps.

a. In the first, after conceding that patent infringement cases had long been tried to juries, the court distinguished between the case as a whole and a particular part of the case:

> This conclusion raises the second question, whether a particular issue occurring within a jury trial (here the construction of a patent claim) is itself necessarily a jury issue, the guarantee being essential to preserve the right to a jury's resolution of the ultimate dispute. In some instances the answer to this second question may be easy because of clear historical evidence that the very subsidiary question was so regarded under the English practice of leaving the issue for a jury.

Markman at 377.

b. The second step involved finding that because these "claims" had over the years become much more technical than they were in 1791, there was in fact no clear historical answer to the Seventh Amendment inquiry:

> But when, as here, the old practice provides no clear answer, we are forced to make a judgment about the scope of the Seventh Amendment guarantee without the benefit of any foolproof test.

Id.

c. Having found that they were writing on a clean slate, the justices engaged in an unusual form of analysis:

> We accordingly consult existing precedent and consider both the relative interpretive skills of judges and juries and the statutory policies that ought to be furthered by the allocation. . . .
>
> Where history and precedent provide no clear answers, functional considerations also play their part in the choice between judge and jury to define terms of art. We said in Miller v. Fenton, 474 U.S. 104 (1985), that when an issue "falls somewhere between a pristine legal standard and a simple historical fact, the fact/law distinction at times has turned on a determination that, as a matter of the sound administration of justice, one judicial actor is better positioned than another to decide the issue in question." So it turns out here, for judges, not juries, are the better suited to find the acquired meaning of patent terms.
>
> The construction of written instruments is one of those things that judges often do and are likely to do better than jurors unburdened by training in exegesis. . . .
>
> Finally, we see the importance of uniformity in the treatment of a given patent as an independent reason to allocate all issues of construction to the court. . . . It was just for the sake of such desirable uniformity that Congress created the Court of Appeals for the Federal Circuit as an

exclusive appellate court for patent cases, [29 U.S.C. §1295 (1981)], observing that increased uniformity would "strengthen the United States patent system in such a way as to foster technological growth and industrial innovation."

Uniformity would, however, be ill served by submitting issues of document construction to juries.

Id. at 384-381.

d. In most infringement cases the only significant question is whether Device A falls within the scope — the "claim" — of Device B and therefore infringes. Only rarely will there be a dispute about whether Device A was actually manufactured. As a result, judges, not juries, decide most significant patent issues — a clear change from the situation in 1791.

e. Note that the functional reasoning — that judges are better than juries at construing written documents — would apply as well to many situations in which juries regularly operate when they construe deeds, contracts, and the like. The *Markman* opinion is careful to limit its holding to the patent area, but its reasoning, if extended, could swallow up a lot of the Seventh Amendment.

9. Though they differ in outcome, *Markman* and *Terry* have an important similarity: Both explore the right to jury trial in the face of statutory silence. The 1991 amendment to the Civil Rights Act, discussed in Note 7(b), contains an explicit statutory provision of jury trial. What if the statute had instead forbidden jury trial? What if it had required jury trial of a clearly equitable claim? For example, could Congress order juries in Title VII cases where the only remedy sought is reinstatement? Is there, in other words, a constitutional right to a nonjury trial? The holdings on this question are sparse, but dicta suggest there is no constitutional right to trial by a judge, even in cases traditionally equitable. See, e.g., Beacon Theatres v. Westover, 359 U.S 500, 510 (1959) ("the right to jury trial is a constitutional one . . . while no similar requirement protects trials by the court"). Assuming that this sentence reflects the law, which of the following situations presents a Seventh Amendment issue?

a. Congress passes a statute creating a new private right of action for sexual harassment and authorizing both injunctive relief and damages. The statute provides that all questions of fact shall be tried by a jury, no matter what remedies are sought.

b. Congress passes the same statute, but it provides that all questions of fact shall be tried by a judge, regardless of the remedies sought.

10. Noticeably absent from the Court's Seventh Amendment opinions has been any discussion of the strengths and weaknesses of the jury as a factfinding body: *Markman* is a rare exception. Such discussions occasionally do, however, creep into opinions.

a. One district court, in a Title VII case, noted that fear of racial prejudice by the jurors, particularly in the South, had led earlier courts to shy away from juries and to construe the Seventh Amendment narrowly in light of those fears. The judge noted that today many plaintiffs are seeking jury trials and that the jury question accordingly ought to be reconsidered. Beesley v. Hartford Fire Insurance Co., 717 F. Supp. 781, on reconsideration, 723 F. Supp. 635 (N.D. Ala. 1989).

b. Contrast the preceding view with United States v. Schay, 746 F. Supp. 877 (E.D. Ark. 1990), which suggests that some judges think jury prejudice is a continuing problem in discrimination cases. The plaintiffs in *Schay* sued for housing discrimination under Title VIII. The principal plaintiff, a law clerk to a federal judge, wished to rent a house in a predominantly white section of Little Rock, Arkansas. He telephoned and was told the house was available, but when he arrived and the broker saw his skin color, the house was declared to be already rented. Returning to the office, the plaintiff asked colleagues to make the same inquiry. They were told the house was still available. At trial, the explanation for these discrepancies was that one Frank Daley had rented it before the plaintiff met the broker but had afterward changed his mind, thus accounting for its subsequent availability. After very brief deliberation, a jury found for the white defendant. The district judge, ruling on motions for judgment notwithstanding the verdict and new trial, found the defendant's witnesses barely credible. He remarked of Mr. Daley, "In respect to the testimony and actions of Frank Daley, it might be an exaggeration to say that he was the least credible witness appearing in this court during the last nine years that the writer of this opinion has held this office, but he would certainly be within the top five." Id. at 884. Because of the factfinding power vested in the jury, however, the judge found himself constrained to let the verdict stand.

11. The law-equity jury trial issue also arises in state courts. Unlike the Sixth Amendment (dealing with criminal juries), the Seventh Amendment does not apply to the states. As a consequence, there is no *federal* constitutional requirement that states accord the right of jury trial in any civil case. State courts may thus reach conclusions under their own laws that differ from those reached by the federal courts under the Seventh Amendment.

a. In many instances state courts have proved substantially less enthusiastic about jury trials in civil cases than have the federal courts. As examples of cases in which state courts rejected claims of entitlement to a jury, consider: C & K Engineering Contractors v. Amber Steel Co., 23 Cal. 3d 1 (1978) (contract actions based on promissory estoppel); Strauss v. Summerhays, 157 Cal. App. 3d 806 (1984) (quiet-title actions);

Robair v. Dahl, 80 Mich. App. 458 (1978) (constructive trusts); State ex rel. Willmam v. Sloan, 574 S.W.2d 421 (Mo. 1978) (calculation of damages after breach of a contractual covenant not to compete); Pelfrey v. Bank of Greer, 270 S.C. 691 (1978) (explicitly rejecting, as a matter of state law, Ross v. Bernhard, 396 U.S. 531 (1970), which held that shareholders' derivative actions were triable to a jury); State Bank of Lehi v. Woolsey, 565 P.2d 413 (Utah 1977) (mortgage foreclosure).

b. Why have state courts embraced the civil jury less warmly than the federal courts have? Two possibilities — one political, one practical — come to mind. First, the special history of the Seventh Amendment, whose absence was thought by some to be so important as nearly to scuttle the ratification of the federal Constitution, might cause the federal courts to err on the side of the jury when in doubt. There was no equivalent controversy in most state constitutional debates: Civil juries were taken to be a matter of course. Second, federal courts can more easily absorb the costs of additional jury trials; not only are federal courts proportionately better financed than their state counterparts, but the federal government, unlike those of the states, can print money to cover budget deficits. Every time a state court creates a new right to civil jury trial, it is adding a strain on court budgets.

c. State independence works both ways, sometimes yielding a jury where federal courts would deny one. In Hodgdon v. Mt. Mansfield Co., 624 A.2d 1122 (Vt. 1992) the Vermont Supreme Court held that under its state constitution claims brought under a state statute closely modeled on federal Title VII were triable to a jury, although the equivalent claim brought in a federal court would not have been (see Note 7b above).

3. Applying the Historical Test to New Procedures

The preceding section has illustrated the difficulty posed by changes in substantive law that have forced the court to grasp at sometimes slippery analogies to causes of action that existed in 1791. Procedural changes have occurred as well, and they create equally challenging problems in applying the Seventh Amendment. Some changes have occurred outside the judicial system, as Congress has created administrative agencies to do things that once were, or could have been, done by courts. Other changes have occurred within the judicial system itself, with the merger of law and equity and the abolition of the writ system. Both kinds of procedural change have created tensions in the doctrine surrounding jury trial.

a. The Seventh Amendment and Changes in Judicial Procedure

At the time of the Seventh Amendment there were, of course, separate courts of law and equity. If a litigant needed relief from both (for example, first the reformation of a contract, then suit for damages on the reformed agreement), he would have to file two suits. Moreover, a good deal of adversarial jockeying could arise, with one party seeking remedies at law while the other sought equitable relief. In such cases, which court took precedence? In American Life Insurance Co. v. Stewart, 300 U.S. 203 (1937), the Court ruled that the way to settle such questions was to grant considerable discretion to the trial court, guided by an appeal to historical practice. The judge sitting in equity might decide to restrain the legal action; alternatively, he might decide to let the jury trial proceed while holding the equitable relief in abeyance. Either decision, Stewart suggested, would be consistent with the Seventh Amendment.

The Federal Rules of Civil Procedure, which resulted in the merger of law and equity, became effective one year after *Stewart*. Cases that were formerly legal or equitable could now arise in one suit, and the courts were given little guidance as to when a jury trial was required in a merged procedure. The constitutional right to jury trial still applied. The trouble was that the right that was "preserved" came from a system that no longer existed — that is, the right was preserved but the underlying procedural system was not. There was no particular difficulty in applying the historical approach to actions that could be denominated as clearly legal or equitable. For example, the typical personal injury suit was cognizable at law, and a suit seeking only injunctive relief was cognizable in equity. In such cases, a jury trial was granted or denied in accordance with the premerger practice.

But what happened when legal and equitable claims and defenses found their way into the same case? Some examples might be helpful:

(1) *Plaintiff joins legal and equitable claims.* For example, plaintiff might sue to enjoin a nuisance and simultaneously seek damages for past harm.

(2) *Plaintiff brings legal claim; defendant has equitable defense.* For example, plaintiff might sue for breach of contract, and defendant might claim mistake and seek reformation of the instrument.

(3) *Plaintiff brings a legal (or equitable) claim; defendant brings equitable (or legal) counterclaim.* For example, plaintiff might sue for damages while defendant seeks specific performance of the agreement.

In each of these situations the legal and equitable phases of the case had common issues: For example, did the defendant's behavior constitute a nuisance? The merger of law and equity forced courts to think about jury trial in situations such as these with little guidance either from the rule makers who had preserved the right but destroyed the system or from the Supreme Court's opinion in *Stewart*. The next case exemplifies the approach finally adopted.

Amoco Oil Co. v. Torcomian
722 F. 2d 1099 (3d Cir. 1983)

BECKER, Circuit Judge.

The question presented by this appeal is whether the district court erred in refusing to afford defendants John Torcomian and Albert Torcomian a jury trial with respect to both the complaint of plaintiff Amoco and the Torcomians' compulsory counterclaim. The basis of the denial was that the claims, which arose out of the parties' dealings concerning an Amoco service station, were equitable in nature. The district court, following a bench trial, found for Amoco on all issues, and the Torcomians appeal. . . . [T]he district court erred in refusing to grant the defendants a jury trial. And because the district court could not properly have granted Amoco a directed verdict on either its claim or the Torcomians' counterclaim, the denial of a jury trial was not harmless error. The defendants' seventh amendment rights were therefore violated. Accordingly, the district court's judgment must be vacated and the entire case remanded for further proceedings.

I. The Record Relevant To The Jury Trial Issue

[The underlying dispute was between Amoco, which owned the service station, and the Torcomians, father and son, who wanted to take the station over from its previous operators and become Amoco's franchised dealers. The Torcomians actually operated the station for some months while negotiations were going on, but they never executed the franchise agreement. The parties disagreed about whether an Amoco representative had ever promised the plaintiffs would be accepted as franchisees and whether they met the stated qualifications for franchisees.]

Amoco originally sought extensive relief including: (1) ejectment of the defendants from the service station; (2) a permanent injunction restraining defendants from continued use, enjoyment and possession of Parkside Amoco; (3) a permanent injunction restraining defendants from use of the Amoco logo, trade name, service mark or trademark; (4) judgment in the amount of $46,675 for profits lost as a result of defendants' wrongful possession and fraudulent misrepresentations; (5) judgment for $12,000 for defendants' mesne profits and wrongful use of the Amoco logo, trade name, service mark or trademark; and (6) attorneys' fees. At the beginning of trial, however, Amoco attempted to orally amend its complaint to delete . . . portions of its complaint that sought money damages other than for mesne profits so as to eliminate any claims that might be construed as legal and to thereby foreclose the defendants' right to a jury trial.

Defendants' pleadings and their submissions in the pre-trial order state a claim that the defendants had a franchise relationship with Amoco at least until July 1984. These claims are based upon negotiations with and representations allegedly made by two Amoco agents. . . . Based on these allegations, the defendants sought "(1) [an] injunction enjoining plaintiff to comply with its franchise agreement with John Torcomian; (2) [a] judgment against plaintiff in an amount in excess of $100,000.00 for profits lost by John Torcomian as a result of plaintiff's failure to comply with its franchise agreement and for plaintiffs fraudulent misrepresentations; [and] (3) [a] judgment against plaintiff in the amount of defendants' reasonable attorneys' fee[s] and other costs involved in defending this action.". . .

II. Were The Components Of Amoco's Claim Legal Or Equitable?

It has long been settled law that neither joinder of an equitable claim with a legal claim nor joinder of a prayer for equitable relief with a claim for legal relief as to a legal claim can defeat an otherwise valid seventh amendment right to a jury trial. See Beacon Theatres, Inc. v. Westover, 359 U.S. 500 (1959); Dairy Queen, Inc. v. Wood, 369 U.S. 469 (1962). Thus, in order to assess the district court's denial of the defendants' demand for a jury trial as to the main claim, we must consider whether it comprised any legal claims seeking legal relief. If we find such claims, we must vacate the judgment, at least as to those claims, unless we are persuaded that Amoco was entitled to a directed verdict on those claims.

At the outset, we note that on its surface Amoco's complaint appears to present a number of essentially legal claims.[6] The complaint sought

6. Defendants apparently admit that at least some of the plaintiffs' claims (such as equitable relief for trademark infringement and restitution of mesne profits) would not require a jury trial if they stood alone. Nothing we say here is intended to prevent the district court from resolving these components of the complaint without a jury. . . .

ejectment, a form of action long regarded as legal. It also sought damages, a form of relief usually treated as legal. Plaintiff offers several theories, however, to counter this surface interpretation.

To rebut the normal rule that ejectment is an action at law, plaintiff cites two Pennsylvania cases. These cases purportedly hold that, where actual title to property is not in doubt, an action for injunction against defendant's continued possession of property leased to plaintiff is equitable. While our preliminary reading of the cited cases suggests that Amoco's interpretation and conclusions are dubious, there is a more telling problem with its argument: Pennsylvania's characterization of ejectment is irrelevant. As the Supreme Court [has] held, "in diversity cases, of course, the substantive dimension of the claim asserted finds its source in state law . . . but the characterization of that state-created claim as legal or equitable for purposes of whether a right to jury trial is indicated must be made by recourse to federal law." And federal law, as we have indicated, unequivocally holds actions seeking ejectment to be legal, not equitable. . . .

III. Were The Components Of The Defendants' Counterclaim Equitable Or Legal?

It is settled law in this Circuit and elsewhere that even an equitable main claim cannot preclude a jury trial on a legal counterclaim, at least when the counterclaim is compulsory.[10] A rule to the contrary would enable the preemptive filing of a complaint by the holder of an equitable claim, coupled with the doctrine of res judicata, to deprive the holder of a legal claim of his seventh amendment right to a jury trial. Accordingly, we must consider whether there was an element present in the counterclaim which would have given rise to a right to jury trial.

Although the defendants did ask for equitable relief in their counterclaim (i.e., fulfillment of Amoco's obligation under the alleged franchise agreement), defendants also sought damages for the past breach of that agreement. A routine claim such as that presented here for damages stemming from breach of contract is legal. As we have noted in Part II of this opinion, the fact that equitable relief is sought in addition to substantial legal relief does not eliminate a right to a jury trial. . . .

---

10. The counterclaim is clearly compulsory here because it arose out of the same transactions and occurrences that were the subject matter of Amoco's claim. See Fed. R. Civ. P. 13(a). The whole case revolves around the parties' dealings with each other in 1981 with respect to Parkside Amoco.

IV.   Was a Directed Verdict Appropriate?

We have now certainly found a sufficient admixture of law in Amoco's main claim and the defendants' counterclaim to render erroneous the district court's denial of a jury trial over at least those elements of the two claims. The error is harmless, however, if we are convinced that the evidence was such that Amoco would have been entitled to a directed verdict anyway.

Unfortunately for Amoco, disposition of both its claim and the counterclaim — which, as Amoco confesses, was in many ways the "mirror image" of the main claim — rested largely on issues of credibility. . . .

Viewing the evidence most favorably to the defendants . . . as a trial judge would be obliged to do in considering a motion for a directed verdict, the district court would have had to conclude that a jury could have found a lease or dealership agreement to have existed between Amoco and the defendants. . . . Consequently, we do not believe that a directed verdict could properly have been granted by the district court in this case on either the claim or counterclaim. . . . Nor can we say that a directed verdict was warranted for Amoco on grounds that Arata and Plocki[, Amoco's agents,] had no authority to bind it. For, according to the testimony of John Torcomian, Arata had said that he (Arata) had "the authority to approve me or anybody else as a dealer," and we cannot say, on the basis of the evidence of the course of dealings between the parties, that a jury could not reasonably have believed that Arata had apparent authority to bind Amoco or that the defendants reasonably relied upon his representations. . . .

V.   Conclusion

We have concluded that both Amoco's main claim and the defendants' counterclaim contained a number of legal components to which the defendants were entitled to a jury trial under the seventh amendment. Accordingly, the judgment of the district court will be vacated and the case remanded for a new trial.

NOTES AND PROBLEMS

1. *Torcomian* involves a review of principles already discussed, a basic holding about a new situation, and some complications.

a. As a quick review of the materials in the preceding section, explain why Amoco thought it might be able to avoid a jury trial by amending its complaint.

b. Now focus on the new aspect of the case. Begin by charting each of plaintiff's claims and each of defendant's counterclaims. Identify each of them as either legal or equitable.

c. Suppose the only claim in the lawsuit was plaintiff's prayer for an injunction preventing defendants from using the Amoco brand on the grounds that they were not official franchisees. Explain why there would have been no right to trial by jury.

d. Now suppose defendants had then filed a single counterclaim, seeking solely an order of specific performance requiring Amoco to honor its alleged agreement with them. Explain why there would have been no right to trial by jury.

e. Finally, suppose that plaintiff amended its complaint to add the claim for ejectment. Explain how this changes the entire complexion of the lawsuit and creates a Seventh Amendment issue.

2. The *Torcomian* opinion makes two statements, both entirely standard, that need to be reconciled.

a. It holds that the district court erred by denying a jury trial.

b. It also says, in footnote 6, "that at least some of the plaintiffs' claims (such as equitable relief for trademark infringement and restitution of mesne profits) would not require a jury trial if they stood alone. Nothing we say here is intended to prevent the district court from resolving these components of the complaint without a jury."

c. How could both propositions be true? The resolution lies in understanding an aspect of *Beacon Theatres*, cited in the opinion as the leading case on this aspect of jury trials. *Beacon* laid no new ground in holding that in a case with overlapping equitable and legal claims and counterclaims, a party could get a jury trial on any legal claims. *Beacon's* importance comes from its second holding: that the jury trial should precede any hearing on the equitable claim and that the jury's findings would control as to any "common" factual issues — disputed issues that might arise both in the legal and in the equitable claims.

d. The negative corollary of *Beacon* is that equitable claims in which there are no such common issues are not subject to jury trial; they will still be decided by the judge alone.

3. To see what these principles mean, apply them to the facts of *Torcomian*. Plaintiff sought ejectment of defendants from the service station premises. Ejectment, held the court, is a legal claim triable to a jury. One of defendants' counterclaims sought a decree of specific

performance, requiring Amoco to comply with its purported franchise agreement. Standing alone, such a claim would not be triable to a jury. Under *Beacon* the jury decides any contested issues of fact in the ejectment action, and the jury's determination of *those issues* will control in the equitable claim.

a. Suppose a jury determined that Amoco's apparently authorized representative did agree that the Torcomians could be its franchisee. That would resolve the claim for ejectment: Amoco could hardly eject a lawful franchisee from its premises. What about defendants' counter-claim for specific performance? The judge, in ruling on that claim, could not retry the facts and find that Amoco did not enter into a franchise agreement. He would, however, still have to weigh the equitable consider-ations required for specific performance. In doing so he *might* reach the conclusion that even though Amoco had agreed to allow the Torcomians to be its franchisee, specific performance was not called for because a legal remedy of damages was adequate or that the difficulties of supervising a franchise between parties already at each other's throats would be too formidable. Such a ruling would respect the jury's finding of an agreement even though it did not grant specific performance.

b. Now consider an alternative scenario. Suppose a jury determined that Amoco's representative had never made such an agreement and that the Torcomians were wrongfully occupying the premises. That would again resolve the ejectment action (this time in plaintiff's favor). But what about plaintiff's claim for $12,000 in mesne profits and wrongful use of the Amoco trademark? The judge would again be bound by the jury's findings that there was no franchise agreement. Footnote 6 suggests that Amoco's claim for restitution remains equitable and could be tried by the judge alone once the jury had resolved the legal claims and made findings on any issues common to the equitable claims.

4. The premise of *Torcomian*, which follows *Beacon* in this respect, is that whichever trier of fact goes first will bind the subsequent trier. Where there are overlapping legal and equitable claims, respect for the jury requires that the jury try *its* claims first. In the preceding example, the ejectment claim was legal. Suppose issues in that claim overlapped with the defendants' claim for specific performance of the alleged fran-chise agreement. In those circumstances the judge would let the jury try the ejectment claim first and would then be bound by the jury's findings on any issues that overlapped with the claim for specific performance.

Sometimes the equitable claim involving the same issue occurs in a completely separate lawsuit. Does it violate the Seventh Amendment to assign preclusive effect to the equitable claim if the same issue arises in a second suit? No, held Parklane Hosiery v. Shore, 439 U.S. 322 (1979), which appears in Chapter XII. The Securities and Exchange Commission (SEC) filed suit for injunctive relief, alleging that a company's proxy solicitation was misleading; the judge ruled for the SEC, finding the proxy misleading. A second suit, brought by a shareholder, sought damages flowing from the same proxy. In this second suit the defendant would be entitled to a jury trial on whatever issues remained unresolved. The defendant maintained that all issues were unresolved because it would violate the Seventh Amendment to give preclusive effect to the judge's finding that the proxy was misleading. The Supreme Court rejected that contention, holding that the judge's finding in the previous equitable suit controlled in the second action. Parklane was entitled to a jury on the issue of damages but could not relitigate the issues decided by the judge in the equitable claim.

5. After holding that the parties' claims and counterclaims contained a mixture of legal and equitable claims, *Torcomian* goes on to ask whether the court could rightly have disposed of the legal claims on a motion for a directed verdict.

a. Why does the court do that? Suppose that it would have been appropriate to grant a directed verdict — to one party or the other — on each of the legal claims. How and why would that have changed the court's holding?

b. Why on these facts was it inappropriate to grant a directed verdict?

6. According to *Beacon* and *Torcomian,* under which of the following circumstances should a timely demand for jury trial be honored?

a. Plaintiff seeks an injunction; defendant denies allegations of the complaint.

b. Plaintiff seeks an injunction; defendant counterclaims for the imposition of a constructive trust.

c. Plaintiff seeks an injunction; defendant counterclaims for damages.

7. Suppose that, after the dispute arose, one of the parties had brought a single claim, seeking declaratory relief, that Amoco had (or had not) entered into an enforceable franchise agreement. The federal Declaratory Judgment Act, 28 U.S.C. §2201, makes it possible to bring a claim even though one is seeking no coercive relief (damages, an injunction). Declaratory relief, like a counterclaim, is a twentieth-century procedural reform; it was not available in 1791. The legislative history of the act suggests that it was not meant to alter the right to trial by jury. How do the courts think about jury trials in such situations?

a. *Beacon* contained language suggesting that a declaratory judgment action was itself a legal remedy. That statement is inconsistent with the act and has not been widely followed, though it has never been expressly disclaimed by the Court.

b. Most federal courts have asked whether a legal claim would have been possible at the time of the suit. "Thus, in a school desegregation case [seeking injunctive relief], the inclusion of a request for a declaratory judgment does not authorize a jury trial." Richard Bourne & John Lynch, Merger of Law and Equity under the Revised Maryland Rules: Does It Threaten Trial By Jury?, 14 U. Balt. L. Rev. 1, 48 (1984). By contrast, if Amoco had brought an action for declaratory judgment on the facts of *Torcomian*, defendants could have argued that any of several imaginable claims for coercive relief — ejectment, fraud — would have been available, thus entitling either party to a jury trial.

8. All the preceding discussion, in this and the previous section, has assumed that one ought to judge the jury triability of a claim on the basis of the pleader's allegations — accepting at face value the parties' statement of their claims. Courts generally do just that, but a word of caution about one wild-card case is in order:

a. Dairy Queen, Inc. v. Wood, 369 U.S. 469 (1962), suggested that the Court might probe beneath the pleadings, recharacterizing the allegations of the pleadings. Plaintiff, owner of the Dairy Queen trademark, licensed defendant to use the trademark and to franchise others to use it in a specified territory in exchange for certain cash payments. After defendant defaulted, plaintiff terminated the contract and canceled the right to use the trademark; defendant apparently continued, however, to operate under the Dairy Queen name. Dairy Queen thereupon brought suit and sought the following: (a) temporary and permanent injunctions to restrain defendant from using the trademark, (b) an accounting to determine how much defendant owed Dairy Queen and a judgment for that amount, and (c) an injunction pending the accounting to prevent defendant from collecting money from Dairy Queen stores in the territory. All of these claims are generally thought to be equitable, and the district court struck defendant's demand for a jury trial. The Supreme Court reversed:

> The most natural construction of the respondents' claim for a money judgment would seem to be that it is a claim that they are entitled to recover whatever was owed them under the contract as of the date of its purported termination plus damages for infringement of their trademark since that date. . . .
>
> The respondents contention that this money claim is "purely equitable" is based primarily upon the fact that their complaint is cast in terms of an "accounting" rather than in terms of an action for "debt" or "damages." But the constitutional right to trial by jury cannot be made to depend upon the choice of words used in the pleadings. The necessary prerequisite to the right to maintain a suit for an equitable accounting, like all other

equitable remedies, is, as we pointed out in *Beacon Theatres*, the absence
of an adequate remedy at law. . ·. . The legal remedy cannot be characterized as inadequate merely because the measure of damages may necessitate
a look into petitioner's business records.

Id. at 476-479.

b. Notice the potential sweep of *Dairy Queen*. First, aren't all claims
and remedies always a function of the way the "complaint is cast"? If
courts freely recharacterize complaints to discover their "real" nature, it
will become quite difficult to predict jury entitlements. Second, because
equitable remedies are available only if legal remedies are inadequate,
could a party seeking a jury trial always argue that there was a *possibility*
that the court would award damages and that she was therefore entitled
to a jury? Consider, for example, the following hypothetical case: S agrees
to sell Blackacre to B for $100,000, but on the appointed day, S refuses
to perform the contract. B brings an action against S and alleges in Count
I his right to specific performance; in Count II, he seeks monetary
damages as an alternative remedy only in the event specific performance
is denied. Cf. Rule 8(e)(2). Does B have a right to jury trial? Does S?

c. There is good news for those whose minds threaten to explode at
this point: Matters have not gone this far. One does not see many cases
in which courts recharacterize pleadings to decide on the basis of what
parties are "really" seeking. Combined with *Beacon*, *Dairy Queen* does
give lower courts some latitude and creates some potential confusion,
but chaos has not resulted.

b. The Seventh Amendment and the Structure of Government

Everyone understands and expects that an amendment about jury trial
would have some effect on litigation. The Seventh Amendment also
poses a broader, structural challenge that emerges if one thinks of the
jury not only as a factfinder but also as an institution of government. Just
as the Constitution would forbid combining the Senate and House of
Representatives into a single legislative chamber, so some have thought
the Seventh Amendment to bar certain changes in the distribution of
government powers. Real exploration of this topic would take us far
from the boundaries of civil procedure, but the student needs a very
brief sketch to understand the importance of the Amendment. One can
briefly capture the debate by asking whether the amendment stands as
a barrier to what is sometimes called the administrative state — a system
that delegates tasks that look like adjudication to agencies other than
courts.

In 1791 government was considerably smaller and less specialized than it is today. By the end of the nineteenth century, however, state and federal governments began to create administrative agencies to regulate and administer large areas of public concern. Congress, in particular, created a number of such agencies dealing with areas ranging from transportation (Interstate Commerce Commission, Federal Aviation Administration) to food (Food and Drug Administration) to public welfare (Social Security Administration) to labor relations (National Labor Relations Board). As these bodies began to appear on the national scene, they raised a number of constitutional questions: How would a Constitution that seemed to establish three branches of government deal with what some have called the fourth branch? Most of these challenges focused on broad issues about the structure of government and lie beyond the province of our discussion. Two, however, bear mention.

You will not be surprised to learn that the Seventh Amendment has not prevented the establishment of administrative agencies, even when those agencies perform adjudication of issues that might, were they in a court setting, trigger jury trial. The issue arises when Congress gives an agency power to resolve the type of question usually decided by a court. For example, was a worker injured in the scope of his employment and thus eligible for federal workers' compensation? Did an employer's actions violate the National Labor Relations Act? Was a workplace unsafe as defined by the Occupational Safety and Health Act? Each of these questions required an agency, usually acting through a hearing officer or administrative law judge, to determine various factual issues and to apply the law to those questions — just the sort of work that a jury might have done had the issue been entrusted to a court. Moreover, such adjudications sometimes resulted in individual liability for money, making the circumstances look even more like traditional adjudication in which juries might be involved.

The Court has spoken with less than complete clarity about this issue. In general, it has upheld the notion of administrative adjudication so long as Congress entirely removes the claim from the court system. To that extent, the Court has endorsed the constitutionality of administrative adjudication (without juries). See, for example, Atlas Roofing v. Occupational Safety & Health Review Commission, 430 U.S. 442 (1977) (holding that the administrative imposition of penalties for violating federal health and safety regulations did not violate the Seventh Amendment):

> At least in cases in which "public rights" are being litigated — e.g., cases in which the government sues in its sovereign capacity to enforce public rights created by statutes within the power of Congress to enact — the Seventh Amendment does not prohibit Congress from assigning the fact-

finding function and initial adjudication to an administrative forum with which the jury would be incompatible. . . .

[But the appellant employer contends that under this reasoning] Congress could utterly destroy the right to a jury trial by always providing for administrative rather than judicial resolution of the vast range of cases that now arise in the courts. The argument is well put, but it overstates the holdings of our prior cases. . . . Our prior cases support administrative factfinding only in those situations involving "public rights," e.g., where the Government is involved in its sovereign capacity. . . . Wholly private tort, contract, and property cases, as well as a vast range of other cases . . . are not at all implicated. . . .

430 U.S. at 450. Although reality is not as neat as this snippet implies, it is clear that administrative adjudication is constitutional under the Seventh Amendment.

The picture begins to cloud when one moves the site of adjudication from something called an agency into something called a court. The most fertile source of conflicts has been bankruptcy. The Constitution allows Congress to establish a bankruptcy regime; it has done so both by passing legislation regulating the distribution of insolvents' assets and by establishing federal bankruptcy courts. Although bankruptcy tribunals are called "courts," they stand in the constitutional scheme halfway between the Article III federal courts and administrative agencies; more germane to our topic, bankruptcy courts operate without juries. A series of Supreme Court cases have sought to sort out the tangle presented by this situation; two of those cases involved the Seventh Amendment.

In Katchen v. Landy, 382 U.S. 323 (1966), a creditor presented his claim to the bankruptcy court seeking to have the claim satisfied out of the assets of the bankrupt's estate. But for the bankruptcy, the claim would have been a legal action for breach of contract, a claim triable to a jury. In bankruptcy, the trustee disallowed the claim in a summary proceeding without a jury. The Supreme Court held this did not violate the Seventh Amendment.

With *Katchen* contrast Granfinanciera, S.A. v. Nordberg, 492 U.S. 33 (1989), which presented facts the converse of *Katchen*. The bankruptcy trustee sued Granfinanciera, alleging that the bankrupt, just before bankruptcy, fraudulently transferred to Granfinanciera assets belonging to the bankruptcy estate, thus depriving other creditors of their fair shares. Granfinanciera denied this fraudulent transfer and demanded a jury trial. The Court held that a jury was required:

It may be that providing jury trials in some fraudulent conveyance actions . . . would impede swift resolution of bankruptcy proceedings and increase the expense of Chapter 11 reorganizations. But "these considerations are insufficient to overcome the clear command of the Seventh Amendment.". . .

492 U.S. at 63. At one level it is easy to reconcile *Katchen* and *Granfinanciera:* a creditor presenting a claim to the bankruptcy trustee doesn't get a jury trial, while a person against whom the trustee asserts a claim does. At another level the cases are in conflict and stand for a larger tension between the institutional aspects of the Seventh Amendment and contemporary administrative practice.

4. The Jury's Integrity: Size, Rules of Decision, and the Reexamination Clause

Preceding sections have suggested how difficult it is to "preserve" an institution as context changes. That point has double force if the characteristics of the institution also change — as the jury's have. The key elements of this change have been jury size, jury "rule of decision" (unanimity or super-majority?) and the courts' ability to overturn jury verdicts.

At early common law a jury consisted of twelve persons; the verdict was required to be unanimous; and the verdict could be attacked only by "attaint," a process in which a second jury, twice as large, considered charges that the first jury had been deliberately untruthful in its verdict. All these characteristics have undergone significant change since the thirteenth century.

In Colgrove v. Battin, 413 U.S. 149 (1973), a widely criticized decision, the Supreme Court constitutionalized six-person civil juries, and such juries are now in widespread use in federal courts and in some states. What difference does it make? Fundamentally, a smaller jury is less "average," less representative. Smaller juries are less likely to include any given point of view or social characteristic — race, political views, and so on. Just as a single individual is more likely to be eccentric than a large group is, so smaller juries are more likely to render aberrant verdicts than larger juries are.

In the federal system, unanimous verdicts are still required unless the parties agree to accept a nonunanimous verdict. See Rule 48. (Some states permit nonunanimous verdicts, usually allowing two or three opposing votes on a twelve-person jury.) Again one can ask what difference it makes. Rules of unanimity will result in more hung juries (a single holdout can block a verdict). Some studies suggest that groups where unanimity is required discuss the evidence with more intensity and in more detail than do groups where a super-majority will suffice.

Notice that, combined, these changes in size and decision rules can magnify each other. Decreasing the size of the jury reduces the likelihood that any given social characteristic will be reflected in the jury's membership. Moreover, abolishing the unanimity requirement lessens the effect that social diversity will have on the jury's verdict: If jurors do not have to render a unanimous verdict, the majority can simply ignore the point of view of one or two individuals.

Finally, there have been substantial changes in the assailability of the jury's verdict. By the time of the federal Constitution, courts had some limited power to overturn jury verdicts. Most observers would agree, however, that verdicts have become more vulnerable to attack in the two centuries since the ratification of the Seventh Amendment. That vulnerability has constitutional implications because the Seventh Amendment has two clauses. After granting the right to a jury trial "in suits at common law," the Amendment provides that "no fact tried by a jury, shall be otherwise reexamined in any Court of the United States, than according to the rules of the common law." This language, referred to as the "reexamination clause," serves to bolster jury power by preventing trial and appellate courts from overturning jury verdicts, except insofar as they traditionally had the power to do so. We shall look at the extent of the courts' power to disturb civil jury verdicts in the next chapter. As you will see, in spite of the language of the reexamination clause, trial and appellate courts today have substantial power to overturn jury verdicts that are found to be without evidentiary support.

5. Choosing Juries

As jury size and decision rules have changed, so have the rules about its composition. At common law, the sheriff was given very wide discretion in summoning jurors, and it was understood that he would summon people with both feet firmly planted in the established order: A medieval sheriff would have greeted the idea of a demographic cross-section first with incomprehension, then with horror. That outlook long prevailed. Not long ago, racial minorities, women, and members of the working class were often omitted from juries, sometimes intentionally. The past forty years have seen vast changes in such practices, both in the states and in the federal system. It is unconstitutional to discriminate on the basis of race or gender in compiling the list from which jurors are summoned. Most jurisdictions go further by statutorily requiring jury selection pools that represent broad cross-sections of the community. See 28 U.S.C. §§1861 et seq. Along with these changes in the idea of the ideal jury have come changes in how much freedom parties have in challenging jurors. Fifty years ago a party could challenge jurors without restraint; today that freedom is more limited — at least in theory.

a.   Assembling and Challenging a Pool of Jurors

Choosing a jury involves two phases: First, a pool of prospective jurors is summoned; second, the members of the trial jury are selected from the pool. Law regulates each phase, but the bodies of law regulating the two phases reflect conflicting pictures of the ideal jury — one striving for inclusiveness, the other allowing the parties to eliminate jurors.

To assemble a pool of prospective jurors, a decision must be made about whom to call to the courthouse. While it is clear that no group of mentally competent adult citizens can be systematically excluded from selection,* the general composition of the jury can differ substantially, depending on the type of list used and the method of choosing whom to summon. For example, summoning jurors exclusively from voters' rolls, lists of Social Security recipients, telephone books, driver's license lists, welfare lists, or college registration rolls would yield juries with substantially different characteristics. The federal courts' policy about jury pools appears at 28 U.S.C. §1861: "[L]itigants . . . entitled to trial by jury shall have the right to . . . juries selected at random from a fair cross section of the community. . . ." What is the theory behind applying such a requirement to civil cases? Why is it not adequate that jurors merely be unbiased? The manner in which such cross-sectional summonses are derived is set forth at 28 U.S.C. §§1863-1864 and §1866. The method for challenging a jury pool appears at 28 U.S.C. §1867(c). Examine these statutes and apply them to the following problems.

NOTES AND PROBLEMS

1. Alberta Student leads a campus demonstration protesting University's failure to discipline students allegedly guilty of acts of sexual harassment.

---

* In Thiel v. Southern Pacific Co., 328 U. S. 217 (1946), the Supreme Court held that the practice of excluding all persons who worked for a daily wage from the jury list was improper. As a consequence, the Court exercised its supervisory power to reverse a judgment for defendant railroad; the fact that the actual jury contained five persons who would identify with workers was irrelevant.

University sues Student in federal court, invoking diversity jurisdiction and seeking damages for University property Student allegedly destroyed while leading the protest.

a. Student's lawyer believes that the facts are very closely balanced and that the composition of the jury may make a significant difference in the outcome. When must Student's lawyer raise this challenge?

b. Pursuant to 28 U.S.C. §1867(d), Student's lawyer presents the affidavit of a demographer stating that college students constitute 5 percent of the population of the district but that a sampling of the list used by the jury commissioner indicates that fewer than 1 percent of those summoned for service are college students. The court must now decide whether "if true, [these allegations] would constitute a substantial failure to comply with the provisions" of §§1861 et. seq. Assume that the judge finds student's statistics trustworthy; the only question to be decided is whether the district's selection processes violate the requirement that juries be "selected at random from a fair cross section of the community." What is the issue? How should the judge rule?

c. Would your answer be different if Student's lawyer had instead shown that women constituted 52 percent of the community but that only 40 percent of those summoned as jurors were women?

2. The judge in University v. Student rules that Student has made a prima facie case under 28 U.S.C. §1867(d), with the consequence that Student may depose the jury commissioner and have access to documentary records. Commissioner testifies that he works from voter registration lists and that many students either do not register to vote or maintain their registration in their hometowns.

a. Should the judge accept this as an adequate response to Student's challenge?

b. If the judge does not accept this response, how should he order the list to be revised or supplemented? See 28 U.S.C. §1863(b)(2).

c. What would happen if the commissioner testified that he sent jury questionnaires (the first step to summoning jurors) to proportional numbers of students, but, having been advised that failure to return the questionnaire usually meant that they would not be called for jury service, the students threw the questionnaires away?

3. At one time many jury service statutes categorically exempted large groups of people, ranging from police officers to mothers to physicians. In recent decades state and federal statutes have dramatically reduced these occupational exemptions. The current federal list exempts only active members of the armed services, police and fire officers, and public officials. The result is jury pools that reflect a broader array of occupations,

education, and wealth. What, if any, effect on verdicts would you expect such changes to have?

b.   Challenging for Cause

Even if the jury pool is impeccably cross-sectional, not all of its members can try every case. Just as judges can be recused, so jurors can be challenged for cause. As an obvious example of this principle, a juror cannot decide a case in which he or she is a party. But how much further does this "principle of the unbiased trier" extend? Is the ideal trier neutral as between the parties but acquainted with the law and with the life situation from which the dispute arises? Or is the ideal trier one who requires education in both the facts and the law? The issue is important both to individual litigants — it is terrifying to have one's case depend on a trier one believes to be biased — and to the system of justice. This section explores the question of the "unbiased trier," and in the process extends the understanding of neutrality we began to explore in the material and of the somewhat different expectations we have of judges and jurors.

Once the pool is chosen, jurors must be selected to sit in a particular case. This selection occurs in a process called *voir dire.** Generally, a certain number of those in the pool are called into a particular courtroom, and twelve are selected to sit in the jury box for initial questioning. After general statements about the parties and issues are given, some jurors may be disqualified from service. Parties are not required to accept all jurors. Each party may challenge any juror for *cause* — that is, may seek to convince the judge that the juror is not qualified to serve.

The law on challenges for cause is not well developed. In practice, once relatives and employees of parties have been eliminated, judges are reluctant to discharge for cause. For example, the parties, witnesses, and attorneys will be identified, and any prospective juror who knows any of them will usually be excluded. If the case involves a particular kind of institution, such as a bank or college, persons who are employed by that kind of institution may be excluded. The final step involves questioning individual jurors to find out something about them and to uncover possible bias or prejudice. Both the general and individual questioning may be conducted by the court, by the parties, or by both. See Rule

---

* The term comes from law French, an artificial blend of English and French terms used in medieval English courts; it means "to speak the truth" and dates to an age when jurors were as much witnesses as they were deciders of fact.

47(a). Keeping in mind the goals of achieving an "unbiased" jury, exercise your intuitions on the following problems.

NOTES AND PROBLEMS

1. Suppose a case involves an auto accident; the defendant is a high school teacher.

a. No judge would grant challenges for cause as to all jurors who had gone to high school.

b. Most judges would grant challenges for cause as to any juror who had been a student of the teacher in question.

c. What is the distinction?

2. Between these two poles lie most challenge-for-cause situations. For example, suppose one of the prospective jurors in the case described above is an elementary school teacher who doesn't know the defendant.

a. If you were the plaintiff's lawyer, how would you articulate a challenge for cause?

b. In such situations — where there is possible but not obvious bias — the judge will often ask the juror whether, in spite of that answer, the prospective juror can keep an open mind and decide the case only on the basis of the evidence presented.

c. If the juror answers "No," the judge will discharge him for cause.

d. But if the juror says, "Yes, I can be objective," most judges will not discharge for cause. Does this response place too much faith in human nature?

e. What about the juror who responds to the question in 2b by saying, "I recognize that I may have some unconscious identification with the defendant, but I will do everything in my power not to let it influence my judgment." Should the judge excuse that juror? Or has the judge just found the ideal juror?

3. What if jurors conceal or lie on voir dire?

a. The first question is how a lawyer would find out. Jurors answer the voir dire questions under oath, but there is no official investigation of their accuracy. Consequently, lawyers find out about anomalies mostly by chance.

b. Once a lawyer determines that a juror was not candid during voir dire, what recourse does she have? The leading case on that question, McDonough Power Equipment v. Greenwood, 464 U.S. 548 (1984), established the standard for challenging a verdict on the basis of inaccurate answers on voir dire:

> We hold that to obtain a new trial in such a situation, a party must first demonstrate that a juror *failed to answer honestly a material question* on voir dire, and then further show that *a correct response would have provided a valid basis for a challenge for cause.*

Id. at 555 (emphasis added).

c. Would you expect many verdicts to be upset under this standard?

4. Challenges for cause are difficult to win. That does not make lawyers less interested in voir dire, which, in practice, has two purposes other than developing challenges for cause.

a. Lawyers use voir dire to begin presenting their cases. They cannot be too overt about this; a question such as "You would be sympathetic to my client, wouldn't you?" would be improper. Nor can lawyers make statements about the facts: "Defendant was blind drunk at the time of the accident." But questions designed to frame the client's story, to get the jurors thinking, for example, about the ways in which injuries had shaped the lives of their families, will generally slide by.

b. The second function of voir dire is to let the parties develop a list of jurors whom they would like to strike as one of the peremptory challenges. Not long ago the lawyers had unfettered freedom in exercising their peremptory challenges; that has now changed, as the next section demonstrates.

c. Peremptory Challenges

Unlike a challenge for cause, a *peremptory challenge* allows lawyers to strike a juror for any reason or for no reason at all. In the federal courts, 28 U.S.C. §1870 gives each side three peremptory challenges and additional challenges if alternate jurors are selected; in a federal six-person jury, all of the initial jury selections can be replaced via peremptory challenges. The court usually has broad discretion to allocate peremptory challenges or to permit additional challenges in multiparty actions.

What is the justification for peremptory challenges? One view is that peremptories in effect allow the parties to choose their juries, thus giving any ensuing verdict legitimacy in their eyes. A softer justification is that peremptories allow parties to excuse a juror about whom they have a hunch that does not rise to the level of a challenge for cause, or whom they may have offended through vigorous (but unsuccessful) voir dire questioning. Taken to the extreme, however, peremptories may conflict with the ideas of the cross-sectional jury embodied in statutes like 28 U.S.C. §1861. If society believes that juries composed of many different viewpoints are desirable, does it make sense to allow parties to negate that goal through the use of peremptories?

It is well established that court officials may not intentionally exclude any group from a jury panel. But can the parties accomplish the same result by the use of peremptory challenges? A party ordinarily need not explain or justify the use of such challenges; a party could, for example, strike all blue-eyed panelists from the jury on the basis of whimsy. War stories among trial lawyers suggest the frequent use of peremptories based on hunches about the predilections of various social groups: Are blue-collar, rural whites of Northern European extraction likely to be more defense-oriented than African-American Catholics? Elderly accountants less generous than young race-car drivers? And so on. How far does this unaccountability extend?

One answer is that unaccountability stops when race enters the picture. In Batson v. Kentucky, 476 U.S. 79 (1986), the Court in a criminal case held that the prosecution's systematic striking of black jurors without a justification based on nonracial factors violated the defendant's right to equal protection. Nothing in *Batson* explicitly limited the application of its principle to criminal cases, but the basis for the holding left its reach beyond the criminal context in doubt. The next case extends *Batson* to the civil context.

Edmonson v. Leesville Concrete Co.

500 U.S. 614 (1991)

Justice KENNEDY delivered the opinion of the Court.

We must decide in the case before us whether a private litigant in a civil case may use peremptory challenges to exclude jurors on account of their race. Recognizing the impropriety of racial bias in the courtroom, we hold the race-based exclusion violates the equal protection rights of the challenged jurors. This civil case originated in a United States District Court, and we apply the equal protection component of the Fifth Amendment's Due Process Clause. See Bolling v. Sharpe, 347 U.S. 497 (1954).

I

Thaddeus Donald Edmonson, a construction worker, was injured in a job-site accident at Fort Polk, Louisiana, a federal enclave. Edmonson sued Leesville Concrete Company for negligence in the United States District Court for the Western District of Louisiana, claiming that a Leesville employee permitted one of the company's trucks to roll backward and pin him against some construction equipment. Edmonson invoked his Seventh Amendment right to a trial by jury.

During voir dire, Leesville used two of its three peremptory challenges authorized by statute to remove black persons from the prospective jury. Citing our decision in Batson v. Kentucky, 476 U.S. 79 (1986), Edmonson, who is himself black, requested that the District Court require Leesville to articulate a race-neutral explanation for striking the two jurors. The District Court denied the request on the ground that Batson does not apply in civil proceedings. As impaneled, the jury included 11 white persons and 1 black person. The jury rendered a verdict for Edmonson, assessing his total damages at $90,000. It also attributed 80% of the fault to Edmonson's contributory negligence, however, and awarded him the sum of $18,000.

Edmonson appealed. . . .

II

A

In Powers v. Ohio, 111 S. Ct. 1364 (1991), we held that a criminal defendant, regardless of his or her race, may object to a prosecutor's race-based exclusion of persons from the petit jury. . . .

That an act violates the Constitution when committed by a government official, however, does not answer the question whether the same act offends constitutional guarantees if committed by a private litigant or his attorney. The Constitution's protections of individual liberty and equal protection apply in general only to action by the government. Racial discrimination, though invidious in all contexts, violates the Constitution only when it may be attributed to state action. Thus, the legality of the exclusion at issue here turns on the extent to which a litigant in a civil case may be subject to the Constitution's restrictions. . . .

The principle that the selection of state officials, other than through election by all qualified voters, may constitute state action applies with even greater force in the context of jury selection through the use of peremptory challenges. Though the motive of a peremptory challenge may be to protect a private interest, the objective of jury selection proceedings is to determine representation on a governmental body. Were it not for peremptory challenges, there would be no question that the entire process of determining who will serve on the jury constitutes state action. The fact that the government delegates some portion of this power to private litigants does not change the governmental character of the power exercised. The delegation of authority that in [Chauffeurs, Teamsters &

Helpers, Local No. 391 v.] *Terry* [supra page 670] occurred without the aid of legislation occurs here through explicit statutory authorization. . . .

. . . Here, as in most civil cases, the initial decision whether to sue at all, the selection of counsel, and any number of ensuing tactical choices in the course of discovery and trial may be without the requisite governmental character to be deemed state action. That cannot be said of the exercise of peremptory challenges, however; when private litigants participate in the selection of jurors, they serve an important function within the government and act with its substantial assistance. . . .

Finally, we note that the injury caused by the discrimination is made more severe because the government permits it to occur within the courthouse itself. Few places are a more real expression of the constitutional authority of the government than a courtroom, where the law itself unfolds. Within the courtroom, the government invokes its laws to determine the rights of those who stand before it. In full view of the public, litigants press their cases, witnesses give testimony, juries render verdicts, and judges act with the utmost care to ensure that justice is done. . . .

B

Having held that in a civil trial exclusion on account of race violates a prospective juror's equal protection rights, we consider whether an opposing litigant may raise the excluded person's rights on his or her behalf. As we noted in *Powers*: "In the ordinary course, a litigant must assert his or her own legal rights and interests, and cannot rest a claim to relief on the legal rights or interests of third parties." We also noted, however, that this fundamental restriction on judicial authority admits of "certain, limited exceptions," and that a litigant may raise a claim on behalf of a third party if the litigant can demonstrate that he or she has suffered a concrete, redressable injury, that he or she has a close relation with the third party, and that there exists some hindrance to the third party's ability to protect his or her own interests. All three of these requirements for third-party standing were held satisfied in the criminal context, and they are satisfied in the civil context as well. . . .

We conclude that courts must entertain a challenge to a private litigant's racially discriminatory use of peremptory challenges in a civil trial.

III

It remains to consider whether a prima facie case of racial discrimination has been established in the case before us, requiring Leesville to offer race-neutral explanations for its peremptory challenges. In *Batson*, we held that determining whether a prima facie case has been established requires consideration of all relevant circumstances, including whether there has been a pattern of strikes against members of a particular race. 476 U.S., at 96-97. The same approach applies in the civil context, and we leave it to the trial courts in the first instance to develop evidentiary rules for implementing our decision.

The judgment is reversed, and the case is remanded for further proceedings consistent with our opinion.

It is so ordered.

Justice O'CONNOR, with whom The CHIEF JUSTICE and Justice SCALIA join, dissenting.

The Court concludes that the action of a private attorney exercising a peremptory challenge is attributable to the government and therefore may compose a constitutional violation. This conclusion is based on little more than that the challenge occurs in the course of a trial. Not everything that happens in a courtroom is state action. A trial, particularly a civil trial, is by design largely a stage on which private parties may act; it is a forum through which they can resolve their disputes in a peaceful and ordered manner. The government erects the platform; it does not thereby become responsible for all that occurs upon it. As much as we would like to eliminate completely from the courtroom the specter of racial discrimination, the Constitution does not sweep that broadly. Because I believe that a peremptory strike by a private litigant is fundamentally a matter of private choice and not state action, I dissent. . . .

Justice SCALIA, dissenting.

I join Justice O'Connor's dissent, which demonstrates that today's opinion is wrong in principle. I write to observe that it is also unfortunate in its consequences.

The concrete benefits of the Court's newly discovered constitutional rule are problematic. It will not necessarily be a net help rather than hindrance to minority litigants in obtaining racially diverse juries. In criminal cases, Batson v. Kentucky, 476 U.S. 79 (1986), already prevents the prosecution from using race-based strikes. The effect of today's decision (which logically must apply to criminal prosecutions) will be to prevent the defendant from doing so — so that the minority defendant can no longer seek to prevent an all-white jury, or to seat as many jurors of his own race as possible. To be sure, it is ordinarily more difficult to prove race-based strikes of white jurors, but defense counsel can generally be relied upon to do what we say the Constitution requires. So in criminal cases, today's decision represents a net loss to the minority litigant. In civil cases that is probably not true — but it does not represent an unqualified gain either. Both sides have peremptory challenges, and they are sometimes used to assure rather than to prevent a racially diverse jury. The concrete costs of today's decision, on the other hand, are not at all doubtful; and they are enormous. We have now added to the duties of already-submerged state and federal trial courts the obligation to assure that race is not included among the other factors (sex, age, religion, political views, economic status) used by private parties in exercising their peremptory challenges. That responsibility would be burden enough if it were not to be discharged through the adversary process; but of course it is. When combined with our decision this Term in Powers v. Ohio, 111 S. Ct. 1364 (1991), which held that the party objecting to an allegedly race-based peremptory challenge need not be of the same race as the challenged juror, today's decision means that both sides, in all civil jury cases, no matter what their race (and indeed, even if they are artificial entities such as corporations), may lodge racial-challenge objections and, after those objections have been considered and denied, appeal the denials — with the consequence, if they are successful, of having the judgments against them overturned. Thus, yet another complexity is added to an increasingly Byzantine system of justice that devotes more and more of its energy to sideshows and less and less to the merits of the case. . . .

NOTES AND PROBLEMS

1. Three years after *Edmonson*, the Court extended the principle to include peremptory strikes based on gender. J.E.B. v. Alabama, 511 U.S. 127(1994).

2. *Edmonson* and *J.E.B.* have several layers.

a. One is doctrinal and has chiefly to do with constitutional law. Both cases are applications of the Fourteenth and Fifth Amendments, which forbid the *state* to deprive one of equal protection. Both courts therefore faced an initial question of whether a peremptory challenge exercised by a private litigant was unconstitutional.

b. As you have seen, *Edmonson* held that it was relying on the judge's role in assisting and validating the peremptory challenge.

c. In *J.E.B.* things were more complicated because the party accused of exercising peremptory challenges in an unconstitutional manner was the State of Alabama itself (in its role as a civil litigant). *J.E.B.* was a five-four decision, and the fifth vote for the majority position, Justice

O'Connor, limited her concurrence to the situation in which the state itself was a litigant.

d. Strictly speaking, then, it is unconstitutional for any civil litigant to exercise a peremptory challenge based on race; it is unconstitutional for the state, but not for a private civil litigant, to exercise such a challenge based on gender.

e. Is this a sensible distinction?

3. Notice that *Batson* and *Edmonson* are decided under the Due Process Clause of the Fourteenth Amendment and therefore, unlike the Seventh Amendment, apply to state as well as to federal courts. The net result is that so far as the federal constitution is concerned, a state need not grant a jury trial in any civil case. But if it does, it may not permit parties to use peremptory challenges in a racially discriminatory way.

4. *Batson*, *Edmonson*, and *J.E.B.* open the door for one party to object to the other's use of peremptory challenges. How do such objections to challenges work? According to *Batson* (whose procedure *Edmonson* endorsed), a party must first make an initial showing (a "prima facie case") that allows a court to infer a pattern based on race or gender. Suppose that Bertha, a dismissed employee of a state university, sues, alleging wrongful discharge. After voir dire comes the time for the parties to exercise their peremptory challenges.

a. Defendant (the state university) exercises its first peremptory challenge against a male African-American juror. Bertha objects, citing *Edmonson*. Explain why her objection will be overruled.

b. Bertha then challenges two male jurors (neither is African-American). Defendant, citing *J.E.B.*, suggests that Bertha's use of challenges suggests a pattern, and asks the judge to require her to justify this pattern. What is Bertha's strongest argument that she should not be required to do so?

c. Defendant then challenges a second African-American juror. Bertha renews her objection, now citing the pattern of peremptory challenges. Should defendant now be required to justify the challenges in nonracial terms?

5. *Batson*, *Edmonson*, and *J.E.B.* open a previously closed procedural door, permitting opponents to question the exercise of peremptories and forcing the parties to give nondiscriminatory justifications. But neither case devotes much consideration to what ought to count as a good excuse, an acceptable alternative reason for an apparently unacceptable use of a peremptory challenge. What will count as an acceptable justification of an apparently racial or gender-based challenge?

a. Imagine a challenged peremptory. Asked to justify what is an apparently race- or gender-based pattern, lawyer responds, "I didn't like the way she looked at me during voir dire." If the court accepts that justification, what becomes of the principles enunciated in *Edmonson* and *J.E.B.*?

b. Alternatively, suppose that counsel replies, "Yes, it's true that both challenged jurors were men [or African-Americans], but my real reason was that they occupied managerial positions, and I am therefore concerned that they will not be sympathetic to my client's claim of wrongful discharge from her job." If courts refuse to accept such justification, they will effectively eliminate peremptory challenges. When voir dire is brief, counsel will rarely have any but stereotypical information on which to base their challenges.

c. In Purkett v. Elem, 514 U. S. 765 (1995), the Supreme Court suggested how relaxed a standard it was prepared to apply to a "race-neutral explanation" under *Batson* and *Edmonson*. In *Purkett* the convicted defendant complained that the prosecutor had offered inadequate explanations for peremptory strikes of black jurors. When asked to explain the peremptories, the prosecutor replied:

> I struck [juror] number twenty-two because of his long hair. He had long curly hair. He had the longest hair of anybody on the panel by far. He appeared not to be a good juror for that fact, the fact that he had long hair hanging down shoulder length, curly, unkempt hair. Also he had a mustache and goatee type beard. Those are the only two people on the jury . . . with facial hair. . . . And I don't like the way they looked, with the way the hair is cut, both of them. And the mustaches and the beards look suspicious to me.

Id. at 766. The Supreme Court summarily affirmed the conviction, reversing the Eighth Circuit, which had found such an explanation insufficient. Justices Breyer and Stevens dissented on the grounds that the Court's summary action had effectively overruled part of *Batson*. Does *Purkett* suggest that the Court is having second thoughts about the difficulty of the inquiry required by *Batson* and *Edmonson*?

d. Requiring any explanation for the exercise of peremptories poses a challenge of courtroom etiquette. Suppose that a lawyer, asked in the jury's presence to justify a proposed peremptory challenge, says, "Frankly, Your Honor, Juror #3 didn't seem very intelligent, and I think I need smart jurors on this case." Having heard this explanation, Juror #3 might well form a substantially negative view of counsel — perhaps so negative that it would be difficult for her to keep an open mind about the case. At that point, the lawyer would have a valid basis for challenging the juror for cause. In order to prevent such sequences, many judges insist that all discussions of peremptory challenges occur at sidebar (out of the jury's hearing) or in chambers.

6. One explanation for *Purkett* in Note 5c is that the Court worked itself into a corner with this series of cases by purporting to preserve the peremptory challenge but hedging its exercise sufficiently to make it difficult to use. One can imagine a range of solutions:

a. Reverse or curtail *Batson*. The *Purkett* dissenters thought that was happening in that case.

b. Expand voir dire. *J.E.B.* hinted at such a development:

> If conducted properly, voir dire can inform litigants about potential jurors, making reliance upon stereotypical and pejorative notions about a particular gender or race both unnecessary and unwise. Voir dire provides a means of discovering actual or implied bias and a firmer basis upon which the parties may exercise their peremptory challenges intelligently.

517 U.S. at 143-144. Behind such a suggestion is the idea that a lawyer, asked to justify a peremptory challenge, could reply, "It's not her race, Your Honor; it's her attitude toward punitive damages." Many courts in busy metropolitan areas do not conduct extensive voir dire. Must they now change this practice?

c. Abolish the peremptory challenge. The reasoning would be that peremptories are necessarily exercised on scant evidence (given the usually cursory nature of voir dire) and therefore reflect no more than the lawyer's stereotypes. Moreover, if it is important to have widely representative juries, the peremptory works at cross purposes with such a goal by encouraging lawyers to exercise group-based stereotypes. Under such a proposal, Congress (or a state legislature) would simply abolish peremptories, thus obviating the inquiry into motive and speeding jury selection.

d. Combine the two previous suggestions — to eliminate peremptories but compensate by expanding the basis for challenges for cause. The argument in favor of this course is that it would eliminate the impermissible bases for voir dire while preserving the legitimate ones. Nancy Marder, Beyond Gender: Peremptory Challenges and the Role of the Jury, 73 Tex. L. Rev. 1041 (1995).

e. Permit peremptory challenges but clarify the basis on which they would be permitted. Such clarification could take the form of legislatively created specifications and examples of acceptable reasons. Because *Edmonson* and *J.E.B.* are constitutional cases, such statutes would themselves be subject to constitutional review, but they would at least dispel some of the confusion.

TRIAL

X

Trials occupy a paradoxical status in American law. They occur infrequently in relation to lawsuits filed, but they shape almost every aspect of procedure. It is common to point out that only about 3 percent of claims filed in the United States end in trials.* Yet the elaborate provisions for discovery have as one of their primary goals the uncovering of information to be presented at trial, and much of the law of evidence is aimed at controlling the flow of information during a trial. Likewise, the emphasis on the presentation of live witnesses (rather than depositions or other documentary evidence) — which brings with it the opportunity for theatrical displays by lawyers — stems from a conception of the trial as the culmination of litigation. Even the adversarial stance of the lawyers — perhaps more marked in Anglo-American law than in other systems — may flow in part from the realization that the whole case rides on a single presentation in a comparatively short time span before a trier of fact. In this chapter we focus on an especially procedural aspect of trial: the extent of the controls placed on the finder of fact, with special focus on the jury. We shall examine the procedural mechanisms that empower and control the jury. In doing so, however, we must not lose sight of a larger question: What conceptions of truth, of justice, of democratic decision making underlie jury power and control?

In some respects, the law treats the judge as a trier of fact in the same way as the jury is a trier of fact. The law seeks to assure that both the judge and the jury will consider the evidence properly presented by the adversaries and will reach conclusions for which there is some rational basis in the evidence that the court allowed to be introduced at the trial. The law also seeks to assure that both judge and jury apply the proper

---

* Be careful not to equate trials with adjudication. As you have already learned, it's possible for a court to pass on the merits of a case without having held a trial: 12(b)(6) dismissals and motions for summary judgment are two of the more common means by which a court may adjudicate a dispute without its having gone to trial. If one adds such adjudicated dispositions to the figure for trials, it appears that approximately 30 percent of filed cases end with an adjudicated disposition — of which only a third are trials.

law. In a nonjury case (often called a bench trial), the judge must set forth the legal conclusions behind her judgment. If those legal conclusions reflect an erroneous view of the law, an appellate court will reverse and typically ask the trial judge to reconsider the decision based on a correct statement of the law. In a jury case, the trial judge instructs the jury on the law it should apply. If the trial judge's instructions do not correctly state the law and the appellate court concludes that there is a likelihood that the error affected the jury's verdict, the judgment will be set aside and a new trial will be ordered.

In other respects, however, the law treats judges as triers of fact very differently from jurors. Judges are required to explain the factual and legal reasoning on which their judgment is based. They must explain what they found to be the facts and what law they actually applied to those facts to arrive at their ultimate judgment. And if that reasoning is flawed, it will be corrected on appeal. In contrast, jurors are typically not asked to explain in any way how they reached their verdict. Indeed, the law recognizes that the system of trial by jury requires to a large extent that the jury be treated as a black box, free from scrutiny by lawyers and judges as to the actual reasoning that led to its verdict. One can view a jury trial, then, as a form of bounded lawlessness. The law controls what evidence the jury will see and hear, and the law requires that a jury verdict be set aside if no reasonable person could rationally draw the inferences necessary to support the jury's verdict. But, with only narrow exceptions, the law protects from judicial scrutiny the jury's actual deliberative process and refuses to set aside a verdict even if every juror comes forward and admits the jury's reasoning was flawed.

A.   The Limits of Rational Inference

Contemporary U.S. procedure aims at assuring that judgments will be based only on inferences that a reasonable person could rationally draw from the evidence presented at trial. Excluded by this formulation are judgments that could only have come from hunch, partiality, whim, and disregard of the law, even when that disregard flows from a sense of higher justice. Substantive law provides the framework for this inferential process; the law of evidence screens out information that might tempt the trier to decide on criteria forbidden by the substantive law. For example, if the law of contract states that good intentions do not excuse a breach, the law of evidence will prevent the defendant from explaining that her failure to make a required payment occurred because she had donated the money to charity.

Guarding the boundaries of rationality is often not so easy as in the preceding example. Tort law says that a defendant shall not be liable for harm unless the plaintiff proves that negligence caused the harm for which he is suing. Suppose that the facts are essentially undisputed; the question then becomes what inferences one can draw from those facts and, more particularly, whether one can infer causation from those facts.

Reid v. San Pedro, Los Angeles & Salt Lake Railroad
39 Utah 617, 118 P. 1009 (1911)

This action was brought by respondent to recover damages for the killing of certain cattle by the trains of appellant. . . .

It is alleged in the first cause of action that appellant's railroad passes through certain lands in Salt Lake County, Utah, owned and improved by private owners; that appellant carelessly and negligently permitted the fence along its line of railroad where the same passes through the lands mentioned to be broken and in poor repair and become down so that cattle had an easy passage through the same; that appellant "carelessly and negligently left and permitted to remain open a gate along the line of said railway at said point and plaintiff (respondent) does not know, and therefore is unable to state, whether the fence was down or the gate left open, and because thereof a three year old heifer of the plaintiff strayed on the right of way of said defendant company, and defendant so carelessly and negligently operated its train that it ran on and over said heifer". . . .

[There was a verdict for plaintiff, and defendant appealed from the judgment entered on the verdict.]

McCARTY, J. (after stating the facts as above).

It is contended on behalf of appellant that the evidence is insufficient to support the verdict because it fails to show where and under what circumstances the cattle sued for got upon the right of way.

The evidence shows that the cow mentioned in the first cause of action was being pastured on land that was fenced, improved, and owned by a private party, and through which appellant's railroad was constructed and maintained; that respondent did not own the land, but was pasturing her stock thereon by permission of the owner at the time the cow was killed; that the fence inclosing appellant's right of way was down and out of repair about one mile west of the point where the cow was killed;

that two gates opening into the right of way in the immediate vicinity of the place where the accident occurred, which were installed and maintained by appellant for the benefit and convenience of the owner of the land through which the railroad passes and upon which the cow was being pastured, had been left open almost continuously prior to the accident.

It is not contended, nor even suggested, that these gates, which were in good condition, were used or left open by appellant. In fact, the evidence, what there is on this point, tends to show that the appellant was in no wise responsible for the gates being left open. Respondent contends that the judgment, in so far as it is based on the first cause of action, should be affirmed regardless of whether the cow got on the right of way through the broken fence or the open gate. In his brief counsel for respondent says: "In the first cause of action the evidence showed the fence down and gate open. . . . It is immaterial whether the heifer strayed on through an inviting open gate or an enticing open fence; . . . either gives the verdict to the plaintiff."

Comp. Laws 1907, §456xl, provides:

Whenever such railroad company shall provide gates for private crossings for the convenience of the owner of the lands through which such railroad passes, such owner shall keep such gates closed at all times when not in actual use, and if such owner fail to keep such gates closed, and in consequence thereof his animal strays upon such railroad, and is killed or injured, such owner shall not be entitled to recover damages therefor.

Under this statute, if the cow entered upon the right of way through the open gate, appellant cannot be held liable for her loss; there being no evidence of negligence on the part of trainmen at the time she was killed.

There is no direct evidence as to where the cow got on to the right of way. It is conceded, however, that she was killed in the immediate vicinity of the gate mentioned, and, as shown by the evidence, about one mile from the point where the fence inclosing the right of way was down and out of repair. The inference, therefore, is just as strong, if not stronger, that she entered upon the right of way through the open gate as it is that she entered through the fence at the point where it was out of repair. The plaintiff held the affirmative and the burden was on her to establish the liability of the defendant by a preponderance of the evidence. It is a familiar rule that where the undisputed evidence of the plaintiff, from which the existence of an essential fact is sought to be inferred, points with equal force to two things, one of which renders the defendant liable and the other not, the plaintiff must fail. So in this case, in order to entitle respondent to recover, it was essential for her to show by a preponderance of the evidence that the cow entered upon the right of way through the broken down fence. This the respondent failed to do.

We are of the opinion that the verdict rendered on the first cause of action is not supported by the evidence, and that the trial court should have directed a verdict for appellant on that cause of action in accordance with appellant's request. . . .

NOTES AND PROBLEMS

1. Start with the substantive law of railroads and livestock in Utah at the turn of the century.

a. If the animal reaches the tracks by coming through an open gate, who bears the loss?

b. If the animal reaches the tracks by coming through a hole in the fence, who bears the loss?

2. The appellate court held that the trial court should have "directed a verdict" for the defendant. As we shall see, that statement is tantamount to saying that a rational trier of fact could not have reached a verdict for the plaintiff.

a. Why not?

b. The animal *could* have been killed in a way that made the railroad liable. Why not let a jury conclude that it was?

3. Notice that all the discussion (that of the court and in the preceding notes) is necessarily hypothetical. We don't know how the jury reached its decision.

a. The jurors might have concluded that railroads as a group were richer than ranchers' widows.

b. They might have decided on the basis of information provided by a rancher-juror, that the cows never went through gates if fences were available.

c. They might have decided, on the basis of information provided by another juror, that the cow was more likely to have come through the fence than the gate because the gap in the fence was near a salt lick (which cows like).

d. They might have misunderstood the judge's instructions.

e. They might have remembered the testimony differently from the judge.

f. The appellate court has no idea what the jurors thought. As you will later see, even if it is available, evidence of juror deliberations is typically unavailable to impeach a verdict. See infra pages 744–751. As a consequence, in considering a directed verdict, a trial or appellate court knows what went into the black box — evidence, instruction, and argument — and what came out — the verdict. In deciding whether a verdict may stand the court must engage in hypothetical reconstruction: Could a rational factfinder have concluded X, given evidence of A, B, and C and law consisting of G and F? If so, the verdict stands. If not, either a directed verdict or a new trial is in order.

4. In *Reid*, what additional evidence should be present before the court can enter judgment on the verdict for the plaintiff?

a. What if the animal were found twenty-five feet from the broken fence and half a mile from the open gate?

b. What if the animal were equidistant between the fence and the gate, but a veterinarian testified that cattle are unlikely to go over a broken fence if there is a nearby open gate?

5. Two taxicab companies, White Cab Co. and Yellow Cab Co., operate in Provo, Utah. White Cab Co. owns approximately 75 percent of the cabs. The physical appearance of the cabs is identical except that the White cabs have a white "in service" light, and the Yellow cabs have a yellow "in service" light. *P* is seriously injured in a hit-and-run accident. *W*, a witness, is sure that *P* was hit by a taxicab.

a. If *P* sues White Cab Co. and there is no other evidence, must a judge enter judgment for White?

b. If you say yes to the hypothetical in a., would your answer be different if White owned 95 percent of the cabs?

c. If you would still enter judgment for White in b., would you change your mind if White owned all cabs in Provo — allowing for the possibility that the cab was from another nearby community or Salt Lake City?

d. Same facts as in a., except *W* says that he got a quick glimpse of the "in service" light and thinks it was white. On cross-examination, *W* says he isn't sure.

e. In the preceding versions of this problem, does your answer change if the plaintiff can also show that he diligently sought, through discovery and investigation, other evidence, such as examining the taxis for dents and marks, seeking witnesses, looking at the accident site for paint chips and the like? Most courts would not permit a plaintiff to offer evidence of his attempts to locate such information, on the ground that it was irrelevant.

6. Although *Reid*'s facts sound quaint, they present a problem with modern implications. Suppose a person dies from a rare form of cancer. The deceased lived in a small town where the only major change in the past decade was the construction of a uranium milling plant. Decedent's family sues the plant for wrongful death. Plaintiff's evidence of liability

consists of medical testimony establishing the decedent's death from the rare cancer in question and that nothing in the health history or habits suggested any special risk. Plaintiff follows this evidence with public health and demographic experts, who establish that the background rate for this form of cancer in the town was three deaths annually per 10,000 persons before defendant's plant was built, and that it is now seven deaths per 10,000, and that some public health and medical studies have linked increases in this form of cancer to inevitable atmospheric discharges of the uranium milling process. Plaintiff rests; defendant moves for a directed verdict. What decision?

7. The initial decision in *Reid* was made by a jury. The result on appeal would have been the same, however, had the initial decision been made in a bench trial by a judge sitting without a jury. When a case is tried by a judge, Rule 52(a) requires that "the court shall find the facts specially and state separately its conclusions of law thereon. . . ." Rule 52(a) further provides that a finding of fact made by a trial judge can be set aside on appeal if it is "clearly erroneous." If it would be irrational speculation for a jury to find that the cow got on the track in a particular way, it would be "clearly erroneous" for a judge to make the same finding.

B. Procedural Control of Rational Proof

Reid asks when a chain of inferences drawn by the factfinder strays beyond the bounds of rationality. In the U.S. legal system courts regularly face that question, but it comes to them embedded in a set of procedural institutions. The most important of these are the tradition of adversarial responsibility for proof and the system of jury trial. Both of these dictate the particular forms by which the system tries to assure rationality — and the limits of those efforts.

1. Juries, Democracy, and Rationality

The contemporary jury embodies several contradictory goals. At one level we speak of it simply as a factfinding body, although finding facts in the midst of conflict and perjury is hardly simple. But we also have other aspirations for it: The jury is the voice of the community, tempering and making acceptable applications of law that might otherwise be resented or resisted. Finally, it is a temporary, lay, and democratic institution that stands at the core of a permanent, professional, and elite institution — the judiciary. The two latter roles conflict at times with factfinding, at least if that task is understood in a limited way. To ask juries to decide cases, then, is to permit them — or perhaps to require them — to do something more than find facts.

If one accepts this proposition, the task of procedure becomes more difficult. The litigation system is dedicated to rationality. It is also, however, committed to a model of factfinding that blends rationality with other goals. How does one frame procedural rules that give juries sufficient leeway to perform the political tasks we have set for them without irreparably compromising the rationality of verdicts?

2.   Adversarial Responsibility for Proof

Part of the answer to the question just posed lies in shifting responsibility from the court to the parties. One hopes that trials frequently arrive at something like truth. But because "[l]itigation is a system for managing doubt."* trial procedure aims at fairness as much as at truth. Trials in the United States are framed not as inquiries but as contests. The adversaries have the opportunity to present competing versions of their stories within the limits permitted by the rules of evidence and other procedural constraints that seek to assure the parties an equal and fair opportunity. Experienced observers of trials can easily recall cases in which an unbiased and credible witness was not called because neither side wanted the whole truth to come out. As a result, a verdict is not an announcement about truth, but a judgment about who presented the more credible version of the case.

One need not be cynical about this approach; experienced observers often report that they think that the result of trial is usually a judgment that comes as close as humanly possible to the truth. The point is rather that any system seeking to bring rationality to this contest has to take into account the adversarial mode by which proof is presented. Throughout the trial the parties take turns: They take turns in conducting voir dire (if the court permits lawyers to ask questions directly of jurors), in exercising peremptory strikes of jurors, and in presenting what they think will be the most convincing evidence from among what is available to them. They take turns in presenting their cases and, within their respective turns, take further turns in examining and cross-examining witnesses. The system seeks to take account of this symmetrical, game-like quality of trial by devising procedures that fit the adversarial presentation of proof.

* Geoffrey C. Hazard, Jr., Res Nova in Res Judicata, 44 S. Cal. L. Rev. 1036, 1042 (1971).

3. Burdens

The most important of these procedures goes under the term "burden of proof." We assign to one of the parties the burden of proving some aspect of the case. Then, if the trier of fact finds that the party has not offered the required proof, that party loses. We are all familiar with one such burden, the burden on the prosecution in a criminal case to prove the guilt of the defendant beyond a reasonable doubt. According to the doctrine, if a trier of fact thinks it is probable but not certain that the defendant is guilty, the defendant should be acquitted.

Burdens in civil cases play a different though no less important role. Lawyers typically distinguish between the two forms that the burden of proof can take, the burden of persuasion and the burden of production.

a. Burden of Persuasion

We start with the burden of persuasion because it is more familiar from the criminal context. The burden of persuasion defines the extent to which a trier of fact must be convinced of some proposition in order to render a verdict for the party who bears it. In civil cases the burden of persuasion is lower than "beyond a reasonable doubt." It is variously defined as "the preponderance of evidence," "more probable than not," or "more likely than not." (In a few specialized circumstances — will contests, fraud — courts or legislation sometimes require "clear and convincing evidence," a standard thought to lie somewhere between preponderance and beyond a reasonable doubt.) As interpreted by the courts, the preponderance standard means that a trier of fact can find for the party with the burden of persuasion if the trier finds the material fact merely "probable." Consider what that means.

NOTES AND PROBLEMS

1. In a negligence case the plaintiff bears the burden of persuading the trier that the defendant was negligent. Such a finding would in turn rest on two subsidiary findings: (a) that the defendant committed some act (or failed to take some precaution) and (b) that the act (or omission) created an unreasonable danger. The strictly factual part of that finding concerns the defendant's act or omission. Imagine a simple case in which the plaintiff claims that the defendant ran a red light and collided with the plaintiff's car. Suppose the trier was prepared to find that *if* the defendant ran the red light, she was negligent. The issue then turns on

whether she did. Further suppose conflicting evidence: The plaintiff testifies that the defendant did run the light; defendant testifies that she didn't; and other witnesses give stories that partially corroborate both parties' stories — in short, a very typical case. The judge instructs the jury on the burden of persuasion in a civil case. An example of such an instruction is:

> Plaintiff has the burden of proving by a preponderance of the evidence all of the facts necessary to establish [the claim.]. . .
>
> "Preponderance of the evidence" means evidence that has more convincing force than that opposed to it. If the evidence is so evenly balanced that you are unable to say that the evidence on either side of an issue preponderates, your finding on that issue must be against the party who had the burden of proving it.

California Jury Instructions: Civil 2.60 (P.G. Breckenridge ed., 8th ed. 1994).

a. The jury sifts the evidence and concludes that it thinks the defendant probably did run the light. The jurors aren't sure, but they think it likely. Explain why the outcome will not depend on which party bears the burden of persuasion.

b. The jury sifts the evidence and concludes that it thinks the defendant probably did *not* run the light. The jurors aren't sure but they think it likely. Explain why the outcome will not depend on which party bears the burden of persuasion.

c. The jury sifts the evidence and concludes that it simply can't decide whether the defendant ran the light. It finds the evidence absolutely evenly balanced. Explain why in this situation — and only in this situation — the outcome will depend on which party bears the burden of persuasion.

d. Now suppose that the defendant were being prosecuted criminally for negligent operation of a motor vehicle. In which of the scenarios would the burden of persuasion determine the outcome of the case? Why?

2. In light of the preceding problem, be prepared to explain why lawyers will tell you that the burden of persuasion in a civil case almost never matters.

b. Burden of Production

By contrast, who bears the burden of production in a civil case often matters a great deal. Unlike the burden of persuasion, which comes into play only when all the evidence is in and the trier of fact has to decide what it all means, the burden of production requires a party to "produce," to find and present evidence in the first place. Because you have examined the pretrial process, you can now understand what this means. Summary judgment relies on this idea. At the heart of Celotex Corp. v. Catrett, supra page 630, lies the proposition that a party with the burden of production can lose even before trial if she fails to demonstrate, among the facts uncovered by investigation and discovery, sufficient evidence to allow a rational trier of fact to find in her favor. For example, if the plaintiff has the burden of production on the question of whether the defendant ran the red light, it is up to him to find the witness, to interview or depose her, to make sure that she comes to court on the day of trial, to conduct the direct examination in a way that makes her statement admissible. If the plaintiff fails in any of these steps, he loses — even though, as a matter of historical fact, the defendant did run the red light. The plaintiff loses because he has failed to satisfy the burden of production — of coming forward with evidence from which a rational trier of fact could conclude some proposition of material fact.

NOTES AND PROBLEMS

1. You have already encountered a case about the burden of production — Reid v. San Pedro, Los Angeles & Salt Lake Railroad (supra page 713).

a. In *Reid* the plaintiff lost because she did not produce — come forward with — evidence that permitted one rationally to conclude that more probably than not the railroad's negligence had caused the death of the animal.

b. By contrast, the plaintiff *had* met her burden of production on the question of whether the railroad was negligent. Explain what evidence satisfied the burden of production on that issue.

2. Different parties may have the burden of production on different issues. For example, in a negligence case, the plaintiff will have the burden of production on the defendant's negligence; by contrast, if the defendant pleads the statute of limitations as a defense, she will have the burden of production as to the facts material to that defense. Suppose that the plaintiff was exposed to some allegedly toxic chemicals, perhaps as a result of the defendant's negligence. More than a year after that exposure, the plaintiff manifested some physical symptoms that she is now alleging resulted from the exposure. The statute of limitations is one year, and the state in question says that the statute runs from the time the plaintiff should reasonably have realized that she was injured.

a. The plaintiff has the burden of producing evidence that the defendant negligently handled or used the chemicals in question and that the exposure caused the symptoms complained of.

b. The defendant has the burden of producing evidence that the plaintiff should reasonably have realized that she was injured more than a year before the case was filed.

c. Under those circumstances both parties have the burden of producing evidence — and therefore the risk of losing if they fail to do so — about material facts best known to the adversary. Whether they can bear their burdens may depend on how well they can use discovery.

d. Finally, integrate your understanding of the burdens of production and persuasion by considering what would happen if *both* parties met their burdens of production in the hypothetical toxic chemical case. Both parties have presented evidence sufficient to allow a rational trier of fact to conclude (a) that the defendant had negligently handled the chemical (which had caused the plaintiff harm) and (b) that more than a year had elapsed between the time the plaintiff should reasonably have realized that she had been harmed and the filing of the case. Given this information, can one determine who wins the case?

e. The answer is that one cannot: To say that a trier of fact *might* rationally conclude X is not to say that it *must* conclude X. Satisfying a burden of production means only that a trier *might* rationally decide the case in one's favor, not that it must. In any given case, it is entirely possible for both parties to have satisfied their burdens of production — to have produced enough evidence that a rational jury could find for either party. To understand that one cannot, you have to take a final step, as described in the next section.

4. Controlling Juries Before the Verdict

To define the boundaries of jury rationality, courts employ five procedural devices. Two of these, the law of evidence and the power of instructing the jury on the law and of commenting on the evidence, are designed to control the flow of information that reaches the jury. Three other devices — the directed verdict, the judgment notwithstanding the verdict, and the grant of new trials — are designed to control what the jury does with that information, and, specifically, to prevent it from drawing the "wrong" conclusions. Each of these latter three devices is triggered by a party's argument that the jury should not be permitted to decide in favor of the other side given the evidence it has heard, or that the jury was subject to improper influences. All three devices thus rest on the idea that under some circumstances a jury could not rationally decide in a particular way.

In reading the materials in this section, you should keep two issues separate: First, consider whether the court is limiting what the jury is to consider or whether it is trying to regulate the jury's process of decision making; second, note which procedural device the court is using.

a. Judgment as a Matter of Law (Directed Verdict)

In the hypothetical case of the negligently handled chemical, suppose the plaintiff has presented all her evidence: that the defendant manufactured toxic chemicals, that the plaintiff has experienced physical symptoms or respiratory distress, and that the symptoms are of a sort that can be caused by the chemical. The defendant believes that the plaintiff has failed to meet her burden of production on the issue of negligence. In so asserting, the defendant is saying that a rational jury could not, from the evidence presented, conclude that the defendant had been negligent either in the manufacture of the chemical or in warning users about precautions.

Procedurally, the defendant makes that assertion by moving for what is commonly known as a directed verdict. Rule 50 permits a party at the close of the other party's case to move for "judgment as a matter of law," sometimes abbreviated as "j.m.l." In so moving, the defendant would be asking the judge to take the case away from the jury to prevent it from considering the evidence and reaching a verdict. The ground for the motion would be that the evidence presented would support only one result: In the words of Rule 50(a), "there is no legally sufficient evidentiary basis for a reasonable jury to find for that party on that issue." That being the case, the judge should save everyone's time by announcing the result that a properly functioning jury would inevitably reach.* To grant such a motion results in final judgment being entered against the party with the burden that she has failed to carry.

The question, of course, is when should the judge do so? The black-letter law is easy to state but quite unhelpful: A judge should direct a verdict only if there is no rational basis for a jury to find in favor of the

---

* Historically, judges accomplished this result by "directing" the jury to bring in a verdict for one party or the other. Most juries were delighted to be spared the trouble of deliberating, but occasional juries have refused. The judge is then faced with various uncomfortable alternatives — hectoring the jurors, threatening them with contempt, and the like. Accordingly, the current version of Rule 50 substitutes the term "judgment as matter of law" for the more traditional "directed verdict." Many states — and most lawyers — still use the older term, whose meaning and significance is identical.

party against whom the verdict is directed. Applying that standard requires courts to define its meaning in widely varying factual situations. Tens of thousands of reported cases have passed on the question whether to grant judgment as a matter of law. One can, at best, acquire a rough sense of the problems, bearing in mind Wigmore's dictum that each case will "depend entirely on the nature of the evidence offered in the case in hand; and it is seldom possible that a ruling can serve as a precedent." 9 J. Wigmore, Evidence §2492, at 296 (3d ed. 1940). Part of the problem comes from the circumstance that a motion for judgment as a matter of law can raise several different issues: credibility (which witness is telling the most convincing story?); inference (what conclusions can one rationally draw from undisputed facts?); evaluation (do the physical facts constitute, for example, negligent behavior?); and substance (for example, is knowledge by the defendant an element of the claim?). Which of these issues does the next case raise?

Pennsylvania Railroad v. Chamberlain

288 U.S. 333 (1933)

Mr. Justice SUTHERLAND delivered the opinion of the Court.

This is an action brought by respondent against petitioner to recover for the death of a brakeman, alleged to have been caused by petitioner's negligence. The complaint alleges that the deceased, at the time of the accident resulting in his death, was assisting in the yard work of breaking up and making up trains and in the classifying and assorting of cars operating in interstate commerce; that in pursuance of such work, while riding a cut of cars, other cars ridden by fellow employees were negligently caused to be brought into violent contact with those upon which deceased was riding, with the result that he was thrown therefrom to the railroad track and run over by a car or cars, inflicting injuries from which he died.

At the conclusion of the evidence, the trial court directed the jury to find a verdict in favor of petitioner. Judgment upon a verdict so found was reversed by the court of appeals, Judge Swan dissenting.

That part of the yard in which the accident occurred contained a lead track and a large number of switching tracks branching therefrom. The lead track crossed a "hump," and the work of car distribution consisted of pushing a train of cars by means of a locomotive to the top of the "hump," and then allowing the cars, in separate strings, to descend by gravity, under the control of hand brakes, to their respective destinations in the various branch tracks. Deceased had charge of a string of two gondola cars, which he was piloting to track 14. Immediately ahead of him was a string of seven cars, and behind him a string of nine cars, both also destined for track 14. Soon after the cars ridden by deceased had passed to track 14, his body was found on that track some distance beyond the switch. He had evidently fallen onto the track and been run over by a car or cars.

The case for respondent rests wholly upon the claim that the fall of deceased was caused by a violent collision of the string of nine cars with the string ridden by deceased. Three employees, riding the nine-car string, testified positively that no such collision occurred. They were corroborated by every other employee in a position to see, all testifying that there was no contact between the nine-car string and that of the deceased. The testimony of these witnesses, if believed, establishes beyond doubt that there was no collision between these two strings of cars, and that the nine-car string contributed in no way to the accident. The only witness who testified for the respondent was one Bainbridge; and it is upon his testimony alone that respondent's right to recover is sought to be upheld. His testimony is concisely stated, in its most favorable light for respondent, in the prevailing opinion below by Judge Learned Hand, as follows:

> The plaintiff's only witness to the event, one Bainbridge, then employed by the road, stood close to the yardmaster's office, near the "hump." He professed to have paid little attention to what went on, but he did see the deceased riding at the rear of his cars, whose speed when they passed him he took to be about eight or ten miles. Shortly thereafter a second string passed which was shunted into another track and this was followed by the nine, which, according to the plaintiff's theory, collided with the deceased's. After the nine cars had passed at a somewhat greater speed than the deceased's, Bainbridge paid no more attention to either string for a while, but looked again when the deceased, who was still standing in his place, had passed the switch and onto the assorting track where he was bound. At that time his speed had been checked to about three miles, but the speed of the following nine cars had increased. They were just passing the switch, about four or five cars behind the deceased. Bainbridge looked away again and soon heard what he described as a "loud crash," not however an unusual event in a switching yard. Apparently this did not cause him at once to turn, but he did so shortly thereafter, and saw the two strings together still moving, and the deceased no longer in sight. Later still his attention was attracted by shouts and he went to the spot and saw the deceased between the rails. Until he left to go to the accident, he had stood fifty feet to the north of the track where the accident happened, and about nine hundred feet from where the body was found.

The court, although regarding Bainbridge's testimony as not only "somewhat suspicious in itself, but its contradiction . . . so manifest as to leave little doubt," held, nevertheless, that the question was one of fact depending upon the credibility of the witnesses, and that it was for the jury to determine, as between the one witness and the many, where the truth lay. The dissenting opinion of Judge Swan proceeds upon the theory that Bainbridge did not testify that in fact a collision had taken place, but inferred it because he heard a crash, and because thereafter the two strings of cars appeared to him to be moving together. It is correctly pointed out in that opinion, however, that the crash might have come from elsewhere in the busy yard and that Bainbridge was in no position to see whether the two strings of cars were actually together; that Bainbridge repeatedly said he was paying no particular attention; and that his position was such, being 900 feet from the place where the body was found and less than 50 feet from the side of the track in question, that he necessarily saw the strings of cars at such an acute angle that it would be physically impossible even for an attentive observer to tell whether the forward end of the nine-car cut was actually in contact with the rear end of the two-car cut. The dissenting opinion further points out that all the witnesses who were in a position to see testified that there was no collision; that respondent's evidence was wholly circumstantial, and the inferences which might otherwise be drawn from it were shown to be utterly erroneous unless all of petitioner's witnesses were willful perjurers. "This is not a case," the opinion proceeds, "where direct testimony to an essential fact is contradicted by direct testimony of other witnesses, though even there it is conceded a directed verdict might be proper in some circumstances. Here, when all the testimony was in, the circumstantial evidence in support of negligence was thought by the trial judge to be so insubstantial and insufficient that it did not justify submission to the jury."

We thus summarize and quote from the prevailing and dissenting opinions, because they present the divergent views to be considered in reaching a correct determination of the question involved. It, of course, is true, generally, that where there is a direct conflict of testimony upon a matter of fact, the question must be left to the jury to determine, without regard to the number of witnesses upon either side. But here there really is no conflict in the testimony as to the *facts*. The witnesses for petitioner flatly testified that there was no collision between the nine-car and the two-car strings. Bainbridge did not say there was such a collision. What he said was that he heard a "loud crash," which did not cause him at once to turn, but that shortly thereafter he did turn and saw the two strings of cars moving together with the deceased no longer in sight; that there was nothing unusual about the crash of cars — it happened every day; that there was nothing about this crash to attract his attention except that it was extra loud; that he paid no attention to it; that it was not sufficient to attract his attention. The record shows that there was a continuous movement of cars over and down the "hump," which were distributed among a large number of branch tracks within the yard, and that any two strings of these cars moving upon the same track might have come together and caused the crash which Bainbridge heard. There is no direct evidence that *in fact* the crash was occasioned by a collision of the two strings in question; and it is perfectly clear that no such fact was brought to Bainbridge's attention as a perception of the physical sense of sight or of hearing. At most there was an inference to that effect drawn from observed facts which gave equal support to the opposite inference that the crash was occasioned by the coming together of other strings of cars entirely away from the scene of the accident, or of the two-car string ridden by deceased and the seven-car string immediately ahead of it.

We, therefore, have a case belonging to that class of cases where proven facts give equal support to each of two inconsistent inferences; in which event, neither of them being established, judgment, as a matter of law, must go against the party upon whom rests the necessity of sustaining one of these inferences as against the other, before he is entitled to recover.

The rule is succinctly stated in Smith v. First National Bank in Westfield, 99 Mass. 605, 611–612, quoted in the *Des Moines National Bank* case [United States F. & G. Co. v. Des Moines National Bank, 145 F. 273, 280 (8th Cir. 1906)]:

> There being several inferences deducible from the facts which appear, and equally consistent with all those facts, the plaintiff has not maintained the proposition upon which alone he would be entitled to recover. There is strictly no evidence to warrant a jury in finding that the loss was occasioned by negligence and not by theft. When the evidence tends equally to sustain either of two inconsistent propositions, neither of them can be said to have been established by legitimate proof. A verdict in favor of the party bound to maintain one of those propositions against the other is necessarily wrong.

That Bainbridge concluded from what he himself observed that the crash was due to a collision between the two strings of cars in question is sufficiently indicated by his statements. But this, of course, proves nothing, since it is not allowable for a witness to resolve the doubt as to which of two equally justifiable inferences shall be adopted by drawing a conclusion, which, if accepted, will result in a purely gratuitous award in favor of the party who has failed to sustain the burden of proof cast upon him by the law.

And the desired inference is precluded for the further reason that respondent's right of recovery depends upon the existence of a particular fact which must be inferred from proven facts, and this is not permissible in the face of the positive and otherwise uncontradicted testimony of unimpeached witnesses consistent with the facts actually proved, from which testimony it affirmatively appears that the fact sought to be inferred did not exist. . . .

Not only is Bainbridge's testimony considered as a whole suspicious, insubstantial and insufficient, but his statement that when he turned shortly after hearing the crash the two strings were moving together is simply incredible, if he meant thereby to be understood as saying that he saw the two in contact; and if he meant by the words "moving together" simply that they were moving at the same time in the same direction but not in contact, the statement becomes immaterial. As we have already seen he was paying slight and only occasional attention to what was going on. The cars were 800 or 900 feet from where he stood and moving almost directly away from him, his angle of vision being only 3°3′ from a straight line. At that sharp angle and from that distance, near dusk of a misty evening (as the proof shows), the practical impossibility of the witness being able to see whether the front of the nine-car string was in contact with the back of the two-car string is apparent. And, certainly, in the light of these conditions, no verdict based upon a statement so unbelievable reasonably could be sustained as against the positive testimony to the contrary of unimpeached witnesses, all in a position to see, as this witness was not, the precise relation of the cars to one another. The fact that these witnesses were employees of the petitioner, under the circumstances here disclosed, does not impair this conclusion. Chesapeake & Ohio Ry. v. Martin, 283 U.S. 209, 216–220. . . .

Leaving out of consideration, then, the inference relied upon, the case for respondent is left without any substantial support in the evidence, and a verdict in her favor would have rested upon mere speculation and conjecture. This, of course, is inadmissible.

The judgment of the Circuit Court of Appeals is reversed and that of the District Court is affirmed.

Mr. Justice STONE and Mr. Justice CARDOZO concur in the result.

NOTES AND PROBLEMS

1. Focus first on the procedural steps that frame the issue.

a. A trial typically consists of the plaintiff's presentation of his case, the defendant's of its case, closing argument, and jury instructions. When in the course of this sequence did the defendant move for a directed verdict? Locate the portion of Rule 50 that permits a party to make a motion at this point.

b. Could the defendant have moved for a directed verdict earlier? When?

2. To understand the force of *Chamberlain*, consider a variation on the facts.

a. Suppose at the time of the accident Bainbridge had not been standing several hundred feet away from the scene on a misty evening but instead had been standing ten feet away. He testifies that he clearly saw the collision and that Chamberlain's death had been caused by the following car string's overtaking his string and crushing him between the cars. But suppose further that at the time of the accident a group of clergy had been taking a tour of the rail yards. These clergy also saw the accident clearly, and all testify under oath that the following string did not come near Chamberlain's and that the deceased fell onto the tracks when he waved to a friend. Would this testimony warrant granting a judgment for defendant?

b. The commonly accepted answer to this question is no. This answer is a result of the courts' insistence that in directing verdicts they not make judgments about the credibility of witnesses, even when the case seems strongly one-sided.

c. Is that black-letter statement consistent with *Chamberlain*?

3. Cases such as *Chamberlain* have been thought to raise two related issues. The first is the precise standard for taking the case from the jury — more particularly, which evidence should be considered. There is general agreement that the court should consider all evidence favorable to the plaintiff, all inferences from that evidence, and all undisputed evidence. But should the court also consider testimonial and disputed evidence in favor of the defendant? Closely related is the matter of evaluating the evidence. Many courts have stated that the basic test is whether reasonable persons could differ; if they could, the court should defer to the jury on the ground that its members are reasonable persons whose verdict represents one of several reasonable views. The leading case articulating the prevailing view is Boeing Co. v. Shipman, 411 F.2d 365, 374–375 (5th Cir. 1969):

> On motions for directed verdict and for judgment notwithstanding the verdict the Court should consider all of the evidence — not just that evidence which supports the non-mover's case — but in the light and with all reasonable inferences most favorable to the party opposed to the motion. If the facts and inferences point so strongly and overwhelmingly in favor of one party that the Court believes that reasonable men could not arrive

at a contrary verdict, granting of the motions is proper. On the other hand, if there is substantial evidence opposed to the motions, that is, evidence of such quality and weight that reasonable and fair-minded men in the exercise of impartial judgment might reach different conclusions, the motions should be denied, and the case submitted to the jury. A mere scintilla of evidence is insufficient to present a question for the jury. The motions for directed verdict and judgment n. o. v. should not be decided by which side has the better of the case, nor should they be granted only when there is a complete absence of probative facts to support a jury verdict. There must be a conflict in substantial evidence to create a jury question. However, it is the function of the jury as the traditional finder of the facts, and not the Court, to weigh conflicting evidence and inferences, and determine the credibility of witnesses.

4. The question in *Chamberlain*, then, is whether, using the standard articulated above, one can construct the evidence presented into a story that makes it reasonable to infer that the fellow workers' negligence caused Chamberlain's death.

a. In constructing such a story, consider a snippet from the opinion below, by Judge Learned Hand:

> It does not appear to us impossible, or indeed improbable, that one in [Bainbridge's] position could tell whether the two strings were together. The intervals between cars in a train are uniform; they may be detected by the straight sides. Certainly a gap of four or five car lengths, when the nine cars came to rest, would have been easily observable; and this was the story of the defendant. What Bainbridge saw, coupled with what he had heard, if uncontradicted, would be enough to support a finding that the nine cars had collided with the deceased's and thrown him off. There is no inherent impossibility in the story.

Chamberlain v. Pennsylvania R.R., 59 F.2d 986, 987 (2d Cir. 1932).

b. Is the Supreme Court in fact making a comparative assessment of witness credibility?

c. As the Supreme Court describes the case, Bainbridge's testimony is suspicious because of his inadequate opportunity to observe, while the fellow workers' contrary testimony is taken at face value. Is there reason to suspect the other workers' testimony? Is there reason to credit Bainbridge's inference that the two strings collided?

5. *Chamberlain* has to avoid questions of credibility because the jury is the undoubted arbiter of credibility. But we ask jurors to do much more than to decide who is telling the truth. We also give to the jury many questions that require them to apply general, open-ended standards to the facts of the case. Was it negligent under these circumstances to be driving five miles faster than the speed limit? Was the behavior of

one of the contracting parties unreasonable? To arrive at answers to such questions, juries may have to decide questions of fact. But even after doing so they must then apply the open texture of law to those facts.

a. Because of this role, courts often give to juries cases where the facts are undisputed. A classic example is Railroad Co. v. Stout, 84 U.S. (17 Wall) 657 (1873). A child was injured while playing on a railroad turntable located at the edge of a sparsely populated rural settlement. The turntable was not locked or fenced. No one contested any of these facts; the case went to the jury, which found negligence. Rejecting the railroad's contentions that the judge should have taken the case from the jury, the Supreme Court wrote:

> Upon the facts proven in such cases, it is a matter of judgment and discretion, of sound inference, what is the deduction to be drawn from the undisputed facts. Certain facts we may suppose to be clearly established from which one sensible, impartial man would infer that proper care had not been used, and that negligence existed; another man equally sensible and equally impartial would infer that proper care had been used, and that there was no negligence. It is this class of cases and those akin to it that the law commits to the decision of a jury. Twelve men of the average of the community, comprising men of education and men of little educa-tion, men of learning and men whose learning consists only in what they have themselves seen and heard, the merchant, the mechanic, the farmer, the laborer; these sit together, consult, apply their separate experience of the affairs of life to the facts proven, and draw a unanimous conclusion. This average judgment thus given it is the great effort of the law to obtain. It is assumed that twelve men know more of the common affairs of life than does one man, that they can draw wiser and safer conclusions from admitted facts thus occurring than can a single judge.

Railroad Co. v. Stout, 84 U.S. at 663. Note that the assumption about the gender of jurors rests on premises since held to be unconstitutional. See supra page 707.

b. Given this practice, can one describe the jury as merely a factfinding body? Isn't the jury's role in such cases very close to making "law"?

b. Excluding Improper Influences

Judges prefer not to enter judgments as a matter of law. It goes against the grain to require citizens to take time from family and work to decide a case only to yank it out from under them. Moreover, someone is going to get bad news at the end of the case, and most judges would rather have the jury deliver it to them. Judges therefore do everything they can to assure that jurors won't reach verdicts that can't be sustained by the evidence. Besides entering a judgment as a matter of law, a judge has some less drastic procedural tools to use.

The process starts before trial gets under way. Screening the jury through voir dire (see pages 700–710 supra) seeks to eliminate jurors whose sympathies or inability to understand the evidence might cause them to reach irrational verdicts. During the trial judges try to assure that jurors will consider only information screened through the law of evidence (many of whose parts can be explained as efforts to insulate jurors from information that might be misleading). Even good faith efforts by jurors that bring to their fellow jurors information not filtered through the evidentiary and adversarial screens may result in new trials. For example, in a case that turned on whether aluminum electrical wiring was dangerous, one juror, after hearing testimony to that effect, went home, examined the wiring in his own home, and reported his findings to his fellow jurors the next day. The appellate court ordered a new trial. In re Beverly Hills Fire Litigation, 695 F. 2d 207 (6th Cir. 1982). Judges try to avoid such outcomes by instructing the jurors not to discuss the case with others and to decide only on the basis of evidence presented in the courtroom. In those extreme instances where the case is the subject of much public discussion, the judge can sequester the jury.

c. Instructions and Comment

The judge also teaches the jury by framing the questions for decision and, perhaps, commenting on the evidence. The judge frames the question by instructing the jury on the law. Rule 51. Instructions explain the substantive law that applies to the case, and the judge explains in a sequential way the decisions the jury must reach in a given case. For example, if the jury determines that the defendant was negligent, it must then decide whether the defendant's negligence caused the injury of which the plaintiff is complaining.

Jury instructions have two audiences. Their first audience is the jury itself, who may have an intuitive understanding of the law (quite likely in a negligence case) or none at all (as, for example, in a patent infringement case). The second audience for jury instructions is the appellate court, which will reverse a case if an instruction misstates the law in a material way. These audiences have essentially incompatible requirements. The jury wants a simplified, easy-to-follow path through the wilderness of evidence to help it distinguish the central from the peripheral and to explain what factors should go into its decision on each question. The appellate court wants a nuanced, perfectly balanced, all-inclusive statement of the law. The clash between these contradictory requirements means that most instructions are compromises.

Besides telling the jury what the law is, the judge can, if she is very careful, tell the jury what she thinks of the evidence. Here the law speaks to the judge with a mixed voice. In federal courts at least, the judge has the theoretical power to comment on the evidence. That power is hedged, however, with many qualifications and with exhortations that the judge not trespass into the jury's autonomous decision making space. Judges who do so egregiously — like the judge who solemnly informed a jury that in his experience witnesses who wiped their hands while testifying were liars, Quercia v. United States, 289 U.S. 466, 468 (1933) — are reversed.

5. Controlling Juries After the Verdict

What does a judge do if, after carefully screening the jury, watching the evidence like a hawk, refraining from impermissible comment, and giving a legally impeccable but easily understood set of instructions, gets an absolutely insupportable verdict from the jury? What can a party on the losing end of such a verdict do about it? If the trial judge committed error at trial, an appeal is a possibility. But suppose there is no such error. In that situation, there are two procedural devices for rectifying the problem: the motion for a judgment notwithstanding the verdict and the motion for a new trial. We consider them in turn.

a. Judgment as a Matter of Law (Judgment Notwithstanding the Verdict)

Suppose a verdict is insupportable because there was simply no evidence from which a rational person could have found for the party who won the verdict. The plaintiff put on evidence of an auto accident and her injuries, but nothing from which one could infer that the defendant had been negligent — yet the jury returned a plaintiff's verdict. How could that happen? An attentive reader of this and the preceding chapters will realize that, in theory, such a case would never reach the jury. If the defendant made a motion for summary judgment, the case would not reach trial. If it did reach trial (perhaps because defendant failed to move for summary judgment), at trial the defendant would move for judgment as a matter of law before the case went to the jury, and the court would grant it, thus ending the case.

Such a scenario is possible, but it doesn't always happen. Judges faced with a pretrial summary judgment motion or a preverdict Rule 50 motion, believing that the party with the burden of production has failed to meet it, will sometimes nevertheless deny the motion. Why? If the judge grants the motion and an appellate court reverses, a whole new trial will be necessary — a big waste of time. If the judge denies the motion, one of two things can happen. If the evidence is as one-sided as the judge believes, the jury will likely return a verdict for the "proper" party without any judicial intervention. If something goes wrong, however, the judge can always rescue the case by granting a judgment notwithstanding the verdict (j.n.o.v.).* — essentially a late ruling on the earlier motion for judgment as a matter of law. The grounds for a j.n.o.v. are identical to those for a preverdict judgment as a matter of law: "that there is 'no legally sufficient evidentiary basis for a reasonable jury to find for th[e] party' " against whom the motion is made. Rule 50(a). Only the timing of the two motions differs — one coming before the verdict, the other after.

NOTES AND PROBLEMS

1. In an automobile negligence case, the plaintiff presents evidence of an accident and of her injuries, and than rests her case. The defendant presents his case, which tends to show that the plaintiff, not the defendant, was negligent. The case goes to a jury, which returns a verdict for the plaintiff. The defendant then moves for judgment notwithstanding the verdict. Why must the judge deny this motion, even though the plaintiff has presented no evidence of the defendant's negligence? Rule 50(b).

2. The requirement of a Rule 50(a) motion (for a directed verdict) before the verdict as a prerequisite for granting a Rule 50(b) motion (for judgment notwithstanding the verdict) after trial has constitutional foundations. The Seventh Amendment provides that "no fact tried by a jury, shall be otherwise reexamined in any court of the United States, than according to the rules of common law."

a. The U.S. Supreme Court has held that common law had an analogue to the directed verdict, but none to the judgment notwithstanding the verdict. Does that make the j.n.o.v. unconstitutional? No, said the Su-

---

* So-called from its Latin initials: judgment non obstante veredicto.

preme Court, if the j.n.o.v. is merely a *delayed* ruling on the motion for a directed verdict. Baltimore & Carolina Line v. Redman, 295 U.S. 654 (1935). For it to be a delayed ruling, however, there must have been a motion preceding the submission of the case to the jury.

b. This rule is enshrined in Rule 50(b). Do not, therefore, in the heat of your first federal trial, forget to make a Rule 50(a) motion before the case is submitted to the jury, or you will have waived the right to make a Rule 50(b) motion and may find yourself having to answer some very unpleasant questions from your client and perhaps your malpractice insurer or the state bar.

b. New Trial

Suppose that the trial judge cannot conscientiously say that there is no evidence to support the jury verdict. She thinks, however, that the case was very strong on one side and very weak on the other, but the wrong side won. Must the verdict stand because the judge could not properly grant a j.n.o.v.? Not necessarily: The judge has another weapon in her arsenal of post-trial motions — the new trial.

Rule 59 governs the granting of new trials, which the judge may order on her own initiative (Rule 59(d)) or on a party's motion. Rule 59 does not specify the grounds for which a new trial may be ordered, but there is a well-developed body of common law on the issue. That law indicates two reasons for granting new trials, one focusing on the procedure leading up to the verdict, the other on the correctness of the verdict itself.

(1) Flawed procedures

New trials may be granted when the judge concludes that the process leading up to the verdict has been flawed. For example, the judge may conclude that a lawyer has made an impermissible argument to the jury. Or, on reflection after the trial is over, the judge may conclude that she erred in admitting a piece of evidence or that she gave the jury erroneous instructions. Or a judge may discover that a juror, although he was properly selected, misbehaved during the trial, perhaps by visiting the accident scene himself. Ordering a new trial gives the judge a chance to correct herself. Thus a judge who admitted evidence or gave an instruction over an objection may, after the verdict, conclude that the ruling was wrong and grant a new trial to cure the error. Rule 59 explicitly gives the judge power to order a new trial even if neither party so moves.

(2)   Flawed verdicts

Even if the trial was perfect, however, the judge may conclude that the result of that trial — the verdict — is unjustifiable. One example is the verdict that splits the difference between two parties when the law says one or the other must take all — the $500 verdict on the $1,000 bad check. Such a verdict tells the judge that the jury either misunderstood or ignored the instructions. But less blatant errors also will provoke the grant of a new trial.

Probably the most common ground for granting a new trial is that the verdict is against the weight of the evidence. Understanding this idea requires a glance back at the directed verdict and j.n.o.v. Although both result from verdicts lacking evidentiary support, it is important to understand the difference between them and the grant of a new trial. In granting a j.n.o.v., a court is saying that the winner of the verdict had no evidentiary support for at least one essential element of the claim or defense. The consequences of each reflect this difference. A j.n.o.v. results not in a new trial but in an immediate entry of judgment for the loser of the verdict. By contrast, the grant of a new trial does not make a winner out of a loser; it merely begins the contest again. The standard is accordingly lower: As most courts would put it, a judge may grant a new trial when the verdict is "against the great weight of the evidence." Those same courts would agree, however, that the trial judge may not simply decide how she would have voted as a juror and order a new trial if the jury disagrees. Where the standard lies between these two poles is hard to say.

Lind v. Schenley Industries

278 F.2d 79 (3d Cir. 1960)

[Lind, a sales manager for the defendant liquor company, alleged that it had promised him an increase in pay and a share of commissions but had then breached that promise. The alleged promises were oral. Lind and his then-secretary, Mrs. Kennan, testified to such promises. Schenley's agents denied making them. The jury found a contract; a damage award followed. Schenley moved both for judgment notwithstanding the verdict and, alternatively, for a new trial. The trial judge granted the j.n.o.v., and, in the alternative, a new trial. The plaintiff appealed.]

BIGGS, C. J. . . .

The district court granted the alternative motion for a new trial because it found the jury's verdict (1) contrary to the weight of the evidence, (2) contrary to law and (3) a result of error in the admission of evidence.

Our conclusion that the verdict was not contrary to law automatically eliminates ground (2).

It is convenient to consider the evidentiary issue relating to point (3) first. [The court held that a tabulated summary of liquor sales had been properly admitted into evidence as a business record.]

The remaining basis for ordering a new trial is that the verdict was against the weight of the evidence. It is frequently stated that a motion for a new trial on this ground ordinarily is nonreviewable because within the discretion of the trial court. But this discretion must still be exercised in accordance with ascertainable legal standards and if an appellate court is shown special or unusual circumstances which clearly indicate an abuse of discretion in that the trial court failed to apply correctly the proper standards, reversal is possible. Concededly appellate courts rarely find that the trial court abused its discretion.

In Commercial Credit Corp. v. Pepper, Judge Borah stated:

> It is a principle well recognized in the federal courts that the granting or refusing of a new trial is a matter resting within the discretion of the trial court. The term "discretion," however, when invoked as a guide to judicial action, means a sound discretion, exercised with regard to what is right and in the interests of justice. And an appellate court is not bound to stay its hand and place its stamp of approval on a case when it feels that injustice may result. Quite to the contrary, it is definitely recognized in numerous decisions that an abuse of discretion is an exception to the rule that the granting or refusing of a new trial is not assignable as error.

Thus an appellate court must still rule upon the propriety of an order for a new trial, even though the grounds for reversal are exceedingly narrow. But before any rational decision can be made, the reviewing court must know what standards the trial judge is bound to apply when ruling upon a motion for a new trial. These standards necessarily vary according to the grounds urged in support of the new trial. There is, however, little authority on what standards are to be applied in ruling on a motion for new trial on the grounds that the verdict is against the weight of the evidence beyond the simple maxim that the trial judge has wide discretion. The few available authorities are conflicting. Professor Moore concludes that while the trial judge has a responsibility for the result at least equal to that of the jury he should not set the verdict aside as contrary to the weight of the evidence and order a new trial simply because he would have come to a different conclusion if he were the trier of the facts. Professor Moore states in this connection:

> [S]ince the credibility of witnesses is peculiarly for the jury it is an invasion of the jury's province to grant a new trial merely because the evidence was

sharply in conflict. The trial judge, exercising a mature judicial discretion, should view the verdict in the overall setting of the trial; consider the character of the evidence and the complexity or simplicity of the legal principles which the jury was bound to apply to the facts; and abstain from interfering with the verdict unless it is quite clear that the jury has reached a seriously erroneous result. The judge's duty is essentially to see that there is no miscarriage of justice. If convinced that there has been then it is his duty to set the verdict aside; otherwise not.

Professor Moore's views are logical and persuasive and buttressed by some decisional authority. . . .

What we have stated demonstrates that there is no consensus of opinion as to the exact standards to be used by a trial court in granting a new trial and that the criteria to be employed by an appellate tribunal charged with reviewing the trial judge's decision in this respect are equally indefinite. New trials granted because (1) a jury verdict is against the weight of the evidence may be sharply distinguished from (2) new trials ordered for other reasons: for example, evidence improperly admitted, prejudicial statements by counsel, an improper charge to the jury or newly discovered evidence. In the first instance given it is the jury itself which fails properly to perform the functions confided to it by law. In the latter instances something occurred in the course of the trial which resulted or which may have resulted in the jury receiving a distorted, incorrect, or an incomplete view of the operative facts, or some undesirable element obtruded itself into the proceedings creating a condition whereby the giving of a just verdict was rendered difficult or impossible. In the latter instances, (2), supra, the trial court delivered the jury from a possibly erroneous verdict arising from circumstances over which the jury had no control. Under these conditions there is no usurpation by the court of the prime function of the jury as the trier of the facts and the trial judge necessarily must be allowed wide discretion in granting or refusing a new trial.

But where no undesirable or pernicious element has occurred or been introduced into the trial and the trial judge nonetheless grants a new trial on the ground that the verdict was against the weight of the evidence, the trial judge in negating the jury's verdict has, to some extent at least, substituted his judgment of the facts and the credibility of the witnesses for that of the jury. Such an action effects a denigration of the jury system and to the extent that new trials are granted the judge takes over, if he does not usurp, the prime function of the jury as the trier of the facts. It then becomes the duty of the appellate tribunal to exercise a closer degree of scrutiny and supervision than is the case where a new trial is granted because of some undesirable or pernicious influence obtruding into the trial. Such a close scrutiny is required in order to protect the litigants' right to jury trial.

Where a trial is long and complicated and deals with a subject matter not lying within the ordinary knowledge of jurors a verdict should be scrutinized more closely by the trial judge than is necessary where the litigation deals with material which is familiar and simple, the evidence relating to ordinary commercial practices. An example of subject matter unfamiliar to a layman would be a case requiring a jury to pass upon the nature of an alleged newly discovered organic compound in an infringement action. A prime example of subject matter lying well within the comprehension of jurors is presented by the circumstances at bar.

The subject matter of the litigation before us is simple and easily comprehended by any intelligent layman. The jury's main function was to determine the veracity of the witnesses: i.e., what testimony should be believed. If Lind's testimony and that of Mrs. Kennan, Kaufman's secretary, was deemed credible, Lind presented a convincing, indeed an overwhelming case. We must conclude that the jury did believe this testimony and that the court below substituted its judgment for that of the jury on this issue and thereby abused its legal discretion.

The judgment of the court below will be reversed and the case will be remanded with the direction to the court below to reinstate the verdict and judgment in favor of Lind.

HASTIE, J., with whom KALODNER, J., joins (dissenting).

. . . I think the majority make a serious mistake when they take the extraordinary additional step of reversing the alternative order of the trial judge, granting a new trial because he considered the verdict against the weight of the evidence.

This court has never before reversed an order of a trial judge granting a new trial because of his conclusion on all of the evidence that the jury had reached an unjust result. At least, neither I nor any of my colleagues can find a precedent in our court for such action. Rather, we have recognized that the function in question is broadly discretionary, "requir[ing] that the trial judge evaluate all significant evidence, deciding in the exercise of his own best judgment whether the jury has so disregarded the clear weight of credible evidence that a new trial is necessary to prevent injustice." The opinions of other courts cited by the majority not only recognize that discretion but also emphasize its extreme breadth.

This traditional conception of the role of the trial judge has provided the one important limitation on the power of the jury to make an unimpeachable decision on the facts, even where the evidence is conflicting. The judge may not substitute the verdict he would have rendered on the evidence for that actually rendered by the jury. But he may avoid what in his professionally trained and experienced judgment is an unjust verdict by vacating it and causing the matter to be tried again by a second jury. Thus, the essential institution of jury trial is respected and an expedient middle ground is maintained between the absence of any control over a jury's verdict on conflicting evidence, on the one hand, and judicial usurpation of the fact finding function, on the other.

Under this scheme the only function of a reviewing court, once the trial court has ordered a new trial, is to see whether there can have been any basis in reason for the trial judge's conclusion as to the weight of the evidence and the injustice of the verdict. The majority do not challenge this view, though they do not state explicitly what their understanding of our role is.

The present record discloses a sharp conflict of testimony whether Kaufman, the metropolitan sales manager, ever promised plaintiff, his subordinate district manager, a 1% commission on all gross sales of agents working under plaintiff. There are several remarkable aspects of this alleged promise which could reasonably have influenced the trial judge on this decisive issue. This commission would have more than quadrupled plaintiff's salary of $150 per week, making him much higher paid than his immediate superior, Kaufman, or any other company executive, except the president. No other sales manager or supervisor received any such commission at all. Moreover, after the alleged promise was made, month after month elapsed with no payment of the 1% commission or indication of any step to fulfill such an obligation. Yet plaintiff himself admits that he made no formal demand for or inquiry about the large obligation for several years, and said nothing even informally about it to anyone for many months save for an occasional passing verbal inquiry said to have been addressed to Kaufman. The trial court may have reasoned that the amount said to have been promised was so abnormally large and plaintiff's concern about nonpayment so unnaturally small as to make it incredible that the promise ever was made. In addition, the very vagueness of the alleged promise and the absence of any mention of time in it may have increased the incredulity of the judge who heard the evidence.

In such circumstances it was neither arbitrary nor an abuse of discretion for the trial judge to grant a new trial. Whether in the same circumstances some other trial judge or any member of this court would have let the verdict stand is beside the point.

The majority think the trial judge usurped the function of the jury. I think it is we who are impinging upon the function and discretion of the trial judge in a way that is serious, regrettable and without precedent in this court.

NOTES AND PROBLEMS

1. Why did the trial court grant a new trial?

2. Why did the appellate court reverse the grant of a new trial?

3. The *Lind* opinion merges three separate issues: (1) what standard the trial court should apply in setting aside verdicts as being against the weight of the evidence, (2) how the trial court should apply that standard to the case at hand, and (3) what standard the appellate court should apply in reviewing new trial rulings. How does the *Lind* court resolve each of these issues?

4. The *Lind* opinion also illustrates another part of the relation between directed verdicts and orders for new trials. Notice that defendant, having lost the verdict, made both motions, and the trial court granted both.

a. Why? If the trial judge granted defendant a j.n.o.v., that would end the case. Why bother also ruling on a motion for a new trial? Rule 50(c) contains the answer, permitting a party moving for a j.n.o.v. to make (and the court to rule on) a *conditional* motion for a new trial. This alternative comes into play only if "the judgment [notwithstanding the verdict] is thereafter vacated or reversed." *Lind* illustrates the point of such a conditional ruling because the j.n.o.v. was in fact reversed. Without Rule 50(c), the defendant would have had to return to the trial court and, perhaps some years after the trial, make its motion for a new trial. Rule 50(c), permitting a losing party to make all its post-trial motions at once, allows the trial judge to rule on them with the case still fresh in mind and allows the appellate court to consider all of them at once — as it did in *Lind*.

b. Notice that while the grant of a judgment as a matter of law constitutes a final judgment from which an appeal may be taken, the grant of a new trial, standing alone, does not create a final judgment — this will not happen until the new trial has occurred.

c. The interaction of the final judgment rule and Rule 50(c) creates four possible combinations of grants and denials of judgment as a matter of law and new trial: denial of both motions (probably the most common result); denial of judgment as a matter of law and grant of a new trial; grant of judgment as a matter of law with conditional denial of a new trial; and grant of judgment as a matter of law with conditional grant of a new trial. Which of these are immediately appealable?

5. Suppose a jury returns a defense verdict. The judge, believing that the evidence strongly favored the plaintiff, orders a new trial. The second jury agrees with the first. Should the judge order still a third trial or simply conclude that he was wrong about the weight of the evidence? Because the new trial order is not appealable, the length of such a sequence is theoretically indefinite. In practice, one of three things is likely to happen: the judge may finally get a jury that agrees with him, or the judge may decide that the juries were right and he was wrong. If neither of these occurs, the defendant might eventually get an appellate court to grant a writ of mandamus (see page 783 infra) to put him out of his misery.

c.   Conditional New Trials

Up to now we have dealt with cases in which grants of new trials involved retrying the entire case. Consider a judge who concludes that the jury reasonably could have reached a verdict for the plaintiff but that its damage calculations are unreasonably low or high. May the judge grant a new trial limited to the issue of damages? The answer is yes, though the problems involved in reaching that answer are considerable.

(1)   New trial limited to damages

Consider the logical underpinnings of such a ruling. To be prepared to order a new trial limited to the issue of damages, the judge must be convinced that whatever influences led the jury astray on damages did not infect the judgment on liability as well. Take, for example, a verdict for the plaintiff combined with clearly insufficient damages. Can the judge be certain that the low award did not reflect considerable jury uncertainty that the plaintiff should recover at all — uncertainty that should have been reflected in a judgment for the defendant? The same doubt can exist in the case of clearly excessive damages; a jury so passionately disposed toward the plaintiff may have been so influenced on the issue of liability as well.

Yet courts do order such partial new trials. Pingatore v. Montgomery Ward & Co., 419 F.2d 1138 (6th Cir. 1969), cert denied, 398 U.S. 928 (1970), serves as an example. A rat leapt on and bit plaintiff's knee while she was leaving the department store premises. She developed complications leading to partial paralysis in an arm and leg. Testimony divided over whether the damage was attributable to the treatment for the bite (a series of rabies inoculations), to "conversion hysteria" or "psychosis," or to "malingering." After a trial in which the plaintiff's attorney ranted and swore at the defendant corporation, the jury awarded plaintiff $126,000 in damages and $25,000 to her husband. The court of appeals reversed the judgment on account of the plaintiff's attorney's misbehavior. But, without explaining more than that "there is substantial evidence to support the verdict of the jury on the question of liability," the court limited the new trial to damages. Why was liability so clear? Because it was obvious that the plaintiff should get *something* for being bitten by a rat?

(2)   Remittitur and additur

Instead of ordering a new trial on damages, could the *Pingatore* court simply have reduced the amount of the damage award to one it thought reasonable? The answer is yes — under some circumstances. In such an action, known as *remittitur*, the judge orders a new trial unless the plaintiff agrees to accept reduced damages. Its damage-increasing analogue is *additur*. Both involve many of the problems inherent in the partial new trial as well as some special difficulties.

If the jury renders a verdict that is arguably excessive, the trial judge faces several questions. These questions apply, in reverse, to additur, the less common of the two devices. Essentially the questions are: first, when should one grant such a reduction (or addition) in damages?; and, second, how does one calculate the amount?

Answering the first question, the courts have suggested a "shock the conscience" test or a "passion, bias, or prejudice" test. Besides its inherent vagueness, this standard has a problem: If the verdict is so excessive, how is the court sure that the problem did not also affect the jury's finding of liability? If the court so concludes, the only remedy would be an entire new trial.

Assuming that remittitur is appropriate, how should the court determine the appropriate amount of damages? The three suggested tests are the highest amount a jury could award, a reasonable amount, and the lowest reasonable amount. See Gorsalitz v. Olin Mathieson Chemical Corp., 429 F.2d 1033, 1047 (5th Cir. 1970). Even courts that use the highest-reasonable-amount test recognize a distinction between cases in which the jury simply awards an excessive amount on its own and cases in which some error of the court (usually in the charge on damages) leads to the unreasonably high verdict. In the latter cases, the remittitur will attempt to require remission of the portion of the verdict traceable to the error — in other words, the court must determine the approximate amount of the error.

Consider the choice to which the grant of remittitur puts a plaintiff. Assume a verdict of $150,000 for the plaintiff that the court orders remitted to $75,000. If the plaintiff refuses the remittitur, the consequence is, of course, that the court will grant a new trial. The Supreme Court has held that a plaintiff must get a choice between a new trial and accepting reduced compensatory damages. Hetzel v. Prince William County, 523 U.S. 208 (1998). What about punitive damages? In several cases (see Chapter V) the Supreme Court has held that due process requires judicial scrutiny of punitive damage awards. One court has found that this line of cases overcomes what would otherwise be a Seventh Amendment requirement that the court give plaintiff a choice between reduced punitive damages and a new trial. Johansen v. Combustion Engineering, Inc., 170 F.3d 1320 (11th Cir. 1999).

Suppose the plaintiff accepts the remittitur. May she condition her acceptance on a right to appeal? If not, may the plaintiff at least raise the matter if the defendant appeals the remitted verdict? The Supreme Court has checked the attempt of a number of lower courts to permit appeals from conditionally accepted verdicts; according to the Court, the plaintiff had a choice: Accept the remittitur or prepare for a new trial. Donovan v. Penn Shipping Co., 429 U.S. 648, 649 (1977).

Are remittitur and additur constitutional? Some years ago, the Supreme Court held that additur violates the Seventh Amendment but that remittitur does not. The theory was that remittitur simply involves modifying a decision actually made by a jury, while additur involves making an award that no jury has ever made. See Dimick v. Schiedt, 293 U.S. 474, 483 (1935). Critics have suggested that this is a distinction without a meaning, but it is still the law in federal courts. Many states permit additur as well as remittitur. See, e.g., Jehl v. Southern Pacific Co., 66 Cal, 2d 821, 427 P.2d 988, 59 Cal. Rptr. 276 (1967).

C.   The Limits of the Law's Control: The Jury as a Black Box

What happens if the evidence admitted at trial provides some basis for finding for either side? Suppose the jury is properly instructed in the law, proceeds to deliberate, and then returns a verdict. Suppose the losing party's attorney interviews all the jurors after the verdict, and all the jurors admit that they misunderstood or disregarded one or more of the jury instructions. Suppose the jurors further say that they would have decided the case for the losing party if they had properly understood or followed the instructions. Suppose the jurors go one step further and each executes a sworn affidavit to that effect. Should the court grant judgment notwithstanding the verdict or grant a new trial to ensure a rational result under the applicable law?

Peterson v. Wilson

141 F.3d 573 (5th Cir. 1998)

WIENER, J. . . .

I. Facts and Proceedings

Peterson filed this suit in district court under 42 U.S.C. §§1983 and 1988, as well as the First, Fifth, and Fourteenth Amendments of the United States Constitution after he was fired as grant director at Texas Southern University (TSU). He claims that his property interest in his employment at TSU was damaged or destroyed when it was arbitrarily and capriciously terminated. . . . After five days of trial, conducted by the magistrate judge with the consent of the parties, the jury found for Peterson and awarded him $152,235 for lost pay and benefits and $35,000 for past and future mental anguish. Following the verdict, Wilson renewed his motion for j.m.l. and supplemented it with his bare-bones alternative motion for a new trial.

Some four months later, in January 1996, the district court granted the new trial, ostensibly in response to Wilson's motion, but in actuality on its own motion: The substantive language of the district court's order granting a new trial eschews any conclusion other than that the ruling was granted sua sponte, and that it was not granted for insufficiency of the evidence or because the jury verdict was against the great weight of the evidence, but rather for the following reason:

> The court concludes, based on the jury's verdict and *comments the jurors made to the court after returning the verdict* [and outside the presence of the parties and their respective counsel], that the jury completely disregarded the Court's instructions. Instead, it appears that the jury considered improper factors in reaching its verdict. Accordingly, the Court deems it in the interest of justice to grant a new trial (emphasis added).

. . . The inference is inescapable that, to impeach the jury's verdict, the district court relied on information gleaned from the jurors themselves during the court's post-verdict, ex parte meeting with the jury. The court voided the verdict because, in the court's own words, the jury "completely disregarded the Court's instructions."

Peterson timely filed a motion for reconsideration, which the district court did not grant. The case was re-tried in June 1996, and ended in a jury verdict in favor of Wilson, rejecting Peterson's claims. . . .

C.   Facts

The jury, as the finder of facts and the maker of all credibility calls, reached its verdict in the first trial on the basis of the following record facts and inferences.

Peterson is well educated, well trained, and widely experienced in his field of concentration, which is grant administration for institutions of higher education. When Peterson joined TSU in 1983 he assumed responsibility for administering grants, principally Title III grants. In addition, he was in charge of student affairs and was responsible for determining the residency status of foreign students. Peterson also supervised finances of the university and was in charge of Institutional Research.

As Title III Director, Peterson generally reported directly to the Vice President for Academic Affairs: first Clarkson, then Moore, and eventually, Wilson. The programs supported by Title III grants included faculty development, equipment purchases, and institutional research, providing millions of dollars annually for expenditures at TSU. . . .

Without reiterating every detail of the relevant testimony and documents, it suffices that the evidence heard and obviously credited by the jury painted a picture of Peterson as a highly principled, apolitical, objective grant administrator who repeatedly refused to "play ball" with high ranking TSU administrators when they attempted to obtain expensive equipment for unauthorized personal use or sought to have unauthorized job positions created and funded with grant money for their special "friends."

The jury also heard and obviously credited testimony of both direct and implied threats by Wilson of adverse job actions, including firing, that Peterson was in jeopardy of incurring if, on reflection, he should fail or refuse to accede to requests that would require the unauthorized expenditure of grant funds.

The termination letter of January 3, 1991, from Wilson to Peterson purported to outline nine items constituting "cause" for the firing, each of which was set forth in a report prepared and submitted on request by one Joyce Deyon with whom, it turned out, Wilson never conferred after receiving the report. Wilson testified that he accepted the report and made his judgment based on it.

The jury heard testimony and saw documents which, if believed — as the jury apparently did — methodically refuted or explained away each of the nine purported causes for termination and revealed that Wilson did not even understand some of the items. The jury also heard evidence which, if credited, was sufficient to support a conclusion that the termination and its purported causes were pretext intended to cover Wilson's retaliation and desire to accomplish his actual or implied threats of getting rid of Peterson and replacing him with a grant director who would be more of a team player, i.e., would be more amenable to funding equipment purchases and job creations for "friends" of the higher-ups in the TSU administration with grant money.

That the jury unquestionably credited the testimony and documentation supporting Peterson's version of the facts and rejected Wilson's is confirmed by the "Yes" answer to Interrogatory No. I-A, "Do you find from a preponderance of the evidence that Dr. Bobby Wilson acted arbitrarily and capriciously in terminating Dr. Peterson?" In the interrogatory that followed, the jury awarded Peterson $152,235 in lost pay and benefits, and $35,000 for past and future mental anguish.

II. Analysis

A. Standard of Review

We review the district court's grant of a new trial for abuse of discretion. "It is a well-settled rule in this circuit that 'a verdict can be against the "great weight of the evidence," and thus justify a new trial, even if there is substantial evidence to support it.' " What courts cannot do — and what the district court here never purported to do — is to grant a new trial "simply because [the court] would have come to a different conclusion than the jury did."

B. The District Court's Ruling

The district court's succinct but cryptic, three-sentence explanation for granting a new trial demonstrates beyond question that, following the verdict, the court impermissibly met with and interrogated the jurors outside the presence of the parties and their respective counsel, and then proceeded to act in direct reliance on the jurors' comments as though they constituted newly discovered evidence of a kind that the court could properly consider. It was not. The conclusion is inescapable that, in impeaching the jury's verdict in this case, the district court relied on information obtained from the jurors in the court's post-verdict, ex parte meeting with them and that, by definition, any information thus obtained had to come directly from their internal deliberations qua jurors.

1. Jury Impeachment

Rule 606(b) of the Federal Rules of Evidence (F.R.E.) tightly controls impeachment of jury verdicts. This rule states, in pertinent part:

> Upon an inquiry into the validity of a verdict . . ., a juror may not testify as to any matter or statement occurring during the course of the jury's deliberations or to the effect of anything upon that or any other juror's mind or emotions as influencing the juror to assent to or dissent from the verdict . . . or concerning the juror's mental processes in connection therewith, except that a juror may testify on the question whether extraneous prejudicial information was improperly brought to the jury's attention or whether any outside influence was improperly brought to the jury's attention or whether any outside influence was improperly brought to bear upon any juror. Nor may a juror's affidavit or evidence of any statement by the juror concerning a matter about which the juror would be precluded from testifying be received for these purposes. . . .

The landmark Supreme Court case on this issue is Tanner v. United States. After acknowledging that "[b]y the beginning of this century, if not earlier, the near-universal and firmly established common-law rule in the United States flatly prohibited the admission of juror testimony to impeach a jury verdict," the Court observed that "Federal Rule of Evidence 606(b) is grounded in the common-law rule against admission of jury testimony to impeach a verdict and the exception for juror testimony relating to extraneous influences." Following *Tanner*, and more closely on point, we held in Robles v. Exxon Corp. that receiving testimony from the jurors after they have returned their verdict, for the purpose of ascertaining that the jury misunderstood its instructions, is absolutely prohibited by F.R.E. 606(b). We underscored that holding by noting that "the legislative history of the rule unmistakably points to the conclusion that Congress made a conscious decision to disallow juror testimony as to the jurors' mental processes or fidelity to the court's instructions." What is pellucid here, from the court's own unequivocal and unambiguous words, is that the jurors' statements to the court related directly to matters that transpired in the jury room, that these matters comprehended the mental processes of the jurors in their deliberations on the case, and that the jurors' statements formed the foundation of the court's impeachment of the verdict grounded in the jury's lack of "fidelity to the court's instructions." We cannot conceive of an example more explicitly violative of *Robles*. . . .

[The Court of Appeals concluded that the district court did not find that the verdict was against the great weight of the evidence and that, even if it had, such a decision was contrary to the record.]

We are thus left with no choice but to reverse the district court's grant of a new trial, vacate the court's judgment rendered on the basis of the jury verdict in the second trial, and reinstate the results of the first trial. We therefore remand this case to the district court for entry of judgment in favor of Peterson and against Wilson in the principal sum of $187,235 ($152,235 for lost pay and benefits and $35,000 for past and future mental anguish), and for the assessment of appropriate interest and costs, including reasonable attorneys' fees incurred by Peterson in both trials and on appeal.

NOTES AND PROBLEMS

1. *Peterson* serves both as a review of the preceding chapter and as an embodiment of an important principle about jury integrity. Begin with reviewing some fundamental propositions:

a. Explain why plaintiff could not appeal after the first trial.

b. Explain why the result would have been different had the appellate court found — as defendant urged it to — that the trial court had granted a new trial because the first verdict was "against the great weight of the evidence."

c. Explain why the trial judge, after interviewing the jurors in the first trial and ascertaining that they had misunderstood the instructions, could not grant judgment as a matter of law (j.n.o.v.) for defendant.

2. The principle elaborated in *Peterson* has to do with the inviolability of jury deliberations.

a. It was not unlawful, though it was unusual, for the trial judge to interview the jurors to ascertain whether they understood the instructions. In the more usual situation the lawyers rather than the judge interview the jurors. Most lawyers are interested in how their case looked through jurors' eyes. Win or lose, they are usually interested in finding out what persuaded the jury. Jurors have no obligation to speak to the lawyers after the trial, but they are often willing to do so, as they did here to the judge.

b. Why, having learned through these interviews that the jury misunderstood instructions, could the trial court not grant a new trial on that basis?

c. Distinguish *Peterson* from In re Beverly Hills Fire Litigation, supra page 732. In the latter case a juror performed home experiments on aluminum electrical wiring (the dangerousness of which was a contested issue at trial) and reported his findings to the other jurors. The appellate court held it an abuse of discretion not to grant a new trial. Why is it erroneous to grant a new trial when a juror misunderstands instructions and erroneous not to grant a new trial when a juror performs such experiments? Explain the distinction.

3. What interests are served by prohibiting impeachment of a jury's verdict through post-verdict statements by the jurors regarding their deliberations?

a. One can explain F.R. Evid. 606 cynically: Too many jury verdicts would fall if we delved into jury deliberations deeply.

b. A different explanation is also possible. As you have already seen, if summary judgment and judgment as a matter of law are operating properly, only close cases — cases that could rationally be decided either way — will go to the jury. In such cases, any verdict should be sustainable. And, some would add, in such cases the soft variables that constitute the jury's sense of justice *should* come into play, even when those variables are hard to justify from the lofty plane of rationalism.

4. Distinguish two issues that courts sometimes conflate: what constitutes jury conduct sufficiently improper to require a new trial; and when the court will hear evidence about jury conduct from a *juror*. F.R. Evid. 606 governs the latter but has nothing to say about the former.

a. To sharpen the distinction, imagine a case in which evidence of jury conduct came from two sources — a bailiff who overheard deliberations while stationed outside the room and a juror herself. Rule 606 bars testimony from the latter but not from the former.

b. In fact, because juries deliberate in private, only in the very rare case will anyone other than a juror know what happened in the jury room.

5. In contrast to information about jury deliberations, Rule 606 does allow a verdict to be impeached by evidence that there was some improper "outside influence" on the jury.

a. Bribery obviously meets that criterion. So do threats to jurors by outsiders.

b. What about evidence that a majority of jurors badgered a holdout juror until the holdout caved in and went along with the majority? Is there any basis for treating an outside threat to a juror differently from a threat by a fellow juror? A survey found the courts divided and could offer only the not very helpful observation that the cases seemed fact-specific. Impeachment of Verdict by Juror's Evidence That He Was Coerced or Intimidated by Fellow Juror, 39 A.L.R. 4th 800 (1996).

6. It may already have occurred to you that one might make jury verdicts less opaque by asking the jury to explain how it reached its

verdict. There are in fact two ways to do just that — the special verdict and the general verdict with special interrogatories. See Rule 49. Which of these procedures was used in *Peterson*?

a. In a special verdict the jury does not render a general verdict at all. Instead it answers a series of questions about the evidence: "Was the defendant negligent? If so, did the defendant's negligence cause the plaintiff's injuries? If so, was the plaintiff also negligent? If so, did the plaintiff's negligence in some part contribute to his injuries?" When the jury has answered all the questions — or all those that are necessary — it delivers them as the verdict. In a general verdict with interrogatories, the jury renders a general verdict but also answers particular questions.

b. The concept of the special verdict and general verdict with interrogatories is simple: One gives the jurors a road map of the relevant legal issues, helping them to focus on each question as (and if) it becomes relevant.

c. The practice surrounding these procedures has been much less happy. Jurors regularly become confused by the questions. The nightmare outcome — one too often realized in the cases — is that juries give inconsistent answers. In one notorious case the jury said (a) that the defendant was negligent but (b) that it was impossible for the defendant to have foreseen any danger from a particular condition on its property — that condition being the only way in which the jury could have found the defendant negligent. Gallick v. B&O Railroad, 372 U.S. 108 (1963). As a consequence of these problems, judges, in whose almost unfettered discretion the decision to allow a special verdict lies, often avoid them.

Though trial by ordeal — drowning, burning, and the like — was abolished by the Lateran Council of 1215, lawyers tell us that even ordinary trials are ordeals of anxiety, weariness, and, for one side, disappointment. The one thing most civil trials are not is dramatic. Witnesses can change their stories and an occasional surprise will appear, but a well prepared civil trial where both sides have made effective use of discovery will not look like a *Perry Mason* episode.

Real trials differ from those in drama in another respect. In drama, the trial is the end of the road: The winners rejoice; the losers slink away in shame or defiance. In litigation the trial is a rare event, but even when it occurs, it is often not the end. In part because trials are so rare, parties who have been unable to settle their differences beforehand are unlikely to do so just because a judge or jury has announced a winner. For many, an appeal lies ahead.

APPEAL

XI

Appeals in U.S. litigation are a booming business. Over the past fifty years federal civil appeals have increased at a rate one and one-half times faster than the increase in lawsuits filed. This increase has come even though one may appeal only from a judgment and, as we have seen, only about a third of civil cases end in a judgment. This increase has come even though most cases are affirmed on appeal — between 80 and 90 percent in the federal system.

Appeals are the setting for particularly fierce battles between two salient goals of civil procedure: fairness and justice. Fairness dictates that parties should win or lose depending on their compliance with procedural rules and the quality of their argument. Justice dictates that the "right" party should prevail, regardless of such technicalities. Because the system embraces both goals, one must frequently yield to the other, and the conflict appears starkly in appellate litigation.

In many respects appealing resembles starting a new lawsuit rather than continuing the same one. Moreover, that "new suit" (the appeal) is brought in a system that often applies procedural rules in a more technical fashion than do the trial courts. Unlike some other legal systems, the U.S. litigation system operates with a heavy presumption that the trial court decision is correct. U.S. appellate courts do not supervise trial courts. They have jurisdiction only to review specific trial court decisions claimed to be in error. And when they do so, they may not always reverse even when they conclude that they would have decided the question differently from the trial court. As a consequence of these restrictions, taking an appeal from a trial court decision is in many respects more like starting a separate lawsuit than entering a new phase of a continuing one.

This chapter focuses on the doctrinal walls that shield U.S. trial court decisions. These walls restrict the availability of review in three ways: They limit the persons who can seek review of a trial court decision; they limit when trial court decisions can be appealed; and they limit the depth of scrutiny an appellate court may exercise even over an appealable decision.

753

Understanding these doctrines has two virtues. It is obviously essential for any lawyer who ever wants to appeal a trial court decision. It is equally important for another reason: Understanding the barriers to appellate review helps one to comprehend that, as a practical matter, the trial court's decision on most procedural and substantive matters is likely to be the only decision. This practical autonomy of the trial court puts enormous weight on the trial judge — to make the right decision — and on the lawyers — to give the judge all the information needed to make the right decision.

A.   Who Can Appeal?

In theory, one could imagine appellate courts functioning as the supervisors of trial courts, randomly reviewing cases to assure both that the result is correct and that the trial judge is following appropriate procedure. Or one might imagine a judicial inspector general who would have the power and duty to bring to the attention of appellate courts instances of where either the process or the result of a trial court decision seem questionable. Administrative systems follow such models, and some civil law systems approximate them.

The U.S. courts do not. Even a blatantly erroneous decision may be appealed only by a party to the lawsuit, a party, that is, who has not settled. Even more striking, a losing party who has not settled may nevertheless be unable to gain appellate reversal of a clearly erroneous trial court decision. Two doctrines create this result: those that allow appeals only by parties who have suffered an adverse decision, and those that deter appeals with various penalties.

1.   A Losing Party: Adversity

A hallmark of modern procedure is the ease with which parties can join multiple claims and theories of recovery in a single lawsuit. This poses a problem for appellate review: If one wins on one theory but loses on others, may the party in such a situation appeal the unsuccessful claims and contentions? Contemporary appellate review is result-oriented, so the answer to this question requires one to look at the relief sought by the party prevailing on one but not all theories. If the relief sought under the other, losing theories was identical to that awarded, no appeal will lie, even if the appellate court thinks the trial court erred. If, on the other hand, the rejected theory would have entitled the appealing party to more or different relief — to a different judgment — then appeal lies. One can describe the principle as the requirement of an "adverse" judgment, a judgment granting relief different from what one requested.

NOTES AND PROBLEMS

1. Apply this principle to the cases below:

a. Tenant is injured when she slips on a pool of water formed as a result of a leaky apartment roof. She sues landlord for personal injuries, invoking two theories under which the landlord had a duty to repair the roof — a duty arising under the lease, and a duty arising under the municipal housing code. (See McKey v. Fairbairn, supra page 650.) The trial court rules that a duty is owed under the lease but that there is no duty under the municipal housing code. The court awards damages for personal injury. May plaintiff appeal, contending that a duty arose under the housing code as well? Plaintiff's lawyers, representing other tenants without leases, will wish to establish a precedent under the housing code. Can they appeal?

b. Plaintiff, alleging that automobile dealer sold her a used car when she paid for a new one, sues. She alleges two theories: that the dealer (1) breached a contract; (2) committed fraud. Contract damages call for the plaintiff to recover the difference between the value of the car she received and a new one — $3,000 in this instance. Punitive damages lie for fraud, and are measured not by plaintiff's loss but by magnitude of the wrong committed by defendant. The court finds that punitive damages are inappropriate, but awards plaintiff damages for breach of contract. May plaintiff appeal?

c. Consider the defendants in the two preceding problems. They have "won" parts of both cases, avoiding liability under the housing code in one case and avoiding punitive damages in the other. May they appeal?

2. The "losing party" principle described above comes under tension when a party has won the judgment but where a theory rejected by the trial court will have collateral consequences. In Aetna Casualty & Surety Co. v. Cunningham, 224 F.2d 478 (5th Cir. 1955), an insurance company sued one of its insureds, a building contractor. The contractor had failed to complete a building project, as a result of which the insurer had been required to pay for its completion. The insurer sought to recover its loss from the contractor, using two theories: (1) that the contractor was required to repay the insurer under the terms of the policy; and (2) that the insured contractor had committed fraud in applying for the policy. The insurer won on the contract theory but lost on the fraud theory. May the insurer appeal?

a. Applying the principle of the adverse judgment, the answer would be no. Since the insurer was seeking only compensatory damages, the amount of recovery on the contract claim was identical to that under the fraud claim. Winning on the fraud count would therefore not have increased the judgment.

b. Insurer argued, however, that the builder was about to file for bankruptcy. In bankruptcy a fraud claim receives more generous treatment than does a contract claim. Consequently the effect of the judgment would be different if the insurer prevailed on the fraud claim. In *Cunningham* the Fifth Circuit accepted the insurer's argument and permitted an appeal as to the fraud theory.

c. Suppose the insurer's lawyer had foreseen the probability of bankruptcy and the difficulty of appealing on an alternative ground. How could the plaintiff have framed the prayer for damages so as to assure appealability if the plaintiff lost on the fraud count? (See Note 1b above.)

d. Consider whether Forney v. Apfel, 524 U.S. 266 (1998), changes your response to the preceding questions. Sandra Forney applied for Social Security disability benefits. The Social Security Administration denied her claim, and she sued in federal district court, seeking either an order compelling payment of benefits or, in the alternative, a new administrative hearing. The district court ruled that the evidence of alternative employment for Ms. Forney was inadequate and remanded for a new administrative hearing. She appealed. The Ninth Circuit held the case unappealable on the grounds that, having won on at least part of her claim, she was a prevailing party. The Supreme Court unanimously reversed:

> [F]rom Forney's perspective, the second "alternative," [remand rather than an order compelling benefits], which means further delay and risk, is only half a loaf. Thus, the District Court's order gives petitioner some, but not all, of the relief she requested; and she consequently can appeal the District Court's order insofar as it denies her the relief she has sought.

Id. at 271.

3. Manufacturer sues Retailer for nonpayment of a bill. Retailer counterclaims for breach of warranty. The trial court enters judgment for Manufacturer on its claim but also awards damages to Retailer on its warranty claim. Retailer appeals. On appeal, Manufacturer will argue the correctness of the trial court's rulings on the claim of nonpayment. Manufacturer may also *cross-appeal*, arguing that the court erred in upholding the breach of warranty claim against it. As to that part of the case Manufacturer has suffered an adverse judgment.

4. Another aspect of the requirement that the judgment be adverse is the doctrine of mootness, which holds that one may not appeal from a

judgment when circumstances have changed in such a way that relief is no longer possible. The doctrine affects not only appeals but also the justiciability of the suit because mootness undercuts the existence of an actual case or controversy required by Article III of the Constitution. There are, however, numerous exceptions to the doctrine.

a. One of the most important exceptions is the case in which the plaintiff's claim has been satisfied despite an adverse ruling by the lower court, but the question raised by the claim is likely to recur, and application of the mootness doctrine would effectively prevent the question from receiving appellate review. In Sosna v. Iowa, 419 U.S. 393 (1975), for example, the plaintiff challenged the Iowa one-year residency requirements for obtaining a divorce. The lower court upheld the requirement, but during the litigation the year passed and the plaintiff became able to obtain her divorce. The Supreme Court nevertheless refused to dismiss the case as moot, reasoning that other plaintiffs would find themselves in the same situation.

b. Mootness can also result from settlement. Parties who settle cannot continue to appeal. Can they, as part of their settlement, ask an appellate court to set aside a lower court's action? The U.S. Supreme Court has said no. In U.S. Bancorp Mortgage Co. v. Bonner Mall, 513 U.S. 18 (1994), supra page 598, a unanimous Court refused the request of a settling party to vacate an appellate decision below. In a slightly different setting the California Supreme Court set aside a trial court judgment when asked by both of the settling parties to do so. Neary v. University of California, 3 Cal. 4th 273, 834 P.2d 119, 10 Cal. Rptr. 2d 859 (1992), supra page 595.

2. Who Raised the Issue Below: Waiver

In Cunningham (the case of the insurer alleging fraud, described in Problem 2 in the preceding section), suppose that at trial the insurer's evidence of fraud consisted not of misstatements by the contractor but of his failure to disclose the extent of his debts. Some jurisdictions accept such nondisclosure as evidence of fraud. Suppose the contractor's lawyer does not object to the evidence, though he strenuously argues that the undisclosed information was not material. If the trial court finds against the defendant on the fraud count, may the contractor challenge the judgment on the basis that nondisclosure was not sufficient to show fraud in that jurisdiction?

Generally not: a party must present to the trial court the contentions on which it wants rulings. Failure to do so results in waiver of the contention. A century ago the party had not only to raise the contention below but then to make a formal "exception" to the trial court ruling in order to preserve the issue for appeal. Rule 46 did away with the need for exceptions; the party need only "make known to the court the action which the party desires the court to take. . . ." The abolition of the formal requirement did not, however, abolish the doctrine of waiver.

NOTES AND PROBLEMS

1. How persistently must one party object? Suppose that in *Cunningham* (the insurance fraud case) the defendant filed a 12(b)(6) motion challenging the complaint on the grounds that it alleged only failure to disclose, not affirmative misrepresentation. Having lost the 12(b)(6) motion, would the defendant thereafter have to object to the plaintiff's evidence in order to preserve the issue for appeal? Yes, at least to be on the safe side:

> To preserve the point the moving party can, and in general is required, upon the trial to renew and support his pleaded objections by objections to evidence, and by requesting rulings and instructions from the Court to the jury which he deems necessary to protect and preserve the point asserted by his motion to dismiss or to strike. In the present case the points asserted by motion were not again presented by any request for instructions, or by any effort to have the Court direct the jury to pass separately upon the question of whether the actions should be merely abated or determined upon its merits. Therefore, since the point was not properly urged and presented, there is no occasion to determine the validity of the fifth defense. Likewise, as to the objections now urged to the charge (which in some portions apparently gave effect to this defense) since no objection was presented to the trial Court, the appellant can not here properly complain of the alleged erroneous instruction. We cannot accept the contention that the assertion of the objection by motion to strik[e] properly presented and preserved the point throughout the proceedings of the subsequent trial.

Mims v. Central Mfrs. Mut. Ins. Co., 178 F.2d 56, 59 (5th Cir. 1949)

2. An appellant cannot on appeal use an argument not made below. How about an appellee, the party seeking to support the judgment? If appellee lost on a defense or claim below and wants to preserve the objection in case the case is reversed, he must cross-appeal. But suppose appellee wants to use a new argument in *support* of the judgment? For an example, recall again the facts of *Cunningham*. Suppose that the insurer contended that the insured's fraud had consisted of failure to disclose certain information. Further suppose there was a question of whether the law of Connecticut (the insurer's base) or Texas (the insured's) applied. At trial insurer argued that Connecticut law applied

and that it recognized nondisclosure as fraud. Insurer wins a judgment on the fraud claim and the defendant appeals.

a. On appeal, appellee insurer wants to argue in support of the judgment that Texas also recognizes nondisclosure as fraud so that an appellate ruling that Texas law applies would not require reversal of the judgment. Can it do so? Yes:

> It is true that a party who does not appeal from a final decree of the trial court cannot be heard in opposition thereto when the case is brought here by appeal of the adverse party. In other words, the appellee may not attack the decree with a view either to enlarging his own rights thereunder or of lessening the rights of his adversary, whether what he seeks is to correct an error to supplement the decree with respect to a matter dealt with below. But it is likewise settled that the appellee may, without taking a cross-appeal, urge in support of a decree any matter appearing in the record, although his argument may involve an attack upon the reasoning of the lower court or an insistence upon a matter overlooked or ignored by it.

United States v. American Ry. Exp. Co., 265 U.S. 425, 435 (1923).

b. The same principle requiring an issue be raised below applies to cross-appeals. If a party who prevails at trial cross-appeals, it can on its cross-appeal raise only those arguments made at trial. Again using *Cunningham* as an example, suppose that the insurer prevailed at trial on the contract but not on the fraud count, and the contractor-defendant appealed. Insurer could cross-appeal, contending that the trial court was correct in awarding judgment on the contract count but that the insurer should also have won on the fraud claim. On this cross-appeal the insurer could make only those contentions made below.

3. Another test of the courts' adherence to the requirement that an appellate issue be raised below comes when there has been a change in the law between the time of trial and the appeal.

a. Arthur applies for Social Security disability benefits, and his claim is denied. He sues, challenging the determination that he is not disabled. He loses in trial court and appeals. While his appeal is pending, a case comes down holding that the administrative procedure by which such claims are determined is unconstitutional. May Arthur on appeal raise this constitutional issue, which he did not raise below?

b. A hard-nosed advocate of the adversary system would say no — that Arthur could have raised such a claim below and cannot now seek to ride on the coattails of a more enterprising or imaginative litigant.

c. Courts waver in their willingness to entertain such late-maturing grounds for appeal. If the change in law is sufficiently fundamental, they may hear an argument on appeal that was not raised below. See Carson Products Co. v. Califano, 594 F.2d 453 (5th Cir. 1979) (drug company challenges FDA determination that product ingredient is not a trade secret; on appeal permitted to raise contention that FDA procedures denied due process). But no litigant should count on this grace.

4. The "plain error" rule is another exception to the general requirement that an issue must be raised in the trial court as a predicate to appeal.

a. The doctrine is most commonly applied to criminal cases, where the courts are thought to have a special duty to assure that defendants are not convicted unfairly. Its basis was nicely stated by Judge Frank in Troupe v. Chicago, Duluth & Georgian Bay Transit Co., 234 F.2d 253, 261 (2d Cir. 1956): "[A] litigant surely has the right to assume that a federal trial judge knows the elementary substantive legal rules, long established by the precedents, and . . . will act accordingly, without prompting by the litigant's lawyer." Before you conclude that such a doctrine will save you from failure to object, note that this ringing endorsement of the principle came in a concurring opinion — in a case where the majority held that the doctrine did not apply to a clearly erroneous jury instruction. The rule is typically invoked "where the error has seriously affected the fairness, integrity, or public reputation of judicial proceedings." 9 Wright and Miller §2558, at 675. For a recent statement of the rule in a civil context, see the following opinion:

> We hold that failure to object timely to a magistrate judge's report and recommendation bars a party, except upon grounds of plain error . . . from attacking on appeal not only the proposed factual findings . . . but also the proposed legal conclusions, accepted . . . by the district court, provided that the party has been served with notice that such consequences will result from a failure to object. . . .

Douglas v. U.S.A.A., 79 F.3d 1415 (5th Cir. 1996).

b. The plain-error doctrine tests how U.S. appellate courts balance the principle of fairness to the parties against the correctness of the result. To say that the failure to object is excused (because an error is "plain") is to say that the appellate courts assume some degree of responsibility for assuring the correctness of the outcome, not just fairness to the parties.

c. In addition to raising the matter in the trial court, counsel usually must also raise an issue in the appellate court before the appellate court will consider it. There are exceptions, however. The matter is discussed in Vestal, Sua Sponte Consideration in Appellate Review, 27 Fordham L. Rev. 477 (1959).

d. Having virtually assaulted the student with the proposition that appellate courts will not consider arguments not made at trial, we should note a glaring exception: Erie Railroad v. Tompkins, supra page 265. In that landmark decision neither party had raised the choice of law question, nor had the Supreme Court granted certiorari to consider it. The Court thus made its landmark decision on a basis not argued or briefed by either party. One can reconcile *Erie* with the preceding discussion: A court may decide on a basis not raised by the parties, but a party must consistently raise an issue he wants to argue. Nevertheless, one might think that the concept of fair notice that applies to the parties might also apply to the court.

5. Recall from Chapter III that there is one issue — the court's subject matter jurisdiction — that the federal courts are required to raise on their own and that may be raised for the first time on appeal by either the parties or the appellate court.

3. Who Was Not Deterred

The increasing rate of appeals has caused many jurisdictions to discourage them. The Supreme Court has never held that there is a constitutional right to appeal a civil case, so a jurisdiction could in theory either forbid civil appeals absolutely or, less dramatically, make all civil appeals a matter of discretion rather than of right. No jurisdiction has to date taken either step. Every jurisdiction in the United States grants the right of at least one appeal in civil cases; further appeal is often discretionary.

Even though they permit appeals, however, judicial systems can discourage them. Are there limits on these burdens? The U.S. Supreme Court has faced that issue in several cases. In Lindsey v. Normet, 405 U.S. 56 (1972), the Court invalidated a state statute that required tenants appealing an eviction judgment to post a bond twice as great as the rent expected to accrue during the appeal. By contrast, in Bankers Life & Casualty Co. v. Crenshaw, 486 U.S. 71 (1988), the Court rejected a similar challenge to a Mississippi statute that imposed a 15 percent penalty on an unsuccessful appeal of a judgment for money damages. The penalty was imposed regardless of the merits of the appeal so long as the appellate court affirmed the damages award without alteration. Bankers Life suffered a $1.6 million punitive damage judgment, which it unsuccessfully appealed, with the appellate court adding a $243,000 penalty to the judgment because the original award was affirmed. Bankers Life argued that the statute had denied it equal protection of the law "because it singles out appellants from money judgments, and because it penalizes all such appellants who are unsuccessful, regardless of the merits of their appeal." 486 U.S. at 81. The Supreme Court rejected this contention in language that revealed its general stance toward appeals:

Under this Court's equal protection jurisprudence, Mississippi's statute is "presumed to be valid and will be sustained if the classification . . . is rationally related to a legitimate state interest." The state interests assertedly served by the Mississippi statute were detailed by the Mississippi Supreme Court in Walters v. Inexco Oil Co., 440 So. 2d 268 (1983). The penalty statute . . . "expresses the state's interest in discouraging frivolous appeals. It likewise expresses a bona fide interest in providing a measure of compensation for the successful appellee, compensation for his having endured the slings and arrows of successful appellate litigation." In a similar vein the statute protects the integrity of judgments by discouraging appellant-defendants from prolonging the litigation merely to "squeeze a favorable settlement out of an impecunious" appellee. Also, the penalty statute "tells the litigants that the trial itself is a momentous event, the centerpiece of litigation, not just a first step weighing station en route to endless rehearings and reconsiderations." Finally, in part because it serves these other goals, the penalty statute furthers the State's interest in conserving judicial resources.

Id. at 81-82. The *Bankers Life* Court distinguished *Lindsey* on the grounds that the Oregon statute in *Lindsey* arbitrarily discriminated against tenants (because it applied only to them among all appellants) and was not needed to effectuate the state's purpose of preserving the property at issue.

Lindsey and *Banker's Life* involved "extra" appellate costs. What about ordinary costs that rest on all litigants? Can they ever be unconstitutional? In M.L.B. v. S.L.J., 519 U.S. 102 (1996), the indigent petitioner sought to appeal from a trial court order terminating her parental rights on the grounds she was unfit as a mother. To appeal the state court decision, M.L.B. would have had to pay filing and transcript fees of about $2,300. The state supreme court refused to waive the fees. The U.S. Supreme Court reversed, basing its decision on a combination of due process ("a family association so undeniably important is at stake") and equal protection, the six-to-three majority held "that Mississippi may not withhold from M.L.B. a record of sufficient completeness to permit proper consideration of her claims."

Read together, *Lindsey, Bankers Life,* and *M.L.B.* suggest that some burden on appeals is constitutional. Should legal systems seek generally to discourage appeals by requiring, for example, that the loser pay the winner's attorneys' fees? Cf. Carter v. Deitz, 519 So. 2d 133 (La.), probable jurisdiction noted sub nom. Modjeski & Master v. Carter, 487 U.S. 1217 (1988), appeal dismissed, 498 U.S. 1129 (1991). Does Louisiana's requirement that security of 150 percent of judgment be posted to stay enforcement of money judgement on appeal violate due process? The federal system does not go even this far. Federal Rule of Appellate Procedure (Fed. R. App. P.) 38 permits a court of appeals to award "just damages and single or double costs to the appellee" if the appellate courts "determine[s] that an appeal is frivolous." One finds occasional invocation of this rule, but it is used far less frequently than is Rule 11, its analogue at the district court level.

A quite different sort of sanction for meritless appeals that is increasingly used by state and federal appellate courts is the summary affirmance or unpublished decision. Such orders, which go under different names in different systems, often involve denial of the right to oral argument, a decision on the briefs and record alone, and either a one-word order ("affirmed") or a short unpublished opinion. For an example, see Haddle v. Garrison, supra page 417. Some would argue that such "appeals" exist in name only. Would it be preferable for courts to impose sanctions?

B. When a Decision May Be Reviewed: "Finality"

The single most significant rule of appellate procedure in the United States is one that purports to be only about the timing of appeal. Under 28 U.S.C. §1291, appeals lie only from final decisions of the district courts (with certain statutory exceptions). Most, but not all, states follow a similar pattern.

The final judgment rule had its origins in a procedural system in which most trial court decisions were made at trial. In such a system, decisions were promptly reviewable because the trial resulted in a judgment from which an appeal would lie. Modern procedure changes that pattern: Discovery and the pretrial process now dominate the procedural landscape. Most rulings entered at this stage do not immediately produce final judgments, and many will never produce final judgments because the case settles. Under such circumstances the final judgment rule does not just defer but eliminates appellate review.

The final judgment rule consequently affects not just the technique of appeal but its availability. What purport to be timing rules are in fact rules that effectively bar appellate review of most trial court decisions. That may be a good thing: Appeals take time, and most are unsuccessful. So the unavailability of appeal may merely make justice faster and cheaper. Alternatively, one can see it as empowering trial judges to be petty dictators who can be secure in the knowledge that most of their rulings will never reach appellate scrutiny.

Any rule that has such effects will generate tensions and exceptions. This section explores the contours of the basic rule and some exceptions generated by the pressure to escape it.

1.   The Final Judgment Rule

A final decision "is one which ends the litigation on the merits and leaves nothing for the court to do but execute the judgment." Catlin v. United States, 324 U.S. 229, 233 (1945). That's the easy part; the hard part is determining which decisions are "final." Although at first glance the problem may seem to center on premature attempts at appeal, which entail unnecessary cost and delay, the more serious problem is late appeals: There are cases in which litigants waited for a document labeled as a "final decree" only to learn that earlier orders disposing of their claims were deemed to be a final judgment and that the time for appeal had run in the meantime. For example, see Dickinson v. Petroleum Conversion Corp., 338 U.S. 507 (1950).

a.   Appellate Jurisdiction and the Final Judgment Rule

Section 1291, which contains the final judgment rule, has two functions: It defines the moment at which an appeal is proper; and it grants jurisdiction for the appellate courts to hear that appeal. The next case demonstrates the consequences that a wrong guess about the first function can have on the second.

Liberty Mutual Insurance Co. v. Wetzel
424 U.S. 737 (1976)

Mr. Justice REHNQUIST delivered the opinion of the Court.

Respondents filed a complaint in the United States District Court for the Western District of Pennsylvania in which they asserted that petitioner's employee insurance benefits and maternity leave regulations discriminated against women in violation of Title VII of the Civil Rights Act of 1964, as amended by the Equal Employment Opportunity Act of 1972. The District Court ruled in favor of respondents on the issue of petitioner's liability under that Act, and petitioner appealed to the Court of Appeals for the Third Circuit. That court held that it had jurisdiction of petitioner's appeal under 28 U.S.C. §1291, and proceeded to affirm on the merits the judgment of the District Court. We granted certiorari and heard argument on the merits. Though neither party has questioned the jurisdiction of the Court of Appeals to entertain the appeal, we are obligated to do so on our own motion if a question thereto exists. Because we conclude that the District Court's order was not appealable to the Court of Appeals, we vacate the judgment of the Court of Appeals with instructions to dismiss petitioner's appeal from the order of the District Court.

Respondents' complaint, after alleging jurisdiction and facts deemed pertinent to their claim, prayed for a judgment against petitioner embodying the following relief:

> (a) requiring that defendant establish non-discriminatory hiring, payment, opportunity, and promotional plans and programs;
> (b) enjoining the continuance by defendant of the illegal acts and practices alleged herein;
> (c) requiring that defendant pay over to plaintiffs and to the members of the class the damages sustained by plaintiffs and the members of the class by reason of defendant's illegal acts and practices, including adjusted backpay, with interest, and an additional equal amount as liquidated damages, and exemplary damages;
> (d) requiring that defendant pay to plaintiffs and to the members of the class the costs of this suit and a reasonable attorney's fee, with interest; and
> (e) such other and further relief as the Court deems appropriate.

After extensive discovery, respondents moved for partial summary judgment only as to the issue of liability. Fed. Rule Civ. Proc. 56(c). The District Court on January 9, 1974, finding no issues of material fact in dispute, entered an order to the effect that petitioner's pregnancy-related policies violated Title VII of the Civil Rights Act of 1964. It also ruled that Liberty Mutual's hiring and promotion policies violated Title VII. Petitioner thereafter filed a motion for reconsideration which was denied by the District Court. Its order of February 20, 1974, denying the motion for reconsideration, contains the following concluding language:

> In its Order the court stated it would enjoin the continuance of practices which the court found to be in violation of Title VII. The Plaintiffs were invited to submit the form of the injunction order and the Defendant has filed Notice of Appeal and asked for stay of any injunctive order. Under these circumstances the court will withhold the issuance of the injunctive order and amend the Order previously issued under the provisions of Fed. R. Civ. P. 54(b), as follows:
>
> > And now this 20th day of February, 1974, it is directed that final judgment be entered in favor of Plaintiffs that Defendant's policy of requiring female employees to return to work within three months of delivery of a child or be terminated is in violation of the provisions of Title VII of the Civil Rights Act of 1964; that Defendant's policy of denying disability income protection plan benefits to female employees for disabilities related to pregnancies or childbirth is in violation of Title VII of the Civil Rights Act of 1964 and that it is expressly directed that Judgment be entered for the Plaintiffs upon these claims of Plaintiffs' Complaint; there being no just reason for delay.

It is obvious from the District Court's order that respondents, although having received a favorable ruling on the issue of petitioner's liability to them, received none of the relief which they expressly prayed for in the portion of their complaint set forth above. They requested an injunction, but did not get one; they requested damages, but were not awarded any; they requested attorneys' fees, but received none.

Counsel for respondents when questioned during oral argument in this Court suggested that at least the District Court's order of February 20 amounted to a declaratory judgment on the issue of liability pursuant to the provisions of 28 U.S.C. §2201. Had respondents sought only a declaratory judgment, and no other form of relief, we would of course have a different case. But even if we accept respondents' contention that the District Court's order was a declaratory judgment on the issue of liability, it nonetheless left unresolved respondents' requests for an injunction, for compensatory and exemplary damages, and for attorneys' fees. It finally disposed of none of respondents' prayers for relief.

The District Court and the Court of Appeals apparently took the view that because the District Court made the recital required by Fed. Rule Civ. Proc. 54(b) that final judgment be entered on the issue of liability, and that there was no just reason for delay, the orders thereby became appealable as a final decision pursuant to 28 U.S.C. §1291. We cannot agree with this application of the Rule and statute in question.

Rule 54(b)[2] "does not apply to a single claim action. . . . It is limited expressly to multiple claims actions in which 'one or more but less than all' of the multiple claims have been finally decided and are found otherwise to be ready for appeal." Sears, Roebuck & Co. v. Mackey.[3]

Here, however, respondents set forth but a single claim: that petitioner's employee insurance benefits and maternity leave regulations discriminated against its women employees in violation of Title VII of the Civil Rights Act of 1964. They prayed for several different types of relief in the event that they sustained the allegations of their complaint, see Fed. Rule Civ. Proc. 8(a)(3), but their complaint advanced a single legal

2. "*Judgment upon multiple claims or involving multiple parties.*"
"When more than one claim for relief is presented in an action, whether as a claim, counterclaim, cross-claim, or third-party claim, or when multiple parties are involved, the court may direct the entry of a final judgment as to one or more but fewer than all of the claims or parties only upon an express determination that there is no just reason for delay and upon an express direction for the entry of judgment. In the absence of such determination and direction, any order or other form of decision, however designated, which adjudicates fewer than all the claims or the rights and liabilities of fewer than all the parties shall not terminate the action as to any of the claims or parties, and the order or other form of decision is subject to revision at any time before the entry of judgment adjudicating all the claims and the rights and liabilities of all the parties."
3. Following *Mackey*, the Rule was amended to insure that orders finally disposing of some but not all of the parties could be appealed pursuant to its provisions. That provision is not implicated in this case, however, to which *Mackey's* exposition of the Rule remains fully accurate.

theory which was applied to only one set of facts.[4] Thus, despite the fact that the District Court undoubtedly made the findings required under the Rule had it been applicable, those findings do not in a case such as this make the order appealable pursuant to 28 U.S.C. §1291.

We turn to consider whether the District Court's order might have been appealed by petitioner to the Court of Appeals under any other theory. The order, viewed apart from its discussion of Rule 54(b), constitutes a grant of partial summary judgment limited to the issue of petitioner's liability. Such judgments are by their term interlocutory, see Fed. Rule Civ. Proc. 56(c), and where assessment of damages or awarding of other relief remains to be resolved have never been considered to be "final" within the meaning of 28 U.S.C. §1292. Thus the only possible authorization for an appeal from the District Court's order would be pursuant to the provisions of 28 U.S.C. §1292.

If the District Court had granted injunctive relief but had not ruled on respondents' other requests for relief, this interlocutory order would have been appealable under §1292(a)(1).[5] As noted above, the court did not issue an injunction. It might be argued that the order of the District Court, insofar as it failed to include the injunctive relief requested by respondents, is an interlocutory order refusing an injunction within the meaning of §1292(a)(1). But even if this would have allowed respondents to then obtain review in the Court of Appeals, there was no denial of any injunction sought by Petitioner and it could not avail itself of that grant of jurisdiction.

Nor was this order appealable pursuant to 28 U.S.C. §1292(b).[6] Although the District Court's findings made with a view to satisfying Rule

4. We need not here attempt any definitive resolution of the meaning of what constitutes a claim for relief within the meaning of the Rules. It is sufficient to recognize that a complaint asserting only one legal right, even if seeking multiple remedies for the alleged violation of that right, states a single claim for relief.

5. The courts of appeals shall have jurisdiction of appeals from:

(1) Interlocutory orders of the district courts of the United States, the United States District Court for the District of the Canal Zone, the District Court of Guam, and the District Court of the Virgin Islands, or of the judges thereof, granting, continuing, modifying, refusing or dissolving injunctions, or refusing to dissolve or modify injunctions, except where a direct review may be had in the Supreme Court.

6. "When a district judge, in making in a civil action an order not otherwise appealable under this section, shall be of the opinion that such order involves a controlling question of law as to which there is substantial ground for difference of opinion and that an immediate appeal from the order may materially advance the ultimate termination of the litigation, he shall so state in writing in such order. The Court of Appeals may thereupon, in its discretion, permit an appeal to be taken from such order, if application is made to it within ten days after the entry of the order Provided, however, That application for an appeal hereunder shall not stay proceedings in the district court unless the district judge or the Court of Appeals or a judge thereof shall so order."

54(b) might be viewed as substantial compliance with the certification requirement of that section, there is no showing in this record that petitioner made application to the Court of Appeals within the 10 days therein specified. And that court's holding that its jurisdiction was pursuant to §1291 makes it clear that it thought itself obliged to consider on the merits petitioner's appeal. There can be no assurance that had the other requirements of §1292(b) been complied with, the Court of Appeals would have exercised its discretion to entertain the interlocutory appeal.

Were we to sustain the procedure followed here, we would condone a practice whereby a district court in virtually any case before it might render an interlocutory decision on the question of liability of the defendant, and the defendant would thereupon be permitted to appeal to the court of appeals without satisfying any of the requirements that Congress carefully set forth. We believe that Congress, in enacting present §§1291 and 1292 of Title 28, has been well aware of the dangers of an overly rigid insistence upon a "final decision" for appeal in every case, and has in those sections made ample provision for appeal of orders which are not "final" so as to alleviate any possible hardship. We would twist the fabric of the statute more than it will bear if we were to agree that the District Court's order of February 20, 1974, was appealable to the Court of Appeals.

The judgment of the Court of Appeals is therefore vacated, and the case is remanded with instructions to dismiss the petitioner's appeal.

It is so ordered.

Mr. Justice BLACKMUN took no part in the consideration or decision of this case.

NOTES AND PROBLEMS

1. The *Wetzel* Court was unanimous. What is so important about the finality principle that it elicits such unanimity of feeling? Some of the states, most notably New York, allow interlocutory appeals in a wide range of situations. Since the Judiciary Act of 1789, the policy in the federal courts has been to wait until a final judgment.

a. The basic argument for the final judgment rule can be explained on a cost-benefit basis. The costs of allowing interlocutory appeals are the costs of an unnecessary extra appeal if the trial judge turns out to have been correct. The costs of not allowing interlocutory appeals are those of an unnecessary or an unnecessarily long trial if the trial judge turns out to have been wrong. Is it possible, before deciding the particular appeal, to determine which of these costs is greater? If we assume that the costs of an unnecessary extra appeal are approximately the same as the costs of the unnecessary or unnecessarily long trial, the overall costs are proportional to the number of times the trial judge is right versus the number of times he is wrong. If trial judges are right more often than they are wrong (measured by eventual reversal when appeal finally occurs), then the general policy should disfavor interlocutory appeals. In fact, trial judges are reversed far less often than they are affirmed (the federal courts report a reversal rate of only 10 percent), and many decisions are not even appealed. Thus the general policy seems to be a wise one.

b. Against this argument one can suggest, first, that some of its premises are wrong: Trials, which require witnesses and sometimes juries, will generally be much more expensive than appeals. Second, in some undetermined number of cases, parties will abandon meritorious positions (that is, settle the case) because they cannot afford to wait for vindication on appeal. To point to the absence of appeal in such cases as evidence of a satisfactory trial is to ignore reality.

c. Beyond that, one can make a historical argument. Whatever one thinks of the original merits of the final judgment rule, its effect has changed dramatically with the advent of modern procedure. Before the Federal Rules (and equivalent state systems' rules of procedure) came into effect, there were essentially two stages in litigation, pleading and trial. If a case ended at the pleading stage, appeal was immediately available. If it didn't, trial would follow shortly, after which appeal was again available to the loser. Modern procedure, with its emphasis on discovery and a multistage pretrial process, adopts many of the main features of equity practice. Unlike the common law, equity permitted appeal from all interlocutory rulings. By adopting equity procedure but retaining the common law rule for appealability, modern process has delegated substantial amounts of unreviewable power to the trial court.

d. As noted, New York has formally rejected the final judgment rule. Its procedural code lists a series of pretrial orders from which a losing party may take immediate appeal, including such broad categories as any order that "involves some part of the merits or . . . affects a substantial right." N.Y. Civ. Prac. L.&R. 5701 (McKinney 1978). Other states may, less formally, have created substantial loopholes by manipulating the availability of the extraordinary writs of mandamus and prohibition (see infra page 783).

2. In *Wetzel*, who raised the question of appealability in the Supreme Court?

a. Because the governing statute, §1291, frames appealability in jurisdictional terms, appellate courts have the power and duty to consider appealability even if both parties seek review.

b. Is that a good idea? If both parties want review, should the courts grant it? Compare Rule 12(h)(3), which provides that the district court may raise questions of subject matter jurisdiction sua sponte.

3. A salient characteristic of modern procedure is its allowance of multiple claims and parties. How should we adapt the final judgment rule to such a situation?

a. One extreme would be to allow no one to appeal until after all claims of all parties had been resolved. Rule 54(b) rejects this solution, allowing the court to enter a final judgment as to "one or more but fewer than all of the claims or parties." If such a judgment is entered, it becomes appealable.

b. Rule 54(b) fits neatly into the analysis in Note 1(a), supra, because it covers situations in which matters that could have been raised separately have been joined in one case under liberal joinder rules.

c. But the Rule requires the judge entering such partial final judgment to exercise discretion and to make "an express determination that there is no just reason for delay" in making the decision appealable.

d. Suppose a case involving several plaintiffs against a single defendant. The court grants summary judgment against one of the plaintiffs. Or imagine a case involving one plaintiff against several defendants in which the court grants summary judgment in favor of one defendant. If the court so certifies under Rule 54(b), the loser can immediately appeal. What should guide the judge's discretion in deciding whether to issue a Rule 54(b) certification in such a case? There are efficiency considerations: If the potential appeal contains an issue that persists in the remaining claims, an appellate decision may clarify them before trial. Or a judge might decide on precisely the opposite grounds — that the issues involved as to the loser are entirely different from those for the remaining case — and a decision won't complicate the case for the remaining parties.

4. If some means existed for identifying cases in which the trial judge is particularly likely to be wrong, such cases might pose exceptions to the final judgment rule. Under 28 U.S.C. §1292(b), discussed in the Wetzel Court's opinion and at further length later in this section, the trial judge may certify (among other things) that her order involves "a controlling question of law as to which there is substantial ground for difference of opinion" and "that an immediate appeal from the order may materially advance the ultimate termination of the litigation." Under such circumstances, the assumptions stated in Note 1(a) no longer apply, and an interlocutory appeal is allowed.

b. Defining the Moment of Judgment

Even when one is alert to the dire jurisdictional consequences of failure to heed the final judgment rule, it is not always easy to locate the precise point at which a judgment becomes final — or even, for that matter, to identify the judicial act that constitutes a judgment. One difficulty is that the judge's belief that she is entering a judgment can be second-guessed by the appellate court. Recall that in *Wetzel*, both parties understandably thought that the judge's announcement that "final judgment be entered" meant what it said, but the Supreme Court ruled otherwise. Consider the matter from the perspective of a party wishing to appeal.

The only step required to bring an appeal from a ruling of the district court is the timely filing of a notice of appeal with the clerk of the district court. Fed. R. App. P. 3(a). That notice must be filed within the time allowed by Fed. R. App. P. 4(a)(1) — 30 days for the typical appeal; 60 days for an appeal involving the United States. The issue of timing is critical, because, as you have seen, the courts of appeals have repeatedly held that the time limits are "jurisdictional" — that is, that the court of appeals has no jurisdiction to hear the appeal if the notice of appeal is filed too late. Two provisions of 28 U.S.C. §2107 and the appellate rules slightly alleviate the problem of late filings. The cited statute and Fed. R. App. P. 4(a)(6) empower the district court to let a trial judge extend this time for a party who did not receive notice of the entry of the judgment in question if no prejudice to other parties results. The cited statute and Fed. R. App. P. 4(a)(5) also allow the district court to extend the time for filing the notice of appeal up to 30 days on a showing of "excusable neglect or good cause."

An equally serious problem confronts litigants who file their appeals *too early*. As we have seen, under 28 U.S.C. §1291, appeals lie "from all final decisions of the district courts." By negative implication appeals *do not lie* from decisions of the district courts that are not final. In the distinction lies what the comments to Fed. R. App. P. 4 term "a trap for an unsuspecting litigant." Before the 1993 amendments, the trap was sprung if the appellant filed a notice of appeal after the judgment but while a post-trial motion for j.n.o.v. or new trial was pending. Until these motions are decided, the final outcome — and judgment — in the case has not occurred. A number of unfortunate would-be appellants discovered this point in sorrow-producing ways. Fed. R. App. P. 4(a)(4) alleviates the difficulty by providing that when a party seeks to appeal from an order that would be final but for the interposition of one of these common post-trial motions, the appeal is held in abeyance until the disposition of these motions, at which point it becomes effective, thus securing the jurisdiction of the court of appeals.

Even with these provisions, timing remains critical, and rulemakers have therefore tried to make the moment of judgment extremely clear. Rule 58 provides that

> Every judgment shall be set forth on a separate document. A judgment is effective only when set forth and entered as provided in Rule 79(a).

Matters can still be confusing.

NOTES AND PROBLEMS

1. In United States v. Indrelunas, 411 U.S. 216 (1973), the Court said that the separate-document requirement must be "mechanically applied."

2. Suppose the judge announces what she and the parties intend as a final judgment; the clerk duly enters that judgment on the docket (as required by Rule 79(a)); but the "separate document" required by Rule 58 never appears. The parties appeal. What result?

In Bankers Trust Co. v. Mallis, 435 U.S. 381, rehg. denied, 436 U.S. 915 (1978), the Court held that the judgment was appealable. It explained:

> We assume, without deciding, that the requirements for an effective judgment set forth in the Federal Rules of Civil Procedure must generally be satisfied before §1291 jurisdiction may be invoked. We nonetheless conclude that it could not have been intended that the separate-document requirement of Rule 58 be such a categorical imperative that the parties are not free to waive it.

Is that statement compatible with the general proposition that parties may not waive federal subject matter jurisdiction?

3. FirsTier Mortgage Co. v. Investors Mortgage Insurance Co., 498 U.S. 269, 272 (1991), took matters even further than *Mallis*. In *Mallis* the judge had announced a final decision but had not embodied it in a separate document. In *FirsTier* the trial judge announced that he would grant summary judgment on all counts for the defendant and asked the parties to submit proposed findings of fact. Before the trial judge had issued his findings, the plaintiff appealed — "close to a month before the entry of judgment."

a. The Court held that Fed. R. App. P. 4(a)(2) ("A notice of appeal filed after the court announces a decision or order but before the entry of the judgment or order is treated as filed on the date of and after the entry") applied, even though the judge had announced only his intent to enter summary judgment, not the summary judgment itself, much less the separate document embodying the judgment.

b. The *FirsTier* opinion evinces a certain amount of nervousness about the implications of its holding:

This is not to say that [Fed.] Rule [App. P.] 4(a)(2) permits a notice of appeal from a clearly interlocutory decision — such as a discovery ruling or a sanction order under Rule 11 of the Federal Rules of Civil Procedure — to serve as a notice of appeal from the final judgment. A belief that such a decision is a final judgment would *not* be reasonable.

(Emphasis added.)

c. Is the rule now that a premature notice of appeal is saved by Fed. R. App. P. 4(a)(2) if the appellant reasonably believed that what the judge had issued was a final order? Is that a workable standard?

2. Exceptions to the Final Judgment Rule

The adoption of the Federal Rules in 1938 created a new stage between pleading and trial, in which substantial numbers of important but nonfinal rulings would occur. That circumstance placed substantial pressure on legislatures and courts to find exceptions to the rule. The efforts to define exceptions without abandoning the rule has not been easy. We survey the major exceptions below, starting with the one that has caused the greatest difficulty.

a. *Practical Finality*

Lauro Lines s.r.l. v. Chasser
490 U.S. 495 (1989)

Justice BRENNAN delivered the opinion of the Court.

We granted certiorari to consider whether an interlocutory order of a United States District Court denying a defendant's motion to dismiss a damages action on the basis of a contractual forum-selection clause is immediately appealable under 28 U.S.C. §1291 as a collateral final order. We hold that it is not.

I

The individual respondents were, or represent the estates of persons who were, passengers aboard the cruise ship Achille Lauro when it was hijacked by terrorists in the Mediterranean in October 1985. Petitioner Lauro Lines s.r.l., an Italian company, owns the Achille Lauro. Respondents filed suits against Lauro Lines in the District Court for the Southern

District of New York to recover damages for injuries sustained as a result of the hijacking, and for the wrongful death of passenger Leon Klinghoffer. Lauro Lines moved before trial to dismiss the actions, citing the forum-selection clause printed on each passenger ticket. This clause purported to obligate the passenger to institute any suit arising in connection with the contract in Naples, Italy, and to renounce the right to sue elsewhere.

The District Court denied petitioner's motions to dismiss, holding that the ticket as a whole did not give reasonable notice to passengers that they were waiving the opportunity to sue in a domestic forum. Without moving for certification for immediate appeal pursuant to 28 U.S.C. §1292(b), Lauro Lines sought to appeal the District Court's orders. The Court of Appeals for the Second Circuit dismissed petitioner's appeal on the ground that the District Court's orders denying petitioner's motions to dismiss were interlocutory and not appealable under §1291. The court held that the orders did not fall within the exception to the rule of nonappealability carved out for collateral final orders in Cohen v. Beneficial Industrial Loan Corp., 337 U.S. 541 (1949). We granted certiorari to resolve a disagreement among the Courts of Appeals. We now affirm.

II

Title 28 U.S.C. §1291 provides for appeal to the courts of appeals only from "final decisions of the district courts of the United States." For purposes of §1291, a final judgment is generally regarded as "a decision by the District Court that 'ends the litigation on the merits and leaves nothing for the court to do but execute the judgment.'" Van Cauwenberghe v. Biard, 486 U.S. 517, 521 (1988), quoting Catlin v. United States, 324 U.S. 229, 233 (1945). An order denying a motion to dismiss a civil action on the ground that a contractual forum-selection clause requires that such suit be brought in another jurisdiction is not a decision on the merits that ends the litigation. On the contrary, such an order "ensures that litigation will continue in the District Court." Gulfstream Aerospace Corp. v. Mayacamas Corp., 485 U.S. 271, 275 (1988). Section 1291 thus permits an appeal only if an order denying a motion to dismiss based upon a forum-selection clause falls within the "narrow exception to the normal application of the final judgment rule [that] has come to be known as the collateral order doctrine." Midland Asphalt Corp. v. United States, 489 U.S. 794, 798 (1989). That exception is for a "small class" of prejudgment orders that "finally determine claims of right separable from, and collateral to, rights asserted in the action, [and that are] too important to be denied review and too independent of the cause itself to require that appellate consideration be deferred until the whole case is adjudicated." Cohen, supra, at 546. We have held that to fall within the *Cohen* exception, an order must satisfy at least three conditions: "It must 'conclusively determine the disputed question,' 'resolve an important issue completely separate from the merits of the action,' and 'be effectively unreviewable on appeal from a final judgment.' " Richardson-Merrell Inc. v. Koller, 472 U.S. 424, 431 (1985), quoting Coopers & Lybrand v. Livesay, 437 U.S. 463, 468 (1978). For present purposes, we need not decide whether an order denying a dismissal motion based upon a contractual forum-selection clause conclusively determines a disputed issue, or whether it resolves an important issue that is independent of the merits of the action, for the District Court's orders fail to satisfy the third requirement of the collateral order test.

We recently reiterated the "general rule" that an order is "effectively unreviewable" only "where the order at issue involves 'an asserted right the legal and practical value of which would be destroyed if it were not vindicated before trial.' " Midland Asphalt Corp., supra, at 798, quoting United States v. MacDonald, 435 U.S. 850, 860 (1978). If it is eventually decided that the District Court erred in allowing trial in this case to take place in New York, petitioner will have been put to unnecessary trouble and expense, and the value of its contractual right to an Italian forum will have been diminished. It is always true, however, that "there is value . . . in triumphing before trial, rather than after it," *MacDonald*, supra, at 860, n.7, and this Court has declined to find the costs associated with unnecessary litigation to be enough to warrant allowing the immediate appeal of a pretrial order. See *Richardson-Merrell Inc.*, supra, at 436 ("the possibility that a ruling may be erroneous and may impose additional litigation expense is not sufficient to set aside the finality requirement imposed by Congress" in §1291). Instead, we have insisted that the right asserted be one that is essentially destroyed if its vindication must be postponed until trial is completed.

We have thus held in cases involving criminal prosecutions that the deprivation of a right not to be tried is effectively unreviewable after final judgment and is immediately appealable. Similarly, in civil cases, we have held that the denial of a motion to dismiss based upon a claim of absolute immunity from suit is immediately appealable prior to final judgment, "for the essence of absolute immunity is its possessor's entitlement not to have to answer for his conduct in a civil damages action." Mitchell v. Forsyth, 472 U.S. 511, 525 (1985). And claims of qualified immunity may be pursued by immediate appeal, because qualified immunity too "is an immunity from suit." Id., at 526.

On the other hand, we have declined to hold the collateral order doctrine applicable where a district court has denied a claim, not that the defendant has a right not to be sued at all, but that the suit against the defendant is not properly before the particular court because it lacks jurisdiction. In Van Cauwenberghe v. Biard, 486 U.S. 517 (1988), a civil defendant moved for dismissal on the ground that he had been immune from service of process because his presence in the United States had been compelled by extradition to face criminal charges. We noted that, after *Mitchell*, "[t]he critical question . . . is whether 'the essence' of the claimed right is a right not to stand trial," 486 U.S., at 524, and held that the immunity from service of process defendant asserted did not amount to an immunity from suit — even though service was essential to the trial court's jurisdiction over the defendant.

Lauro Lines argues here that its contractual forum-selection clause provided it with a right to trial before a tribunal in Italy, and with a concomitant right not to be sued anywhere else. This "right not to be haled for trial before tribunals outside the agreed forum," petitioner claims, cannot effectively be vindicated by appeal after trial in an improper forum. There is no obviously correct way to characterize the right embodied in petitioner's forum-selection provision: "all litigants who have a meritorious pretrial claim for dismissal can reasonably claim a right not to stand trial." *Van Cauwenberghe*, supra, at 524. The right appears most like that to be free from trial if it is characterized — as by petitioner — as a right not to be sued at all except in a Neapolitan forum. It appears less like a right not to be subjected to suit if characterized — as by the Court of Appeals — as "a right to have the binding adjudication of claims occur in a certain forum." 844 F.2d, at 55. Cf. *Van Cauwenberghe*, supra, at 526-27. Even assuming that the former characterization is proper, however, petitioner is obviously not entitled under the forum-selection clause of its contract to avoid suit altogether, and an entitlement to avoid suit is different in kind from an entitlement to be sued only in a particular forum. Petitioner's claim that it may be sued only in Naples, while not perfectly secured by appeal after final judgment, is adequately vindicable at that stage — surely as effectively vindicable as a claim that the trial court lacked personal jurisdiction over the defendant — and hence does not fall within the third prong of the collateral order doctrine.

Petitioner argues that there is a strong federal policy favoring the enforcement of foreign forum-selection clauses, citing The Bremen v. Zapata Off-Shore Co., 407 U.S. 1 (1972), and that "the essential concomitant of this strong federal policy . . . is the right of immediate appellate review of district court orders denying their enforcement." A policy favoring enforcement of forum-selection clauses, however, would go to the merits of petitioner's claim that its ticket-agreement requires that any suit be filed in Italy and that the agreement should be enforced by the federal courts. Immediate appealability of a prejudgment order denying enforcement, insofar as it depends upon satisfaction of the third prong of the collateral order test, turns on the precise contours of the right asserted, and not upon the likelihood of eventual success on the merits. The Court of Appeals properly dismissed petitioner's appeal, and its judgment is affirmed.

Justice SCALIA, concurring.

I join the opinion of the Court, and write separately only to make express what seems to me implicit in its analysis.

The reason we say that the right not to be sued elsewhere than in Naples is "adequately vindicable," by merely reversing any judgment obtained in violation of it is, quite simply, that the law does not deem the right important enough to be vindicated by, as it were, an injunction against its violation obtained through interlocutory appeal. The importance of the right asserted has always been a significant part of our collateral order doctrine. When first formulating that doctrine in Cohen v. Beneficial Industrial Loan Corp. we said that it permits interlocutory appeal of final determinations of claims that are not only "separable from, and collateral to, rights asserted in the action," but also, we immediately added, "*too important* to be denied review" (emphasis added). Our later cases have retained that significant requirement. . . .

While it is true, therefore, that the "right not to be sued elsewhere than in Naples" is not fully vindicated — indeed, to be utterly frank, is positively destroyed — by permitting the trial to occur and reversing its outcome, that is vindication enough because the right is not sufficiently important to overcome the policies militating against interlocutory appeals. We have made that judgment when the right not to be tried in a particular court has been created through jurisdictional limitations established by Congress or by international treaty, see Van Cauwenberghe, supra. The same judgment applies — if anything, a fortiori — when the right has been created by private agreement.

NOTES AND PROBLEMS

1. *Lauro Lines* indicates that it is one of a series of cases delineating judicially created exceptions to the final judgment rule. The attraction of such an exception is easy to understand: Some district court decisions seem to cry out for reversal before trial is over. The difficulties of creating exceptions are equally obvious: Can one define a coherent set of cases that will be entitled to review before the final judgment? If not, one has neither the draconian simplicity of a final judgment rule nor the "accuracy" of immediate review; rather, one has constant bickering that comes from the necessity of deciding which cases fall on which side of an indistinct line.

2. The Court in *Lauro Lines* held that the order was not appealable and therefore did not decide whether the forum selection clause was valid. That ruling has the same practical effect as holding the order appealable but affirming the trial court decision on the merits. In some cases it is difficult to overcome the sense that denials of review are made with at least an over-the-shoulder glance at the merits. Such a glance may be particularly important in a case like *Lauro Lines*. Such cases are very unlikely to go to trial, and a settlement will not be appealable. Thus the interlocutory review of the court order is likely to be the only review. Is this the point of Justice Scalia's concurrence?

3. The cases that have posed the most severe problems in defining "practical finality" have been those concerning the official immunity defense for government officials. As you may recall from Chapter VI, government officials sued for violating the constitutional rights of citizens have a powerful defense: "official immunity." That doctrine spares them from liability if they reasonably believed they were acting constitutionally. More germane to the present inquiry, that defense not only frees them from liability but also from the obligation to stand trial — including the necessity to endure discovery.

But, as *Lauro Lines* recognizes, the "right not to stand trial," can only be vindicated if immediate appeal lies from a trial court order that — erroneously — holds that official immunity does not apply. Two cases have so held. Nixon v. Fitzgerald, 457 U.S. 731 (1982) (immediate appeal of trial court refusal to dismiss, on grounds of absolute official immunity in a suit brought against the president of the United States); Mitchell v. Forsyth, 472 U.S. 511 (1985) (immediate appeal of trial court refusal to dismiss, on the ground of qualified official immunity in a suit brought against a former attorney general of the United States).

a. *Nixon* and *Mitchell* opened Pandora's box. Like *Lauro Lines*, they deal with defendants who argue that they have the "right not to stand trial." If one conceives of such a right, then its vindication *after* trial and final judgment seems futile and self-defeating. But one could describe many defendants in such terms. For example, any defendant who moves to dismiss on any of the grounds listed in Rule 12 (and loses the motion), could argue that her "right not to stand trial" has been violated. Likewise, so could a defendant who made an unsuccessful motion for summary judgment. The defendant in *Lauro Lines* unsuccessfully made such an argument, to the effect that it had, at least, the right not to stand trial anywhere but in Naples.

b. In applying *Mitchell*, the Supreme Court has sought to draw a line between two kinds of cases in which immunity might be asserted. In Johnson v. Jones, 515 U.S. 304 (1995), the court held *not* immediately appealable a rejection of the official immunity defense that turned on facts rather than on the law — what the court called a "we didn't do it" case. In holding that no appeal lay from a denial of defendants' motion for summary judgment, the Court recognized that it might prove difficult to separate immediately reviewable "law" cases from the "fact" cases that would be reviewable only on final judgment. Almost immediately, the Court had to make such a distinction. In Behrens v. Pelletier, 516 U.S. 299 (1996), another qualified immunity case, the Court held that the official asserting immunity was entitled to not one but two interlocutory appeals. The defendant had first asserted his immunity at the pleading stage and had appealed the trial court's rejection of this contention. The appellate court affirmed, and the case proceeded to discovery and a summary judgment motion. When defendant lost that motion, he again sought a *Cohen* appeal. The Ninth Circuit ruled that one interlocutory appeal was enough, but the Supreme Court disagreed. It distinguished *Johnson* on the grounds that the case at hand involved a determination by the district court that, as a matter of law, the official's conduct "constituted a violation of clearly established law." Will this distinction — which, you'll recall — is jurisdictional, prove sustainable?

4. An incomplete list of other orders that have been held to be practically final under the *Cohen* doctrine includes:

a. *Cohen* itself: A trial court decision declining to apply in federal court a state statute requiring the posting of a bond in shareholder derivative actions brought by plaintiffs owning small amounts of stock. Cohen v. Beneficial Industrial Corp., 337 U.S. 541 (1949).

b. Orders vacating the attachment of a vessel. Swift & Co. v. Compania Columbiana de Caribe, 339 U.S. 684 (1950).

c. Orders denying a party leave to proceed in forma pauperis. Roberts v. United States District Court, 339 U.S. 844 (1950).

d. An order remanding a diversity action on grounds of abstention. Quackenbush v. Allstate Insurance Co., 517 U.S. 706 (1996).

e. An order requiring the disclosure of documents as to which attorney-client privilege and work product protection was claimed. Kelly v. Ford Motor Co., 110 F.3d 1391 (3d Cir. 1997).

5. Contrast with the cases listed in Note 4 a series of cases in which the Court, as in *Lauro Lines*, has held the order in question not to be practically final:

a. Orders refusing to certify class actions. Coopers & Lybrand v. Livesay, 437 U.S. 463 (1978). As the next section explains, this ruling has partly been reversed by an amendment to Rule 23.

b. Orders disqualifying or refusing to disqualify trial counsel for alleged conflicts of interest. Richardson-Merrell v. Koller, 472 U.S. 424 (1985);

Flanagan v. United States, 465 U.S. 259 (1984); Firestone v. Risjord, 449 U.S. 368 (1981).

c. Orders denying permission to intervene as of right under Rule 24(a) while granting permissive intervention under Rule 24(b). Stringfellow v. Concerned Neighbors in Action, 480 U.S. 370 (1987).

d. Orders denying a motion to dismiss on grounds of immunity from service of process and forum non conveniens. Van Cauwenberghe v. Biard, 486 U.S. 517 (1988).

e. Orders requiring class action defendants to bear the cost of notifying members of the class. Eisen v. Carlisle & Jacquelin, 417 U.S. 156 (1974). (See Chapter XIII.)

f. Judicial rescission of a dismissal pursuant to settlement. Digital Equipment Corp. v. Desktop Direct, Inc., 511. U.S. 863 (1994).

6. The difficulty of satisfactorily distinguishing between the cases in the two preceding notes may have led to a 1990 amendment to 28 U.S.C. §2072. Congress extended the Supreme Court's rulemaking power under the Rules Enabling Act to include rules "defin[ing] when a ruling of a district court is final for the purposes of appeal under section 1291 of this title." Is the invitation to engage in rulemaking perhaps a subtle suggestion that, in writing the rules, the Court eliminate some of the twists and turns in the *Cohen* doctrine by overruling some decisions in this line? No Rule has to date taken up Congress's challenge. One Rule, 23(f), discussed below, takes a half-step in this direction by creating a new category of interlocutory appeals for class action certification decisions.

b. Injunctions

An important exception to the final judgment rule appears in 28 U.S.C. §1292(a), which allows appeals from interlocutory orders of the district courts "granting, continuing, modifying, refusing or dissolving injunctions, or refusing to dissolve or modify injunctions." Recall that this was one of the argued grounds for appealability in *Wetzel,* supra page 764. Such review is thought to be appropriate because of the special nature of injunctions and their potential for harm.

NOTES AND PROBLEMS

1. Section 1292(b) does not apply to a temporary restraining order, though it does to a preliminary injunction. Presumably the basis for this distinction is the short duration of a TRO — 10 days under Rule 65.

2. The Supreme Court has held that denial of summary judgment in favor of one seeking a permanent injunction does not give rise to the right to immediate appeal under this section because the ruling is simply a step on the way to trial rather than a rejection of the claim on the merits. Switzerland Cheese Association v. E. Horne's Market, Inc., 385 U.S. 23 (1966).

3. Suppose a district court, acting pursuant to Rule 16, orders the parties to refrain from any discovery while they discuss settlement or submit to court-ordered mediation. Is that an injunction? Or just an unappealable pretrial order?

c. Interlocutory Appeals

Efforts to release some of the tension created by the final judgment rule are found in several statutes. The terms of 28 U.S.C. §1292(b) permit a district court to certify interlocutory appeals from nonfinal judgments. A district court judge wishing to create the possibility for such an interlocutory appeal must certify that the order "involves a controlling question of law as to which there is a substantial ground for difference of opinion" and that "an immediate appeal from the order may materially advance the ultimate termination of the litigation." For the interlocutory appeal to occur, not only must the district court judge so certify, but the appellate court must agree.

The statute is not heavily used. A study at the close of the 1980s, a period when overall appeals increased dramatically, revealed that in an average year only about 300 §1292(b) were certified by district courts, and of those only about a third, 100 cases, were accepted by the courts of appeals. These numbers are minuscule when compared to the 40,000+ federal appeals filed annually. Michael Solomine, Revitalizing Interlocutory Appeals in the Federal Courts, 58 Geo. Wash. L. Rev. 1165 (1990).

Given parties' (and sometimes judges') almost feverish efforts to escape the rigidities of the final judgment rule, why are there not more interlocutory appeals? One possibility is that the same period in which interlocutory appeals were available coincides with exploding appellate caseloads and increased interest in trial judge management. The latter development may make appellate courts reluctant to add to their docket; the former may make trial courts more reluctant to release cases to the interference of appellate courts. Professor Solomine's study found that appellate courts were restricting interlocutory appeals to "big, exceptional" cases — mass torts, class actions, and the like — where proceedings are likely to be protracted. Id. at 1173.

Another possibility for the "failure" of §1292(b) is its requirement that both trial and appellate courts agree that the question is worth certification. A headstrong or defiant judge will not seek appellate review, and an indecisive or timorous one will be seen by appellate judges as a nuisance. If this hypothesis is correct, amended Rule of Civil Procedure 23(f) may yield better — or at least different — results. As noted in Note 6, page 780 supra, 28 U.S.C. §2072(c) permits Rules to define "when a ruling of a district court is final for purposes of appeal." Acting pursuant to that authority, Rule 23(f) in 1998 was amended to give a court of appeals "discretion to permit an appeal from an order of a district court granting or denying class certification. . . ." The district court need not agree. Should §1292(b) be amended in a similar fashion? Or should Congress await the experience under Rule 23(f)?

NOTES AND PROBLEMS

1. Probably the most common ground for rejecting certification under §1292(b) is that resolution of the issue in question will not in fact "materially advance the ultimate termination of the litigation." For example, in Atlantic City Electric Co. v. General Elec. Co., 337 F.2d 844 (2d Cir. 1964), the court refused to hear an appeal after certification by the trial judge of an issue concerning discovery in antitrust litigation. The judge had refused discovery relating to the defense of "passing on" (the defense, now generally not available, that the plaintiff was not injured by the defendant's price fixing because the plaintiff passed the price increases on to its customers). The availability of the defense had not been settled at that time. The court of appeals emphasized that the case would be a simple one if discovery did not take place and that the error, if any, could be cured quickly on final review. If the trial court had granted discovery, would appeal have been appropriate?

2. In which of the cases considering finality — Liberty Mutual Insurance Co. v. Wetzel and Lauro Lines s.r.l. v. Chasser — would §1292(b) review have been appropriate if the trial judge had certified the issue under the statutory procedure?

3. In addition to 28 U.S.C. §1292(b), other statutes regulating particular areas make certain trial court orders immediately appealable. For example, 9 U.S.C. §15(a) makes a trial judge's refusal of an order to arbitrate immediately appealable. Section (b) of the same statute makes unappealable an order directing arbitration unless it is certified under §1292(b).

4. Suppose the parties agree that a trial court ruling cries out for interlocutory review, but the trial court refuses to certify it, perhaps in the belief that a difficult case will settle if the judge holds the parties'

feet to the fire. Is there any way in which the parties can force the trial judge to certify an interlocutory appeal? Consider whether the next section casts light on that question.

d. Mandamus

A *writ of mandamus*, obtained in an original proceeding in the court that issues the writ, orders a public official to perform an act required by law. The public official may be a judge of a lower court. For example, in LaBuy v. Howes Leather, 352 U.S. 249 (1957), where the district court had referred an antitrust case to a master for trial, the court of appeals had issued the writ, and it was upheld by the Supreme Court. The Seventh Circuit had previously expressed its displeasure with referral of such cases to masters, and the Supreme Court was even more emphatic in describing the district court's action as an "abdication of the judicial function."

The difficulty with mandamus arises because it can become a tempting route for the avoidance of the rules against interlocutory appeals explored in the preceding material. To prevent this evasion of the final judgment rule, the availability of the writ must be limited:

> The remedy of mandamus is a drastic one, to be invoked only in extraordinary situations. As we have observed, the writ "has traditionally been used in the federal courts only 'to confine an inferior court to a lawful exercise of its prescribed jurisdiction or to compel it to exercise its authority when it is its duty to do so.'" And, while we have not limited the use of mandamus by an unduly narrow and technical understanding of what constitutes a matter of "jurisdiction," the fact still remains that "only exceptional circumstances amounting to a judicial 'usurpation of power' will justify the invocation of this extraordinary remedy."

Kerr v. United States District Court, 426 U.S. 394, 402 (1976).

In spite of such limitations, one does find cases where appellate courts are prepared to issue writs of mandate. One area in which mandamus seems freely available, with little discussion of the usual stated limitations, is that in which the trial judge has denied a jury trial. Thus in Beacon Theatres v. Westover, 359 U.S. 500 (1959) (granting a jury trial in a case combining legal and equitable claims; see Chapter IX), the propriety of interlocutory appellate intervention was largely ignored. Another exception to the general stinginess of the courts in issuing the writ is to prevent the transfer of a case, under 28 U.S.C. §1404(a), out of the circuit. The rationale is that the statutory basis for the writ, 28 U.S.C. §1651, authorizes writs to be issued by courts "in aid of their respective jurisdictions." Because a transfer out of the circuit would deprive the court of appeals of its eventual jurisdiction on appeal, the appellate court has jurisdiction to consider the propriety of such a transfer order. The Seventh Circuit has adopted an apparently unique use of mandamus. In seeking the recusal of judges under 28 U.S.C. §455(a) (on the broad ground that "impartiality might reasonably be questioned"), that Circuit requires parties to use mandamus rather than appeal. The Circuit's theory is that in such broadly based recusal motions, an aggrieved party will never be able to demonstrate an effect on his "substantial rights." As you will see in the next section, only such an effect will constitute reversible error; therefore, in order to create some avenue by which §455(a) can be vindicated, mandamus is available. However tortured the Seventh Circuit's reasoning, the result makes sense: In most cases mandamus will be sought early in the case, before time has been wasted on proceedings that must be set aside.

NOTES AND PROBLEMS

1. Reconsider the problem posed at the end of the preceding section: should an appellate court issue mandamus to force a district court to certify an interlocutory appeal under §1292(b)? Can one frame that refusal in such terms as to invoke mandamus?

2. One way in which an appellate court might have its cake and eat it too — refuse to issue mandamus but achieve the same practical effect — is to write an opinion refusing the writ and in the process discussing the course it "hopes" the district court will take. One can find several Supreme Court opinions taking such a tack.

a. In Kerr v. United States District Court, supra, the Supreme Court upheld the Ninth Circuit's refusal to issue mandamus requiring the district court to vacate a discovery order that would have required the California prison system to turn over all of its personnel files. The defendant prison system resisted on grounds that the files were covered by various privileges. The Supreme Court "upheld" the refusal of the writ in terms that came close to granting it:

> Petitioners ask in essence only that the District Court review the challenged documents in camera before passing on whether each one individually should or should not be disclosed. But the Court of Appeals' opinion dealing with the Adult Authority files did not foreclose the possible necessity of such in camera review. . . . The court apparently left open the opportunity for petitioners to return to the District Court, assert the privilege more specifically . . . and then have their request for an in camera review . . . reconsidered in a different light. . . .

Theoretically, the district court remains free after this opinion to refuse in-camera review of the files. Do you suppose it would so refuse after reading this opinion?

b. A similar approach was used in Schlagenhauf v. Holder, studied in Chapter VII (supra page 516). The principal issue in *Schlagenhauf* was whether the district court could order a series of mental and physical examinations of a defendant bus driver whose bus had collided with another vehicle that he later claimed he did not see. The Supreme Court ruled that, of the numerous examinations ordered by the district court, only the eye examination was justified. The court of appeals had refused to issue a writ of mandamus ordering the district court to rescind its order for the additional examinations. One would therefore expect the Supreme Court to remand to the court of appeals for it to issue the writ of mandamus. Instead the Court remanded the case to the district court for proceedings consistent with its opinion. The Court did not note that the mandamus action before it, being an original action in the court of appeals, could not be remanded to the district court and that the original action was still in the district court.

c. Why are procedural rules bent in order to avoid issuance of the writ of mandamus, at least at the Supreme Court level? There may be a number of factors involved, but two are prominent. First, if extraordinary circumstances must be shown in order for the court of appeals to issue the writ, its issuance can be read as a censure of the district judge. Second, the appellate standard of review — that is, the standard that the Supreme Court applies in reviewing the action of the court of appeals — is abuse of discretion, because issuance of the writ is said to be discretionary. Under appropriate circumstances, finding an abuse of discretion may not be too difficult when the court of appeals rules that there are extraordinary circumstances and the Supreme Court thinks that there are not. Ordering the court of appeals to issue the writ requires a finding that there were extraordinary circumstances in the district court and, further, that, given those circumstances, the court of appeals abused its discretion in failing to use the writ of mandamus in response. How much easier it is to affirm denial of the writ but hint broadly at the proper outcome of the dispute in the district court.

C. Scope of Review

Even if a decision is final or otherwise reviewable, and even if the lower court decision is flawed, it does not follow that an appellate court will disturb the judgment. For that to happen, the error must fall into a sometimes elusive category.

1.   Law and Fact

Anderson v. Bessemer City

470 U.S. 564 (1985)

Justice WHITE delivered the opinion of the Court.

[A] District Court's finding of discriminatory intent in an action brought under Title VII of the Civil Rights Act of 1964 . . . is a factual finding that may be overturned on appeal only if it is clearly erroneous. In this case, the Court of Appeals for the Fourth Circuit concluded that there was clear error in a District Court's finding of discrimination and reversed. Because our reading of the record convinces us that the Court of Appeals misapprehended and misapplied the clearly-erroneous standard, we reverse.

I

[Bessemer City sought a new Recreation Director. Ms. Anderson was the only woman to apply for the job. A five-member committee (chaired by its only female member) interviewed the eight applicants and chose a male. Ms. Anderson sued.]

. . . After a 2-day trial, during which the court heard testimony from petitioner, Mr. Kincaid [the successful applicant], and the five members of the selection committee, the court issued a brief memorandum of decision setting forth its finding that petitioner . . . had been denied the position . . . on account of her sex. . . . [The judge also requested] that petitioner's counsel submit proposed findings of fact and conclusions of law expanding upon those set forth in the memorandum. . . . [This procedure led to several rounds of proposed findings by plaintiff and objections by defendant. Finally] the court issued its own findings of fact and conclusions of law.

. . . [T]he court's finding that petitioner had been denied employment . . . because of her sex rested on a number of subsidiary findings[: (1) that Ms. Anderson "had been better qualified than Mr. Kincaid" (the court detailed the careers of each); (2) that "male committee members had in fact been biased against" Ms. Anderson because she was a woman, a finding based "in part on the testimony of one of the committee members that he believed it would have been 'real hard' for a woman to handle the job and that he would not want his wife to have to perform" its duties; (3) that Ms. Anderson "alone among the applicants . . . had been asked whether she realized the job would involve night work and travel and whether her husband approved of her applying for the job" (there was some dispute about whether Mr. Kincaid was asked an analogous question but the trial court concluded that it was "not a serious inquiry"); and (4)] that the reasons offered by the male committee members for their choice of Mr. Kincaid were pretextual. The court rejected the proposition that Mr. Kincaid's degree in physical education justified his choice, as the evidence suggested that where male candidates were concerned, the committee valued experience more highly than formal education. . . .

The Fourth Circuit reversed . . . [holding that three of] the District Court's crucial findings were clearly erroneous: the finding that petitioner was the most qualified candidate, the finding that petitioner had been asked questions that other applicants were spared, and the finding that the male committee members were biased against hiring a woman. . . .

II

We must deal at the outset with the Fourth Circuit's suggestion that "close scrutiny of the record in this case [was] justified by the manner in which the opinion was prepared" — that is, by the District Court's adoption of petitioner's proposed findings of fact and conclusions of law.

We too, have criticized courts for their verbatim adoption of findings of fact prepared by prevailing parties. . . . Nonetheless, our previous discussions of the subject suggest that even when the trial judge adopts the proposed findings verbatim, the findings are those of the court and may be reversed only if clearly erroneous. . . .

In any event, the District Court in this case does not appear to have uncritically accepted findings prepared without judicial guidance. . . .

III

Because a finding of intentional discrimination is a finding of fact, the standard governing appellate review . . . is that set forth in Federal Rule of Civil Procedure 52(a): "Findings of fact shall not be set aside unless clearly erroneous, and due regard shall be given to the opportunity of the trial court to judge the credibility of the witnesses.". . .

Although the meaning of the phrase "clearly erroneous" is not immediately apparent, certain general principles . . . may be derived from our cases. The foremost of these principles, as the Fourth Circuit itself recognized, is that a "finding is 'clearly erroneous' when although there is evidence to support it, the reviewing court on the entire evidence is left with the definite and firm conviction that a mistake has been committed." United States v. United States Gypsum Co., 333 U.S. 364, 395 (1948). . . . Where there are two permissible views of the evidence, the factfinder's choice between them cannot be clearly erroneous.

This is so even when the district court's findings do not rest on credibility determinations, but are based instead on physical or documentary evidence or inferences from other facts. To be sure, various Courts of Appeals have on occasion asserted the theory that an appellate court may exercise de novo review over findings not based on credibility determinations. . . .

The rationale for deference to the original finder of fact is not limited to the superiority of the trial judge's position to make determinations of credibility. The trial judge's major role is the determination of fact, and with experience in fulfilling that role comes expertise. Duplication of the trial judge's efforts in the court of appeals would very likely contribute only negligibly to the accuracy of fact determination at a huge cost in diversion of judicial resources. . . . As the Court has stated in a different context, the trial on the merits should be "the 'main event' . . . rather than a 'tryout on the road.'" Wainwright v. Sykes, 433 U.S. 72, 90 (1977). . . .

IV

Application of the foregoing principles to the facts of the case lays bare the errors committed. . . . [T]he Fourth Circuit improperly conducted what amounted to a de novo weighing of the evidence in the record. The District Court's finding was based on essentially undisputed evidence regarding the respective backgrounds of petitioner and Mr. Kincaid and the duties . . . of Recreation Director. The District Court, after considering the evidence, concluded that the position . . . carried with it broad responsibilities for creating and managing a recreation program involving not only athletics, but also other activities for citizens of all ages and interests. The court determined that petitioner's more varied educational and employment background and her extensive involvement in a variety of civic activities left her better qualified to implement such a rounded program. . . .

The Fourth Circuit, reading the same record, concluded that the basic duty of Recreation Director was to implement an athletic program. . . . Accordingly, it seemed evident to the Court of Appeals that Mr. Kincaid was in fact better qualified than [Ms. Anderson].

Based on our reading of the record, we cannot say that either interpretation of the facts is illogical or implausible. Each has support in inferences that may be drawn from the facts in the record. . . . The question we must answer, however, is not whether the Fourth Circuit's interpretation of the facts was clearly erroneous, but whether the District Court's finding was clearly erroneous. . . .

Somewhat different concerns are raised by the Fourth Circuit's treatment of the District Court's finding that petitioner, alone among the applicants . . ., was asked questions regarding her spouse's feelings. . . . Here the error of the Court of Appeals was its failure to give due regard to the ability of the District Court to interpret and discern the credibility of oral testimony. . . . The Court of Appeals rested its rejection of the District Court's finding . . . on its own interpretation of testimony by Mrs. Boone. . . .

Mrs. Boone's testimony on this point, which is set forth in the margin,[3] is certainly not free from ambiguity. But Mrs. Boone several times stated that other candidates had not been questioned about the reaction of their wives — at least "not in the same context.". . . Whether the judge's

---

3. Q. Did the committee members ask that same kind of question of the other applicants?
A. Not that I recall. . . .
Q. Do you deny that the other applicants, aside from the plaintiff, were asked about the prospect of working at night in that position?
A. Not to my knowledge.
Q. Are you saying they were not asked that?
A. They were not asked, not in the context that they were asked of Phyllis. I don't know whether they were worried because Jim wasn't going to get his supper or what. You know that goes both ways.
Q. Did you tell Phyllis Anderson that Donnie Kincaid was not asked about night work?
A. He wasn't asked about night work.
Q. That answers one question. Now, let's answer the other one. Did you tell Phyllis Anderson that, that Donnie Kincaid was not asked about night work?
A. Yes, after the interviews — I think the next day or sometime, and I know — may I answer something?
Q. If it's a question that has been asked; otherwise no. It's up to the Judge to say.
A. You asked if there was any question asked about — I think Donnie was just married, and I think I made the comment to him personally — and your new bride won't mind.
Q. So you asked him yourself about his wife's reaction?
A. No, no.
Q. That is what you just said.
Mr. Gibson: Objection, Your Honor.
[The] Court: Sustained. You don't have to rephrase the answer.

App. 108a, 120a-121a.

interpretation is actually correct is impossible to tell from the paper record, but it is easy to imagine that the tone of voice in which the witness related her comment, coupled with her immediate denial that she had questioned Mr. Kincaid on the subject, might have conclusively established that the remark was a facetious one. We therefore cannot agree that the judge's conclusion that the remark was facetious was clearly erroneous. . . .

The Fourth Circuit's refusal to accept the District Court's finding that the committee members were biased against hiring a woman was based to a large extent on its rejection of the finding that petitioner had been subjected to questioning that the other applicants were spared. Given that that finding was not clearly erroneous, the finding of bias cannot be termed erroneous. . . .

Our determination that the findings of the District Court regarding petitioner's qualifications, the conduct of her interview, and the bias of the male committee members were not clearly erroneous leads us to conclude that the court's finding that petitioner was discriminated against on account of her sex was also not clearly erroneous. . . .

In so holding, we do not assert that our knowledge of what happened 10 years ago in Bessemer City is superior to that of the Court of Appeals; nor do we claim to have greater insight than the Court of Appeals into the state of mind of the men on the selection committee. . . . Even the trial judge, who has heard the witnesses directly . . . cannot always be confident that he "knows" what happened. Often, he can only determine whether the plaintiff has succeeded in presenting an account of the facts that is more likely to be true than not. Our task — and the task of appellate tribunals generally — is more limited still: we must determine whether the trial judge's conclusions are clearly erroneous. On the record before us, we cannot say that they are. Accordingly, the judgment of the Court of Appeals is reversed.

[The concurring opinion of Justice POWELL and the dissent of Justice BLACKMUN are omitted.]

NOTES AND PROBLEMS

1. Consider two readings of *Anderson*:

a. The Court's holding might rest on the empirical belief that the trial judge is more likely than an appellate court to be correct in his judgments about which witnesses are telling the truth. If so, then the holding could be challenged by a showing that people in general, even judges, are in fact rather bad at detecting lies, even when they see the witness face to face. There is some empirical evidence that most people do lack the capacity to detect untruth. Indeed, that same evidence suggests that people are *better* at detecting lies when they read a transcript than when they hear and see the witnesses. Guy Wellborn, Demeanor, 76 Cornell L. Rev. 1075 (1991) (reviewing a substantial body of essentially unanimous social science literature). If the clearly-erroneous rule rests on such an empirical belief, it is itself clearly erroneous.

b. Alternatively, the holding may have a different justification. Under Rule-driven procedure, cases that get to trial will have evidence supporting both sides, or else summary judgment would have occurred. So in such cases a rational trier of fact could come down on either side. Notwithstanding this uncertainty, a judgment has to be rendered. Precisely because of this uncertainty, it makes sense to adopt the view of the first hearer of the case unless there is powerful reason for thinking him wrong. Is that what the "clearly erroneous" rule is about?

2. *Anderson* grows out of a practice that has its roots in the distinction between law and equity. Because cases in equity were originally considered only on a written record and the appellate court was as able to read the record as the trial court, the rule evolved in equity that the appellate court reviewed equity decisions de novo. That standard came to dominate appellate review not just of decisions in equity but of all decisions by a judge sitting without a jury. An example of the stance is Orvis v. Higgins, 180 F.2d 537, 539-540 (2d Cir.), cert. denied, 340 U.S. 810 (1950):

> We must sustain a general or a special jury verdict when there is some evidence which the jury might have believed, and when a reasonable inference from that evidence will support the verdict, regardless of whether that evidence is oral or by deposition. In the case of findings by an administrative agency, the usual rule is substantially the same as that in the case of a jury, the findings being treated like a special verdict. Where a trial judge sits without a jury, the rule varies with the character of the evidence: (a) If he decides a fact issue on written evidence alone, we are as able as he to determine credibility, and so we may disregard his finding. (b) Where the evidence is partly oral and the balance is written or deals with undisputed facts, then we may ignore the trial judge's finding and substitute our own, (1) if the written evidence or some undisputed fact renders the credibility of the oral testimony extremely doubtful, or (2) if the trial judge's finding must rest exclusively on the written evidence or the undisputed facts, so that his evaluation of credibility has no significance. (c) But where the evidence supporting his finding as to any fact issue is entirely oral testimony, we may disturb that finding only in the most unusual circumstances.

Which of these assertions does *Anderson* overrule?

3. Rule 52(a) now codifies one of *Anderson*'s points: "Findings of fact, *whether based on oral or documentary evidence*, shall not be set aside unless clearly erroneous." (Emphasis added.)

4. Cooter & Gell v. Hartmarx Corp., 469 U.S. 384 (1990), divided into three layers the appellate scrutiny of a trial court's decision to apply Rule 11 sanctions: (a) determinations of historical fact (what investigation did the lawyer do before filing the complaint?); (b) determinations of legal sufficiency (was the complaint warranted by existing law or a good faith extension thereof?); and (c) the fashioning of the sanction. The Court held that the first determination (correctness of factual findings) was reviewable under the clearly-erroneous standard (citing *Anderson*). The second and third were reviewable under an abuse-of-discretion standard. The Court also held that in this context all three standards were essentially identical. Justifying the application of the abuse-of-discretion standard to the second question, the Court ruefully noted the difficulty of determining between legal and factual questions.

5. As in *Cooter & Gell*, many decisions are up to the sound discretion of the trial judge. Appellate courts can review such decisions for abuse of discretion. As in *Anderson*'s insistence that factual findings be reversed only if clearly erroneous, the Supreme Court has expressed its impatience with appellate courts that "cheat" on the abuse-of-discretion standard by applying it too stringently. In General Electric v. Joiner, 522 U.S. 136 (1997), a trial court had refused to allow some expert witnesses to testify. Such decisions are within the court's discretion. The Eleventh Circuit reversed, citing a generalized preference for admissibility, and conceding that it was applying a particularly stringent standard of review. The Supreme Court reversed, ordering that the usual abuse-of-discretion standard be applied.

6. When a jury rather than a judge has found the fact in question, the principle of *Anderson* may be constitutionally required. The "reexamination clause" of the Seventh Amendment provides that "no fact, tried by a jury, shall be otherwise reexamined in any Court of the United States, than according to the rules of common law." The Supreme Court has said that this clause permits *trial* court scrutiny of jury verdicts via Rules 50 and 59 motions. The Court has also suggested, however, that the same reexamination by an appellate court, because it has not been historically sanctioned, is at least doubtful. Gasperini v. Center for the Humanities, Inc., supra page 297. Does this come close to saying that the clearly erroneous rule is required by the Seventh Amendment in a jury case?

7. *Anderson* deals with one side of the law-fact distinction, holding that findings of fact are entitled to a deferential standard of review. The

other side of that distinction is equally important: the proposition that trial court conclusions of law are not entitled to any deference. That statement may seem to be obvious, but in at least one application it has not been clear to many courts of appeals. Diversity actions often involve interpretations of state law. In such cases *Erie* puts the appellate court in the same position as the district court — seeking to predict how the state courts would decide the question. In such circumstances some courts of appeals have deferred to the district courts, whose judges usually come from the state in question, on the ground that they are in a better position to predict state law rulings. These courts are in effect treating questions of state law as factual for purposes of appellate review. In Salve Regina College v. Russell, 499 U.S. 225 (1991), the Supreme Court held that such deference was inappropriate: "We conclude that a court of appeals should review de novo a district court's determination of state law."

a. Isn't *Salve Regina* the mirror image of *Anderson*? One requires that appellate courts defer to district courts on questions of fact, even when the appellate court thinks it could do a better job; the other requires appellate courts not to defer to district courts, even when the appellate court does not think it can do a better job.

b. Is either rule sensible?

2. Harmless Error

Even if an appellate court applying the appropriate standard of review determines that the trial court committed error, it will not necessarily reverse. Federal courts are forbidden to reverse for "errors or defects that do not affect the substantial rights of the parties." 28 U.S.C. §2111. This statute was enacted to reverse the so-called Exchequer Rule,* which had presumed that any error was harmful and required reversal. As a consequence of §2111, a court must, after concluding there was error, also decide whether that error was harmful.

Courts typically do so by speculating about the likely outcome of the case in the absence of the error. One can see the difficulty inherent in such speculation in Mehojah v. Drummond, 56 F.3d 1213 (10th Cir. 1995). Plaintiffs had been injured when their car struck cattle that had wandered onto the road. The case turned on whether the fencing was unreasonably inadequate. Plaintiffs sought to introduce into evidence testimony showing that, the day after the accident, the fencing had been

---

* So-called from the name of the English court that had originated the practice.

improved. The trial judge excluded this testimony; the majority regretted this exclusion but thought it harmless:

> While we conclude that the court should not have excluded the evidence, we do not believe that the exclusion constituted reversible error. . . .
>
> Having reviewed the entire record including the pleadings, we are of the view that the dispositive fact question in this trial was whether the [defendant] was negligent in placing cattle in a pasture where one end was secured only by a water gap fence. Indeed, at trial, [plaintiff's] counsel stated that the "negligence . . . is not so much the lack of Drummond building the fence, the negligence is placing the cattle on property which was improperly maintained. . . ." Given the material issue at trial, the evidence about construction of the wing fence by Mr. Fairweather (the non-party property owner) the following day would not have helped the [plaintiff's] case. . . .
>
> 28 U.S.C. §2111 requires us to "give judgment after an examination of the record without regard to errors or defects which do not affect the substantial rights of the parties." See also Fed. R. Civ. P. 61. The statute applies to both criminal and civil cases. Applying the nonconstitutional standard for harmless error, we are satisfied that the erroneous exclusion of the evidence did not have a substantial influence on the verdict, nor do we have grave doubt as to whether it had such an effect.

The dissent agreed that the evidentiary ruling was error but thought it harmful:

> Incredibly, the majority holds that the evidence should have been admitted for all purposes, including proof of negligence, but then finds that the error was harmless. How the majority can conclude that the plaintiffs were deprived of their legal right to show graphically both negligence and control by the act of Mr. Fairweather and then conclude that both of these deprivations singly and cumulatively are harmless is beyond me. . . . Since the [defendant] had a non-delegable duty to take reasonable care, it was essential for the jury to know if it would have been feasible for the [defendant] to do more than it did (i.e., inspect the fence) (and, under the majority view, for the jury to be told that they could consider the subsequent actions in determining negligence). . . .
>
> Since the exclusion of the evidence and the resulting impression essentially removed the question of negligence from the jury, the error affected a substantial right of the plaintiffs, and thus, was far from harmless. In fact, since the judge properly instructed the jury that, under Oklahoma law, the defendants had a non-delegable duty to keep the cattle from escaping, I am unable to discern any other basis for the jury to have found for the defendants. I would therefore vacate the judgment and remand for a new trial.

NOTES AND PROBLEMS

1. How should an appellate court decide such questions?

a. A statute, 28 U.S.C. §2111, tells appellate courts not to be trigger-happy in reversing.

b. In the absence of evidence about how the jury actually reached its decision, how does a court responsibly speculate about "what would have happened if . . . ?" An appellate judge with extensive trial court experience might have some basis for a guess; a judge without such experience is likely to be clueless.

2. Should certain kinds of errors, such as errors affecting jury deliberations, be considered intrinsically more serious than others, such as confusing jury instructions? Not all errors affecting jury deliberation are found to constitute prejudicial error.

a. In Gertz v. Bass, 59 Ill. App. 180, 208 N.E.2d 113 (1965), the appellate court reversed because a jury asked to decide whether defendant's behavior was "willful" or "wanton," had obtained from a bailiff a dictionary containing definitions of those terms that differed from the definitions in the jury instructions.

b. In Aetna Casualty & Surety Co. v. Perez, 360 S.W.2d 157 (Tex. Civ. App. 1962), the decision of the lower court was affirmed even though the bailiff had said to some of the jurors, "If you guys are just a couple of thousand dollars apart why don't you settle it?" and "What in the world is the matter with you in there; are you fighting over two or three thousand dollars?" None of the jurors discussed the comments with each other or the other jurors. It should be noted that Texas allows examination of the jurors after the trial for evidence of impropriety and that such an investigation was undertaken in Perez. Should that matter?

c. Extrinsic policies occasionally dictate that an error be considered reversible even though no prejudice is demonstrated. In Javis v. Board of Education, 393 Mich. 689, 227 N.W.2d 543 (1975), for example, the Michigan Supreme Court ruled that failure to give any of the Michigan Standard Jury Instructions that are (1) requested by a party, (2) relevant to the case, and (3) a correct statement of the law is presumed to be prejudicial (and therefore reversible error) even if another instruction, otherwise correct and adequate, is given.

RESPECT FOR JUDGMENTS

XII

Procedural rules serve two masters. They aim to air disputes completely and to reach an accurate and just outcome. They also seek to lay disputes to rest efficiently even if the resting condition is less than optimal. Writers sometimes loftily describe this latter goal as "finality" or "repose." Several branches of law serve the goal of finality. Statutes of limitations forbid litigation entirely if it begins too late. And, as we saw in the preceding chapter, appellate courts have only limited power to overturn trial court findings. This chapter focuses on two other doctrines that serve to bring lawsuits to an end: *claim preclusion* and *issue preclusion.*

Both doctrines are part of the broader topic of *former adjudication* — the effect of judgments on subsequent litigation. These doctrines provide an answer to a pair of related questions: What does it mean for a lawsuit to be over? What does a concluded lawsuit decide? Suppose, for instance, that Pamela sues Donald for injuries sustained in an auto accident, and the case goes to a final judgment. The loser can, of course, appeal. But can there be a second lawsuit? For example, may Pamela bring a second suit concerning the same accident, this time seeking recovery for damage to her automobile? Today, most states would say no, citing the principles of claim preclusion. Claim preclusion forbids a party from relitigating a claim that should have been raised in former litigation.

Issue preclusion comes into play when a claim is not barred but when some issue involved in that claim has been previously litigated. If Pamela and Donald had the misfortune to become involved in a second collision the week after the first, Pamela's suit against Donald for injuries sustained in the first accident would not prevent her from bringing suit concerning the second one. But she and Donald might find themselves prevented from relitigating issues decided in that first suit that are relevant to the second, such as whether at the time of the accidents either was required to wear corrective lenses while driving.

Much of this chapter will be devoted to exploring the conditions that enable a party to invoke issue or claim preclusion. You will find that in examining these questions courts sometimes use an older set of terminology to refer to these concepts. They refer to claim preclusion as *res judicata* and to issue preclusion as *collateral estoppel*. They also occasionally use "res judicata" to refer to the entire topic of former adjudication. The underlying ideas are identical; only the terminology varies.

A.   Claim Preclusion

Claim preclusion has several goals: efficiency, finality, and the avoidance of inconsistency. Efficiency comes most strongly into play when a party that should have raised a claim in previous litigation failed to do so. Only the naive would believe, however, that the exact point at which one claim stops and another begins is always clear; thus this section pays close attention to the scope of a cause of action. Although consistency and economy are the chief policies behind applications of claim preclusion, other policies come into play as well. Suppose a court dismisses a case as punishment for plaintiff's refusal to comply with discovery orders. To be effective sanctions, such dismissals must be "with prejudice," thereby preventing further litigation.

1.   Precluding the "Same" Claim

The standard doctrinal formulation says that claim preclusion bars the same claim from relitigation. Thus stated, the principle sounds both uncontroversial and obvious. In practice, matters become much more interesting because claim preclusion has two goals — the fostering of efficiency and the prevention of inconsistency. In pursuit of these goals doctrines of claim preclusion go a good deal further than a simple statement of the doctrine might suggest.

a.   Efficiency

Claim preclusion grows from pleading. A common law pleader could not combine different writs in a single suit. Because it seemed unfair to block a second suit if the pleader's only mistake lay in selecting the wrong writ, common law courts precluded a plaintiff only from bringing a second claim on the same writ; the plaintiff remained free to try a different writ on the same facts. This narrow scope of preclusion thus flowed from narrow joinder of claims rules at common law.

The two great pleading reforms of the past 150 years, the Field Codes in the nineteenth century and the Federal Rules in the twentieth, freed pleaders from the confines of the writs. But to the extent they thereby made pleading easier, they made claim preclusion more difficult. A pleader under the Codes or the Rules was free to combine different claims. Did she therefore *have* to do so at the risk of finding them precluded? To put the problem at its most extreme, under Rules 8 and 18, a pleader may state as many claims as she has against the opposing party: If she brings only one such claim, are all others forever precluded? No court has ever gone this far, but, short of this extreme, how broadly should preclusion sweep? In the next case the court contrasts two answers to that question.

Frier v. City of Vandalia

770 F.2d 699 (7th Cir. 1985)

EASTERBROOK, Circuit Judge.

The City of Vandalia is fairly small (the population is less than 2,500), and apparently its police have maintained informal ways. When Charles Frier parked one of his cars in a narrow street, which forced others to drive on someone else's lawn to get around Frier's car, the police left two notes at Frier's house asking him to move the car. That did not work, so an officer called a local garage, which towed the car back to the garage. The officer left a note, addressed to "Charlie," telling him where he could find the car. The officer did not issue a citation for illegal parking, however; he later testified that he wanted to make it easier for Frier to retrieve the car.

Frier balked at paying the $10 fee the garage wanted. He also balked at keeping his cars out of the street. The police had garages tow four of them in 1983 — a 1963 Ford Falcon, a 1970 Plymouth Duster, a 1971 Opal GT, and a 1971 Dodge van. Instead of paying the garages, Frier filed suits in the courts of Illinois seeking replevin. Each suit named as defendants the City of Vandalia and the garage that had towed the car.

One of the suits (which sought to replevy two cars) was dismissed voluntarily when Frier got his cars back. We do not know whether he paid for the tows and the subsequent daily storage fees or whether the garage thought it cheaper to surrender the cars than to defend the suit. The other two cases were consolidated and litigated. The police testified to the circumstances under which they had called for the tows. The court concluded that the police properly took the cars into the City's possession to remove obstructions to the alley, and it declined to issue the writ of replevin because the City had the right to remove the cars from the street. Frier then retrieved another car;[1] so far as we can tell, a garage still has the 1970 Plymouth Duster.

After losing in state court, Frier turned to federal court. His complaint maintained that the City had not offered him a hearing either before or after it took the cars and that it is the "official policy" of the City not to do so. The complaint invoked the Due Process Clause of the Fourteenth Amendment and 42 U.S.C. §1983, and it sought equitable relief in addition to $100,000 in compensatory and $100,000 in punitive damages. The district court, after reviewing the transcript of the replevin action, dismissed the complaint for failure to state a claim on which relief may be granted. (Because the judge considered the transcript he should have treated the motion to dismiss as one for summary judgment. We analyze the decision as if he had done so.) The court found that Frier had notice of each tow and knew how to get his cars back. Frier also had a full hearing in the replevin action on the propriety of the tows. Although the judicial hearing came approximately one month after the tows, the court thought the delay permissible.

A month is a long wait for a hearing when the subject is an automobile. The automobile is "property" within the meaning of the Due Process Clause, and the City therefore must furnish appropriate process. Sutton v. City of Milwaukee, 672 F.2d 644 (7th Cir. 1982), holds that a hearing is not necessary before the police tow a car but suggests that one must be furnished promptly after the tow. *Sutton* also suggests, in line with many other cases, that the City must establish the process and tender an opportunity for a hearing; it may not sit back and wait for the aggrieved person to file a suit.

The City, for its part, maintains that a few isolated tows without hearings are not the "policy" of the City and may not be imputed to it, and that anyway a month's delay in holding a hearing about seized property is permissible. . . .

A court ought not resolve a constitution[al] dispute unless that is absolutely necessary. Here it is not. Frier had his day in court in the replevin action. The City has argued that this precludes further suits. (The City raised this argument in the motion to dismiss, which is irregular but not fatally so. See Fed. R. Civ. P. 8(c).) The district court bypassed this argument because, it believed, Frier could not have asserted his constitutional arguments in a replevin action. This is only partially correct.

Frier could not have obtained punitive damages or declaratory relief in a suit limited to replevin. But he was free to join one count seeking

---

1. One garage told Frier he could come and get his car any time he wanted, without paying a fee.

such relief with another seeking replevin. See Welch v. Brunswick Corp., 10 Ill. App. 3d 693 (1st Dist. 1973), revd. in part on other grounds, 57 Ill. 2d 461 (1974); Hanaman v. Davis, 20 Ill. App. 2d 111 (2d Dist. 1959), both of which allow one count seeking replevin to be joined with another count seeking different relief. As we show below, the law of Illinois, which under 28 U.S.C. §1738 governs the preclusive effect to be given to the judgment in the replevin actions, see Marrese v. American Academy of Orthopaedic Surgeons, 470 U.S. 373 (1985), would bar this suit. The City therefore is entitled to prevail on the ground of claim preclusion, although the district court did not decide the case on that ground. See Massachusetts Mutual Life Insurance Co. v. Ludwig, 426 U.S. 479 (1976).

Illinois recognizes the principles of claim preclusion (also called res judicata or estoppel by judgment). Jones v. City of Alton, 757 F.2d 878, 884-85 (7th Cir. 1985) (summarizing the law of preclusion in Illinois). One suit precludes a second "where the parties and the cause of action are identical." Redfern v. Sullivan, 111 Ill. App. 3d 372, 376 (4th Dist. 1982). "Causes of action are identical where the evidence necessary to sustain a second verdict would sustain the first, i.e., where the causes of action are based upon a common core of operative facts." Ibid. Two suits may entail the same "cause of action" even though they present different legal theories, and the first suit "operates as an absolute bar to a subsequent action . . . 'not only as to every matter which was offered and received to sustain or defeat the claim or demand, but as to any other admissible matter which might have been offered for that purpose.' " People v. Bone, 82 Ill. 2d 282, 287 (1980), cert. denied, 454 U.S. 839 (1981), quoting Cromwell v. County of Sac, 94 U.S. 351, 352 (1877). More[over], as we pointed out in *Hagee* [v. City of Evanston], 729 F.2d 510, 513 [(7th Cir. 1984)], some cases in Illinois recognize preclusion when both suits arise out of the same transaction. This ground of preclusion is potentially broader than the "same evidence" ground.

The City was a defendant in each replevin action. Frier could have urged constitutional grounds as reasons for replevin.[2] He also could have joined a constitutional claim seeking punitive damages and declaratory relief to his demand for replevin, and therefore he had a full and fair opportunity to litigate (unlike Jones v. City of Alton, where procedural obstacles impeded litigation of the federal claim). The actions also involve both the same "common core of operative facts" and the same transac-

2. At one point in the argument before the state court, Frier's lawyer invoked the constitution, saying that the towing was "the taking of a man's property without due process of law and . . . they have taken [the cars] illegally and are holding [them] illegally" (Tr. 48). This is too fleeting to amount to a formal request for a constitutional ruling, but it does show the pertinence of the constitution to the replevin action.

tions. Frier argues that the City towed his cars wrongfully. Each complaint seeking replevin asserted [that] Frier owned each car and that it had not been "seized under lawful process" — in other words, that there had been no citation and no hearing at which anyone had found that the cars were illegally parked. The replevin statute requires a plaintiff to show that the property was taken without "lawful process." Ill. Rev. Stat., ch. 110, §19-104. "Process," even in its technical sense, initiates or follows a hearing. Had there been process and a hearing at which a magistrate found the cars to have been illegally parked, Frier would have had no claim for replevin no matter how strongly he contested the substantive issue. The "operative facts" in the replevin and §1983 actions therefore are the same. Frier urges that he owned the car (the property interest) and that the City did not offer him a hearing to adjudicate the legality of his parking (the absence of due process).

The replevin actions diverged from the path of this §1983 suit only because the state judge adjudicated on the merits the propriety of the seizures. Having found the seizures proper, the judge had no occasion to determine whether the City should have offered Frier an earlier hearing. But this divergence does not mean that the two legal theories require a different "core of operative facts." The courts of Illinois sometimes put the inquiry as whether the two theories of relief "allege the same conduct" by the defendant. Kenny v. Interim General Superintendent, 112 Ill. App. 3d 342, 349 (1st Dist. 1983). Frier has attacked the "same conduct" — towing and detaining the cars without a determination of a parking violation — in all of his suits.

To an extent there is any doubt about this, we look (as we did in *Hagee*) to the purpose of doctrines of preclusion. Claim preclusion is designed to impel "parties to consolidate all closely related matters into one suit" (*Hagee*, 729 F.2d at 514; note omitted). This prevents the oppression of defendants by multiple cases, which may be easy to file and costly to defend. There is no assurance that a second or third case will be decided more accurately than the first and so there is no good reason to incur the costs of litigation more than once. When the facts and issues of all theories of liability are closely related, one case is enough. Here the replevin theory contained the elements that make up a due process theory, and we are therefore confident that the courts of Illinois would treat both theories as one "cause of action."

The final question is whether it makes a difference that only two of the replevin actions went to judgment, while here Frier challenges the towing of four cars. Under Illinois law the answer is no. The defendant may invoke claim preclusion when the plaintiff litigated in the first suit a subset of all available disputes between the parties. See Baird & Warner, Inc. v. Addison Industrial Park, Inc., 70 Ill. App. 3d 59 (1st Dist. 1979), which holds that a suit on three of six disputed parcels of land precludes a subsequent suit on all six. We doubt that Illinois would see difference between three lots out of six and two cars out of four.

If Frier had filed the current suit in state court, he would have lost under the doctrine of claim preclusion. Under 28 U.S.C. §1738 he therefore loses in federal court as well.

Affirmed.

SWYGERT, Senior Circuit Judge, concurring in the result.

In my view, the majority has simply applied the wrong analysis to the problem at hand. Rather than trying to squeeze a res judicata solution into a mold that does not fit, I would review the facts to determine whether Frier's procedural due process claims could withstand a summary judgment motion. Because I believe the City was entitled to summary judgment, I concur in the result.

I

In determining whether the disposition of a claim in State court precludes a subsequent suit on the same claim in federal court, the federal court must apply the State's law of res judicata. Allen v. McCurry, 449 U.S. 90, 96 (1980). Because Illinois continues to adhere to the narrow, traditional view of claim preclusion, as opposed to the broader approach codified in the Restatement (Second) of Judgments §§24, 25 (1982), I would hold that Frier's substantive traffic law claim does not preclude this subsequent procedural due process claim. Under the more modern view of the new Restatement, all claims arising from a single "transaction" — broadly defined to include matters related in time, space, origin, and motivation — must be litigated in a single, initial lawsuit, or be barred from being raised in subsequent litigation. There was only one transaction in the case at bar: the seizure of Frier's cars. Accordingly, Frier should have raised both his substantive and procedural objections to the seizure in one initial lawsuit.

Illinois, however, has not adopted the view of the new Restatement.[1] Rather, as the majority recognizes, the Illinois courts focus on the similarities between the causes of action alleged in both suits, not on whether there is a common factual transaction. One suit precludes a second "where the parties and the cause of action are identical." Redfern v.

---

1. No Illinois court has ever cited the new Restatement. The first Restatement, which follows the traditional "cause of action" approach, see Restatement of Judgments §61 (1942), has been cited several times. E.g., Hilti, Inc. v. Griffith, 68 Ill. App. 3d 528, 386 N.E.2d 63, 65-66, 24 Ill. Dec. 859 (1979); Pierog v. H. F. Karl Contractors, Inc., 39 Ill. App. 3d 1057, 351 N.E.2d 249, 252 (1976).

Sullivan, 111 Ill. App. 3d 372, 444 N.E.2d 205, 208 (1983). "Causes of action are identical where the evidence necessary to sustain a second verdict would sustain the first, i.e., where the causes of action are based upon a common core of operative facts." Id. The allusion to a "common core of operative facts" is not an attempt to adopt the transactional view of the new Restatement. Indeed the court in *Redfern* cites with approval a section of a legal encyclopedia that expressly repudiates the transactional view. Id. (citing 23A Ill. L. & Prac. Judgments §331 (1979) ("causes of action which are distinct and independent, although growing out of the same . . . transaction . . . may be sued on separately"); accord Fountas v. Breed, 118 Ill. App. 3d 669, 455 N.E.2d 200, 203 (1983) ("Two claims are not necessarily the same cause of action merely because they arose out of the same general transaction or set of facts."). Rather, the "common core of operative facts" is defined by the previous clause, which refers to an identity of evidence. This requires the court to focus on the various elements of two causes of action to determine whether the same evidence is necessary to sustain both.

In sum, the common set of facts that must be shown to invoke Illinois' doctrine of claim preclusion is defined as those facts necessary to sustain the cause of action, not as those facts that could be conveniently litigated in one lawsuit. This focus on the elements of the causes of action and the proofs at trial — rather than on the policy advantages of trying both actions in one suit — dooms any attempt to invoke claim preclusion in the case at bar. To be sure, both actions arise from the same seizure of the same cars. Yet, both the theory of recovery and focus of factual inquiry are dramatically different in each case. Frier's replevin claim was substantive in nature; to replevy property, the claimant must show his superior possessory rights. Frier's possessory rights turned on the legality of his parking. Because the trial court found that "the officer reasonably believed and had a right to believe that . . . [Frier's] vehicle obstructed the free use and passage way of that street at that time," it concluded that, therefore, Frier did not enjoy the "superior right to possession of the property" necessary to sustain a replevin action.

Frier's procedural due process claim requires an entirely different factual showing. The legality or reasonableness of the seizure is irrelevant. Because of the "risk of error inherent in the truth-finding process," an individual is entitled to certain procedural safeguards regardless of whether the deprivation of property was substantively justified. The focus of the inquiry, then, is the adequacy of procedures attending the seizure, not the seizure itself.

The majority urges that Frier could have joined a separate constitutional claim to his replevin action. This precise argument was rejected in *Fountas*, 455 N.E.2d at 204. There, the court held that although the plaintiff-administrator could have joined a wrongful death action with the decedent's personal injury action, the dismissal of the personal injury action did not preclude a subsequent wrongful death action, unless such joinder was mandatory. Illinois law focuses on the similarities and differences between the various causes of action. That two wholly-different causes of action arising out of the same transaction could be joined together as one convenient trial unit is irrelevant for the purposes of Illinois law, though this would be dispositive under the new Restatement. See Restatement (Second) of Judgments §24(2) (1982). . . .

Somewhat more persuasive is the majority's reliance on a line of Illinois cases that appear to adopt a more transactional approach by focusing on whether the same "conduct" underlies both lawsuits. In Hagee v. City of Evanston, 729 F.2d 510 (7th Cir. 1984), this court extensively reviewed Illinois' law of res judicata and concluded that some appellate courts had begun to diverge from the strict traditional test by emphasizing the need to compare the "underlying" or "operative" facts of the various lawsuits. Relying on decisions of the Illinois Supreme Court, this court defined Illinois law to include two rules that modify the strict traditional test. A party may not maintain two suits based on the "same set of facts" by (1) "limiting the theories of recovery advanced in the first" or (2) "altering the claims for relief from one suit to the next." Id. at 514.

Although it is true that Frier "limit[ed] the theories of recovery advanced in the first [suit]," his second suit is not precluded because it is not based on the "same set of facts." The common operative facts required for claim preclusion are those facts necessary to sustain the cause of action, not those facts that can be conveniently litigated in one lawsuit. *Hagee*, then, merely repudiated those appellate court cases that relied on technical differences between theories of relief or remedies to avoid invoking claim preclusion despite a substantial overlap in the operative facts necessary to sustain both actions. This court did not, and could not, repudiate Illinois' consistent emphasis on the underlying cause of action, as opposed to the underlying transaction.

Here, in contrast to *Hagee*, there is a significant divergence in the facts necessary to sustain Frier's two claims. Accordingly, the Illinois courts would not find claim preclusion in the case at bar.

II

It was established at Frier's replevin trial that the City police caused various service station owners to tow four of Frier's cars and, in lieu of a traffic citation, left written notice of the reason for the towing and the whereabouts of the cars. Frier eventually recovered two of his cars. Thus, the replevin action, and this action, concern only two of the cars. Frier could have recovered one of those cars immediately by paying a $10.00 towing fee to the owner of the service station that towed the car. However, Frier was informed that any further delay in reclaiming the car would result in a $2.50 per day storage charge. Frier was free to reclaim the other car without paying any fee. I would hold that, on the basis of these uncontested facts, the City was entitled to summary judgment against Frier's procedural due process claim. . . .

[Judge Swygert went on to analyze plaintiff's claim under the line of cases interpreting the Due Process Clause.]

I would hold, then, that notice of towing, the availability of an expedited State tort suit that can make the petitioner whole, and the ability to reclaim the towed cars immediately at a cost of $10.00 together constitute adequate postdeprivation process as long as the $10.00 fee does not present a financial hardship. This holding would not necessarily conflict with recent decisions of other courts reqiring more immediate and elaborate postdeprivation process. More elaborate process may well be required in those cases because the towing practices of the various municipalities were more burdensome on the respective petitioners: Immediate reclamation required significantly more than $10.00 and the litigants had standing to represent indigents who could afford no fee. We need not reach such troublesome issues in the case at bar.

I would find, as a matter of law, no procedural due process violation under these facts. Accordingly, I concur with the majority's decision to affirm the judgment below.

NOTES AND PROBLEMS

1. Why does Frier lose?

a. Does the majority reject his constitutional claim?

b. Does anyone assert that he actually litigated his constitutional claim in the first lawsuit?

c. If not, is it fair now to prevent him from doing so in a second action?

2. The majority and concurrence debate the difference (if any) between the Illinois definition of "claims" for purposes of preclusion and that of the Restatement (Second) of Judgments §24.

a. What is the point of that debate?

b. Notice that the doctrines of claim preclusion discussed in *Frier* do not flow from the Rules but from common law. One could imagine an amendment to Rule 8 stating that a final judgment on a claim barred the refiling of that claim or any other arising from the same transaction or occurrence. Should the Rules explicitly so state? Would such an amendment violate the Rules Enabling Act, 28 U.S.C. §2072(b), which specifies that the Rules may not "abridge, enlarge, or modify any substantive right"?

c. The Restatement (Second), which seeks to summarize the common law of claim and issue preclusion, sets forth a broad definition of "claims":

> (1) When a valid and final judgment rendered in an action extinguishes a plaintiff's claim pursuant to the rules of merger or bar . . ., the claim extinguished includes all rights of the plaintiff to remedies against the defendant with respect to all or any part of the transaction, or series of connected transactions, out of which the claim arose.
>
> (2) What factual grouping constitutes a "transaction," and what groupings constitute a "series," are to be determined pragmatically, giving weight to such considerations as whether the facts are related in time, space, origin, or motivation, whether they form a convenient trial unit, and whether their treatment as a unit conforms to the parties' expectations or business understanding or usage.

d. What considerations ought to determine whether a given jurisdiction adopts a transactional test or a narrower one?

e. Should it matter whether the jurisdiction uses a broad, general definition of "claim" for pleading purposes (like that set forth in Rule 8) or a narrower, more focused one? Illinois employs a variation on Code pleading:

> (a) All pleadings shall contain a plain and concise statement of the pleader's *cause of action*, counterclaim, defense or reply.

Ill. Ann. Stat. ch. 110, para. 2-603 (Smith-Hurd 1983) (emphasis supplied). Does the reference to "cause of action" focus more on the legal theory than on the underlying transaction and thus justify a narrow doctrine of preclusion?

3. The opinion identifies some of the bases of claim preclusion:

> Claim preclusion is designed to impel "parties to consolidate all closely related matters into one suit[.]" This prevents the oppression of defendants by multiple cases, which may be easy to file and costly to defend. There is no assurance that a second or third case will be decided more accurately than the first and so there is no good reason to incur the costs of litigation more than once.

Would any of these principles be violated by permitting Frier to raise his constitutional challenge to Vandalia's towing practices?

4. If the purpose of claim preclusion is to prevent inefficiency by forcing a party to bring all its closely related claims together, who is the intended beneficiary of this efficiency — the courts, the opposing party,

or both? If the doctrine of claim preclusion is intended to protect the courts, why can it be waived by the opposing side? See Rule 8(c).

5. Many states and the federal court system use the transactional definition of "claim" for preclusion purposes. Both *Frier* opinions seem to agree that, under the transactional test, Frier's second claim would have been precluded. Is this a sensible result? Assuming that plaintiff wants to challenge the city's entire procedure for towing cars, should he have to do so when he tried to retrieve his car from the garage? Would it make as much sense to permit him to get his car back and then bring a second, broad-based constitutional challenge to the underlying process?

6. The standard answer to the questions posed in the preceding Note is that forcing a plaintiff to combine all the claims arising out of a transaction does not force the court to try all those claims in a single suit. Rule 42(b) (or an equivalent state rule) gives the trial court authority to sever parts of a complaint for trial. One can imagine a court's wishing to separate the question whether Frier could have his car back from the question whether the city's towing process was unconstitutional. If that is so, however, it casts some doubt on whether the two claims should be treated as one for preclusion purposes. Notice that Restatement (Second) of Judgments §24(b) specifies that "whether [the claims] form a convenient trial unit" is one of the factors to be considered in deciding whether they ought to be precluded.

7. When courts conclude that a second claim ought to be precluded under the applicable test for preclusion, they often describe the precluded plaintiff as trying to split her claim between two lawsuits. Most "splitting" cases are analyzed as involving (a) different theories of recovery, (b) arithmetical splitting, or (c) splitting of relief.

a. Common examples of separate theories are attempts to recover in contract in one action and in quasi-contract in a second, or in conversion in the first action and restitution in the second. For a modern example, see Ley v. Boron Oil Co., 454 F. Supp. 448 (W.D. Pa. 1978) (first action determined that defendant's inquiries about plaintiff did not violate the Fair Credit Reporting Act; second action based on invasion of privacy barred by claim preclusion). Is *Frier* an example of a split theory? Most would answer no because, unlike the standard instances of split theories, Frier sought different remedies in his two claims: replevin to get the cars back, then §1983 for damages.

b. Arithmetical splitting occurs when a plaintiff tries to recover for separate damages from the same incident in separate actions. Clearly, if a plaintiff is injured in an accident, he cannot seek damages for a broken hand in one action and a broken foot in another. Similarly, most courts would not permit a plaintiff to sue for personal injuries and property damage in separate actions. See Rush v. City of Maple Heights in Chapter I. In the case of a series of obligations, such as installment payments on a debt or rent, a plaintiff is required to sue for all installments already due at the time of bringing the action. If the contract has a so-called acceleration clause that makes all installments due if one or two are missed, plaintiff must sue for all installments. This rule does not apply if the acceleration is optional and the option has not been exercised; nor does it apply if the installment obligations are represented by separate notes. Why are separate notes given this treatment?

c. Splitting of relief occurs when a plaintiff asserts one remedy in one action and seeks an alternative or supplemental remedy in a second action. *Frier* has elements of such splitting: There the plaintiff sought one remedy (replevy of his cars) in the first suit and then, deploying constitutional theories in a second suit, sought damages for the same acts of allegedly unlawful towing. In another example, a plaintiff who lost a contract action could not later bring an action to reform the same contract. Gatzemeyer v. Vogel, 589 F.2d 360 (8th Cir. 1978). Similarly, a plaintiff who sues to enjoin State University from charging him out-of-state tuition would not be allowed to sue again to recover past overcharges.

8. Having grasped the counter-intuitive idea that unlitigated claims can be precluded, do not overstate the principle. Before a claim can be precluded by a lawsuit, it must *be* a claim at the time of that suit. The rule that installments not yet due need not be joined (see Note 7(b)) thus illustrates the broader principle that any claims that could not be brought in an action will not be deemed to be merged into it. The principle in question is not limited to issues of a claim's ripeness; they may also involve the first tribunal's competency. For example, claims for equitable relief would not be precluded as a result of a suit in a court that had no power to grant equitable relief.

9. The transactional definition of claims does not extend to claims by different parties but arising from the same episode. For example, if H and W were injured when a car they were riding in was hit by T's truck, each can sue T separately. The Supreme Court of New Hampshire has suggested that a compulsory joinder of parties rule might be desirable in certain cases. But in Reid v. Spadone Machine Co., 119 N.H. 198, 400 A.2d 54 (1979), the court, noting that no such compulsory joinder rule exists, allowed a wife to sue for loss of consortium after her husband had won a claim for an employment-related injury. Would such a rule create problems that do not exist for compulsory joinder of claims?

10. What happens when two cases are proceeding at the same time? Frier, for example, might have filed his Illinois replevin action and

simultaneously brought his civil rights claim in federal court. Courts of one state will often give precedence to a suit pending in another state or country if the latter was brought first. But courts sometimes do not do so. What happens then? Without entering fully into this complex area, which courses in conflict of laws and federal courts explore more fully, it is possible to sketch the problem and some standard answers.

a. Suppose Court A enters judgment first, and a party now argues that this judgment precludes the claim pending in Court B. Court B will have to decide this question, using the principles we have just explored (is it the same claim, etc.?). The Restatement 2d, Judgments §26(1)(a) treats a defendant's failure to object to the simultaneous pendency of related suits as an agreement to allow plaintiff to split his claim.

b. Suppose Court B decides the first judgment does not preclude the second claim, on which it now enters judgment. Further suppose that the judgments of the two courts conflict, with one holding defendant liable, the other not. What should the parties do now?

The standard answer is that the party who lost on her preclusion argument in the second suit should appeal, if necessary all the way to the U.S. Supreme Court. She has federal grounds for such an appeal because Article IV, §1 of the U.S. Constitution orders states to give "full faith and credit" to judgments of sister states. (28 U.S.C. §1738 gives the same command to federal courts.) Her argument on appeal will be that Court A would have viewed the first judgment as precluding the second suit and that Court B was bound to give full faith and credit to the judgment. If an appellate court agrees, it will reverse the second judgment and order Court B to recognize Court A's judgment and dismiss the second suit.

c. Having worked through this logic, one can understand what a third court should do when faced with conflicting judgments of A and B: It should follow the *second* judgment. Why? Because if that second judgment (rejecting preclusion) had been erroneous, it could have been appealed. If it was not (or if it was but was affirmed), it must be correct. Restatement 2d, Judgments §15.

b.   Consistency — The Logical Implications of the Former Judgment

Claim preclusion encourages parties to bring claims in efficiently large packages — by threatening them with preclusion if they do not. The same doctrine also aspires to prevent at least the most egregious forms of inconsistency in successive judgments.

Common law had no compulsory counterclaim rule. Thus, while the Federal Rules could remain silent on compulsory joinder of claims, an explicit rule was needed for counterclaims. Review Rule 13(a). In *Martino*, which follows, the court considers the scope of Rule 13(a) and an application of the principles of preclusion, raising issues of consistency and efficiency.

Martino v. McDonald's System, Inc.

598 F.2d 1079 (7th Cir.), cert. denied, 444 U.S. 966 (1979)

PELL, J.

The plaintiffs, Louis J. Martino and McDonald's Drive-In of Ottumwa, Iowa, Inc. (McDonald's Ottumwa) appeal from the district court's entry of summary judgment against them on one count of their two count antitrust complaint against the defendants, McDonald's System, Inc. (McDonald's System) and Franchise Realty Interstate Corporation (FRIC). The only issue before this court is whether a 1973 consent judgment against Martino precludes the cause of action set forth in Count I of the present complaint. The district court held that both res judicata and the compulsory counterclaim rule of Fed. R. Civ. P. 13(a) barred the plaintiffs from suing on their first cause of action.

In 1962 the plaintiff Louis Martino and three brothers not involved in this action entered into a franchise and lease agreement with the defendants.[1] Martino and his brothers then organized McDonald's Ottumwa, the corporate plaintiff here, to operate the business. The contract to which Martino and the defendants were parties provided that neither Martino nor a member of his immediate family would acquire a financial interest in a competing self-service food business without the written consent of McDonald's System and FRIC. In 1968 Martino's son purchased a Burger Chef franchise in Pittsburg, Kansas. Martino financed this transaction.

On the basis of this transaction FRIC and McDonald's System brought a federal diversity action in Iowa against Martino and his three brothers, charging that Martino had violated the contract provision restricting acquisitions described above. This lawsuit, commenced in 1972, ended in 1973 with a consent judgment to which the district court appended findings of fact and conclusions of law. The court order also provided that the parties had entered an agreement for the sale of McDonald's Ottumwa franchise to FRIC for $140,000. The sale was completed ac-

---

1. The defendant McDonald's System, Inc. licensed the McDonald's franchise, and the defendant FRIC leased the property for the franchise.

cording to the terms of the agreement. Martino's brothers later canceled their stock in McDonald's Ottumwa, leaving Martino as the sole shareholder.

Martino and McDonald's Ottumwa brought this action in 1975. Count I of their complaint alleges that the enforcement of the restriction on acquisition in the franchise and lease agreements violated Section 1 of the Sherman Act, 15 U.S.C. §1. As a basis for damages, Martino claims profits he would have earned as owner of the McDonald's franchise. Both plaintiffs claim damages for having had to sell the franchise, allegedly below its market value.

The defendants have presented two theories for barring Count I of the plaintiffs' antitrust complaint. The first theory is based on the preclusive effect of Fed. R. Civ. P. 13(a), applying to compulsory counterclaims. The second theory is based on the principle of res judicata. We shall now consider the merits of each theory.

The defendants argue that the district court correctly held that Count I is precluded by Fed. R. Civ. P. 13(a).[2] Claims coming within the definition of "compulsory counterclaim" are lost if not raised at the proper time. According to the defendants, Rule 13(a) required Martino to raise this antitrust challenge to the contract provision in the earlier suit based on the same provision. If Rule 13(a) were applicable to these facts, the defendants' argument might have merit.[3] Rule 13(a), however, by its own terms does not apply unless there has been some form of pleading.

The rule expressly says that "a *pleading* shall state as a counterclaim any claim which at the time of serving the *pleading* the *pleader* has against any opposing party. . . ." (Emphasis added.) In the prior Iowa action at issue here, Martino filed no pleading as the word is defined in Fed. R. Civ. P. 7(a).[4] For this reason, Martino argues that we must

2. Rule 13(a) provides in pertinent part:

A pleading shall state as a counterclaim any claim which at the time of serving the pleading the pleader has against any opposing party, if it arises out of the transaction or occurrence that is the subject matter of the opposing party's claim and does not require for its adjudication the presence of third parties of whom the court cannot acquire jurisdiction.

3. Martino argues, however, [that] Mercoid Corp. v. Mid-Continent Investment Co., 320 U.S. 661 (1944), requires special treatment of antitrust counterclaims. We consider this argument as it applies to the res judicata theory of preclusion, infra. Because we decline to apply Rule 13(a) in the circumstances of this case, we do not consider the merits of Martino's argument that *Mercoid* requires that all antitrust counterclaims be treated as permissive counterclaims under Fed. R. Civ. P. 13(b).

4. Rule 7(a) defines the following as pleadings: an answer, a reply to a counterclaim, an answer to a cross-claim, a third party complaint, and a third party answer.

not apply Rule 13(a) to the claim stated in Count I of his complaint. We agree.

Rule 13(a) is in some ways a harsh rule. It forces parties to raise certain claims at the time and place chosen by their opponents, or to lose them. The rule, however, is the result of a balancing between competing interests. The convenience of the party with a compulsory counterclaim is sacrificed in the interest of judicial economy. We do not believe that the drafters of Rule 13 chose the term "pleading" unadvisedly. It no doubt marks, although somewhat arbitrarily, a point at which the judicial burden of the earlier lawsuit outweighs the opposing party's interest in bringing an action when and where it is most convenient. The earlier action between these parties was terminated by a consent judgment before the answer was filed. We see little sense in applying the broad bar established in Rule 13(a) to an action that ended with virtually no burden on the judicial calendar. . . .

Although Rule 13(a) does not dispose of Martino's antitrust claim, longstanding principles of res judicata establish a narrowly defined class of "common law compulsory counterclaims." See Restatement (Second) of Judgments §56.1(2)(b), Reporter's Note on Comment f (Tent. Draft No. 1, 1973). We hold that the antitrust claim set forth in Count I of Martino's complaint falls within this narrow class of claims and that the res judicata effect of the earlier consent judgment is a bar to raising it now.

The principle of res judicata at issue here treats a judgment on the merits as an absolute bar to relitigation between the parties and those in privity with them of every matter offered and received to sustain or defeat the claim or demand and to every matter which might have been received for that purpose.

The conclusion of the earlier contract lawsuit with a consent judgment does not prevent the earlier judgment from having a res judicata effect. . . . Although the earlier judgment at issue here was entered pursuant to the agreement of the parties, it was accompanied by judicial findings of fact and conclusions of law that go to the merits of the controversy. The court described Martino's actions as "a material breach of the agreements sufficient to justify termination." The trial "court is not properly a recorder of contracts, but is an organ of government constituted to make judicial decisions and when it has rendered a consent judgment it has made an adjudication." 1B Moore's Federal Practice ¶0.409[5] at 1030 (2d ed. 1974).

Having determined that the prior consent judgment is an adjudication on the merits, we conclude that this judgment precludes Count I of the antitrust action. As a predicate for our discussion of the res judicata effect of the prior judgment we turn to the basis of Martino's present antitrust claim.

The gravamen of Count I of Martino's antitrust complaint is the 1973 lawsuit. In paragraph 12 of Count I, the complaint describes the 1973 lawsuit seeking termination of the franchise. Paragraph 15 alleges that

> By enforcing the provisions of the franchise agreement and the sub-lease that prohibited the acquisition of any financial interest in a non-McDonald's self service food and beverage establishment against plaintiffs, defendants discouraged competition and unreasonably restrained trade and commerce in violation of Section 1 of the Sherman Act (15 U.S.C. §1).

Paragraph 16 concludes Count I, alleging that Martino lost profits he would have earned as owner of the McDonald's franchise and that Martino was forced to sell the franchise at below its market value.

It is impossible to interpret this count as anything but a direct challenge to the outcome of the 1973 lawsuit. The 1973 lawsuit concluded that termination was justified. The plaintiff now contends that termination was not justified, because the federal antitrust laws forbade it. If Martino's antitrust theory had merit, it would have been a defense in 1973, changing the outcome of the litigation.

The well-settled rule for the purpose of determining the res judicata effect of a judgment is that a "cause of action" comprises defenses, such as the alleged antitrust violation here, that were or might have been raised. As the Supreme Court said long ago:

> [A judgment on the merits] is a finality as to the claim or demand in controversy, concluding parties, and those in privity with them, not only as to every matter which was offered and received to sustain or defeat the claim or demand, but as to any other admissible matter which might have been offered for that purpose. Thus, for example, a judgment rendered on a promissory note is conclusive as to the validity of the instrument and the amount due upon it, although it be subsequently alleged that perfect defenses actually existed, of which no proof was offered, such as forgery, want of consideration, or payment. If such defenses were not presented in the action, and established by competent evidence, *the subsequent allegation of their existence is of no consequence.*

Cromwell v. County of Sac, 94 U.S. 351, 352 (1876) (emphasis added).

Because the alleged antitrust violation constitutes a separate ground for recovery as well as a defense to the suit to terminate the franchise, however, Martino argues that Count I of this action constitutes a different "cause of action" for the purpose of res judicata and that the prior judgment does not preclude relitigation of the defendants' termination rights under the antitrust laws. For cases like this one, to which Rule

13(a) is inapplicable, Martino's argument correctly states the general rule. When facts form the basis of both a defense and a counterclaim, the defendant's failure to allege these facts as a defense or a counterclaim "does not preclude him from relying on those facts in an action subsequently brought by him against the plaintiff." Restatement (Second) of Judgments §56.1(1), Comment b (Tent. Draft No. 1, 1973). The logic of this rule in circumstances not subject to Rule 13(a) is manifest. Should the earlier litigation end in its very first stage, no great burden on the courts results from permitting a counterclaim to be raised at a more convenient time and place. Notions of judicial economy give way to fairness. The defendant in the earlier action has his day in court when and where he sees fit.

The rule is not absolute, however. Both precedent and policy require that res judicata bar a counterclaim when its prosecution would nullify rights established by the prior action. Judicial economy is not the only basis for the doctrine of res judicata. Res judicata also preserves the integrity of judgments and protects those who rely on them. McDonald's System and FRIC have terminated and repurchased Martino's franchise in reliance on the trial court's 1973 judgment telling them they were justified in doing so. Now Martino seeks to impose significant financial liability on the defendants for these actions. We cannot hold that the counterclaim exception to the res judicata rule, based merely on notions of convenience, permits the plaintiff here to wage this direct attack on the rights established by the prior judgment.

A comparison between two Supreme Court decisions illustrates the rule and the exception to the rule we have discussed. In Chicot County Drainage District v. Baxter State Bank, 308 U.S. 371 (1940), a case similar in relevant respects to the one before us, the Supreme Court applied res judicata to preclude a claim. In Chicot County the Court held that a judgment effecting a plan of readjustment of indebtedness, resulting in a cancellation of certain bonds, precluded a subsequent suit on the same bonds. The subsequent suit on the bonds alleged the unconstitutionality of the 1934 Readjustment Act, which was the basis of the prior action. Although the question of constitutionality in Chicot County, like the antitrust issue here, was not actually litigated in the earlier action, and although the suit to recover on the bonds, like the antitrust claim here, was a different cause of action, the Supreme Court applied the principle of res judicata to bar the second action. The Court explained:

> As parties, these bondholders had full opportunity to present any objections to the proceeding. . . . Apparently no question of validity was raised and the cause proceeded to decree on the assumption by all parties and the court itself that the statute was valid. . . . If the general principles

governing the defense of res judicata are applicable, these bondholders, having the opportunity to raise the question of invalidity, were not the less bound by the decree because they failed to raise it.

303 U.S. at 375.

The unfairness of subjecting the issuer of the bonds in *Chicot County* to inconsistent obligations was manifest, and res judicata precluded that result. In contrast, in Virginia-Carolina Chemical Co. v. Kirven, 215 U.S. 252 (1909), a purchaser sued for damages to his crops caused by the defendant's fertilizer. The defendant chemical company argued that its earlier successful suit against the purchaser for the price was a bar to the present suit. The Supreme Court held that the purchaser was entitled to bring the action for damages, drawing a distinction between claims which is crucial to the result in this case. A claim for crop damage in the earlier action for the purchase price would merely have effected a set-off to the Chemical Company's recovery of the purchase price. The claim for crop damage "[did not] go to the validity of the [Chemical Company's] demand [for the price] in its inception . . . such as . . . forgery, want of consideration, or payment." Concluding that Martino's claim set forth in Count I of his complaint is a direct attack on the termination rights established in the earlier judgment, we hold that Martino is barred from raising that claim. . . .

Accordingly, the judgment of the district court is affirmed.

NOTES AND PROBLEMS

1. Martino asserted that the contractual provision barring his relatives from owning competing franchises violated the U.S. antitrust laws.
   a. Did any court ever rule on the merits of that contention?
   b. If not, why was the claim barred?
2. *Martino* analyzes two problems: the operation of Rule 13(a) and the operation of the "common law compulsory counterclaim" in the absence of Rule 13(a).
   a. First work through the analysis of Rule 13(a). If Rule 13(a) applied to this case, why would it have barred the second claim?
   b. Why didn't Rule 13(a) apply?
3. If Rule 13(a) does not apply, why is the second claim barred?
   a. The *Martino* court refers to "a narrowly defined class of common law 'compulsory counterclaims.' " The court appears to mean that in some cases the common law of claim preclusion operates *as if* the defendant had omitted a compulsory counterclaim.

b. Is it more accurate to say that the plaintiff lost the antitrust claim not because of failure to plead it but because the previous judgment upholding termination of the lease would be inconsistent with a later finding that the termination would violate the antitrust laws?

c. If the argument implied in Note 3b is valid, then the doctrines of claim preclusion are at least in part concerned not just with efficiency but with preventing inconsistent judgments.

4. Consent judgments sometimes recite that the agreement is without prejudice to the parties' other legal rights, but one must choose language with care. In Coker v. Jay Hambridge Art Foundation, 144 Ga. App. 660, 242 S.E.2d 323 (1978), the defendant foundation had sought in a previous action to enjoin the present plaintiffs from occupying a cottage on the defendant's property. The previous case was settled with an agreement that an injunction would issue after one month. The agreement further recited that "nothing herein contained shall preclude either party from pursuing against the other any legal remedy the respective parties hereto may have, if any." In the cited action plaintiffs sued the defendant foundation on their employment contract. It was admitted that the claim would have been compulsory but for the language just quoted. The Georgia Court of Appeals held the second action was barred and upheld the trial court's interpretation of the language as allowing the present plaintiffs to have asserted their contract claim as a counterclaim in the original suit but not as a claim in a separate action. Should the intent of the parties control? If so, is it likely that the parties would actually intend, without saying, that the employment issue be raised in the first action but not in a second?

2. Between the "Same" Parties

Most commonly, claim preclusion will operate only between those who were the parties to both the first and second lawsuits; by contrast, different parties possess different claims for preclusion purposes, even when those claims arise out of the same transaction. The proposition that claim preclusion operates only between the same parties has, however, several exceptions. Imagine, for example, that the owner of Suburbanacre sues Neighbor for trespass, and the court rules that Neighbor enjoys a permanent easement over Owner's land. If Owner sells Suburbanacre to Buyer, Buyer will be bound by the judgment, even though he was not a party to the action. Courts go further than this: they sometimes note that it is possible for someone not formally named as a party to be so closely connected to a suit that it is appropriate to treat her as if she were named. When they do so, they often describe the party bound as "in privity" with the party to the first suit. That term is harmless as long as one understands that it merely expresses the conclusion that the person whose name was not on the caption of the first case should nevertheless be bound. When that should happen is the issue in the next case.

Searle Brothers v. Searle
588 P.2d 689 (Utah 1978)

[Edlean Searle sued Woodey Searle for a divorce. In that case, the court determined that a piece of property known as the Slaugh House, which was recorded in Woodey's name, was part of the marital property; Woodey argued that he had a one-half interest in the property and that the other half was owned by a partnership with his sons as partners. The court awarded the entire property to Edlean.

This action was brought against Edlean by the partnership (Searle Bros.), which claimed an undivided one-half interest in Slaugh House. It was alleged that Slaugh House had been paid for with partnership funds. The trial court held that claim and issue preclusion barred this action.]

ELLETT, C.J.:

Appellants [the partnership] have appealed this judgment, claiming that the trial court erred in that the appellants were not parties to the divorce action and could not be bound by the decree entered therein.

In general, a divorce decree, like other final judgments, is conclusive as to parties and their privies and operates as a bar to any subsequent action. In order for res judicata to apply, both suits must involve the same parties or their privies and also the same cause of action; and this precludes the relitigation of all issues that could have been litigated as well as those that were, in fact, litigated in the prior action. If the subsequent suit involves different parties, those parties cannot be bound by the prior judgment.

Collateral estoppel, on the other hand, arises from a different cause of action and prevents parties or their privies from relitigating facts and issues in the second suit that were fully litigated in the first suit. This means that the plea of collateral estoppel can be asserted only against a party in the subsequent suit who was also a party or in privity with a party in the prior suit.

In Bernhard v. Bank of America Natl. Trust & Savings Assoc. the California Supreme Court considered the question of the applicability of res judicata as a basis for applying the collateral estoppel doctrine and identified the following three tests as being determinative:

1. Was the issue decided in the prior adjudication identical with the one presented in the action in question?
2. Was there a final judgment on the merits?
3. Was the party against whom the plea is asserted a party or in privity with a party to the prior adjudication?

In a subsequent opinion, the California Supreme Court recognized the necessity for a fourth test: "Was the issue in the first case competently, fully, and fairly litigated?" These four tests have been adopted by the majority of jurisdictions as the correct standard to apply. As to the second test above, there is no dispute that the divorce decree rendered in the former suit was a final judgment on the merits. Points One and Four will be discussed infra. Under the third test, it is clear that the appellants in this action were not parties to the first action; hence, the only way they can be barred or estopped from pursuing the second suit is if they were "in privity" with the parties to the divorce action.

The legal definition of a person in privity with another, is a person so identified in interest with another that he represents the same legal right. This includes a mutual or successive relationship to rights in property. Our Court has said that as applied to judgments or decrees of court, privity means "one whose interest has been legally represented at the time."

In the case before us, appellants' interest was neither mutual nor successive. They claim no part of the interest owned by Woodey B. Searle, but assert their own, independent and separate partnership interest in 50 percent of the property involved. The rights are similar but not identical. The property interest arose before the commencement of the first action, not subsequent thereto, so that appellants cannot be regarded as in privity and subject to the judgment rendered therein. Furthermore, under U.C.A. [Utah Code Ann.], 1953, as amended, 48-1-22(1), partners are co-owners of specific partnership property which is directly opposite to successive interests.

The first and fourth tests previously outlined also do not permit the application of collateral estoppel in this case. The partnership interest was not legally represented in the prior divorce suit. Woodey B. Searle, the defendant in the prior action, was acting in his individual capacity as the husband of the plaintiff and was not acting in a representative capacity for the partnership. Respondent urges that Woodey B. Searle was acting as *agent* for the partnership; hence, the partnership is bound by his action or inaction in the prior litigation. However, the general rule is that agents and principals do not have any mutual or successive relationship to rights of property and are not, as a consequence thereof, in privity with each other. Therefore, the principal is not bound by any judgment obtained against an agent, unless the principal became a party or privy thereto by actually and openly defending the action.

The right to intervene as a party in the prior suit does not bind the party in the subsequent suit where he failed to so intervene. 46 Am. Jur. 2d, Judgments, Sec. 530 discusses this point as follows:

> A party to the principal case is regarded as a stranger to the judgment rendered in the previous action where he was not directly interested in the subject matter thereof, and had no right to make defense, adduce testimony, cross-examine witnesses, control the proceedings or appeal from the judgment, even though he could have made himself a party to the previous action. The right to intervene in an action does not, in the absence of its exercise, subject one possessing it to the risk of being bound by the result of the litigation, under the doctrine of res judicata. . . .

The foregoing rule has been adopted by this Court.[13]

Collateral estoppel is not available to defeat appellants' claim since the partners were not made parties to the first suit and there is not sufficient evidence in the record to show that the interest of the partnership in the "Slaugh House" was ever litigated. The standard rule was reiterated by this Court earlier this year in Ruffinengo v. Miller when we said: "Collateral estoppel is not a defense against a litigant who was not a party to the action and judgment claimed to have created an estoppel.". . .

Appellants cannot be bound by the decree entered in the previous suit nor are they estopped from litigating their own claim against the property in a subsequent suit since they were not parties or privies in the first action, and the issue raised in the second action was never litigated in the prior proceeding. The trial court erred in holding that the doctrines of res judicata and collateral estoppel barred the appellants from pursuing their suit. In making this ruling, we do not express an opinion as to whether or not the property in question was an asset of the partnership.

The judgment is reversed and remanded for trial. Costs are awarded to appellants.

WILKINS and HALL, JJ., concur.

---

13. [C]f. also Rule 19(b), Utah Rules of Civil Procedure which provides that persons who ought to be made parties but who are nonetheless outside the jurisdiction of the court, are not affected by any judgment rendered therein.

CROCKETT, J. (dissenting):

I am unable to agree with the main opinion that the trial court erred when it held that the doctrine of collateral estoppel barred the plaintiffs. It is my judgment that the ruling was in conformity with principles of equity and justice.

It is to be conceded that the judgment in the divorce action would not normally bar the plaintiffs' action here because they were not parties thereto. However, upon a survey of the total circumstances I think the trial court was justified in its ruling. The main opinion correctly indicates that the doctrine of collateral estoppel is applicable when it is shown that: (1) the prior judgment is on the same issue and the same facts; (2) the issue thus litigated was essential to support the prior judgment; and (3) that it was between parties who were the same, or in privity with them.

As to (1) there can be no question but that this "Slaugh House," which is the subject of this suit, was one of the assets about which there was dispute in the divorce proceeding. Therein counsel for the plaintiffs' father, Woodey B. Searle, asserted that the Slaugh House property was owned one-half by the parties and the other half by the parties' sons as a result of a claimed partnership between the father and the sons (these plaintiffs). He also urged that the father should be awarded that property.

Neither is there any question as to (2) above because it is obvious that determination as to the ownership of the house was a predicate to awarding it to the mother (plaintiff therein Edlean Searle).

The more critical question is to whether these plaintiffs, the sons of the parties to the divorce action, were sufficiently involved and interested therein that they should properly be regarded as parties in privity thereto.

It appears that this matter was submitted to the trial court on the basis of the testimony given in the divorce action. The court's order recited that "The transcript of testimony of the previous divorce action between the plaintiff's parents was referred to" and that "after full consideration . . . the court further finds that the doctrine of collateral estoppel . . . is a bar to plaintiff's claim." It is incontestably plain that the members of the family, including the plaintiffs herein, were actively involved in that suit, which in turn involved whatever interest any of them had in the family assets. Further, they were fully aware of the adverse claims being asserted to the Slaugh House which is the subject of this suit. Two of the sons, Randy and Rhett, were called to testify on behalf of their father in that trial.

It is not contended that there was ever any written partnership agreement. In his testimony plaintiff Rhett Searle characterized it as an informal arrangement. The father stated that this Slaugh House had been purchased with funds of such a partnership and that its being recorded in his name only was but an oversight. He also stated that he kept the rents collected therefrom in an account which he could spend on his own as he desired, but with the intention of putting it back.

This is a situation where the plaintiffs are seeking the aid of equity to assert ownership in property which stood of record only in their father's name. Even under the facts as contended by them, he was the managing partner of the claimed partnership, who had control of the property in dispute and the income therefrom; and he thus should be regarded as representing and protecting whatever interests they and the claimed partnership had therein.[2] Further, plaintiffs themselves were fully aware of the disputation concerning the ownership of this property. They actively participated in that lawsuit, but asserted no claim for themselves. Instead of doing so, they stood by until the determination was made adverse to their father's (and their own) interests. Such claim as they have in contesting the record title to the property is based solely upon supposed oral declarations made within the family, and self-serving declarations at that.

The purpose of the doctrine of collateral estoppel is to protect a party from being subjected to harassment by being compelled to litigate the same controversy more than once. This case impresses me as being a very good example of a situation where the trial court was justified in applying that doctrine and, consistent therewith, concluding that in equity and good conscience the plaintiffs should now be estopped from seeking the relief they asked against their mother.

For the reasons stated above I would affirm the dismissal of the case. MAUGHAN, J., concurs in the views expressed in the dissenting opinion of CROCKETT, J.

NOTES AND PROBLEMS

1. The majority opinion speaks both in terms of res judicata (claim preclusion) and collateral estoppel (issue preclusion). One can make an argument for both labels. On the one hand, claim preclusion requires an identity of causes of action, and different parties are generally thought to have different causes of action. Thus one might conclude that claim preclusion is not the question and that issue preclusion must be. On the other hand, if the parties to the present litigation were in fact in privity with those to the former litigation, one can think of them as legally identical, eliminating the objection to the claim preclusion label.

2. That family relationship is one factor which may be considered in determining whether privity exists, see 46 Am. Jur. 2d, Judgments, Section 532 and cases cited therein.

As far as privity is concerned, the label doesn't matter. Thus the following Notes freely mix cases referring to claim preclusion and issue preclusion. A detailed consideration of issue preclusion, which comes later in the chapter, should not be necessary to understand the cases.

2. We do not ordinarily preclude witnesses from bringing claims similar to those in the case in which they testified. For example, if two cars collide and Passenger testifies when Driver One sues Driver Two, Passenger remains free to bring her own lawsuit.

a. The Searle brothers were asserting that they were, in effect, just like Passenger — mere witnesses in the first lawsuit who should not be barred from bringing a suit on their own behalf. What does that characterization leave out?

b. Can the brothers make convincing arguments that they did not have an opportunity to litigate fully the question of ownership in the first action? As nonparties, could they have appealed the first judgment?

3. The case holds that Randy and Rhett can sue their mother. If the outcome of that suit matches the prior one — ruling that Slaugh House was Woodey's sole property — there is no problem except the added expense to Edlean from having to litigate twice.

a. Suppose, however, that the second court sides with the sons. Edlean, who now has less property than the first court awarded her, seeks to reopen the marital property decree to have Woodey turn over assets matching the half interest in Slaugh House of which she has now been deprived. In this action Woodey can successfully argue that he is not bound by the judgment in the litigation between Edlean and the two sons. Explain why.

b. Now suppose that Edlean's lawyer had seen this train wreck of litigation approaching and realized that what was needed was a proceeding in which all four family members were parties. That can't be done in a divorce action; however interested children may be in such litigation, they are not parties. Can you construct a lawsuit to which all four would be parties — a suit settling the ownership of the property — whose results could then be used in the marital property litigation?

4. *Searle* stands for the proposition that a strong legal relationship is required to bind someone to a judgment in a case to which he was not a party. The Supreme Court has reminded us that this proposition has a constitutional dimension. Richards v. Jefferson County, 517 U.S. 793 (1996), arose from an Alabama county's imposition of a "occupation tax" to finance construction of a new civic center. Several lawsuits challenging the legality of the tax were filed. The first of these, Bedingfield v. Jefferson County, 520 So. 2d 1270 (Ala. 1988), went to the Alabama Supreme Court, which upheld the tax. When Richards filed a second action,

raising federal law challenges to the tax, the Alabama Supreme Court held "that the federal chaims as well as the state claims were barred by the adjudication in *Bedingfield* . . . [because a] judgment is generally 'res judicata not only as to all matters litigated and decided by it, but as to all relevant issues which could have been but were not raised and litigated in the suit,'" quoting Jefferson County v. Richards, 662 So. 2d 1127 (Ala. 1995).

a. As a quick review, explain why the Alabama Supreme Court was on solid ground in this part of its ruling. Which case in this chapter is most squarely on point?

b. The U.S. Supreme Court disagreed: Even though the Alabama Court was entirely conventional in its statement of claim preclusion doctrine, the U.S. Supreme Court reversed. It did so because Alabama had applied claim preclusion not to the original parties in the suit but to new parties. The Alabama Supreme Court had applied claim preclusion to new plaintiffs on the grounds that there was "substantial identity of the parties" to the first and second lawsuits — *Bedingfield* and *Richards*.

> State courts are generally free to develop their own rules for protecting against the relitigation of common issues or the piecemeal resolution of disputes. We have long held, however, that extreme applications of the doctrine of res judicata may be inconsistent with a federal right that is "fundamental in character." . . .
>
> The limits on a state court's power to develop estoppel rules reflect the general consensus "'in Anglo-American jurisprudence that one is not bound by a judgment in personam in a litigation in which he is not designated as a party or to which he has not been made a party by service of process.' Hansberry v. Lee, [infra page 982] . . . This rule is part of our 'deep-rooted historic tradition that everyone should have his own day in court.'" Martin v. Wilks, [infra page 948]. . . .
>
> Of course, these principles do not always require one to have been a party to a judgment in order to be bound by it. Most notably, there is an exception when it can be said that there is "privity" between a party to the second case and a party who is bound by an earlier judgment. For example, a judgment that is binding on a guardian or trustee may also bind the ward or the beneficiaries of a trust. Moreover, although there are clearly constitutional limits on the "privity" exception, the term "privity" is now used to describe various relationships between litigants that would not have come within the traditional definition of that term. See generally Restatement (Second) of Judgments, ch. 4 (1980). . . .
>
> We begin by noting that the parties to the *Bedingfield* case failed to provide petitioners with any notice that a suit was pending which would conclusively resolve their legal rights. That failure is troubling because, as we explained in Mullane v. Central Hanover Bank & Trust Co. [supra

page 175], the right to be heard ensured by the guarantee of due process "has little reality or worth unless one is informed that the matter is pending and can choose for himself whether to appear or default, acquiesce or contest.". . .

Nevertheless, respondents ask us to excuse the lack of notice on the ground that petitioners, as the Alabama Supreme Court concluded, were adequately represented in *Bedingfield*. . . .

Even assuming that our opinion in *Hansberry* may be read to leave open the possibility that in some class suits adequate representation might cure a lack of notice, it may not be read to permit the application of res judicata here. Our opinion explained that a prior proceeding, to have binding effect on absent parties, would at least have to be "so devised and applied as to insure that those present are of the same class as those absent and that the litigation is so conducted as to insure the full and fair consideration of the common issue." 311 U.S. at 43. It is plain that the *Bedingfield* action, like the prior proceeding in *Hansberry* itself, does not fit such a description. . . .

. . . [T]here is no reason to suppose that the *Bedingfield* court took care to protect the interests of petitioners in the manner suggested in *Hansberry*. Nor is there any reason to suppose that the individual taxpayers in *Bedingfield* understood their suit to be on behalf of absent county taxpayers. Thus, to contend that the plaintiffs in *Bedingfield* somehow represented petitioners, let alone represented them in a constitutionally adequate manner, would be "to attribute to them a power that it cannot be said that they had assumed to exercise." *Hansberry*, 311 U.S. at 46. . . .

Of course, we are aware that governmental and private entities have substantial interests in the prompt and determinative resolution of challenges to important legislation. We do not agree with the Alabama Supreme Court, however, that, given the amount of money at stake, respondents were entitled to rely on the assumption that the *Bedingfield* action "authoritatively established" the constitutionality of the tax. A state court's freedom to rely on prior precedent in rejecting a litigant's claims does not afford it similar freedom to bind a litigant to a prior judgment to which he was not a party. That general rule clearly applies when a taxpayer seeks a hearing to prevent the State from subjecting him to a levy in violation of the Federal Constitution.

Id. at 797-805.

c. First focus on the implication of the holding in *Richards*. At a minimum it means that Randy and Rhett Searle, had the Utah Supreme Court not decided in their favor, could have appealed to the U.S. Supreme Court on due process grounds (assuming, of course, they had not waived that contention by failing to raise it below). *Richards* does not, of course, hold that the Searle brothers would have prevailed on such an appeal. They had notice of the prior suit, and the argument that their father had represented them was much stronger than for the litigants in *Richards*. The difficult question is where the line between constitutional and unconstitutional representation lies.

5. As *Richards* notes, courts regularly bind nonparties to judgments in a number of circumstances. Three broadly defined situations result in binding a nonparty to the results of a lawsuit. Explain whether and why each of these passes the test of due process.

a. *Substantive legal relationships.* Successive owners of property supply a common example. Alice owns Blackacre. During her ownership a lawsuit between her and Ben establishes that Ben has a prescriptive easement in Blackacre. Ben records that judgment on the title of Blackacre. When Caroline buys Blackacre, she takes subject to the easement. Restatement 2d, Judgments §44.

Other such substantive relationships can lead to similar results. In Albright v. R.J. Reynolds Tobacco Co., 463 F. Supp. 1220 (W.D. Pa. 1979), the court held that an action for injuries (brought by a person who later died) was the same claim as a wrongful death action brought by the person's survivors. The court further decided that the administrator of the decedent's estate was in privity with the decedent, so that the administrator's wrongful death action was barred by the decedent's previous loss of an action against the same defendant for the same acts causing injury. Other such substantive relationships include beneficiary and trustee and heirs and executors of estates. By contrast, in Arsenault v. Carrier, 390 A.2d 1048 (Me. 1978), a child was allowed to sue his father for support through his mother as "next friend" even though the mother had previously settled an action against the father. The rights of the mother and child for support were held to be distinct.

Co-ownership, joint obligation, vicarious liability (like that of an employer for the acts of an employee), and indemnification present some special problems. But the principles are the same as with successive owners of property: *If* the substantive law of the relationship treats A as a substitute for B, B will be bound by the results of a lawsuit in which A participated. Thus, in Jones v. Bradley, 366 So. 2d 1266 (Fla. Dist. Ct. App. 1979), an insurance company was barred from suing an alleged tortfeasor on a subrogation theory after the insured, to whom the company was subrogated, had previously lost an action against the tortfeasor.

b. *Express agreement to be bound by a decision to which one is not a party.* Ann and Ben, both passengers in a car, are injured in a collision with a vehicle driven by Charles, against whom they bring separate lawsuits. In return for Charles's agreement not to contest the extent of her injuries, Ann agrees to be bound by the court's determination of

Charles's liability in the suit brought by Ben. Restatement (Second) of Judgments §40.

c. *Instances of "procedural representation."* In contrast to the previous categories, here the binding effect is the result not of the substantive law or agreement, but of something that happens in the lawsuit itself. Examples include guardians ad litem appointed by the court to represent an incompetent or minor, class actions (considered at length in the next chapter), and an ephemeral category sometimes called "virtual representation."

Classically, courts of equity used virtual representation to determine future or contingent interests in property. Suppose many contingent beneficiaries of a trust, all with identical interests. It may be impossible to locate or identify all of them. If a sufficient number can be identified and appear in the suit to determine their interests, the others will be bound because they are "virtually represented." In re Estate of Lange, 75 N.J. 464, 383 A.2d 1130 (1978) (potential takers from an estate who could not be identified and who might not even have been born at the time of litigation were represented by other members of the same class of takers who could be identified at the time of litigation). See Mullane v. Central Hanover Bank & Trust, supra page 175.

Courts have occasionally used the term "virtual representation" to describe another situation, in which someone, though not a party to a lawsuit, so guides and controls it that a court treats him as if he were a party. For example, in Rynsburger v. Dairymen's Fertilizer Cooperative, 266 Cal. App. 2d 269, 72 Cal. Rptr. 102 (1968), the court barred a homeowners' group from bringing an action to enjoin an alleged nuisance when the group had earlier gathered evidence and requested that the city bring a similar action and where some of the group's members had testified in the city's action. In Montana v. United States, 440 U.S. 147 (1979), the United States was held to be bound by a previous judgment upholding the constitutionality of a state tax imposed on contractors for public but not private construction projects. The United States was bound, the Court ruled, because the issues were the same and the previous litigation (brought by a contractor) had been financed and controlled by the United States. Is *Searle* distinguishable?

3. After a Final Judgment

It is sometimes said that the doctrine of claim preclusion requires a prior final judgment. Like the proposition that claim preclusion applies only between the same parties, the final judgment requirement does not receive a completely literal interpretation. Thus, certain kinds of administrative determinations may be entitled to claim-preclusion effect. For example, see South Bend Federation of Teachers v. National Education Association, 180 Ind. App. 299, 389 N.E.2d 23 (1979).

A more important question involving finality is the effect of an appeal on a judgment's status. The usual rule is that a judgment is final even though an appeal is pending; in a few states, however, the mere pendency of an appeal voids a judgment. What should be done if a judgment is given claim-preclusion effect and then reversed on appeal? Some courts solve the problem by postponing the decision on claim preclusion until the appeal is resolved. For another approach see Rule 60(b)(5). Should the trial in the second action go forward although the issue of claim preclusion is being held in abeyance?

4. After a Judgment "on the Merits"

Not all final judgments, even though they involve the same claim and the same parties, receive preclusive effect. For example, all agree that a judgment after a full trial is undoubtedly entitled to preclusive effect. Short of that, however, when ought preclusive effect to attach? The problem is difficult because courts might want to assign preclusive effect to a judgment for at least two quite different reasons. One reason, of course, is that the court considered and decided the merits of the lawsuit. A different reason would be that the party had misbehaved (for example, refused to obey court orders) and the court dismissed the suit as a sanction; such a dismissal would have nothing to do with the merits of the complaint, but the sanction would be futile unless it barred the refiling of the suit. Unfortunately, courts sometimes discuss this problem by stating that preclusive effect ought to attach only to judgments "on the merits." This phrase conceals more than it explains, because it entirely begs the real question: For what reasons should we attach preclusive effect to a judgment?

NOTES AND PROBLEMS

1. As a matter of principle, which of the following stages of litigation ought to preclude filing of a second suit by the same party on the same claim?
   a. Full jury trial.
   b. Directed verdict.

c. Summary judgment.

d. Dismissal after a Rule 12(b)(6) motion for failure to state a claim.

e. Dismissal after a Rule 12(b)(2) motion for want of personal jurisdiction.

f. Dismissal for failure to prosecute.

2. Consider whether Rule 41 changes your answers to the previous Note. Rule 41(b) provides:

> Unless the court in its order for dismissal otherwise specifies, a dismissal under this subdivision and any dismissal not provided for in this rule, other than a dismissal for lack of jurisdiction, for improper venue, or for failure to join a party under Rule 19, operates as an adjudication on the merits.

3. How did you answer problem 1(d)? That problem — how to treat a judgment following a dismissal for failure to state a claim upon which relief can be granted under Rule 12(b)(6) — creates difficulties, which arise because one can see such a dismissal in two ways. On the one hand, it can be for essentially formal reasons: The plaintiff's lawyer forgot that one must allege an agreement as part of a breach of contract suit. If the underlying facts suggest an agreement, it seems unjust to preclude when a sentence added to the pleading would cure the problem. On the other hand, if the plaintiff's lawyer has alleged all that can truthfully be alleged and the complaint is still dismissed, isn't that a statement about the merits of a claim?

a. Is the question answered for the federal courts by Rule 41(b)? Does the argument that a complaint should not be dismissed for failure to state a claim unless there is no possible basis for relief have anything to do with the issue? In Federated Department Stores v. Moitie, 452 U.S. 394 (1981), the Supreme Court wrote a footnote that, in its entirety, reads: "The dismissal for failure to state a claim under Fed. Rule Civ. Proc. 12(b)(6) is a 'judgment on the merits.' " Id. at 399 n.3. The statement was necessary to the decision of the case and is thus a holding, but it was unexplained and unelaborated.

b. A further justification for treating Rule 12(b)(6) dismissals as claim-preclusive is the ease of amendment. It is axiomatic that a trial court should not dismiss a pleading for failure to state a claim without granting plaintiff at least one leave to amend. Suppose plaintiff does amend, and the trial court nevertheless dismisses the amended complaint. Is the opportunity to amend — after being instructed by the trial court what was wrong with the original complaint — a sufficient assurance that plaintiff has stated any possible claim, and therefore justification for assigning preclusive effect?

c. Not all states adhere to the same rule. For example, see In re Estate of Cochrane, 72 Ill. App. 3d 812, 391 N.E.2d 35 (1979) (under Illinois procedural law, which differs somewhat from the Federal Rules, dismissal for failure to plead enough facts to state a claim does not bar a second suit with the necessary facts added; presumably it would bar bringing a suit based on an identical complaint); Keidatz v. Albany, 39 Cal. 2d 826, 249 P. 2d 264 (1952) (dismissal on demurrer bars subsequent action on complaint alleging same facts but does not bar claim raising new issues or new facts in support of same claim). Is it possible to decide which rule is preferable without taking into account the pleading regime of the jurisdiction in question?

4. Finally, test the implicit theory developed in the preceding questions with the issue in the next case: Should a court assign preclusive effect to a dismissal based solely on failure to comply with discovery orders?

Gargallo v. Merrill, Lynch, Pierce, Fenner & Smith
918 F.2d 658 (6th Cir. 1990)

RYAN, J.

This case presents the interesting dual questions 1) whether a federal court must apply federal or state claim preclusion law in deciding 2) whether a prior state court judgment upon subject matter over which only a federal court has jurisdiction is a bar to a subsequent federal court claim upon the identical cause of action. . . . The district court dismissed the suit below on grounds of res judicata as to Merrill Lynch. . . .

I

Miguel Gargallo opened a "margin brokerage account" with Merrill Lynch in 1976. He maintained the account until 1980, when his investments apparently went awry and losses occurred, resulting in a debt of some $17,000 owed to Merrill Lynch. . . . When the obligation was not paid, the brokerage firm filed suit for collection in the Court of Common Pleas, Franklin County, Ohio. In response, Mr. Gargallo filed an answer and counterclaim against Merrill Lynch, alleging that Merrill Lynch caused his losses through "negligence, misrepresentations, and churning," and that the firm had violated . . . federal securities laws. After a considerable history of discovery difficulties, the state court dismissed Mr. Gargallo's counterclaim "with prejudice," citing Ohio Civil Rule 37 [substantially identical to Federal Rule 37], for refusal to comply with Merrill Lynch's discovery requests and the court's discovery orders. . . .

Mr. Gargallo . . . then filed a complaint in the United States District Court, Southern District of Ohio, charging Merrill Lynch and its account executive, Larry Tyree, with violating [federal securities laws] . . . based on the same transactions at issue in the state litigation. After preparing a thoughtful written opinion, the district court dismissed the suit against Merrill Lynch on res judicata grounds, finding that the "issues, facts and evidence to sustain this action are identical to the claims asserted [against the brokerage firm] in [Mr. Gargallo's] counterclaim that was dismissed with prejudice by the state court." This appeal followed.

II

There is no dispute in this case about the essential facts relating to the summary judgment, and the ultimate issue is: whether the district court correctly dismissed the plaintiff's claims on res judicata . . . grounds. . . .

A. Claim Preclusion

The federal securities law violations asserted against Merrill Lynch . . . in this litigation are the same, for all practical purposes, as those Mr. Gargallo previously asserted in the counterclaim he filed in the Franklin County court. For reasons we shall discuss shortly, Ohio claim preclusion law ultimately determines the outcome of this case. Consequently, we must decide whether the Franklin County court judgment dismissing Mr. Gargallo's first lawsuit would operate as a bar, under Ohio claim preclusion rules, to the action brought in the district court, now under review, had it been brought in an Ohio court. . . .

In Ohio, the requirements for application of the doctrine of claim preclusion, or res judicata as the earlier Ohio court termed it, are the same as those applicable in a federal court:

> The doctrine of res judicata is that an existing final judgment rendered upon the merits, without fraud or collusion, by a court of competent jurisdiction, is conclusive of rights, questions and facts in issue, as to the parties and their privies, in all other actions in the same or any other judicial tribunal of concurrent jurisdiction.

Norwood v. McDonald, 142 Ohio St. 299, 305, 52 N.E.2d 67, 71 (1943).

Under Ohio law, the dismissal with prejudice of Mr. Gargallo's Common Pleas Court counterclaim for noncompliance with Ohio's Civil Rule 37 was a "final judgment rendered upon the merits."[1]

. . . [W]hether a final judgment upon one claim precludes the filing of another claim in Ohio depends on whether the second claim embodies the same cause of action as the first. . . . Mr. Gargallo's suit against the defendants in the district court complained of the same transactions, alleged violation of the same federal securities law, and added alleged violations of certain Securities and Exchange Commission regulations. We agree with the district court that the "issues, facts, and evidence to sustain this action are identical to the claims asserted . . . in [plaintiff's state] counterclaim," and we are satisfied that the federal claim or cause of action giving rise to this appeal is the same claim or cause of action that was asserted in the counterclaim dismissed in the state court litigation.

Thus, we have no question that, absent any regard for subject matter jurisdiction, Ohio claim preclusion law would bar the claim asserted in Mr. Gargallo's district court complaint had it been filed in an Ohio court.

B.   Federal Exclusivity

However, the district court in which plaintiff brought his claim is not an Ohio court but a federal tribunal. Consequently, we are faced with the more difficult issue of whether a federal district court may give claim preclusive effect to an Ohio judgment regarding federal securities laws that are within the exclusive jurisdiction of the federal courts. The first rule in determining whether a prior state court judgment has preclusive effect in a federal court is that the full faith and credit statute, 28 U.S.C. §1738,[3] requires a federal court to give a state court

---

1. In *Austin* [v. Miami Valley Hosp, 483 N.E.2d. 1185 (Ohio Ct. App. 1984)], the Court of Appeals for Montgomery County, Ohio, was asked whether a medical malpractice claim filed May 20, 1983, against Miami Valley and one of its doctors was barred by . . . the doctrine of res judicata since an identical action between the same parties was dismissed for discovery noncompliance on February 17, 1981 . . ., the court said:

> Even if the prior dismissal was premised on Civ. R. 37 for appellant's failure to comply with the discovery order, Civ. R. 41(B)(3) states the effect of such a dismissal is an adjudication on the merits unless the trial court expressly states otherwise in its dismissal entry. The dismissal entry in the instant case did not include the language "otherwise than upon the merits" or "without prejudice."

Consequently, that court held that the trial court did not err in dismissing the second claim as barred by the statute of limitations and the doctrine of res judicata.

3. In pertinent part, 28 U.S.C. §1738 provides that "the Acts of the legislature of any State, Territory, or Possession of the United States" and "the records and judicial proceedings of any court of any such State, Territory or Possession . . . shall have the same full faith and credit in every court within the United States and its Territories and Possessions as they have by law or usage in the courts of such State, Territory or Possession from which they are taken."

judgment the same preclusive effect such judgment would have in a state court. . . .

In Marrese v. [American] Academy of Orthopaedic Surgeons, 470 U.S. 373 (1985), the Court [held] . . . that federal courts are required under 28 U.S.C. §1738 to determine the preclusive effect of prior state court judgments, pursuant to the law of the state in which the judgment was entered, even as to claims within the exclusive jurisdiction of the federal courts. *Marrese* requires, therefore, that a federal court must determine whether to give claim preclusive effect to a state court judgment upon a cause of action over which the state court had no subject matter jurisdiction by determining whether the state court would give preclusive effect to such a judgment. . . .

Ohio appears to subscribe to the Restatement (Second) of Judgments position that a judgment rendered by a court lacking subject matter jurisdiction ought not be given preclusive effect. . . . It seems clear, therefore, that in Ohio a final judgment by a court of that state, upon a cause of action over which the adjudicating court had no subject matter jurisdiction, does not have claim preclusive effect in any subsequent proceedings. . . .

In summary, we hold that the Ohio court judgment, dismissing, with prejudice, Mr. Gargallo's federal securities law claims against Merrill Lynch . . . may not be given claim preclusive effect in a subsequent federal court action asserting those same claims because Ohio courts would not give claim preclusive effect to a prior final judgment upon a cause of action over which the Ohio court had no subject matter jurisdiction. . . .

[Reversed and remanded.]

NOTES AND PROBLEMS

1. *Gargallo* has two aspects: (1) whether the original dismissal was "on the merits" for purposes of claim preclusion; and (2) how the jurisdictional defect in the first proceeding ought to affect claim preclusion.

2. Start with the first aspect. Cases like *Gargallo* are easier to understand if one does not become distracted by the misleading phrase "on the merits."

a. Explain why it is fair — and probably necessary — to assign pre-clusive effect to the dismissal for failure to comply with discovery orders.

b. Explain why it is fair to do so although no one in his right mind would say that the prior suit determined the merits of Gargallo's claim in the ordinary sense of that phrase.

3. To understand the force of the principle illustrated in *Gargallo*, suppose that Mr. Gargallo had not waited to be sued by his brokerage and had instead brought his federal securities claims against Merrill, Lynch in a federal court. Further imagine that Mr. Gargallo had been as uncooperative in discovery in federal court as he was in the Ohio courts and suffered a dismissal under Rules 37 and 41 for failure to comply with discovery orders. Now suppose he refiled that suit in federal court — what result?

4. Turn now to the jurisdictional defect in Gargallo's state court counterclaim. Would it be fair to say that Mr. Gargallo's ignorance (in filing his federal securities claim in the wrong court) saved him from the consequences of his behavior (failure to comply with discovery)? The underlying principle may be just — is the result?

5. What procedures did defendant use to raise its argument of claim preclusion?

a. Former adjudication is an affirmative defense. See Rule 8(c).

b. Having raised this defense, how did defendant get a judicial ruling on the question of whether the first suit precluded the second?

c. Why is such a case decided on a motion for summary judgment rather than on the pleadings? What "facts" are needed for the court to decide if the claim is precluded?

B.   Issue Preclusion

Issue preclusion has a narrower but deeper bite than claim preclusion. If the conditions for claim preclusion are met, a party will find *all* her contentions barred from relitigation — those she actually advanced in the first case as well as those that she did not advance. The preclusive effect, however, extends only to the same claim. By contrast, issue preclusion bars from relitigation only those issues actually litigated and determined. But they will be barred from relitigation in all subsequent claims between the parties — and, according to recent doctrine, in some claims that do not involve both parties.

The black letter of issue preclusion is simple:

> When [1] an issue of fact or law is [2] actually litigated and determined by [3] a valid and final judgment, and [4] the determination is essential to the judgment, the determination is conclusive in a subsequent action between the parties, whether on the same or a different claim.*

---

* Restatement (Second) of Judgments §27.

Each of these four conditions, however, involves some difficulties that we shall examine in turn. We shall first look briefly at what it means for an issue to be the same in successive cases. Second comes an exploration of the boundaries between issue and claim preclusion and an effort to define the conditions under which one can say that an issue has been "actually litigated and determined." Then we examine the meaning of "essentiality to the judgment." Finally, we turn to a body of doctrine that severely limits the last of the stated conditions — that the subsequent case be "between the parties."

1. The Same Issue

A threshold question in all issue-preclusion cases will be the identity of the issue to be precluded. Sometimes the analysis of that question will be easy. For example, suppose the United States sues Student civilly, seeking nonpayment of two student loans, both signed on the same day and containing identical and allegedly fraudulent statements. Student defends on the grounds that the statements in the loan documents are true. If Student loses the first lawsuit, the fraudulence of the statements in question will be precluded in the second suit as well.

But matters can be subtler. Suppose that in the student loan lawsuits, the government prevails, establishing fraudulent misstatements. The United States then prosecutes Student criminally, asserting that he obtained the loans fraudulently. Student defends on grounds that the statements are true. Does the government's previous victory in the civil lawsuit preclude Student from his defense? No: Civil and criminal proceedings operate under different burdens of proof. To prevail, as the government did, on a civil burden of preponderance of the evidence does not mean that one can establish the same issue beyond a reasonable doubt. One must, then, build into one's definition of the "issue" not only its substantive contours but the procedural conditions under which it was determined.

NOTES AND PROBLEMS

1. The federal government criminally prosecutes an IRS agent, accusing her of stealing tax revenues. She is acquitted. The government then sues Agent in a civil suit to recover funds allegedly embezzled in the same criminal acts. Agent seeks to invoke preclusion on the grounds that the previous case demonstrates the acts did not occur. Preclusion?

2. Reverse the order of the civil and criminal actions in the preceding example. Suppose the civil action came first, and the government prevailed, winning a judgment against Agent on the ground that she had embezzled funds. The government now prosecutes Agent criminally, charging her with the same acts of embezzlement. Why doesn't the first case preclude Agent from relitigating the question of embezzlement?

3. Suppose in Problem 1 Agent had been convicted in the criminal prosecution. In the subsequent civil case could the government take advantage of preclusion against Agent?

2. An Issue "Actually Litigated and Determined"

Even if one concludes that the issue at stake in the first and second lawsuits is identical, one must ask a further question: Was that issue actually litigated and determined in the first case? In Gargallo v. Merrill, Lynch, supra page 830, Larry Tyree, a Merrill stockbroker sued by Gargallo, sought to use the issues established in the first suit against Gargallo in the second, federal suit. The court's answer was swift and clear:

> With respect to the summary judgment in favor of Larry Tyree, since Mr. Gargallo's counter claim was dismissed in the state court as a sanction for discovery violations, none of the factual or legal issues he raised were actually litigated and decided. Consequently, the doctrine of collateral estoppel, or issue preclusion, is not applicable.

Gargallo v. Merrill, Lynch, 918 F.2d 658, 664 (6th Cir. 1990) The answer is not always so easy.

Illinois Central Gulf Railroad v. Parks
181 Ind. App. 141, 390 N.E.2d 1078 (1979)

LYBROOK, J.

[Jessie and Bertha Parks were injured when a car driven by Jessie in which Bertha was a passenger collided with an Illinois Central train. Bertha and Jessie sued Illinois Central; Bertha sought compensation for her injuries, and Jessie sought damages for loss of Bertha's services and consortium. Bertha recovered a $30,000 judgment on her claim, and judgment was rendered for Illinois Central on Jessie's claim.

Jessie then sued Illinois Central for his own injuries. On Illinois Central's motion for summary judgment, the trial court held that Jessie's claim was not barred by claim preclusion and that the prior action did not preclude Jessie on the issue of contributory negligence. Illinois Central took an interlocutory appeal.]

. . . Illinois Central Gulf's first allegation of error is an attempt to apply estoppel by judgment [the court's term for claim preclusion] in the case at bar, but the railroad concedes its own argument by admitting that Jessie's cause of action for loss of services and consortium as a derivative of Bertha's personal injuries is a distinct cause of action from Jessie's claim for damages for his own personal injuries.

Estoppel by judgment precludes the relitigation of a *cause of action* finally determined between the parties, and decrees that a judgment rendered is a complete bar to any subsequent action on the *same claim or cause of action*. Jessie's cause of action in the case at bar is a different cause of action from the one he litigated in the companion case; therefore, estoppel by judgment does not apply.

Estoppel by verdict [the court's term for issue preclusion], however, does apply. Using Judge Shake's terminology, the causes of action are not the same but, if the case at bar were to go to trial on all the issues raised in the pleadings and answer, some facts or questions determined and adjudicated in the companion case would again be put in issue in this subsequent action between the same parties.

To protect the integrity of the prior judgment by precluding the possibility of opposite results by two different juries on the same set of facts, the doctrine of estoppel by verdict allows the judgment in the prior action to operate as an estoppel as to those facts or questions actually litigated and determined in the prior action. The problem at hand, then, is to determine what facts or questions were actually litigated and determined in the companion case.

We agree with three concessions made by Illinois Central Gulf as to the effect of the verdict in the prior case: (1) that the verdict in favor of Bertha established, among other things, that the railroad was negligent and that its negligence was a proximate cause of the accident and Bertha's injuries; (2) that, inasmuch as Jessie's action for loss of services and consortium was derivative, if Jessie sustained any such loss it was proximately caused by the railroad's negligence; and (3) that, in order for the jury to have returned a verdict against Jessie, it had to have decided that he either sustained no damages or that his own negligence was a proximate cause of his damages.

This third proposition places upon the railroad the heavy burden outlined by Judge Shake in [Flora v. Indiana Service Co., 222 Ind. App. 253, 256–257 (1944)]:

> . . . [W]here a judgment may have been based upon either or any of two or more distinct facts, a party desiring to plead the judgment as an estoppel by verdict or finding upon the particular fact involved in a subsequent

suit must show that it went upon that fact, or else the question will be open to a new contention. The estoppel of a judgment is only presumptively conclusive, when it appears that the judgment could not have been rendered without deciding the particular matter brought in question. It is necessary to look to the complete record to ascertain what was the question in issue.

The railroad argues that, because Jessie's evidence as to his loss of services and consortium was uncontroverted, the jury's verdict had to be based upon a finding of contributory negligence. Illinois Central Gulf made this same argument in the companion case in relation to a related issue and Jessie countered, as he does here, with his contention that, although the evidence was uncontroverted, it was minimal and, thus, could have caused the jury to find no compensable damages. We reviewed the complete record in the companion case and held that the jury verdict against Jessie in that cause could mean that he had failed his burden of proving compensable damages. . . .

We hold that Illinois Central Gulf has failed its burden of showing that the judgment against Jessie in the prior action could not have been rendered without deciding that Jessie was contributorily negligent in the accident which precipitated the two lawsuits. Consequently, the trial court was correct in granting partial summary judgment estopping the railroad from denying its negligence and in limiting the issues at trial to whether Jessie was contributorily negligent, whether any such contributory negligence was a proximate cause of the accident, and whether Jessie sustained personal injuries and compensable damages. . . .

NOTES AND PROBLEMS

1. *Parks* causes potential confusion for the reader who has just completed the preceding section on claim preclusion.

a. If one were told the facts in the first lawsuit (Bertha and Jessie v. Railroad) and were further told that the railroad asserted a defense of former adjudication in the second suit, what would one expect that defense to be?

b. Why wasn't claim preclusion available to the railroad in Indiana? Indiana applies a definition of claim preclusion that is narrower than that set forth in Restatement (Second) of Judgments §24, supra page 807.

2. Now focus on why Jessie was not precluded from relitigating the issue of his contributory negligence in the second lawsuit. Why did the court reject the railroad's contention that the jury's verdict demonstrated that Jesse was contributorily negligent?

a. Isn't it plausible — indeed, likely — that the jury decided that Jessie was contributorily negligent? So why doesn't the court so conclude?

b. What is the other way a jury could have reached its verdict in the first suit? Should the court interview the jury about how it actually reached its decision?

3. What is the purpose of issue preclusion? A typical opinion explains, "[a]pplication of the doctrine of [issue preclusion] represents a decision that the needs of judicial finality and efficiency outweigh the possible gains of fairness or accuracy from continued litigation of an issue that previously has been considered by a competent tribunal." Nasem v. Brown, 595 F.2d 801 (D.C. Cir. 1979). Are such reasons credible?

a. Professor Martin Shapiro has argued that "it must always be remembered that the basic aim of a trial is to resolve a conflict or to impose social controls, not to find the facts. Much of what may appear to be unsatisfactory as pure fact-finding, if we were applying general scientific canons for empirical inquiry, may be quite satisfactory in the specific context of trials." * If Professor Shapiro's analysis is correct, courts are understandably hesitant to transplant the "findings" to a second dispute because it is a *different* dispute. The requirements that hedge issue preclusion thus grow from courts' understandable reluctance to equate findings with facts.

b. Does this analysis omit something? Do courts have a right to prevent two successive judgments from finding that fact X both did and did not occur? Is more than judicial face-saving at stake?

4. Assume that Illinois Central had not asserted Jessie's contributory negligence in the first action. Would Illinois Central be precluded from asserting it when Jessie sued for his own injuries? Most courts would say no. Unlike claim preclusion, under which theories are barred even if not raised, issue preclusion only estops issues actually decided in the prior action. Why? What is it about a new claim that makes it fair to preclude only those issues in the previous claim that were actually litigated?

5. Apply the lesson of *Parks*. Suppose A and B are involved in an accident in a state that has no compulsory counterclaim rule. A sues B alleging negligence, and B pleads contributory negligence as an affirmative defense. A general verdict is rendered for B. B then sues A for damages from the same accident. What — if any — issues are precluded?

6. Should a litigant be allowed to use evidence extrinsic to the record to establish what issues were actually determined in the previous litigation? The answer is yes, according to Restatement (Second) of Judgments

* Shapiro, Courts: A Comparative and Political Analysis 44 (1981).

§27 Comment f. What kind of extrinsic evidence would be useful to show which issues were determined by previous litigation?

7. What happens if the first action involved a default judgment?

a. Note 4 would imply that no issues are collaterally estopped because no issues were actually decided. Some jurisdictions do recognize an exception for facts that it would have been necessary to prove in the defaulted proceedings if they had been contested. For example, see Braxton v. Litchalk, 55 Mich. App. 708, 223 N.W.2d 316 (1974). This rule seems to arise in cases like *Martino*, supra, wherein the use to which the fact is to be put in the second case would be logically inconsistent with the original judgment.

b. Can there ever be reasons for giving preclusive effect to an issue *not* actually litigated and determined in a prior proceeding? Consider the facts of In re Sammy Daily, 47 F.3d 365 (9th Cir. 1995). The Federal Deposit Insurance Corporation, as receiver for bank loans, sued Daily, alleging he had fraudulently obtained the loans. Daily answered the complaint, then engaged in "a deliberate, dilatory course of conduct" constituting "a strategy of delay and evasiveness . . . [that] significantly prejudiced the plaintiffs [and] the judicial process." As a sanction for this behavior, the trial court, invoking Rule 37, "ordered all allegations of the complaint deemed admitted and entered a default judgment in favor of the FDIC." In the meantime, Daily had filed for bankruptcy. Bankruptcy does not discharge debts resulting from fraudulent acts. The FDIC sought to have the bankruptcy court rule that the judgment could not be discharged in bankruptcy on grounds of fraud. Daily argued that the prior judgment did not establish fraud, because those claims had not been "actually litigated." The Ninth Circuit conceded that ordinarily a default judgment could not serve as a basis for issue preclusion, but ruled that this judgment was different:

> The judgment entered in the [prior] action was not an ordinary default judgment. Daily did not simply decide the burden of litigation outweighed the advantages of opposing the FDIC's claim and fail to appear. He actively participated in the litigation, albeit obstructively, for two years before judgment was entered against him. A party who deliberately precludes resolution of factual issues through normal adjudicative procedures may be bound, in subsequent, related proceedings involving the same parties and issues, by a prior judicial determination reached without completion of the usual process of adjudication. In such a case the "actual litigation" requirement may be satisfied by substantial participation in an adversary contest in which the party is afforded a reasonable opportunity to defend himself on the merits but chooses not to do so.

Id. at 368.

The opinion cited no case directly establishing this proposition; *Gargallo,* quoted in the introduction to this section, supra page 830, is to the contrary. Is the result nevertheless reasonable?

3.   An Issue "Essential to the Judgment"

In *Parks* the court declined to apply preclusion because the opacity of the general verdict made it difficult to determine what the first judgment had decided. Sometimes courts face the opposite problem: too many findings in support of a judgment. In a trial to the bench, Rule 52(a) requires the judge to set forth findings of fact and conclusions of law. Imagine that the trial in *Parks* had taken place before a judge, who had determined (1) that Illinois Central had not been negligent *and* (2) that Jessie Parks had been contributorily negligent. Under these circumstances, should the court in a subsequent claim between the same parties hold Jessie precluded from relitigating both those issues? Or neither one? That question, though it occurs infrequently, uncovers the values underlying the doctrine. It is also a question debated among judges and academics. The first Restatement of Judgments took the position that when alternative grounds for decision existed, *both* should be precluded in subsequent litigation. The Restatement (Second) of Judgments §27 Comment i opines that *neither* determination should be binding in subsequent litigation:

> It might be argued that the judgment should be conclusive with respect to both issues. The matter has presumably been fully litigated and fairly decided; the determination does support, and is in itself sufficient to support, the judgment for the prevailing party; and the losing party is in a position to seek reversal of the determination from an appellate court. Moreover, a party who would otherwise urge several matters in support of a particular result may be deterred from doing so if a judgment resting on alternative determinations does not effectively preclude relitigation of particular issues.
>
> There are, however, persuasive reasons for analogizing the case to that of the nonessential determination. . . . First, a determination in the alternative may not have been as carefully or rigorously considered as it would have if it had been necessary to the result, and in that sense it has some of the characteristics of dicta. Second, and of critical importance, the losing party, although entitled to appeal from both determinations, might be dissuaded from doing so because of the likelihood that at least one of them would be upheld and the other not even reached. If he were to appeal solely for the purpose of avoiding the application of the rule of issue preclusion, then the rule might be responsible for increasing the

burdens of litigation on the parties and the courts rather than lightening those burdens.

As if to show just how close the question is, a later comment to the same section qualifies the suggested rule:

[Comment] o [to §27]. Effect of an appeal. . . .

If the judgment of the court of first instance was based on a determination of two issues, either of which standing independently would be sufficient to support the result, and the appellate court upholds both of these determinations as sufficient, and accordingly affirms the judgment, the judgment is conclusive as to both determinations. In contrast to the case discussed in Comment i, the losing party has here obtained an appellate decision on the issue, and thus the balance weighs in favor of preclusion.

If the appellate court upholds one of these determinations as sufficient but not the other, and accordingly affirms the judgment, the judgment is conclusive as to the first determination.

If the appellate court upholds one of these determinations as sufficient and refuses to consider whether or not the other is sufficient and accordingly affirms the judgment, the judgment is conclusive as to the first determination.

To get a grasp of the issues at stake, imagine that in federal district court a defendant makes a pretrial motion seeking to dismiss a case, citing alternative grounds for its decision — lack of federal subject matter jurisdiction and lack of personal jurisdiction. See, for example, Ruhrgas AG v. Marathon Oil, 119 S. Ct. 1563 (1999), noted supra page 233. The district court dismisses and the plaintiff refiles the suit in state court. When he does so, the defendant invokes issue preclusion based on the prior decision.

NOTES AND PROBLEMS

1. Consider several variations on *Ruhrgas*, beginning with the simplest. Suppose the district court had dismissed solely on grounds that federal subject matter jurisdiction was lacking. Under those conditions, what effect will the prior decision have on the state court suit?

2. Now suppose that the federal district court had dismissed solely on grounds that personal jurisdiction was lacking. What effect will the prior decision have on the state court suit?

3. Now suppose that the federal district court had dismissed, citing both grounds, ruling in a written opinion that personal and subject matter

jurisdiction were both lacking. What effect should that ruling have in the second lawsuit?

4. Finally, suppose that after the federal district court had dismissed, citing both grounds, the plaintiff had appealed. Suppose the court of appeals affirms.

a. If the appellate court affirms the absence of subject matter jurisdiction without reaching the question of personal jurisdiction, what effect in the second lawsuit?

b. If the appellate court affirms both grounds for dismissal, what effect on the second suit?

5. What idea is behind the importance that the Restatement Second attaches not just to the opportunity to appeal but to actual appellate litigation of alternative grounds? Does this suggest a lack of confidence in trial court decisions, or is there something else at work? Put yourself in the position of the plaintiff in the hypothetical lawsuit. You have just lost big in federal district court, with the judge throwing your lawsuit out of court on two alternative grounds. One of those grounds was that the defendant had insufficient contacts with the state to permit personal jurisdiction. You are offended by that finding, so you go to your lawyer and say, "We should appeal."

a. Your lawyer will explain why an appeal claiming that the personal jurisdiction ruling was erroneous has little chance of success. Why?

b. Isn't the Restatement (Second) position based on an image of litigation not as a search for truth but as a set of incentives and disincentives? In that world a judge will have less reason to be careful about any particular finding if there are other independent grounds leading to the same result. The losing litigant will have less incentive to appeal any particular finding if it seems likely that the appellate court will affirm on the basis of the other, independent grounds for decision. Under those circumstances, the theory goes, too few people have an incentive to make sure the findings are accurate. That being the case, we should be reluctant to import them into a second lawsuit.

4. Between Which Parties?

We have thus far dealt with situations in which the former and the present lawsuits involve the same parties. At common law this identity of parties (called "mutuality") was a requirement for both claim preclusion and issue preclusion. It continues to be a requirement for claim preclusion; in recent decades, however, many courts have abandoned this requirement for issue preclusion.

a. The "Victim" of Preclusion

To see how such a scheme might operate, consider a variation on the facts in Illinois Central Gulf Railroad v. Parks. Wife sues Railroad for injuries suffered in a crossing collision. Wife wins a judgment. Husband now sues for his injuries, sustained in the same accident. Railroad cannot argue that his claim is precluded by the first lawsuit: Biologically separate individuals possess separate claims, and no rule compels such individuals, even when married to each other, to prosecute their claims together. So Husband's suit can go forward.

In Husband v. Railroad, can either party take advantage of issue preclusion? Fifty years ago, the answer was a clear no. Like claim preclusion, issue preclusion applied only if both parties had been in the first suit, and, because Husband was not a party to that first lawsuit, the conditions for issue preclusion were not met. The last several decades have seen that principle of mutuality erode. Many courts would today permit Husband, even though he had not been a party to the first suit, to take advantage of an issue fully litigated and determined in that suit. In this case Railroad's negligence, causation, and proximate causation would all be candidates for preclusion in the second action. The rationale for that extension of issue preclusion is that the "victim" of issue preclusion (here, the railroad) had a full and fair opportunity to litigate the matter in the first suit.

Now change one factor: what if Railroad had won the first suit, demonstrating to the jury's satisfaction that it was not negligent? Could it take advantage of that determination in a second action brought by Husband? The answer is no. Whether they attribute this result to simple fairness or to due process, all agree that a party who has never had an opportunity to litigate an issue cannot be precluded from doing so. The abandonment of mutuality thus creates a potential asymmetry: If Railroad loses the first case brought by Wife, it will be saddled by that loss in subsequent litigation with Husband. If it wins against Wife, however, it must still defend against Husband. The anomaly has its logic; as one pioneering decision put it:

> The criteria for determining who may assert a plea of [issue preclusion] differ fundamentally from the criteria for determining against whom [such] a plea . . . may be asserted. The requirements of due process of law forbid the assertion of a plea of . . . [issue preclusion] against a party unless he was bound by the earlier litigation in which the matter was decided. He is bound by that litigation only if he has been a party thereto or in privity with a party thereto. There is no compelling reason, however, for requiring that the party asserting the plea . . . must have been a party, or in privity with a party, to the earlier litigation.

No satisfactory rationalization has been advanced for the requirement of mutuality. Just why a party who was not bound by a previous action should be precluded from asserting it as res judicata against a party who was bound by it is difficult to comprehend. (See 7 Bentham's Works, Bowring's Ed., 171.)

Bernhard v. Bank of America, 19 Cal. 2d 807, 811-812, 122 P.2d 892, 894-895 (1942) (Traynor, J.). Despite this reasoning, the asymmetrical availability of nonmutual preclusion has made some courts and commentators uneasy. The next case explores the problem.

b. The Precluder

Parklane Hosiery Co. v. Shore
439 U.S. 322 (1979)

Mr. Justice STEWART delivered the opinion of the Court.

This case presents the question whether a party who has had issues of fact adjudicated adversely to it in an equitable action may be collaterally estopped from relitigating the same issues before a jury in a subsequent legal action brought against it by a new party.

The respondent brought this stockholder's class action against the petitioners in a Federal District Court. The complaint alleged that the petitioners, Parklane Hosiery Co., Inc. (Parklane), and 13 of its officers, directors, and stockholders, had issued a materially false and misleading proxy statement in connection with a merger.[1] The proxy statement, according to the complaint, had violated §§14(a), 10(b), and 20(a) of the Securities Exchange Act of 1934, as well as various rules and regulations promulgated by the Securities and Exchange Commission (SEC). The complaint sought damages, rescission of the merger, and recovery of costs.

Before this action came to trial, the SEC filed suit against the same defendants in the Federal District Court, alleging that the proxy statement that had been issued by Parklane was materially false and misleading in essentially the same respects as those that had been alleged in the respondent's complaint. Injunctive relief was requested. After a four-day

---

1. The amended complaint alleged that the proxy statement that had been issued to the stockholders was false and misleading because it failed to disclose (1) that the president of Parklane would financially benefit as a result of the company's going private; (2) certain ongoing negotiations that could have resulted in financial benefit to Parklane; and (3) that the appraisal of the fair value of Parklane stock was based on insufficient information to be accurate.

trial, the District Court found that the proxy statement was materially false and misleading in the respects alleged, and entered a declaratory judgment to that effect. The Court of Appeals for the Second Circuit affirmed this judgment.

The respondent in the present case then moved for partial summary judgment against the petitioners, asserting that the petitioners were collaterally estopped from litigating the issues that had been resolved against them in the action brought by the SEC.[2] The District Court denied the motion on the ground that such an application of collateral estoppel would deny the petitioners their Seventh Amendment right to a jury trial. The Court of Appeals for the Second Circuit reversed, holding that a party who has had issues of fact determined against him after a full and fair opportunity to litigate in a nonjury trial is collaterally estopped from obtaining a subsequent jury trial of these same issues of fact. The appellate court concluded that "the Seventh Amendment preserves the right to jury trial only with respect to issues of fact, [and] once those issues have been fully and fairly adjudicated in a prior proceeding, nothing remains for trial, either with or without a jury." Because of an inter-Circuit conflict, we granted certiorari.

I

The threshold question to be considered is whether quite apart from the right to a jury trial under the Seventh Amendment, the petitioners can be precluded from litigating facts resolved adversely to them in a prior equitable proceeding with another party under the general law of collateral estoppel. Specifically, we must determine whether a litigant who was not a party to a prior judgment may nevertheless use that judgment "offensively" to prevent a defendant from relitigating issues resolved in the earlier proceeding.[4]

2. A private plaintiff in an action under the proxy rules is not entitled to relief simply by demonstrating that the proxy solicitation was materially false and misleading. The plaintiff must also show that he was injured and prove damages. Mills v. Electric Auto-Lite Co., 396 U.S. 375, 386-390. Since the SEC action was limited to a determination of whether the proxy statement contained materially false and misleading information, the respondent conceded that he would still have to prove these other elements of his prima facie case in the private action. The petitioners' right to a jury trial on those remaining issues is not contested.

4. In this context, offensive use of collateral estoppel occurs when the plaintiff seeks to foreclose the defendant from litigating an issue the defendant has previously litigated unsuccessfully in an action with another party. Defensive use occurs when a defendant seeks to prevent a plaintiff from asserting a claim the plaintiff has previously litigated and lost against another defendant.

A

Collateral estoppel, like the related doctrine of res judicata,[5] has the dual purpose of protecting litigants from the burden of relitigating an identical issue with the same party or his privy and of promoting judicial economy by preventing needless litigation. Blonder-Tongue Laboratories, Inc. v. University of Illinois Foundation, 402 U.S. 313, 328-329. Until relatively recently, however, the scope of collateral estoppel was limited by the doctrine of mutuality of parties. Under this mutuality doctrine, neither party could use a prior judgment as an estoppel against the other unless both parties were bound by the judgment. Based on the premise that it is somehow unfair to allow a party to use a prior judgment when he himself would not be so bound,[7] the mutuality requirement provided a party who had litigated and lost in a previous action an opportunity to relitigate identical issues with new parties.

By failing to recognize the obvious difference in position between a party who has never litigated an issue and one who has fully litigated and lost, the mutuality requirement was criticized almost from its inception.[8] Recognizing the validity of this criticism, the Court in Blonder-Tongue Laboratories, Inc. v. University of Illinois Foundation, supra, abandoned the mutuality requirement, at least in cases where a patentee seeks to relitigate the validity of a patent after a federal court in a previous lawsuit has already declared it invalid. The "broader question" before the Court, however, was "whether it is any longer tenable to afford a litigant more than one full and fair opportunity for judicial resolution of the same issue." The Court strongly suggested a negative answer to that question:

> In any lawsuit where a defendant, because of the mutuality principle,
> is forced to present a complete defense on the merits to a claim which

5. Under the doctrine of res judicata, a judgment on the merits in a prior suit bars a second suit involving the same parties or their privies based on the same cause of action. Under the doctrine of collateral estoppel, on the other hand, the second action is upon a different cause of action and the judgment in the prior suit precludes relitigation of issues actually litigated and necessary to the outcome of the first action.

7. It is a violation of due process for a judgment to be binding on a litigant who was not a party or a privy and therefore has never had an opportunity to be heard. Blonder-Tongue Laboratories, Inc. v. University of Illinois Foundation.

8. This criticism was summarized in the Court's opinion in Blonder-Tongue Laboratories, Inc. v. University of Illinois Foundation, supra. The opinion of Justice Traynor for a unanimous California Supreme Court in Bernhard v. Bank of America Natl. Trust & Savings Assn., made the point succinctly: "No satisfactory rationalization has been advanced for the requirement of mutuality. Just why a party who was not bound by a previous action should be precluded from asserting it as res judicata against a party who was bound by it is difficult to comprehend."

the plaintiff has fully litigated and lost in a prior action, there is an arguable misallocation of resources. To the extent the defendant in the second suit may not win by asserting, without contradiction, that the plaintiff had fully and fairly, but unsuccessfully, litigated the same claim in the prior suit, the defendant's time and money are diverted from alternative uses — productive or otherwise — to relitigation of a decided issue. And, still assuming that the issue was resolved correctly in the first suit, there is reason to be concerned about the plaintiff's allocation of resources. Permitting repeated litigation of the same issue as long as the supply of unrelated defendants holds out reflects either the aura of the gaming table or "a lack of discipline and of disinterestedness on the part of the lower courts, hardly a worthy or wise basis for fashioning rules of procedure." Although neither judges, the parties, nor the adversary system performs perfectly in all cases, the requirement of determining whether the party against whom an estoppel is asserted had a full and fair opportunity to litigate is a most significant safeguard.[10]

B

The *Blonder-Tongue* case involved defensive use of collateral estoppel — a plaintiff was estopped from asserting a claim that the plaintiff had previously litigated and lost against another defendant. The present case, by contrast, involves offensive use of collateral estoppel — a plaintiff is seeking to estop a defendant from relitigating the issues which the defendant previously litigated and lost against another plaintiff. In both the offensive and defensive use situations, the party against whom estoppel is asserted has litigated and lost in an earlier action. Nevertheless, several reasons have been advanced why the two situations should be treated differently.

First, offensive use of collateral estoppel does not promote judicial economy in the same manner as defensive use does. Defensive use of collateral estoppel precludes a plaintiff from relitigating identical issues by merely "switching adversaries." Bernhard v. Bank of America Natl. Trust & Savings Assn.[12] Thus defensive collateral estoppel gives a plaintiff a strong incentive to join all potential defendants in the first action if possible. Offensive use of collateral estoppel, on the other hand, creates

10. The Court also emphasized that relitigation of issues previously adjudicated is particularly wasteful in patent cases because of their staggering expense and typical length. Under the doctrine of mutuality of parties an alleged infringer might find it cheaper to pay royalties than to challenge a patent that had been declared invalid in a prior suit, since the holder of the patent is entitled to a statutory presumption of validity.

12. Under the mutuality requirement, a plaintiff could accomplish this result since he would not have been bound by the judgment had the original defendant won.

precisely the opposite incentive. Since a plaintiff will be able to rely on a previous judgment against a defendant but will not be bound by that judgment if the defendant wins, the plaintiff has every incentive to adopt a "wait and see" attitude, in the hope that the first action by another plaintiff will result in a favorable judgment. Thus offensive use of collateral estoppel will likely increase rather than decrease the total amount of litigation, since potential plaintiffs will have everything to gain and nothing to lose by not intervening in the first action.[13]

A second argument against offensive use of collateral estoppel is that it may be unfair to a defendant. If a defendant in the first action is sued for small or nominal damages, he may have little incentive to defend vigorously, particularly if future suits are not foreseeable. The Evergreens v. Nunan; cf. Berner v. British Commonwealth Pac. Airlines (application of offensive collateral estoppel denied where defendant did not appeal an adverse judgment awarding damages of $35,000 and defendant was later sued for over $7 million). Allowing offensive collateral estoppel may also be unfair to a defendant if the judgment relied upon as a basis for the estoppel is itself inconsistent with one or more previous judgments in favor of the defendant.[14] Still another situation where it might be unfair to apply offensive estoppel is where the second action affords the defendant procedural opportunities unavailable in the first action that could readily cause a different result.[15]

C

We have concluded that the preferable approach for dealing with these problems in the federal courts is not to preclude the use of offensive

13. The Restatement (Second) of Judgments §88(3) (Tent. Draft No. 2, Apr. 15, 1975) provides that application of collateral estoppel may be denied if the party asserting it "could have effected joinder in the first action between himself and his present adversary."

14. In Professor Currie's familiar example, a railroad collision injures 50 passengers all of whom bring separate actions against the railroad. After the railroad wins the first 25 suits, a plaintiff wins in suit 26. Professor Currie argues that offensive use of collateral estoppel should not be applied so as to allow plaintiffs 27 through 50 automatically to recover. Currie, [Mutuality of Collateral Estoppel: Limits of the *Bernhard* Doctrine], 9 Stan. L. Rev. [281, 304 (1957)]. See Restatement (Second) of Judgments §88(4).

15. If, for example, the defendant in the first action was forced to defend in an inconvenient forum and therefore was unable to engage in full scale discovery or call witnesses, application of offensive collateral estoppel may be unwarranted. Indeed, differences in available procedures may sometimes justify not allowing a prior judgment to have estoppel effect in a subsequent action even between the same parties, or where defensive estoppel is asserted against a plaintiff who has litigated and lost. The problem of unfairness is particularly acute in cases of offensive estoppel, however, because the defendant against whom estoppel is asserted typically will not have chosen the forum in the first action. See, id., at §88(2) and Comment d.

collateral estoppel, but to grant trial courts broad discretion to determine when it should be applied.[16] The general rule should be that in cases where a plaintiff could easily have joined in the earlier action or where, either for the reasons discussed above or for other reasons, the application of offensive estoppel would be unfair to a defendant, a trial judge should not allow the use of offensive collateral estoppel.

In the present case, however, none of the circumstances that might justify reluctance to allow the offensive use of collateral estoppel is present. The application of offensive collateral estoppel will not here reward a private plaintiff who could have joined in the previous action, since the respondent probably could not have joined in the injunctive action brought by the SEC even had he so desired.[17] Similarly, there is no unfairness to the petitioners in applying offensive collateral estoppel in this case. First, in light of the serious allegations made in the SEC's complaint against the petitioners, as well as the foreseeability of subsequent private suits that typically follow a successful Government judgment, the petitioners had every incentive to litigate the SEC lawsuit fully and vigorously.[18] Second, the judgment in the SEC action was not inconsistent with any previous decision. Finally, there will in the respondent's action be no procedural opportunities available to the petitioners that were unavailable in the first action of a kind that might be likely to cause a different result.[19]

We conclude, therefore, that none of the considerations that would

16. This is essentially the approach of [the Restatement (Second) of Judgments] at §88, which recognizes that "the distinct trend if not the clear weight of recent authority is to the effect that there is no intrinsic difference between 'offensive' as distinct from 'defensive' issue preclusion, although a stronger showing that the prior opportunity to litigate was adequate may be required in the former situation than the latter." Id., Reporter's Note, at 99.

17. SEC v. Everest Management Corp. ("the complicating effect of the additional issues and the additional parties outweighs any advantage of a single disposition of the common issues"). Moreover, consolidation of a private action with one brought by the SEC without its consent is prohibited by statute. 15 U.S.C. §78u(g).

18. After a four-day trial in which the petitioners had every opportunity to present evidence and call witnesses, the District Court held for the SEC. The petitioners then appealed to the Court of Appeals for the Second Circuit, which affirmed the judgment against them. Moreover, the petitioners were already aware of the action brought by the respondent, since it had commenced before the filing of the SEC action.

19. It is true, of course, that the petitioners in the present action would be entitled to a jury trial of the issues bearing on whether the proxy statement was materially false and misleading had the SEC action never been brought — a matter to be discussed in Part II of this opinion. But the presence or absence of a jury as factfinder is basically neutral, quite unlike, for example, the necessity of defending the first lawsuit in an inconvenient forum.

justify a refusal to allow the use of offensive collateral estoppel is present in this case. Since the petitioners received a "full and fair" opportunity to litigate their claims in the SEC action, the contemporary law of collateral estoppel leads inescapably to the conclusion that the petitioners are collaterally estopped from relitigating the question of whether the proxy statement was materially false and misleading.

II

The question that remains is whether, notwithstanding the law of collateral estoppel, the use of offensive collateral estoppel in this case would violate the petitioners' Seventh Amendment right to a jury trial. . . . The Seventh Amendment has never been interpreted in the rigid manner advocated by the petitioners. On the contrary, many procedural devices developed since 1791 that have diminished the civil jury's historic domain have been found not to be inconsistent with the Seventh Amendment. . . .

The *Galloway* case [Galloway v. United States, 319 U.S. 372 (1943)] is particularly instructive. There the party against whom a directed verdict had been entered argued that the procedure was unconstitutional under the Seventh Amendment. In rejecting this claim, the Court said: "The Amendment did not bind the federal courts to the exact procedural incidents or details of jury trial according to the common law in 1791, any more than it tied them to the common-law system of pleading or the specific rules of evidence then prevailing. Nor were 'the rules of the common law' then prevalent, including those relating to the procedure by which the judge regulated the jury's role on questions of fact, crystallized in a fixed and immutable system." . . .

The law of collateral estoppel, like the law in other procedural areas defining the scope of the jury's function, has evolved since 1791. Under the rationale of the *Galloway* case, these developments are not repugnant to the Seventh Amendment simply for the reason that they did not exist in 1791. Thus if, as we have held, the law of collateral estoppel forecloses the petitioners from relitigating the factual issues determined against them in the SEC action, nothing in the Seventh Amendment dictates a different result, even though because of lack of mutuality there would have been no collateral estoppel in 1791. . . .

[The Court held that the Seventh Amendment was not a bar to successful assertion of issue preclusion.

Justice REHNQUIST dissented on the ground that preclusion under these circumstances violated the Seventh Amendment.]

NOTES AND PROBLEMS

1. Think of *Parklane* as a variation on Illinois Gulf Central v. Parks.

a. Without joining her husband Jessie, Bertha Parks sues the railroad, alleging its negligence as a cause of her injuries. Bertha wins. In *Parklane*, which party is Bertha and which is the railroad?

b. Jessie Parks now sues the railroad, alleging its negligence as a cause of his injuries. Jessie wants to treat the determination of the railroad's negligence and causation as precluded from relitigation. That issue is identical, was actually litigated and determined, and was essential to the judgment in the first case. In *Parklane*, which party to the second lawsuit is in the same position as Jessie, and what issue did that party want to preclude from relitigation?

c. In fact, the *Parklane* opinion suggests a reason for thinking that *Parks* is a *weaker* case for preclusion than is *Parklane* itself. What opportunity did Jessie Parks have that Shore (the plaintiff in the second *Parklane* suit) did not have? Under *Parklane*, would that opportunity have been sufficient reason for denying Jessie the use of nonmutual-issue preclusion?

2. Consider the following situations in which parties might wish to take advantage of preclusion. In which should they be able to do so?

a. The Rushes, riding on a motorcycle, are thrown off when the cycle hits a pothole. Mrs. Rush, the owner of the cycle, sues the city for $1,000 in damages to the machine. See Rush v. City of Maple Heights, supra page 57. Mrs. Rush brings the suit in municipal court, which uses an abbreviated system of discovery and has a jurisdictional limit of $5,000. City loses. Mr. Rush sues for disabling spinal injuries suffered in the same accident; he seeks damages of $1.5 million. Mr. Rush seeks to invoke preclusion on the issue of City's negligence.

b. An airplane crashes. The National Transportation Safety Board investigates the accident in a proceeding in which it calls various witnesses (but in which Airline does not have the right to cross-examine). The NTSB makes a finding that the crash occurred as a result of Airline's negligent failure to train its pilots for a particular predictable emergency situation. Passenger's executor sues, invoking the finding as conclusive of Airline's negligence.

c. Finally, a nonmutual variation on a hypothetical case considered earlier in this section. The federal government accuses an IRS agent of certain criminal acts. She is acquitted. The government then sues Accomplice to recover funds allegedly embezzled in the same criminal acts. Accomplice seeks to invoke preclusion on the grounds that the previous case demonstrates the acts did not occur. Standefer v. United States, 447 U.S. 10 (1980) (no preclusion).

d. These hypothetical cases emphasize a point that should by now be familiar: Lawsuits do not decide "what happened" in the abstract; instead, they decide who, given the procedural setting of the case, made a better showing. If one keeps this point in mind, it is easier to understand why procedural settings that differ significantly may supply a reason not to apply preclusion.

3. *Parklane* joins a number of state cases in permitting nonmutual preclusion. Like *Parklane*, these cases generally cite both efficiency and fairness as grounds for applying preclusion. To this judicial enthusiasm for issue preclusion there is, however, one glaring exception: the federal government. In United States v. Mendoza, 464 U.S. 154 (1984), the Court held that the United States could not be subjected to nonmutual-issue preclusion. The ordinary rules of issue preclusion apply if Party and the United States are involved in two successive lawsuits, but if A sues the United States and prevails, B may not in a later suit use against the United States those issues determined in A's favor. Otherwise put, the principles of *Parklane* do not apply to the United States. Why not? The *Mendoza* Court did not do a remarkably good job of justifying its result, but one can imagine two reasons.

a. There is a practical problem. At present the United States appeals selectively, choosing only those cases in which some principle of law or fact important to the United States is at stake. (The office of the Solicitor General makes these discretionary judgments.) The *Mendoza* court worried that applying *Parklane* to the United States would force the government to appeal virtually every case it lost, for fear of its effect in subsequent cases. Note, however, that this same problem afflicts other large litigants — state governments, Microsoft, General Motors, large insurers — but no such exception has been carved out for them.

b. The United States faces another problem. Many of the suits to which it is a party involve constitutional questions. As things now stand, an unappealed decision of a district court involving a constitutional question affects only those involved in the case itself. It does not even bind other courts in the same district. If one applied *Parklane* to the United States, all that would change. A single district court decision against the United States on a constitutional issue would become — by virtue of issue preclusion — a kind of superprecedent that would bind all other courts, including the U.S. Supreme Court. For example, suppose a district court in the course of a criminal trial ruled that all searches of automobiles without a warrant were unconstitutional. If that ruling stood, it could be applied against the United States by all subsequent defendants. Moreover, unlike ordinary precedent, the ruling would not be subject to reconsideration or "overruling" by the U.S. Supreme Court. Is this a good enough reason not to extend *Parklane* to the United States? Or does it suggest a narrower exception involving only questions of constitutional law?

4. The widespread move to various forms of comparative negligence raises several questions of issue preclusion.

a. Consider a fairly simple case. Two cars collide; Passenger is riding in one of them. The two drivers sue each other and the case goes to judgment. The jury finds that both drivers were negligent and apportions fault at 70 percent to Driver A and 30 percent to Driver B. If Passenger now sues (assuming the state permits such claims), the apportionment of fault from the former suit will bind both drivers. The reasoning is that both had a fair opportunity to litigate an issue essential to the judgment.

b. But what happens if Passenger sues only one driver, perhaps because she is uncertain about the other's negligence and wishes not to complicate an otherwise clear case? May Passenger take advantage of the finding of negligence as against Driver A alone? Presumably so. Is she limited to collecting only 70 percent of her damages? That will depend on the state's regime of joint and several liability, but in many states Passenger (assuming no fault on her part) will be able to collect her total damage bill from Driver A, who may have an action for equitable indemnification against Driver B.

c. Suppose Passenger is in a state that has modified the common law rules of joint and several liability so that she may collect from each driver only in proportion to his fault. Must Passenger accept the finding that Driver A was only 70 percent at fault, or is she free to show that his proportion was greater? Can Passenger have the sweet without the bitter — the determination of liability without the limitation as to its amount?

5. For those who argue that mutuality is an unnecessary constraint on preclusion, there is a nightmare case: several plaintiffs with essentially identical claims against the same defendant. The typical example is a bus or train crash, with multiple suits brought by injured passengers. Why is this example a nightmare? — Because it illuminates the extent to which everything turns on the outcome of the first case.

a. If the plaintiff won the first case and the second through fiftieth plaintiffs now seek to invoke preclusion, what result under the doctrine of *Parklane*?

b. If the defendant won the first case and now seeks to invoke preclusion against subsequent plaintiffs, what result?

c. Lest you think such situations are confined to the teeming brains of law teachers, consider the next case.

State Farm Fire & Casualty Co. v. Century Home Components

275 Or. 97, 550 P.2d 1185 (1976)

HOLMAN, J.

Defendant appeals from judgments entered in 13 actions for damages resulting from a fire. These actions were among 48 cases consolidated for a single hearing in the court below on the issue of collateral estoppel. The ruling of the trial court that defendant was collaterally estopped from contesting liability in each of the 48 actions forms the basis for defendant's appeal.

The fire giving rise to this litigation started early one Sunday morning in the summer of 1968. Defendant constructed prefabricated housing in a large shed. Plaintiffs' property was stored in a warehouse which was located approximately 60 feet from defendant's shed and which was connected thereto by a wooden loading dock. On the side of defendant's shed was a wooden box, called a skip box, into which sawdust from a neighboring saw was customarily deposited. On the Saturday evening preceding the fire, defendant's janitor had dumped a mix of linseed oil and dry sawdust into the box. No employees were present at the time the fire started. Whatever its cause and point of origin, and these are in dispute, the fire spread via the loading dock and caused substantial damage to defendant's shed, the warehouse and its contents.

Shortly thereafter various actions, eventually totaling over 50, were filed against defendant to recover for losses from the fire. Three of these actions proceeded separately through trial to final judgment. In each case the plaintiffs alleged essentially that defendant was negligent with respect to both the start and spread of the fire. The first case to come to trial resulted in a jury verdict for defendant. On appeal this court reversed the judgment for error in failing to compel defendant to produce a statement needed by the plaintiff for purposes of impeaching a defense witness, and remanded for a new trial. Pacific N.W. Bell v. Century Home. During the pendency of the foregoing appeal the second case was tried and produced another jury verdict for defendant. Sylwester v. Century Home Components, Inc. No appeal was taken from that judgment and it became final. Shortly thereafter the third case was tried and a jury verdict was returned for the plaintiff. This judgment was affirmed on appeal. Hesse v. Century Home. The *Pacific N. W. Bell* case was subsequently retried, this time to the court sitting without a jury, and the court found for the plaintiff. We affirmed on appeal.

Following entry of final judgment in both *Hesse* and *Pacific N.W. Bell*, the present plaintiffs filed amended and supplemental complaints, conforming their allegations to those in the foregoing cases, and asserted that the judgments therein should operate to preclude defendant from again litigating the question of liability. Defendant alleged in defense that it would be unfair to bar relitigation in view of the similarity of issues between those cases and *Sylwester* and of the existence of the jury verdict and judgment in defendant's favor in *Sylwester*. In the consolidated hearing on the question of collateral estoppel the parties submitted the records and transcripts of all three cases. The trial court rendered its ruling in favor of plaintiffs, finding inter alia: "That the allegations of the second amended and supplemental complaint raising the issue of collateral estoppel have been established by the greater weight of the evidence, and that the affirmative allegations of the answer thereto have not been established by the evidence. . . ."

To summarize the posture of these cases, the question of defendant's negligence has been tried four times and three final judgments have been rendered. Defendant has procured one favorable judgment (and two jury verdicts) and the claimants have received two judgments. The present plaintiffs, who were not parties to any of the previous actions, seek to utilize the prior claimants' judgments to establish conclusively defendant's negligence and its responsibility for any loss caused by the fire. . . .

The "multiple-claimant anomaly" was first hypothesized by Brainerd Currie as one instance where, absent mutuality, the unrestrained application of collateral estoppel might produce unfair results. Currie, Mutuality of Collateral Estoppel: Limits of the Bernhard Doctrine, 9 Stan. L. Rev. 281 (1957). Currie posed the situation of a train wreck resulting in 50 separate claims being filed against the railroad for negligence. If the defendant railroad won the first 25 cases and subsequently lost the 26th, Currie characterized as an "absurdity" the notion that the remaining 24 claimants could ride in on the strength of the 26th plaintiff's judgment and estop the defendant on the issue of negligence. The reason was that the 26th judgment would clearly seem to be an aberration. Currie then reasoned that, if we should be unwilling to give preclusive effect to the 26th judgment, we should not afford such effect to an adverse judgment rendered in the *first* action brought because "we have no warrant for assuming that the aberrational judgment will not come as the first in the series." Currie, supra. Currie thus concluded that, absent mutuality, collateral estoppel should not be applied where a defendant potentially faces more than two successive actions.

Those courts which have discarded the rule of mutuality and permit the offensive assertion of collateral estoppel have generally rejected Currie's solution to the multiple-claimant anomaly in situations where the *first* judgment is adverse to the defendant, and have precluded a defendant from relitigating multiple claims where it has been concluded that the defendant had in actuality the incentive and complete opportunity to contest the issue fully in the first action. Currie's reservations were based on the apprehension that the first judgment might well be an aberration, but this view failed to recognize that the very notion of collateral estoppel demands and assumes a certain confidence in the integrity of the end result of our adjudicative process. There is no foundation in either experience or policy for accepting the suggestion that a decision rendered after a full and fair presentation of the evidence and issues should be considered either substantially suspect or infected with variables indicating the question might be decided differently in another go-around. Currie subsequently conceded the untenability of his initial position and retreated from it, stating that "so long as we retain sufficient faith in the institution of trial by jury to retain it for civil cases at all, what warrant is there for mistrusting the verdict for purposes of collateral estoppel when there is no suggestion that there has been compromise or other impropriety?" Currie, Civil Procedure: The Tempest Brews, 53 Calif. L. Rev. 25, 36 (1965). . . .

As the foregoing discussion would indicate, however, we are not free to disregard incongruous results when they are looking us in the eye. If the circumstances are such that our confidence in the integrity of the determination is severely undermined, or that the result would likely be different in a second trial, it would work an injustice to deny the litigant another chance. Thus, where it is apparent that the verdict was the result of a jury compromise, the losing party should not be precluded by the judgment. Berner v. British Commonwealth Pacific Airlines, Ltd.; Restatement (Second) of Judgments §88(5) (Tent. Draft No. 2, 1975). In *Berner* the additional circumstance that the award of damages of $35,000 was so small in comparison to the $500,000 prayer of the complaint might well have caused the airlines to consider the judgment an actual "victory" and to accept that determination rather than incur the additional expense of appealing for a new trial to rectify whatever errors may have been committed during the course of the trial. It has also been held that if the prior determination was manifestly erroneous the judgment should not be given preclusive effect. Restatement (Second) of Judgments §88(7) and Comment i. (Tent. Draft No. 2, 1975). And the existence of newly discovered or crucial evidence that was not available to the litigant at the first trial would provide a basis for denying preclusion where it appears the evidence would have a significant effect on the outcome.

Those courts and commentators[4] which have considered the question are in virtually unanimous agreement that where outstanding determinations are actually inconsistent on the matter sought to be precluded, it would be patently unfair to estop a party by the judgment it lost. Although Currie's initial perceptions provoked much discussion, the problem has remained largely academic because inconsistent verdicts are rarely encountered. Our research has disclosed only one case where inconsistent determinations by separate trial courts were asserted as a reason for denying collateral estoppel. . . .

We agree with the commentators to the extent at least that, where there are extant determinations that are inconsistent on the matter in issue, it is a strong indication that the application of collateral estoppel would work an injustice. There seems to be something fundamentally offensive about depriving a party of the opportunity to litigate the issue again when he has shown beyond a doubt that on another day he prevailed.[5] As stated by the Tentative Draft of Restatement (Second) of Judgments:

> Giving a prior determination of an issue conclusive effect in subsequent litigation is justified not merely as avoiding further costs of litigation but also by underlying confidence that the result reached is substantially correct. Where a determination relied on as preclusive is itself inconsistent with some other adjudication of the same issue, that confidence is generally unwarranted. The inference, rather, is that the outcomes may have been based on equally reasonable resolutions of doubt as to the probative strength of the evidence or the appropriate application of a legal rule to the evidence. That such a doubtful determination has been given effect in the action in which it was reached does not require that it be given effect against the party in litigation against another adversary. Restatement (Second) of Judgments §88(4), Comment f. (Tent. Draft No. 2, 1975).

---

4. Currie, Mutuality of Collateral Estoppel: Limits of the *Bernhard* Doctrine, 9 Stan. L. Rev. 281, 285 (1957); Eizenstat, Mutuality: Is This Doctrine Really Necessary?, 3 Harv. Legal Comm. 83, 93 (1966); Hazard, Res Nova in Res Judicata, 44 S. Cal. L. Rev. 1036, 1044 (1971); James, Civil Procedure 601-02, §11.34 (1965) (the result is "offensive to the sense of justice"); Semmel, Collateral Estoppel, Mutuality and Joinder of Parties, 68 Colum. L. Rev. 1457, 1466-67 (1968) ("[T]he common defendant should never be bound if he wins the first and then loses a later trial; there is no policy which commands that either judgment should be available to non-parties to the actions in such a situation. Both judgments should be ignored in the subsequent actions, not because of lack of mutuality or offensive-defensive distinctions, but because of common sense."); Note, Res Judicata: The Shield Becomes a Sword, 1964 Duke L.J. 402, 404. But see Comment, Privity and Mutuality in the Doctrine of Res Judicata, 35 Yale L.J. 607, 611-12 (1926).

5. We do not mean to say that one favorable determination can never be overcome and estoppel never applied despite the number of subsequent determinations to the contrary.

Plaintiffs in the present case contend that the determinations are not "inconsistent" because the issues in *Hesse* and *Pacific N.W. Bell* were not identical with the issues in *Sylwester*. It is true, as plaintiffs point out, that the phrasing of the allegations of negligence differed and that certain specifications of negligence were not submitted to the jury in *Sylwester*. We do not give much weight to variations in the wording of the pleadings, however, where essentially the same acts and omissions are alleged. To concentrate on slight discrepancies in the allegations of negligence would put defendant at a distinct disadvantage, for claimants could modify the wording after each judgment for defendant until one claimant prevailed, after which all remaining claimants could conform their complaints to that of the prevailing claimant and could then successfully claim that the prior judgments for defendant were based upon different issues.

The thrust of plaintiffs' argument must be that the jury in *Hesse* and the court in *Pacific N.W. Bell* adjudicated defendant negligent in respects which were not considered by the jury in *Sylwester*. The records of the cases, however, do not permit such a conclusion. Since the jury in *Hesse* returned a general verdict, we do not know in which respects it found defendant negligent and, given the substantial similarity of some of the allegations and the basic thrust of the negligence alleged, we are unable to conclude that it found defendant negligent on the basis of conduct not submitted to the jury in *Sylwester*. In *Pacific N. W. Bell* the court specifically found that the fire started in defendant's skip box; and that defendant was negligent in failing at the close of the preceding work day to remove combustible materials from its plant, in storing them in a box which was not a suitable receptacle or bin, in placing inflammable wastes in such a manner that defendant knew or should have known that any fire in the skip box was likely to spread to adjacent structures, and in failing to empty the trash box before leaving the premises unattended for the night. Allegations of essentially the same conduct were submitted to the jury in *Sylwester* under proper instructions by the court, and the jury obviously found that defendant was not negligent in the respects specified by the court in *Pacific N.W. Bell*. . . .

We conclude that the prior determinations are basically inconsistent and that the circumstances are such that it would be unfair to preclude defendants from relitigating the issue of liability.

Reversed and remanded.

NOTES AND PROBLEMS

1. The court concludes that because there were several lawsuits with varying verdicts, issue preclusion should not apply.

a. Could one argue that this was a *stronger* case for issue preclusion than in the ordinary case because here one had several verdicts, most pointing in one direction?

b. Does *Century Home Components* suggest that issue preclusion rests as much on the desire to prevent inconsistency as it does on the goal of efficiency?

2. Suppose Baker sues Welch and invokes prior judgments involving identical issues against Welch and in favor of Slater and Schultz. The trial court denies issue-preclusion effect to the earlier judgments, and the action is tried to the jury. Welch prevails. On appeal, Baker demands that the appellate court set aside the judgment of the trial court and order it to enter judgment in Baker's favor. What result? If the appellate court grants Baker's requests, would it thereby promote efficiency and consistency, the twin goals of issue preclusion?

3. Professor Currie doubtless was correct when he observed a certain inconsistency between disallowing issue preclusion (in favor of the plaintiff) when the defendant wins the first nine cases but loses the tenth and allowing it when the defendant loses the first action. Is such a system unfair to the defendant?: "Heads I win; tails we play over and over until I win." Another way of putting the point is to say that the rules of nonmutual preclusion make it very difficult for the defendant to place a value on litigation while it is in progress: A loss can have devastating consequences, but a victory's value is confined to a single case.

4. One solution to the problem posed by *Century Home Components* lies in judicial control of dockets. In many jurisdictions, claims arising out of the same episode — a large building fire, an airplane crash — will be assigned to the same judge for consolidated proceedings. That judge's management of the case can have substantial implications for the application of preclusion.

a. Suppose such consolidation had occurred in *Century Home Components* and that the second *Pacific N.W. Bell* case (recall that plaintiffs contended this was the best-tried of all the cases) had come first. At that point the judge would have been writing on a clean slate: one case, well-tried, with a plaintiff's verdict resulting. Preclusion might have seemed like an attractive possibility.

b. To avoid the premature use of preclusion, some judges faced with these circumstances will purposely set several cases for trial to see if the results are inconsistent or if a pattern develops. Is this a better approach?

5. *Century Home Components* involved a single occurrence affecting several parties; the analogy to a transportation disaster seems apt. But there are other patterns of mass torts, one of the most common of which is the mass product liability case. One of the major areas of such litiga-

tion has been claims of asbestos-related injuries. The general fact patterns are similar: Workers in factories, shipyards, or in mining, years after exposure to various forms of asbestos, develop one of several forms of lung disease.

a. One might imagine that such litigation would present an occasion for applying issue preclusion against defendant producers of asbestos. But the courts have not typically done so. Should they?

b. As the asbestos cases have developed, a variation on preclusion has occurred. As hundreds of cases have been tried over a number of years, the lawyers on both sides have come to recognize patterns of verdicts. These patterns include both determinations of liability (was the plaintiff's death caused by, for example, smoking rather than by asbestos?) and of damages. Using these patterns of verdicts, lawyers and judges have begun to develop bases for settling the cases relatively quickly, sometimes without any formal court proceedings.

c. Is such a development a triumph or a failure of the system? On the one hand, it seems clear that the pattern of verdicts provides a much more reliable basis for assessment than a single case, no matter how well tried. On the other hand, the litigants whose cases have produced that pattern have "paid" for the information, sometimes quite literally with their lives.

6. The position of the Restatement (Second) of Judgments on mutuality is as follows:

§29. Issue Preclusion in Subsequent Litigation with Others

A party precluded from relitigating an issue with an opposing party, in accordance with §§27 and 28,* is also precluded from doing so with another person unless he lacked full and fair opportunity to litigate the issue in the first action or other circumstances justify affording him an opportunity to relitigate the issue. The circumstances to which considerations should be given include those enumerated in §28 and also whether:

(1) Treating the issue as conclusively determined would be incompatible with an applicable scheme of administering the remedies in the actions involved;

(2) The forum in the second action affords the party against whom preclusion is asserted procedural opportunities in the presentation and determination of the issue that were not available in the first action and that could likely result in the issue being differently determined;

(3) The person seeking to invoke favorable preclusion, or to avoid unfavorable preclusion, could have effected joinder in the first action between himself and his present adversary;

---

* See supra page 834 and infra pages 865–867 et seq. — ED.

(4) The determination relied on as preclusive was itself inconsistent with another determination of the same issue;

(5) The prior determination may have been affected by relationships among the parties to the first action that are not present in the subsequent action, or apparently was based on a compromise verdict or finding;

(6) Treating the issue as conclusively determined may complicate determination of issues in the subsequent action or prejudice the interests of another party thereto;

(7) The issue is one of law and treating it as conclusively determined would inappropriately foreclose opportunity for obtaining reconsideration of the legal rule upon which it was based;

(8) Other compelling circumstances make it appropriate that the party be permitted to relitigate the issue.

Restatement (Second) of Judgments. Do any of these factors justify the result in *Century Home Components?* Is there a common thread running through these exceptions?

7. Should issue preclusion apply if the first case is a criminal proceeding? In Teitelbaum Furs, Inc. v. Dominion Insurance Co., 58 Cal. 2d 601, 375 P.2d 439, 25 Cal. Rptr. 559 (1962), cert. denied, 372 U.S. 966 (1963), Teitelbaum Furs sued to recover on a theft insurance policy. The insurance company sought to invoke a criminal judgment convicting Teitelbaum, plaintiff's president, of stealing the furs. The court applied issue preclusion, finding that Teitelbaum was the alter ego of the company and had been "afforded a full opportunity to litigate the issue of his guilt with all the safeguards afforded the criminal litigant, and . . . he had every possible motive to make as vigorous a defense as possible." 58 Cal. 2d at 606-607, 375 P.2d at 441, 25 Cal. Rptr. at 661. Teitelbaum's decision not to testify was, according to the court, a matter of trial strategy not affecting issue preclusion. Is this an adequate resolution of the differences between civil and criminal proceedings?

C. The Boundaries of Preclusion

With *Century Home Components* we have already begun to approach the topic of this section — the point at which preclusion doctrines should yield. Both claim and issue preclusion are judge-made doctrines, and neither is engraved in stone. With the exception of the full faith and credit issues, to be considered in the next section, and the due process restrictions on the excessive use of either doctrine, neither has significant consititutional dimensions. Thus it is not surprising that other policies should occasionally challenge the applications of either doctrine.

1. Claim Preclusion

Claim preclusion, or res judicata, has more stringent requirements than issue preclusion and therefore presents fewer opportunities for anomalous results. Section 26 of the Restatement (Second) of Judgments lists some straightforward reasons for declining to apply claim preclusion: where the parties have expressly or implicitly agreed to allow claim splitting; where a court has in the first action reserved plaintiff's right to bring the second; or where jurisdictional limitations prevented plaintiff from seeking certain forms of relief now sought. Past that point, the Restatement enters uncertain ground:

§26. Exceptions to the General Rule Concerning Splitting

(1) When any of the following circumstances exists, the general rule of §24 does not apply to extinguish the claim, and part or all of the claim subsists as a possible basis for a second action by the plaintiff against the defendant:. . . .

(d) The judgment in the first action was plainly inconsistent with the fair and equitable implementation of a statutory or constitutional scheme, or it is the sense of the scheme that the plaintiff shoud be permitted to split his claim; or

(e) For reasons of substantive policy in a case involving a continuing or recurrent wrong, the plaintiff is given an option to sue once for the total harm, both past and prospective, or to sue from time to time for the damages incurred to the date of suit, and chooses the latter course; or

(f) It is clearly and convincingly shown that the policies favoring preclusion of a second action are overcome for an extraordinary reason, such as the apparent invalidity of a continuing restraint or condition having a vital relation to personal liberty or the failure of the prior litigation to yield a coherent disposition of the controversy.

The situation imagined in (d) typically involves a broadly applicable law as to which interpretation has changed. Imagine that in the years before Brown v. Board of Education, 347 U.S. 483 (1954), a school child sues seeking racial integration of her school. She loses. The next year *Brown* is decided. It has to be possible for the plaintiff, otherwise bound by the now rejected interpretation of the Constitution, to take advantage of the changed law. Section 26(e) seeks the same result for situations involving repeated interactions between the same parties.

The final catchall exception is designed to help courts out of messes that inconsistent prior decisions can lead to. One prominent example is Adams v. Pearson, 411 Ill. 431, 104 N.E.2d 267 (1952). Adams sold a farm to Pearson for a down payment of $4,000 and a balance of $14,600, to be paid when Pearson sold a farm in Indiana. The contract required

Adams and his wife to sign a warranty deed. When Mrs. Adams refused to sign, Adams sought rescission of the contract in a counterclaim to Pearson's suit for specific performance, with various suggested means of protecting Mrs. Adams's dower rights. The court denied specific performance because it was unavailable in Illinois at that time in cases in which the wife had not waived her dower right. The court also denied the counterclaim, however, because there was no showing of fraud on Pearson's part. Pearson had been in possession of the farm since the time of the signing of the contract but had refused to pay the balance of the contract price without the warranty deed. Adams then brought an action in ejectment; Pearson counterclaimed for specific performance in the form of a warranty deed signed by Adams alone. Both parties pleaded claim preclusion as a defense to the claim of the other. As the Illinois Supreme Court noted, application of the doctrine would have been standard under most circumstances but would have left Pearson, after ten years of litigation, with possession but not title, and Adams, after ten years, with title but no money. The court decided that application of claim preclusion was inappropriate and that the equities of the case lay with Pearson, who was allowed to prevail in his counterclaim for a warranty deed signed by Adams but not his wife.

Apart from these rather unusual circumstances, courts take claim preclusion very seriously, even when the prior decision has obviously been erroneous. Recall Gargallo v. Merrill, Lynch, Pierce, Fenner & Smith, supra page 830, in which the Sixth Circuit was prepared to give preclusive effect to a state court judgment on a claim over which federal courts have exclusive jurisdiction. Matsushita Elec. Industrial Co. v. Epstein, supra page 583, provides another example. Again, there was a state court judgment embodying a settlement of a securities claim over which the federal courts have exclusive jurisdiction. For the majority in Matsushita, the only question to be discussed was whether the state courts would assign preclusive effects to such a judgment.

Should there be exceptions to the ordinary principles of claim preclusion for certain kinds of claims? One candidate might be federal civil rights claims, which have their genesis in congressional distrust of state courts. Should state court litigation — in which federal civil rights claims are not raised — preclude their later litigation in federal court? Yes, said the U.S. Supreme Court in Migra v. Warren City School District, 465 U.S. 75 (1984). In Migra the plaintiff brought a state court contract action challenging her dismissal as a teacher. After that case went to judgment, she brought a federal civil rights action alleging that her dismissal had been motivated by her role in preparing for desegregation of the schools. The Court held that the federal civil rights claim would be barred in federal court if the state courts would bar it. The Court reasoned that a plaintiff who wanted a federal forum for her civil rights claim was free to bring the original lawsuit in federal court; if she chose instead to use the state courts, then state preclusion law ought to apply, even if that meant barring unlitigated federal civil rights claims. Congress was free, said the court, to provide for statutory exceptions to the common law of claim preclusion, but it hadn't done so. Isn't the very existence of federal rights statutes an indication that Congress did not entirely trust state courts to be fair with such claims?

2. Issue Preclusion

Exceptions to the application of issue preclusion, or collateral estoppel, are more numerous than exceptions to claim preclusion. The Restatement (Second) of Judgments §28, excerpts of which are reprinted below, provides a guide to the terrain:

§28. Exceptions to the General Rule of Issue Preclusion

Although an issue is actually litigated and determined by a valid and final judgment, and the determination is essential to the judgment, relitigation of the issue in a subsequent action between the parties is not precluded in the following circumstances:

> (1) The party against whom preclusion is sought could not, as a matter of law, have obtained review of the judgment in the initial action. . . .

An example of this principle may be found in Murphy v. Andrews, 465 F. Supp. 511 (E.D. Pa. 1979), in which the plaintiff charged various police officials with violation of his civil rights by beating him in an attempt to obtain a confession from him. In the criminal proceedings against him, plaintiff sought to suppress his confession on those grounds but lost the motion on a finding that illegal duress had not taken place. Subsequently, another party confessed to the murder, and plaintiff was acquitted. Plaintiff then brought the civil action in question, and defendants argued that the ruling in the criminal case settled the question of the legality of the interrogation. The court ruled otherwise, suggesting that even if plaintiff had appealed the denial of the suppression order, the appeal would have been useless because of the acquittal. Note that this latter rationale suggests a principle somewhat broader than that set out in §28 of the Restatement. The original draft of this section specified that the review of the judgment should be "by an appellate court"; the deletion presumably indicates that the drafters may have had in mind proceedings in which a federal district court reviews a magistrate judge's findings or in which a trial court reviews an administrative agency's findings.

> (2) The issue is one of law and (a) the two actions involve claims that are substantially unrelated, or (b) a new determination is warranted in order to take account of an intervening change in the applicable legal context or otherwise to avoid inequitable administration of the laws. . . .

In Commissioner v. Sunnen, 333 U.S. 591 (1948), a device for attributing certain income to a wife instead of her husband (in order to pay a lower rate on it) had been upheld by a decision of the Board of Tax Appeals. The device was used for many years, and the IRS challenged it again after a series of decisions had undercut the reasoning of the original decision. The Supreme Court denied application of issue preclusion against the IRS on several grounds, including the change in the applicable law. Why is *Sunnen* an issue-preclusion rather than a claim-preclusion case?

> (3) A new determination of the issue is warranted by differences in the quality or extensiveness of the procedures followed in the two courts or by factors relating to the allocation of jurisdiction between them. . . .

Newport News Shipbuilding and Drydock Co. v. Director, 583 F.2d 1273 (4th Cir. 1978), illustrates the point relating to jurisdiction of the two courts. Plaintiff had sought damages for a work-related lung disease from the Virginia Industrial Commission. He lost on a finding that the injury did not arise in the course of employment. The plaintiff subsequently sought compensation in federal court under the federal Longshoremen's and Harbor Workers' Compensation Act. The finding of the state industrial commission that the injury did not arise out of the plaintiff's employment was not given issue-preclusion effect because of the commission's limited jurisdiction. By law the commission was limited to claims under the state workers' compensation law.

In another common application of this principle, actions in small claims or traffic courts to not have issue-preclusion effect. Thus the defendant's conviction in traffic court for speeding will not give rise to issue preclusion in a subsequent negligence action. This result is a practical recognition of the informal procedures and lack of adequate opportunity for discovery that often prevail in such courts.

> (4) The party against whom preclusion is sought had a significantly heavier burden of persuasion with respect to the issue in the initial action than in the subsequent action; the burden has shifted to his adversary; or the adversary has a significantly heavier burden than he had in the first action. . . .

Newport News Shipbuilding also illustrates this principle, because the worker had the burden of showing by a preponderance of the evidence before the state industrial board that his injury arose out of his employment, while his burden in the federal action was much weaker.

> (5) There is a clear and convincing need for a new determination of the issue (a) because of the potential adverse impact of the determination on the public interest or the interests of persons not themselves parties in the initial action, (b) because it was not sufficiently foreseeable at the time of the initial action that the issue would arise in the context of a subsequent action, or (c) because the party sought to be precluded, as a result of the conduct of his adversary or other special circumstances, did not have an adequate opportunity or incentive to obtain a full and fair adjudication in the initial action.

Points (b) and (c) are discussed in both *Parklane Hosiery* and *Century Home Components.* Point (a) was an alternative basis for the holding for the *Sunnen* tax case: The public interest in the evenhanded application of the tax laws suggested that a taxpayer should not be able to take perpetual advantage of an earlier superseded decision. A similar rationale has been applied to decisions categorizing goods for import duty purposes. Assume A and B import the same products. A engages in litigation with the government and obtains a favorable ruling concerning import duties, and B litigates with the government and receives an unfavorable decision. Giving permanent issue-preclusion effect to A's judgment will give A a permanent competitive advantage over B. United States v. Stone & Downer Co., 274 U.S. 225 (1927). Note also that the public interest may also call for application of issue preclusion and even the abandonment of mutuality. The decision in *Blonder-Tongue*, discussed extensively in *Parklane Hosiery*, was based partially on the public interest in consistent adjudications with respect to the same patent: If some manufacturers are bound by a patent while others have won adjudications of its invalidity, the market will be distorted by the unequal costs of the suppliers, some of whom have to pay royalties while others do not.

3.   The Law of the Case and "Judicial Estoppel"

Two doctrines logically and technically distinct from claim and issue preclusion sometimes play roles resembling them: the law of the case and "judicial estoppel" (also sometimes known as preclusion of inconsistent positions). A brief survey may help to clarify their rather narrow roles and to distinguish them from claim and issue preclusion.

The law of the case functions within a single case to prevent relitigation of decided points of law. Suppose that plaintiff seeks injunctive
relief concerning an allegedly unconstitutional municipal hiring
practice — perhaps a requirement that city police officers be residents
of the city. The district court grants a preliminary injunction, and, pursuant to 28 U.S.C. §1292(a)(1), the loser appeals. The appellate court
affirms the district court's interpretation of the law and remands for a
trial on final injunctive relief. Neither the doctrine of precedent nor the
doctrine of issue preclusion would prevent the loser from seeking to re-
argue his position on remand to the district court nor on a subsequent
appeal of the final judgment. Precedent would not apply because it is
the same case, and issue preclusion would not apply because there would
as yet be no final judgment. Enter the law of the case, which serves to
stabilize such a legal ruling once it has been made. That doctrine essentially says that the parties get a single appellate shot at their legal contentions and that, once they have achieved such an appellate ruling, it continues to govern in subsequent trial and appellate proceedings. If the loser
does not like the initial appellate ruling, his remedy lies in a petition for
certiorari to the U.S. Supreme Court. What he may not do is to continue
to argue the question in the lower courts.

The doctrine of judicial estoppel (or preclusion of inconsistent positions) lacks the sharp definition of the law of the case. Not all courts
apply it, and those that do cannot entirely agree on its definition. One
commentator has bluntly if inaccurately described it as a prohibition on
lying. Comment: Raising the Cost of Lying: Rethinking *Erie* for Judicial
Estoppel, 64 U. Chi. L. Rev. 873 (1997). Courts typically invoke judicial
estoppel when a party has taken a sworn position in a prior proceeding,
benefited from that position by receiving a judgment or other official
award, and now seeks to take a differing position in the present proceeding
in order to win a judgment that would rest on a basis inconsistent with
his prior position. One court has sought to describe judicial estoppel by
contrasting it with issue preclusion:

> Collateral estoppel forecloses "the relitigation of issues of fact or law that
> are identical to issues which have been actually determined and necessarily
> decided in prior litigation in which the party against whom [issue preclu-
> sion] is asserted had a full and fair opportunity to litigate." For collateral
> estoppel to apply, the proponent must establish that: (1) the issue sought
> to be precluded is identical to one previously litigated; (2) the issue must
> have been actually determined in the prior proceeding; (3) determination
> of the issue must have been a critical and necessary part of the decision
> in the prior proceeding; (4) the prior judgment must be final and valid;
> and (5) the party against whom estoppel is asserted must have had a full
> and fair opportunity to litigate the issue in the previous forum. . . .

. . . [By contrast, "j]udicial estoppel precludes a party from adopting a position that is inconsistent with a stance taken in prior litigation," John S. Clark Co. v. Faggert & Frieden P.C., 65 F.3d 26, 28 (4th Cir. 1995), and is designed to prevent a party from "playing fast and loose" with the courts and "protect the essential integrity of the judicial process." Allen v. Zurich Ins. Co., 667 F.2d 1162, 1166 (4th Cir. 1982). Although "courts have had difficulty in formulating a specific test for determining when judicial estoppel should be applied," at least three elements must always be satisfied. Lowery v. Stovall, 92 F.3d 219, 223-24 (4th Cir. 1996), cert. denied, 117 S. Ct. 954 (1997). First, the party sought to be estopped must assert a position inconsistent with that taken in prior litigation and the position must be one of fact rather than law or legal theory. Second, the prior inconsistent position must have been accepted by the court. Id. And third, the party sought to be estopped must intentionally have misled the court to gain unfair advantage.

Sedlack v. Braswell Services Group Inc., 134 F.3d 219 (4th Cir. 1998). Note that with issue preclusion an issue must have been contested and decided *against* the party burdened with preclusion; with judicial estoppel the party burdened has typically *prevailed* in the prior litigation. Further note that even if a court does not apply judicial estoppel, the opposing party remains perfectly free to present evidence of prior sworn, inconsistent statements to the trier of fact. The doctrine thus serves primarily to prevent a second factfinder from overlooking or disregarding a party's prior inconsistent position.

A number of recent cases have invoked judicial estoppel in the context of successive actions by former employees who have obtained Social Security benefits — on grounds of total disability — and then have sued their employers under the Americans with Disabilities Act (ADA) or the Age Discrimination in Employment Act, alleging fitness for employment. One influential, but criticized, case is McNemar v. Disney Store, Inc., 91 F.3d 610 (3d Cir. 1996). Plaintiff, dismissed from his job, sought and received disability benefits on grounds of total disability. He then sued under the ADA, alleging ability to work given appropriate accommodation. As a test of your understanding, see why issue preclusion would not apply here: The plaintiff had prevailed in the first proceedings against the Social Security Administration and was now suing a different party, the former employer. Ordinarily issue preclusion applies when a contention has been forced on the party to be burdened; here the plaintiff had prevailed. Responding to this situation, the Third Circuit issued a ruling that has been interpreted as a "per se" rule of estoppel: The successful receipt of benefits based on an allegation of total disability bars subsequent actions in which an allegation of ability to work is required.

The U.S. Supreme Court has subsequently held that the definitions of "disability" under the Social Security Act (SSA) and the ADA are sufficiently different that such a per se rule is inappropriate:

> We believe that, in context, these two seemingly divergent statutory contentions are often consistent, each with the other. Thus pursuit, and receipt, of SSDI benefits does not automatically estop the recipient from pursuing an ADA claim. Nor does the law erect a strong presumption against the recipient's success under the ADA. Nonetheless, an ADA plaintiff cannot simply ignore her SSDI contention that she was too disabled to work. To survive a defendant's motion for summary judgment, she must explain why that SSDI contention is consistent with her ADA claim that she could "perform the essential functions" of her previous job, at least with "reasonable accommodation.". . .
>
> This case does not involve . . . directly conflicting statements about purely factual matters, such as "The light was red/green," or "I can/cannot raise my arm above my head." An SSA representation of total disability differs from a purely factual statement in that it often implies a context-related legal conclusion, namely "I am disabled for purposes of the Social Security Act." And our consideration of this latter kind of statement consequently leaves the law related to the former, purely factual, kind of conflict where we found it. . . .
>
> Nonetheless, in some cases an earlier SSDI claim may turn out genuinely to conflict with an ADA claim. Summary judgment for a defendant is appropriate when the plaintiff "fails to make a showing sufficient to establish the existence of an element essential to [her] case, and on which [she] will bear the burden of proof at trial." Celotex Corp. v. Catrett, [supra page 630]. An ADA plaintiff bears the burden of proving that she is a "qualified individual with a disability" — that is, a person "who, with or without reasonable accommodation, can perform the essential functions" of her job. And a plaintiff's sworn assertion in an application for disability benefits that she is, for example, "unable to work" will appear to negate an essential element of her ADA case — at least if she does not offer a sufficient explanation. For that reason, we hold that an ADA plaintiff cannot simply ignore the apparent contradiction that arises out of the earlier SSDI total disability claim. Rather, she must proffer a sufficient explanation. . . .
>
> When faced with a plaintiff's previous sworn statement asserting "total disability" or the like, the court should require an explanation of any apparent inconsistency with the necessary elements of an ADA claim. To defeat summary judgment, that explanation must be sufficient to warrant a reasonable juror's concluding that, assuming the truth of, or the plaintiff's good faith belief in, the earlier statement, the plaintiff could nonetheless "perform the essential functions" of her job, with or without "reasonable accommodation."

Cleveland v. Policy Management Systems, 119 S Ct. 1597 (1999).

Note that judicial estoppel, whatever its exact contours, is in some tension with Rule 8(e)(2), which permits a party to state as many claims as it has, "regardless of consistency." As you have seen, the explanation of this rule lies in the parties' uncertainty about which set of facts they will be able persuasively to present. Can one reconcile the apparent conflict between Rule 8(e)(2) and the doctrine of judicial estoppel? Judicial estoppel applies not to pleadings but to sworn positions taken in actual proceedings. Many courts further limit it to situations in which those sworn statements have resulted in a judgment or award to the party now taking the inconsistent position. Are the values protected by judicial estoppel sufficiently important to warrant its elaboration? Or can we rely on the opposing party and factfinder's good sense to discredit parties who talk — under oath — out of both sides of their mouths?

D. Repose: Collateral Attack and Reopened Judgments

This chapter has focused on a pair of common law doctrines that prevent subsequent lawsuits from undermining judgments. Claim preclusion, by preventing subsequent litigation on the same claim, requires the parties to include related grievances in the same suit. Issue preclusion prevents inconsistent findings when subsequent litigation is permitted. We turn now to two principles that ensure that courts heed the doctrines of former adjudication without producing unfair hardship.

To see their relationship, consider a hypothetical case. Motorists from New York and New Jersey collide with each other. New Jersey plaintiff sues New York defendant in New Jersey state court and loses. Could plaintiff try again by going to New York and suing there in either state or federal court? Or suppose that after the original case has gone to judgment, plaintiff discovers a witness who supplies the crucial missing evidence of defendant's negligence; moreover, plaintiff discovers that defendant knew of the witness but failed to reveal his existence in response to interrogatories. Can plaintiff somehow bring this evidence before the court? The doctrines of claim preclusion do not answer the first question because, as common law doctrines, they speak only to the courts of a given jurisdiction. As the next section shows, principles of full faith and credit back up the common law by insisting that courts of one jurisdiction heed the judgments of another. But the doctrines of former adjudication, reinforced by full faith and credit, have the potential to work injustice if they perpetuate defendant's fraudulent concealment of evidence in the second case. To prevent that, legislatures have created the opportunity, in limited circumstances, to reopen a judgment.

1.   Full Faith and Credit as a Bar to Collateral Attack

The common law doctrines of claim and issue preclusion require courts of any given political unit to heed the judgments of courts of that unit. However, they give no guidance respecting the judgments of sister jurisdictions — other states or the federal government. Two provisions of law fill that silence. Section 1738 of 28 U.S.C. demands that federal courts give the same full faith and credit to state court judgments as those states would give. Though the statute does not mention full faith and credit to federal court judgments, that requirement has always been assumed and is not questioned. The Constitution itself, in Article IV, places the same obligation on state courts to recognize sister-state judgments.

If one puts these provisions together with the common law of preclusion, they create an apparently seamless web. Within any given political unit, the law of preclusion prevents attacks on the judgment: Anything that was or could have been litigated in the previous case may not be relitigated. Across the boundaries of political units, the principles of full faith and credit require that the courts of one unit give to sister courts' judgments the same credence they would have in the unit that rendered them. We have already seen these principles in operation in Gargallo v. Merrill, Lynch, Pierce, Fenner & Smith and Matsushita Elec. Industrial Co. v. Epstein, supra pages 830 and 583.

There is, however, a hole — of indeterminate size — in this doctrinal tapestry. That hole is created by a nineteenth century doctrine that has been eroded but not entirely eliminated. As you will recall from the study of jurisdiction, under some circumstances one may collaterally attack a judgment on the grounds that the court rendering it lacked jurisdiction. (That is one of the holdings of Pennoyer v. Neff, supra page 77.) Nineteenth century courts often asserted this proposition in sweeping terms, saying that a judgment entered without jurisdiction was "void." One implication of that proposition was that such a judgment was not entitled to full faith and credit.

Put in the most general terms, the objection that a judgment was invalid for want of jurisdiction created a sizable hole in the doctrines of finality. Twentieth century courts have begun, cautiously, to patch some of the hole. The next case describes the extent of this patching.

Durfee v. Duke
375 U.S. 106 (1963)

Mr. Justice STEWART delivered the opinion of the Court.

The United States Constitution requires that "Full Faith and Credit shall be given in each State to the . . . judicial Proceedings of every other State." The case before us presents questions arising under this constitutional provision and under the federal statute enacted to implement it.

In 1956 the petitioners brought an action against the respondent in a Nebraska court to quiet title to certain bottom land situated on the Missouri River. The main channel of that river forms the boundary between the States of Nebraska and Missouri. The Nebraska court had jurisdiction over the subject matter of the controversy only if the land in question was in Nebraska. Whether the land was Nebraska land depended entirely upon a factual question — whether a shift in the river's course had been caused by avulsion or accretion.[3] The respondent appeared in the Nebraska court and through counsel fully litigated the issues, explicity contesting the court's jurisdiction over the subject matter of the controversy.[4] After a hearing the court found the issues in favor of the petitioners and ordered that title to the land be quieted in them. The respondent appealed, and the Supreme Court of Nebraska affirmed the judgment after a trial de novo on the record made in the lower court. The State Supreme Court specifically found that the rule of avulsion was applicable, that the land in question was in Nebraska, that the Nebraska courts therefore had jurisdiction of the subject matter of the litigation, and that title to the land was in the petitioners. The respondent did not petition this Court for a writ of certiorari to review that judgment.

Two months later the respondent filed a suit against the petitioners in a Missouri court to quiet title to the same land. Her complaint alleged that the land was in Missouri. The suit was removed to a Federal District Court by reason of diversity of citizenship. The District Court after hearing evidence expressed the view that the land was in Missouri but held that all the issues had been adjudicated and determined in the Nebraska litigation, and that the judgment of the Nebraska Supreme Court was res judicata and "is now binding upon this court." The Court of Appeals reversed, holding that the District Court was not required to give full faith and credit to the Nebraska judgment, and that normal res judicata principles were not applicable because the controversy involved land and a court in Missouri was therefore free to retry the question of the Nebraska court's jurisdiction over the subject matter. We granted certiorari to consider a question important to the administration of justice in our federal system. For the reasons that follow, we reverse the judgment before us.

3. Throughout this litigation there has been no dispute as to the controlling effect of this factual issue.

4. This is, therefore, not a case in which a party, although afforded an opportunity to contest subject-matter jurisdiction, did not litigate the issue. Cf. Chicot County Drainage Dist. v. Baxter State Bank, 308 U.S. 371.

The constitutional command of full faith and credit, as implemented by Congress, requires that "judicial proceedings . . . shall have the same full faith and credit in every court within the United States . . . as they have by law or usage in the courts of such State . . . from which they are taken." Full faith and credit thus generally requires every State to give to a judgment at least the res judicata effect which the judgment would be accorded in the State which rendered it. "By the Constitutional provision for full faith and credit, the local doctrines of res judicata, speaking generally, become part of national jurisprudence, and therefore federal questions cognizable here."

It is not questioned that the Nebraska courts would give full res judicata effect to the Nebraska judgment quieting title in the petitioners. It is the respondent's position, however, that whatever effect the Nebraska courts might give to the Nebraska judgment, the federal court in Missouri was free independently to determine whether the Nebraska court in fact had jurisdiction over the subject matter, i.e., whether the land in question was actually in Nebraska.

In support of this position the respondent relies upon the many decisions of this Court which have held that a judgment of a court in one State is conclusive upon the merits in a court in another State only if the court in the first State had power to pass on the merits — had jurisdiction, that is, to render the judgment. As Mr. Justice Bradley stated the doctrine in the leading case of Thompson v. Whitman, 18 Wall. 457 [(1873)], "we think it clear that the jurisdiction of the court by which a judgment is rendered in any State may be questioned in a collateral proceeding in another State, notwithstanding the provision of the fourth article of the Constitution and the law of 1790, and notwithstanding the averments contained in the record of the judgment itself." The principle has been restated and applied in a variety of contexts.

However, while it is established that a court in one State, when asked to give effect to the judgment of a court in another State, may constitutionally inquire into the foreign court's jurisdiction to render that judgment, the modern decisions of this Court have carefully delineated the permissible scope of such an inquiry. From these decisions there emerges the general rule that a judgment is entitled to full faith and credit — even as to questions of jurisdiction — when the second court's inquiry disclosed that those questions have been fully and fairly litigated and finally decided in the court which rendered the original judgment.

With respect to questions of jurisdiction over the person,[8] this principle was unambiguously established in Baldwin v. Iowa State Traveling Men's

---

8. It is not disputed in the present case that the Nebraska courts had jurisdiction over the respondent's person. She entered a general appearance in the trial court, and initiated the appeal to the Nebraska Supreme Court.

Assn., 283 U.S. 522 [(1931)]. There it was held that a federal court in Iowa must give binding effect to the judgment of a federal court in Missouri despite the claim that the original court did not have jurisdiction over the defendant's person, once it was shown to the court in Iowa that that question had been fully litigated in the Missouri forum. "Public policy," said the Court, "dictates that there be an end of litigation; that those who have contested an issue shall be bound by the result of the contest, and that matters once tried shall be considered forever settled as between the parties. We see no reason why this doctrine should not apply in every case where one voluntarily appears, presents his case and is fully heard, and why he should not, in the absence of fraud, be thereafter concluded by the judgment of the tribunal to which he has submitted his cause."

Following the *Baldwin* case, this Court soon made clear in a series of decisions that the general rule is no different when the claim is made that the original forum did not have jurisdiction over the subject matter. In each of these cases the claim was made that a court, when asked to enforce the judgment of another forum, was free to retry the question of that forum's jurisdiction over the subject matter. In each case this Court held that since the question of subject-matter jurisdiction had been fully litigated in the original forum, the issue could not be retried in a subsequent action between the parties. . . .

In *Treinies* [v. Sunshine Mining Co., 308 U.S. 66 (1939)], the rule was succinctly stated: "One trial of an issue is enough. 'The principles of res judicata apply to questions of jurisdiction as well as to other issues,' as well to jurisdiction of the subject matter as of the parties."

The reasons for such a rule are apparent. In the words of the Court's opinion in Stoll v. Gottlieb, [305 U.S. 165, 172 (1938)],

> We see no reason why a court, in the absence of an allegation of fraud in obtaining the judgment, should examine again the question whether the court making the earlier determination on an actual contest over jurisdiction between the parties, did have jurisdiction of the subject matter of the litigation. . . . Courts to determine the rights of parties are an integral part of our system of government. It is just as important that there should be a place to end as that there should be a place to begin litigation. After a party has his day in court, with opportunity to present his evidence and his view of the law, a collateral attack upon the decision as to jurisdiction there rendered merely retries the issue previously determined. There is no reason to expect that the second decision will be more satisfactory than the first.

To be sure, the general rule of finality or jurisdictional determinations is not without exceptions. Doctrines of federal pre-emption or sovereign immunity may in some contexts be controlling. Kalb v. Feuerstein, 308

U.S. 433 [(1940)]; United States v. United States Fidelity Co., 309 U.S. 506 [(1940)].[12] But no such overriding considerations are present here. . . .

It is to be emphasized that all that was ultimately determined in the Nebraska litigation was title to the land in question as between the parties to the litigation there. Nothing there decided, and nothing that could be decided in litigation between the same parties or their privies in Missouri, could bind either Missouri or Nebraska with respect to any controversy they might have, now or in the future, as to the location of the boundary between them, or as to their respective sovereignty over the land in question. Either State may at any time protect its interest by initiating indepennt judicial proceedings here.

For the reasons stated, we hold in this case that the federal court in Missouri had the power and, upon proper averments, the duty to inquire into the jurisdiction of the Nebraska courts to render the decree quieting title to the land in the petitioners. We further hold that when that inquiry disclosed, as it did, that the jurisdictional issues had been fully and fairly litigated by the parties and finally determined in the Nebraska courts, the federal court in Missouri was correct in ruling that further inquiry was precluded. Accordingly the judgment of the Court of Appeals is reversed, and that of the District Court is affirmed.

It is so ordered.

Mr. Justice BLACK, concurring.

Petitioners and respondent dispute the ownership of a tract of land adjacent to the Missouri River, which is the boundary between Nebraska

---

12. It is to be noted, however, that in neither of these cases had the jurisdictional issues actually been litigated in the first forum.

The Restatement of Conflict of Laws recognizes the possibility of such exceptions:

> Where a court has jurisdiction over the parties and determines that it has jurisdiction over the subject matter, the parties cannot collaterally attack the judgment on the ground that the court did not have jurisdiction over the subject matter, unless the policy underlying the doctrine of res judicata is outweighed by the policy against permitting the court to act beyond its jurisdiction. Among the factors appropriate to be considered in determining that collateral attack should be permitted are that
> (a) the lack of jurisdiction over the subject matter was clear;
> (b) the determination as to jurisdiction depended upon a question of law rather than of fact;
> (c) the court was one of limited and not of general jurisdiction;
> (d) the question of jurisdiction was not actually litigated;
> (e) the policy against the court's acting beyond its jurisdiction is strong.

Restatement, Conflict of Laws, §451(2) (Supp. 1948). See Restatement, Judgments, §10 (1942).

and Missouri. Resolution of this question turns on whether the land is in Nebraska or Missouri. Neither State, of course, has power to make a determination binding on the other as to which State the land is in. U.S. Const., Art. III, §2; 28 U.S.C. §1251(a). However, in a private action brought by these Nebraska petitioners, the Nebraska Supreme Court has held that the disputed tract is in Nebraska. In the present suit, brought by this Missouri respondent in Missouri, the United States Court of Appeals has refused to be bound by the Nebraska court's judgment. I concur in today's reversal of the Court of Appeal's judgment, but with the understanding that we are not deciding the question whether the respondent would continue to be bound by the Nebraska judgment should it later be authoritatively decided, either in an original proceeding between the States in this Court or by a compact between the two States under Art. I, §10, that the disputed tract is in Missouri.

NOTES AND PROBLEMS

1. Begin by framing the issue clearly.

a. *Durfee* seems to be a simple case: The contesting party appeared, specifically litigated the issue of jurisdiction (both at trial and on appeal), and lost. There had been a full judicial airing of the contested matter.

b. Suppose that the question a party sought to relitigate was an ordinary factual one: the date of a purported deed conveying the land. If a Nebraska court had decided that question, ordinary preclusion doctrine would bar its relitigation in any subsequent action between the same parties. The Full Faith and Credit clauses would require that a Missouri court (or a federal court) give the same effect to that decided issue as a Nebraska court.

c. In fact the Nebraska court had decided an issue — whether it had jurisdiction over the subject matter of the case.

d. So why did Duke think he could relitigate the question in another court?

2. Suppose the Missouri parties had not appeared in the Nebraska action (believing that the Nebraska court had no jurisdiction over them or their property), and the Nebraska parties did not appear in the Missouri federal court proceedings on a similar ground. Each court, believing the land to be located within its jurisdiction, could claim jurisdiction based on the fact that ownership of the land was directly in dispute (citing Shaffer v. Heitner. See Chapter II). But neither side could invoke the principle of *Durfee*, could it? What would be the result if the Nebraska court ordered its sheriff to protect the possession of the Nebraska parties

and the federal court ordered the federal marshal to evict the Nebraska parties?

3. Suppose the Missouri parties had appeared in the Nebraska proceedings but failed to raise the jurisdictional issue. There would be no issue preclusion because the issue was not actually litigated and determined. Is there nevertheless waiver of the jurisdictional defense?

The answer to that question is cloudy because of the maneuvering room created by nineteenth century courts that had declared that judgments entered without jurisdiction were "void," with the corollary that they could be attacked (or ignored) in subsequent litigation. Because the issue decided in the Missouri proceeding could be described as jurisdiction, Duke could argue that he was free to challenge it collaterally.

4. Understanding this maneuvering room requires a review of the half-steps by which the Court has almost — but not quite — assimilated jurisdictional challenges to other preclusion doctrine.

a. The starting point is Pennoyer v. Neff, which states that an unnotified party over whom the court lacks personal jurisdiction may collaterally challenge the resulting judgment.

b. The opposite proposition — that a party who appears and contests personal jurisdiction is bound by the court's decision on the jurisdictional question — was decided in Baldwin v. Iowa State Travelling Men's Assn., described in the *Durfee* opinion.

c. *Durfee* itself extends the *Baldwin* holding to subject matter jurisdiction: A party who appears and litigates a challenge to subject matter jurisdiction is bound by the resulting decision.

d. Defendants who appear but fail to raise a challenge to personal jurisdiction are universally treated as having waived their objections. Rule 12(h).

5. The principles thus far described leave gaps: How does one treat a defendant who was properly notified but failed to raise an objection to subject matter jurisdiction? (One might further subdivide matters by distinguishing between defendants who defaulted and those who appeared but defended on other, nonjurisdictional grounds.) It is here that the Supreme Court has wavered — almost but not quite endorsing the ordinary rules of preclusion — that would preclude relitigation of jurisdictional issues under these circumstances.

a. The Court's nearest approach to this "ordinary principles of preclusion" position came in Chicot County Drainage District v. Baxter State Bank, 308 U.S. 371 (1940). In that case two defendants were notified of the action but did not appear. The Court held that they were bound by the resulting decree even though the statute under which that decree was rendered was declared to be unconstitutional.

b. Had matters remained there, *Durfee* might have been a brief per curiam opinion. But in the same term as *Chicot County* the Court decided Kalb v. Feuerstein, 308 U.S. 433 (1940). In *Kalb* the Court held that a properly notified defendant who had not appeared could nevertheless challenge the decree collaterally, because the statute specifically created an exception to the principles forbidding collateral attack. Thus stated, *Kalb* sounds easy to reconcile with *Chicot County.* The difficulty is that the statute did not state in unequivocal — or even in equivocal — terms that it overcame preclusion; instead the Court implied the exception to preclusion from the statute's purposes.

c. There matters stand. One can say that a litigant who litigates jurisdiction, whether subject matter or personal, is bound by the decision. One can say that a defendant who does not appear can raise a collateral challenge to personal jurisdiction and that a defendant who appears but does not challenge personal jurisdiction thereby waives her objection. One cannot, however, be certain about collateral challenges to subject matter jurisdiction. *Chicot County* suggests that ordinary preclusion rules will apply to bar afterthought challenges. *Kalb* stands as a reminder that there will be exceptions, either by virtue of specific statutory exemptions or those implied by the importance of the jurisdictional challenge.

d. One may not collaterally attack subject matter jurisdiction for failure of diversity, Des Moines Navigation & Railroad v. Iowa Homestead Co., 123 U.S. 552 (1887), even though a court may dismiss sua sponte for lack of diversity on appeal in the original case, Capron v. Van Noorden, 6 U.S. 126 (1804).

e. Conversely, states may choose to declare judgments of their own courts void when they lack subject matter jurisdiction; such judgments are subject to attack at any time. See the discussions in Gargallo v. Merrill, Lynch, Pierce, Fenner & Smith, supra page 830. Under the full faith and credit statute, 28 U.S.C. §1738, and its requirement to give the "same" full faith and credit as the rendering state, the second state must look to the effect that the first state gives its own judgments from courts lacking subject matter jurisdiction.

f. Even if a court has jurisdiction over the defendant and the subject matter, the defendant may collaterally attack the judgment in another state by showing that it was procured fraudulently, Bondeson v. Pepsico, Inc., 573 S.W.2d 842 (Tex. Civ. App. 1978) (summary judgment in favor of plaintiff on Florida judgment denied where defendant alleged that plaintiff had promised to dismiss the Florida action and not prosecute it further).

6. Fraud aside, the requirement of full faith and credit to judgments is a strict one, as illustrated by Fauntleroy v. Lum, 210 U.S. 230 (1908).

The parties had made a contract in Mississippi that was illegal (in fact, criminal) under Mississippi law. Plaintiff sued defendant in Mississippi but voluntarily dismissed the case before judgment on the merits. Then plaintiff sued in Missouri, apparently on the basis of transient jurisdiction, and the Missouri courts enforced the contract. It is likely that if the illegality of the contract had been raised in the Missouri proceedings, the principle requiring full faith and credit to the laws (as opposed to the judgments) of another state would have required Missouri to apply Mississippi law and to refuse enforcement of the contract. Nonetheless, plaintiff took his Missouri judgment to Mississippi for enforcement. The Mississippi courts balked, but the Supreme Court ruled that they were required to enforce the Missouri judgment because the Missouri court had jurisdiction. In effect, the Court said that all but the jurisdictional questions had to be raised and appealed in the first action.

7. Although by ignoring several bases for refusing enforcement of the Missouri judgment, *Fauntleroy* establishes a strict principle for judgments, the law of recognition of equitable decrees is not nearly so severe. The majority of American courts holds that a decree is entitled to full faith and credit with respect to the circumstances and issues as of the time of the decree. But since decrees are generally modifiable because of changed circumstances in the courts that rendered them, changed circumstances subsequent to the rendition of the decree allow its modification in another state. See, for example, Ashwood v. Ashwood, 371 So. 2d 924 (Ala. Civ. App. 1979) ("best interests" of a child in a custody determination can never be finally determined).

The changed-circumstance rule plays a large role in one of the most frequent and bitter disputes over interstate enforcement of equitable decrees — battles over child custody and support decrees. The intensity of the parties' feelings and the frequency of changed residence of at least one party combine to create opportunity for contest and bitterness. Several legislative efforts have sought to alleviate at least the jurisdictional battles arising from these unhappy circumstances. The adoption of the Uniform Reciprocal Enforcement of Support Act and the Uniform Child Custody Jurisdiction Act by some states has had a limited effect in solving problems of interstate jurisdiction and relitigation of facts in cases involving children. Federal legislation — 28 U.S.C. §§1738A and 1738B — requires state courts to enforce without modification a decree entered by another court if that court has met certain prerequisites. Those prerequisites include not only the obvious — jurisdiction — but also that the decree have been entered in the child's home state (except under unusual circumstances).

8. Foreign country judgments present special problems. If the United States and the foreign nation have entered into a treaty requiring reciprocal enforcement of each other's judgments, that treaty binds state and federal courts. In the absence of such a treaty, neither state nor federal courts are required to give full faith and credit under the terms of 28 U.S.C. §1738 or Article IV of the Constitution. In Hilton v. Guyot, 159 U.S. 113 (1895), however, the Supreme Court applied notions of comity and reciprocity to give some effect to foreign country judgments. Specifically it held that if a foreign country judgment resulted from proceedings that comported with broad notions of due process, the judgment would be enforced if the foreign country recognized American judgments. As noted above, comity describes the voluntary recognition of judgments. The limitation to judgments of countries that recognize American judgments is called *reciprocity*. State courts are usually held not to be bound by Hilton v. Guyot — for example, Nicol v. Tanner, 310 Minn. 68, 256 N.W.2d 796 (1976). Should the federal courts be bound by the state rule in a diversity case? Note that *Hilton* was decided before *Erie*.

2. The Reopened Judgment as an Alternative to Collateral Attack

Claim and issue preclusion combine with requirements of full faith and credit to force litigants and courts to honor judgments. In the great majority of cases, litigants wishing to challenge the correctness of a judgment must appeal the decision to a higher court rather than file a second lawsuit. This principle, intended to force challenges into regular channels, can itself work injustice. Consider the case of a litigant who discovers that her opponent has won a victory by unlawful means: Perhaps he failed to serve her with process and thus obtained a default judgment; perhaps he concealed a crucial piece of evidence by failing to produce it in response to an appropriate discovery request. In such a case appeal will not work because the original court committed no error; the complaint is instead about evidence that never reached the court's attention. But if the plaintiff simply begins a second lawsuit, she will face the defense of claim preclusion.

The escape from this dilemma lies in the opportunity to reopen a judgment. See Rule 60(b). We approach this subject gingerly because any discussion of it tends to overstate its practical availability. The basic mechanisms for correcting errors are post-trial motions in the trial court and appeals. To the extent that another postjudgment remedy is available, it necessarily undercuts the appellate system. For this reason, courts insist repeatedly that relief under Rule 60(b) is not a substitute for appeal. See, for example, Marshall v. Board of Education, 575 F.2d 417, 424 (3d Cir. 1978).

Scan Rule 60(b) and note the different grounds for which relief may be granted. Consider its effort to define the line between finality of adjudication and the sense that an injustice has occurred. Now consider what should happen, under Rule 60, if, after a final judgment, the losing litigant discovers that the opposition has failed during discovery to produce highly relevant, perhaps dispositive, materials in its possession. Compare your intuition to the results of the next case.

United States v. Beggerly

524 U.S. 38 (1998)

Chief Justice REHNQUIST delivered the opinion of the Court.

[In assembling the lands for a National Seashore, the federal government in 1979 brought a quiet title action (the *Adams* litigation) in the Southern District of Mississippi against respondents. The case turned on whether, before the date of the Louisiana Purchase in 1803, the land had been deeded to a private individual. If so, it would belong to Beggerly, and the United States would have to purchase it; if not, the U.S. government would already own it. That case settled on the eve of trial for a relatively modest sum, reflecting the uncertainty of Beggerly's title.] Judgment was entered based on this settlement agreement. In 1994, some 12 years after that judgment, respondents sued in the District Court to set aside the settlement agreement and obtain a damage award for the disputed land. . . .

During discovery in the *Adams* litigation, respondents sought proof of their title to the land. Government officials searched public land records and told respondents that they had found nothing proving that any part of Horn Island had ever been granted to a private landowner. Even after the settlement in the *Adams* litigation, however, respondents continued to search for evidence of a land patent that supported their claim of title. In 1991 they hired a genealogical record specialist to conduct research in the National Archives in Washington. The specialist found materials that, according to her, showed that on August 1, 1781, Bernardo de Galvez, then the Governor General of Spanish Louisiana, granted Horn Island to [a private party].

Armed with this new information, respondents filed a complaint in the District Court on June 1, 1994. They asked the court to set aside the 1982 settlement agreement and award them damages. . . . The

District Court concluded that it was without jurisdiction to hear respondents' suit and dismissed the complaint.

The Court of Appeals reversed. It concluded that there were two jurisdictional bases for the suit. First, the suit satisfied the elements of an "independent action," as the term is used in Federal Rule of Civil Procedure 60(b). . . .

The Government's primary contention is that the Court of Appeals erred in concluding that it had jurisdiction over respondents' 1994 suit. It first attacks the lower court's conclusion that jurisdiction was established because the suit was an "independent action" within the meaning of Rule 60(b). . . . [The Government argued that although] the District Court had jurisdiction over the original Adams litigation because the United States was the plaintiff, 28 U.S.C. §1345, there was no statutory basis for the Beggerlys' 1994 action, and the District Court was therefore correct to have dismissed it.

We think the Government's position is inconsistent with the history and language of Rule 60(b). Prior to the 1937 adoption of the Federal Rules of Civil Procedure, the availability of relief from a judgment or order turned on whether the court was still in the same "term" in which the challenged judgment was entered. . . . If the term had expired, resort had to be made to a handful of writs, the precise contours of which were "shrouded in ancient lore and mystery.". . .

The 1946 Amendment [to Rule 60] . . . made clear that nearly all of the old forms of obtaining relief from a judgment, i.e., coram nobis, coram vobis, audita querela, bills of review, and bills in the nature of review, had been abolished. The revision made equally clear, however, that one of the old forms, i.e., the "independent action,"[2] still survived. The Advisory Committee notes confirmed this, indicating that "if the right to make a motion is lost by the expiration of the time limits fixed in these rules, the only other procedural remedy is by a new or independent action to set aside a judgment upon those principles which have heretofore been applied in such an action.". . .

The Government is therefore wrong to suggest that an independent action brought in the same court as the original lawsuit requires an independent basis for jurisdiction. This is not to say, however, that the requirements for a meritorious independent action have been met here. If relief may be obtained through an independent action in a case such as this, where the most that may be charged against the Government is a failure to furnish relevant information that would at best form the basis for a Rule 60(b)(3) motion, the strict 1-year time limit on such motions

---

2. This form of action was also referred to as an "original action."

would be set at naught. Independent actions must, if Rule 60(b) is to be interpreted as a coherent whole, be reserved for those cases of "injustices which, in certain instances, are deemed sufficiently gross to demand a departure" from rigid adherence to the doctrine of res judicata. Hazel-Atlas Glass Co. v. Hartford-Empire Co., 322 U.S. 238 (1944).

Such a case was Marshall v. Holmes, 141 U.S. 589 (1891), in which the plaintiff alleged that judgment had been taken against her in the underlying action as a result of a forged document. The Court said:

> According to the averments of the original petition for injunction . . . the judgments in question would not have been rendered against Mrs. Marshall but for the use in evidence of the letter alleged to be forged. The case evidently intended to be presented by the petition is one where, without negligence, laches or other fault upon the part of petitioner, [respondent] has fraudulently obtained judgments which he seeks, against conscience, to enforce by execution.

Id., at 596.

The sense of these expressions is that, under the Rule, an independent action should be available only to prevent a grave miscarriage of justice. In this case, it should be obvious that respondents' allegations do not nearly approach this demanding standard. Respondents allege only that the United States failed to "thoroughly search its records and make full disclosure to the Court" regarding the Boudreau grant. Whether such a claim might succeed under Rule 60(b)(3) we need not now decide; it surely would work no "grave miscarriage of justice," and perhaps no miscarriage of justice at all, to allow the judgment to stand. We therefore hold that the Court of Appeals erred in concluding that this was a sufficient basis to justify the reopening of the judgment in the *Adams* litigation.[4]

The judgment of the Court of Appeals is therefore reversed, and the case is remanded for further proceedings consistent with this opinion.

[Justice STEVENS's concurring opinion is omitted.]

NOTES AND PROBLEMS

1. *Beggerly* deals with several distinct problems in reopening judgments. Start with the issue that faced the plaintiff and the Supreme Court. The plaintiffs had found significant evidence not disclosed by their adversary in the prior litigation that might well have led to the award of damages many times the amount for which they had settled twelve years previously.

---

4. We therefore need not address the additional requirement that evidence of the Boudreau grant would have changed the outcome of the original action.

a. Examine Rule 60(b) carefully and explain why "an independent action," described in the Court's opinion, was the *only* avenue of relief open to them under the Rule.

b. Now explain the basis for the federal district court's jurisdiction to hear this "independent action."

c. Finally, approach the merits. Why does the Court conclude that these facts do not satisfy the criteria for reopening the judgment under the murky criteria for an independent action? Why does it not work a "grave miscarriage of justice" for the federal government to have taken the plaintiffs' land for an alleged fraction of its value?

d. The materials bearing on the case were apparently in the National Archives, which are open to anyone armed with the determination, bibliographic, and linguistic skills to make use of them. Would the case have come out differently if the same information had existed solely in confidential or secret files, such as those of the Federal Bureau of Investigation or Central Intelligence Agency?

2. Return now to the text of Rule 60(b) and consider how it might have applied had the Beggerlys uncovered the archival evidence within months after the first judgment.

a. Which sections of the Rule might apply?

b. The opinion mentions Rule 60(b)(3). Is that the most obvious one?

3. As implied in *Beggerly*, courts treat the one-year statute of limitations applying to sections (1)-(3) as meaning what it says.

a. Consider the case of the unfortunate Lorenzo Brandon:

Lorenzo Brandon sought Rule 60 relief from a judgment entered against him for failure to prosecute his case. The district court denied relief and Brandon now appeals. The facts are unusual. Indeed, Brandon claims they are unique. Brandon filed his Americans with Disabilities action against the Chicago Board of Education on August 2, 1995. His attorneys, Paul F. Peters and James C. Reho, entered appearances in the case, listing as their address the Law Offices of Paul F. Peters, One North LaSalle Street, Chicago. It is undisputed that in docketing the case, the Clerk of the United States District Court erroneously entered Paul A. Peters, another Chicago attorney, who is located at 10 South LaSalle Street, Chicago, as attorney for the plaintiff. As a result of this error, subsequent mailings from the court were directed to the wrong attorney at the wrong address. . . .

A little more than a year passed before plaintiff's counsel began to wonder what happened to the case. Upon visiting the Clerk's office in late 1996, he discovered his case had been quite active without him. Included in the court's file was . . . the order dismissing the case for want of prosecution.

Brandon v. Chicago Board of Education, 143 F.3d 293 (7th Cir. 1998). The Court of Appeals affirmed the dismissal. It held that a case can fall into only a single category of Rule 60(b) and that this one fell into 60(b)(1). Because it fell into (b)(1), it could not also fall into (b)(6). The one-year limit applicable to (b)(1) but not (b)(6) was therefore in effect, and because Brandon's lawyer had filed the Rule 60 motion three days after the one-year period had run, the motion was barred.

b. Can Brandon recover against his lawyer for malpractice?

4. What principles or values justify holdings like those in *Beggerly* and *Brandon*? It is easy to pillory the courts for adhering to mindless technicality in upholding unjust judgments.

a. Consider the consequences of an opposite rule: that a judgment could be reopened at any time a party had additional relevant information to present.

b. Once one rejects such a rule, there is going to be a difficult line-drawing problem. Does Rule 60 draw its lines in the right places?

5. Underlying some decisions in the Rule 60 area is realism (or cynicism) about the limits of adversarial factfinding and advocacy — a line between, if you will, litigation and science. In scientific inquiry, no evidence ever comes in too late, and no conclusion is barred from reexamination.

a. Litigation is different. We bring some disputes to an end not because we're sure we're right, but because we're sure there has to be an end to the dispute so people can move on with their lives. In such a view only a genuinely egregious mistake (and perhaps one that the other side caused) is enough to upset the judgment.

b. Moreover, the passage of time itself confers legitimacy: Old law is good law in part because we develop reliance on it.

6. Such responses seem most convincing, however, only if the litigant seeking relief has had at least one fair shot at the adversarial system.

a. Perhaps as a consequence, although the Rule itself does not make any distinction between judgments entered at different stages of the litigative process, the courts have made a very sharp distinction between default judgments and others. The effect has been to make it comparatively easy to open a default judgment on the showing of some negligence and meritorious defense. Numerous decisions state, in one way or another, a very strong policy against judgments without consideration of the merits. For example, see Caruso v. Drake Motor Lines, 78 F.R.D. 586 (E.D. Pa. 1978). Indeed, this policy is so strong that some practitioners advise against taking a default judgment unless there is absolutely no alternative. These lawyers have seen too many default judgments taken and defended in clear and justifiable circumstances, only to be set aside in the trial court or on appeal. The net result is considerable expense and a multi-year delay in the litigation.

b. As *Brandon* suggests, plaintiffs may have a somewhat harder time. Even so, when the client herself seems not to have been at fault in such circumstances, courts often grant relief. Typical may be Boughner v. Secretary of Health, Education and Welfare, 572 F.2d 976 (3d Cir. 1978), an action for black-lung benefits. The court vacated summary judgment for HEW, pursuant to Rule 60(b)(1), on finding that plaintiffs' attorney had failed to respond to motions in fifty-two cases, that some plaintiffs had been given relief under Rule 60(b) by another judge, and that plaintiffs were not at fault.

7. As a review, imagine that P and D are involved in an automobile accident. P sues D, claiming that D was intoxicated at the time and that the accident resulted from D's failure to keep a proper lookout and his inability to keep the car in his lane. At the trial, P and D testify, and the jury renders a verdict for D. Within one year, P moves to set aside the judgment. Under which of the following circumstances should it be vacated?

a. D bribed the judge.

b. D lied when he said he had been at home prior to the accident; in fact, D had just left his girlfriend's apartment.

c. W witnessed the event and observed D's negligent driving and intoxicated state. P had taken the deposition of X, who was at the scene of the accident, but X said he did not see anything and no other person was there. It now turns out that X lied because W told X he didn't want to get involved.

d. Same facts except W actually testified at the trial that he didn't see anything.

e. In any of the preceding cases, would the answer differ if the motion had been made more than one year after judgment?

PART C

EXPANDING THE FRAMEWORK OF
LITIGATION: ADDITIONAL CLAIMS
AND PARTIES

This section combines the approaches taken in the two sections that precede it. Part A took a top-down view in looking at the ways in which the U.S. Constitution establishes constraints for civil litigation. Part B started at the bottom, taking the individual lawsuit as its unit of examination.

We turn now to opportunities and problems that arise when procedural rules open the confines of a lawsuit. Our forum for that examination is the rules of joinder, the principles that allow parties to modern civil litigation to combine claims and add additional parties. Those principles constitute one of the respects in which contemporary civil litigation differs sharply from its predecessors: A modern lawsuit can, to a large extent, aim at resolving an entire dispute by encompassing all the claims and all the parties involved.

Those same principles, however, challenge both the jurisdictional scheme elaborated in Part A and the litigation process explored in Part B. In many cases jurisdictional problems will either limit or defeat joinder that would otherwise be available. From one standpoint, these limitations are undesirable restrictions on a lawsuit that would otherwise provide a comprehensive resolution to a dispute. From another standpoint, jurisdictional limits prevent what might otherwise become a litigational monster from devouring both the court system and the litigants swept into it. Joinder poses a similar issue for the design of the procedural system. Flexible joinder rules permit parties to frame issues broadly and to include everyone who has a stake in the resolution of those issues. Carried to its logical conclusion, however, this principle of inclusion can create a lawsuit that cannot resolve anything — because it is unmanageable. The Rules consequently establish a fine line by seeking broad inclusion but trying to define circumstances under which inclusiveness does not prevent resolution of the dispute.

The issues thus raised require the student to review much of the course. At the threshold of many cases will be both a pleading problem and a jurisdictional problem. The pleading problem will require the student to consider whether the party or claim fits within the joinder rule's definition. If it does, there will sometimes be a second level of inquiry: Assuming that the party or claim can be joined as a matter of pleading, does the court's jurisdictional reach extend sufficiently far to encompass this joinder? Just beyond the pleading and jurisdictional inquiries may lie a question about preclusion: Joinder is often sought in order to achieve claim or issue preclusion, and the preclusive effects of the case may supply an additional reason for joining (or not joining) a claim or party. This interplay among principles already explored makes joinder challenging — and useful as a test of one's grasp of the preceding material.

JOINDER

XIII

Modern civil procedure in the United States has two distinguishing features. One, discovery, increases the depth of any given lawsuit. The other, broad *joinder* of claims and parties, increases the breadth of a suit. To achieve this breadth, modern process turned from the single-mindedness of common law procedure and focused on the transaction rather than on the writ or legal theory. This focus permits parties to combine various claims and to add additional parties. The advantage of a larger litigative "package" is that it allows a single suit to adjudicate multiple claims against multiple parties and permits litigation to reflect some of life's complexity. Disadvantages can also flow from this freedom: Litigation can become intricate, and considerable procedural skirmishing can occur long before the merits come into view, as parties dispute whether a given effort at joinder is permitted.

A. Joinder of Claims

In our exploration of procedure up to this point, we have for the most part assumed a simple case in which one plaintiff had a single claim against one defendant, and the defendant did not have a claim against the plaintiff. But, as the reader will already have seen, many lawsuits are not that simple: A plaintiff may have more than one claim against a defendant, and a defendant may have claims against the plaintiff. We first consider joinder issues in the context of a lawsuit between a single plaintiff and a single defendant. The ensuing sections will examine the questions that arise when additional parties are joined.

891

1.   Joinder of Claims by Plaintiff

a.   *Historical Background*

At common law the rules governing joinder of claims were simple: Plaintiff could join only claims using the same writ but could do so regardless of whether the claims were factually related. For example, plaintiff could join claims for assaults on two separate occasions or a slander on one day and an act of negligence months later (both actions on the case), but could not join a claim for assault with a claim for slander, even if both were part of the same incident, because the writ for assault was trespass and the writ for slander was case. Plaintiff also could join alternative versions of the same grievance by alleging each in a separate count, as if each count referred to a separate occurrence. But, again, each version had to be within the same form of action; plaintiff could not set forth one count in assumpsit and another in trover. This principle becomes more understandable if one remembers that different writs used different forms of pretrial and trial process and that the goal of much common law procedure was to frame a single, straightforward question for the jury. Also bear in mind that the scope of former adjudication was correspondingly narrow (see supra page 798).

At common law a mistake in joinder had severe consequences. Misjoinder could lead to a successful demurrer or even the upsetting of a verdict; the defect was not waived by failure to make an early objection. One can find cases as late as the early part of this century throwing out verdicts for plaintiff because of misjoinder. See, e.g., Dean v. Cass, 73 Vt. 314, 50 A. 1085 (1901).

Equity was more relaxed than common law; indeed, this broader scope was one reason for parties' resort to equity. Although standards for joinder in equity were never made completely clear, joinder was generally permitted when claims shared a transactional relationship and raised common issues. There were limits, however, and a bill in equity could be found objectionable for *multifariousness*, meaning that it combined too many claims.

b.   *Federal Rules*

The Rules changed all this: They eliminated all barriers to joinder of claims by a plaintiff. Read Rule 18. A single plaintiff can join any and all claims he has against a single defendant. This freedom can create trial management problems. If one imagines a case between Microsoft and one of its major business partners, the possibilities are mind-boggling.

The Rules solve this problem by permitting the judge, under Rule 42(b), to sever claims for trial convenience. Such severed claims may, of course, be as distinct for pretrial and trial purposes as if the plaintiff had brought entirely separate suits.

Although Rule 18 permits joinder, it does not compel it. So far as the *Rules* are concerned there is no compulsory joinder of claims. The Rules do not, however, tell the whole story. First, the principles of former adjudication, explored in Chapter XII, often require a plaintiff to join related claims, especially when they arise out of the same incident. Moreover, a plaintiff's own interest is often served by joinder of all claims, or at least all related claims, he has against a defendant. The combination of these two factors creates a powerful incentive for plaintiffs to join claims, even in the absence of a Rule requiring that they do so. If preclusion and litigative strategy encourage broad joinder, jurisdiction often supplies an obstacle.

c.   Joinder and Jurisdiction

The most difficult joinder issues often involve jurisdictional considerations. Review of a few fundamental propositions may be helpful in setting the stage.

Assume A, a citizen of Illinois, sues B, also a citizen of Illinois, on a federal claim. Can A join a state claim against B? That question poses two subquestions: (1) Do the principles of joinder, governed by the Rules, permit combining these claims; and (2) Assuming that joinder is allowed by the rules, does the federal court have jurisdiction over the state claim thus joined?

Rule 18 creates no joinder problem in this situation. Recall that the Rule permits a plaintiff to join as many claims as she wishes, whether related or unrelated. The problem is jurisdictional: The court may lack subject matter jurisdiction over A's state law claim.

Such problems will rarely matter in state courts using the Federal Rules as a model, but they often prove important in federal litigation. The basic proposition to bear in mind is that federal courts are tribunals of limited jurisdiction: They do not have jurisdiction unless a provision of the Constitution and a statute grant it to them. In the example, the basis for jurisdiction over the plaintiff's original claim is straightforward: It arises under federal law, over which Article III and 28 U.S.C. §1331 confer jurisdiction.

Jurisdiction over the state law claim is more difficult. There is no diversity of citizenship between plaintiff and defendant. The claim arises under state rather than federal law, so there is no original federal question jurisdiction. If there is jurisdiction, it exists, therefore, only by virtue of the supplemental jurisdiction conferred by 28 U.S.C. §1367. Reread that statute and consider what question would have to be answered to resolve the jurisdictional issue here.

Section 1367 has a particularly important feature for our exploration of joinder. Its grant of supplemental jurisdiction depends on three variables: (1) the basis of the original jurisdiction over the case; (2) the identity of the party — plaintiff or defendant — seeking to invoke supplemental jurisdiction; and (3) the Rule authorizing the joinder of the party or claim over whom supplemental jurisdiction is sought. In the sections below we shall have repeated occasion to explore these variables; in order to gain a basic orientation, consider some elementary problems. In answering each, be prepared to explain which provision of §1367 governs and how you believe that section resolves the question.

NOTES AND PROBLEMS

1. In this and the next four problems, assume the litigation occurs in federal district court. A, a citizen of Illinois, sues B, also a citizen of Illinois, alleging that B violated federal civil rights statutes in firing her. A seeks to add a state law claim alleging that her firing also violated a state wrongful discharge law. Is there supplemental jurisdiction?

2. A, a citizen of Illinois, sues B, also a citizen of Illinois, alleging that B violated federal civil rights statutes in firing her. A seeks to add a state law claim alleging that B caused her injuries when his car backed into hers in the company parking lot. Is there supplemental jurisdiction?

3. A, a citizen of Illinois, sues B, also a citizen of Illinois, alleging that B violated federal civil rights statutes by permitting co-workers to engage in sexual harassment. A seeks to join C, a co-worker, who actually engaged in the harassment. State tort law is the basis of A's claim against C. Because C is not A's employer, the claim against him does not arise under federal law. Assume that the claim against C presents sufficiently common issues to qualify for joinder under Rule 20. Is there supplemental jurisdiction over the claim against C?

4. A, a citizen of Illinois, sues B, a citizen of Wisconsin, alleging breach of an employment contract and seeking a recovery in excess of $75,000. A seeks to join C, a citizen of Illinois; A alleges that C conspired with B to breach the employment contract. Assume that the claim against C presents sufficiently common issues to qualify for joinder under Rule 20. Is there supplemental jurisdiction over the claim against C?

5. We have focused on the interplay between joinder rules and federal subject matter jurisdiction. As you will see, joinder can also raise issues

of personal jurisdiction. In the hypothetical case explored above, suppose that A, a citizen of Illinois, wants to sue B, a citizen of Wisconsin, and C, a citizen of Illinois, on a federal civil rights claim. Joinder will present no problem if the claims against the two defendants arise from the same transaction and share common questions of law and fact; subject matter jurisdiction will present no obstacle because the claim arises under federal law. But if the suit is brought in Illinois, there may be a question of whether the court has personal jurisdiction over B, the citizen of Wisconsin.

6. Such a problem of personal jurisdiction will also affect a state court considering a joinder problem. State courts will also — very occasionally — need to consider issues of federal subject matter jurisdiction in connection with joinder. Suppose in a state court operating under the Federal Rules plaintiff sues a publisher for breach of contract, alleging defendant failed to publish her book as promised.

a. Plaintiff then proposes in an amended complaint to add a breach of copyright infringement claim. Does Rule 18 pose any problem?

b. What is the objection to this claim? See 28 U.S.C. §1338(a); cf. Gargallo v. Merrill Lynch, supra page 830.

2. Claims by the Defendant: Counterclaims

In examining pleading we considered the responses that defendant might make to plaintiff's complaint, but we did not explore the possibility that defendant might have claims against plaintiff. At common law the rules governing such claims were simple: They did not exist. The defendant who had such a claim could bring a separate suit or, in a limited number of cases, "set off" her claim against the plaintiffs (that is, reduce the plaintiff's recovery) but could not herself recover in the original action. Today Rule 13 permits defendants to assert such claims. Rule 13 divides counterclaims into two categories, *compulsory* and *permissive*. As you read the next case, consider what it means for a counterclaim to be compulsory and why it matters.

Plant v. Blazer Financial Services
598 F.2d 1357 (5th Cir. 1979)

RONEY, J.:

In this truth-in-lending case, we resolve . . . important issues to this field of the law. First, we decide that an action on the underlying debt in default is a compulsory counterclaim that must be asserted in a suit by the debtor on a truth-in-lending cause of action. . . .

On July 17, 1975 plaintiff Theresa Plant executed a note in favor of defendant Blazer Financial Services, Inc. for $2,520.00 to be paid in monthly installments of $105.00. No payments were made on the note. In March 1976 plaintiff commenced a civil action under §1640 of the Truth-in-Lending Act, 15 U.S.C.A. §1601 et seq., for failure to make disclosures required by the Act and by Regulation Z, 12 C.F.R. §226.1 et seq. (1978) promulgated thereunder. Defendant counterclaimed on the note for the unpaid balance. Based on defendant's failure to disclose a limitation on an after-acquired security interest, the trial court held the disclosure inadequate and awarded plaintiff the statutory penalty of $944.76 and $700.00 in attorney's fees. . . .

I.   Counterclaim

Plaintiff challenges the trial court's ruling that defendant's counterclaim on the underlying debt was compulsory. The issue is jurisdictional. A permissive counterclaim must have an independent jurisdictional basis, while it is generally accepted that a compulsory counterclaim falls within the ancillary jurisdiction of the federal courts even if it would ordinarily be a matter for state court consideration. In the instant case there is no independent basis since neither federal question nor diversity jurisdiction is available for the counterclaim. Consequently, if the counterclaim were to be treated as permissive, defendant's action on the underlying debt would have to be pursued in the state court.

The issue of whether a state debt counterclaim in a truth-in-lending action is compulsory or permissive is one of first impression in this Circuit, has never, to our knowledge, been decided by a court of appeals, and has received diverse treatment from a great number of district courts. . . .

Rule 13(a), Fed. R. Civ. P., provides that a counterclaim is compulsory if it "arises out of the transaction or occurrence" that is the subject matter of plaintiff's claim. Four tests have been suggested to further define when a claim and counterclaim arise from the same transaction:

> 1) Are the issues of fact and law raised by the claim and counterclaim largely the same?
> 2) Would res judicata bar a subsequent suit on defendant's claim absent the compulsory counterclaim rule?
> 3) Will substantially the same evidence support or refute plaintiff's claim as well as defendant's counterclaim?
> 4) Is there any logical relation between the claim and the counterclaim?

6 Wright & Miller, Federal Practice and Procedure §1410 at 42 (1971). An affirmative answer to any of the four questions indicates the counterclaim is compulsory.

The test which has commended itself to most courts, including our own, is the logical relation test. Revere Copper & Brass, Inc. v. Aetna Casualty & Surety Co., 426 F.2d at 714; 6 Wright & Miller at 48. The logical relation test is a loose standard which permits "a broad realistic interpretation in the interest of avoiding a multiplicity of suits." "The hallmark of this approach is its flexibility."

In *Revere Copper & Brass* this Court added a third tier to the counterclaim analysis by further defining "logical relationship" to exist when the counterclaim arises from the same "aggregate of operative facts" in that the same operative facts serve as the basis of both claims or the aggregate core of facts upon which the claim rests activates additional legal rights, otherwise dormant, in the defendant.

Applying the logical relationship test literally to the counterclaim in this case clearly suggests its compulsory character because a single aggregate of operative facts, the loan transaction, gave rise to both plaintiff's and defendant's claims. Because a tallying of the results from the district courts which have decided this question, however, shows that a greater number have found such a counterclaim merely permissive, we subject the relationship between the claims to further analysis.

The split of opinion on the nature of debt counterclaims in truth-in-lending actions appears to be, in large part, the product of competing policy considerations between the objectives of Rule 13(a) and the policies of the Truth-in-Lending Act, and disagreement over the extent to which federal courts should be involved in state causes of action for debt. While Rule 13(a) is intended to avoid multiple litigation by consolidating all controversies between the parties, several courts and commentators have observed that accepting creditors' debt counterclaims may obstruct achievement of the goals of the Truth-in-Lending Act.

Various arguments are made compositely as follows: The purpose of the Act is

> to assure a meaningful disclosure of credit terms so that the consumer will be able to compare more readily the various credit terms available to him and avoid the uninformed use of credit.

15 U.S.C.A. §1601. This purpose is effectuated by debtors' standing in the role of private attorneys general not merely to redress individual injuries but to enforce federal policy. The success of this private enforcement scheme would be undermined if debtors were faced with counterclaims on debts often exceeding the limits of their potential recovery under the Act. The purpose of the Act would suffer further frustration if federal courts were entangled in the myriad factual and legal questions essential to a decision on the debt claims but unrelated to the truth-in-

lending violation. In Roberts v. National School of Radio & Television Broadcasting, the court also noted the incongruity of enlisting the federal court's resources to assist in debt collection by the very target of the legislation which gives the plaintiff its cause of action.

Several other factors have been cited to offset the attractiveness of treating all related disputes in a single action under Rule 13. For example, courts have predicted a flood of debt counterclaims, greatly increasing the federal court workload. Furthermore, permitting debt counterclaims might destroy truth-in-lending class actions by interjecting vast numbers of individual questions. The judicial economy of consolidated litigation might be countered by the delay of having to provide a jury trial for the debt claim though none is available to the truth-in-lending plaintiff. Other courts have suggested that regarding such debt counterclaims as compulsory would infringe on the power of states to adjudicate disputes grounded in state law.

Courts which have concluded debt counterclaims to be permissive have found the nexus between the truth-in-lending violation and debt obligation too abstract or tenuous to regard the claims as logically related. One claim, they reason, involves the violation of federal law designed to deter lender nondisclosure and facilitate credit shopping and the other concerns merely a default on a private duty.

After careful consideration of the factors relied upon in these cases to find counterclaims permissive, we opt for the analysis applied by district courts in Louisiana, Alabama, Texas and Georgia in determining debt counterclaims to be compulsory. . . .

The results reached in *Carter* [v. Public Finance Corp.] were found "inescapable" in George v. Beneficial Finance Co. of Dallas. Emphasizing the goal of judicial economy furthered by a single presentation of facts, the court observed that "suits on notes will inevitably deal with the circumstance of the execution of the notes and any representation made to 'induce' the borrowing.". . .

We add to these arguments the observation that one of the purposes of the compulsory counterclaim rule is to provide complete relief to the defendant who has been brought involuntarily into the federal court. Absent the opportunity to bring a counterclaim, this party could be forced to satisfy the debtor's truth-in-lending claim without any assurance that his claims against the defaulting debtor arising from the same transaction will be taken into account or even that the funds he has been required to pay will still be available should he obtain a state court judgment in excess of the judgment on the truth-in-lending claim. In addition, a determination that the underlying debt was invalid may have a material effect on the amount of damages a debtor could recover on a truth-in-lending claim.

To permit the debtor to recover from the creditor without taking the original loan into account would be a serious departure from the evenhanded treatment afforded both parties under the Act. Truth-in-lending claims can be brought in either state or federal court. To the extent this dual jurisdiction was intended to permit litigation of truth-in-lending claims in actions on the debt, it reflects a purpose that the debt claim and the truth-in-lending claims be handled together. To the extent it was intended to relieve federal courts of any of this litigation, the purpose would be frustrated by providing a sanctuary from the creditor's claims in one jurisdiction but not in the other. State courts would always have jurisdiction of a creditor's counterclaim. Had Congress intended to insulate recovery in truth-in-lending actions in federal court from the counterclaims of creditors, of which it surely was aware, it could have easily done so.

We conclude that the obvious interrelationship of the claims and rights of the parties, coupled with the common factual basis of the claims, demonstrates a logical relationship between the claim and counterclaim under the test of *Revere Copper & Brass*.[13] We affirm the trial court's determination that the debt counterclaim is compulsory. . . .

NOTES AND PROBLEMS

1. What is the practical significance of this decision?

a. If Plant had not paid the loan, why had Blazer not already brought suit?

b. Suppose the court had decided that the counterclaim was not compulsory. So what? Rule 13(b) permits a defendant to bring as a permissive counterclaim any claim, related or unrelated, against a plaintiff. What difference would it have made to Blazer if the court had called the debt a permissive rather than a compulsory counterclaim?

13. State courts, which share jurisdiction over truth-in-lending actions, have considered the nexus between such claims in the opposite procedural posture. Where creditors bring actions on the debt, state courts have split on the question of whether the debtor may assert a truth-in-lending counterclaim otherwise barred by the Act's one-year statute of limitations. 15 U.S.C.A. §1640(e). Where the counterclaim can be regarded as arising from the same transaction as the claim, courts have permitted the counterclaim as a "recoupment" or "setoff" without regard to the statute of limitations. The similarity between the requirements for recoupment and those for Rule 13(a) compulsory counterclaims has been noted. . . .

c. What difference would it have made to permit Plant to maintain her action without Blazer's counterclaim rather than require her to defend against the counterclaim?

2. The opinion refers to "competing policy considerations between the objectives of Rule 13(a) and the Truth-in-Lending Act."

a. Articulate the policies underlying those two laws in a way that puts them in conflict in this case.

b. The Seventh Circuit addressed a similar question in the context of another statute regulating credit, the Consumer Leasing Act, 15 U.S.C. §1667–1667e. Discussing whether a counterclaim for an unpaid lease should be compulsory to a claim for violating the Act's disclosure regulations (and therefore within the grant of supplemental jurisdiction), the court said:

> Plaintiffs contend — presumably invoking [28 U.S.C.] §1367(c)(4), though they do not discuss it — that a court should not entertain a counterclaim on the lease because the threat of an adverse judgment [on the counterclaim] would unduly discourage enforcement of the Consumer Leasing Act.

Channell v. Citicorp Nat'l Services, Inc. 89 F.3d 379, 386 (7th Cir. 1996)

c. As a sample of the reasoning that led one court to reach a conclusion opposite that of *Plant*, consider Whigham v. Beneficial Finance Co. of Fayetteville, 599 F.2d 1322, 1323–1324 (4th Cir. 1979):

> We conclude that a lender's claim for debt against a borrower who sues for violation of the Truth-in-Lending Act has none of the characteristics associated with a compulsory counterclaim. First, the lender's counterclaim raises issues of fact and law significantly different from those presented by the borrower's claim. The only question in the borrower's suit is whether the lender made disclosures required by the federal statute and its implementing regulations. The lender's counterclaim, on the other hand, requires the court to determine the contractual rights of the parties in accordance with state law.
>
> Second, the evidence needed to support each claim differs. The borrower need produce only the loan documents for consideration in light of the federal requirements. The lender, however, must verify the obligation and prove a default on loan payments.
>
> Third, the claim and the counterclaim are not logically related. The lender's counterclaim alleges simply that the borrower has defaulted on a private loan contract governed by state law. The borrower's federal claim involves the same loan, but it does not arise from the obligations created by the contractual transaction. Instead, the claim invokes a statutory penalty designed to enforce federal policy against inadequate disclosure by lenders. To let the lender use the federal proceedings as an opportunity to pursue

private claims against the borrower would impede expeditious enforcement of the federal penalty and involve the district courts in debt collection matters having no federal significance.

3. Notice that *Whigham* and *Blazer* reach opposite conclusions while quoting the same "test" — whether a counterclaim arises out of the same transaction or occurrence and is therefore compulsory. *Blazer* sets forth four such tests. How helpful are these formulations?

a. Aren't the first and the third tests mirror images of each other? That is, if there is significant overlap of law and fact (test 1), doesn't it follow that the same evidence would be relevant (test 3)?

b. Isn't the second test just a restatement of the question? That is, *if* both claims arise out of the same transaction or occurrence, they *will* involve the same claim and *therefore* will be subsequently barred.

c. Isn't the fourth test essentially meaningless as interpreted by the court? There is no logical relationship between a Truth-in-Lending claim and one for an unpaid debt, if "logical" refers to an analytically strict set of relationships like those of formal logic. If "logical" instead means "sensibly related," then this test, like the second, becomes a restatement of the question: Just what claims are "sensibly related" to each other?

4. *Blazer* posits that two consequences flow from deciding a counterclaim is compulsory.

a. First, it must be brought at the risk of losing it.

b. Second, if it is brought, supplemental jurisdiction extends to cover it. As you will see, the enactment of 28 U.S.C. §1367 may give courts slightly more jurisdictional flexibility, but the basic proposition still holds true.

c. Under those circumstances, there is a penalty for omitting a counterclaim that is later held to be compulsory, but no penalty for including a counterclaim that is found not to be compulsory. Do you see why?

d. As a result of this asymmetrical penalty, most cases presenting the issue whether a counterclaim is compulsory or permissive do not arise in situations in which defendant has omitted the counterclaim in one action and attempted to assert it in a later action. Martino v. McDonald's System, Inc., Chapter XII, is a rare exception. Instead, most cases are similar to *Plant*, in which plaintiff asserts a federal claim; defendant interposes a counterclaim under state law for which there is no independent federal jurisdiction; plaintiff moves to dismiss the counterclaim for lack of subject matter jurisdiction; and defendant argues that the counterclaim is a compulsory one within the supplemental jurisdiction of the federal court. Such an attack is, of course, based on the premise that there is no supplemental jurisdiction over permissive counterclaims.

5. At the time of *Plant*, supplemental jurisdiction was a product of case law. Today it is codified in 28 U.S.C. §1367. That statute speaks of supplemental jurisdiction's extending to any claims that "form part of the same case or controversy under Article III." (The reference to the case or controversy requirement is taken from United Mine Workers v. Gibbs, which appears in Chapter III.) Consult the statute and consider the issues it raises with respect to counterclaims.

a. If the statutory allusion to *Gibbs* means that Congress intends to apply the *Gibbs* test, then §1367 will presumably not change the result of cases such as *Plant* that purport to apply the *Gibbs* test.

b. If, however, the reference to case or controversy is meant to be broader than "same transaction or occurrence" or "common nucleus of operative facts," then it will change some results in cases presenting issues analogous to those in *Plant*. It will do so wherever joinder rules are more liberal than the existing jurisdictional rules. In the case of counterclaims, Rule 13(b) permits joinder of any counterclaim, regardless whether related to plaintiff's claim. Does §1367 extend supplemental jurisdiction to all such counterclaims? To some of them?

c. Section 1367(b) proposes a narrower role for supplemental jurisdiction in cases based solely on diversity jurisdiction. But this narrowing does not apply to counterclaims by defendants. Why?

6. *Plant* represents a straightforward, if subtle, counterclaim problem. To test your understanding of the doctrine, consider a complex manifestation of the doctrine found in Great Lakes Rubber Corp. v. Herbert Cooper Co., 286 F.2d 631 (3d Cir. 1961). This case arose after two key employees of Great Lakes left to form Herbert Cooper. An active competition for contracts relating to the manufacture of flexible rubber tubing followed. Initially, Great Lakes sued Herbert Cooper for (1) unfair competition in stealing trade secrets and customers, (2) unfair competition in bidding for contracts on the basis of prices that would involve infringing patents, and (3) disparagement of Great Lakes's product. Cooper then interposed an antitrust counterclaim alleging that Great Lakes was trying to monopolize the relevant market by (1) making false statements to Cooper's suppliers that the suppliers were contributory infringers and (2) bringing a series of unjustified lawsuits to harass Cooper. Great Lakes's claim was dismissed for lack of jurisdiction, but the antitrust counterclaim, with an independent basis for federal jurisdiction, remained. Great Lakes then interposed essentially the same allegations in the form of a counterclaim to the antitrust claim, and the court found the counterclaim compulsory:

> We have indicated that a counterclaim is compulsory if it bears a "logical relationship" to an opposing party's claim. . . . The phrase "logical rela-

tionship" is given meaning by the purpose of the rule which it was designed to implement. Thus, a counterclaim is logically related to the opposing party's claim where separate trials on each of their respective claims would involve a substantial duplication of effort and time by the parties and the courts. Where multiple claims involve many of the same factual issues, or the same factual and legal issues, or where they are offshoots of the same basic controversy between the parties, fairness and considerations of convenience and of economy require that the counterclaimant be permitted to maintain his cause of action. Indeed the doctrine of res judicata compels the counterclaimant to assert his claim in the same suit for it would be barred if asserted separately, subsequently.

Cooper alleges that the claims originally asserted in Great Lakes' amended complaint, reiterated in substance in its counterclaim, are "unjustified" and were brought in "bad faith and without color of right with the sole object of harassing and preventing defendant [Cooper] from competing in the manufacture and sale of flexible hose." These are the only allegations set out by Cooper's counterclaim which demonstrate a relationship within the purview of Rule 13(a) to Great Lakes' amended complaint or counterclaim. But that they do demonstrate a relationship is unquestionable. It is clear that a determination that Cooper's claims that the claims asserted in Great Lakes' amended complaint and reiterated in substance in its counterclaim are harassing will entail an extensive airing of the facts and the law relating to Great Lakes' counterclaim. It follows that the court below was in error in dismissing Great Lakes' counterclaim on the ground that it was permissive. We hold that Great Lakes' counterclaim was a compulsory one within the meaning of Rule 13(a). ·

Id. at 634. Would the result have been different if Cooper's complaint had not alleged the unjustified lawsuits?

7. Some limitations on the doctrine of compulsory counterclaims are illustrated in the following questions:

a. In 1998, B purchased a house from S and gave a promissory note for $50,000, payable on January 2, 2000, for the unpaid balance of the purchase price. In 1999, alleging numerous defects in the house, B sued S for breach of contract and breach of warranty. Is S's claim on the unpaid promissory note a compulsory counterclaim?

b. Same facts as in (a), except that the suit was brought in February 2000 after S had commenced an action on the note in another court.

8. Assume Passenger is injured in a collision between Driver 1 and Driver 2 and brings suit against both. Driver 1 may have no counterclaim against Passenger but may have her own claim against Driver 2.

a. The Rules refer to Driver 1's claim against Driver 2 as a *cross-claim*. See Rule 13(g).

b. Some states do not make such fine distinctions in their joinder terminology. California, for example, uses "cross-claim" to refer both to what a federal court would call a "counterclaim" and to what a federal court would call a "cross-claim."

B.   Joinder of Parties

1.   By Plaintiffs

Mosley v. General Motors Corp.
497 F.2d 1330 (8th Cir. 1974)

Ross, J.

Nathaniel Mosley and nine other persons joined in bringing this action individually and as class representatives alleging that their rights guaranteed under 42 U.S.C. §2000e et seq. and 42 U.S.C. §1981 were denied by General Motors and Local 25, United Automobile, Aerospace and Agriculture Implement Workers of American [Union] by reason of their color and race. Each of the ten named plaintiffs had, prior to the filing of the complaint, filed a charge with the Equal Employment Opportunity Commission [EEOC] asserting the facts underlying these claims. Pursuant thereto, the EEOC made a reasonable cause finding that General Motors, Fisher Body Division and Chevrolet Division, and the Union had engaged in unlawful employment practices in violation of Title VII of the Civil Rights Act of 1964. Accordingly, the charging parties were notified by EEOC of their right to institute a civil action in the appropriate federal district court. . . .

In each of the first eight counts of the twelve-count complaint, eight of the ten plaintiffs alleged that General Motors, Chevrolet Division, had engaged in unlawful employment practices by: "discriminating against Negroes as regards promotions, terms and conditions of employment"; "retaliating against Negro employees who protested actions made unlawful by Title VII of the Act and by discharging some because they protested said unlawful acts"; "failing to hire Negro employees as a class on the basis of race"; "failing to hire females as a class on the basis of sex"; "discharging Negro employees on the basis of race"; and "discriminating against Negroes and females in the granting of relief time." Each additionally charged that the defendant Union had engaged in unlawful employment practices "with respect to the granting of relief time to Negro and female employees" and "by failing to pursue 6a grievances." The remaining two plaintiffs made similar allegations against General Motors, Fisher Body Division. All of the individual plaintiffs requested injunctive relief, back pay, attorneys fees and costs. Counts XI and XII of the complaint were class action counts against the two individual divisions of General Motors. They also sought declaratory and injunctive relief, back pay, attorneys fees and costs. . . .

The district court ordered that "insofar as the first ten counts are concerned, those ten counts shall be severed into ten separate causes of action," and each plaintiff was directed to bring a separate action based upon his complaint, duly and separately filed. . . .

In reaching this conclusion on joinder, the district court followed the reasoning of Smith v. North American Rockwell Corp. which, in a somewhat analogous situation, found there was no right to relief arising out of the same transaction, occurrence or series of transactions or occurrences, and that there was no question of law or fact common to all plaintiffs sufficient to sustain joinder under Federal Rule of Civil Procedure 20(a). Similarly, the district court here felt that the plaintiffs' joint actions against General Motors and the Union presented a variety of issues having little relationship to one another; that they had only one common problem, i.e., the defendant; and that as pleaded the joint actions were completely unmanageable. Upon entering the order, and upon application of the plaintiffs, the district court found that its decision involved a controlling question of law as to which there is a substantial ground for difference of opinion and that any of the parties might make application for appeal under 28 U.S.C. §1292(b). We granted the application to permit this interlocutory appeal and for the following reasons we affirm in part and reverse in part.

Rule 20(a) of the Federal Rules of Civil Procedure provides:

> All persons may join in one action as plaintiffs if they assert any right to relief jointly, severally, or in the alternative in respect of or arising out of the same transaction, occurrence, or series of transactions or occurrences and if any question of law or fact common to all these persons will arise in the action. . . .

Additionally, Rule 20(b) and Rule 42(b) vest in the district court the discretion to order separate trials or make such other orders as will prevent delay or prejudice. In this manner, the scope of the civil action is made a matter for the discretion of the district court, and a determination on the question of joinder of parties will be reversed on appeal only upon a showing of abuse of that discretion. To determine whether the district court's order was proper herein, we must look to the policy and law that have developed around the operation of Rule 20.

The purpose of the rule is to promote trial convenience and expedite the final determination of disputes, thereby preventing multiple lawsuits. 7 C. Wright, Federal Practice and Procedure §1652 at 265 (1972). Single trials generally tend to lessen the delay, expense and inconvenience to all concerned. Reflecting this policy, the Supreme Court has said: "Under the Rules, the impulse is toward entertaining the broadest possible scope of action consistent with fairness to the parties; joinder of claims, parties and remedies is strongly encouraged." United Mine Workers of America v. Gibbs, 383 U.S. 715 (1966).

Permissive joinder is not, however, applicable in all cases. The rule imposes two specific requisites to the joinder of parties: (1) a right to relief must be asserted by, or against, each plaintiff or defendant relating to or arising out of the same *transaction or occurrence, or series of transactions or occurrences;* and (2) some *question of law or fact common* to all the parties must arise in the action.

In ascertaining whether a particular factual situation constitutes a single transaction or occurrence for purposes of Rule 20, a case by case approach is generally pursued. 7 C. Wright, Federal Practice and Procedure §1653 at 270 (1972). No hard and fast rules have been established under the rule. However, construction of the terms "transaction or occurrence" as used in the context of Rule 13(a) counterclaims offers some guide to the application of this test. For the purposes of the latter rule, " 'Transaction' is a word of flexible meaning. It may comprehend a series of many occurrences, depending not so much upon the immediateness of their connection as upon their logical relationship." Moore v. New York Cotton Exchange, 270 U.S. 593 (1926). Accordingly, all "logically related" events entitling a person to institute a legal action against another generally are regarded as comprising a transaction or occurrence. 7 C. Wright, Federal Practice and Procedure §1653 at 270 (1972). The analogous interpretation of the terms as used in Rule 20 would permit all reasonably related claims for relief by or against different parties to be tried in a single proceeding. Absolute identity of all events is unnecessary.

This construction accords with the result reached in United States v. Mississippi, 380 U.S. 128 (1965), a suit brought by the United States against the State of Mississippi, the election commissioners, and six voting registrars of the State, charging them with engaging in acts and practices hampering and destroying the right of black citizens of Mississippi to vote. The district court concluded that the complaint improperly attempted to hold the six county registrars jointly liable for what amounted to nothing more than individual torts committed by them separately against separate applicants. In reversing, the Supreme Court said:

> But the complaint charged that the registrars had acted and were continuing to act as part of a state-wide system designed to enforce the registration laws in a way that would inevitably deprive colored people of the right to vote solely because of their color. On such an allegation the joinder of all the registrars as defendants in a single suit is authorized by Rule 20(a) of the Federal Rules of Civil Procedure. . . . These registrars were alleged to be carrying on activities which were part of a series of transactions or occurrences the validity of which depended to a large extent upon "question[s] of law or fact common to all of them."

Here too, then, the plaintiffs have asserted a right to relief arising out of the same transactions or occurrences. Each of the ten plaintiffs alleged that he had been injured by the same general policy of discrimination on the part of General Motors and the Union. Since a "state-wide system designed to enforce the registration laws in a way that would inevitably deprive colored people of the right to vote" was determined to arise out of the same series of transactions or occurrences, we conclude that a company-wide policy purportedly designed to discriminate against blacks in employment similarly arises out of the same series of transactions or occurrences. Thus the plaintiffs meet the first requisite for joinder under Rule 20(a).

The second requisite necessary to sustain a permissive joinder under the rule is that a question of law or fact common to all the parties will arise in the action. The rule does not require that *all* questions of law and fact raised by the dispute be common. Yet, neither does it establish any qualitative or quantitative test of commonality. For this reason, cases construing the parallel requirement under Federal Rule of Civil Procedure 23(a) provide a helpful framework for construction of the commonality required by Rule 20. In general, those cases that have focused on Rule 23(a)(2) have given it a permissive application so that common questions have been found to exist in a wide range of contexts. 7 C. Wright, Federal Practice and Procedure §1763 at 604 (1972). Specifically, with respect to employment discrimination cases under Title VII, courts have found that the discriminatory character of a defendant's conduct is basic to the class, and the fact that the individual class members may have suffered different effects from the alleged discrimination is immaterial for the purposes of the prerequisite. Hicks v. Crown Zellerbach Corp. In this vein, one court has said:

> [A]lthough the actual effects of a discriminatory policy may thus vary throughout the class, the existence of the discriminatory policy threatens

the entire class. And whether the Damoclean threat of a racially discriminatory policy hangs over the racial class is a question of fact common to all
the members of the class.

The right to relief here depends on the ability to demonstrate that
each of the plaintiffs was wronged by racially discriminatory policies
on the part of the defendants General Motors and the Union. The
discriminatory character of the defendants' conduct is thus basic to each
plaintiff's recovery. The fact that each plaintiff may have suffered different
effects from the alleged discrimination is immaterial for the purposes of
determining the common question of law or fact. Thus, we conclude
that the second requisite for joinder under Rule 20(a) is also met by
the complaint.

For the reasons set forth above, we conclude that the district court
abused its discretion in severing the joined actions. The difficulties in
ultimately adjudicating damages to the various plaintiffs are not so overwhelming as to require such severance. If appropriate, separate trials
may be granted as to any particular issue after the determination of
common questions.

The judgment of the district court disallowing joinder of the plaintiffs'
individual actions is reversed and remanded with directions to permit
the plaintiffs to proceed jointly. . . .

NOTES AND PROBLEMS

1. *Mosley* is an unusual case in at least one respect: The district and
appellate courts thought the issue of joinder important enough to certify
an interlocutory appeal, something that happens only about 100 times
each year among the 250,000 civil suits filed annually in the federal
system. Why did the litigants think the question important?. If you were
the plaintiffs' lawyer, would you rather try these cases together or separately? If you were General Motors' lawyer, which would you prefer?

2. If the decision about joinder is going to make it much more likely
that plaintiffs will prevail, it becomes important to be sure that the decision is right. Is it?

a. The court says "[e]ach of the ten plaintiffs alleged that he had been
injured by the same general policy of discrimination on the part of
General Motors and the Union."

b. Consider who the plaintiffs are:

- African-Americans who worked for GM but alleged they had not
  been promoted;

- African-American workers who alleged they had been punished for protesting unlawful actions by GM;
- African-Americans who had applied for but not been hired by GM;
- Women (presumably both African-American and white) who had applied for jobs but not been hired by GM;
- African-American employees who had been fired;
- African-Americans and women employees who alleged they had not been granted "relief time" on the same terms as white males.

What "question of law or fact common to all those persons will arise in the action"? (Rule 20.)

c. The Eighth Circuit reversed the district court, ordering joinder. Suppose the case proceeds, with discovery focusing on the defendant's alleged refusal to hire or promote African-Americans and women. Imagine the suit goes to trial (or, more likely a settlement that is embodied in a consent decree, which has the same preclusive effect as a judgment). Thereafter, one of the female plaintiffs brings a second suit alleging that GM's maternity leave policies during the period at issue in the first lawsuit constituted a violation of Title VII, the same statute invoked in the first suit. Is that claim precluded? Could GM argue that the breadth of joinder in the first suit meant that it precluded relitigation of any claim involving prohibited race- or gender-based discrimination?

d. What would have happened in *Mosley* if the court had found joinder improper? See Rule 21.

e. Courts are not always so flexible as *Mosley* in finding common links among plaintiffs:

> The Plaintiffs in this case, all female, are employed by or were formerly employed by AT&T as sales persons in a small, distinct business organization within AT&T known as the Profile Initiative Program (PIP). The Plaintiffs are residents of five different cities and four different states who worked in four separate AT&T offices located in three states. While the Plaintiffs were directly supervised by different managers in each office, it appears they were indirectly supervised by the same centralized PIP upper management group. The Plaintiffs contend the PIP management systematically discriminated against them because of their sex and allege discriminatory actions by some of the same individuals in PIP management. However, the Plaintiffs identify no specific discriminatory policy or practice to which they were all subjected. In addition to the claims of sex discrimination, Plaintiff Harryman asserts claims of race, age, and national origin discrimination, while Plaintiff Bryan asserts a claim of age discrimination. All the Plaintiffs also assert various state law claims against the Defendants. Thus, AT&T is faced with five individual Plaintiffs asserting a total of more than twenty claims against it. . . .

> AT&T contends the Plaintiffs are misjoined and request that this Court sever the claims of each Plaintiff and proceed with five separate trials. . . . AT&T argues the jury may improperly conclude that it is guilty of wrongdoing simply because so many Plaintiffs will complain of discrimination and so many different witnesses will testify in support of the Plaintiffs' claims. AT&T further contends that in a single trial, the jury will hear evidence that may be relevant to the claims of one Plaintiff, but that is completely irrelevant and prejudicial to the claims of the remaining Plaintiffs. According to AT&T, a single trial will unnecessarily complicate evidentiary rulings and will deprive this Court of its discretion to rule on the admissibility of marginally relevant but highly prejudicial evidence.

Henderson v. AT&T Corp., 918 F. Supp. 1059, 1061 (S.D. Tex. 1996). Recognizing that *Mosley* was the leading case on joinder of plaintiffs in employment discrimination cases, the court allowed the joinder under Rule 20 but went on to sever three of the five cases for pretrial and trial.

3. *Henderson* (supra) reminds us that joinder is a game that three can play.

a. Initially plaintiff has the choice, subject to the constraints of Rule 20.

b. Like in *Mosley* and *Henderson*, defendant can challenge joinder of parties, with the result, under Rule 21, that the parties found to be improperly joined will have their cases severed.

c. The third player is the judge, who rules on any challenges to joinder under Rule 20 but also exercises independent power to consolidate and sever claims under Rule 42. Suppose that the *Mosley* plaintiffs had filed nine separate lawsuits and the trial judge had concluded that they were in fact closely related and should be consolidated. Under Rule 42(a) the judge can order "a joint hearing or trial of any or all matters in issue in the actions."

d. Conversely, even if the parties are content with the party structure as it stands, a court acting under the authority of Rule 42(b) may sever claims.

e. Finally, in many federal districts there are local rules that require parties to identify a case that is factually related to any other case currently pending in the district. The purpose of this identification is to allow consolidation of related claims — and to prevent judge-shopping by filing several similar claims and then dismissing all but the one that draws the friendliest judge.

f. Given this judicial discretion, is Rule 20 necessary? Should there be unlimited joinder of parties — just as there is of claims — with the question of joinder treated as one of trial convenience? Are Rules 20 and 21 consistent with Rule 42? A concrete way of putting this question is to ask whether, after the *Mosley* opinion, the trial court, invoking the authority of Rule 42, could still sever the claims for trial.

4. Assume *A* has similar claims against *B* and *C*. What is the practical difference between one action by *A* against *B* and *C* and consolidation of separate actions by *A* v. *B* and *A* v. *C* under Rule 42(a)? Some possible differences include requirements of serving papers, Rules 5(a), 30(b)(1); right to cross-examine at depositions, cf. Rule 30(c); and right of discovery by *B* against *C* and vice versa, Rules 33, 34, 35. In practice, the court consolidating the two cases may order that *B* and *C* be treated as co-parties for such matters, thus minimizing the differences.

2.   By Defendants: Third-Party Claims

Although modern procedure accords plaintiffs great autonomy, it does not give them the last word about parties to the suit. The next case illustrates defendants' ability to join additional parties — and the limits to that ability.

Watergate Landmark Condominium Unit Owners' Association v. Wiss, Janey, Elstner Associates
117 F.R.D. 576 (E.D. Va. 1987)

ELLIS, J. . . .

This multiparty construction litigation raises the question whether third party claims are permissible in the absence of derivative or secondary liability. They are not; Rule 14(a), Fed. R. Civ. P., by its terms, and established authority make unmistakably clear that a third party complaint is appropriate only where the third party defendant would be secondarily or derivatively liable to the defendant in the event the defendant is held liable to the plaintiff. . . .

[A condominium association hired a real estate management firm to oversee maintenance of the units. When owners reported that their balconies were crumbling, the real estate management firm hired an engineering firm — Wiss, Janey, Elstner Associates (the defendants) — to draw specifications for repairing the balconies. On the basis of those specifications the condo association hired Brisk Waterproofing to do the repairs. When the repairs failed to satisfy the owners, they invoked diversity jurisdiction and sued the engineering firm and the real estate management firm but not the waterproofers.]

In response to the complaint, [the real estate managers,] Legum & Norman[,] filed an answer, a cross-claim against Wiss, Janey and a third party complaint against Brisk Waterproofing Company (Brisk), the company that performed the repairs. . . . The amended third party complaint

alleges that Brisk negligently performed the repairs and is solely liable
to the Association. Brisk has moved pursuant to Rule 12(b)(6), Fed. R.
Civ. P. to dismiss the amended third party complaint. For the reasons set
forth here, the motion is granted and the amended third party complaint is
dismissed without prejudice.

Analysis

The question presented is whether Legum & Norman's third party claim
is maintainable under Rule 14(a), Fed. R. Civ. P. Central to this question
is whether the third party claim asserts that Brisk's liability is derivative
of, or secondary to, Legum & Norman's liability to the Association.
Legum & Norman does not claim that Brisk is derivatively or secondarily
liable. Nor indeed could such a claim be made, for the Association's
complaint concedes that the repair work was performed non-negligently
in accordance with the specifications. Whether Brisk's work was negligent
is not part of the main claim of the Association against Legum & Norman.
Thus, Legum & Norman's claim against Brisk is independent of the
outcome of the main claim. Given this, the third party claim against
Brisk is manifestly inappropriate in this case.

It is settled beyond dispute that a third party claim can be maintained
only if the liability it asserts is in some way derivative of the main claim.
Typically, proper third party claims involve one joint tortfeasor impleading another, an indemnitee impleading an indemnitor, or a secondarily
liable party impleading one who is primarily liable. Absent such derivative
liability, a third party claim must fail. As one district court succinctly
put it:

> It is no longer possible under Rule 14, as it was prior to the 1948 amend-
> ment to the rule, to implead a third party claimed to be solely liable to the
> plaintiff. . . . A proposed third-party plaintiff must allege facts sufficient to
> establish the derivative or secondary liability of the proposed third-party
> defendant. . . . Thus, under Rule 14(a), a third-party complaint is appro-
> priate only in cases where the proposed third-party defendant would be
> secondarily liable to the original defendant in the event the latter is held
> to be liable to the plaintiff.

Barab v. Menford, 98 F.R.D. 455, 456 (E.D. Pa. 1983) (citations omitted).

Numerous courts have echoed this principle. To be sure, further factual
development may suggest that the repair work, as Legum & Norman
alleges, was the sole cause of the problem. But even so, this would not
save the third party claim, for "[u]nder Rule 14(a), a third-party defendant
may not be impleaded merely because he may be liable to the *plaintiff*."
Owen Equip. & Erection Co. v. Kroger, 437 U.S. 365, 368 n.3 (1978)

(emphasis in original). Derivative liability is central to the operation of Rule 14. It cannot be used as a device to bring into a controversy matters which merely happen to have some relationship to the original action.

Other courts' use of the Rule 14 derivative liability principle confirms the inappropriateness of the claim against Brisk in this case. Thus, in Struss v. Renault, U.S.A., Inc., 108 F.R.D. 691 (W.D. Pa. 1985), a plaintiff, whose two minor children were injured in an auto accident, sued the auto manufacturer on a crashworthiness theory. The manufacturer's effort to implead the driver failed where it was based on the theory that the driver's neligence was the sole cause. Similarly, in the *Barab* case, impleader was held improper where plaintiff claimed defendant was the seller of the doormat that caused her injuries and defendant denied this and claimed that the proposed third party defendant was the actual seller of the accused doormat. In other words, a third party claim is not appropriate where the defendant and putative third party plaintiff says, in effect, "It was him, not me." Such a claim is viable only where a proposed third party plaintiff says, in effect, "If I am liable to plaintiff, then my liability is only technical or secondary or partial, and the third party defendant is derivatively liable and must reimburse me for all or part (one-half, if a joint tortfeasor) of anything I must pay plaintiff." Legum & Norman's claim against Brisk is a "him, not me" situation and therefore must fail.[2]

Legum & Norman cannot avoid this result by claiming that it is seeking contribution from Brisk. Although a right of contribution is generally a proper basis on which to file a third party complaint, Virginia's contribution statute does not apply to this action.[3] Section 8.01-34 provides that, "Contribution among wrongdoers may be enforced when the wrong results from negligence and involves no moral turpitude." Legum & Norman and Brisk are not joint wrongdoers within the meaning of the statute.

The statute has been held to give a right of contribution "only where the person injured . . . has a right of action against two persons for the

2. The inappropriateness of Rule 14 impleader in this context is vividly illustrated by the differing types of proof each party would pursue and the resultant high potential for jury confusion. While the Association would focus on inadequate specifications, Legum & Norman and Brisk would focus on the workmanship, a topic the Association would claim was irrelevant. Conceivably, the Association might fail to prevail on its specifications claim, while Legum & Norman might, at the same time, prevail on its negligent workmanship claim. In that event, however, no damages could be awarded to the Association because the main claim would have failed.

3. Rule 14 creates no new substantive rights: litigants must look to some other rule of law on which to base a third-party complaint. Uptagrafft v. United States, 315 F.2d 200, 202-03 (4th Cir.), cert. denied, 375 U.S. 818 (1963).

same indivisible injury." Laws v. Spain, 312 F. Supp. 315, 318 (E.D. Va. 1970). Here, the acts which are involved in the main claim are separate and distinct from the acts alleged to give rise to the third party claim. The main claim against Legum & Norman involves the hiring of Wiss, Janey and the delivery of the specifications. Legum & Norman is alleged to have breached its contract with the Association and its duties as an agent of the Association. The third party complaint deals with Brisk's alleged negligent performance of the repairs, a separate event which occurred later in time and, significantly, an event that is specifically disclaimed by the complaint as a basis for the action. Brisk is not alleged to have participated in the selection of Wiss, Janey or in the failure to deliver information to the Association. Thus, because Legum & Norman and Brisk did not share a common duty to the Association and the acts giving rise to the main claim and third party claim were separate in time, place and consequences, the alleged injuries to plaintiff were not indivisible. There is no joint liability between Legum & Norman and the Association for plaintiff's claims and therefore no duty on Brisk's part to contribute to any recovery of damages against Legum & Norman.

Accordingly, Legum & Norman's third party complaint against Brisk is dismissed. This Court, of course, intimates no view as to whether Legum & Norman's theory that Brisk's negligence caused plaintiff's damages may provide a defense to the main claim.[4] Similarly, no view is expressed here on the merits of any separate claim the Association or Legum & Norman may have against Brisk for negligent workmanship. And finally, it may be worth noting that a different result would obtain here had the Association's claim been broad enough to include a claim for recovery based on inadequate workmanship.

An appropriate order has been entered.

NOTES AND PROBLEMS

1. *Watergate* is an unusual case in one respect: Plaintiff chose not to sue all those who might conceivably be liable for the injuries alleged. As a rule plaintiffs like multiple defendants because of the litigation dynamics of such cases: The defendants begin to point the finger at each other, thus easing the plaintiff's burden and framing the question as one of which defendant is liable rather than whether anyone is. Why didn't the plaintiff pursue that route in this case?

---

4. Even if the specifications are shown to be inadequate, the proximate cause of the harm claimed by the Association may be negligent workmanship.

a. One possibility is that after investigation plaintiff simply decided that there was no basis for liability — that Brisk had competently fulfilled its contract. If that was the plaintiff's view, suing Brisk risked not only defeat on the merits but Rule 11 sanctions.

b. Another possibility is jurisdictional obstacles. This was a diversity case. If Brisk and the plaintiff were citizens of the same state (and recall that both the state of incorporation *and* the principal place of business count), naming Brisk as a defendant would destroy complete diversity. There is no such obstacle to naming Brisk as a third-party defendant. Even if defendant/third-party plaintiff and Brisk did not fulfill diversity requirements, supplemental jurisdiction would attach. Reread 28 U.S.C. §1367 and identify the phrases that give the court broad supplemental jurisdiction over a properly impleaded third-party defendant.

Nor would personal jurisdiction be an obstacle. Explain why on the facts of *Watergate Landmark* it is clear that Brisk could be sued in the state where he performed the work in question.

2. Impleader is a powerful idea but limited. *Watergate Landmark* emphasizes the limits. Two variations on its facts will illustrate the power of impleader.

a. The *Watergate Landmark* Condominium Association, which owned the property, had itself hired the waterproofers. Suppose the condominium association had not taken such a hands-on approach but had simply instructed the real estate management firm to "fix the problem." Further suppose the real estate management firm had then hired the engineers (to draw the specifications) and the waterproofers (to perform the work). The balconies still leaked, and the condominium association sued the real estate management firm. Under *those* circumstances the real estate management firm would have a good basis under Rule 14 to join both the engineering firm and the waterproofers as third-party defendants. What makes this situation different from that of the actual case?

b. At this point one would have a plaintiff (the condominium association), a defendant (the real estate management firm) and two third-party defendants (the engineers and the waterproofers). Matters might not end there. Suppose Brisk, the waterproofer, believed the problem lay in defective roofing paper it had bought from one of its suppliers. Rule 14 would permit Brisk to implead the supplier, with the result that a third-party defendant would implead another third-party defendant. The supplier, alleging that the flaws in the paper stemmed from a defective batch of chemicals purchased from ChemCo, could in turn implead ChemCo.

c. Closer to the facts of the original case, suppose that the condominium association had sued only the real estate management firm. Recall that the real estate firm had hired the engineers. If the real estate management firm had thought that the leaks resulted from faulty specifications provided by the engineers, it could have impleaded them.

3. Return to the stated facts of the case itself.

a. Can defendants, without impleading Brisk, continue to assert that it was Brisk's poor work, not defendant's specifications, that caused the continuing problems?

b. What is the difference between asserting Brisk's responsibility as a defense and asserting it as the basis of a third-party claim?

4. Impleader solves what would otherwise be a problem of nonpreclusion of issues. Suppose Bert sues Ernie, alleging Ernie's negligence caused the auto accident that injured Bert. Ernie has auto liability insurance, but his insurer after investigating concludes that Ernie was not driving the borrowed car and that the policy therefore does not cover him.

a. In a world without (or before) impleader, Bert might sue Ernie and recover — prevailing in his contention that Ernie was the driver. Ernie, now saddled with the judgment, could then sue Insurer. But Insurer, because it was not a party to the first suit, would not be bound by its finding that Ernie was the driver, and might successfully defend, maintaining that he was not.

b. Explain how impleader solves this problem. On the stated facts, what would Ernie do in the first lawsuit?

5. Because Rule 14 permits impleader only where the substantive law permits the defendant to "pass on" liability to another party, most of the difficult problems in impleader cases are substantive: Does the substantive law require the third-party defendant to indemnify or share the liability of the defendant/third-party plaintiff?

a. That means joinder possibilities will shift as substantive law changes. Suppose Winters was seriously injured when a snowblower he was using blasted snow in his face, causing him to fall down and hit his head against a tree stump. Assume that Winters has potential claims against Dealer both for failing to adjust the blower properly and for failing to show Winters how to operate it, and against Manufacturer for faulty design. If Winters sues Dealer, Dealer can implead Manufacturer on the grounds that its design led to the problem. If Winters instead sues Manufacturer, can Manufacturer implead Dealer either on the theory that the accident would not have occurred if Dealer had checked the snowblower or on the theory that Dealer was at least equally at fault? Absent a *right of contribution*, the answer is no, because there is no liability running from Dealer to Manufacturer. If Dealer is liable at all, it is only to Winters directly.

Assume now that the state provides for contribution among joint tortfeasors. If Winters sues Manufacturer, can Manufacturer implead Dealer? If the answer is yes, the right of contribution not only has reallocated the loss among those involved but also has substantially reduced the plaintiff's control over the action.

b. In recent years the spread of comparative negligence in several forms, combined with redefined rights of contribution, have triggered a number of impleader cases. As an illustration of how impleader arises from an everyday situation, consider a three-car accident among Paul, Dan, and Donna. Paul sues Dan. (Nothing obligates plaintiff to sue both defendants.) Dan can in the lawsuit argue that Paul was entirely responsible for the accident or that Donna was. In some states the jury will determine the relative fault of all three persons — including Donna, *who is not a party*. But, in most states, Dan will be jointly and severally liable for *all* of the damages, including the harm for which the jury has said Donna is responsible. Moreover, although Dan can sue Donna for a contribution to any damage judgment he has paid, Donna, as a non-party, will not be bound by the jury's determination of her proportionate fault. Do you see why Dan will have a powerful incentive to implead Donna?

6. In which of the following cases could the defendant implead a third-party defendant?

a. Landlord hires Building Maintenance Company to inspect and maintain his apartment. Tenant falls down the stairs when the handrail breaks. Tenant sues Landlord for her injuries. May Landlord implead Building Maintenance Co.?

b. Recall Beeck v. Aquaslide, Chapter VI, supra page 470. Beeck sues Aquaslide for injuries sustained when sliding down a swimming pool slide, alleging that the slide was defective. May Aquaslide implead Pool-slides, Inc., on the ground that it, not Aquaslide, manufactured the slide in question?

7. As the *Watergate Landmark* opinion says, the present Rule 14 rejects allegations that "It was him, not me" as a basis for impleader. It was not always so. As the case also notes, the original version of Rule 14(a), which has been retained by some states that base their procedures on the Federal Rules, permitted a defendant to force an additional defendant into the suit, even if the plaintiff originally chose not to sue that defendant. See 6 Wright, Miller & Kane, Civil 2d §1441, at 287-288. More recently, the view has prevailed that the plaintiff should have the right to select from available defendants those he wants to sue. In Rose v. Chicago, Rock Island & Pacific Railroad, 308 F. Supp. 1357, 1361 (W.D. Okla. 1970), this view was expressed as follows:

> The result [of permitting a Defendant to bring in a joint tortfeasor under Rule 14(a)] is to cause the Plaintiff to litigate his claim in an action into which the Defendant has brought one whom the Plaintiff has not seen fit to proceed against for one reason or another. A Plaintiff should not

only be allowed to select his forum if appropriate, but should also have
some proper measure of control over the parties whom he elects to litigate
with in regard to an injury received by him.

Temple v. Synthes, Chapter I, manifests a similar respect for plaintiff
autonomy. Why should the plaintiff have this choice?

8. Note that in order to implead a third-party defendant, the impleading
party need not show liability conclusively; it is enough to show that the
third-party defendant "may be" liable for all or part of the damages sought
from the defendant. Rule 14 provides only a procedural route by which
to bring that potential indemnifier into the suit; the Rule does not in
itself create substantive liability.

3. More Complex Litigation

Thus far, we have considered what may be called single-issue joinder
problems involving a single rule. Many cases, however, involve combinations of the joinder provisions already discussed. Consider one such case.
Sidney purchases a new Ford from Dan's Auto Sales, and, after a small
down payment, Sidney and his wife Wanda sign a note for the balance
of the purchase price. The car doesn't work, and Sidney sues Dan.

NOTES AND PROBLEMS

1. If Dan wants to counterclaim against Sidney for the debt, can he
join Wanda as a codefendant on the counterclaim? Yes: Rule 13(h)
permits additional parties to a counterclaim if the Rule 20 joinder tests
are satisfied, and, given the obligation of both Sidney and Wanda on the
same note, Rule 20 would here be satisfied.

2. Assume Dan makes a third-party claim against Ford, claiming that
Ford is liable to indemnify Dan for any damages Dan must pay Sidney.
Can Dan also make a claim against Ford for failure to reimburse Dan
for warranty work on cars other than Sidney's? So far as the Rules are
concerned, the answer is yes. Once Dan can make a third-party claim
against Ford under Rule 14(a), he can make any other claim he has
against Ford. Remember that Rule 18 permits joinder of all claims,
whether related or unrelated.

3. Assume Sidney sues both Dan and Ford. Can Ford cross-claim
against Dan for failure to repay a loan?

a. No: Ford's cross-claim does not arise out of the "transaction or occurrence" that is the subject of Sidney's claim, as required by Rule 13(g).

b. Why doesn't Rule 18, permitting the joinder of all claims, counter-claims, and cross-claims, whether or not related, permit Ford to bring its claim against Dan? Harmonizing Rules 13, 14, and 18 requires careful analysis. Rule 18 provides that a "party asserting a claim . . . as an original claim, counterclaim, cross-claim, or third-party claim, may join, either as independent or as alternate claims, as many claims, legal, equita-ble, or maritime as he has against an opposing party." But Rule 13(g) contains a more restrictive provision, limiting cross-claims to those "aris-ing out of the transaction or occurrence that is the subject matter either of the original action or of a counterclaim therein. . . ." Rule 14(a) similarly restricts claims by third-party defendants. Does Rule 18 eliminate the restrictions created by Rules 13 and 14? No; the key to reconciliation lies in the difference between the requirements for the *first* cross-claim or third-party-defendant claim and any subsequent ones. So, in the hypo-thetical case of Ford's cross-claim against Dan, the original cross-claim had to meet the requirements of Rule 13(g); if it did, then Rule 18 would permit the cross-claimant to add as many additional claims, whether or not related, as it wished.

4. The problems in this Note have thus far focused on the propriety of joinder under the Rules. As we have already seen, federal courts facing joinder questions must often confront a second problem beyond the issue of the propriety of joinder — jurisdiction.

a. If a claim carries with it an independent jurisdictional basis, that question is quickly resolved. For example, if a cross-claim arises under federal law, there will be no problem. Similarly, if a defendant/third-party plaintiff and a third-party defendant meet the requirements of diversity of citizenship, there will be no difficult jurisdictional issue.

b. But what happens if the federal court would not otherwise have jurisdiction over a compulsory counterclaim, third-party claim, or cross-claim? Does supplemental jurisdiction extend to cover these essentially defensive claims? In many circumstances, the answer is yes. Section §1367 of the Judiciary Code (28 U.S.C.) permits many, but not all, such claims to come in under the umbrella of supplemental jurisdiction.

c. Locating the line between permissible and impermissible extensions of supplemental jurisdiction requires (1) a close reading of the statute and (2) a consideration of the concept underlying the statute. It also involves thinking strategically along with the parties as they invoke the Rules and the principles of jurisdiction. The next case, which we examine in several separate phases, explores both the possibilities of impleader and a jurisdictional barrier to its deployment.

Kroger v. Omaha Public Power District

523 F.2d 161 (8th Cir. 1975)

NANGLE, J. . . . .

Plaintiff-Appellant, Geraldine Kroger . . . as administratrix of the estate of James Kroger, brought suit based on diversity jurisdiction for damages resulting from decedent's wrongful death by electrocution.

Appellant's decedent was employed by Paxton & Vierling Steel Company at its factory in Carter Lake, Iowa. On January 18, 1972, decedent was involved in the movement of a large steel tank by means of a crane with a 60-foot boom. While one man drove the crane and another operated the boom, decedent walked alongside the tank to steady it. During this maneuver, the boom came close enough to high-tension lines that electricity from those lines arced over to the boom. Another arc of electricity arced from the tank over to decedent and killed him. . . .

NOTES AND PROBLEMS

1. Put yourself in the position of plaintiff's lawyer. Your client has suffered a terrible loss and any success in a lawsuit will be of great help to a young family. You survey potential defendants and learn the following:

> The crane involved was owned by the Owen Equipment and Erection Company, and leased by Paxton & Vierling Steel Company (hereafter "Paxton") for heavy lifting.

Kroger v. Owen Equipment & Erection Co., 558 F.2d 417, 418 (8th Cir. 1977).

> Omaha Public Power District [OPPD], a public corporation of the state of Nebraska, had at one time owned the transmission lines involved. On November 14, 1966, however, OPPD sold the lines and equipment to Paxton & Vierling, OPPD thereafter sold electricity to Paxton & Vierling and when so requested made repairs upon the lines and equipment.

Kroger v. Omaha Public Power District, 523 F.2d 161, 162 (8th Cir. 1975). You have, then, three possible defendants: Omaha Public Power, Paxton & Vierling Steel, and Owen Equipment & Erection.

a. If one assumes that each of these entities has assets sufficient to satisfy a judgment, which seems intuitively to be liable for Mr. Kroger's death — if anyone is?

b. Paxton might seem a promising defendant. But in most states, workers' compensation laws give employees the right to receive compensation for on-the-job injuries and death without the necessity of proving fault. In return for this right, workers' compensation laws bar tort suits against employers.

    c. Can you identify any reason for not suing Owen Equipment?

    d. Mrs. Kroger's lawyer in fact sued only Omaha Public Power District.

    2. Now imagine yourself as the lawyer for Omaha Power. Look back at the facts above. Your client has been sued on a claim for which you believe it has no liability.

    a. What is your basic strategy for a defense?

    b. Explain why, on these facts, it would be plausible to implead Owen Equipment. Why would such a use of impleader not violate the "It was him, not me" stance rejected in *Watergate Landmark*, supra page 911?

    c. Having used impleader as a form of "litigation insurance," Omaha Power returned to its central defense — denial of liability — and successfully sought summary judgment:

> The District Court based its order of summary judgment on the fact that ownership of the transmission lines lay indisputably with Paxton & Vierling, that OPPD had no duty to maintain the lines, that OPPD had not been requested to discontinue the flow of electricity on the date of the accident and that OPPD had not been put on notice that a crane was being operated in the vicinity of the lines. As a result, there was no duty owed by OPPD to decedent, the breach of which would give rise to liability.

Kroger v. Omaha Public Power District, 523 F.2d 161 at 162. The Eighth Circuit affirmed.

    3. Switch sides again and return to your original representation of Mrs. Kroger. Omaha Power has impleaded Owen Equipment. Although you did not sue this defendant originally, it is now in the case and you decide to take advantage of the opportunity.

    a. Read Rule 14(a) with care and identify the sentence that makes it possible for you to assert a claim against Owen Equipment.

    b. Mrs. Kroger's complaint, let us assume, complied with Rule 8(a)(1) by asserting that plaintiff was a citizen of Iowa and that Owen Equipment was a Nebraska corporation with its principal place of business in that state and otherwise satisfied the requirements of 28 U.S.C. §1332. Owen answered Kroger's complaint as follows:

> 1. Admits that Owen Equipment and Erection Company is a corporation organized and existing under the Laws of the State of Nebraska.
>
> 2. Denies each and every other allegation contained in said Amended Complaint, except those allegations which would be in the nature of admissions against the interest of the plaintiff.

Kroger v. Owen Equipment & Erection Co., 558 F.2d 417, 429 (8th Cir. 1977).

c. Read Rule 8(b), which governs answers, and recall Zielinski v. Philadelphia Piers, Inc., supra page 457. Does this answer — quoted in its entirety — comply with the Rule? Has defendant conceded jurisdiction?

4. Two years after these pleadings — and after Omaha Power had won its summary judgment motion — trial began, with Owen Equipment as the sole defendant. That trial saw a dramatic development:

> So stood the description of the parties until noon on the third day of the trial. At this juncture, defendant Owen elicited from witness Petersen, Secretary of Owen, that Owen's principal place of business was in Carter Lake, Iowa. Having done so, defendant the same afternoon challenged the jurisdiction of the court on the ground of lack of diversity.

Kroger v. Owen Equipment & Erection Co., 558 F.2d 417 at 419.

a. Note that this evidence does not squarely contradict the answer, which admitted that defendant was a Nebraska corporation and generally — but vaguely — denied everything else, including, by inference, that defendant's principal place of business was in Nebraska.

b. Before asking whether the court should grant Owen's motion, consider why that motion came only at trial. Rule 12(h)(3) specifies that jurisdictional challenges are not waived and can be raised at any time. But why wait? What advantages might accrue to Owen by waiting two years to make this motion?

5. The district court refused to grant Owen's motion to dismiss.

a. The Court of Appeals affirmed. The opinion discussed but did not expressly rely on reasoning like that used in *Zielinski* to the effect that defendant was estopped from relying on an ambiguous and deceptive pleading. The court said, "The doctrine of the perpetual availability of jurisdictional challenge furnishes no sanctuary to appellant in the light of such conduct." Kroger v. Owen Equipment & Erection Co., 558 F.2d 417 at 427.

b. But the Court of Appeals devoted most of its opinion to another ground. The case, which preceded the enactment of 28 U.S.C. §1367, raises one of the problems the statute now addresses — extending supplemental jurisdiction to a claim asserted by a plaintiff against a nondiverse third-party defendant. The Court of Appeals held that supplemental jurisdiction did extend to Mrs. Kroger's claim against Owen Equipment; the U.S. Supreme Court disagreed.

Owen Equipment & Erection Co. v. Kroger

437 U.S. 365 (1978)

Mr. Justice STEWART delivered the opinion of the Court. . . .

The relevant statute in this case, 28 U.S.C. §1332(a)(1), confers upon federal courts jurisdiction over "civil actions where the matter in controversy exceeds the [requisite amount in controversy] . . . and is between . . . citizens of different States." This statute and its predecessors have consistently been held to require complete diversity of citizenship. That is, diversity jurisdiction does not exist unless *each* defendant is a citizen of a different State from *each* plaintiff. Over the years Congress has repeatedly reenacted or amended the statute conferring diversity jurisdiction, leaving intact this rule of complete diversity. Whatever may have been the original purposes of diversity of citizenship jurisdiction, this subsequent history clearly demonstrates a congressional mandate that diversity jurisdiction is not to be available when any plaintiff is a citizen of the same State as any defendant.

Thus it is clear that the respondent could not originally have brought suit in federal court naming Owen and OPPD as codefendants, since citizens of Iowa would have been on both sides of the litigation. Yet the identical lawsuit resulted when she amended her complaint [to assert a claim against Owen]. Complete diversity was destroyed just as surely as if she had sued Owen initially. In either situation, in the plain language of the statute, the "matter in controversy" could not be "between . . . citizens of different States."

It is a fundamental precept that federal courts are courts of limited jurisdiction. The limits upon federal jurisdiction, whether imposed by the Constitution or by Congress, must be neither disregarded nor evaded. Yet under the reasoning of the Court of Appeals in this case, a plaintiff could defeat the statutory requirement of complete diversity by the simple expedient of suing only those defendants who were of diverse citizenship and waiting for them to implead nondiverse defendants.[17] If, as the Court of Appeals thought, a "common nucleus of operative fact" were the only requirement for ancillary jurisdiction in a diversity case, there would be no principled reason why the respondent in this case could not have joined her cause of action against Owen in her original complaint as ancillary to her claim against OPPD. Congress' requirement of complete diversity would thus have been evaded completely.

---

17. This is not an unlikely hypothesis, since a defendant in a tort suit such as this one would surely try to limit his liability by impleading any joint tortfeasors for indemnity or contribution. Some commentators have suggested that the possible abuse of third-party practice could be dealt with under 28 U.S.C. §1359, which forbids collusive attempts to create federal jurisdiction. See, e.g., 3 J. Moore, Federal Practice para. 14.27[1], p. 14-571 (2d ed. 1974); 6 C. Wright & A. Miller, Federal Practice and Procedure §1444, pp. 231-232 (1971); Note, Rule 14 Claims and Ancillary Jurisdiction, 57 Va. L. Rev. 265, 274-275 (1971). The dissenting opinion today also expresses this view. Post, at 383. But there is nothing necessarily collusive about a plaintiff's selectively suing only those tortfeasors of diverse citizenship, or about the named defendants' desire to implead joint tortfeasors. Nonetheless, the requirement of complete diversity would be eviscerated by such a course of events.

It is true, as the Court of Appeals noted, that the exercise of ancillary jurisdiction over nonfederal claims has often been upheld in situations involving impleader, cross-claims or counterclaims. But in determining whether jurisdiction over a nonfederal claim exists, the context in which the nonfederal claim is asserted is crucial. And the claim here arises in a setting quite different from the kinds of nonfederal claims that have been viewed in other cases as falling within the ancillary jurisdiction of the federal courts.

First, the nonfederal claim in this case was simply not ancillary to the federal one in the same sense that, for example, the impleader by a defendant of a third-party defendant always is. A third-party complaint depends at least in part upon the resolution of the primary lawsuit. Its relation to the original complaint is thus not mere factual similarity but logical dependence. The respondent's claim against the petitioner, however, was entirely separate from her original claim against OPPD, since the petitioner's liability to her depended not at all upon whether or not OPPD was also liable. Far from being an ancillary and dependent claim, it was a new and independent one.

Second, the nonfederal claim here was asserted by the plaintiff, who voluntarily chose to bring suit upon a state-law claim in a federal court. By contrast, ancillary jurisdiction typically involves claims by a defending party haled into court against his will, or by another person whose rights might be irretrievably lost unless he could assert them in an ongoing action in a federal court. A plaintiff cannot complain if ancillary jurisdiction does not encompass all of his possible claims in a case such as this one, since it is he who has chosen the federal rather than the state forum and must thus accept its limitations. "[T]he efficiency plaintiff seeks so avidly is available without question in the state courts."[20]

It is not unreasonable to assume that, in generally requiring complete diversity, Congress did not intend to confine the jurisdiction of federal courts so inflexibly that they are unable to protect legal rights or effectively to resolve an entire, logically entwined lawsuit. Those practical needs are the basis of the doctrine of ancillary jurisdiction. But neither the convenience of litigants nor considerations of judicial economy can suffice to justify extension of the doctrine of ancillary jurisdiction to a plaintiff's cause of action against a citizen of the same State in a diversity case. Congress has established the basic rule that diversity jurisdiction exists under 28 U.S.C. §1332 only when there is complete diversity of citizenship. "The policy of the statute calls for its strict construction."

20. Whether Iowa's statute of limitations would now bar an action by the respondent in an Iowa court is, of course, entirely a matter of state law.

To allow the requirement of complete diversity to be circumvented as it was in this case would simply flout the congressional command.[21]

Accordingly, the judgment of the Court of Appeals is reversed.

It is so ordered.

Mr. Justice WHITE, with whom Mr. Justice BRENNAN joins, dissenting.

The Court today states that "[i]t is not unreasonable to assume that, in generally requiring complete diversity, Congress did not intend to confine the jurisdiction of federal courts so inflexibly that they are unable . . . effectively to resolve an entire, logically entwined lawsuit." In spite of this recognition, the majority goes on to hold that in diversity suits federal courts do not have the jurisdictional power to entertain a claim asserted by a plaintiff against a third-party defendant, no matter how entwined it is with the matter already before the court, unless there is an independent basis for jurisdiction over that claim. Because I find no support for such a requirement in either Art III of the Constitution or in any statutory law, I dissent from the Court's "unnecessarily grudging" approach. . . .

We have previously noted that "[s]ubsequent decisions of this Court indicate that *Strawbridge* is not to be given an expansive reading." State Farm Fire & Cas. Co. v. Tashire. In light of this teaching, it seems to me appropriate to view §1332 as requiring complete diversity only between the plaintiff and those parties he actually brings into the suit. Beyond that, I would hold that in a diversity case the District Court has power, both constitutional and statutory, to entertain all claims among the parties arising from the same nucleus of operative fact as the plaintiff's original, jurisdiction-conferring claim against the defendant. Accordingly, I dissent from the Court's disposition of the present case.

NOTES AND PROBLEMS

1. Recall that *Kroger* preceded the enactment of 28 U.S.C. §1367. Consider the statute's effect on the factual situation.

a. First confirm the proposition that 28 U.S.C. §1367 codifies *Kroger*. What phrase in what section of the statute codifies the Supreme Court's views in *Kroger*?

---

21. Our holding is that the District Court lacked power to entertain the respondent's lawsuit against the petitioner. Thus, the asserted inequity in the petitioner's alleged concealment of its citizenship is irrelevant. Federal judicial power does not depend upon "prior action or consent of the parties." American Fire & Cas. Co. v. Finn.

b. Contrast the statute's handling of federal question claims. Suppose that Mrs. Kroger's claim had been based on federal rather than state law, in which she alleged that OPPD had violated federal job-site safety regulations and that the violation caused decedent's death. OPPD then impleaded Owen Equipment, alleging that it was directly responsible for the violations, and, once Owen Equipment was in the suit, Mrs. Kroger asserted a claim directly against Owen Equipment. Explain why on those facts there *would be* supplemental jurisdiction over Mrs. Kroger's claim against Owen.

2. The Supreme Court almost — but not quite — ignored the question that had so exercised the district and circuit courts: Owen's misleading answer to the jurisdictional allegations and its late raising of the jurisdictional defense.

a. Footnote 21 suggests, though it does not quite hold, that there could be no such "jurisdictional estoppel." Is that a sound ruling?

b. Could one distinguish between cases in which a party simply failed to raise a jurisdictional defense and those like *Kroger*, in which a party misled the court and other parties? If federal question jurisdiction is a fundamental political boundary line, party behavior should make no difference, should it?

3. Congress, in enacting §1367, could have reversed the result in *Kroger*.

a. As a quick review, explain why Congress had that power.

b. Why do you suppose Congress did not do so? One possibility is the concern about collusive suits, in which A wishing to sue C but lacking jurisdiction to do so, instead sues B, who A knows will implead C, against whom A can then assert a claim under Rule 14(a). Is this a big concern?

4. Test your analysis on a variation on the facts of *Kroger*. Suppose that the third-party defendant had first made a claim against the plaintiff — perhaps an allegation that Mr. Kroger had been vandalizing the crane at the time of the accident.

a. As a matter of pleading, that claim is allowable. Rule 14(a) provides that a third-party defendant "may assert any claim against the plaintiff arising out of the transaction or occurrence that is the subject matter of the plaintiff's claim" against the original defendant. Would supplemental jurisdiction also attach to such a claim? See §1367(b).

b. Now suppose that *after* Owen Equipment asserted such a claim, Mrs. Kroger filed her claim for wrongful death. As a matter of pleading such a claim is again allowable, whether analyzed under 14(a) or under 13(a). (Do you see why both of these sections might plausibly apply?) Would supplemental jurisdiction attach to Mrs. Kroger's claim in these circumstances?

In answering that question, consider the relevance of a passage from *Kroger*:

> [I]n determining whether jurisdiction over a nonfederal claim exists, the context in which the nonfederal claim is asserted is crucial. . . .
>
> [T]he nonfederal claim here was asserted by the plaintiff, who voluntarily chose to bring suit upon a state-law claim in a federal court. By contrast [supplemental] jurisdiction typically involves claims by *a defending party* haled into court against his will. . . . (Emphasis added.)

When Owen Equipment asserts a claim against Mrs. Kroger, does she then become "a defending party" entitled to invoke supplemental jurisdiction? The straightforward language of the statute suggests not: This is a claim by a plaintiff against a third-party defendant. The rationale of *Kroger* might lead one to a different decision. The statute is more recent than *Kroger*, and Congress has the power to supersede the case law on a matter not governed by the Constitution. But the statutory history of §1367 suggests it intended to codify *Kroger*, not to supersede it. So does one read into the statute *Kroger*'s gloss on the statute? Or follow the text alone?

5. Finally, let us return to the travails of Mrs. Kroger. Having lost on the merits against Omaha Power and against Owen Equipment on a belatedly raised jurisdictional defense, what remedies did she have?

a. The Supreme Court suggested a state court lawsuit. There would be no jurisdictional barrier to such a suit, but what defense could her lawyer anticipate?

b. Iowa, like some but not all states, has "savings statutes" that grant relief from the statute of limitations under some conditions. Such statutes are aimed, among other things, at jurisdictional dismissals. Iowa's statute provides:

> If, after the commencement of an action, the plaintiff, for any cause except negligence in its prosecution, fails therein, and a new one is brought within six months thereafter, the second shall, for the purposes herein contemplated, be held a continuation of the first.

Iowa Code Ann. §614.10 (1997). Would Mrs. Kroger's claim be saved by this statute? About what clauses might her lawyer be worried?

c. As it happens, Mrs. Kroger's legal travails came to an end that was, if not happy, at least less disastrous than their beginning. Rumor has it that during the pendency of the several phases of the suit, she remarried and moved to Texas. She filed suit again, successfully invoked the Iowa savings statute as an answer to the statute of limitations defense, and settled the case for what is reported to be somewhat more than the original jury had awarded.

4.   Compulsory Joinder

This chapter has thus far concentrated on who can be joined in a suit if someone already a party seeks joinder. We now consider whether there are those who must be joined — even if neither they nor those already in the suit desire to see them there. The topic, sometimes rather confusingly described in terms of "necessary and indispensable parties," has its roots in eighteenth century equity practice. Chancery developed the perfectly sensible notions that: (1) litigation often affected people who weren't formal parties; and (2) if the effects were serious enough and the affected persons could be joined, they should be. Rule 19 now embodies these propositions.

Thus stated and broadly applied, these principles would collide head-on with the assumptions about party autonomy otherwise basic to the procedural system. In its broadest imaginable application, such a rule would require a court in every case to consider whether to join additional parties; in practice, the Rule does not come even close to embracing such a proposition. It does not, for example, require the joinder of anyone who might be affected by precedent:

> We are not sure what the district court means by the phrase "persuasive precedent." To the extent it involves the doctrine of stare decisis, we are not inclined to hold that any potential effect the doctrine may have on an absent party's rights makes the absent party's joinder compulsory under Rule 19(a) whenever "feasible." Such a holding would greatly expand the class of "necessary" or compulsory parties Rule 19(a) creates. Moreover, to whatever extent the rule's phrase "as a practical matter impair or impede" has broader meaning than that given by principles of issue preclusion, we think the effect of the federal decision must be more direct and immediate than the effect a judgment in Shepard Niles' favor would have on Underwood here. They are, after all, separate corporate entities. In any event, we do not believe any possibility of a "persuasive precedent" requires joinder under subsection 19(a)(2)(i).

Janney Montgomery Scott, Inc. v. Shepard Niles, Inc., 11 F.3d 399, 407 (3d Cir. 1993).

Nor does the Rule require that lawsuits be brought in efficient packages. Recall the facts of Temple v. Synthes, Chapter I, supra page 32. Billy Temple, injured by unsuccessful back surgery, brought two lawsuits — a state court action against his physicians and hospital and a federal diversity action against the manufacturer of an allegedly defective steel plate implanted in his back. The federal defendant invoked Rule 19, arguing that it would be much more efficient to have all the claims resolved in a single suit. The district court agreed and dismissed the suit when plaintiff refused to bring the other defendants into the federal suit. The Supreme Court reversed in a curt per curiam opinion:

> In his petition for certiorari to this Court, Temple contends that it was error to label joint tortfeasors as indispensable parties under Rule 19(b) and to dismiss the lawsuit with prejudice for failure to join those parties. We agree. Synthes does not deny that it, the doctor, and the hospital are potential joint tortfeasors. It has long been the rule that it is not necessary for all joint tortfeasors to be named as defendants in a single lawsuit. Nothing in the 1996 revision of Rule 19 changed that principle.

Temple v. Synthes, 498 U.S. 5, 7 (1990).

Given these background understandings, the necessary parties rules therefore typically operate only when "there is some connection of property ownership, contract rights, or obligations between those who are initially made parties and those who have not been joined." James, Hazard & Leubsdorf at 526. Rule 19 seeks to describe the circumstances under which courts should overcome the ordinary presumptions of party autonomy. Read it and apply it to an elementary problem.

NOTES AND PROBLEMS

1. Buyer enters into a contract with Husband and Wife to purchase Blackacre. The sellers fail to convey the land at the appointed time and Buyer sues Husband, seeking a decree of specific performance. Assume that the jurisdiction in question requires the signatures of both Husband and Wife to convey ordinary, clean title.

a. According to Rule 19(a), should Wife be joined if that is feasible?

b. Be prepared to explain, using the categories of the Rule, why Wife's joinder is desirable (or not desirable).

2. Notice that Rule 19 is somewhat coy about who is to raise the question of joining additional parties. Unlike rules that empower one of the parties to make a motion, this one says, "a person . . . shall be joined as a party," suggesting the court has independent power (and perhaps a duty) to make inquiry. In practice, courts will do so only in a few quite well-defined circumstances. More frequently, one of the parties, typically the defendant, will raise the objection. The defendant's motive for doing so is frequently less than altruistic, as you will see if you study Rule 19(b).

a. What do you suppose the typical defendant is hoping will happen as a result of a Rule 19 motion?

b. Consider again the case of Buyer's suit for specific performance against Husband. Suppose that the court concludes that (1) Wife should be joined; but (2) the court lacks jurisdiction over her. What should the court do? Dismiss Buyer's suit? Something else?

c. In analyzing the preceding question, consider especially the language in Rule 19(b) requiring the court to think about "the extent to which, by protective provisions in the judgment, by the shaping of relief, or other measures, the prejudice can be lessened or avoided. . . ." Buyer wants Blackacre as contracted for, with a clean title. Husband and Wife are entitled to the purchase price, but Wife is not a party to the suit. About whom should the court be concerned and what can it do to alleviate these concerns if it goes forward with the suit?

3. In the typical Rule 19 case, the indispensable party issue is raised in the trial court, and it is a given that the assertedly desirable party is not subject to jurisdiction. The question is then whether it is possible and fair to proceed in his absence. *Helzberg's* is an example of such a case.

Helzberg's Diamond Shops v. Valley West Des Moines Shopping Center

564 F.2d 816 (8th Cir. 1977)

ALSOP, J.

On February 3, 1975, Helzberg's Diamond Shops, Inc. (Helzberg), a Missouri corporation, and Valley West Des Moines Shopping Center, Inc. (Valley West), an Iowa corporation, executed a written Lease Agreement. The Lease Agreement granted Helzberg the right to operate a full line jewelry store at space 254 in the Valley West Mall in West Des Moines, Iowa. Section 6 of Article V of the Lease Agreement provides:

> [Valley West] agrees it will not lease premises in the shopping center for use as a catalog jewelry store nor lease premises for more than two full line jewelry stores in the shopping center in addition to the leased premises. This clause shall not prohibit other stores such as department stores from selling jewelry from catalogs or in any way restrict the shopping center department stores.

Subsequently, Helzberg commenced operation of a full line jewelry store in the Valley West Mall.

Between February 3, 1975 and November 2, 1976 Valley West and two other corporations entered into leases for spaces in the Valley West Mall for use as full line jewelry stores. Pursuant to those leases the two corporations also initiated actual operation of full line jewelry stores.

On November 2, 1976, Valley West and Kirk's Incorporated, Jewelers, an Iowa corporation, doing business as Lord's Jewelers (Lord's), entered into a written Lease Agreement. The Lease Agreement granted Lord's the right to occupy space 261 in the Valley West Mall. Section I of Article V of the Lease Agreement provides that Lord's will use space 261

> . . . only as a retail specialty jewelry store (and not as a catalogue or full line jewelry store) featuring watches, jewelry (and the repair of same) and incidental better gift items.

However, Lord's intended to open and operate what constituted a full line jewelry store at space 261.

In an attempt to avoid the opening of a fourth full line jewelry store in the Valley West Mall and the resulting breach of the Helzberg-Valley West Lease Agreement, Helzberg instituted suit seeking preliminary and permanent injunctive relief restraining Valley West's breach of the Lease Agreement. The suit was filed in the United States District Court for the Western District of Missouri. Subject matter jurisdiction was invoked pursuant to 28 U.S.C. §1332 based upon diversity of citizenship between the parties and an amount in controversy which exceeded $10,000. Personal jurisdiction was established by service of process on Valley West pursuant to the Missouri "long arm" statute, Rev. Stat. Mo. §506.500 et seq. (1977). Rule 4(e), Fed. R. Civ. P.

Valley West moved to dismiss pursuant to Rule 19 because Helzberg had failed to join Lord's as a party defendant. That motion was denied. The district court went on to order that

> pending the determination of [the] action on the merits, that [Valley West] be, and it is hereby, enjoined and restrained from allowing, and shall take all necessary steps to prevent, any other tenant in its Valley West Mall (including but not limited to Kirk's Incorporated, Jewelers, d/b/a Lord's Jewelers) to open and operate on March 30, 1977, or at any other time, or to be operated during the term of [Helzberg's] present leasehold, a fourth full line jewelry store meaning a jewelry store offering for sale at retail a broad range of jewelry items at various prices such as diamonds and diamond jewelry, precious and semi-precious stones, watches, rings, gold jewelry, costume jewelry, gold chains, pendants, bracelets, belt buckles, tie tacs, tie slides and earrings, provided, however, nothing contained herein shall be construed to enjoin [Valley West] from allowing the opening in said Valley West Mall of a small store, known by [Valley West] as a boutique, which sells limited items such as only Indian jewelry, only watches, only earrings, or only pearls.

From this order Valley West appeals.

It is clear that Valley West is entitled to appeal from the order granting preliminary injunctive relief. 28 U.S.C. §1292(a)(1). However, Valley West does not attack the propriety of the issuance of a preliminary injunction directly; instead, it challenges the District Court's denial of its motion to dismiss for failure to join an indispensable party and argues that the District Court's order fails for lack of specificity in describing the acts of Valley West to be restrained. . . .

[The opinion quotes Rule 19.]

Because Helzberg was seeking and the District Court ordered injunctive relief which may prevent Lord's from operating its jewelry store in the Valley West Mall in the manner in which Lord's originally intended, the District Court correctly concluded that Lord's was a party to be joined if feasible. See Rule 19(a)(2)(i), Fed. R. Civ. P. Therefore, because Lord's was not and is not subject to personal jurisdiction in the Western District of Missouri, the District Court was required to determine whether or not Lord's should be regarded as indispensable. After considering the factors which Rule 19(b) mandates be considered, the District Court concluded that Lord's was not to be regarded as indispensable. We agree. . . .

Rule 19(b) requires the court to look first to the extent to which a judgment rendered in Lord's absence might be prejudicial to Lord's or to Valley West. Valley West argues that the District Court's order granting preliminary injunctive relief does prejudice Lord's and may prejudice Valley West. We do not agree.

It seems axiomatic that none of Lord's rights or obligations will be ultimately determined in a suit to which it is not a party. Even if, as a result of the District Court's granting of the preliminary injunction, Valley West should attempt to terminate Lord's leasehold interest in space 261 in the Valley West Mall, Lord's will retain all of its rights under its Lease Agreement with Valley West. None of its rights or obligations will have been adjudicated as a result of the present proceedings, proceedings to which it is not a party. Therefore, we conclude that Lord's will not be prejudiced in a way contemplated by Rule 19(b) as a result of this action.

Likewise, we think that Lord's absence will not prejudice Valley West in a way contemplated by Rule 19(b). Valley West contends that it may be subjected to inconsistent obligations as a result of a determination in this action and a determination in another forum that Valley West should proceed in a fashion contrary to what has been ordered in these proceedings.

It is true that the obligations of Valley West to Helzberg, as determined in these proceedings, may be inconsistent with Valley West's obligations to Lord's. However, we are of the opinion that any inconsistency in those obligations will result from Valley West's voluntary execution of two Lease Agreements which impose inconsistent obligations rather than from Lord's absence from the present proceedings.

Helzberg seeks only to restrain Valley West's breach of the Lease Agreement to which Helzberg and Valley West were the sole parties. Certainly, all of the rights and obligations arising under a lease can be adjudicated where all of the parties to the lease are before the court. Thus, in the context of these proceedings the District Court can determine all of the rights and obligations of both Helzberg and Valley West based upon the Lease Agreement between them, even though Lord's is not a party to the proceedings.

Valley West's contention that it may be subjected to inconsistent judgments if Lord's should choose to file suit elsewhere and be awarded judgment is speculative at best. In the first place, Lord's has not filed such a suit. Secondly, there is no showing that another court is likely to interpret the language of the two Lease Agreements differently from the way in which the District Court would. Therefore, we also conclude that Valley West will suffer no prejudice as a result of the District Court's proceeding in Lord's absence. Any prejudice which Valley West may suffer by way of inconsistent judgments would be the result of Valley West's execution of Lease Agreements which impose inconsistent obligations and not the result of the proceedings in the District Court.

Rule 19(b) also requires the court to consider ways in which prejudice to the absent party can be lessened or avoided. The District Court afforded Lord's an opportunity to intervene in order to protect any interest it might have in the outcome of this litigation. Lord's chose not to do so. In light of Lord's decision not to intervene we conclude that the District Court acted in such a way as to sufficiently protect Lord's interests.

Similarly, we also conclude that the District Court's determinations that a judgment rendered in Lord's absence would be adequate and that there is no controlling significance to the fact that Helzberg would have an adequate remedy in the Iowa courts were not erroneous. It follows that the District Court's conclusion that in equity and good conscience the action should be allowed to proceed was a correct one.

In sum, it is generally recognized that a person does not become indispensable to an action to determine rights under a contract simply because that person's rights or obligations under an entirely separate contract will be affected by the result of the action. This principle applies to an action against a lessor who has entered into other leases which also may be affected by the result in the action in which the other lessees are argued to be indispensable parties. We conclude that the District

Court properly denied the motion to dismiss for failure to join an indispensable party. . . .

In view of the foregoing, it follows that the judgment of the District
Court is affirmed.

NOTES AND PROBLEMS

1. What is the fight about in *Helzberg's*?

a. Assume the suit proceeds without Lord's, and the court enters a
permanent injunction forbidding Valley West to rent to Lord's. When
Valley West proceeds to evict Lord's, Lord's sues, alleging that the eviction
will be a breach of its lease with Valley West. Valley West points to the
injunction, arguing that the court's construction of the lease is binding.
What is Lord's response to that contention?

b. Suppose that in Lord's suit against Valley West the court construes
the lease differently from the first court and holds that Lord's is entitled
to conduct its business in the mall. At this point Valley West is under
two conflicting court orders: one requiring that it evict Lord's, the other
that it honor its lease with Lord's. Both decrees are valid; what should
Valley West do?

c. The opinion in *Helzberg's* seems to concede implicitly that the
scenario just sketched is possible. What is its response to the dilemma
in which Valley West may find itself?

d. What would have been the alternative to proceeding with the suit
in federal district court in Missouri?

e. In light of this alternative, articulate an argument that the court
improperly applied Rule 19.

2. With *Helzberg's* contrast Clinton v. Babbitt, 180 F.3d 1081 (9th
Cir., June 17, 1999), involving what the court described "as claims to
exclusive use [of land] . . . between the Hopi Tribe and the Navajo
Nation, producing what became known as " 'the greatest title problem
in the West.' "

a. Members of the Navajo Tribe living on lands that a settlement had
awarded to the Hopi Nation sued the Secretary of the Interior, alleging
unconstitutional discrimination in the terms of the leases given them as
part of the settlement. The secretary argued that the Hopi Nation, which
stood to lose large sums of money if the settlement fell apart, was a
necessary party. But, the argument continued, the Hopi Nation could
not be joined because of sovereign immunity — and the suit must therefore be dismissed. The Ninth Circuit agreed:

> The plaintiffs seek, at a minimum, a declaration that Secretary Babbitt
> cannot constitutionally approve any individual leases between HPL Nava-
> jos and the Hopi Tribe that use the standard terms of the [settlement].

Such a declaration would prohibit the Tribe from fulfilling its obligations under the Settlement Agreement to enter into such leases and would deprive the Tribe of substantial compensation from the United States (over $25 million and the creation of additional trust lands), which is conditioned on Secretary Babbitt's approval of certain numbers of such leases. The Hopi Tribe, therefore, has a legally protected interest relating to the subject of the action as defined by Rule 19(a)(2). . . .

. . . Although no alternative forum exists for the plaintiffs to seek relief, we conclude that the Hopi Tribe's interest in maintaining its sovereign immunity outweighs the interest of the plaintiffs in litigating their claim. See *Quileute*, 18 F.3d at 1460-61 (" '[A p]laintiff's interest in litigating a claim may be outweighed by a tribe's interest in maintaining its sovereign immunity [because] society has consciously opted to shield Indian tribes from suit without congressional or tribal consent.' " (citations omitted)). . . .

Clinton at 1089–1090.

b. *Helzberg's* differs from *Clinton* in an important way: The former case rejected arguments that an outside party should be joined, while the latter held that it should be joined. A further contrast is that in *Helzberg's* the court, having rejected arguments for compulsory joinder, proceeded to judgment with the existing parties; in *Clinton* the court, having held that the outsider should be joined but could not be, dismissed the entire case, leaving the plaintiff with no forum for his claim. Notice the striking result of the necessary-parties doctrine in such conditions: Because the court cannot do perfect justice, it decides it will do nothing at all. Before it takes such an action, should a court be sure that it is not doing a worse injustice to the existing parties by dismissing than it would do to the unjoined party by proceeding in its absence? Consider a footnote in *Clinton*:

Whether the allegations of the plaintiffs' equal protection claim are sufficient to state a claim upon which relief may be granted is a question we need not reach in this appeal. We note, however, the apparent lack of substance to the claim. First, the plaintiffs admit they are in the unique position of being offered free leases to remain on land to which they have no right, and fail to allege that they are being treated less favorably than any similarly situated individuals. Second, even if the plaintiffs make the threshold showing of disparate treatment they fail to show that this treatment is not rationally related to legitimate legislative goals, such as the peaceful settlement of the Navajo-Hopi land dispute:

[The 1996 Settlement Act] will implement a settlement [which is] a consensual resolution of an age old problem. It creates a way for Navajo families now residing on Hopi land to lawfully remain at the homesites where their families have lived for many generations. At the same time, it preserves the Hopi Tribe's right to exercise jurisdiction over its land. It is based on princi-

> ples of self-determination for the Tribes and human dignity for all tribal
> members. With this settlement, both tribes now will be able to devote
> their efforts and resources to important educational, health, and economic
> developments for the Navajo and Hopi people.

Navajo-Hopi Land Dispute Settlement Act of 1996: Signing Statement of
President William J. Clinton.

Clinton at 1087, n.4. Does this footnote constitute an effort to assure
readers that the court has not lost sight of what Rule 19(b) calls "equity
and good conscience"?

3. In *Helzberg's* the asserted jurisdictional obstacle to joinder was
personal jurisdiction. In *Clinton* the obstacle was the sovereign immunity
of an Indian tribe. Because claims of sovereign immunity will be rare,
and the reach of modern long-arm jurisdiction is long, the more common
objection is want of subject matter jurisdiction.

a. Take, for example, a variation on the facts of *Helzberg's*. Suppose
that Helzberg's and Lords were both Missouri corporations. Under those
circumstances Helzberg's could invoke diversity jurisdiction in its suit
against Valley West (an Iowa corporation); joining Lord's as a defendant
would, however, destroy diversity.

b. Should the federal courts extend supplemental jurisdiction to cover
this situation?

c. In cases relying entirely on diversity jurisdiction, 28 U.S.C. §1367(b)
explicitly excludes from supplemental jurisdiction "claims by plaintiff
against persons made parties under Rule 14, 19, 20, or 24 . . . or over
claims by persons proposed to be joined as plaintiffs under Rule 19 . . .
or seeking to intervene as plaintiffs under Rule 24." What is the theory
underlying denial of supplemental jurisdiction where there is no independent basis for diversity jurisdiction? Sometimes it is said that if the courts
permitted ancillary jurisdiction in this situation, it would open the door
to collusive manipulation of jurisdiction: A, wishing to sue B and C but
lacking complete diversity, would sue just B, hoping that she would plead
C's absence and insist on joinder under Rule 19; if ancillary jurisdiction
extended to cover this situation, A could achieve an otherwise impermissible lawsuit.

d. Another section of the same statute (28 U.S.C. §1367(a)), however,
suggests that supplemental jurisdiction *will* extend to such parties if the
plaintiff is not asserting claims against them or if there is a ground for
federal jurisdiction other than diversity. Is there a theory underlying
such a discrepancy between the treatment of plaintiffs invoking diversity
jurisdiction and others?

4. Should federal courts be more willing under Rule 19(b) to dismiss
cases in which the reason for nonjoinder is a problem with subject
matter jurisdiction than when the difficulty is personal jurisdiction? The

argument for such a result would be that there will always be a state court where subject matter jurisdiction is not a problem, but (because the state and federal courts have substantially identical reaches under personal jurisdiction) there may not be a state court that can resolve the lawsuit.

5. Arguments for compulsory joinder are most common in the following situations:

a. Cases involving an obligation on which two or more persons are, originally or by assignment, either joint obligees or joint obligors, but not all joint obligees or joint obligors are joined as parties.

b. Cases involving ownership of, or interests in, real or personal property in which some persons claiming an interest (for example, joint owners, lessees, mortgagees, mortgagors, lienors, and holders of equity of redemption) are not included as parties.

c. Cases involving representative parties in which either the representative or some of the parties being represented are not included.

d. Cases involving claims to a limited fund or pool of assets, such that potential claimants who are not parties will find the funds depleted when their cases are heard.

6. Practice your analysis of compulsory joinder with the following problems:

a. Joseph Axt is a well-known attorney in Atlanta, Georgia. He was recently divorced from his first wife, Susan, and married his present wife, Mary. The local phone directory contains the following entries: for Susan, "Mrs. Joseph Axt"; for Mary, "Mary (Mrs. Joseph) Axt." Mary brings an action against the Georgia Telephone Co. seeking damages for defamation (by suggesting that she was party to a bigamous marriage) and intentional infliction of mental suffering. Is there something the phone company can do?

b. Larry is the income beneficiary of a spendthrift trust, and his children have the remainder interest. The trustee has a power to appoint the trust to Larry at any time. Larry, a California resident, sues the trustee, an Illinois resident, seeking a declaration that the trustee abused his power by not appointing the trust to him. Any problems?

c. Prior to 1990, H was married to W1 and procured an insurance policy with I Co. payable to "my wife." In 1990, H obtains a Mexican divorce and marries W2. After H's death in 1994, W1 brings an action against I claiming: (a) H never was properly divorced; and (b) even if H were divorced, his intention was to have the policy payable to her. I moves to dismiss for failure to join W2. What result?

d. Homer, husband of Wilma, is injured in a collision between a car driven by Wilma (in which he was a passenger) and a car driven by Triandos. The accident occurs in a comparative negligence state in which each joint tortfeasor is liable only for the portion that his own fault contributed to the accident. Homer sues Triandos, and Triandos moves to dismiss for failure to join Wilma as an indispensable party. What result?

7. Possible prejudice to the defendant and to the absent party are among the factors specified in Rule 19(b). Consider these in turn.

a. The court probably should consider the defendant's ability to join the third party under Rule 14(a) or by using the interpleader device. See Brown v. Chaffee, 612 F.2d 497, 503 (10th Cir. 1979) (in suit against insurer for breach of duty to defend prior action, attorneys who conducted defense are not necessary parties because an adverse decision is not binding on them; insurer could join attorneys under Rule 14(a) and avoid any possible risk of an inconsistent decision).

b. What about the absent party? In its analysis of Rule 19 the *Helzberg's* court dismisses concerns about Lord's (the absent party) by noting that Lord's had the chance to intervene in the proceedings (an opportunity it passed up). The court reasoned that Lord's interests were adequately protected by that chance to intervene. In so stating, the court was taking up a suggestion in a prior case, Provident Tradesmens Bank & Trust v. Patterson, 390 U.S. 102 (1968); in *Martin v. Wilks*, infra page 948, however, the Supreme Court rejects that proposition. *Wilks's* holding makes it more difficult for a court to find that the unjoined party's interests are adequately protected. Does *Wilks* make it more likely that future courts will hold that joinder (or dismissal) is necessary under Rule 19?

C. Intervention

The joinder devices thus far explored have a common characteristic: They serve to bring into a lawsuit a party who does not want to be there. We turn now to a doctrine with the opposite function: to permit an unjoined party to elbow her way into a suit where no one wants her. Like the doctrines of compulsory joinder, the principles of intervention flow from a recognition that lawsuits may have effects on persons not joined. The effects will not be those of formal preclusion — due process forbids binding one who was not a party — but judgments have broader ripple effects than the formal binding effect of the decree.

To take a common example, suppose that Developer and Zoning Board are engaged in litigation over whether Developer can build an office building on a plot of land bordering a residential area. If Developer wins the suit, Homeowner, whose property lies next to the plot in question, will be affected. If Developer loses the suit, Landowner, who owns another adjacent plot of land that would be more valuable if it can be commercially developed, will be adversely affected. The resulting judgment will not formally bind either Homeowner or Landowner, but it will affect them. Both might wish to influence the outcome of the suit. If they were entitled to intervene, they would thereby become parties to the suit, with the right to present evidence and arguments in the same way as Developer and Zoning Board.

Notice that Developer and Zoning Board (and perhaps the judge as well) may be notably unenthusiastic about intervention. From the standpoint of the existing parties, it complicates and perhaps weakens their litigating strategy. Even an intervenor who seeks the same outcome as one of the parties will have a different perspective and perhaps a different strategy. Moreover, additional parties may make settlement more difficult. Conceptually, intervention means further erosion of the principle of party autonomy, and, carried to a logical extreme, turns every lawsuit into a town meeting at which anyone even distantly "interested" in the topic of litigation becomes a party. The principles of intervention seek to allow some — but not all — who might wish to be involved in a lawsuit to join it. Read Rule 24.

Note the structure of the Rule. It is subdivided into two major categories: intervention of right (Rule 24(a)) and permissive intervention (Rule 24(b)). Intervention of right is designed to give to those with strong interests in the litigation the power to insist on joinder. The terms of Rule 24(a)(2) echo those of Rule 19(a)(2) — "an interest relating to" the pending litigation and a situation in which "disposition of the action may as a practical matter" harm the would-be intervenor. Permissive intervention is the weaker counterpart, as it is designed to capture those with weaker bases for insisting on joinder. As the terms imply, an applicant who meets the criteria of Rule 24(a) must be allowed to join the lawsuit. An applicant who meets only the criteria of Rule 24(b) may be allowed to join, with the judge's decision reviewed only for abuse of discretion.

Most of the reported cases focus on Rule 24(a), the general criteria for intervention as of right. That section contains four requirements. The intervention must be timely — the intervenor may not lie in wait until the litigation is on the brink of resolution. The intervenor must have an "interest" in the property or transaction that is the subject of the suit, and that interest must be in some strong way at risk. Finally, even an applicant meeting all these criteria will be denied intervention if those already in the lawsuit are adequately representing the interest. The next case assumes that intervention is timely and analyzes the other three criteria.

Natural Resources Defense Council v. United States Nuclear Regulatory Commission
578 F.2d 1341 (10th Cir. 1978)

DOYLE, J.

The American Mining Congress and Kerr-McGee Nuclear Corporation seek review of the order of the United States District Court for the District of New Mexico denying their motions to intervene [as] a matter of right or on a permissive basis, pursuant to Rule 24(a)(2) and (b), Fed. R. Civil Proc.

The underlying action in which the movants requested intervention was instituted by the Natural Resources Defense Council, Inc., and others. In the action, declaratory and injunctive relief is directed to the United States Nuclear Regulatory Commission (NRC) and the New Mexico Environmental Improvement Agency (NMEIA), prohibiting those agencies from issuing licenses for the operation of uranium mills in New Mexico without first preparing environmental impact statements. Kerr-McGee and United Nuclear are potential recipients of the licenses.

Congress, in the Atomic Energy Act of 1954, has authorized the NRC to issue such licenses. NMEIA is involved because under §274(b) of the Act, the NRC is authorized to enter into agreements with the states allowing the states to issue licenses. Such agreements have been made with about 25 states including New Mexico. Thus, the action below in effect seeks to prevent the use of §274(b) of the Act so as to avoid the requirement of an impact statement for which provision is made in the National Environmental Policy Act.

42 U.S.C. §4332(2)(C) (1970) requires that a detailed environmental impact statement must be prepared by all federal agencies "in every recommendation or report on proposals for legislation and other major Federal actions significantly affecting the quality of the human environment." The complaint cites this requirement and alleges that an environmental impact statement would ordinarily be required here as a prerequisite to the issuance of licenses for the operation of uranium mills were it not for the arrangement which gives jurisdiction to the state. It further alleges that such statements are now prepared by the NRC in states that have not entered into agreements with the NRC, but that the NRC does not prepare such statements where there is an agreement with a state such as New Mexico. Plaintiff contends that the granting of licenses by state agencies predicated on delegation of authority from the NRC causes the NRC to consider the aspect of "major federal action" to be thereby eliminated. The New Mexico agency, NMEIA, which grants the license, does not prepare environmental impact statements since it is not

a federal agency and is not required either by its agreement with NRC or by state law to prepare such a statement.

The relief sought by the plaintiffs' complaint is, first, that NRC's involvement in the licensing procedure in New Mexico is, notwithstanding the delegation to the state, sufficient to constitute major federal action, whereby the impact statement requirement is not eliminated. Second, that if an impact statement is not required in connection with the granting of licenses, the New Mexico program is in conflict with §274(d)(2) of the Atomic Energy Act of 1954.

The motion of United Nuclear Corporation to intervene is not opposed by the parties and was granted. On May 3, 1977, the date that the complaint herein was filed, NMEIA granted a license to United Nuclear to operate a uranium mill at Church Rock, New Mexico. The complaint seeks to enjoin the issuance of the license thus granted.

It was after that that Kerr-McGee Nuclear Corporation, Anaconda Company, Gulf Oil Corporation, Phillips Petroleum Company, and the American Mining Congress filed motions to intervene. These motions, insofar as they sought intervention as of right, were denied on the ground that the interests of the parties or movants would be adequately represented by United Nuclear. Permissive intervention was also denied. Kerr-McGee and the American Mining Congress both appeal denial of both intervention as of right and permissive intervention.

Our issue is a limited one. We merely construe and weigh Rule 24(a) of the Fed. R. Civ. P. (intervention as of right) and decide in light of the facts and considerations presented whether the denial of intervention was correct. [The court quoted Rule 24(a).]

We do not have a subsection (1) situation involving a statutory conferring of right to intervene. Accordingly, we must consider the standards set forth in subsection (2), which are:

1. Whether the applicant claims an interest relating to the property or transaction which is the subject of the action.

2. Whether the claimants are so situated that the disposition of the action may as a practical matter impair or impede their ability to protect that interest.

3. Whether their interest is not adequately represented by existing parties.

The district court's order denying intervention by the several corporations focused on whether the interest of the party seeking to intervene was adequately represented by a fellow member of the industry. . . . The court decided that the interests of the movants were adequately protected by United Nuclear, which possessed the necessary experience and knowledge in a complex area of business, whereby the representative's capability was competent to meet the demands. The court thought that to allow the intervention would engender delay and produce unwieldy procedure; and that the movants' requirements were met by allowing the filing of amicus curiae briefs.

Our conclusion is that the interests of movants in the subject matter is sufficient to satisfy the requirements of Rule 24 and that the threat of loss of their interest and inability to participate is of such magnitude as to impair their ability to advance their interest.

I

The position adopted by the trial court that Kerr-McGee was adequately represented dispensed with the need for the court to consider the question whether Kerr-McGee had an interest in the litigation before the court. Plaintiffs-appellees maintain that the appellants do not have the requisite interest because they are not directly involved; that the controversy centers on the effort of Natural Resources Defense Council, Inc. to prevent the issuance of a license to United Nuclear unless and until an environmental impact statement is issued. The question then is whether the contention made is a correct concept of interest. Strictly to require that the movant in intervention have a *direct* interest in the outcome of the lawsuit strikes us as being too narrow a construction of Rule 24(a)(2). Kerr-McGee argues that the meaning of interest is one which, if they do not prevail in the intervention, threatens them with a disposition of the action which may, as a practical matter, impair or impede their efforts to protect the interest. Thus, we are asked to interpret interest in relationship to the second criterion in Rule 24(a)(2), impairment or impeding ability to protect the interest.

The Supreme Court has said that the interest must be a significantly protectable interest. See Donaldson v. United States, 400 U.S. 517 (1971). The Supreme Court held that a taxpayer did not have a right to intervene in a judicial enforcement proceeding seeking issuance of an Internal Revenue summons ordering production of business records of his employer. The narrowness of the *summons proceeding* was noted, and it was said that an objection of the taxpayer could be raised at the proper time in a subsequent trial.

Cascade Natural Gas Corp. v. El Paso Natural Gas Co., 386 U.S. 129, 135-36 (1967), held that the interest claimed by the applicant in intervention did not have to be a direct interest in the property or transaction at issue provided that it was an interest that would be impaired by the outcome. There Cascade's source of supply would have been a new company created by an antitrust divestiture, a significant change. In view of this consequence of the litigation, it was held that Cascade had a sufficient interest. See also Allard v. Frizzell. In *Allard* it was ruled that the applicant in intervention did not have a sufficient interest. Movant's interest there was general and somewhat abstract.

In our case the matter of immediate interest is, of course, the issuance and delivery of the license sought by United Nuclear. However, the consequence of the litigation could well be the imposition of the requirement that an environmental impact statement be prepared before granting any uranium mill license in New Mexico, or, secondly, it could result in an injunction terminating or suspending the agreement between NRC and NMEIA. Either consequence would be felt by United Nuclear and to some degree, of course, by Kerr-McGee, which is said to be one of the largest holders of uranium properties in New Mexico. It operates a uranium mill in Grants, New Mexico, pursuant to an NMEIA license, which application for renewal is pending. A decision in favor of the plaintiffs, which is not unlikely, could have a profound effect upon Kerr-McGee. Hence, it does have an interest within the meaning of Rule 24(a)(2). This interest of Kerr-McGee is in sharp contrast to the minimal interest which was present in *Allard*, wherein it was an interest of environmental groups in the protection of living birds. This was considered insufficient to justify intervention in a case involving feathers which are part of Indian artifacts. Their interest was said to be limited to a general interest in the public. The interest asserted on behalf of Kerr-McGee and the American Mining Congress is one which is a genuine threat to Kerr-McGee and the members of the American Mining Congress to a substantial degree.

We do not suggest that Kerr-McGee could expect better treatment from state authorities than federal. We do recognize that a change in procedure would produce impairing complications.

II

The next question is whether, assuming the existence of an interest, the chance of impairment is sufficient to fulfill the requirement of Rule 24(a)(2).

As already noted, the question of impairment is not separate from the question of existence of an interest. The appellants both claim an interest in licenses that are now before NMEIA or will be in the future. If the relief sought by the plaintiffs is granted, there can be little question but that the interests of the American Mining Congress and of Kerr-McGee would be affected. Plaintiffs contend, however, that appellants would not be bound by such a result if they are not participants. Kerr-McGee points

out that even though it may not be res judicata, still it would have a
stare decisis effect. Moreover, with NRC and NMEIA as parties, the
result might be more profound than stare decisis.

It should be pointed out that the Rule refers to impairment "as a
practical matter." Thus, the court is not limited to consequences of a
strictly legal nature. The court may consider any significant legal effect
in the applicant's interest and it is not restricted to a rigid res judicata
test. Hence, the stare decisis effect might be sufficient to satisfy the
requirement. It is said that where, as here, the case is of first impression,
the stare decisis effect would be important.

Finally, the considerations for requiring an environmental impact statement will be relatively the same in respect to the issuance of a uranium
mining license in every instance. Hence, to say that it can be repeatedly
litigated is not an answer, for the chance of getting a contrary result in a
case which is substantially similar on its facts to one previously adjudicated
seems remote.

We are of the opinion, therefore, that appellants have satisfied the
impairment criterion.

III

The final question is whether the trial court was correct in its conclusion
that United Nuclear would adequately represent Kerr-McGee and the
American Mining Congress.

The finding and conclusion was that the representation would be
adequate because United Nuclear, a fellow member of the industry, has
interests which were the same as those of the appellants and possessed the
same level of knowledge and experience with the ability and willingness to
pursue the matter and could adequately represent Kerr-McGee and the
members of the American Mining Congress.

We have held in accordance with Trbovich v. UMW, 404 U.S. 528,
538 n. 10 (1972), that the burden continues to be on the petitioner or
movant in intervention to show that the representation by parties may
be inadequate. National Farm Lines v. ICC. We have also recognized
the holding in *Trbovich* that the burden is minimal; that it is enough to
show that the representation "may be" inadequate.

United Nuclear is situated somewhat differently in this case than are
the other members of the industry since it has been granted its license.
From this it is urged by Kerr-McGee that United Nuclear may be ready
to compromise the case by obtaining a mere declaration that while
environmental impact statements should be issued, this requirement need
be prospective only, whereby it would not affect them. While we see this
as a remote possibility, we gravely doubt that United Nuclear would opt

for such a result. It is true, however, that United Nuclear has a defense of laches that is not available to Kerr-McGee or the others.

7A C. Wright & A. Miller, Federal Practice & Procedure, §1909, at 524 (1972), says:

> [I]f [an applicant's] interest is similar to, but not identical with, that of one of the parties, a discriminating judgment is required on the circumstances of the particular case, but he ordinarily should be allowed to intervene unless it is clear that the party will provide adequate representation for the absentee.

While the interest of the two applicants may appear similar, there is no way to say that there is no possibility that they will not be different and the possibility of divergence of interest need not be great in order to satisfy the burden of the applicants under *National Farm Lines*.

There are other reasons for allowing intervention. There is some value in having the parties before the court so that they will be bound by the result. American Mining Congress represents a number of companies having a wide variety of interests. This can, therefore, provide a useful supplement to the defense of the case. The same can be said of Kerr-McGee.

The trial court was concerned that the addition of these movants would make the litigation unwieldy. If the intervenors are limited to this group, unwieldiness does not become a problem which the trial court cannot control. It does not appear that there would be a need for additional parties in view of the presence of the American Mining Congress. While we do not express an opinion on the possibilities of further additions, we wish to make clear that the present holdings that the two applicants should be allowed to intervene does not say that others should be added. The two appellants here have satisfied their burden of the three requirements of Rule 24(a)(2). Consequently, they should be and they are hereby allowed to intervene. Accordingly, we need not determine whether the district court erred in denying permissive intervention under Rule 24(b).

The order of the district court is reversed and the cause is remanded with instructions to the trial court to grant the appellants, Kerr-McGee's and American Mining Congress', motions to intervene.

NOTES AND PROBLEMS

1. Focus on each of the intervenors separately.

a. United Nuclear's motion to intervene was granted without objection. Why? Analyze United Nuclear's position and explain why it met the categories of Rule 24.

b. Kerr-McGee sought to intervene as of right; the trial court denied the motion. Why? How does the court of appeals deal with the trial court's reason for denying Kerr McGee's motion?

c. How was the position of the American Mining Congress different from that of any of the other intervenors? Was its case for intervention stronger or weaker than that of Kerr McGee?

d. Construct an argument that the correct result on these facts was to grant intervention to United Nuclear and the American Mining Congress, but to deny Kerr-McGee's motion.

e. The court holds that all of the would-be intervenors met the criteria of Rule 24(a). Suppose it had come to a different decision. It would then have had to review the decision of the trial court to deny the intervenors permissive intervention under Rule 24(b). Explain why it is likely that the appellate court would have affirmed the trial court's denial of permissive intervention.

2. In Trbovich v. United Mine Workers, 404 U.S. 528 (1972), a union member sought to intervene in an action by the Secretary of Labor to set aside a union election. The Court held that the union member could not intervene to allege additional grounds to set aside the election or to propose safeguards for a future election but could intervene "to present evidence and argument in support of the Secretary's [challenge to the election.]" Id. at 537. In answer to the contention that the Secretary's representation was adequate, the Court stated that "[t]he requirement of the Rule [relating to adequacy of representation] is satisfied if the applicant shows that representation of his interest" may be "inadequate; and the burden of making that showing should be treated as minimal." Id. at 538 n.10. The Court then found this "minimal" burden was satisfied, as the Secretary represented the interests of both the union members *and* the public; thus, the union member might intervene to assure protection of the union member's interest alone. Does this approach present a difficulty? Is it consistent with *Natural Resources Defense Council*?

3. Rule 24 applies not only to competing claimants to property but, as *Natural Resources Defense Council* indicates, goes far beyond such a situation. How far?

a. Assume A and B were both injured in a fireworks display held at Memorial Stadium. A sues Memorial Stadium and alleges that the stadium was negligent in handling the fireworks, and, in the alternative, that the fireworks display was an extrahazadrous activity for which the stadium has absolute liability. B seeks to intervene, claiming liability on similar grounds.

b. Plaintiff sues Auto Manufacturer claiming that a defective design led to her injury. Substantial discovery occurs, followed by a settlement agreement that includes a provision requiring that the materials uncovered by plaintiff in discovery remain confidential. Sixteen persons, each claiming injuries in unrelated accidents involving the same design feature, seek to intervene to challenge the protective order that is part of the settlement. See Jochims v. Isuzu Motors, Ltd., 148 F.R.D. 624 (S.D. Iowa 1993) (permissive intervention granted for purpose of challenging motion for protective order).

4. As already noted, intervention under Rule 24 and the compulsory joinder of parties under Rule 19 deal with related problems.

a. The texts of the two Rules closely resemble each other; more fundamentally, the two rules address similar issues, Rule 19 from the viewpoint of those already in the lawsuit, Rule 24 from that of those outside it. How should a court address the problem that arises when someone who might have been joined — but was not — and might have intervened — but did not — now complains of harm suffered from the judgment entered without her participation?

b. Occasionally courts have hinted that knowledge of a pending action in which one could intervene would suffice to make the judgment binding on such a person, even though she had not in fact intervened. *Helzberg's Diamond Shops*, supra page 930, has language so suggesting. In Provident Tradesmens Bank & Trust, 390 U.S. 101, 114 (1968), the court remarked:

> [I]t might be argued that [a certain nonparty] should be bound by the previous decision because, although technically a nonparty, he had purposely bypassed an adequate opportunity to intervene. We do not now decide whether such an argument would be correct. . . .

Parklane Hosiery v. Shore, supra page 845, contained a similar hint. Explaining why it was prepared to allow nonmutual issue preclusion, the *Parklane* Court noted:

> The application of offensive collateral estoppel will not here reward a private plaintiff who could have joined in the previous action, since the respondent probably could not have joined in the injunctive action brought by the SEC even had he so desired.

11439 U.S. at 331.

In spite of these hints, neither *Provident Tradesmens* nor *Parklane* decided squarely whether one could bind parties who had knowledge of a suit in which their interests were at stake in a lawsuit but who failed to intervene. When the Supreme Court faced that question squarely, it did not go in the direction suggested by its previous hints. The dispute involved a challenge by racial minorities to the hiring practices of Birmingham, Alabama, a city that had in the preceding generation been at the center of the struggle against racial segregation.

Martin v. Wilks

490 U.S. 755 (1989)

Chief Justice REHNQUIST delivered the opinion of the court. . . .

The litigation [that gave rise to the present lawsuit] began in 1974, when the Ensley Branch of the NAACP and seven black individuals filed separate class-action complaints against the City [of Birmingham] and the Board [that made hiring decisions for public employees]. They alleged that both had engaged in racially discriminatory hiring and promotion practices in various public service jobs in violation of Title VII of the Civil Rights Act of 1964, 42 U.S.C. §2000e et seq., and other federal law. After a bench trial on some issues, but before judgment, the parties entered into two consent decrees, one between the black individuals and the City and the other between them and the Board. These proposed decrees set forth an extensive remedial scheme, including long-term and interim annual goals for the hiring of blacks as firefighters. The decrees also provided for goals for promotion of blacks within the department.

The District Court entered an order provisionally approving the decrees and directing publication of notice of the upcoming fairness hearings. Notice of the hearings, with a reference to the general nature of the decrees, was published in two local newspapers. At that hearing, the Birmingham Firefighters Association (BFA) appeared and filed objections as amicus curiae. After the hearing, but before final approval of the decrees, the BFA and two of its members also moved to intervene on the ground that the decrees would adversely affect their rights. The District Court denied the motions as untimely and approved the decrees. Seven white firefighters, all members of the BFA, then filed a complaint against the City and the Board seeking injunctive relief against enforcement of the decrees. The seven argued that the decrees would operate to illegally discriminate against them; the District Court denied relief. . . .

A new group of white firefighters, the *Wilks* respondents, then brought suit against the City and the Board in District Court. They too alleged that, because of their race, they were being denied promotions in favor of less qualified blacks in violation of federal law. The Board and the City admitted to making race conscious employment decisions, but argued the decisions were unassailable because they were made pursuant to the consent decrees. A group of black individuals, the *Martin* petitioners, were allowed to intervene in their individual capacities to defend the decrees.

The defendants moved to dismiss the reverse discrimination cases as impermissible collateral attacks on the consent decrees. . . . After trial the District Court granted the motion to dismiss. . . .

On appeal, the Eleventh Circuit reversed. It held that "[b]ecause . . . [the *Wilks* respondents] were neither parties nor privies to the consent decrees, . . . their independent claims of unlawful discrimination are not precluded." . . .

We granted certiorari and now affirm the Eleventh Circuit's judgment. All agree that "[i]t is a principle of general application in Anglo-American jurisprudence that one is not bound by a judgment in personam in a litigation in which he is not designated as a party or to which he has not been made a party by service of process." Hansberry v. Lee, 311 U.S. 32, 40 (1940) [see infra page 982]. This rule is part of our "deep-rooted historic tradition that everyone should have his own day in court." 18 C. Wright, A. Miller, & E. Cooper, Federal Practice and Procedure §4449, p. 417 (1981) (18 Wright). A judgment or decree among parties to a lawsuit resolves issues as among them, but it does not conclude the rights of strangers to those proceedings.[2]

Petitioners argue that, because respondents failed to timely intervene in the initial proceedings, their current challenge to actions taken under the consent decree constitutes an impermissible "collateral attack." They argue that respondents were aware that the underlying suit might affect them and if they chose to pass up an opportunity to intervene, they should not be permitted to later litigate the issues in a new action. The position has sufficient appeal to have commanded the approval of the great majority of the Federal Courts of Appeals, but we agree with the contrary view expressed by the Court of Appeals for the Eleventh Circuit in this case.

We begin with the words of Justice Brandeis in Chase National Bank v. Norwalk, 291 U.S. 431 (1934):

> The law does not impose upon any person absolutely entitled to a hearing the burden of voluntary intervention in a suit to which he is a stranger. . . .
> Unless duly summoned to appear in a legal proceeding, a person not a privy may rest assured that a judgment recovered therein will not affect his legal rights. Id. at 441.

While these words were written before the adoption of the Federal Rules of Civil Procedure, we think the Rules incorporate the same princi-

---

2. We have recognized an exception to the general rule when, in certain limited circumstances, a person, although not a party, has his interests adequately represented by someone with the same interests who is a party. See Hansberry v. Lee, 311 U.S. 32, 41-42 (1940) ("class" or "representative" suits); Fed. Rule Civ. Proc. 23 (same); Montana v. United States, 440 U.S. 147, 154-155 (1979) (control of litigation on behalf of one of the parties in the litigation). Additionally, where a special remedial scheme exists expressly foreclosing successive litigation by nonlitigants, as for example in bankruptcy or probate, legal proceedings may terminate pre-existing rights if the scheme is otherwise consistent with due process. See NLRB v. Bildisco & Bildisco, 465 U.S. 513, 529-530, n. 10 (1984) ("proof of claim must be presented to the Bankruptcy Court . . . or be lost"); Tulsa Professional Collection Services, Inc. v. Pope, 485 U.S. 478 (1988) (nonclaim statute terminating unsubmitted claims against the estate). Neither of these exceptions, however, applies in this case.

ple; a party seeking a judgment binding on another cannot obligate that person to intervene; he must be joined. . . . Against the background of permissive intervention set forth in *Chase National Bank*, the drafters cast Rule 24, governing intervention, in permissive terms. See Fed. Rule Civ. Proc. 24(a) (intervention as of right) ("[u]pon timely application anyone shall be permitted to intervene"); Fed. Rule Civ. Proc. 24(b) (permissive intervention) ("[u]pon timely application anyone may be permitted to intervene"). They determined that the concern for finality and completeness of judgments would be "better [served] by mandatory joinder procedures." 18 Wright §4452, p. 453. Accordingly, Rule 19(a) provides for mandatory joinder in circumstances where a judgment rendered in the absence of a person may "leave . . . persons already parties subject to a substantial risk of incurring . . . inconsistent obligations. . . ." Rule 19(b) sets forth the factors to be considered by a court in deciding whether to allow an action to proceed in the absence of an interested party.

Joinder as a party, rather than knowledge of a lawsuit and an opportunity to intervene, is the method by which potential parties are subjected to the jurisdiction of the court and bound by a judgment or decree.[6] The parties to a lawsuit presumably know better than anyone else the nature and scope of relief sought in the action, and at whose expense such relief might be granted. It makes sense, therefore, to place on them a burden of bringing in additional parties where such a step is indicated, rather than placing on potential additional parties a duty to intervene when they acquire knowledge of the lawsuit. The linchpin of the "impermissible collateral attack" doctrine — the attribution of preclusive effect to a failure to intervene — is therefore quite inconsistent with Rule 19 and Rule 24. . . .

Petitioners . . . rely on our decision in *Provident Tradesmans Bank*, supra, as authority for the view which they espouse. In that case we discussed Rule 19 shortly after parts of it had been substantially revised, but we expressly left open the question of whether preclusive effect might be attributed to a failure to intervene.

---

6. The dissent argues on the one hand that respondents have not been "bound" by the decree but rather, that they are only suffering practical adverse affects from the consent decree. On the other hand, the dissent characterizes respondents' suit not as an assertion of their own independent rights, but as a collateral attack on the consent decree which, it is said, can only proceed on very limited grounds. Respondents in their suit have alleged that they are being racially discriminated against by their employer in violation of Title VII: either the fact that the disputed employment decisions are being made pursuant to a consent decree is a defense to respondents' Title VII claims or it is not. If it is a defense to challenges to employment practices which would otherwise violate Title VII, it is very difficult to see why respondents are not being "bound" by the decree.

Petitioners contend that a different result should be reached because the need to join affected parties will be burdensome and ultimately discouraging to civil rights litigation. Potential adverse claimants may be numerous and difficult to identify; if they are not joined, the possibility for inconsistent judgments exists. Judicial resources will be needlessly consumed in relitigation of the same question.

Even if we were wholly persuaded by these arguments as a matter of policy, acceptance of them would require a rewriting rather than an interpretation of the relevant Rules. But we are not persuaded that their acceptance would lead to a more satisfactory method of handling cases like this one. It must be remembered that the alternatives are a duty to intervene based on knowledge, on the one hand, and some form of joinder, as the Rules presently provide, on the other. No one can seriously contend that an employer might successfully defend against a Title VII claim by one group of employees on the ground that its actions were required by an earlier decree entered in a suit brought against it by another, if the later group did not have adequate notice or knowledge of the earlier suit.

The difficulties petitioners foresee in identifying those who could be adversely affected by a decree granting broad remedial relief are undoubtedly present, but they arise from the nature of the relief sought and not because of any choice between mandatory intervention and joinder. Rule 19's provisions for joining interested parties are designed to accommodate the sort of complexities that may arise from a decree affecting numerous people in various ways. We doubt that a mandatory intervention rule would be any less awkward. As mentioned, plaintiffs who seek the aid of the courts to alter existing employment policies, or the employer who might be subject to conflicting decrees, are best able to bear the burden of designating those who would be adversely affected if plaintiffs prevail; these parties will generally have a better understanding of the scope of likely relief than employees who are not named but might be affected. Petitioners' alternative does not eliminate the need for, or difficulty of, identifying persons who, because of their interests, should be included in a lawsuit. It merely shifts that responsibility to less able shoulders.

Nor do we think that the system of joinder called for by the Rules is likely to produce more relitigation of issues than the converse rule. The breadth of a lawsuit and concomitant relief may be at least partially shaped in advance through Rule 19 to avoid needless clashes with future litigation. And even under a regime of mandatory intervention, parties who did have adequate knowledge of the suit would relitigate issues. Additional questions about the adequacy and timeliness of knowledge would inevitably crop up. We think that the system of joinder presently contemplated by the Rules best serves the many interests involved in the run of litigated cases, including cases like the present one.

. . . A voluntary settlement in the form of a consent decree between one group of employees and their employer cannot possibly "settle," voluntarily or otherwise, the conflicting claims of another group of employees who do not join in the agreement. . . .

For the foregoing reasons we affirm the decision of the Court of Appeals for the Eleventh Circuit. . . .

Justice STEVENS, with whom Justice BRENNAN, Justice MARSHALL, and Justice BLACKMUN join, dissenting.

As a matter of a law there is a vast difference between persons who are actual parties to litigation and persons who merely have the kind of interest that may as a practical matter be impaired by the outcome of a case. Persons in the first category have a right to participate in a trial and to appeal from an adverse judgment; depending on whether they win or lose, their legal rights may be enhanced or impaired. Persons in the latter category have a right to intervene in the action in a timely fashion, or they may be joined as parties against their will. But if they remain on the sidelines, they may be harmed as a practical matter even though their legal rights are unaffected. One of the disadvantages of sideline-sitting is that the bystander has no right to appeal from a judgment no matter how harmful it may be.

In this case the Court quite rightly concludes that the white firefighters who brought the second series of Title VII cases could not be deprived of their legal rights in the first series of cases because they had neither intervened nor been joined as parties. . . . There is no reason, however, why the consent decrees might not produce changes in conditions at the white firefighters' place of employment that, as a practical matter, may have a serious effect on their opportunities for employment or promotion even though they are not bound by the decrees in any legal sense. The fact that one of the effects of a decree is to curtail the job opportunities of nonparties does not mean that the nonparties have been deprived of legal rights or that they have standing to appeal from that decree without becoming parties. . . .

Regardless of whether the white firefighters were parties to the decrees granting relief to their black co-workers, it would be quite wrong to assume that they could never collaterally attack such a decree. If a litigant has standing, he or she can always collaterally attack a judgment for certain narrowly defined defects. See, e.g., Klapprott v. United States, 335 U.S. 601 (1949). See also Korematsu v. United States, 584 F. Supp. 1406 (N.D. Cal. 1984) (granting writ of coram nobis vacating conviction based on Government concealment of critical contradictory evidence in Korematsu v. United States, 323 U.S. 214 (1944)). On the other hand, a district court is not required to retry a case — or to sit in review of another courts' judgment — every time an interested nonparty asserts that *some* error that might have been raised on direct appeal was committed. Such a broad allowance of collateral review would destroy the integrity of litigated judgments, would lead to an abundance of vexatious litigation, and would subvert the interest in comity between courts. . . .

NOTES AND PROBLEMS

1. Consider both the sequence of litigative events and the identity of the parties involved. The basic lawsuit involved one "entity plaintiff" (the NAACP) and seven individual plaintiffs suing a pair of entity defendants (the City and the County Personnel Board, which was apparently responsible for staffing firehouse positions).

a. The plaintiffs and defendants engaged in considerable litigation — including a trial of some issues — before arriving at a settlement.

b. There were then three separate efforts to challenge the settlement, each by a slightly different set of individual and entity parties. What actions did these groups take, at what stages of the lawsuit, and by what procedural means?

2. Now put yourself in the position of the original parties. They have fought each other to exhaustion and have arrived at a settlement that they are prepared to live with. Now comes a group not previously involved in the litigation, who contend that the terms of the settlement disadvantage them in an unlawful way.

a. Explain why both original parties to the suit would be unhappy about this development.

b. Describe the argument — ultimately rejected by the Court — that the original parties used to explain why the white firefighters should be bound by the settlement agreement, even though they had not participated in the lawsuit or in the settlement negotiations. Though it was rejected by the majority, this argument got four votes. Why?

3. *Wilks* can be understood as a question of who has the responsibility to ensure that the requisite interests are represented in the lawsuit. One view, rejected by the majority, is that the absentees have the burden of invoking Rule 24 to intervene. On this view the penalty for failing to intervene is that one must subsequently suffer under any unfavorable result. The other view, adopted in *Wilks*, is that those in the suit share with the court the responsibility for joining the absentees. On this view

the penalty for failing to locate and join all absentee interests is that one must face the prospect of subsequent litigation when the absentees do assert their interests. As a matter of either good judicial administration or due process, is the choice between the two paths clear?

4. The problem in *Wilks* can also be seen as one of respect for judgments as well as of joinder of parties. How one reacts to the first will affect one's response to the second. If one believes that parties should be encouraged or required to intervene in a pending action in which their interests may be affected, one will be tempted to enforce that belief by refusing to hear a later action. If, on the other hand, one believes strongly in party autonomy, one may be reluctant to require intervention in the original suit and accordingly to permit the later action.

5. *Wilks* shifts the "burden of joinder" to the parties in the original action. Consider a similar case arising after the decision in *Wilks*. A group of Hispanic employees sues its employer, alleging discrimination in employment. Both sides agree only that the claims will be difficult to prove. After some discovery, the parties begin to talk about settling. The terms of the tentative settlement may work some practical disadvantage on non-Hispanic employees.

a. Should the parties move to join the non-Hispanic employees on the ground that failure to do so will render any settlement open to challenge?

b. If one or both parties move to join another group, how should that be done? By moving to join them under Rule 19? What happens if the potential opposition is not organized? Can the court simply name one or several non-Hispanic employees and treat them as representing the rest?

c. If the non-Hispanic employees join the lawsuit, either voluntarily or as compulsorily joined parties, how much control do they have over the settlement? May they block the settlement simply by stating that it is disadvantageous to them and that they will not agree to it? Or, in order to prevent the settlement, must they demonstrate that, if adopted, it would result in unlawful discrimination against them?

d. Arriving at a settlement under these conditions will probably be more difficult than it would be with only the original parties. On the other hand, a settlement satisfactory to all the interests will probably be more durable. Do you suppose the Court considered such matters? Should it?

6. In the wake of *Wilks*, Congress enacted and the president signed legislation aimed at, among other things, reversing the holding of the case. S. 1745, 102d Cong., 1st Sess. §108 (1991). The statute prohibits a collateral challenge to a consent decree in a civil rights case complaining of employment discrimination if the challenger is "a person who, prior

to the entry of [the consent decree] had — (i) actual notice . . . of the proposed judgment. . . ; and (ii) a reasonable opportunity to present objections to such judgment or order; or (iii) . . . a person whose interests were adequately represented" in the first action.

a. Explain why, on the facts of *Wilks*, this statute would lead to a result different from that decision.

b. The legislation applies only to employment discrimination consent decrees. It would not apply, for example, to an antitrust consent decree. Should Congress seek to dictate different procedural rules for particular substantive areas?

c. What is the source of law for the decision in *Wilks*? Is it an interpretation of Rule 19 or is it based on the Due Process Clause? If *Wilks* is based on the Due Process Clause, a statute that sought to overrule *Wilks* would itself be unconstitutional.

D. Interpleader

In discussing necessary parties, we looked briefly at a case in which a husband made a life insurance policy payable to "my wife." The couple subsequently divorced. Husband remarried and later died. Both wives claimed the proceeds of the policy. If both wives bring separate suits on the policy, it is possible that, to the consternation of the insurance company, both will win. In the past, any possible resolution of the insurance company's dilemma had to overcome two difficulties: (a) the unavailability of an effective procedural device to join both claimants, and (b) jurisdictional and venue limitations in using available procedural devices. Interpleader provides a procedure by which a "stakeholder" — often a bank or insurer — could require the competing claimants to litigate their rights to the fund or property in question. Typically the stakeholder invokes interpleader, joining the claimants as parties. Such a proceeding will, however, fail to yield a stable resolution of the dispute if the forum lacks jurisdiction over the claimants.

As an illustration of the difficulties such limitations could pose, consider New York Life Insurance Co. v. Dunlevy, 241 U.S. 518 (1916). Father, in Pennsylvania, bought an insurance policy that paid a lump sum amount after a set number of years. The sum came due, but Father and Daughter disagreed about whether he or she was entitled to the sum. One of Daughter's creditors brought suit in Pennsylvania. The insurer, knowing of the dispute between Father and Daughter, interpleaded Father, Daughter, and Creditor. The Pennsylvania court ruled that Father was entitled to the proceeds. Daughter, dissatisfied by this result, sued the insurer in California. Insurer contended that the Pennsylvania suit precluded Daughter's claim. Wrong, held the U.S. Supreme Court — because Pennsylvania had not acquired personal jurisdiction over Daughter, who lived in California. The insurer was thus liable — a second time — for the policy proceeds.

Congress responded to the procedural uncertainties and the jurisdictional issues presented in cases like *Dunlevy* by enacting the Federal Interpleader Act, codified at 28 U.S.C. §§1335, 1397, and 2361. This legislation accomplishes several tasks:

a. The Interpleader Act broadens the circumstances in which interpleader is available, eliminating some restrictions that older equity doctrines had imposed. See §1335.

b. The Act removes limitations on federal subject matter jurisdiction. How does it do this? See §1335(a).

c. The Act permits nationwide service of process. See §2361. Thus, in *Dunlevy*, Daughter would be subject to the jurisdiction of the federal courts in Pennsylvania, which could thus resolve all the parties' conflicting claims.

d. The Act expands venue provisions to permit venue where any claimant resides. See §1397. The provisions of Rule 22 closely resemble those of the Interpleader Act. Like the Interpleader Act, Rule 22 eliminates, either explicitly or by implication, each of the four common law restrictions on equitable interpleader. But it is subject to the normal rules for subject matter jurisdiction (diversity between all plaintiffs and all defendants); personal jurisdiction (jurisdiction within the state); and venue (all defendants, or where the claim arises). In practice, Rule 22 interpleader is used when the stakeholder is a citizen of one state and all claimants are citizens of a second state. In such a case, there is no jurisdiction under the Interpleader Act because no two claimants are of diverse citizenship. In such cases, however, the normal rules for jurisdiction and venue can be satisfied by an action in the state of all claimants.

The table on page 957, opposite, illustrates some differences between statutory interpleader and Rule 22 interpleader.

Would statutory or Rule interpleader best have suited the situation described in the next case? The setting of the case involved international politics as well as personal greed. Ferdinand Marcos was the president (and some claimed the corrupt dictator) of the Republic of the Philippines between 1972 and 1986. After Marcos's overthrow, allegations surfaced that he and his wife Imelda had converted government funds to their personal use and had used those funds to acquire everything from 3,000 pairs of shoes for Imelda to real estate and art objects in several nations. Some of those objects are the subject of the next case.

Issue	Statutory	Rule 22
Subject Matter Jurisdiction		
— Diversity	Minimal diversity; determined as between claimants	Complete diversity; stakeholder on one side and claimants on the other
— Amount	$500 in controversy	$75,000+
Personal Jurisdiction; service of process	Nationwide service of process	Need personal jurisdiction; service under Rule 4
Venue	Residence of one or more claimants	Residence of any claimants (if all from one state); district where dispute arose; district where property is; district where any claimant found if no other basis for venue
Injunctions	Statutory authority for injunctions (28 U.S.C. §2361)	Only basis is provision in 28 U.S.C. §2283 for stay "where necessary in aid of . . . jurisdiction."

Cohen v. The Republic of the Philippines

146 F.R.D. 90 (S.D.N.Y. 1993)

CONNER, J.

This is an interpleader action initiated by Marc Cohen and Marc Cohen & Co. (collectively "Cohen") against Klaus Braemer (Braemer) and The Republic of the Philippines (the Philippines). The action is presently before the Court on the motion of Imelda R. Marcos (Marcos) for leave to intervene. The motion is granted subject to the conditions outlined below.

Background

At issue in this action is the ownership of four paintings whose total value is nearly $5,000,000.[1] In late 1991 or early 1992, Cohen received the

---

1. The paintings at issue are Georges Braque's "Guitar Valse," Henri Matisse's "Head of a Woman," Pierre Auguste Renoir's "Jeune Fille au Chien," and Pierre Auguste Renoir's "Jeunes Filles au bord de l'eau" (collectively "the paintings").

paintings on consignment from Braemer, who was Marcos's agent entrusted to run her New York home in which the paintings had previously hung. Braemer demanded return of the paintings in March of 1992, but Cohen refused because he was uncertain who actually owned the paintings. Consequently, Cohen brought this interpleader action against Braemer and the Philippines.

Braemer claims that Marcos authorized him to sell the paintings, and he asserts a direct interest in the paintings originating from a $300,000 loan made to Marcos and a $500,000 loan which Braemer guaranteed for Marcos, both of which were collateralized by the paintings. The Philippines claims that the paintings were acquired with Philippine Government funds for the benefit of the Philippines, or that the paintings were acquired with funds which Marcos or her husband illegally obtained during Ferdinand Marcos's tenure as President of the Philippines. In either case, the Philippines claims to be the rightful owner of the paintings. Marcos now seeks to intervene in this action, claiming that the paintings were acquired with her personal funds and remain her property. She denies that a lien or security interest in the paintings was given to Braemer and, in the alternative, claims a right to the paintings after payment of the amount due Braemer. . . .

Discussion

Marcos's motion for leave to intervene in this action is granted with conditions because she has complied with the requirements of Rule 24(a), Fed. R. Civ. P. Rule 24(a)(2) allows anyone, upon timely application, to intervene in an action if

> [t]he applicant claims an interest relating to the property or transaction which is the subject of the action and the applicant is so situated that the disposition of the action may as a practical matter impair or impede the applicant's ability to protect that interest, unless the applicant's interest is adequately represented by existing parties.

Marcos's intervention motion is timely; Marcos has an interest in the paintings that are the subject of this interpleader action; Marcos's interest is likely to be prejudiced by the action; and the existing parties are unlikely to adequately protect Marcos's interest.

Timeliness

Timeliness is a flexible determination made in the discretion of the Court. Among the factors to be considered in determining whether a motion to intervene is timely are (1) how long the applicant knew of his interest before making the motion; (2) prejudice to the existing parties from any such delay; (3) prejudice to applicant if the motion is denied; (4) other unusual circumstances. Marcos's decision to apply for intervention was made approximately five months after the initial complaint was filed. However, all parties knew of Marcos's potential intervention from the inception of the action, and the delay was caused by settlement discussions between Marcos and the Philippines in a California action which may have disposed of this matter as well. We believe Marcos's delay was not unreasonable given the complex and politically sensitive international implications of this action. The existing parties have not been unduly prejudiced by the delay because the addition of Marcos does not require altering a scheduled trial date on which they may have relied. However, as stated below, Marcos's interest is very likely to be prejudiced if her intervention is denied.

Interest

Marcos has an interest in the paintings in question. She has filed an affidavit with her motion which claims that the paintings were acquired with her personal funds and hung in her Olympic Tower residence in New York City. In addition, Marcos disputes Braemer's alleged lien on the paintings. The Philippines has submitted a default judgment of July 1987 which indicates that Marcos's Olympic Tower residence was held in a constructive trust for the Philippines. However, this judgment does not make any reference to the contents of the premises, nor do we wish to try the merits of Marcos's interest in determining this motion. Marcos has alleged and affirmed an interest in the paintings sufficient to support her motion to intervene.

Possible Prejudice and Lack of Adequate Representation

Marcos's interest may be impaired by the action and is not adequately protected by the existing parties. Marcos's alleged interest is contrary to the interest of both existing parties. Marcos claims an interest in the paintings superior to that of the Philippines, and she disputes Braemer's alleged security interest in the paintings. Thus, Braemer can not adequately protect Marcos's interest. Furthermore, the Philippines asserts that a joint tentative settlement of this action and the Sotheby's action has been reached and that Marcos's intervention will destroy this agreement. If Braemer were adequately protecting Marcos's interests in these negotiations, the addition of Marcos as a party would not disrupt the agreement. However, since the loan at issue in the Sotheby's action is under-collateralized while the loan at issue here is over-collateralized, we believe that this over-collateralization will be somehow divided among the existing parties to both actions pursuant to the joint settlement agreement. If Marcos has an interest in either the paintings or the over-collateralized portion thereof, this settlement will defeat that interest. We will not deprive Marcos of her day in court simply to allow the speedy but possibly unjust disposition of the two actions before us.[3]

Conclusion

Marcos fulfills all the requirements of Rule 24(a)(2), and her motion to intervene is, therefore, granted subject to the following conditions:

(1) Marcos must make all necessary applications to the Philippine Government to allow her to travel to New York for a deposition in this matter at least 7 days before trial.

(2) If the Government of the Philippines grants her the right to travel, Marcos must appear for a deposition in New York at least 7 days before trial.

(3) If the Government of the Philippines denies Marcos the right to travel to New York for this deposition, Marcos must make herself available for a deposition in the Philippines at least 30 days before trial.

SO ORDERED.

NOTES AND PROBLEMS

1. Consider first the case as things stood before Marcos's intervention.

a. Cohen, the art dealer, had the paintings.

b. He also had two parties, Braemer and the Republic of the Philippines, asserting ownership to them.

c. Suppose Cohen sought your counsel at this stage. What risk would you point out to him?

d. How did Cohen's next procedural move seek to avoid that risk?

e. What is the obstacle — surmounted by the time we read the case — to the use of that procedure?

2. As things turned out, still another party — Marcos — also asserted that she owned the paintings and intervened to protect that interest. The court permitted her to do so. For our purposes the case becomes even more interesting had she not intervened.

---

3. The Philippines claims that Marcos's interest will not be adversely affected by this action because she is free to pursue her interests in other actions in the Philippines or elsewhere. However, a requirement that Marcos institute a separate action is too great a burden on her interest.

a. Suppose the case went to judgment, awarding the paintings to Braemer. Marcos now sues Braemer, alleging that he stole them from her. Can he point to the judgment as proof that they belong to him? Why not?

b. What if Cohen sought to interplead Mrs. Marcos as well as Braemer and the Philippines? As a matter of pleading, she easily satisfies the criteria for a "claimant." But she is located in the Philippines. Nationwide service of process does not reach her. Is there jurisdiction based on her previous residence in New York City, where the paintings were hung?

c. If Cohen knew that the Philippines and Marcos, as well as Braemer, claimed the paintings as theirs, why didn't he try to interplead Marcos as well as the other two claimants?

d. Note that the Philippines objected to Marcos's intervention. From a purely analytic standpoint, it might have wished her presence in the suit, if only to establish ownership firmly. In real life, the Philippines might not have been too worried about a suit by Marcos. Where would such a suit have taken place?

3. Arthur had an insurance policy with Prudential Life Insurance Co. payable to Barbara. The policy terms did not permit him to change beneficiaries. Sometime before his death, Arthur changed the beneficiary to Grace; and, because of a clerical error, the company did not realize that no changes were permitted. Arthur died, and both Barbara and Grace claimed the proceeds of the policy. In Trowbridge v. Prudential Insurance Co., 322 F. Supp. 190 (S.D.N.Y. 1971), the court held interpleader improper on the ground that Prudential's liability to Barbara was not inconsistent with its also being liable to Grace. This was because liability to Barbara was for failure to follow instructions, and liability to Grace was on the policy. Since both claimants were not claiming the same thing, and Prudential's liability to each was independent, the requirements for interpleader were not met.

4. Imagine that Chicago National Bank holds funds claimed by both Fred, a Kansas resident, and Greta, a Nebraska resident. In which federal courts can the bank file an interpleader action under the Interpleader Act? Under Rule 22? What is the outcome if Fred first sued Chicago National Bank in the U.S. District Court for the District of Kansas?

5. What is the relationship between Rule 19 and interpleader? For example, assume Haas (an Ohio citizen) claimed certain shares of common stock of Jefferson National Bank (for diversity purposes a Florida citizen), pursuant to an agreement with Glueck (an Ohio citizen) for joint purchase of the shares. Assume the shares were held by the bank at the time. Haas maintains that he performed his part of the bargain, the bank had knowledge of his interest, and Glueck requested transfer of the shares to Haas but the bank refused. Jefferson claims it refused

because Glueck had owed the bank a debt for which the stock was collateral and that Glueck then withdrew the transfer request and pledged the stock to the bank. On closely related facts, the court in Haas v. Jefferson National Bank, 442 F.2d 394 (5th Cir. 1971), held Glueck an indispensable party based on the possibility that "Glueck, not being bound by res judicata, could theoretically succeed in later litigation against the Bank in asserting ownership of the whole." 442 F.2d at 398. If you had represented Haas, what argument might you have made in response to the court's belief that it had to dismiss the case because the bank risked double liability?

6. Finally, consider a situation that stretches the concept of interpleader to the breaking point. A bus collides with a pickup truck, injuring numerous passengers. The driver of the truck has a liability policy with a maximum of $20,000 in coverage, an amount that will be exhausted many times over if driver is found to be negligent.

a. Can the insurance company interplead all the actual and potential plaintiffs (the bus passengers)? Unlike the usual interpleader situation, there is here no danger that the insurer will be subject to multiple liability: It may have a duty to defend its insured in multiple suits and to minimize his liability, but the insurer's duty to indemnify is limited to the face value of the policy. The virtue of interpleader in this situation is that it assures that the plaintiffs will share proportionately in the policy proceeds rather than have the total amount go to the first plaintiff whose case comes to judgment.

b. Under these circumstances the U.S. Supreme Court said that interpleader would lie. The plaintiffs could not be required to litigate the question of liability in the interpleader action, but interpleader could be used to distribute the policy proceeds equitably. State Farm Fire & Casualty Co. v. Tashire, 386 U.S. 523 (1967).

c. *Tashire* is also notable for an entirely different reason: It held, squarely and definitively, that the requirement of complete diversity was statutory rather than constitutional. The necessary implication is that Congress can amend §1332 to permit federal jurisdiction when some but not all parties are of diverse citizenship.

E.   Class Actions

1.   Introduction

A class action permits, in the words of Rule 23, one or more parties to "sue or be sued as representative parties on behalf" of all those similarly situated. The underlying concept is simple: If many persons find themselves in the same situation, advantages may flow from aggregating many lawsuits into one. In practice, the class action has stimulated comments as favorable as "one of the most socially useful remedies in history" and as negative as "legalized blackmail."* Technically a joinder device, the class action has a potential effect on the judicial system and the substantive law unmatched by other joinder devices discussed in this chapter. The class action repays study: It raises some of the most challenging procedural issues on the current legal scene, and it raises questions that lie close to the heart of civil litigation — the nature of representation and the purpose of a lawsuit.

Although one can trace collective litigation into the mists of the common law, the modern class action traces its immediate pedigree only to 1966.** The revision of Rule 23 in that year sparked a new interest in and widespread use of class actions, prompting reaction of the type quoted earlier. Class actions clearly differ from the normal litigation model in which an individual plaintiff seeks redress from an individual defendant. The difference is not merely quantitative. For reasons that will become clear in the following materials, the ability to aggregate large numbers of litigants tends to shift the focus from the client to the lawyer, from damages to attorneys' fees, and from litigation to settlement.

The effect of class actions on the substantive law is subtler. It is not that the availability of class actions literally changes the statutes or the content of the case law, but, rather, that rules devised for one-on-one litigation have different effects in the context of mass litigation. For example, in Katz v. Carte-Blanche Corp., 496 F.2d 747 (3d Cir.), cert. denied, 419 U.S. 885 (1974), a background issue was whether minimum statutory damages of $100 should be available to each person in a class containing hundreds of thousands of members. More generally, when the availability of class actions increases the number of claims that are brought rather than simply facilitating the bringing of large numbers of claims that would have been brought separately, the impact of the underlying substantive law may be greatly heightened. Some have argued that this effect is a regrettable aspect of the rule. Others have argued that the increased potential for deterring wrongdoers and forcing wider compliance with the law is a powerful argument in favor of the device.

---

* The former comment comes from Pomerantz, New Developments in Class Actions — Has Their Death Knell Been Sounded?, 25 Bus. Law. 1259 (1970); the latter characterization appears in Handler, The Shift from Substantive to Procedural Innovations in Anti-Trust Suits, 71 Colum. L. Rev. 1, 9 (1971).

** See generally Stephen C. Yeazell, From Medieval Group Litigation to the Modern Class Action (1987).

2.   Statutory Requirements

To understand the furor, one has first to see how the contemporary class action operates. The starting point is, as always, the text of the Rule. That text establishes a series of hurdles for class actions to surmount, on their way to "certification," a process described in Rule 23(d). To become certified, a class action must meet both the requirements of Rule 23(a) and also fit into one of the three categories of Rule 23(b).

Practitioners refer to the four requirements of Rule 23(a) as numerosity, commonality, typicality, and adequacy of representation. To establish a case as a class action, the person seeking to represent the class must show that each of these requirements is satisfied.

Numerosity (Rule 23(a)(1)) is established if the class representative can show that enough persons are in the class to make joining them as individuals impractical. Courts occasionally certify classes as small as a few score, but typically classes consist of at least hundreds of persons.

Commonality is jargon for the idea that the class should be a class — that it should consist of persons who share characteristics that matter in terms of the substantive law involved. This chapter has already encountered this idea in Mosley v. General Motors, supra page 904. *Mosley* discussed commonality as a requirement for joining individual plaintiffs under Rule 20. The requirement of cohesiveness recurs in class actions. For example, a "class" consisting of all persons who have claims against the United States would not have much in common: One person would be seeking an income tax refund, another compensation for an accident involving a postal truck, and a third might be seeking Social Security benefits. A much-litigated question is whether the members of the class have *enough* in common to justify class certification. Since virtually all classes proposed will have some characteristics in common and some unshared characteristics, there is much room for argument.

Typicality is the requirement that class representatives stand, in significant respects, in the same shoes as the average class member. For example, in a case alleging mismanagement of a pension plan, if most members of the class have lost a few hundred dollars, it would raise a typicality problem if the class representative alleged losses of tens of thousands. The premise underlying the typicality requirement is that the class representative will be controlling the litigation, making the decisions that a client would be making in a one-client suit. In order to protect the interests of the absent class members, one would want the representative client to have the same incentives and motivations as the average class member. In practice, the class representatives have proved far less significant than the lawyers, and judges have consequently been willing to bend the requirements of typicality if they are assured that the last requirement — adequacy of representation — is fulfilled.

Courts have measured adequacy in several ways. The class representative herself must have some stake in the litigation. The representative's relation to the lawyer should be straightforward. For example, the class representative should not be an employee or a relative of the lawyer — relationships that would conflict with the representative's decisions about the litigation. The lawyer should have no conflicts that would cloud the representation. For example, some class representatives have been found inadequate because their real reason for pursuing the class action was to gain additional leverage for an individual client's case. Finally, the lawyer has to be sufficiently skillful and equipped with sufficient support and resources to handle the case. To use an extreme example, it is unlikely that a young laywer with the ink still drying on her bar certificate would be found to be an adequate representative in a complex class action. Conversely, decisions certifying adequacy typically recite the lawyer's experience with previous similar cases. Decisions also note the lawyer's and firm's financial ability to finance protracted litigation.

Having surmounted the hurdles of Rule 23(a), the lawyer seeking class certification still has to show that the litigation fits within one of the three categories of Rule 23(b). One might ask why: If the case fits the requirements of Rule 23(a), should it not be a class action? The drafters of the Rule were understandably unsure about the potential of the class action — for good or for harm. They had two fairly clear cases in mind that they thought should usually be treated as class actions — the situations described in Rule 23(b)(1) and 23(b)(2) — and a residual category — the (b)(3) cases — where they wanted courts to proceed cautiously.

The first situation — the 23(b)(1) class — is essentially a mass-production version of Rule 19. For example, suppose a city proposes to issue bonds to build a new civic auditorium. One group of citizens sues to block the issuance of the bonds; another group sues the city to insist that it go forward with the bonds and the project. If those suits proceed separately, the city might find itself the subject of incompatible judicial rulings: Issue the bonds; do not issue the bonds. By grouping the challengers and the supporters into classes, the court prevents a situation in which "varying adjudications with respect to individual members of the class" (the taxpayers) "would establish incompatible standards of conduct for the party opposing the class" (the city). Or, to take another example, suppose that a number of claimants all seek to collect on claims that exceed insurance coverage. Under such circumstances Rule 23(b)(1) provides a way to assure that similarly situated parties are treated alike.

Rule 23(b)(2) provides for class actions where the party opposing the class has acted or refused to act "on grounds generally applicable to the class." The advisory committee notes to the Rule make clear that the drafters had in mind civil rights claims, where the plaintiff class would be alleging that defendants were acting on a racially motivated basis. Note that the availability of Rule 23(b)(2) is limited to cases in which the plaintiffs are seeking injunctive or declaratory relief. Again, such a description fits the standard civil rights case, where the typical relief sought is an injunction requiring some action — voter registration, school integration, changes in employment practices — by a defendant. An often litigated question is how much monetary relief a 23(b)(2) class can seek before the action ceases to be primarily injunctive and therefore ineligible for 23(b)(2) treatment.

The final category of class actions — those brought under Rule 23(b)(3) — has proved the most controversial. It comprises all class actions not captured in 23(b)(1) and 23(b)(2). In particular it includes all claims in which the plaintiffs are seeking primarily money damages. In practice, those actions can be subdivided into two groups. One group consists of what one might call "small claims" lawsuits: actions in which many persons allege small amounts of damage. Examples include such diverse lawsuits as one in which all purchasers of blue jeans in California were alleged to have been overcharged by a dollar or two and a claim in which 5 million purchasers and sellers of small lots of stock were alleged to have been overcharged by an average of $70. Notice that such claims are probably not worth any individual plaintiff's time or money to bring and that only the class action device makes them viable. Notice too that in such actions, the defendant is, as a practical matter, immune from liability unless a class is certified.

At the other end of the scale of Rule 23(b)(3) actions lies what is often called the "mass tort" — an airplane crash, a hotel fire, the exposure of hundreds of thousands of workers to asbestos fibers. The drafters of Rule 23 suggested in the Advisory Committee notes that such cases would not usually be appropriate for class treatment, but in the past decade courts have increasingly — and controversially — certified class actions in mass torts. Because of the amount of potential damages, each of the individual plaintiffs will have a viable lawsuit. Such lawsuits in the aggregate may, however, drag on for many years and, in extreme cases, threaten to bankrupt the defendants and overwhelm the courts. In these suits the incentives for a class action change. To plaintiffs they continue to offer the increased bargaining power that comes from aggregation and the prospect of a single overwhelming damage judgment. In contrast to the small claims cases, they also offer some advantages to defendants — consolidation (of suits that would have been brought even without the class action), efficiency, and the possibility of a global settlement.

Placing a class action in one of the Rule 23 categories is more than a matter of analytical neatness. Whole cases may stand or fall as a result of the classification. This unexpected consequence flows from two sources. First, Rule 23(b)(3) requires the certifying judge to engage in a complicated weighing of advantages and disadvantages — as a result of which he may rule against certification. Second, Rule 23(c)(2) requires individual notice to class members in all 23(b)(3) cases but not in the other two categories. Because the Supreme Court has held that the representative plaintiff must initially pay for such notice, inability to bear these costs may end the suit. Eisen v. Carlisle & Jacquelin, 417 U.S. 156 (1974).

The notes that follow ask you to consolidate this elementary discussion of Rule 23.

NOTES AND PROBLEMS

1. The regents of State University announce a tuition increase that applies only to out-of-state students. Two thousand such students stand to have their tuition increased. The president of the Student Association, an in-state student, announces that she is filing suit, on behalf of the affected students, to enjoin the regents from implementing the increase.

a. With which of the requirements of Rule 23(a) will the prospective class action have most difficulty?

b. What additional information will the court likely require in order to decide whether the suit meets the criteria of 23(a)?

c. Suppose that after some rearrangement, the court rules that the class meets the requirements of Rule 23(a); into what category of Rule 23(b) would it fall?

2. Assume that the tuition increase described in the preceding note has gone into effect and has been paid by the out-of-state students. One enterprising such student discovers that the regents adopted the increase at a closed meeting — in violation of state law — and that it is therefore unlawful. He proposes to file suit as representative of a class of all out-of-state students.

a. Student (as class representative) proposes to seek refunds in the form of reduced tuition in the following school year. Do you see why such a plan for relief may cause the court to find Student an inadequate representative (and perhaps an atypical one) for at least some members of the class?

b. Suppose Student proposes to remedy the adequacy of representation problems exposed in 2a by seeking cash refunds to all students, present and former, who paid the allegedly unlawful higher fees. What will this change in remedy do to the classification of the lawsuit under Rule 23(b)? What consequences will that change in classification have? (See Rule 23(c)(2).)

c. Suppose Student finally decides to seek certification of a Rule 23(b)(3) class seeking cash refunds to all students who paid the higher fees. The costs of notifying the class are estimated to be in the neighborhood of $10,000. How might this fact cause a court that was otherwise satisfied that Student met the criteria of Rule 23(a)(4) to reconsider its decision and to decertify the class?

3. With these relatively elementary issues under your belt, consider courts struggling with certification in more complex situations.

Communities for Equity v. Michigan High School Athletic Assn.

1999 U.S. Dist. LEXIS 5780 (W.D. Mich. 1999)

ENSLEN, C.J.

This matter is before the Court on the Plaintiffs' Motion for Class Certification. For the reasons which follow, the motion will be granted.

Plaintiffs bring this suit against the Michigan High School Athletic Association and its Representative Council, alleging that they have been excluded from opportunities to participate in interscholastic athletic programs and have received unequal treatment and benefits in these programs. They contend that this putative exclusion and unequal treatment constitute gender discrimination, in violation of (1) Title IX of the Education Amendments of 1972; (2) the Equal Protection Clause of the Fourteenth Amendment; and (3) Mich. Comp. Laws §§37.2302 and 37.2402. The alleged discrimination is made manifest, according to Plaintiffs, in MHSAA's: (1) refusing to sanction girls' ice hockey and water polo; (2) requiring that the Plaintiff Class play its sports in non-traditional seasons; (3) operating shorter athletic seasons for some girls' sports than for boys' sports; (4) scheduling the competitions of the Plaintiff Class on inferior dates; (5) providing, assigning, and operating inferior athletic facilities to the Plaintiff Class in which to play MHSAA-sanctioned games; (6) requiring that the Plaintiff Class play some sports under rules and/or conditions different from those in the NCAA or other governing organizations, unlike boys; and (7) allocating more resources for the support and promotion of male interscholastic athletic programs than for female programs.

Plaintiffs' Motion for Class Certification asks the Court to define the proposed class as follows: all present and future female students enrolled in MHSAA member schools who participate in interscholastic athletics or who are deterred from participating in interscholastic athletics because of Defendants' discriminatory conduct and who are adversely affected by that conduct.

Standard for Class Certification

According to the United States Supreme Court, this Court must conduct a "rigorous analysis" into whether the prerequisites of Federal Rule of Civil Procedure 23 are met before certifying a class action. General Tel. Co. v. Falcon, 457 U.S. 147, 161 (1982). . . . The "rigorous analysis requirement" means that a class is not maintainable merely because the complaint parrots the legal requirements of Rule 23. Although a hearing prior to the class determination is not always required, "it may be necessary for the court to probe behind the pleadings before coming to rest on the certification question." *Falcon* [at 160.] In this case, the extensive briefing filed by the parties, the Court's past review of motions, and the documentary evidence and affidavits filed make the hearing of evidence unnecessary because the Court is able to probe behind the pleadings without additional evidence or argument.[1] . . .

Class Certification

Rule 23(a)(1) — Numerosity/Impracticability of Joinder. . . .

In this case, the numbers themselves justify a conclusion of numerosity and impracticability of joinder. Under Plaintiffs' theory of liability, thousands of female high school athletes and would-be athletes are subjected to Defendants' alleged discriminatory practices. . . . The Court concludes that the numerosity requirement is satisfied by the proposed class. . . .

---

1. Defendants raise a number of liability arguments in their briefing. While these may carry the day ultimately, that day has not yet arrived. The certification determination is not concerned with a plaintiff's success on the merits. See Eisen v. Carlisle & Jacquelin, 417 U.S. 156 (1974) (stating that certification question concerns Rule 23 factors and not an assessment of the merits).

Rule 23(a)(2) — Commonality

Next, the Rule requires commonality — that there are questions of law and fact common to class members. Not every common question suffices. What is necessary for certification are common issues the resolution of which will advance the litigation. In cases involving the question of whether a defendant has acted through an illegal policy or procedure, commonality is readily shown because the common question becomes whether the defendant in fact acted through the illegal policy or procedure. Where the nature of the legal claims are such that individuals would have to submit separate proofs to establish liability, class actions are disapproved due to lack of commonality. See, e.g., *Sprague* [v. General Motors Corp.], 133 F.3d at 398 (class action disapproved as to estoppel which would require individual proof of reliance). However, the presence of individual questions need not defeat certification. See In re Prudential Ins. Co. of America Sales Lit., 148 F.3d 283, 310 (3rd Cir. 1998). This should be obvious, since Rule 23 requires common questions, not the absence of individual ones. Once it is determined that there are common questions of law and fact as to a legal claim, differences in damages sustained by class members will usually not defeat certification.

Here, the common questions of fact and law are obvious enough. The overarching question is, did MHSAA and its Representative Council act in a manner inconsistent with Title IX, the Equal Protection Clause of the Fourteenth Amendment; and/or Mich. Comp. Laws §§37.2302 and 37.2402? The answer turns on the resolution of factual questions regarding Defendants' decisionmaking process and outcomes, and determination of the legal consequences of those facts.

Rule 23(a)(3) — Typicality. . . .

The typicality requirement is the one demanding the closest attention in this matter. The Court must determine whether, on the facts of this case, the Supreme Court's *Falcon* decision precludes a finding of typicality, given the breadth of Plaintiffs' claims. In *Falcon*, a Mexican-American employee who alleged that he had been denied a promotion because of race discrimination brought a class action against his employer. The class included all Mexican-American employees and Mexican-American applicants for employment who had not been hired. The class was certified pursuant to a Fifth Circuit rule which permitted "across-the-board" attacks on all racially discriminatory employment practices. The Fifth Circuit had held that it was permissible for " 'an employee complaining of one employment practice to represent another complaining of another practice, if the plaintiff and the members of the class suffer from essentially the same injury. In this case, all of the claims are based on discrimination because of national origin.'" The Supreme Court reversed, holding that:

> Respondent's complaint provided an insufficient basis for concluding that the adjudication of his claim of discrimination in promotion would require the decision of any common question concerning the failure of petitioner to hire more Mexican-Americans. Without any specific presentation identifying the questions of law or fact that were common to the claims of respondent and of the members of the class he sought to represent, it was error for the District Court to presume that respondent's claim was typical of other claims against petitioner by Mexican-American employees and applicants. If one allegation of specific discriminatory treatment were sufficient to support an across-the-board attack, every Title VII case would be a potential company wide class action.

At first blush, the Supreme Court's criticism of the class certification challenged in *Falcon* appears applicable in a case such as this. After all, a number of different harms are alleged here, which have not been suffered uniformly among the proposed class representatives. There are two reasons, however, that *Falcon* does not bar the certification of this class.

First, the various discrete harms alleged by Plaintiffs are all allegedly suffered by members of Communities for Equity, a proposed class representative. "Numerous decisions have recognized the ability of associations, both incorporated and unincorporated, to act as class representatives under Rule 23. . . ." Upper Valley Assoc. For Handicapped Citizens v. Mills, 168 F.R.D. 167, 171 (D. Vt. 1996). . . .

More importantly, however, the mere fact of some distinction between the particular claims of named Plaintiffs and the diverse manifestations of discrimination alleged here is insufficient to extinguish typicality. The *Falcon* Court provided for the possibility of broad-based attacks on discrimination if there were proof of an underlying policy of discrimination. Here, the variety of alleged manifestations of discrimination, such as inequitable facilities, scheduling, sanctioning, and rules, present a sufficient case of an underlying policy or practice of discrimination.[2] The Court determines that differences between sanctioning water polo and scheduling basketball are less significant in this matter than the typicality of claims that female high school athletes are discriminated against in violation of the various laws invoked by Plaintiffs. . . .

---

2. If it should be shown by the conclusion of the litigation that such a policy were absent, there might be cause to remove the individual Plaintiffs as representatives for lack of typicality. CFE, however, might remain a viable representative.

Rule 23(a)(4) — Adequacy of Representation

Rule 23(a) requires that the class members and their counsel be prepared to provide fair and adequate representation to the class. In Senter v. General Motors Corp., 532 F.2d 511, 525 (6th Cir. 1976), the Sixth Circuit Court of Appeals articulated two criteria for determining adequacy of representation: "1) the representative must have common interests with unnamed members of the class, and 2) it must appear that the representatives will vigorously prosecute the interests of the class through qualified counsel." . . . Two issues in this matter raise the potentiality for conflict.

First, it is quite possible that members of the class have no desire to pursue this action, and are not unhappy with the status quo. However, the proposed class purports to include only those who are "adversely affected." . . . As well, even without the limiting language, this sort of putative conflict generally fails to bar class certification. See Newberg at §3.30 ("the class member who wishes to remain a victim of unlawful conduct does not have a legally cognizable conflict with the class representative"). . . .

Moreover, as suggested by Plaintiffs, the interests of those class members who do not consider themselves adversely affected will be adequately represented by Defendants." As long as both those seeking to uphold and those desiring to strike the particular regulations are adequately represented, the suit may proceed as a class action." 7A Charles Alan Wright, Arthur R. Miller, & Mary Kay Kane, Federal Practice and Procedure §1768 (2nd ed. 1986).

A second type of potential conflict may be that achieving certain types of relief in this case could come at the expense of other types. For instance, MHSAA may experience legally justifiable financial constraints which make it impossible for it to sanction tournaments in both ice hockey and water polo. Should a conflict arise from the limited availability of resources, however, it may be resolved by the creation of subclasses. In this case, the Court believes that the appropriate course is to defer consideration of any subclasses until the relief stage, if any, of this litigation. . . . To the extent that the underlying issue in this case is one of unequal treatment and discrimination, the matter of whether to sanction a particular sport appears to be one relating to relief, rather than liability.

Adequacy of representation is also measured by the quality of class counsel. There is no argument here that counsel for Plaintiffs are unqualified. They are experienced in both Title IX litigation, and litigation generally. The Court determines that the requirements of Rule 23(a)(4) are satisfied.

Rule 23(b)(2) — Injunctive or Declaratory Relief. . . .

Defendants argue that a class is unnecessary, because relief granted to named Plaintiffs would inure to the benefit of the class. The Sixth Circuit has disclaimed any necessity requirement for Rule 23(b)(2) certification. Even if such a requirement existed, mootness concerns would suggest the necessity of certification.

To the extent that Defendants discriminate against female high school athletes through unequal treatment, Defendants act or refuse to act on grounds generally applicable to the class. Injunctive relief is, of course, an appropriate remedy for discriminatory treatment. Rule 23(b)(2) certification is therefore appropriate. . . .

Therefore, it is the conclusion of this Court that the Motion for Class Certification shall be granted. An order shall issue consistent with this Opinion.

Order

In accordance with the Court's Opinion of this date;

IT IS HEREBY ORDERED that the Plaintiffs' Motion for Class Certification is GRANTED and that the Court certifies this matter as a class action pursuant to Federal Rule of Civil Procedure 23(b)(2). The class action is certified as to the following class: all present and future female students enrolled in MHSAA member schools who participate in interscholastic athletics or who are deterred from participating in interscholastic athletics because of Defendants' discriminatory conduct and who are adversely affected by that conduct.

NOTES AND PROBLEMS

1. Why a class action? Consider the situation before the lawsuit started. The athletes and parents disadvantaged by the association's decisions want to challenge their legality; the association, imagining turmoil if existing arrangements have to be altered, wants to maintain them.

a. A single student or a small group could sue, seeking an injunction. If the court agreed with their claims, the injunction would, as a practical matter, forbid the association and its member schools from conducting women's athletics in the manner the plaintiffs had successfully challenged. If that is so, why should the plaintiffs bother jumping through the class action hoops? Why not just plunge into the merits?

b. Consider the same problem from the defendants' standpoint. It is obvious that there is a group of very unhappy students and parents who will mount a legal challenge to existing arrangements. If that's a given, why not welcome the class action as a way of getting the dispute over with, once and for all, in a way that will bind all concerned?

c. Part of the answer on the plaintiffs' side has to do with mootness. Litigation can drag on, and students graduate or leave sports programs. The plaintiffs don't want to be on the verge of a decision only to find that a student's departure for college moots the whole issue. In many similar circumstances plaintiff classes find themselves involved with institutional defendants on a temporary basis; a class action, by defining the group as those currently involved, prevents mootness.

d. But another part of the answer probably lies outside the courtroom. If you were the defendant, would you rather be dealing with an adversary who, with judicial approval, could describe herself as representing all the women high school athletes in Michigan? — Or would you rather be dealing with a dozen plaintiffs whom you could, perhaps with some accuracy, describe as malcontents?

2. The opinion described the question of typicality as the most difficult on these facts.

a. Another district court came to a different certification decision on similar facts, citing concerns about adequacy of representation:

> In this case, there is unrebutted evidence of a conflict of interests between the named plaintiffs and other members of the class which precludes certification under Rule 23. The results of the survey related to the court by defendant's expert indicate that plaintiffs do not adequately represent the interests of all the members of their class and that plaintiffs' claims are not typical of their class. A majority of the female public school athletes surveyed expressed a desire to preserve the status quo, meaning that most would not favor the injunctive relief sought by plaintiffs. There is a clear division in the class between those girls whose schools have already been subject to reclassification and those girls whose schools could, potentially, at some future time, be subject to reclassification. Those who have never experienced reclassification prefer not to have the entire system changed to suit the student athletes who have had to stop playing one or more of their preferred sports due to reclassification. Logically, if statewide realignment occurred, many more girls would be faced with the necessity of changing which sports they play. . . .
>
> This conflict prevents plaintiffs from satisfying the typicality requirement as well as the adequacy of representation requirement. Plaintiffs have presented nothing to dispel the defendant's suggestion that there is a schism between girls who may benefit from reclassification and those who are injured by reclassification. A girl who could not previously play two sports because they occurred in the same season may be able to play those two

sports when a school is reclassified and the seasons for some sports change. Such girls would not bring claims like the ones brought here by plaintiffs. Thus it cannot be said that as goes the claim of these plaintiffs, so go the claims of all others in the class.

Alston v. Virginia High School League, Inc., 184 F.R.D. 574, 579 (W.D. Va. 1999). Is this point well taken? Suppose that the Virginia arrangements for women high school athletes violate federal law: does it matter that a number of athletes are satisfied with those arrangements?

b. What factual difference arguably makes *Alston* distinguishable from *Communities for Equity*?

c. The *Communities for Equity* court had three different solutions to the possibility that some women athletes might not share the goals of the class representatives. Explain what they were.

d. Notice that such intraclass conflicts will be particularly severe in 23(b)(1) and (b)(2) cases because those classes lack the possibility of opting out, which is offered by Rule 23(c)(2) for (b)(3) classes. They are necessarily "trapped" in the class.

3. Some conflicts are like those asserted in the *Alston* opinion: Do all the class members want to challenge the legality of the practice in question?

a. Other class conflicts have a more objective quality. In Kohl v. Association of Trial Lawyers, 183 F.R.D. 475 (D. Md. 1998), a former employee challenged the way in which a pension plan made certain distributions; she argued they should include a cost-of-living increase. Her original complaint sought to represent "all . . . who received or who will be eligible to receive in the future" such distributions. That definition thus included present as well as former employees. Defendant objected on grounds of inadequate representation:

> Defendants argue that to the extent that Plaintiff is successful in her suit and obtains some monetary relief, she would be depriving the Plan of a portion of its "finite pool of resources." According to Defendants, if Plaintiff is successful in this lawsuit, and damages are granted, "she will take money [from ATLA employees] that could be used for pay raises and enhanced benefits away from current employees." Thus, Defendants argue that a conflict of interest would exist between Plaintiff and those members of the class that are still employed. . . .
>
> This Court . . . has no real evidence before it that Plaintiff's interests may be antagonistic to the interests of current ATLA employees/future retirees. However, the Court finds no problem with Plaintiff representing the interests of current retirees, like herself.

Id. at 485.

b. The *Kohl* decision just quoted dealt with a potential conflict by narrowing the class. Another technique is to create subclasses, a technique that can be used to deal both with conflicts and with commonality and typicality problems. Of course, if the subclasses become numerous, the whole action threatens to become unmanageable.

c. Notice an odd feature of all such cases. It is the defendant who raises arguments that ostensibly seek to insure that plaintiffs have the best possible representation. In fact, defendants are seeking to avoid class certification and thus to eliminate the lawsuit entirely.

4. The *Communities for Equity* opinion is a typical class action certification decision. The requirement for "rigorous analysis" means that each class certification will travel over the categories of Rule 23(a) and then locate the case in one of the three 23(b) categories. As with this case, sometimes the category requires only cursory discussion, sometimes more.

a. A frequently litigated question is whether the existence of a damage claim alongside a prayer for injunctive relief moves the case from the b(2) to the (b)(3) category:

> An action seeking monetary damages cannot fall under (b)(2) unless the final injunctive relief or corresponding declaratory relief is the primary relief sought. . . . The plaintiffs are seeking all the remedies provided by the statute. Consequently, the difficult issue in this case is whether the monetary relief is incidental to the plaintiffs' request for final injunctive or declaratory relief.

Israel v. Avis Rent-A-Car Systems, Inc., 185 F.R.D. 372, 382 (S.D. Fla. 1999). Why do the litigants care?

> An action for money damages and injunctive relief can be certified under Rule(b)(3). To be certified under Rule 23(b)(3), however, the class must meet two prerequisites, neither of which is applicable under (b)(2): (1) the questions of law or fact common to the members of the class must predominate over any questions affecting only individual members; and (2) the class action must be superior to other available methods for the fair and efficient adjudication of the controversy. Actions brought under (b)(3) are also subject to the provisions in Rule 23(c)(2) requiring that notice be given to all members who can be identified through reasonable effort and each member has the option to be excluded from the class.

Id. at 384.

b. Another recurrent question in class actions is a choice of law problem that some practitioners refer to as the "fifty states" issue. In a nationwide class there can be persons who stand in similar factual circumstances but to whom different state laws apply. For example, suppose a proposed class consisting of cigarette smokers who claim that tobacco is a "defective" or unreasonably dangerous product. In considering whether the claims of such persons have sufficient commonality, a court might conclude that the product liability regimes of the states are sufficiently diverse as to deprive the proposed class of cohesiveness. Costano v. American Tobacco Co., 84 F.3d 734 (5th Cir. 1996) (class certification reversed for failure to consider how variations in state law affect predominance and superiority). A frequent counter to such arguments is the assertion either that state laws are converging or that a class action can resolve a number of common issues before the divergences are encountered.

5. As you will have gathered, the decision to certify (or to refuse to certify) a proposed class action is often critical for the outcome of the litigation. Certification gives the class representative immense bargaining power, refusal to certify means that the defendant is facing only a single plaintiff or a handful of plaintiffs, with much less at stake.

a. Until 1998 a district court's decision on certification was not appealable. If it certified the class, there was no final judgment. If it refused to certify the class, the action, though practically dead, still continued, in theory, as the claim of the representative plaintiff. As a consequence, there is less appellate law than one might think on the question of appropriately certifiable classes.

b. Rule 23(f) changes that situation. Read the Rule to see how. But the amendment also poses an interesting question: When should an appellate court take such appeals?

6. As you can see, even an "ordinary" class action certification has some knotty issues. Consider one made more complicated by procedural maneuvering.

Heaven v. Trust Company Bank

18 F.3d 735 (11th Cir. 1997)

BURNS, J.:

Background

Plaintiff . . . Ranae Heaven . . . leased a Ford Taurus from Sun Trust, signing a preprinted lease form provided by Sun Trust. . . . Later, she brought this action alleging that Sun Trust failed to comply with the strict disclosure requirements of the C[Consumer] L[easing] A[ct], 15 U.S.C. §§1667-67e] and Regulation M [implementing the Act]. Heaven sued for the statutory penalty and attorney fees but alleged no actual damages. She sought to certify a class pursuant to Fed. R. Civ. P. 23(a) and (b)(3).[3]

Sun Trust counterclaimed on the alternative grounds that individual class members had (a) defaulted on the terms of their lease agreements, and/or (b) made false statements in their lease applications. The district court denied certification of the class. . . .

Standard of Review

The district court's decision whether to certify a class may only be overturned if it constitutes an abuse of discretion. . . .

Discussion. . . .

The district court ruled that Heaven had established the four prerequisites of Rule 23(a). We see no need to revisit that aspect of the court's ruling. The district court concluded Heaven had not established that her action met the requirements of subdivision (b)(3). . . .

The district court recognized that the question of appropriateness of class certification in this case was very close. We agree with that assessment. The court engaged in a lengthy and thoughtful analysis and determined that several factors taken together tipped the balance against certification.

First, the court determined that Sun Trust's counterclaims were compulsory under Fed. R. Civ. P. 13(a). We agree that this conclusion is compelled by the case law of this circuit. See Plant v. Blazer Financial Services, Inc., [supra page 895] (Holding that debt counterclaims are compulsory in Truth In Lending Act (TILA) cases).

Heaven does not dispute that debt counterclaims are compulsory in TILA and CLA cases as a general matter. However, she contends that the presence of counterclaims cannot be a basis for denying class certification. Heaven apparently asserts that Roper v. Consurve, Inc., 578 F.2d 1106 (5th Cir. 1978), aff'd, 445 U.S. 326, (1980) stands for the proposition that Fed. R. Civ. P. 13(a) has no application at all in class certification analysis. We do not believe that *Roper* states such a universal rule. . . .

---

3. Heaven defined the class she sought to represent as:

all persons who satisfy the following criteria: (a) They signed a lease [with Sun Trust] prepared using the same printed form [that Heaven used]; (b) The total payments on the lease were less than $ 25,000; (c) The lease was for more than four months; (d) The lease is marked as a consumer purpose lease; and (e) The leases were outstanding within one year prior to the filing of this action.

The court below considered the nature of SunTrust's counterclaims and determined that individual lessee counterclaim defendants would be compelled to come forward with individual defenses. This would require the court to engage in multiple separate factual determinations, a proper factor for consideration under Rule 23(b)(3)(D). The court also determined that the interests of some individual class members in controlling their own case would be compromised. Their exposure as counterclaim defendants could well exceed the amount they might recover for statutory penalties as class members. The statutory claims asserted by the class would be against the interests of these individual class members. This is a proper factor for consideration under Rule 23(b)(3)(A). . . .

If this panel had faced the class certification issue in the first instance, we may well have found it appropriate to certify the class or to establish subclasses. However, where the district court has given due consideration to all the relevant factors within the context of a rigorous analysis and has not relied on impermissible factors, we are unable to find an abuse of discretion. If, after such an evaluation, the district court is convinced that a class action is not superior to other available methods for the fair and efficient adjudication of the controversy, we cannot second guess that conclusion under the applicable standard of review.[7] . . .

Affirmed.

NOTES AND PROBLEMS

1. Explain why the district court declined to certify the class. On what part of Rule 23 did the proposed action founder? Why?

2. There were presumably hundreds of leases in question here, and evidently some substantial number of consumers had not paid in accordance with their lease terms. As to these, SunTrust counterclaimed.

    a. If the leases were unpaid, why had SunTrust not already brought suit?

    b. Was it improper to do so after the class action was filed?

3. Citing Plant v. Blazer Financial Services, supra page 895, *Heaven* takes it as established that the district court has jurisdiction over the compulsory counterclaim, thus making class certification questionable

---

7. We do not intend to suggest that compulsory counterclaims should preclude the maintenance of class actions in cases under the CLA as a general rule. We rule only that it is a proper exercise of discretion for the district court to evaluate the nature of the counterclaims and the difficulties they present and to consider the usefulness of breaking the proposed class into subclasses to avoid those difficulties.

because of the manageability problems. In a case presenting very similar issues, a court declined to exercise supplemental jurisdiction precisely *because* its exercise would make the class unmanageable:

> The parties did not raise and the court did not address, however, whether the court should decline to exercise jurisdiction pursuant to 28 U.S.C. §1367(c). This court raises the issue sua sponte, and for the reasons set· forth below, declines to exercise supplemental jurisdiction over ECS's counterclaims. See 28 U.S.C. §1367(c)(4). Pursuant to section 1367(c)(4): "The district courts may decline to exercise supplemental jurisdiction over a claim under subsection (a) if . . . (4) in exceptional circumstances, there are other compelling reasons for declining jurisdiction."
>
> The court finds that there are compelling reasons for public policy embodied in the [federal disclosure legislation] for declining jurisdiction in this case.
>
> To allow a debt collector defendant to seek to collect the debt in the federal action to enforce the [disclosure statute] might well have a chilling effect on persons who otherwise might and should bring suits such as this. . . . Given the remedial nature of the [statute] and the broad public policy it serves, federal courts should be loath to become immersed in the debt collection suits [brought by] the target of the very legislation under which the . . . plaintiff states a cause of action.

Ballard v. Equifax Check Servs., 1999 U.S. Dist. LEXIS 4071 (E.D. Cal. 1999).

4. The decision to certify or not to certify a proposed class action can have dramatic consequences for both parties.

a. In one category of case — the "small claims" class — that decision is usually dispositive. In such cases, typically (b)(3) actions, a large number of persons seek damages for claims that are individually small. If the individual claims carry no attorneys' fee provision, the plaintiffs will rarely find it economically worthwhile to pursue their claims individually. In such cases a refusal to certify will end not just the class but any individual actions. Conversely, the decision to certify may face the defendant with a potentially huge liability claim, one it feels compelled to settle almost without regard to the merits.

b. Certifying a class has another important consequence. As you will see in the next section, an adequately represented class is bound by a judgment or settlement. Use the facts of *Communities for Equity*, supra page 968, to see this proposition at work. The trial judge certified the case over defendants' objections. The defendants' unhappiness would change, however, if the trial court proceeded, as footnote 1 hinted it might, to find that the defendants' actions were entirely lawful. At that point — if we assume the plaintiffs were adequately represented — no present or future woman high school athlete could challenge Michigan's arrangements on grounds of gender inequity. Do you see why this is so?

5. Because of the important consequences of class certification, Rule 23(c)(1) requires that the court shall determine whether to certify case as a class action "as soon as practicable after the commencement of the action." Because the certification is difficult, however, and because it so sharply changes the dynamics of the litigation, sometimes parties and judges drag their feet, leaving the class uncertified even after a decision on the merits.

a. In Pabst Brewing Co. v. Corrao, 161 F.3d 434 (7th Cir. 1988) plaintiff managed to snatch defeat from the jaws of victory by such a delay. Pabst, in financial difficulty, told its retirees that it would discontinue its long practice of paying their health insurance. To establish the legality of this new policy, Pabst sought a declaratory judgment and took the unusual step of naming a defendant class consisting of all retired workers. Rule 23 speaks of defendant classes, but difficulties of assuring adequate representation make them rare. The named defendants' representative decided to fight fire with fire and brought a counterclaim for health benefits on behalf of himself and of all similarly situated retirees. For reasons that are unclear, the district court failed to act on the class certification but proceeded to the merits, awarding Pabst a victory. Some of that victory evaporated on appeal, however, as the Seventh Circuit noted, sua sponte, that the absence of class certification required the court to treat the case as that of the individual class representative; by treating the suit as that of an individual, the court left open the claims of other retirees. Unfortunately for those retirees, the court went on to rule on the merits of the case for that individual, affirming the district court and thus establishing not claim preclusion but a strong precedent against any member of the putative class who would seek to challenge the decision.

b. What's the difference between being bound by precedent and being bound by claim preclusion? As a formal matter, the distinction is that one can at least try to convince the court that there are arguments it overlooked in its former decision or that the precedent itself is wrong and should be overruled. In claim preclusion the only question that matters is whether this is the same claim between the same parties.

3.   The Class Action and the Constitution

Above the controversy surrounding the class action stand a pair of constitutional arguments that both enable and limit the procedure. Both flow from the Due Process Clause. One argument entails whether a party can be bound by litigation to which he is not a party. The other asks whether due process requires certain procedures within the class action in order for it to be a valid adjudication of the absentees' rights.

a.   Representative Adequacy

Fundamental to the class action is the idea that a suit, conducted by a representative on behalf of a number of persons who are not formal parties, may nevertheless bind the entire represented class. In that respect it represents a departure from the ordinary proposition that one may be bound only by litigation to which one is a party. One might cite any number of cases for this proposition, including *Martin v. Wilks*, supra page 948. The next case works out the conditions under which such a representative may bind those who are not parties. It limits the class action, but at the same time it gives the class action, thus limited, great potential power.

Hansberry v. Lee
311 U.S. 32 (1940)

Mr. Justice STONE delivered the opinion of the Court.

The question is whether the Supreme Court of Illinois, by its adjudication that petitioners in this case are bound to a judgment rendered in an earlier litigation to which they were not parties, has deprived them of the due process of law guaranteed by the Fourteenth Amendment. . . .

[The case was decided before Shelley v. Kraemer, 334 U.S. 1 (1948), holding racially restrictive covenants unenforceable. The Hansberrys, a black family, bought a house in an area of Chicago allegedly covered by a racially restrictive covenant. The covenant said it did not take effect unless signed by owners of 95 percent of the frontage. In fact, the signers represented only 54 percent. Lee brought an action to enjoin breach of the covenant, naming as defendants both the Hansberrys, who had purchased a home allegedly in violation of the covenant, and the people from whom the Hansberrys had bought the property. One of the Hansberrys' defenses was that the covenant was unenforceable because not enough owners had signed it. Plaintiff countered by referring to Burke v. Kleiman, an earlier suit to enforce the same covenant. In *Burke* a property owner "in behalf of herself and other property owners in like situation" sued four named individuals allegedly in violation of the covenant. *Burke* was litigated in the Illinois courts, where the parties had *stipulated* (falsely) that the requisite 95 percent had signed, and the earlier court had adopted that stipulation in its findings. *Burke* upheld the covenant. The Supreme Court of Illinois in the present case determined that *Burke* had been a class action, that the Hansberrys and their vendors were members of the class of *plaintiffs* in *Burke,* and that they were therefore bound by the findings in the previous action even though those findings were factually erroneous.]

To the defense that the agreement had never become effective because owners of 95 percent of the frontage had not signed it, respondents pleaded that that issue was res judicata by the decree in an earlier suit. To this petitioners pleaded, by way of rejoinder, that they were not parties to that suit or bound by its decree, and that denial of their right to litigate, in the present suit, the issue of performance of the condition precedent to the validity of the agreement would be a denial of due process of law guaranteed by the Fourteenth Amendment. It does not appear, nor is it contended that any of petitioners is the successor in interest to or in privity with any of the parties in the earlier suit.

The [state] . . . court, after a trial on the merits, found that owners of only about 54 per cent of the frontage had signed the agreement, and that the only support of the judgment in the *Burke* case was a false and fraudulent stipulation of the parties that owners of 95 per cent had signed. But it ruled that the issue of performance of the condition precedent to the validity of the agreement was res judicata as alleged and entered a decree for respondents. . . .

From this the Supreme Court of Illinois concluded in the present case that Burke v. Kleiman was a "class" or "representative" suit, and that in such a suit, "where the remedy is pursued by a plaintiff who has the right to represent the class to which he belongs, other members of the class are bound by the results in the case unless it is reversed or set aside on direct proceedings"; that petitioners in the present suit were members of the class represented by the plaintiffs in the earlier suit and consequently were bound by its decree. . . .

State courts are free to attach such descriptive labels to litigations before them as they may choose and to attribute to them such consequences as they think appropriate under state constitutions and laws, subject only to the requirements of the Constitution of the United States. But when the judgment of a state court, ascribing to the judgment of another court the binding force and effect of res judicata, is challenged for want of due process it becomes the duty of this Court to examine the course of procedure in both litigations to ascertain whether the litigant whose rights have thus been adjudicated has been afforded such notice and opportunity to be heard as are requisite to the due process which the Constitution prescribes.

It is a principle of general application in Anglo-American jurisprudence that one is not bound by a judgment in personam in a litigation in which he is not designated as a party or to which he has not been made a party by service of process. Pennoyer v. Neff. A judgment rendered in such circumstances is not entitled to the full faith and credit which the Constitution and statutes of the United States prescribe, Pennoyer v. Neff; and judicial action enforcing it against the person or property of the absent party is not that due process which the Fifth and Fourteenth Amendments require.

To these general rules there is a recognized exception that, to an extent not precisely defined by judicial opinion, the judgment in a "class" or "representative" suit, to which some members of the class are parties, may bind members of the class or those represented who were not made parties to it.

The class suit was an invention of equity to enable it to proceed to a decree in suits where the number of those interested in the subject of the litigation is so great that their joinder as parties in conformity to the usual rules of procedure is impracticable. Courts are not infrequently called upon to proceed with causes in which the number of those interested in the litigation is so great as to make difficult or impossible the joinder of all because some are not within the jurisdiction or because their whereabouts is unknown or where if all were made parties to the suit its continued abatement by the death of some would prevent or unduly delay a decree. In such cases where the interests of those not joined are of the same class as the interests of those who are, and where it is considered that the latter fairly represent the former in the prosecution of the litigation of the issues in which all have a common interest, the court will proceed to a decree. . . .

[T]here is scope within the framework of the Constitution for holding in appropriate cases that a judgment rendered in a class suit is res judicata as to members of the class who are not formal parties to the suit. Here, as elsewhere, the Fourteenth Amendment does not compel state courts or legislatures to adopt any particular rule for establishing the conclusiveness of judgments in class suits, nor does it compel the adoption of the particular rules thought by this Court to be appropriate for the federal courts. With a proper regard for divergent local institutions and interests, this Court is justified in saying that there has been a failure of due process only in those cases where it cannot be said that the procedure adopted, fairly insures the protection of the interests of absent parties who are to be bound by it.

It is familiar doctrine of the federal courts that members of a class not present as parties to the litigation may be bound by the judgment where they are in fact adequately represented by parties who are present, or where they actually participate in the conduct of the litigation in which members of the class are present as parties, or where the interest of the members of the class, some of whom are present as parties, is joint, or where for any other reason the relationship between the parties present and those who are absent is such as legally to entitle the former to stand in judgment for the latter.

In all such cases, so far as it can be said that the members of the class who are present are, by generally recognized rules of law, entitled to stand in judgment for those who are not, we may assume for present purposes that such procedure affords a protection to the parties who are represented, though absent, which would satisfy the requirements of due process and full faith and credit. Nor do we find it necessary for the decision of this case to say that, when the only circumstance defining the class is that the determination of the rights of its members turns upon a single issue of fact or law, a state could not constitutionally adopt a procedure whereby some of the members of the class could stand in judgment for all, provided that the procedure were so devised and applied as to insure that those present are of the same class as those absent and that the litigation is so conducted as to insure the full and fair consideration of the common issue. We decide only that the procedure and the course of litigation sustained here by the plea of res judicata do not satisfy these requirements.

The restrictive agreement did not purport to create a joint obligation or liability. If valid and effective its promises were the several obligations of the signers and those claiming under them. The promises ran severally to every other signer. It is plain that in such circumstances all those alleged to be bound by the agreement would not constitute a single class in any litigation brought to enforce it. Those who sought to secure its benefits by enforcing it could not be said to be in the same class with or represent those whose interest was in resisting performance, for the agreement by its terms imposes obligations and confers rights on the owner of each plot of land who signs it. If those who thus seek to secure the benefits of the agreement were rightly regarded by the state Supreme Court as constituting a class, it is evident that those signers or their successors who are interested in challenging the validity of the agreement and resisting its performance are not of the same class in the sense that their interests are identical so that any group who had elected to enforce rights conferred by the agreement could be said to be acting in the interest of any others who were free to deny its obligation.

Because of the dual and potentially conflicting interests of those who are putative parties to the agreement in compelling or resisting its performance, it is impossible to say, solely because they are parties to it, that any two of them are of the same class. Nor without more, and with the due regard for the protection of the rights of absent parties which due process exacts, can some be permitted to stand in judgment for all.

It is one thing to say that some members of a class may represent other members in a litigation where the sole and common interest of the class in the litigation, is either to assert a common right or to challenge an asserted obligation. It is quite another to hold that all those who are free alternatively either to assert rights or to challenge them are of a single class, so that any group, merely because it is of the class so constituted, may be deemed adequately to represent any others of the class in litigating their interests in either alternative. Such a selection of representatives for purposes of litigation, whose substantial interests are not necessarily or even probably the same as those whom they are deemed to represent, does not afford that protection to absent parties which due process requires. The doctrine of representation of absent parties in a class suit has not hitherto been thought to go so far. Apart from the opportunities it would afford for the fraudulent and collusive sacrifice of the rights of absent parties, we think that the representation in this case no more satisfies the requirements of due process than a trial by a judicial officer who is in such situation that he may have an interest in the outcome of the litigation in conflict with that of the litigants.

The plaintiffs in the *Burke* case sought to compel performance of the agreement in behalf of themselves and all others similarly situated. They did not designate the defendants in the suit as a class or seek any injunction or other relief against others than the named defendants, and the decree which was entered did not purport to bind others. In seeking to enforce the agreement the plaintiffs in that suit were not representing the petitioners here whose substantial interest is in resisting performance. The defendants in the first suit were not treated by the pleadings or decree as representing others or as foreclosing by their defense the rights of others; and, even though nominal defendants, it does not appear that their interest in defeating the contract outweighed their interest in establishing its validity. For a court in this situation to ascribe to either the plaintiffs or defendants the performance of such functions on behalf of petitioners here, is to attribute to them a power that it cannot be said that they had assumed to exercise, and a responsibility which, in view of their dual interests it does not appear that they could rightly discharge.

Reversed.

Mr. Justice McREYNOLDS, Mr. Justice ROBERTS and Mr. Justice REED concur in the result.

NOTES AND PROBLEMS

1. In The History Behind Hansberry v. Lee, 20 U.C. Davis L. Rev. 481 (1987), Allen Kamp reveals that the case was one step in a long struggle over the desegregation of Chicago neighborhoods. The Hansberry family itself gave the nation considerably more than a leading case: Lorraine Hansberry, the daughter of the named party, was a leading playwright whose best-known work is *Raisin in the Sun*. In reminiscences about her father she recalled the terrible toll that this fight had on her and her family:

> [T]wenty-five years ago, [my father] spent a small personal fortune, his considerable talents, and many years of his life fighting, in association with NAACP attorneys, Chicago's "restrictive covenants" in one of this nation's ugliest ghettos.
>
> That fight also required that our family occupy with disputed property in a hellishly hostile "white neighborhood" in which literally howling mobs surrounded our house. . . . One of these missiles almost took the life of the then eight-year-old signer of this letter. My memories of this "correct" way of fighting white supremacy in America include being spat at, cursed and pummeled in the daily trek to and from school. And I also remember my desperate and courageous mother, patrolling our household all night with a loaded German [L]uger [pistol], doggedly guarding her four children, while my father fought the respectable part of the battle in the Washington court.

Id. at 488, quoting L. Hansberry, To Be Young, Gifted and Black 20-21 (adapted by R. Nemiroff, 1969).

2. *Hansberry*'s doctrinal equation is simple to state: a judgment in a class action binds absentee members of a class only if they have been adequately represented. For example, imagine that the homeowners in the area had brought a class suit against the property tax assessor, alleging that improper assessment principles had been used in figuring taxes on the tract. Assume the class lost on the merits. If the class of plaintiffs had been adequately represented, a single member of the class would be barred from bringing a second suit challenging the same assessment.

3. Much harder to work out is the application of that principle to the facts of *Hansberry*.

a. Were the Hansberrys and their vendors "represented" in the earlier class action, according to the Illinois courts?

b. On which side? The only plausible class was a group of persons seeking to enforce the covenant against those who wished to buy or sell property free of racial restrictions. Surely the Hansberrys weren't represented by this class.

c. If there had been a defendant class in Burke v. Kleiman as well — a class consisting of all those who challenged the validity of the covenant — one could at least begin to discuss whether the Hansberrys were members of that class. But the defendants in *Burke* were four named individuals who purported to represent only themselves. So on its face it represents massive confusion to describe Burke v. Kleiman as a class suit that bound the Hansberrys.

4. At this point the U.S. Supreme Court had a problem. The Court doesn't have jurisdiction to correct confusion within state courts unless that confusion falls within its jurisdiction. The only way the Court could reach the Illinois judgment was to find a constitutional error.

a. What was the constitutional error?

b. The *Hansberry* opinion tells us that the Illinois Supreme Court deemed the earlier action to have been a class action even though it was not conducted with any real attention to the interests of the "class" members. Couldn't the result in *Hansberry* have rested on the much narrower ground that due process is denied when binding effect is given to a judgment in an action in which no attempt was made to consider the problems of representing a group of absentees? Isn't the real problem that no one tried to represent the Hansberrys' interests in the earlier suit?

5. In explaining why the prior litigation did not bind the Hansberrys, the Court contrasted appropriate class actions with inappropriate ones:

> It is one thing to say that some members of a class may represent other members in a litigation where the sole and common interest of the class in the litigation is either to assert a common right or to challenge an asserted obligation. It is quite another to hold that all those who are free alternatively either to assert rights or to challenge them are of a single class, so that any group, merely because it is of the class so constituted, may be deemed adequately to represent any others of the class in litigating their interests in either alternative.

311 U.S. at 44-45.

a. In the context of the *Hansberry* case itself, the statement has special force. Professor Kamp's research revealed that the Burke family, who sold to the Hansberrys, had been the leaders of the plaintiff class in the first lawsuit and then later changed their minds about the covenant:

> The Court's words, "free to assert or deny" [rights] did not refer to an abstract possibility — that is exactly what had happened. The party enforcing the covenant in *Burke* was the wife of the person who had sold his house to Carl Hansberry. . . . Although the language is so sweeping it could apply to and invalidate every class action, what actually happened

in *Burke* and *Hansberry* was unique — that husband of the class representative in the first action had become a defendant and sought to subvert the goals of the plaintiff class.

20 U.C. Davis L. Rev. 481, 497 (1987).

b. Assume that Rule 23 had been in effect in the Illinois courts that heard Burke v. Kleiman. What portion of that Rule would have been most relevant to the conduct of the case?

6. Removed from the specific facts of *Hansberry*, the problem of the binding effect of a class action is a difficult one. It should be no surprise that named parties to the action are bound by the judgment. It also is hard to find a denial of due process to unnamed parties in giving them the benefit of a victory by the class of which they are a part. But if the same unnamed parties are not bound by a loss, isn't the one-way effect of the judgment unfair to the defendant in the class action? By including the opt-out provision of Rule 23(c)(2), the 1966 amendment to Rule 23 attempted to prevent a more blatant case of such one-sidedness: the case in which the class member sits out until the merits of the case have been determined in favor of his class. Under the new provision, "the judgment, whether favorable or not, will include all members who do not request exclusion." Note that the quoted language does not go quite so far as to say that it will not include, if favorable, those who do request exclusion. Is that a logical implication? Consider:

A brings a class action against D under Rule 23(b)(3). X is a member of the plaintiff class and receives notice. X requests exclusion. The class wins the litigation. X then sues D and claims that D is bound by the previous litigation by collateral estoppel. Most commentators (and one leading case) would not allow the person opting out to take advantage of a favorable judgment later by issue preclusion. See, e.g., Kaplan, Continuing Work of the Civil Committee: 1966 Amendments of the Federal Rules of Civil Procedure (I), 81 Harv. L. Rev. 356, 391-392 n. 136 (1967); Parklane Hosiery v. Shore, Chapter XII. On the other side, see Homburger, State Class Actions and the Federal Rule, 71 Colum. L. Rev. 609, 647 (1971).

7. The problem of the binding power of a class action usually boils down to a question of fairness to parties who may not have been adequately represented. Although the court in the first action can help to ensure adequate representation of such parties, no ruling to that effect in the first action should bind them if in fact they were not adequately represented. (An analogy can be made to attacks on the personal jurisdiction of a court: Recall from pages 872–899 that if the defendant appears in the first action and either raises or has an opportunity to raise the jurisdictional

issue, he is bound by the court's determination that it has jurisdiction. But if the defendant does not appear in the first action, no jurisdictional ruling of the first court can bind him.) Thus, *Hansberry* can also be cited for the proposition that a person asserted to be bound by former class litigation has the right collaterally to challenge the adequacy of the representation in the class suit.

A good illustration of this point is Gonzales v. Cassidy, 474 F.2d 67 (5th Cir. 1973), in which an unnamed member of a class was not precluded from bringing a later action even though an earlier class action had failed. The named plaintiff in the earlier action had succeeded in securing relief for himself; at that point, the second court ruled, he had become an inadequate representative of the class by failing to appeal. Failure of the plaintiff in the second action to intervene in the first action for the purpose of appealing was held not to be fatal to his argument that the first decision should not bind him.

b.   Jurisdiction

Hansberry tells us that for a class action to bind absentees the representation of the class must be adequate. Does due process place further constraints on the operation of the class action?

Phillips Petroleum v. Shutts
472 U.S. 797 (1985)

REHNQUIST, J.

[Phillips produces and sells natural gas. During the 1970s it acquired some of this gas by leasing gas-producing lands from others, paying royalties on the gas it extracted from each parcel of leased land. The royalty was based on the price for which the gas was finally sold, and increases in the selling price required approval by a federal agency. While regulatory approval was pending, however, Phillips sold the gas at higher prices but paid royalties only on the lower, already approved prices, paying the incremental royalties only when and if the increase met with regulatory approval. Phillips's defense of this practice rested on the difficulty of obtaining rebates from the royalty owners if the price increases were not approved.

Plaintiff Irl Shutts filed a suit on behalf of himself and 33,000 small royalty owners, claiming that they were entitled to interest on the money during the period when Phillips was awaiting approval of its price increases. The average claim of the class members was $100. Suit was filed in Kansas state court, which certified the action under a state provision substantially resembling Federal Rule of Civil Procedure 23.]

After the class was certified respondents provided each class member with notice through first-class mail. The notice described the action and informed each class member that he could appear in person or by counsel; otherwise each member would be represented by Shutts and the Andersons, the named plaintiffs. The notices also stated that class members would be included in the class and bound by the judgment unless they "opted out" of the lawsuit by executing and returning a "request for exclusion" that was included with the notice. The final class as certified contained 28,100 members; 3,400 had "opted out" of the class by returning the request for exclusion, and notice could not be delivered to another 1,500 members, who were also excluded. Less than 1,000 of the class members resided in Kansas. Only a minuscule amount, approximately one quarter of one percent, of the gas leases involved in the lawsuit were on Kansas land. [After some procedural skirmishing over the class action issue, the case went to trial. On the merits the Court held "as a matter of Kansas equity law" that Phillips owed the royalty owners interest and entered judgment for the plaintiff class.]

Petitioner raised two principal claims in its appeal to the Supreme Court of Kansas. It first asserted that the Kansas trial court did not possess personal jurisdiction over absent plaintiff class members as required by International Shoe Co. v. Washington and similar cases. Related to this first claim was petitioner's contention that the "opt-out" notice to absent class members, which forced them to return the request for exclusion in order to avoid the suit, was insufficient to bind class members who were not residents of Kansas or who did not possess "minimum contacts" with Kansas. Second, petitioner claimed that Kansas courts could not apply Kansas law to every claim in the dispute. The trial court should have looked to the laws of each State where the leases were located to determine, on the basis of conflict of laws principles, whether interest on the suspended royalties was recoverable, and at what rate.

The Supreme Court of Kansas held that the entire cause of action was maintainable under the Kansas class-action statute and the court rejected both of petitioner's claims. . . .

Reduced to its essentials, petitioner's argument is that unless out-of-state plaintiffs affirmatively consent, the Kansas courts may not exert jurisdiction over their claims. Petitioner claims that failure to execute and return the "request for exclusion" provided with the class notice cannot constitute consent of the out-of-state plaintiffs; thus Kansas courts may exercise jurisdiction over these plaintiffs only if the plaintiffs possess the sufficient "minimum contacts" with Kansas as that term is used in cases involving personal jurisdiction over out-of-state defendants. E.g., International Shoe Co. v. Washington, Shaffer v. Heitner, World-Wide Volkswagen Corp. v. Woodson. Since Kansas had no prelitigation contact with many of the plaintiffs and leases involved, petitioner claims that Kansas has exceeded its jurisdictional reach and thereby violated the due process rights of the absent plaintiffs.

[The opinion summarized *International Shoe*.]

The purpose of this test, of course, is to protect a defendant from the travail of defending in a distant forum, unless the defendant's contacts with the forum make it just to force him to defend there. As we explained in *Woodson*, supra, the defendant's contacts should be such that "he should reasonably anticipate being haled" into the forum. In Insurance Corp. of Ireland v. Compagnie des Bauxites de Guinée [supra page 160], we explained that the requirement that a court have personal jurisdiction comes from the Due Process Clause's protection of the defendant's personal liberty interest, and said that the requirement "represents a restriction on judicial power not as a matter of sovereignty, but as a matter of individual liberty."

Although the cases like *Shaffer* and *Woodson* which petitioner relies on for a minimum contacts requirement all dealt with out-of-state defendants or parties in the procedural posture of a defendant, petitioner claims that the same analysis must apply to absent class-action plaintiffs. In this regard petitioner correctly points out that a chose in action is a constitutionally recognized property interest possessed by each of the plaintiffs. Mullane v. Central Hanover Bank & Trust Co. An adverse judgment by Kansas courts in this case may extinguish the chose in action forever through res judicata. Such an adverse judgment, petitioner claims, would be every bit as onerous to an absent plaintiff as an adverse judgment on the merits would be to a defendant. Thus, the same due process protections should apply to absent plaintiffs: Kansas should not be able to exert jurisdiction over the plaintiffs' claims unless the plaintiffs have sufficient minimum contacts with Kansas.

We think petitioner's premise is in error. The burdens placed by a State upon an absent class-action plaintiff are not of the same order or magnitude as those it places upon an absent defendant. An out-of-state defendant summoned by a plaintiff is faced with the full powers of the forum State to render judgment *against* it. The defendant must generally hire counsel and travel to the forum to defend itself from the plaintiff's claim, or suffer a default judgment. The defendant may be forced to participate in extended and often costly discovery, and will be forced to respond in damages or to comply with some other form of remedy imposed by the court should it lose the suit. The defendant may also face liability for court costs and attorney's fees. These burdens are substantial, and the minimum contacts requirement of the Due Process Clause prevents the forum State from unfairly imposing them upon the defendant.

A class-action plaintiff, however, is in quite a different posture. The Court noted this difference in Hansberry v. Lee which explained that a "class" or "representative" suit was an exception to the rule that one could not be bound by judgment *in personam* unless one was made fully a party in the traditional sense. Ibid., citing Pennoyer v. Neff. As the Court pointed out in *Hansberry*, the class action was an invention of equity to enable it to proceed to a decree in suits where the number of those interested in the litigation was too great to permit joinder. The absent parties would be bound by the decree so long as the named parties adequately represented the absent class and the prosecution of the litigation was within the common interest.[1]

Modern plaintiff class actions follow the same goals, permitting litigation of a suit involving common questions when there are too many plaintiffs for proper joinder. Class actions also may permit the plaintiffs to pool claims which would be uneconomical to litigate individually. For example, this lawsuit involves claims averaging about $100 per plaintiff; most of the plaintiffs would have no realistic day in court if a class action were not available.

In sharp contrast to the predicament of a defendant haled into an out-of-state forum, the plaintiffs in this suit were not haled anywhere to defend themselves upon pain of a default judgment. As commentators have noted, from the plaintiffs' point of view a class action resembles a "quasi-administrative proceeding, conducted by the judge."

A plaintiff class in Kansas and numerous other jurisdictions cannot first be certified unless the judge, with the aid of the named plaintiffs and defendant, conducts an inquiry into the common nature of the named plaintiffs and the absent plaintiffs' claims, the adequacy of representation, the jurisdiction possessed over the class, and any other matters that will bear upon proper representation of the absent plaintiffs' interest. See, e.g., Kan. Stat. Ann. §60-223 (1983), Fed. Rule Civ. Proc. 23. Unlike a defendant in a civil suit, a class-action plaintiff is not required to fend for himself. See Kan. Stat. Ann. §60-223(d) (1983). The court and named plaintiffs protect his interest. Indeed, the class-action defendant itself has a great interest in ensuring that the absent plaintiffs' claims are properly

---

1. The holding in *Hansberry*, of course, was that petitioners in that case had not a sufficient common interest with the parties to a prior lawsuit such that a decree against those parties in the prior suit would bind the petitioners. But in the present case there is no question that the named plaintiffs adequately represent the class, and that all members of the class have the same interest in enforcing their claims against the defendant.

before the forum. In this case, for example, the defendant sought to avoid class certification by alleging that the absent plaintiffs would not be adequately represented and were not amenable to jurisdiction.

The concern of the typical class-action rules for the absent plaintiffs is manifested in other ways. Most jurisdictions, including Kansas, require that a class action, once certified, may not be dismissed or compromised without the approval of the court. In many jurisdictions such as Kansas the court may amend the pleadings to ensure that all sections of the class are represented adequately. Kan. Stat. Ann. §60-223(d) (1983); see also e.g., Fed. Rule Civ. Proc. 23(d).

Besides this continuing solicitude for their rights, absent plaintiff class members are not subject to other burdens imposed upon defendants. They need not hire counsel or appear. They are almost never subject to counterclaims or cross-claims, or liability for fees or costs.[2] Absent plaintiff class members are not subject to coercive or punitive remedies. Nor will an adverse judgment typically bind an absent plaintiff for any damages, although a valid adverse judgment may extinguish any of the plaintiff's claim which was litigated.

Unlike a defendant in a normal civil suit, an absent class-action plaintiff is not required to do anything. He may sit back and allow the litigation to run its course, content in knowing that there are safeguards provided for his protection. In most class actions an absent plaintiff is provided at least with an opportunity to "opt out" of the class, and if he takes advantage of that opportunity he is removed from the litigation entirely. This was true of the Kansas proceedings in this case. . . .

Petitioner contends, however, that the "opt out" procedure provided by Kansas is not good enough, and that an "opt in" procedure is required to satisfy the Due Process Clause of the Fourteenth Amendment. Insofar as plaintiffs who have no minimum contacts with the forum State are concerned, an "opt in" provision would require that each class member affirmatively consent to his inclusion within the class.

Because States place fewer burdens upon absent class plaintiffs than they do upon absent defendants in nonclass suits, the Due Process Clause need not and does not afford the former as much protection from state-court jurisdiction as it does the latter. The Fourteenth Amendment does protect "persons," not "defendants," however, so absent plaintiffs as well as absent defendants are entitled to some protection from the jurisdiction

2. Petitioner places emphasis on the fact that absent class members might be subject to discovery, counterclaims, cross-claims or court costs. Petitioner cites no cases involving any such imposition upon plaintiffs, however. We are convinced that such burdens are rarely imposed upon plaintiff class members, and that the disposition of these issues is best left to a case which presents them in a more concrete way.

of a forum State which seeks to adjudicate their claims. In this case we hold that a forum State may exercise jurisdiction over the claim of an absent class-action plaintiff, even though that plaintiff may not possess the minimum contacts with the forum which would support personal jurisdiction over a defendant. If the forum State wishes to bind an absent plaintiff concerning a claim for money damages or similar relief at law,[3] it must provide minimal procedural due process protection. The plaintiff must receive notice plus an opportunity, to be heard and participate in the litigation, whether in person or through counsel. The notice must be the best practicable, "reasonably calculated, under all the circumstances, to apprise interested parties of the pendency of the action and afford them an opportunity, to present their objections." *Mullane.* The notice should describe the action and the plaintiffs' rights in it. Additionally, we hold that due process requires at a minimum that an absent plaintiff be provided with an opportunity to remove himself from the class by executing and returning an "opt out" or "request for exclusion" form to the court. Finally, the Due Process Clause of course requires that the named plaintiff at all times adequately represent the interests of the absent class members. . . .

We think that the procedure followed by Kansas, where a fully descriptive notice is sent first-class mail to each class member, with an explanation of the right to "opt out," satisfies due process. . . .

In this case over 3,400 members of the potential class did "opt out," which belies the contention that "opt out" procedures result in guaranteed jurisdiction by inertia. Another 1,500 were excluded because the notice and "opt out" form was undeliverable. We think that such results show that the "opt out" procedure provided by Kansas is by no means pro forma, and that the Constitution does not require more to protect what must be the somewhat rare species of class member who is unwilling to execute an "opt out" form, but whose claim is nonetheless so important that he cannot be presumed to consent to being a member of the class by his failure to do so. Petitioner's "opt in" requirement would require the invalidation of scores of state statutes and of the class-action provision of the Federal Rules of Civil Procedure, and for the reasons stated we do not think that the Constitution requires the State to sacrifice the obvious advantages in judicial efficiency resulting from the "opt out" approach for the protection of the rara avis portrayed by petitioner.

3. Our holding today is limited to those class actions which seek to bind known plaintiffs concerning claims wholly or predominantly for money judgments. We intimate no view concerning other types of class-action lawsuits, such as those seeking equitable relief. Nor, of course, does our discussion of personal jurisdiction address class actions where the jurisdiction is asserted against a *defendant* class.

We therefore hold that the protection afforded the plaintiff class members by the Kansas statute satisfies the Due Process Clause. The interests of the absent plaintiffs are sufficiently protected by the forum State when those plaintiffs are provided with a request for exclusion that can be returned within a reasonable time to the court. Both the Kansas trial court and the Supreme Court of Kansas held that the class received adequate representation, and no party disputes that conclusion here. We conclude that the Kansas court properly asserted personal jurisdiction over the absent plaintiffs and their claims against petitioner. . . .

The Kansas courts applied Kansas contract and Kansas equity law to every claim in this case, notwithstanding that over 99 percent of the gas leases and some 97 percent of the plaintiffs in the case had no apparent connection to the State of Kansas except for this lawsuit. Petitioner protested that the Kansas courts should apply the laws of the States where the leases were located, or at least apply Texas and Oklahoma law because so many of the leases came from those States. The Kansas courts disregarded this contention and found petitioner liable for interest on the suspended royalties as a matter of Kansas law, and set the interest rates under Kansas equity principles. . . .

. . .We make no effort to determine for ourselves which law must apply to the various transactions involved in this lawsuit, and we reaffirm our observation in *Allstate* that in many situations a state court may be free to apply one of several choices of law. But the constitutional limitations laid down in cases such as Allstate and Home Insurance Co. v. Dick must be respected even in a nationwide class action.

We therefore affirm the judgment of the Supreme Court of Kansas insofar as it upheld the jurisdiction of the Kansas courts over the plaintiff class members in this case, and reverse its judgment insofar as it held that Kansas law was applicable to all of the transactions which it sought to adjudicate. We remand the case to that Court for further proceedings not inconsistent with this opinion.

Justice POWELL took no part in the decision of this case.

Justice STEVENS [concurred with the majority opinion on the class action issue and dissented only on the choice of law question.]

NOTES AND PROBLEMS

1. Start by admiring the defendant's fiendishly clever argument.

a. According to the defendant, how did the plaintiff class members in this case resemble defendants in ordinary cases?

b. According to the defendant, what implication did that resemblance have for the conduct of the class action?

c. How did the Supreme Court disagree with defendant?

2. Now turn to *Shutts*'s implications for our understanding of due process and the class action. What does *Shutts* hold?

a. Does its ruling apply only to class actions in which the members are scattered about the nation? That will include many, but by no means all, class actions.

b. Or does the *Shutts* ruling apply to all class actions, even where the class members are not distant from the forum site? If the latter, *Shutts* has broad implications.

c. The question matters because Rule 23(c)(2) requires individual notice to all members of 23(b)(3) classes but does not apply to (b)(1) and (b)(2) classes. In Eisen v. Carlisle & Jacquelin, 417 U.S. 156 (1974) the U.S. Supreme Court read Rule 23(c)(2) as an inflexible requirement: In all (b)(3) classes, all members of the class must receive individual notice and a chance to opt out of the class. The Kansas courts, operating under an analogous state rule, apparently interpreted the notice requirements for (b)(3) actions in the same way as the *Eisen* court had.

d. *Shutts* might mean that the holding in *Eisen* was constitutionally required — that anything less than individualized notice in (b)(3) classes denies due process.

e. But is that an accurate reading of the case? Does *Shutts* hold that the provisions of Rule 23(c)(2) are the minimum necessary to satisfy the Constitution, or just that they are sufficient to do so? To illustrate, imagine that Kansas had mailed notice to a random sample of the 33,000 class members and taken out ads on radio and television stations where large numbers of them lived. Would that have satisfied the requirements of due process?

3. Another version of the same question would have arisen if Kansas, instead of excluding the 1,500 royalty owners who could not be located, had included them in the class. Would these unnotified absentees have been bound by the resulting judgment? *Shutts* suggests not, but recall the facts of Mullane v. Central Hanover Bank & Trust (Chapter II). In that case the Court held that a number of unnotified trust beneficiaries would be bound by a judgment because they had been adequately represented by those who were notified. If *Mullane* is good law, then notice to those who can't easily be located is not required. But is that part of *Mullane* still good law after *Shutts*?

4. *Shutts* contains a curious footnote indicating that its decision reaches only class actions involving money damages primarily or

exclusively — that is, Rule 23(b)(3) actions. Why this limitation? There seem to be at least two possibilities:

a. The Court may merely be exercising traditional common law restraint in not deciding cases not before it.

b. Or there may be something special about the nature of injunctive relief that makes the requirement of notice and an opportunity to opt out less important or significant than in other cases. If the latter, did that impulse lead the Rules' drafters to treat 23(b)(3) cases differently from the other two sorts?

c. The question of which reading of *Shutts* is correct has substantial implications. If one thinks that *Shutts*'s concerns apply to Rule 23(b)(1) and (b)(2) actions as well as to (b)(3) cases, then Rule 23 provides insufficient constitutional protections to the members of (b)(1) and (b)(2) classes. Such a reading would mean that a court conducting such an action should require some notice (perhaps not individualized notice) to the members of those classes even though the Rule does not require such notice. A few courts have done so in some cases; most have not.

NOTE: CLASS ACTIONS IN FEDERAL COURTS

As *Hansberry* and *Shutts* indicate, the federal courts have no monopoly on class actions, but the federal courts have played a particularly important role in the development of the modern class action.

The original Federal Rules of Civil Procedure provided for class actions but did so in a Rule so opaque and confusing that the device was little used before the 1966 revision to Rule 23, in which that Rule took essentially the shape it now has. That revision brought the class action into modern prominence, and since that time the courts and Congress have debated whether the class action is an entirely good thing.

The federal courts have seemed uncertain about how to think about jurisdiction over the class action. Well before the Federal Rules, Supreme Tribe of Ben-Hur* v. Cauble, 255 U.S. 356 (1921), held that for purposes of complete diversity, courts should look to the citizenship only of the class representatives and ignore the class members. *Supreme Tribe* thus lowers jurisdictional barriers to the class action. By contrast, on the issue of the amount in controversy, the Court has proved much less accommodating. Snyder v. Harris, 394 U.S. 332 (1969), held that one

---

* The Supreme Tribe was a fraternal organization whose life insurance program was the subject of the lawsuit.

could not aggregate the claims of all class members for purposes of satisfying the amount in controversy. Zahn v. International Paper Co., 414 U.S. 291 (1973), went further by requiring that not just named plaintiffs but each member of the class satisfy the amount in controversy. Several appellate courts have held that 28 U.S.C. §1367 reverses the result in *Zahn*, though not in *Snyder*. Their reasoning is that §1367(a) extends supplemental jurisdiction to all but the cases designated in §1367(b), whose exceptions do not cover the class action situation. Compare Free v. Abbott Laboratories, 51 F.3d 524 (5th Cir. 1995) (supplemental jurisdiction over plaintiff class members) with Leonhardt v. Western Sugar Co., 160 F.3d 631 (10th Cir. 1998) (1367 does not overrule *Zahn*).

None of these rulings affect class actions based on federal law. Congress, however, has spoken sharply in one such area. For several years class actions based on alleged violations of federal securities laws have proved controversial. In 1995 Congress, believing that some of these suits lacked merit, acted to tighten pleading requirements for claims alleging violations of federal securities laws. 15 U.S.C. §78u4(b)(1)(B).

Three years later, citing evidence that plaintiffs had reacted to this change by moving their lawsuits to state courts, Congress enacted the Uniform Securities Litigation Standards Act of 1998, 15 U.S.C.§77p(c). That Act uses an interesting repertory of procedural devices to restrict state law securities class actions. First, it states that federal law preempts state securities laws, but only in class actions alleging fraud in the purchase and sale of securities. Second, it provides that all class actions filed in state courts and alleging securities fraud shall be removable to federal district courts without regard to diversity or amount in controversy. Once removed, they should be dismissed unless they fall into a narrow range of permitted claims. The result of this two-step procedure — removal followed by dismissal — essentially eliminates all class actions based on violations of state securities laws.

The student of procedure will find several features of the statute remarkable. Congress has undoubted power to preempt state securities laws. Here, however, Congress has achieved both more and less than preemption. The Act achieves less than preemption because it applies only to class actions rather than to all state law securities claims. It achieves more than ordinary preemption because it assures that all "preempted" claims will be dismissed. With ordinary substantive preemption, Congress relies on state courts to recognize and enforce the preemptive effect of federal law. The Supreme Court acts as the only federal enforcer of preemptive federal law by granting certiorari if state courts fail to recognize federal preemption. But the Supreme Court can hear only about 100 cases a year and thus allows for considerable slippage in the enforcement of preemptive federal laws. In the Act's scheme, removal solves this slippage problem. The federal district courts, not the Supreme Court, enforce federal preemption. *Every* class action involving state securities laws is removable, thus assuring a federal forum for this federal "defense." The Act demonstrates both the significance of the class action and the use of federal jurisdiction to control it.

4.   Settlement of Class Actions and the "Settlement Class"

The student will already have understood that the effect of the class action is more than the simple gathering together of similar cases. That proposition is particularly true at the settlement stage — the way in which most class actions end. Settlement presents several difficult problems unique to the class action. Most of those problems flow from the circumstance that, in many class actions (especially those created by Rule 23(b)(1) and (b)(3)), the litigative group is organized only for purposes of the lawsuit. In the most extreme cases the "group" may exist only in the abstract — as, for example, the sharers of some hypothesized interest. Yet many of the ordinary rules of litigation assume a client who hires a lawyer, guides the case, authorizes settlement, and benefits directly from the relief, if any.

a.   Fees

In most litigation the client pays the lawyer's fee because she has agreed to do so. While the named representative party in a class action may have such an agreement, that contract does not bind absentees. Yet it may seem that the lawyer whose work has benefited the class should be paid for that work. In class actions that recover money damages, courts apply the "common fund" doctrine, described supra pages 351–352. According to this doctrine, a plaintiff whose efforts create a fund is entitled to have those who benefit contribute to his lawyer's fee. In class actions that create funds for distribution to class members, the doctrine is applied more directly: Courts regularly award the class lawyer a fee taken directly from the fund created by the litigation.

How should the court calculate such a fee? One school holds that a simple percentage is appropriate, using the analogy of contingent fee arrangements. Others point out that the key ingredient in a contingent fee calculation — the agreement between lawyer and client — is missing in the class action context. They argue instead that the proper way to calculate fees is to start with the appropriate hourly rate of the lawyer and then adjust that according to various factors — such as special risks, novelty of the issues, and the like. In practice, the two methods may often arrive at similar results.

Setting these fees presents problems, because most class actions settle, and the fee award is made in the context of a settlement approval hearing required by Rule 23(e). At that hearing the representatives of the plaintiff and defendant, who will have agreed on an appropriate amount of fees, are unlikely to raise questions casting doubt on the agreed amount. The Rule addresses this problem by requiring notice to the absent class members and permitting them to come forward to object to the settlement terms. The idea is that they will have an incentive to do so because the lawyer's fee is coming out of a fund, the remainder of which will be distributed to the class. In a number of cases objectors have come forward. Consider how some representative problems should be solved.

NOTES AND PROBLEMS

1. Solo Practitioner brings a class action on behalf of a group of plaintiffs, alleging they were overcharged for their automobiles. The case is settled after three years, during which time Solo has devoted a third of her professional hours to it. The suit grants injunctive relief and $100,000 in compensatory damages. The two hundred members of the class will share in whatever remains of the proceeds after Solo's fee is paid. The judge finds that Solo spent more than 1,500 hours on the case. The court also finds that in her other legal work Solo billed clients at $75 an hour. Finally, the court finds that similarly skilled lawyers working in larger firms typically bill for such work at not less than $150 per hour.

a. Should the court use Solo's actual hourly rate or the higher rate for comparable big-firm lawyers?

b. This was Solo's first piece of comparably complex litigation. The judge finds that a more experienced practitioner would have devoted 200 fewer hours to the case. Should the judge subtract this amount from the hours Solo actually expended?

c. Even using the lower billing rate and a lower number of hours, multiplying the hours times the rate will yield a sum nearly as great as the $100,000 recovery. What should the court do?

2. In a class action seeking several millions of dollars in damages, the defendant offers to settle for a total sum of $100,000, with $95,000 allocated to lawyers' fees and $5,000 to the 500 plaintiffs.

a. Should such separately negotiated attorneys' fees be ethical?

b. If they are, how should the judge decide whether to approve such an offer?

3. A few courts have approached the fee problem in a novel way — by putting the legal work in class actions out to bid. In this system, which has several variations, the district court certifies a class and announces that the court will take bids from firms interested in taking on the representation. See, e.g., Sherleigh Assoc. LLC v. Sherleigh Associates, Inc., Profit-Sharing Plan, 186 F.R.D. 669 (S.D. Fla. 1999). Should this be a requirement of Rule 23?

b. Damages and Injunctive Relief

In class actions, damages pose an issue that rarely arises in ordinary cases: making sure that the class recovery finds its way into the hands of the class members. Class members often are unaware of the class action and subsequent recovery and consequently don't claim damages. The nature of some types of class actions makes notice difficult. One proposed solution to the problem is the *fluid class recovery*, under which, in the case of a class consisting of past consumers that dealt with a company, damages would be distributed to future consumers through rate reductions lasting long enough to exhaust the recovery. That was the approach taken in Daar v. Yellow Cab Co., 433 P.2d 732 (Cal. 1967), in which the class consisted of overcharged taxicab customers in Los Angeles. The court said it would be appropriate to require the defendant to lower its rates to all customers until the damages had been "paid." At least one district court suggested this approach, which was firmly rejected by the Second Circuit. Eisen v. Carlisle & Jacquelin, 479 F.2d 1003 (1973). Note that the ordinary purpose of litigation — compensation of the plaintiff for a wrong suffered — is not served by the fluid class recovery because some of the beneficiaries are not the people who have suffered the harm but merely people similar to them. Fluid class recovery thus serves to deter the defendants but not to compensate the plaintiffs. Is that a problem? Or is it a virtue?

Rule 23 is silent on the cost of efforts to contact class members after a judgment against a defendant. Should the defendant be required to bear the cost? If so, can such a requirement be squared with the fact that defendants in ordinary litigation bear no analogous cost? Should the cost be deducted from the damages claimed by those who are contacted? Should it come from the entire recovery — even the portion that will not be claimed?

If the relief sought is declaratory or injunctive rather than damages, the problems just discussed do not arise. Instead, problems for class members who do not receive notice relate to the due process issues discussed earlier. For example, what should be the binding effect of a school busing order on parent members of the plaintiff class who do not wish their children to be bused?

c. Settlement and Dismissal

Class actions are supposed to bind members of the class, so it is particularly important that class members be informed, if possible, of settlement proposals. Rule 23(e) requires court approval for dismissal or compromise, and "notice . . . in such manner as the court directs." What happens when someone objects? Rule 23(e) requires the court to approve any settlement or dismissal. Courts have interpreted this as a requirement that they consider the "fairness" of the proposed settlement, which is often a difficult task, and one that is not aided by the circumstance that the previously adverse parties are now both urging approval of the settlement. At fairness hearings a court will typically consider testimony from the plaintiff about how weak her case was — and thus why the settlement is favorable from her standpoint — and from the defendant about how diligent and creative plaintiff was — showing why one could not expect more. If there has been substantial discovery in the case, the judge may be able to make some independent judgment about such matters. What, however, if the parties have conducted little or no discovery? In such a case the judge will have little more than each party's word that the settlement is fair. The most dramatic such problems are presented in the so-called settlement class, in which the motion for class certification is presented simultaneously with a proposed settlement. A celebrated and controversial example follows.

Amchem Products, Inc. v. Windsor
521 U.S. 591 (1997)

Justice GINSBURG delivered the opinion of the Court.

This case concerns the legitimacy under Rule 23 of the Federal Rules of Civil Procedure of a class-action certification sought to achieve global settlement of current and future asbestos-related claims. The class proposed for certification potentially encompasses hundreds of thousands, perhaps millions, of individuals tied together by this commonality: each was, or some day may be, adversely affected by past exposure to asbestos products manufactured by one or more of 20 companies. Those companies, defendants in the lower courts, are petitioners here. . . .

I

A

The settlement-class certification we confront evolved in response to an asbestos-litigation crisis. A United States Judicial Conference Ad Hoc Committee on Asbestos Litigation, appointed by The Chief Justice in September 1990, described facets of the problem in a 1991 report:

> [This] is a tale of danger known in the 1930s, exposure inflicted upon millions of Americans in the 1940s and 1950s, injuries that began to take their toll in the 1960s, and a flood of lawsuits beginning in the 1970s. On the basis of past and current filing data, and because of a latency period that may last as long as 40 years for some asbestos related diseases, a continuing stream of claims can be expected. The final toll of asbestos related injuries is unknown. Predictions have been made of 200,000 asbestos disease deaths before the year 2000 and as many as 265,000 by the year 2015.
>
> The most objectionable aspects of asbestos litigation can be briefly summarized: dockets in both federal and state courts continue to grow; long delays are routine; trials are too long; the same issues are litigated over and over; transaction costs exceed the victims' recovery by nearly two to one; exhaustion of assets threatens and distorts the process; and future claimants may lose altogether.

Report of The Judicial Conference Ad Hoc Committee on Asbestos Litigation 2-3 (Mar. 1991).

Real reform, the report concluded, required federal legislation creating a national asbestos dispute-resolution scheme. . . . To this date, no congressional response has emerged.

In the face of legislative inaction, the federal courts — lacking authority to replace state tort systems with a national toxic tort compensation regime — endeavored to work with the procedural tools available to improve management of federal asbestos litigation. Eight federal judges, experienced in the superintendence of asbestos cases, urged the Judicial Panel on Multidistrict Litigation (MDL Panel), to consolidate in a single district all asbestos complaints then pending in federal courts. Accepting the recommendation, the MDL Panel transferred all asbestos cases then filed, but not yet on trial in federal courts to a single district, the United States District Court for the Eastern District of Pennsylvania; pursuant to the transfer order, the collected cases were consolidated for pretrial proceedings before Judge Weiner. The order aggregated pending cases only; no authority resides in the MDL Panel to license for consolidated proceedings claims not yet filed.

B

After the consolidation, attorneys for plaintiffs and defendants formed separate steering committees and began settlement negotiations. . . .

Settlement talks . . . concentrated on devising an administrative scheme for disposition of asbestos claims not yet in litigation. In these negotiations, counsel for masses of inventory plaintiffs [*] endeavored to represent the interests of the anticipated future claimants, although those lawyers then had no attorney-client relationship with such claimants.

Once negotiations seemed likely to produce an agreement purporting to bind potential plaintiffs, CCR[, a consortium of defendants,] agreed to settle, through separate agreements, the claims of plaintiffs who had already filed asbestos-related lawsuits. . . . After settling the inventory claims, CCR, together with the plaintiffs' lawyers CCR had approached, launched this case, exclusively involving persons outside the MDL Panel's province — plaintiffs without already pending lawsuits.[3]

C

The class action thus instituted was not intended to be litigated. Rather, within the space of a single day, January 15, 1993, the settling parties — CCR defendants and the representatives of the plaintiff class described below — presented to the District Court a complaint, an answer, a proposed settlement agreement, and a joint motion for conditional class certification.

The complaint identified nine lead plaintiffs, designating them and members of their families as representatives of a class comprising all persons who had not filed an asbestos-related lawsuit against a CCR defendant as of the date the class action commenced, but who (1) had

---

* [As the opinion elsewhere explained, the steering committees referred to persons who had already filed claims as "inventory plaintiffs," distinguishing them from those who had not yet filed claims, to whom they referred as "exposure-only" cases. — ED.]

3. It is basic to comprehension of this proceeding to notice that no transferred case is included in the settlement at issue, and no case covered by the settlement existed as a civil action at the time of the MDL transfer.

been exposed — occupationally or through the occupational exposure of a spouse or household member — to asbestos or products containing asbestos attributable to a CCR defendant, or (2) whose spouse or family member had been so exposed. Untold numbers of individuals may fall within this description. All named plaintiffs alleged that they or a member of their family had been exposed to asbestos-containing products of CCR defendants. More than half of the named plaintiffs alleged that they or their family members had already suffered various physical injuries as a result of the exposure. The others alleged that they had not yet manifested any asbestos-related condition. The complaint delineated no subclasses; all named plaintiffs were designated as representatives of the class as a whole.

The complaint invoked the District Court's diversity jurisdiction. . . . .

A stipulation of settlement accompanied the pleadings; it proposed to settle, and to preclude nearly all class members from litigating against CCR companies, all claims not filed before January 15, 1993, involving compensation for present and future asbestos-related personal injury or death. An exhaustive document exceeding 100 pages, the stipulation presents in detail an administrative mechanism and a schedule of payments to compensate class members who meet defined asbestos-exposure and medical requirements. The stipulation describes four categories of compensable disease: mesothelioma; lung cancer; certain "other cancers" (colon-rectal, laryngeal, esophageal, and stomach cancer); and "non-malignant conditions" (asbestosis and bilateral pleural thickening). Persons with "exceptional" medical claims — claims that do not fall within the four described diagnostic categories — may in some instances qualify for compensation, but the settlement caps the number of "exceptional" claims CCR must cover. . . . .

For each qualifying disease category, the stipulation specifies the range of damages CCR will pay to qualifying claimants. Payments under the settlement are not adjustable for inflation. Mesothelioma claimants — the most highly compensated category — are scheduled to receive between $20,000 and $200,000. The stipulation provides that CCR is to propose the level of compensation within the prescribed ranges; it also establishes procedures to resolve disputes over medical diagnoses and levels of compensation.

Class members are to receive no compensation for certain kinds of claims, even if otherwise applicable state law recognizes such claims. . . . . Although not entitled to present compensation, exposure-only claimants and pleural claimants may qualify for benefits when and if they develop a compensable disease and meet the relevant exposure and medical criteria. Defendants forgo defenses to liability, including statute of limitations pleas.

Class members, in the main, are bound by the settlement in perpetuity, while CCR defendants may choose to withdraw from the settlement after ten years. A small number of class members — only a few per year — may reject the settlement and pursue their claims in court. Those permitted to exercise this option, however, may not assert any punitive damages claim or any claim for increased risk of cancer. Aspects of the administration of the settlement are to be monitored by the AFL-CIO and class counsel. Class counsel are to receive attorneys' fees in an amount to be approved by the District Court.

D

On January 29, 1993, as requested by the settling parties, the District Court conditionally certified, under Federal Rule of Civil Procedure 23(b)(3), an encompassing opt-out class. . . . Judge Weiner assigned to Judge Reed, also of the Eastern District of Pennsylvania, "the task of conducting fairness proceedings and of determining whether the proposed settlement is fair to the class." Various class members raised objections to the settlement stipulation, and Judge Weiner granted the objectors full rights to participate in the subsequent proceedings. . . .

Objectors raised numerous challenges to the settlement. They urged that the settlement unfairly disadvantaged those without currently compensable conditions in that it failed to adjust for inflation or to account for changes, over time, in medical understanding. They maintained that compensation levels were intolerably low in comparison to awards available in tort litigation or payments received by the inventory plaintiffs. And they objected to the absence of any compensation for certain claims, for example, medical monitoring, compensable under the tort law of several States. . . .

Strenuous objections had [also] been asserted regarding the adequacy of representation, a Rule 23(a)(4) requirement. Objectors maintained that class counsel and class representatives had disqualifying conflicts of interests. In particular, objectors urged, claimants whose injuries had become manifest and claimants without manifest injuries should not have common counsel and should not be aggregated in a single class. Furthermore, objectors argued, lawyers representing inventory plaintiffs should not represent the newly-formed class. . . .

Declaring class certification appropriate and the settlement fair, the District Court preliminarily enjoined all class members from commenc-

ing any asbestos-related suit against the CCR defendants in any state or
federal court.

E

The Court of Appeals [reversing] . . . found that "serious intra-class
conflicts precluded the class from meeting the adequacy of representation
requirement" of Rule 23(a)(4). . . .

In the Third Circuit's view, the "most salient" divergence of interests
separated plaintiffs already afflicted with an asbestos-related disease from
plaintiffs without manifest injury (exposure-only plaintiffs). The latter
would rationally want protection against inflation for distant recoveries.
They would also seek sturdy back-end opt-out rights and "causation
provisions that can keep pace with changing science and medicine, rather
than freezing in place the science of 1993." Already injured parties, in
contrast, would care little about such provisions and would rationally
trade them for higher current payouts. These and other adverse interests,
the Court of Appeals carefully explained, strongly suggested that an
undivided set of representatives could not adequately protect the discrete
interests of both currently afflicted and exposure-only claimants. . . .

II

Objectors assert in this Court, as they did in the District Court and Court
of Appeals, an array of jurisdictional barriers. Most fundamentally, they
maintain that the settlement proceeding instituted by class counsel and
CCR is not a justiciable case or controversy within the confines of Article
III of the Federal Constitution. In the main, they say, the proceeding is
a nonadversarial endeavor to impose on countless individuals without
currently ripe claims an administrative compensation regime binding on
those individuals if and when they manifest injuries. . . .

[Like the Third Circuit, the Supreme Court] declined to reach these
issues because they "would not exist but for the [class action] certification.". . .

III

To place this controversy in context, we briefly describe the characteristics
of class actions for which the Federal Rules provide. Rule 23, governing
federal-court class actions, stems from equity practice and gained its
current shape in an innovative 1966 revision. . . .

In the decades since the 1966 revision of Rule 23, class action practice has become ever more "adventuresome" as a means of coping with claims too numerous to secure their "just, speedy, and inexpensive determination" one by one. See Fed. Rule Civ. Proc. 1. The development reflects concerns about the efficient use of court resources and the conservation of funds to compensate claimants who do not line up early in a litigation queue. . . .

Among current applications of Rule 23(b)(3), the "settlement only" class has become a stock device. Although all Federal Circuits recognize the utility of Rule 23(b)(3) settlement classes, courts have divided on the extent to which a proffered settlement affects court surveillance under Rule 23's certification criteria. . . .

IV

We granted review to decide the role settlement may play, under existing Rule 23, in determining the propriety of class certification. The Third Circuit's opinion stated that each of the requirements of Rule 23(a) and (b)(3) "must be satisfied without taking into account the settlement." That statement, petitioners urge, is incorrect.

We agree with petitioners to this limited extent: settlement is relevant to a class certification. The Third Circuit's opinion bears modification in that respect. But, as we earlier observed, the Court of Appeals in fact did not ignore the settlement; instead, that court homed in on settlement terms in explaining why it found the absentees' interests inadequately represented. The Third Circuit's close inspection of the settlement in that regard was altogether proper.

Confronted with a request for settlement-only class certification, a district court need not inquire whether the case, if tried, would present intractable management problems, see Fed. Rule Civ. Proc. 23(b)(3)(D), for the proposal is that there be no trial. But other specifications of the rule — those designed to protect absentees by blocking unwarranted or overbroad class definitions — demand undiluted, even heightened, attention in the settlement context. Such attention is of vital importance, for a court asked to certify a settlement class will lack the opportunity, present when a case is litigated, to adjust the class, informed by the proceedings as they unfold. See Fed. Rule Civ. Proc. 23(c),(d).[16]

---

16. Portions of the opinion dissenting in part appear to assume that settlement counts only one way — in favor of certification. To the extent that is the dissent's meaning, we disagree. Settlement, though a relevant factor, does not inevitably signal that class action certification should be granted more readily than it would be were the case to be litigated. For reasons the Third Circuit aired, proposed settlement classes sometimes warrant more, not less caution on the question of certification.

And, of overriding importance, courts must be mindful that the rule as now composed sets the requirements they are bound to enforce. Federal Rules take effect after an extensive deliberative process involving many reviewers: a Rules Advisory Committee, public commenters, the Judicial Conference, this Court, the Congress. The text of a rule thus proposed and reviewed limits judicial inventiveness. Courts are not free to amend a rule outside the process Congress ordered, a process properly tuned to the instruction that rules of procedure "shall not abridge . . . any substantive right." §2072(b).

Rule 23(e), on settlement of class actions, reads in its entirety: "A class action shall not be dismissed or compromised without the approval of the court, and notice of the proposed dismissal or compromise shall be given to all members of the class in such manner as the court directs." This prescription was designed to function as an additional requirement, not a superseding direction, for the "class action" to which Rule 23(e) refers is one qualified for certification under Rule 23(a) and (b). . . .

The safeguards provided by the Rule 23(a) and (b) class-qualifying criteria, we emphasize, are not impractical impediments — checks shorn of utility — in the settlement class context. . . .

Federal courts, in any case, lack authority to substitute for Rule 23's certification criteria a standard never adopted — that if a settlement is "fair," then certification is proper. Applying to this case criteria the rulemakers set, we conclude that the Third Circuit's appraisal is essentially correct. Although that court should have acknowledged that settlement is a factor in the calculus, a remand is not warranted on that account. The Court of Appeals' opinion amply demonstrates why — with or without a settlement on the table — the sprawling class the District Court certified does not satisfy Rule 23's requirements. . . .

A

We address first the requirement of Rule 23(b)(3) that "[common] questions of law or fact . . . predominate over any questions affecting only individual members." The District Court concluded that predominance was satisfied based on two factors: class members' shared experience of asbestos exposure and their common "interest in receiving prompt and fair compensation for their claims, while minimizing the risks and transaction costs inherent in the asbestos litigation process as it occurs presently in the tort system.". . .

The predominance requirement stated in Rule 23(b)(3), we hold, is not met by the factors on which the District Court relied. The benefits asbestos-exposed persons might gain from the establishment of a grand-scale compensation scheme is a matter fit for legislative consideration, but it is not pertinent to the predominance inquiry. That inquiry trains on the legal or factual questions that qualify each class member's case as a genuine controversy, questions that preexist any settlement. . . .

B

Nor can the class approved by the District Court satisfy Rule 23(a)(4)'s requirement that the named parties "will fairly and adequately protect the interests of the class." The adequacy inquiry under Rule 23(a)(4) serves to uncover conflicts of interest between named parties and the class they seek to represent. . . .

As the Third Circuit pointed out, named parties with diverse medical conditions sought to act on behalf of a single giant class rather than on behalf of discrete subclasses. In significant respects, the interests of those within the single class are not aligned. Most saliently, for the currently injured, the critical goal is generous immediate payments. That goal tugs against the interest of exposure-only plaintiffs in ensuring an ample, inflation-protected fund for the future. . . .

The settling parties, in sum, achieved a global compromise with no structural assurance of fair and adequate representation for the diverse groups and individuals affected. Although the named parties alleged a range of complaints, each served generally as representative for the whole, not for a separate constituency. . . .

The Third Circuit found no assurance here — either in the terms of the settlement or in the structure of the negotiations — that the named plaintiffs operated under a proper understanding of their representational responsibilities. That assessment, we conclude, is on the mark.

C . . .

Because we have concluded that the class in this case cannot satisfy the requirements of common issue predominance and adequacy of representation, we need not rule, definitively, on the notice given here. In accord with the Third Circuit, however, we recognize the gravity of the question whether class action notice sufficient under the Constitution and Rule 23 could ever be given to legions so unselfconscious and amorphous.

V

The argument is sensibly made that a nationwide administrative claims processing regime would provide the most secure, fair, and efficient means of compensating victims of asbestos exposure. Congress, however, has not adopted such a solution. And Rule 23, which must be interpreted with fidelity to the Rules Enabling Act and applied with the interests of absent class members in close view, cannot carry the large load CCR, class counsel, and the District Court heaped upon it. As this case exemplifies, the rulemakers' prescriptions for class actions may be endangered by "those who embrace [Rule 23] too enthusiastically just as [they are by] those who approach [the rule] with distaste." C. Wright, Law of Federal Courts 508 (5th ed. 1994). . . .

Justice O'CONNOR took no part in the consideration or decision of this case.

Justice BREYER, with whom Justice STEVENS joins, concurring in part and dissenting in part.

Although I agree with the Court's basic holding that "settlement is relevant to a class certification," I find several problems in its approach that lead me to a different conclusion. First, I believe that the need for settlement in this mass tort case, with hundreds of thousands of lawsuits, is greater than the Court's opinion suggests. Second, I would give more weight than would the majority to settlement-related issues for purposes of determining whether common issues predominate. Third, I am uncertain about the Court's determination of adequacy of representation, and do not believe it appropriate for this Court to second-guess the District Court on the matter without first having the Court of Appeals consider it. Fourth, I am uncertain about the tenor of an opinion that seems to suggest the settlement is unfair. And fifth, in the absence of further review by the Court of Appeals, I cannot accept the majority's suggestions that "notice" is inadequate. . . .

The issues in this case are complicated and difficult. The District Court might have been correct. Or not. Subclasses might be appropriate. Or not. I cannot tell. And I do not believe that this Court should be in the business of trying to make these fact-based determinations. That is a job suited to the district courts in the first instance, and the courts of appeal on review. But there is no reason in this case to believe that the Court of Appeals conducted its prior review with an understanding that the settlement could have constituted a reasonably strong factor in favor of class certification. For this reason, I would provide the courts below with an opportunity to analyze the factual questions involved in certification by vacating the judgment, and remanding the case for further proceedings.

NOTES AND PROBLEMS

1. *Amchem* exposes numerous issues, some of which challenge the most basic assumptions about the nature of civil litigation. In that respect

it is a fitting close both to this chapter on joinder and to the student's exploration of civil procedure.

2. Start by defining the respects in which *Amchem* is an unusual case, even within the category of class actions, which are themselves unusual if measured by ordinary litigation standards.

a. In a typical class action the plaintiff files a complaint; there is a battle over class certification, followed (if the class is certified) by discovery, perhaps a summary judgement motion, and settlement discussions. What happened in *Amchem*?

b. In many ordinary, single-plaintiff-single-defendant cases, the parties settle before any suit is filed. To use the asbestos context, a lawyer for a former shipyard worker alleging injuries from inhalation of asbestos dust could approach an asbestos manufacturer and settle the case without ever filing so much as a complaint. Why didn't the parties do so in *Amchem*? Why *couldn't* they do so if they wanted the settlement to have the intended effect?

c. What did the parties — in particular the defendants — want to get from class certification that they could not have gotten in any other way?

3. To answer Problem 2c, one must be clear about the definition of the class. The persons involved in the *Amchem* litigation comprised two groups.

a. There were individual claimants who had filed complaints against various asbestos manufacturers (the so-called inventory claimants). These cases had been consolidated (under the provision for Multidistrict Litigation, 28 U.S.C. §1407). These claims could have been settled without regard to class certification; indeed, it was the discussion of their settlement that led to the proposed class action.

b. Who, then, were the members of the class?

c. Put yourself in the position of a defendant. Why would you have wanted the class certification and settlement before being willing to settle the "inventory" of individual cases?

4. You are now in a position to understand the ethical dimension of *Amchem*.

a. The same group of lawyers represented both the individual, already-filed, "inventory" cases and the class of unfiled, often unidentified "exposure-only" cases.

b. What's the problem (which lawyers would refer to as "a conflict")?

c. Why is this problem discussed at length in an opinion on whether a class action should be certified (as opposed, for example, to a state bar disciplinary proceeding against one of the lawyers)? What, in other words, makes this problem part of the law of class actions as well as of professional ethics?

d. The Supreme Court has emphasized that it meant what it said in *Amchem* about the avoidance of conflicts of interest by lawyers representing classes. Striking down another asbestos settlement class in Ortiz v. Fibreboard Corp., 119 S. Ct. 2295 (1999), the Court said:

> One may take a settlement amount as good evidence of the maximum available if one can assume that parties of equal knowledge and negotiating skill agreed upon the figure through arms-length bargaining, unhindered by any considerations tugging against the interests of the parties ostensibly represented in the negotiation. But no such assumption may be indulged in this case, or probably in any class action settlement with the potential for gigantic fees. In this case, certainly, any assumption that plaintiffs' counsel could be of a mind to do their simple best in bargaining for the benefit of the settlement class is patently at odds with the fact that at least some of the same lawyers representing plaintiffs and the class had also negotiated the separate settlement of 45,000 pending claims, the full payment of which was contingent on a successful global settlement agreement or the successful resolution of the insurance coverage dispute. . . . Class counsel thus had great incentive to reach any agreement in the global settlement negotiations that they thought might survive a Rule 23(e) fairness hearing, rather than the best possible arrangement for the substantially unidentified global settlement class. Cf. Cramton, Individualized Justice, Mass Torts, and "Settlement Class Actions": An Introduction, 80 Cornell L. Rev. 811, 832 (1995) ("Side settlements suggest that class counsel has been laboring under an impermissible conflict of interest and that it may have preferred the interests of current clients to those of the future claimants in the settlement class"). The resulting incentive to favor the known plaintiffs in the earlier settlement was, indeed, an egregious example of the conflict noted in *Amchem* resulting from divergent interests of the presently injured and future claimants. See 521 U.S. at 626-627 (discussing adequacy of named representatives under Rule 23(a)(4)).

Id. at 2317-2318.

5. In *Amchem* the district court's response to the adequacy-of-representation problem took two forms. It examined the length and serious quality of the negotiations among counsel, the "maturity" of asbestos litigation (a term used to describe the many litigated cases, whose outcome made it easier to value individual claims), and the relationship of the amounts that had previously been awarded in asbestos verdicts to the amounts proposed to be paid to future claimants. Looking at all these factors, the district judge concluded that the negotiations had led to a fundamentally fair result — and that counsel had therefore been adequate.

a. What part of that reasoning did the Supreme Court attack?

b. Does the majority opinion rest on a conviction that the procedure was fundamentally unfair?

6. In the background of *Amchem* is the question of whether any settlement class can ever be approved under Rule 23.

a. Like *Amchem*, Ortiz v. Fibreboard Corp., supra Note 4d, rejected a global settlement class but, also like *Amchem*, did so in terms that stressed the deficiencies of the particular procedure rather than any inherent unlawfulness of the idea:

> This case turns on the conditions for certifying a mandatory settlement class on a limited fund theory under Federal Rule of Civil Procedure 23(b)(1)(B). We hold that applicants for contested certification on this rationale must show that the fund is limited by more than the agreement of the parties, and has been allocated to claimants belonging within the class by a process addressing any conflicting interests of class members.

Ortiz at 2302.

Besides the problem of conflicts of interest among the lawyers representing classes with divergent interests, *Fibreboard* emphasizes the problem of certifying for settlement a 23(b)(1) class. As you will recall, the rationale for (b)(1) classes is that an inherently limited fund must be distributed; the function of the class action is to assure the parties share equitably in the fund. In *Fibreboard* the "limitedness" of the fund resulted from an agreement among two insurance companies and the defendant that they would contribute only a certain amount to settle these claims. For the Supreme Court, this wasn't enough to create a limited fund.

b. Have there been approved settlement classes? Yes. For an example, see Hanlon v. Chrysler Corp., 150 F.3d 1011, 1020-1021 (9th Cir. 1997), in which plaintiffs sued an auto manufacturer alleging a defective latch in a van's door. Affirming the district court's approval of a settlement class, the Ninth Circuit carefully distinguished *Amchem*:

> At the heart of *Amchem* was concern over settlement allocation decisions; asbestos manufacturers had a designated amount of money that was not fairly distributed between present and future claimants. The *Amchem* settlement eliminated all present and future claims against asbestos manufacturers, with class counsel attempting to represent both groups of plaintiffs. The Supreme Court found this dual representation to be particularly troubling, given that present plaintiffs had a clear interest in a settlement that maximized current funds, while future plaintiffs had a strong interest in preserving funds for their future needs and protecting the total fund against inflation.
>
> Unlike the class in *Amchem*, this class of minivan owners does not present an allocation dilemma. Potential plaintiffs are not divided into conflicting discrete categories, such as those with present health problems and those who may develop symptoms in the future. Rather, each potential plaintiff has the same problem: an allegedly defective rear latchgate which requires repair or commensurate compensation. The differences in severity

of personal injury present in Amchem are avoided here by excluding personal injury and wrongful death claims. Similarly, there is no structural conflict of interest based on variations in state law, for the named representatives include individuals from each state, and the differences in state remedies are not sufficiently substantial so as to warrant the creation of subclasses. Representatives of other potential subclasses are included among the named representatives, including owners of every minivan model. However, even if the named representatives did not include a broad cross-section of claimants, the prospects for irreparable conflict of interest are minimal in this case because of the relatively small differences in damages and potential remedies.

Is this an adequate response?

7. As one can gather from the disagreement between majority and dissent, the judiciary, academia, and the bar are divided on the desirability of settlements like *Amchem* and *Fibreboard.*

a. One experienced observer of the legal scene described such cases as violations of due process and "the sale of res judicata — at a bargain basement price."

b. Others have praised them as embodying the highest traditions of judicial creativity and lawyers' cooperation.

c. In part, one's assessment may depend on one's assumptions about the alternatives. If one thinks that the alternative is an expeditiously conducted civil trial, much of the straining to find that the settlement did not breach either the principles of due process or of professional ethics will seem unnecessary and undesirable. One can find some evidence to support the thesis that the "ordinary" litigation system was developing methods of coping with the asbestos cases.

d. If one thinks that the alternative is the death or financial destitution of those waiting in line for such a civil trial, then the district courts' action in *Amchem* and *Fibreboard* will seem both humane and sensible. One can find some evidence that the litigation system was drowning in asbestos litigation and that litigation expenses, including lawyers' fees, were consuming two-thirds of the amounts recovered.

8. Beyond this level of debate is a subsidiary one about legal institutions. Some who would accept the argument that courts were doing badly with asbestos litigation would nevertheless say that there were other institutions that could and should have responded.

a. One candidate was Congress, which could have created an administrative system (like that for workers' compensation) for dealing with the asbestos claims. The Black Lung Benefits Act, 30 U.S.C. §§901 et seq. might have provided a model. Under the Act, funded by a tax on coal, miners who show disability produced by exposure to coal dust collect benefits from a federal agency. As the opinion in *Amchem* noted, Congress has not acted in a similar way in the case of asbestos. Does that mean that the courts should act on their own? Or has the courts' search for solutions taken the political heat off Congress and thereby thwarted a legislative solution?

b. Another candidate was the bankruptcy courts. John Coffee (who testified — without fee — as an expert in *Amchem*) argues that bankruptcy courts are in the business of collective litigation: They regularly resolve cases in which large numbers of creditors have claims against an entity. Moreover, they are expressly vested with the power to do the sort of quasi-administrative tasks achieved by the proposed settlement. Finally, Coffee argues, the history of a large asbestos bankruptcy suggests that the claimants would get more (and the lawyers less) than under the settlement. One theoretical objection to the settlement class in *Fibreboard* was that by using Rule 23(b)(1) and a limited fund rationale, the defendants were seeking the sort of protection they might have achieved in bankruptcy without subjecting themselves to the powers of a bankruptcy proceeding that might have dug much more deeply into their pockets.

9. As a nice summation of your grasp of civil procedure, be prepared either to defend or to attack the *Amchem* settlement — and explain your grounds for doing so — both as a matter of procedural law and of political theory.

TABLE OF CASES

TABLE OF CITATIONS TO THE JUDICIAL CODE (28 U.S.C.)

§133(a)	197
§144	656, 665
§372	662
§455	656, 661-665, 784
§636	432, 511
§651	604
§657	605
§1253	68
§1254	68
§1255	68
§1256	68
§1257	68
§1258	68
§1291	65, 368, 511,573, 763, 764, 770, 771, 780
§1292(a)	368, 780, 868
§1292(b)	257, 560, 770, 780-784
§1331	7, 214, 216, 893
§1332	7, 214, 220, 232-237, 242, 921, 962
§1332(c)	235, 236
§1332(d)	235, 236
§1333	214
§1334	214
§1335	188, 233, 956
§1338	214, 895
§1359	235
§1367	233, 243, 244, 249-251, 258, 894, 901, 902, 915, 917, 922, 925, 926, 999
§1391	14, 197, 198, 201
§1392	197
§1397	956
§1404	94, 203-205, 212, 299, 783
§1406	211, 212
§1407	212, 1013
§1441	251, 252, 257, 258
§1442	258
§1445	258
§1446	251, 257
§1447	251, 252
§1631	211
§1651	783
§1652	262
§1738	586, 594, 810, 872, 879, 881
§1738A	156, 873
§1738B	880
§1861	697-699, 702
§1863	698, 699
§1864	698
§1866	698
§1867	698, 699
§1870	702
§1920	356
§1961	321
§2072	293, 780, 782, 807
§2106	602
§2107	771
§2111	793, 795
§2201	223, 691
§2202	223
§2361	145, 184, 196, 956
§2412	354

TABLE OF CITATIONS TO THE FEDERAL RULES OF CIVIL PROCEDURE

26(d)	497	45	37, 38, 42, 502
26(f)	497, 503, 504, 507	47(a)	700, 701
26(g)	498, 505-508, 546, 560	48	696
28	498	49	751
29	507	50	56, 628, 723, 729, 734, 792
30	38, 498	50(a)	50, 51, 723, 734
30(b)	499, 500	50(b)	52, 734, 735
30(d)	499, 500	50(c)	741
31	498, 499	51	51, 732
32	498	52(a)	717, 792, 841
33	38, 498	54	356, 770
33(b)	499	55	49, 566, 567
33(c)	537	55(b)	568
34	37, 42, 501, 502	55(c)	571
35	38, 503, 508, 515, 524	56	43, 55, 627
36	49, 504	56(c)	43, 627, 628
37	498, 505, 506 507, 546, 834, 840	56(e)	629, 636
37(a)	354, 499, 507, 511	56(f)	39
37(b)	506, 560	57	339
37(c)	504, 506	59	32, 735, 792
37(d)	506, 511, 547	59(d)	735
37(g)	506	60	881, 886
38	299, 678	60(b)	52, 190, 392, 561, 567, 571,
41	829, 834		828, 881, 882, 885, 886, 887
41(a)	49, 462, 573-575, 580	65(a)	367
41(b)	49, 566, 572, 581, 829	65(b)	293, 380
42	30, 910	65(c)	367
42(b)	808, 893	68	355-357
44.1	167		

TABLE OF AUTHORITIES

Abolition of Diversity of Citizenship Jurisdiction, H.R. Rep. No. 893, 95th Cong., 2d Sess. 2, 3-5 (1978), 220, 230

Adams, World-Wide Volkswagen v. Woodson — The Rest of the Story, 72 Neb. L. Rev. 1122 (1993), 128

Annual Report of the Director of the Administrative Office of the United States Courts (1998), 310, 609

Blackstone, W., Commentaries on the Laws of England 436 (1768), 392

Borchers, The Origin of Diversity Jurisdiction, the Rise of Legal Positivism, and a Brave New World for *Erie* and *Klaxon*, 72 Texas L. Rev. 79 (1993), 279

Bourne & Lynch, Merger of Law and Equity Under the Revised Maryland Rules: Does It Threaten Trial By Jury? 14 U. Balt. L. Rev. 1 (1984), 692

Brazil, The Adversary Character of Civil Discovery: A Critique and Proposals for Change, 31 Vand. L. Rev. 1295 (1978), 545

Brickman, Horowitz, & O'Connell, Rethinking Contingency Fees (Manhattan Institute 1994), 348

Bridwell, R. & R.U. Whitten, The Constitution and the Common Law (1977), 279

Carrington & Haagen, Contract & Jurisdiction, 1996 Sup. Ct. Rev. 331, 610

Clermont & Eisenberg, Xenophilia in American Courts, 109 Harv. L. Rev. 1120 (1996), 167

Comment, Raising the Cost of Lying: Rethinking *Erie* for Judicial Estoppel, 64 U. Chi. L. Rev. 873 (1997), 868

Eskridge, Jr., The New Textualism, 37 UCLA L. Rev. 621 (1990), 240

Feltham, Tortious Interference with Contractual Relations: The Texaco Inc. v. Pennzoil Litigation, 33 N.Y. L. Sch. L. Rev. 111 (1988), 575

Fink & Tushnet, Federal Jurisdiction: Policy and Practice 168 (1984), 223, 263

Fiss, The Civil Rights Injunction (1978), 332

Freyer, Harmony and Dissonance: The *Swift* and *Erie* Cases in American Federalism (1982), 279

Grinfeld, Justice on Loan, 19 Calif. Lawyer 39 (1999), 346

Gross & Syverud, Getting to No: A Study of Settlement Negotiations and the Selection of Cases for Trial, 90 Mich. L. Rev. 319 (1991), 565

_____, The Georgia Domestic Relations Long-Arm Statute: An Appraisal, 189 Ga. L. Rev. 691-692 (1984), 158

_____, Pierce v. Cook & Co.: Rule 60(b) (6) Relief from Judgment for Change of State Law in a Diversity Case, 62 Va. L. Rev. 414 (1976), 302

Ostrom, et al., State Court Caseload Statistics: Annual Report 1995 (National Center for State Courts 1996), 310, 329, 565

Pomerantz, New Developments in Class Actions — Has Their Death Knell Been Sounded?, 25 Bus. Law. 1259 (1970), 963
Pomeroy, Code Remedies (5th ed. 1929), 397

Rendleman, The Inadequate Remedy at Law: Prerequisite for an Injunction, 33 U. Fla. L. Rev. 346 (1980), 334
Resnik, Managerial Judges, 96 Harv. L. Rev. 374 (1982), 644
_____, "Naturally" Without Gender: Women, Jurisdiction, and the Federal Courts, 66 N.Y.U.L. Rev. 1682 (1991), 235
_____, Whose Judgment? Vacating Judgments, Preferences for Settlement, and the Role of Adjudication at the Close of the Twentieth Century, 41 UCLA Rev. 1471 (1994), 601
Restatement (Second) of Conflict of Laws (1971), 115
Restatement (Second) of Contracts, 321
Restatement (Second) of Judgments (1982), 227, 806-809, 810, 826, 827, 834, 838, 841, 861-863, 865
Restatement (Second) of Torts, 307, 821, 823
Rizzi, _Erie_ Memoirs Reveal Drama, Tragedy, 63 Harv. L. Rev. 2 (Sept. 24, 1976), 250
Rosenberg, The Pre-trial Conference and Effective Justice (1964), 649
Rubenstein, The Myth of Superiority, 16 Const. Commentary 599 (2000), 215

S.1745, 102d Cong. 1st Session §108 (1991), 954
Shapiro, M., Courts: A Comparative and Political Analysis 44 (1981), 839
_____, D., Federal Rule 16: A Look at the Theory and Practice of Rulemaking, 137 U. Pa. L. Rev. 1969 (1990), 608
Silberman, Shaffer v. Heitner: The End of an Era, 53 N.Y.U.L. Rev. 33 (1978), 87
Solomine, Revitalizing Interlocutory Appeals in the Federal Courts, 58 Geo. Wash. L. Rev. 1165 (1990), 781
Stevens, Venue Statutes: Diagnosis and Proposed Cure, 49 Mich. L. Rev. 307 (1951), 195
Stewart, Forum Non Conveniens: A Doctrine in Search of a Role, 14 Cal. L. Rev. 1259 (1986), 210
Storing, What the Anti-Federalists Were For: The Political Thought of the Opponents of the Constitution (1981), 666
Subrin, How Equity Conquered Common Law: The Federal Rules of Civil Procedure in Historical Perspective, 135 U. Pa. L. Rev. 909 (1987), 395

Uniform Child Custody Jurisdiction Act, 874
Uniform Enforcement of Foreign Judgments Act, 875

INDEX

1035